WOOD ENGINEERING AND CONSTRUCTION HANDBOOK

Library of Congress Cataloging-in-Publication Data

Wood engineering and construction handbook / Keith F. Faherty, editor, Thomas G. Williamson, editor. — 2nd ed.
p. cm.

Includes bibliographical references and index.
ISBN 0-07-019911-6
1. Building, Wooden. I. Faherty, Keith F. II. Williamson, Thomas G.
TA666.W63 1995
624.1′89—dc20 94-38030
CIP

3 4 5 6 7 8 9 DOC/DOC 9 0 9 8 7 6

ISBN 0-07-019911-6

The sponsoring editor for this book was Larry S. Hager, the editing supervisor was Paul R. Sobel, and the production supervisor was Suzanne W. Babeuf. It was set in Times Roman by PRO-Image Corporation, Techna-Type Div., York, PA

Printed and bound by R.R. Donnelly & Sons Company.

This book is printed on acid-free paper.

CONTENTS

CONTRIBUTORS

R. Richard Avent, Ph.D., P.E., *Professor and Chairman of Civil Engineering and Environmental Engineering, Louisiana State University, Baton Rouge, Louisiana* (CHAP. 12)

E.D. Diekmann, S.E., *Consulting Structural Engineer, Kensington, California* (CHAP. 8)

D.W. Ebeling, P.E., *Dick W. Ebeling, Inc., Portland, Oregon (Deceased)* (CHAP. 10)

Keith F. Faherty, Ph.D., P.E., *Professor of Civil and Environmental Engineering, Marquette University, Milwaukee, Wisconsin,* (CHAP. 5)

Alan D. Freas, P.E., *Retired Assistant Director, Forest Products Laboratory, Madison, Wisconsin,* (CHAP. 1)

Robert K. Kaseguma, P.E., *KAS Engineering, Unadilla, New York,* (CHAP. 9)

S.K. Malholta, Ph.D., P.E., *Dean of Graduate Studies and Professor of Civil Engineering, Technical University of Nova Scotia, Nova Scotia, Canada, (Deceased)* (CHAP. 3)

Alfred R. Mangus, P.E., *Civil Engineer, Sacramento, California,* (CHAP. 11)

Thomas E. McLain, *Professor of Timber Engineering and Head, Department of Forest Products, Oregon State University, Corvallis, Oregon,* (CHAP. 7)

David G. Pollock, Jr., P.E., *Former Director of Engineering, American Forest and Paper Association, Washington, D.C.,* (CHAP. 3)

Michael A. Ritter, P.E., *Research Engineer, Engineered Wood Products and Structures, Forest Products Laboratory, Madison, Wisconsin,* (CHAP. 10)

Erwin L. Schaffer, Ph.D., P.E., *Retired Assistant Director, Wood Products Research, USDA-Forest Service, Forest Products Laboratory, Madison, Wisconsin,* (CHAP. 2)

Kenneth Smetts, P.E., *K.D. Smetts Consulting Engineers, Inc., Lafayette, California,* (CHAP. 4)

Trus Joist MacMillan, *Boise, Idaho,* (CHAP. 6)

Thomas G. Williamson, P.E., *Executive Vice President, APA-The Engineered Wood Association, Tacoma, Washington,* (CHAP. 4)

PREFACE

The principal objective of this Handbook was to provide the information and procedures needed to design virtually any type of wood structure, or structural wood component. Included are design equations, design procedures including numerous examples, and design data. Design examples are provided for columns, beams, beam-columns, bents, pole structures, wood foundations, perma-frost foundations, arches, domes, shearwalls, diaphragms, composite beams, composite structures, timber bridges, and many other wood systems.

Basic information is provided on the physical and mechanical properties of wood, commercial lumber and other wood product standards, preservatives, and fire-resistive designs. Numerous connection design examples are provided illustrating the use of nails, screws, lag screws, bolts, shear plates, and split rings. In addition, an extensive discussion is included on the do's and don'ts of joint design.

Information and design examples have been provided for glued-laminated columns, beams, tapered beams, arches, and domes. A chapter each has been devoted to structural panel products, adhesives, shearwalls and diaphragms, and trusses. Each of these include extensive basic product information, design data, and design examples. The second edition of the *Wood Engineering and Construction Handbook* is consistent with the 1991 National Design Specification® for wood construction as published by the American Forest and Paper Association. The coverage on timber bridges has been extensively expanded to include state-of-the-art information and design examples.

Each chapter has been carefully reviewed to minimize duplication, to arrange its content in a logical order, and to insure that useful design examples and design data were included. The editors gratefully acknowledge the many hours of painstaking effort taken by the authors in preparation of their chapter manuscripts, their cooperation during our editing of their work, and their patience. A sincere thanks is extended to Judith A. Scholl for typing the manuscript changes for the second edition. A special thanks is extended to our wives, Joan M. Faherty and Barbara L. Williamson for their patience and encouragement over the many years it took to make this Handbook a reality.

Keith F. Faherty
Thomas G. Williamson

WOOD ENGINEERING AND CONSTRUCTION HANDBOOK

CHAPTER 1
WOOD PROPERTIES

Alan D. Freas, P.E.

1.1 INTRODUCTION

1.1.1 Background

For many centuries, wood has been a natural material of construction for homes and other buildings, for bridges and waterfront structures, for poles and pole frames, for electric and telephone lines, and for many other uses. Today wood remains important to the engineer, the architect, and the builder by reason of improved technology. Modern technology has increased the durability of wood, spurred a host of new wood products such as plywood, particleboard, and other panel products, largely removed the limitations of size and form through the glue-laminating process, and developed improved fasteners with greater load-carrying capacity.

In the United States, approximately 100 species of wood are available to the user, but not all are in a single locale nor in a range of qualities and sizes. Of these 100 species, about 60 are of major commerical importance, although only a few play a strong role in construction. About 30 species are imported, some in the form of logs or cants and some in the form of lumber, veneer, or finished products.

As is true of other construction materials, wood products, including lumber, are available in a range of qualities (grades) and in a series of standardized sizes. Manufacturers of most wood products have joined together into associations in order to standardize grades and sizes and to ensure that standards and quality are maintained. Treatment processes are similarly standardized and are subject to quality control. These aspects will be discussed more fully in later chapters. A brief description of wood and some of its important characteristics is given in this chapter.

1.1.2 Wood Formation

A cross section of a tree (Fig. 1.1) shows several distinct features. From the outside in, there is first the bark—both the outer corky dead part and the inner thin living part. Next is the wood, which in the merchantable sizes of most species can be differentiated into sapwood and heartwood. Finally, there is the pith, a small central core which represents the primary growth in a stem or a branch.

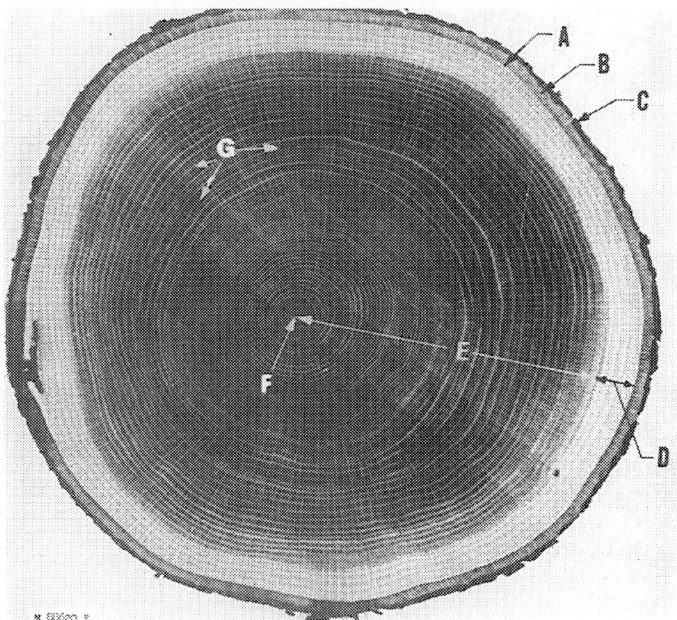

FIG. 1.1 Cross section of tree trunk. *A*—Cambium layer (microscopic) is inside inner bark and forms wood and bark cells. *B*—Inner bark is moist, soft, and contains living tissue; carries prepared food from leaves to all growing parts of tree. *C*—Outer bark containing corky layers is composed of dry dead tissue; gives general protection against external injuries; inner and outer barks are separated by bark cambium. *D*—Sapwood contains both living and dead tissues; is light-colored wood beneath bark; carries sap from roots to leaves. *E*—Heartwood (inactive) is formed by gradual change in sapwood. *F*—Pith is soft tissue about which first wood growth takes place in newly formed twigs. *G*—Wood rays connect various layers from pith to bark for storage and transfer of food. (*Courtesy of U.S. Forest Products Laboratory, Madison, Wisc.*)

Between the bark and the wood is a layer of thin-walled cells called the *cambium.* New wood cells are formed on the inside of the cambium and new bark cells on the outside. Thus growth in diameter results from the formation of new cells, not from growth of the wood already formed. Similarly, growth in the length of branches and stems is the result of the addition of cells at the ends of the stem and the branches.

Wood cells are of various sizes, shapes, and functions. The majority of cells are elongated and pointed at the ends and are customarily called *fibers* or *tracheids:* they impart strength to the wood. In addition to fibers, hardwoods contain a series of cells of large diameter called *vessels,* which function as the main arteries for the longitudinal movement of sap. In softwoods, the same function is performed by the tracheids. Other types of cells, some arranged horizontally in the tree, perform specialized functions.

1.1.3 Growth Rings

In temperate climates there is, with most species, sufficient difference between the wood formed early in the growing season and that formed later in the growing season to produce distinct annual growth rings (see Fig. 1.1). The age of a tree may be determined by counting the growth rings at the stump. Drought, defoliation by insects, and other factors may interrupt diameter growth or change its pattern, and such variations have been used to determine the age of very old structures such as the pueblos in the southwestern part of the United States. In tropical climates, growth is more or less continuous, but concentric demarcations may still occur as a result of fluctuations in growth activity. Such demarcations do not indicate the limits of annual growth.

1.1.4 Earlywood and Latewood

As indicated, the wood formed early in the growing season and that formed later are different. That formed early is called *earlywood* or *springwood,* and that formed later is called *latewood* or *summerwood.* The earlywood, formed during the most active period of growth, is composed of cells having relatively large cavities and thin walls, while that formed later has smaller cavities and thicker walls. Because of the lesser proportion of wood substance, the earlywood is lighter in weight, softer, and weaker than the latewood. Because of the greater density and strength of latewood, the proportion of latewood is sometimes used as an indicator of the quality or strength of wood.

1.1.5 Sapwood and Heartwood

The outer portion of the tree stem, the *sapwood,* located next to the cambium, functions primarily in the storage of food and the mechanical transport of sap. It varies in thickness, is usually light-colored, and is less resistant to decay than is the heartwood. The *heartwood* in many species is somewhat darker than the sapwood, its cells have become inactive, various materials (commonly called *extractives*) have become deposited in its cells, and it functions mainly in the mechanical support of the tree. In general, there is no difference in mechanical properties between heartwood and sapwood; that is, the strength of a piece of wood is determined principally by the conditions which exist when the wood is formed, not by the changes that take place during the growth of the tree.

1.1.6 Hardwood and Softwood

Tree species generally are divided into two large groups commonly referred to as *hardwoods* and *softwoods.* The hardwoods have broad leaves and lose their leaves in the fall or during the winter. The softwoods are the coniferous species and have needlelike or scalelike leaves which, except for a couple of species, remain on the tree throughout the year. The terms *hardwood* and *softwood* are only vaguely related to the actual hardness of the wood, since some softwoods are actually harder than some hardwoods. Typical softwood species are the pines, firs, spruces, and redwoods, while typical hardwood species include the oaks, maples, and birches.

1.1.7 Chemical Composition

Dry wood is made up chiefly of cellulose and lignin, with smaller amounts of other chemicals such as hemicelluloses, extractives, and ash-forming minerals. Cellulose is the major constituent, making up about half the wood substance by weight. It is a high-molecular-weight linear polymer which is arranged in a series of elements which make up the cell walls of wood fibers. Lignin, an extremely complex material, makes up about one-fourth to one-third the weight of wood and serves to bind the fibers together. While the extractives are not part of the wood structure, they do contribute to various wood properties, including decay resistance. They also contribute to density but play a minor role in the strength of wood.

1.1.8 Anisotropy

The arrangement of fibers in wood, with the long axes of the fibers parallel to the axis of the trunk, suggests that wood may have different characteristics in the various directions within itself. This is indeed true, and thus wood is anisotropic rather than isotropic, as are many other materials such as metals. Specifically, wood is considered to be orthotropic, having unique and independent properties in the direction of three mutually perpendicular axes. The axes (Fig.1.2) are longitudinal, or parallel to the length of the fibers; radial, or perpendicular to the length of the fibers and in a direction radial to the growth rings; and tangential, or perpendicular to the fiber length and in a direction tangential to the growth rings. The strength, the modulus of elasticity, and other characteristics such as shrinkage and swelling differ in the three directions.

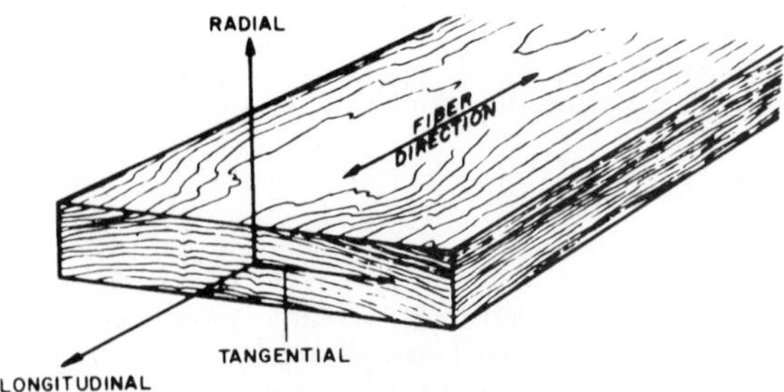

FIG. 1.2 Three principal axes of wood growth with respect to grain direction and growth rings. (*Courtesy of U.S. Forest Products Laboratory, Madison, Wisc.*)

1.2 PHYSICAL PROPERTIES

1.2.1 Density

The density of wood is determined principally by two factors—the amount of wood substance per unit volume and the moisture content. Other factors, such as the content of extractives and minerals, have minor effects on density. The density of wood, exclusive of water, differs greatly within as well as between species. Typically, density falls in the range of 20 to 45 lbm/ft^3 (320 to 720 kg/m^3). The range actually extends from something like 10 lbm/ft^3 (160 kg/m^3) for balsa to more than 65 lbm/ft^3 (1040 kg/m^3) for some other tropical species. Density values for a number of species can be obtained from the specific gravity values given in Table 5.2. Many characteristics of wood are affected by density. Since it is the wood substance in the fibers that imparts strength and stiffness, wood of high density is stronger and stiffer than wood of low density, other factors such as moisture content being equal. Woods of high density typically shrink and swell more with changes in moisture content than do woods of low density.

1.2.2 Moisture in Wood

Wood in the living tree is associated with moisture. The moisture content of the wood varies widely among species, among individual trees of a single species, and between sapwood and heartwood. In the green wood, the moisture content varies from as little as 30 percent (based on the ovendry weight of the wood) to about 200 percent. Most uses of wood require that the moisture content be fairly low, with the general rule being that before use, the wood should be dried to a moisture content as close as possible to that which it will be expected to reach in service. Thus flooring for use in homes in the northern part of the United States would be dried to a lower moisture content than would bevel siding for the same home.

Moisture in green wood is partly adsorbed in the cell walls and partly present in the cell cavities. As wood dries, the cell walls do not give off moisture until the cell cavities are empty. The condition in which the cell walls are fully saturated and the cell cavities are empty is known as the *fiber saturation point.* The fiber saturation point varies with the species but is commonly taken to be at a moisture content of about 30 percent.

Any piece of wood will give off or take on moisture from the surrounding atmosphere (i.e., wood is hygroscopic) until the moisture in the wood has come to a balance with that in the atmosphere. The moisture in the wood at the point of balance is called the *equilibrium moisture content* (EMC). The EMC is closely related to the relative humidity and the temperature of the surrounding atmosphere, although differences in temperature do not have a strong effect on the EMC, as illustrated by Table 1.1.

Relationships such as those shown in Table 1.1 can be used to estimate the moisture content to be expected in service from the characteristics of the atmosphere in which the wood will be exposed. Thus the in-service moisture content in an arid atmosphere such as that of the American Southwest will be different from that to be expected along the Gulf Coast.

The moisture content is commonly determined using electrical instruments, which work on the principle that some electrical chracteristic such as resistance is

TABLE 1.1 Moisture Content of Wood in Equilibrium with Stated Dry-Bulb Temperature and Relative Humidity

Temperature, dry-bulb, °F	Relative Humidity, %																			
	5	10	15	20	25	30	35	40	45	50	55	60	65	70	75	80	85	90	95	98
30	1.4	2.6	3.7	4.6	5.5	6.3	7.1	7.9	8.7	9.5	10.4	11.3	12.4	13.5	14.9	16.5	18.5	21.0	24.3	26.9
40	1.4	2.6	3.7	4.6	5.5	6.3	7.1	7.9	8.7	9.5	10.4	11.3	12.3	13.5	14.9	16.5	18.5	21.0	24.3	26.9
50	1.4	2.6	3.6	4.6	5.5	6.3	7.1	7.9	8.7	9.5	10.3	11.2	12.3	13.4	14.8	16.4	18.4	20.9	24.3	26.9
60	1.3	2.5	3.6	4.6	5.4	6.2	7.0	7.8	8.6	9.4	10.2	11.1	12.1	13.3	14.6	16.2	18.2	20.7	24.1	26.8
70	1.3	2.5	3.5	4.5	5.4	6.2	6.9	7.7	8.5	9.2	10.1	11.0	12.0	13.1	14.4	16.0	17.9	20.5	23.9	26.6
80	1.3	2.4	3.5	4.4	5.3	6.1	6.8	7.6	8.3	9.1	9.9	10.8	11.7	12.9	14.2	15.7	17.7	20.2	23.6	26.3
90	1.2	2.3	3.4	4.3	5.1	5.9	6.7	7.4	8.1	8.9	9.7	10.5	11.5	12.6	13.9	15.4	17.3	19.8	23.3	26.0
100	1.2	2.3	3.3	4.2	5.0	5.8	6.5	7.2	7.9	8.7	9.5	10.3	11.2	12.3	13.6	15.1	17.0	19.5	22.9	25.6
110	1.1	2.2	3.2	4.0	4.9	5.6	6.3	7.0	7.7	8.4	9.2	10.0	11.0	12.0	13.2	14.7	16.6	19.1	22.4	25.2
120	1.1	2.1	3.0	3.9	4.7	5.4	6.1	6.8	7.5	8.2	8.9	9.7	10.6	11.7	12.9	14.4	16.2	18.6	22.0	24.7
130	1.0	2.0	2.9	3.7	4.5	5.2	5.9	6.6	7.2	7.9	8.7	9.4	10.3	11.3	12.5	14.0	15.8	18.2	21.5	24.2
140	0.9	1.9	2.8	3.6	4.3	5.0	5.7	6.3	7.0	7.7	8.4	9.1	10.0	11.0	12.1	13.6	15.3	17.7	21.0	23.7
150	0.9	1.8	2.6	3.4	4.1	4.8	5.5	6.1	6.7	7.4	8.1	8.8	9.7	10.6	11.8	13.1	14.9	17.2	20.4	23.1
160	0.8	1.6	2.4	3.2	3.9	4.6	5.2	5.8	6.4	7.1	7.8	8.5	9.3	10.3	11.4	12.7	14.4	16.7	19.9	22.5
170	0.7	1.5	2.3	3.0	3.7	4.3	4.9	5.6	6.2	6.8	7.4	8.2	9.0	9.9	11.0	12.3	14.0	16.2	19.3	21.9
180	0.7	1.4	2.1	2.8	3.5	4.1	4.7	5.3	5.9	6.5	7.1	7.8	8.6	9.5	10.5	11.8	13.5	15.7	18.7	21.3
190	0.6	1.3	1.9	2.6	3.2	3.8	4.4	5.0	5.5	6.1	6.8	7.5	8.2	9.1	10.1	11.4	13.0	15.1	18.1	20.7
200	0.5	1.1	1.7	2.4	3.0	3.5	4.1	4.6	5.2	5.8	6.4	7.1	7.8	8.7	9.7	10.9	12.5	14.6	17.5	20.0
210	0.5	1.0	1.6	2.1	2.7	3.2	3.8	4.3	4.9	5.4	6.0	6.7	7.4	8.3	9.2	10.4	12.0	14.0	16.9	19.3

related to the moisture content of the wood. Moisture meters have a limited range within which the measured moisture content has high accuracy, but fortunately, this range is generally within the range of moisture contents commonly expected in service.

One of the reasons wood is dried to a moisture content near that expected in service is that wood shrinks as its moisture content drops below the fiber saturation point. Conversely, swelling occurs when dry or partially dry wood adsorbs moisture. Thus a piece of wood machined to a particular size when green will be smaller than that size when it reaches equilibrium in most conditions of service except, of course, those which involve more or less continuous exposure to very high humidity or to water, such as piles and cooling towers. Since every piece of wood does not shrink and swell by exactly the same amount, it is desirable to machine wood products to finished size when they are near the moisture content to be expected in service. In addition, wood shrinks and swells at a different rate in the various directions with respect to the fiber direction—least longitudinally (parallel to grain), most tangentially, and intermediate radially. Thus changes in grain direction within a piece of wood, such as the localized cross grain around knots, can result in differences in shrinkage, which, in turn, can cause warp of various forms (Fig. 1.3). Some abnormal types of wood, such as compression wood and wood formed early in the life of the tree (juvenile wood), commonly have abnormally high longitudinal shrinkage. A piece of lumber which has a portion of its width composed of such wood is likely to warp

Table 1.2 lists average values of shrinkage for a few species. Average shrinkage values for a considerably larger number of species are given in Chap. 3 of the *Wood Handbook.*[1] These values may be used to estimate dimensional changes associated with changes in moisture content, assuming that the relationship of shrinkage to

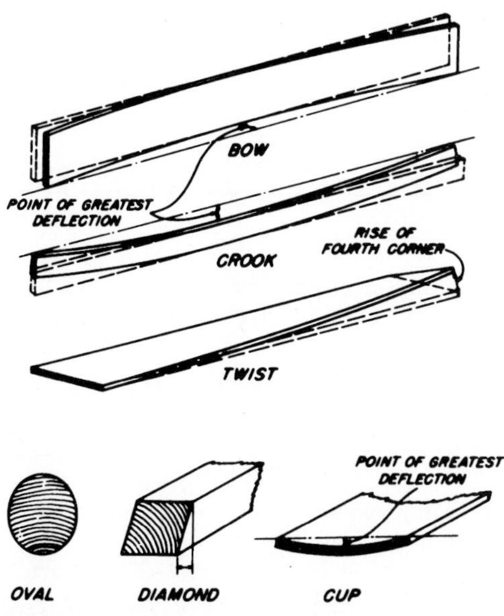

FIG. 1.3 Various kinds of warp. *(Courtesy of U.S. Forest Products Laboratory, Madison, Wisc.)*

TABLE 1.2 Shrinkage Values for Selected Domestic Woods

Species	Shrinkage from green to ovendry moisture content, %		
	Radial	Tangential	Volumetric
Cedar			
Western red cedar	2.4	5.0	6.8
Douglas fir			
Coast	4.8	7.6	12.4
Interior north	3.8	6.9	10.7
Interior west	4.8	7.5	11.8
Fir			
Grand	3.4	7.5	11.0
Noble	4.3	8.3	12.4
White	3.3	7.0	9.8
Hemlock			
Eastern	3.0	6.8	9.7
Mountain	4.4	7.1	11.1
Western	4.2	7.8	12.4
Larch			
Western	4.5	9.1	14.0
Pine			
Eastern white	2.1	6.1	8.2
Loblolly	4.8	7.4	12.3
Lodgepole	4.3	6.7	11.1
Longleaf	5.1	7.5	12.2
Ponderosa	3.9	6.2	9.7
Shortleaf	4.6	7.7	12.3
Western white	4.1	7.4	11.8
Spruce			
Black	4.1	6.8	11.3
Engelmann	3.8	7.1	11.0
Red	3.8	7.8	11.8
Sitka	4.3	7.5	11.5

moisture-content change is linear and that shrinkage begins at a moisture content of 30 percent except for a few species. Dimensional change estimates may be made with the following equation:

$$\Delta D = \frac{D_I(M_F - M_I)}{\dfrac{30(100)}{S_T} - 30 + M_I} \qquad (1.1)$$

where ΔD = change in dimension
D_I = dimension at start of change
M_F = moisture content at end of change, percent
M_I = moisture content at start of change, percent
S_T = tangential shrinkage from green to ovendry, percent (Table1.2)

Radial shrinkage S_R should be used when shrinkage in the radial direction is desired. If a maximum estimate for dimensional change is desired, tangential shrinkage S_T should be used.

1.2.3 Thermal Properties

Wood, as is common with other materials, expands when heated, but not generally to the same degree as do materials such as metals. The thermal coefficient of expansion for wood parallel to grain may, for example, be as little as one three-hundredth that for steel. Coefficients perpendicular to grain may be on the order of 5 to 10 times that parallel to grain.

Wood is a good insulator; that is, it has a high resistance to heat flow. In normal wood, thermal conductivity is about the same in either the radial or the tangential direction, but it is 2 to 3 times greater in the longitudinal direction. The average thermal conductivity perpendicular to grain for moisture contents of up to about 40 percent may be expressed by the following empirical equation:

$$k = S(1.39 + 0.028M) + 0.165 \tag{1.2}$$

where k = thermal conductivity, Btu·in/h·ft^2·°F
S = specific gravity based on volume at current moisture content and weight when ovendry
M = moisture content expressed as percentage of ovendry weight

Values of specific gravity for a large number of species may be found in Table 5.2 and Chap. 4 of the *Wood Handbook.*[1] For wood at moisture contents greater than 40 percent, thermal conductivity may be expressed by

$$k = S(1.39 + 0.038M) + 0.165 \tag{1.3}$$

The thermal conductivity of wood is much less than that of many other structural materials. Values of thermal conductivity for a few materials are shown in Table 1.3. It may be seen that the thermal conductivity of wood is only about one-sixteenth that of sand and gravel concrete and only about one four-hundredth that of steel.

1.2.4 Electrical Properties

The most important electrical property of wood as it relates to structural use is its resistance to the passage of electric current. At low moisture content, wood is classified as an electric insulator rather than a conductor. This is important in such uses as power-line poles and in tool handles for equipment in use around electric lines. The dc electric resistance varies greatly with the moisture content, especially below the fiber saturation point. It decreases as the moisture content increases, changing tenfold, for example, as the moisture varies from about 25 to 7 percent. This is the principle used in many electric moisture meters. Effects of a few factors, such as temperature and species, must be taken into account when using moisture meters, but methods of adjustment for the factors are provided with commercial meters.

TABLE 1.3 Thermal Properties of Building Materials Used in Wall Construction

Material*	Thermal conductivity, k, Btu/h·°F†	Thermal resistance $1/k$, °F/Btu·h‡	Relative efficiency, % (wood = 100)
Air	0.168	5.95	476.0
Wood (average coniferous)	0.80	1.25	100.0
Clay brick	4.8	0.208	16.5
Limestone	6.5	0.154	12.3
Sandstone	12.0	0.083	6.6
Concrete			
Sand and gravel	12.6	0.079	6.3
Lightweight			
120-lb/ft³ density	5.2	0.192	15.4
80-lb/ft³ density	2.5	0.400	32.0
40-lb/ft³ density	1.15	0.870	69.6
Steel	312.0	0.0032	0.25
Aluminum	1416.0	0.000707	0.06

*A 1-ft² panel, 1 in thick is assumed.

†Thermal conductivity is conventionally expressed as heat energy in British thermal units transmitted each hour through a panel of material 1 ft² and 1 in thick for each 1°F temperature differential on opposite sides of the panel.

‡Thermal resistance is conventionally expressed as the temperature differential in degrees Fahrenheit required to effect a transfer of 1 Btu/h through a panel of material 1 ft² and 1 in thick.

1.2.5 Acoustical Properties

The most important acoustical property of wood to be used in construction is its ability to dampen vibrations. Wood has a much greater damping capacity than do most other materials. Therefore, wood is a preferred material for structural components in which vibration is undesirable.

In sound-conditioning a room, both the sound-absorption capability of floor, wall, and ceiling materials and the sound-transmission resistance of the materials are important. The sound absorption of finished wood is about the same as that of brick, glass, and plaster. Wood can be striated to improve its absorption properties. Wood frame walls have been found to provide good sound barriers in buildings and have found some application as sound barriers on highways.

1.2.6 Behavior in Fire

Wood is combustible. It is also a good insulator, as is the char formed during combustion. As a consequence, the wood just inside the char is at a comparatively low temperature as compared with that at the fire-exposed surface. Because of these insulating layers of wood and char, the rate of charring is low—on the order of 1½ in/h (0.038 m/h)—and wood members of large cross sections retain substantial proportions of their original load-carrying capacity for relatively long periods during fire exposure.

The exposure of wood to elevated temperatures results in a loss of unit strength. With short-time exposure there may be no lasting effect, but long-time exposure causes a permanent loss in unit strength, the degree of loss being dependent on both the temperature and the duration of exposure. However, because wood just below the char line has experienced only a moderate rise in temperature, a large proportion of the unburned part of the member retains its original unit strength, with a thin layer next to the char retaining most of its original strength. Thus, in many cases, particularly in fires of short duration, the loss of load-carrying capacity may be only the loss that results from a reduced effective cross section. For conservatively designed members, rehabilitation after a fire may require only the removal of char. In the case of glued-laminated bending members, which have special tension laminations, the loss of a large proportion of such high-quality laminations may change the overall allowable design stress greatly. This effect as well as the effect of change in cross section must be considered in evaluating the residual load-carrying capacity of the member. This subject is discussed in detail in Chap. 4 of Ref. 2.

The rate of surface flame spread can be materially reduced by impregnating the wood with suitable chemicals. Impregnation with waterborne salts will reduce flame spread by reducing the amount of flammable products released during combustion. The treatment also reduces the amount of heat released in the volatiles during the early stages of combustion and results in the wood being self-extinguishing if the source of heat is removed. This type of treatment is commonly applied to wood panel products where the rapidity of flame spread is of major concern. Treatment will not, however, prevent thermal decomposition and charring of the wood, and the rate of fire penetration is about the same as for untreated wood. However, the salt treatment reduces the wood strength, and this effect must be considered in design. There are some commercial fire retardants not based on salts which do not cause a strength loss.

1.2.7 Resistance to Chemicals

Wood is naturally resistant to many chemicals. As a consequence, it is the preferred material for numerous applications in industries where chemicals are used in processes, as in tanks and other containers, and for structures where chemicals are used or stored. Wood is widely used in cooling towers where the hot water to be cooled contains boiler-conditioning chemicals and dissolved chlorine for the suppression of algae. It is also commonly used in the construction of buildings for bulk chemical storage where the wood will be in direct contact with the chemicals.

Certain species have greater resistance to chemicals than do others, and generally the heartwood is more resistant to chemical attack than is the sapwood. Thus the heartwoods of cypress, southern pine, Douglas fir, and redwood are preferred for water tanks. Heartwood of the first three is preferred where resistance to chemical attack is essential. All four species combine moderate to high resistance to water penetration with moderate to high resistance to chemical attack and decay.

Two general types of action account for most effects of chemical solutions on wood. The first, generally completely reversible, involves swelling of the wood structure. The second, which is irreversible, causes permanent change in the wood due to an alteration of its chemical constituents.

In the first, water, alcohols, and some other organic liquids swell the wood without degradation. Removal of the liquid permits the wood to return to its original condition. Petroleum oils and creosote do not cause swelling.

In the second, permanent changes result from the hydrolysis of cellulose and hemicelluloses by acids or acidic salts, the oxidation of wood substance by oxidizing agents, or the delignification and solution of hemicelluloses by alkalies or alkaline salt solutions. Highly acidic salts tend to hydrolyze wood when present in high concentrations. However, even when present in low concentrations, migration of the salts may result in high concentrations under certain conditions, such as in railroad ties in hot, arid regions.

Iron salts develop at points of contact with tie plates, bolts, and other connectors and can degrade wood, especially in the presence of moisture. The softening and discoloration of wood around corroded iron fastenings are common. They are especially prominent in acidic woods such as oaks and in woods such as redwood which contain large amounts of tannin and related compounds. The use of corrosion-resistant fasteners avoids the problem.

Certain types of treatments may be used to enhance the natural resistance of wood to chemicals. Impregnants which increase the resistance of the wood to the penetration of moisture are helpful. Impregnation with phenol-formaldehyde resin-forming systems or with a monomeric resin such as methyl methacrylate followed in both cases by polymerization has shown good results in improving chemical resistance.

1.2.8 Durability

Wood, like other materials, is subject to attack by various destructive agents. As an organic material, it is subject to attack by certain organisms. In general, wood that remains dry is relatively immune to attack by many of the destructive agents, although the color of the wood may be slightly changed by exposure to air and sunlight, and erosion may occur, albeit at a very slow rate, from the slow breakdown of surface elements which are then washed away by rain. Nonetheless, there are numerous examples of centuries-old wood structures, especially in Europe and Asia. In the United States, many wood houses built early in the colonial history of the country still stand and are in use. In Salt Lake City, the famed Great Tabernacle of the Mormons, built in 1863, is still in regular use.

Decay is one of the principal hazards faced by wood. It results from the action of certain types of fungi, which use the wood substance as a food source. Wood-destroying fungi require favorable conditions of moisture, temperature, and access to air as well as access to wood. Lack of any of these will inhibit the growth of the fungi. The simplest of these factors to control is the moisture content. Thus keeping wood dry (i.e., below about 20 percent moisure content) is the most effective way of preventing decay. Wood fully saturated with water does not decay, so that piles constantly submerged in fresh water will have long life, as will foundation piles in locations where the groundwater level is above the tops of the piles. Wood species differ greatly in the resistance of their heartwood to decay. Of all species, sapwood has only limited resistance to decay. For use under conditions conducive to decay, either a species of high natural resistance to decay should be selected or the wood should be treated with preservative chemicals.

The fungi that cause mold and stain do not attack the wood substance in the cell walls but obtain their nutrients from materials in cell cavities. Thus they have minor effects, if any, on the mechanical properties.

Bacteria in water may attack the cell walls, reducing strength and increasing porosity. As a result of increased porosity, excessive amounts of preservative chemicals may be adsorbed during preservative treatment.

A number of insects and borers attack wood and destroy it, with termites probably being the most destructive, especially in the southern United States. Carpenter ants and others may be quite destructive, although they use the wood only for shelter rather than for food, as do termites. Carpenter ants require moist wood, so that keeping the wood dry will prevent damage from their attack. The same preservatives that control decay also will generally control insects. In salt or brackish waters, marine borers may be active and cause rapid destruction of piles and other wood members. Heavy treatment with creosote is generally effective, except for *Limnoria,* where a dual treatment of the wood, first with waterborne salts and then with creosote, is more effective.

The chemicals commonly used for preservative treatment of wood have little or no effect on its strength. The pressures and temperatures used in the treating process, however, may reduce strength and thus are limited in standards for the treating processes, such as those developed by the American Wood Preservers Association. Strict attention must be paid to the control of the processes, and the results are commonly evaluated by measuring the depth of penetration and by assaying samples to evaluate the amount of preservative that has been put into the wood. The effects of preservative treatment on the mechanical properties are discussed in Sec. 1.4.

1.3 MECHANICAL PROPERTIES

1.3.1 Directional Characteristics

As discussed in Sec. 1.1.8, the properties in various directions with respect to the direction of the fibers are different. Thus the mechanical properties parallel to grain are greatly different from those perpendicular to grain. Compressive strength parallel to grain may be 5 to 10 times as great as that perpendicular to grain, and the difference in tensile strengths will be much greater. The modulus of elasticity parallel to grain is likely to be on the order of 10 to 25 times that perpendicular to grain. Differences in the perpendicular-to-grain direction are likely to be minor between properties parallel (tangent) to the growth rings and those perpendicular (radial) to the growth rings. Detailed information on property differences in the various directions can be found in Chap. 4 of the *Wood Handbook.*[1] Directional differences in the mechanical properties must be taken into account in the design of wood structures. The low levels of some properties must be considered carefully in design, particularly where tensile stress perpendicular to grain develops under service loads.

1.3.2 Resistance to Compressive and Tensile Loads

The crushing strength of wood is an important characteristic in posts, columns, piles, and truss chords and in those web members of trusses which are subjected to compressive stress. For longer compressive members, however, the member may reach its load-bearing limit by buckling rather than by crushing. End-to-end bearing will depend on the crushing strength only if a metal plate is inserted between the two ends. When wood-to-wood end bearing occurs, latewood may bear on earlywood, and crushing may occur at stresses below the crushing strength of the wood. The crushing strength depends greatly on moisture content, with dry wood being substantially stronger in compression than moist wood. Design values for end-grain bearing are presented in the Appendix.

When wood is compressed under high loads perpendicular to grain, the cell cavities are eliminated, and cell wall bears on cell wall. Eventually, the wood becomes greatly densified, and its compressive strength across the grain becomes very high. However, the crushing which takes place with increasing loads may produce deformation, which is unacceptable. Design stresses in compression perpendicular to grain, therefore, are commonly set at the level of proportional limit stress (i.e., they are set at a level that limits deformation). When a piece of wood is loaded in compression perpendicular to grain over a porton of its area, the fibers extending from adjacent nonloaded areas give support to the loaded fibers, and thus the unit stress which it sustains is higher than if the full face of the piece had been loaded. This effect is accounted for in design by allowing increases for partially loaded areas, such as under washers and plates.

The compressive strength of wood at angles intermediate between parallel to grain and perpendicular to grain is intermediate between the strengths parallel and perpendicular to grain.

The tensile strength parallel to grain is the highest strength property of wood. Because of a sensitivity to irregularities of grain, edge knots, notches, and other stress risers, it is difficult to realize this superior strength in structural members of commercial lumber.

The tensile strength perpendicular to grain, on the other hand, is one of the lowest strength properties of wood. Besides its weakness when loaded in this direction, this property is sensitive to stress concentrations. In some instances, such as in some joint details, it is not possible to avoid tensile stress perpendicular to grain. Care should be taken in such cases to keep the stresses as low as possible. In general, however, it is best to avoid carrying loads in such a way as to generate tensile stresses perpendicular to grain.

Strength values at intermediate angles may be estimated by means of the Hankinson formula, which is discussed in Sec. 1.4.4.

1.3.3 Resistance to Bending Loads

Wood develops high strengths in the extreme fiber in bending and has a high strength-to-weight ratio in comparison with other materials. Research has shown that the modulus of rupture is less for large beams than for small beams, so an adjustment for size may be required in design. The bending strength increases markedly with drying, but this gain is offset by the development of drying defects. For this reason, credit for the effect of drying on strength is usually limited to material less than about 4 in thick, in which the effect of drying defects is less than in material of larger cross sections.

1.3.4 Resistance to Deformation

The tendency of a piece of wood to deform under stress is indicated by the modulus of elasticity. The use of the modulus of elasticity in standard engineering formulas, however, gives only the immediate, or elastic, deformation. Wood under long-continued load will continue to deform, a deformation which is generally nonrecoverable. Creep, or sag, will generally be greater if the wood is wet when the load is applied and then dries during the time the load is on the member. Typically, creep deformation may be expected to be about equal to the initial deformation if environmental conditions do not change. Creep deflections under bending load at several stress levels are shown in Fig.1.4. A 50°F increase in temperature can result in an increase in creep deformation of as much as 2 to 3 times. Green wood may creep as much as 4 to 5 times the initial deformation as it dries. Upon removal of loads, a member will immediately recover the elastic deformation, and after some period of time, it will recover about one-half the creep deformation. Creep does not indicate a change in the modulus of elasticity. It has been found that the relation of unit stress to unit strain for increments of load applied or removed is the same after long-time loading as it was before the load was applied. Only a modest increase in the modulus of elasticity results from drying.

1.3.5 Resistance to Shear Loads

Shear stress is particularly critical at connections and near reactions and load points, so the shear strength of wood is an important characteristic. The shear strength parallel to grain has a relatively low value, and it is sensitive to stress concentrations. The shear strength across the grain is never considered in design, since its value is high and failure will always occur first in shear parallel to grain. The sensitivity of shear strength to stress concentrations requires that care be used in design to avoid stress concentrations such as those caused by notches or other sudden changes in cross section.

1.3.6 Resistance to Repeated Loads

Fatigue properties are generally of little concern in many applications of wood but can become important in applications where there are many repetitions of stress, as in railroad bridges or in propellers such as those being developed for the generation of electricity from wind power. Data on the fatigue properties of wood are somewhat limited. However, tests have shown that after 2 million cycles of bending, clear straight-grained wood will have 60 percent of the strength of similar specimens tested under static conditions. In similar fatigue tests, specimens with small knots had 50 percent of the static strength of clear straight-grained wood, specimens

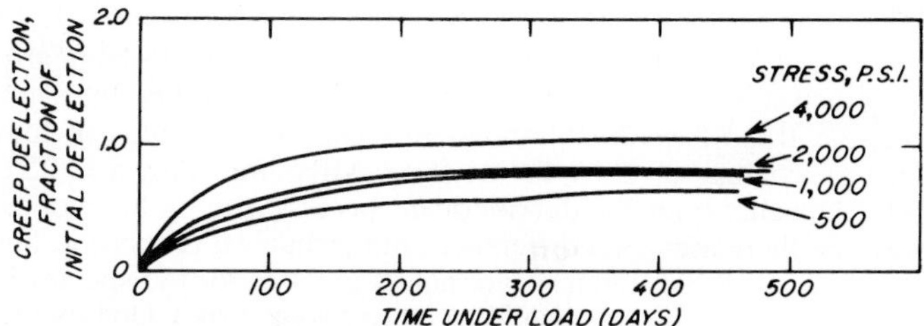

FIG. 1.4 Creep as influenced by four levels of stress. (*Courtesy of U.S. Forest Products Laboratory, Madison, Wisc.*)

with 1/12 slope of grain had 45 percent, and specimens with both knots and sloping grain had 30 percent of the static strength of clear straight-grained wood (see also Sec. 2.4).

1.3.7 Resistance to Torsional Loads

Torsional loads are generally not important in the design of wood structures, but data are available that permit the calculation of properties for use in such instances. Torsional shear strength, for example, may be taken as equal to that for shear parallel to grain. If torsional deformation becomes a problem, data on moduli of rigidity in the various planes are available in Chap. 4 of the *Wood Handbook*[1] for the necessary calculations.

1.3.8 Resistance to Rapidly Applied or Long-Continued Loads

The load that will cause failure in a member that must carry loads continuously for a long period is much less than the load that would cause failure in a few minutes. For example, a wood member under the continuous action of bending stress for 10 years will carry only about 60 percent of the load under which the same member would fail in a few minutes.

Conversely, if the duration of stress is very short, the load-carrying capacity will be much higher than normally published strength properties. The load that will produce failure in 1 s is approximately 25 percent higher than that causing failure in a few minutes. It is this effect that permits disregarding impact stresses up to 100 percent greater than the usual allowable values.

Most data on the effect of the duration of stress are based on information from tests of clear straight-grained wood. There is some indication that the duration effect may be different for material containing knots, cross grain, and other characteristics found in commercial lumber. However, no change in the design procedure has been formulated at the present time.

1.4 EFFECT OF VARIOUS FACTORS ON MECHANICAL PROPERTIES

1.4.1 Species

Different species of wood have characteristically different mechanical properties. Some of the greatest extremes are found in woods not native to the United States. For example, the *Wood Handbook*[1] shows in Chap. 4 a modulus of rupture at 12 percent moisture content of 2800 lb/in^2 (19.3 MPa) for balsa and 22,600 lb/in^2 (156 MPa) for lapacho, both South American species. Among the woods grown in the United States, there are again differences in mechanical properties, but for those most commonly used, the differences are not as great as for the species mentioned. For example, again from data in the *Wood Handbook,* coast Douglas fir shows a modulus of rupture at 12 percent moisture content of 12,400 lb/in^2 (85.5 MPa), loblolly pine a value of 12,800 lb/in^2 (88.3 MPa), and eastern hemlock a value of

8900 lb/in^2 (61.4 MPa). Thus woods from different species are adaptable to various uses, depending on their mechanical and other properties.

Even within species there are differences in mechanical properties. Some result from variations in structure, while others may result from differences in growth conditions. Trees grown in relatively arid areas, for example, will have different mechanical properties from those of the same species grown in areas of relatively high rainfall. Even within trees, variations in mechanical properties may occur dependent on the climatic conditions during the life of the tree.

1.4.2 Density

Much of the difference in properties between and within species can be attributed to differences in density. The specific gravity of the wood substance is essentially constant at about 1.50, so the specific gravity of a piece of wood is effectively a measure of the proportion of the volume occupied by wood substance. Since it is the wood substance that imparts strength to a piece of wood, the greater the proportion of wood substance (i.e., the higher the specific gravity), the higher the mechanical properties may be expected to be. For example, the green specific gravities of the two South American species mentioned in the preceding section are 0.17 and 0.92.

The relation between mechanical properties and specific gravity has the form

$$S = KG^n \tag{1.4}$$

where S = the value of any particular mechanical property
G = specific gravity
K, n = constants depending on the particular property being considered

For differences between species, the values of n range from 1.00 to 2.25, and for within-species variation, they range from 1.25 to 2.50. Some equations for a variety of properties are given in Table 4.8 of the *Wood Handbook.*[1]

1.4.3 Moisture

Changes in moisture content below the fiber saturation point (Sec. 1.2.2) result in changes in the mechanical properties, with higher properties at the lower moisture contents, except that properties related to impact (toughness, work to maximum load in static bending, and height of drop in impact bending) may remain the same or may actually decrease at the lower moisture contents. Estimates of the effect of moisture differences on the properties of clear wood such as those given in the *Wood Handbook*[1] may be obtained by the following equation:

$$P_M = P_a \left(\frac{P_a}{P_g}\right)^{-(M-a)/(M_p-a)} \tag{1.5}$$

where P_M = property at some moisture content M
P_a = property at some moisture content a
P_g = value of property for all moisture contents greater than moisture content M_p (slightly below fiber saturation point), at which property changes due to drying are first observed

Since mechanical property values are commonly given for the green condition and at a moisture content of 12 percent, a may be taken as 12 and

$$P_M = P_{12}\left(\frac{P_{12}}{P_g}\right)^{-(M-12)/(M_p-12)} \tag{1.6}$$

Values of M_p for a few species are given in Table 1.4. For species not listed, M_p may be taken as 25 percent. Approximations of changes in properties may be made using the approximate percentage changes of properties shown in Table 1.5.

1.4.4 Strength-Reducing Characteristics

Knots. Knots are portions of branches which have become incorporated into the bole of the tree during growth. They reduce strength for several reasons. First, the fibers in the knot run generally at right angles to the fiber direction in the wood member. Since the strength perpendicular to grain is lower than that parallel to grain, the strength in the area of the knot is lower than that in the wood surrounding the knot, and thus the overall strength is lessened. Second, the knot represents a discontinuity, and thus stress concentrations result. Third, the grain direction of the wood surrounding the knot is distorted, with the strength suffering because of the local cross grain that results from this distortion. Thus a knot represents a distinct area of weakness in members stressed parallel to grain and must be limited in members in which strength is important. In general, the strength-reducing effect of knots depends on the portion of the cross section that they occupy. In bending members, however, the location of the knot in the cross section is also important. Knots near the extreme fibers are more critical than those near the center of depth. When loads are applied perpendicular to grain, knots actually increase both the hardness and the strength, but they may be objectionable in such applications because they result in uneven wear or stress concentrations.

TABLE 1.4 Moisture Content at Which Properties Change, Due to Drying, for Selected Species

Species	M_p, %
Ash, white	24
Birch, yellow	27
Chestnut, American	24
Douglas fir	24
Hemlock, western	28
Larch, western	28
Pine, loblolly	21
Pine, longleaf	21
Pine, red	24
Redwood	21
Spruce, red	27
Spruce, Sitka	27
Tamarack	24

TABLE 1.5 Approximate Percentage Increase (or Decrease) in Mechanical Properties for 1 Percent Decrease (or Increase) in Moisture Content

Property	Change per 1% change in moisture content,* %
Static bending	
Fiber stress at proportional limit	5
Modulus of rupture	4
Modulus of elasticity	2
Work to proportional limit	8
Work to maximum load	0.5
Impact bending	
Height of drop to cause complete failure	0.5
Compression parallel to grain	
Fiber stress at proportional limit	5
Maximum crushing strength	6
Compression perpendicular to grain	
Fiber stress at proportional limit	5.5
Shear parallel to grain	
Maximum shearing strength	3
Tension perpendicular to grain	
Maximum tensile strength	1.5
Hardness	
End	4
Side	2.5

*Corrections to properties should be made successively for each 1% change in moisture content until the total change has been covered. For example, for a 3% change in moisture content, the calculation would be, for change in modulus of rupture, $(1.04)^3 = 1.125$, or the percentage change is 12.5%.

Grain Direction. The fiber direction may not be parallel to the axis of a structural member for a number of reasons. First, the piece may not have been cut parallel to the fiber direction when it was sawed from the log. Second, the fiber direction may not have been parallel to the axis of the log. In some cases, the fibers in a tree form a spiral rather than being parallel to the length of the trunk. A piece sawn parallel to the axis of a log from such a tree will have the fiber direction at an angle to its axis. Of course, there also may be local irregularities in the grain direction, such as might result if the log were crooked. Whatever the cause, however, cross grain can reduce strength, since a stress parallel to the axis of the piece will have components both parallel and perpendicular to the fiber (grain) direction. Since the strength perpendicular to grain is much smaller than that parallel to grain (Sec. 1.3.1) the perpendicular-to-grain component will limit the strength in a direction parallel to the axis. The steeper the grain slope, the lower the strength parallel to the axis will be, as indicated by the empirical Hankinson equation:

$$N = \frac{PQ}{P \sin^n \theta + Q \cos^n \theta} \tag{1.7}$$

where N is the strength at an angle θ to the grain, and P and Q are the strengths parallel and perpendicular to the grain, respectively. The exponent n is an empirically derived constant ranging from about 1.5 to 2.5. Ranges of n for various properties are given in Chap. 4 of the *Wood Handbook.*[1]

The strengths of wood members loaded at an angle to the grain as a percentage of the strength of a straight-grained member are given in Fig. 1.5 for several properties. The data on which the curves are based came from Chap. 4 of the *Wood Handbook.*[1] and represent strength tests of cross-grained wood.

Ring Orientation. Stresses perpendicular to grain may be oriented at any angle to the annual rings ranging from 0 (tangential direction in the tree or log) to 90° (radial direction). The values of compressive strength perpendicular to grain given in the *Wood Handbook*[1] are derived from tests in which the load is applied in the tangential direction, while the values of tension perpendicular to grain are averages of test values in the tangential and radial directions. The modulus of elasticity is least for the 45° orientation, greatest for the 90° orientation, and intermediate for the 0° orientation. The value of proportional limit stress in compression increases gradually as the ring orientation increases from 0 to 90°.

Longitudinal Separations. Checks, shakes, and splits may result from stresses in the growing tree, from stresses occurring in drying from the green condition, or from mechanical forces. In each case, the longitudinal separations, whether in the longitudinal-radial or in the longitudinal-tangential planes, will result in the loss of strength when a member containing them is subjected to shear, as in a beam or at a mechanical connection.

Reaction Wood. Abnormal woody tissue may occur in the trunk of the growing tree where the trunk has been leaning from the vertical, or it may occur in the branches of the tree. In softwood this abnormal wood is commonly called *compression wood* because it occurs in areas where the stress is compressive, as on the lower side of branches. The reaction wood in hardwoods is commonly called *tension wood* because it occurs in areas of tensile stress in the tree.

Many properties of reaction wood differ from those of normal wood. For example, reaction wood is generally denser than normal wood, with compression wood frequently being 30 to 40 percent higher in specific gravity and tension wood somewhat less high. Compression wood may be somewhat stronger than normal wood, particularly in compression, but it is less strong than normal wood of comparable specific gravity. Both compression wood and tension wood shrink more longitudinally with a change in moisture content than does normal wood. Because of the abnormal properties of reaction wood, it is frequently desirable to restrict or forbid its use in structural members.

Compression Failures. Excessive bending of standing trees by wind or snow, by felling across obstacles, or by rough handling of logs or lumber may result in excessive compressive stresses along the grain, which can cause minute failures. These failures may be evident as lines resulting from crumpling or buckling of the fibers, or they may be invisible to the naked eye. Material containing visible compression failures can have markedly reduced strength in tension and thus in bending and in its ability to withstand shock loads. The tensile strength has been found to be as low as one-third the strength of wood free from compression failures. Even compression failures that cannot be detected visually may cause serious losses of

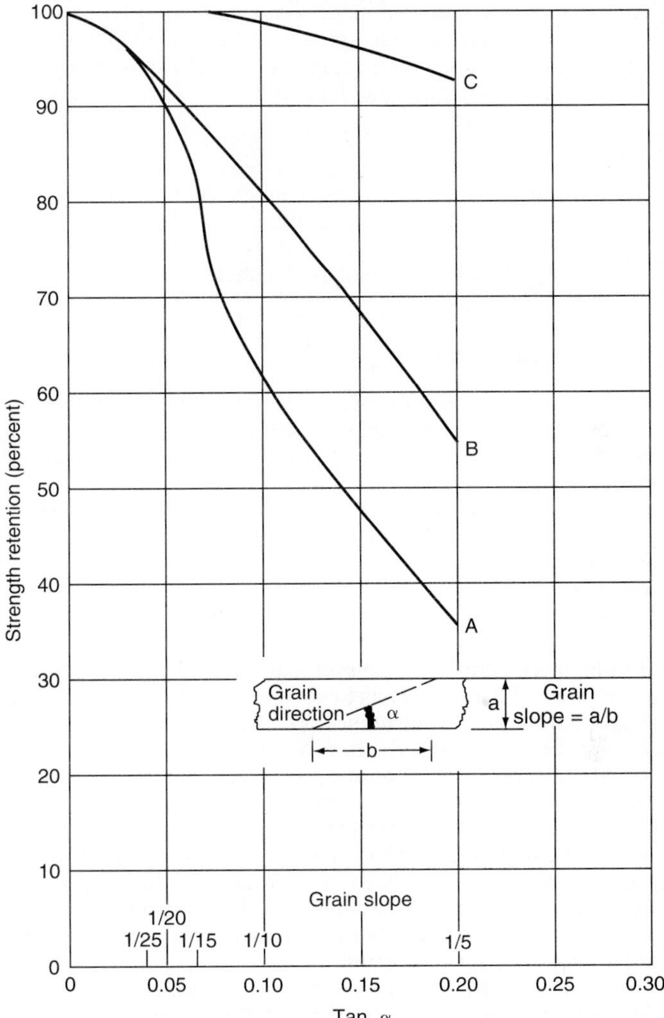

FIG. 1.5 Strengths of wood members with various grain slopes conpared to strength of straight-grained member, expressed as percentages. *A*—Impact bending, height of drop causing complete failure (50-lb hammer); *B*—modulus of rupture; *C*—compression parallel to grain, maximum crushing strength. (*Adapted from* Wood Handbook, *Table 4-9. Courtesy of U.S. Forest Products Laboratory, Madison, Wisc.*)

strength. Because of the difficulty of detecting compression failures, special methods are required in inspection, such as the use of light impinging on the surface at a very low angle and wetting of the surface with a fluid that changes the angle of refraction and emphasizes compression failures.

Pitch Pockets. Pitch pockets generally have relatively small effects on strength, but where they are present in large numbers, deficient bond between annual growth layers may have occurred, and pieces that contain pitch pockets in large number should be inspected for separations along the grain. Pitch may exude from the pockets in service, and while the exudation does not affect the mechanical properties, it may be unsightly and may damage finishes.

1.4.5 Extremes of Temperature

The strength of wood varies with its temperature, although the effects are small enough in the normal temperature range that they may generally be disregarded. Thus, within the usual range to be expected in structures, no special consideration need be given in design to temperature effects.

In general, mechanical properties at temperatures below the normal range are higher than in the normal range. For example, tests at temperatures of about −300°F (−184°C) have shown that the important mechanical properties of dry wood, including shock resistance, are higher than in the normal temperature range. It is this characteristic which led to the structural use of wood in ships designed to transport liquefied gas.

Exposure to high temperatures, however, can weaken wood. This effect may be evidenced in two ways. First, wood has lower strength at elevated temperatures than at normal temperatures. This is an immediate effect while the wood is at the elevated temperature. For short periods of exposure, the wood returns to its normal strength on cooling. If, however, exposure to elevated temperatures is sustained for an extended period, there is a permanent effect. Thus, if a primary structural member is in a position where it will be exposed to elevated temperatures for long periods, this fact must be reflected in design. A girder just above a boiler, for example, would be designed at a lower stress than one which is in a more normal exposure. Wet wood suffers greater strength loss than does dry wood. Thus a beam near a cooking vat emitting steam at high temperature would suffer more than would a similar beam subjected to dry heat.

The approximate immediate effects of temperature on several mechanical properties are illustrated in Figs. 1.6 to 1.8. The effect of dry heat for extended periods on the modulus of rupture is illustrated in Fig. 1.9.

Extremes of temperature are obviously reached when a wood member is subjected to fire, and a fire-exposed face of a wood member will, eventually, flame and become charred, the char having little strength. However, both wood and char are good insulators, and the wood just beyond the char-wood interface will be subjected to temperatures well below those of the flame. The behavior of wood when exposed to fire is discussed in Sec. 1.2.6.

1.4.6 Chemicals

As discussed in Sec. 1.2.7, chemicals may degrade wood, with the degree of degradation being reflected in varying degrees of loss in mechanical properties. Some

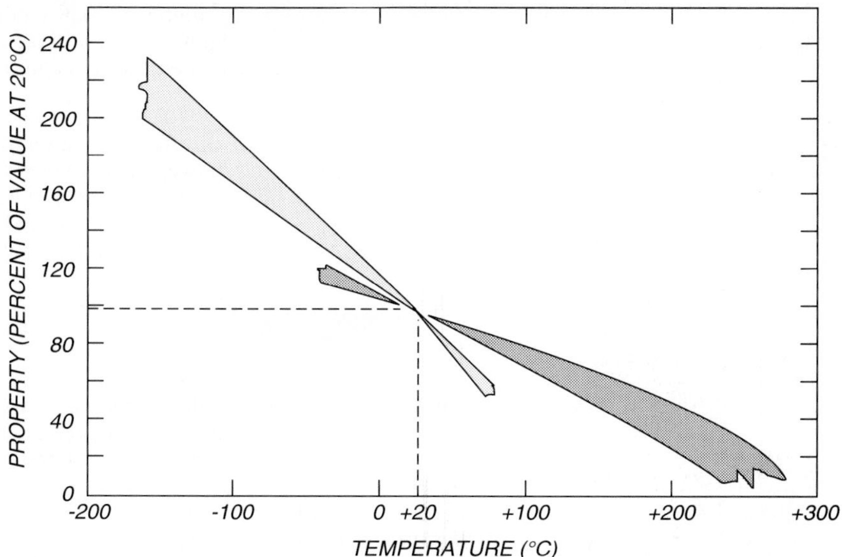

FIG. 1.6 Immediate effect of temperature on strength properties, expressed as percentage of value at 68°F. Trends illustrated are composites from studies on three strength properties—modulus of rupture in bending, tensile strength perpendicular to grain, and compressive strength parallel to grain—as examined by several investigators. Variability in reported results is illustrated by widths of bands. *(Courtesy of U.S. Forest Products Laboratory, Madison, Wisc.)*

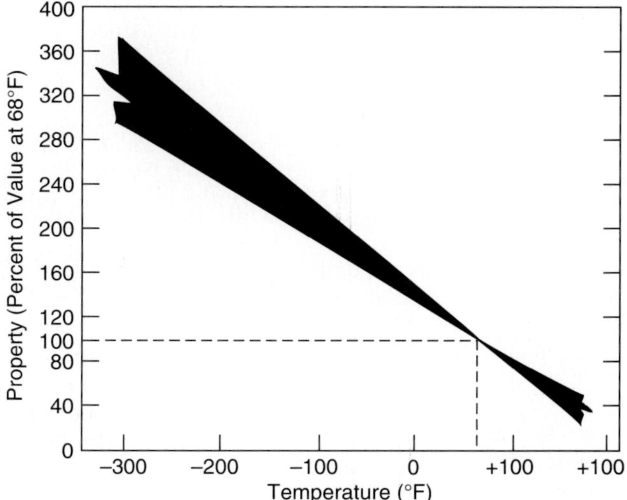

FIG. 1.7 Immediate effect of temperature on proportional limit in compression perpendicular to grain at approximately 12 percent moisture content relative to value at 68°F. Variability in the reported results of several investigators is illustrated by width of band. *(Courtesy of U.S. Forest Products Laboratory, Madison, Wisc.)*

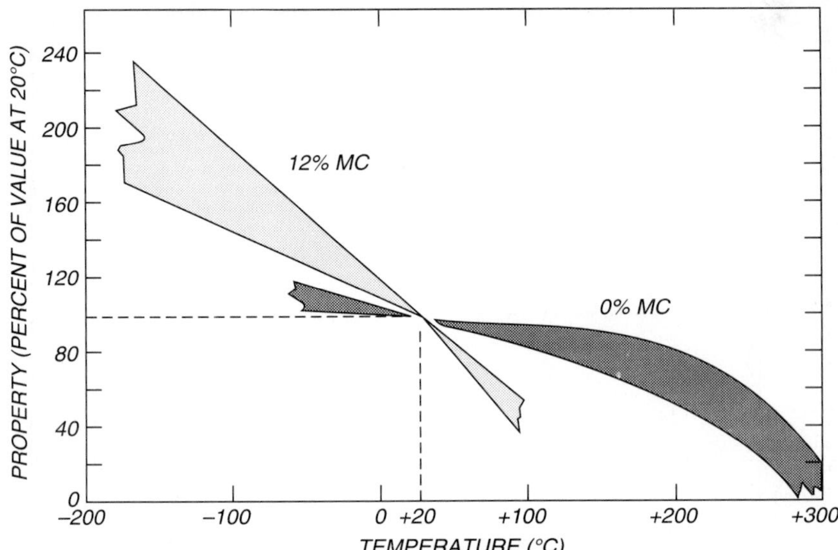

FIG. 1.8 Immediate effect of temperature on modulus of elasticity relative to value at 68°F. Plot is a composite of studies on modulus as measured in bending, tension parallel to grain, and compression parallel to grain by several investigators. Variability in reported results is illustrated by width of bands. (*Courtesy of U.S. Forest Products Laboratory, Madison, Wisc.*)

typical strength loss data are given in Table 1.6. Unfortunately, it is not possible to calculate the service life or the amount of strength loss associated with the length of time a wood member is in contact with a chemical. "Corrosion" rates for wood are simply not available. From knowledge of the factors that affect the rate and amount of chemical reactions, some general ranges may be described. Thus service conditions suitable for the use of wood in contact with chemicals are (1) when the pH of the solution is between 2 and 11, (2) when the temperature is usually less than 122°F (50°C), and (3) when there is no contact with oxidizing chemicals. The service life is shortened at extremes of the pH range, particularly at elevated temperatures.

Fire retardants based on salts are impregnated into wood in high concentrations and have a substantial effect on its strength. For example, the allowable unit stresses for solid structural lumber treated with waterborne salts must be decreased 10 percent. For glued-laminated members, the effect on strength must be determined for each treatment.

1.4.7 Organisms

Decay fungi can cause substantial loss in mechanical properties. This can be quite evident when decay is highly advanced, such as, for example, when the wood has become friable and light in weight. For stages intermediate between the initiation of decay and highly advanced decay, there is no way of estimating accurately the loss in strength and related properties. It is known, however, that marked effects

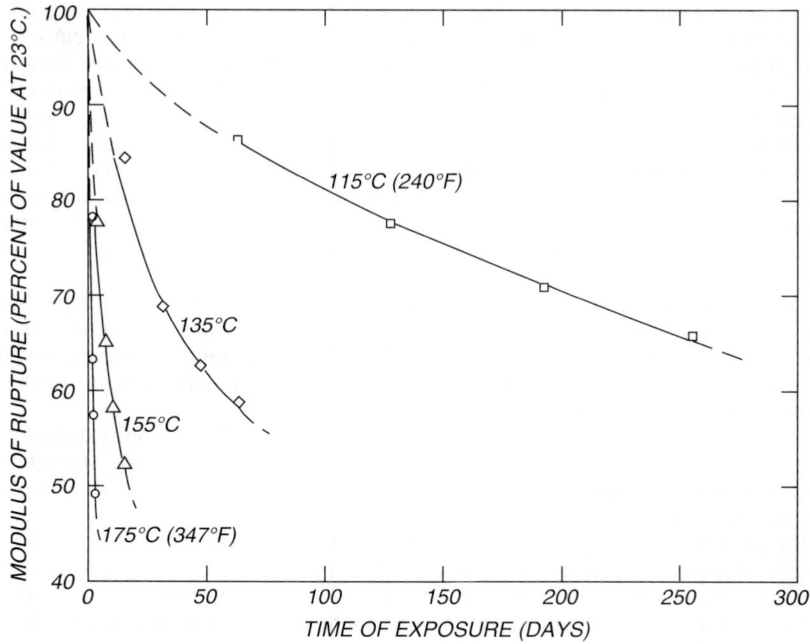

FIG. 1.9 Permanent effect of oven heating at four temperatures on modulus of rupture, based on four softwood and two hardwood species. (*Courtesy of U.S. Forest Products Laboratory, Madison, Wisc.*)

TABLE 1.6 Strength Retention after Chemical Exposure as a Percentage of Water-Soaked Control

Concentration, %	Nitric, %	Sulfuric, %	Acetic, %	Caustic, %
		Douglas fir		
2	80	92	90	22
6	60	89	88	0
		White oak		
2	44	80	101	20
6	13	60	101	0

Source: Ref. 2; used with permission.

TABLE 1.8 Estimated Values for Strength Loss in Softwoods and Hardwoods at Early Stages of Decay (Indicated by Weight Loss) by Brown-Rot and White-Rot Fungi as a Percentage of Values for Nondecayed Samples*

Approximate weight loss, %	Toughness	Impact bending	Static bending: General bending strength	Static bending: Work to maximum load	Static bending: Modulus of rupture	Static bending: Modulus of elasticity	Compression, perpendicular (radial)	Compression, parallel	Tension, parallel	Shear, parallel	Hardness
White rot											
Softwoods											
1	55	—	—	—	—	—	—	—	—	—	—
2	—	—	—	—	—	—	10–20	—	4–38	—	—
4	—	—	—	—	—	—	—	—	8–43	—	—
6	75	—	—	—	—	—	32–61	—	10–49	—	—
8	—	—	—	—	—	—	—	—	14–58	—	—
10	85	—	—	—	—	—	—	—	20–63	—	—
Hardwoods											
1	—	21	—	—	—	—	4	—	—	—	—
2	—	26	—	28–35	13–14	4	5	—	22–42	—	—
4	70	44	—	38	20	—	—	—	17–44	—	—
6	75	50	—	45–53	20–27	10	12–27	14	12–58	—	18
8	—	—	—	—	—	—	—	—	14–49	—	—
10	85	60	—	58	24	14	35	20	20–50	—	25

*Values obtained from published experimental results and adjusted to equivalent weight-loss levels.
Source: After Ref. 3.

snow when evaluating the load-carrying capacity for such structures for continued use.

REFERENCES

1. Forest Products Laboratory, *Wood Handbook,* Agriculture Handbook 72, Forest Service, U.S. Dept. of Agriculture, Washington, D.C., 1987.
2. *Evaluation, Maintenance and Upgrading of Wood Structures—A Guide and Commentary,* Committee on Wood, American Society of Civil Engineers, New York, 1982.
3. W. W. Wilcox, "Review of Literature on the Effects of Early Stages of Decay on Wood Strength," *Wood and Fiber* **9**(4):252–257 (1978).

FURTHER READING

Wood Structures—A Design Guide and Commentary, Committee on Wood, American Society of Civil Engineers, New York, 1975.

CHAPTER 2
PRELIMINARY DESIGN CONSIDERATIONS

Erwin L. Schaffer, Ph.D., P.E

2.1 SPECIES, GRADES, AND SIZES OF LUMBER

2.1.1 Availability

Lumber is probably the most readily available of all building materials, since there are lumber dealers in nearly every community. The stock from which to select, however, varies with the section of the country. As a result, a given species, grade, cross-sectional size, and length which is abundant in one part of the country may not be in another. The designer should contact a local supplier to determine what lumber is commonly stocked and proceed accordingly. In selecting from the available lumber, one often can achieve the same design objectives with a substantial savings in cost. Species that are abundant for use in construction include Douglas fir, western hemlock, southern pine, larch, ponderosa pine, spruce, white pine, white fir, and lodgepole pine. For grading purposes, some species are combined into species groups (e.g., spruce-pine-fir is the spruce, white pine, and eastern fir species; and hem-fir is the West Coast hemlock and white fir species). A complete listing of species and species groups used in construction in the United States and Canada is given in Table 2.1.

2.1.2 Sawn Lumber

Lumber in North America is subdivided into three types based on thickness:

1. *Boards:* Less than 2 in (38.1 mm*) in nominal thickness
2. *Dimension:* From 2 to 4½ in (38.1 to 101.6 mm) in nominal thickness
3. *Timber:* Nominal thickness of 5 in (114.3 mm) or more

*All SI units shown for sawn lumber are for the actual net dimensions corresponding to the nominal dimension indicated. In all example problems, SI units are provided only for given data and the final problem answer or answers. No intermediate values or data are expressed in SI units.

FIG. 2.3 LVL used for flanges in wood I beams. *(Courtesy of Trus Joist MacMillan Corp.)*

TABLE 2.3 Typical Allowable Design Properties for Commercially Available Laminated Veneer Lumber under Dry Conditions of Use (i.e., Moisture Content < 15%)

Property	Range in allowable design stresses, lb/in^2
Bending F_b	1950–3100
Tension F_t	1400–2600
Compression	
Parallel to grain F_c	1950–2850
Perpendicular to grain $F_{c\perp}$	350–775
Shear	
Horizontal	160–250
Across grain	150–285
Modulus of elasticity (MOE), $\times 10^6$	1.8–2.2

Note: 1000 lb/in^2 = 6.895 MPa.

FIG. 2.3 LVL used for flanges in wood I beams. *(Courtesy of Trus Joist MacMillan Corp.)*

TABLE 2.3 Typical Allowable Design Properties for Commercially Available Laminated Veneer Lumber under Dry Conditions of Use (i.e., Moisture Content < 15%)

Property	Range in allowable design stresses, lb/in^2
Bending F_b	1950–3100
Tension F_t	1400–2600
Compression	
Parallel to grain F_c	1950–2850
Perpendicular to grain $F_{c\perp}$	350–775
Shear	
Horizontal	160–250
Across grain	150–285
Modulus of elasticity (MOE), $\times 10^6$	1.8–2.2

Note: 1000 lb/in^2 = 6.895 MPa.

FIG. 2.2 Parallel-strand lumber product produced from long strips of veneer. *(Courtesy of Trus Joist MacMillan Corp.)*

Design property levels for each SCL product commercially produced are available from the manufacturer. Typical allowable design values for commercially available SCL material are given in Table 2.3.

2.1.4 Grading

Sawn lumber quality is more difficult to control than is the quality of many other engineering materials. Even though the wood chemical composition is fixed by nature, tree growth characteristics and the processing of the tree into lumber create lumber of varying quality. To sort lumber into use classes, grading rules have been devised for the various species and species groups. The resulting "grades" provide both a quality basis for the purchase and sale of the material and a means of assessing the structural quality of several classes of lumber. Boards, dimension lumber, and timber are graded for quality.

FIG. 2.1 Laminated veneer lumber of 5¼- and 7½-in depth. *(Courtesy of Trus Joist MacMillan Corp.)*

lumber of the desired depth and length is resawn. The product is produced under both heat and pressure. This normally results in a densification of the wood used. Another structural composite lumber product produced from long strips of veneer (Fig. 2.2) has been developed recently. SCL currently finds specialty use as scaffold planks, headers and beams, chords for trusses, ridge beams in mobile homes, and flanges in I beams (Fig. 2.3).

SCL is available as both "boards" and "dimension," to conform with the definitions for sawn lumber. It is produced in dimensions essentially compatible with sawn lumber sizes. In addition, it can be obtained in widths of up to 24 in (610 mm) net on order.

SCL quality is more easily controlled than that of sawn lumber. This is largely due to the control of strength-reducing characteristics such as slope of grain, knots, and splits allowed in the veneer used to produce the material as well as to the homogenizing effect of laminating many layers, which results in a random dispersal of the defects throughout the member. SCL is graded into strength-stiffness classes by the producer. It is purchased by selecting SCL with properties suitable for the intended end use. Industry standards for SCL are still under development. Individual manufacturers have obtained acceptance of their product by the governing building code bodies.

The term *nominal* is derived from the dimension resulting from the rough sawing of unseasoned (green) lumber. Subsequent planing or seasoning results in a product of smaller cross section, but the nominal original dimension is still applied. A nominal 2- by 4-in stud, for example, is 1½ by 3½ in (38.1 by 88.9 mm) in the fully dried and planed state. The nominal and minimum dressed sizes of lumber are given in Table 2.2.

2.1.3 Structural Composite Lumber (SCL)

One type of structural composite lumber, generically called *laminated veneer lumber* (LVL), has been available since 1971 (Fig. 2.1). Dried veneer or veneer strips are laminated into thick panels [as wide as 4 ft (1.22 m)] and of continuous length parallel to the grain using exterior-quality adhesive. From these panels, structural

TABLE 2.2 American Standard Lumber Sizes (inches) for Stress-Graded and Non-Stress-Graded Lumber for Construction

Item	Nominal thickness*	Minimum dressed thickness		Nominal face width*	Minimum dressed face width	
		Dry	Green		Dry	Green
Boards	1	¾	25⁄32	2	1½	1 9⁄16
	1¼	1	1 1⁄32	3	2½	2 9⁄16
	1½	1¼	1 9⁄32	4	3½	3 9⁄16
				5	4½	4⅝
				6	5½	5⅝
				7	6½	6⅝
				8	7¼	7½
				9	8¼	8½
				10	9¼	9½
				11	10¼	10½
				12	11¼	11½
				14	13¼	13½
				16	15¼	15½
Dimension	2	1½	1 9⁄16	2	1½	1 9⁄16
	2½	2	2 1⁄16	3	2½	2 9⁄16
	3	2½	2 9⁄16	4	3½	3 9⁄16
	3½	3	3 1⁄16	5	4½	4⅝
	4	3½	3 9⁄16	6	5½	5⅝
	4½	4	4 1⁄16	8	7¼	7½
				10	9¼	9½
				12	11¼	11½
				14	13¼	13½
				16	15¼	15½
Timbers	5 and greater		½ less than nominal	5 and greater		½ less than nominal

Note: 1 in = 25.4 mm.
*Nominal sizes are used for convenience. No inference should be drawn that they represent actual sizes.

TABLE 2.1 Species and Species Groups Used in the United States and Canada

Species or species group	Region
Aspen	Northeast, North Central, Northwest
Balsam fir	North Central, Northeast
Black cottonwood	Canada
California redwood	California
Coast Sitka spruce	Canada
Coast species	Canada
Douglas fir–larch	South Dakota and West
Douglas fir–larch (north)	Canada
Douglas fir (south)	Southwest
Eastern hemlock–tamarack	North Central, Northeast
Eastern hemlock–tamarack (north)	Canada
Eastern spruce	North Central, Northeast
Eastern white pine	North Central, Northeast
Eastern white pine (north)	East Canada
Eastern woods	North Central, Northeast
Engelmann spruce–alpine fir	West
Engelmann spruce–lodgepole pine	West
Hem-fir	West
Hem-fir (north)	Canada
Idaho white pine	West
Lodgepole pine	West
Mountain hemlock	Northwest
Mountain hemlock–hem-fir	Northwest
Northern aspen	Canada
Northern pine	North Central, Northeast
Northern species	Canada
Northern white cedar	Northeast
Ponderosa pine	Canada
Ponderosa pine–lodgepole pine	West
Ponderosa pine–sugar pine	West
Red pine	Canada
Sitka spruce	Northwest
Southern pine	South Central, Southeast
Spruce-pine-fir	Canada
Western cedars	West
Western cedars (north)	Canada
Western hemlock	West
Western white pine	Canada
Western woods	West
White woods	West

Source: 1966 National Design Specification for Wood Construction.

CHAPTER 2
PRELIMINARY DESIGN CONSIDERATIONS

Erwin L. Schaffer, Ph.D., P.E

2.1 SPECIES, GRADES, AND SIZES OF LUMBER

2.1.1 Availability

Lumber is probably the most readily available of all building materials, since there are lumber dealers in nearly every community. The stock from which to select, however, varies with the section of the country. As a result, a given species, grade, cross-sectional size, and length which is abundant in one part of the country may not be in another. The designer should contact a local supplier to determine what lumber is commonly stocked and proceed accordingly. In selecting from the available lumber, one often can achieve the same design objectives with a substantial savings in cost. Species that are abundant for use in construction include Douglas fir, western hemlock, southern pine, larch, ponderosa pine, spruce, white pine, white fir, and lodgepole pine. For grading purposes, some species are combined into species groups (e.g., spruce-pine-fir is the spruce, white pine, and eastern fir species; and hem-fir is the West Coast hemlock and white fir species). A complete listing of species and species groups used in construction in the United States and Canada is given in Table 2.1.

2.1.2 Sawn Lumber

Lumber in North America is subdivided into three types based on thickness:

1. *Boards:* Less than 2 in (38.1 mm*) in nominal thickness
2. *Dimension:* From 2 to 4½ in (38.1 to 101.6 mm) in nominal thickness
3. *Timber:* Nominal thickness of 5 in (114.3 mm) or more

*All SI units shown for sawn lumber are for the actual net dimensions corresponding to the nominal dimension indicated. In all example problems, SI units are provided only for given data and the final problem answer or answers. No intermediate values or data are expressed in SI units.

2.2 COMMERCIAL LUMBER STANDARDS

2.2.1 Sawn Lumber

The standards by which lumber is graded are commonly referred to as the *grade rules* for the species or species group. A separate grade-rule manual exists for each of the species groups listed in Table 2.1.

Lumber intended for use in furniture, window and door casings, siding, and a number of specialty materials is graded on the basis of the expected yield of clear, usable material. Lumber graded in this way is not intended to be used for strictly structural applications in an engineering design sense. Some boards are graded in this manner, but such lumber may have unreliable strength properties and is not recommended for use where structural lumber is specified.

Lumber to be used in structural applications is graded on an estimated strength and stiffness property basis. Though the softwood species most commonly comprise structurally graded lumber, a few hardwoods (aspen, yellow poplar, and cottonwood) are structurally graded as well. One can expect to see more hardwoods graded for this use in the future. Dimension lumber and timbers are sorted into structural grades.

Boards, dimension lumber, and timbers are all graded using a "visual" grading technique; that is, the surface of each piece is examined visually by trained and experienced technicians who assess the influence of natural wood characteristics on the end use of the piece. Dimension lumber and timbers are primarily graded based on the influence and these characteristics will have on their strength and stiffness in a given structural use. In this case, structural lumber is defined as being visually stress-graded.

Increasing amounts of structural lumber are also being machine stress-rated (MSR) in addition to being visually stress-rated. The combined visually stress-graded and MSR technique allows the strength and stiffness to be defined more narrowly, thereby increasing the reliability of performance. The organizational responsibilities and techniques for grading are discussed in what follows.

Organizational Responsibilities for Stress Grades. An orderly, voluntary, but circuitous system of responsibilities has evolved in the United States for the development, manufacture, and merchandizing of most stress-graded lumber. The system is shown schematically in Fig. 2.4. Stress-grading principles are developed from research findings and engineering concepts, often within committees and subcommittees of the American Society for Testing and Materials (ASTM).

The National Institute of Standards and Technology cooperates with lumber producers, distributors, and users through an American Lumber Standards Committee (ALSC) to assemble a voluntary softwood standard of manufacture, called the *American Softwood Lumber Standards*. PS 20-94.[1] The *American Softwood Lumber Standards* and the related *National Grading Rule* prescribe the ways in which stress-grading principles can be used to formulate grading rules said to be American Standard.

Most commercial softwoods are stress-graded under standard practice in the United States. The principles of stress grading also can be applied to hardwoods, several of which are graded under provisions of the *American Softwood Lumber Standards*.

Lumber found in the marketplace may be stress-graded by methods approved by the ALSC or by some other grading rule, or it may not be stress-graded. Stress grades that meet the requirements of the voluntary *American Softwood Lumber*

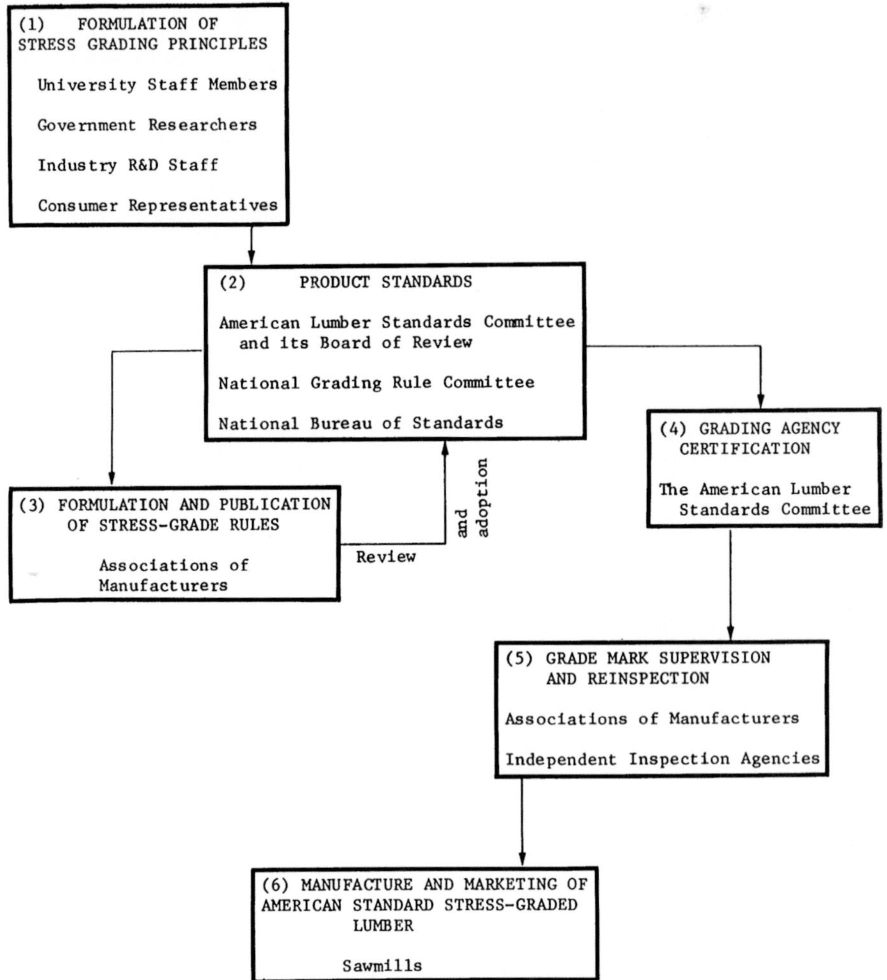

FIG. 2.4 Voluntary system of responsibility for stress grading under the *American Softwood Lumber Standard.*

Standards are developed by the principles that have been described in this chapter, and only these stress grades are discussed here.

Stress grading under the auspices of the ALSC is applied to many of the sizes and several of the patterns of lumber meeting the provisions of the *American Softwood Lumber Standards*. A majority of stress-graded lumber is dimension, however, and a uniform procedure, the *National Grading Rules,* is used for writing grading rules for this size lumber. Grade rules for other sizes may vary by grading agencies or species.

The *American Softwood Lumber Standards*[1] provide for a national grading rule for lumber from 2 in (38.1 mm) up to, but not including, 5 in (114 mm) in nominal thickness (dimension lumber). All American Standard lumber in that size range is required to conform to the *National Grading Rules,* except for special products such as scaffold planks.

The *National Grading Rules* establish the lumber classifications and grade names for visually stress-graded lumber as shown in Table 2.4. The approximate minimum bending strength ratio is also shown to provide a comparative index of quality. The corresponding visual descriptions of the grades can be found in the grading rule books of most of the softwood rule-writing agencies listed in Table 2.5. Grades of lumber that meet these requirements should have about the same appearance regardless of species. They will not have the same allowable properties. The allowable strength properties for each species and grade are given in the appropriate rule books and in the *National Design Specification* (NDS).[11]

The *National Grading Rules* also establish limitations on the sizes of permissible edge knots and other visual characteristics for American Standard lumber that is graded by a combination of mechanical and visual methods.

Some species are commonly grouped together, and the lumber from them is treated as equivalent. This usually has been done for species that have about the same mechanical properties, for the wood of two or more species that are very similar in appearance, or for marketing convenience. For visual stress grades, ASTM D 2555, *Standard Methods for Establishing Clear Wood Strength Values,*[2] contains rules for calculating clear wood properties for groups of species. The properties assigned to a group by such a procedure often will not be identical with any one of the species that make up the group. The group will display a unique identity with nomenclature approved by the ALSC. The grading association under whose auspices the lumber was graded should be contacted if the identities, properties, and characteristics of individual species of the group are desired.

In the case of mechanical stress grading, the inspection agency that supervises the grading certifies by test that the allowable properties in the grading rule are appropriate for the species or species group and the grading process.

Lumber Stress-Grade Development. A stress grade is characterized by

1. One or more sorting criteria
2. A set of allowable properties for engineering design
3. A unique grade name

Discussed here are sorting criteria for two stress-grading methods, along with the philosophy of how allowable properties are derived. The allowable properties depend on the particular sorting criteria and on additional factors that are independent of the sorting criteria. Allowable properties are different from, and usually much lower than, the properties of clear straight-grained wood.

From one to six allowable properties are associated with a stress grade—modulus of elasticity and stresses in tension and compression parallel to grain, in compression perpendicular to grain, in shear parallel to grain, and in extreme fiber in bending. As with any structural material, the strength properties used to derive the five allowable stresses must be inferred or measured nondestructively to avoid damage to pieces of lumber. Any nondestructive test provides both sorting criteria and a means of calculating appropriate mechanical properties.

The philosophies outlined are used by a number of organizations to develop commercial stress grades. The exact procedures used and the resulting allowable stresses are not detailed, but reference to them is given.

TABLE 2.4 Strength Ratios, Quality Factors, and Special Adjustments

Category	Grade	$F_b^{a,b}$ Strength ratio	$F_b^{a,b}$ Depth[c]	F_t Strength ratio	F_t Special reduction[d]	Strength ratio F_c	Strength ratio F_v	Strength ratio $F_{c\perp}$	Quality factor Q
Structural light framing	Select structural	67	0.9397	67		78	50	100	100
	No. 1	55	0.9397	55		62	50	100	100
	No. 2	45	0.9397	45		49	50	100	90
	No. 3	26	0.9397	26		30	50	100	80
Light framing	Construction	34	0.9397	34		56	50	100	80
	Standard	19	0.9397	19		46	50	100	80
	Utility	9	0.9397	9		30	50	100	80
Studs	Studs (2 to 4 in wide)	26	0.9397	26		30	50	100	80
	Studs (5 to 6 in wide)	26	0.8937	26	0.80				
Structural joists and planks	Select structural	65	0.8254	65	1.00	69	50	100	100
	No. 1	55	0.8254	55	1.00	62	50	100	100
	No. 2	45	0.8254	45	0.80	52	50	100	90
	No. 3	26	0.8254	26	0.80	33	50	100	80
Beams and stringers	Strength ratio 86	86	[e]	86	NA[f]	90	50	100	100
	Strength ratio 72	72	0.8195	72	NA	80	50	100	100
	Select structural	65	0.7743	65	NA	75	50	100	100
	No. 1	55		55	NA	62	50	100	100
Posts and timbers	Strength ratio 86	86	[e]	86	NA	90	50	100	100
	Strength ratio 72	72	0.8195	72	NA	80	50	100	100
	Select structural	65	0.7743	65	NA	75	50	100	100
	No. 1	55		55	NA	62	50	100	100

[a]For multiple-member use, see "Allowable Unit Stresses for Lumber Grades" in Ref. 12

[b]The strength ratios shown are the minimum ratios specified by the *National Grading Rule* for each grade category. The depth factor reflects adjustment for maximum width. Actual practice most commonly deviates from this simplified presentation.

[c]These depth adjustments assume dry ALS sizes, except as noted.

[d]No adjustment required for 2- to 4-in width. Where a factor is given, it applies to 5- and 6-in nominal widths only. For 8-in width, the factors are 0.90 for select structural, 0.80 for No. 1, and 0.64 for Nos. 2 and 3. For 10 in and wider, use 0.80 for select structural, 0.60 for No. 1, and 0.48 for Nos. 2 and 3.

[e]0.8195 applies to actual widths 12 in and less; 0.7743 applies to actual widths 12 to 20 in.

[f]NA = not applicable.

TABLE 2.5 Organizations Promulgating Softwood Grades

Name and address	Species covered by grading rules
National Hardwood Lumber Association 58 East Van Buren Street Chicago, IL 60605	Baldcypress, eastern redcedar
Northeastern Lumber Manufacturers Association, Inc. 13 South Street Glens Falls, NY 12801	Balsam fir, eastern white pine, red pine, eastern hemlock, black spruce, white spruce, red spruce, pitch pine, tamarack, jack pine, northern white cedar
Northern Hardwood and Pine Manufacturers Association Suite 207, Northern Building Green Bay, WI 54301	Bigtooth aspen, quaking aspen, eastern white pine, red pine, jack pine, black spruce, white spruce, red spruce, balsam fir, eastern hemlock, tamarack
Red Cedar Shingle and Handsplit Shake Bureau 5510 White Building Seattle, WA 98101	Western redcedar (shingles and shakes)
Redwood Inspection Service 617 Montgomery Street San Francisco, CA 94111	Redwood
Southern Cypress Manufacturers Association P.O. Box 5816 Jacksonville, FL 32207	Baldcypress
Southern Pine Inspection Bureau Box 846 Pensacola, FL 32502	Longleaf pine, slash pine, shortleaf pine, loblolly pine, Virginia pine, pond pine, pitch pine
West Coast Lumber Inspection Bureau Box 25406 1750 SW. Skyline Boulevard Portland, OR 97225	Douglas fir, western hemlock, western redcedar, incense cedar, Port Orford cedar, Alaska cedar, western true firs, mountain hemlock, Sitka spruce
Western Wood Products Association 700 Yeon Building Portland, OR 97204	Ponderosa pine, western white pine, Douglas fir, sugar pine, western true firs, western larch, Engelmann spruce, incense cedar, western hemlock, lodgepole pine, western redcedar, mountain hemlock, red alder

Visual-Sorting Criteria. Visual grading is the oldest stress-grading method. It is based on the premise that mechanical properties of lumber differ from mechanical properties of clear wood because of characteristics that can be seen and judged by eye. These visual characteristics are used to sort the lumber into stress grades. The following are major visual-sorting criteria.

Density. Strength is related to the weight or the density of clear wood. Properties assigned to lumber are sometimes modified by using the rate of growth and the percentage of latewood as measures of density. Selection for rate of growth requires that the number of annual rings per inch be within a specified range. It is possible to eliminate some very low strength pieces from a grade by excluding those which are exceptionally light in weight.

Decay. Decay in most forms should be severely restricted or prohibited in stress grades because its extent is difficult to determine and its effect on strength is often greater than visual observation would indicate. Limited decay of the pocket type (e.g., *Fomes pini*) can be permitted to some degree in stress grades, as can decay that occurs in knots but does not extend into the surrounding wood.

Heartwood and Sapwood. Heartwood and sapwood of the same species have equal mechanical properties, and no heartwood requirement needs to be made in stress grading. Since heartwood of some species is more resistant to decay than sapwood, heartwood may be required if the untreated wood is to be exposed to a decay hazard. On the other hand, sapwood takes preservative treatment more readily and should not be limited in lumber that is to be treated.

Slope of Grain. In zones of cross grain, the direction of the wood fibers is not parallel to the edges of the lumber. Cross grain reduces the mechanical properties of lumber. Severely cross-grained pieces are also undesirable because they tend to warp with changes in moisture content. Stresses caused by shrinkage during drying are greater in structural lumber than in small, clear specimens and are increased in zones of sloping or distorted grain.

Knots. Knots interrupt the direction of grain and cause localized cross grain with steep slopes. Intergrown or live knots resist some kinds of stress, but encased knots or knotholes transmit little or no stress. On the other hand, distortion of grain is greater around an intergrown knot than around an encased or dead knot. As a result, overall strength effects are roughly equalized, and often no distinction is made in stress grading between live knots, dead knots, and knotholes.

The zone of distorted grain (cross grain) around a knot has less "parallel to piece" stiffness than straight-grained wood. Thus localized areas of low stiffness are often associated with knots. Such zones generally comprise only a minor part of the total volume of a piece of lumber, however, and overall piece stiffness reflects the character of all parts.

The presence of a knot in a piece modifies some of the clear wood strength properties more than it affects the overall stiffness. The effect of a knot on strength depends approximately on the proportion of the cross section of the piece of lumber occupied by the knot, on knot location, and on the distribution of stress in the piece. Limits on knot sizes are therefore made in relation to the width of and location on the face in which the knot appears. Compression members are stressed about equally throughout, and no limitation related to the location of knots is imposed. In tension, knots along the edge of a member produce an eccentricity that induces bending stresses and are therefore restricted more than knots away from the edge. In structural members subjected to simple span bending, stresses are greater in the middle part of the length and in the outer fibers of the tension and compression zones. These facts can be recognized by differing limitations on the sizes of knots in different locations.

Shake. Shake in members subjected to bending reduces the resistance to shear and therefore is limited most closely in those parts of a bending member where shear stresses are highest. In a member subjected only to tension or compression, a shake does not greatly affect its strength. However, there may be a limit because of appearance and because it permits entrance of moisture, which may result in decay.

Checks and Splits. While a shake indicates a weakness of fiber bond that is presumed to extend lengthwise without limit, checks and splits are rated only by the area of actual opening. An end split is considered equal to an end check that extends through the full thickness of the piece. The effects of checks and splits on strength and the principles of their limitation are the same as for a shake.

Wane. Requirements of appearance, fabrication, or the need for ample bearing or nailing surfaces generally impose stricter limitations on wane than does strength. Wane is therefore limited in structural lumber on these bases.

Pitch Pockets. Pitch pockets ordinarily have so little effect on structural lumber that they can be disregarded in stress grading if they are small and limited in number. The presence of a large number of pitch pockets, however, may indicate a shake or a weakness of bond between annual rings.

Developing Mechanical Grades. The mechanical stress grading of lumber is the assignment of an allowable stress to lumber intended for structural use by nondestructively measuring several other physical properties that are correlated. A common, popularly used term for mechanically stress-graded lumber is *MSR lumber*. As generally used, mechanical stress grading, including MSR, is based on an observed relation between the modulus of elasticity and the bending strength, tensile strength, or compressive strength parallel to grain. The modulus of elasticity of the lumber is the sorting criterion used in this method of grading. Mechanical devices operating at relatively high rates of speed measure the modulus of elasticity or stiffness for sorting into a series of stress grades.

Mechanical-Sorting Criteria. The modulus of elasticity used as a sorting criterion for mechanical properties of lumber can be measured in a variety of ways. Usually the apparent modulus or a stiffness-related deflection is the actual measurement used. Because lumber is heterogeneous, the apparent modulus of elasticity depends on span, orientation (edgewise or flatwise in bending), mode of test (static or dynamic), and method of loading (tension, bending, concentrated, uniform, etc.). Any of the apparent moduli can be used as long as the grading machine is calibrated properly to give the appropriate strength property. Most grading machines in the United States are designed to detect the lowest flatwise bending stiffness that occurs in any approximately 4-ft (1.22-m) span of the piece.

Deriving Properties of Mechanically Graded Lumber. A stress grade derived for mechanically graded lumber relates allowable strength in bending and in compression and tension parallel to grain to the modulus of elasticity levels by which the grade is identified. This relationship between properties is selected so that 95 percent of the pieces encountered will be at least as strong as indicated by the grading process. Figure 2.5 shows an example of a relationship between bending strength and the modulus of elasticity as measured in flatwise bending over an 80-in (2.03-m) span.

As in visual grading, the modulus of elasticity assigned to a grade is intended to be an average value for the grade. However, because the basis for mechanical stress grading is the sorting of lumber by modulus of elasticity classes, machines can be adjusted so that the modulus for a grade varies less in a mechanical stress grade than in a visual stress grade.

Strengths in shear parallel to grain and in compression perpendicular to grain have not been shown to be well correlated with the modulus of elasticity. Therefore, in mechanical stress grading these properties are still handled in relation to clear wood properties and the visually assessed characteristics of lumber.

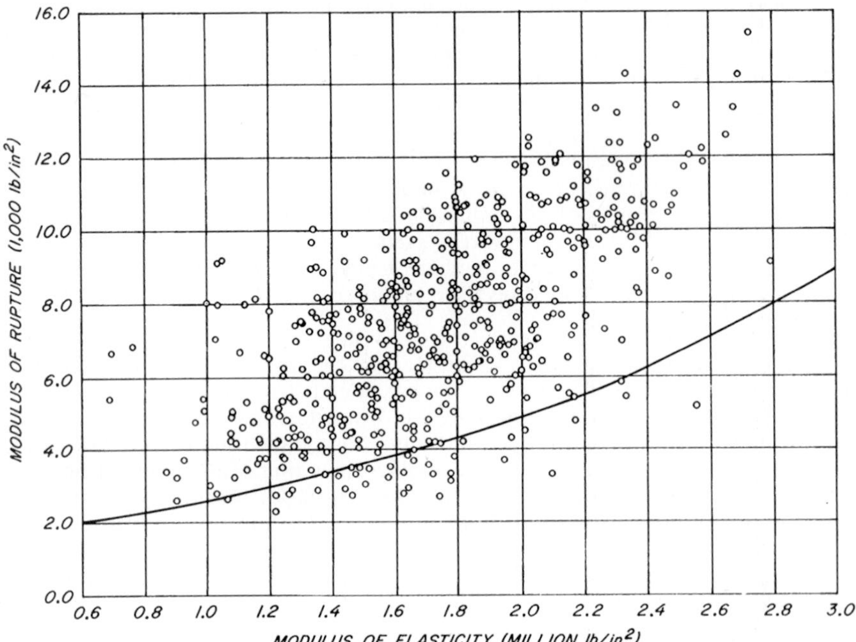

FIG. 2.5 Modulus of elasticity as a predictor of modulus of rupture (———, 5 percent exclusion line).

Most commercial mechanical-grading practices in the United States combine a modified strength ratio procedure with the measured modulus of elasticity as a predictor of grade properties. Emphasis is placed on edge defects when deriving the limitations to visual characteristics of the grade. It has been shown that the strength ratio and the measured modulus of elasticity used together provide a more reliable strength prediction than either by itself.

Allowable Properties for Design. The derivation of mechanical properties of visually graded lumber is based on clear wood properties and on the lumber characteristics allowed by the visual-sorting criteria. The influence of the sorting criteria is handled with *strength ratios* for the strength properties of wood and with *quality factors* for the modulus of elasticity.

From piece to piece, there is variation both in the clear wood properties and in the occurrence of the property-modifying characteristics. The influence of this variability on lumber properties is handled differently for strength than it is for the modulus of elasticity.

Once the clear wood properties have been modified for the influence of sorting criteria and variability, additional modifications for size, moisture content, and load duration are applied.

The visual lumber-grading system employed in the United States and Canada is based on two key standards, ASTM D 2555[2] and ASTM D 245, *Standard Methods for Establishing Structural Grades and Related Allowable Properties for Visually*

Graded Lumber.[3] These standards function in sequence, with clear wood properties cataloged and grouped by ASTM D 2555 and the adjustments for design derived from ASTM D 245. These ASTM standards are equally applicable to hardwoods and to softwoods, although they have been applied much more generally to softwoods.

This discussion cannot cover all possible aspects of the derivation process. (In fact, the ASTM standards also fail to do that.) When these procedures become "institutionalized" through repetitive use by a lumber rule-writing agency, key decisions must be made that relate practical concerns for uniformity and standardization to the procedures permitted by ASTM. For example, the strength ratios used by grading agencies for specific lumber grade-size combinations sometimes exceed those nominally assigned to a grade because the critical defect (for uniformity or efficiency) is more limiting (smaller) than that required by the *National Grading Rules.*

There are no specific strength-ratio requirements under PS 20-94[1] for sizes other than dimension. Consequently, a grade of timber (beams and stringers or posts and timbers) defined by one grading agency may differ slightly from that of another. In southern pine, for example, timber is graded uniformly along the length. By contrast, some western timber has particular restrictions on the middle third of the piece, corresponding to the presumed region of maximum bending moment in end use as a simple span beam. Such differences are permitted under PS 20-70.[1] Similar interpretations of ASTM standards are important, but all cannot be chronicled here.

In the application of ASTM D 245[3] under American Lumber Standard PS 20-70,[1] lumber nominally 2 through 4½ in (38.1 through 101.6 mm) thick, termed *dimension,* is governed by the *National Grading Rules.* One feature that must be followed uniformly between agencies is the minimum strength ratio in bending applicable to a grade. Strength ratios for other properties are consistent as well, because the *National Grading Rules* also specify knots and other characteristics permitted in dimension lumber.

It is frequently desirable for marketing purposes to combine or group species that have relatively similar properties. ASTM procedures seek equitable treatment for each species in a group or combination by weighting factors based on standing timber volume. A species weighting factor is the ratio of the individual species volume to the combined volume of all species in the combination.

The allowable properties in design for bending, tension parallel to grain, compression parallel to grain, and shear are based on the lower 5 percent exclusion level of each clear wood property, as cataloged in ASTM D 2555,[2] with adjustments as follows:

$$\begin{matrix}\text{5\% exclusion}\\ \text{value of}\\ \text{clear wood}\end{matrix} \times \begin{matrix}\text{seasoning}\\ \text{increase}\end{matrix} \times \begin{matrix}\text{general adjust-}\\ \text{ment factor}\end{matrix} \times \begin{matrix}\text{size}\\ \text{effect}\end{matrix} \times \begin{matrix}\text{strength}\\ \text{ratio}\end{matrix}$$

For compression perpendicular to grain and the elastic modulus, the allowable properties are derived from average clear wood properties as follows:

$$\begin{matrix}\text{Clear wood}\\ \text{average}\\ \text{value}\end{matrix} \times \begin{matrix}\text{seasoning}\\ \text{increase}\end{matrix} \times \begin{matrix}\text{general adjust-}\\ \text{ment factor}\end{matrix} \times \begin{matrix}\text{grade}\\ \text{factor}\end{matrix}$$

These factors will be discussed in turn.

Clear Wood Stresses. This section shows how for clear, unseasoned wood, stresses are assigned for individual species and for marketing groups. The modulus of rupture, tension and compression parallel to grain, and shear strength are near minimum property values (5 percent exclusion limits). Compression perpendicular to grain and the modulus of elasticity are average values.

The lower 5th percentile exclusion limits (EL) for individual species are calculated as

$$\mathrm{EL} = \bar{x} - 1.645s \tag{2.1}$$

where $\bar{x}$ and s are estimates of species averages and standard deviation, respectively, as taken from ASTM D 2555.[2] This estimates wood property levels which would be exceeded 95 percent of the time. Exclusion limits for species combinations are the lower 5th percentile of the volume-weighted frequency distribution (see ASTM D 2555,[2] paragraphs 5.2.2.2 and 5.3.2.2).

Some softwood clear wood stresses and their standard deviations are given in Table 2.6.

In-Grade Testing. In 1978, the lumber industry in cooperation with the USDA Forest Service, Forest Products Laboratory, began an extensive program of testing on full-size dimension lumber members. The objective of the study was to evaluate the properties of commercially produced structural lumber. Specimens to be tested were selected from within the existing lumber grades—thus the term *in-grade*.

Approximately 73,000 specimens were tested in bending, tension, and compression parallel to grain. Tests were conducted in accordance with ASTM D 4761, *Standard Test Methods for Mechanical Properties of Lumber and Wood-Base Structural Material*. The data were analyzed using ASTM D 1990, *Standard Practice for Establishing Allowable Properties for Visually Graded Dimension Lumber from In-Grade Tests of Full-Size Specimens*. In June 1991, new allowable properties were approved by the ALSC for all species sold as structural lumber in the United States.

The principal changes that resulted from the in-grade testing program for dimension lumber are

1. There is now a different allowable design value for each width of member. For example, 2 × 4s, 2 × 6s, 2 × 8s, 2 × 10s, and 2 × 12s each have different design values.
2. All dimension lumber has one moisture designation, KD19.

A comparison of the design stresses given in the 1991 NDS Supplement with those published in the 1986 NDS Supplement shows the following:

1. Design values for bending and tension parallel to grain for the narrow widths (2 × 4) and the highest grades are generally higher in the 1991 NDS.
2. Most design values for bending for the wide widths (2 × 10) and wider are lower in the 1991 NDS.
3. Many of the values for the modulus of elasticity E are slightly lower in the 1991 NDS, particularly for the lower lumber grades.
4. Compression parallel to grain design values are significantly higher in the 1991 NDS.

TABLE 2.6 Clear Wood Strength Values Unadjusted for End Use and Measures of Variation for Commercial Species of Wood in the Unseasoned Condition

Species	Modulus of rupture,* lb/in^2		Modulus of elasticity, 1000 lb/in^2		Compression parallel to grain, crushing strength, maximum, lb/in^2		Shear strength, lb/in^2		Compression perpendicular to grain, fiber stress at proportional limit, lb/in^2	
	Average	Standard deviation	Average	Standard deviation	Average	Standard deviation	Average	Standard deviation	Average	Standard deviation
Douglas fir (Canada)	7540	1206	1613	355	3610	650	922	129	460	129
Western hemlock (United States)	6637	1088	1307	258	3364	615	864	105	282	79
Idaho white pine (United States)	5220	835	1168	257	2650	477	635	89	238	67
Sitka spruce (United States)	5660	906	1230	271	2670	481	757	106	279	78

Note: 1000 lb/in^2 = 6.895 MPa.
*For clear wood tension, use modulus of rupture values.

The in-grade testing program did not include timbers, members with a nominal cross section of 5 × 5 inches or greater. Design values for these remain essentially the same in the 1991 and 1986 NDSs.

Seasoning and General Adjustment Factors. The following adjustment factors apply to sawn lumber.

Seasoning Adjustments. Most wood structures become seasoned in the service environment and remain quite dry. This increases their strength and elastic properties over the unseasoned values. Table 2.7 lists permissible increases for various properties of unseasoned lumber for use conditions of 19 percent moisture content or less. The increases are variable according to species, but the percentages given can be safely applied to most North American species.

Modification for Density. Strength properties may be increased by 17 percent and the modulus of elasticity by 5 percent for lumber qualifying as dense.

General Adjustment Factor. For each property, this factor brings together two or more conditions which differentiate test values from commercial wood values, as listed in Table 2.8 and discussed hereafter.

Duration of Load. Wood strength properties are dependent on the rate of loading.[4,5] Ultimate strengths are higher if loading is rapid. Wood will resist high load for short time periods and low load for very long time periods. Figure 2.6 is a load-duration curve showing the relationship between the ultimate bending strength by the short-term laboratory test and that for longer time periods.

Allowable strength properties are established for a cumulative duration of maximum load of 10 years during the total life of a structure, which is generally accepted as good practice for most building conditions. For example, the 10-year strength for softwoods in bending is 62.5 percent of the laboratory test values, as shown by Fig. 2.6.

The relationship is similar for other ultimate properties: 67 percent for compression parallel to grain and 62.5 percent for tension and shear parallel to grain. For compression perpendicular to grain, a proportional limit property value of 110 percent is used. The elastic modulus is not affected by load duration for general structural applications.

The 110 percent for compression perpendicular to grain warrants further clarification. This factor is applied to an average proportional limit property to produce an average ultimate property, and it contains an increase component to account for

TABLE 2.7 Increase of Properties of Unseasoned Lumber for Use Conditions of 19 Percent Moisture or Less

Property	Permissible increase, %
Bending	25
Modulus of elasticity	14
Tension parallel to grain	25
Compression parallel to grain	50
Shear parallel to grain	8
Compression perpendicular to grain	50

TABLE 2.8 General Adjustment Factors and Their Components

Property	Duration of load	Manufacture and use	Stress concentration	End position	Shear strain	General adjustment factor	Applied to
Bending	0.625	0.769	—	—	—	0.481	5% EV*
Compression parallel to grain	0.667	0.800	—	—	—	0.533	5% EV
Tension parallel to grain	0.625	0.769	—	—	—	0.481	5% EV
Shear parallel to grain	0.625	0.888	0.444	—	—	0.246	5% EV
Compression perpendicular to grain	1.100	0.909	—	0.667	—	0.667	Average
Elastic modulus	1.000	1.000	—	—	1.064	1.064	Average

*EV = exclusion value.

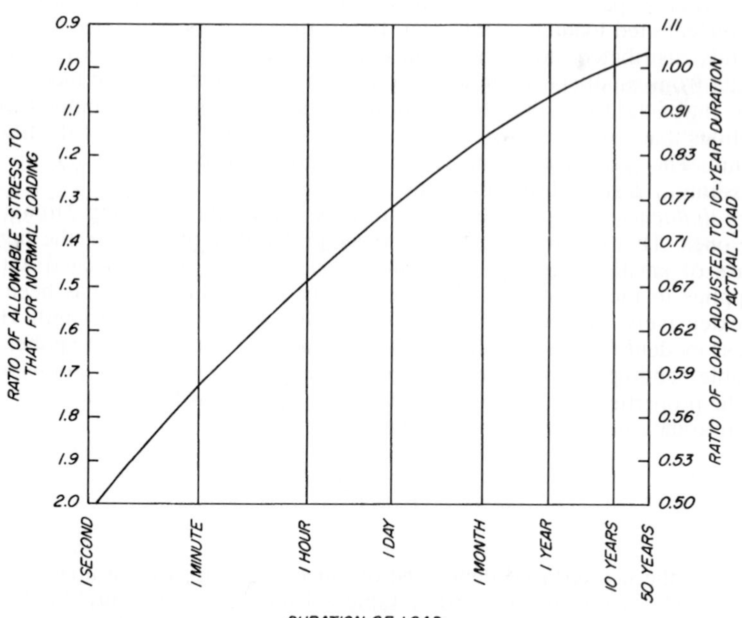

FIG. 2.6 Relation of strength to duration of load.

TABLE 2.10 Allowable Clear Wood Properties for Western Hemlock for Use at 19% Maximum Moisture Content

Property	5% exclusion value, lb/in²	Seasoning increase	General adjustment factor	Size effect	Clear wood allowable
Bending	4847	1.25	0.481	0.86	2506
Compression parallel to grain	2352	1.50	0.533	—	1880
Tension parallel to grain	4847	1.25	0.481	—	2914
Shear parallel to grain	691	1.08	0.246	—	184
Compression perpendicular to grain	282*	1.50	0.667	—	282
Elastic modulus	1,307,000*	1.14	1.064	—	1,585,339

Note: 1000 lb/in² = 6.895 MPa.
*Average values.

used for all widths, and the grade descriptions are written for defect size limitations that will introduce compensation for wider or narrower lumber.

The clear wood allowable properties are then multiplied by the strength ratios to obtain the grade allowable properties, as shown in Table 2.11. Some rounding, according to ASTM D 245,[3] is allowed. The resulting properties are those published for western hemlock graded by the Western Wood Products Association (WWPA), with two exceptions. The tension properties for No. 2 and No. 3 grades published

TABLE 2.11 Allowable Properties for Visually Stress-Graded Structural Joists and Planks of Western Hemlock for Use at 19% Maximum Moisture Content

Property	Select structural	No. 1	No. 2	No. 3
Bending,* lb/in²	1550	1350	1100	650
Compression parallel to grain, lb/in²	1300	1150	975	625
Tension parallel to grain, lb/in²	1050	900	750	425
Shear parallel to grain, lb/in²	90	90	90	90
Compression perpendicular to grain, lb/in²	280	280	280	280
Elastic modulus/1000, lb/in²	1600	1600	1400	1300

Note: 1000 lb/in² = 6.895 MPa.
*May be increased 15% for multiple-member use.

by WWPA are slightly lower. These values were reduced on the basis of studies by that organization which indicated that more conservative values were in order. Rules-writing agencies are always allowed to take more conservative positions if they wish to do so. Also, the published shear property is one-half the derived value as an additional provision for the possible occurrence of an end split after grading.

Machine Stress Grades. The determination of allowable design properties for machine stress grades recognizes the same adjustment factors, except strength ratios for bending, tension, and compression parallel to grain. For these properties, the defined relationship between the strength properties and the elastic modulus replaces the function of the strength ratio. This relationship is established from the testing of full-sized lumber of structural quality. The 5 percent exclusion level for residuals from regression is determined and used in place of the 5 percent exclusion level for clear wood specimens. The moisture-content adjustment is not required if the regression is for seasoned lumber, as is usually the case. The values of shear and compression perpendicular to grain, which are constant for all visual grades, are also constant for all machine stress grades and are determined by the strength-ratio method.

The elastic modulus is measured by the machine directly and does not need to be estimated. The size effect is introduced by proper machine calibration for each width setting.

The 900f-1.0*E* through 3300f-2.6*E* grades given in Table 2.12 are typical machine stress grades.

Repetitive Member Systems. Roof and floor systems are usually supported by multiples of joists or rafters closely spaced and connected to a load-distributing deck or bridging. This forces the joists and rafters to deflect together rather than singly. Since the joists and rafters vary in elastic properties, they assume loads in proportion to their stiffness. Thus, since strength is related directly to elastic properties, the stronger members carry the higher loads.

When the spacing between members is 24 in or less, it is customary to increase the bending strength for design by 15 percent. This increase is generally taken for floor and roof systems and for tongue-and-groove–connected deck planks.

2.2.2 Structural Composite Lumber (SCL)

Design Properties. ASTM D 5456-93 Standard Specifications for Evaluation of Structural Composite Lumber Products (24) is the first common standard developed for these products. Based on the provisions at ASTM D 5456 individual manufacturers have obtained acceptance of their product by the governing building code bodies and maintain a quality-control program to ensure continued product quality. Design property levels for each SCL product commercially produced are available from the manufacturer. Typical allowable design properties for commercially available SCL are given in Table 2.3. These values typically exceed those assigned to the select structural, dense, grade species of structural sawn lumber.

General Adjustment Factors. The behavior of SCL compared with sawn lumber is still undergoing examination. Until definition of behavior, the general adjustment factors applicable to sawn lumber are assumed to apply to SCL design stresses. These include the effects of

TABLE 2.12 Machine Stress Grades of Lumber, 2 in or Less Thick, All Widths*

Grade name	Allowable bending stress, lb/in² Single	Allowable bending stress, lb/in² Multiple	Allowable tension lb/in²	Allowable compression, lb/in²	Elastic modulus, 1000 lb/in²
900f-1.0*E*	900	1050	350	725	1000
1200f-1.2*E*	1200	1400	600	950	1200
1500f-1.4*E*	1500	1750	900	1200	1400
1800f-1.6*E*	1800	2050	1175	1450	1600
2100f-1.8*E*	2100	2400	1575	1700	1800
2400f-2.0*E*	2400	2750	1925	1925	2000
2700f-2.2*E*	2700	3100	2150	2150	2200
3000f-2.4*E*	3000	3450	2400	2400	2400
3300f-2.6*E*	3300	3800	2650	2650	2600

Species	Allowable horizontal shear, lb/in²	Allowable compression, perpendicular to grain, lb/in²
Cedars	75	425
Douglas fir–larch	95	625
Douglas fir (south)	90	520
Southern pine	90	565
Hem-fir	75	405
Western hemlock	90	410
Englemann spruce	70	320
Pine and mixed species	70	315

Note: 1000 lb/in² = 6.895 MPa.

*Properties in table are for dry use. Allowable compression perpendicular to grain and shear are the same for each grade, but are species-related. Cedars = western red cedar and incense cedar; pine = Idaho white; mixed species = all species graded by West Coast Lumber Inspection Bureau.

Duration of load

Fatigue

Size influence

Moisture content

See Secs. 2.3 and 2.4 for adjustments of duration of load and fatigue effects.

As with sawn lumber and glued-laminated members, the allowable bending stress is adjusted for the depth d of the member under flexure. The allowable bending stresses for SCL have been generated based on 12-in-deep members.

To adjust this level for shallower or deeper members, the allowable bending stress is multiplied by the size effect factor C_F, which is discussed in Sec. 2.2.3 with an experimental value as determined by end manufacturer in accordance with the provisions of ASTM D 5456 being used.

The allowable design stresses for SCL are developed for dry end-use conditions. This is assuming that the SCL in use will not have a moisture content exceeding 15 percent. For higher moisture contents, the allowable design properties should be reduced in proportion to the increase above 15 percent. Section 2.5.1 discusses this adjustment procedure.

2.2.3 Glued-Laminated Timber

Glued-laminated (glulam) timber finds its major application for flexural members, columns, arches, truss members, and decking. Because a degree of homogenization is achieved when glue laminating structural lumber into larger sections, glulam structural members and products have higher allowable stresses and more reliable stiffness than sawn timber. In addition, they are available in curved or rectilinear forms of larger cross sections and longer lengths than sawn timber. Glulam is produced of kiln-dried lumber and hence does not have nearly the magnitude of problems of shrinkage and secondary stress generation that often occurs in the joints from sawn timbers.

Glulam timbers utilize graded structural lumber as the laminate materials, which are bonded with wet-use adhesives.

Grading. In addition to the grading rules for structural lumber previously described, the rules for the visual grading of structural-laminating lumber are more restrictive with respect to skip and the amount of wane permitted. For western species, six laminating grades of lumber (descending in overall strength and quality) are identified as 302, L1, L1C, L2D, L2, and L3 (D denotes dense and C denotes close grain). Southern pine uses the structural lumber grades as the basis. The 302 grade is specifically used to sort for tension-zone laminations in bending members and is universally graded for all species.

To obtain a better view of how the L grades of Douglas fir compare with Douglas fir structural lumber graded as joists and planks, a comparison is shown in Table 2.13.

Mechanical grading (E-rated) combined with visual grading [defined as visual stress rating (VSR)] of laminating lumber is being used increasingly to sort for higher-stiffness lumber. The laminating grades 302 are being increasingly selected using both VSR and E-rating techniques.

Derivation of Allowable Properties for Design. Though one can generate allowable properties for the use of sawn structural lumber as previously described, the procedure for glulam must take into account the processing of the laminations and their combination into a composite section. The processing permits a selective placement of laminations in members as a function of the required strength or stiffness. Individual laminations may or may not be single lengths of sawn lumber. Structural end joints (e.g., finger joints, scarf joints) are introduced as needed to

TABLE 2.13 Lamination Grades of Douglas Fir Structural-Laminating Lumber Approximately Compared with Douglas Fir Joists and Plank Structural Lumber

Laminating grade	Structural grade
L1	Dense select structural
L2D	Select structural
L2	No. 1 or No. 2
L3	No. 3

generate lengths of laminations equivalent to the length of the glulam timber desired. These joints provide locations having tensile strengths less than the tensile strength of the lumber joined.

An ASTM standard (D 3737) and computer models based on this standard have been developed which predict the strength and stiffness of glulam timbers. These experimentally validated models are used to generate combinations for the layup order of glulam members. These combinations are used by glulam manufacturers and are given in American Institute of Timber Construction (AITC) Standard 117 and American Wood Systems (AWS) NER report.[4]

The process for the establishment of design stresses for glulam is described in ASTM D 3737.[5] It basically details the selection of visually graded or *E*-rated lumber for the glulam; the calculation of strength ratios for bending, compression and tension parallel to grain, and horizontal shear–governed members; adjustment of stresses for end use; and the calculation of design stress levels using clear wood design strengths as the base.

The equations for generating the allowable design stresses for bending (horizontally laminated), tension, and compression members are similar to those for sawn structural lumber, and the allowable stress is obtained using adjustments as follows:

$$\begin{matrix}\text{Clear wood}\\ \text{design}\\ \text{stress}\end{matrix} \times \begin{matrix}\text{general ad-}\\ \text{justment}\\ \text{factor}\end{matrix} \times \begin{matrix}\text{moisture}\\ \text{content in}\\ \text{use factor}\end{matrix} \times \begin{matrix}\text{volume}\\ \text{effect}\end{matrix} \times \begin{matrix}\text{strength}\\ \text{ratio}\end{matrix} \tag{2.3}$$

Clear Wood Design Strength. The determination of clear wood strengths is discussed in the structural lumber section. Clear wood strengths for green lumber are used to generate such properties. Based on these properties, allowable clear wood design strengths are determined. These modifications are addressed in the following material. Green clear wood properties and their variations are given in ASTM D 2555[2] for all commercial species.

Basically, the lower 5th percentile or average green wood level of the strength property desired is determined. This is multiplied by a seasoning factor to correct the stress level from the green to a dry (12 percent moisture content) condition and divided by an appropriate factor of safety for the strength property. Table 2.14 lists the strength properties and the corresponding multiplier factors. Other comments, adjustments, or procedures applicable for a given property follow.

TABLE 2.14 Adjustment Factors for Clear Wood Stresses

Property	Average or 5th percentile	Safety factor multiplier		Seasoning factor for 12% moisture content
		Softwood	Hardwood	
Bending strength	5th percentile	0.476	0.435	1.35
Compression				
Parallel to grain	5th percentile	0.526	0.476	1.75
Perpendicular to grain	Average	0.667	0.667	1.50
Horizontal shear	5th percentile	0.244	0.222	1.13
Modulus of elasticity	Average	1.095	1.095	1.20

Bending. The property generated requires multiplication by 0.743 to adjust the stress to that for a uniformly loaded 12-in (305-mm) simple beam with a 21:1 span-to-depth ratio. Clear dry wood design stress values are given in Table 2.15 for three species groups.

Tension. The tensile clear wood design stress is defined as five-eighths of the clear wood design strength in bending of 12-in (0.305-m)-deep members.

Modulus of Elasticity. The factor in Table 2.14 adjusts the E value to that for a beam of 100:1 span-to-depth ratio and uniformly loaded. Table 2.15 may be used for E values for the species groups given.

Modulus of Rigidity. The modulus of rigidity G can be considered as a constant fraction of the minimum modulus of elasticity E of all the laminations in a glulam member. For design purposes, this is

$$G = \frac{E}{16} \tag{2.4}$$

Horizontal Shear. The procedure is as indicated for structural lumber, with the exception that the clear wood design stress is fixed at established levels of 165 lb/in² (1.14 MPa) for Douglas fir medium grain, close grain, and dense and at 200 lb/in² (1.38 MPa) for southern pine. Coarse-grain Douglas fir and southern pine are assigned a value of 140 lb/in² (0.965 MPa). For other softwood species, the 5th percentile horizontal shear clear wood stress is calculated (ASTM D 2555[2]) and multiplied by 0.244. This is then adjusted using Eq. (2.3) to obtain the allowable horizontal shear stress.

TABLE 2.15 Clear Wood Design Stresses in Bending Based on Large Beam Tests

Species	Growth classification*	Clear wood design stress in bending†		Modulus of elasticity	
		lb/in²	MPa	10^6 lb/in²	MPa
Douglas fir	Medium grain	3000	20.7	1.9	13,100
	Close grain	3250	22.4	2.0	13,800
	Dense	3500	24.2	2.1	14,500
Southern pine	Coarse grain‡	2000	13.8	1.5	10,300
	Medium grain	3000	20.7	1.8	12,400
	Dense	3500	24.1	2.0	13,800
Hem-fir	Medium grain	2560	17.7	1.7	11,700
	Dense§	3000	20.7	1.8	12,400

*Classification for "dense" wood shall follow ASTM D 245.[3]

†Values shown are derived from full-sized beam tests. Beams designed using these values and tested according to ASTM D 198, *Methods of Static Tests of Timbers in Structural Sizes,* will yield strength values such that the lower 5th percentile will exceed the design bending stress by a factor of 2.1 with 75% confidence. Analysis of test data assumed a log-normal distribution. For unsymmetric combinations, tests have shown that values up to 30% higher than those listed may be applied to the compression side of bending members.

‡Also applicable to minor species of southern pine regardless of growth.

§Specific gravity, based on ovendry weight and volume at 12% moisture content, must equal or exceed 0.39.

Lamination Effects. For bending members of vertically laminated lumber comprised of two or more laminations, the allowable design bending stress f_b is given by

$$f_b = \overline{E}\left(\frac{f}{E}\right)_{\min} \tag{2.5}$$

where $\overline{E}$ is the thickness-weighted average of the component lamination E values, and $(f/E)_{\min}$ is the lowest value of the ratios of the allowable design stress f to the modulus of elasticity E for each grade of lumber in the beam.

Average E values applicable to horizontally laminated bending members are 95 percent of the values calculated using transformed section analysis. The average E values applicable to vertically laminated beams are 95 percent of the average of the laminations. Vertically and horizontally laminated bending members are illustrated in Fig. 2.7.

Radial Tension (Perpendicular to Grain). This is defined as one-third of the value for horizontal shear to obtain the clear wood design value. Douglas fir and larch are limited, however, to 15 lb/in^2 (0.103 MPa) for loads other than from wind or earthquake loading.

Compression (Perpendicular to Grain). The allowable stress level is that of the structural lamination, tension, or compression face subjected to that load condition.

Strength Ratios. As with graded structural lumber, knot location and size, slope of grain, and splits determine the reduction to be applied to clear wood stress levels.

The following procedures have been developed for members comprised of visually stress-graded lumber. The same procedures apply to E-rated lumber as well, except that horizontally laminated bending members employing E-rated lumber have strength ratios not less than the strength ratios given in Table 2.16 for members 15 in (381 mm) or less in depth. The strength ratio is assumed to be at least 0.5 for members of greater depth.

Vertically laminated bending members shall establish the strength ratio assuming that the coefficient of variation of E-rated lumber is less than that of visually stress-graded lumber. A value of 0.24 is specified for E-rated lumber as compared with

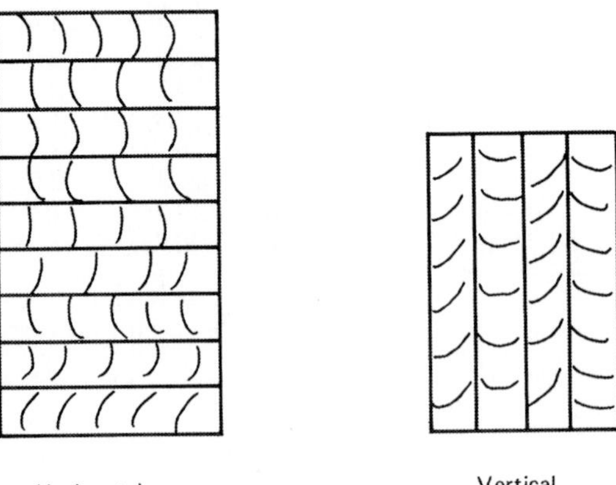

FIG. 2.7 Horizontally and vertically laminated beam cross sections.

TABLE 2.16 Minimum Bending and Compression Parallel-to-Grain Strength Ratios for Members of *E*-Rated Lumber

E-grade designation*	Horizontally laminated members	Vertically laminated members	Compression† parallel to grain
⅙-1.9*E*	0.70	0.70	0.71
⅙-2.1*E*	0.69	0.69	0.69
⅙-2.3*E*	0.68	0.68	0.69
⅙-2.5*E*	0.67	0.67	0.69
¼-1.3*E*	0.64	0.64	0.69
¼-1.6*E*	0.64	0.64	0.69
½-1.3*E*	0.50	0.26	0.50
½-1.6*E*	0.50	0.26	0.50
½-1.9*E*	0.50	0.26	0.50
½-2.1*E*	0.50	0.26	0.50
½-2.3*E*	0.50	0.26	0.50
½-2.5*E*	0.50	0.26	0.50

*The first part of the *E*-grade designation indicates the fraction of cross section that can be occupied by edge characteristics, which include knots, knotholes, burls, distorted grain, or decay partially or wholly at edges of wide faces. The second part indicates *E* in units of 10^6 lb/in^2.

†Values are for members of two or more laminations.

0.36 for visually stress-graded lumber. This use of *E*-rated lumber effectively increases the strength ratio for a member using *E*-rated lumber in the tension or compression zone.

Slope of Grain. Strength ratios for a varying slope of grain are given in Table 2.17 as a function of the locations of tension or compression in members.

Knots. For laminated beams, the influence of knots located throughout the beam is accounted for by considering the location of the knots as measured from the neutral axis. Knots affect strength less if located near the neutral axis. The influence of the knots is best measured by their moment of inertia I_k. Tests of glulam

TABLE 2.17 Parallel-to-Grain Strength Ratios (%) Associated with Slope of Grain for Designing Glulam Combinations

Slope of grain	Tension	Compression
1:4	27	46
1:6	40	56
1:8	53	66
1:10	61	74
1:12	69	82
1:14	74	87
1:16	80	100
1:18	85	100
1:20	100	100

beams have provided an empirical relationship between the moment of inertia I_k when knots are present within 6 in of a cross section and the gross cross-sectional moment of inertia I_g. Procedures to determine these are specified in ASTM D 3737.[5]

The strength ratio in bending SR_b for a horizontally laminated beam is given by

$$SR_b = (1 + 3R)(1 - R)^3\left(1 - \frac{R}{2}\right) \tag{2.6}$$

where $R = I_k/I_g$.

The knot-influenced bending strength ratio for vertically laminated members is given by

$$SR = C_1(SR_1^{0.81})(N^{\alpha})\left(1 - \frac{1.645\Omega_1}{N^{1/2}}\right) \tag{2.7}$$

where C_1 = empirical constant dependent upon SR_1 level
SR_1 = strength ratio for individual piece of lumber loaded on edge (taken from ASTM D 245)[3]
$\alpha = 0.329\ (1 - 1.049\ SR_1)$
N = number of laminations (not to exceed five); use $N = 5$ for members with five or more laminations
Ω_1 = coefficient of variation in bending strength for one lamination; 0.36 for visually graded structural lumber and 0.24 for machine stress-graded lumber

The compression parallel-to-grain knot-strength ratio is governed by the percentage of the cross section occupied by the largest knot for individual laminations. The knot-strength ratio is given by

$$SR_k = (1/4)(Y^3 - 4Y^2 - Y + 4) \tag{2.8}$$

where Y is the knot size expected at the 99.5th percentile of the distribution of knots for a given grade of structural lumber. Its diameter is expressed as a fraction of the dressed width of lumber used for the lamination.

The strength ratio in tension parallel to the grain as governed by knots is given by

$$SR_k = 1 - Y_2 \tag{2.9}$$

where Y_2 is the maximum edge knot size permitted in the laminating grade, expressed as a fraction of the dressed width of the wide face of the lumber used.

Splits. Splits, cracks in lumber, or gaps generated by wane at lamination joints reduce horizontal shear strength. However, shakes, splits, and wane are so restricted through grading that the strength ratio for horizontal shear in horizontally laminated beams can be assumed to be 1.0. In vertically laminated members, one of every four laminations is assumed to have a shake or split that limits the single lamination to a strength ratio in shear of 0.5. The weighted strength ratio for the four laminates combined is 0.875. For two or three laminations, the weighted shear-strength ratios are 0.75 and 0.83, respectively. When species having different shear properties are combined into vertically laminated members, a weighted average of clear wood shear stresses is used to establish a single clear wood shear stress level.

TABLE 2.18 Glulam Wet-Use Adjustment Factors

Type of stress	Wet-use factor
Bending	0.80
Compression parallel to grain	0.73
Tension parallel to grain	0.80
Modulus of elasticity	0.833
Horizontal shear	0.875
Compression perpendicular to grain	0.667
Tension perpendicular to grain	0.875

Moisture Content in Use Factor. The standard condition for nonadjustment of stresses for glulam is 12 percent average moisture content of the member and approximately 70°F (21°C) ambient temperature environs.

Two different moisture conditions in use are recognized for glulam members, dry use and wet use. Dry use is a service condition where the moisture content of the glulam remains below 16 percent; in wet use, the glulam member is at a moisture content of 16 percent or more. Stresses are modified for the wet-use condition only. These reduction factors are given in Table 2.18.

Volume Effect. The volume of a glulam structural element influences the member strength in bending. This volume effect C_v is calculated using the following equation:

$$C_v = K_L \left(\frac{21}{L}\right)^{1/x} \left(\frac{12}{d}\right)^{1/x} \left(\frac{5.125}{b}\right)^{1/x} \leq 1.0 \tag{2.10}$$

where L = length of bending member between points of zero moment, in feet
d = depth of bending member, in inches.
b = width of bending member, in inches. For multiple piece width lay-ups, b = width of widest piece used in lay-up; thus $b \leq 10.75$ in.
x = 20 for southern pine, 10 for all other species
K_L = loading condition coefficient (see Table 2.19)

The volume factor C_v is not applied simultaneously with the beam stability factor C_L.

TABLE 2.19 Loading Condition Coefficients K_L for Structural Glued-Laminated Bending Members

Loading condition	K_L
Single concentrated load at midspan	1.09
Uniformly distributed load	1.0
Third-point loads	0.96
Continuous beam or cantilever, all loading conditions	1.00

General Adjustment Factors

Duration of Load. As with structural lumber, the allowable design properties (except elastic modulus) are adjusted for the duration of load if the cumulative design load application is less than or greater than 10 years' duration. Properties are adjusted in the same manner as already discussed under structural lumber.

Curvature. Glulam members can be fabricated having laminations curved with constant or varying degrees of curvature. This curvature magnifies the bending and axial stress in service, and the allowable design levels must be reduced. Bending and axial stresses are modified by the factor

$$C_c = 1 - 2000\left(\frac{t}{R}\right)^2 \tag{2.11}$$

where C_c = curvature factor
t = individual lamination thickness
R = radius of curvature in equivalent units

Beams and arches are generally produced with t/R ratios not exceeding 1/125 for softwoods and 1/100 for heartwoods to minimize breakage of laminations during fabrication.

Shear Deformation. The average E values for glulam beams calculated per recommendations in this chapter are applicable for a span-to-depth ratio of 21:1. Included herein is the assumption that up to 5 percent of the deflection will be due to shear and the rest due to bending when uniformly loaded. These E values may be applied to beams for span-to-depth ratios as small as 14:1 and will result in estimating the maximum deflection within 5 percent or less. For more precise deflection calculations and calculations for span-to-depth ratios less than 14:1, shear deflection contribution should be considered separately.

Design Values for Glulam Members. Appropriate stress values for specific glulam members can be obtained by multiplying the member clear wood strengths by the strength ratios and modifications for end use discussed in the previous sections.

Final property levels should be rounded to three significant digits for stresses and to two significant digits for E values. Values for various species and lamination combinations are given in AITC 117.[4]

2.2.4 Poles and Piles

Wood poles are used in electric transmission and distribution lines as well as in building construction. They are used extensively in marine construction and foundation systems. The prime factors governing the selection of a particular species for pole or pile are the quantity available, the strength and weight, the natural shape of the tree, and the ability of the wood to receive and retain commercial preservative treatments.

All species can be used for both poles and piles. However, the hardwoods are used less than the softwoods due to a lack of experience in treatment and their higher weight per unit volume. Douglas fir, southern pine, western red cedar, and lodgepole pine comprise the highest percentage of poles treated in the United States, with the southern pines being predominant. Oak is a common species for driven piles.

Pole and pile weight depends on the species, size, moisture content, and preservative treatment. Poles may be in the green moisture condition when produced, but the portion of the pole above ground will dry to less than 30 percent in use.

Pole Design Values. Species, class, and length are characteristics specified for poles to be used for transmission and distribution lines as well as in buildings. Specifications for round timber poles for transmission and distribution lines are given in American National Standards Institute (ANSI) Standard 05.1.[6] Utilities use fiber stress values for pole design which are based on an extensive ASTM wood pole research program conducted in the 1950s and was supplemented by more recent tests. Strength test procedures are as specified in ASTM D 1036.[8]

ANSI 05.1 assumes that wood poles are governed in use by strength in bending. Pole classes are established based on their circumference measured 6 ft (1.83 m) from the butt end and maximum fiber stress at the groundline in bending as a simple cantilever. As a result, poles of a given class and length have approximately the same load-carrying capacity, regardless of species.

The ultimate fiber stresses specified for a given transmission or distribution pole class are reduced by a safety factor consistent with the end use of the pole. For electric utility structure uses, reductions are given in the *National Electrical Safety Code,* Handbook 81 of the National Institute of Standards and Technology.[9]

The basic principles applied to develop design values for round timber poles used in building construction are given in ASTM D 3200, and values are given in Table 11.8.

Pile Design Values. Wood piling continues to play an important role in building, bridge, marine, and wharf construction. Characteristics that contribute significantly to this are sufficient strength and straightness to withstand driving forces and resistance to degradation as provided by preservative treatment. Piles used for temporary construction or located permanently below fresh water do not require preservative treatment.

The specification for selecting round poles for use as piles is given in ASTM D 25.[10] Timber piles are designed at a critical section as governed by tip size, butt size, or an intermediate cross section.

Controlled characteristics of pile timber are decay presence, taper, length, circumference at tip and butt, sapwood presence to enhance treatment, straightness, twist of grain, extent of bark removal, knots, holes, or scars, and checks, shakes, and splits.

The bearing capacity of a timber pile is governed by subsoil stratum types. Depending on the soil substructure, a pile or group of piles may be designed assuming earth friction along the length and circumference, bearing on the tip, or a proportioned combination of both. A rock stratum would allow full-tip bearing to be developed.

For wood poles that are fully tip bearing, the compressive stress parallel to the grain governs the allowable applied load. For wood poles depending on side friction, the friction forces developed are a function of the stability of the soil. Often such poles do not develop the ultimate strength of the pile but instead are controlled by the soil properties and the length or diameter of the pile.

A pile extending above the ground is usually limited by compression parallel to the grain as a column of some nonlaterally supported length or in combination with bending due to side loading. Bracing to provide lateral restraint or to withstand side loads by reducing the unsupported column length is common. Unbraced piles used in soils incapable of lateral support require design as columns.

Engineering design procedures are available to estimate the load-carrying capacity of piles. Among these are the rate of penetration of the piles under blows from the driving hammer, static load tests, and experience or observation of the behavior of piles under similar conditions.

Recommendations for setting the working stresses or allowable design stresses for piles are given in model building codes as derived from recommendations in ASTM D 2899.[7] Factors influencing the allowable design stress levels were previously indicated. Basic clear wood strength values (from ASTM D 2555[2]) are adjusted from short-time test conditions to normal 10-year duration-of-load conditions to a lower compressive strength for the pile tip, increased for lower strength variability because of using the whole tree bole, and for growth and shape characteristics. No reduction is made for preservative treatment.

ASTM D 2899[7] establishes the procedures for calculating design values for green untreated piles. The properties determined are compression parallel to grain, bending, horizontal shear, and compression perpendicular to grain. Design values are given in Table 11.8.

A size effect is encountered that reduces the bending strength when the pile circumference exceeds 43 in (1.09 m) at the critical cross section. Hence a size-effect factor must be applied to the allowable bending stress for this condition. This can be calculated using Eq. (2.2).

Design values for bending and compression parallel to grain apply strictly to piles used in clusters where load sharing between adjacent piles is achieved. If a single pile is supporting a specific load, an increased factor of safety is needed: 1.25 for compression parallel to grain and 1.30 for bending stress.

Published design values (see Table 11.8) include an adjustment to compensate for strength reduction due to conditioning prior to treatment. If this is not done, values other than E may be increased by factors dependent on the species.

These multiplying factors are as follows:

Pacific Coast Douglas fir, red oak, and red pine	1.11
Southern pine	1.18

The reduction in strength of a wood column resulting from crook, eccentric loading, or any other condition that will result in combined bending and compression is not as great as may be expected. Tests have shown that a timber, when subjected to combined bending and compression, develops a higher stress at both the proportional limit and the maximum load than when subjected to compression only. This does not imply that crook and eccentricity should be without restriction, but it should relieve anxiety as to the influence of crook such as that found in piles.

2.3 DURATION OF LOAD

2.3.1 Wood Response to Load with Time

The time period during which a load acts on wood members is an important characteristic in determining the load a member can carry safely. This effect is termed the *duration-of-load* or *duration-of-stress influence.* The reader is referred to Secs. 1.3.8 and 1.4.8 for additional descriptions of the time effect.

As has been stated earlier, the allowable design stress levels as given in the NDS[11] have been adjusted to a base of a 10-year cumulative application of the design load, called *normal loading.* Figure 2.6 shows the ratio of the expected strength at any period of applied load to that of 10-year application.

There is evidence that an intermittent load produces a cumulative effect on strength. Hence the total accumulated duration of an intermittent full-load condition should be used to calculate the duration-of-load effect. Theory that describes the wood response and limited structural evaluation of trusses after 15-year loading indicates that one may not detect any significant strength reduction in a timber member after relatively long periods of loading. The property is not reduced linearly with increasing duration of load but can be expected to drop dramatically as the end of the period is approached. As a result, conducting tests of timber that has been subjected to various load levels often does not exhibit any detectable strength loss. Strength loss is detected from tests in which the applied load level is greater than 85 percent of the 5-minute strength; however, failure usually occurs almost immediately.

NDS[11] recommends that when the load duration is other than normal, the allowable stesses be multiplied by the following factors:

0.90 for permanent load (more than 10 years)

1.15 for 2 months' duration of load, as for snow

1.25 for 7 days' duration of load

1.60 for wind or earthquake

2.00 for impact

In many design circumstances there are several loads on the structure, some acting simultaneously, and each with a different duration. Each increment of time during which the total load is constant should be treated separately, with the most severe condition governing the design. Either the allowable stress or the total design load (but not both) can be adjusted using Fig. 2.6.

2.3.2 Deflection

The recommended duration-of-load factors apply only to stresses and not to the modulus of elasticity E. Hence for members or structures which may be controlled by deflection, as in beams or trusses, no duration-of-load effect is applied to the E value. Wood members and structures do creep deflect with time in addition to the initial elastic deformation which occurs on the application of load. The reader is referred to Sec. 1.3.4 for a more complete description of creep deflection.

How the stress level affects this time-dependent deflection, or creep, response is illustrated in Fig. 1.4. Note that a high dead-load stress condition [one that generates a stress level of 500 lb/in^2 (3.46 MPa)] can increase deflection by about 50 percent with the passing of a year or two. The NDS requires short-term elastic deformation to be increased to account for creep. The increase factor is 1.5 for dry and 2.0 for wet service conditions. The American Institute of Timber Construction and American Wood System recommend that a camber be provided in glulam members equal to 1½ times the elastic dead-load deflection to compensate for long-term creep deflection.

moisture contents of 16 percent or more, a wet-use adjustment factor is applied to the design values. These adjustment factors are given in Table 2.18.

Fasteners. The fastener strength is reduced with increasing moisture content due to a decrease in the strength and stiffness of wood and not that of the fastener. The dry condition for fasteners is defined as any location where wood has a moisture content of 19 percent or less.

Because joints in lumber and timber are influenced by shrinkage to a degree that varies with the seating of the fastener (tightness of fit), the adjustment factors for fastener design values also vary with the fastener type. No adjustment is necessary for fasteners installed in dry wood and placed in dry condition of service. Fastener load modification factors are given in Chap. 5, "Mechanical Fasteners and Connectors." Wire nails and spikes are severely reduced in withdrawal resistance (a factor of 0.25) when used in dry wood connections that are employed in the wet state. Emplacing connectors in wet wood and using the assembly in the dry condition result in at least a 20 percent reduction in strength.

2.6 PRESERVATIVES

2.6.1 Protective Measures

When lumber is used in exposed conditions, it may attain a moisture content conducive to decay or to insect attack. Moisture contents in excess of 20 percent are recognized to make wood especially vulnerable to attack. As a result, protective measures should be taken. Either the heartwood of a naturally resistant species should be used or the wood should be treated with preservative chemicals, applied by a recognized and acceptable process, to give the wood the necessary degree of resistance. A number of such chemicals are available.

2.6.2 Standard Preservatives

The following preservatives are recognized in the standards of the American Wood Preservers' Association (AWPA):

Preservative oils

- Creosote
- Creosote–coal-tar solutions
- Creosote-petroleum solutions

Oilborne preservatives

- Pentachlorophenol
- Copper naphthenate

Waterborne preservatives

- Chromated zinc chloride (CZC)
- Fluor chrome arsenate phenol (FCAP)
- Tanalith (Wolman salts)
- Celcure

- Chemonite
- Greensalt (Eradlith)
- Boliden salts

2.6.3 Treatment Methods

The selection of the proper method of treatment is as important as the selection of the proper preservative. The best preservative known will not increase the life of wood appreciably if it is not injected effectively into the wood. The increased life thereby obtained, moreover, is in direct proportion to the thoroughness with which the treatment has been carried out. Methods of treatment may be divided into two general classes: (1) pressure processes and (2) nonpressure processes.

2.6.4 Pressure Processes

For maximum protection, pressure processes are recommended because they permit the greatest penetration of the preservative. Wood products to be treated by a pressure process are loaded on tram cars (Fig. 2.8) and rolled into long steel cylinders. The cylinders are then sealed and filled with the preservative. Through established combinations of temperature, vacuum, and pressure, the preservative is injected into the wood. Two basic methods, known as the *full-cell* (Bethell) *process* and the *empty-cell* (Rueping or Lowry) *process,* are available.

Treatment by the full-cell process leaves the cells of the woods, within the depth of penetration, full of preservative. It is used in treating all material for marine construction and also if a specified retention is greater than that which can be obtained by the empty-cell process.

The empty-cell process leaves the cell walls saturated but with no free liquid preservative in the cell cavities. This process yields a drier product and permits maximum penetration for any specified weight of treatment.

Except for marine structures, the empty-cell process is generally specified for oil preservatives. Salt preservatives are usually injected by the full-cell process. Oilborne pressure-treated material may be used without further seasoning immediately after it comes from the retort. Wood treated with salt preservatives, however, may require seasoning after treatment to a moisture content suitable for the intended end use of the material, should seasoning in service be undesirable.

2.6.5 Nonpressure Processes

Nonpressure processes cover all modifications of immersion or dip treatments at atmospheric pressures. They range from the hot-and-cold bath, which essentially creates pressure differences by expelling some of the air in the wood, to the spray or brush treatment.

If the decay hazard is small or the application is not essential to building safety, protection by nonpressure processes may prove satisfactory, even if not as effective as that by pressure processes, which provide greater penetration and retention of chemicals. Effectiveness usually can be increased by a higher degree of seasoning of the wood, by lengthening the time of immersion, and by utilizing a natural vacuum such as in the hot-and-cold bath process.

FIG. 2.8 Pressure processing.

Spray and brush treatments should be used only for on-the-job localized care for areas that have been exposed by boring or grooving after initial treatment by other methods.

2.6.6 Preparation for Treatment

Wood that is resistant to penetration by preservatives is sometimes incised before treatment to permit deeper and more uniform penetration. Sawn or hewed material is passed through a machine having horizontal and vertical rollers equipped with teeth that cut into the wood to a predetermined depth, usually ½ to ¾ in. The teeth are spaced to give the desired distribution of the preservative with the minimum number of incisions. A machine of different design is required for incising the butts of poles. The effectiveness of incising is based on the fact that preservatives usually penetrate into wood much farther in a longitudinal direction than in a direction perpendicular to the face of the stock. By exposing end-grain surfaces, the incisions permit such penetration. They are especially effective in improving penetration in the heartwood portions of sawn or hewed surfaces.

All possible cutting, framing, and boring of holes should be done before treatment. Cutting into the wood in any way after treatment may expose the untreated or lesser treated portions of the timber and thus permit ready access to destructive fungi or insects. When such cutting cannot be avoided, an aftertreatment of the area by soaking it with several applications of hot preservative is recommended. The end grain of wood, such as pile cutoffs, can be treated effectively by setting up a mud or sheet metal dam around the end and filling it several times with hot preservative. Holes can be treated by inserting a plug at one end and a pressure gun at the other to force the hot preservative into the wood. The aftertreatment preservative should be the same as that originally used on the whole member.

2.6.7 Choice of Preservation Process

Many factors must be considered in selecting the proper treatment process and chemical for a specific situation. The conditions of exposure, the aftertreatment surface required (such as for staining or painting), the estimated useful life of the structure, and the availability of special treating equipment are but a few. Wood used in permanent structures in direct contact with the ground, such as piling, poles, or foundation timbers, requires the best treatment possible. Items that are protected from leaching by paint or other surface finish, such as window sashes and exterior trim, can be given sufficient protection with a dip treatment. The possibilities of leaching and corrosion of metal fastenings are factors to be considered when salt-type preservatives are used. Salt treatment of wood that remains dry or is only occasionally wet in service causes little trouble. Under conditions of exposure to moisture, however, corrosion of steel fasteners or leaching of salts can be severe.

2.6.8 Specifications

Federal Specification TT-W-571[13] presents a conservative guide for specifiers and users of pressure-treated wood. Table 2.21, excerpted from this specification, recommends the types of preservatives applicable to different classes of material and varying locations of use. Minimum retention of preservative per cubic foot is stipulated, and the standard AWPA specification for the applicable treating process is described.

Waterborne Preservatives. One major advantage of many waterborne preservatives is their resistance to leaching by water. These particular metallic salts undergo hydrolytic reduction upon contact with the reducing sugars found in wood. In this process, known as *fixation,* the cell wall is oxidized, and subsequently, strength is affected. At most usable concentrations, these preservatives are sufficiently acidic

TABLE 2.21 Preservative Types, Retention by Assay of Treated Wood (lb/ft^3), and Applicable AWPA Standards[a,b]

Material and usage	Oilborne preservatives: Creosote[e]	Creosote, coal tar[e]	Creosote, petroleum	Pentachlorophenol[c]	Waterborne preservatives[c,d]: Acid copper chromate (ACC)[c]	Ammoniacal copper arsenate (ACA)	Chromated copper arsenate (CCA)	Chromated zinc chloride (CZC)	Fluor chrome arsenate phenol (FCAP)	AWPA standards[f]
Lumber and plywood										
Above ground	8[g]	8[g]	8[g]	0.40	0.25	0.25	0.25	0.45	0.25	C2/C9[h]
Ground contact										
Nonstructural	10[g]	10[g]	10[g]	0.50	0.50	0.40	0.40	NR[i]	NR	C2/C9[h]
Structural	12[g]	12[g]	12[g]	0.60	NR	0.60	0.60	NR	NR	C2/C9[h]
In saltwater	25	25	NR	NR	NR	2.5	2.5	NR	NR	C2/C9[h]
Piles										
Land or freshwater use and foundations	12	12	12	0.60	NR	0.80	0.80	NR	NR	C3
Saltwater, prevalent marine organism:										
Teredo only	20	20	NR	NR	NR	2.5 and 1.5[j]	2.5 and 1.5[j]	NR	NR	C18
Pholads only	20	20	NR	NR	NR	NR	NR	NR	NR	C18
Limnoria tripunctata only	NR	NR	NR	NR	NR	2.5 and 1.5[j]	2.5 and 1.5[j]	NR	NR	C18
For both pholads and Limnoria tripunctata, use dual treatment:										
First treatment	—	—	—	—	—	1.0	1.0	—	—	C18
Second treatment	20	20	—	—	—	—	—	—	—	C18
Poles										
Utility	7.5	7.5	7.5	0.38	NR	0.60	0.60	NR	NR	C4
Normal	9.0	9.0	9.0	0.45	NR	0.60	0.60	NR	NR	C4
Severe service conditions (high incidence of decay or termite attack)										
Building poles, structural	9.0	NR	NR	0.45	NR	0.60	0.60	NR	NR	C3

Posts										
Fence, guide, and sight										
Round, half-round, and quarter-round	8	8	8	0.40	0.50	0.40	0.40	NR	NR	C14
Sawn four sides	10	10	10	0.50	0.62	0.50	0.50	NR	NR	C14
Guardrail and sign (including spacer blocks)										
Round	10	10	10	0.50	NR	0.50	0.50	NR	NR	C14
Sawn four sides	12	12	12	0.60	NR	0.60	0.60	NR	NR	C14
All-weather wood foundation system	NR	NR	NR	NR	NR	0.60	0.60	NR	NR	[k]

[a]Southern pine protected from the weather or exposed in a manner not to permit water to stand for any appreciable length of time does not require preservative treatment. Building codes generally require that wood floors closer than 18 in, or wood girders closer than 12 in, to exposed ground be pressure-treated (preservative).

[b]AWPA standards detail plant-operating procedures for pressure treatment of wood. These standards include minimum vacuum, pressure, and penetration requirements, maximum steaming and temperature allowances. AWPA also details retention and assay zone requirements for each commodity, preservative, and wood species. AWPA standards make it unnecessary for specifications to include detailed requirements on penetration and allowable processes. Generally, it is desirable to specify the preservative desired, the intended application, and necessary retention, and to reference appropriate AWPA standards. AWPA C1 applies to each of the treating processes and all types of material.

[c]Pentachlorophenol in suitable solvents or waterborne preservatives can provide a clean, paintable, odorless, dry surface. When one or more of these features are required, the processor should be so advised when the order is placed.

[d]Trade names of waterborne preservatives (*Reg. U.S. Patent Office):

Acid copper chromate (ACC):
  Celcure*
Ammoniacal copper arsenate (ACA):
  Chemonite*
Chromated copper arsenate, type A (CCA type A):
  Greensalt
Chromated copper arsenate, type B (CCA type B):
  Boliden* CCA
  Koppers CCA-B
  Osmose K-33*
Chromated zinc chloride (CZC)
Chromated copper arsenate; type C (CCA type C):
  Chrome-Ar-Cu (CAC)*
  Langwood*
  Osmose K-33
  Wolman* CCA
  Wolmanac* CCA
  Wood Last* CCA-C
Fluor chrome arsenate phenol (FCAP):
  Osmosalts* (Osmosar*)
  Tanalith
  Wolman* salts FCAP
  Wolman* salts FMP

[e]When these preservatives are specified for materials to be used in saltwater, the creosote coal tar shall conform to AWPA P2 or P12, and the creosote shall conform to AWPA P1 or P13.

[f]These retentions are taken from among those given in various standards of the American Wood Preservers' Association (AWPA) and have been selected by SFPA on the basis of structural importance.

[g]Not recommended where cleanliness and freedom from odor are necessary.

[h]AWPA C2, Lumber, AWPA C9, Plywood.

[i]NR—Not recommended.

[j]The assay retentions are based on two assay zones—0 to 0.50 in and 0.50 to 2.0 in.

[k]American Wood Preservers' Bureau (AWPB), FDN standard.

or alkaline to cause some cell-wall hydrolysis. Most waterborne preservative salts increase the hygroscopicity of the wood. This causes an increased equilibrium moisture content which may reduce strength.

With waterborne treatments such as CCA or ACA, most treated dimension lumber is dried twice. Lumber must be dry to achieve adequate waterborne preservative penetration, so the material is kiln-dried before treatment, and then the treated lumber often is kiln-dried a second time to remove residual water remaining from the waterborne preservative treatment process and to finalize the fixation process. Limited research has been done to investigate the effects of this second drying process. The effects are probably not the same as those due to the initial drying process because the combination of hydrolytic chemicals and high temperature may be substantially more degrading to strength properties. In general, waterborne preservative treatments have no apparent effect on E; they reduce the modulus of rupture, T (tensile strength), and FSPL (fiber stress at the proportional limit) by about 5 percent; reduce WML (work to maximum load) by about 20 percent; and reduce toughness by about 30 percent. The magnitude of these effects can be increased or decreased by controlling the severity of treating and the processing parameters.

Preservative formulations that contain copper and chromium salts reportedly promote afterglow in treated wood subjected to fire. Once the treated wood starts to burn or glow, the wood may continue to glow until the entire member is consumed, even when no flame is present. This characteristic can cause serious problems in utility poles, fenceposts, highway signs, and structures that might be subjected to accidental fires or controlled ground fire, which is used as an agricultural management tool.

2.6.10 Handling and Seasoning Timber after Preservative Treatment

Treated timber should be handled with sufficient care to avoid penetrating through the treated areas. The use of pikes, cant hooks, picks, tongs, or other pointed tools that dig deeply into the wood should be prohibited. Handling heavy loads of lumber or sawn timber in rope or cable slings may crush the corners or edges of the outside pieces. Breakage or deep abrasions also may result from throwing the lumber or dropping it. If damage results, the exposed place should be retreated as thoroughly as conditions permit. Long storage of treated wood before installation should be avoided because such storage encourages deep and detrimental checking and also may result in a significant loss of some preservatives. Treated wood that must be stored before use should be covered for protection from the elements.

Although cutting wood after treatment should be avoided, this is not always possible. When cutting is necessary, the damage may be partly overcome in timber for land or freshwater use by a thorough application of a grease containing 10 percent pentachlorophenol. This provides a protective reservoir of preservative on the surface, some of which may slowly migrate into the end grain of the wood. Thoroughly brushing the cut surfaces with two coats of hot creosote is also helpful, although brush coating cut surfaces gives little protection against marine borers. A special device is available for pressure treating bolt holes bored after treatment. For wood treated with waterborne preservatives, where the use of creosote or pentachlorophenol solution on the cut surfaces is not practicable, a 5% solution of the waterborne preservative being used should be substituted.

For treating the end surfaces of piles where they are cut off after driving, at least two heavy coats of creosote should be applied. A coat of asphalt or similar material may be applied over the creosote, followed by some protective sheet material, such as metal, roofing felt, or saturated fabric fitted over the pile head and brought down the sides far enough to protect against damage to the top treatment and against the entrance of storm water. Providing a protective sheet material is not recommended for those installations where the sheet may be damaged and moisture can enter, such as posts on bridge railings. The protective covering will provide a barrier to the drying of the post and thus increase the rate at which decay takes place. AWPA M4[14] contains instructions for the care of pressure-treated wood after treatment.

Petroleum-Based Preservatives. Petroleum-based chemicals such as creosote and pentachlorophenol in oil are also used as wood preservatives. These organic preservatives are inert toward the cell-wall substance and do not seem to cause any appreciable strength losses. Because of the higher treating temperatures commonly used with organic preservatives, however, strength losses have been attributed to the treatment conditions (high temperature and pressure) rather than to the organic preservative chemicals given above.

2.7 FIRE-RESISTIVE DESIGN

There are many approaches for providing fire safety in any structure. This involves a combination of (1) preventing fire occurrence, (2) controlling fire growth, and (3) providing protection to life and property. All need systematic attention in order to provide a high degree of fire safety economically. The building design professional can control fire growth within the structure by generating plans that include such features as protecting occupants either confined to or exiting the structure, confining fire in compartmented areas, and incorporating fire suppression and smoke-heat venting devices at critical locations.

Controlling construction features to facilitate rapid egress, protection of occupants in given areas, and the prevention of fire growth or spread are regulated by codes as a function of building occupancy. If the design professional rationally blends protection solutions for these items with the potential use of a fire-suppression system (sprinklers, for example), economical fire protection can be achieved.

Though attention could be given to all the protection techniques available to the building design professional, the scope here will be limited to the provisions that prevent fire growth and limit the fire to compartments.

2.7.1 Planning

Generating the plans for a building of prescribed occupancy is a challenge due to the varying requirements of the three major regional building codes: Building Officials Conference of America (BOCA), National; International Conference of Building Officials (ICBO), Uniform; and Southern Building Code Congress International, Inc. (SBCCI), Standard. Canada is regulated by a separate code. As a first step, the code covering the local jurisdiction where a proposed building is to be constructed must be consulted for the requirements of the specific design project. This normally concerns the type of construction desired as well as allowable building areas and heights for each construction type.

The buildings constructed using wood are generally code classified under types as type I, type III, type IV, type V, type V (111), and type V (000).

Type I. Type I construction is generally required to be of noncombustible materials having fire endurance ratings of up to 4 h, depending on the size and location of the building. Some circumstances provide for the use of wood in the walls of noncombustible wall wood joist and noncombustible types of construction. The *Uniform Building Code,* for example, allows the use of fire-retardant–treated wood framing for nonbearing walls if such walls are over 5 ft (1.52 m) from the property line. Exceptions to the use of noncombustible materials in the noncombustible-type buildings are sometimes made for heavy timber members. Heavy timber members often can be used for roof members more than 25 ft (7.62 m) above the floor, balcony, or gallery in one-story noncombustible-type buildings.

Type III. Type III construction has exterior walls of noncombustible materials and roofs, floors, and interior walls and partitions of wood frame. As in wood frame, they are also subdivided into two classes that are either protected or unprotected.

Type IV. Type IV construction consists of exterior walls of noncombustible materials and columns, floors, roofs, and interior partitions of wood of a minimum size. These sizes are listed in Table 2.22.

Type V. Type V construction is defined as having exterior walls, bearing walls, partitions, floors, and roofs of wood stud and joist framing of 2-in (38.1-mm) nominal dimension. These are subdivided into two classes, type V (111) or type V (000) construction. Protected construction calls for having load-bearing assemblies of 1-h fire endurance.

Besides having protected and unprotected subclasses for each building type, increases in floor area and height of the building are allowed when sprinkler protection systems are included. For example, protected wood frame educational occupancies can be increased in height due to the presence of sprinklers to three stories instead of two, and the floor area in the first two stories may be doubled or even tripled under some conditions.

To assist the designer, allowable height and area information for eight occupancy classifications in each of the major codes has been assembled by the American Forest and Paper Association, and this information is presented clearly in *Code Conforming Wood Design.*[15] Similar information for the Canadian building code is contained in the Canadian Wood Council's *Wood and Fire Safety* manual.[16]

TABLE 2.22 Minimum Sizes of Wood for Type IV Construction

Roof decking	
Lumber (thickness)	2 in nominal
Plywood (thickness)	$1\frac{1}{8}$ in net
Floor decking (thickness)	3 in nominal
Roof framing	4 by 6 in nominal
Floor framing	6 by 10 in nominal
Columns	8 by 8 in nominal

Note: 1 in = 25.4 mm.

2.7.2 Fire-Rated Assemblies

It was shown in the preceding section that some occupancies require the use of fire-rated assemblies or members to prevent collapse or fire spread from one compartment of a building to another or from one building to another.

Members and assemblies are rated for their ability either to continue to carry design loads during fire exposure or to prevent the passage of fire through them. Such rating is done by either calculation or experiment for both members and assemblies. The fire exposure is defined as that given in ASTM E 119.[17]

A 1-h fire-resistance rating for wall, floor, and floor-ceiling assemblies incorporating nominal 2-in structural lumber can be accomplished through the use of noncombustible surfaces (such as gypsum wallboard). Fastening of these surface materials is critical for ceiling membranes, however, and is carefully specified. For some wood assemblies, 2-h ratings have been achieved.

Experimentally Rated Members and Assemblies. Experimentally rated members and assemblies are listed in several useful publications:

National Building Code of Canada, Part 9

NBCC Supplement No. 2: *Fire Performance Ratings Listings of Underwriters' Laboratories of Canada Ltd.*

Listings of Underwriters' Laboratories Incorporated (U.S.)

Listings of the International Conference of Building Officials (ICBO)

Listings of the Building Officials Conference of America (BOCA)

Fire Resistance Design Manual of the Gypsum Association[18]

National Fire Protection Association Fire Protection Handbook[19]

Experimental ratings are also obtained independently on assemblies and members by materials and structural member producers. For a given assembly type incorporating proprietary components, the company supplying the component also can be contacted to obtain the fire rating of the assembly. Typically rated floor-ceiling assemblies are shown in Fig. 2.9.

Analytically Rated Members and Assemblies. In lieu of experimentally rating the fire endurance of members and assemblies, the major codes will accept engineering calculations of the expected fire endurance as based on engineering principles and material properties. This applies to the rating of previously untested members or assemblies or in cases where it is desired to substitute one material or component for another.

Though calculation procedures may be conservative, they have the advantage of being able to rate an assembly or member quickly and allow interpolation or some extrapolation of expected performance.

Walls and Floors. An additive protection calculation procedure for both load-bearing and non-load-bearing wall wood stud frame assemblies has been advanced and is accepted by a number of building codes.[15] The 2- by 4-in nominal (38.1- by 88.9-mm) studs spaced 16 in (406 mm) on center are assigned a minimum incremental 20-min fire endurance with any surface on both sides. The incremental times assigned to other interior wallboard membranes are given in Table 2.23. Additional constraints to using this information are

Typical One-Hour Fire-Resistive Floor-Ceiling Assemblies

Double Lumber Floor; Ceiling Nailed Directly to Joists

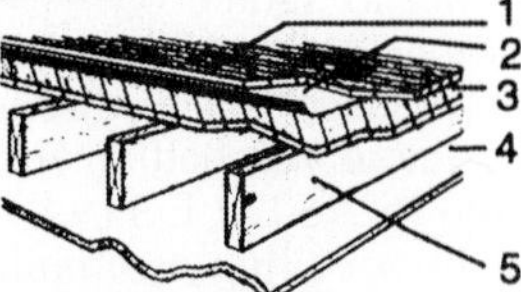

(1) 1″ wood flooring; (2) building paper; (3) 1x6 T&G boards or ½″ standard grade plywood with ext. glue; (4) 5/8″ type X gypsum board ceiling or ½″ special fire-resistive gypsum board ceiling (may be attached to resilient acoustical channels or nailed directly to joists); (5) joists 16″ o.c.**

Double Plywood Floor; Ceiling Suspended in T-Bar Grid

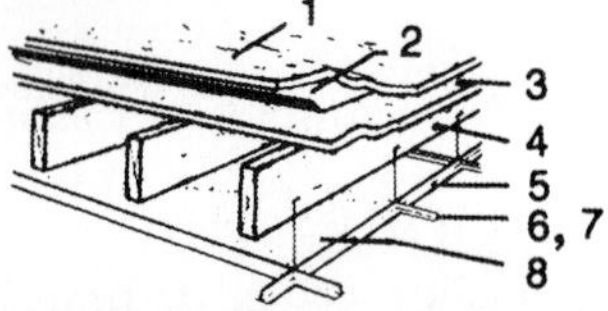

(1) 5/8″ T&G underlayment grade plywood; (2) building paper; (3) ½″ standard grade plywood with ext. glue; (4) joists 16″ o.c.**; (5) T-bar grid ceiling system; (6) main runners 48″ o.c.; (7) cross-tees 24″ o.c.; (8) ½″x48″x24″ mineral acoustical ceiling panels (install with hold-down clips).

Gypsum Underlayment Compound on Plywood Subfloor; Ceiling Resilient Acoustical Channels

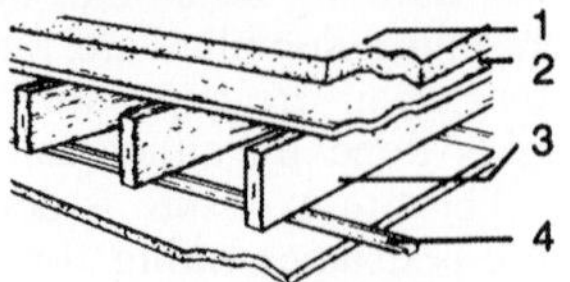

(1) gypsum underlayment compound; (2) ½″ T&G underlayment grade plywood; (3) joists 16″ o.c.**; (4) 5/8″ type X or ½″ fire-resistive type gypsum board ceiling on resilient acoustical channels.

Two-Hour Fire-Resistive Floor-Ceiling Assembly

Double Wood Floor; Double Gypsum Board Ceiling

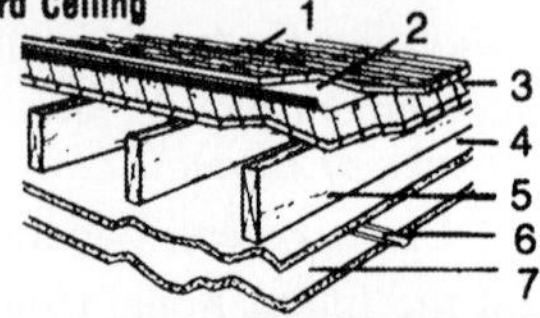

(1) 1″ wood flooring; (2) building paper; (3) 1x6 T&G boards; (4) 5/8″ type X gypsum board nailed directly to joists; (5) joists 16″ o.c.**; (6) resilient acoustical channels; (7) 5/8″ type X gypsum board, second layer applied on channels.

** Fire tests conducted with 2″x10″ joists.

FIG. 2.9 Typical 1- and 2-h fire-resistive floor-ceiling assemblies. (*Courtesy of Western Wood Products Association.*)

TABLE 2.23 Incremental Time Assigned to Wallboard Membranes

Description of finish	Time, min
⅜-in Douglas fir plywood, phenolic bonded	5
½-in Douglas fir plywood, phenolic bonded	10
⅝-in Douglas fir plywood, phenolic bonded	15
⅜-in gypsum wallboard	10
½-in gypsum wallboard	15
⅝-in gypsum wallboard	20
½-in type X gypsum wallboard	25
⅝-in type X gypsum wallboard	40
Double ⅜-in gypsum wallboard	25
½- + ⅜-in gypsum wallboard	35
Double ½-in gypsum wallboard	40

- Gypsum wallboard shall be installed with its long dimension parallel to framing members, and joints shall be finished.
- Where fire endurance is expected to occur on only one side of a wall, as on the interior side of an exterior wall, the wall is assigned a rating based on the interior membrane materials. The membrane on the outside or non-fire-exposed side may consist of sheathing, sheathing paper, and siding assigned an incremental time for fire endurance of 15 min or more or of a combination from Table 2.24.
- Calculations can only be used to determine ratings of up to the limits specified in the codes.
- Add 15 min to the rating of wood stud walls if the spaces between the studs are filled with rock wool or slag mineral wool batts weighing not less than ¼ lb/ft² (12.0 Pa) of wall surface.
- Add 5 min to the rating of non-load-bearing wood stud walls if the spaces between the studs are filled with glass fiber batts weighing not less than ¼ lb/ft² of wall surface.

EXAMPLE 2.1 Calculate the fire endurance of a stud wall having a construction of

2- × 4-in (38.1- × 88.9-mm) studs, 16 in (406 mm) on center

Interior membrane: ½-in (12.7-mm) gypsum wallboard.

Exterior membrane: ½-in (12.7-mm) fiberboard and ⅝-in (15.9-mm) exterior sheathing siding plywood.

Insulation: Rock wool of ¼ lb/ft² (12.0 Pa) of wall surface.

Rating calculation:

2 × 4 studs	20 min
Insulation	15 min
½-in gypsum	15 min
Total	50 min

TABLE 2.24 Membrane on Exterior Face of Wood Stud Walls

Sheathing	Paper	Exterior finish
⅝-in T&G lumber 5/16-in exterior grade plywood ½-in gypsum wallboard ⅝-in gypsum wallboard None	Sheathing paper	Lumber siding Wood shingles and shakes ¼-in plywood exterior grade ¼-in hardboard Metal siding Stucco on metal lath Masonry veneer ⅜-in exterior grade plywood

Check exterior membrane:

½-in fiberboard	5 min	
⅝-in exterior plywood	15 min	
Total	20 min > 15 min	OK

The calculated rating is 50 min.

In a similar fashion, the additive procedure is acceptable for wood floor and roof joist assemblies exposed to fire from below and having joists or rafters spaced 16 in (406 mm) on center and nominal thickness dimension of 2 in (38.1 mm). In this case, the joists or rafters are assigned an incremental rating of 10 min. The flooring or roofing shall be at least that given in Table 2.25. This coincides with the rating assigned to unprotected joist floor assemblies found in one- and two-family dwellings.

Incremental rating times for the protective ceiling membrane may be taken from Table 2.23. Hence, to achieve a 1-h protected joist floor fire endurance rating, at least two layers of ½-in (12.7-mm) type X gypsum wallboard (2 × 25 min = 50 min) would need to be attached to joists 16 in on center (10-min increment). Experimentally tested assemblies using specific improved fastening means can achieve 1-h ratings with one layer of ⅝-in (15.9-mm) type X wallboard. This illustrates both the conservative nature of the calculation procedure and the benefit achieved by giving attention to the manner and type of fastening used to attach the ceiling membrane to the joists. No benefit is assigned to the presence of insulation in the cavity between joists or rafters.

Beams and Columns. Heavy timber construction traditionally has been recognized to provide a fire-resistant building. This is due primarily to the large size of the members, the connection details, and the lack of concealed spaces. Such a construction type often has satisfied the fire-resistive requirement in all codes by simple prescription. While it has not been "rated" in the United States, Canada has determined that it can be assigned a 45-min fire endurance rating.

Some local codes in the United States have accepted the heavy timber type as having a 1-h rating if the minimum timber or lumber depth and thickness given in Sec. 2.7.1 are increased to the next nominal dimension.

TABLE 2.25 Flooring or Roofing over Wood Framing

Assembly	Structural members	Subfloor or roof deck	Finish flooring or roofing
Floor	Wood	½-in plywood or 11⁄16-in T&G softwood	Hardwood or softwood flooring on building paper Resilient flooring, parquet floor, felted-synthetic-fiber floor coverings, carpeting, or ceramic tile on ⅜-in-thick panel-type underlay Ceramic tile on 1¼-in mortar bed
Roof	Wood	½-in plywood or 11⁄16-in T&G softwood	Finish roofing material with or without insulation

Glulam timber columns and beams can be designed for desired fire endurance rating levels in the United States and Canada using calculations.

The fire endurance rating R, in minutes, is determined for beams or columns exposed to fire on either three or four sides by the following equation:

$$R = 2.54(ZbG) \tag{2.12}$$

where Z = factor dependent on load applied and member type, from Fig. 2.10
b = width dimension of cross section of beam or of larger dimension of a column before exposure to fire, inches
G = beam or column cross-sectional factor, from Table 2.26

The allowable load on a beam or column is determined by employing the allowable stresses and the procedures given in the NDS.[11,12]

EXAMPLE 2.2 What is the fire endurance rating for a glulam beam of cross section 8.75 in wide by 16.5 in deep, carrying a uniform load, that develops 100 percent of its allowable design stress in bending and is subjected to exposure to fire on two sides and at the bottom? (A deck covers the top.)

From Figure 2.10, $Z = 1.0$, so

$$b/d = 8.75/16.5 = 0.530$$

$$G = 4 - b/d = 3.47$$

$$R = 2.54Zb(4 - b/d) = 2.54(1.0)(8.75)(3.47) = 77 \text{ min}$$

More precise procedures to allow glulam beams and columns to be designed to achieve given fire endurance ratings, as a function of laminate grade ordering and placement, are under development.

2.7.3 Fire and Draft Stopping

In all construction, no greater emphasis can be placed on the control of construction to reduce the fire growth hazard than the emplacement of fire and draft stops in concealed spaces. The spread of fire and smoke through these concealed openings within large rooms or between rooms has been a continuous cause of major life and property loss. As a result, most codes enforce their use. Detailing of fire and draft stops within building plans should be done and checked.

Recommendations for fire and draft stopping in wood construction have been developed by the American Forest and Paper Association. Refer to their brochure, *Improved Fire Safety: Design of Firestopping and Draft-Stopping for Concealed Spaces.* Fire stops considered acceptable are

- 2-in (38.1-mm) nominal lumber
- Two thicknesses of 1-in (19.0-mm) nominal lumber
- One thickness of ¾-in (19.0-mm) plywood with joints backed with ¾-in (19.0-mm) plywood

Draft stops do not require the fire resistance of fire stops, and therefore, they are not required to be as thick. Typical draft-stop materials and their minimum thicknesses are

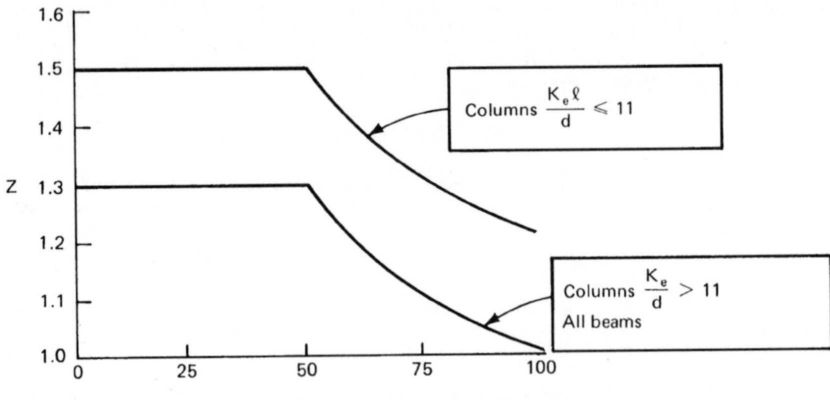

Buckling modes						
Theoretical K_e value	0.5	0.7	1.0	1.0	2.0	2.0
Recommended design K_e when ideal conditions approximated	0.65	0.80	1.2	1.0	2.10	2.4
End condition code		Rotation fixed, translation fixed				
		Rotation free, translation fixed				
		Rotation fixed, translation free				
		Rotation free, translation free				

Effective column length

FIG. 2.10 Determination of Z factor.

- ½-in (12.7-mm) gypsum wallboard
- ⅜-in (9.52-mm) plywood

Building codes have considered an area between draft stops of 1000 ft² (92.9 m²) as reasonable. Concealed spaces consisting of open-web floor truss components

TABLE 2.26 Cross-Sectional Factor G for Beams or Columns Exposed to Fire on Three and Four Sides

	Three sides	Four sides
Beam	$4 - b/d$	$4 - 2b/d$
Column	$3 - b/2d$	$3 - b/d$

Note: b = width of beam or larger side of column before exposure to fire, inches; d = depth of beam or smaller side of column before exposure to fire, inches.

in protected floor-ceiling assemblies are an important location to draft-stop parallel to the component. Areas of 500 ft^2 (46.4 m^2) in single-family dwellings and 1000 ft^2 (92.9 m^2) in other buildings are recommended, and between family compartments they are absolutely necessary.

Other important locations to fire-stop in wood frame construction are in concealed spaces

- of stud walls and partitions at ceiling and floor levels
- at intersections between concealed horizontal and vertical spaces such as occur at soffits
- at the top and bottom of stairs between stair stringers
- at openings around vents, pipes, ducts, chimneys (and fireplaces at ceiling and floor levels) with noncombustible fire stops

Critical draft-stop locations are in concealed spaces in

- floor-ceiling assemblies
- attics of multifamily dwellings when separation walls do not extend to the roof sheathing above

Draft stopping is not required where approved sprinklers are provided.

2.7.4 Flame Spread

The regulation of the materials used on the interior building surfaces (and sometimes exterior surfaces) of other than one- and two-family structures is provided to minimize the danger of rapid flame spread.

ASTM E 84[20] gives the method used to obtain the flame-spread property for regulatory purposes of paneling materials. Materials are classified as having a flame spread of more than or less than that of red oak, which has a base of 100. A noncombustible inorganic reinforced cement board has a base number of zero. A list of accredited flame-spread ratings for various commercial woods and wood products is given in Table 2.27. Note that most wood products lie in the 75 to 200 range of flame spread.

TABLE 2.27 ASTM E 84 Flame-Spread Classifications for Wood and Wood Products

Lumber, 1-in nominal thickness	
Yellow birch	105–110
Eastern red cedar (½ in)	110
Pacific Coast yellow cedar	78
Western red cedar	73, 70
Cottonwood	115
Cypress	145–150
Douglas fir	70–100
Douglas fir (½ in)	100
Red gum	140–155
West Coast hemlock	60–75
Maple flooring	104
Red or white oak	100
White pine	73
Eastern white pine	85
Idaho white pine	72
Lodgepole pine	93
Ponderosa pine*	154
Ponderosa pine (½ in)	105–200
Red pine	142
Southern yellow pine	130–195
Southern yellow pine (½ in)	130–190
Western white pine	75
Poplar	170–185
Redwood	70
Redwood (⅜ in nominal)	95
Redwood (½ in)	70–95
Northern spruce	65
Western spruce	100
White spruce	65
Spruce (½ in)	75–110
Teak	76
Walnut	130–140
Composite products	
Fiberboard, 16 lb/ft^3, ½ in	200–350
Fiberboard, 18 lb/ft^3, ½ in	54
Flakeboard, 42–47 lb/ft^3, ½ in, four types	71, 127, 147, 189
Flakeboard, red oak, 40 lb/ft^3, 1$\frac{1}{16}$ in	108
Hardboard, 60 lb/ft^3, ¼ in	130–200
Hardboard, 60 lb/ft^3, 0.2 in	153
Particleboard, phenolic or urea binder, ⅜–¾ in	145–200
Plywood, phenolic or urea glue, ⅜ in or thicker	75–200
Plywood, 0.1 in	228
Plywood, 0.2 in	205
Plywood, lauan, three-ply, $\frac{11}{64}$ in	167
Plywood, lauan, three-ply, $\frac{3}{16}$ in	69–271
Plywood, lauan, three-ply, urea glue, ¼ in	110
Plywood, Douglas fir, ¼ in	118
Plywood, redwood, ⅝ in	75
Plywood, redwood, ⅜ in	95
Plywood, walnut, ¾ in	130
Plywood, western species, 1⅛ in	56

*Mean value.

2.7.5 Fire-Retardant Treatments

It is possible to make wood highly resistant to the spread of fire by pressure impregnating it with one of the approved chemical formulations. Wood will char if exposed to fire or fire temperatures even if it is treated with a fire-retardant solution, but the rate of its destruction and the transmission of heat can be retarded by chemicals. The most significant contribution chemicals make, however, consists of reducing the spread of the fire. Wood that has absorbed adequate amounts of one of the recognized compounds will not support combustion nor contribute fuel and will cease to burn as soon as the source of ignition is removed.

The two general methods of improving the resistance of wood to fire are (1) impregnation with an effective chemical and (2) coating the surface with a layer of noncombustible paint. The first method is more effective. However, it is not recommended for use with certain products such as glued laminated timber. For interiors or locations protected from the weather, impregnation treatments can be considered permanent. Some coatings and fire-resistant paints, nevertheless, have considerable value in preventing ignition. These surface applications offer the principal means of increasing the fire-retardant properties of existing structures. They may, however, require periodic renewal if an effective coating is to be maintained.

Fire-retardant chemicals are injected into wood by the same pressure processes used in treatments to prevent decay.

2.7.6 Fire Retardants

Salts such as sodium tetraborate, diammonium phosphate, trisodium phosphate, diammonium sulfate, and salts of boric acid have long been used as fire retardants. Fire-retardant treatments or coatings are used to obtain wood products with flame-spread ratings below 75. Treated products with a special UL designation FR-5 have a flame-spread classification of not over 25 and no evidence of significant progressive combustion in an extended 30-min ASTM E 84 test. Flame-spread ratings for other proprietary products are listed by UL.

In the past, the only effective chemicals were water soluble, making fire-retardant treatments unadaptable to weather exposure. Impregnated fire retardants that are more resistant to both high humidity and exterior exposures are becoming increasingly available on the market for treated lumber and plywood products. The chemicals are bound to the wood structure and cross-linked to enhance their durability. The majority of these treatments are patented and trademarked.

Many fire-retardant salt treatments are very hygroscopic. Accordingly, most formulations are not recommended for use where relative humidity is over 80 percent. Recently, fire-retardant resin treatments have been developed that largely overcome hygroscopic and corrosion problems, but because they are proprietary, little is known of their nature.

Several studies have investigated the relationships between strength properties and fire-retardant salt treatments. The chemicals used in fire-retardant (FR) treatments are thermally stable for short periods at temperatures up to 330°F. However, recent Forest Products Laboratory research has shown that over extended exposure, the limit of thermal stability for fire-retardant–treated material is between 130 and 150°F.

While fire-retardant–treated lumber and plywood have been used successfully in structures exposed to temperatures less than 100°F for nearly 50 years, field failures have occurred in buildings that used fire-retardant–treated plywood as roof sheathing. These failures show that elevated temperatures induced by solar radiation caused some commercial fire-retardant formulations to undergo thermal decomposition.

Design Guidelines. Designers intending to use fire-retardant–treated materials in areas of elevated temperatures, such as roof decks, should ask suppliers the following questions:

1. Does the fire-retardant formulator-treater warranty the fire-retardant–treated material for the intended use?

2. What are the initial effects of the fire-retardant formulation on wood strength, stiffness, and fastener corrosion?

3. Has the material been tested at elevated temperatures?

4. Has an approved third-party inspection agency certified compliance with all existing standards?

5. Was the material dried after treatment to required moisture content levels? These moisture content levels are required for proper structural performance. AWPA has implemented new drying requirements.

6. Will precautions be used during shipping and at the job site to prevent moisture from rewetting the material and to allow proper drying if exposed?

2.8 SOUND CONTROL

Sound control in wood structures is closely related to providing fire resistance. Procedures which produce excellent fire-resistive performance also provide high resistance to sound transmission. This is largely because heat transmission and fire movement are controlled by construction and material properties that influence sound transmission in the same way.

Noise is transmitted from one compartment to another as airborne, structure-borne, or impact noise, and measures are needed for each. The difference in vibrational energy transferred from one side of a barrier to another determines its effectiveness in insulating against noise. It is important to isolate a wall assembly from a ceiling or a floor assembly. Leaks through cracks at the boundaries that provide a path for airborne sound are significant reducers of sound barrier effectiveness.

Structureborne noise is normally that due to vibrations generated from fans, compressors, water movement in pipes, air movement in ducts, and so on, which are not isolated from the structure.

For convenience in specifying the sound-insulating qualities, a single number, called the *sound transmission class* (STC), is determined for various wall, ceiling, and floor assemblies. The higher the number, the better the sound barrier. Values of 55 to 65 are commonly cited for good barriers. The way a sound barrier like a wall or floor affects acoustical privacy is illustrated in Fig. 2.11. In this case, the STC is about 50.

The STC rating system is based on measurements using ASTM E 90.[21]

To minimize the transmission of sound through floor-ceiling assemblies from the movement of people or objects on floors separating two living units, impact

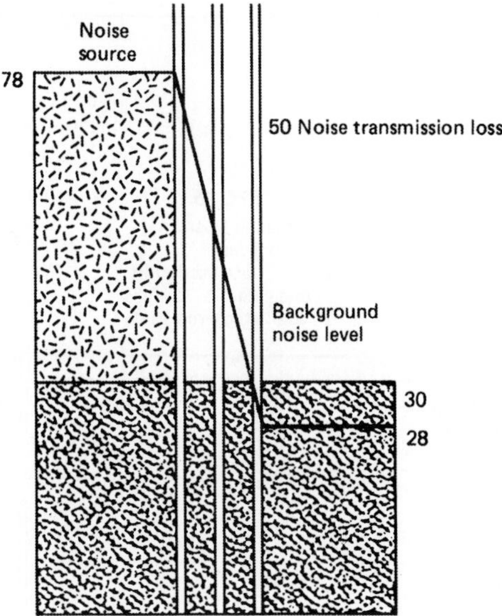

FIG. 2.11 Sound barrier effectiveness. A good sound barrier should reduce the noise originating in one room to below the background noise level in an adjacent room.

insulation is needed. The U.S. Housing and Urban Development *Guide to Noise Control in Multifamily Dwellings*[22] discusses the incorporation of such control. Impact insulation classes (IIC) are determined for floor-ceiling assemblies and are similar in concept to the STC airborne noise rating. ASTM D 492 provides the description and interpretation of a tapping test to generate IIC numbers. From a design standpoint, one first establishes the airborne noise insulating class for a floor-ceiling assembly and then selects the floor covering to obtain the appropriate IIC rating. Often a floor-ceiling assembly with a STC rating of 50 also will have an acceptable IIC rating near 50. The IIC rating from no carpet to a heavy carpet can increase by about 20 dB.

Sound transmission levels for some windows, doors, walls, and floor-ceiling assemblies are illustrated in Figs. 2.12 and 2.13. Note that gypsum wallboard wall coverings on studs and as ceilings on joist floors provide STC levels only between 30 and 35. Additional isolation of the two surfaces or the addition of batt insulation is needed to reach more desirable STC levels of 45 to 50. Single-pane windows and hollow-core doors are known to be poor sound insulators.

Impact sound insulation is required by the major U.S. codes for floor-ceiling assemblies between separate units or guest rooms. Floor coverings, such as carpet, may be included in the assembly to achieve required impact IIC insulation levels of at least 45.

Sound transmission levels for various assemblies are given in the *Fire Resistance Design Manual,*[18] and both STCs and IICs for wall and floor-ceiling assemblies are listed in a California Department of Health Services catalog.[23]

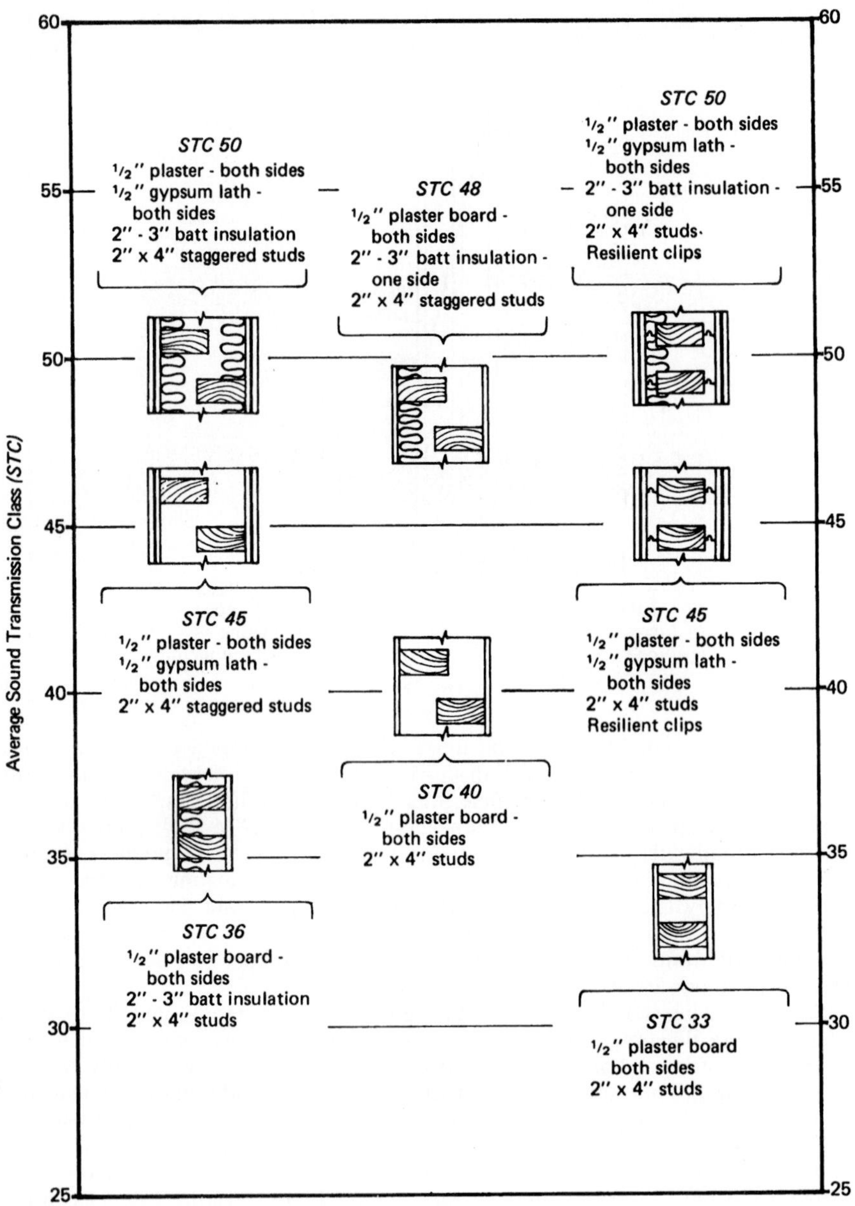

FIG. 2.12 Sound transmission class ratings—walls.

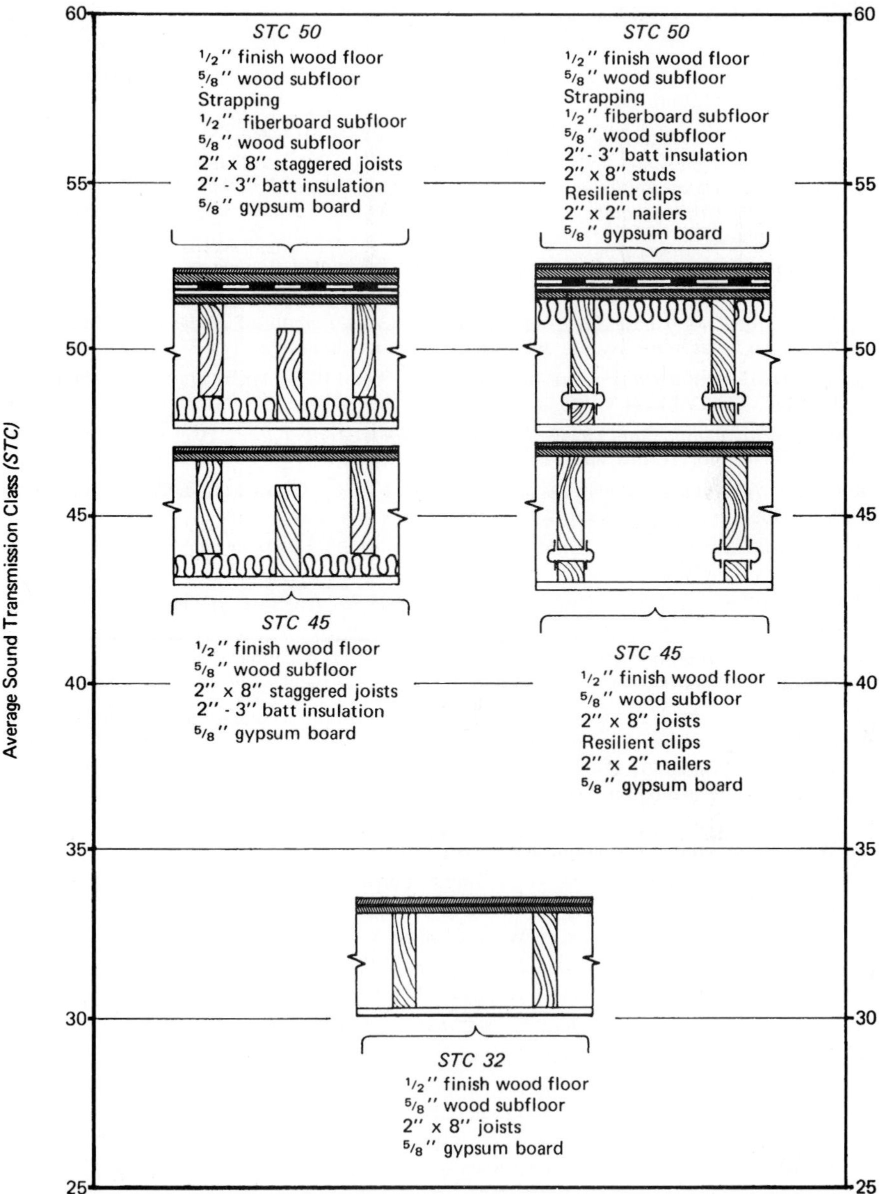

FIG. 2.13 Sound transmission class ratings—floors.

REFERENCES

1. *American Lumber Standards,* U.S. Products Standard PS 20-94, U.S. Department of Commerce, Washington, D.C.
2. *Standard Methods for Establishing Clear Wood Strength Values,* ASTM D 2555, American Society for Testing and Materials, Philadelphia, Pa.
3. *Standard Methods for Establishing Structural Grades and Related Allowable Properties for Visually Graded Lumber,* ASTM D 245, American Society for Testing and Materials, Philadelphia, Pa.
4. *Standard Specifications for Structural Glued Laminated Timber of Softwood Species,* AITC 117, American Institute of Timber Construction, Englewood, Colo.
5. *Method for Establishing Stresses for Structural Glued Laminated Timbers,* ASTM D 3737, American Society for Testing and Materials, Philadelphia, Pa.
6. *Specifications and Dimensions for Wood Poles,* ANSI 05.1, American National Standards Institute, New York, N.Y.
7. *Method for Establishing Design Stresses for Round Timber Piles,* ASTM D 2899, American Society for Testing and Materials, Philadelphia, Pa.
8. *Method for Static Test of Wood Poles.* ASTM D 1036, American Society for Testing and Materials, Philadelphia, Pa.
9. *National Electrical Safety Code,* Handbook 81, National Institute of Standards and Technology, Gaithersburg, Md.
10. *Specifications for Round Timber Poles,* ASTM D 25, American Society for Testing and Materials, Philadelphia, Pa.
11. *National Design Specification for Wood Construction,* American Forest and Paper Association, Washington, D.C.
12. *Design Values for Wood Construction—A Supplement to the National Design Specification for Wood Construction,* American Forest and Paper Association, Washington, D.C.
13. *Wood Preservative Treating Practices,* Federal Specification TT-W-571, U.S. Federal Supply Service, Washington, D.C.
14. *Standard for the Care of Preservative-Treated Wood Products,* AWPA M4, American Wood Preservers' Association, Stevensville, Md.
15. *Code Conforming Wood Design,* American Forest and Paper Association, Washington, D.C.
16. *Wood and Fire Safety,* Canadian Wood Council, Ottawa, Canada.
17. *Method for Fire Tests of Building Construction and Materials,* ASTM E 119, American Society for Testing and Materials, Philadelphia, Pa.
18. *Fire Resistance Design Manual,* Gypsum Association, Evanston, Ill.
19. *Fire Protection Handbook,* National Fire Protection Association, Boston, Mass.
20. *Test Method for Surface Burning Characteristics of Building Materials,* ASTM E 84, American Society for Testing and Materials, Philadelphia, Pa.
21. *Method for Laboratory Measurement of Airborne-Sound Transmission Loss of Building Partitions,* ASTM E 90, American Society for Testing and Materials, Philadelphia, Pa.
22. R. D. Berendt et al., *A Guide to Airborne Impact and Structure-Borne Noise Control in Multifamily Dwellings,* Rep. FT/TS-24, U.S. Department of Housing and Urban Development, Washington, D.C.
23. R. B. DuPree, *Catalog of STC and IIC Ratings for Wall and Floor/Ceiling Assemblies,* California Department of Health Services, Berkeley, Calif.
24. *Standard Specifications for Evaluation of Structural Composite Lumber Products,* ASTM D 5456, American Society for Testing and Materials, Philadelphia, Pa.

CHAPTER 3
COLUMNS

David G. Pollock, Jr., P.E.
S. K. Malhotra, Ph.D., P.E.

3.1 COLUMN BEHAVIOR

3.1.1 General

A column is a compression member whose length is usually many times greater than its cross-sectional dimensions. Wood columns may be divided into three general classes: simple solid columns, spaced columns, and built-up columns. The types of wood columns used most frequently are the simple solid columns, which consist of a single solid piece or of pieces properly glued together to form a single member. Spaced columns are assemblies of two or more individual members joined longitudinally with timber connectors and separated at the ends and middle points of their length by blocking. Built-up columns (excluding spaced columns) are fabricated by joining individual pieces with mechanical fastenings along the length.

Depending on the relationship between length and cross-sectional dimensions of the column, termed the *slenderness ratio,* the design of wood columns is limited by a combination of stiffness and compression parallel to grain strength.

3.1.2 Slenderness Ratio and Shape of Cross Section

In its traditional form, the *slenderness ratio* is defined as the ratio of the unbraced, or unsupported, length to the least radius of gyration r, in which $r = \sqrt{I/A}$, where I is the moment of inertia of the cross section about the weak axis and A is the area of cross section. For rectangular wood columns, the slenderness ratio is expressed as the ratio of the unbraced column length to the least dimension of the column. If the unbraced length of the column is not the same about both the strong and weak axes, when considering buckling about these two axes of the section (Fig. 3.1), the larger of the two slenderness ratios L_1/d_1 and L_2/d_2 is used for design calculations. In cases where buckling is effectively prevented about one axis, the slenderness ratio to be taken in the design is determined by taking the unbraced length for the other axis. Such a case can exist in studs in a bearing wall (Fig. 3.2). If adequate sheathing is properly fastened to the studs, buckling is prevented about the weak axis of the stud (axis 2–2), and only the slenderness ratio about axis

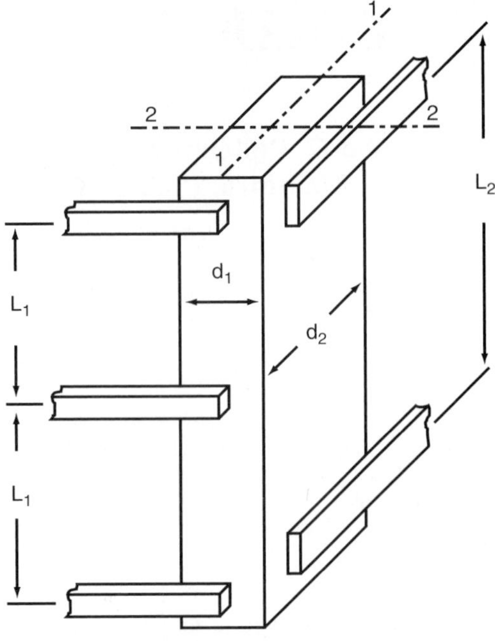

FIG. 3.1 Slenderness ratios in simple solid column.

1–1 needs to be evaluated. The slenderness ratio is not permitted to exceed 50 for simple solid columns or built-up columns and 80 for individual members of spaced columns, except that the slenderness ratio is permitted to approach 75 for simple solid columns or built-up columns used as temporary bracing during construction.

The design formula for columns having rectangular cross sections can be used for other column shapes, such as circular or I section, by substituting $r\sqrt{12}$ for d

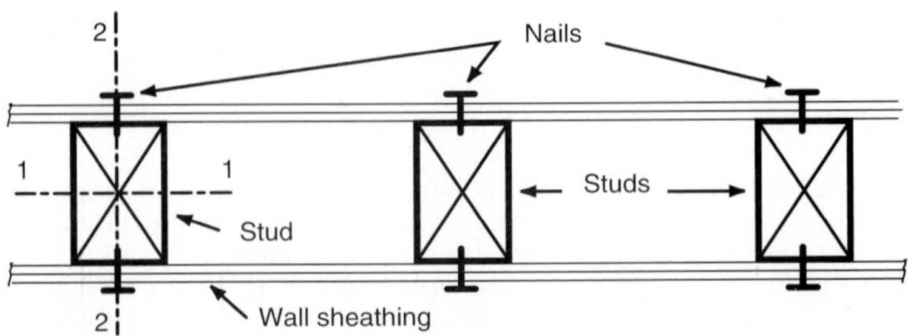

FIG. 3.2 Column buckling in stud wall.

in the formula; where r is the applicable radius of gyration of the column cross section. Thus the design load for a column of round cross section is the same as that for a square column with equivalent cross-sectional area. Multiplying the diameter of the round column by 0.886 gives the dimension d of the equivalent square column.

For a column of rectangular cross section, tapered at one or both ends, the dimension d for calculating the slenderness ratio in each plane of the column (Fig. 3.3) is taken as

$$d = d_{\min} + (d_{\max} - d_{\min}) \left[a - 0.15 \left(1 - \frac{d_{\min}}{d_{\max}} \right) \right] \tag{3.1}$$

where $d_{\min}$ = the minimum dimension for that plane of the column
$d_{\max}$ = the maximum dimension for that plane of the column

Support Conditions

$a = 0.7$ Large end fixed, small end unsupported or simply supported
$a = 0.3$ Small end fixed, large end unsupported or simply supported
$a = 0.5$ Both ends simply supported, tapered toward one end
$a = 0.7$ Both ends simply supported, tapered toward both ends

For all other support conditions, the dimension d is taken as

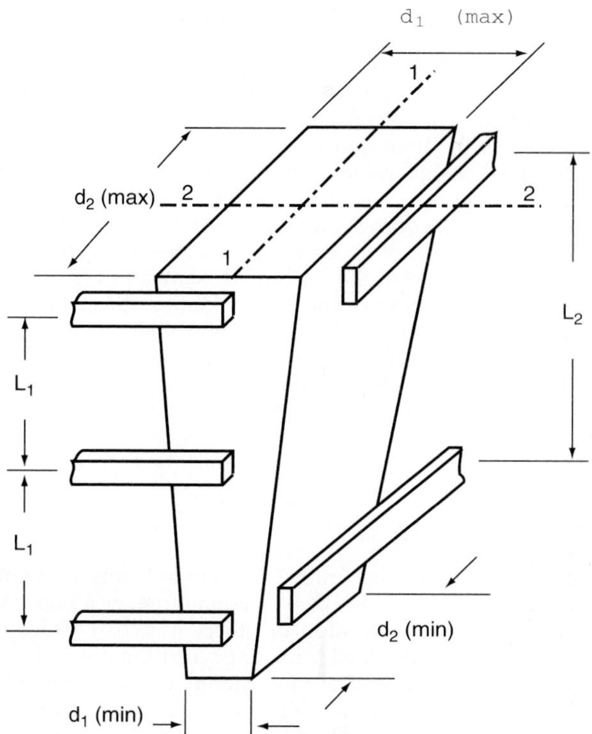

FIG. 3.3 Slenderness ratios in tapered rectangular column.

$$d = d_{\min} + \frac{1}{3}(d_{\max} - d_{\min}) \tag{3.2}$$

The design value in compression parallel to grain, adjusted for lateral stability using the slenderness ratio, applies to the cross-sectional area of the tapered column corresponding to the dimension d used in the calculation. A column with a round cross section, tapered at one or both ends, is treated like a square column of the same cross-sectional area and having the same degree of taper. In addition, the design value in compression parallel to grain (without adjustment for lateral stability) should not be exceeded at any cross section in a tapered column.

3.1.3 End-Restraint Conditions

The load capacity of a column is dependent on its end-restraint conditions. Generally, a column held in position and restrained against rotation at both its ends (fixed ends) is much stronger than a pin-end column that is rotation-free but translation-fixed and of the same length and cross section. The design formulas for simple solid columns are given for pin-end conditions. The effect of column end restraints is recognized in the design procedure by the introduction of the effective-length concept.

When column-end conditions are different than pin-end, the effective length of the column for design can be determined in accordance with good engineering practice. The effective length L_e is taken as the distance between the points of inflection on the buckled column. An inflection point represents a point of zero moment and is a location of reverse curvature on the deflected shape of the column. Thus it can be considered as a pinned end for the column analysis. The effective length of a column with square-end conditions fixed against translation is usually taken to be the same as the unbraced length.

Commonly accepted design values and theoretical values of effective length for various end-restraint conditions are given in Fig. 3.4. Some of the design values are somewhat higher than the corresponding theoretical values. Since a perfect fixed end condition seldom occurs, it is common practice to increase the theoretical values for use in design. Three of the conditions, shown in Fig. 3.4*a* to *c*, represent columns that undergo no sidesway, and the remaining three, Fig. 3.4*d* to *f*, have sidesway. The identification of a column that will undergo sidesway depends on the type of system provided to resist lateral forces. For example, columns in a rigid frame without bracing will undergo sidesway if the columns buckle (Fig. 3.5). However, sidesway is prevented in columns of a frame with adequate bracing to resist lateral forces.

3.1.4 Effects of Eccentricity

The design equations given in the following sections apply to columns subjected to axial compression only. The concept of a column under a concentric axial load is only an idealized case. Compression members in actual structures have some unavoidable eccentricities of the load with respect to the column axis created due to initial curvature, nonhomogeneity of the material, or construction tolerances. The magnitude of the bending moment developed by this eccentric loading is generally unknown. In many practical cases, ignoring this moment effect may be justifiable

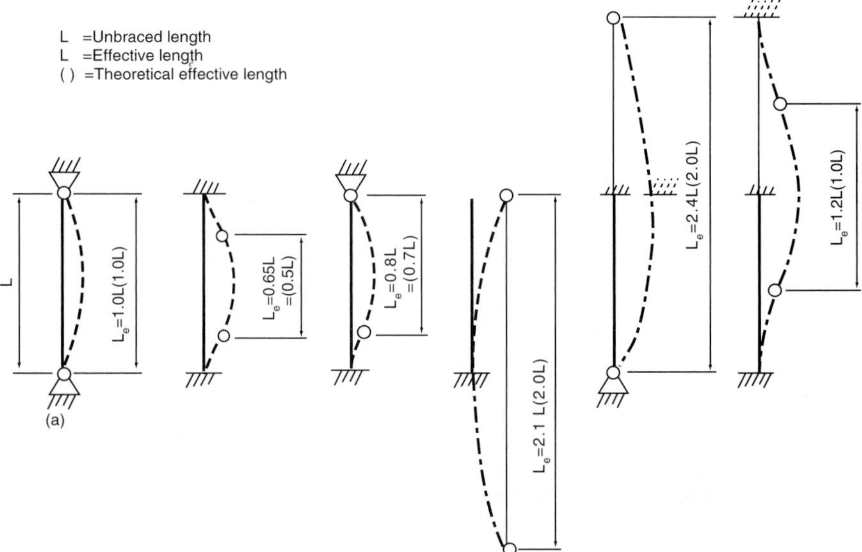

FIG. 3.4 Effective length for columns with various end-restraint conditions. (*a–c*) Columns without sidesway; (*d–f*) columns with sidesway.

because it is compensated for by safety adjustments included in the published design equations and design values.

It has been suggested by Gurfinkel[1] that wood columns should be designed for some minimum unavoidable eccentricity, as is the practice in the design of axially loaded reinforced concrete columns. However, there is no requirement in the *National Design Specification for Wood Construction* (NDS)[2] that wood columns must be designed for this minimum eccentricity. The inclusion or exclusion of a minimum eccentric moment in the design of a wood column is left to the judgment of the designer.

Besides the above-mentioned minimum unavoidable eccentricity, a column may be subjected to intentional eccentric loading. The design of columns under eccentric or side loading is dealt with in Sec. 3.7.

3.2 COLUMN DESIGN FORMULAS

3.2.1 Design Equations

Columns are designed to resist failure in direct compression (crushing of wood fibers) and buckling. Adjusted design values for wood columns are determined by

$$F'_c = F^*_c \left\{ \frac{1 + (F_{cE}/F^*_c)}{2c} - \sqrt{\left[\frac{1 + (F_{cE}/F^*_c)}{2c}\right]^2 - \frac{F_{cE}/F^*_c}{c}} \right\} \tag{3.3}$$

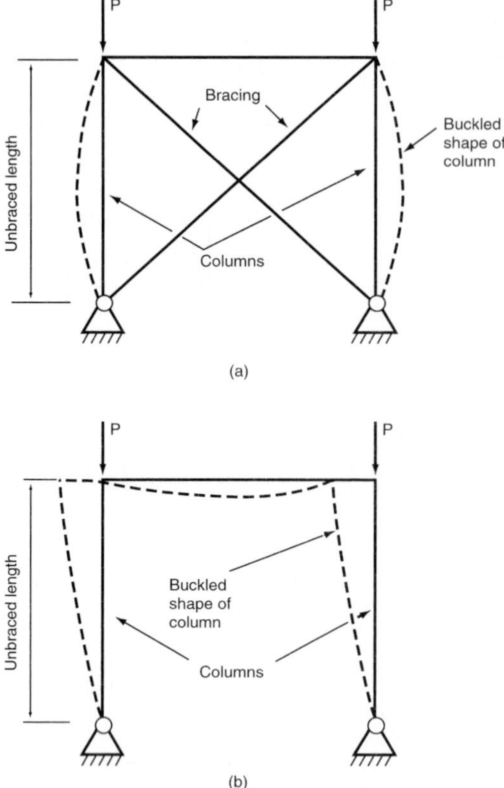

FIG. 3.5 Systems showing columns (*a*) without and (*b*) with sidesway.

where F'_c = allowable compression parallel to grain design value adjusted for service conditions, size effect, and lateral stability

F^*_c = compression parallel to grain design value adjusted for service conditions (moisture, temperature, load duration) and size effect

F_{cE} = critical buckling design value

c = 0.8 for sawn lumber, 0.85 for round timber poles and piles, 0.9 for glued-laminated timber and structural composite lumber

The critical buckling design value is determined by the well-known Euler column formula:

$$F_{cE} = \frac{K_{cE}E'}{(L_e/d)^2} \tag{3.4}$$

where E' = allowable modulus of elasticity adjusted for service conditions (moisture, temperature)

d = dimension of column in plane of lateral support (see Sec. 3.1.2)

L_e = effective column length in plane of lateral support (see Sec. 3.1.3)
K_{cE} = 0.300 for products with $COV_E = 0.25$, such as visually graded lumber and round timber poles and piles; 0.384 for products with $COV_E = 0.15$, such as machine evaluated lumber (MEL); 0.418 for products with $COV_E \leq 0.11$, such as machine stress-rated (MSR) lumber, glued-laminated timber, and structural composite lumber

The Euler buckling coefficient K_{cE} increases with decreasing coefficient of variation in modulus of elasticity COV_E, thus providing increased column design values for products with lower variability.

Equation (3.3) provides a continuous curve which describes the interaction between crushing and buckling in columns with various slenderness ratios. Figure 3.6 shows the variation in column design values with increasing slenderness ratio. Columns which are fully braced against buckling ($L_e/d = 0$) are controlled by direct compression (crushing) strength of the material. As the slenderness ratio L_e/d increases, column design values are controlled more and more by buckling strength, until at high L_e/d ratios Eq. (3.3) approaches the critical Euler buckling curve.

The constant c in Eq. (3.3) accounts for material nonhomogeneity and initial eccentricity associated with member warp, providing increased column design values for products which are straighter and more homogeneous. The magnitude of c for visually graded lumber was established by empirically fitting Eq. (3.3) to test data for lumber columns of various species, grades, and sizes. Tests of glued-laminated timber and structural composite lumber columns are currently underway to assess the appropriate magnitudes of c for these products.

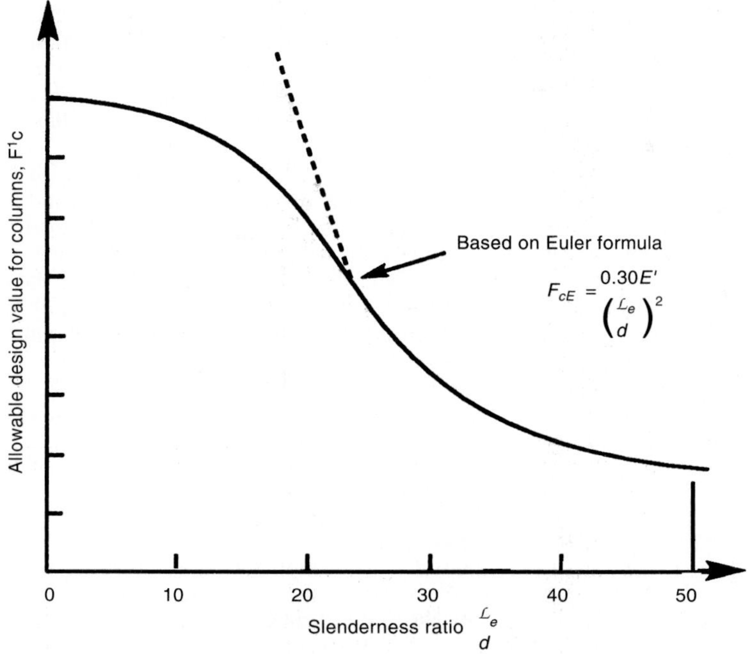

FIG. 3.6 Column design stress versus slenderness ratio.

Equations (3.3) and (3.4) apply to simple solid columns. Modified forms of these equations are provided later in this chapter for spaced columns and built-up columns.

3.2.2 Net Section

The allowable design value F'_c applies to the full column section, except that it is applied to the net column section for the case in which the reduced section occurs in the critical portion of the column length that is most subject to potential buckling. Furthermore, the unit stress developed in any column based on the net column section at any point in the column length is not to exceed the design value F^*_c adjusted for all conditions except lateral stability.

3.3 SIMPLE SOLID SAWN COLUMNS

Simple solid sawn columns are designed according to Eqs. (3.3) and (3.4). The design of columns is a trial-and-error process. The length of the column and the axial load it has to carry are given. A member must be selected with a cross-sectional area such that the unit compressive stress developed by the applied load does not exceed the allowable column stress for the column material and conditions of use. However, the allowable column stress depends on the slenderness ratio and cannot be determined until the cross-sectional dimensions are known. Thus the design has to be carried out by investigating trial sections. A trial section is assumed, and the allowable load for the section is calculated. If the calculated (allowable) value of the load is less than the applied load, or if it is too large, leading to an uneconomical size, another trial section is assumed. This process is continued until a satisfactory cross section is determined. The stepwise procedure outlined below may be followed.

Step 1. Note the values of E and F_c for the assumed column material from appropriate design tables. Adjust these values for applicable service conditions.

Step 2. Assume a trial section, based on the applicable design load and the tabulated F_c value for assumed species and applicable service conditions.

Step 3. Determine the effective length of the column, depending on the column end conditions. Compute the slenderness ratio L_e/d for the trial section; it must not exceed 50 unless the column is being used as temporary bracing during construction in which case it may not exceed 75.

Step 4. Compute the value of F_{cE} and F'_c using Eqs. (3.3) and (3.4).

Step 5. By using F'_c, the value of allowable stress in the column calculated from Step 4, the allowable axial load is determined as

$$P = F'_c A$$

in which A is the area of the column cross section.

Step 6. If the calculated value of P from Step 5 is equal to or slightly greater than the applied axial load on the column, the trial section is accepted. If the calculated value is either less than or significantly larger than the applied load, repeat the process (Steps 1 to 6) for another trial section.

EXAMPLE 3.1 Calculate the maximum allowable load that a nominal 6- by 6-in (139.7- by 139.7-mm)* sawn lumber column, 16 ft (4.88 m) long, can carry. The applied loading is combined dead and snow loads. The column is effectively held in position at both ends and is restrained against rotation at one end. Assume the tabulated design values to be E = 1,300,000 lb/in² (8963 MPa) and F_c = 975 lb/in² (6723 kPa).[1]

SOLUTION: Given section:

$$\text{Dressed dimensions} = 5.5 \times 5.5 \text{ in}$$
$$A = 30.25 \text{ in}^2$$

Allowable stresses:

$$E' = 1{,}300{,}000 \text{ lb/in}^2$$
$$F_c^* = 975 \times 1.15 = 1121 \text{ lb/in}^2$$

Effective length:

$$L_e = 0.8L = 0.8 \times 16 = 12.8 \text{ ft}$$

Slenderness ratio:

$$\frac{L_e}{d} = \frac{12.8 \times 12}{5.5} = 27.9 < 50 \qquad \text{OK}$$

Allowable design value:

$$F_{cE} = \frac{0.30E'}{(L_e/d)^2} = \frac{0.30 \times 1{,}300{,}000}{27.9^2} = 501 \text{ lb/in}^2$$

$$\frac{F_{cE}}{F_c^*} = \frac{501}{1121} = 0.447$$

$$F_c' = 1121\left[\frac{1 + 0.447}{2 \times 0.8} - \sqrt{\left(\frac{1 + 0.447}{2 \times 0.8}\right)^2 - \frac{0.447}{0.8}}\right] = 443 \text{ lb/in}^2$$

Maximum allowable load:

$$P = F_c'A = 443 \times 30.25 = 13{,}405 \text{ lb (59.6 kN)}$$

EXAMPLE 3.2 Determine the size of a sawn lumber column of unbraced length of 12 ft (3.66 m) to carry an axial load of 45 kips (220.2 kN). Assume end conditions of the column to be square ends and loading as combined dead and snow loads. Use nominal 6-in (139.7-mm) or wider material for the column. Assume the tabulated design values to be E = 1,700,000 lb/in² (11,722 MPa) and F_c = 1350 lb/in² (9808 kPa).

*All SI units shown for sawn lumber are for the actual net dimensions corresponding to the nominal dimension indicated. In all example problems, SI units are only provided for given data and the final problem answer or answers. No intermediate values or data are expressed in SI units.

SOLUTION: Try nominal 6×6 in:

$$\text{Dressed dimensions} = 5.5 \times 5.5 \text{ in}$$
$$A = 30.25 \text{ in}^2$$

Allowable stresses:

$$E' = 1{,}700{,}000 \text{ lb/in}^2$$
$$F_c^* = 1350 \times 1.15 = 1552 \text{ lb/in}^2$$

Effective length:

$$L_e = 1.0L = 12 \text{ ft}$$

Slenderness ratio:

$$\frac{L_e}{d} = \frac{12 \times 12}{5.5} = 26.2 < 50 \qquad \text{OK}$$

Allowable design value:

$$F_{cE} = \frac{0.30E'}{(L_e/d)^2} = \frac{0.30 \times 1{,}700{,}000}{26.2^2} = 743 \text{ lb/in}^2$$

$$\frac{F_{cE}}{F_c^*} = \frac{743}{1552} = 0.479$$

$$F_c' = 1552 \left[\frac{1 + 0.479}{2 \times 0.8} - \sqrt{\left(\frac{1 + 0.479}{2 \times 0.8}\right)^2 - \frac{0.479}{0.8}} \right] = 650 \text{ lb/in}^2$$

Allowable axial load:

$$P = F_c'A = 650 \times 30.25$$
$$= 19{,}660 \text{ lb} = 19.66 \text{ kips} < 45 \text{ kips} \qquad \text{SECTION NOT ADEQUATE}$$

Try nominal 8×8 in

$$\text{Dressed dimensions} = 7.5 \times 7.5 \text{ in}$$
$$A = 56.25 \text{ in}^2$$

Design values (E' and F_c^*) for the new trial section are the same as for the first.

Slenderness ratio:

$$\frac{L_e}{d} = \frac{12 \times 12}{7.5} = 19.2 < 50 \qquad \text{OK}$$

Allowable design value:

$$F_{cE} = \frac{0.30E'}{(L_e/d)^2} = \frac{0.30 \times 1{,}700{,}000}{19.2^2} = 1383 \text{ lb/in}^2$$

$$\frac{F_{cE}}{F_c^*} = \frac{1383}{1552} = 0.891$$

$$F_c' = 1552 \left[\frac{1 + 0.891}{2 \times 0.8} - \sqrt{\left(\frac{1 + 0.891}{2 \times 0.8}\right)^2 - \frac{0.891}{0.8}} \right] = 1009 \text{ lb/in}^2$$

Allowable axial load:

$$P = F_c'A = 1009 \times 56.25$$
$$= 56{,}760 \text{ lb } (252.5 \text{ kN}) = 56.76 \text{ kips} > 45 \text{ kips} \qquad \text{OK}$$

Use an 8- × 8-in (190.4- × 190.4-mm) column section.

EXAMPLE 3.3 Determine the maximum allowable axial load a round column 8 in (203.2 mm) in diameter and 12 ft (3.66m) long can carry for the tabulated design values of $E = 1{,}700{,}000$ lb/in² (11,722 MPa) and $F_c = 1200$ lb/in² (8274 kPa). The base of the column is effectively held in position and restrained against rotation, and the top is restrained neither against rotation nor against horizontal movement. The duration of load is normal.

SOLUTION: Given section:

$$\text{Column diameter} = 8 \text{ in}$$
$$\text{Equivalent } d = 0.886 \times 8 = 7.09 \text{ in}$$
$$A = 50.27 \text{ in}^2$$

Allowable stresses:

$$E' = 1{,}700{,}000 \text{ lb/in}^2$$
$$F_c^* = 1200 \text{ lb/in}^2$$

Effective length:

$$L_e = 2.1L = 2.1 \times 12 = 25.2 \text{ ft}$$

Slenderness ratio:

$$\frac{L_e}{d} = \frac{25.2 \times 12}{7.09} = 42.65 < 50 \qquad \text{OK}$$

Allowable design value:

$$F_{cE} = \frac{0.30E'}{(L_e/d)^2} = \frac{0.30 \times 1{,}700{,}000}{42.65^2} = 280 \text{ lb/in}^2$$

$$\frac{F_{cE}}{F_c^*} = \frac{280}{1200} = 0.233$$

$$F_c' = 1200 \left[\frac{1 + 0.233}{2 \times 0.85} - \sqrt{\left(\frac{1 + 0.233}{2 \times 0.85} \right)^2 - \frac{0.233}{0.85}} \right] = 268 \text{ lb/in}^2$$

Maximum allowable load:

$$P = F_c'A = 268 \times 50.27$$
$$= 13{,}470 \text{ lb (59.9 kN)}$$

3.4 GLUED-LAMINATED COLUMNS

Glulam columns are designed according to Eqs. (3.3) and (3.4). The use of seasoned lumber for the laminations and a more even distribution of defects within the fabricated member result in less variability in mechanical properties than for sawn lumber and thus permit higher F_c' values for glulam columns. Tables of design values for various structural glulam timbers are given in the NDS.[2]

EXAMPLE 3.4 Check the adequacy of an 8½- by 12⅜-in (215.9- by 314.3-mm) glulam column of 16-ft 6-in (5.03-m) unbraced length to carry an axial load of 165 kips (733.9 kN) (Fig. 3.7). Assume the tabulated design values for a southern pine laminating combination A-51 to be E = 1,700,000 lb/in² (11,722 MPa) and F_c =

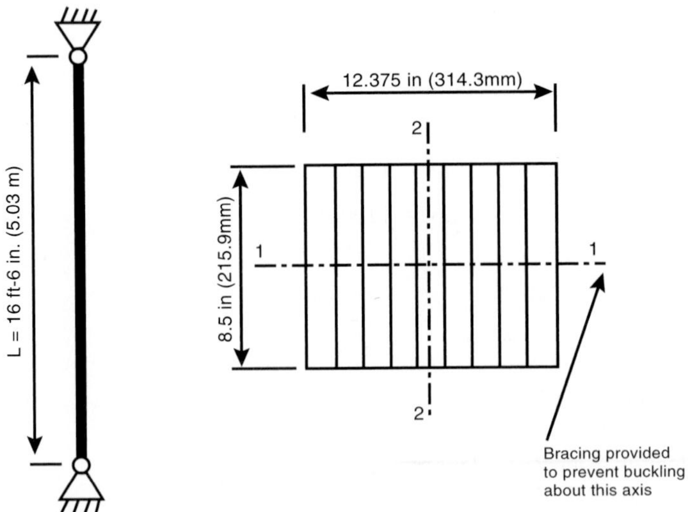

FIG. 3.7 Glued-laminated column in Example 3.4.

1900 lb/in^2 (13,100 kPa). The service condition is dry use, and the duration of load is normal. Consider end conditions of the column as pin-ends. The column is braced in such a manner that buckling is prevented about the weak axis of the cross section (axis 1–1 in Fig. 3.7).

SOLUTION: Given section:

$$\text{Net dimensions} = 8.5 \times 12.375 \text{ in}$$
$$A = 105.2 \text{ in}^2$$

Allowable stresses:

$$E' = 1{,}700{,}000 \text{ lb/in}^2$$
$$F_c^* = 1900 \text{ lb/in}^2$$

Effective length:

$$L_e = 1.0L = 16.5 \text{ ft}$$

Slenderness ratio:

$$\frac{L_e}{d} = \frac{16.5 \times 12}{12.375} = 16.0 < 50 \qquad \text{OK}$$

Allowable design value:

$$F_{cE} = \frac{0.418E'}{(L_e/d)^2} = \frac{0.418 \times 1{,}700{,}000}{16^2} = 2776 \text{ lb/in}^2$$

$$\frac{F_{cE}}{F_c^*} = \frac{2776}{1900} = 1.46$$

$$F_c' = 1900\left[\frac{1 + 1.46}{2 \times 0.9} - \sqrt{\left(\frac{1 + 1.46}{2 \times 0.9}\right)^2 - \frac{1.46}{0.9}}\right] = 1655 \text{ lb/in}^2$$

Allowable load:

$$P = F_c'A = 1655 \times 105.2$$
$$= 174{,}100 \text{ lb (774.5 kN)} = 174.1 \text{ kips} > 165 \text{ kips} \qquad \text{OK}$$

EXAMPLE 3.5 Design a glulam column having a 12-ft (3.66-m) length to carry an axial load of 46 kips (204.6 kN). Assume that a Douglas fir–larch laminating combination A-1 is to be used and the column is to be built of 1½-in (38.1-mm)-thick by 6¾-in (171.5-mm)-wide laminations. Assume wet service conditions and a duration of load of 2 months. The end conditions of the column are taken as pin-ends. The tabulated design values for this column are E = 1,500,000 lb/in^2 (10,342 MPa) with a wet-use factor of 0.833 and F_c = 1550 lb/in^2 (10,687 kPa) with a wet-use factor of 0.73.

SOLUTION: Try 6¾ × 7½ in:

$$\text{Net dimensions} = 6.75 \times 7.5 \text{ in}$$
$$A = 50.62 \text{ in}^2$$

Allowable stresses:

$$E' = 1{,}500{,}000 \times 0.833 = 1{,}249{,}500 \text{ lb/in}^2$$
$$F_c^* = 1550 \times 0.73 \times 1.15 = 1301 \text{ lb/in}^2$$

Effective length:

$$L_e = 1.0L = 12 \text{ ft}$$

Slenderness ratio:

$$\frac{L_e}{d} = \frac{12 \times 12}{6.75} = 21.3 < 50 \qquad \text{OK}$$

Allowable design value:

$$F_{cE} = \frac{0.418E'}{(L_e/d)^2} = \frac{0.418 \times 1{,}249{,}500}{21.3^2} = 1151 \text{ lb/in}^2$$

$$\frac{F_{cE}}{F_c^*} = \frac{1151}{1301} = 0.885$$

$$F_c' = 1301 \left[\frac{1 + 0.885}{2 \times 0.9} - \sqrt{\left(\frac{1 + 0.885}{2 \times 0.9}\right)^2 - \frac{0.885}{0.9}} \right] = 924 \text{ lb/in}^2$$

Allowable axial load:

$$P = F_c'A = 924 \times 50.62$$
$$= 46{,}800 \text{ lb (208 kN)} = 46.8 \text{ kips} > 46 \text{ kips} \qquad \text{OK}$$

Use 6¾- × 7.5-in (171.5- × 190.5-mm) glulam section.

EXAMPLE 3.6 Evaluate the adequacy of a 1.75- by 3.5-in (44.4- by 88.9-mm) structural composite lumber column 7 ft 6 in (2.29 m) long to carry an axial load of 7 kips (31.1 kN). Assume end conditions of the column to be pin-ends, buckling of the column prevented about the weak axis of the cross section, and loading as combined dead and snow loads. Assume the tabulated design values to be E = 2,000,000 lb/in² (13,790 MPa) and F_c = 2800 lb/in² (19,306 kPa). Structural composite lumber generally has a coefficient of variation (COV) of less than 11 percent for its mechanical properties.

SOLUTION: Given section:

$$\text{Net dimensions} = 1.75 \times 3.5 \text{ in}$$
$$A = 6.12 \text{ in}^2$$

Allowable stresses:

$$E' = 2{,}000{,}000 \text{ lb/in}^2$$

$$F_c^* = 2800 \times 1.15 = 3220 \text{ lb/in}^2$$

Effective length:

$$L_e = 1.0L = 7.5 \text{ ft}$$

Slenderness ratio:

$$\frac{L_e}{d} = \frac{7.5 \times 12}{3.5} = 25.7 < 50 \qquad \text{OK}$$

Allowable design value:

$$F_{cE} = \frac{0.418E'}{(L_e/d)^2} = \frac{0.418 \times 2{,}000{,}000}{25.7^2} = 1266 \text{ lb/in}^2$$

$$\frac{F_{cE}}{F_c^*} = \frac{1266}{3220} = 0.393$$

$$F_c' = 3220 \left[\frac{1 + 0.393}{2 \times 0.9} - \sqrt{\left(\frac{1 + 0.393}{2 \times 0.9}\right)^2 - \frac{0.393}{0.9}} \right] = 1195 \text{ lb/in}^2$$

Allowable load:

$$P = F_c'A = 1195 \times 6.12$$

$$= 7310 \text{ lb (32.5 kN)} = 7.31 \text{ kips} > 7 \text{ kips} \qquad \text{OK}$$

3.5 SPACED COLUMNS

Spaced columns consist of two or more individual members with their longitudinal axes parallel and separated at the ends and at the middle of their lengths by blocking (Fig. 3.8). The individual components are joined at the ends by connectors capable of developing the required shear between the members and blocking (end blocks). If only a single spacer blocker is provided at the center of the column, only bolts need to be used. When two or more spacer blocks are used, timber connectors are required. Spaced columns are used as compression chords and web members in trusses and as supporting columns. When compression chords of a truss are considered as spaced columns, panel points which are stayed laterally are taken as the ends of spaced columns. The truss web members between the individual components of the assembly can function as end blocks.

3.5.1 General Design Considerations and Formulas

The design of spaced columns is similar to that of a simple solid column of rectangular cross section with end-fixity conditions. The only spaced-column action that is recognized in the NDS[2] is that developed by joining end blocks to the individual column components with timber connectors.

The connectors used in conjunction with bolts at each end of the spaced column provide a degree of restraint against rotation depending on the location of the centroid of the connector group. Two end-fixity conditions, conditions *a* and *b*, are recognized in the NDS[2] (Fig. 3.8). Condition *a* refers to the case when the centroid of the end-spacer-block connector group is located not more than $L_1/20$ from the end of the column. For condition *b*, the centroid of the connector group in the end blocks is between $L_1/20$ and $L_1/10$ from the end of the column. Distance L_1 is measured between lateral supports that provide restraint perpendicular to the wide face of the individual members. It is taken as the distance from center to center of lateral supports of continuous columns, as in compression chords of trusses and multistory buildings, and from end to end of simple spaced columns, as in one-story building columns. For the two fixity conditions, effective length values and the corresponding fixity factors are shown in Fig. 3.9.

The individual members in a spaced column act together to carry the load on the column. Each member is designed separately on the basis of its slenderness ratio, which is calculated as L_1/d_1, where d_1 is the least cross-sectional dimension of an individual member. The maximum slenderness ratio L_1/d_1 permitted for spaced columns is 80, whereas for simple columns it is 50. A greater slenderness ratio is allowed for a spaced column because of the end fixity created by the provisions of connectors and end blocks. This fixity is effective only in the direction

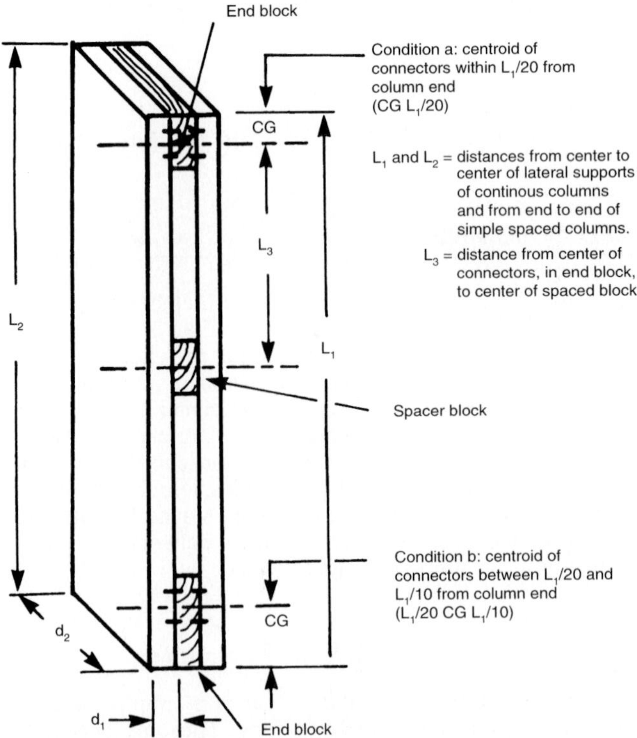

FIG. 3.8 Spaced column, end-fixity conditions *a* and *b*.

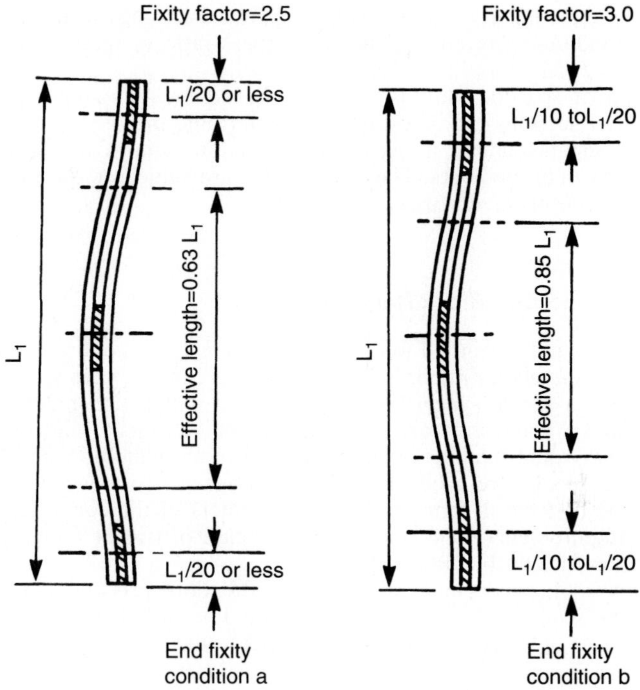

FIG. 3.9 Degree of restraint against rotation of spaced column ends.

parallel to dimension d_1. The slenderness ratio in the other direction, L_2/d_2, is subject to the provisions for simple solid columns. The value of d_2 is the dimension of the wide face of an individual member, and L_2 is the distance between the lateral supports which provide restraint in the direction parallel to dimension d_2.

The design formulas for spaced columns are developed by applying a fixity coefficient K_x to the critical buckling design value for simple solid columns, Eq. (3.4), as follows:

$$F_{cE} = \frac{K_{cE}K_xE'}{(L_1/d_1)^2} \tag{3.5}$$

where K_x = 2.5 for fixity condition *a*
K_x = 3.0 for fixity condition *b*

The F_{cE} value for spaced columns is used in Eq. (3.3) to determine the allowable design value F_c'.

In case the allowable design values F_c' for the two individual members of a spaced column are different on account of the members being of different thicknesses, grades, or species, the lesser value of F_c' is applied to both members.

The allowable design values determined for spaced-column action in accordance with Eqs. (3.3) and (3.5) are not to exceed the allowable design values for the individual members taken as simple solid columns without regard to fixity; that is, the pin-end conditions are taken. The slenderness ratio of these simple solid columns, taken as L_2/d_2, should not exceed 50.

The design of spaced columns is accomplished by following a trial-and-error procedure. Trial sections are investigated to determine their safe load-carrying capacities. The design load for a spaced column is the sum of the design loads for each of its individual members. The unit stresses are subject to the limitations with respect to net sections as discussed in Sec. 3.2.2.

3.5.2 Spacer and End-Block Requirements

The ratio L_3/d_1 is not permitted to exceed 40, where L_3 is the distance between the centroid of the connectors in an end block and the center of the spacer block (see Fig. 3.8). When a single spacer block is provided within the middle tenth of the column length L_1, connectors are not required for this block, and the connection between the individual members and the block can be made by using bolts. If two or more spacer blocks are used, the distance between two adjacent blocks should not exceed one-half the distance between the centers of the connection in the end blocks. The requirements for connectors in the case of two or more spacer blocks are the same as for end blocks.

The thickness of spacers and end blocks should not be less than that of individual members of the spaced column. The blocks should be sufficient in width and length to maintain adequate end and edge distances and spacings of the required connectors.

3.5.3 End-Block Constants for Spaced Columns

Each end block of the spaced column requires connectors to resist the shearing forces between individual members and blocking. These forces are taken as equal to the cross-sectional area of the individual member multiplied by an end-spacer constant, which depends on the L_1/d_1 ratio and the species of wood for the member. The end-block constant can be determined from Fig. 3.10 for various groups of species (for groupings, see NDS[2]). This graph is plotted on the basis of data tabulated in the NDS.[2]

The size and number of connectors in each mutually contacting surface of each block and individual member at each end of a spaced column must be such as to provide a load capacity at least equal to the force determined by using the end-spacer-block constant. For spaced columns that are part of a truss system or other similar framing, the connectors should be checked against the values calculated by applying the concept of end-block constant (see Fig. 3.10).

EXAMPLE 3.7 A spaced column 10 ft (3.05 m) long consists of two 3- by 8-in (63.5- by 184.1-mm) individual members separated by 3-in (63.5-mm)-thick blocks. The connectors and bolts are located in end blocks to provide fixity condition *a*. Calculate the allowable load on the spaced column. Assume the loading to be combined dead and live (snow) loads. Column material is No. 1 Douglas fir–larch (group B species) with tabulated design values of E = 1,700,000 lb/in^2 (11,722 MPa) and F_c for 1450 lb/in^2 (9997 kPa) and a size factor adjustment for F_c of 1.05.

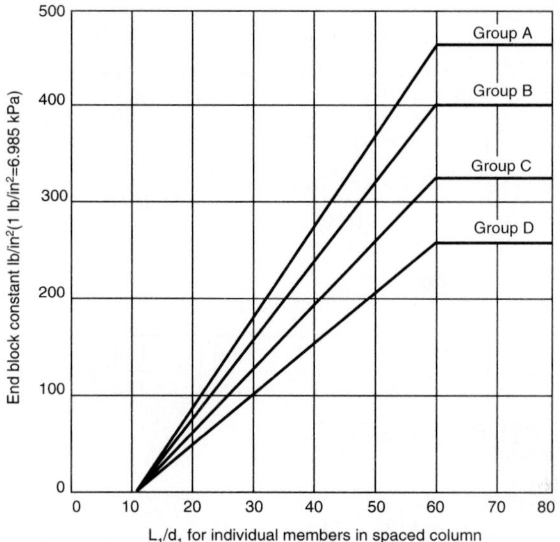

FIG. 3.10 End-spacer-block constants for spaced columns.

SOLUTION: Given section:

$$\text{Dressed dimensions} = 2.5 \times 7.25 \text{ in each}$$

$$A = 2 \times 18.12 = 36.25 \text{ in}^2$$

Allowable stresses:

$$E = 1{,}700{,}000 \text{ lb/in}^2$$

$$F_c^* = 1450 \times 1.15 \times 1.05 = 1751 \text{ lb/in}^2$$

1. *Spaced-column action:*

Slenderness ratio:

$$\frac{L_1}{d_1} = \frac{10 \times 12}{2.5} = 48 < 80 \qquad \text{OK}$$

Allowable design value:

$$F_{cE} = \frac{0.30 K_x E'}{(L_1/d_1)^2} = \frac{0.30 \times 2.5 \times 1{,}700{,}000}{48^2} = 553 \text{ lb/in}^2$$

$$\frac{F_{cE}}{F_c^*} = \frac{553}{1751} = 0.316$$

$$F_c' = 1751 \left[\frac{1 + 0.316}{2 \times 0.8} - \sqrt{\left(\frac{1 + 0.316}{2 \times 0.8} \right)^2 - \frac{0.316}{0.8}} \right] = 511 \text{ lb/in}^2$$

2. *Check as solid column using wide-face dimension:*

Slenderness ratio:

$$\frac{L_2}{d_2} = \frac{10 \times 12}{7.25} = 16.6 < 50 \qquad \text{OK}$$

Allowable design value:

$$F_{cE} = \frac{0.30E'}{(L_2/d_2)^2} = \frac{0.30 \times 1{,}700{,}000}{16.6^2} = 1851 \text{ lb/in}^2$$

$$\frac{F_{cE}}{F_c^*} = \frac{1851}{1751} = 1.06$$

$$F_c' = 1751 \left[\frac{1 + 1.06}{2 \times 0.8} - \sqrt{\left(\frac{1 + 1.06}{2 \times 0.8} \right)^2 - \frac{1.06}{0.8}} \right] = 1245 \text{ lb/in}^2$$

Therefore, $F_c' = 511$ lb/in^2 controls.

Allowable load:

$$P = F_c'A = 511 \times 36.25$$

$$= 18{,}500 \text{ lb} = 18.5 \text{ kips (82.3 kN)}$$

3. *Check connectors for spaced-column action:*

$L_1/d_1 = 48$, group B. From Fig. 3.10, end-block constant = 300.

$$\text{Total connector load} = 300 \times 18.12 = 5436 \text{ lb}$$

Allowable load per 4-in split ring (see Chap. 5):

$$5000 \times 1.15 = 5750 \text{ lb (25.6 N)}$$

Therefore, one 4-in (101.6-mm) split ring is needed in each face.

EXAMPLE 3.8 Design a spaced column 14 ft (4.27 m) long, consisting of No. 2 southern pine, S-Dry (group B species), to carry an axial load of 10.8 kips (48.0 kN). The duration of load is 2 months under dry service conditions. Consider fixity condition *b* in the design. Use nominal 3-in (63.5-mm)-thick by 6-in (139.7-mm) or wider material for the column. The tabulated design values are $E = 1{,}600{,}000$ lb/in^2 (11,032 MPa) and $F_c = 1600$ lb/in^2 (11,032 kPa).

SOLUTION: Try two members, nominal 3 × 6 in:

$$\text{Dressed dimensions} = 2.5 \times 5.5 \text{ in each}$$

$$A = 2 \times 13.75 = 27.5 \text{ in}^2$$

Allowable stresses:

$$E' = 1{,}600{,}000 \text{ lb/in}^2$$

$$F_c^* = 1600 \times 1.15 = 1840 \text{ lb/in}^2$$

1. *Spaced-column action:*

Slenderness ratio:

$$\frac{L_1}{d_1} = \frac{14 \times 12}{2.5} = 67.2 < 80 \qquad \text{OK}$$

Allowable design value:

$$F_{cE} = \frac{0.30K_xE'}{(L_1/d_1)^2} = \frac{0.30 \times 3.0 \times 1{,}600{,}000}{67.2^2} = 319 \text{ lb/in}^2$$

$$\frac{F_{cE}}{F_c^*} = \frac{319}{1840} = 0.173$$

$$F_c' = 1840 \left[\frac{1 + 0.173}{2 \times 0.8} - \sqrt{\left(\frac{1 + 0.173}{2 \times 0.8}\right)^2 - \frac{0.173}{0.8}}\right] = 306 \text{ lb/in}^2$$

Total allowable load:

$$P = F_c'A = 306 \times 27.5$$

$$= 8415 \text{ lb} = 8.42 \text{ kips} < 10.8 \text{ kips} \qquad \text{SECTION NOT ADEQUATE}$$

Try two members, nominal 3 × 8 in:

$$\text{Dressed dimensions} = 2.5 \times 7.25 \text{ in each}$$

$$A = 2 \times 18.125 = 36.25 \text{ in}^2$$

The tabulated compression parallel to grain design value is $F_c = 1550$ lb/in^2. The values of L_1/d_1 and F_{cE} are the same as for the first trial section.

Allowable design value:

$$F_c^* = 1550 \times 1.15 = 1780 \text{ lb/in}^2$$

$$\frac{F_{cE}}{F_c^*} = \frac{319}{1780} = 0.179$$

$$F_c' = 1780 \left[\frac{1 + 0.179}{2 \times 0.8} - \sqrt{\left(\frac{1 + 0.179}{2 \times 0.8}\right)^2 - \frac{0.179}{0.8}}\right] = 306 \text{ lb/in}^2$$

Total allowable load:

$$P = F_c'A = 306 \times 36.25$$

$$= 11{,}090 \text{ lb} = 11.09 \text{ kips} > 10.8 \text{ kips} \qquad \text{OK}$$

2. *Check as solid column using wide-face dimension:*

Slenderness ratio:

$$\frac{L_2}{d_2} = \frac{14 \times 12}{7.25} = 23.2 < 50 \qquad \text{OK}$$

Allowable design value:

$$F_{cE} = \frac{0.30E'}{(L_2/d_2)^2} = \frac{0.30 \times 1{,}600{,}000}{23.2^2} = 892 \text{ lb/in}^2$$

$$\frac{F_{cE}}{F_c^*} = \frac{892}{1780} = 0.501$$

$$F_c' = 1780 \left[\frac{1 + 0.501}{2 \times 0.8} - \sqrt{\left(\frac{1 + 0.501}{2 \times 0.8} \right)^2 - \frac{0.501}{0.8}} \right] = 773 \text{ lb/in}^2$$

Total allowable load:

$$P = F_c'A = 773 \times 36.25$$

$$= 28{,}000 \text{ lb (125 kN)} = 28.0 \text{ kips} > 10.8 \text{ kips} \qquad \text{OK}$$

3. *Check connectors for spaced-column action:*

$L_1/d_1 = 67.2$, group B. From Fig. 3.10, end-block constant = 399.

Total connector load = 399 × 18.12 = 7230 lb

Allowable load per 4-in split ring (see Chap. 5):

5000 × 1.15 = 5750 lb (25.6 kN)

Therefore, two 4-in (101.6-mm) split rings are required in each face.

3.6 BUILT-UP COLUMNS

This section deals with built-up columns, excluding spaced columns, which have been covered in Sec. 3.5. Built-up wood columns are often fabricated by joining together individual pieces with mechanical fasteners, such as nails, spikes, bolts, or other types of mechanical fasteners. Many different configurations of such columns can be built. Some common forms are shown in Fig. 3.11.

It has been noted[4–6] that no arrangement of pieces with any type of mechanical fasteners can make a built-up column fully equal in strength to its equivalent solid column. *Equivalent solid column* refers to a one-piece solid column of the same overall dimensions, end conditions, and material as those of the built-up column. The allowable design value F_c' of a built-up column is less than that of its equivalent solid column but considerably greater than that of an unconnected assembly in which individual members are treated as independent columns without any sharing of load between them. Details on behavior, analysis, and potential design procedures for various types of built-up columns are given in Refs. 3, 4, and 7.

The strength of a built-up column can be expressed as a percentage of the strength of its equivalent solid column. For the two types of arrangements shown in Fig. 3.11*a* and *b*, this strength ratio is given in Table 3.1.[6] The first arrangement consists of parallel planks and cover plates, and the second is planks boxed around a solid core. For slenderness ratios L/d of 11 or greater, the strength of the column is independent of whether the individual pieces are full-length or butt-jointed. In case of short columns (L/d less than 11), individual pieces butted end to end fail at 75 to 80 percent of the crushing strength of full-length pieces.

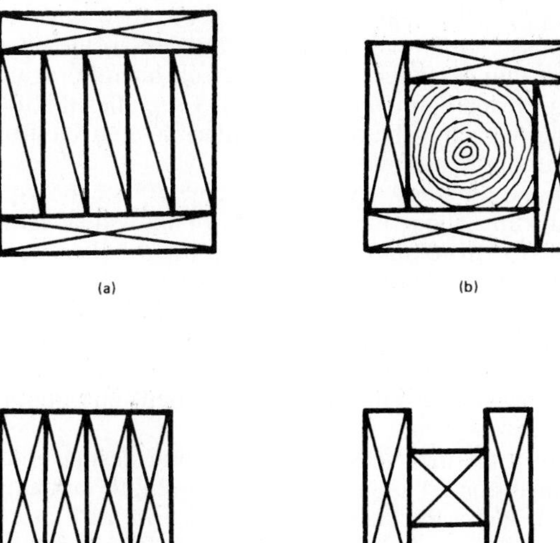

FIG. 3.11 Cross sections of built-up columns. (*a*) Parallel planks and cover plates; (*b*) boxed solid core; (*c*) layered column; (*d*) H column.

The percentage values given in Table 3.1 apply only if the individual pieces of a built-up section are adequately fastened to develop composite action of the assembly. Individual planks should not be wider than 5 times their thickness. When the planks are joined together with spikes, the spikes are to penetrate through two planks well into the third piece. The longitudinal spacing of spikes should not exceed 6 times the plank thickness. Lumber used for the fabrication of built-up columns should be well seasoned, that is, kiln-dried.

Layered built-up columns (see Fig. 3.11*c*) with full-length laminations may be conservatively designed by treating the individual laminations as independent columns which carry proportional shares of the applied load. This methodology is typically applied to built-up compression members which have full lateral bracing

TABLE 3.1 Strength of Built-up Columns as Percentage of Solid Column Strength

Slenderness ratio L/d	Percentage of strength of equivalent solid column
6	82
10	77
14	71
18	65
22	74
26	82

to prevent buckling of individual laminations about their weak axis (e.g., built-up studs or built-up truss chords with sheathing attached to the edge of each lamination). For built-up columns which do not have full lateral bracing to prevent weak axis buckling of individual laminations, the NDS specifies the following procedure for determining the capacity of bolted or nailed layered built-up columns which meet specified fastening requirements:

Step 1. Determine the allowable design value F'_c for the equivalent solid column, assuming buckling about the weak axis of individual laminations. Apply a reduction factor of 0.75 to obtain the F'_c value for a bolted built-up column or a reduction factor of 0.60 to obtain the F'_c value for a nailed built-up column.

Step 2. Determine the allowable design value F'_c for the equivalent solid column, assuming buckling about the strong axis of individual laminations. Do not apply a reduction to this F'_c value.

Step 3. The allowable design value for the built-up column is the lesser F'_c value obtained from steps 1 and 2.

In order to qualify for the NDS built-up column design procedures, a layered built-up column must consist of two to five full-length laminations, each having identical face widths and a thickness of at least 1.5 in, and fastened in accordance with the following nailing or bolting requirements.

Nailed Built-up Columns

1. Adjacent nails are driven from opposite sides of the column.
2. Nails penetrate all laminations, including at least three-quarters of the thickness of the last lamination.
3. The end distance between the nearest nail and the end of the column is between 15 and 18 times the nail diameter.
4. The spacing between adjacent nails in a row, measured along the longitudinal axis of the column, is greater than 20 times the nail diameter and less than 6 times the thickness of the thinnest lamination.
5. The spacing between rows of nails, measured across the wide face of a lamination, is between 10 and 20 times the nail diameter.
6. The distance from the nearest nail to the edge of the column is between 5 and 20 times the nail diameter.
7. When the face width of a lamination is greater than 3 times the thickness of the thinnest lamination, two or more longitudinal rows of nails are provided. When only one longitudinal row of nails is required, adjacent nails are staggered about the longitudinal axis of the column. When three or more longitudinal rows of nails are used, nails in adjacent rows are staggered.

Bolted Built-up Columns

1. A metal plate or washer is provided between the wood and the bolt head and between the wood and the nut. Nuts are tightened to ensure that faces of adjacent laminations are brought into contact.
2. The end distance between the nearest bolt and the end of the column is between 7 and 8.4 times the bolt diameter for softwood laminations or between 5 and 6 times the bolt diameter for hardwood laminations.

3. The spacing between adjacent bolts in a row, measured along the longitudinal axis of the column, is greater than 4 times the bolt diameter and less than 6 times the thickness of the thinnest lamination.

4. The spacing between rows of bolts, measured across the wide face of a lamination, is between 3 and 10 times the bolt diameter.

5. The distance from the nearest bolt to the edge of the column is between 4 and 10 times the bolt diameter.

6. When the face width of a lamination is greater than 3 times the thickness of the thinnest lamination, two or more longitudinal rows of bolts are provided.

EXAMPLE 3.9 Determine the allowable load on a 16-ft (4.88-m)-long layered built-up column made of five nominal 2- by 8-in (38- by 184-mm) pieces connected by two rows of ½-in (12.7-mm) bolts. Adjacent bolts in a row are spaced 8 in (203 mm) apart, each bolt is 2 in (50.8 mm) from the edge of the column, and the end bolts in each row are 4 in (102 mm) from the end of the column. Assume column pin-end conditions, dry service conditions, and normal duration of loading. The tabulated design values are assumed to be $E = 1{,}700{,}000$ lb/in² (11,722 MPa) and $F_c = 1650$ lb/in² (11,376 kPa).

SOLUTION: Given section of equivalent solid column:

$$\text{Dressed dimensions} = 7.5 \times 7.25 \text{ in}$$

$$A = 54.4 \text{ in}^2$$

Allowable stresses:

$$E' = 1{,}700{,}000 \text{ lb/in}^2$$

$$F_c^* = 1650 \text{ lb/in}^2$$

1. *Check buckling about weak axis of individual laminations:*

Effective length:

$$L_{e2} = 1.0L_2 = 16 \text{ ft}$$

Slenderness ratio:

$$\frac{L_{e2}}{d_2} = \frac{16 \times 12}{7.5} = 25.6 < 50 \qquad \text{OK}$$

Allowable design value:

$$F_{cE2} = \frac{0.30E'}{(L_{e2}/d_2)^2} = \frac{0.30 \times 1{,}700{,}000}{25.6^2} = 778 \text{ lb/in}^2$$

$$\frac{F_{cE2}}{F_c^*} = \frac{778}{1650} = 0.4715$$

$$F_c' = 0.75 \times 1650 \left[\frac{1 + 0.4715}{2 \times 0.8} - \sqrt{\left(\frac{1 + 0.4715}{2 \times 0.8}\right)^2 - \frac{0.4715}{0.8}} \right] = 511 \text{ lb/in}^2$$

2. *Check buckling about strong axis of individual laminations:*

Effective length:

$$L_{e1} = 1.0L_1 = 16 \text{ ft}$$

Slenderness ratio:

$$\frac{L_{e1}}{d_1} = \frac{16 \times 12}{7.25} = 26.5 < 50 \qquad \text{OK}$$

Allowable design value:

$$F_{cE1} = \frac{0.30E'}{(L_{e1}/d_1)^2} = \frac{0.30 \times 1{,}700{,}000}{26.5^2} = 726 \text{ lb/in}^2$$

$$\frac{F_{cE1}}{F_c^*} = \frac{726}{1650} = 0.44$$

$$F'_c = 1650 \left[\frac{1 + 0.44}{2 \times 0.8} - \sqrt{\left(\frac{1 + 0.44}{2 \times 0.8} \right)^2 - \frac{0.44}{0.8}} \right] = 644 \text{ lb/in}^2 > 511 \text{ lb/in}^2$$

Therefore, $F'_c = 511 \text{ lb/in}^2$ controls.

Allowable load:

$$P = F'_c A = 511 \times 54.4 = 27{,}800 \text{ lb} = 27.8 \text{ kips (124 kN)}$$

3.7 COMBINED LOADINGS FOR COLUMNS

In many instances, columns must be designed to resist combined axial compression stresses and bending moment stresses. Moments may be caused by eccentric end loads or by side loads such as may occur when a column is designed to withstand lateral wind forces. The following general formula has been developed (see Refs. 2 and 10) for the design of pin-end columns of square or rectangular cross section subjected to an eccentric axial load and side loads on orthogonal faces of the column (biaxial bending):

$$\left(\frac{f_c}{F'_c}\right)^2 + \frac{f_{b1} + f_c(6e_1/d_1)\,[1 + 0.234\,(f_c/F_{cE1})]}{F'_{b1}[1 - (f_c/F_{cE1})]}$$

$$+ \frac{f_{b2} + f_c(6e_2/d_2)\left(1 + 0.234\left\{\left(\dfrac{f_c}{F_{cE2}}\right) + \left[\dfrac{f_{b1} + f_c(6e_1/d_1)}{F_{bE}}\right]^2\right\}\right)}{F'_{b2}\left\{1 - \left(\dfrac{f_c}{F_{cE2}}\right) - \left[\dfrac{f_{b1} + f_c(6e_1/d_1)}{F_{bE}}\right]^2\right\}} \le 1.0 \qquad (3.6)$$

For columns with a concentric axial load and side loads on orthogonal faces (biaxial bending), the following simplified formula applies:

$$\left(\frac{f_c}{F'_c}\right)^2 + \frac{f_{b1}}{F'_{b1}[1 - (f_c/F_{cE1})]} + \frac{f_{b2}}{F'_{b2}[1 - (f_c/F_{cE2}) - (f_{b1}/F_{bE})^2]} \leq 1.0 \quad (3.7)$$

For columns with a concentric axial load and a side load applied to only one face (uniaxial bending), the formula may be further simplified for either a side load applied to the narrow face, Eq. (3.8), or a side load applied to the wide face, Eq. (3.9):

$$\left(\frac{f_c}{F'_c}\right)^2 + \frac{f_{b1}}{F'_{b1}[1 - (f_c/F_{cE1})]} \leq 1.0 \quad (3.8)$$

$$\left(\frac{f_c}{F'_c}\right)^2 + \frac{f_{b2}}{F'_{b2}[1 - (f_c/F_{cE2})]} \leq 1.0 \quad (3.9)$$

Simplified formulas for additional combinations of eccentric axial load and side loads are provided in Refs. 2 and 11. The following definitions apply to the nomenclature used in Eqs. (3.6) through (3.9):

F_{cE1} = critical buckling design value for buckling about the strong axis
F_{cE2} = critical buckling design value for buckling about the weak axis
F_{bE} = critical buckling design value for bending members (see Chap. 4)
f_c = compression stress parallel to grain induced by axial load
f_{b1} = edgewise bending stress induced by side loads on narrow face only
f_{b2} = flatwise bending stress induced by side loads on wide face only
F'_c = allowable compression design value parallel to grain that would be permitted if axial compressive stress only existed
F'_{b1} = allowable edgewise bending design value that would be permitted if edgewise bending stress only existed
F'_{b2} = allowable flatwise bending design value that would be permitted if flatwise bending stress only existed
d_1 = wide face dimension
d_2 = narrow face dimension
e_1 = eccentricity, measured parallel to wide face from centerline of column to centerline of axial load
e_2 = eccentricity, measured parallel to narrow face from centerline of column to centerline of axial load

The load-duration factor associated with the shortest duration load in a combination of loads should be used to determine F'_c, F'_{b1} and F'_{b2} in Eqs. (3.6) through (3.9). Thus, for a column which supports an axial load (due to dead plus snow) and a strong axis bending load (due to wind), Eq. (3.8) would apply with F'_c and F'_{b1} computed using the wind load-duration factor. In addition, the column capacity should be checked using Eqs. (3.3) and (3.4) and the snow load-duration factor to determine F'_c.

In addition to columns designed for combined loading due to bending moments induced by eccentric end loads located at the top of the column or by side loads applied normal to the column axis, columns also may be subjected to loads applied through brackets attached to the column somewhere below its top. Figure 3.12 illustrates the typical use of a side bracket. An exact solution to a side bracket load

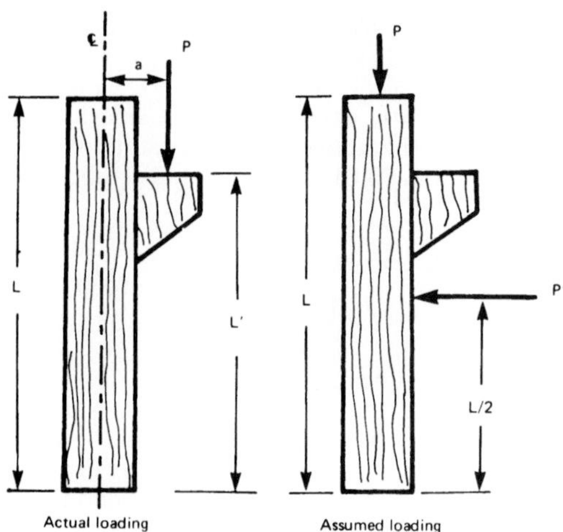

FIG. 3.12 Columns with side bracket loading.

is difficult, but the following procedure allows a safe analysis and is quite accurate for brackets located in the upper quarter of the length of the column.

Assume that a bracket load P, at a distance a from the center of the column (Fig. 3.12), is replaced by the same load P applied centrally at the top of the column, plus a side load P' applied at midheight. Determine P' from the following formula:

$$P' = 3 \times \frac{L'}{L} \times \frac{a}{L} P = \frac{3aL'P}{L^2} \tag{3.10}$$

where a = horizontal distance from load on bracket to center of column
L = total length of column
L' = distance measured vertically from point of load application on bracket to farther end of column
P = actual load on bracket
P' = assumed horizontal side load placed at center of height of column

The assumed centrally applied load P should be added to other concentric column loads, and the calculated side load P' is used to determine bending stress f_b for use in the formula for concentric axial loading and side loading, Eq. (3.8) or (3.9).

EXAMPLE 3.10 Determine the adequacy of an 8¾- by 12-in (222.2- by 304.8-mm) giulam column to resist a concentric end load (dead load plus snow load) of 20 kips (89 kN) and a wind load applied uniformly over the length of the column of 0.50 kips/ft (7.3 kN/m). Assume the column has pin-ends, is 20 ft (6.10 m) in length, and is oriented with the 8¾-in (222.2-mm) dimension parallel to the applied wind load. Assume the column is a Douglas fir–larch A-2 laminating combination with tabulated design values of E = 1,700.000 lb/in^2 (11,722 MPa), F_{b2} = 1800 lb/in^2 (12,411 kPa), F_c = 1900 lb/in^2 (13,100 kPa), and a flat use factor adjustment for F_{b2} of 1.04.

SOLUTION: Given section:

$$\text{Net dimensions} = 8.75 \times 12 \text{ in}$$
$$A = 105 \text{ in}^2$$
$$S = 153.12 \text{ in}^3$$

Allowable stresses:

$$E' = 1{,}700{,}000 \text{ lb/in}^2$$
$$F'_{b2} = 1800 \times 1.6 \times 1.04 = 2995 \text{ lb/in}^2$$
$$F_c^* = 1900 \times 1.15 = 2185 \text{ lb/in}^2 \textit{ for axial load only}$$
$$F_c^* = 1900 \times 1.6 = 3040 \text{ lb/in}^2 \textit{ for combined loading}$$

Effective length:

$$L_e = 1.0\, L = 20 \text{ ft}$$

Slenderness ratio:

$$\frac{L_{e2}}{d_2} = \frac{20 \times 12}{8.75} = 27.4 < 50 \qquad \text{OK}$$

Allowable compression design values:
For axial load only:

$$F_{cE2} = \frac{0.418E'}{(L_{e2}/d_2)^2} = \frac{0.418 \times 1{,}700{,}000}{27.4^2} = 946.5 \text{ lb/in}^2$$

$$\frac{F_{cE2}}{F_c^*} = \frac{946.5}{2185} = 0.433$$

$$F'_c = 2185 \left[\frac{1 + 0.433}{2 \times 0.9} - \sqrt{\left(\frac{1 + 0.433}{2 \times 0.9}\right)^2 - \frac{0.433}{0.9}}\right] = 886 \text{ lb/in}^2$$

$$P = F'_cA = 886 \times 105$$
$$= 93{,}030 \text{ lb (414 kN)} = 93.0 \text{ kips} > 20 \text{ kips} \qquad \text{OK}$$

For combined loading:

$$\frac{F_{cE2}}{F_c^*} = \frac{946.5}{3040} = 0.311$$

$$F'_c = 3040 \left[\frac{1 + 0.311}{2 \times 0.9} - \sqrt{\left(\frac{1 + 0.311}{2 \times 0.9}\right)^2 - \frac{0.311}{0.9}}\right] = 907 \text{ lb/in}^2$$

Induced stresses due to applied loads:

$$M_{wL} = \frac{W_{wL}L^2}{8} = \frac{500 \times 20^2}{8} = 25{,}000 \text{ ft} \cdot \text{lb}$$

$$f_b = \frac{M_{wL}}{S} = \frac{25{,}000 \times 12}{153.12} = 1959 \text{ lb/in}^2$$

$$f_c = \frac{P}{A} = \frac{20{,}000}{105} = 190 \text{ lb/in}^2$$

Combined stresses:

$$\left(\frac{f_c}{F'_c}\right)^2 + \frac{f_{b2}}{F'_{b2}\left[1 - \left(\frac{f_c}{F_{cE2}}\right)\right]} =$$

$$\left(\frac{190}{907}\right)^2 + \frac{1959}{2995\left[1 - \left(\frac{190}{946.5}\right)\right]} = 0.86 \le 1.0 \qquad \text{OK}$$

EXAMPLE 3.11 Determine the adequacy of a nominal 8- by 8-in (190.5- by 190.5-mm), 10-ft (3.05-m)-long sawn timber pin-ended column subjected to an axial load P of 10 kips (44.5 kN) applied to a bracket located 2 ft (0.61 m) below the top of the column. The distance of load P from the centerline of the column is 9 in (228.5 mm). Assume dry-use conditions and duration of load 2 months. Assume that the column has tabulated design values of E = 1,400,000 lb/in² (9653 MPa), F_b = 1100 lb/in² (7584 kPa), and F_c = 625 lb/in² (4309 kPa).

SOLUTION:

$$P' = \frac{3aL'P}{L^2} = \frac{3 \times 9 \times 96 \times 10{,}000}{120^2} = 1800 \text{ lb}$$

Therefore, design column for an axial concentric load of 10,000 lb and a side load of 1800 lb located at the midheight of the column.
Given section:

$$\text{Net dimensions} = 7.5 \times 7.5 \text{ in}$$
$$A = 56.25 \text{ in}^2$$
$$S = 70.31 \text{ in}^3$$

Allowable stresses:

$$E' = 1{,}400{,}000 \text{ lb/in}^2$$
$$F'_b = 1100 \times 1.15 = 1265 \text{ lb/in}^2$$
$$F^*_c = 625 \times 1.15 = 719 \text{ lb/in}^2$$

Effective length:

$$L_e = 1.0L = 10.0 \text{ ft}$$

Slenderness ratio:

$$\frac{L_e}{d} = \frac{10 \times 12}{7.5} = 16.0 < 50 \qquad \text{OK}$$

Allowable compression design value:

$$F_{cE} = \frac{0.3E'}{(L_e/d)^2} = \frac{0.3 \times 1{,}400{,}000}{16^2} = 1641 \text{ lb/in}^2$$

$$\frac{F_{cE}}{F_c^*} = \frac{1641}{719} = 2.28$$

$$F_c' = 719 \left[\frac{1 + 2.28}{2 \times 0.8} - \sqrt{\left(\frac{1 + 2.28}{2 \times 0.8} \right)^2 - \frac{2.28}{0.8}} \right] = 638 \text{ lb/in}^2$$

Induced stresses due to applied loads:

$$M_P = \frac{P'L^2}{4} = \frac{1800 \times 10}{4} = 4500 \text{ ft} \cdot \text{lb}$$

$$f_b = \frac{M_P}{S} = \frac{4500 \times 12}{70.31} = 768 \text{ lb/in}^2$$

$$f_c = \frac{P}{A} = \frac{10{,}000}{56.25} = 178 \text{ lb/in}^2$$

Combined stresses:

$$\left(\frac{f_c}{F_c'} \right)^2 + \frac{f_b}{F_b' \left[1 - \left(\frac{f_c}{F_{cE}} \right) \right]} = \left(\frac{178}{638} \right)^2 + \frac{768}{1265 \left[1 - \left(\frac{178}{1641} \right) \right]}$$

$$= 0.76 \leq 1.0 \qquad \text{OK}$$

3.8 TABLES OF ALLOWABLE UNIT STRESSES FOR COLUMNS

As previously noted, the design of wood columns is a trial-and-error, indirect process. A total cross section is assumed and then investigated for suitability to carry the applied loads. Design aids, such as design tables and charts, eliminate the necessity for solving the column design formulas, thereby facilitating the verification of the assumed sections.

Tables 3.2 and 3.3 are provided here as an aid to wood column design. These tables are compiled from data given in Ref. 9. They offer a simplified approach for determining design loads on simple solid columns. Similar tables are available in Ref. 9 for spaced columns.

TABLE 3.2 Allowable Design Values F'_c for Simple Solid Columns with L_e/d from 2 to 30

E' lb/in²	F^*_c lb/in²	2	8	12	15	18	20	22	24	26	28	30
		L_e/d										
2100000	4000	3979	3588	2884	2234	1695	1419	1199	1023	882	767	673
	3800	3781	3432	2802	2197	1679	1409	1193	1019	879	765	671
	3600	3583	3274	2714	2156	1660	1398	1185	1014	876	763	669
	3400	3385	3112	2619	2110	1639	1385	1177	1009	872	760	667
	3200	3187	2948	2518	2058	1615	1370	1168	1002	867	757	665
	3000	2988	2781	2409	2000	1588	1353	1157	995	862	753	662
	2800	2790	2611	2294	1935	1556	1333	1144	986	856	749	659
	2600	2591	2439	2172	1862	1518	1309	1129	976	850	744	656
	2400	2393	2265	2042	1779	1475	1281	1110	964	841	738	651
	2200	2194	2088	1906	1688	1423	1248	1088	950	831	731	646
	2000	1995	1908	1762	1586	1362	1207	1062	931	819	722	640
	1800	1796	1727	1612	1473	1291	1158	1028	909	803	711	632
	1600	1597	1543	1455	1349	1206	1097	986	879	782	696	621
	1400	1397	1357	1292	1214	1107	1022	931	841	755	677	607
	1200	1198	1169	1123	1068	993	931	862	790	718	650	587
2000000	3600	3582	3254	2660	2089	1597	1341	1135	970	837	728	639
	3400	3384	3095	2571	2047	1578	1329	1128	965	833	726	637
	3200	3186	2933	2475	2000	1557	1316	1119	959	830	723	635
	3000	2988	2768	2373	1947	1532	1301	1109	953	825	720	633
	2800	2789	2600	2262	1887	1503	1283	1098	945	820	716	630
	2600	2591	2430	2145	1819	1470	1262	1084	936	813	712	627
	2400	2392	2257	2020	1743	1430	1237	1068	925	806	706	623
	2200	2193	2081	1887	1657	1383	1207	1049	912	797	700	618
	2000	1995	1903	1748	1560	1328	1170	1024	896	786	692	613
	1800	1796	1722	1600	1452	1261	1125	994	876	772	682	605
	1600	1597	1540	1446	1333	1182	1069	956	849	753	669	596
	1400	1397	1354	1285	1202	1089	1000	907	815	729	652	583
1900000	3600	3582	3232	2602	2018	1532	1283	1084	926	798	694	609
	3400	3384	3076	2519	1981	1516	1273	1078	921	795	692	607
	3200	3185	2916	2429	1938	1496	1261	1070	916	791	689	605
	3000	2987	2754	2332	1890	1474	1247	1061	910	787	686	603
	2800	2789	2588	2227	1835	1449	1232	1051	903	782	683	601
	2600	2590	2420	2115	1773	1419	1213	1039	895	777	679	598
	2400	2392	2248	1995	1702	1383	1191	1025	886	770	674	594
	2200	2193	2074	1867	1622	1341	1164	1007	874	762	669	590
	2000	1994	1897	1731	1532	1290	1131	986	860	752	662	585
	1800	1795	1718	1587	1430	1229	1090	959	842	740	653	579
	1600	1596	1536	1436	1316	1156	1039	925	818	724	641	570
	1400	1397	1352	1278	1189	1069	976	880	787	702	626	559
	1200	1198	1165	1113	1051	965	896	821	745	672	604	543
	1000	999	976	941	901	844	797	744	687	629	573	520

TABLE 3.2 Allowable Design Values F_c' for Simple Solid Columns with L_e/d from 2 to 30 *(Continued)*

E' lb/in²	F_c^* lb/in²	L_e/d 2	8	12	15	18	20	22	24	26	28	30
1800000	3400	3383	3054	2461	1910	1451	1215	1027	877	756	657	576
	3200	3185	2897	2377	1872	1434	1205	1020	872	753	655	575
	3000	2986	2737	2286	1829	1414	1193	1013	867	749	653	573
	2800	2788	2574	2188	1779	1392	1179	1004	861	745	650	571
	2600	2590	2408	2081	1723	1365	1162	993	854	740	646	568
	2400	2391	2238	1966	1658	1333	1142	980	846	734	642	565
	2200	2193	2066	1843	1584	1296	1119	965	835	727	637	562
	2000	1994	1891	1712	1500	1250	1089	946	823	718	631	557
	1800	1795	1713	1573	1404	1195	1053	922	807	707	623	551
	1600	1596	1532	1425	1296	1128	1007	891	786	693	613	544
	1400	1397	1349	1270	1175	1047	950	851	758	674	599	534
	1200	1198	1163	1107	1041	949	876	798	721	647	580	520
	1000	999	975	938	894	833	783	727	668	609	552	500
	800	799	784	761	735	699	669	634	594	552	510	468
1700000	3200	3184	2875	2320	1802	1369	1147	969	828	713	621	544
	3000	2986	2718	2235	1764	1352	1136	963	823	710	618	543
	2800	2788	2558	2143	1719	1332	1124	955	818	707	616	541
	2600	2589	2394	2043	1669	1309	1110	946	812	702	613	539
	2400	2391	2227	1934	1610	1281	1092	935	804	697	609	536
	2200	2192	2057	1817	1543	1247	1072	921	795	691	605	533
	2000	1994	1883	1691	1465	1207	1046	904	784	683	599	529
	1800	1795	1707	1556	1375	1157	1014	883	770	674	592	524
	1600	1596	1528	1413	1273	1096	973	856	752	661	584	517
	1400	1397	1345	1261	1158	1022	921	821	728	644	572	509
	1200	1198	1160	1101	1029	931	854	773	695	621	555	497
	1000	998	973	933	886	821	768	709	648	587	531	479
	800	799	783	759	731	692	659	621	580	536	493	451
	600	599	591	577	563	543	526	506	484	458	431	403
1600000	3200	3183	2850	2256	1728	1303	1088	918	783	674	586	514
	3000	2985	2697	2178	1694	1288	1079	912	779	671	584	512
	2800	2787	2540	2093	1655	1270	1068	905	774	668	582	511
	2600	2589	2379	2000	1610	1250	1056	897	769	664	579	509
	2400	2390	2214	1898	1557	1226	1041	888	762	660	576	506
	2200	2192	2046	1787	1497	1196	1022	876	755	655	572	503
	2000	1993	1875	1667	1426	1161	1000	861	745	648	567	500
	1800	1795	1700	1537	1343	1117	972	843	733	640	561	496
	1600	1596	1522	1398	1248	1062	936	820	717	629	554	490
	1400	1397	1342	1250	1139	994	890	788	696	614	543	483
	1200	1198	1158	1093	1015	910	829	746	667	594	529	472
	1000	998	971	928	877	807	750	688	625	564	508	457
	800	799	782	756	725	683	648	608	564	519	474	432
	600	599	590	576	560	538	520	499	475	447	419	389

TABLE 3.2 Allowable Design Values F'_c for Simple Solid Columns with L_e/d from 2 to 30 *(Continued)*

E' lb/in²	F_c^* lb/in²	L_e/d 2	8	12	15	18	20	22	24	26	28	30
1500000	3000	2984	2672	2115	1620	1221	1020	861	734	632	549	482
	2800	2786	2519	2037	1586	1206	1011	855	730	629	547	480
	2600	2588	2361	1951	1546	1189	1000	848	725	626	545	478
	2400	2390	2200	1857	1500	1168	987	839	720	622	542	476
	2200	2191	2034	1752	1446	1142	971	829	713	617	539	474
	2000	1993	1865	1639	1382	1111	952	817	705	612	535	471
	1800	1794	1693	1515	1307	1073	928	801	694	605	530	467
	1600	1595	1517	1381	1219	1024	897	781	681	595	523	462
	1400	1396	1337	1238	1117	964	856	754	662	583	514	456
	1200	1197	1155	1085	1000	887	802	717	637	565	502	447
	1000	998	969	923	867	791	730	665	601	539	483	434
	800	799	781	752	719	673	635	592	546	500	454	412
	600	599	589	574	557	533	514	490	464	435	405	375
	400	400	395	389	382	373	365	356	345	333	320	305
1400000	2800	2785	2494	1974	1512	1140	952	803	685	590	513	449
	2600	2587	2341	1896	1478	1125	943	797	681	587	511	448
	2400	2389	2182	1809	1437	1107	932	790	676	584	508	446
	2200	2191	2020	1713	1390	1085	918	782	670	580	506	444
	2000	1992	1854	1606	1333	1058	902	771	663	575	502	442
	1800	1794	1684	1489	1266	1025	881	758	654	569	498	438
	1600	1595	1510	1362	1186	983	854	740	643	561	492	434
	1400	1396	1332	1223	1092	929	819	717	627	550	484	429
	1200	1197	1151	1075	982	860	772	685	606	535	474	421
	1000	998	967	916	855	772	708	640	574	513	458	410
	800	799	779	748	712	662	621	575	526	479	433	392
	600	599	588	572	553	528	506	481	452	422	390	359
	400	400	395	388	381	370	362	352	340	327	313	297
1300000	2800	2784	2465	1902	1433	1071	892	751	639	550	478	419
	2600	2586	2316	1833	1404	1058	884	746	636	548	476	417
	2400	2388	2162	1755	1369	1043	875	740	632	545	474	416
	2200	2190	2004	1667	1328	1025	863	733	627	542	472	414
	2000	1992	1841	1568	1279	1002	850	724	621	537	469	412
	1800	1793	1673	1459	1220	974	832	712	614	532	465	409
	1600	1595	1502	1338	1149	938	809	698	604	526	460	406
	1400	1396	1326	1206	1063	891	779	678	591	517	454	401
	1200	1197	1147	1063	961	830	739	651	573	504	445	395
	1000	998	964	908	841	751	682	612	546	485	432	385
	800	799	777	744	704	649	604	555	505	456	411	370
	600	599	587	570	549	521	497	469	439	406	374	342
	400	400	395	387	379	368	358	347	335	320	304	287
	200	200	199	197	195	193	191	188	186	183	180	176

TABLE 3.2 Allowable Design Values F'_c for Simple Solid Columns with L_e/d from 2 to 30 *(Continued)*

E' lb/in²	F^*_c lb/in²	L_e/d 2	8	12	15	18	20	22	24	26	28	30
1200000	2600	2585	2287	1761	1325	990	824	693	590	508	441	387
	2400	2387	2138	1692	1296	977	816	688	587	506	439	385
	2200	2189	1984	1613	1261	962	807	682	583	503	437	384
	2000	1991	1825	1524	1219	943	795	675	578	499	435	382
	1800	1793	1661	1424	1168	919	780	666	572	495	432	380
	1600	1594	1492	1311	1106	889	762	654	564	489	428	377
	1400	1396	1319	1186	1029	849	736	637	553	482	423	373
	1200	1197	1142	1049	936	797	702	615	538	472	415	368
	1000	998	960	899	825	726	653	582	515	456	404	360
	800	799	775	738	694	633	584	532	480	431	387	347
	600	599	586	567	544	512	486	456	423	389	356	324
	400	400	394	386	377	364	354	342	328	312	295	276
	200	200	199	197	195	192	190	187	185	181	178	173
1100000	1800	1792	1646	1381	1110	861	727	617	529	457	398	350
	1600	1594	1481	1278	1056	836	711	607	522	452	395	347
	1400	1395	1311	1161	990	803	691	594	513	446	391	344
	1200	1196	1136	1031	907	758	662	576	501	438	385	340
	1000	998	956	888	805	697	621	549	483	425	376	333
	800	798	773	731	682	614	561	507	454	405	361	323
	600	599	585	563	538	502	473	440	405	370	336	304
	400	400	393	384	374	360	349	335	319	302	283	264
	200	200	198	196	194	191	189	186	183	179	175	170
1000000	1800	1791	1627	1330	1045	799	670	568	485	418	364	320
	1600	1593	1466	1238	1000	778	658	560	480	415	362	318
	1400	1395	1300	1131	943	752	641	549	473	410	358	315
	1200	1196	1128	1010	871	715	618	534	463	403	353	311
	1000	997	952	874	780	664	585	512	448	393	346	306
	800	798	770	723	667	591	535	478	425	377	335	298
	600	599	583	559	530	490	457	421	384	348	314	283
	400	400	393	383	371	356	342	327	309	290	270	250
	200	200	198	196	193	190	188	184	181	177	172	167
900000	1600	1592	1449	1188	936	717	602	510	436	376	328	287
	1400	1394	1287	1094	890	696	589	502	431	372	325	285
	1200	1196	1119	983	829	667	571	490	423	367	321	283
	1000	997	945	856	750	625	545	473	411	359	315	278
	800	798	766	713	648	564	504	446	393	346	306	272
	600	599	581	554	520	475	438	399	360	324	290	260
	400	400	392	381	368	350	334	317	297	276	255	234
	200	200	198	195	193	189	186	182	178	173	168	162

TABLE 3.3 Allowable Design Values F'_c for Simple Solid Columns with L_e/d from 30 to 50

E' lb/in²	F^*_c lb/in²	L_e/d 30	32	34	36	38	40	42	44	46	48	50
2100000	4000	673	594	529	473	426	386	350	320	293	270	249
	3800	671	593	528	473	426	385	350	320	293	269	249
	3600	669	592	527	472	425	385	350	319	293	269	248
	3400	667	590	526	471	424	384	349	319	292	269	248
	3200	665	589	524	470	423	383	349	318	292	269	248
	3000	662	587	523	469	422	383	348	318	291	268	248
	2800	659	584	521	467	421	382	347	317	291	268	247
	2600	656	582	519	466	420	381	346	317	290	267	247
	2400	651	578	517	464	419	379	346	316	290	267	246
	2200	646	575	514	462	417	378	344	315	289	266	246
	2000	640	570	510	459	415	376	343	314	288	265	245
	1800	632	564	506	455	412	374	341	312	287	264	244
	1600	621	556	500	451	408	371	339	310	285	263	243
	1400	607	546	492	445	404	368	336	308	283	261	242
	1200	587	531	481	436	397	362	332	305	281	259	240
2000000	3600	639	565	503	450	405	367	333	304	279	256	237
	3400	637	564	502	449	405	366	333	304	279	256	236
	3200	635	562	500	448	404	366	332	304	278	256	236
	3000	633	560	499	447	403	365	332	303	278	256	236
	2800	630	558	498	446	402	364	331	303	277	255	236
	2600	627	556	496	445	401	363	331	302	277	255	235
	2400	623	553	493	443	400	362	330	301	276	254	235
	2200	618	549	491	441	398	361	329	300	276	254	234
	2000	613	545	488	438	396	359	327	299	275	253	234
	1800	605	540	484	435	393	357	326	298	274	252	233
	1600	596	533	478	431	390	355	324	296	272	251	232
	1400	583	523	471	426	386	351	321	294	271	250	231
1900000	3600	609	538	478	428	385	349	317	289	265	244	225
	3400	607	537	477	428	385	348	317	289	265	244	225
	3200	605	535	476	427	384	348	316	289	265	243	225
	3000	603	534	475	426	383	347	316	288	264	243	224
	2800	601	532	474	425	383	346	315	288	264	243	224
	2600	598	530	472	423	382	346	314	287	263	242	224
	2400	594	527	470	422	380	345	314	287	263	242	223
	2200	590	524	468	420	379	344	313	286	262	241	223
	2000	585	520	465	418	377	342	312	285	262	241	222
	1800	579	515	461	415	375	340	310	284	261	240	222
	1600	570	509	457	411	372	338	308	282	259	239	221
	1400	559	501	450	407	368	335	306	280	258	238	220
	1200	543	489	442	400	363	331	303	278	256	236	218
	1000	520	472	429	390	356	325	298	274	252	233	216

TABLE 3.3 Allowable Design Values F'_c for Simple Solid Columns with L_e/d from 30 to 50 *(Continued)*

E' lb/in²	F^*_c lb/in²	L_e/d 30	32	34	36	38	40	42	44	46	48	50
1800000	3400	576	509	453	406	365	330	300	274	251	231	213
	3200	575	508	452	405	365	330	300	274	251	231	213
	3000	573	507	451	404	364	329	299	273	251	231	213
	2800	571	505	450	403	363	329	299	273	250	230	213
	2600	568	503	448	402	362	328	298	273	250	230	212
	2400	565	501	447	401	361	327	298	272	249	230	212
	2200	562	498	445	399	360	326	297	271	249	229	212
	2000	557	495	442	397	358	325	296	270	248	228	211
	1800	551	491	439	395	356	323	295	269	247	228	210
	1600	544	485	435	391	354	321	293	268	246	227	210
	1400	534	478	429	387	351	319	291	266	245	226	209
	1200	520	468	421	381	346	315	288	264	243	224	207
	1000	500	453	410	372	339	310	284	261	240	222	205
	800	468	428	392	358	328	301	277	255	236	218	202
1700000	3200	544	481	428	383	345	312	284	259	237	218	201
	3000	543	480	427	382	344	312	283	259	237	218	201
	2800	541	478	426	381	344	311	283	258	237	218	201
	2600	539	477	425	380	343	310	282	258	236	217	201
	2400	536	475	423	379	342	310	282	257	236	217	200
	2200	533	472	421	378	341	309	281	257	235	217	200
	2000	529	469	419	376	339	308	280	256	235	216	200
	1800	524	466	416	374	338	306	279	255	234	215	199
	1600	517	461	413	371	335	304	277	254	233	215	198
	1400	509	454	408	367	332	302	276	252	232	214	198
	1200	497	445	401	362	328	299	273	250	230	212	196
	1000	479	432	391	355	322	294	269	247	228	210	195
	800	451	411	375	342	313	287	263	242	224	207	192
	600	403	374	346	320	296	273	252	234	217	201	187
1600000	3200	514	454	404	361	325	294	267	244	223	206	190
	3000	512	453	403	361	325	294	267	244	223	205	189
	2800	511	451	402	360	324	293	267	243	223	205	189
	2600	509	450	401	359	323	293	266	243	223	205	189
	2400	506	448	399	358	322	292	266	242	222	205	189
	2200	503	446	398	357	321	291	265	242	222	204	188
	2000	500	443	396	355	320	290	264	241	221	204	188
	1800	496	440	393	353	319	289	263	241	221	203	188
	1600	490	436	390	351	317	287	262	240	220	202	187
	1400	483	431	386	347	314	285	260	238	219	202	186
	1200	472	423	380	343	311	283	258	236	217	200	185
	1000	457	411	371	336	306	278	255	234	215	199	184
	800	432	393	357	326	297	272	249	229	212	196	181
	600	389	360	333	306	282	260	240	222	205	191	177

TABLE 3.3 Allowable Design Values F_c' for Simple Solid Columns with L_e/d from 30 to 50 *(Continued)*

E' lb/in²	F_c^* lb/in²	L_e/d 30	32	34	36	38	40	42	44	46	48	50
1500000	3000	482	425	378	339	305	276	251	229	210	193	178
	2800	480	424	378	338	304	275	250	228	209	192	178
	2600	478	423	377	337	304	275	250	228	209	192	177
	2400	476	421	375	336	303	274	249	228	209	192	177
	2200	474	420	374	335	302	273	249	227	208	192	177
	2000	471	417	372	334	301	273	248	227	208	191	177
	1800	467	415	370	332	300	272	247	226	207	191	176
	1600	462	411	367	330	298	270	246	225	207	190	176
	1400	456	406	364	327	296	269	245	224	206	189	175
	1200	447	400	359	323	293	266	243	222	204	188	174
	1000	434	390	351	318	288	263	240	220	202	187	173
	800	412	374	339	308	281	257	235	216	199	184	171
	600	375	346	318	292	268	247	227	210	194	180	167
	400	305	289	273	256	240	224	209	195	182	170	159
1400000	2800	449	397	353	316	284	257	234	213	196	180	166
	2600	448	396	352	315	284	257	233	213	195	180	166
	2400	446	395	351	315	283	256	233	213	195	179	166
	2200	444	393	350	314	283	256	233	212	195	179	165
	2000	442	391	349	313	282	255	232	212	194	179	165
	1800	438	389	347	311	281	254	231	211	194	178	165
	1600	434	386	344	309	279	253	230	211	193	178	164
	1400	429	382	341	307	277	251	229	210	192	177	164
	1200	421	376	337	304	275	249	227	208	191	176	163
	1000	410	367	331	299	271	246	225	206	190	175	162
	800	392	354	320	291	265	242	221	203	187	173	160
	600	359	330	302	277	254	233	214	198	183	169	157
	400	297	280	263	246	229	214	199	185	172	161	150
1300000	2800	419	370	329	294	265	239	217	198	182	167	154
	2600	417	369	328	293	264	239	217	198	182	167	154
	2400	416	368	327	293	264	238	217	198	181	167	154
	2200	414	366	326	292	263	238	216	198	181	167	154
	2000	412	365	325	291	262	237	216	197	181	166	153
	1800	409	363	323	290	261	237	215	197	180	166	153
	1600	406	360	321	288	260	236	214	196	180	165	153
	1400	401	357	319	286	258	234	213	195	179	165	152
	1200	395	352	315	283	256	233	212	194	178	164	152
	1000	385	345	310	279	253	230	210	192	177	163	151
	800	370	333	301	273	248	226	207	190	175	161	149
	600	342	313	286	261	239	219	201	185	171	158	147
	400	287	270	252	234	218	202	188	174	162	151	141
	200	176	172	167	162	157	151	145	139	132	126	120

TABLE 3.3 Allowable Design Values F_c' for Simple Solid Columns with L_e/d from 30 to 50 *(Continued)*

E' lb/in²	F_c^* lb/in²	30	32	34	36	38	40	42	44	46	48	50
		L_e/d										
1200000	2600	387	341	303	271	244	221	201	183	168	154	142
	2400	385	340	303	271	244	221	200	183	168	154	142
	2200	384	339	302	270	243	220	200	183	167	154	142
	2000	382	338	301	269	243	220	200	182	167	154	142
	1800	380	336	299	268	242	219	199	182	167	153	142
	1600	377	334	298	267	241	218	198	181	166	153	141
	1400	373	331	296	265	239	217	198	181	166	153	141
	1200	368	327	293	263	238	216	196	180	165	152	140
	1000	360	321	288	260	235	213	195	178	164	151	139
	800	347	312	281	254	231	210	192	176	162	149	138
	600	324	295	268	244	223	204	187	172	159	147	136
	400	276	258	240	222	206	190	176	163	152	141	131
	200	173	169	164	158	152	146	140	133	127	120	114
1100000	1800	350	309	276	247	222	201	183	167	153	141	130
	1600	347	308	274	246	221	201	182	167	153	141	130
	1400	344	305	272	244	220	200	182	166	152	140	129
	1200	340	302	270	242	219	198	181	165	152	140	129
	1000	333	297	266	240	217	197	179	164	151	139	128
	800	323	289	260	235	213	194	177	162	149	138	127
	600	304	275	250	227	207	189	173	159	146	135	125
	400	264	245	226	209	193	178	164	152	141	131	121
	200	170	165	160	153	147	140	133	127	120	113	107
1000000	1800	320	282	251	225	203	183	167	152	139	128	118
	1600	318	281	250	224	202	183	166	152	139	128	118
	1400	315	279	249	223	201	182	166	151	139	128	118
	1200	311	276	247	221	200	181	165	151	138	127	117
	1000	306	273	244	219	198	180	164	150	137	127	117
	800	298	266	239	216	195	177	162	148	136	126	116
	600	283	255	231	209	190	173	159	146	134	124	115
	400	250	230	212	195	179	165	152	140	129	120	111
	200	167	161	155	148	141	134	127	119	113	106	100
900000	1600	287	254	226	202	182	165	150	137	125	115	106
	1400	285	253	225	202	182	164	149	137	125	115	106
	1200	283	250	223	200	181	164	149	136	125	115	106
	1000	278	247	221	199	179	162	148	135	124	114	106
	800	272	243	217	196	177	161	146	134	123	113	105
	600	260	234	211	191	173	158	144	132	121	112	104
	400	234	214	196	179	164	151	138	128	118	109	101
	200	162	155	148	141	133	126	119	111	105	98	92

For a given value of slenderness ratio L_e/d and given values for the modulus of elasticity E' and compression parallel to grain F_c^*, the allowable design value F_c' for a column is taken from the applicable table. The slenderness ratio is determined as discussed in Sec. 3.1.2. Before applying the design values of E' and F_c^* to the tables, they should be modified by the applicable factors to reflect the conditions in which the wood will be used. It should be noted that the design value of E is not adjusted for duration of load. In the case of lumber, allowable stresses, or design values, for E' and F_c^* are dependent on lumber cross-sectional dimensions. When trial sections of different dimensions are investigated in a design, it should be ensured that the allowable stresses appropriate for the cross-sectional size being investigated are used in the computations.

The total design load on a column is equal to the appropriate F_c' value taken from the applicable table times the cross-sectional area of the column. Values of F_c' for slenderness ratios L_e/d or L_1/d_1 intermediate to those given in the tables may be determined by straight-line interpolation. A similar procedure may be used for determining F_c' for intermediate F_c^* values.

EXAMPLE 3.12 Using the tables for allowable design values, design a solid column 11-ft 8-in (3.56-m) long to carry an axial load of 36 kips (160 kN). The duration of load is 7 days, and service conditions are dry. Assume the tabulated design values for column material to be $E = 1{,}300{,}000$ lb/in^2 (8963 MPa) and $F_c = 1050$ lb/in^2 (7240 kPa). Assume the column has pin-ends.

SOLUTION: Try nominal 6 × 6 in:

$$\text{Dressed dimensions} = 5.5 \times 5.5 \text{ in}$$

$$A = 30.25 \text{ in}^2$$

Allowable stresses:

$$E' = 1{,}300{,}000 \text{ lb/in}^2$$

$$F_c^* = 1050 \times 1.25 = 1312 \text{ lb/in}^2$$

Effective length:

$$L_e = 1.0L = 11.67 \text{ ft}$$

Slenderness ratio:

$$\frac{L_e}{d} = \frac{11.67 \times 12}{5.5} = 25.5 < 50 \qquad \text{OK}$$

Use Table 3.2 to determine F_c'. For $E' = 1{,}300{,}000$ lb/in^2, interpolating for $F_c^* = 1312$ lb/in^2 between 1200 and 1400, and interpolating for $L_e/d = 25.5$ between 24 and 26:

$$573 + (112/200)(591 - 573) = 583 \text{ lb/in}^2 \qquad \text{for } L_e/d \text{ of } 24$$

$$504 + (112/200)(517 - 504) = 511 \text{ lb/in}^2 \qquad \text{for } L_e/d \text{ of } 26$$

$$511 + (0.5/2.0)(583 - 511) = 529 \text{ lb/in}^2 \qquad \text{for } L_e/d \text{ of } 25.5$$

$$F_c' = 529 \text{ lb/in}^2$$

Allowable axial load:

$$P = F_c'A = 529 \times 30.25$$

$$= 16{,}000 \text{ lb} = 16.0 \text{ kips} < 36 \text{ kips} \qquad \text{SECTION NOT ADEQUATE}$$

Try nominal 6 × 8 in:

$$\text{Dressed dimensions} = 5.5 \times 7.5 \text{ in}$$

$$A = 41.25 \text{ in}^2$$

F_c' is the same as for the first trial section.
Allowable axial load:

$$P = F_c'A = 529 \times 41.25$$

$$= 21{,}800 \text{ lb} = 21.8 \text{ kips} < 36 \text{ kips} \qquad \text{SECTION NOT ADEQUATE}$$

Try nominal 8 × 8 in:

$$\text{Dressed dimensions} = 7.5 \times 7.5 \text{ in}$$

$$A = 56.25 \text{ in}^2$$

Slenderness ratio:

$$\frac{L_e}{d} = \frac{11.67 \times 12}{7.5} = 18.7 < 50 \qquad \text{OK}$$

Use Table 3.2 to determine F_c'. For E′ = 1,300,000 lb/in², interpolating for $F_c^* = 1312$ lb/in² between 1200 and 1400, and interpolating for $L_e/d = 18.7$ between 18 and 20:

$$830 + (112/200)(891 - 830) = 864 \text{ lb/in}^2 \qquad \text{for } L_e/d \text{ of } 18$$

$$739 + (112/200)(779 - 739) = 761 \text{ lb/in}^2 \qquad \text{for } L_e/d \text{ of } 20$$

$$761 + (1.3/2.0)(864 - 761) = 828 \text{ lb/in}^2 \qquad \text{for } L_e/d \text{ of } 18.7$$

$$F_c' = 828 \text{ lb/in}^2$$

Allowable axial load:

$$P = F_c'A = 828 \times 56.25$$

$$= 46{,}600 \text{ lb (207 kN)} = 46.6 \text{ kips} > 36 \text{ kips} \qquad \text{OK}$$

Use nominal 8- by 8-in (190.5- by 190.5-mm) column section.

REFERENCES

1. G. Gurfinkel, *Wood Engineering,* Southern Forest Products Association, New Orleans, La., 1981.
2. *National Design Specification for Wood Construction,* 1991 ed., American Forest and Paper Association, Washington, D.C., 1991.
3. S. K. Malhotra and A. P. Sukumar, "A Simplified Design Procedure for Built-up Wood Compression Members," Presented at the Canadian Society for Civil Engineering Annual Conference, June 1989.

4. S. K. Malhotra and D. B. Van Dyer, "Rational Approach to the Design of Built-up Timber Columns," *Wood Science* **9**(4):174–186 (1977).
5. *Wood Handbook: Wood as an Engineering Material,* Agriculture Handbook 72, Forest Products Laboratory, U.S. Department of Agriculture, Washington, D.C., 1987.
6. *Wood Handbook,* Agriculture Handbook 72, Forest Products Laboratory, U.S. Department of Agriculture, Washington, D.C., 1955.
7. J. R. Goodman and R. M. Gutkowski, "Composite Construction in Wood and Timber," in G. M. Sabnis (ed.), *Handbook of Composite Construction Engineering,* Van Nostrand Reinhold, New York, 1979.
8. L. W. Wood, "Formulas for Columns with Side Loads and Eccentricity," Report 1782, Forest Products Laboratory, U.S. Department of Agriculture, Madison, Wisc., 1961.
9. *Wood Structural Design Data,* 1986 ed. with 1992 revisions. American Forest and Paper Association, Washington, D.C., 1993.
10. J. J. Zahn, "Design of Wood Members Under Combined Load," *Journal of Structural Engineering* **112**(9):2109–2126 (1986).
11. *Commentary on the National Design Specification for Wood Construction,* American Forest and Paper Association, Washington, D.C., 1993.

CHAPTER 4
BENDING MEMBERS

Kenneth Smetts, P.E.
Thomas G. Williamson, P.E.

4.1 INTRODUCTION

Bending members represent some of the most common structural timber elements, and their proper design involves a number of considerations, most not generally required for the design of the supporting walls, posts, and columns. The theory of beam flexure, deflection, and shear is well covered by various textbooks. As such, only those features of particular concern to the designer working with wood beams are presented. The proper design of a wood beam requires an understanding of both the theory and the practical consequences of the following considerations with regard to wood flexural members:

1. Flexural design stresses and corresponding moment resistance capacity
2. Induced horizontal shear stresses as a function of vertical shear forces
3. Deflection characteristics related to both short-term and long-term performance
4. Bearing strength at end and interior bearing locations
5. Allowable stress adjustments, which are corrections or limitations that become part of the "art" necessary to correctly analyze a wood beam to meet structural design, serviceability, performance, and economic requirements. These adjustments are discussed in Chap. 2 and are categorized as follows:
   - **a.** Duration of load
   - **b.** Moisture adjustments related to in-service conditions
   - **c.** In-service conditions other than moisture, including need for preservative treatment and effects of temperature
   - **d.** Size or volume effect
   - **e.** Lateral stability considerations
   - **f.** Curvature or shape effects

Note: In all example problems, SI units are provided only for given data and the final problem answer or answers. No intermediate values or data are expressed in SI units.

4.1.1 Flexural Considerations

The flexural strength of a beam is generally the primary structural consideration of the designer. Although lack of proper consideration of the other factors listed may cause failure or unsatisfactory performance, the improper determination of the flexural capacity will typically result in a more serious form of damage. This concept can be stated simply by saying that any beam design should first be approached by providing adequate flexural capacity. After this basic task has been satisfied, other design considerations need to be taken into account, and the "art" of wood beam design begins. Following conventional beam theory, the resisting moment is based on the relationship of the structural section capacity (section modulus) and the allowable material strength (allowable stress in bending). This relationship is shown as

$$\text{Resisting moment} = \text{section modulus} \times \text{allowable bending stress}$$

or

$$M = S \times F_b$$

For the common rectangular timber beam section.

$$S = \frac{bd^2}{6}$$

where b is the width and d the depth of the member.

This calculation determines the resistance side of the design analysis, which is then related to the given loading and span conditions which determine the actual bending moment to be resisted. In practice, it is convenient to make use of tables and formulas for moments, shears, and deflections, which have been published for the most common design conditions. It is important to note that in determining the resistance side of the design analysis of wood beams, it is necessary to apply certain modifications to either the allowable bending stresses or the section modulus based on anticipated in-service conditions.

The simple task of selecting the allowable bending stress F_b can be a complex problem for the designer. To properly determine F_b, the designer must first know the species, grade, and approximate size of the member. The designer must understand that a simple beam consisting of a 2× member will have different values for F_b depending on whether the beam has a nominal depth of 4 in or less or whether its nominal depth is 5 in or greater. The selection of a purlin or small beam is further complicated by the fact that a 4× member will have a different allowable value than a 5× member and furthermore that a 6 × 8 will have a different value than a 6 × 12. All this assumes specifications of the same species and grade of lumber. A designer becoming involved in timber design must become familiar with the lumber grading rules and rely on the actual size definitions rather than the function or use terminology assigned by the grading agencies.

All structural lumber with nominal sizes of 2×, 3×, or 4× is graded in accordance with the *American Softwood Lumber Standard,* PS20-70,[1] and as such is uniform throughout the United States and Canada. This information is repeated in the publications of the various regional grading agencies. *Design Values for Wood Construction,*[2] a supplement to the *National Design Specification for Wood Construction* (NDS),[3] provides tabular allowable stress data for virtually all wood species and grades available in the United States. Excerpts from this publication of stress values for commonly used species are given in the Appendix, "Reference Data."

When the anticipated beam size exceeds that normally available in solid sawn members, the selection of a glued-laminated (glulam) timber member or structural composite lumber section typically becomes the next option to the designer. For glulam timbers, the allowable stress F_b, as well as all other design stresses, is based on a classification system involving "combination" numbers and species identification. For structural composite lumber, the designer must reference the manufacturer's proprietary literature for size, allowable stress, and structural capacity information.

The American Forest and Paper Association publishes allowable stresses for a wide range of glulam combinations in their publication *Design Value for Wood Construction.*[2] A summary of commonly used values from this reference is also given in the Appendix, "Reference Data." The primary species used by the laminating industry are Douglas fir–larch and southern pine, although other species may be used. Since it is difficult to determine species availability on a regional basis, it is recommended that the designer determine the allowable stresses required to satisfy the design requirements and specify that the laminated timber supplier select a species and stress combination that will satisfy these required stresses. This relieves the designer of the need to know what species are available in a given geographic location and allows the supplier to select the most economical species-grade combination for the given design. Specifying a species-grade combination that may not be available in a given geographic area can result in an unnecessary cost premium assessed the buyer-owner.

4.1.2 Deflection and Related Stiffness Control

The theory of beam action provides the basis for calculating the theoretical deflection or vertical movement under load of a wood beam in either a simple-span design or the more involved cantilever or continuous-span designs. This theory assigns part of the deflection to the elongation of the wood fibers due to bending and part to shear deformation. To simplify calculations, the allowable or recommended modulus of elasticity E values have been reduced by about 10 percent to automatically include shear deflection in flexural deflection calculations. Since the shear deformation in most flexural members is small in relationship to the flexural effect, this is a practical solution. However, in short-span heavily loaded members, shear deflections may exceed 10 percent and, if necessary, could be calculated separately using virtual work or other methods for calculating deflections due to shear.

For sawn lumber and glulam members, the published E values are average values and are further affected by in-service moisture conditions, particularly with regard to the tendency for increased observed deflection when the design load is applied to a green or unseasoned sawn member which seasons or dries in place under load. Thus the designer is faced with having to adjust the calculations for solid sawn unseasoned beams to reflect this particular material characteristic. In addition, the rather large coefficient of variation associated with the average E values of sawn timbers also can influence in-service deflection performance.

For glulam timbers, the published E values, while still averages, have a much lower coefficient of variation than for sawn timbers and provide a greater degree of predictability of in-service deflections. Also, glulam members are fabricated using kiln-dried lumber which has a maximum moisture content at the time of gluing of 16 percent. Thus they have an initial moisture content at the time of installation that is much closer to the final in-service equilibrium moisture conditions than that of solid sawn timbers. To accomplish this element of the beam design, namely (1) to control deflection, (2) to provide adequate stiffness for the intended use, and (3) to provide for moisture content changes, if applicable, requires the designer to consider the following:

1. Selection of allowable modulus of elasticity E from published tables for an anticipated species and grade (sawn timbers) or stress combination (glulam).

2. Calculation of deflection based on the previously selected E values and given load and span conditions as defined by the designer to truly represent the in-service use of members.

3. Establishment of deflection control limits that have shown by experience to provide acceptable performance. Unfortunately, such limits are often assigned in various building codes on a somewhat arbitrary basis and are not necessarily as restrictive as needed. It is absolutely essential to properly control in-service deflections, and thus appropriate limitations to ensure this control may not be reflected by the limits published by the most commonly accepted building codes. A suggested set of deflection criteria are given in Table 4.1.

4. Consideration of long-term deflection characteristics and their effect on stiffness and camber performance. This is an important factor for such considerations as prevention of "ponding," general feel or sense of adequacy of floors, vibration, storm drainage, and residual camber. The term *camber,* which is essentially a reverse curvature built into the beam to offset the anticipated vertical deflection of the beam, is important to understand, in particular as it relates to glulam timbers. Obviously, it is impossible to camber a sawn wood member, except for the minor effect of placing the "crown up" in simple-beam applications. It is important to understand that camber is related to stiffness control but at the same time is completely independent. The correct design of a glulam timber beam involves consideration of both stiffness limitations and practical camber practice. However, camber cannot compensate adequately for a beam in which proper stiffness control has not been provided. Recommended minimum cambers for glulam timber beams are as given in Table 4.2. The American Wood Systems Technical Note, *Glulam Beam Camber,*[4] provides a detailed discussion of camber considerations and gives a table of camber values for various spans and radius of curvatures.

4.1.3 Shear Considerations

In the typical horizontal beam, vertical shear stress results from vertically placed loads. This shear stress is not a failure mode in wood flexural members. However, vertical shear stress always induces a horizontal shear stress which is parallel to the grain of the wood and must be considered in design. For the wood beam used as a simple-span member, the horizontal shear stress is maximum at the supports and at or near the neutral axis, becoming zero at the top and bottom faces of the member. The theoretical formula to determine horizontal shear stresses is

$$F_v = \frac{VQ}{It} \tag{4.1}$$

TABLE 4.1 Recommended Beam Deflection or Stiffness Limits

Use	Glulam		Solid sawn	
	LL only	TL	LL only	TL
Roof				
Industrial				
Purlins		$\ell/180$		$\ell/240$
Beams		$\ell/120$		
Commercial				
Purlins		$\ell/240$		$\ell/360$
Beams		$\ell/180$		
Commercial—ceilings				
Purlins		$\ell/240$		$\ell/360$
Beams		$\ell/240$		
Commercial—plaster				
Purlins	$\ell/360$	$\ell/240$		$\ell/360$
Beams	$\ell/360$	$\ell/240$		
Floor				
Short span <20 ft	$\ell/360$		$\ell/360$	
Medium span 20–30 ft	$\ell/480$		$\ell/480$	
Long span >30 ft	*			

*Deflection limitations for long spans require specific consideration of acceptable deflection magnitudes for each individual case. Since these suggested limitations or criteria have to be modified by each designer's personal engineering judgment, the designer should review completed projects, particularly those involving longer spans, to determine their actual performance history. A designer should be alerted to floor loading conditions that vary both the loading and the span from what has been experienced previously.

where V = vertical shear
Q = static moment of area outside level of desired shear about neutral axis
I = moment of inertia
t = width of beam at level of desired shear stress

For a rectangular section, this formula reduces to

$$F_v = \frac{1.5V}{A} \tag{4.2}$$

where V is the vertical shear and A the cross section of the beam.

Note that the beam is checked for vertical shear as determined from the usual shear diagram, but the actual shear stress is investigated as horizontal shear, which is the mode of shear failure for wood.

Since shear seldom governs design except in cases of short spans with heavy loading, such as high-snow-load mountain areas or heavily loaded floor beams, or in cantilevered or continuous-span beam designs, certain refinements in both anal-

TABLE 4.2 Recommended Minimum Cambers for Glulam Beams

Roof beams*	1.5 times dead-load deflection
Floor beams†	1.5 times dead-load deflection
Bridge beams‡	
Long span	2 times dead-load deflection
Short span	2 times dead-load deflection plus one-half of applied load deflection

**Roof beams:* The minimum camber of 1.5 times dead-load deflection will produce a nearly level member under dead load alone after plastic deformation has occurred. Additional camber may be provided to improve appearance or provide necessary roof drainage. Roof beams should have a positive slope or camber equivalent to 0.25 in per foot of horizontal distance between the level of the drain and the high point of the roof. In addition, on long spans, level roof beams may not be desirable because of the optical illusion that the ceiling is sagging. This condition may also apply to floor beams in multistory buildings.

†*Floor beams:* The minimum camber of 1.5 times dead-load deflection will produce a nearly level member under dead load along after plastic deformation has occurred. For warehouse or similar floors where live load may remain for long periods, additional camber should be provided to give a level floor under the permanently applied load.

‡*Bridge beams:* Bridge members are normally cambered for dead load only on multiple spans to obtain acceptable riding qualities.

ysis and adjustment of allowable stress are not often utilized. In the case of sawn timber beams, the NDS[3] and the regional grade rules permit increases in the allowable shear stress if end splits can be controlled. This end-split control places the designer in the difficult position of having to know the expected seasoning performance of the members in service as well as the initial condition of the members at the time of fabrication. This knowledge of production practices and job-site conditions may be beyond the designer's area of expertise.

Often overlooked or assumed to be not directly tied to shear is the question of a shear-type mode of failure caused or aggravated by severe end notches, which should be avoided, and shaping or placement of connectors. Examples of such end treatment are shown in Fig. 4.1, and additional related considerations such as the effect of a bolted-only connection with bolts placed near the unloaded face are given in Chap. 5.

4.1.4 Bearing Considerations

Provision of adequate bearing area at supports is another design consideration requiring the attention of the designer. However, this design is relatively simple, and the consequence of design error causing structural problems is generally minimal. The allowable bearing stress values $F_{c\perp}$ have recently been increased significantly to recognize their past ultraconservative nature. Even with these increases, an expected mode of failure would be localized deformation as contrasted to a catastrophic type of failure.

Glulam timbers add some confusion to this design stress by the use of different compression perpendicular to grain values for compression and tension faces of glulam members. The NDS[3] lists such dual values for all the combinations contained in that reference (see the Appendix, "Reference Data," for similar information). It is noted that in some combinations the value is the same. By reviewing these tables, it becomes apparent that the factor accounting for these possibly different compression perpendicular to grain stresses is the presence of denser lumber laminations placed on these outer faces. For a combination such as Douglas fir 24F-

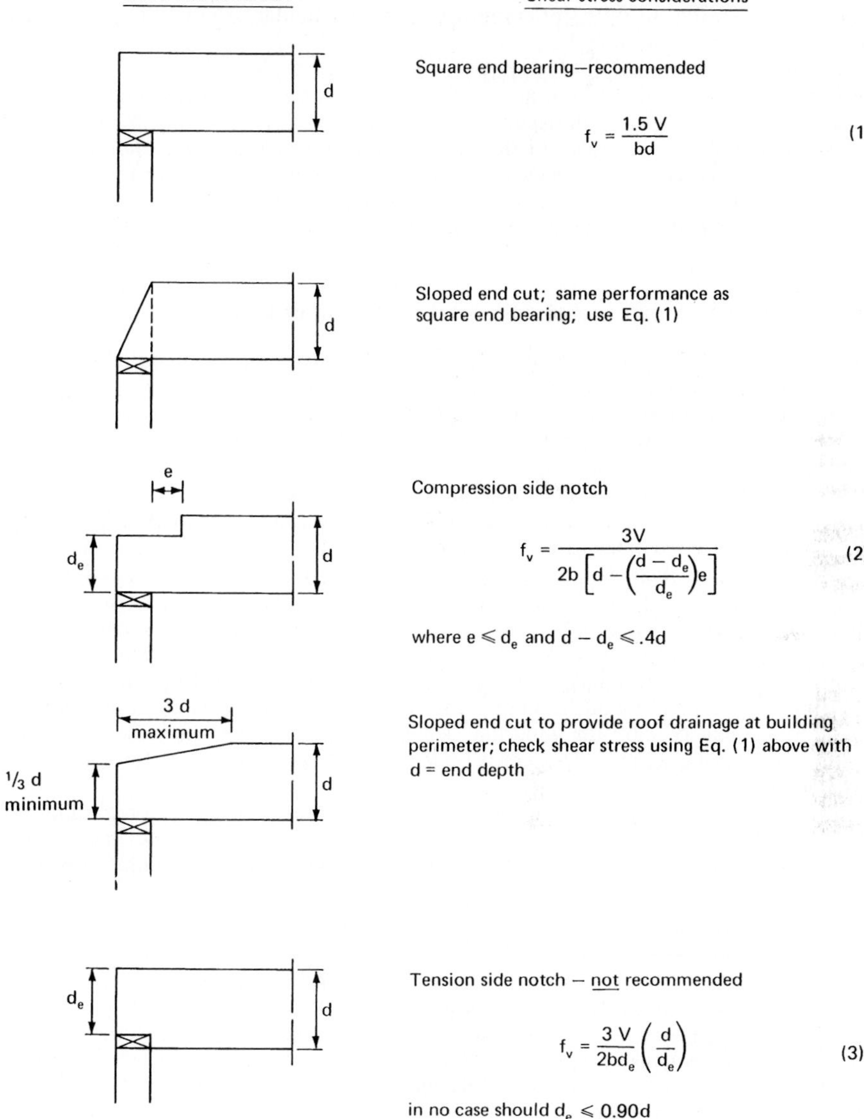

FIG. 4.1 Typical beam bearing conditions.

V8, the end use assumes that negative moments or continuity will exist as well as the normal positive moments so that the beam is manufactured as a balanced section and uses high-density laminations in both top and bottom faces. Conversely, there are combinations such as Douglas fir 24F-V3, which assume a simple-span condition as the end use with high-density laminations required only on the lower or tension face of the bending member and less dense material allowed for the top face, thus resulting in different compression perpendicular to grain stresses for the top and bottom of the member.

From a design standpoint, it is possible to have a simple beam designed for $F_{c\perp} = 650$ lb/in^2 (4481.8 kPa) at a wall pilaster seat yet supporting a concentrated load on the top face near midspan having an allowable $F_{c\perp} = 560$ lb/in^2 (3861.2 kPa). A review of the tables in the NDS[3] shows considerable differences in $F_{c\perp}$ values due to variations in species and in density within a given species. It should be noted that the duration-of-load adjustments are not applicable to allowable compression perpendicular to grain values for either sawn or glulam timbers.

4.1.5 Allowable Stress Adjustments—Duration of Load

The duration-of-load adjustments discussed in Chap. 2 are reviewed here as they affect bending-member design. This adjustment is related primarily to roof-load conditions but applies to any loading pattern where the time period of actual loading is different from what is defined as normal loading, that is, fully loaded for 10 years. Floor loads are generally considered to be normal duration-of-load applications, although permanent floor loadings such as a water tank floor or a heavy industrial warehouse floor can occur and should be treated as long-term loading. The ability of wood fiber to accept overstress for a short period of time has long been an accepted fact, but its application to actual design has on occasion been misunderstood. The permissible overstress is inversely proportional to the time of maximum loading. The NDS[3] provides an explanation of this adjustment and includes not only stresses but also fasteners and other design considerations as well. Using this reference as a base, Table 4.3 indicates how this adjustment factor should be applied to typical wood framing. It must be noted that the use of a duration-of-load adjustment of 1.60 for wind and seismic events has not been adopted by all code jurisdictions, and the designer is referred to the applicable code for verification of this factor.

Although an established concept, some concerns have been raised regarding the use of the 1.25 factor when applied to roof systems without snow loading and where the minimum roof load is further reduced due to the contributing area sup-

TABLE 4.3 Duration of Load Adjustments, C_D

Typical loading	Period of loading[a]	Permitted adjustment
Normal	10 years[b]	1.0 (no increase)
Short term	7 days[a]	1.25
Snow	2 months[d]	1.15
Wind or seismic	10 minutes	1.60[f]
Permanent	[e]	0.90

[a]Period of loading is cumulative during entire life of structure, or 50 years. Period relates to time of loading at maximum design load shown.

[b]Fully loaded for 10 years with both dead load and live load.

[c]7 days' loading, such as normal roof load with no snow.

[d]2 months' loading, such as snow load.

[e]Full application of design live load and dead load for a period of time greater than 10 years.

[f]Check with local code for verification of this factor.

ported by the beam. In areas of the country not subjected to snow loading, the area of concern has been related to the use of a 12-lb/ft^2 (574.56-Pa) live load associated with relatively high dead loads and the application of the 1.25 duration-of-load increase. There are no code explanations of any limitations related to various combinations of live and dead loads, and the following criteria are suggested as possible design limitations to control potential overstress conditions associated with relatively light roof design loads.

For a live load of 12 lb/ft^2 (574.56 Pa) and a dead load of 14 lb/ft^2 (670.32 Pa) or less, use a load duration factor of 1.25.

For a live load of 12 lb/ft^2 (574.56 Pa) and a dead load of 19 lb/ft^2 (909.72 Pa) maximum, use a load duration factor of 1.15.

For a live load of 12 lb/ft^2 (574.56 Pa) and a dead load of 20 lb/ft^2 (957.60 Pa) or more, use a load duration factor of 1.00.

The load-duration factor is a permissive adjustment and applies to allowable stresses for wood, except for compression perpendicular to grain and modulus of elasticity. It is also applicable to most connector design values.

4.1.6 Adjustment Considerations—Seasoning

Since the designer is working either with wood fiber in a sawn member as cut from the log, for example, joists, purlins, beams, or stringers, or with glued wood products such as produced from manufactured lumber or veneers, that is, glulam timber or structural composite lumber (SCL), seasoning or change of moisture content in service is a physical fact. The designer cannot prevent seasoning, which will typically occur in service, but by proper design and detailing may be able to limit or control the effects of this in-service seasoning. This requires certain adjustments to allowable stresses to reflect the expected initial and final in-place equilibrium moisture conditions. Such adjustments may be either a decrease or an increase in stresses, depending on the anticipated character of the change in moisture content of the wood fibers (i.e., increase or decrease in moisture content).

For glulam timbers, industry manufacturing standards require a maximum moisture content of the individual laminations at the time of manufacture not to exceed 16 percent, and the published stress values have been developed based on this assumed dry condition. If the in-service conditions produce an equilibrium moisture content greater than 16 percent, the published allowable values require that the "wet-use" reduction factors be applied. These reduction factors are typically listed as percentages of the normal stresses and vary for different types of stresses. In addition, when the equilibrium moisture content will be greater than 16 percent, waterproof or exterior-use adhesives must be used in the manufacture of glulam. If the moisture content exceeds approximately 20 percent, there is an additional concern regarding the wood's resistance to decay or insect attack, and the individual laminations or the completed member must be pressure preservatively treated to control these hazards.

For sawn wood beams such as joists and purlins there are many possible variations or adjustments due to seasoning. Although properly described in the regional grading rules, there are many questions regarding availability of the material at the moisture contents listed. For example, the use of sawn lumber designated "S-dry" at 19 percent and "MC15" at 15 percent moisture content can be of great help in controlling the shrinkage of wood members in floors and can provide increased strength and stiffness. Such material is normally limited to 2- by 4-in material up to 2- by 12-in sizes and occasionally in 3× material and usually only for "S-dry." The grading rules list this material for 2× , 3× , and 4× with no size limitations. Any attempt to specify this drier material for 4× and wider material is not recommended unless local suppliers are able to assure both quality and availability.

The importance of knowing the availability of "dry" sawn lumber is related to the practicality of utilizing the higher allowable stresses and improved *E* available with the lower moisture content. The adjustments related to size and moisture content limitations are shown in the grading rules. For sawn timber members surfaced dry but used in an atmosphere producing an equilibrium moisture content greater than 19 percent, the stresses must be adjusted by the reductions shown in the grading rules. Obviously, changes of moisture content can result in either a bonus or a penalty. These can be determined from the allowable stress tables for lumber, portions of which are given in the Appendix, "Reference Data." The assumed conditions for seasoning or moisture content are as follows:

1. If "S-dry" material has been dried to a moisture content of 19 percent or less and then planed to finished size and used in service with an atmosphere producing an equivalent moisture content of 19 percent or less. Then allowable stresses for "dry" may be used.

2. If surfaced to finished size in the green or undried condition (S-GRN)—a common marketing condition for larger timbers—the member is assumed to season in place prior to application of the full design loads. To compensate for this seasoning in place, the finished size in the green condition is larger than that permitted for "dry" so that after in-service shrinkage takes place, the net dimensions remaining approach that of the "dry" material.

3. Section properties for 2× , 3× , and 4× material are based on the "dry" surfaced size, and all sizes, green or dry, are identified by nominal sizes. Stress values are calculated based on the permitted net sizes for "S-dry."

4.1.7 Adjustment Considerations—Service Conditions Other Than Moisture

There are a number of potential nontypical service conditions other than normal moisture and seasoning that may need to be considered. The related adjustments are specified in the NDS[3] and include such items as

1. *Temperature effects:* High temperature and humidity (penalty); low temperature (bonus)
2. *Pressure treatments:* For resistance to decay and insects (normally no stress adjustment required) and for resistance to fire (a reduction varying with treatment)
3. *End splits:* Allowable increases in horizontal shear values if degree of split can be controlled.

The first two adjustments are considered as special cases which the designer should consider for each specific project to determine their applicability. The last adjustment, for end splits, is a means to improve shear capacity of sawn timbers by as much as 100 percent. To use this adjustment requires the designer to have a good understanding of both manufacturing standards and in-place atmospheric conditions. From a designer's viewpoint, there are opportunities for these bonus values for the smaller sections seasoned before surfacing to a moisture content of less than 19 percent. Any other condition introduces unknowns not normally controllable by the designer. For a detailed discussion of these variables, the designer is referred to the NDS.[3]

4.1.8 Adjustment Considerations—Effect of Member Size

There are several stress reductions which may be applicable to the allowable stress in bending, namely, the effect of member size, member curvature, or lateral stability considerations. Member size is accounted for by applying a size-effect factor C_F to the published bending stresses for sawn timbers and a volume factor C_v to the bending stresses for glulam. The size effect factor $C_F = (12/d)^{1/9}$ is applied to sawn timber having a nominal width of 5 in or greater and a depth of 12 in or greater. For example, the bending stress for a 6 × 16 would be reduced by applying a factor of 0.97. A size factor is also applied to the bending, tension, and compression parallel to grain design stresses for visually graded dimension lumber 2 to 4 in thick in accordance with the regional grading rule provisions. These size factors are given in the NDS Supplement, *Design Values for Wood Construction* (see Appendix, "Reference Data").

For glulam members, a volume-effect factor is used to account for member size. This factor is calculated using the following equation:

$$C_V = K\left(\frac{12}{d}\right)^{1/x}\left(\frac{5.125}{w}\right)^{1/x}\left(\frac{21}{\ell}\right)^{1/x} \tag{4.3}$$

where K is a factor to account for loading condition (often assumed to be unity for simplicity of calculation) and d, w, and ℓ are the depth, width, and length of the member, in inches for d and w and in feet for ℓ. The term x in the exponent is 20 for southern pine and 10 for western species used in the manufacture of glulam. The value of C_V is limited to a maximum of 1.0.

The designer of wood bending members is cautioned to verify the applicable size- or volume-effect factor at the time of design. For example, the volume-effect factor is only applied to glulam bending members when the load is applied perpendicular to the wide face of the laminations. For glulam members on which the load is applied parallel to the wide face of the laminations, the size-effect factor is applicable.

The size- or volume-effect factor can be applied in two procedures. The first approach requires the designer to estimate the expected size and thus depth of the beam, reduce the allowable stress in bending F_b by the appropriate factor, and then determine the actual size or depth required. This requires a trial-and-error solution. An alternate procedure utilizes section modulus values that have already been reduced to reflect the reduction due to the size factor. A simple formula of required or actual bending moment (in inch-pounds) divided by the allowable F'_b, with appropriate adjustments for duration of load, moisture content, and other applicable factors, equals the required section modulus[5] as modified by the size-effect factor C_F. This is shown as

$$\frac{M}{F'_b} = SC_F = S_{\text{adj}} \tag{4.4}$$

This concept also can be expressed as

$$f_b = \frac{M}{S_{\text{adj}}} \tag{4.5}$$

that is, the actual bending stress is equal to the moment divided by the reduced section modules accounting for the size effect factor. Since the volume-effect factor also includes the length of the member as a design parameter, S_{adj} values can only be tabulated for a specific ℓ/d ratio and must be further modified for other ℓ/d conditions.

4.1.9 Adjustment Considerations—Effect of Curvature or Shape

This group of adjustments is not a consideration for bending members having straight rectangular cross sections, used for conventional industrial or commercial structures. The effect of curvature is applicable to glulam timbers such as curved beams, PTC beams, and arches and relates to the thickness of the individual laminations and the radius of the member. This factor is discussed in detail in Chap. 2 and is calculated by the equation

$$\text{Curvature factor } C_c = 1.0 - 2000\left(\frac{t}{R}\right)^2 \tag{4.6}$$

where t is the net lamination thickness and R is the inside radius of curvature, both in inches.

For normal camber requirements, the curvature adjustment typically can be neglected as the radius will be relatively large.

The second form of adjustments is related to the shape of the member. These are discussed in Chap. 2, and since they are seldom applicable, they are not discussed in this chapter.

4.2 LATERAL STABILITY CONSIDERATIONS

Before considering the adjustment for member slenderness or lateral stability, it is important to note that the volume-effect factor is related to a tension mode of failure. This is an important consideration, since the slenderness concept relates to a compression mode of failure. Due to the different modes of failure, these two major adjustments to bending capacity are not applied cumulatively for glulams, but rather the one that results in the greatest reduction in allowable bending stress controls design. For sawn members, the two factors are applied in a cumulative manner.

For those framing systems where the floor or roof sheathing is not attached directly to the top of the beams or where the beams are not braced by closely spaced secondary framing members such as joists, it may be necessary to reduce the allowable bending stress due to possible buckling of the compression edge. The reduction is represented by the beam-stability factor and represents the loss of beam resistance when the compression zone of a wood bending member is not positively supported against lateral buckling. Continuous or cantilever beams also require investigation in the negative moment areas when the compression zone is at the bottom of the beam where there is normally no attachment of subframing members or sheathing to brace the member against lateral buckling.

4.2.1 Effective Span Length

Determining the beam-stability factor is an empirical process. It requires the determination of an effective span length, a beam slenderness ratio, and then the beam-stability factor. The first parameter to be determined is the effective span length, which is a function of the unbraced length. For example, a common framing system for warehouses utilizes cantilever beams framed over the top of glulam girders. This system provides two conditions where the beam-stability factor must be investigated. The first condition occurs in the cantilever member where a negative moment exists in the area at the top of the beam. In this area, the effective unbraced length between points of lateral support must be determined, and from these data the effective span length can be calculated. The second condition occurs in the girder itself, where the only effective top edge support for this simple-span member exists at its end supports and at the point of support for the beam cantilevered over the top of the girder. These locations thus determine the unbraced lengths needed to determine the effective span length.

TABLE 4.4 Effective Length ℓ_e for Bending Members

Cantilever*	When $\ell_u/d < 7$	When $\ell_u/d \geq 7$
Uniformly distributed load	$\ell_e = 1.33\ell_u$	$\ell_e = 0.90\ell_u + 3d$
Concentrated load at unsupported end	$\ell_e = 1.87\ell_u$	$\ell_e = 1.44\ell_u + 3d$
Single-span beam*	**When $\ell_u/d < 7$**	**When $\ell_u/d \geq 7$**
Uniformly distributed load	$\ell_e = 2.06\ell_u$	$\ell_e = 1.63\ell_u + 3d$
Concentrated load at center with no intermediate lateral support	$\ell_e = 1.80\ell_u$	$\ell_e = 1.37\ell_u + 3d$
Concentrated load at center with lateral support at center	$\ell_e = 1.11\ell_u$	
Two equal concentrated loads at ⅓ points with lateral support at ⅓ points	$\ell_e = 1.68\ell_u$	

*For single-span or cantilevered bending members with loading conditions not specified in Table 4.4.

$$\ell_e = 2.06\ell_u \quad \text{when } \ell_u/d < 7$$
$$\ell_e = 1.63\ell_u + 3d \quad \text{when } 7 \leq \ell_u/d \leq 14.3$$
$$\ell_e = 1.84\ell_u \quad \text{when } \ell_u/d > 14.3$$

The value selected is a combination of the actual unbraced length defined as ℓ_u and a factor reflecting the mode of loading and end support. Table 4.4 shows these various factors for several loading and support conditions for simple-span and cantilevered beams. The NDS[3] provides more extensive effective length factors.

4.2.2 Slenderness Ratio

The formula for the slenderness ratio R_B is given as

$$R_B = \sqrt{\frac{\ell_e d}{b^2}} \tag{4.7}$$

where R_b = slenderness ratio
b = beam width
d = beam depth
ℓ_e = effective length of unsupported compression flange, in

the slenderness ratio for bending members shall not exceed 50.

4.2.3 Beam-Stability Factor

The beam-stability factor C_L is calculated by the following relationship:

$$C_L = \frac{1 + (F_{bE}/F_b^*)}{1.9} - \sqrt{\left[\frac{1 + (F_{bE}/F_b^*)}{1.9}\right]^2 - \frac{(F_{bE}/F_b^*)}{0.95}} \tag{4.8}$$

where F_b^* = tabulated allowable bending design value multiplied by all applicable adjustment factors
$F_{bE} = K_{bE}E'/R_B^2$

where R_B = slenderness ratio determined from Eq. (4.7)
K_{BE} = 0.438 for visually graded lumber
K_{BE} = 0.609 for wood products with a COV $\leq$ 0.11 for MOE
E' = tabulated modulus of elasticity value multiplied by all applicable adjustment factors.

The following example illustrates use of the beam-stability factor for the analysis of a glulam beam.

EXAMPLE 4.1 Assume a glulam timber beam is to be used to support a skylight framing system in which the beam will be unbraced over its full length and will carry only a concentrated load at midspan. Assume the following design span and loadings:

Span = 32 ft (9.75 m).

Concentrated load P at midspan = 11,000 lb (48,930 N), resulting from a combination of dead load and snow load; therefore, use duration-of-load increase of 1.15.

Allowable Δ_{TL} = 1 in (2.54 cm) (per skylight manufacturer's recommendation).

Assume a 24F-V3 southern pine glulam combination will be used having the following allowable design values: F_{bx} = 2400 lb/in^2 (16,548 kPa), F_v = 200 lb/in^2 (1379 kPa), E_x = 1,800,000 lb/in^2 (12,400,000 kPa), and E_y = 1,600,000 lb/in^2 (11,000,000 kPa).

Assume a beam weight of 40 lb/ft (583.8 N/m).

Estimate beam size based on bending:

$$M = \frac{PL}{4} + \frac{wL^2}{8} = \frac{11{,}000 \times 32}{4} + \frac{40 \times 32^2}{8} = 93{,}120 \text{ ft·lb}$$

$$S_{\text{req}} = \frac{M}{F'_b} = \frac{93{,}120 \times 12}{2400 \times 1.15 \times 0.90} = 450 \text{ in}^3$$

where 0.90 represents an assumed value for C_V. Try a 6¾- by 24-in glulam section having the following properties:

$$A = 162.0 \text{ in}^2 \qquad S = 648.0 \text{ in}^3 \qquad I = 7776.0 \text{ in}^4$$

Check shear stress:

$$f_v = \frac{1.5V}{A} = \frac{1.5 \times 6060}{162} = 56.1 \text{ lb/in}^2 \text{ (386.8 kPa)}$$

$$\ll F'_y = 200 \times 1.15 = 230 \text{ lb/in}^2 \text{ (1585.8 kPa)}$$

Check bending stress: Since the beam is fully unbraced, it must be checked for lateral stability considerations. Determine the effective span length ℓ_e:

$$\ell_e = 1.37\ell_u + 3d = (1.37 \times 32 \times 12) + (3 \times 24) = 598.1 \text{ in}$$

where ℓ_u is the unbraced length and 1.37 is the lateral support factor from Table 4.4.

Determine the slenderness ratio R_B:

$$R_B = \sqrt{\frac{\ell_e d}{b^2}} = \sqrt{\frac{598.1 \times 24}{6.75^2}} = 17.7$$

Determine the beam-stability factor C_L:

$$F_{bE} = \frac{0.609 \times 1{,}600{,}000}{(17.7)^2} = 3110 \text{ lb/in}^2$$

$$C_L = \frac{1 = (2760/3110)}{1.9} - \sqrt{\left[\frac{1 + (2760/3110)}{1.9}\right]^2 - \frac{(2760/3110)}{0.95}}$$

$$= 0.765$$

$$F'_b = 2400(0.765) = 1836 \text{ lb/in}^2$$

Determine F'_b based on the volume-effect factor:

$$F'_b = F_b C_V = 2400 \times 1.15 \times 0.933 = 2575 \text{ lb/in}^2$$

Therefore, use $F'_b = 1836$ lb/in² based on lateral stability.

Determine the actual bending stress f_b,

$$f_b = \frac{M}{S} = \frac{93{,}120 \times 12}{648}$$

$$= 1724 \text{ lb/in}^2 \text{ (11,887 kPa)} < F'_b = 1836 \text{ lb/in}^2 \text{ (12,660 kPa)}$$

Note that the approximate weight of a 6¾- by 24-in (17.1- by 61.0-cm) glulam beam is 40 lb/ft (583.76 N/m), which agrees with the original assumption. If the weight is considerably different, the moment calculation should be rechecked.

Check deflection:

$$\Delta_{TL} = \frac{P\ell^3}{48EI} + \frac{5w\ell^4}{384EI}$$

$$= \frac{11{,}000 \times 32^3 \times 1728}{48 \times 1{,}800{,}000 \times 7776}$$

$$+ \frac{5 \times 40 \times 32^4 \times 1728}{384 \times 1{,}800{,}000 \times 7776}$$

$$= 0.995 \text{ in (2.53 cm)} = 1.0 \text{ in (2.54 cm)} = \Delta \text{ (allowable)}$$

Therefore, the beam size is adequate.

For sawn lumber joist systems and secondary beams, this detailed process for lateral stability is seldom used. Instead, arbitrary controls found in the model building codes and the NDS[3] are substituted as design guides. These limitations are in the form of acceptable depth-to-width ratios d/b based on nominal sizes such as follows:

A ratio of 2/1, such as for a 2 × 4, requires no lateral support.

A ratio of 5/1, such as for a 2 × 10, requires one edge to be held in line for its full length.

A ratio of 6/1, such as for a 2 × 12, needs effective full-length compression flange support via proper sheathing and requires effective lateral end support or restraint to prevent rotation.

A ratio of 7/1, such as for a 2 × 14, needs both edges held in line for their entire length.

A more detailed discussion of these guidelines is given in the NDS.[3] While these guidelines are recommendations, they are not based on any specific testing or research. These limits on d/b ratios have been used for years without any indication of hindering performance or economics.

It is noted that d/b ratios of greater than 7/1 are permissable for members such as glulam assuming that the lateral stability considerations of this section are satisfied.

4.3 TORSION

Wood bending members are not typically loaded in such a manner as to induce torsional stresses, i.e., stresses that result when the applied load tends to twist the member. However, there are specific instances where torsional stresses may need to be considered by the designer. One such design situation exists in the case of a carrying beam supporting a relatively large eccentric load applied to one side of the member only.

For square or rectangular cross sections, the shear center is the same as the centroid of the cross section. The torsional stress in a rectangular member can be determined by

$$f_S = \frac{T(3a + 1.8b)}{8a^2b^2} \tag{4.11}$$

where f_s = torsional stress at midpoint of long side, lb/in^2
T = applied torque, in·lb
a = longest side dimension divided by 2, in
b = shortest side dimension divided by 2, in

One of the difficulties in analyzing a wood beam subjected to torsional loading is the limited information available for assigning allowable torsional stresses. For sawn members, the *Wood Handbook*[5] recommends using the torsional shear strength F_s equal to the shear strength parallel to the grain. For glulam timber beams, a value for F_s equal to the allowable radial tension stress is recommended.

Due to the uncertainty associated with assigning allowable torsional shear stress values, it is recommended that the designer avoid those design situations which result in a twisting or rotation of the member, causing torsional stresses. One way to eliminate the torsional effects of an eccentric side load is to design the steel hanger used to transmit this load in such a manner as to resist inducing torsional stress, as illustrated in Chap. 5.

EXAMPLE 4.2: TORSIONAL STRESS CALCULATION Assume that a southern pine 20F-V2 combination glulam beam having a cross section of 6.75 by 24 in (17.15 by 60.96 cm) must resist a torque of 10,000 in·lb (57.10 N·m). For southern pine, the allowable torsional stress is $F_V/3 = 200/3 = 66.7$ lb/in^2 (459.9 kPa). Assume the member is a floor beam and the duration-of-load factor is 1.0.

Therefore, using Eq. (4.11),

$$a = 24/2 = 12$$

$$b = 6.75/2 = 3.375$$

$$f_s = \frac{10{,}000\ [(3 \times 12 + 1.8 \times 3.375)]}{8 \times 12^2 \times 3.375^2}$$

$$= 32.0 \text{ lb/in}^2 \text{ (220.6 kPa)} < F_s = 66.7 \text{ lb/in}^2 \text{ (459.9 kPa)}$$

4.4 GENERAL DESIGN PROCEDURES FOR PRISMATIC BENDING MEMBERS

The best way to illustrate the techniques of designing wood bending members having a constant cross section is to outline the steps involved and, by example, to develop the required formulas, stress adjustments, and engineering judgments needed to produce a successful beam design. It must be kept in mind that the design seldom is limited to a single member but rather involves a number of beams having different loading and span conditions that, in turn, function as a structural system. Thus the design of any particular component must be considered as it affects the design of adjacent members. The importance of this interrelationship between members in a structural system cannot be overstated. The basic design procedure, modified as required to suit either solid sawn wood beams or manufactured wood members such as glulam or structural composite lumbers (SCL), can be listed as follows:

1. Determination of applicable design loads, including live, dead, wind, snow, earthquake, equipment, and other types and their combinations as mutually existent loadings
2. Determination of available species, grades, and lengths of sawn timbers and stress combinations and lengths of manufactured timbers
3. Selection of the most practical framing system or options for structural requirements, as well as providing adequate roof drainage and satisfying architectural requirements
4. Selection of the allowable stresses for each design element for the material identified in step 2
5. Selection of proper allowable stress adjustments as related to step 4, job-site conditions, and end-use conditions
6. Preparation of structural design of framing system, including options
7. Refinement of design in step 6 to include proper drainage, camber, stiffness, field limitations, durability, and service conditions

Step 1: Determination of Design Loads

Live loads: This task is generally a matter of reviewing the applicable building code and local ordinances or other requirements. These values are stated as a minimum condition, and there may be individual projects where the designer may elect to increase these minimum values based on experience. For roof live loads and floor loads, building codes have provisions for reduction of live loads dependent on the contributing area supported by a particular structural element. Thus it is common to design for more than one live load for different members in the same structural system, i.e., a larger or basic live load applied to the design of joists, a slightly smaller live load used to design secondary beams, and a minimum live load value applied to the design of primary members supporting large contributing areas.

As an example, in the southwestern areas of the United States, where snow load is not a typical design consideration, the basic live load for roofs is generally stated as 20 lb/ft^2 (957.6 Pa) for beams supporting up to 200 ft^2 (18.58 m^2) of contributing area, with a reduction to 16 lb/ft^2 (766.1 Pa) when the contributing area is between 200 and 600 ft^2 (18.58 and 46.45 m^2) and a further reduction to a minimum of 12 lb/ft^2 (574.6 Pa) when the contributing area is over 600 ft^2 (55.74 m^2). It must be understood that these reductions are not permitted when the member is designed for snow loading, and no reductions should be made in roof loads resulting from snow, based on tributary area.

Dead loads: These values reflect the actual weight of the construction materials supported by a particular framing element. In determining such values, there will normally be one value for the subframing members such as joists, another still larger value for the secondary beams supporting the joists, and another slightly larger value for the primary beams supporting these secondary beams. These values may be best expressed in pounds per square foot, with subtotals developed for each of the framing elements. It is very easy to establish an office standard for minimum dead-load values for the various elements to simplify preliminary designs and to aid in preventing simple errors in this most important task.

Step 2: Determination of Available Resources. Determination of the available sawn species and grades and of glulam stress combinations and their attendant available lengths is generally based on past experience. Assistance in this selection process may be requested from a number of available sources, such as the local building official, local contractors, specialty wood framing subcontractors, local suppliers, and local designers or by inspection of existing and under-construction buildings of similar function. To avoid specifying a species, grade, or stress combination that is not readily available in a given geographic area, the designer can specify the allowable stress value which must be met to satisfy a particular design situation and rely on the material supplier to meet these stress requirements.

For proprietary framing materials such as prefabricated wood I joists or structural composite lumber, the designer must rely on information available from manufacturers of these products.

Step 3: Selection of the Most Practical Framing System. This selection involves such considerations as economy of erection, economic spans and spacing, economic lengths and sizes of materials, relationships between joist spacing and structural panel thickness, and related requirements to tie the beam framing system to the overall structural system.

The selection of an inefficient framing system by the designer can result in such problems as a project over budget subjected to delays due to nonavailability of material, with added costs for redesigning the structural elements.

An example of joist framing systems could include such input as the following:

1. A wider joist spacing, such as a 24-in (60.96-cm) spacing, may be preferred over a closer joist spacing, such as a 16-in (40.64-cm) spacing. While the joists may need to be slightly deeper, there will be fewer members to install, and thus reduced labor and hanger or connection costs will result. The extra weight of the joist is not normally a factor in the cost of construction, whereas there is usually a saving in board footage of lumber when wider spacings are used. The use of wood I joists is particularly suited to these wider on-center spacings.

2. Except for special ordering and potentially higher costs, joists in the 2× size are generally limited to 2 × 14s with lengths up to 24 ft (7.32 m). Once beyond this limit, the designer should investigate either 3× or 4× material. Availability of 3× structural material is generally limited, and 4× members are the more practical choice. When faced with these longer spans and heavier loading conditions, the designer must investigate the practicality of options using manufactured bending members such as glulam purlins, structural composite lumber beams, wood trusses, and wood I joists.

For glulam timber framing options, the overall function and size of the building will normally control the design. For a small building, say 50 ft (15.24 m) from wall to wall, the choices are limited. In such cases, there is little economy to be gained by not using clear-span framing without any interior columns that would interfere with the function of the building. A glulam beam at 16- to 24-ft (4.88- to 7.32-m) centers spanning the 50 ft (15.24 m) would be an economical solution. The choice of framing between these members could be 2× joists for the 16-ft (4.88-m) on-center beam spacing, with other types of framing such as wood trusses, sawn timbers, resawn glulam purlins, or prefabricated wood I joists being used for the 24-ft (7.32-m) on-center spacing of the main members. When the building becomes larger, selection of the framing systems becomes more complex. Unless the function of the building can justify the higher construction costs, the first option involves one or more rows of columns spaced to optimize span usage with the beams in the individual rows utilizing a cantilever–suspended-beam system with either a secondary joist system between them or more commonly an adaptation of a preformed panelized system using purlins and subjoists between the laminated beams.

If the distance between columns in any particular row exceeds approximately 45 ft (13.72 m), this cantilever pattern will be more practical than the use of simple-span glulam beams spanning from column to column. For even larger buildings, the need may arise to utilize a laminated girder layout supporting laminated beams, which may be either simple-span or a cantilever system. Obviously, there are a large number of possible framing plans that can be generated by the designer, but overall economics of the system will normally dictate the final selection of the framing system. Examples and general tables of common layouts with related dimensions are presented in the design examples of this chapter.

Step 4: Selection of Allowable Stresses. The selection of the allowable stresses for each design element was discussed in Sec. 4.1.1. This process starts with the basic selection of the grades, species, and other combinations determined in step 2 but conditioned by the knowledge that different-sized (i.e., cross section) wood members of the same species and grade do not necessarily have the same allowable values. As previously discussed, the designer must become familiar with the regional lumber grading rules to simplify the selection of allowable stresses for sawn members.

Step 5: Applicable Stress Adjustments. Selection of the allowable adjustments to be made to the stresses determined in step 4 is an important decision. This step in the design procedure requires an initial checklist type of approach covering all possible combinations of adjustments. The NDS[3] provides this type of checklist in the form of a table listing all applicable adjustment factors. Of the adjustments discussed previously, duration-of-load, moisture condition, and size- or volume-effect factors are the most commonly applied. However, the designer must be able to identify those applications where the other stress adjustments must be considered. Of these adjustments, duration-of-load and in-service moisture conditions require the most subjective judgment by the designer.

Step 6: Structural Analysis of the Framing System. Preparation of the structural design of the framing system and of alternate framing schemes when applicable is the next step in the design sequence. In many ways this step in the procedure is no different from that which occurs when designing a similar project using other construction materials. The need for determining loads, bending moments, shear, and deflection is universal, with certain additional requirements needed for wood due to its unique characteristics. To convert a simple design example into a satisfactory building design requires the art of understanding that a complete structural system is involved and not just isolated members. More than simple mathematics is required, and successful designers soon learn to coordinate the entire system into their thinking as they consider the design of any single element. In this chapter some of the examples will attempt to isolate some of these interrelationships, but no design reference can replace actual design experience.

Step 7: Design Refinement. Refinement of the design as developed in step 6 involves a number of tasks needed to consider the project as a whole system. Preliminary beam sizes are refined to account for actual dead loads, changes in span or spacing, the effect of secondary framing, the need for roof drainage, the need for proper cambering if glued-laminated members are used, the need to control shrinkage and long-term deflection, and the need for proper connection details to integrate the beam system with the overall structure. Due to these varied interrelationships, this process of refinement may involve more than one revision in the design and may perhaps require a change in the basic selection of some members. Hopefully, during the early stage of this refinement of design the designer will review the overall project for serviceability, service conditions that might need changes in either design or detailing, or any in-place condition for the wood framing system selected.

4.4.1 Sawn Lumber Beams

The design of typical sawn lumber beams is illustrated by the following examples.

EXAMPLE 4.3: SAWN LUMBER ROOF JOISTS

Assumed loads:

Live load: 20 lb/ft^2 (957.6 Pa) (no snow load)

Dead load:		
	tar and gravel	= 6.0 lb/ft^2 (287.3 Pa)
	½-in plywood	= 1.5 lb/ft^2 (71.8 Pa)
	2 × 10 at 24 in	= 1.5 lb/ft^2 (71.8 Pa)
	Miscellaneous	= 0.5 lb/ft^2 (23.9 Pa)
	Ceiling	= none
	Sprinkler	= none
	Total	= 9.5 lb/ft^2 (454.9 Pa)

Use 10.0 lb/ft^2 (478.8 Pa).

Deflection criteria: $\ell/180$ for total load.

Species, grade, and size: Assume Douglas fir–larch, No. 1, S-dry, 2 × 12.

For a nonsnow live load of 20 lb/ft^2 and a dead load of 10 lb/ft^2, use a 1.25 duration of load increase.

Allowable adjusted stresses:

$$F'_b = F_b \times C_D \times C_r \times C_F$$

$$F_b = 1000 \times 1.25 \times 1.15 \times 1.0 = 1437 \text{ lb/in}^2 \text{ (9908 kPa)}$$

$$F_v' = F_v \times C_D$$

$$F_v = 95 \times 1.25 = 118.8 \text{ lb/in}^2 \text{ (818.8 kPa)}$$

$$f_{c\perp} = 625 \text{ lb/in}^2 \text{ (4309.2 kPa)}$$

$$E = 1{,}700{,}000 \text{ lb/in}^2 \text{ (11,721,500 kPa)}$$

Assume 24 in (60.96 cm) on center spacing:

$$w = 2(20 + 10) = 60 \text{ lb/ft (875.6 N/m)}$$

Assume design span: 19.5 ft (5.94 m)
Bending moment:

$$M = \frac{wL^2}{8} = \frac{60 \times 19.5^2}{8} = 2852 \text{ ft·lb} = 34{,}224 \text{ in·lb}$$

End reaction:

$$R = \frac{wL}{2} = \frac{60 \times 19.5}{2} = 585 \text{ lb}$$

$$\text{Design V} = 585 - 60(11.25/12) = 529 \text{ lb}$$

Section properties for surfaced, seasoned 2 × 12 joists (see the Appendix, "Reference Data"):

$$A = 16.88 \text{ in}^2 \qquad S = 31.64 \text{ in}^3 \qquad I = 178.0 \text{ in}^4$$

$$f_b = \frac{M}{S} = \frac{34{,}224}{31.64} = 1082 \text{ lb/in}^2 \text{ (7460 kPa)} < F_b' = 1437 \text{ lb/in}^2 \text{ (9908 kPa)}$$

$$f_V = \frac{1.5V}{A} = \frac{1.5 \times 529}{16.88} = 47 \text{ lb/in}^2 \text{ (324 kPa)} < F_V' = 118.8 \text{ lb/in}^2 \text{ (818.8 kPa)}$$

Required bearing length:

$$L_{brg} = \frac{585}{1.5 \times 625} = 0.62 \text{ in (1.57 cm)}$$

Deflection calculation:

$$\Delta_{TL} = \frac{5wl^4 \times 1728}{384EI}$$

$$= \frac{5 \times 60 \times 19.5^4 \times 1728}{384 \times 1{,}700{,}000 \times 178.0} = 0.65 \text{ in (1.64 cm)}$$

$$\textit{Allowable deflection} = \frac{\ell}{180} = \frac{19.5 \times 12}{180}$$

$$= 1.3 \text{ in } (3.30 \text{ cm}) > 0.65 \text{ in } (1.64 \text{ cm})$$

Comments. Bending stress: Repetitive member bending stress may be used for members 24 in (60.96 cm) or less on center and when there are three or more members. See NDS[3] for a description of this adjustment.

Shear stress: The design shear was decreased by an amount equal to the uniform load located within the joist depth of the face of the support. For preliminary sizing, this load reduction is often ignored.

Required bearing length: 0.62 in (1.58 cm). Check hanger requirements or bearing seat for adequacy; generally not critical for this size member and loading conditions.

Deflection: Design meets assumed deflection criteria but should be further investigated as it relates to other structural elements in the system. If a more restrictive criterion is deemed necessary, the 2 × 12 joist at 24 in (60.96 cm) on center may not be acceptable. Increasing the grade quality to achieve a higher allowable E value and a correspondingly lower deflection is one design option. Another solution would be to use No. 2 Douglas fir–larch 2 × 14 joists at 24 in (60.96 cm) on center. Other member selection options also could be considered by varying grades, sizes, and on-center spacing. It also may be desirable to increase the deflection due to dead load by 50 percent to determine the effect of long-term deflection which may result from creep.

The techniques or procedures for the design of secondary sawn timber purlins are very similar to those used for joists or subpurlins, although the live load may be affected by the contributing area if such reductions are permitted by the local code. The process of determining allowable stresses may be more complex when the proposed beam is 4×- or 6×-in size due to the changing stresses and the resulting grade rule classification of the member. Although not as serious for roof framing as for floor framing, these larger sawn timber members introduce the added concern of shrinkage and the need to control any potential damage due to a change in dimension that could result due to the shrinkage process. These larger sawn timbers are seldom available in the dry condition most desired for construction since commercial dry kiln production is not economically feasible. The availability of aged, salvaged material is limited; thus the designer should consider all such sawn timber beams to be "green" with respect to selecting allowable stresses and detailing these members.

The presence of potential shrinkage is particularly critical where the beam in question is repeated at a number of building levels combined with a support condition at the end of the beam which has little or no shrinkage potential. The consideration of in-service shrinkage extends to the selection of joists or small-beam hangers. For sawn members, an acceptable practice is to place the top of the beam slightly above the floor framing. While this may initially result in slight humps in the surface prior to in-service seasoning of these sawn members, the final result should be a level surface.

EXAMPLE 4.4: SAWN TIMBER PURLINS Assume sawn timber roof purlins are placed at 8-ft (2.44-m) centers. Assume these purlins span between glulam girders spaced 28 ft (8.53 m) on center, resulting in a design span of 27 ft 6 in (8.38 m) center to center of purlin hanger.

Assumed loads:

Live load: 20 lb/ft^2 (957.6 Pa) (no snow load).
Contributing area = 8 × 28 = 224 ft^2 (20.81 m^2) > 200 ft^2 (18.58 m^2).
Therefore, use live load = 16 lb/ft^2 (766.1 Pa).

For roof live load, use duration-of-load factor c_D of 1.25.

Dead load:		
	Tar and gravel roofing	= 6.0 lb/ft^2 (287.3 Pa)
	½-in plywood	= 1.5 lb/ft^2 (71.8 Pa)
	2 × 4 joists at 24 in on center	= 0.7 lb/ft^2 (33.5 Pa)
	6 × 16 at 8 ft on center	= 2.6 lb/ft^2 (124.5 Pa)
	Sprinklers	= 1.5 lb/ft^2 (71.8 Pa)
	Miscellaneous	= 0.5 lb/ft^2 (23.9 Pa)
	Total	= 12.8 lb/ft^2 (612.9 Pa)

Use 13 lb/ft^2 (622.4 Pa).
Uniformly distributed load:

$$w_{TL} = w \times 8 = (16 + 13)8 = 232 \text{ lb/ft } (3385.8 \text{ N/m})$$

Deflection criteria: $\ell/240$ for total load
Species, grade, and size: Assume Douglas fir–larch No. 1, beam and stringer, 6 × 16
Allowable stresses, with applicable adjustments:

$$F'_b = F_b \times C_D \times C_F$$
$$F_b = 1350 \times 1.25 \times 0.965 = 1628 \text{ lb/in}^2 \text{ (11.228 kPa)}$$
$$F'_v = \text{F}_v \times C_D$$
$$F_v = 85 \times 1.25 = 106 \text{ lb/in}^2 \text{ (730.9 kPa)}$$
$$F_{c\perp} = 625 \text{ lb/in}^2 \text{ (4309.4 kPa)}$$
$$E = 1{,}600{,}000 \text{ lb/in}^2 \text{ (11,000,000 kPa)}$$

Bending moment:

$$M = \frac{w\ell^2}{8} = \left(\frac{232 \times 27.5^2}{8}\right) \times 12 = 263{,}175 \text{ in·lb}$$

End reaction:

$$R = \frac{232 \times 27.5}{2} = 3190 \text{ lb}$$

$$\text{Design V} = 3190 - (15.5/12)(232) = 2890 \text{ lb}$$

Required bearing length:

$$L_{brg} = \frac{3190}{5.5 \times 625} = 0.93 \text{ in}$$

Allowable deflection at total load:

$$\frac{\ell}{240} = \frac{27.5 \times 12}{240} = 1.38 \text{ in}$$

For assumed 6- by 16-in sawn timber:

$$A = 85.25 \text{ in}^2 \qquad s = 220.2 \text{ in}^3 \qquad I = 1706.8 \text{ in}^4$$

$$f_b = \frac{M}{S} = \frac{263{,}175}{220.2} = 1195 \text{ lb/in}^2 \text{ (8239.5 kPa)} < F'_b = 1628 \text{ lb/in}^2 \text{ (11.228 kPa)}$$

$$f_v = \frac{1.5V}{A} = \frac{1.5 \times 2890}{85.25} = 51 \text{ lb/in}^2 \text{ (350.6 kPa)} < F'_v = 106 \text{ lb/in}^2 \text{ (730.9 kPa)}$$

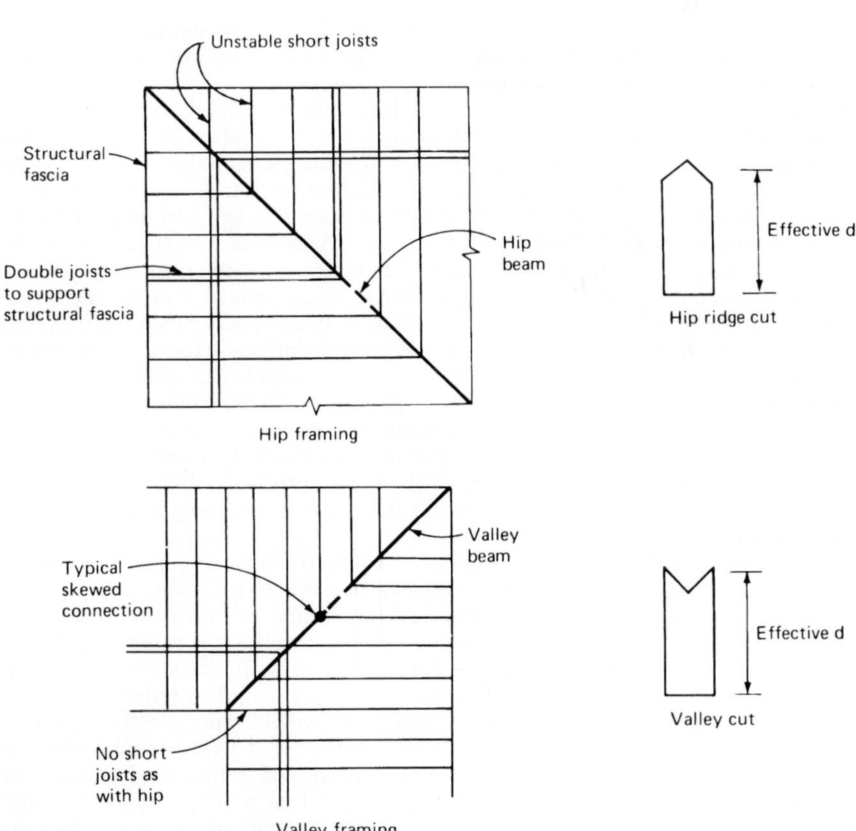

FIG. 4.2 Hip and valley beam framing.

Actual deflection at total load;

$$\Delta_{TL} = \frac{5 \times 232 \times 27.5^4 \times 1728}{384 \times 1{,}600{,}000 \times 1706.8}$$

$$= 1.09 \text{ in } (2.77 \text{ cm}) < \ell/240 = 1.38 \text{ in } (3.51 \text{ cm})$$

Dead load only deflection:

$$\Delta_{DL} = \frac{13}{29 \times 1.09} = 0.49 \text{ in } (1.24 \text{ cm})$$

Comments. Bending stress: The member is only stressed to 73% of its capacity. The designer may wish to review the design using a smaller size, such as a 4 × 16 or a 6 × 14, with the same species and grade, i.e., Douglas fir–larch No. 1, or with the same size but a lower grade, such as Douglas fir–larch No. 2.

Shear stress: Is low and well within the allowable values. Again, a smaller size or lower grade could be specified.

Bearing length: Seldom governs but should be checked with the specified hanger details and other seat or bearing details.

Stiffness: Deflection limits meet the suggested values shown in Table 4.1 and, as discussed in Example 4.3 for the joist design, is not controlled by the building code. With these larger sawn timber beams delivered to the job site "green," deflection anticipated to occur under dead load only and in the early life of the structure as the framing shrinks and seasons under the applied dead load becomes an important design consideration. The *Wood Handbook*[5] and the *Uniform Building Code*[6] both recommend that the calculated deflection for dead load only be increased by a factor of 2 to account for deflections resulting from long-term creep. Thus in this example the predicted long-term deflection is 2 × 0.49 = 1 in. This increased deflection must be considered when establishing the slope or gradient for the roof drainage. While the 2 × multiplier is an acceptable average approach to determine deflection of the unseasoned timbers, occasionally sawn members may have even greater deflection. A partial explanation of this excessive deflection is due to the fact that the published values for the modulus of elasticity for sawn timbers are average values and are not 5 percent exclusion limits such as utilized in establishing some of the other allowable wood stresses. The designer is thus faced with a stiffness capacity dependent on a wide range of average modulus of elasticity values and material quality. This is a controllable element for roof systems, but becomes a serious limitation for floor systems utilizing large, unseasoned sawn timber beams.

There are many other framing applications which utilize simple-span sawn lumber bending members that are not positioned in a horizontal plane.

One common application is an inclined roof rafter. For relatively low pitches, the span is taken as the horizontal distance from the wall to the ridge with the dead and live loads applied over this span length. When the pitch increases to steeper than, say, 4 on 12, the design dead load must be increased to reflect the inclined length of the rafter and the associated increase in weight represented as applied to the horizontal span measurement. This increase in dead load becomes more important with increased pitch and percentage of dead load to total load. Sloped rafter framing must utilize either a ridge beam designed as a simple-span member to support the contributing area or a ridge board that results in a thrust at the top of the wall from the inclined joists. Resistance to this outward thrust may be provided by ceiling joists placed parallel with the roof rafters and adequately connected to

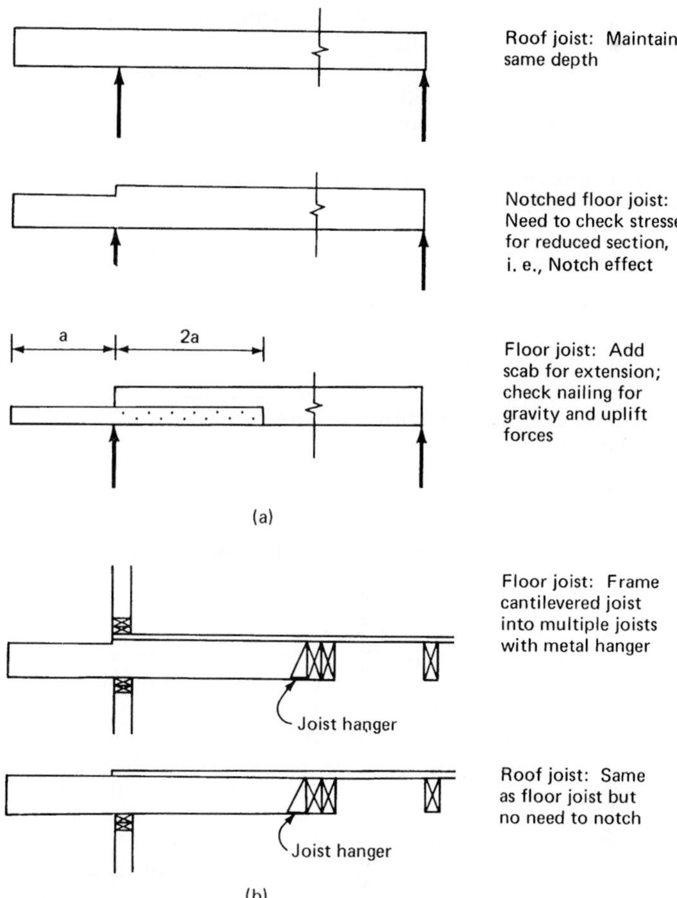

FIG. 4.3 Typical cantilevered joist framing (*a*) Cantilevered joists parallel to joist system; (*b*) cantilevered joists perpendicular to joist system.

them, or by the use of a collar tie located at the top of the wall or some distance above the top of the wall, or by the cantilever action of the wall itself.

In the first case, the ridge beam may become large and relatively expensive as the length of the room or building increases. In the second situation, the normal presence of the ceiling joists makes this the most practical solution, particularly for small structures. When collar ties replace the ceiling joists, the top of the wall must provide enough beam action to resist this thrust with their span equal to the spacing of the collar ties. The rafters themselves must be investigated for the effect of bending about the connection point. This, in fact, becomes the main design problem, how to attach the collar tie for the required force without damaging the joist's bending capacity.

Other examples of sloped simple-span bending members are hip beams and valley beams. A review of Fig. 4.2 shows that the main design features are the skewed connection of the joists to the hip, the unstable nature of the joist near the intersecting corner, and the resulting potential deflection of the fascia near the corner of the overhang. Hips without overhangs do not have these deflection problems. Consideration also should be given to the effect of the required top bevel cut when a steep pitch occurs, since the structural properties of the members, i.e., area, section modulus, and moment of inertia, must be reduced proportionately, as shown in Fig. 4.2.

Valley members, as shown in Fig. 4.2, are similar to hips in that a triangular loading pattern occurs and skewed joist connections are necessary. However, the valley members, unlike the hip members, typically do not have a problem with unstable joists.

Cantilevered rafters in lighter frame construction pose a problem related to detailing and construction problems rather than theoretical design. A few examples are shown in Fig. 4.3, with alternate solutions to show the "art" necessary to produce a successful cantilever system.

4.4.2 Design of Glued-Laminated Timber Bending Members

In general, the design task for glulam beams is similar to that of sawn joists or timber beams. Due to their normally larger span and on-center spacing, the consequences of design error are much more obvious and demand more attention to detail. The many options available in framing a large building require extensive preliminary study before beginning the actual structural design of the individual bending members to ensure an optimum design solution.

Seven general design considerations for wood bending members were given at the beginning of this section. For specific application to glulam beam design, these steps are expanded on as follows:

Determination of Design Loads. This is a continuation of the task of accurately identifying the load carried by each element. An additional requirement for cantilever systems, which are quite common forms of glulam framing, is that unbalanced loading conditions often control design.

Determination of the Most Practical Species and Stress Combinations. The first variable, regional species, is primarily geographic; that is, typically, it might be expected that a western species might be more readily available for a project located on the West Coast of the United States, whereas southern pine might be an obvious selection for a project located in the southeastern United States. However, these assumptions of species availability may not necessarily be applicable, and the designer is encouraged to develop design criteria that are not species-dependent whenever possible. The next variable normally concerns allowable stresses, basically the allowable bending stress F_b and the modulus of elasticity E. For members primarily loaded in bending and with a depth estimated to be 12 in (30.5 cm) or deeper, the most economical member is typically produced with an F_b of either 2400 or 2000 lb/in^2 (16,548 or 13,790 kPa) and an E of 1,800,000 or 1,700,000 lb/in^2 (12,400,000 or 11,700,000 kPa). The NDS[3] lists a number of species options for these stress levels. Thus before proceeding with the design calculations, the designer should inquire from local glulam suppliers which stress levels are the most readily available.

Assume the designer has selected the required preliminary single-span beam sections which produce the following design stresses, adjusted for normal duration of load and other applicable service conditions:

$$f'_b = 2325 \text{ lb/in}^2 \text{ (16,030.8 kPa)}$$

$$f'_v = 155 \text{ lb/in}^2 \text{ (1068.7 kPa)}$$

$$f'_{c\perp} = 440 \text{ lb/in}^2 \text{ (3033.8 kPa)}$$

$$E' = 1{,}650{,}000 \text{ lb/in}^2 \text{ (11,400,000 kPa)}$$

Shown below are possible laminating combinations that will satisfy these design stresses:

	Allowable Stresses, lb/in²					
	Western species			Southern pine		
Combination symbol	24F-V3	24F-V4	24F-V5	24F-V1	24F-V2	24F-V3
F_b	2400	2400	2400	2400	2400	2400
F_v	165	165	155	200	200	200
$F_{c\perp}$	650	650	650	650	650	650
$E \times 10^6$	1.8	1.8	1.7	1.7	1.7	1.8

Note: 1 lb/in² = 6.895 kPa.

Thus by specifying a choice of western species having combination symbols of 24F-V3, V4, or V5 or southern pine having combination symbols 24F-V1, V2, or V3, the design requirements will be satisfied and the owner will receive the economic benefit of being able to select or order from the largest possible number of combinations available in the local market. The following example illustrates the design of glulam beams for a typical building configuration using both simple-span and cantilevered systems.

EXAMPLE 4.5: GLULAM BEAM SYSTEM Design a glulam beam system for a warehouse to be located in Arizona, having a partial roof framing plan as shown in Fig. 4.4. Three framing schemes *A*, *B*, and *C* will be evaluated. Assume *Uniform Building Code*[6] provisions are applicable.

Assume the following design loads:

Live load:	20 lb/ft² (nonsnow load)	
Dead load:	Roofing	= 6.0 lb/ft² (287.3 Pa)
	½-in plywood	= 1.5 lb/ft² (71.8 Pa)
	2 × 4 at 24 in on center	= 0.7 lb/ft² (33.5 Pa)
	4 × 14 at 8 ft on center	= 1.5 lb/ft² (71.8 Pa)
	Sprinkler	= 1.5 lb/ft² (71.8 Pa)
	Ceiling	= none
	Miscellaneous	= 0.3 lb/ft² (14.4 Pa)
	Weight of glulam	= 2.0 lb/ft² (95.8 Pa)
	Total	= 13.5 lb/ft² (646.4 Pa)

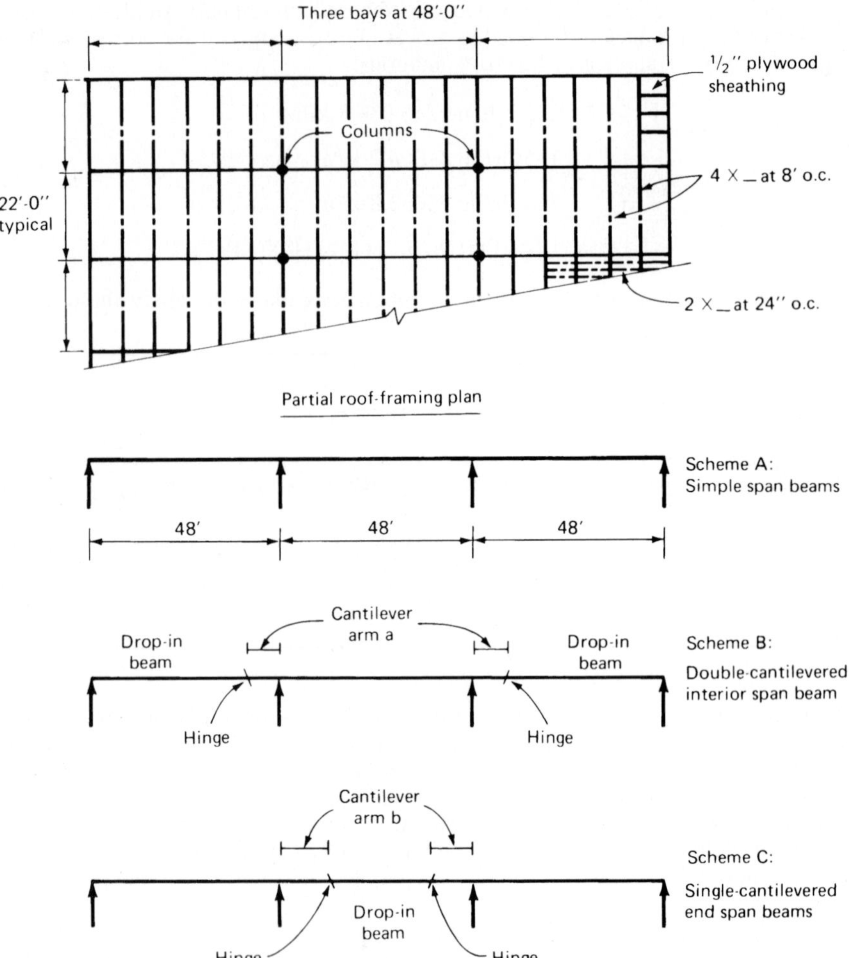

FIG. 4.4 Roof framing plan for glulam beam system design.

Tributary area = 48 by 22 ft = 1056 ft² (98.1 m²). Therefore, use a design live load for glulam beams of 12 lb/ft² (574.6 Pa) per *Uniform Building Code*.[6] The total uniformly distributed design load w is thus

$$w = (12 + 13.5)22 = 561 \text{ lb/ft } (8187.2 \text{ N.m})$$

Assume the following allowable design stresses for western species glulam beams:

$$F'_b = 2400 \times 1.25 = 3000 \text{ lb/in}^2\text{*} \ (20{,}685 \text{ kPa})$$

$$F'_V = 140 \times 1.25 = 175 \text{ lb/in}^2\text{*} \ (1206.6 \text{ kPa})$$

$$E = 1{,}500{,}000 \text{ lb/in}^2 \ (10{,}300{,}000 \text{ kPa})$$

Note that relatively low values for F'_v and E have been specifically selected to permit the use of the most possible western species glulam combinations as given in the NDS.[3]

Assume allowable total-load deflection of $\ell/180$.

Framing Scheme A: Simple Span Beams

$$M = \frac{w\ell}{8} = \frac{561 \times 48^2 \times 12}{8} = 1.940 \times 10^6 \text{ in·lb}$$

$$R = \frac{w\ell}{2} = \frac{561 \times 48}{2} = 13{,}464 \text{ lb}$$

$$S_{\text{req}} = \frac{M}{F'_h C_V} = \frac{1.94 \times 10^6}{2400 \times 1.25 \times 0.90} = 718.5 \text{ in}^3$$

Note: For preliminary size determination, a value for C_v must be assumed.

$$A_{\text{req}} = \frac{1.5V}{F'_V} = \frac{1.5 \times 13{,}464}{140 \times 1.25} = 115.4 \text{ in}^2$$

Note: For preliminary size determination, no reduction has been taken for loads located within a distance equal to the depth of the member from its end.

$$I_{\text{req}} = \frac{337.5WL^3}{E} = 13{,}959 \text{ in}^4$$

Try a 5⅛- by 33-in glulam section:

$$A = 169.1 \text{ in}^2 \qquad S = 930.2 \text{ in}^3 \qquad I = 15{,}350 \text{ in}^4$$

Check actual shear stress:

$$f_V = \frac{1.5V}{A}$$

where

$$V = R - w\left(\frac{d}{12}\right) = 13{,}464 - 561\left(\frac{33}{12}\right) = 11{,}921 \text{ lb}$$

$$f_V = \frac{1.5 \times 11{,}921}{169.1} = 105.7 \text{ lb/in}^2 < F'_v = 175 \text{ lb/in}^2$$

*The applicable duration-of-load increase is 1.25. Assume beams fully braced by roof decking such that lateral buckling is not a design consideration.

Check actual bending stress:

$$f_b = \frac{M}{SC_V} = \frac{1.94 \times 10^6}{930.2 \times 0.832} = 2507 \text{ lb/in}^2 < F'_b = 3000 \text{ lb/in}^2$$

where

$$C_V = (12/33)^{1/10}(5.125/5.125)^{1/10}(21/48)^{1/10} = 0.832$$

Check deflection:

$$\Delta_{TL} = \frac{5w\ell^4}{384EI} = \frac{5 \times 561 \times 48^4 \times 1728}{384 \times 1{,}500{,}000 \times 15{,}350}$$

$$= 2.91 \text{ in} < \text{allowable } \Delta = \ell/180 = 3.20 \text{ in}$$

$$\Delta_{DL} = \frac{13.5}{25.5} \times 2.91 = 1.54 \text{ in}$$

Recommended camber $= 1.5\Delta_{DL} = 2.3$ in; use 2¼-in camber at beam centerline.

Comments. Due to the relatively low E value selected, stiffness governs this design. By specifying a glulam combination with $E = 1{,}800{,}000$ lb/in² (12,400,000 kPa), the required I value is reduced to 11,633 in⁴ (484,202 cm⁴). For $I = 11{,}633$ in⁴, a 5⅛- by 30-in (13.0- by 76.2-cm) section having $I = 11{,}531$ in⁴ (479,956 cm⁴) could be used. For a 5⅛- by 30-in (13.0- by 76.2-cm) section, $f_b = (1.94 \times 10^6)/(768.7 \times 0.840) = 3004$ lb/in² (20,716 kPa), which is approximately equal to $F'_b = 3000$ lb/in² (20,685 kPa) so that the reduced section would be adequate.

If $E = 1{,}500{,}000$ lb/in² (10,300,000 kPa) is used, a glulam combination having a lower F_b could be selected while still maintaining this E value. For example, a 20F-V2 Hem-Fir combination has $F_b = 2000$ lb/in² (13,790 kPa) and $E = 1{,}500{,}000$ lb/in² (10,300,000 kPa) (see NDS[3]).

The allowable $F'_b = 2000 \times 1.25 = 2500$ lb/in² (17,237.5 kPa), which is approximately equal to $f_b = 2507$ lb/in² (17,280 kPa). Therefore, the designer has the option of specifying a combination having a higher E value, such as a 24F-V4 Douglas fir–larch, and reducing the beam size to 5⅛ by 30 in (13.0 by 76.2 cm). Another option is to retain the calculated beam size of 5⅛ by 33 in (13.0 by 83.8 cm) and specify a combination having a lower F_b value, such as a 20F-V2 Hem-Fir, while still maintaining the specified E value. Both decisions will result in reduced cost and should be considered as design options.

Framing Scheme B: Double-Cantilevered Center Beam with Drop-in Beams in End Bays. The optimum length a of the cantilever is from 0.15 to 0.17 times the length of the main span, or $0.15 \times 48 = 7.2$ ft (2.19 m) to $0.17 \times 48 = 8.15$ ft (2.48 m). Thus, for preliminary design use, cantilever length $a = 7.5$ ft (2.29 m).

The tributary area for the drop-in beam is $(48 - 7.5)22 = 891$ ft² (82.8 m²). Thus use a live load of 12 lb/ft² (574.6 Pa).

Note that for this system of cantilever and drop-in beams, depending on the ratio of dead load to total load, the drop-in beams often require a greater depth than the cantilevered beam. Economic selection of sizes may then require the cantilever arm a to be increased to bring the depth of the drop-in to the same depth or less than the cantilever beam.

Based on a cantilever length of 7.5 ft (2.29 m), as assumed for this example, the resulting beam sizes are

Drop-in beams: 5⅛ by 25½ in (13.0 by 64.8 cm)

Cantilever beam: 5⅛ by 24 in (13.0 by 61.0 cm)

The calculation of these sizes follows the same procedure as outlined for framing scheme *C*, which follows.

Framing Scheme C: End-Bay Beams Cantilevered (Single Cantilever) with Drop-in Beam in Center Bay. The optimum length b of the cantilever is approximately 0.20 to 0.25 times the length of the main span, or $0.20 \times 48 = 9.6$ ft (2.92 m) to $0.25 \times 48 = 12.0$ ft (3.66 m). This varies depending on the ratio of dead load to total load, as discussed for framing scheme *B*.

The general design procedure for these cantilevered systems is as follows:

1. By trial and error, adjust cantilever arm b so that the following are as near equal as practical:
   - ***a.*** The negative moment of the cantilever with full live load + dead load on all spans
   - ***b.*** The positive moment near midspan of the main or interior span with full live load + dead load on the main span and cantilever overhang and dead load only on the drop-in beam
2. Determine the adequacy for horizontal shear stresses, which are normally maximum at the interior support.
3. Determine the maximum deflection for both cantilevered beams and drop-in beams under full live load + dead load and compare with assumed deflection controls. In most cases, the cantilever beam will not be governed by deflection whereas the drop-in beam often will be.
4. Determine the required cambers based on calculated deflections.
5. Determine the bearing requirement at interior supports, cantilever hinges, and end supports based on calculated reactions.

For this case, assume the same loading conditions and allowable stresses as used for framing scheme *A*.

Try cantilever arm $b = 11.5$ ft (3.51 m). For these conditions, shear and moment diagrams for the cantilevered beam are shown in Fig. 4.5.

Check bending stresses:

$$M_{max} = 1{,}489{,}702 \text{ in·lb}$$

$$S_{req} = \frac{1{,}489{,}702}{2400 \times 1.25 \times 0.85} = 584.2 \text{ in}^3$$

Note: A value of 0.85 has been assumed for the volume-effect factor C_V. For calculation of the actual volume effect, use the actual member width and depth in inches and the member length in feet, with the length being taken as the distance from point of zero moment to point of zero moment.

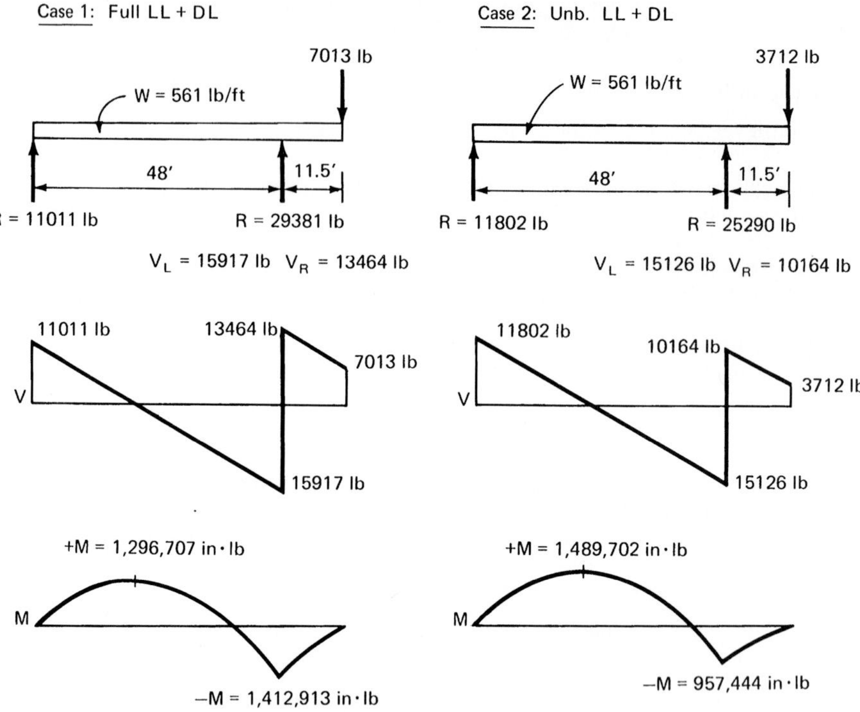

FIG. 4.5 Shear and moment diagrams for the cantilevered beam in Example 4.5.

Try 5.125 by 27 in, $S = 622.7$ in^3, and $I = 8406$ in^4,

$$+f_b = \frac{1,489,702}{622.7 \times 0.85} = 2815 \text{ lb/in}^2$$

$$-f_b = \frac{1,412,913}{622.7 \times 0.91} = 2493 \text{ lb/in}^2$$

$$F'_b = 2400 \times 1.25 = 3000 \text{ lb/in}^2 \text{ (20,680 kPa)} > f_b$$

$$= 2815 \text{ lb/in}^2 \text{ (19,410 kPa)}$$

Therefore, select a glulam combination which has an allowable F_b of 2400 lb/in^2 for both the tension and the compression zones, i.e., a "balanced" lay-up, since both $+f_b$ and $-f_b$ are approximately equal.

Check shear:

$$V_{\text{max}} = 15,917 \text{ lb}$$

$$V_{\text{design}} = 15,917 - 561 \times \frac{27}{12} = 14,655 \text{ lb}$$

$$f_v = \frac{1.5 \times 14{,}655}{5.125 \times 27} = 159 \text{ lb/in}^2$$

$$F'_V = 140 \times 1.25 = 175 \text{ lb/in}^2 > f_v = 159 \text{ lb/in}^2$$

Check deflection:

$$\Delta_{TL} \text{ (free end of cantilever)} = 0.73 \text{ in}$$

$$\Delta_{TL} \text{ (near midspan of main beam)} = 3.55 \text{ in}$$

Note: Deflections were calculated using formulas published in various reference documents for various deflection, span, and loading conditions. They also can be determined by various energy methods.

Since Δ_{TL} near midspan of the main beam is greater than the allowable deflection based on the assumed criterion of $\Delta_{TL} = \ell/180 = 3.2$ in, select a glulam combination having an E value of 1,700,000 lb/in². Based on $E = 1{,}700{,}000$ lb/in², the following deflections result:

$$\Delta \text{ (free end of cantilever)} = \frac{1{,}500{,}000}{1{,}700{,}000} \times 0.73 = 0.64 \text{ in}$$

$$\Delta \text{ (midspan of main beam)} = \frac{1{,}500{,}000}{1{,}700{,}000} \times 3.55 = 3.13 \text{ in} < \ell/180 = 3.2 \text{ in}$$

Determine camber based on $1.5\Delta_{DL}$.

$$\text{Camber (end of cantilever)} = 1.5 \times 0.64 \times \left(\frac{13.5}{25.5}\right) = 0.51 \text{ in}$$

$$\text{Camber (midspan of main beam)} = 1.5 \times 3.13 \times \left(\frac{13.5}{25.5}\right) = 2.5 \text{ in}$$

Therefore, use 2½-in positive camber at midspan and a reverse camber of ½ in at the free end of the cantilever.

Determine the length of the bearings required,

$$R \text{ (end)} = 11{,}801 \text{ lb} \qquad \ell_b = \frac{11.801}{650 \times 5.125} = 3.5 \text{ in}$$

$$R \text{ (interior)} = 29{,}381 \text{ lb} \qquad \ell_b = \frac{29{,}381}{650 \times 5.125} = 8.8 \text{ in}$$

Note: The designer also should check the cantilevered beam for lateral buckling over support unless bracing of the bottom of the beam is provided. If no bracing of the compression side of the beam is provided, the unbraced length is taken as the distance from the point of zero moment to the end of the cantilever.

Drop-in beam design: The drop-in beam is designed as a simple-span bending member following the same procedure as for the member designed under framing scheme *A*. In this case, the span of the drop-in beam is

$$L = 48 - (2 \times 11.5) = 25 \text{ ft (7.62 m)}$$

For $L = 25$ ft (7.62 m), the tributary area is $25 \times 22 = 550$ ft² (51.1 m²) < 600 ft² (55.7 m²). Therefore, the allowable live-load reduction per *Uniform Building Code*[6] is $25 \times 22 \times 0.08 = 44\% > 40\%$ maximum. Therefore, use 40 percent reduction.

The design live load is

$$20 - (20 \times 0.4) = 20 - 8 = 12 \text{ lb/ft}^2 \text{ (574.6 Pa)}$$

The drop-in beam size required is then 5⅛ by 16½ in (13.0 by 41.9 cm).

4.4.3 Curved Beams

In addition to having virtually unlimited span and load-carrying capacity when used as straight beams, glulam members also can be fabricated in curved shapes, such as curved beams, radial arches, tudor arches, and other curved configurations. The design of curved beams is addressed in this section, while that of curved sections used as arches is presented in Chap. 9.

As noted in Sec. 4.1.9, when wood members are curved, the allowable stress in bending must be reduced by multiplying by the curvature factor C_c. In glulam timbers, the amount of curvature R is limited as follows:

$$t/R < 1/100 \text{ for hardwoods and southern pine}$$

$$t/R < 1/125 \text{ for other softwoods}$$

where t is the thickness of individual laminations used and R is the radius of curvature of the inside face of lamination, both in inches. Thus for a 1.5-in (3.8-cm)-thick lamination, the minimum radius of curvature that could be used is 12 ft 6 in (3.81 m) for hardwoods or southern pine and 15 ft 7.5 in (4.77 m) for other softwoods. These are values which could be achieved under optimal conditions, and more conservative values are typically used in production. The resulting curvature factors C_c for these conditions would be 0.80 and 0.87, respectively, which illustrates the relative magnitude that could be expected for this modifying factor. It is noted that it is customary to use thinner laminations when bending members to relatively tight radii to minimize the effect of this strength-reducing parameter and more readily achieve the curvature required.

In addition to the application of the curvature factor, curved bending members also must be designed to resist radial stresses which are induced when the member is subjected to a bending moment. These radial stresses occur as stresses acting perpendicular to the grain of the member along the neutral axis. If the moment is such that it increases the radius of curvature, the stress is in tension, whereas if the moment reduces the radius of curvature, the stress is in compression. Radial stresses can be determined from the relationship

$$f_r = \frac{3M}{2R_m bd} \tag{4.12}$$

where M = bending moment, in·lb
R_m = radius of curvature, in (at neutral axis or centerline of member)
b = width of member, in
d = depth of member, in

If the radial stress is a compression stress, the allowable radial stress F_r is limited to the allowable compression perpendicular to grain stress $F_{c\perp}$, and if tension, the allowable stress is limited to the allowable radial tension stress F_{rt}.

The allowable radial tension stress shall be limited to one-third the design value in horizontal shear stress for southern pine and California redwood for all load conditions and for Douglas fir–larch, Douglas fir–south, hem-fir, and western woods subjected to wind and earthquake loadings. The limit shall be 15 lb/in^2 (103.4 kPa) for Douglas fir–larch. Douglas fir–south, hem-fir, and western woods for other conditions of loading. These values are subject to modification for the duration of load.

The following example illustrates the design of a curved glulam beam.

EXAMPLE 4.6: CURVED BEAM DESIGN Assume a curved glulam beam, combination 24F-V2 southern pine, is to be used to form an entryway roof in a shopping mall. Assume the following geometry and design loads:

Span = 40 ft (12.19 m).

Spacing = 12 ft on center (3.66 m).

Radius = 40 ft (12.19 m); therefore use 1.5-in (3.81-cm) laminations.

Live load (snow) = 30 lb/ft^2 (1436.4 Pa).

Dead load = 15 lb/ft^2 (718.2 Pa) including weight of beam.

Assume the following base allowable stresses:

$$F_b = 2400 \text{ lb/in}^2 \text{ (16,548 kPa)}$$

$$F_V = 200 \text{ lb/in}^2 \text{ (1379 kPa)}$$

$$E = 1{,}700{,}000 \text{ lb/in}^2 \text{ (11,700,000 kPa)}$$

Determine the minimum beam size for bending,

$$w_{TL} = 45 \times 12 = 540 \text{ lb/ft}$$

$$M = \frac{wL^2}{8} = \frac{540 \times 40^2}{8}$$

$$= 108{,}000 \text{ ft·lb}$$

$$F'_b = 2400\, C_V C_c C_D$$

$$\text{where } C_v = \left(\frac{12}{d}\right)^{1/20} \times \left(\frac{5.125}{b}\right)^{1/20} \times \left(\frac{21}{L}\right)^{1/20}$$

Note: The exponential factor of 1/20 is only applicable for the design of southern pine glulam.

$$C_c = 1 - 2000\left(\frac{t}{R}\right)^2 = 1 - 2000\left(\frac{1.5}{40 \times 12}\right)^2 = 0.98$$

$$C_D = 1.15 \text{ for snow loading}$$

Then $S = \dfrac{M}{F'_b} = \dfrac{108{,}000 \times 12}{2400 \times 0.98 \times 1.15\ C_V}$

Therefore, assume $C_V = 0.90$ for preliminary design.

$$S = 532.4 \text{ in}^3$$

Try a 5.125- by 25.5-in section, $S = 555.4$ in^3.
Check beam for bending stress:

$$f_b = \frac{10800 \times 12}{555.4 \times 0.93} = 2509 \text{ lb/in}^2 \text{ (17,299 kPa)} < F'_b$$

$$= 2400 \times 0.98 \times 1.15$$

$$= 2705 \text{ lb/in}^2 \text{ (18,651 kPa)}$$

Check beam for radial stress:

$$f_r = \frac{3M}{R_m bd} = \frac{3 \times 108{,}000 \times 12}{2 \times 492.75 \times 5.125 \times 25.5} = 30.2 \text{ lb/in}^2$$

Since the induced moment causes an increase in the radius of curvature (tends to straighten the member), it is a radial tension stress. For southern pine, the allowable radial tension stress is

$$F'_{rt} = \left(\frac{F_v}{3}\right) 1.15 = \left(\frac{200}{3}\right) 1.15 = 77 \text{ lb/in}^2 \text{ (530.9 kPa)} > f_v$$

$$= 30.2 \text{ lb/in}^2 \text{ (208.2 kPa)}$$

Check beam for shear:

$$V = 540\left(\frac{40}{2} - \frac{25.5}{12}\right) = 9652.5 \text{ lb}$$

$$f_v = 1.5\left(\frac{9652.5}{5.125 \times 25.5}\right) = 110.8 \text{ lb/in}^2 \text{ (764.0 kPa)} < F'_v = 200 \times 1.15$$

$$= 230 \text{ lb/in}^2 \text{ (1585.8 kPa)}$$

Check beam for deflection:

$$\Delta_{TL} = \frac{5w\ell^4}{384EI} = \frac{5 \times 540 \times 40^4 \times 1728}{384 \times 1{,}700{,}000 \times 7082} = 2.58 \text{ in (6.55 cm)}$$

For a commercial roof beam it is recommended that the allowable total load deflection be limited to $\ell/240$:

$$\Delta_{TL} \text{ (allowable)} = \frac{40 \times 12}{240} = 2.0 \text{ in (5.08 cm)} < \Delta_{TL} = 2.58 \text{ in (6.55 cm)}$$

Therefore, increase the member size to maintain $\Delta_{TL} < 2.0$ in,

$$I_{req} = \frac{5w\ell^4}{384EI} = \frac{5 \times 540 \times 40^4 \times 1728}{384 \times 1{,}700{,}000 \times 2.0} = 9148 \text{ in}^4$$

Use 5.125- by 28.5-in (13.0- by 72.4-cm) glulam, $I = 9887$ in^4 (411,528 cm^4).

$$\Delta_{TL} = 1.85 \text{ in (4.70 cm)} < \ell/240 = 2.0 \text{ in (5.08 cm)}$$

4.5 WOOD BENDING MEMBERS HAVING NONPRISMATIC CROSS SECTIONS

4.5.1 Straight Tapered Beams

Often it is desirable to taper wood beams to satisfy architectural requirements, provide pitched roofs, facilitate drainage, and lower wall height requirements at the end supports. Figure 4.6 illustrates some of the shapes that these beams may take; however, othe shapes are possible. In most cases, these shapes are created using glulam timbers, although it is possible to saw some amount of taper into solid sawn timbers. When glulam is used, it is recommended that any sawn taper cuts be made only on the compression face of tapered beams, with the individual laminations running parallel to the tension face of the member. An exception is a taper cut on the top face of a cantilevered beam over a support.

If camber is required for tapered glulam beams, it may be provided by specifying camber on the tension face in the same manner as for nontapered beams and by sawing camber into the compression face. For single-taper straight beams, the required camber is typically built into the tension face as well as being sawn into the taper face. For double-taper straight beams, the camber is usually built into the tension face, and if this camber exceeds 2 in (5.08 cm), one-fourth the centerline camber also should be sawn into the tapered face. The designer should specify any required camber for both the tension side and the sawn compression side. Camber is typically not provided for custom beams by the fabricator unless specified by the designer.

The design methods for straight tapered beams are based on the information presented in Ref. 9. The solutions presented in this research study are based on the assumption of the Bernoulli-Euler theory of bending for a beam of isotropic material. While this results in an approximate solution for wood beams which are orthotropic, it is considered to be somewhat conservative and is thus satisfactory for design purposes.

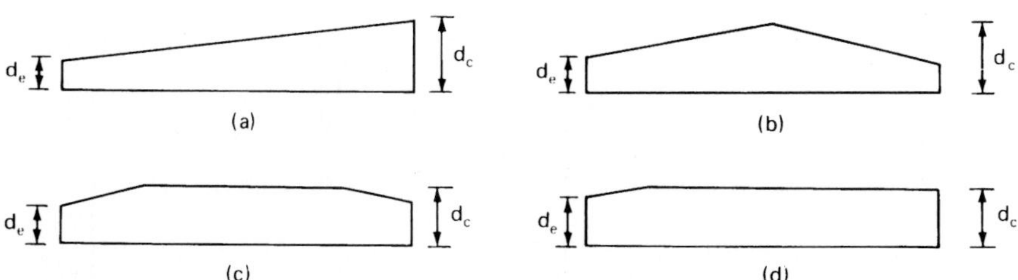

FIG. 4.6 Typical tapered beam shapes. (*a*) Single-tapered straight; (*b*) double-tapered straight; (*c*) tapered both ends; (*d*) tapered one end.

Stresses in Tapered Beams. In a tapered section, with the top and bottom of the member not parallel to each other, consideration must be given to the interaction effects of flexural compression perpendicular to grain and shear parallel to grain stresses. The classic presentation of the distribution of the shear stresses existing in a tapered beam is given in Fig. 4.7. This clearly illustrates the variation of this stress along the length of the beam, as contrasted with the traditional parabolic distribution which occurs at the end of the members. To account for the combined effect of these stresses, an interaction formula is applied that considers these stresses to occur simultaneously, thus reducing the member's load-carrying capacity below that which it would have if each of these stresses were considered to act independently. Such an interaction equation expressing the effects of these combined stresses, which is used for materials other than wood, takes the form

$$\frac{f_x^2}{F_x^2} + \frac{f_y^2}{F_y^2} + \frac{f_{xy}^2}{F_{xy}^2} < 1 \tag{4.13}$$

In the case of a wood beam, these stresses can be given as

$f_x = f_b$ = actual bending stress, lb/in^2

$f_y = f_{c\perp}$ = actual compression stress perpendicular to grain, lb/in^2, assuming taper cut is on the compression face

$f_{xy} = f_v$ = actual shear stress, lb/in^2

$F_x = F_b$ = tabular design value in bending, lb/in^2, adjusted by all applicable modifiers except size factor C_F, interaction stress factor C_I, and lateral stability factor C_L

$F_y = F_{c\perp}$ = tabular design value in compression perpendicular to grain, lb/in^2, adjusted by all applicable modifiers

$F_{xy} = F_V$ = tabular design value in horizontal shear, lb/in^2, adjusted by all applicable modifiers

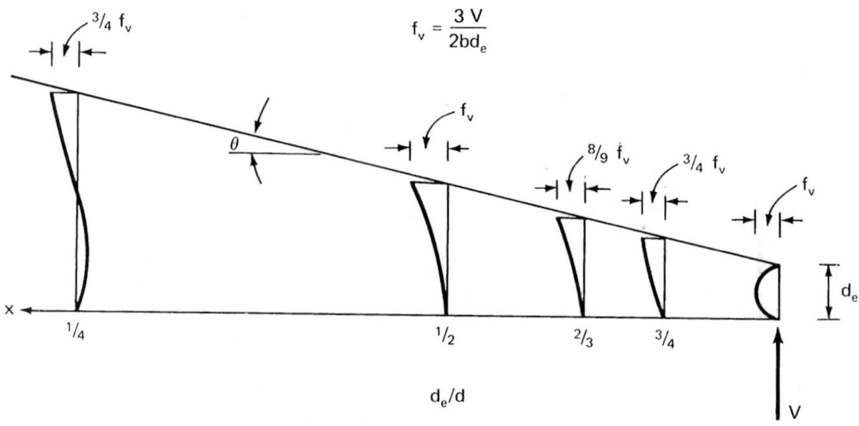

FIG. 4.7 Shear-stress distribution for tapered beam.

For tapered beams, the actual stresses existing at the tapered edge can be expressed as a function of the bending stress f_b,

$$f_v = f_b \tan \theta \tag{4.14}$$

$$f_c = f_b \tan^2 \theta \tag{4.15}$$

where tan θ is the slope of the tapered face.

Since the interaction stress equation is somewhat cumbersome to use in design, its application can be simplified by the use of an interaction stress factor C_I, which is dependent only on the stress properties of the material and the slope of the tapered face. By assuming an optimal design (the interaction stress equation is set equal to 1), it is possible to write the interaction equation as

$$\frac{f_b^2}{F_b^2} + \frac{f_b^2 \tan^2 \theta}{F_V^2} + \frac{f_b^2 \tan^4 \theta}{F_c^2} < 1 \tag{4.16}$$

Setting $f_b = F_b C_I$ and solving for C_I gives

$$C_I = \sqrt{\frac{1}{1 + [F_b(\tan \theta)/F_V]^2 + [F_b(\tan^2 \theta)/F_c]^2}} \tag{4.17}$$

Therefore, to account for the interaction stresses in design, the design value in bending is modified by C_I, or

$$F_b' = F_b C_I \qquad \text{or} \qquad f_b < F_b C_I$$

where F_b' is the tabular design value in bending modified by all applicable modifiers except C_L and C_V as previously defined.

Assuming the taper cut is on the compression side of the beam, C_I is cumulative with adjustments for lateral stability C_L but is not cumulative with adjustments for the volume effect C_V. If the taper cut is on the tension side of beams, *which is not recommended*, C_I is cumulative with C_V but not C_L. Since C_I is dependent only on the slope of the tapered face and the member material properties, tabular values of C_I as a function of tan θ can be developed. Table 4.5 presents this type of information for some of the more commonly used glulam stress combinations as given in the Appendix, "Reference Data."

Thus, the designer may readily determine C_I from this table and compare it to C_V for a given design situation. The allowable bending stress is then multiplied by whichever of these factors results in the lowest allowable bending stress. In the calculation of stresses and interaction of stresses it is necessary to determine the location of the maximum stress condition. As noted, the shear stress f_v and the perpendicular to grain stress $f_{c\perp}$ are functions of the bending stress f_b. Thus determination of the location of the maximum bending stress also will locate the position of maximum values for f_v and $f_{c\perp}$. In some members the location of the point of maximum stress can be obtained by simple calculation or by inspection. However, in others, depending on the shape of the member and loading conditions, it may be necessary to divide the member into a number of finite sections and calculate the maximum bending stress at each of these cross sections to locate the maximum stress condition.

TABLE 4.5 Interaction Stress Factor C_I* as a Function of tan θ; F_c = 560 lb/in²

	F_b = 2400 lb/in²		F_b = 2000 lb/in²	
tan θ	F_v = 165 lb/in²	F_v = 200 lb/in²	F_v = 165 lb/in²	F_v = 200 lb/in²
0.02	0.960	0.972	0.972	0.981
0.025	0.940	0.958	0.957	0.970
0.03	0.910	0.941	0.940	0.958
0.035	0.891	0.922	0.921	0.944
0.04	0.864	0.902	0.900	0.928
0.045	0.837	0.880	0.878	0.912
0.05	0.809	0.857	0.855	0.894
0.055	0.781	0.835	0.832	0.876
0.06	0.753	0.811	0.809	0.857
0.065	0.727	0.788	0.785	0.838
0.07	0.701	0.766	0.762	0.819
0.075	0.676	0.743	0.740	0.800
0.08	0.652	0.721	0.718	0.781
0.085	0.629	0.700	0.696	0.762
0.09	0.607	0.679	0.676	0.743
0.095	0.586	0.659	0.656	0.725
0.100	0.566	0.640	0.636	0.707
0.105	0.548	0.621	0.618	0.689
0.110	0.530	0.604	0.600	0.672
0.115	0.513	0.586	0.583	0.656
0.120	0.497	0.570	0.566	0.640
0.125	0.482	0.554	0.551	0.624
0.150	0.416	0.485	0.482	0.554
0.200	0.325	0.384	0.381	0.446

Note: 1000 lb/in² = 6.895 MPa.

*Applicable when taper cut is on compression side only. Taper cutting on the tension side is *not* permitted except at cantilevered ends.

Most tapered beams are either single-tapered or symmetrically double-tapered with uniformly distributed loads. For these members, the determination of the location of maximum stress is given by the equation

$$d = 2d_e \frac{d_e + l \tan \theta}{2d_e + l \tan \theta} \tag{4.18}$$

where d = depth of member at point of maximum stress, in
d_e = depth of member at its shallow end, in
ℓ = length of member, in
θ = slope of tapered face

This formula can be reduced to the following equations for ease of computation.

For single-tapered beams,

$$d = 2d_e\left(\frac{d_c}{d_e + d_c}\right) \tag{4.19}$$

For symmetrical double-tapered beams,

$$d = \frac{d_e}{d_c}(2d_c - d_e) \tag{4.20}$$

The bending stress f_b at this point of maximum stress for both types of beams referred to above can be determined by the following formula for a uniform load:

$$f_b = \frac{3WL}{4bd_e(d_e + \ell \tan \theta)} \tag{4.21}$$

where W is the total uniform load, in pounds, and ℓ is the span in inches. The other terms are as defined previously.

For single-tapered straight beams this formula can be written as

$$f_b = \frac{3WL}{4bd_cd_e} \tag{4.22}$$

For double-tapered symmetrical straight beams this formula becomes

$$f_b = \frac{3WL}{4bd_e(2d_c - d_e)} \tag{4.23}$$

Another frequently encountered loading is that of a single concentrated load. For this condition the depth at which maximum stress occurs can be determined by the formula

$$d = 2d_e \tag{4.24}$$

when d lies between the end of the beam and the point of application of the concentrated load. When d, as determined from the formula $d = 2d_e$, does not occur between the end of the beam and the point of application of the concentrated load, the depth at which maximum bending stress occurs is at the load point. If the depth d under the load point is such that $\frac{4}{3}d_e < d < 2d_e$, the maximum shear at the section also occurs on the tapered surface. If the depth d under the load point is such that $d_e < d < \frac{4}{3}d_e$, the maximum value of shear stress lies within the beam, but because the stresses along the taper are those considered in the interaction equation, the value of shear stress as determined by the formula $f_v = f_b \tan \theta$ is still applicable for use in the interaction equation.

The stresses at the tapered surface can be determined by the following formulas:

$$f_b = \frac{6M}{bd^2} \tag{4.25}$$

$$f_v = f_b \tan \theta \tag{4.26}$$

$$f_c = f_b \tan^2 \theta \tag{4.27}$$

where M = moment at point where depth d occurs, in·lb
b = width at point where depth d occurs, in

d = depth where maximum bending stress occurs, in

It is noted that for a tapered beam loaded with either a uniformly distributed load or by a single concentrated point load, the value f_v as calculated for the interaction stress equation will normally be less than the shear at the end of the member. Thus the designer is cautioned to check the member for stress at the end using the minimum value for beam end depth, as would be done for a nontapered beam design.

When a tapered member is designed to resist load combinations other than a uniform load or a single concentrated load, or if the member is not symmetrical in shape, the simplified formulas for determining the depth at which the maximum stress occurs do not apply. In these cases it is generally necessary to subdivide the member into a number of finite divisions and to determine f_b at these various points along the member to locate the point of maximum bending stress. Once the maximum bending stress f_b has been obtained, f_v and $f_{c\perp}$ can be calculated at that cross section, and the interaction stresses at that location can be checked.

Similarly, when beams are continuous or cantilevered over a support, the same principles of interaction still apply. However, the simplified procedures for simply supported beams as previously discussed do not apply. Thus the point of maximum bending stress must be determined and the interaction stress factor applied at that point. In some cases the maximum bending stress may occur over a support.

For a beam cantilevered over a support, as shown in Fig. 4.8, the shear at the support which is calculated by the usual shear formula should not be added to the shear determined by the interaction formula. In this case the taper is on the tension side of the beam, and the stress perpendicular to the grain is tension. The interaction stress factor C_I cannot be used for this situation because C_I is calculated using $F_{c\perp}$ and f_c in the interaction formula. Therefore the interaction formula must be used.

Occasionally, straight beams are designed with short tapers on one or both ends to facilitate drainage, meet architectural requirements, or reduce wall height requirements. In most cases the interaction of stresses along the tapered-end cut does not control the design. However, these stresses should be checked using the interaction equation. The bending stress could be calculated at very close increments along the tapered end, such as for every foot of the tapered section, but usually this is not necessary. One or two calculations will generally suffice.

Typically, the design of these beams is controlled by bending or deflection at midspan or shear at the end.

It is noted that for a glulam member having a short end taper, the usual practice is to cut through the higher-grade lamination to the lower-grade inner laminations. For example, the lowest acceptable laminating grade of Douglas fir is an L3 grade, which has an allowable F_b of only 1500 lb/in^2 for nine or more laminations, as given in the Appendix "Reference Data." Therefore, the designer is cautioned to

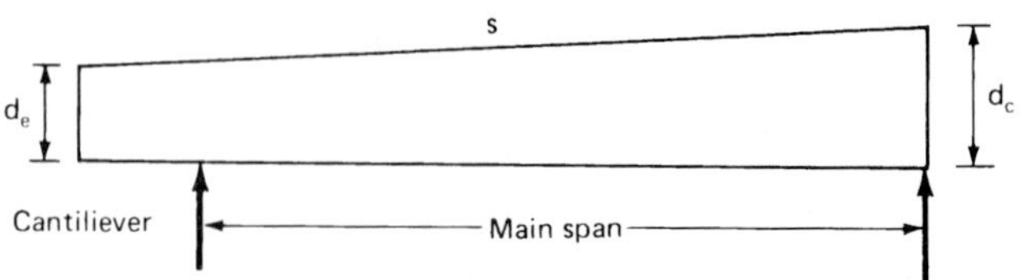

FIG. 4.8 Cantilevered tapered beam.

evaluate correctly the allowable bending stresses to be used in the interaction stress analysis for this type of member.

Deflection of Tapered Beams. The deflection of any wood member loaded in bending is composed of the components caused by both bending and shear. The modulus of elasticity E as published for both sawn grades of lumber and glulam has been modified by a factor that reflects the effect of shear on deflection for a member having an ℓ/d of 21, which approximates the average ℓ/d of members in service. Thus using the published values for E in the standard deflection formulas takes into account the deflection due to shear as well as for bending, and separate calculations for these two components are not typically required. While it is possible to develop correction factors for ℓ/d values other than 21, such refinements are seldom justified.

The shear deflection is larger in tapered members than in prismatic members, and the resulting total deflection, including both bending deflection and shear deflection, is slightly larger than that obtained by the customary methods of calculating deflection in prismatic members.

If both shear deflection and bending deflection are to be calculated, the published allowable values of E should be increased by 10 percent to obtain the true bending modulus of elasticity. In extreme tapers, tests indicate that shear deflection could account for up to 25 percent of the total deflection of a tapered member. Since only 10 percent is accounted for as shear deflection in the published values, members with high tapers should be checked using both the shear-deflection formula and the bending-deflection formula. While exact calculation of the deflection of tapered beams is relatively complex, acceptable accuracy in determining the deflection of tapered members can be obtained by determining the deflection of an equivalent prismatic member. The depth of an equivalent member of constant cross section of the same width that will have an approximately equal deflection as a tapered beam can be determined by the formula

$$d = C_{dt}d_e \qquad (4.28)$$

where d_e is the end depth of a double-tapered symmetrical beam or the shallower end depth of a single-tapered beam, and C_{dt} is a constant derived from the relationship of the formulas for deflection or tapered beams and straight prismatic beams as follows. For a uniformly loaded symmetrical double-tapered beam,

$$C_{dt} = 1 + 0.66C_y \qquad \text{when } 0 < C_y < 1 \qquad (4.29)$$

$$C_{dt} = 1 + 0.62C_y \qquad \text{when } 1 < C_y < 3 \qquad (4.30)$$

For a uniformly loaded single-tapered straight beam,

$$C_{dt} = 1 + 0.46C_y \qquad \text{when } 0 < C_y < 1.1 \qquad (4.31)$$

$$C_{dt} = 1 + 0.43C_y \qquad \text{when } 1.1 < C_y < 2 \qquad (4.32)$$

$$C_y = \frac{d_c - d_e}{d_e} \qquad (4.33)$$

Having thus determined the equivalent depth d, the calculation of deflection is then based on the standard engineering equation for a uniformly loaded beam. The calculation of the deflection of tapered beams with other than uniform loads becomes somewhat more complicated. In many cases the actual moment diagram approximates the moment diagram for a uniform load, and thus a close approximation of the deflection can be obtained by calculating the equivalent uniform load deflection. When this approach will not result in the desired accuracy, it is recommended that one of the energy methods of determining deflection, such as the virtual work (dummy load) method, be used.

EXAMPLE 4.7: DOUBLE-TAPERED BEAM DESIGN Design a double-tapered straight glulam roof beam to meet the requirements shown below. Roof decking is assumed to be applied directly to the top of the member to provide continuous lateral support and the ends are assumed to be fixed against rotation.

Span = 50 ft (15.24 m)

Spacing = 12 ft (3.66 m)

Roof slope = 2:12

Snow load = 30 lb/ft² (1436.4 Pa)

Dead load = 20 lb/ft² (957.6 Pa), including weight of member

Assume that the following allowable stresses as obtained from the Appendix, "Reference Data," are applicable:

$$F_b = 2400 \text{ lb/in}^2 \text{ (16,548.0 kPa)}$$

$$F_V = 165 \text{ lb/in}^2 \text{ (1137.7 kPa)}$$

$$F_{c\perp} \text{ (top)} = 560 \text{ lb/in}^2 \text{ (3861.2 kPa)}$$

$$F_{c\perp} \text{ (bottom)} = 650 \text{ lb/in}^2 \text{ (4481.7 kPa)}$$

$$E = 1{,}700{,}000 \text{ lb/in}^2 \text{ (11,700,000 kPa)}$$

$$\text{Allowable } \Delta_{TL} = \frac{\ell}{180} = \frac{50 \times 12}{180} = 3.33 \text{ in (8.46 cm)}$$

Since this is an interior application, dry conditions of use are applicable.

Determine minimum end depth for shear. Since this is a trial calculation, loads occurring within a distance d of the end will not be neglected. Assume width of member = 5.125 in.

$$R = V = \frac{w\ell}{2} = \frac{(30 + 20)12 \times 50}{2} = 15{,}000 \text{ lb}$$

The required end depth is

$$d_e = \frac{3V}{2bF'_v} = \frac{3 \times 15{,}000}{2 \times 5.125 \times 165 \times 1.15} = 23.1 \text{ in}$$

Use 24 in.

Determine preliminary centerline depth based on geometry:

$$d_c = d_e + (\text{roof slope})(\text{span}/2) = 24 + \left(\frac{2}{12}\right)\left(\frac{50}{2}\right) 12 = 74 \text{ in}$$

Note that $d_c/b = 74/5.125 = 14.4$, which is considerably greater than industry-recommended d/b ratios for straight prismatic beams.

While there are no specific industry recommendations regarding the maximum d/b ratio for tapered members, the designer is cautioned to use judgment. Typically, the value of $d/b < 7$ is a reasonable guideline to follow for tapered beams, with d being the depth at the point of maximum bending stress. Therefore, try $b = 6.75$ in (17.15 cm). Check the actual stresses based on trial sizes of

$b = 6.75$ in (17.15 cm) $\quad d_e = 18$ in (45.72 cm) $\quad d_c = 68$ in (172.72 cm)

Determine shear stress at the end:

$$V = 600 \left(\frac{L}{2} - \frac{d_e}{12}\right) = 14{,}100 \text{ lb}$$

$$f_v = \frac{1.5 \times 14{,}100}{6.75 \times 18} = 174 \text{ lb/in}^2$$

$$F'_V = 165 \times 1.15 = 190 \text{ lb/in}^2 \text{ (1310 kPa)} > f_v = 174 \text{ lb/in}^2 \text{ (1200 kPa)}$$

Determine maximum stresses at depth d, using Eq. (4.20):

$$d = \frac{d_e}{d_c}(2d_c - d_e) = \left(\frac{18}{68}\right)(136 - 18) = 31.2 \text{ in}$$

$$\frac{d}{b} = \frac{31.2}{6.75} = 4.6 < 7$$

Determine the bending stress at $d = 31.2$ in, using Eq. (4.23):

$$f_b = \frac{3WL}{4bd_e(2d_c - d_e)} = \frac{3 \times 600 \times 50 \times 50 \times 12}{4 \times 6.75 \times 18(136 - 18)} = 942 \text{ lb/in}^2$$

Determine shear stress at $d = 31.2$ in, using Eq. (4.26):

$$f_V = f_b \tan\theta = 942(2/12) = 157 \text{ lb/in}^2$$

$$F'_V = 190 \text{ lb/in}^2 \text{ (1310 kPa)} > f_v = 157 \text{ lb/in}^2 \text{ (1083 kPa)}$$

Determine compression perpendicular to grain stress at $d = 31.2$ in, using Eq. (4.27):

$$f_{c\perp} = f_b \tan^2\theta = 942(2/12)^2 = 26 \text{ lb/in}^2$$

$$F_{c\perp} = 560 \text{ lb/in}^2 \text{ (3861 kPa)} > f_{c\perp} = 26 \text{ lb/in}^2 \text{ (179 kPa)}$$

The effects of combined stresses should be checked at the point of maximum stress by either the interaction formula or use of the interaction stress factor C_I.

Determine the interaction stress factor C_I:

$$\tan\theta = 2/12 = 0.167$$

C_I (from Table 4.5) $= 0.385$
Determine the volume-effect factor C_V:

$$C_V = \left(\frac{12}{31.2}\right)^{1/10} \times \left(\frac{5.125}{6.75}\right)^{1/10} \times \left(\frac{21}{50}\right)^{1/10} = 0.81$$

$C_I < C_F$; therefore, C_I controls.

$$F'_b = F_b C_I = 2400 \times 1.15 \times 0.385 = 1063 \text{ lb/in}^2 \text{ (7329 kPa)} > f_b$$

$$= 942 \text{ lb/in}^2 \text{ (6495 kPa)}$$

Determine deflection:

$$C_y = \frac{d_c - d_e}{d_c} = \frac{68 - 18}{18} = 2.78$$

$$C_{dt} = 1 + (0.62 \times 2.78) = 2.724$$

$$d = 2.724 \times 18 = 49 \text{ in}$$

$$\Delta_{TL} = \frac{5 \times 600 \times 50^4 \times 1728}{384 \times 1{,}700{,}000 \times 66{,}178} = 0.75 \text{ in}$$

$$\Delta_{TL} \text{ (allowable)} = \frac{\ell}{240} = 2.5 \text{ in (6.35 cm)} > \Delta_{TL} = 0.75 \text{ in (1.90 cm)}$$

Determine the amount of camber: Dead-load deflection is

$$\Delta_{DL} = \Delta_{TL}\left(\frac{w_{DL}}{w_{TL}}\right) = 0.75\left(\frac{240}{600}\right) = 0.30 \text{ in}$$

Centerline camber is

$$1.5\Delta_{DL} = 1.5 \times 0.30 = 0.45 \text{ in (1.14 cm)}$$

Use ½ in (1.27 cm). No compression face camber is required because this camber is less than 2 in.

4.5.2 Pitched and Curved Beams

A number of different shapes of curved bending members can be manufactured from glulam timbers in addition to the curved beams discussed in Sec. 4.4.3. Some of the more common shapes are shown in Fig. 4.9. Each of these shapes has unique design requirements, but probably the most complex member to analyze is the double-tapered pitched and curved beam, often referred to as a *PTC beam.* This shape of glulam beam is one of the most popular types of structural roof member where a sloped roof, maximum interior clearance, and aesthetic appearance are desired. In these members the top edge slopes from the apex at the centerline toward the supports at an angle to the horizontal defined as ϕ_T, and the lower edge is

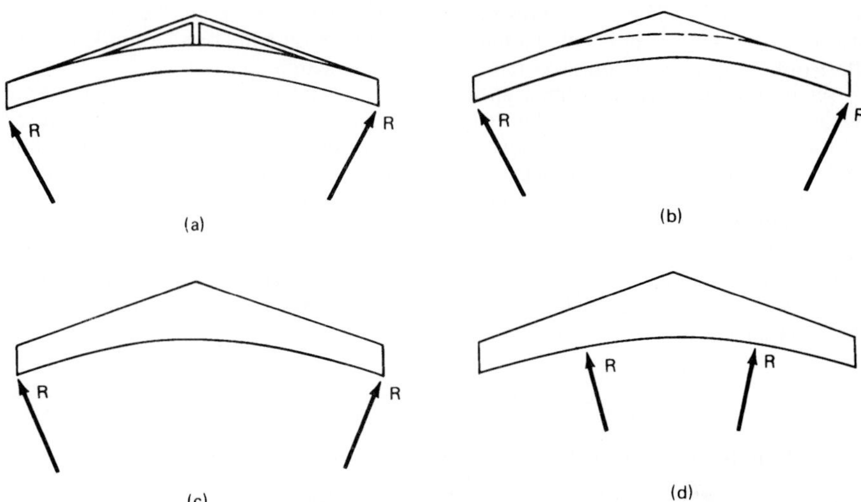

FIG. 4.9 Typical shapes of pitched and curved beams. (*a*) Double-pitched and curved, constant-cross-section framed haunch; (*b*) double-pitched and tapered, constant-cross-section mechanically attached haunch; (*c*) double-pitched and curved, constant radius; (*d*) double-tapered-pitched and curved.

curved between the tangent points (TP) and slopes at an angle ϕ_B between tangent point and support (Fig. 4.10). The portion between the tangent point and the support end of the member is usually tapered but may be of constant cross section. The tangent points are usually located near the quarter points, but the location can vary from a point located as close to the center as the minimum radius of curvature permits to a point at the end support. The optimal design of a PTC beam is when all architectural requirements are satisfied using the smallest volume of wood.

The design of PTC beams is similar to that of straight prismatic beams, with the exception that radial stresses are induced in the curved portion and the distribution of the bending stresses about the assumed neutral axis varies from that in a prismatic member. The need to design for radial stresses as discussed in Sec. 4.4.3 has long been recognized in the design of curved members.

The bending and radial stresses which develop in double-tapered pitched beams are a function of the variable shape of the cross section, and their exact determi-

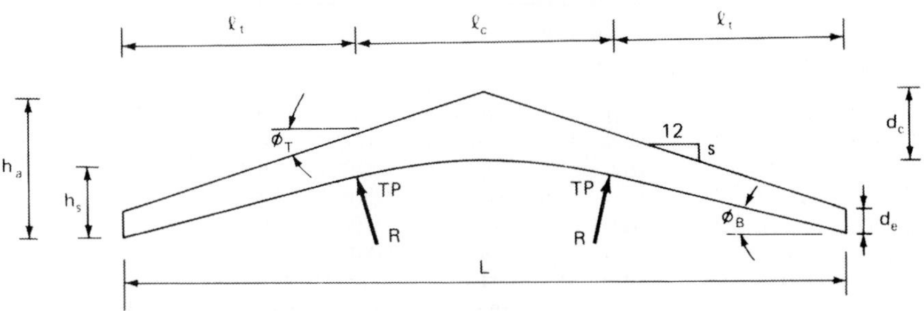

FIG. 4.10 Typical PTC beam geometry.

nation is complex. The procedures presented in this handbook are based on extensive research on glulam beams having this configuration and are a simplification of the more complex procedures derived from this research.[10]

As in straight tapered beams, an interaction of stresses on the top tapered cut of these type members occurs, but it is usually very small and is generally ignored with no significant loss in accuracy. Since the factors for determining bending and radial tension stresses are a function of the geometric configuration of the member, they cannot be determined accurately until the final size and shape of the member have been established, and thus an iterative trial-and-error method must be used for the design. As previously noted, Fig. 4.10 defines the geometric nomenclature associated with this shape of beam. When analyzing a curved bending member having a variable cross section, such as a PTC beam, the radial stress f_r is computed by the equation

$$f_r = K_r C_r \left(\frac{6M}{bd_c^2} \right) \tag{4.34}$$

where K_r is the radial stress factor calculated from

$$K_r = A + B\left(\frac{d_c}{R_m} \right) + C\left(\frac{d_c}{R_m} \right)^2 \tag{4.35}$$

Values for constants A, B, and C are given in Table 4.6. K_r also can be determined from Fig. 4.11. Other terms in this equation are defined as

M = bending moment at midspan, in·lb

b = width of cross section, in

d_c = depth of cross section at centerline, in

C_r = reduction factor, which is a function of the shape of the member and is defined in Figs. 4.12 to 4.15

R_m = radius of curvature of member at centerline of midspan depth, in

The radial stress factor K_r varies with the ratio of the slope of the bottom face

TABLE 4.6 Constants for Polynomial Approximation to K_r

Top slope ϕ_T, deg	A	B	C
2.5	0.0079	0.1747	0.1284
5.0	0.0174	0.1251	0.1939
7.5	0.0279	0.0937	0.2162
10.0	0.0391	0.0754	0.2119
15.0	0.0629	0.0619	0.1722
20.0	0.0893	0.0608	0.1393
25.0	0.1214	0.0605	0.1238
30.0	0.1649	0.0603	0.1115

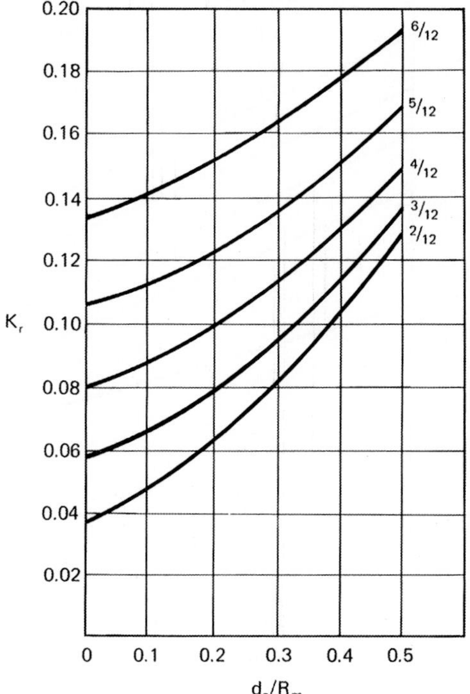

FIG. 4.11 Plot of K_r versus d_c/R_m.

to the slope of the top face, ϕ_B/ϕ_T. In order to reduce the design complexity, a fixed ϕ_B/ϕ_T ratio was selected in developing Fig. 4.11, which results in a slightly conservative design for other ϕ_B/ϕ_T ratios. Allowable radial stress values are given in Sec. 4.4.3. If the calculated stress exceeds the applicable design value indicated, the design should be reevaluated by modifying the geometry of the section in such a way as to reduce this radial tension stress. As an alternate procedure for Douglas fir–larch, Douglas fir–south, hem-fir, and western woods, mechanical reinforcement may be used. When mechanical reinforcement is used, it must be designed to resist the full magnitude of the calculated radial tension stress. With radial reinforcement, the calculated radial tension stress is limited to one-third of the horizontal shear stress for Douglas fir–larch, Douglas fir–south, hem-fir, and western woods for all loading conditions subject to modification for the duration of load.

In analyzing the members for flexure, the stress in bending f_b is a function of a bending stress factor K_θ, which results from the shape of the member. Thus

$$f_b = K_\theta\left(\frac{6M}{bd_c^2}\right) \tag{4.36}$$

where M = moment at midspan, in·lb
b = width, in
d_c = depth at midspan, in

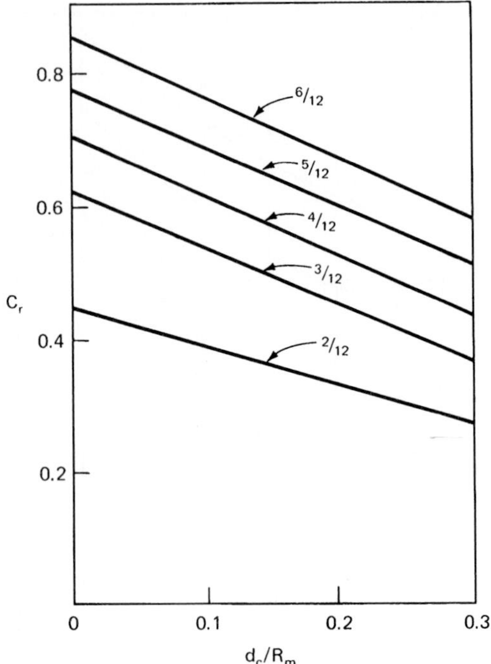

FIG. 4.12 Plot of C_r versus d_c/R_m for $L/L_c = 1.0$.

and

$$k_\theta = A + B\left(\frac{d_c}{R_m}\right) + C\left(\frac{d_c}{R_m}\right)^2 \tag{4.37}$$

where A, B, and C are dimensionless factors from Table 4.7, and the other terms are as defined previously.

The deflection of the member is also affected by its shape, making its exact calculation very complex. The following equation, which considers only bending deflection, provides a close approximation of the actual deflection as computed by an energy-deformation method correlated to research test data:

$$\Delta_c = \frac{5W\ell^3}{384E_b d b_{eb}^3} \tag{4.38}$$

where Δ_c = deflection at midspan, in
W = total uniform load, lb
ℓ = span, in
E_b = modulus of elasticity adjusted by appropriate modifiers
b = member width, in

and

$$d_{eb} = (d_e + d_c)(0.5 + 0.735 \tan \phi_T) - 1.41d_c \tan \phi_B \tag{4.39}$$

Other more exact methods of determining deflection, such as the virtual work method, also may be used if a precise determination of deflection is required. An accurate evaluation of vertical deflection can become a significant factor if the

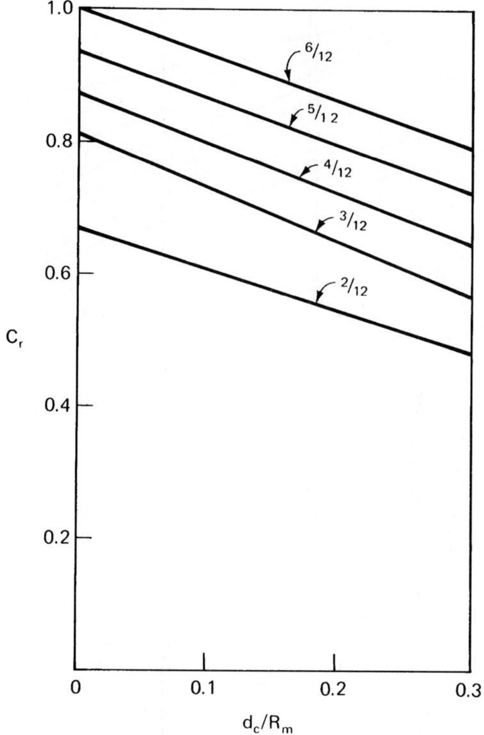

FIG. 4.13 Plot of C_r versus d_c/R_m for $L/L_c = 2.0$.

magnitude of horizontal movement, which is a function of the vertical deflection, is a major design consideration.

EXAMPLE 4.8: PITCHED AND TAPERED CURVED BEAM DESIGN This example illustrates the various steps involved in the design procedure for double-tapered pitched and curved beams. See Fig. 4.16 for span and loading conditions.

Assume a 24F-V3 southern pine glulam combination with the following stresses:

$$F_b = 2400 \text{ lb/in}^2 \text{ (16,548.0 kPa)}$$

$$F_V = 200 \text{ lb/in}^2 \text{ (1379.0 kPa)}$$

$$F_{c\perp} = 650 \text{ lb/in}^2 \text{ (4481.7 kPa)}$$

$$E = 1{,}800{,}000 \text{ lb/in}^2 \text{ (12,400,000 kPa)}$$

Determine minimum end depth d_e based on shear: For preliminary trial purposes, use the full span in determining the vertical end shear:

$$d_e = \frac{3V}{2bF'_V}$$

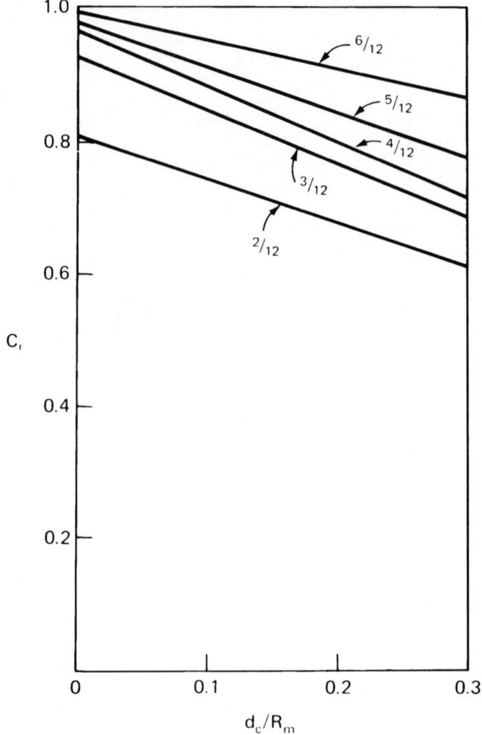

FIG. 4.14 Plot of C_r versus d_c/R_m for $L/L_c = 3.0$.

where V = shear, lb
b = beam width (assumed), in
F'_v = tabular design value in shear, lb/in², adjusted by appropriate modifying factors

Assume $b = 8\frac{1}{2}$ in (21.59 cm):

$$d_e = \frac{3 \times 45(60/2)12}{2 \times 8.5 \times 200 \times 1.15} = 12.4 \text{ in}$$

Try $d_e = 16\frac{1}{2}$ in.

Determine approximate centerline depth d_{cb} required to meet bending-stress limitations:

$$d_{cb} = \sqrt{\frac{6MA}{bF_b}}$$

where A = coefficient obtained from Table 4.7
M = maximum bending moment, in·lb
F_b = tabular design value in bending, lb/in², adjusted by appropriate factors
b = width of member, in

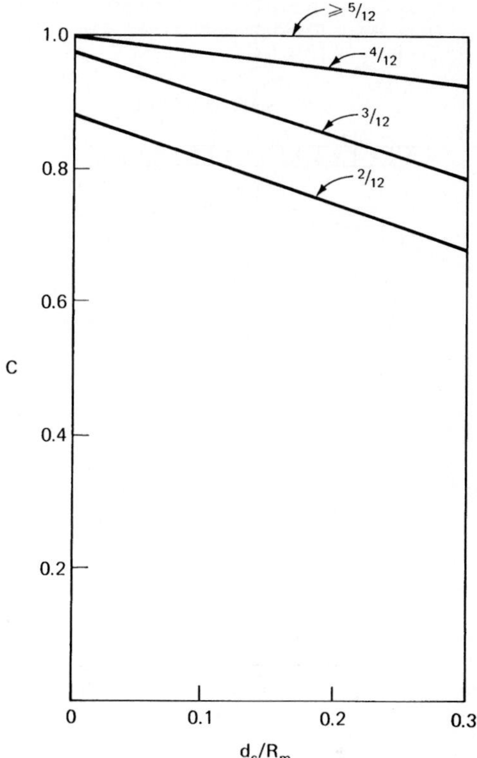

FIG. 4.15 Plot of C_r versus d_c/R_m for L/L_c = 4.0.

TABLE 4.7 Coefficients for Determining K_θ*

Top slope ϕ_T, deg	A	B	C
2.5	1.042	4.247	6.201
5	1.149	2.036	−1.825
10	1.330	0.0	0.927
15	1.738	0.0	0.0
20	1.961	0.0	0.0
25	2.625	−2.829	3.538
30	3.062	−2.954	2.440

*For intermediate values of A, B, or C, use straight-line interpolation.
Source: From Ref. 8.

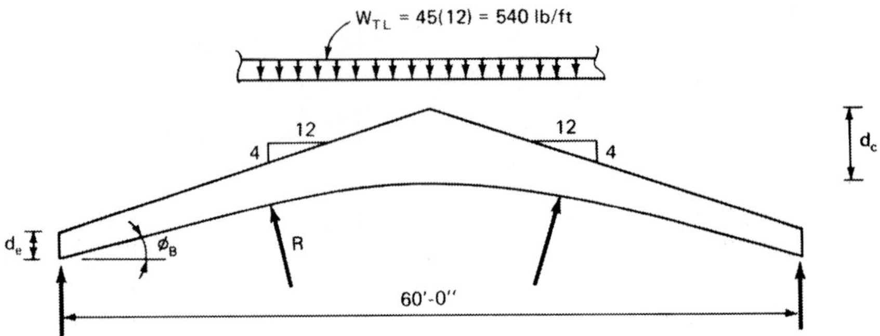

FIG. 4.16 Beam geometry and loading for Example 4.8.

Thus $$d_{cb} = \sqrt{\frac{6 \times 243{,}000 \times 12 \times 1.891}{8.5 \times 2400 \times 1.15 \times 0.90}} = 39.6 \text{ in}$$

where 0.90 is an assumed value for C_V.

Determine approximate centerline depth $d_{c\Delta}$ to meet deflection limitations of $\ell/240$ for total load: First, determine an approximate effective centerline depth d_{eff} for use in calculating $d_{c\Delta}$:

$$d_{\text{eff}} = \sqrt[3]{\frac{W\ell^3}{6.4Eb\Delta_{\max}(\cos \phi_T)^3}}$$

where W = total uniform load, lb
ℓ = span, in
E = tabular design value for modular of elasticity, lb/in², adjusted by applicable modifiers
b = width of member, in
ϕ_T = slope of top face, deg
$\Delta_{\max}$ = allowable deflection = $\ell/240$ for total load

Thus $$d_{\text{eff}} = \sqrt[3]{\frac{32{,}400 \times 720^3}{6.4 \times 1{,}800{,}000 \times 8.5 \times 3.0 \times 0.949^3}} = 36.3 \text{ in}$$

The approximate centerline depth is then calculated as

$$d_{c\Delta} = 2d_{\text{eff}} - d_e = (2 \times 36.3) - 16.5 = 56.1 \text{ in}$$

Determine the trial minimum centerline depth d_{crt} due to radial tension stress limitations:

$$d_{crt} = \sqrt{\frac{6MK_r}{bF'_{rt}}}$$

where K_r = value obtained from Fig. 4.11
d_c = depth of beam at centerline, in
R_m = radius of curvature at neutral axis, in
M = maximum bending moment, in·lb
F'_{rt} = allowable value for radial tension, adjusted by appropriate modifying factors

The determination of K_r requires an estimate of d_c/R_m. It is recommended that an initial trial value of K_r be determined by taking d_c as the greater of the trial values of d_{cb} or $d_{c\Delta}$. Select an initial trial value for R_m equal to the span:

$$\frac{d_c}{R_m} = \frac{56}{60 \times 12} = 0.078$$

$$K_r = 0.087$$

$$d_{crt} = \sqrt{\frac{6 \times 243{,}000 \times 12 \times 0.087}{8.5 \times 67 \times 1.15}} = 48.2 \text{ in (332.3 cm)}$$

Determine beam geometry: Determine the height of the apex point h_a, the height of the soffit at midspan h_s, a trial bottom slope ϕ_B, and a soffit radius R as follows:

$$h_a = d_e + \frac{L}{2}(\tan \phi_T)$$

where L is the span length in inches, and ϕ_T is the top slope in degrees. Therefore,

$$h_a = 16.5 + \frac{60}{2}(12)(\tan 18.44°) = 136.5 \text{ in}$$

$$h_s = h_a - d_c$$

where d_c is the largest of d_{cb}, $d_{c\Delta}$, or d_{crt}. Therefore, use $d_c = d_{c\Delta} = 56.1$ in, or 56 in:

$$h_s = 136.5 - 56 = 80.5 \text{ in (204.5 cm)}$$

Determine $\phi_{B\,\max}$ from the equation

$$\phi_{B\,\max} = \sin^{-1}\left(\frac{4Lh}{L^2 + 4h_s^2}\right) = \sin^{-1}\left(\frac{4 \times 60 \times 80.5 \times 12}{720^2 + (4 \times 80.5^2)}\right) = 25.21°$$

If $\phi_{B\,\max} < \phi_T$, set $\phi_{B\,\max} = \phi_T$. Therefore, use $\phi_{B\,\max} = 18.44°$.
Determine $\phi_{B\,\min}$ from the equation

$$\phi_{B\,\min} = \sin^{-1}\left(\frac{R_{\min}}{a}\right) - \tan^{-1}\left(\frac{\nu}{L/2}\right)$$

where $y = R_{min} - h_s$ and $a = \sqrt{y^2 + (L/2)^2}$. For 1½-in laminations, use R_{min} = 27 ft 6 in. For ¾-in laminations, use R_{min} = 9 ft 4 in. For this example, use R_{min} = 27 ft 6 in:

$$y = (27.5 \times 12) - 80.5 = 249.5 \text{ in}$$

$$a = 438 \text{ in}$$

$$\phi_{B\ min} = \sin^{-1}\left(\frac{27.5 \times 12}{438}\right) - \tan^{-1}\left(\frac{249.5}{360}\right) = 14.16°$$

Choose the trial bottom slope as $\phi_B = 0.45(\phi_{B\ max} + \phi_{B\ min})$, but not less than $\phi_{B\ min} = 14.6°$. Therefore, use $\phi_B = 0.45(18.44° + 14.16) = 14.67°$.

Determine the trial soffit radius R as

$$R = \frac{h_s - \ell/2 \tan \phi_B}{1 - \cos \phi_B - \sin \phi_b \tan \phi_b} = 33.98 \text{ ft}$$

Use $R = 34$ ft.

Determine the following values using the calculated values for ϕ_B and R. Length of tapered leg:

$$\ell_t = \frac{\ell}{2} - R \sin \phi_B = 21.39 \text{ ft}$$

Ratio of span length to distance between tangent points:

$$\frac{\ell}{\ell_c} = \frac{\ell}{\ell - 2\ell_t} = \frac{60}{60 - (2 \times 21.39)} = 3.48$$

Depth of beam at tangent point,

$$d_t = d_e + \ell_t(\tan \phi_T - \tan \phi_b)$$

$$= 16.5 + (21.39 \times 12)(\tan 18.44° - \tan 14.67°) = 34.9 \text{ in}$$

$$\frac{d_c}{R_m} = \frac{d_c}{R + d_c/2} = \frac{56}{(34 \times 12) + 56/2} = 0.128$$

Check capacity of trial beam: The reference stress at centerline used for convenience in the calculation is

$$f_0 = \frac{6M}{bd_c^2}$$

where M is the maximum bending moment at centerline in inch-pounds:

$$f_0 = \frac{6 \times 243{,}000 \times 12}{8.5 \times 56^2} = 656 \text{ lb/in}^2$$

Check bending stresses: Determine the extreme fiber bending stress at the apex centerline. Determine the bending stress factor K_θ from Table 4.7 corresponding to ϕ_T and d_c/R_m. For $\phi_T = 18.44°$ and $d_c/R_m = 0.128$,

$$K_\theta = A + B\left(\frac{d_c}{R_m}\right) + C\left(\frac{d_c}{R_m}\right)^2 = 1.891$$

$$f_b = K_\theta f_0 = 1.891 \times 656 = 1240 \text{ lb/in}^2 \text{ (8550 kPa)}$$

which is smaller than $F'_b = F_b \times C_D \times C_V = 2400 \times 1.15 \times 0.86 = 2373$ lb/in^2 (16,362 kPa).

Determine the extreme fiber bending stress at the tangent point:

$$f_{bt} = \frac{6M_t}{bd_t^2} = \frac{6 \times 222{,}984 \times 12}{8.5 \times 34.9^2} = 1551 \text{ lb/in}^2 \text{ (10,694 kPa)}$$

where M_t is the bending moment at a distance L_t from the end, in inch-pounds:

$$F'_b = F_b \times C_D \times C_V = 2400 \times 1.15 \times 0.88$$

$$= 2428 \text{ lb/in}^2 \text{ (16,741 kPa)}$$

$$> f_{bt} = 1551 \text{ lb/in}^2 \text{ (10,694 kPa)}$$

Note: If $f_{bt} \approx F'_{bt}$, the designer may need to check bending stresses for additional points between the tangent point and the end of the member.

Check the maximum radial stress: Determine the radial stress factor K_r corresponding to d_c/R_m for the given ϕ_T from Fig. 4.11. Determine the reduction factor C_r corresponding to L/L_c for the given ϕ_T from Figs. 4.12 to 4.15. For values of L/L_c between those shown in the figures, use straight-line interpolation:

$$f_{rt} = K_r C_r F_0 = 0.091 \times 0.915 \times 656$$

$$= 54.6 \text{ lb/in}^2 \text{ (376.5 kPa)} < F'_{rt} = \left(\frac{200}{3}\right) 1.15 = 77 \text{ lb/in}^2 \text{ (530.9 kPa)}$$

Check deflection at the centerline:

$$d_{eb} = (d_e + d_c)(0.5 + 0.735 \tan \phi_T) - 1.41 d_c \tan \phi_B = 33.3 \text{ in}$$

$$\Delta_c = \frac{5W\ell^3}{32Ebd_{eb}^3} = \frac{5 \times 32{,}400 \times 720^3}{32 \times 1{,}800{,}000 \times 8.5 \times 33.3^3} = 3.35 \text{ in (8.51 cm)}$$

$$\Delta \text{ (allowable)} = \frac{\ell}{240} = \frac{60 \times 12}{240} = 3.0 \text{ in (7.62 cm)} < \Delta_c = 3.35 \text{ in (8.51 cm)}$$

Note: If either the deflection or the radial stress limitations cannot be met, redesign by increasing the depth d_c. If only the bending stress at the tangent point does not meet the limitations, revise the geometry by decreasing the angle ϕ_B (maintain $\phi_B \geq \phi_{B\,\min}$).

Since all design requirements for this example are satisfied with the exception of the deflection limitation of $\ell/240$, the designer may wish to consider using a deflection limitation of $\ell/180$ for the total load which satisfies industry recommendations. Otherwise, the depth of the beam at the centerline must be increased.

Determine the horizontal movement at the supports Δ_H using the formula

$$\Delta_H = \frac{2h\Delta_c}{\ell}$$

where h = rise in centroidal axis from end to center, in; $= h_a - d_c/2$
ℓ = span length, in
Δ_c = centerline deflection as previously calculated

Then $$\Delta_H = \frac{2 \times 108.5 \times 3.35}{720} = 1.01 \text{ in} \approx 1 \text{ in (2.54 cm)}$$

Note: Horizontal movement should be provided for by the use of a slotted connection with a suitable frictionless bearing pad. See Chap. 5 for typical connection details using slotted holes.

Radial Reinforcement. Since the allowable radial stress is only 15 lb/in² (103.4 kPa) (adjusted by applicable modifiers) for Douglas fir–larch, Douglas fir–south, hem-fir, or western woods, the typical design procedure for these species is to use radial reinforcement to resist radial tension stresses. While various types of reinforcements designed on the basis of sound engineering principles could be used, two types of mechanical reinforcements have proven to be effective based on field experience. These are lag bolts mechanically attached to the wood or deformed bars (such as rebars) bonded by adhesive to transfer these radial tension stresses from the wood to the reinforcements throughout the entire depth of embedment. The adhesive used to bond the reinforcement to the wood should be of a durable quality and capable of developing the required tensile strength of the reinforcement. Other than designing the radial reinforcement, the general design procedures for PTC beams as illustrated by Example 4.8 still apply. The following example illustrates this additional design requirement.

EXAMPLE 4.9: PTC BEAM WITH RADIAL REINFORCEMENT. Assume a Douglas fir glulam PTC beam is to be designed for the same geometry and loading conditions as given for Example 4.8 for southern pine. Assume the following allowable stresses from the Appendix, "Reference Data," are applicable:

$$F_b = 2400 \text{ lb/in}^2 \text{ (16,548 kPa)}$$

$$F_V = 165 \text{ lb/in}^2 \text{ (1137.7 kPa)}$$

$$F_{rt} = 15 \text{ lb/in}^2 \text{ (103.4 kPa) without mechanical reinforcement}$$

$$F_{rt} = 55 \text{ lb/in}^2 \text{ (379.2 kPa) with mechanical reinforcement}$$

$$E = 1{,}800{,}000 \text{ lb/in}^2$$

$$F_{c\perp} = 650 \text{ lb/in}^2$$

A comparison of these allowable stresses with those given for the southern pine beams in Example 4.8 indicates that only the allowable F_V and F_{rt} values are lower for the Douglas fir beam. Thus, by inspection, the designer need only reanalyze the beam for horizontal shear and radial tension.

It is noted that a standard width for Douglas fir is 8¾ in (22.22 cm), compared with the 8½-in (21.59-cm) width used for southern pine.

Check shear stresses:

$$V = 540\left(\frac{60}{2} - \frac{16.5}{12}\right) = 15{,}458 \text{ lb}$$

$$f_v = \frac{1.5V}{A} = \frac{1.5 \times 15{,}458}{8.75 \times 16.5}$$

$$= 161 \text{ lb/in}^2 \text{ (1110 kPa)} < F'_v = 165 \times 1.15 = 190 \text{ lb/in}^2 \text{ (1310 kPa)}$$

Check radial tension stresses: $f_{rt} = 54.6$ lb/in² from Example 4.8. Therefore, for Douglas fir beam,

$$f_{rt} = 54.6\left(\frac{8.5}{8.75}\right) = 53 \text{ lb/in}^2$$

Since $F'_{rt} = 15 \times 1.15 = 17.25$ lb/in² (118.9 kPa) $< f_{rt} = 53$ lb/in² $< 55 \times 1.15 = 63.25$ lb/in² (436.1 kPa), use of radial reinforcement is required.

Design radial reinforcement: The radial tension force per inch is 53 × 8.75 = 464 lb/in. Assume 1-in threaded lag bolts will be used.

From Table 4.8, the allowable steel tension capacity is 9560 lb and the allowable withdrawal load is 558 lb per inch of penetration. Lag bolts are installed from the top of the member and are designed to extend to within 2 in of the soffit face. From Table 4.8, the maximum length for a 1-in lag bolt is 60 in. The length of the lag bolt is

$$d_c - 2 = 56 - 2 = 54 \text{ in (137.2 cm)} < 60 \text{ in (152.4 cm)}$$

Effective thread penetration is $d_c/2 - 2 = 56/2 - 2 = 26$ in. Therefore, the allowable withdrawal load is 26 × 558 = 14,508 lb. Maximum spacing controlled by withdrawal is 14,508/464 = 31 in, and maximum spacing controlled by steel

TABLE 4.8 Radial Reinforcement Design Data[a]

Lag bolt design values[b]			Dowel design values[f]		
Diameter, in	Design value, lb/in of penetration[c,d]	Capacity controlled by steel,[e] lb	Rebar, number	Design value, lb/in of penetration	Capacity controlled by steel,[g] lb
¾	449	5,270	3	552	3,980
⅞	504	7,330	4	648	7,070
1	558	9,560	5	754	11,040

[a]For additional design information, see AITC 404–92[9].

[b]For ease of installation, limit length of lag bolts as follows: 36 in for ¾ in; 48 in for ⅞ in; 60 in for 1 in.

[c]For normal duration of load.

[d]Based on specific gravity of 0.51 as for Douglas fir; values shown are 85 percent of those obtained from NDS[3] to allow for slightly oversize lead holes.

[e]Based on unit tensile stress of 20,000 lb/in².

[f]Design values based on qualifying dowel system in accordance with AITC 404-86.[11]

[g]Based on rebars with minimum yield strength of 60,000 lb/in².

Source: Courtesy of American Institute of Timber Construction.

stress is 9560/464 = 20.6 in. Therefore, use 1-in threaded lag bolts spaced 18 in on center.

The mechanical reinforcement should extend from tangent point to tangent point and be spaced symmetrically about the centerline of the PTC beam as shown in Fig. 4.17.

Note: If the design of this beam has been controlled by bending stresses at either midspan or the tangent points, it would be necessary for the designer to recheck the member at these points based on a reduced section modulus allowing for the wood removed by the mechanical reinforcement.

Alternate Design Procedure for PTC Beams. Due to the relative complexity of designing PTC beams, an alternate design procedure has been developed. In this procedure, the haunch portion is mechanically attached to the member rather than being integrally bonded by adhesives and is not considered to act as part of the structural section. This procedure reduces the radial tension stresses considerably and is thus particularly applicable to glulam PTC beams manufactured using western species, such as Douglas fir–larch. The remainder of the structural section is designed as a curved beam of constant cross section with the tangent points assumed to be located at the quarter point of the span (Fig. 4.17). The following example illustrates this alternate design procedure.

EXAMPLE 4.10: SIMPLIFIED PTC BEAM DESIGN Assume a Douglas fir glulam PTC beam is to be designed for the same loading and geometry conditions as given for Example 4.8. Assume the applicable allowable stresses are the same as those given in Example 4.9.

Determine the soffit radius assuming the tangent point at $L/4$:

$$R = \frac{L/4}{\sin \phi_T} = \frac{60/4}{\sin 18.44°} = 47.4 \text{ ft}$$

Since $R > 27$ ft 6 in, which is the minimum radius for 1½-in laminations, use 1½-in laminations:

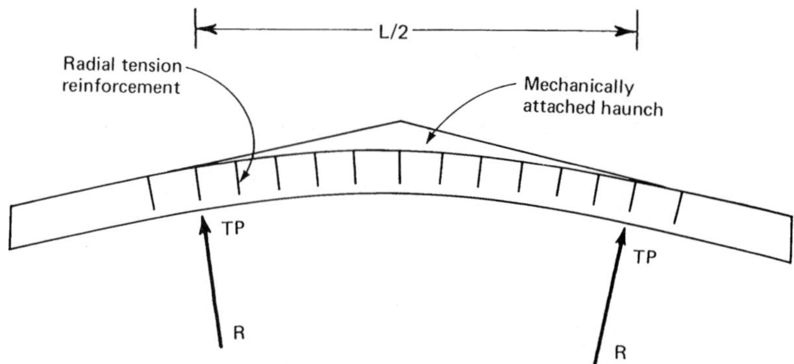

FIG. 4.17 PTC beam with mechanically attached haunch and radial reinforcement.

$$C_c = 1 - 2000\left(\frac{t}{R}\right)^2 = 1 - 2000\left(\frac{1.15}{568.8}\right)^2 = 0.986$$

Determine a trial size assuming a constant-cross-section curved beam:

$$V = \frac{wL}{2} = \frac{540 \times 60}{2} = 16{,}200 \text{ lb}$$

$$A = \frac{1.5V}{E'_v} = \frac{1.5 \times 16{,}200}{165 \times 1.15} = 128 \text{ in}^2$$

Note that this area is slightly conservative since the full design span was used to calculate the shear.

$$M = \frac{wL^2}{8} = \frac{540 \times 60^2}{8} = 243{,}000 \text{ ft·lb}$$

$$S = \frac{M}{F'_b} = \frac{243{,}200 \times 12}{2400 \times 1.15 \times 0.986 \times 0.90} = 1192 \text{ in}^3$$

Note that the 0.90 value is an assumed value for C_v

$$\Delta_{TL} \text{ (allowable)} = \ell/180 = \frac{60 \times 12}{180} = 4.0 \text{ in}$$

$$I = \frac{5WL^4}{384E\Delta_{TL}} = \frac{5 \times 540 \times 60^4 \times 1728}{384 \times 1{,}800{,}000 \times 4.0} = 21{,}870 \text{ in}^4$$

From the Appendix, "Reference Data," select a 6¾- by 34½-in member which has the following section properties:

$$A = 232.9 \text{ in}^2 \qquad S = 1339 \text{ in}^3 \qquad I = 23{,}100 \text{ in}^4$$

Check bending stress:

$$f_b = \frac{M}{S} = \frac{243{,}200 \times 12}{1339} = 2178 \text{ lb/in}^2 \text{ (15,017 kPa)}$$

$$F'_b = 2400 \times 1.15 \times 0.986 \times C_v$$

$$= 2400 \times 1.15 \times 0.986 \times 0.79$$

$$= 2150 \text{ lb/in}^2 \text{ (14,824 kPa)} \approx f_b = 2178 \text{ lb/in}^2 \text{ (15,017 kPa)}$$

Check shear stress:

$$V = 540\left(\frac{\ell}{2} - \frac{d}{12}\right) = 540\left(\frac{60}{2} - \frac{34.5}{12}\right) = 14{,}647 \text{ lb}$$

$$f_V = \frac{1.5V}{A} = \frac{1.5 \times 14{,}647}{232.9} = 94.3 \text{ lb/in}^2$$

$$F'_V = 165 \times 1.15 = 190 \text{ lb/in}^2 \text{ (1310 kPa)} > f_V = 94.3 \text{ lb/in}^2 \text{ (650 kPa)}$$

Check deflection:

$$\Delta_{TL} = \frac{5 \times 540 \times 60^4 \times 1728}{384 \times 1{,}800{,}000 \times 23{,}100}$$

$$= 3.79 \text{ in } (9.63 \text{ cm}) < \Delta_{TL\ \text{allow.}} = 4.0 \text{ in } (10.2 \text{ cm})$$

Check radial tension stresses:

$$R_m = R + \frac{d}{2} = 568.8 + \frac{34.5}{2} = 586 \text{ in}$$

$$f_{rt} = \frac{3M}{2R_m bd} = \frac{3 \times 243{,}000 \times 12}{2 \times 586 \times 6.75 \times 34.5} = 32 \text{ lb/in}^2$$

Since $F'_V = 15 \times 1.15 = 17.25$ lb/in^2 $< f_{rt} = 32$ lb/in^2 $< 55 \times 1.15 = 63.25$ lb/in^2, use radial reinforcement. The design of the radial reinforcement would follow the same procedure as given in Example 4.9.

Determine horizontal displacement:

$$\Delta_H = \frac{2h\Delta_c}{L}$$

where Δ_c = vertical centerline deflection, in
L = span, ft
h = rise in centroidal axis from end, in

$$h = \tan\phi_T\left(\frac{L}{4}\right) + (1 - \cos\phi_T)R_m$$

$$= \tan 18.44\left(\frac{60}{4}\right) 12 + (1 - \cos 18.44°)586 = 90.1 \text{ in}$$

and

$$\Delta_H = \frac{2 \times 90.1 \times 3.79}{60 \times 12} = 0.95 \text{ in } (2.41 \text{ cm})$$

The final beam cross section is shown in Fig. 4.17.

It is noted that the haunch is typically attached to the curved beam using ¾-in threaded lag bolts spaced 48 in on center with 12 in of penetration into the curved section. This may vary by supplier.

Also, while this procedure may result in a slightly less effective beam section than that obtained using the more rigorous analysis described previously, it is usually satisfactory for most design cases.

4.6 MEMBERS SUBJECTED TO BENDING ABOUT BOTH AXES

Occasionally, the designer is confronted with a design situation in which a wood member is subjected to bending stresses acting simultaneously about both axes of the member. This is typically referred to as *biaxial bending*. In these cases, bending stresses induced in the member become additive, and it is necessary to account for this through the use of the following interaction equation:

$$\frac{f_{bx}}{F'_{bx}} + \frac{f_{by}}{F'_{by}} < 1 \tag{4.40}$$

For sawn lumber members, the allowable bending stresses in both the x and y axes are assumed to be the same. For glulam and some other composite wood bending members, the bending stresses in these two axes may be different, and the designer is cautioned to use the appropriate allowable bending stresses in the interaction equation. One common example of a bending member subjected to bending stresses about both axes is an oblique roof purlin such as that illustrated in Fig. 4.18.

It should be noted that an oblique roof purlin will always be required to carry the component of load normal to the roof w_N. In addition, depending on the roof

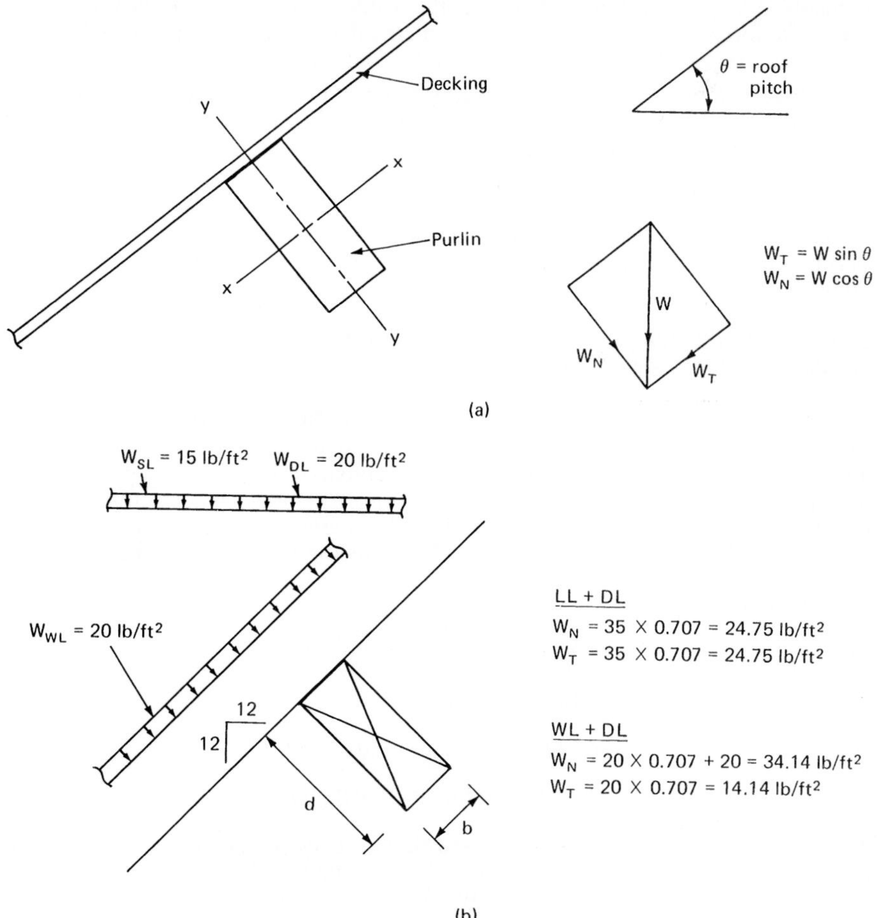

FIG. 4.18 Oblique purlin design.

construction, it also may be required to support all or a part of the tangential component w_T. For pitched roofs, the following guidelines may be used to determine the portion of tangential load which must be carried by the purlins:

1. If plywood or other wood panel sheathing is adequately nailed to all supporting members, it is generally considered to act as a structural diaphragm and carries the tangential component directly to the wall framing. In this case, the purlin can be designed as a simple bending member resisting only the normal load component.

2. If wood decking is used, it may not be able to develop full diaphragm action in transmitting the tangential load to the perimeter framing. However, if properly nailed to the supporting members, wood decking is typically assumed to have adequate capacity to transmit the tangential forces to the ridge purlin and eave purlin or side wall through tension or compression, respectively. In this case, the ridge and eave purlins must be designed as biaxial bending members to resist the normal component of bending forces as well as the bending stresses due to the cumulative tangential forces distributed to them. The intermediate purlins can again be designed as simple span bending members subjected to only the normal load component.

3. If sheathing is not adequate to transfer the tangential force component as described in 1 or 2, sag rods or intermediate lines of blocking can be introduced to transfer these forces to the ridge or eave purlins or side walls. The intermediate purlins must then be designed to carry their normal load component plus the appropriate portion of the tangential load between lines of blocking or sag rods.

4. The conservative solution to the design of oblique purlins is to assume each purlin supports its tributary area of both the normal and tangential force components.

Example 4.11 illustrates the use of the interaction equation for biaxial bending as applied to the design of an oblique roof purlin assuming condition 4 above.

EXAMPLE 4.11: BIAXIAL BENDING IN OBLIQUE ROOF PURLINS Assume an oblique roof purlin is to be used on a $^{12}/_{12}$ roof pitch as shown in Fig. 4.18*a*. Assume each purlin is to carry the normal and tangential load forces equally with no allowance given to diaphragm action. However, assume roof decking does provide lateral support to the top of the member over its full length such that lateral buckling is not a design consideration. Assume a 20F-V2 southern pine glulam beam combination having the following allowable stresses (see Appendix, "Reference Data") is to be used:

$$F_{bx} = 2000 \text{ lb/in}^2 \text{ (13,790.0 kPa)}$$

$$F_{by} = 1450 \text{ lb/in}^2 \text{ (9997.7 kPa)}$$

$$E_x = 1{,}600{,}000 \text{ lb/in}^2 \text{ (11,000,000 kPa)}$$

$$E_y = 1{,}400{,}000 \text{ lb/in}^2 \text{ (9,650,000 kPa)}$$

Assume the following span, spacing, and design loads as shown in Fig. 4.18*a* are applicable with the snow load and dead load applied to the horizontal projection and the wind load applied normal to the roof slope:

Span = 24 ft (7.32 m)

Spacing = 8 ft (2.44 m) o.c.

Snow load = 15 lb/ft^2 (718.2 Pa)

Dead load = 20 lb/ft^2 (957.6 Pa) including weight of purlin

Wind load = 20 lb/ft^2 (957.6 Pa)

Determine bending moments: Snow load plus dead load give

$$M_N = \frac{24.75(8)(24)^2}{8} = 14.256 \text{ ft·lb}$$

$$M_T = M_N = 14.256 \text{ ft·lb}$$

Wind load plus dead load give

$$M_N = \frac{34.14 \times 8 \times 24^2}{8} = 19.665 \text{ ft·lb}$$

$$M_T = \frac{14.14 \times 8 \times 24^2}{8} = 8145 \text{ ft·lb}$$

Determine approximate section required assuming volume effect factor of 1.0: Snow load plus dead load give

$$S_x = \frac{M_N}{F'_{bx}} = \frac{14{,}256 \times 12}{2000 \times 1.15} = 74.4 \text{ in}^3$$

$$S_y = \frac{M_T}{F'_{by}} = \frac{14{,}256 \times 12}{1450 \times 1.15} = 102.6 \text{ in}^3$$

Wind load plus dead load give

$$S_x = \frac{M_N}{F'_{bx}} = \frac{19{,}665 \times 12}{2000 \times 1.33} = 88.7 \text{ in}^3$$

$$S_y = \frac{M_T}{F'_{by}} = \frac{8145 \times 12}{1450 \times 0.90} = 74.9 \text{ in}^3$$

Try a 6.75- × 21-in section

$$S_x = 496.1 \qquad S_y = 159.5$$

$$I_x = 5209.3 \qquad I_y = 538.2$$

$$C_V = 0.95 \qquad C_F = 1.0$$

Check combined bending stresses by Eq. (4.40):

$$\frac{f_{bx}}{F'_{bx}} + \frac{f_{by}}{F'_{by}} < 1$$

Snow load plus dead load give

$$\frac{(14256 \times 12)/496.1}{2000 \times 1.15 \times 0.95} + \frac{(14256 \times 12)/159.5}{1450 \times 1.15 \times 1.0} = 0.16 + 0.68 = 0.84 < 1$$

Wind load plus dead load give

$$\frac{(19665 \times 12)/496.1}{2000 \times 1.33 \times 0.95} + \frac{(8145 \times 12)/159.5}{1450 \times 0.90 \times 1.0} = 0.19 + 0.49 = 0.68 < 1$$

Determine deflection due to snow load plus dead load loading: Total deflection can be determined by

$$\Delta_T = \sqrt{\Delta_x^2 + \Delta_y^2}$$

$$\Delta_x = \frac{5 \times 24.75 \times 8 \times 24^4 \times 1728}{384 \times 1{,}600{,}000 \times 5209.3} = 0.18 \text{ in} \tag{4.41}$$

$$\Delta_y = \frac{5 \times 24.75 \times 8 \times 24^4 \times 1728}{384 \times 1{,}400{,}000 \times 538.2} = 1.96 \text{ in}$$

$$\Delta_T = \sqrt{0.18^2 + 1.96^2} = 1.97 \text{ in (5.0 cm)}$$

The designer may wish to increase the width of the member to increase I_y if this amount of calculated deflection is considered to be excessive.

4.7 MEMBERS SUBJECTED TO COMBINED BENDING AND AXIAL STRESSES

It is not uncommon to have design situations which result in wood bending members being subjected to bending stresses acting in combination with either axial tension or compression stresses. One example of a beam-column, i.e., a member subjected to combined bending and axial compression stresses, would be the compression chord of a truss. The use of an eave purlin acting as a tension tie for a hip roof is an example of a design which would result in a combined bending–axial-tension member. As with members subjected to biaxial bending stresses, as described in Sec. 4.6, the accumulation of the combined effects of these forces is accounted for through the use of appropriate interaction equations.

For a bending member subjected to both bending and axial compression, the interaction equation is given as

$$\left(\frac{f_c}{F'_c}\right)^2 + \frac{f_{b1}}{F'_{b1}\left[1 - \left(\frac{f_c}{F_{cE1}}\right)\right]} + \frac{f_{b2}}{F'_{b2}\left[1 - \left(\frac{f_c}{F_{cE2}}\right) - \left(\frac{f_{b1}}{F_{bE}}\right)^2\right]} \le 1.0 \tag{4.42}$$

where $f_c < F_{cE1} = \dfrac{K_{cE}E'}{(\ell_{e1}/d_1)^2}$ for either uniaxial or biaxial bending

$f_c < F_{cE2} = \dfrac{K_{cE}E'}{(\ell_{e2}/d_2)^2}$ for biaxial bending

$$f_{b1} < F_{bE} = \frac{K_{bE}E'}{(R_B)^2} \text{ for biaxial bending}$$

f_{b1} = actual edgewise bending stress (bending load applied to narrow face of member

f_{b2} = actual flatwise bending stress (bending load applied to wide face of member)

d_1 = wide face dimension or member depth

d_2 = narrow face dimension or member width

$R_B = \sqrt{\frac{\ell_e d}{b^2}}$ and where E is the modulus of elasticity and F_c is the allowable compression parallel to grain stress, both in pounds per square inch

Effective column lengths ℓ_{e1} and ℓ_{e2} and F'_c, F_{cE1}, and F_{cE2} shall be determined in accordance with the provisions of Chap. 3. F_{b1}, F'_{b2}, and F_{bE} shall be determined in accordance with the provisions of Sec. 4.2. The load-duration factor C_D associated with the shortest-duration load in a combination of loads shall be permitted to be used to calculate F'_c, F'_{b1}, and F'_{b2}. All applicable load combinations shall be evaluated to determine the critical load combination.

For the typical case of bending about the primary axis only, this equation reduces to

$$\left(\frac{f_c}{F'_c}\right)^2 + \frac{f_{b1}}{F'_{b1}[1 - (f_c/f_{cE1})]} \tag{4.43}$$

where all terms are the same as for Eq. (4.42).

The designer is referred to Parts III and XV of the NDS[3] for further information regarding the design of beam columns. For a bending member subjected to both bending and axial tension stresses, the design should be checked in accordance with the following equations:

$$\frac{f_t}{F'_t} + \frac{f_b}{F'_b} < 1 \tag{4.44}$$

and

$$\frac{f_b - f_t}{F'_b} < 1 \tag{4.45}$$

where f_t = actual tension parallel to grain stress, lb/in²

f_b = actual bending stress, lb/in²

F'_t = allowable tension parallel to grain stress, lb/in²

F'_b = allowable bending stress, lb/in²

The following example illustrates the design of bending members subjected to combined bending and axial stresses. The designer is referred to Chaps. 3 and 6 for additional examples illustrating this type of design analysis.

EXAMPLE 4.12: MEMBERS SUBJECTED TO COMBINED BENDING AND AXIAL STRESSES Determine the size of laminated veneer lumber (LVL) required for the hip beam and perimeter tie beam shown in Fig. 4.19 (see page 4.69 of the first edition of this Handbook). Assume the plywood roof sheathing is nailed directly to these members providing lateral bracing. Subframing members are 2 × dimension lumber in hangers. Assume the following design loads as applied to the horizontal projection of the roof framing:

Snow load = 30 lb/ft² (1436.4 Pa)

Dead load = 15 lb/ft² (718.2 Pa) including weight of the LVL

Assume the LVL has the following allowable stresses:

$$F_b = 2800 \text{ lb/in}^2 \text{ (19,306.0 kPa)}$$

$$F_y = 285 \text{ lb/in (1965.1 kPa)}$$

$$F_t = 1850 \text{ lb/in}^2 \text{ (12,755.7 kPa)}$$

$$F_C = 2700 \text{ lb/in}^2 \text{ (18,616.5 kPa)}$$

$$E = 2{,}000{,}000 \text{ lb/in}^2 \text{ (13,800,000 kPa)}$$

$$M = 0.1283WL = 0.1283(5062.5)(21.2) = 13770 \text{ ft·lb}$$

Try two pieces of 1¾- by 11⅞-in LVL:

$$S = 82.2 \text{ in}^3 \qquad A = 41.6 \text{ in}^2$$

Check combined bending and axial compression stresses by Eq. (4.43):

$$\left(\frac{f_c}{F'_c}\right)^2 + \frac{f_{bx}}{F'_{bx}[1 - (f_c/F_{cE1})]} < 1$$

In the direction perpendicular to the bending load, the member is assumed to be braced laterally. In calculating F_{cE1}, use K_{cE} equal to 0.418 because LVL products have a COV for modulus of elasticity of less than 0.11. The combined stresses are

$$\left(\frac{15006/41.6}{2700 \times 1.15}\right)^2 + \frac{(13770 \times 12)/82.2}{2800 \times 1.15[1 - (360.7/1821.5)]}$$

$$= 0.013 + 0.778 = 0.791 < 1$$

Shear and deflection will typically not be design controls in hip roof member design, but the designer may wish to check these design parameters.

Design tie beam: Assume tie beams act as 20-ft simple span bending members. Use allowable deflection of $\ell/180$ for total load.

$$\text{Tension force} = \frac{H/2}{0.707} = \frac{14{,}310/2}{0.707} = 10{,}120 \text{ lb}$$

$$R_L = 1453 \text{ lb} \qquad R_R = 2484 \text{ lb} \qquad \text{(see Fig. 4.19)}$$

$$V = 0 \qquad \text{at 11.36 ft from left support}$$

$$M = (1453 \times 11.36) - \frac{1453 \times 11.36}{3} = 11{,}004 \text{ ft·lb}$$

Try two pieces of 1¾- by 11⅞-in LVL:

$$A = 41.6 \text{ in}^2 \qquad S = 82.2 \text{ in}^3 \qquad I = 488.4 \text{ in}^4$$

Check combined bending and axial tension stresses by Eqs. (4.44) and (4.45):

$$\frac{f_b}{F'_b} + \frac{f_t}{F'_t} = \frac{(11{,}004 \times 12)/82.2}{2800 \times 1.15} + \frac{10{,}120/41.6}{1850 \times 1.15} = 0.50 + 0.11 = 0.61 < 1$$

$$\frac{f_b - f_t}{F'_b} = \frac{[(11{,}004 \times 12)/82.2] - (10120/41.6)}{F'_b} = \frac{1606 - 243}{2800 \times 1.15} = 0.42 < 1$$

Check shear:

$$V_{\max} = R_R = 2484 \text{ lb}$$

$$f_V = \frac{1.5 \times 2484}{41.6} = 89.6 \text{ lb/in}^2 \text{ (618 kPa)} < f'_v = 328 \text{ lb/in}^2 \text{ (2262 kPa)}$$

Check deflection based on equivalent uniform loading:

$$W_{\text{equiv}} = \frac{8 \times 11{,}004}{20^2} = 220 \text{ lb/ft}$$

$$\Delta = \frac{5 \times 220 \times 20^4 \times 1728}{384 \times 2{,}000{,}000 \times 488.4}$$

$$= 0.81 \text{ in (2.06 cm)} < \frac{\ell}{180} = 1.33 \text{ in (3.38 cm)}$$

Therefore, use two pieces of 1¾- by 11⅞-LVL for hip beams and tie beams. It is noted that LVL is not typically a cambered product, and the designer may need to add an additional piece of LVL or increase the depth of the LVL for the tie beam if the calculated deflection of 0.81 inches is determined to be unacceptable from a visual aspect.

4.8 PONDING CONSIDERATIONS

A common use of wood bending members is in relatively flat roof building construction. Unless properly designed and constructed, these flat roof systems can develop an accumulation of water or water combined with snow and ice leading to a condition typically referred to as *ponding*. Ponding can lead to excessive accumulations of loads combined with progressively increasing deflections, which may overload and cause the wood roof system to fail.

The most effective way to prevent ponding is to provide adequate roof slope to achieve the required drainage of water. It is recommended that all wood roof systems be designed to have a minimum slope of ¼ in per foot of horizontal distance between any point of the roof and a drain. This ¼ in/ft should be a residual slope which exists after long-term deflection of the beams has occurred. Considerations of the positioning of drains, number of drains, type of drain to minimize clogging, etc. are beyond the scope of this handbook, but the designer is cautioned that all these factors related to the actual design of the drains are critical to the performance of the structural roof system.

When roof slope is not adequate to provide recommended drainage, the roof system should be checked to determine if it can sustain potential ponding loads. Typically, ponding is a greater concern for roofs using relatively long-span bending members. In addition, roofs designed for relatively light live loads, such as occur in areas not subjected to snow loading, are also more susceptible to ponding problems.

One criterion for determining the relative stiffness of roof beams to resist ponding loads is to determine the deflection which will be caused by a uniformly distributed load of 5 lb/ft^2 (239.4 Pa) which is approximately the weight of 1 in (2.54 cm) of water. This is commonly referred to as the *spring constant* of the member. A criterion which has been adopted for the design of wood roof systems is to restrict the deflection caused by this 5 lb/ft^2 (239.4 Pa) load to ½ in (1.27 cm) or less. This can be expressed as

$$\Delta_{5\ \mathrm{lb/ft^2}} < \tfrac{1}{2}\ \mathrm{in} \tag{4.46}$$

It is noted that all roof framing components should satisfy this criterion because water accumulations can occur between framing members or over subframing members which could result in a progressive accumulation of water being carried to the main framing elements.

In addition to satisfying the criterion expressed by Eq. (4.46), the potential effects of ponding also should be determined by calculating the ponding magnification factor and applying this to the member stresses determined by design loading. This procedure accounts for the stresses which can be expected to develop due to existing or design loads in combination with ponding effects. The *ponding magnification factor* C_p is determined by the relationship

$$C_p = \frac{1}{1 - W'\ell^3/\pi^4 EI} \tag{4.47}$$

where W' = total load of 1 in of water on the roof area supported by the member, lb
ℓ = span of member, in
E = modulus of elasticity of member, lb/in^2
I = moment of inertia of member, in^4

The following example illustrates the use of the spring constant and magnification factor calculations in determining the potential effects of ponding on a roof beam.

EXAMPLE 4.13: PONDING DESIGN Assume a simple span glulam beam is to be used in a flat roof system in which adequate drainage of ¼ in/ft cannot be provided due to architectural constraints. Assume the following load-span conditions:

Snow load = 25 lb/ft^2 (1197.0 Pa)

Dead load = 18 lb/ft^2 (861.8 Pa)

Span = 40 ft (12.19 m)

Spacing = 18 ft (5.49 m) o.c.

Assume the glulam beam is a combination 24F-V2 hem-fir, having the following allowable stresses:

$$F_b = 2400 \text{ lb/in}^2 \text{ (16,548.0 kPa)}$$

$$F_V = 155 \text{ lb/in (1068.7 kPa)}$$

$$E = 1{,}500{,}000 \text{ lb/in}^2 \text{ (10,300,000 kPa)}$$

Determine member size based on design loading:

$$w = (25 + 18)\ 18 = 774 \text{ lb/ft}$$

$$M = \frac{774 \times 40^2}{8} = 154{,}800 \text{ ft·lb}$$

$$S_{\text{req}} = \frac{M}{F_b'} = \frac{154{,}800 \times 12}{2400 \times 1.15 \times 0.90} = 748 \text{ in}^3$$

where 0.90 is an assumed value for the volume-effect factor.

$$R = \frac{774 \times 40}{2} = 15{,}480 \text{ lb}$$

$$A_{\text{req}} = \frac{15{,}480 \times 1.5}{155 \times 1.15} = 130 \text{ in}^2$$

Assume allowable deflection $\Delta_{TL} = \ell/240 = (40 \times 12)/240 = 2.0$ in:

$$I_{\text{req}} = \frac{5 \times 774 \times 40^4 \times 1728}{384 \times 1{,}500{,}000 \times 2.0} = 14{,}860 \text{ in}^4$$

Try 5⅛- by 33-in (13.0- by 83.8-cm) section, where $A = 169.1$ in^2 (1090.9 cm^2), $S = 930.2$ in^3 (15,243.2 cm^2), and $I = 15{,}350$ in^4 (638,915 cm^4):

$$f_b = \frac{154{,}800 \times 12}{930.2} = 1997 \text{ lb/in}^2$$

$$F_b' = 2400 \times 1.15 \times C_V$$

$$= 2400 \times 1.15 \times 0.85 = 2346 \text{ lb/in}^2 \text{ (16,176 kPa)} > f_b$$

$$= 1997 \text{ lb/in}^2 \text{ (13,769 kPa)}$$

$$V = 15{,}480 - 774 \times \frac{33}{12} = 13{,}351 \text{ lb}$$

$$f_V = \frac{1.5 \times 13{,}351}{169.1} = 118.4 \text{ lb/in}^2 \text{ (816.4 kPa)}$$

$$F'_V = 155 \times 1.15 = 178.2 \text{ lb/in}^2 \text{ (1229 kPa)} > f_v$$

$$= 118.4 \text{ lb/in}^2 \text{ (816.4 kPa)}$$

$$\Delta_{TL} = \frac{5 \times 774 \times 40^4 \times 1728}{384 \times 1{,}500{,}000 \times 15{,}350}$$

$$= 1.94 \text{ in (493 cm)} < \Delta_{\text{allow.}} = 2.0 \text{ in (5.08 cm)}$$

Check effects of ponding:

$$\Delta_{5 \text{ lb/ft}^2} = \frac{5 \times 18}{774} \times 1.94 = 0.23 \text{ in (0.58 cm)} < \tfrac{1}{2} \text{ in (1.27 cm)}$$

$$W' = 5 \times 18 \times 40 = 3600 \text{ lb}$$

$$C_p = \frac{1}{1 - [(3600 \times 480^3)/(\pi^4 \times 1{,}500{,}000 \times 15{,}350)]} = \frac{1}{0.823} = 1.216$$

$$f_b = 1997 \times 1.216 = 2428 \text{ lb/in}^2 \text{ (16,741 kPa)} > 2346 \text{ lb/in}^2 \text{ (16,176 kPa)}$$

$$f_V = 118.4 \times 1.216 = 144 \text{ lb/in}^2 \text{ (992.9 kPa)} < 178 \text{ lb/in}^2 \text{ (1227 kPa)}$$

$$\Delta_{TL} = 1.94 \times 1.216 = 2.36 \text{ in (5.99 cm)} > 2.0 \text{ in (5.08 cm)}$$

Therefore, member size must be increased to satisfy bending and deflection criteria. Note that an increase in I also will change the value of C_p.

Try a 5⅛- by 34½-in member with $S = 1016.7$ in^3, $I = 17{,}538$ in^4, and $C_p = 1.184$:

$$f_b = 1827 \times 1.184 = 2163 \text{ lb/in}^2 \text{ (14,914 kPa)} < F'_b$$

$$= 2339 \text{ lb/in}^2 \text{ (16,127 kPa)}$$

$$\Delta_{TL} = 2.36 \times \frac{15{,}350}{17{,}538} \times \frac{1.184}{1.216}$$

$$= 2.01 \text{ in (5.10 cm)} \simeq \frac{\ell}{240}$$

Thus, to provide for potential ponding, the member depth must be increased by one lamination, or 1½ in (3.81 cm). It is noted that the published tabular values for E are average values. Depending on the type of wood member, these values of E can have different degrees of variability. For example, typical values for the coefficient of variation in modulus of elasticity for three types of wood products are 0.25 for visually graded lumber, 0.11 for machine stress-rated lumber, and 0.10 for glued-laminated timbers consisting of six or more laminations.

Since the ponding analysis is very sensitive to the member stiffness, the designer may wish to use a value of E other than the average. The variation of E in wood approaches a normal statistical distribution for a given species or grade. Assuming that the designer wishes to calculate the fifth percentile value of E, it can be determined from the following equation:

$$E_{0.05} = E - 1.645EC_v \tag{4.48}$$

where E = average modulus of elasticity, lb/in^2
C_v = coefficient of variation
1.645 = a statistical constant for determining fifth percentile value of normal distribution

An example of the difference between the fifth percentile value of E and the average E for a given member is illustrated by the following example.

EXAMPLE 4.15: DETERMINATION OF THE FIFTH PERCENTILE VALUE OF MODULUS OF ELASTICITY $E_{0.05}$ Assume a glued-laminated timber beam has a published average E of 1,800,000 lb/in^2 (12,410 kPa). The coefficient of variation of E for this member is 0.10. Therefore, the value of E at the fifth percentile assuming a normal distribution is

$$\begin{aligned} E_{0.05} &= 1{,}800{,}000 - 1.645 \times 1{,}800{,}000 \times 0.10 \\ &= 1{,}504{,}000 \text{ lb/in}^2 \ (10{,}370 \text{ kPa}) \end{aligned}$$

Thus, in the case of this glulam beam, the use of the fifth percentile value of E instead of the average E value could have a significant effect on the ponding analysis. This effect of variability of E also can be an important design consideration in the analysis of single-member columns which carry heavy structural loads.

4.9 CONNECTION CONSIDERATIONS

The detailed structural analysis of a timber bending member is of little value unless the designer can develop appropriate connection details to transmit the loads from the beam to the supporting structure. In addition to understanding the various mechanical fasteners which can be used to connect wood members, wood has several unique characteristics with which the designer must be familiar to effectively develop beam connection details. Three of these characteristics which will be briefly discussed here are (1) shrinkage effects, (2) effects of notching, and (3) effects of exposure to the elements. The designer is referred to Chap. 5 for a complete discussion of mechanical fasteners and connectors as used in wood design. Chapter 13 provides a discussion of the use of adhesives related to timber connection design.

4.9.1 Shrinkage Effects

It is universally recognized that wood will undergo dimensional changes due to shrinkage and swelling of the wood fibers as they are subjected to moisture cycling. The designer is referred to Chap. 1 for a complete discussion of these effects. Of particular concern related to timber connection detailing are the dimensional changes which take place perpendicular to the grain of the member. These changes can result in a change in member cross section which can affect the overall building configuration depending on the type of connection detailing specified.

The effects of shrinkage also can result in structural concerns. If the connection detail used tends to restrain the natural dimensional changes of the member, cross-grain tension may result which can result in a horizontal shear type of failure. Several examples of this type of connection are illustrated in Chap. 5. In addition, shrinkage of the member also can cause seasoning checks. Typically, these seasoning checks are not considered to have an effect on the structural integrity of the beam. However, in extreme situations, these checks can progress until they become splits. If these splits develop along the neutral axis of the member near the end bearing, they can affect the structural capacity of the member, resulting in a cross-grain tension type of failure. The designer is referred to American Wood System Technical Notes EWS R465[11] and EWS R475[12] for further information on the effect of checking as it relates to structural integrity of wood members.

4.9.2 Effects of Notching

As previously discussed in Sec. 4.1.3, notching of wood bending members can have a serious effect on the structural integrity of the member. Examples of end-bearing conditions with various degrees of notching are shown in Fig. 4.1. In addition, Chap. 5 provides a discussion of various connection details which can result in a notch type of effect and which should be avoided by the designer. Lastly, the designer is cautioned to avoid the use of any connection detail which would result in a notch occurring in the highly stressed tension zone of a wood bending member. The paper "Strength and Stiffness Reduction of Large Notched Beams"[12] provides an excellent discussion of the effects of notching on a wood beam. American Wood Systems Technical Note EWS S560[13] provides some practical guidelines on drilling and notching of glulam beams.

4.9.3 Exposure to the Elements

Often overlooked by the designer is the effect that exposure to the elements or high ambient moisture conditions can have on an otherwise properly designed connection. If the connection detail specified is such that it tends to entrap moisture, the result may be the development of a condition conducive to the growth of decay fungi. Thus the designer is cautioned to avoid this type of detail. Chapter 5 contains several examples of proper details for members exposed to high potential moisture conditions which would help avoid this situation. In addition to properly detailing the connections associated with the design of members exposed to the elements, the designer is cautioned to specify proper pressure preservative treatment of these members as discussed in Chap. 2.

In addition, any structural element subjected to these high moisture content environments is also likely to undergo significant degrees of moisture cycling. As discussed in Sec. 4.9.1, these moisture changes can result in dimensional changes which must be accounted for in the connection design.

REFERENCES

1. *American Softwood Lumber Standard,* PS20-93, Voluntary Product Standard, U.S. Dept. of Commerce, Washington, D.C., 1970; amended 1993.
2. *Design Values for Wood Construction,* a supplement to the 1991 National Design Specification for Wood Construction, American Forest and Paper Association, Washington, D.C., 1991.
3. *National Design Specification for Wood Construction,* American Forest and Paper Association, Washington, D.C., 1991.
4. *Glulam Beam Camber,* Technical Note EWS S 550A, American Wood Systems, Tacoma, Wash., 1993.
5. *Wood Handbook, Wood as an Engineering Material,* Agricultural Handbook 76, Forest Service, U.S. Dept. of Agriculture, Washington, D.C., 1987.
6. *Uniform Building Code,* International Conference of Building Officials, Whittier, Calif., 1991.
7. A. C. Maki and E. W. Kuenzi, "Deflection and Stresses of Tapered Wood Beams," U.S. Forest Service Research Paper FPL 34, U.S.D.A., Forest Products Laboratory, U.S. Dept. of Agriculture, Madison, Wisc., 1965.
8. V. J. A. Gopu, J. R. Goodman, M. D. Vanderbilt, E. G. Thompson, and J. Bodig, "Behavior and Design of Double-Tapered Pitched and Curved Glulam Beams," Structural Research Rep. 16, Colorado State University, Ft. Collins, Colo., 1976.
9. *Standard for Radially Reinforcing Curved Glued Laminated Timber Members to Resist Radial Tension,* AITC 404-92, American Institute of Timber Construction, Englewood, Co., 1992.
10. *Checking in Glued Laminated Timber,* AWS Technical Note EWS R465, American Wood Systems, Tacoma, Wash., 1992.
11. *Evaluation of Check Size in Glued Laminated Timber Beams,* AWS Technical Note EWS R475, American Wood Systems, Tacoma, Wash., 1993.
12. J. F. Murphy, "Strength and Stiffness Reduction of Large Notched Beams," *J. Struct. Eng.* **112** (1986).
13. *Field Notching and Drilling of Glued Laminated Timber Beams,* AWS Technical Note EWS S560, American Wood Systems, Tacoma, Wash., 1993.

CHAPTER 5
MECHANICAL FASTENERS AND CONNECTORS

Keith F. Faherty, Ph.D., P.E.

5.1 INTRODUCTION

Fasteners and connectors for wood have been improved over the years, and reliable design standards have been developed. Joints can now be designed with the same accuracy as other parts of the structure. However, poor design or construction practices have often resulted in the connector controlling the strength or serviceability of a structural unit or system.

Many types of fasteners and connectors are available for use in attaching one structural unit to another. Some of these, such as nails, screws, lag screws, dowels, drift pins, drift bolts, and bolts, have been available for many years. Other types of fasteners and connectors available to the designer are special nails, staples, split rings, shear plates, spike grids, toothed sheet-steel plates, clamping plates, framing anchors, joist and purlin hangers, and many other types of special fasteners and connectors. Some of these are shown in Fig. 5.1.

Nails are generally used when loads are light. They are used for light-frame construction, diaphragms, and shear walls. Screws are not commonly used as fasteners in structural joints of wood. However, they are more satisfactory than nails under vibratory or withdrawal loads, since they have less tendency to work loose.

Lag screws, bolts, and timber connectors are used when loads of relatively large magnitude need to be transmitted through a joint. They are used in heavy-timber construction and in light-frame construction when large loads are anticipated.

Bolts are less efficient than split rings or shear plates; however, they are often adequate. Lag screws are used when bolts are undesirable, when the member is too thick, or when one face of the member is not accessible for the installation of washers and nuts. Lag screws also can be used in conjunction with split rings and shear plates. They also can be especially effective when withdrawal loads of large magnitude are anticipated.

Split rings and shear plates are used for joints in heavy timber construction. They also may be used for joint connections in wood trusses when spans are rel-

Note: All SI units shown for sawn lumber are for the actual net dimensions corresponding to the nominal dimension indicated. In all example problems, SI units are only provided for given data and the final problem answer or answers. No intermediate values or data are expressed in SI units.

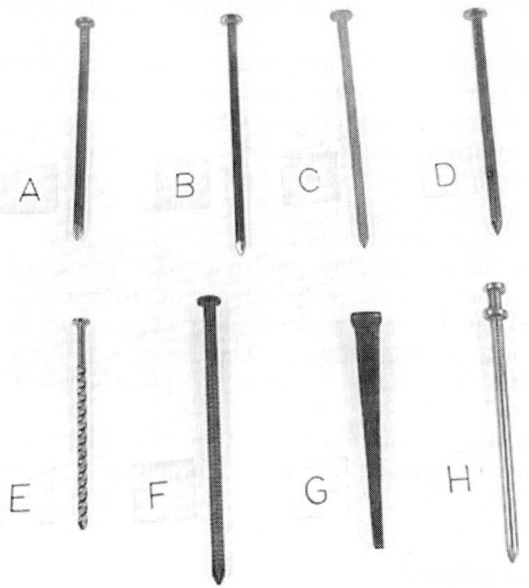

FIG. 5.2 Nails: (*A*) common wire nail; (*B*) box nail; (*C*) zinc-coated; (*D*) cement-coated; (*E*) helically threaded; (*F*) annularly threaded; (*G*) cut nail; (*H*) double-headed construction nail.

TABLE 5.1 Nail and Spike Sizes

		Wire diameter, in			
Penny-weight	Length, in	Box nails	Common wire nails	Threaded hardened-steel nails	Common wire spikes
6d	2	0.099	0.113	0.120	—
8d	2½	0.113	0.131	0.120	—
10d	3	0.128	0.148	0.135	0.192
12d	3¼	0.128	0.148	0.135	0.192
16d	3½	0.135	0.162	0.148	0.207
20d	4	0.148	0.192	0.177	0.225
30d	4½	0.148	0.207	0.177	0.244
40d	5	0.162	0.225	0.177	0.263
50d	5½	—	0.244	0.177	0.283
60d	6	—	0.263	0.177	0.283
70d	7	—	—	0.207	—
80d	8	—	—	0.207	—
90d	9	—	—	0.207	—
5⁄16 in	7	—	—	—	0.312
3⁄8 in	8½	—	—	—	0.375

Note: 1 in = 25.4 mm.

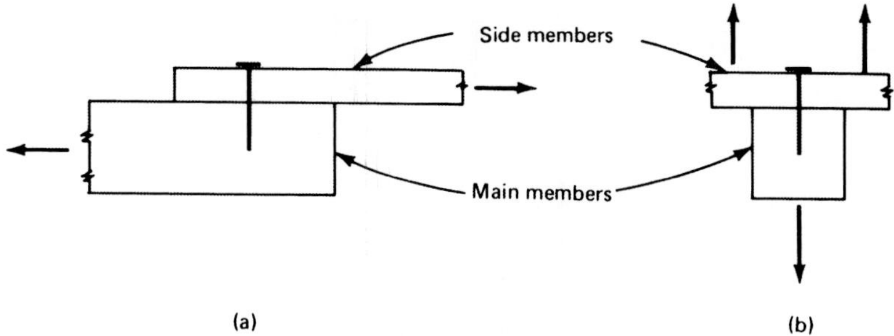

FIG. 5.3 Type of loading on nails. (*a*) Lateral loading; (*b*) withdrawal loading.

4. End-grain withdrawal (nails driven into wood parallel with the fibers) is not generally recommended. If used, design should be based on supporting research data.

Design Values. The design values given in Tables 5.3, 5.4*a*, 5.4*b*, 5.5*a*, and 5.5*b* are for common steel wire nails and spikes, box nails, and threaded hardened-steel nails which meet the minimum size given in Table 5.1 before the application of any protective finish or coating. Threaded, hardened-steel nails and spikes are to

TABLE 5.2 Specific Gravity of Some Commonly Used Wood Species

Species of wood	Specific gravity G
Aspen	0.39
Coast sitka spruce	0.39
Douglas fir–larch	0.50
Douglas fir–larch (north)	0.49
Douglas fir–south	0.46
Eastern hemlock	0.41
Eastern softwoods	0.36
Eastern spruce	0.41
Hem-fir	0.43
Hem-fir (north)	0.46
Mixed southern pine	0.51
Mountain hemlock	0.47
Ponderosa pine	0.43
Redwood, close grain	0.44
Redwood, open grain	0.37
Sitka spruce	0.43
Southern pine	0.55
Spruce-pine-fir	0.42
Spruce-pine-fir (south)	0.36
Western hemlock	0.47
Western hemlock (north)	0.46
Western white pine	0.40

TABLE 5.3 Nail and Spike Withdrawal Design Values (W)*

Tabulated withdrawal design values (W) are in pounds per inch of penetration into side grain of main member.

Specific gravity G	Common wire nails, box nails and common wire spikes, diameter D, in															Threaded nails, wire diameter D, in				
	0.099	0.113	0.128	0.131	0.135	0.148	0.162	0.192	0.207	0.225	0.244	0.263	0.283	0.312	0.375	0.12	0.135	0.148	0.177	0.207
0.55	31	35	40	41	42	46	50	59	64	70	76	81	88	97	116	41	46	50	59	70
0.50	24	28	31	32	33	36	40	47	50	55	60	64	69	76	91	32	36	40	47	55
0.43	17	19	21	22	23	25	27	32	35	38	41	44	47	52	63	22	25	27	32	38
0.42	16	18	20	21	21	23	26	30	33	35	38	41	45	49	59	21	23	26	30	35

*Tabulated withdrawal design values W for nail or spike connections shall be multiplied by all applicable adjustment factors.

Note: 1 in = 25.4 mm; 1 lb = 4.45 N.

Source: This table provided courtesy of American Forest and Paper Association, Washington, D.C.

TABLE 5.4*a* Common Wire Nail Design Values (Z) for Single-Shear* *(Two-Member) Connections with Both Members of Identical Species*

Side member thickness t_s, in	Nail length L, in	Nail Diameter D, in	Penny weight	$G = 0.55$ Southern pine, Z, lb	$G = 0.50$ Douglas fir–larch, Z, lb	$G = 0.43$ Hem-fir, Z, lb	$G = 0.42$ Spruce-pine-fir, Z, lb
½	2	0.113	6d	67	59	49	47
	2½	0.131	8d	85	76	63	61
	3	0.148	10d	101	90	75	73
	3¼	0.148	12d	101	90	75	73
	3½	0.162	16d	117	105	89	87
	4	0.192	20d	137	124	105	103
	4½	0.207	30d	148	134	115	112
	5	0.225	40d	162	147	126	123
	5½	0.244	50d	166	151	130	127
	6	0.263	60d	188	171	147	144
⅝	2	0.113	6d	76	66	53	52
	2½	0.131	8d	94	82	67	65
	3	0.148	10d	110	97	80	77
	3¼	0.148	12d	110	97	80	77
	3½	0.162	16d	126	112	93	90
	4	0.192	20d	146	130	109	106
	4½	0.207	30d	156	140	118	115
	5	0.225	40d	169	151	128	125
	5½	0.244	50d	173	155	132	129
	6	0.263	60d	194	175	149	145
¾	2½	0.131	8d	104	90	73	70
	3	0.148	10d	121	105	85	83
	3¼	0.148	12d	121	105	85	83
	3½	0.162	16d	138	121	99	96
	4	0.192	20d	157	138	114	111
	4½	0.207	30d	166	147	122	119
	5	0.225	40d	178	158	132	129
	5½	0.244	50d	182	162	136	132
	6	0.263	60d	203	181	152	149
1	3	0.148	10d	128	118	99	96
	3¼	0.148	12d	128	118	99	96
	3½	0.162	16d	154	141	113	109
	4	0.192	20d	183	159	128	124
	4½	0.207	30d	192	167	135	131
	5	0.225	40d	202	177	144	140
	5½	0.244	50d	207	181	148	143
	6	0.263	60d	227	199	164	159
1¼	3¼	0.148	12d	128	118	102	100
	3½	0.162	16d	154	141	122	120
	4	0.192	20d	185	170	145	140
	4½	0.207	30d	203	186	152	147
	5	0.225	40d	224	200	160	155
	5½	0.244	50d	230	204	163	158
	6	0.263	60d	256	222	179	174

TABLE 5.4*a* Common Wire Nail Design Values (*Z*) for Single-Shear* *(Continued)* *(Two-Member) Connections with Both Members of Identical Species*

Side member thickness t_s, in	Nail length *L*, in	Nail Diameter *D*, in	Penny weight	*G* = 0.55 Southern pine, *Z*, lb	*G* = 0.50 Douglas fir–larch, *Z*, lb	*G* = 0.43 Hem-fir, *Z*, lb	*G* = 0.42 Spruce-pine-fir, *Z*, lb
1½	3½	0.162	16d	154	141	122	120
	4	0.192	20d	185	170	147	144
	4½	0.207	30d	203	186	161	158
	5	0.225	40d	224	205	178	172
	5½	0.244	50d	230	211	181	175
	6	0.263	60D	262	240	197	191

Note: 1 in = 25.4 mm; 1 lb. = 4.45 N.

*Tabulated lateral design values (*Z*) for nailed connections shall be multiplied by all applicable adjustment factors. Tabulated lateral design values (*Z*) are for common wire nails inserted in side grain with nail axis perpendicular to wood fibers, and with the following nail bending yield strengths (F_{yb}):

F_{yb} = 100,000 psi for 0.113 and 0.131 in diameter common wire nails

F_{yb} = 90,000 psi for 0.148 and 0.162 in diameter common wire nails

F_{yb} = 80,000 psi for 0.192, 0.207, and 0.225 in diameter common wire nails

F_{yb} = 70,000 psi for 0.244 and 0.263 in diameter common wire nails

Source: This table provided courtesy of American Forest and Paper Association, Washington, D.C.

be made of high-carbon steel wire, headed, pointed, annularly or helically threaded, and heat-treated and tempered to provide greater strength than is developed by common wire nails of corresponding size.

When more than one nail or spike is used in a joint, the total design value for the joint in withdrawal or lateral resistance is the sum of the design values for the individual nails or spikes.

When using a prebored hole having a diameter not exceeding nine-tenths that of the nail or spike for wood with a specific gravity greater than 0.6 or three-fourths for wood with a specific gravity of 0.6 or less, the design values for the same-size fastener, without a prebored hole, apply in withdrawal and lateral resistance.

Prebored Holes. The design values given in Tables 5.3 or 5.4 apply either with or without predrilling holes in the wood. When a predrilled hole is desired to prevent splitting of wood, the diameter of the hole drilled should not exceed the values given below:

Specific gravity *G*	Percent of nail or spike diameter
$G > 0.6$	90
$G \leq 0.6$	75

Table 5.2 provides specific gravity values for commonly used wood species.

TABLE 5.4*b* Common Wire Spike Design Values (Z) for Single-Shear* (Two-Member) Connections with Both Members of Identical Species

Side member thickness t_s, in	Spike length L, in	Spike Diameter D, in	Penny weight	$G = 0.55$ Southern pine, Z, lb	$G = 0.50$ Douglas fir–larch, Z, lb	$G = 0.43$ Hem-fir, Z, lb	$G = 0.42$ Spruce-pine-fir, Z, lb
½	3	0.192	10d	137	124	105	103
	3¼	0.192	12d	137	124	105	103
	3½	0.207	16d	148	134	115	112
	4	0.225	20d	162	147	126	123
	4½	0.244	30d	166	151	130	127
	5	0.263	40d	188	171	147	144
	5½	0.283	50d	201	183	158	155
	6	0.283	60d	201	183	158	155
⅝	3	0.192	10d	146	130	109	106
	3¼	0.192	12d	146	130	109	106
	3½	0.207	16d	156	140	118	115
	4	0.225	20d	169	151	128	125
	4½	0.244	30d	173	155	132	129
	5	0.263	40d	194	175	149	145
	5½	0.283	50d	208	187	160	156
	6	0.283	60d	208	187	160	156
¾	3¼	0.192	12d	157	138	114	111
	3½	0.207	16d	166	147	122	119
	4	0.225	20d	178	158	132	129
	4½	0.244	30d	182	162	136	132
	5	0.263	40d	203	181	152	149
	5½	0.283	50d	217	194	163	159
	6	0.283	60d	217	194	163	159
	7	0.312	5/16	257	231	196	191
	8½	0.375	⅜	319	287	244	238
1	3½	0.207	16d	192	167	135	131
	4	0.225	20d	202	177	144	140
	4½	0.244	30d	207	181	148	143
	5	0.263	40d	227	199	164	159
	5½	0.283	50d	243	214	176	171
	6	0.283	60d	243	214	176	171
	7	0.312	5/16	283	250	207	202
	8½	0.375	⅜	348	309	257	250
1¼	4	0.225	20d	224	200	160	155
	4½	0.244	30d	230	204	163	158
	5	0.263	40d	256	222	179	174
	5½	0.283	50d	275	239	193	186
	6	0.283	60d	275	239	193	186
	7	0.312	5/16	316	276	224	217
	8½	0.375	⅜	386	338	276	268
1½	4½	0.244	30d	230	211	181	175
	5	0.263	40d	262	240	197	191
	5½	0.283	50d	281	257	212	205
	6	0.283	60d	281	257	212	205
	7	0.312	5/16	342	305	244	236
	8½	0.375	⅜	428	373	299	290

TABLE 5.4*b* Common Wire Spike Design Values (*Z*) for Single-Shear* (Two-Member) Connections with Both Members of Identical Species *(Continued)*

Side member thickness t_s, in	Spike length *L*, in	Spike Diameter *D*, in	Penny weight	*G* = 0.55 Southern pine, *Z*, lb	*G* = 0.50 Douglas fir–larch, *Z*, lb	*G* = 0.43 Hem-fir, *Z*, lb	*G* = 0.42 Spruce-pine-fir, *Z*, lb
2½	6	0.283	60d	281	257	223	219
	7	0.312	5⁄16	342	313	271	266
	8½	0.375	3⁄8	428	391	340	332
3½	8½	0.375	3⁄8	428	391	340	332

Note: 1 in = 25.4 mm; 1 lb. = 4.45 N.

*Tabulated lateral design values (*Z*) for spike connections shall be multiplied by all applicable adjustment factors. Tabulated lateral design values (*Z*) are for common wire spikes inserted in side grain with spike axis perpendicular to wood fibers, and with the following spike bending yield strengths (F_{yb}):
F_{yb} = 80,000 psi for 0.192, 0.207, and 0.225 in diameter common wire spikes
F_{yb} = 70,000 psi for 0.244 and 0.263 in diameter common wire spikes
F_{yb} = 60,000 psi for 0.283 and 5⁄16 in diameter common wire spikes
F_{yb} = 45,000 psi for 3⁄8 in diameter common wire spikes

Source: This table provided courtesy of American Forest and Paper Association, Washington, D.C.

Placement. It has often been the practice in the past to let the placement of nails be determined on the job. However, in present-day design, this may not be satisfactory. While some guidance is available on the placement of nails in wood, the recommendations are not consistent. The following recommendations have been obtained from the literature:†

1. *Wood Handbook*[1]

End distance* = 15d

End distance = 12d

Edge distance = 10d

2. *Uniform Building Code*[2]

End distance* = one-half required penetration of nail

Edge distance* = one-half required penetration of nail

Spacing in row* = required penetration of nail

3. *Timber Design and Construction Handbook.*[3] Softwoods:

End distance = one-half nail length

Edge distance = one-fourth nail length

Spacing = one-half nail length

†*Note:* d = diameter of nail and * refers to distance in direction of stress.

TABLE 5.5a Common Wire Nail Design Values (Z) for Single-Shear* (Two-Member) Connections with ASTM A446, Grade A Steel Side Plate

Steel side plate	Nail length L, in	Nail diameter D, in	Penny weight	$G = 0.55$ Southern pine, Z, lb	$G = 0.50$ Douglas fir–larch, Z, lb	$G = 0.43$ Hem-fir, Z, lb	$G = 0.42$ Spruce-pine-fir, Z, lb
3 gauge	5½	0.244	50d	263	245	218	214
$t_s = 0.239$ in	6	0.263	60d	291	271	241	237
7 gauge	4	0.192	20d	203	189	168	165
$t_s = 0.179$ in	4½	0.207	30d	217	202	179	176
	5	0.225	40d	234	217	193	189
	5½	0.244	50d	240	223	198	194
	6	0.263	60d	268	249	221	217
10 gauge	2	0.113	6d	90	84	75	74
$t_s = 0.134$ in	2½	0.131	8d	115	107	95	94
	3	0.148	10d	137	127	113	111
	3¼	0.148	12d	137	127	113	111
	3½	0.162	16d	160	149	132	129
	4	0.192	20d	188	174	155	152
	4½	0.207	30d	203	188	167	163
	5	0.225	40d	221	205	181	178
	5½	0.244	50d	227	210	186	183
	6	0.263	60d	256	237	210	206
11 gauge	2	0.113	6d	87	81	72	71
$t_s = 0.12$ in	2½	0.131	8d	112	104	92	90
	3	0.148	10d	133	123	109	107
	3¼	0.148	12d	133	123	109	107
	3½	0.162	16d	156	145	128	126
	4	0.192	20d	184	171	151	148
	4½	0.207	30d	199	185	163	160
	5	0.225	40d	218	202	178	175
	5½	0.244	50d	224	207	183	180
	6	0.263	60d	253	234	207	203
12 gauge	2	0.113	6d	83	78	69	68
$t_s = 0.105$ in	2½	0.131	8d	108	100	89	87
	3	0.148	10d	129	120	106	104
	3¼	0.148	12d	129	120	106	104
	3½	0.162	16d	152	141	125	123
	4	0.192	20d	181	168	148	145
	4½	0.207	30d	196	182	161	158
	5	0.225	40d	215	199	176	173
	5½	0.244	50d	221	205	181	177
	6	0.263	60d	251	232	205	201
14 gauge	2	0.113	6d	78	72	64	63
$t_s = 0.075$ in	2½	0.131	8d	103	95	84	83
	3	0.148	10d	124	115	101	99
	3¼	0.148	12d	124	115	101	99
	3½	0.162	16d	147	136	120	118
	4	0.192	20d	176	163	144	141
	4½	0.207	30d	192	178	157	154

TABLE 5.5*a* Common Wire Nail Design Values (*Z*) for Single-Shear* (Two-Member) Connections with ASTM A446, Grade A Steel Side Plate *(Continued)*

Steel side plate	Nail length L, in	Nail diameter D, in	Penny weight	$G = 0.55$ Southern pine, Z, lb	$G = 0.50$ Douglas fir–larch, Z, lb	$G = 0.43$ Hem-fir, Z, lb	$G = 0.42$ Spruce-pine-fir, Z, lb
14 gauge	5	0.225	40d	212	196	172	169
$t_s = 0.075$ in	5½	0.244	50d	218	202	177	174
	6	0.263	60d	248	229	201	198
16 gauge	2	0.113	6d	76	70	62	61
$t_s = 0.06$ in	2½	0.131	8d	101	94	83	81
	3	0.148	10d	122	113	100	98
	3¼	0.148	12d	122	113	100	98
	3½	0.162	16d	146	135	119	116
	4	0.192	20d	175	162	142	140
	4½	0.207	30d	191	177	156	153
18 gauge	2	0.113	6d	75	69	61	60
$t_s = 0.048$ in	2½	0.131	8d	100	93	82	80
	3	0.148	10d	121	112	99	97
	3¼	0.148	12d	121	112	99	97
	3½	0.162	16d	145	134	118	116
20 gauge	2	0.113	6d	75	69	61	59
$t_s = 0.036$ in	2½	0.131	8d	100	92	81	80
	3	0.148	10d	121	112	98	96

Note: 1 in = 25.4 mm; 1 lb. = 4.45 N.

*Tabulated lateral design values (*Z*) for nailed connections shall be multiplied by all applicable adjustment factors. Tabulated lateral design values (*Z*) are for common wire nails inserted in side grain with nail axis perpendicular to wood fibers, and with the following nail bending yield strengths (F_{yb}):

F_{yb} = 100,000 psi for 0.113 and 0.131 in diameter common wire nails, F_{yb} = 80,000 psi for 0.192, 0.207, and 0.225 in diameter common wire nails.

F_{yb} = 90,000 psi for 0.148 and 0.162 in diameter common wire nails, F_{yb} = 70,000 psi for 0.244 and 0.263 in diameter common wire nails.

Tabulated lateral design values (*Z*) are based on a dowel bearing strength F_e of 45,000 psi for ASTM A446, Grade A steel.

Source: This table provided courtesy of American Forest and Paper Association, Washington, D.C.

4. *Wood Technology in the Design of Structures*[4]
Without prebored holes:

$$\text{End distance} = 20d$$

$$\text{Edge distance} = 5d$$

$$\text{Perpendicular-to-grain spacing} = 10d$$

$$\text{Parallel-to-grain spacing} = 20d$$

With prebored holes:

$$\text{End distance} = 10d$$

$$\text{Edge distance} = 5d$$

TABLE 5.5*b* Common Wire Spike Design Values (Z) for Single-Shear* (Two-Member) Connections with ASTM A446, Grade A Steel Side Plate

Steel side plate	Spike length L, in	Spike diameter D, in	Penny weight	$G = 0.55$ Southern pine, Z, lb	$G = 0.50$ Douglas fir–larch, Z, lb	$G = 0.43$ Hem-fir, Z, lb	$G = 0.42$ Spruce-pine-fir, Z, lb
3 gauge $t_s = 0.239$ in	4½	0.244	30d	263	245	218	214
	5	0.263	40d	291	271	241	237
	5½	0.283	50d	312	291	259	254
	6	0.283	60d	312	291	259	254
	7	0.312	5⁄16	367	342	304	298
	8½	0.375	3⁄8	454	423	375	368
7 gauge $t_s = 0.179$ in	3	0.192	10d	203	189	168	165
	3¼	0.192	12d	203	189	168	165
	3½	0.207	16d	217	202	179	176
	4	0.225	20d	234	217	193	189
	4½	0.244	30d	240	223	198	194
	5	0.263	40d	268	249	221	217
	5½	0.283	50d	288	267	237	233
	6	0.283	60d	288	267	237	233
	7	0.312	5⁄16	343	318	282	277
	8½	0.375	3⁄8	426	395	350	344
10 gauge $t_s = 0.134$ in	3	0.192	10d	188	174	155	152
	3¼	0.192	12d	188	174	155	152
	3½	0.207	16d	203	188	167	163
	4	0.225	20d	221	205	181	178
	4½	0.244	30d	227	210	186	183
	5	0.263	40d	256	237	210	206
	5½	0.283	50d	274	254	225	221
	6	0.283	60d	274	254	225	221
	7	0.312	5⁄16	330	306	270	265
	8½	0.375	3⁄8	411	381	337	330
11 gauge $t_s = 0.12$ in	3	0.192	10d	184	171	151	148
	3¼	0.192	12d	184	171	151	148
	3½	0.207	16d	199	185	163	160
	4	0.225	20d	218	202	178	175
	4½	0.244	30d	224	207	183	180
	5	0.263	40d	253	234	207	203
	5½	0.283	50d	271	251	222	218
	6	0.283	60d	271	251	222	218
	7	0.312	5⁄16	327	303	267	262
	8½	0.375	3⁄8	408	378	334	327
12 gauge $t_s = 0.105$ in	3	0.192	10d	181	168	148	145
	3¼	0.192	12d	181	168	148	145
	3½	0.207	16d	196	182	161	158
	4	0.225	20d	215	199	176	173
	4½	0.244	30d	221	205	181	177
	5	0.263	40d	251	232	205	201
	5½	0.283	50d	269	249	219	215
	6	0.283	60d	269	249	219	215
	7	0.312	5⁄16	325	301	265	260
	8½	0.375	3⁄8	406	376	331	324

TABLE 5.5*b* Common Wire Spike Design Values (Z) for Single-Shear* (Two-Member) Connections with ASTM A446, Grade A Steel Side Plate *(Continued)*

Steel side plate	Spike length L, in	Spike diameter D, in	Penny weight	$G = 0.55$ Southern pine, Z, lb	$G = 0.50$ Douglas fir–larch, Z, lb	$G = 0.43$ Hem-fir, Z, lb	$G = 0.42$ Spruce-pine-fir, Z, lb
14 gauge	3	0.192	10d	176	163	144	141
$t_s = 0.075$ in	3¼	0.192	12d	176	163	144	141
	3½	0.207	16d	192	178	157	154
	4	0.225	20d	212	196	172	169
	4½	0.244	30d	218	202	177	174
	5	0.263	40d	248	229	201	198
	5½	0.283	50d	266	246	216	212
	6	0.283	60d	266	246	216	212
	7	0.312	5⁄16	323	298	262	257
	8½	0.375	⅜	404	373	328	321
16 gauge	3	0.192	10d	175	162	142	140
$t_s = 0.06$ in	3¼	0.192	12d	175	162	142	140
	3½	0.207	16d	191	177	156	153

Note: 1 in = 25.4 mm; 1 lb. = 4.45 N.

*Tabulated lateral design values (Z) for spike connections shall be multiplied by all applicable adjustment factors. Tabulated lateral design values (Z) are for common wire spikes inserted in side grain with spike axis perpendicular to wood fibers, and with the following nail bending yield strengths (F_{yb}):

F_{yb} = 80,000 psi for 0.192, 0.207, and 0.225 in diameter common wire spikes
F_{yb} = 70,000 psi for 0.244 and 0.263 in diameter common wire spikes
F_{yb} = 60,000 psi for 0.283 and 5⁄16 in diameter common wire spikes
F_{yb} = 45,000 psi for ⅜ in diameter common wire spikes

Tabulated lateral design values (Z) are based on a dowel bearing strength F_e of 45,000 psi for ASTM A446, Grade A steel.

Source: This table provided courtesy of American Forest and Paper Association, Washington, D.C.

$$\text{Perpendicular-to-grain spacing} = 3d$$

$$\text{Parallel-to-grain spacing} = 10d$$

The recommended values for nail placement as given in the four references listed above show considerable variation. For example, the recommended values for end distance can vary from approximately 5*d* to 20*d*. Minimum spacing as well as end and edge distances are necessary to prevent the wood from splitting as the nail is driven in. The density, moisture content, straight grain versus interlocking grain, and the tangential versus radial grain orientation of the wood and the diameter of the shank and type of point of the nail all have an effect on the splitting of the wood as the nails are driven in.

5.2.2 Withdrawal Resistance

Predesign. Withdrawal loading results from a force or force component which is applied parallel to the axis of the nail, as shown in Fig. 5.3*b*. If possible, nails and spikes should be laterally loaded and withdrawal loading avoided.

The withdrawal resistance of nail or spike shanks is greatly affected by such factors as the type of nail point, type of shank, surface coatings, length of time nail remains in the wood, and changes in moisture content of the wood. The equation used by the *National Design Specification*[5] (NDS) to obtain allowable design values is

$$P = 1380G^{5/2}D \tag{5.1}$$

where P = allowable design value per inch of penetration in member holding point of nail
G = specific gravity of wood
D = diameter of nail, in

Equation (5.1) provides allowable values for normal duration of load which are somewhat less than one-sixth the ultimate value for short-term loading. Values obtained by NDS[5] using Eq. (5.1) are given in Table 5.3.

Table 5.3 gives design values per inch of penetration of the nail. The table values are for

1. Nails driven into wood without splitting
2. Seasoned wood which remains dry, or unseasoned wood which remains wet
3. Normal load duration
4. Nails driven into the side grain
5. Normal temperature

Common wire nails or spikes are not to be loaded in withdrawal from the end grain of wood.

If the conditions assumed in Table 5.2 are not satisfied in a joint under consideration, then adjustments need to be made. The conditions which need to be considered are

1. Load duration
2. Moisture condition in service
3. Fire-retardant treatment
4. Wood temperature

The duration-of-load adjustment is the same as that which applies to allowable design stresses and is given in Table 4.3. The moisture condition adjustments are given in Table 5.30*a*. If the wood is treated with a fire-retardant chemical, it may be necessary to reduce the allowable design values of Table 5.3 by as much as 25 percent or in accordance with recommendations of the manufacturer of the treatment. Temperature adjustments are given in Table 5.33.

EXAMPLE 5.1: WITHDRAWAL LOADING OF NAILS. Four 20d common wire nails are driven into a wood beam of Douglas fir (Fig. 5.4). The wood is unseasoned but will season with use. Determine the allowable withdrawal dead load.

SOLUTION: Specific gravity of wood = 0.50 (see Table 5.2).
Length of nail = 4 in (see Table 5.1).
Penetration of nail = 4 − 0.5 = 3.5 in.
Load-duration factor, C_D = 0.9 (see Sec.2.3).

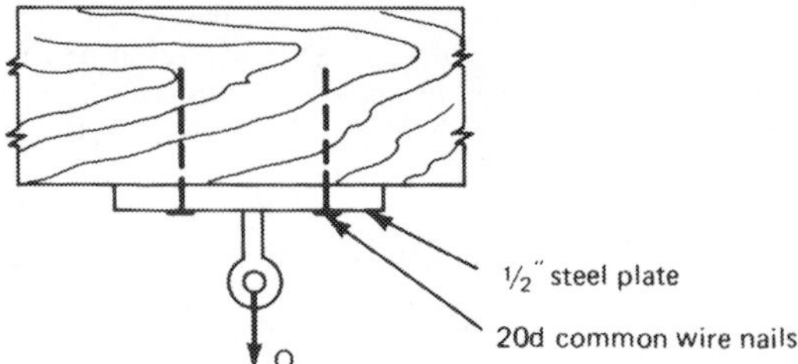

FIG. 5.4 Example 5.1.

Condition-of-use factor, $C_M = 0.25$ (see Table 5.30*a*).
Allowable load per inch of nail penetration: $q = 40$ lb (see Table 5.2)

$$Q \text{ (allowable)} = q \times \text{penetration} \times C_D \times C_M \times \text{number of nails}$$

$$Q \text{ (allowable)} = 47 \times 3.5 \times 0.9 \times 0.25 \times 4 = \underline{148 \text{ lb}} \text{ (0.658 kN)}$$

5.2.3 Lateral Resistance

Predesign. Lateral loading results from a force or force component which is applied perpendicular to the axis of the nail or spike as shown in Fig. 5.3*a*. A typical load-slip curve for an 8d nail is shown in Fig. 5.5.

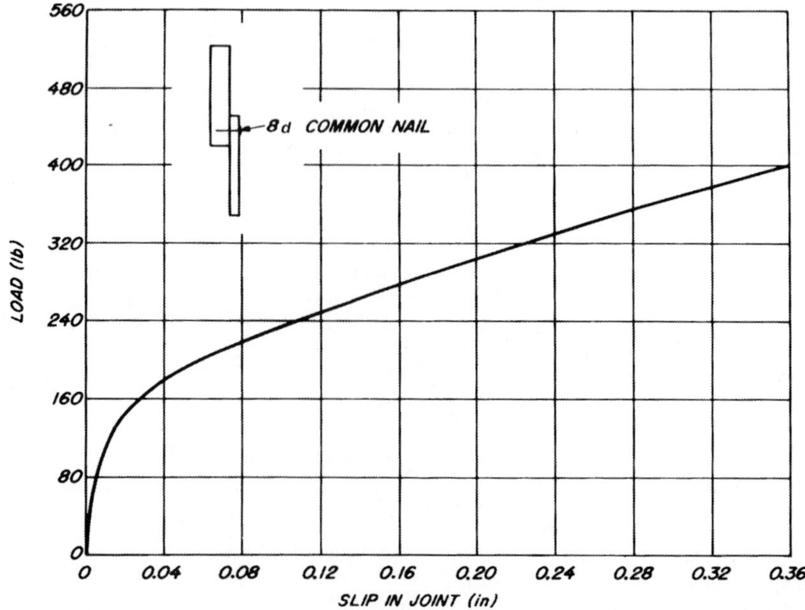

FIG. 5.5 Typical relation between load and slip in joint.

5.2.3 Lateral Resistance

The ultimate lateral load capacity of a nail or spike in single shear (two members) will be dependent on several material and dimensional properties of the connection. These include the thicknesses of the two joined members, the crushing strength of the wood, and the diameter and yield strength of the nail or spike.

The European yield model (EYM) theory provides four possible failure modes for a two-member connection in single shear. The model assumes that the bearing capacity is reached when either the wood crushes under the nail or spike or one or two plastic hinges are formed in the nail or spike. Shown below are the four yield modes and the equations which provide the allowable lateral load value for each of the yield modes. The controlling value for a particular joint is the lowest value obtained from the four equations.

Nominal nail or spike lateral design value Z shall be lesser of

	Yield mode
$Z = \dfrac{Dt_sF_{es}}{K_D}$	Mode I_s
$Z = \dfrac{k_1DpF_{em}}{K_D(1 + 2R_e)}$	Mode III_m
$Z = \dfrac{k_2Dt_sF_{em}}{K_D(2 + R_e)}$	Mode III_s
$Z = \dfrac{D^2}{K_D}\sqrt{\dfrac{2F_{em}F_{yb}}{3(1 + R_e)}}$	Mode IV

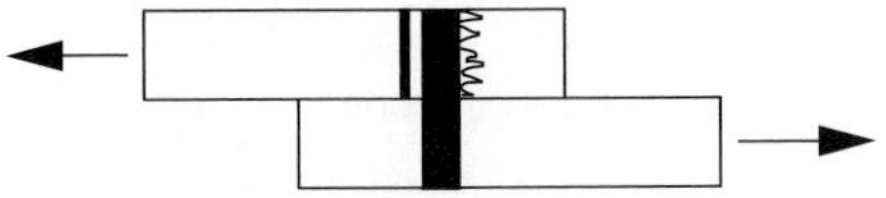

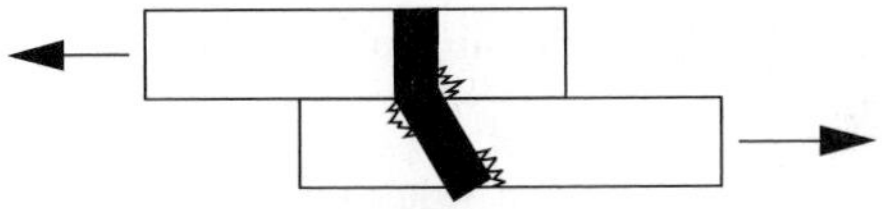

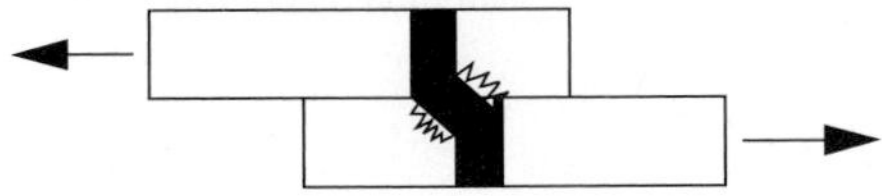

where $k_1 = -1 + \sqrt{2(1 + R_e) + \dfrac{2F_{yb}(1 + 2R_e)D^2}{3F_{em}t_s^2}}$

$$k_2 = -1 + \sqrt{\frac{2(1 + R_e)}{R_e} + \frac{2F_{yb}(1 + 2R_e)D^2}{3F_{em}t_s^2}}$$

$R_e = F_{em}/F_{es}$

p = penetration, main member, in

t_s = thickness side member, in

F_{em} = dowel bearing strength, main member, lb/in^2 (Table 5.34)

F_{es} = dowel bearing strength, side member, lb/in^2 (Table 5.34)

D = nail or spike diameter, in (use root diameter for threaded nails)

K_D = 2.2 for $D \leq 0.17$ in, $K_D = 10D + 0.5$ for $0.17 \text{ in} < D < 0.25$ in, $K_D = 3.0$ for $D \geq 0.25$ in

Lateral design values have been obtained using the yield model equations by NDS[5]

and are given in Tables 5.4*a*, 5.4*b*, 5.5*a*, and 5.5*b*. These tables provide values for box nails, common wire nails and spikes, and hardened steel nails.

If a connection does not qualify under the geometry and material properties given in Tables 5.4*a*, 5.4*b*, 5.5*a* and 5.5*b* then the four yield model equations may be used to obtain a lateral design value *Z*. Table 5.34 in the Appendix may be used to obtain the dowel bearing strengths, F_{em} and F_{es} needed in solving these equations. These equations have a built-in factor of safety of about 3½ for softwoods; however, the deflection as shown in Fig. 5.5 at ultimate load is about 20 times the proportional limit value which is about at the design value.

The load-carrying capacity of most fastenings is affected considerably by the large variations in the properties of wood along and across the wood grain. However, the lateral load values for nails are approximately the same regardless of the direction of bearing on the side grain of the wood.[6] Yet there is some indication that for the larger-diameter spikes, the parallel and perpendicular to grain proportional-limit values may not be the same.[7]

Tables 5.4*a*, 5.4*b*, 5.5*a* and 5.5*b* give design values of lateral loads for nails or spikes. The values are for

1. Nails driven into wood without splitting
2. Seasoned wood which remains dry in service
3. Normal load duration
4. A nail or spike in single shear
5. Full penetration
6. Nail inserted in side grain
7. Normal temperature
8. Wood or steel side plates

If the conditions assumed in Table 5.3 are not satisfied in a joint under consideration, then adjustments need to be made. The conditions which need to be considered are

1. Load duration C_D
2. Moisture condition at time of fabrication and in service C_M
3. Double shear
4. Length of penetration C_d
5. End-grain lateral loading C_{eg}
6. Fire-retardant treatment
7. Temperature in service C_t
8. Diaphragm factor C_{di}
9. Toe-nail C_{tn} (see Sec. 5.24)

The adjustments recommended for load duration, moisture condition in service, and temperature given in Tables 4.3, 5.30*a*, and 5.33 respectively. See manufacturers recommendations on adjustment for fire-retardant treatments.

Double Shear. Lateral design values Z for nails or spikes in double shear (three-member joints) in wood-to-wood connections are 2 times the least value of Z determined for each shear plane provided $t_m > 6D$, where t_m is the thickness of main (center) member, and D is the shank diameter of nail. In addition, the penetration depth factor is applied based on the penetration of the nail in the member containing the point of the nail, except that $C_d = 1.0$ for nails not exceeding 12d size when the nail extends at least 3 diameters beyond the side member and is clinched and the side members are at least ⅜ in thick.

Length of Penetration. The design values given in Tables 5.4*a*, 5.4*b*, 5.5*a*, and 5.5*b* apply only where the depth of penetration of the nail or spike into the member holding the point is 12 times the nail or spike diameter, $p = 12D$. When penetration is less than specified, the design value may be determined by using the equation $C_d = p/12D \leq 1.0$, except that the minimum penetration permit p is $6D$.

Lateral Resistance in End Grain. The design value in lateral resistance for a nail or spike into the end grain (parallel to wood fibers) is only two-thirds ($C_{eg} = 0.67$) of the design value given for lateral load when the nail or spike is driven into the side grain.

Diaphragm and Shearwalls. Nails and spikes used in diaphragm and shearwall construction may be increased 10 percent, $C_{di} = 1.1$. Other appropriate adjustments also should be applied.

Variation in Specific Gravities of Joined Members. When the connected members are sawed lumber of different species groups, an appropriate design value Z can be calculated using the four yield model equations given above. Separate dowel bearing strengths are to be used for the main and side members.

EXAMPLE 5.2: LATERAL LOAD ON NAIL Determine the number and size of common wire nail needed to transfer a 900-lb (4.00-kN) (dead load plus snow load) load from the diagonal to the vertical (Fig. 5.6). Wood is seasoned Douglas fir which will remain dry.

SOLUTION: Try 16d spikes = 3.5 in, $D = 0.162$ in (Table 5.1).

Penetration needed to use full lateral load design value = $12D = 1.94$. Actual penetration = $3.50 - 1.50 = 2.00$ in.

$$P \text{ (allowable)} = 154 \text{ lb} \qquad \text{(see Table 5.4}a\text{)}$$

$$P \text{ (adjusted)} = 154 \times C_D \times C_M \times C_d \times C_t$$

$$C_d = \frac{2.00}{1.94} = 1.03 > 1.0 \text{ use } C_d = 1.0$$

$$P \text{ (adjusted)} = 141 \times 1.15 \times 1.0 \times 1.0 \times 1.0 = 177 \text{ lb}$$

Number of spikes required = $900/1.77 = 5.1$.

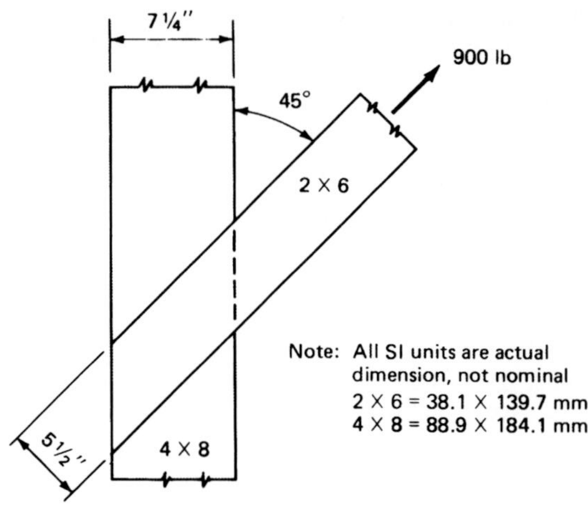

FIG. 5.6 Example 5.2.

ANSWER: Use six 16d nails.

EXAMPLE 5.3: NAILS, LATERAL LOAD, STEEL SIDE PLATES Steel gusset plates are used to transfer the load Q through the joint shown (Fig. 5.7). If twelve 8d wire nails are used per side as shown, what is the allowable load assuming only dead load is carried? Wood is unseasoned spruce-pine-fir which will be used in a dry location.

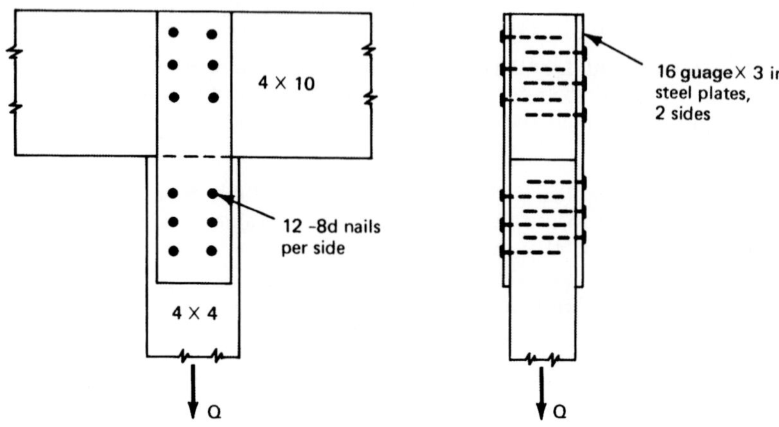

Note: 4 X 4 = 88.9 X 88.9 mm
4 X 10 = 88.9 X 235.0 mm

FIG. 5.7 Example 5.3.

SOLUTION: For 8d nail, $l = 2.50$ in, $D = 0.131$ in (see Table 5.1).
Penetration needed to use full design value $= 12D = 1.57$ in.

$$\text{Actual penetration} = 2.50 - 0.0598 = 2.44 > 1.57$$

$$P\ (\text{allowable}) = 81\ \text{lb} \qquad (\text{Table 5.5}a)$$

$$P\ (\text{adjusted}) = 81 \times C_D \times C_M \times C_t$$

$$P\ (\text{adjusted}) = 81 \times 0.90 \times 0.75 \times 1.0 = 55\ \text{lb per nail}$$

$$Q = 55 \times 12 = 660\ \text{lb}$$

Steel Side Plates. It is unlikely that steel side plates will control the design of joints using nails or screws. However, if there is some doubt, the steel side plates must be checked. The following is provided as an example of that which needs to be checked.

$$A\ (\text{net}) = 0.0598\ (3.0 - 2 \times 0.131) \times 2 = 0.327\ \text{in}^2$$

$$Q = A\ (\text{net}) \times F\ (\text{steel}) = 0.327 \times 22{,}000 = 7190\ \text{lb}$$

$$Q\ (\text{max}) = \underline{660\ \text{lb}}\ (2.94\ \text{kN}) < 7190\ \text{lb} \qquad \text{OK}$$

EXAMPLE 5.4: NAILS, LATERAL LOAD, PLYWOOD SIDE PLATES A tension splice is constructed of seasoned southern pine lumber and southern pine plywood which will remain dry. Determine the number, size, and placement of common wire nails needed to transmit the 1800-lb (8.01-kN) load (dead load plus wind load) through the joint shown (Fig. 5.8*a*).

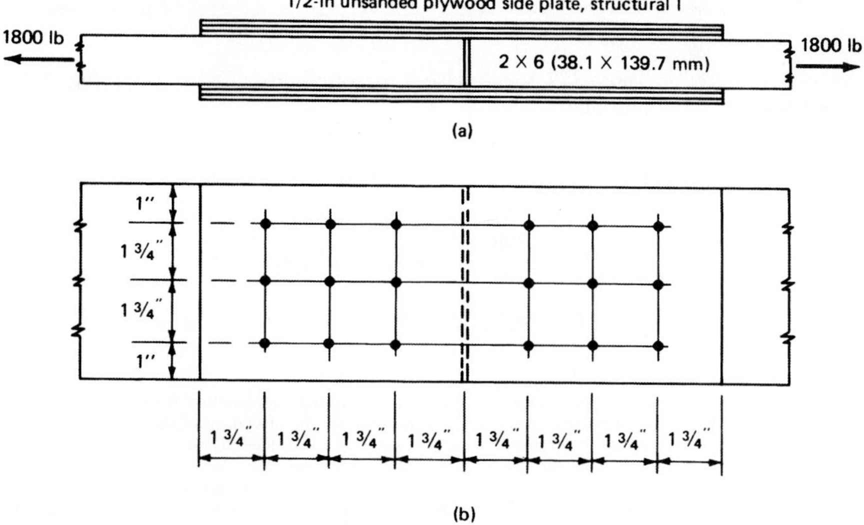

FIG. 5.8 Example 5.4. (*a*) Side view; (*b*) placement.

Note: Research[8] has shown that ½-in (12.7-mm) plywood when used as a side member (one side) will develop approximately the full bearing strength of a 10d nail (as shown in the table below) assuming the holding member is of adequate thickness and approximately equal density to that of the plywood.

Plywood thickness,* in (mm)	Common wire nail size
5⁄16 (7.94)	6d
3⁄8 (9.52)	8d
1⁄2 (12.70)	10d
5⁄8 (15.88)	16d

*Minimum plywood thickness needed to develop approximately the full bearing strength of the nail given.

SOLUTION: Try 10d nails; length = 3.00 in, D = 0.148 in; clinch if possible.
Protruding length required for clinching = $3D$ = 3 × 0.148 = 0.444 in.
Length protruding = 3.00 − 2.50 = 0.50 > 0.444; thus clinching may be used.
Thickness of main member will control design, t = 1.5 in.
Penetration needed to use full design value = $12D$ = 1.78 in.

$$P \text{ (allowable)} = 82 \qquad \text{(see Table 5.4}a\text{)}$$

$$P \text{ (adjusted)} = 101 \times C_D \times C_M \times C_t \times C_d$$

$$\times \text{ clinching adjustment (for double shear)}$$

$$P \text{ (adjusted)} = 101 \times 1.60 \times 1.0 \times 1.0 \times \frac{1.50}{1.78} \times 2.0 = 272 \text{ lb per nail}$$

Number required = 1800/272 = 6.6. Use 9 for simplicity of placement (Fig. 5.8*b*).
Check plywood side plates:*

$$A \text{ (net)} = \frac{2.175}{12.00} \times 5.5 \times 2 = 1.99 \text{ in}\dagger$$

$$f_t = \frac{P}{A \text{ (net)}} = \frac{1800}{1.99} = 904 \text{ psi} < F_t \text{ (plywood)}$$

$$F_t \text{ (plywood)} = 1650 \times 1.33 = 2194 \text{ psi (15.1 MPa)}$$

*The gross area of all plies parallel to the load is an appropriate assumption for the net area of the plywood side plate. The worst possible condition was assumed for the placement of the plywood side plate (face plies placed perpendicular to the member axis). Structural I unsanded plywood with S-2 stress level was assumed in selecting the allowable tensile stress for the plywood. All values for area and stress used are from the American Plywood Association publication *Plywood Design Specification.*[9]

†In some cases, it may be necessary to predrill holes to three-fourths of the nail shank diameter to avoid splitting. If threaded hardened-steel nails are used, clinching is not required to justify the design value used. But if nails are not clinched, the protruding portion may be a safety hazard.

5.2.4 Toenails

Toenailing is often used to fasten studs and joists to plates. The nail is driven as shown in Fig. 5.9. It is recommended that the nail be driven at an angle of 30° with the member and that it be started approximately one-third the length of the nail from the end of the piece. Because of the quality of the work and material needed to provide a good-quality toenail, the author recommends that toenailing be avoided in engineering structures when possible.

Withdrawal Loading. The design value for withdrawal loading at a toenail should not exceed two-thirds of the side-grain withdrawal value.

Lateral Loading. The design value for a toenail subjected to a lateral load should not exceed five-sixths of that permitted for a nail driven in side grain and laterally loaded.

Adjustments—Toenails. All adjustment factors which apply to lateral and withdrawal values for side grain also apply to toenails (see Secs. 5.2.2 and 5.2.3), except the wet-service factor C_M does not apply for toenails loaded in withdrawal.

5.2.5 Special Nails

Special nails is a term used to designate all nails which are not common wire nails or spikes. These include box nails and all surface-coated and deformed shank nails. Little or no structural advantage is gained by using special nails under normal loading and use conditions. In fact, because of the smaller diameter of special nails, the allowable design values given by NDS are generally equal to or less than those for common wire nails and spikes for both lateral and withdrawal loads.

Special nails may provide an improved design if

1. Normal penetration is not possible.
2. A change in moisture content is likely to take place.
3. Vibrations are present.
4. Splitting is a problem.

Nails with deformed shanks are less likely to work loose under changes in moisture content or under vibratory loads. Allowable values in withdrawal as given by NDS (see Table 5.3) for threaded nails are about 6 to 10 percent greater than

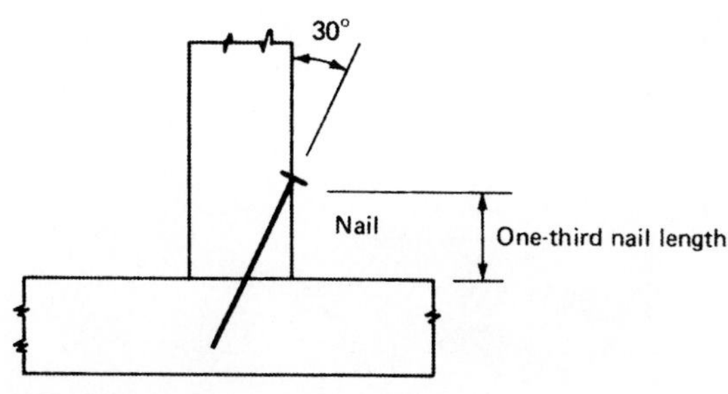

FIG. 5.9 Toenail.

the values given for common wire nails or box nails of equal diameter. Special hardened-steel nails may permit the use of a smaller-diameter nail and thus most likely will cause less splitting.

The design and analysis procedure for joints using special nails such as a ring shank is the same as that given in the example problems for common wire nails and spikes.

Appropriate withdrawal load design values can be obtained for nonstandard nails from those given by NDS for common wire nails and spikes and box nails. It is recommended that the design value (in withdrawal) be selected from Table 5.3 for a shank diameter equal to or nearly equal to the nonstandard nail. Lateral load design values can be obtained by using the equations of Sec. 5.2.3. All adjustment factors given for common wire nails and spikes also apply.

5.3 STAPLES

Staples are usually U-shaped wire fasteners with two same-size pointed or pointless legs connected by a common crown. They are designed to be driven by strike, pneumatic, electric, manual, or spring tools and to hold two or more pieces together.

If hammer-driven into wood or wood-base materials, these staples have to be relatively stout to prevent buckling during driving. If tool-driven, the staples can be relatively slender, since they are driven at a rapid rate while laterally supported by the tool's guide body. Tool-driven staples are usually provided with flats along their legs to facilitate tight collating into strips, as shown in Fig. 5.10. They are often coated with polymers in order to decrease the staple's driving resistance.

Table 5.6 gives the sizes of collated and cohered heavy-wire steel staples that are typically available. Allowable loads for staples can be reasonably taken to be equal to twice the value for a nail with a shank diameter equal to that of one leg of the staple.

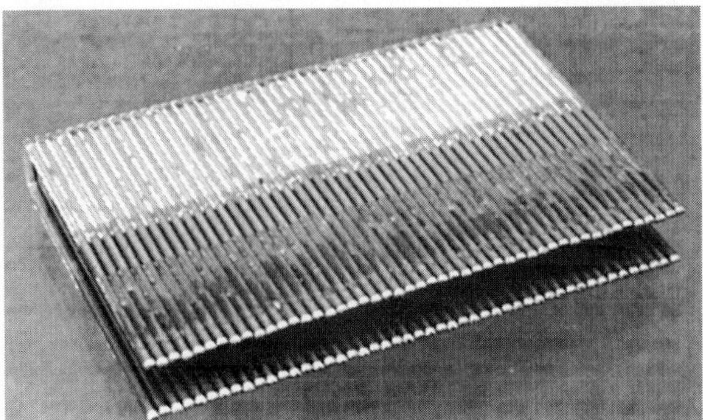

FIG. 5.10 Staples.

TABLE 5.6 Available Sizes of Standard, Collated, and Cohered Heavy-Wire Steel Staples*

		Crown width, in													
		0.18	0.25	0.38	0.44	0.44	0.50	0.75	0.88	0.94	1.00	1.00	1.38	1.56	2.12
Leg length, in	Wire sizes:	18	18	18 16 14	16 15	14	16 15 14	16 14	16 14	16 14	16 14	10	12	12	10
1.00		x	x		x	x	x	x	x	x	x				
1.12		x	x	x	x	x	x	x	x	x	x				
1.25		x	x	x	x	x	x	x	x	x	x				
1.38				x	x	x	x	x	x	x	x				
1.50		x	x	x	x	x	x	x	x	x	x				
1.62				x	x	x	x	x	x				x	x	x
1.75				x	x	x	x	x	x			x			
1.88					x	x	x	x	x						
2.00					x	x	x	x	x			x			
2.25					x	x	x								
2.50					x	x	x								
2.75						x	x								
3.00						x	x								
3.25						x	x								
3.50						x									

Note: 1 in = 25.4 mm.
*Outside crown width is given.

5.4 WOOD SCREWS

5.4.1 Introduction

The general procedure for the design of joints using wood screws is very similar to that used for nails. There are some notable differences in construction practices. Lead holes are to be drilled, and screws are to be inserted by turning and are not to be driven with a hammer.

The common types of wood screws and their principal parts are shown in Fig. 5.11. Screws are designated by gauge (diameter of shank) and their overall length. For example, a No. 9, 2-in (50.8-mm) wood screw would have a shank diameter of 0.177 in (4.50 mm) and a total length of 2.00 in (5.08 mm). Table 5.7 gives some typical available screw sizes. It is adequate for design purposes to assume that two-thirds of the screw length is threaded. Lubricating the surface of a screw with wax or soap will facilitate insertion and will have little effect on the allowable load. If possible, the structural design should avoid using wood screws in withdrawal from end grain.

5.4.2 Withdrawal Resistance

Predesign. Withdrawal tests on wood screws have shown that the ultimate load for a screw inserted into the side grain of seasoned wood may be expressed by the equation

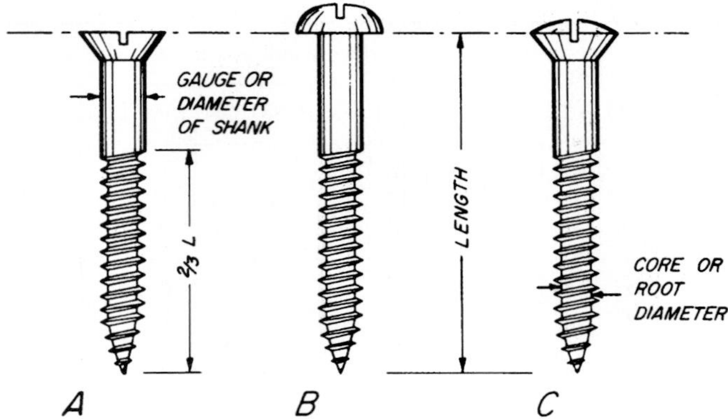

FIG. 5.11 Common types of wood screws: (*A*) flathead; (*B*) roundhead; (*C*) ovalhead.

$$P = 15{,}700G^2DL \tag{5.2}$$

where P = maximum withdrawal load, lb
G = specific gravity of wood
D = shank diameter of screw, in
L = length of penetration of threaded part of screw

The equation used to obtain the allowable design value given in the NDS was

$$P' = 2840G^2D \tag{5.3}$$

where P' is the allowable design value, per inch of penetration of threaded part of screw, and G and D are as defined for Eq. (5.2). Equation (5.3) provides allowable values for normal duration of load which are somewhat less than one-sixth of that given by Eq. (5.2) which is for short-term ultimate loading.

Table 5.8 gives the design values in withdrawal loading for a wood screw obtained by using Eq. (5.3). The table is for

TABLE 5.7 Some Lengths and Gauges of Available Wood Screws

Length, in	Gauge limits	Length, in	Gauge limits
½	2 to 8	2	8 to 20
⅝	3 to 10	2¼	9 to 20
¾	4 to 11	2½	12 to 20
⅞	6 to 12	2¾	14 to 20
1	6 to 14	3	16 to 20
1¼	7 to 16	3½	18 to 24
1½	6 to 18	4	18 to 24
1¾	8 to 20		

Note: 1 in = 25.4 mm.

TABLE 5.8 Cut Thread or Rolled Thread Wood Screw Withdrawal Design Values (W)*

Tabulated withdrawal design values (W) are in pounds per inch of thread penetration into side grain of main member. Thread length is approximately two-thirds the total wood screw length (see Ref. 4).

Specific gravity G	*Wood screw gauge*										
	6g	*7g*	*8g*	*9g*	*10g*	*12g*	*14g*	*16g*	*18g*	*20g*	*24g*
0.55	119	130	141	152	163	186	208	231	253	275	320
0.50	98	107	117	126	135	154	172	191	209	228	264
0.43	73	79	86	93	100	114	127	141	155	168	196
0.42	69	76	82	89	95	108	121	134	147	161	187

Note: 1 in = 25.4 mm; 1 lb = 4.45 N.

*Tabulated withdrawal design values (W) for wood screw connections shall be multiplied by all applicable adjustment factors.

Source: This table provided courtesy of the American Forest and Paper Association, Washington, D.C.

1. Seasoned wood which remains dry in service
2. Normal load duration
3. Screw turned into side grain
4. Normal temperature

If the conditions assumed in Table 5.8 are not satisfied in a joint under consideration, then adjustments need to be made. The conditions which need to be considered are:

1. Moisture condition in service
2. Load duration
3. Fire-retardant treatment
4. Wood temperature

The adjustment recommended for moisture condition in service, load duration, and fire-retardant treatment is given in Table 5.24*a*.

The wood screw used should have a tensile strength at net (root) section greater than the applied load. Failure should occur in the wood rather than in the metal.

Number of Wood Screws. The design value when more than one wood screw is used is equal to the sum of the design values permitted for each screw.

Lead Holes. Lead holes should be bored as follows:

Specific gravity G	Percent of root diameter
$G > 0.6$	90
$0.5 \leq G \leq 0.6$	70
$G \leq 0.5$	No lead hole required

Penetration. The effective penetration to be used is the length of the threaded portion of the screw in the member receiving the point.

End Grain. Wood screws should not be loaded in withdrawal from the end grain of the wood.

EXAMPLE 5.5: WITHDRAWAL LOAD, WOOD SCREWS Determine the size and number of wood screws needed to support a 900-lb (3.56-kN) load for 2 months (Fig. 5.12). The wood is seasoned hem-fir which remains dry.

SOLUTION: Try No. 12 × 2½-in wood screws.
Specific gravity of wood = 0.43 (see Table 5.2)
Penetration = 2.50 − 0.50 = 2.00 in.
Threaded length approximately = ⅔ × length screw = ⅔ × 2.50 = 1.67 in < 2.00; use 1.67 in.

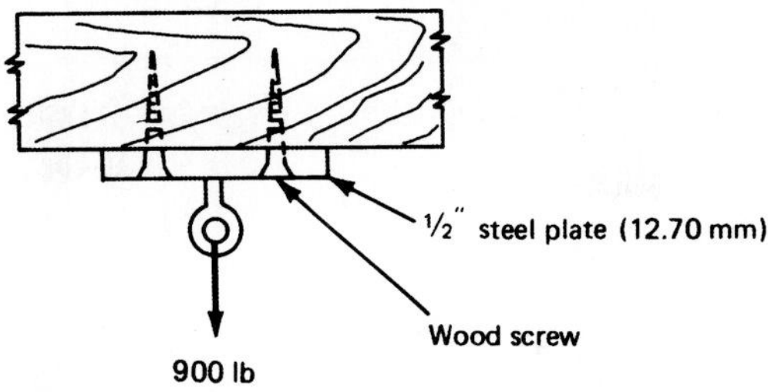

FIG. 5.12 Example 5.5.

$$P \text{ (allowable)} = 114 \text{ lb/in of threaded length (Table 5.7).}$$

$$P \text{ (adjusted)} = 114 \times C_D \times C_M \times C_t \times \text{threaded length}$$

$$P \text{ (adjusted)} = 108 \times 1.15 \times 1.0 \times 1.0 \times 1.67 = 219 \text{ lb}$$

Number required = 900/219 = 4.11; assume that four screws are desirable.
Try No. 12 × 3-in wood screws.
Penetration = 3.00 − 0.50 = 2.50 in.
Threaded length = ⅔ × 3.00 = 2.00 in < 2.50; use 2.00 in.

$$P \text{ (allowable)} = 114 \times 1.15 \times 2.0 = 262 \text{ lb}$$

Number required = 900/262 = 3.44.

ANSWER: Use four No. 12 × 3-in wood screws (5.49 × 76.2 mm).

5.4.3 Lateral Resistance

The ultimate lateral load capacity of a wood screw in single shear (two members) is dependent on several material and dimensional properties of the connection. These include the thickness of the two joined members, the crushing strength of the wood, and the diameter and yield strength of the wood screw.

The European yield model (EYM) theory provides three possible failure modes for a two-member wood screw connection in single shear. The model assumes that the bearing capacity is reached when either the wood crushes under the wood screw or one or two plastic hinges are formed in the wood screw. Shown below are the three yield modes and the equations which provide the allowable lateral load value for each yield mode. The controlling value for a particular joint is the lowest value obtained from the three equations.

Nominal screw lateral design value Z shall be lesser of

	Yield mode	
$Z = \dfrac{Dt_s F_{es}}{K_D}$	Mode I_s	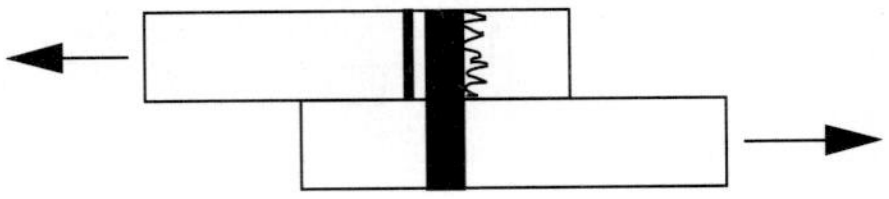
$Z = \dfrac{kDt_s F_{em}}{K_D(2 + R_e)}$	Mode III_s	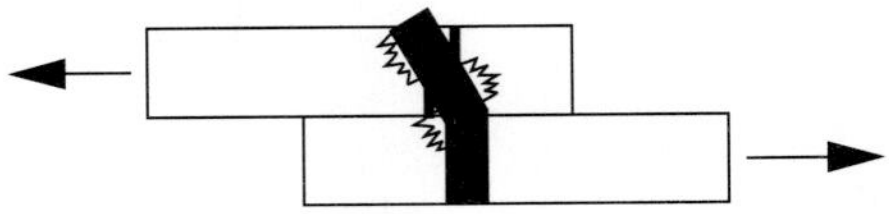
$Z = \dfrac{D^2}{K_D}\sqrt{\dfrac{1.75F_{em}F_{yb}}{3(1 + R_e)}}$	Mode IV	

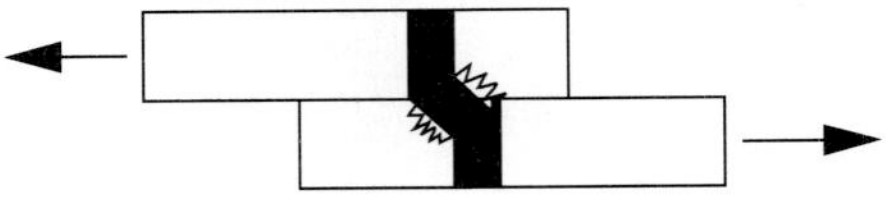

where $K = -1 + \sqrt{\dfrac{2(1 + R_e)}{R_e} + \dfrac{F_{yb}(2 + R_e)D^2}{2F_{em}t_s^2}}$

$R_e = F_{em}/F_{es}$
t_s = thickness side member, in
F_{em} = dowel bearing strength of main member, psi
F_{es} = dowel bearing strength of side member, psi
F_{yb} = bending yield strength of wood screw, psi
D = unthreaded shank diameter of wood screw, inches
K_D = 2.2 for $D \leq 0.17$ in, $10D + 0.5$ for 0.17 in $< D <$ 0.25 in, and 3.0 for $D \geq 0.25$ in

Lateral design values have been obtained using the yield model equations by NDS[5] and are given in Table 5.9 for wood-to-wood joints and in Table 5.10 for wood-to-metal joints.

If a connection does not qualify under the geometry and materials properties given in Tables 5.9 and 5.10 then the three yield model equations may be used to obtain a lateral design value Z. Table A.13 in the Appendix may be used to obtain the dowel bearing strengths, F_{em} and F_{es} needed in solving these equations. These equations have a built-in factor of safety of about equal to that provided for nails.

Tables 5.9 and 5.10 give the lateral load design values for a wood screw. The tables are for

1. Seasoned wood which remains dry in service
2. Normal load duration
3. A screw in single shear
4. Full penetration ($7D$ as given in the tables)
5. Screw inserted in side grain
6. Normal temperature

TABLE 5.9 Cut Thread Wood Screw Design Values (Z)* for Single-Shear (Two-Member) Connections with Both Members of Identical Species

Side member thickness t_s, in	Wood screw diameter D, in	Wood screw gauge g	G = 0.55 Southern pine, Z, lb	G = 0.50 Douglas fir–larch, Z, lb	G = 0.43 Hem-fir, Z, lb	G = 0.42 Spruce-pine-fir, Z, lb
½	0.138	6d	85	75	62	60
	0.151	7d	95	84	70	68
	0.164	8d	108	96	81	79
	0.177	9d	119	107	90	87
	0.190	10d	122	109	92	90
	0.216	12d	138	124	105	103
	0.242	14d	146	132	112	110
	0.268	16d	171	155	133	130
	0.294	18d	190	172	148	145
⅝	0.138	6d	95	83	67	65
	0.151	7d	105	92	75	73
	0.164	8d	119	105	86	83
	0.177	9d	130	114	95	92
	0.190	10d	133	117	97	94
	0.216	12d	147	131	109	106
	0.242	14d	155	138	116	113
	0.268	16d	179	161	136	132
	0.294	18d	199	178	151	147
¾	0.138	6d	106	92	73	71
	0.151	7d	117	102	82	79
	0.164	8d	132	114	92	90
	0.177	9d	142	124	101	98
	0.190	10d	145	127	103	100
	0.216	12d	159	140	115	112
	0.242	14d	166	146	121	118
	0.268	16d	190	169	141	137
	0.294	18d	210	187	156	152
	0.320	20d	242	216	182	177
	0.372	24d	283	252	212	207
1	0.138	6d	110	101	87	84
	0.151	7d	125	115	97	93
	0.164	8d	148	135	108	104
	0.177	9d	167	147	117	113
	0.190	10d	171	150	119	115
	0.216	12d	186	161	129	125
	0.242	14d	193	168	135	131
	0.268	16d	217	190	154	150
	0.294	18d	240	210	171	166
	0.320	20d	272	239	196	190
	0.372	24d	317	279	229	222

TABLE 5.9 Cut Thread Wood Screw Design Values (Z)* for Single-Shear (Two-Member) Connections with Both Members of Identical Species *(Continued)*

Side member thickness t_s, in	Wood screw diameter D, in	Wood screw gauge g	G = 0.55 Southern pine, Z, lb	G = 0.50 Douglas fir–larch, Z, lb	G = 0.43 Hem-fir, Z, lb	G = 0.42 Spruce-pine-fir, Z, lb
1¼	0.138	6d	110	101	87	86
	0.151	7d	125	115	99	97
	0.164	8d	148	135	117	115
	0.177	9d	167	152	132	129
	0.190	10d	171	157	136	132
	0.216	12d	200	183	147	142
	0.242	14d	213	193	153	147
	0.268	16d	249	215	172	166
	0.294	18d	275	238	190	184
	0.320	20d	308	268	215	208
	0.372	24d	359	312	251	243
1½	0.138	6d	110	101	87	86
	0.151	7d	125	115	99	97
	0.164	8d	148	135	117	115
	0.177	9d	167	152	132	129
	0.190	10d	171	157	136	133
	0.216	12d	200	183	159	155
	0.242	14d	213	195	170	166
	0.268	16d	255	233	192	185
	0.294	18d	284	260	212	204
	0.320	20d	336	300	238	230
	0.372	24d	394	349	277	268

Note: 1 in = 25.4 mm; 1 lb. = 4.45 N.

*Tabulated lateral design values (Z) for wood screw connections shall be multiplied by all applicable adjustment factors. Tabulated lateral design values (Z) are for cut thread wood screws inserted in side grain with wood screw axis perpendicular to wood fibers, and with the following wood screw bending yield strengths (F_{yb}):

F_{yb} = 100,000 psi for 6d wood screws

F_{yb} = 90,000 psi for 7d, 8d, and 9d wood screws

F_{yb} = 80,000 psi for 10d and 12d wood screws

F_{yb} = 70,000 psi for 14d and 16d wood screws

F_{yb} = 60,000 psi for 18d and 20d wood screws

F_{yb} = 45,000 psi for 24d wood screws

Source: This table provided courtesy of American Forest and Paper Association, Washington, D.C.

If the conditions assumed in Tables 5.9 and 5.10 are not satisfied in a joint under consideration, then adjustments need to be made. The conditions which need to be considered are

1. Moisture condition in service
2. Load duration
3. Length of penetration
4. End-grain lateral loading

TABLE 5.10 Cut Thread Wood Screw Design Values (Z)* for Single-Shear (Two-Member) Connections with ASTM A446, Grade A Steel Side Plate

Steel side plate	Wood screw diameter D, in	Wood screw gauge g	$G = 0.55$ Southern pine, Z, lb	$G = 0.50$ Douglas fir–larch, Z, lb	$G = 0.43$ Hem-fir, Z, lb	$G = 0.42$ Spruce-pine-fir, Z, lb
3 gauge	0.242	14d	241	225	200	197
$t_s = 0.239$ in	0.268	16d	275	256	228	224
	0.294	18d	304	283	252	248
	0.320	20d	348	325	289	283
	0.372	24d	407	379	337	331
7 gauge	0.190	10d	184	171	152	150
$t_s = 0.179$ in	0.216	12d	204	190	169	166
	0.242	14d	215	200	178	174
	0.268	16d	248	231	205	201
	0.294	18d	276	256	228	223
	0.320	20d	320	297	264	259
	0.372	24d	374	347	308	302
10 gauge	0.138	6d	114	107	95	93
$t_s = 0.134$ in	0.151	7d	128	119	106	104
	0.164	8d	147	137	122	119
	0.177	9d	162	151	134	132
	0.190	10d	166	155	137	135
	0.216	12d	188	175	155	152
	0.242	14d	199	185	164	161
	0.268	16d	234	217	192	188
	0.294	18d	260	241	213	209
	0.320	20d	304	282	250	245
	0.372	24d	356	330	292	286
11 gauge	0.138	6d	110	103	91	89
$t_s = 0.12$ in	0.151	7d	124	115	102	100
	0.164	8d	143	133	118	115
	0.177	9d	158	147	130	128
	0.190	10d	162	151	133	131
	0.216	12d	184	171	152	149
	0.242	14d	196	182	161	158
	0.268	16d	230	214	189	185
	0.294	18d	256	238	210	206
	0.320	20d	301	279	246	242
	0.372	24d	352	326	288	283
12 gauge	0.138	6d	106	99	88	86
$t_s = 0.105$ in	0.151	7d	119	111	98	97
	0.164	8d	138	129	114	112
	0.177	9d	154	143	127	124
	0.190	10d	158	147	130	127
	0.216	12d	181	168	148	145
	0.242	14d	192	178	158	155
	0.268	16d	227	211	186	182
	0.294	18d	253	234	207	203
	0.320	20d	298	276	243	239
	0.372	24d	348	323	285	279

TABLE 5.10 Cut Thread Wood Screw Design Values (Z)* for Single-Shear (Two-Member) Connections with ASTM A446, Grade A Steel Side Plate *(Continued)*

Steel side plate	Wood screw diameter D, in	Wood screw gauge g	$G = 0.55$ Southern pine, Z, lb	$G = 0.50$ Douglas fir–larch, Z, lb	$G = 0.43$ Hem-fir, Z, lb	$G = 0.42$ Spruce-pine-fir, Z, lb
14 gauge $t_s = 0.075$ in	0.138	6d	100	93	82	80
	0.151	7d	113	105	92	91
	0.164	8d	132	122	108	106
	0.177	9d	148	137	121	119
	0.190	10d	152	141	124	122
	0.216	12d	176	163	144	141
	0.242	14d	188	174	153	150
	0.268	16d	223	207	182	178
	0.294	18d	249	230	203	199
16 gauge $t_s = 0.06$ in	0.138	6d	98	90	80	78
	0.151	7d	111	103	90	89
	0.164	8d	130	120	106	104
	0.177	9d	146	135	119	117
	0.190	10d	150	139	122	120
18 gauge $t_s = 0.048$ in	0.138	6d	97	89	79	77
	0.151	7d	110	101	89	88
	0.164	8d	129	119	105	103

Note: 1 in = 25.4 mm; 1 lb. = 4.45 N.

*Tabulated lateral design values (Z) for wood screw connections shall be multiplied by all applicable adjustment factors. Tabulated lateral design values (Z) are for cut thread wood screws inserted in side grain with wood screw axis perpendicular to wood fibers, and with the following wood screw bending yield strengths (F_{yb}):

F_{yb} = 100,000 psi for 6d wood screws

F_{yb} = 90,000 psi for 7d, 8d, and 9d wood screws

F_{yb} = 80,000 psi for 10d and 12d wood screws

F_{yb} = 70,000 psi for 14d and 16d wood screws

F_{yb} = 60,000 psi for 18d and 20d wood screws

F_{yb} = 45,000 psi for 24d wood screws

Source: This table provided courtesy of American Forest and Paper Association, Washington, D.C.

5. Fire-retardant treatment
6. Wood temperature

The adjustments recommended for load duration, moisture condition in service and temperature are given in Tables 4.3, 5.30*a*, and 5.33 respectively. See manufacturers recommendations on adjustments for fire retardant treatments.

Number of Wood Screws. The design value when more than one wood screw is used is equal to the sum of the design values permitted for each screw.

Lead Holes

Specific gravity G	Part of screw	Percent of diameter of screw
$G > 0.6$	Shank	100
	Thread	100
$G \leq 0.6$	Shank	87.5
	Thread	87.5

Penetration. For lateral resistance, the penetration of the screw into the main member should be approximately 7 times the shank diameter. If the penetration is less than 7 diameters, the design value should be reduced in proportion to its reduced penetration using the equation $C_d = p/7D \leq 1.0$. The minimum penetration should not be less than four shank diameters.

Angle of Load to Grain. The design values for wood screws apply to any angle of load to grain for wood or steel side plates.

End Grain. Design values for lateral resistance, when the wood screw is inserted into the end grain and the screw is laterally loaded, should be reduced to two-thirds of the values in Tables 5.9 and 5.10.

5.4.4 Combined Lateral and Withdrawal Loads

When a wood screw is inserted perpendicular to the wood fibers and is subjected to both lateral and withdrawal loadings, the equation given in Sec. 5.7.5 may be used to obtain a design value.

EXAMPLE 5.6: LATERAL LOAD ON WOOD SCREW Determine the allowable wind load Q for the joint shown (Fig. 5.13). Wood is seasoned southern pine which is exposed to the weather.

SOLUTION: Wood specific gravity = 0.55 (see Table 5.2).
For No. 12 × 1¾-in wood screws: $\ell = 1.75$ in, and $D = 0.216$ in (see Table 5.10).
Penetration needed to use full design value = $7D = 1.512$ in.
Minimum penetration permitted = $4D = 0.864$ in.
Actual penetration = $1.75 - 0.105 = 1.645 > 7D$; thus $C_d = 1.0$.

$$P \text{ (allowable)} = 181 \text{ lb} \qquad \text{(see Table 5.10)}$$

$$P \text{ (adjusted)} = 181 \times C_D \times C_M \times C_d$$

$$P \text{ (adjusted)} = 181 \times 1.6 \times 0.75 \times 1.0 \times 1.0 = 217 \text{ lb}$$

$$Q = 217 \times 8 = \underline{1736 \text{ lb}} \text{ (7.72 kN)*}$$

*It is unlikely that steel side plates will control the design of joints using nails or screws. However, if there is some doubt, the steel side plates must be checked (see Example 5.3).

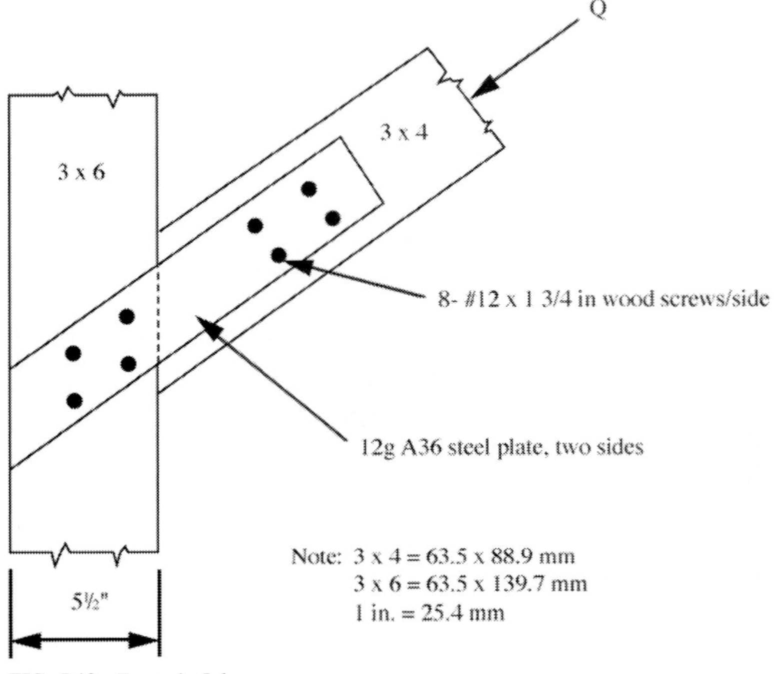

FIG. 5.13 Example 5.6.

5.5 HANKINSON FORMULA

Wood is not as strong or as stiff perpendicular to its grain as it is parallel to its grain. Elastic properties in directions other than parallel or perpendicular to the grain of the wood can be approximated by using the Hankinson formula:

$$F_n = \frac{F_{e\parallel} F_{e\perp}}{F_{e\parallel} \sin^2\theta + F_{e\perp} \cos^2\theta} \tag{5.4}$$

where F_n = dowel bearing strength at inclination θ with direction of grain
$F_{e\parallel}$ = dowel bearing strength parallel to grain
$F_{e\perp}$ = dowel bearing strength perpendicular to grain
θ = angle between direction of grain and direction of desired property

Allowable values for some fasteners and connectors are dependent on the direction of the applied load. For example, the allowable design value for a bolt is considerably less when the bolt is loaded perpendicular to the grain of the wood than when it is loaded parallel to the grain. The Hankinson formula can be used to obtain the allowable design value when the load is applied at an angle between 0° (parallel to grain) and 90° (perpendicular to grain). The Scholten nomograph is a graphic plot of the Hankinson formula; it is given in Fig. 5.14. To use the nomo-

The Hankinson formula may be solved graphically through use of the charts on this page.

The compressive strength of wood depends on the direction of the grain with respect to the direction of the applied load. It is highest parallel to the grain, and lowest perpendicular to the grain. The variation in strength, at angles between parallel and perpendicular, is determined by the Hankinson formula. The Scholten nomographs, shown here, are a graphical solution of this formula which is–

$$F_n = \frac{F_e F_{e1}}{F_e \sin^2\theta + F_{e1}\cos^2\theta}$$

F_e = Dowel bearing strength parallel to the grain.

F_{e1} = Dowel bearing strength perpendicular to the grain.

θ = Angle between the direction of grain and direction of load normal to the face considered.

F_n = Dowel bearing strength at inclination θ with the direction of grain.

The difference between the two charts is in scale, the one on the right to units of 1000 pounds, and the one on the left to units of 100 pounds. These units may be applied to design values in pounds per square inch, or to total loads in the case of bolts, timber connectors or lag screws.

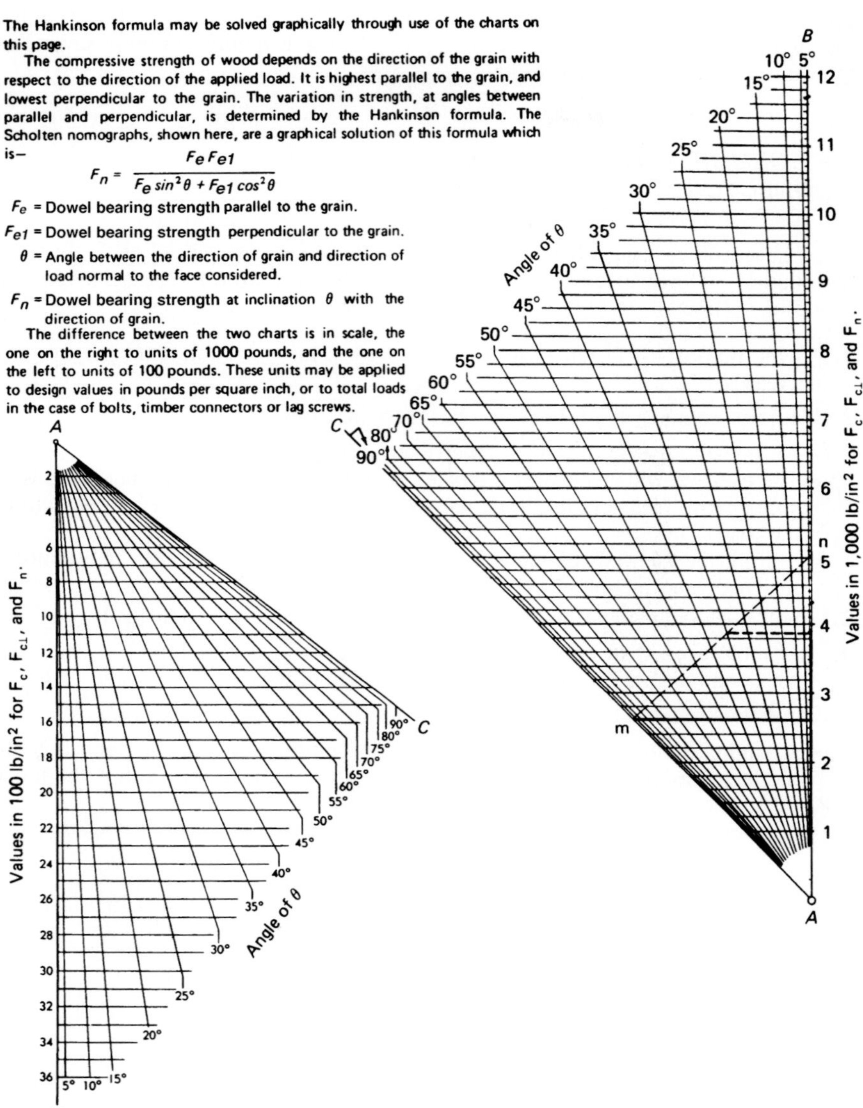

FIG. 5.14 Solution of Hankinson formula. *(Courtesy of American Forest and Paper Association, Washington, D.C.)*

graph requires only that the load values parallel and perpendicular to the grain and the angle of load-to-grain direction be known. Its use is demonstrated in several of the example problems which follow.

5.6 GROUP ACTIONS OF FASTENERS AND CONNECTORS

Tests have shown that when more than two fasteners are placed in a row, the distribution of force to the fasteners in the row is not uniform. The behavior of a group of fasteners in a joint is as given in Ref. 10.

1. As the number of fasteners in a row increases, the allowable load per fastener decreases.

2. If a joint contains more than two fasteners in a row,
   - An uneven distribution of fastener load occurs.
   - The two end fasteners carry a greater load than the interior fasteners, and with six or more fasteners in a row, the two end fasteners carry over 50 percent of the load.
   - The elastic strength of the joint will not increase significantly if additional fasteners (more than six) are added to a row.

3. Small misalignment of bolt holes may cause large shifts in bolt loads.

4. The most even distribution of bolt loads occurs in a butt joint in which the extensional stiffness of the main member is equal to that of both side plates.

5. Ultimate strength tests show that
   - A slight redistribution of the load from the more heavily loaded end bolts to the less heavily loaded interior bolts when crushing under the bolt is the mode of failure.
   - A partial specimen failure occurs before substantial redistribution takes place if final failure is in shear.

Therefore, it is necessary in the design of a joint with more than two fasteners in a row to include a group action factor C_g. This factor is applied only to *lag screws, bolts,* and *connectors.*

$$C_g = \left[\frac{m(1 - m^{2n})}{n[(1 + R_{EA}m^n)(1 + m) - 1 + m) - 1 + m^{2n}]}\right]\left(\frac{1 + R_{EA}}{1 - m}\right) \tag{5.5}$$

where n = number of fasteners in a row
R_{EA} = the lesser of E_sA_s/E_mA_m or E_mA_m/E_sA_s
E_m = modulus of elasticity of main member, psi
E_s = modulus of elasticity of side member, psi
A_m = gross cross-sectional area of main member, in^2
A_s = sum of gross cross-sectional area of side member, in^2
$m = u - \sqrt{u^2 - 1}$
$u = 1 + \gamma \frac{s}{2}\left(\frac{1}{E_mA_m} + \frac{1}{E_sA_s}\right)$
s = center-to-center spacing between adjacent fasteners in a row, in
γ = load/slip modulus for connection, lb/in

γ = 500,000 lb/in for 4-in split-ring or shear-plate connectors
γ = 400,000 lb/in for 2½-in split-ring or 2⅝-in shear-plate connections
$\gamma = (180{,}000)(D^{1.5})$ for bolts or lag screws in wood-to-wood connections
$\gamma = (270{,}000)(D^{1.5})$ for bolts or lag screws in wood-to-metal connections
D = Diameter of bolt or lag screw, in

5.6.1 Allowable Load

If the fasteners are of same type and size,

$$P_r = P_{sg} = Pn_fC_g \tag{5.6}$$

where P_r = allowable load on row of fasteners
P_s = sum of values for individual fasteners in row
P = allowable load for single fastener
n_f = number of fasteners in row
C_g = group action factor

C_g is selected based on the type of side members, the size of the members, and the number of fasteners in a row from Table 5.26, 5.27, 5.28, or 5.29

$$P_T = \Sigma P_r \tag{5.7}$$

where P_T is total allowable load for the group of fasteners.

5.6.2 Cross-Sectional Areas

In order to obtain the modification factor C_g from tabular data provided in Table 5.26, 5.27, 5.28, or 5.29, it is first necessary to determine the cross-sectional areas which contribute to the extensional stiffness of the members joined.

1. Load applied parallel to grain: Use the gross cross-sectional area of the member.
2. Load applied perpendicular to grain: The equivalent cross-sectional area is the product of member thickness and overall width of the fastener group. If only one row of fasteners is used, use the minimum parallel-to-grain spacing of the fasteners as the width of the fastener group.
3. Load applied at an angle to grain: No guidance is provided by NDS; however, based on engineering judgment, appropriate cross-sectional areas can be determined.

5.6.3 Row of Fasteners

The following are considered to be a row of fasteners:

1. Two or more bolts of the same diameter loaded in single or multiple shear.
2. Two or more connector units or lag bolts of the same type and size loaded in single shear.
3. Adjacent staggered rows of fasteners which are spaced apart less than one-quarter the spacing between the fasteners in a row. See Fig. 5.15*a*.

Examples of fasteners which are staggered are shown in Fig. 5.15, and these apply to lag screws, bolts, or connectors.

EXAMPLE 5.7: GROUP OF FASTENERS LOADED PARALLEL TO GRAIN Determine the group action factor and the allowable load for the bolted butt joint shown (Fig. 5.16). Assume an allowable load (excluding group action reduction) of $P_s = 2500$ lb (11.1 kN) per bolt (double shear).

SOLUTION:

$$A_m\ (3 \times 6) = 2.5 \times 5.5 = 13.75\ \text{in}^2$$

$$A_s\ (\text{two } 2 \times 6\text{s}) = 2 \times (1.5 \times 5.5) = 16.50\ \text{in}^2$$

$$\frac{A_m}{A_s} = \frac{13.75}{16.50} = 0.833 \qquad \text{since } A_s/A_m > 1.0$$

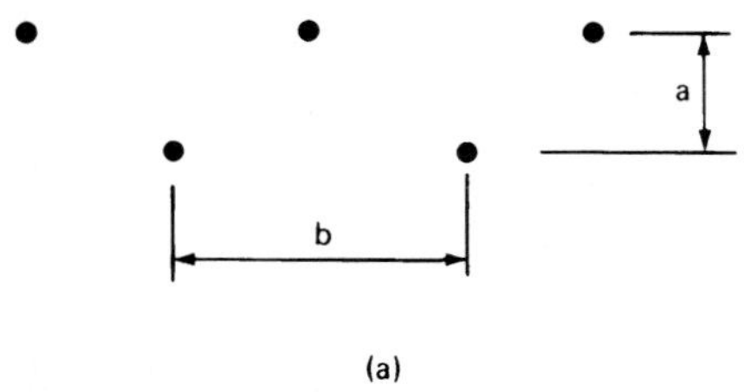

(a)

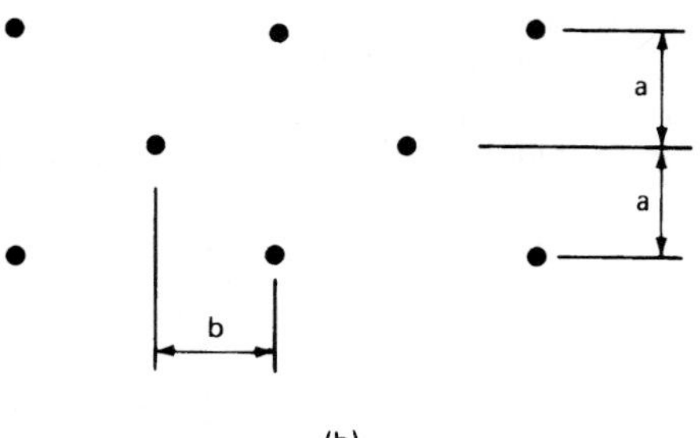

(b)

FIG. 5.15 Staggered fasteners. (*a*) If $a < b/4$, single row; if $a > b/4$, two rows. (*b*) If $a < b/4$, top two lines act as one row and bottom lines acts as a second row; if $a > b/4$, consider as three rows.

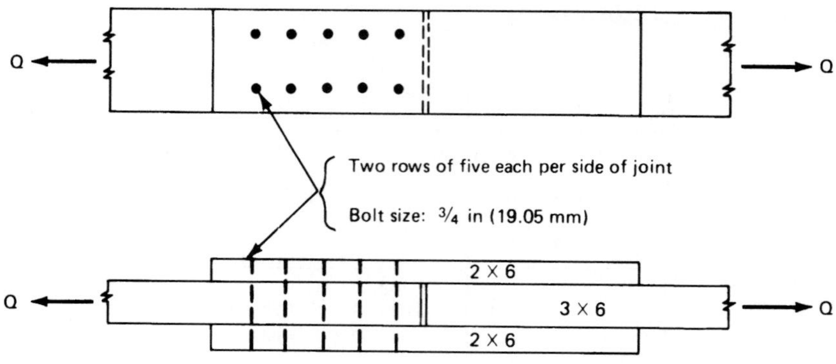

FIG. 5.16 Example 5.7.

Interpolating from Table 5.26,

$$C_g = 0.87 + 0.06\ (0.333/0.50) = 0.91$$

$$P_r = P_s \times n_f \times C_g = 2500 \times 5 \times 0.91 = 11{,}375 \text{ lb per row}$$

$$P_t = \Sigma P_r = 2 \times 11{,}375 = \underline{22{,}750 \text{ lb}}\ (101.2 \text{ kN})$$

EXAMPLE 5.8: GROUP OF FASTENERS LOADED PERPENDICULAR TO GRAIN Determine the group reduction factor and the allowable load for the bolted joint (Fig. 5.17). Assume an allowable load (excluding group reduction factor) of P_s = 1250 lb (5.560 kN) per bolt (double shear).

SOLUTION: An equivalent area for the 4- by 12-in piece is (see Sec. 5.6.2)

$$A_m = 2.5 \times 2 \times 3.5 = 17.5 \text{ in}^2$$

where 2.5 × 2 = overall width of fastener group and 3.5 is the thickness of the main member.

$$A_s = (\text{two } 3 \times 8\text{s}) = 2 \times 18.125 = 36.25 \text{ in}^2$$

$$\frac{A_m}{A_s} = \frac{17.5}{36.25} = 0.48$$

Extrapolating from Table 5.26, C_g = 0.92.

$$P_r = P_s \times n_f \times C_g = 1250 \times 4 \times 0.92 = 4600 \text{ lb per row}$$

$$P_T = \Sigma P_r = 3 \times 4600 = \underline{13{,}800 \text{ lb}}\ (61.4 \text{ kN})$$

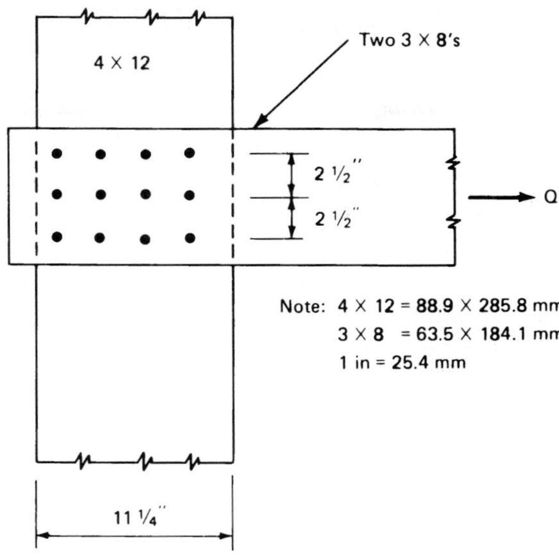

FIG. 5.17 Example 5.8.

5.7 LAG SCREWS

5.7.1 Introduction

Lag screws (lag bolts) are typically used for convenience or where bolts are impossible to install or undesirable to use. The size of a lag screw is designated by its shank diameter D_s and its nominal length L (see Fig. 5.18). Table 5.11 provides typical data on lag screw sizes and dimensions. The holding power for a lag screw is dependent on factors similar to those of both the wood screw and the bolt.

Lag screws are turned into prebored holes. The recommended diameter of the hole is dependent on the density of the wood and the diameter of the shank of the lag screw. The total length of the hole drilled should be equal to the total nominal

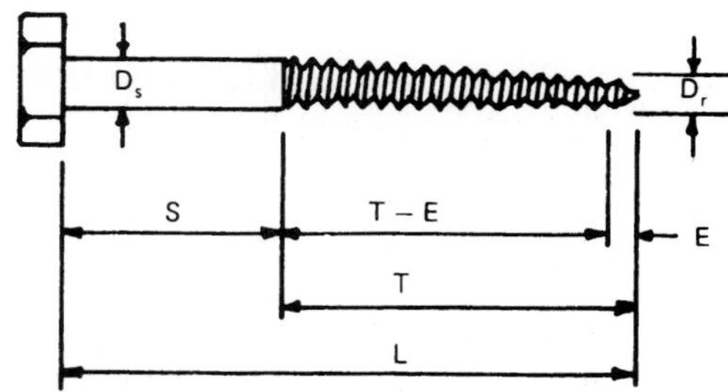

FIG. 5.18 Lag screw dimensions. *Note:* All terms are defined in Table 5.11.

TABLE 5.11 Typical Dimensions of Standard Lag Screws for Wood

All dimensions in inches.

D = nominal diameter
$D_s = D$ = diameter of shank
D_r = diameter at root of thread
W = width of head across flats
H = height of head
L = nominal length
S = length of shank
T = length of thread
E = length of tapered tip
N = number of threads per inch

Nominal length L, in*	Item	Nominal diameter D												
		3/16	1/4	5/16	3/8	7/16	1/2	9/16	5/8	3/4	7/8	1	1 1/8	1 1/4
All lengths	$D_s = D$	0.190	0.250	0.3125	0.375	0.4375	0.500	0.5625	0.625	0.750	0.875	1.000	1.125	1.250
	D_r	0.120	0.173	0.227	0.265	0.328	0.371	0.435	0.471	0.579	0.683	0.780	0.887	1.012
	E	5/32	3/16	1/4	1/4	9/32	5/16	3/8	3/8	7/16	1/2	9/16	5/8	3/4
	H	9/64	11/64	13/64	1/4	19/64	21/64	3/8	27/64	1/2	19/32	21/32	3/4	27/32
	W	9/32	3/8	1/2	9/16	5/8	3/4	7/8	15/16	1 1/8	1 5/16	1 1/2	1 11/16	1 7/8
	N	11	10	9	7	7	6	6	5	4 1/2	4	3 1/2	3 1/4	3 1/4
1	S	1/4	1/4	1/4	1/4	1/4	1/4							
	T	3/4	3/4	3/4	3/4	3/4	3/4							
	$T - E$	19/32	9/16	1/2	1/2	15/32	7/16							
1 1/2	S	3/8	3/8	3/8	3/8	3/8	3/8							
	T	1 1/8	1 1/8	1 1/8	1 1/8	1 1/8	1 1/8							
	$T - E$	31/32	15/16	7/8	7/8	27/32	13/16							
2	S	1/2	1/2	1/2	1/2	1/2	1/2	1/2	1/2					
	T	1 1/2	1 1/2	1 1/2	1 1/2	1 1/2	1 1/2	1 1/2	1 1/2					
	$T - E$	1 11/32	1 5/16	1 1/4	1 1/4	1 7/32	1 3/16	1 1/8	1 1/8					
2 1/2	S	1	1	7/8	7/8	3/4	3/4	3/4	3/4					
	T	1 1/2	1 1/2	1 5/8	1 5/8	1 3/4	1 3/4	1 3/4	1 3/4					
	$T - E$	1 11/16	1 5/16	1 3/8	1 3/8	1 15/32	1 7/16	1 3/8	1 3/8					
3	S	1	1	1	1	1	1	1	1	1	1	1		
	T	2	2	2	2	2	2	2	2	2	2	2		
	$T - E$	1 27/32	1 13/16	1 3/4	1 3/4	1 23/32	1 11/16	1 5/8	1 5/8	1 9/16	1 1/2	1 7/16		
4	S	1 1/2	1 1/2	1 1/2	1 1/2	1 1/2	1 1/2	1 1/2	1 1/2	1 1/2	1 1/2	1 1/2	1 1/2	1 1/2
	T	2 1/2	2 1/2	2 1/2	2 1/2	2 1/2	2 1/2	2 1/2	2 1/2	2 1/2	2 1/2	2 1/2	2 1/2	2 1/2
	$T - E$	2 11/32	2 5/16	2 1/4	2 1/4	2 7/32	2 3/16	2 1/8	2 1/8	2 1/16	2	1 15/16	1 7/8	1 3/4

TABLE 5.11 Typical Dimensions of Standard Lag Screws for Wood *(Continued)*

All dimensions in inches.

Nominal length L, in*	Item	Nominal diameter D												
		3/16	1/4	5/16	3/8	7/16	1/2	9/16	5/8	3/4	7/8	1	1 1/8	1 1/4
5	S	2	2	2	2	2	2	2	2	2	2	2	2	2
	T	3	3	3	3	3	3	3	3	3	3	3	3	3
	$T - E$	2 27/32	2 13/16	2 3/4	2 3/4	2 23/32	2 11/16	2 5/8	2 5/8	2 9/16	2 1/2	2 7/16	2 3/8	2 1/4
6	S	2 1/2	2 1/2	2 1/2	2 1/2	2 1/2	2 1/2	2 1/2	2 1/2	2 1/2	2 1/2	2 1/2	2 1/2	2 1/2
	T	3 1/2	3 1/2	3 1/2	3 1/2	3 1/2	3 1/2	3 1/2	3 1/2	3 1/2	3 1/2	3 1/2	3 1/2	3 1/2
	$T - E$	3 11/32	3 5/16	3 1/4	3 1/4	3 7/32	3 3/16	3 1/8	3 1/8	3 1/16	3	2 15/16	2 7/8	2 3/4
7	S	3	3	3	3	3	3	3	3	3	3	3	3	3
	T	4	4	4	4	4	4	4	4	4	4	4	4	4
	$T - E$	3 27/32	3 13/16	3 3/4	3 3/4	3 23/32	3 11/16	3 5/8	3 5/8	3 9/16	3 1/2	3 7/16	3 3/8	3 1/4
8	S	3 1/2	3 1/2	3 1/2	3 1/2	3 1/2	3 1/2	3 1/2	3 1/2	3 1/2	3 1/2	3 1/2	3 1/2	3 1/2
	T	4 1/2	4 1/2	4 1/2	4 1/2	4 1/2	4 1/2	4 1/2	4 1/2	4 1/2	4 1/2	4 1/2	4 1/2	4 1/2
	$T - E$	4 11/16	4 5/16	4 1/4	4 1/4	4 7/32	4 3/16	4 1/8	4 1/8	4 1/16	4	3 15/16	3 7/8	3 3/4
9	S	4	4	4	4	4	4	4	4	4	4	4	4	4
	T	5	5	5	5	5	5	5	5	5	5	5	5	5
	$T - E$	4 27/32	4 13/16	4 3/4	4 3/4	4 23/32	4 11/16	4 5/8	4 5/8	4 9/16	4 1/2	4 7/16	4 3/8	4 1/4
10	S	4 3/4	4 3/4	4 3/4	4 3/4	4 3/4	4 3/4	4 3/4	4 3/4	4 3/4	4 3/4	4 3/4	4 3/4	4 3/4
	T	5 1/4	5 1/4	5 1/4	5 1/4	5 1/4	5 1/4	5 1/4	5 1/4	5 1/4	5 1/4	5 1/4	5 1/4	5 1/4
	$T - E$	5 3/32	5 1/16	5	5	4 31/32	4 15/16	4 7/8	4 7/8	4 13/16	4 3/4	4 11/16	4 5/8	4 1/2
11	S	5 1/2	5 1/2	5 1/2	5 1/2	5 1/2	5 1/2	5 1/2	5 1/2	5 1/2	5 1/2	5 1/2	5 1/2	5 1/2
	T	5 1/2	5 1/2	5 1/2	5 1/2	5 1/2	5 1/2	5 1/2	5 1/2	5 1/2	5 1/2	5 1/2	5 1/2	5 1/2
	$T - E$	5 11/32	5 9/32	5 1/4	5 1/4	5 7/32	5 3/16	5 1/8	5 1/8	5 1/16	5	4 15/16	4 7/8	4 3/4
12	S	6	6	6	6	6	6	6	6	6	6	6	6	6
	T	6	6	6	6	6	6	6	6	6	6	6	6	6
	$T - E$	5 27/32	5 13/16	5 3/4	5 3/4	5 23/32	5 11/16	5 5/8	5 5/8	5 9/16	5 1/2	5 7/16	5 3/8	5 1/4

Note: 1 in = 25.4 mm.

*Length of thread T on intervening bolt lengths is the same as that of the next shorter length listed. The length of thread T on standard lag screw lengths L in excess of 12 in is equal to one-half the lag screw length, $L/2$.

Source: This table provided courtesy of the American Forest and Paper Association, Washington, D.C.

length of the lag screw. Table 5.12 gives the required values for both diameter and length of hole. When loaded primarily in withdrawal, ⅜-in and smaller-diameter lag screws may be inserted into a member of specific gravity $G \leq 0.5$ without a lead or clearance hole provided that spacings, end distances, and edge distances are such as to prevent unusual splitting.

The threaded portion of the screw is to be turned into its lead hole and not driven in by a hammer. Soap or other lubricant is recommended to facilitate insertion and to prevent damage to the lag screw.

The design values apply to lag screws conforming to ASTM Standard A307, *Low-Carbon Steel Externally and Internally Threaded Standard Fasteners.* For lag screws having other metal properties, the design values of Tables 5.13, 5.14,, and 5.15 may be adjusted in proportion to the square roots of the yield point stresses of the lag screw material.

5.7.2 Withdrawal Resistance

Predesign. An empirical equation which can be used to calculate the maximum withdrawal load of a lag screw from seasoned wood is

$$P = 8100G^{1.5}D_s^{0.75}T \tag{5.8}$$

where P = maximum withdrawal load, lb
G = specific gravity of wood
D_s = shank diameter, in
T = length of penetration of the threaded part, in

P is for short duration of load, and G is based on ovendry weight and volume taken at 12 percent moisture content.

Allowable design values are given by Table 5.13 as force per inch of penetration of the threaded part into the member holding point. These allowable values are about one-fifth of the ultimate values obtained by using Eq. (5.8).

Lag screws loaded in withdrawal can, if long enough, develop loads in excess of the yield strength of the steel. Therefore, the length allowed in calculating the withdrawal load is assumed to be approximately 8 times the shank diameter.

Table 5.13 gives the design value in withdrawal load for a lag screw. The table is for

1. Seasoned wood which remains dry

TABLE 5.12 Recommended Diameter and Length of Holes for Lag Screws

Part of hole	Length of hole*	Specific gravity of wood G	Diameter of hole†
Shank	S	All	D_s
Threaded	$T - E$	$G > 0.6$	65–85% of D_s
		$0.5 < G \leq 0.6$	60–75% of D_s
		$G \leq 0.5$	40–70% of D_s

*See Fig. 5.18 for dimensions of lag screw.
†Larger percentages for larger diameter of lag screws.

TABLE 5.13 Lag Screw Withdrawal Design Values (*W*)*

Tabulated withdrawal design values (W) are in pounds per inch of thread penetration into side grain of main member. Length of thread penetration in main member shall not include the length of the tapered tip.

Specific gravity G	Lag screw unthreaded shank diameter, D, in										
	1/4	5/16	3/8	7/16	1/2	5/8	3/4	7/8	1	1 1/8	1 1/4
0.55	260	307	352	395	437	516	592	664	734	802	868
0.50	225	266	305	342	378	447	513	576	636	695	752
0.43	179	212	243	273	302	357	409	459	508	554	600
0.42	173	205	235	264	291	344	395	443	490	535	579

Note: 1 in = 25.4 mm; 1 lb = 4.45 N.

*Tabulated withdrawal design values (*W*) for lag screw connections shall be multiplied by all applicable adjustment factors.

Source: This table provided courtesy of the American Forest and Paper Association, Washington, D.C.

TABLE 5.14 Lag Screw Design Values (Z) for Single-Shear (Two-Member) Connections* with Both Members of Identical Species

Side member thickness t_s, in	Lag screw diameter D, in	$G = 0.55$ Southern pine			$G = 0.50$ Douglas fir–larch			$G = 0.43$ Hem-fir			$G = 0.42$ Spruce-pine-fir		
		$Z_{\parallel}$, lb	$Z_{s\perp}$, lb	$Z_{m\perp}$, lb	$Z_{\parallel}$, lb	$Z_{s\perp}$, lb	$Z_{m\perp}$, lb	$Z_{\parallel}$, lb	$Z_{s\perp}$, lb	$Z_{m\perp}$, lb	$Z_{\parallel}$, lb	$Z_{s\perp}$, lb	$Z_{m\perp}$, lb
1/2	1/4	170	130	130	160	110	120	150	90	110	150	90	110
	5/16	240	140	180	220	130	170	190	100	150	180	100	150
	3/8	290	160	220	260	140	200	230	110	180	220	110	180
5/8	1/4	180	130	140	170	120	130	160	110	120	150	110	110
	5/16	250	180	190	240	160	180	220	130	160	210	120	160
	3/8	310	200	230	290	170	210	270	140	190	270	130	190
3/4	1/4	200	140	150	180	130	140	160	110	120	160	110	120
	5/16	270	190	200	250	170	190	230	150	170	220	150	160
	3/8	330	220	240	310	210	220	280	170	200	280	160	200
1	1/4	230	160	180	210	150	160	190	130	140	190	120	140
	5/16	300	210	230	280	190	210	250	160	190	250	160	180
	3/8	370	240	270	350	220	250	310	190	220	300	190	220
1 1/4	1/4	230	180	180	220	170	170	210	140	150	200	140	150
	5/16	340	230	250	320	210	240	280	180	210	280	170	210
	3/8	420	270	300	390	240	290	350	210	250	340	200	250

TABLE 5.14 Lag Screw Design Values (Z) for Single-Shear (Two-Member) Connections* with Both Members of Identical Species *(Continued)*

Side member thickness t_s, in	Lag screw diameter D, in	$G = 0.55$ Southern pine			$G = 0.50$ Douglas fir–larch			$G = 0.43$ Hem-fir			$G = 0.42$ Spruce-pine-fir		
		$Z_{\parallel}$, lb	$Z_{s\perp}$, lb	$Z_{m\perp}$, lb	$Z_{\parallel}$, lb	$Z_{s\perp}$, lb	$Z_{m\perp}$, lb	$Z_{\parallel}$, lb	$Z_{s\perp}$, lb	$Z_{m\perp}$, lb	$Z_{\parallel}$, lb	$Z_{s\perp}$, lb	$Z_{m\perp}$, lb
1½	¼	230	180	180	220	170	170	210	150	150	200	150	150
	5/16	340	250	250	320	230	240	300	200	210	300	190	210
	⅜	420	300	300	400	270	290	370	230	260	370	220	260
	7/16	570	350	400	540	320	380	480	270	340	470	270	330
	½	710	420	500	660	380	460	580	330	400	570	320	400
	⅝	980	570	680	920	530	620	820	420	550	810	410	540
	¾	1320	660	880	1240	590	820	1120	460	720	1100	450	710
	⅞	1710	720	1110	1620	630	1040	1470	500	920	1450	490	900
	1	2170	770	1370	2060	680	1290	1800	540	1150	1760	530	1130
	1⅛	2590	810	1670	2360	710	1560	2030	570	1400	1980	560	1380
	1¼	2880	860	2000	2630	750	1860	2250	600	1670	2200	580	1650
2½	¼	230	180	180	220	170	170	210	150	150	200	150	150
	5/16	340	250	250	320	240	240	300	210	210	300	210	210
	⅜	420	300	300	400	290	290	370	260	260	370	260	260
	7/16	570	400	400	550	380	380	510	340	340	500	340	340
	½	750	520	520	710	480	480	660	420	440	650	410	430
	⅝	1170	700	780	1120	630	730	1030	540	660	1020	530	650
	¾	1680	870	1090	1570	800	1020	1390	690	910	1360	680	890
	⅞	2100	1080	1400	1950	1000	1280	1740	830	1110	1710	810	1090
	1	2560	1280	1660	2390	1130	1530	2140	900	1340	2110	880	1320
	1⅛	3080	1350	1950	2880	1180	1800	2600	960	1590	2560	930	1560
	1¼	3650	1440	2270	3430	1250	2100	3110	1000	1850	3070	970	1820

Note: 1 in = 25.4 mm; 1 lb = 4.45 N.

*Tabulated lateral design values (Z) for lag screw connections shall be multiplied by all applicable adjustment factors. Tabulated lateral design values (Z) are for "full diameter" lag screws (see Ref. 3) inserted in side grain with lag screw axis perpendicular to wood fibers, and with the following lag screw bending yield strengths (F_{yb}):

F_{yb} = 70,000 psi for D = ¼ in
F_{yb} = 60,000 psi for$D$ = 5/16 in
F_{yb} = 45,000 psi for $D \geq$ ⅜ in

Source: This table provided courtesy of the American Forest and Paper Association, Washington, D.C.

TABLE 5.15 Lag Screw Design Values (Z) for Single Shear (Two-Member) Connections* with ¼-in ASTM A36 Steel Side Plate or ASTM A446, Grade A Steel Side Plate (for t_s < ¼ in)

Steel side plate t_s, in	Lag screw diameter D, in	$G = 0.55$ Southern pine		$G = 0.50$ Douglas fir–larch		$G = 0.43$ Hem-fir		$G = 0.42$ Spruce-pine-fir	
		$Z_{\parallel}$, lb	$Z_{\perp}$, lb	$Z_{\parallel}$, lb	$Z_{\perp}$, lb	$Z_{\parallel}$, lb	$Z_{\perp}$, lb	$Z_{\parallel}$, lb	$Z_{\perp}$, lb
¼	¼	310	230	300	220	280	200	280	190
	5⁄16	410	290	400	280	370	250	370	250
	⅜	510	350	490	330	460	300	450	290
	7⁄16	650	430	620	400	580	370	580	360
	½	810	520	780	490	730	440	720	430
	⅝	1190	720	1140	680	1070	610	1060	610
	¾	1660	960	1600	910	1490	820	1480	810
	⅞	2220	1240	2130	1170	1990	1050	1980	1030
	1	2870	1540	2750	1460	2570	1310	2550	1300
	1⅛	3610	1880	3460	1770	3230	1600	3200	1580
	1¼	4440	2260	4260	2120	3970	1910	3930	1880
3 gauge	¼	270	210	260	190	250	180	250	170
$t_s = 0.239$ in	5⁄16	370	270	360	250	340	230	340	230
	⅜	460	320	440	300	420	270	410	270
7 gauge	¼	250	180	240	170	220	160	220	160
$t_s = 0.179$ in	5⁄16	340	240	330	230	310	210	310	210
	⅜	420	290	410	270	380	250	380	250
10 gauge	¼	230	170	220	160	210	150	210	140
$t_s = 0.134$ in	5⁄16	330	230	310	220	290	200	290	190
	⅜	400	280	390	260	360	240	360	230
11 gauge	¼	250	170	220	160	200	140	200	140
$t_s = 0.12$ in	5⁄16	320	230	310	210	290	190	290	190
	⅜	400	270	380	260	360	230	360	230
12 gauge	¼	220	170	210	160	200	140	200	140
$t_s = 0.105$ in	5⁄16	320	220	310	210	290	190	280	190
	⅜	400	270	380	250	360	230	350	230
14 gauge $t_s = 0.075$ in	¼	220	160	210	150	200	140	190	140

Note: 1 in = 25.4 mm; 1 lb = 4.45 N.

*Tabulated lateral design values (Z) for lag screw connections shall be multiplied by all applicable adjustment factors. Tabulated lateral design values (Z) are for "full diameter" lag screws (see Ref. 3) inserted in side grain with lag screw axis perpendicular to wood fibers, and with the following lag screw bending yield strengths (F_{yb}):

F_{yb} = 70,000 psi for D = ¼ in
F_{yb} = 60,000 psi for$D$ = 5⁄16 in
F_{yb} = 45,000 psi for $D \geq$ ⅜ in

Tabulated lateral design values (Z) are based on dowel bearing strengths (F_e) of 58,000 psi for ASTM A36 steel and 45,000 psi for ASTM A446, Grade A steel.

Source: This table provided courtesy of the American Forest and Paper Association, Washington, D.C.

2. Normal load duration
3. Withdrawal from side grain

If the conditions assumed in Table 5.13 are not satisfied in a joint under consideration, then adjustments need to be made. The conditions which need to be considered are

1. Moisture condition in service
2. Load duration
3. Fire-retardant treatment

Moisture-condition, temperature and load duration adjustments can be found for lag screws in Table 5.30*a*, 5.33 and 4.3 respectively duration and fire-retardant treatment adjustment should be obtained from the manufacturer.

Number of Lag Screws. When more than one lag screw is loaded in withdrawal, the allowable load is the sum of the allowable values for each lag screw.

End Grain. If possible, the design should avoid withdrawal from end grain of wood. When this condition cannot be avoided, the design value in withdrawal from the grain should be multiplied by an end-grain factor $C_{eg} = 0.75$.

5.7.3 Lateral Resistance

The ultimate lateral load capacity of a lag screw in single shear (two members) is dependent on several material and dimensional properties of the connection. These include the thickness of the two joined members, the crushing strength of the wood, and the diameters (shank and root) and yield strength of the lag screw.

The European yield model (EYM) theory provides three possible failure modes for a two-member lag screw connection in single shear. The model assumes that the bearing capacity is reached when either the wood crushes under the lag screw or one or two plastic hinges are formed in the lag screw. Shown below are the three yield modes and the equations which provide the allowable lateral load value for each yield mode. The controlling value for a particular joint is the lowest value obtained from the three equations.

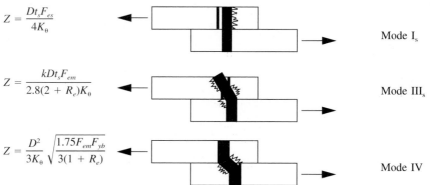

	Yield mode
$Z = \dfrac{Dt_sF_{es}}{4K_\theta}$	Mode I_s
$Z = \dfrac{kDt_sF_{em}}{2.8(2 + R_e)K_\theta}$	Mode III_s
$Z = \dfrac{D^2}{3K_\theta}\sqrt{\dfrac{1.75F_{em}F_{yb}}{3(1 + R_e)}}$	Mode IV

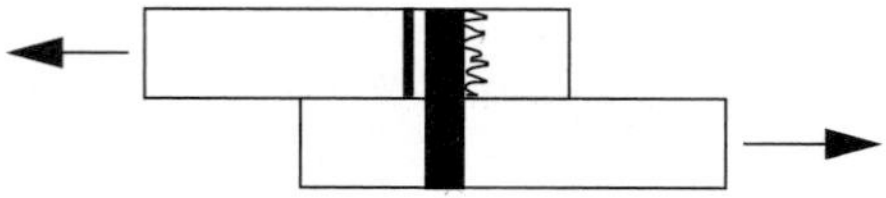

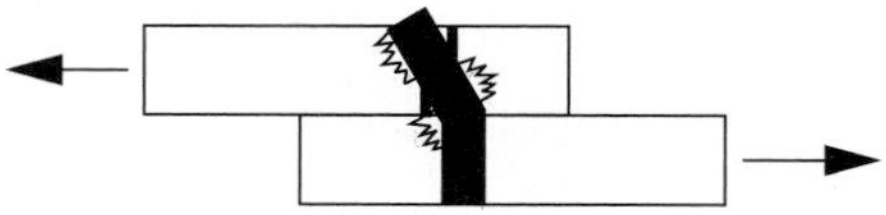

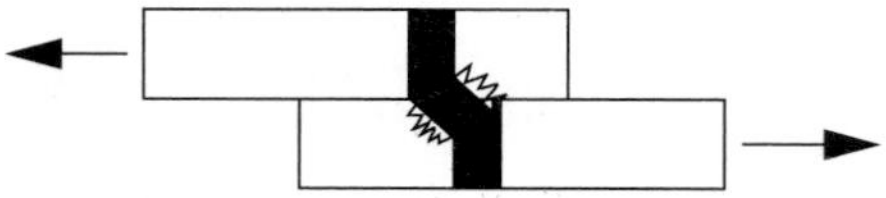

where $K = -1 + \sqrt{\dfrac{2(1 + R_e)}{R_e} + \dfrac{F_{yb}(2 + R_e)D^2}{2F_{em}t_s^2}}$

$R_e = F_{em}/F_{es}$

t_s = thickness of side member, inches

F_{em} = dowel bearing strength of main member (member holding point), psi

F_{es} = dowel bearing strength of side member, psi

F_{yb} = bending yield strength of lag screw, psi

D = unthreaded shank diameter of lag screw, inches

$K_\theta = 1 + (\theta_{max}/360°)$

θ_{max} = maximum angle of load to grain ($0° \le \theta \le 90°$) for any member in a connection.

Lateral design values have been obtained using the yield model equations by NDS[5] and are given in Table 5.14 for wood-to-wood joints and in Table 5.15 for wood-to-metal joints. Design values are given in both tables for loading applied parallel to grain ($Z_{\parallel}$) and perpendicular to grain ($Z_{\perp}$).

If a connection does not qualify under the geometry and materials properties given in Tables 5.14 and 5.15, then the three yield model equations may be used to obtain a lateral design value Z. Table 5.36 in the Appendix may be used to obtain the dowel bearing strength $F_{e\parallel}$ and $F_{e\perp}$ needed in solving EYM equations. These equations will provide a design value of about one-fifth the ultimate capacity of the lag screw.

For other angles of loading, the allowable load may be computed from values parallel and perpendicular to the grain by using the Hankinson formula or the Scholten nomograph. Both the Hankinson formula and the Scholten nomograph are given in Sec. 5.5.

Table 5.14 gives allowable design values for lateral load when side plates are wood of ½- to 2½-in (12.7- to 63.5-mm) thickness. When side plates are steel from 14 gauge to ¼ in (1.99 to 6.35 mm), values can be obtained from Table 5.15. Allowable values are provided for both parallel and perpendicular to grain loading. The tables are based on

1. Seasoned wood which remains dry in service
2. Normal load duration
3. One lag screw, in single shear
4. Lag screw laterally loaded parallel or perpendicular to grain

If the conditions assumed in Tables 5.14, and 5.15 are not satisfied in a joint under consideration, then adjustments need to be made. The conditions which need to be considered are

1. Moisture condition in service
2. Load duration
3. Side plates of greater thickness than those given in Tables 5.14 and 5.15
4. Multiple lag screws in a row
5. Angle of load to grain if other than 0° or 90°
6. Penetration of less than $8D$

The adjustments recommended for moisture condition, temperature and load duration are given in Tables 5.30*a* and *b*, 5.33 and 4.3 respectively. See manufacturers recommendations for fire retardant treated wood adjustments.

Penetration Depth Factor. Lateral loading design values for lag screws are based on a penetration of lag screw (not including length of tapered tip) into the main member of eight times the shank diameter of the lag screw, $p = 8D$. The minimum lag screw penetration for a reduced design value is four times the diameter of the lag screw shank; when $4D \leq p \leq 8D$, the design value should be multiplied by C_d, where $C_d = p/8D \leq 1.0$.

Metal Side Plates. If the metal side plates are thicker than ¼ in (6.35 mm), then the allowable value for a lag screw should be reduced in proportion to the lesser penetration of the lag screw. No increase is allowed for side plates thinner than ¼ inch (6.35 mm). Metal side plates must be of ample strength to carry imposed loads.

Multiple Lag Screws in a Row. If more than one lag screw is placed in a row, then it is necessary to apply a group reduction. The procedure for this has been discussed in Sec. 5.6.

Angle of Load to Grain. Tables 5.14 and 5.15 give the allowable value for a lag screw loaded parallel or perpendicular to the grain of the wood (0° and 90°, respectively). When the load acts at other than 0° and 90° with the grain and the lag screw is inserted into the side grain of the wood, the design value can be obtained by using the Hankinson formula or the Scholten nomograph. See Sec. 5.5.

Lag Screw in End Grain. When the loads act perpendicular to the grain and the lag screw is inserted parallel to the fibers (i.e., in the end grain of the member), design values for lateral resistance should be multiplied by the end-grain factor $C_{eg} = 0.67$.

5.7.4 Placement

The recommended spacing, end distances, edge distances, and net section for lag screws are the same as those given for a bolt diameter equal to the shank diameter of the lag screw. These are given in Sec. 5.9.6.

5.7.5 Combined Lateral and Withdrawal Loads

When a lag screw is subjected to a combined lateral and withdrawal loading (see Fig. 5.19), it is recommended that the allowable design value be obtained by using the equation

$$Z'_\alpha = \frac{(W'p)Z'}{W'p\cos^2\alpha + Z'\sin^2\alpha}$$

where α = angle between the wood surface and the direction of applied load
p = length of thread penetration in main member
Z' = allowable lateral design load
W' = allowable withdrawal design load

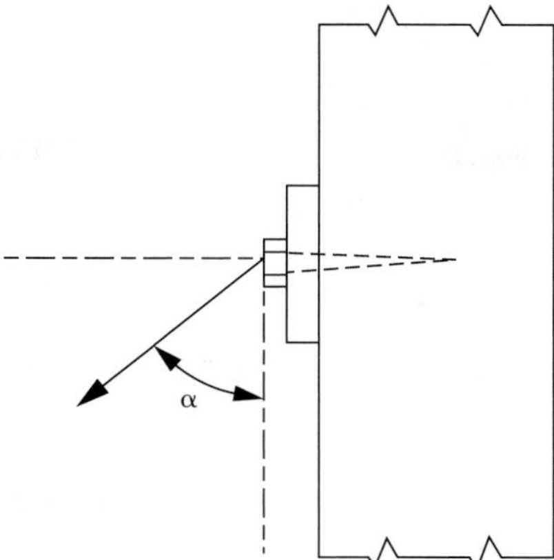

FIG. 5.19 Combined lateral and withdrawal loading.

EXAMPLE 5.9: LAG SCREWS LOADED AT AN ANGLE TO THE GRAIN Determine the allowable load Q (dead load plus earthquake load) for the joint shown (Fig. 5.20). The wood is No. 1 Douglas fir surfaced green and is used in a dry-service condition.

SOLUTION: Specific gravity = 0.50 (see Table 5.2).
$Z_{\|} = 1570$ lb, $Z_{m\perp} = 1020$ lb (from Table 5.14).
Check penetration of lag screw:

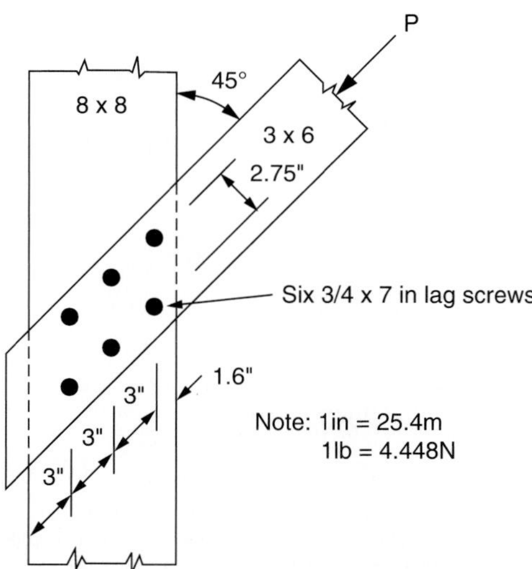

FIG. 5.20 Example 5.9.

$$p = 7.0 - 2.5 = 4.5 \text{ in}$$

$$C_d = \frac{p}{8D} \leq 1.0$$

$$= \frac{4.5}{(8 \times 3/4)} = 0.75$$

$$Z_{\|}^1 = Z_{\|} \times C_d = 1570 \times 0.75 = 1178 \text{ lb}$$

$$Z_{m\perp}^1 = Z_{m\perp} \times C_d = 1020 \times 0.75 = 765 \text{ lb}$$

$$P_s = P_{45°} = 928 \text{ lb}$$

(by Hankinson formula using Scholten nomograph; see Sec. 5.5).

Group reduction factor:

$$A_m = 3.25 \times 4.50 = 14.62 \text{ in}^2\text{*}$$

$$A_s = 2.5 \times 5.5 = 13.75 \text{ in}^2$$

$$\frac{A_m}{A_s} = \frac{14.62}{13.75} > 1.0 \qquad \text{(see footnotes to Table 5.26)}$$

Therefore, use $A_m/A_s = 13.75/14.62 = 0.94$ and use $A_m = 14.62 \text{ in}^2$. $C_g = 0.99$ by interpolation from Table 5.26. $C_m = 0.4$ (see Table 5.30).
Allowable load:

$$Q = n\Sigma P_s \times C_g \times C_D \times C_M$$

$$= 2 \times 3 \times 928 \times 0.99 \times 1.6 \times 0.4$$

$$= \underline{3660 \text{ lb}} \text{ (16.28 kN)}$$

Check net area (3 × 6):

$$A_{\text{net}} = 13.75 - (2 \times 2.5 \times 0.75) = 10.00 \text{ in}^2$$

$$F_c' = F_c \times C_F \times C_M \times C_D$$

$$= 1450 \times 1.1 \times 0.8 \times 1.6$$

$$= 2040 \text{ psi}$$

$$P \text{ (allowable)} = F_c \times A_{\text{net}}$$

$$= 2040 \times 10.00$$

$$= 20{,}400 \text{ lb (90.8 kN)} > 3660 \qquad \text{OK}$$

*The group reduction factor C_g is partially based on the extensional stiffness of the connected members. Therefore, since the load is not parallel or perpendicular to the grain, it is appropriate to use an equivalent width slightly larger than the spacing between rows and a thickness equal to the penetration of the lag screw into the main member for the effective area of the main member. The use of a wider width is justified based upon the fact that wood when loaded at an angle to the grain (not including 90°) has a greater extensional stiffness than when loaded perpendicular to the grain.

5.8 DOWELS, DRIFT PINS, AND DRIFT BOLTS

5.8.1 Introduction

Dowels, drift pins, and drift bolts are hammer-driven or pressed into tight-fitting or slightly undersized holes. They are designed primarily to transmit shear loads from member to member. Drift pins are also used to align members. Dowels, drift pins, and drift bolts may be made of metal, wood, or high-strength plastics.

The performance of dowels, drift pins, and drift bolts depends to a considerable extent on their bending stiffness and shear resistance as well as on their bearing areas and the bearing resistance of the fastened members. Because of their tight fit, multiples of these fasteners in a joint, designed to transmit shear loads, act like multiple lag screws.

So that a tight fit of the fastener is maintained in the hole, the shrinkage and swelling of the fastener, if any, and that of the surrounding wood must be similar. Thus, the moisture content of the wood surrounding the fastener should be similar to that of the fastener at the time of installation if the fastener is made of wood.

5.8.2 Dowels

Dowels may be plain rods or squares, twisted squares, longitudinally or helically fluted rods, or helically threaded rods. The deformed rods are commonly known as *spiral dowels*. Dowels are headless and normally are not pointed. They may be inserted flush with the outer faces of the fastened members or reach only to or near to the end of the predrilled hole. If plain or deformed, they may be adhesively bonded to the surrounding material. Wood dowels are cut to length from dowel stock which ranges in size from ¼ to 1 in (6.35 to 25.4 mm) in diameter. The stock length is usually 3 ft (0.914 m). The stock sizes of available spiral dowels are given in the table below:

Available sizes of spiral dowels

Outside diameter, in	¼	5⁄16	⅜	7⁄16	½	⅝
Minimum length, in	2½	3	3½	3½	4	4
Maximum length, in	6	6½	10	12	18	24

Spiral dowels come in length increments of ½ in up to 8 in and 1-in length increments for lengths over 8 in. The diameter of a spiral dowel is measured across its greatest dimension after it has been formed.

Lead holes for spiral dowels should be drilled to about 75 percent of the dowel's outside diameter. This hole size will permit easy driving and is small enough so that the screwlike action of the spiral dowel can occur.

If the dowel is bonded to the members as a result of friction, by deformations of the dowel surface, or by an adhesive, the dowels may tie adjoining members to each other and/or reduce or even prevent their splitting.

5.8.3 Drift Pins

Drift pins are plain or helically fluted headless rods with a tapered point end. They are installed with both ends flush with or protruding from the outer faces of the fastened members.

The lead hole for a drift pin or drift bolt should be 1⁄16 in less than the diameter of the drift pin. This should prevent splitting and allow for the full strength of the drift pin to be developed.

5.8.4 Drift Bolts

Drift bolts—at times referred to as *drift pins*—are plain headless and pointless cylindrical fasteners. They are installed with both ends protruding from the outer faces of the fastened members. If solid, both ends may be swedged, and if made of tube or pipe, both ends may be flared. When steel sleeve or side plates are used, a practice often used in the field is to weld the ends of the drift bolt to the steel. Care must be taken so that the wood will not be burned during welding. Washers should be provided below the swedges and flares if steel sleeve or plates are not used.

5.8.5 Design Values for Dowels, Drift Pins, and Drift Bolts

Joints assembled with dowels, drift pins, and drift bolts are designed in a manner similar to that used for bolts. An appropriate design value for a dowel can be obtained from Table 5.16. For a drift pin or drift bolt an appropriate design value can be obtained by using 75 percent of the design value for a common bolt of the same diameter and length in main member. If however, the drift pin or drift bolt is used in a manner similar to a lag screw, the design value should be taken to be that of a lag screw with shank diameter equal to that of the drift pin or drift bolt. It is recommended that some additional penetration of the pin into members be provided to offset the lack of the washer, head, and nut of a common bolt.

A typical example of the use of a spiral dowel is shown in Fig. 5.21, which illustrates a concealed connection of a wood beam to a wood column. Table 5.16 gives allowable design values for spiral dowels for both lateral loads and withdrawal loads. Table 5.17 gives adjustment factors for varying conditions of moisture content at fabrication and in service.

Samsalone and White[11] give design values for dowels placed in the end grain of glue-laminated timber for monotonic, repeated, and sustained loads.

TABLE 5.16 Allowable Design Values for Spiral Dowels

Diameter of spiral dowel, in	Group I	Group II	Group III	Group IV
Lateral resistance in pounds per spiral dowel				
1/4	128	111	96	76
5/16	201	173	150	119
3/8	289	250	216	172
7/16	393	340	294	234
1/2	514	444	384	305
9/16	650	562	486	386
5/8	803	693	600	477
3/4	1156	998	863	686
7/8	1573	1359	1175	934
1	2055	1775	1535	1220
1 1/8	2600	2246	1943	1544
1 1/4	3211	2773	2398	1906
Withdrawal resistance in pounds per inch of penetration				
Side grain				
1/4	154	104	70	38
5/16	181	122	83	45
3/8	207	140	95	52
7/16	233	158	107	58
1/2	258	174	118	64
9/16	281	190	129	71
5/8	305	206	140	75
3/4	349	236	160	87
7/8	392	265	180	99
1	434	293	199	109
1 1/8	473	320	217	119
1 1/4	512	346	235	128
End grain				
1/4	88	59	40	22
5/16	103	70	47	25
3/8	119	81	54	29
7/16	133	90	61	32
1/2	148	99	67	36
9/16	160	108	74	40
5/8	173	117	79	43
3/4	200	135	92	50
7/8	223	151	103	56
1	247	167	113	61
1 1/8	270	184	124	67
1 1/4	292	198	135	74

Note: 1 in = 25.4 mm; 1 lb = 4.45 N.

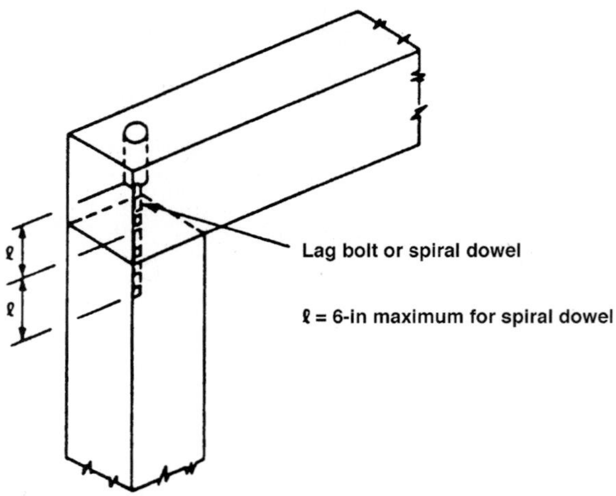

FIG. 5.21 Concealed type—girder to wood column.

5.9 BOLTS

5.9.1 Introduction

Although bolts do not have as great a load-carrying capacity as timber connectors, in many cases they provide more than adequate strength. Bolts are more easily installed, since it is not necessary to cut grooves and the members being joined do not need to be separated.

The bolt most typically used is the standard ASTM A307 grade. As will be shown later, the use of a high-strength bolt such as an A325 grade may or may not increase the allowable design value. Standard bolts range in size from ¼ to 1½ in (6.35 to 25.4 mm) in diameter and from 1 to 16 in (25.4 to 406 mm) in length, as is shown in Table 5.18.

TABLE 5.17 Adjustment of Spiral Dowel Load Values for Service, Seasoning, and Use Conditions

Condition of lumber		Percentage of withdrawal load value	Percentage of lateral load value
When installed	In service		
Seasoned*	Seasoned	100	100
Unseasoned (m.c. 30%)	Seasoned	25	100
Seasoned or unseasoned	Exposed to weather	25	70
Seasoned or unseasoned	Always wet	100	60
Use condition: spiral dowel in end grain		See Table 5.16	60

*Seasoned solid sawed lumber has a maximum moisture content of 19 percent. Glued-laminated timber has a maximum moisture content of 16 percent.

TABLE 5.18 Some Available Sizes of Standard Regular-Stock Steel Bolts

Diameter, in	Lengths, in*
1/4	1 to 8
5/6	1 to 8 and 8½ to 10
3/8	1 to 8 and 8½ to 11½
7/16	1 to 8 and 8½ to 11½
1/2	1 to 8 and 8½ to 11½
5/8	1 to 8 and 8½ to 11½
3/4	1 to 8 and 8½ to 11½
7/8	1¼ to 8 and 8½ to 11½
1	1½ to 8 and 8½ to 11½
1⅛	1½ to 8 and 8½ to 11½
1¼	1½ to 8 and 8½ to 11½

Note: 1 in = 25.4 mm.

*Bolt lengths vary by ¼ in from 1 to 8 in and by ½ in from 8½ to 11½ in.

Steel bolts can be electroplated or galvanized. Special bolts for a variety of purposes may be made of aluminum, bronze, stainless steel, Monel, or specialized wood products like Permali.

Bolts are placed in holes predrilled from 1/32 to 1/16 in (0.794 to 1.588 mm) larger than the bolt diameter with the larger value applying to the larger-diameter bolts. Shrinkage of the bolt hole will be about 5 to 8 percent of bolt diameter across the grain; therefore, the larger hole size will prevent future splitting of the wood as it dries to an equilibrium moisture content in place. It also facilitates field installation.

Washers are to be used with all bolts when the head or the nut will bear against the wood. If they are not used, then the head or nut will be drawn into the wood when the bolt is tightened. Allowable design values are not based on washers bearing firmly on wood. It is recommended, however, that all nuts be tight (snug) at the time of installation and that they be retightened after the wood has reached its equilibrium moisture content.

If bolt holes are not properly aligned, a considerable shift in the distribution of load to the bolts may occur, and excessive deflections may result. However, it has been found that normal fabrication tolerances have been sufficient to make bolted structures perform in an acceptable manner even if exposed to vibrations, shocks, and earthquakes.

5.9.2 Loads on Bolts

Loads applied to bolts are placed perpendicular to the axis of the bolt as a lateral load. Loads can be applied either parallel, perpendicular, or at an angle to the grain of the wood members being joined.

The ultimate load capacity of a bolted joint, in single, double, or multiple shear, is dependent on several material and dimensional properties and the number of bolt shear planes.

The European yield model (EYM) theory provides six possible modes of failure for bolted connections in single shear, as shown in Fig. 5.22. EYM theory provides four modes of failure for double-shear connections which are also shown in Fig. 5.22. The models assume that failure occurs when the wood crushes under the bolt or when one, two, or four plastic hinges are formed in the bolt.

The controlling value for a two-member connection (single shear) is the least value of Z obtained by solving the six equations given below:

Equation	Yield mode
$Z = \dfrac{Dt_m F_{em}}{4K_\theta}$	Mode I_m
$Z = \dfrac{Dt_s F_{es}}{4K_\theta}$	Mode I_s
$Z = \dfrac{k_1 Dt_s F_{es}}{3.6K_\theta}$	Mode II
$Z = \dfrac{k_2 Dt_m F_{em}}{3.2(1 + 2R_e)K_\theta}$	Mode III_m
$Z = \dfrac{k_3 Dt_s F_{em}}{3.2(2 + R_e)K_\theta}$	Mode III_s
$Z = \dfrac{D^2}{3.2K_\theta}\sqrt{\dfrac{2F_{em}F_{yb}}{3(1 + R_e)}}$	Mode IV

where $k_1 = \sqrt{\dfrac{R_e + 2R_e^2(1 + R_t + R_t^2) + R_t^2 R_e^3 - R_e(1 + R_t)}{(1 + R_e)}}$

$$k_2 = -1 + \sqrt{2(1 + R_e) + \frac{2F_{yb}(1 + 2R_e)D^2}{3F_{em}t_m^2}}$$

$$k_3 = -1 + \sqrt{\frac{2(1 + R_e)}{R_e} + \frac{2F_{yb}(2 + R_e)D^2}{3F_{em}t_s^2}}$$

$R_e = F_{em}/F_{es}$
$R_t = t_m/t_s$
t_m = thickness of main (thicker) member, in
t_s = thickness of side (thinner) member, in
F_{em} = dowel bearing strength of main (thicker) member, psi
F_{es} = dowel bearing strength of side (thinner) member, psi
F_{yb} = bending yield strength of bolt, psi
D = nominal bolt diameter, in
$K_\theta = 1 + (\theta_{max}/360°)$
θ_{max} = maximum angle of load to grain ($0° \leq \theta \leq 90°$) for any member in a connection.

The controlling value for a three-member connection (double shear) is the least value of Z obtained by solving the four equations given below:

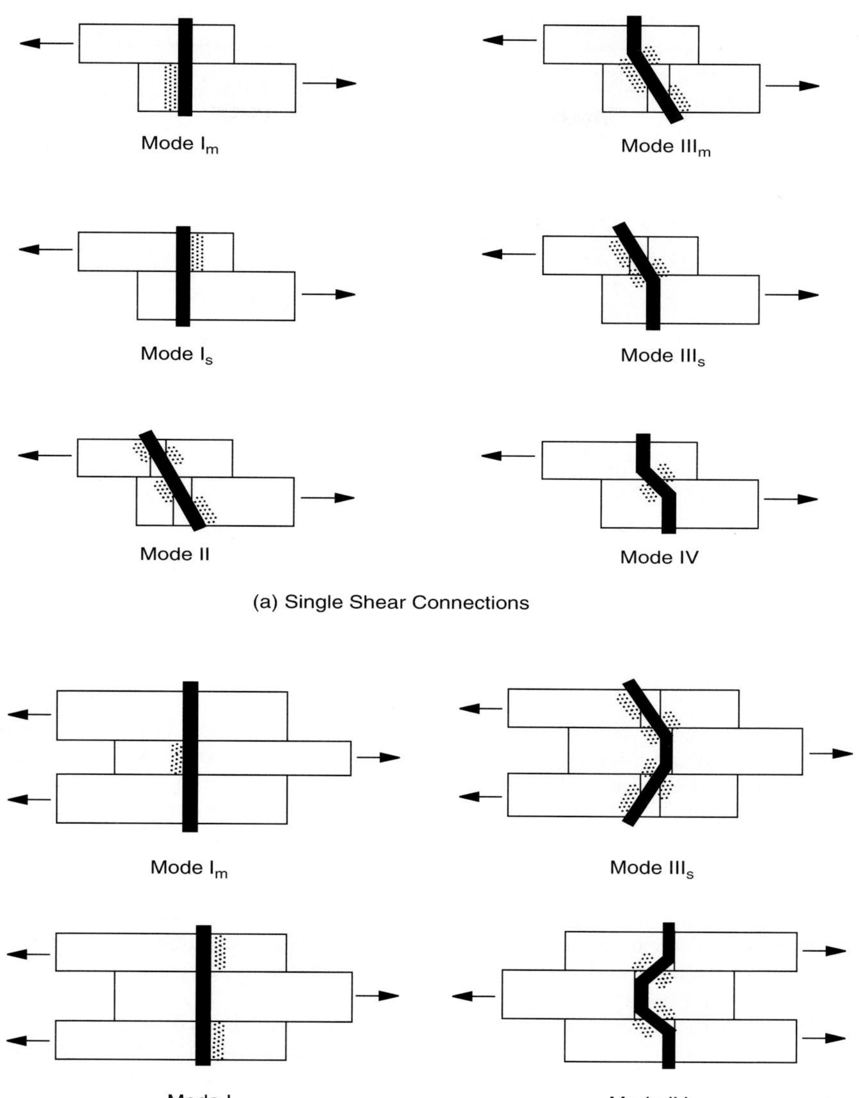

FIG. 5.22 Modes of failure bolted joins in single and double shear.

Equation	Yield mode
$Z = \dfrac{Dt_m F_{em}}{4K_\theta}$	Mode I_m
$Z = \dfrac{Dt_s F_{es}}{2K_\theta}$	Mode I_s
$Z = \dfrac{k_3 D t_s F_{em}}{1.6(2 + R_e)K_\theta}$	Mode III_s
$Z = \dfrac{D^2}{1.6K_\theta}\sqrt{\dfrac{2F_{em}F_{yb}}{3(1 + R_e)}}$	Mode IV

where $k_3 = -1 + \sqrt{\dfrac{2(1 + R_e)}{R_e} + \dfrac{2F_{yb}(2 + R_e)D^2}{3F_{em}t_s^2}}$

$R_e = F_{em}/F_{es}$
t_m = thickness of main (center) member, in
t_s = thickness of side member, in
F_{em} = dowel bearing strength of main (center) member, psi
F_{es} = dowel bearing strength of side members, psi
F_{yb} = bending yield strength of bolt, psi
D = nominal bolt diameter, in
$K_\theta = 1 + (\theta_{max}/360°)$
θ_{max} = maximum angle of load to grain ($0° \leq \theta \leq 90°$) for any member in a connection.

A typical load-deformation curve is shown in Fig. 5.23 for a joint with a ½-in (12.7-mm) bolt and three members. The two splice plates are steel. As can be seen, the first part of the curve is linear, and little slip takes place in the joint. At the proportional limit, slip begins to increase rapidly with load, the curve finally flattens out, and slip becomes very large for little or no load increase.

Test results have shown that joints having a seasoned wood main member and two splice plates of steel have a bearing stress parallel to the grain at proportional limit loads of about 60 percent of the crushing strength for softwoods and 80 percent for hardwoods. When wood side plates are used, each equal to one-half the thickness of the main member, the bearing stress is about 80 percent of that obtained for steel splice plates.

The proportional limit value is less for a bolted joint loaded perpendicular to the grain than it is when the joint is loaded parallel to the grain. This is due to the lower crushing strength of the wood perpendicular to the grain.

5.9.3 Quality of Bolt Hole

The bearing strength of wood under a bolt is affected to a considerable extent by the size and quality of the hole into which the bolt is inserted. If too large a hole is bored, the bearing strength under the bolt will not be uniform, and if the hole is too small, the wood will split when the bolt is driven in or as it dries to equilibrium moisture content.

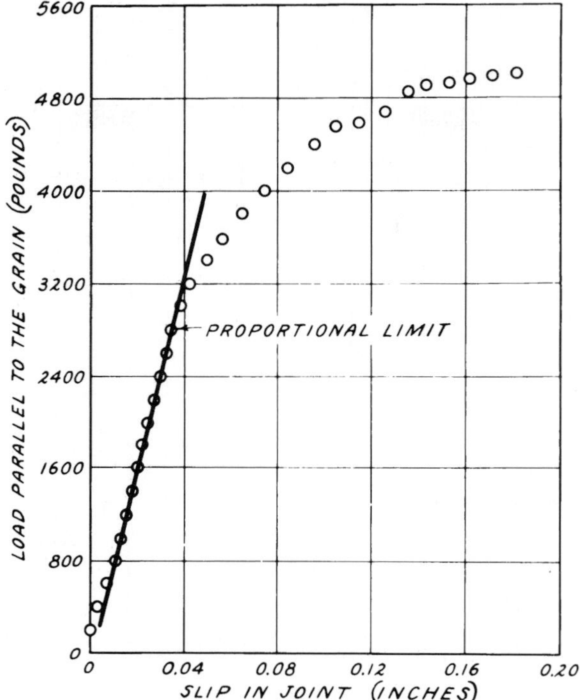

FIG. 5.23 Variation of load parallel to the grain and slip in joint.

A smooth hole will give higher bearing values than a rough-cut hole, as shown in Fig. 5.24. Also, deformations as a result of load will increase with an increase in the roughness of the bolt hole surface. Rough surfaces are caused by using dull bits and improper rates of feed and drill speed.

5.9.4 Allowable Loads

Allowable design values for bolts laterally loaded are given in Tables 5.19 and 5.20 for both parallel and perpendicular to grain for single-shear (two-member) connections (see Fig. 5.25*a*). Separate values are given for loading of side or main member perpendicular to grain. Table 5.19 provides allowable design values for sawn lumber when both members are of identical species. Table 5.20 gives allowable design values when a ¼-in A36 steel side plate is used with a sawn wood member. Allowable design values when glued-laminated timber members are used in conjunction with a sawn lumber side member or a ¼-in A36 steel side member are given in similar tables in the NDS.[5]

Tables 5.21 and 5.22 provide bolt design values for double-shear (three-member) connections when the load is applied parallel to grain or perpendicular to side or main member (see Fig. 5.25*b*). Table 5.21 is for main and side members of identical

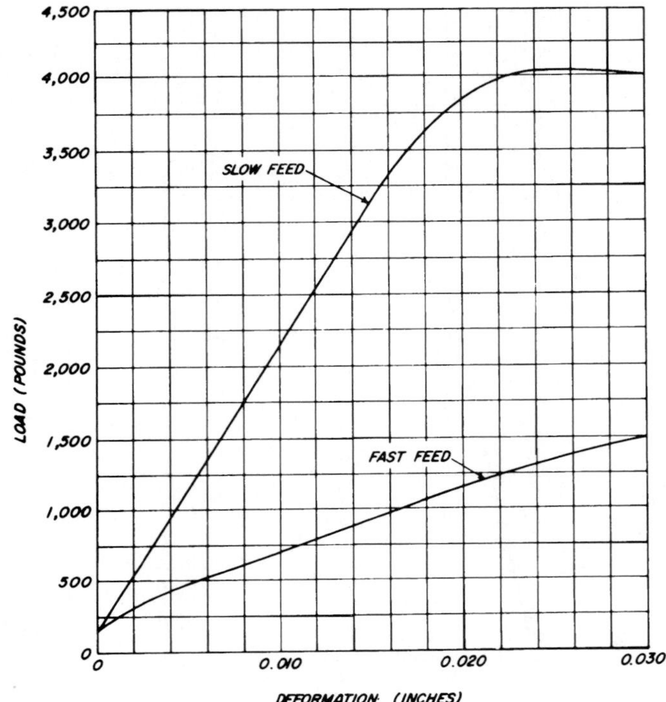

FIG. 5.24

FIG. 5.24 Effects of surface condition of bolt holes, resulting from a fast feed rate and a slow feed rate of drill bit, on load deformation of bolted joints.

species, whereas Table 5.22 is for a connection with side members of ¼-in A36 steel. For allowable design values when the main member is glued-laminated timber and the side members are sawn lumber of species identical to the glued-laminated timber or ¼-in A36 steel side plates, see tables in the NDS.[5]

Allowable values for angles of load between 0° (parallel to grain) and 90° (perpendicular to grain) can be obtained from parallel and perpendicular values by using the Hankinson formula or the Scholten nomograph. If a connection does not qualify under the geometry and materials properties given in Tables 5.19–5.22, then the six or four yield model equations may be used to obtain a lateral design value Z. Table 5.37 in the Appendix may be used to obtain the dowel bearing strength F_{em} and F_{es} needed in solving these equations.

As stated earlier, allowable values given in Tables 5.19–5.22 are applicable whether or not nuts have been tightened.

A plot of allowable values both parallel and perpendicular to grain for two bolt sizes for three-member (double-shear) connections is shown in Fig. 5.26. As can be seen, these values first increase proportionally (in general) with the thickness of side members and main member. However, they then reach a maximum value because the bolt reaches its yield strength or the wood crushes under the bolt.

TABLE 5.19 Bolt Design Values (Z) for Single-Shear (Two-Member) Connections* for Sawn Lumber with Both Members of Identical Species

Thickness			$G = 0.55$ Southern pine			$G = 0.50$ Douglas fir–larch			$G = 0.43$ Hem-fir			$G = 0.42$ Spruce-pine-fir		
Main member t_m, in	Side member t_s, in	Bolt diameter D, in	$Z_{\parallel}$, lb	$Z_{s\perp}$, lb	$Z_{m\perp}$, lb	$Z_{\parallel}$, lb	$Z_{s\perp}$, lb	$Z_{m\perp}$, lb	$Z_{\parallel}$, lb	$Z_{s\perp}$, lb	$Z_{m\perp}$, lb	$Z_{\parallel}$, lb	$Z_{s\perp}$, lb	$Z_{m\perp}$, lb
1½	1½	½	530	330	330	480	300	300	410	250	250	410	240	240
		⅝	660	400	400	600	360	360	520	300	300	510	290	290
		¾	800	460	460	720	420	420	620	350	350	610	340	340
		⅞	930	520	520	850	470	470	720	390	390	710	380	380
		1	1060	580	580	970	530	530	830	440	440	810	430	430
2½	1½	½	660	400	420	610	370	370	550	320	310	540	320	300
		⅝	930	560	490	850	520	430	730	420	360	710	410	350
		¾	1120	660	560	1020	590	500	870	460	410	850	450	400
		⅞	1300	720	620	1190	630	550	1020	500	450	1000	490	440
		1	1490	770	680	1360	680	610	1160	540	500	1140	530	490
3	1½	½	660	400	470	610	370	420	550	320	350	540	320	330
		⅝	940	560	550	880	520	480	790	420	400	780	410	390
		¾	1270	660	620	1190	590	550	1020	460	450	1000	450	440
		⅞	1520	720	690	1390	630	610	1190	500	500	1160	490	490
		1	1740	770	750	1590	680	670	1360	540	550	1330	530	540
3½	1½	½	660	400	470	610	370	430	550	320	380	540	320	370
		⅝	940	560	620	880	520	540	790	420	440	780	410	430
		¾	1270	660	690	1200	590	610	1100	460	500	1080	450	480
		⅞	1680	720	770	1590	630	680	1370	500	550	1340	490	540
		1	2010	770	830	1830	680	740	1570	540	600	1530	530	590
	3½	½	750	520	520	720	490	490	660	440	440	660	430	430
		⅜	1170	780	780	1120	700	700	1040	600	600	1020	590	590
		¾	1690	960	960	1610	870	870	1450	740	740	1420	730	730
		⅞	2170	1160	1160	1970	1060	1060	1690	910	910	1660	890	890
		1	2480	1360	1360	2260	1230	1230	1930	1030	1030	1890	1000	1000

TABLE 5.19 Bolt Design Values (Z) for Single-Shear (Two-Member) Connections* for Sawn Lumber with Both Members of Identical Species *(Continued)*

Thickness: Main member t_m, in	Thickness: Side member t_s, in	Bolt diameter D, in	$G = 0.55$ Southern pine $Z_\parallel$, lb	$Z_{s\perp}$, lb	$Z_{m\perp}$, lb	$G = 0.50$ Douglas fir–larch $Z_\parallel$, lb	$Z_{s\perp}$, lb	$Z_{m\perp}$, lb	$G = 0.43$ Hem-fir $Z_\parallel$, lb	$Z_{s\perp}$, lb	$Z_{m\perp}$, lb	$G = 0.42$ Spruce-pine-fir $Z_\parallel$, lb	$Z_{s\perp}$, lb	$Z_{m\perp}$, lb
4½	1½	⅝	940	560	640	880	520	590	790	420	530	780	410	520
		¾	1270	660	840	1200	590	750	1100	460	600	1080	450	590
		⅞	1680	720	930	1590	630	820	1460	500	660	1440	490	640
		1	2150	770	1000	2050	680	890	1800	540	720	1760	530	710
	3½	⅝	1170	780	780	1120	700	730	1040	600	660	1020	590	650
		¾	1690	960	1090	1610	870	1000	1490	740	840	1480	730	820
		⅞	2300	1160	1300	2190	1060	1160	1950	920	960	1920	910	940
		1	2870	1390	1440	2610	1290	1290	2240	1140	1070	2190	1120	1050
5½	1½	⅝	940	560	640	880	520	590	790	420	530	780	410	520
		¾	1270	660	850	1200	590	790	1100	460	700	1080	450	690
		⅞	1680	720	1090	1590	630	980	1460	500	780	1440	490	760
		1	2150	770	1190	2050	680	1060	1800	540	860	1760	530	830
	3½	⅝	1170	780	780	1120	700	730	1040	600	660	1020	590	650
		¾	1690	960	1090	1610	870	1030	1490	740	920	1480	730	900
		⅞	2300	1160	1410	2190	1060	1260	1950	920	1030	1920	910	1010
		1	2870	1390	1550	2660	1290	1390	2370	1140	1150	2330	1120	1120
7½	1½	⅝	940	560	640	880	520	590	790	420	530	780	410	520
		¾	1270	660	850	1200	590	790	1100	460	700	1080	450	690
		⅞	1680	720	1090	1590	630	1010	1460	500	900	1440	490	890
		1	2150	770	1350	2050	680	1270	1800	540	1130	1760	530	1110
	3½	⅝	1170	780	780	1120	700	730	1040	600	660	1020	590	650
		¾	1690	960	1090	1610	870	1030	1490	740	920	1480	730	910
		⅞	2300	1160	1450	2190	1060	1360	1950	920	1210	1920	910	1180
		1	2870	1390	1830	2660	1290	1630	2370	1140	1340	2330	1120	1300

Note: 1 in = 25.4 mm; 1 lb = 4.45 N.

*Tabulated lateral design values (Z) for bolted connections shall be multiplied by all applicable adjustment factors. Tabulated lateral design values (Z) are for "full diameter" bolts (see Ref 3) with a bending yield strength (F_{yb}) of 45,000 psi.

Source: This table provided courtesy of the American Forest and Paper Association, Washington, D.C.

TABLE 5.20 Bolt Design Values (Z) for Single-Shear (Two-Member) Connections* for Sawn Lumber with ¼-in ASTM A36 Steel Side Plate

Thickness			$G = 0.55$ Southern pine		$G = 0.50$ Douglas fir–larch		$G = 0.43$ Hem-fir		$G = 0.42$ Spruce-pine-fir	
Main member t_m, in	Steel side plate t_s, in	Bolt diameter D, in	$Z_{\parallel}$, lb	$Z_{\perp}$, lb	$Z_{\parallel}$, lb	$Z_{\perp}$, lb	$Z_{\parallel}$, lb	$Z_{\perp}$, lb	$Z_{\parallel}$, lb	$Z_{\perp}$, lb
1½	¼	½	570	310	530	270	470	240	460	230
		⅝	710	350	660	320	590	270	580	270
		¾	860	390	800	360	700	310	690	300
		⅞	1000	440	930	400	820	340	810	340
		1	1140	480	1060	440	940	380	920	370
2½	¼	½	780	440	750	390	700	320	690	310
		⅝	1100	500	1010	440	880	370	860	360
		¾	1320	550	1210	490	1050	410	1030	400
		⅞	1540	610	1410	540	1230	450	1210	440
		1	1760	650	1620	590	1410	490	1380	480
3	¼	½	780	500	750	450	710	370	700	360
		⅝	1170	580	1130	510	1040	420	1020	410
		¾	1560	640	1430	570	1240	470	1220	460
		⅞	1830	700	1670	620	1450	510	1420	500
		1	2090	750	1910	670	1660	560	1630	540
3½	¼	½	780	500	750	470	710	430	700	410
		⅝	1170	670	1130	580	1050	480	1040	470
		¾	1650	730	1580	650	1440	530	1410	520
		⅞	2120	800	1940	710	1680	570	1640	560
		1	2420	850	2210	760	1910	630	1880	610

TABLE 5.20 Bolt Design Values (Z) for Single-Shear (Two-Member) Connections* for Sawn Lumber with 1/4-in ASTM A36 Steel Side Plate *(Continued)*

Thickness			$G = 0.55$ Southern pine		$G = 0.50$ Douglas fir–larch		$G = 0.43$ Hem-fir		$G = 0.42$ Spruce-pine-fir	
Main member t_m, in	Steel side plate t_s, in	Bolt diameter D, in	$Z_{\parallel}$, lb	$Z_{\perp}$, lb	$Z_{\parallel}$, lb	$Z_{\perp}$, lb	$Z_{\parallel}$, lb	$Z_{\perp}$, lb	$Z_{\parallel}$, lb	$Z_{\perp}$, lb
4 1/2	1/4	5/8	1170	710	1130	660	1050	600	1040	580
		3/4	1650	920	1580	820	1480	660	1470	640
		7/8	2220	1010	2130	880	1990	710	1970	700
		1	2880	1070	2760	950	2440	770	2390	750
5 1/2	1/4	5/8	1170	710	1130	660	1050	600	1040	600
		3/4	1650	950	1580	900	1480	790	1470	770
		7/8	2220	1220	2130	1070	1990	860	1970	830
		1	2880	1290	2760	1150	2580	930	2550	900
7 1/2	1/4	5/8	1170	710	1130	660	1050	600	1040	600
		3/4	1650	950	1580	900	1480	810	1470	800
		7/8	2220	1240	2130	1160	1990	1040	1970	1030
		1	2880	1540	2760	1460	2580	1250	2550	1210
9 1/2	1/4	3/4	1650	950	1580	900	1480	810	1470	800
		7/8	2220	1240	2130	1160	1990	1040	1970	1030
		1	2880	1540	2760	1460	2580	1310	2550	1290
11 1/2	1/4	7/8	2220	1240	2130	1160	1990	1040	1970	1030
		1	2880	1540	2760	1460	2580	1310	2550	1290
13 1/2	1/4	1	2880	1540	2760	1460	2580	1310	2550	1290

Note: 1 in = 25.4 mm; 1 lb = 4.45 N.

*Tabulated lateral design values (Z) for bolted connections shall be multiplied by all applicable adjustment factors. Tabulated lateral design values (Z) are for "full diameter" bolts (see Ref. 3) with a bending yield strength (F_{yb}) of 45,000 psi. Tabulated lateral design values (Z) are based on a dowel bearing strength (F_e) of 58,000 psi for ASTM A36 steel.

Source: This table provided courtesy of the American Forest and Paper Association, Washington, D.C.

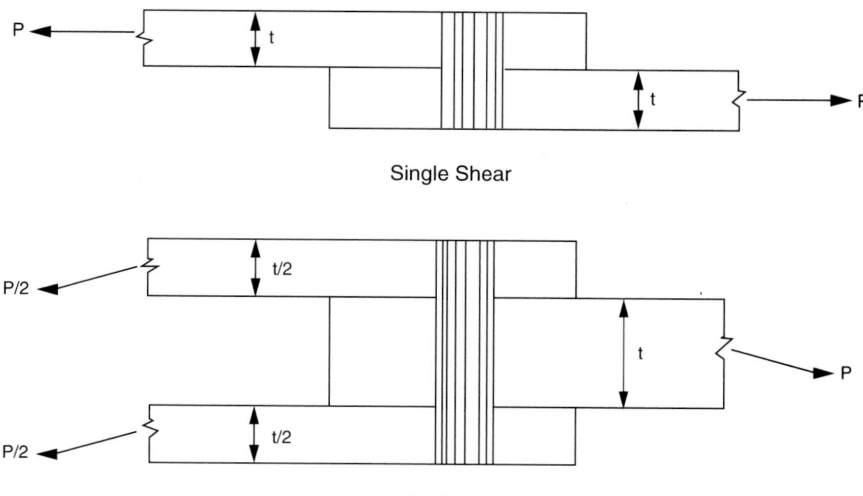

FIG. 5.25 Bolt in single and double shear.

If the wood members being joined are of different species, the allowable design value should be selected based on the species with the least dowel bearing strength. This is typically the species of least wood specific gravity (see Table 5.37).

Design values for large-diameter bolts (more than 1 in) may or may not be justified based on their behavior in actual structures and the results of research conducted. The designer is cautioned before selecting large-diameter bolts as fasteners to check current design information.

5.9.5 Miscellaneous Topics

Wood-to-Concrete Connections. A wood-to-concrete connection is composed of a single wood member which is attached to concrete or masonry by bolts which are embedded in the concrete or masonry. The allowable design value should be selected from the single-shear wood-to-wood connections (Table 5.19) using the following:

$$t_m = 2t_s = \text{twice thickness of wood member}$$

$$F_{em} = F_{es} = \text{dowel bearing strength of wood member}$$

The concrete or masonry should be checked to ensure that it has adequate strength to support the applied loads.

Multiple Shear Planes. Joints with more than two shear planes are best explained by an example problem which is given later (see Example 5.10).

TABLE 5.21 Bolt Design Values (Z) for Double-Shear (Three-Member) Connections* for Sawn Lumber with Both Members of Identical Species

Thickness		Bolt diameter	$G = 0.55$ Southern pine			$G = 0.50$ Douglas fir–larch			$G = 0.43$ Hem-fir			$G = 0.42$ Spruce-pine-fir		
Main member t_m, in	Side member t_s, in	D, in	$Z_{\parallel}$, lb	$Z_{s\perp}$, lb	$Z_{m\perp}$, lb	$Z_{\parallel}$, lb	$Z_{s\perp}$, lb	$Z_{m\perp}$, lb	$Z_{\parallel}$, lb	$Z_{s\perp}$, lb	$Z_{m\perp}$, lb	$Z_{\parallel}$, lb	$Z_{s\perp}$, lb	$Z_{m\perp}$, lb
1½	1½	½	1150	800	550	1050	730	470	900	650	380	880	640	370
		⅝	1440	1130	610	1310	1040	530	1130	840	420	1100	830	410
		¾	1730	1330	660	1580	1170	590	1350	920	460	1320	900	450
		⅞	2020	1440	720	1840	1260	630	1580	1000	500	1540	970	490
		1	2310	1530	770	2100	1350	680	1800	1080	540	1760	1050	530
2½	1½	½	1320	800	910	1230	730	790	1100	650	640	1080	640	610
		⅝	1870	1130	1020	1760	1040	880	1590	840	700	1570	830	690
		¾	2550	1330	1110	2400	1170	980	2190	920	770	2160	900	750
		⅞	3360	1440	1200	3060	1260	1050	2630	1000	830	2570	970	810
		1	3840	1530	1280	3500	1350	1130	3000	1080	900	2940	1050	880
3	1½	½	1320	800	940	1230	730	860	1100	650	760	1080	640	740
		⅝	1870	1130	1220	1760	1040	1050	1590	840	840	1570	830	830
		¾	2550	1330	1330	2400	1170	1170	2190	920	920	2160	900	900
		⅞	3360	1440	1440	3180	1260	1260	2920	1000	1000	2880	970	970
		1	4310	1530	1530	4090	1350	1350	3600	1080	1080	3530	1050	1050
3½	1½	½	1320	800	940	1230	730	860	1100	650	760	1080	640	740
		⅝	1870	1130	1290	1760	1040	1190	1590	840	980	1570	830	960
		¾	2550	1330	1550	2400	1170	1370	2190	920	1080	2160	900	1050
		⅞	3360	1440	1680	3180	1260	1470	2920	1000	1160	2880	970	1130
		1	4310	1530	1790	4090	1350	1580	3600	1080	1260	3530	1050	1230
	3½	½	1500	1040	1040	1430	970	970	1330	880	880	1310	870	860
		⅝	2340	1560	1420	2240	1410	1230	2070	1190	980	2050	1170	960
		¾	3380	1910	1550	3220	1750	1370	2980	1490	1080	2950	1460	1050
		⅞	4600	2330	1680	4290	2130	1470	3680	1840	1160	3600	1810	1130
		1	5380	2780	1790	4900	2580	1580	4200	2280	1260	4110	2240	1230

4½	1½	⅝	1870	1130	1290	1760	1040	1190	1590	840	1050	1570	830	1040
		¾	2550	1330	1690	2400	1170	1580	2190	920	1380	2160	900	1350
		⅞	3360	1440	2170	3180	1260	1890	2920	1000	1500	2880	970	1460
		1	4310	1530	2300	4090	1350	2030	3600	1080	1620	3530	1050	1580
	3½	⅝	2340	1560	1560	2240	1410	1460	2070	1190	1270	2050	1170	1240
		¾	3380	1910	1990	3220	1750	1760	2980	1490	1380	2950	1460	1350
		⅞	4600	2330	2170	4390	2130	1890	3900	1840	1500	3840	1810	1460
		1	5740	2780	2300	5330	2580	2030	4730	2280	1620	4660	2240	1580
5½	1½	⅝	1870	1130	1290	1760	1040	1190	1590	840	1050	1570	830	1040
		¾	2550	1330	1690	2400	1170	1580	2190	920	1400	2160	900	1380
		⅞	3360	1440	2170	3180	1260	2030	2920	1000	1800	2880	970	1780
		1	4310	1530	2700	4090	1350	2480	3600	1080	1980	3530	1050	1930
	3½	⅝	2340	1560	1560	2240	1410	1460	2070	1190	1320	2050	1170	1310
		¾	3380	1910	2180	3220	1750	2050	2980	1490	1690	2950	1460	1650
		⅞	4600	2330	2650	4390	2130	2310	3900	1840	1830	3840	1810	1780
		1	5740	2780	2810	5330	2580	2480	4730	2280	1980	4660	2240	1930
7½	1½	⅝	1870	1130	1290	1760	1040	1190	1590	840	1050	1570	830	1040
		¾	2550	1330	1690	2400	1170	1580	2190	920	1400	2160	900	1380
		⅞	3360	1440	2170	3180	1260	2030	2920	1000	1800	2880	970	1780
		1	4310	1530	2700	4090	1350	2530	3600	1080	2270	3530	1050	2240
	3½	⅝	2340	1560	1560	2240	1410	1460	2070	1190	1320	2050	1170	1310
		¾	3380	1910	2180	3220	1750	2050	2980	1490	1850	2950	1460	1820
		⅞	4600	2330	2890	4390	2130	2720	3900	1840	2450	3840	1810	2420
		1	5740	2780	3680	5330	2580	3380	4730	2280	2700	4660	2240	2630

Note: 1 in = 25.4 mm; 1 lb = 4.45 N.

*Tabulated lateral design values (Z) for bolted connections shall be multiplied by all applicable adjustment factors. Tabulated lateral design values (Z) are for "full diameter" bolts (see Ref 3) with a bending yield strength (F_{yb}) of 45,000 psi.

Source: This table provided courtesy of the American Forest and Paper Association, Washington, D.C.

TABLE 5.22 Bolt Design Values (Z) for Double-Shear (Three-Member) Connections* for Sawn Lumber with ¼-in ASTM A36 Steel Side Plates

Thickness			$G = 0.55$ Southern pine		$G = 0.50$ Douglas fir–larch		$G = 0.43$ Hem-fir		$G = 0.42$ Spruce-pine-fir	
Main member t_m, in	Steel side plate t_s, in	Bolt diameter D, in	$Z_\parallel$, lb	$Z_\perp$, lb	$Z_\parallel$, lb	$Z_\perp$, lb	$Z_\parallel$, lb	$Z_\perp$, lb	$Z_\parallel$, lb	$Z_\perp$, lb
1½	¼	½	1150	550	1050	470	900	380	880	370
		⅝	1440	610	1310	530	1130	420	1100	410
		¾	1730	660	1580	590	1350	460	1320	450
		⅞	2020	720	1840	630	1580	500	1540	490
		1	2310	770	2100	680	1800	540	1760	530
2½	¼	½	1570	910	1510	790	1410	640	1400	610
		⅝	2350	1020	2190	880	1880	700	1840	690
		¾	2880	1110	2630	980	2250	770	2200	750
		⅞	3360	1200	3060	1050	2630	830	2570	810
		1	3840	1280	3500	1130	3000	900	2940	880
3	¼	½	1570	1000	1510	940	1410	770	1400	740
		⅝	2350	1220	2250	1050	2110	840	2090	830
		¾	3300	1330	3150	1170	2700	920	2640	900
		⅞	4040	1440	3680	1260	3150	1000	3080	970
		1	4610	1530	4200	1350	3600	1080	3530	1050
3½	¼	½	1570	1000	1510	940	1410	860	1400	840
		⅝	2350	1420	2250	1230	2110	980	2090	960
		¾	3300	1550	3170	1370	2960	1080	2940	1050
		⅞	4440	1680	4260	1470	3680	1160	3600	1130
		1	5380	1790	4900	1580	4200	1260	4110	1230

4½	¼	⅝	2350	1420	2250	1330	2110	1200	2090	1190
		¾	3300	1910	3170	1760	2960	1380	2940	1350
		⅞	4440	2170	4260	1890	3980	1500	3940	1460
		1	5750	2300	5520	2030	5150	1620	5110	1580
5½	¼	⅝	2350	1420	2250	1330	2110	1200	2090	1190
		¾	3300	1910	3170	1800	2960	1610	2940	1590
		⅞	4440	2470	4260	2310	3980	1830	3940	1780
		1	5750	2810	5520	2480	5150	1980	5110	1930
7½	¼	⅝	2350	1420	2250	1330	2110	1200	2090	1190
		¾	3300	1910	3170	1800	2960	1610	2940	1590
		⅞	4440	2470	4260	2320	3980	2080	3940	2060
		1	5750	3090	5520	2910	5150	2620	5110	2590
9½	¼	¾	3300	1910	3170	1800	2960	1610	2940	1590
		⅞	4440	2470	4260	2320	3980	2080	3940	2060
		1	5750	3090	5520	2910	5150	2620	5110	2590
11½	¼	⅞	4440	2470	4260	2320	3980	2080	3940	2060
		1	5750	3090	5520	2910	5150	2620	5110	2590
13½	¼	1	5750	3090	5520	2910	5150	2620	5110	2590

Note: 1 in = 25.4 mm; 1 lb = 4.45 N.

*Tabulated lateral design values (Z) for bolted connections shall be multiplied by all applicable adjustment factors. Tabulated lateral design values (Z) are for "full diameter" bolts (see Ref. 3) with a bending yield strength (F_{yb}) of 45,000 psi. Tabulated lateral design values (Z) are based on a dowel bearing strength (F_e) of 58,000 psi for ASTM A36 steel.

Source: This table provided courtesy of the American Forest and Paper Association, Washington, D.C.

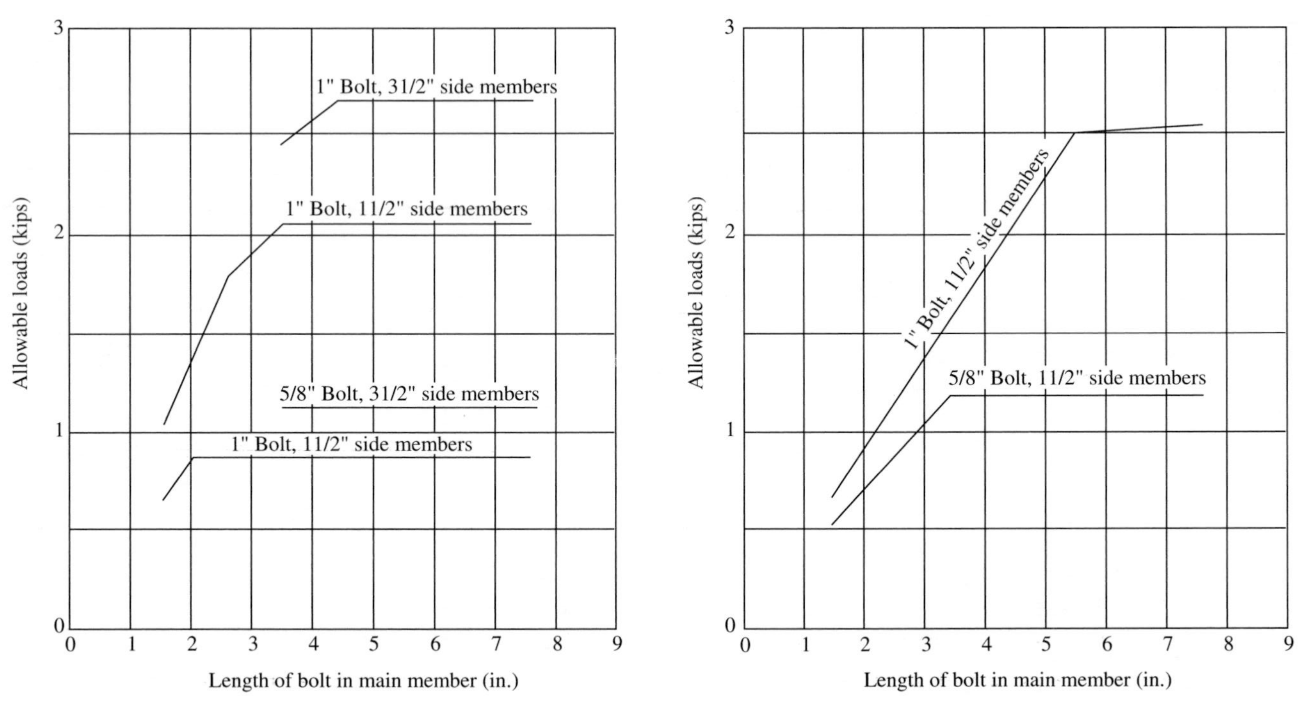

(a) For three member connection (double shear) with specific gravity of 0.5 and load applied parallel to gain

(b) For three member (double shear with specific gravity of 0.5 and load applied perpendicular-to-grain of main member.

FIG. 5.26 Allowable bolt load as given by the 1991 NDS for Wood Connection.

5.9.6 Placement

In the placement of bolts, it is necessary to consider the following:

1. End distance: tension or compression
2. Edge distance: loaded and unloaded
3. Spacing in a row
4. Spacing between rows

Since it may be necessary to determine the placement of bolts in both the parallel and the perpendicular to grain directions, and it may even be necessary in some cases to consider a load applied at an angle to grain; the calculation of all dimensions can be a considerable task. NDS gives values for spacings when loads are applied either parallel or perpendicular to the grain. No spacing values are given for placement of the bolt when loads are applied at an angle to grain, although "uniform stress in main members and a uniform distribution of load to all bolts...requires that the gravity axis of the members shall pass through the center of resistance of the bolt group."[5] It is easiest to show the NDS requirements for the placement of bolts by providing a drawing which shows these (Fig. 5.27). Most values of distances are based on the bolt diameter D and are given from center to center of bolt hole.

The l/D ratio is defined as the length l of the bolt in the member divided by the bolt diameter D. The length of the bolt l is the lesser of the thickness of the main member or the thickness of the side(s) members. For example,

1. In two-member connection with t_s = 1.5 in, t_m = 2.5 in, and D = 0.75 in,

$$l/D = 1.5/0.75 = \underline{2.0 \text{ controls}}$$

$$l_m/D = 2.5/0.75 = 3.33$$

2. In three-member connection with $t_s = 2 \times 1.5$ in, t_m = 2.5 in, and D = 0.75 in,

$$l_s/D = 2 \times 1.5/0.75 = 4.0$$

$$l_m/D = 2.5/0.75 = \underline{3.33 \text{ controls}}$$

The NDS[5] permit end distances and spacings in a row for bolts to be reduced if the design load applied to the connection is less than its design capacity. These are given below; however, it is recommended that the spacings given in Fig. 5.27 be maintained when the use of these spacings will not significantly influence the overall cost of the connection.

If an end distance or spacing is reduced, the allowable design value should be reduced by multiplying the design value from Table 5.19 through 5.22 by the geometry factor C_Δ as defined in Table 5.23.

On occasion, designers select relatively large diameter washers. Care must be taken so that adequate spacing is provided between the bolts to prevent an overlap of washers.

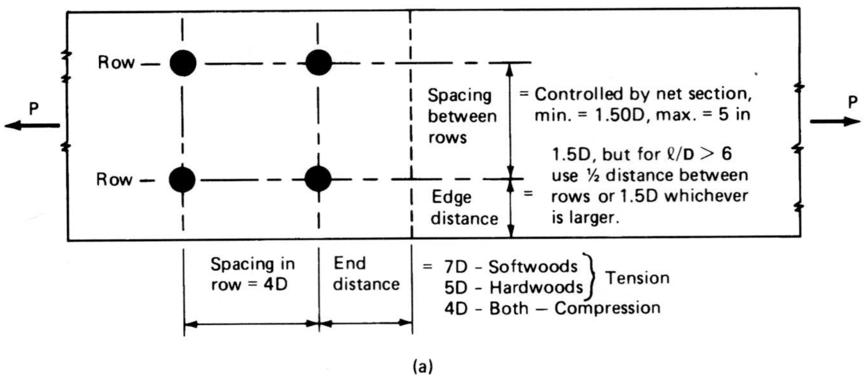

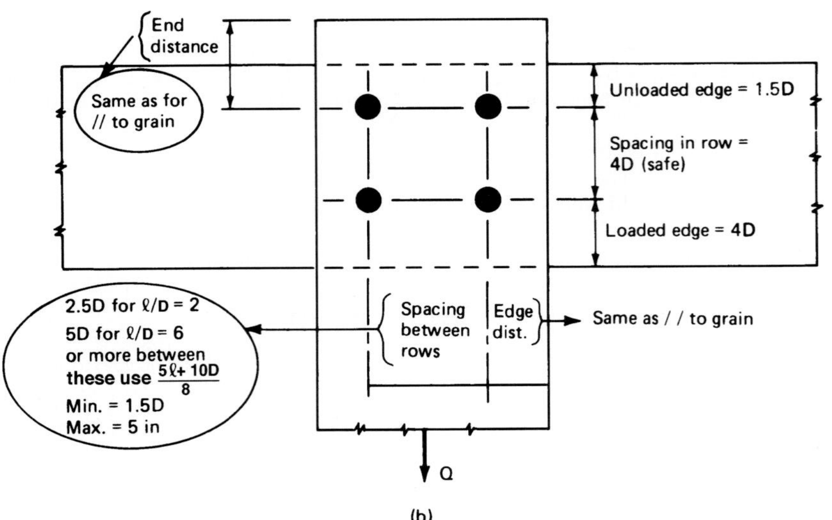

FIG. 5.27 Placement of bolts. (*a*) Parallel to grain; (*b*) perpendicular to grain. *Note:* All values are minimum unless otherwise stated.

5.9.7 Net Section

Members must be checked for load-carrying capacity at the critical net section of the joints. The gross cross-sectional area of the member must be reduced for holes. In tension and compression members, the required net area, in square inches, is determined by dividing the total load transferred through the critical net section by the allowable design stress for the species and grade of material used. When the bolts are staggered, adjacent bolts or lag screws should be considered as being placed in the critical section unless the bolts in a row are spaced at least eight diameters apart.

TABLE 5.23*a* End Distance for Bolts

Direction of loading	Minimum end distance	
	For reduced design value	For full design value
⊥ to grain	$2D$	$4D$
∥ to grain,		
• Compression	$2D$	$4D$
• Tension		
Softwoods	$3.5D$	$7D$
Hardwoods	$2.5D$	$5D$

$$C_\Delta = \frac{\text{actual end distance}}{\text{full design value end distance}}$$

TABLE 5.23*b* Spacing for Bolts in Row

Direction of loading	Minimum spacing	
	For reduced design value	For full design value
∥ to grain	$3D$	$4D$
⊥ to grain	$3D$	Required spacing for attached member(s)

$$C_\Delta = \frac{\text{actual spacing}}{\text{full design value spacing}}$$

5.9.8 Adjustments to Allowable Values

After the allowable value has been selected from Table 5.19 through 5.22, adjustments must be made to account for conditions in the joint that are not in agreement with those assumed by NDS[5] in establishing these values. Adjustments that should be considered are

1. Load duration C_D (see Chap. 2)
2. Moisture condition in service C_M (see Table 5.30*a*)
3. Temperature of wood in service C_t (see Table 5.33)
4. Group action factor C_g (see Sec. 5.6)
5. Fire-retardant treatment (see manufacturers recommendations)
6. Geometry of bolt placement C_Δ (see Sec. 5.9.6)

EXAMPLE 5.10: BOLTS, MULTIPLE MEMBERS, LOAD DISTRIBUTION Assume a 1-in (25.40-mm) bolt is used to connect the members shown (Fig. 5.28). Wood is seasoned southern pine which remains dry. Loading is of normal duration. Determine the maximum force which can be distributed through the joint if

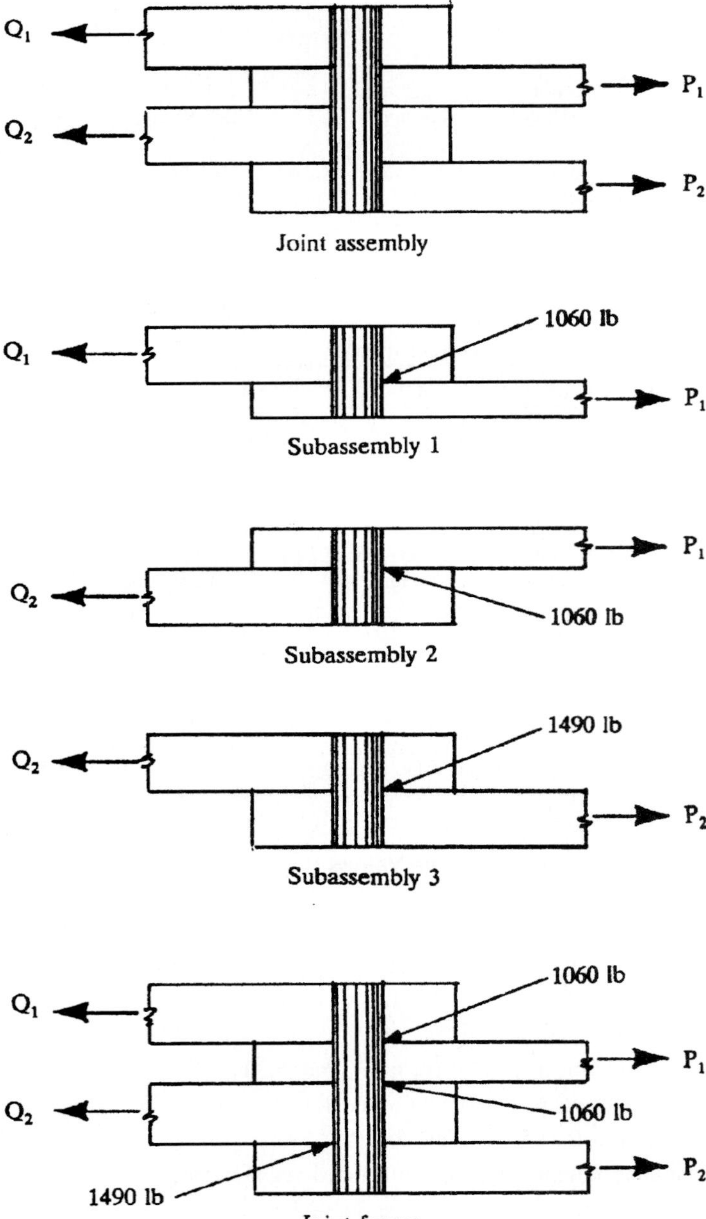

FIG. 5.28 Example 5.10.

1. The distribution of force to each member is not known.

2. The distribution of force to each member is known.

Note: All values are minimum, unless otherwise stated. The solution of this joint requires that it be analyzed as three separate two-member joints as shown below.

Subassembly 1. Bottom member, 2 × 6 controls the allowable value, since it is thinner member:

$$P_1 \text{ (allowable)} = 1060 \text{ lb (4.71 kN)}$$

Subassembly 2. Top member, 2 × 6 controls the allowable value, since it is thinner member:

$$P_2 \text{ (allowable)} = 1060 \text{ lb (4.71 kN)}$$

Subassembly 3. Both members of equal thickness, thus 3 × 6 controls allowable value for this shear plane:

$$P_3 \text{ (allowable} = 1490 \text{ lb (6.63 kN)}$$

Controlling allowable values for each shear plane is shown below.

SOLUTION: Part A: When the distribution of force to each member in the joint is not known, the maximum design force for the joint is obtained by multiplying the smallest force for any shear plane by the total number of shear planes in the joint:

$$Z(\text{max}) = 3 \times P_1 = 3180 \text{ lb (14.1 kN)}$$

SOLUTION: Part B: When the distribution of force in each member in the joint is known, the maximum design force for the joint is obtained by summing the allowable shear force for each shear plane.

$$Z(\text{max}) = P_1 + P_2 + P_3 = 1060 + 1060 + 1490 = 3610 \text{ lb (16.1 kN)}$$

EXAMPLE 5.11: BOLT, PARALLEL TO GRAIN LOAD, PLACEMENT Determine the size, number, and placement of bolts needed to transfer the 7500-lb (33.4-kN) load (dead load plus snow load) through the butt joint shown (Fig. 5.29). Wood is seasoned No. 1 Douglas fir, which will remain dry in service.

SOLUTION: Size of member:

$$A \text{ (required)} = \frac{P}{F_t} = \frac{7500}{675 \times 1.15 \times 1.2^*} = 8.05 \text{ in}^2$$

Try 2 by 8 in, $A = 10.875$ in^2, for both main member and side plates. Select bolts: Try ⅝-in bolts.

$$P \text{ (allowable)} = 1310 \text{ pounds per bolt (Table 5.21)}$$

$$P \text{ (adjusted)} = P \times C_D \times C_M = 1310 \times 1.15 \times 1.0 = 1506 \text{ lb}$$

$$\text{Number required} = 7500/1506 = 4.98$$

Try six ⅝-in bolts, two rows of three each.

---

*Assume that lumber would be 8-in nominal (Table 4, Supplement, footnote 3 of NDS[5] allowable stresses).

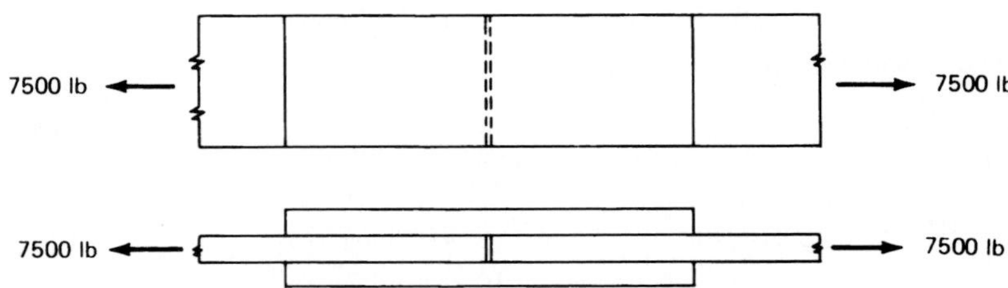

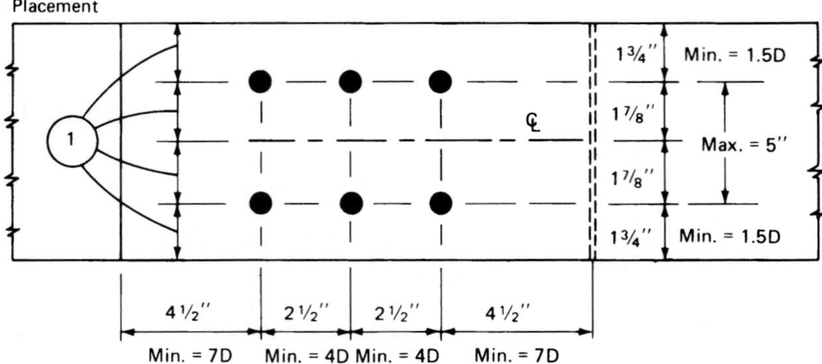

Notes: (1) As closely as possible make these values all equal for uniform distribution of stress across the section.
(2) 1 in = 25.4 mm

FIG. 5.29 Example 5.11.

Group reduction:

$$A_m = 1.5 \times 7.25 = 10.875 \text{ in}^2$$

$$A_s = 2 \times 10.875 = 21.75 \text{ in}^2$$

$$\frac{A_s}{A_m} = \frac{21.75}{10.875} = 2 > 1.0 \qquad \text{Thus use}$$

$$\frac{A_m}{A_s} = \frac{10.875}{21.75} = 0.5$$

and use A_m in place of A_s. Thus

$$C_g = 0.96 \qquad \text{(see Table 5.26)}$$

$$Q = 1506 \times 0.96 \times 2 \times 3$$

$$= 8674 \text{ lb (38.6 kN)} > 7500 \text{ lb (33.4 kN)} \qquad \text{OK}$$

Net section:

$$A \text{ (net)} = 10.875 - (2 \times 0.984)^*$$
$$= 8.90 \text{ in}^2 > 7.05 \text{ in}^2 \qquad \text{OK}$$

EXAMPLE 5.12: BOLT, PERPENDICULAR TO GRAIN LOADING, PLACEMENT Determine the size, number, and placement of bolts needed to transfer the 6000-lb (26.7-kN) (2-month duration) load through the joint shown (Fig. 5.30). Wood is seasoned No. 1 Douglas fir which will remain dry.

SOLUTION: Select bolts: Try 1-in bolts:

$$\left.\begin{aligned} P_{\perp}\ (4 \times 10) &= 1580 \text{ lb per bolt} \\ P_{\parallel}\ (2 \times 1\tfrac{1}{2}) &= 4090 \text{ lb per bolt} \end{aligned}\right\} \quad \text{(see Table 5.21)}$$

$$\text{Number required} = \frac{6000}{1580 \times 1.15} = 3.30$$

Try two rows of two each
Note: No group reduction factor required for two or fewer in a row.
Net section:

$$A \text{ (net)} = (8.25 \times 2) - (2 \times 1.59 \times 2)^{**} = 10.14 \text{ in}^2$$

$$A \text{ (required)} = \frac{6000}{F_t} = \frac{6000}{675 \times 1.3 \times 1.15}$$

$$= 6.21 \text{ in}^2 \text{ (4010 mm}^2\text{)} < 10.14 \text{ in}^2 \text{ (6774 mm}^3\text{)}$$

Note: Net section applies only to member loaded parallel to grain.

1. Percent full load capacity of bolts = 3.45/4 × 100 = 86 percent.

$$4D \times 0.86 = 3.44 \text{ in} \qquad \text{(spacing in row)}$$

2. For l/D, use lesser of l_m/D or l_s/D:

$$l_m/D = 3.5/1.0 = 3.5$$
$$l_s/D = 3.0/1.0 = 3.0 \text{ (controls)}$$

Minimum spacing between rows is given by the equation $l_{\min} = (5l + 10D)/8$ (see Fig. 5.27) when $2 < l/D < 6$; thus

$$l_{\min} = (5 \times 3 + 10 \times 1)/8 = 3.12 \text{ in} \qquad \text{(see Fig. 5.30)}$$

Required width = 1.5 + 3.12 + 1.5 = 6.12 in; thus need 2 × 8.

ANSWER: Use two 2 × 8s (38.1 by 184.2 mm) for vertical members.

Note: Since width of member was changed to 8-in nominal, a reduction is required in allowable stress F_t. Therefore,

$$A \text{ (required)} = \frac{6000}{675 \times 1.2} = 6.44 \text{ in}^2 \qquad \text{OK}$$

---

*1.5 × 21/32 = 0.984 = area removed by bolt hole, which is drilled 1/32 in larger than bolt diameter.
**1.5 × 17/16 = 1.59 = area removed by bolt hole.

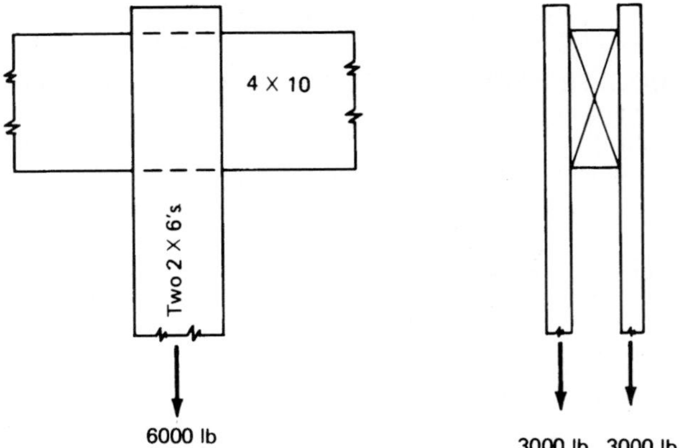

Placement

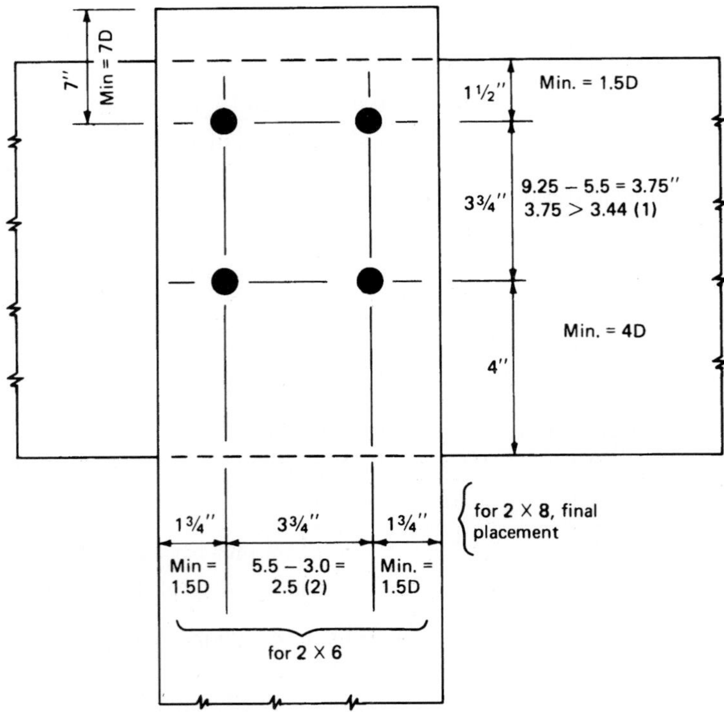

FIG. 5.30 Example 5.12.

EXAMPLE 5.13: BOLT, METAL SIDE PLATE, ANALYSIS Determine the allowable load Q (dead load + construction load) for the joint shown using a C_D of 1.25 (Table 4.3). Wood is seasoned No. 1 hem-fir which will remain dry. All bolt spacings, ends, and edge distances are assumed to be adequate.

SOLUTION: Analysis of diagonal member:

$$P_{\parallel} = 4200 \text{ lb per bolt} \qquad \text{(see Table 5.22)}$$

$$Q = P_{\parallel} \times C_D \times \text{number of bolts}$$

$$= 4200 \times 1.25 \times 2 = \underline{10{,}500 \text{ lb}}$$

$$\text{Net section} = 12.25 - (17/16 \times 3.5) = 8.53 \text{ in}^2$$

$$Q = 8.53 \times 550 \times 1.5 \times 1.25 = \underline{8800}$$

Analysis of vertical member:

$$P_{\parallel} = 4200 \text{ lb per bolt}$$

$$P_{\perp} = 1260 \text{ lb per bolt}$$

$$P_{30^\circ} = 2650 \text{ lb} \quad \text{(see Fig. 5.14)}$$

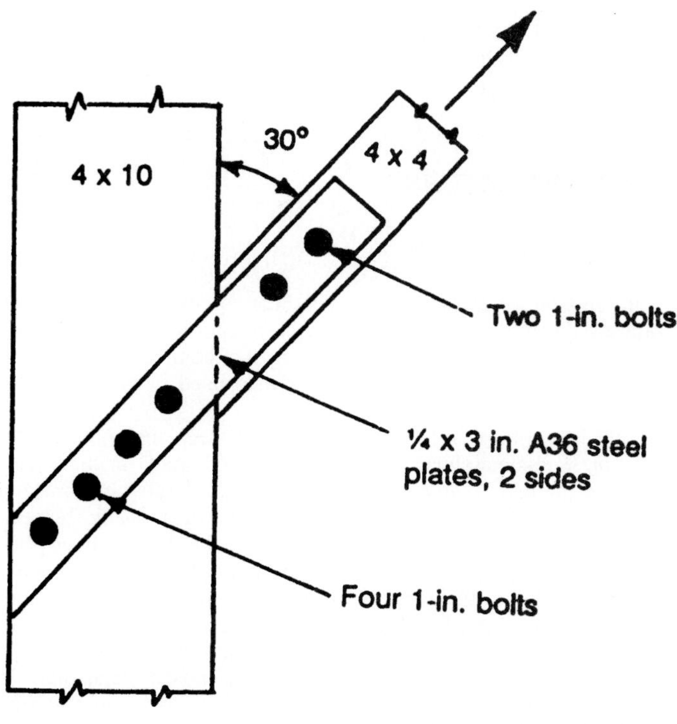

FIG. 5.31 Example 5.13.

Group reduction: $A_m = 3.5 \times 6 = 21.0$, assumed width equal to minimum spacing between rows, ($3.5D = 3.5$ in) plus some additional distance to account for load not acting perpendicular to grain (see footnote to Example 5.9 and bolt placement chart).

$$A_s = 0.5 \times 3.0 \times 2 = 3.0 \text{ in}^2 \text{ (steel side plates)}$$

$$\frac{A_m}{A_s} = \frac{21.0}{3.0} = 7.0$$

$$C_g = 0.94 \quad \text{(see Table 5.29)}$$

$$Q = P_{30°} \times C_D \times C_g \times \text{number of bolts}$$

$$= 2650 \times 1.25 \times 0.94 \times 4 = \underline{12{,}450 \text{ lb}}$$

Check steel side plates:

$$\text{Net width} = 3 - 1\tfrac{1}{16} = 1.94 \text{ in}$$

$$A \text{ (net)} = 1.94 \times \tfrac{1}{4} \times 2 = 0.97 \text{ in}^2$$

$$Q \text{ (allowable)} = A \text{ (net)} \times F_{t(\text{steel})}$$

$$= 0.97 \times 22{,}000 = 21{,}340 \text{ lb}$$

Therefore, Q (max) = 8800 lb (39.1 kN) and is controlled by the net section of wood in the diagonal member.

5.10 TIMBER CONNECTORS

5.10.1 Shear Plates

Shear plates are capable of transferring large shear forces. They are used to attach beams to columns through steel straps, in the fabrication of heavy timber trusses by using steel splice plates, and quite extensively for connections between glulam members of timber structures. Shear plates are also used in pairs to make wood-to-wood connections.

Two types of shear plates are available: pressed steel and malleable iron (see Fig. 5.32). The pressed-steel shear plate is 2⅝ in (66.7 mm) in diameter and can be obtained in two gauges, regular and light. The total depths are 27⁄64 and 11⁄32 in (10.7 and 8.73 mm) for the regular- and light-gauge shear plates, respectively. A ¾-in (19.0-mm) bolt or lag screw is to be used with the 2⅝-in shear plate.

The malleable-iron shear plate is 4 in (102 mm) in diameter with a total depth of 41⁄64 in (16.3 mm). A ¾- or ⅞-in (19.0- or 22.2-mm) bolt or lag screw is to be used with the 4-in shear plate. See Figs. 5.36*b* through 5.38*b* for all dimensions.

Shear plates require that a groove be cut and a hole be drilled by using a special tool. The shear plate does not provide a wedge fit; thus a shear-plate joint will allow greater slip than a split-ring joint and is less likely to cause a wood member to split as a result of shrinkage due to seasoning of the wood in service. The bolt or lag screw in a shear-plate joint serves a dual function of clamping the joint together and assisting in transferring the load.

FIG. 5.32 Shear plates: pressed steel, malleable iron, and fiberglass.

5.10.2 Split Rings

Split rings are also capable of transferring large shear forces. They may be used in virtually any wood-to-wood joint requiring the transfer of high shear forces and were traditionally used in the fabrication of heavy timber trusses. In the past, they also were successfully used on occasion for light wood trusses.

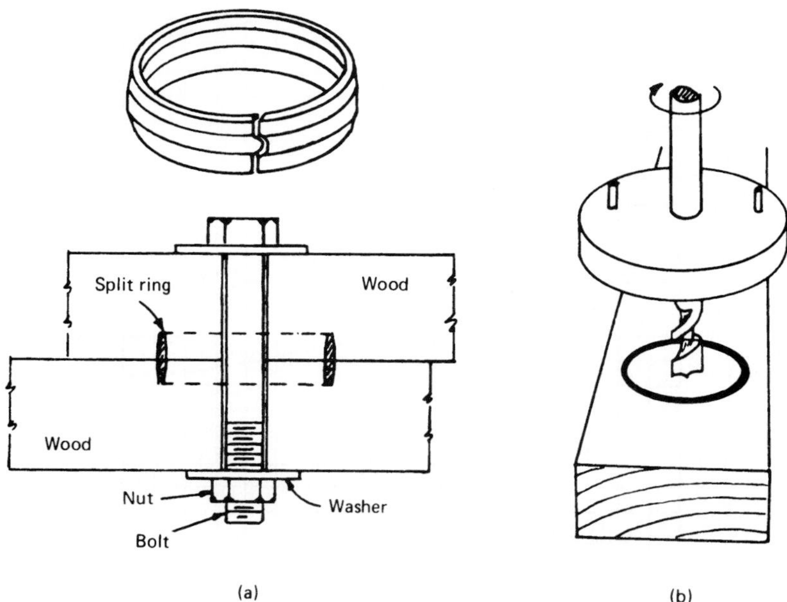

FIG. 5.33 (*a*) Split-ring connector and (*b*) grooving tool.

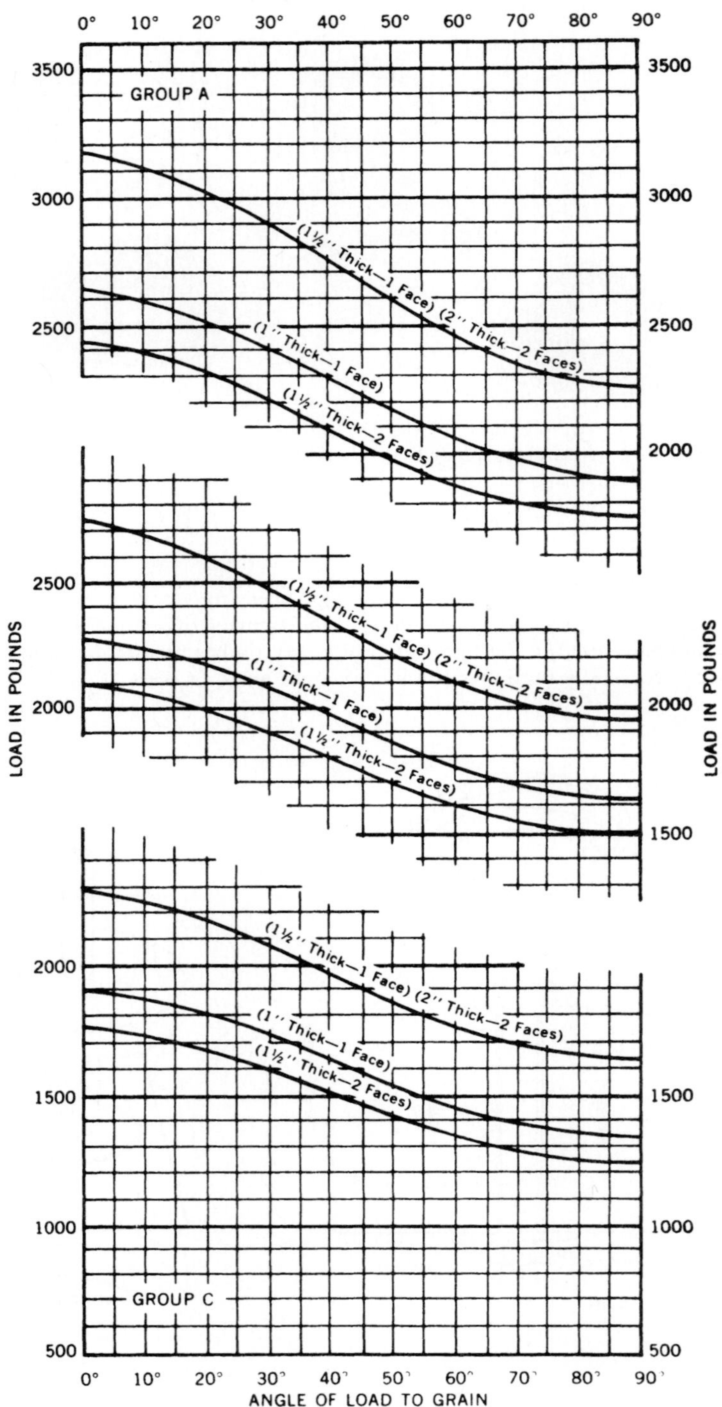

FIG. 5.34*a* Load chart for normal loading; one 2½-in split ring and bolt in single shear. *(Courtesy of TECO Products and Testing Corporation.)*

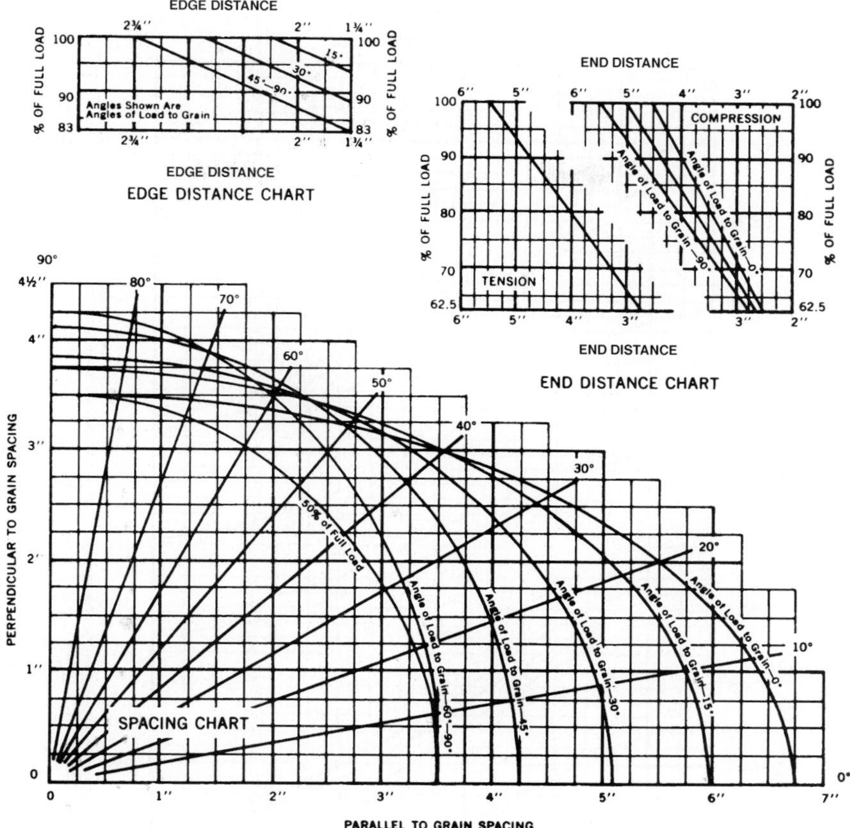

FIG. 5.34*b* Placement of 2½-in split ring. *(Courtesy of TECO Products and Testing Corporation.)*

Split ring—dimensions	
Inside diameter at center when closed, in	2½
Inside diameter at center when installed, in	2.54
Thickness of ring at center, in	0.163
Thickness of ring at edge, in	0.123
Depth, in	¾
Lumber, minimum dimensions allowed	
Width, in	3½
Thickness, rings in one face, in	1
Thickness, rings opposite in both faces, in	1½
Bolt, diameter, in	½
Bolt hole, diameter, in	9/16
Projected area for portion of one ring within a member, in^2	1.10
Washers, minimum	
Round, cast, or malleable iron, diameter, in	2⅛
Square plate	
Length of side, in	2
Thickness, in	⅛
(For trussed rafters and similar light construction standard wrought washers may be used.)	

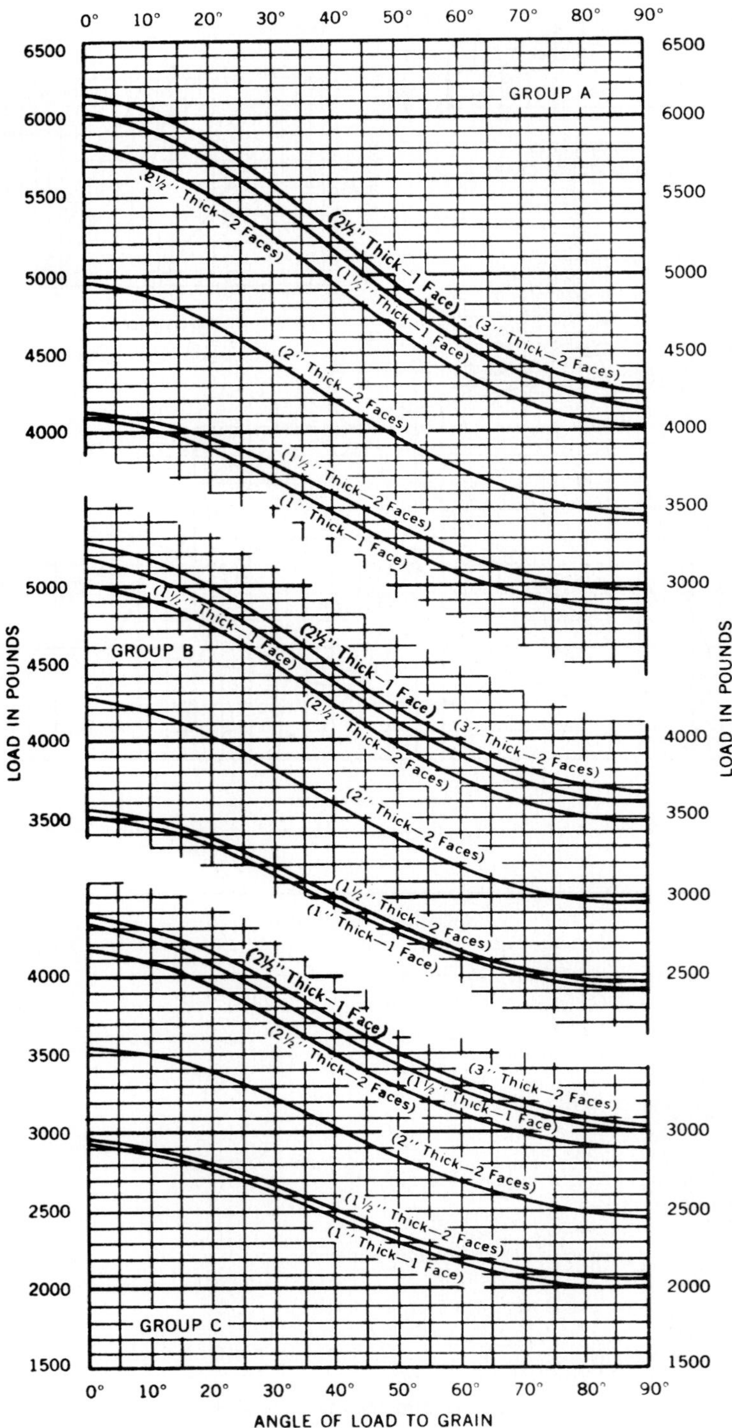

FIG. 5.35*a* Load chart for normal loading; one 4-in split ring and bolt in single shear. *(Courtesy of TECO Products and Testing Corporation.)*

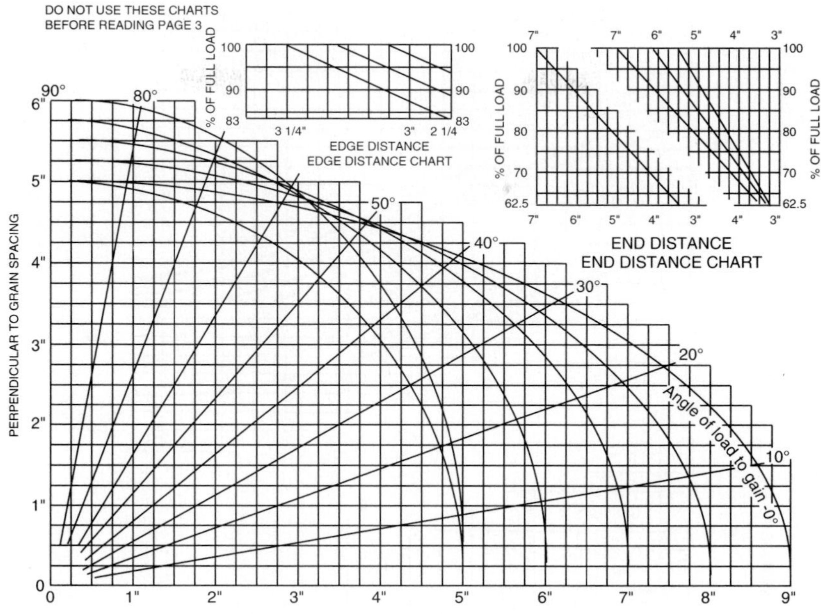

FIG. 5.35*b* Placement of 4-in split ring. *(Courtesy of TECO Products and Testing Corporation.)*

Split ring—dimensions	
Inside diameter at center when closed, in	4
Inside diameter at center when installed, in	4.06
Thickness of ring at center, in	0.193
Thickness of ring at edge, in	0.133
Depth, in	1
Lumber, minimum dimensions allowed	
Width, in	5½
Thickness, rings in one face, in	1
Thickness, rings opposite in both faces, in	1½
Bolt, diameter, in	¾
Bolt hole, diameter, in	13/16
Projected area for portion of one ring within a member, in^2	2.24
Washers, minimum	
Round, cast, or malleable iron, diameter, in	3
Square plate	
Length of side, in	3
Thickness, in	3/16
(For trussed rafters and similar light construction standard wrought washers may be used.)	

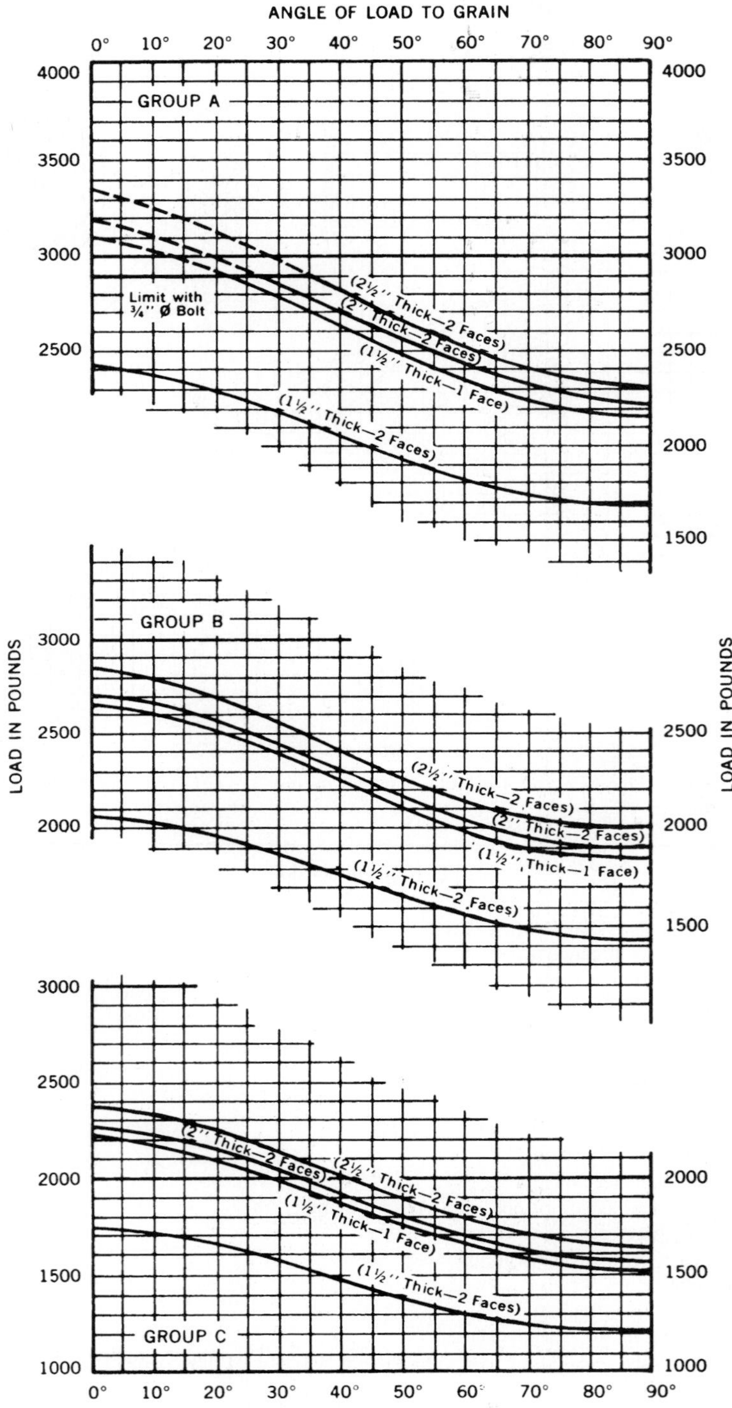

FIG. 5.36*a* Load chart for normal loading; one 2⅝-in shear plate and bolt single shear. *(Courtesy of TECO Products and Testing Corporation.)*

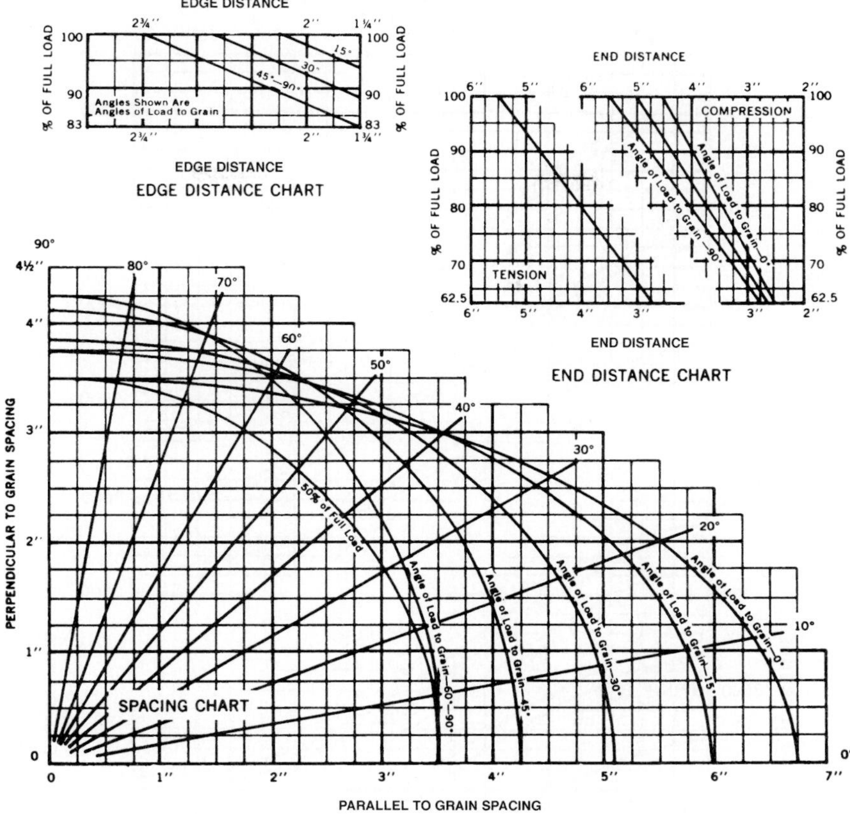

FIG. 5.36*b* Placement of 2⅝-in shear plates. *(Courtesy of TECO Products and Testing Corporation.)*

Pressed steel		
	Reg.	Lt. Ga.
Shear plates, dimensions		
Diameter of plate, in	2.62	2.62
Diameter of bolt hole, in	0.81	0.81
Depth of plate, in	0.42	0.35
Lumber, minimum dimensions		
Face, width, in	3½	3½
Thickness, plates in one face only, in	1½	1½
Thickness, plates opposite in both faces, in	1½	1½
Steel shapes or straps (thickness required when used with shear plates)		
Thickness of steel side plates shall be determined in accordance with A.I.S.C. recommendations.		
Hole, diameter in steel straps or shapes, in	13/16	13/16
Bolt, diameter, in	¾	¾
Bolt hole, diameter in timber, in	13/16	13/16
Washers, standard, timber to timber connections only		
Round, cast, or malleable iron, diameter in	3	3
Square plate		
Length of side, in	3	3
Thickness, in	¼	¼
(For trussed rafters and other light structures wrought washers may be used.)		
Projected area, for one shear plate, in^2	1.18	1.00

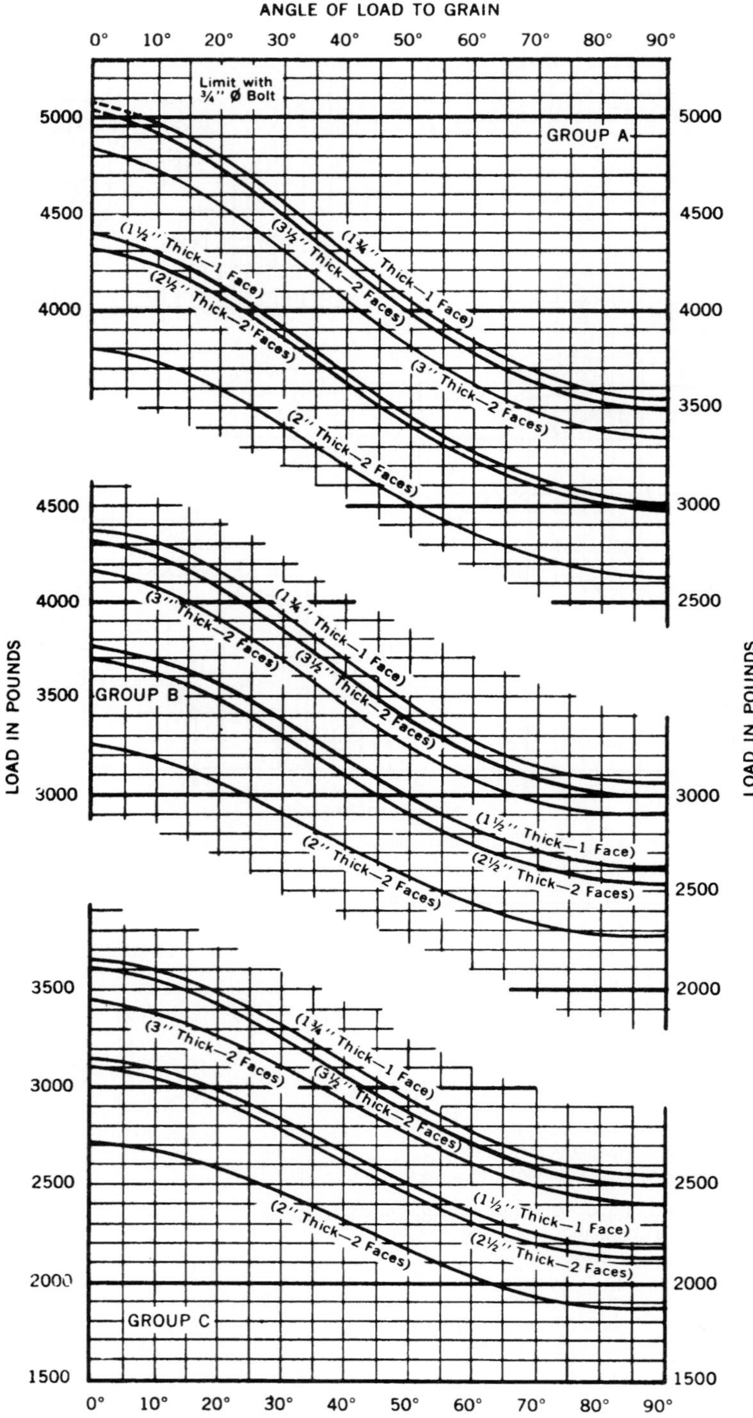

FIG. 5.37*a* Load chart for normal loading; one 4-in shear plate (wood-to-wood) and bolt in single shear. *(Courtesy of TECO Products and Testing Corporation.)*

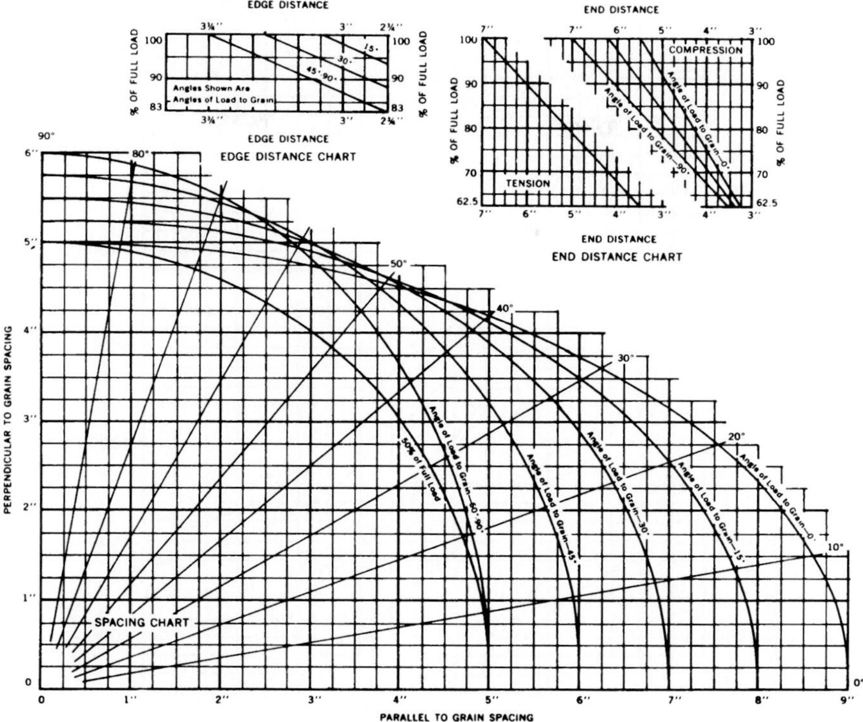

FIG. 5.37*b* Placement of 4-in shear plates (wood-to-wood). *(Courtesy of TECO Products and Testing Corporation.)*

	Malleable iron	Malleable iron
Shear plates, dimensions Material		
Diameter of plate, in	4.03	4.03
Diameter of bolt hole, in	0.81	0.94
Depth of plate	0.64	0.64
Lumber, minimum dimensions		
Face, width, in	5½	5½
Thickness, plates in one face only, in	1½	1½
Bolt, diameter, in	¾	⅞
Bolt hole, diameter in timber, in	13/16	15/16
Washers, standard, timber to timber connections only		
Round, cast, or malleable iron, diameter, in	3	3½
Square plate		
Length of side, in	3	3
Thickness, in	¼	¼
(For trussed rafters and other light structures standard wrought washers may be used.)		
Projected area for one shear plate, in^2	2.58	2.58

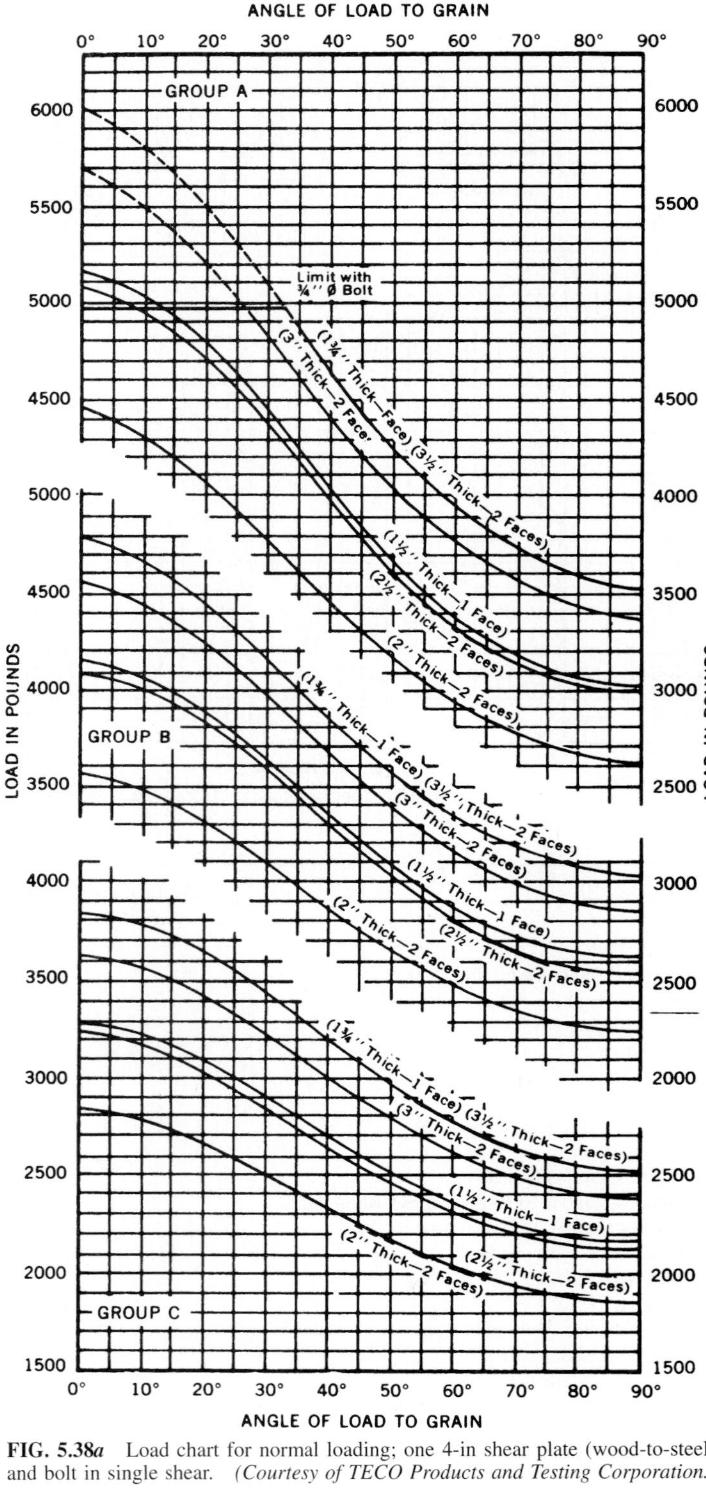

ANGLE OF LOAD TO GRAIN

0° 10° 20° 30° 40° 50° 60° 70° 80° 90°

GROUP A

Limit with ¾″ Ø Bolt

(1¾″ Thick—Face) (3½″ Thick—2 Faces)

(3″ Thick—2 Faces)

(1½″ Thick—1 Face)

(2½″ Thick—2 Faces)

(2″ Thick—2 Faces)

GROUP B

(1¾″ Thick—1 Face) (3½″ Thick—2 Faces)

(3″ Thick—2 Faces)

(1½″ Thick—1 Face)

(2½″ Thick—2 Faces)

(2″ Thick—2 Faces)

GROUP C

(1¾″ Thick—1 Face) (3½″ Thick—2 Faces)

(3″ Thick—2 Faces)

(1½″ Thick—1 Face)

(2½″ Thick—2 Faces)

(2″ Thick—2 Faces)

LOAD IN POUNDS

0° 10° 20° 30° 40° 50° 60° 70° 80° 90°

ANGLE OF LOAD TO GRAIN

FIG. 5.38*a* Load chart for normal loading; one 4-in shear plate (wood-to-steel) and bolt in single shear. *(Courtesy of TECO Products and Testing Corporation.)*

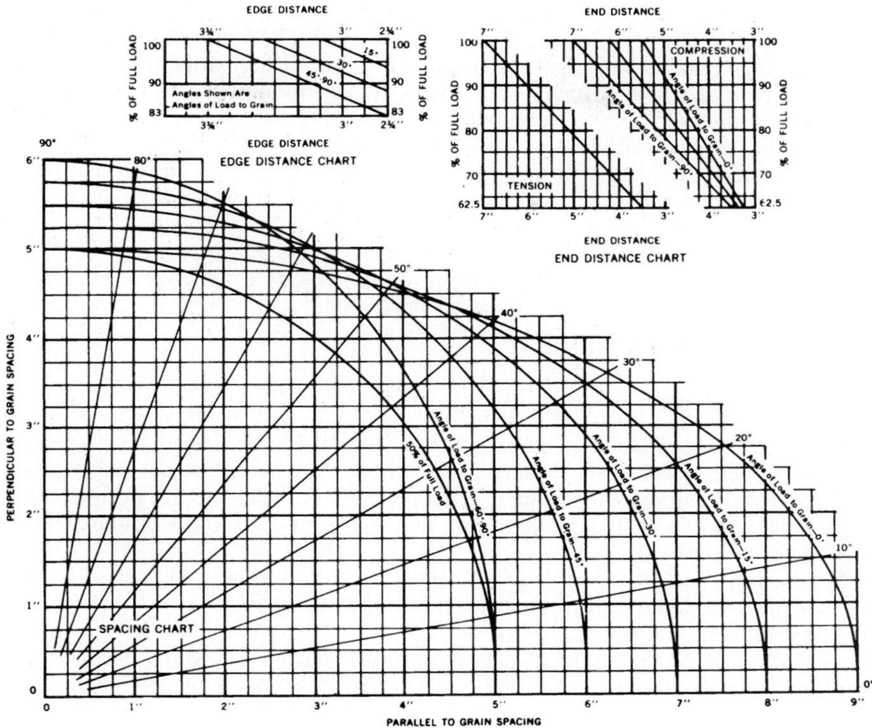

FIG. 5.38*b* Placement of 4-in shear plates (wood-to-steel). *(Courtesy of TECO Products and Testing Corporation.)*

	Malleable iron	Malleable iron
Shear plates, dimensions		
Diameter of plate, in	4.03	4.03
Diameter of bolt hole, in	0.81	0.94
Depth of plate	0.64	0.64
Lumber, minimum dimensions		
Face, width, in	5½	5½
Thickness, plates in one face only, in	1½	1½
Steel shapes or straps (thickness required when used with shear plates)		
Thickness of steel side plates shall be determined in accordance with A.I.S.C. recommendations		
Hole, diameter in steel straps or shapes, in	13/16	15/16
Bolt, diameter, in	3/4	7/8
Bolt hole, diameter in timber, in	13/16	15/16
Projected area, for one shear plate, in²	2.58	2.58

Split rings are available in two sizes, 2½ and 4 in (63.5 and 102 mm), and are to be used with ½ and ¾-in (12.7- and 19.0-mm) bolts, respectively. The depth of the split ring is ¾ in (19.0 mm). See Figs. 5.34*b* and 5.35*b* for all dimensions.

Split rings require that a groove be cut by a special tool in both faces of the mating pieces of wood (see Fig. 5.33). At the same time the groove is cut, a hole is bored for the bolt. As the name implies, a split ring has a split which allows it to expand as it is placed in the groove, thus allowing it to fit tightly in the groove. Therefore, very little slip will take place as load is applied. Because of the extra effort needed to install split rings properly and the potential shrinkage problems, most designers prefer to use shear plates.

The bolt in a split-ring joint serves merely to clamp the two pieces of wood together, thereby keeping the split ring in place. The bolt does not assist in the transfer of load as do the bolts in a shear-plate joint.

5.10.3 Solid Rings

Solid ceramic rings are used in place of steel split-ring connectors for special-purpose structures where environmental conditions are such that the use of non-metallic and/or corrosion-resistant fasteners is required. They are 2¾ in (69.8 mm) in diameter and ⅞ in (22.2 mm) wide, and a 31/32-in (24.6-mm) central hole is drilled for bolt insertion.

These rings are placed in a groove precut with a special tool. The rings are located and used like split-ring connectors. They are designed for shear load transfer in wood-to-wood joints.

Tests conducted by private industry have shown that solid ceramic rings perform as well under load as steel split rings. Therefore, the allowable design value for a solid ceramic ring may be taken to be the equivalent to that of a steel split ring of equal diameter.

5.10.4 Factors Which Affect Load: Shear Plates and Split Rings

Factors which affect the strength of a connector joint in wood loaded parallel to grain are

1. Size and type of connector
2. Type of wood used
3. Load duration
4. Moisture content of wood
5. Width of member
6. Thickness of member
7. End and edge distances
8. Spacing between connectors parallel and perpendicular to grain
9. Net section of member
10. Number of connectors in a row
11. Metal side plates (applicable to 4-in shear plates only)

Tests show that similar factors affect the strength of the connector loaded perpendicular to grain. Figures 5.39, 5.40, and 5.41[13] show the effect that spacing, thickness, and end distance have on the maximum load for a 4-in (102-mm) split ring.

5.10.5 Allowable Loads: Shear Plates and Split Rings

Figure 5.42 shows the results of a test on a 4-in (102-mm) split ring with a ¾-in (19.0-mm) bolt when loaded parallel to grain. The wood was clear, seasoned, and free of checks. As can be seen, while the load was applied, an initial tightening of the joint (slip) took place as the ring came into full bearing. The proportional limit defines the end of the linear relationship. The load at this point is approximately 24 kips (107 kN) at a slip of 0.06 in (1.52 mm), and it will generally be about one-half to two-thirds of the ultimate. Considerable additional slip takes place in the joint before the ultimate load is reached. For the test shown, the ultimate load was 40 kips (178 kN) at a slip of 9.45 in (240 mm). This provides considerable ductility for the joint.

Allowable loads for split rings and shear plates were obtained by applying a reduction factor to the ultimate test load. It was found that a factor of 4 gave loads that would not exceed ⅝ of the proportional-limit test load. This does not, however, imply a factor of safety of 4. Because of the reduction needed from the short-duration load (test) to the long-duration load (9⁄16) and a factor to account for the variability of wood (¾), the true factor of safety is more likely about 1.75 for a long-duration load.

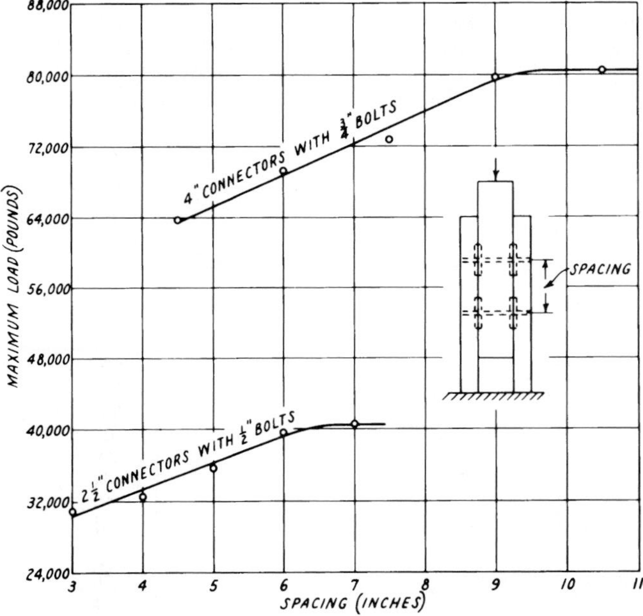

FIG. 5.39 Effect of spacing on load parallel to grain for joint consisting of four connectors and two bolts.

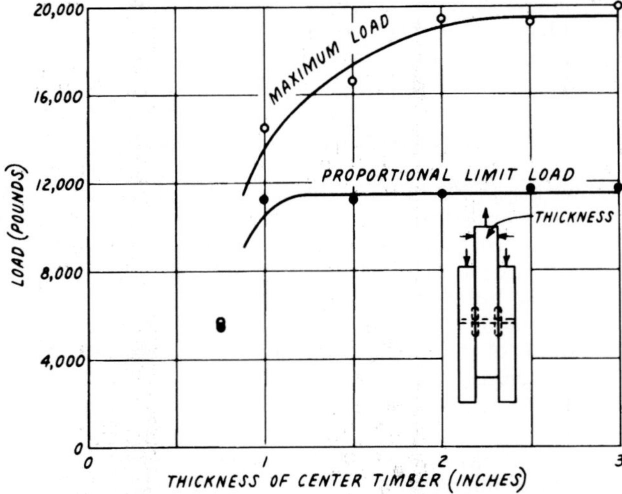

FIG. 5.40 Effect of thickness of center member on load parallel to

Allowable values for perpendicular to grain loading were based on a relationship that was established between parallel and perpendicular values. Some tests were made on joints loaded perpendicular to grain upon which this relationship was established.

Allowable values for split rings and shear plates are given by Figs. 5.34 through 5.38, which give values for parallel and perpendicular to grain loading and for loads at angle to grain (not parallel or perpendicular). Values for angle of load are based on the Hankinson formula. The allowable value for a connector installed into the

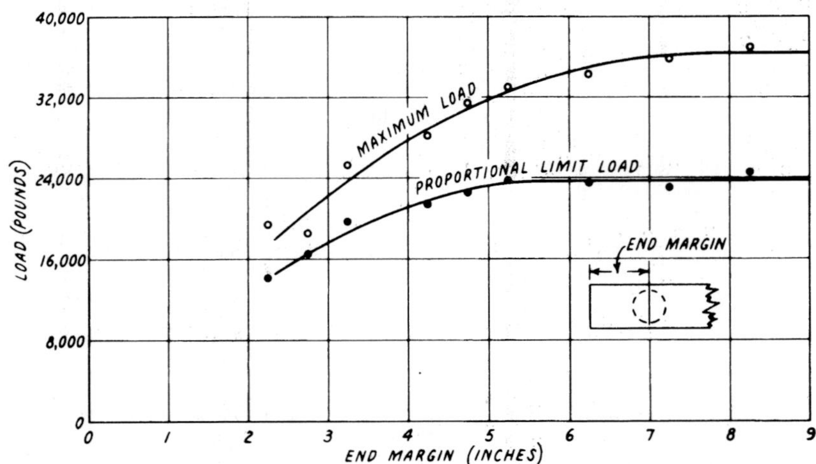

FIG. 5.41 Effect of end distance on load parallel to grain for a 4-in split ring.

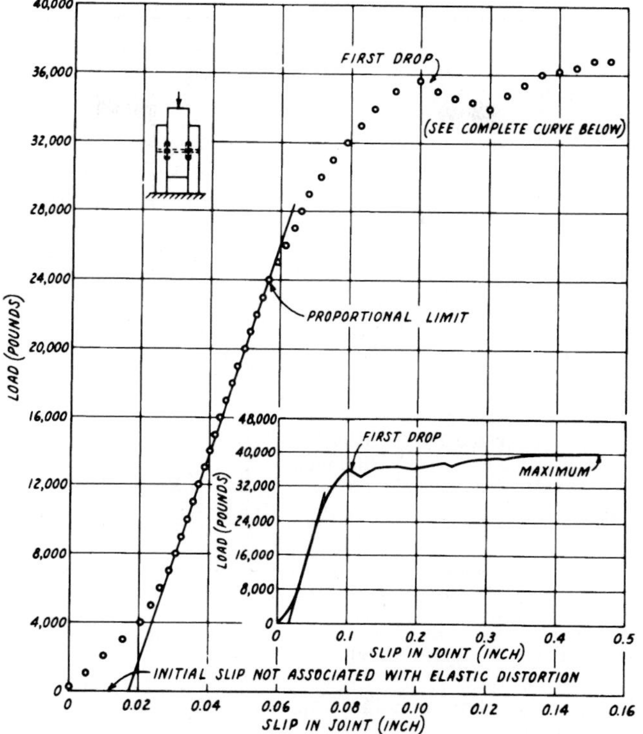

FIG. 5.42 Load-slip relationship of a 4-in split-ring connector joint with ¾-in bolt when loaded parallel to grain.

end grain of a member should be taken as 60 percent of the allowable value obtained for a load applied perpendicular to the grain (90°) of the wood. When the connector is located on a sloping cut end and the direction of the load lies in a plane that contains the neutral axis of the member, the allowable value may be determined by using the Hankinson formula.

Lag screws may be used in connector joints when it is not desirable or possible to use a bolt. The design value given for a connector is modified by the factor obtained from Table 5.24, and its use is demonstrated in Example 5.17.

A booklet prepared by Timber Engineering Company (TECO)[14] is most useful in obtaining allowable loads for timber connectors for any angle of load to grain. Its use is highly recommended, and values from this booklet are given in Figs. 5.34 through 5.38 and in Table 5.31 and have been used in solving problems dealing with shear plates and split rings.

5.10.6 Definition of Terms: Shear Plates and Split Rings

In order to use split rings and shear plates in design, it is necessary that several terms be understood.

TABLE 5.24 Modification Factors for Connectors Used with Lag Screws*

Connector size and type	Side plate	Penetration	Penetration of lag screw into member receiving point (number of shank diameters) Fasteners species group (see Table 5.25) A	B	C	D	Modification factor†
2½-in split ring, 4-in split ring, 4-in shear plate	Wood or metal	Standard Minimum	7 3	8 3½	10 4	11 4½	1.00 0.75
2⅝-in shear plate	Wood	Standard Minimum	4 3	5 3½	7 4	8 4½	1.00 0.75
2⅝-in shear plate	Metal	Standard and minimum	3	3½	4	4½	1.00

*Factors apply to design values tabulated for connector units used with bolts.
†Use straight-line interpolation for intermediate penetrations.
Source: This table provided courtesy of the American Forest and Paper Association, Washington, D.C.

Species groups are A, B, C, and D and are dependent on the density of the wood (Table 5.25).

Angle of load to grain is the angle θ the load makes with the axis of the member, as shown in Fig. 5.43.

Angle of axis to grain is the angle β, a line drawn through the center of connectors makes with the axis of the member, as shown in Fig. 5.44.

Spacing is the distance from center to center of connectors measured either parallel or perpendicular to grain of wood.

Edge distance is the distance from the center of the connector to the edge of the member measured perpendicular to the edge, as shown in Fig.5.45. The loaded edge is the edge toward which the load acts; the unloaded edge is the opposite edge.

End distance is the distance from the center of the connectors to the end of a square-cut piece of lumber, as shown in Fig. 5.46*a*. For a member cut on a bias, the end distance is taken as shown in Fig. 5.46*b*.

5.10.7 Design Considerations: Shear Plates and Split Rings

Adjustment of Allowable Values. After the allowable value has been determined from Figs. 5.34 through 5.38, adjustments must be made to account for conditions in the joint that are not in agreement with those assumed by NDS.

TABLE 5.25 Species Groups for Split-Ring and Shear-Plate Connectors

Group A	Group B	Group C	Group D
Beech-birch-hickory	Douglas fir–larch	Douglas fir–south	Apsen
Douglas fir–larch (dense)	Douglas fir–larch (north)	Eastern hemlock–tamarack (north)	Balsam fir
Mixed oak	Mixed maple	Hem-fir	Coast sitka spruce
Northern red oak	Mixed southern pine	Hem-fir (north)	Cottonwood
Red oak	Red maple	Mountain hemlock	Eastern hemlock
Southern pine (dense)	Southern pine*	Northern pine	Eastern hemlock–tamarack
White oak		Ponderosa pine	Eastern softwoods
		Red pine	Eastern spruce
		Redwood (close grain)	Eastern white pine
		Sitka spruce	Northern species
		Spruce-pine-fir	Northern white cedar
		Western hemlock	Redwood (open grain)
		Western hemlock (north)	Spruce-pine-fir (south)
		Yellow poplar	Western cedars
			Western cedars (north)
			Western white pine
			Western woods

*Coarse grain southern pine, as used in some glued-laminated timber combinations, is in group C.
Source: This table provided courtesy of the American Forest and Paper Association, Washington, D.C.

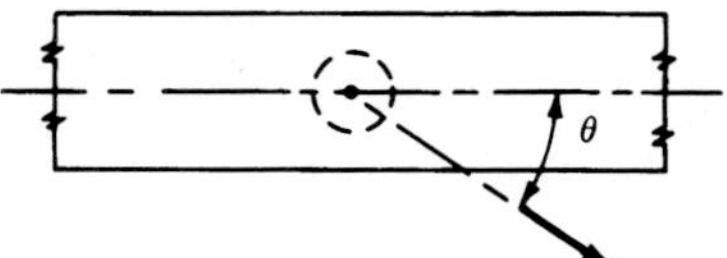

FIG. 5.43 Angle of load to grain.

Adjustments That Should Be Considered

1. Load duration
2. Moisture condition in service
3. Group action factor
4. Fire-retardant treatment
5. End or edge distances less than those required for 100 percent load
6. Spacing less than that required for 100 percent load
7. Net section
8. Metal side plates (applicable to 4-in shear plates only)

General Considerations

1. The controlling member in a split-ring joint is that member which has the smallest allowable load. It is usually the member with the largest angle of load to grain.
2. Two-and-a-half-inch (63.5-mm) split rings are more generally used in 2-in (nominal) (38.1-mm net) lumber and truss spans to 50 ft (15.2 m). Four-inch (102-mm) split rings are more often used in thicker lumber and in longer truss spans. The same general guidelines would apply to shear plates. There are often exceptions to these general guidelines, and the actual selection is dependent on the magnitude of forces to be transferred through the joint and the space available for placing the connectors.
3. If split rings or shear plates have a parallel to grain spacing of less than their diameter, they shall be considered as being in one cross section.
4. When multiple connectors are used in a joint, it is often easiest to determine placement by drawing the joint to a large scale.

EXAMPLE 5.14: SHEAR PLATES Determine the allowable load of a 4-in (102-mm) shear plate (wood to steel) when it is loaded at an angle of load to grain of (1) 0°, (2) 30°, (3) 60°, and (4) 90°.

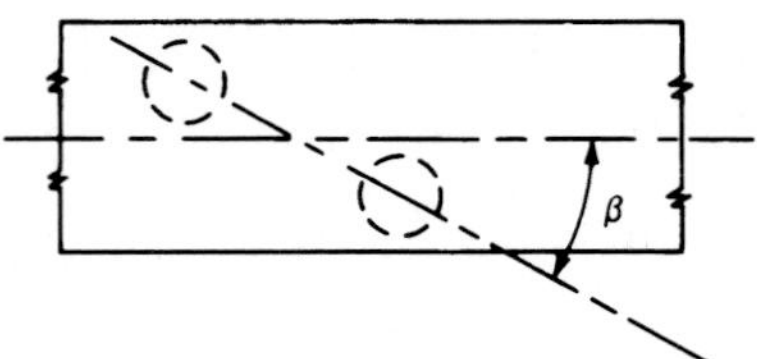

FIG. 5.44 Angle of axis to grain.

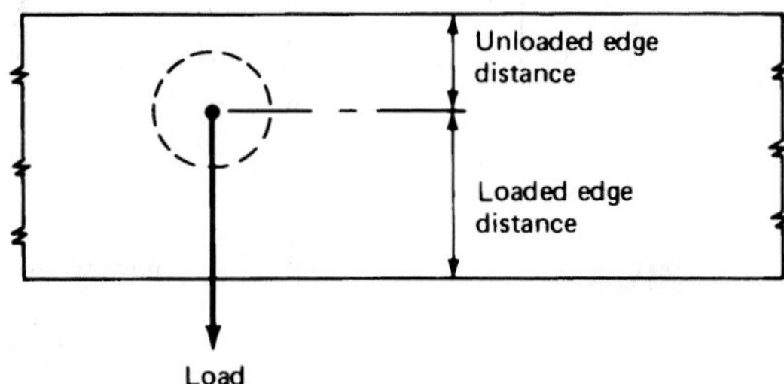

FIG. 5.45 Edge distances.

SOLUTION: Assume a group A wood and 3-in (nominal) (63.5-mm) lumber with shear plates in two faces and edge distances of 2¾ in (69.8 mm) for the unloaded edge and 3¾ in (95.2 mm) for the loaded edge. A 3/4-in (19.0-mm) bolt is used. Use Fig.5.38*a*.

ANSWERS: (1) 4970 lb (22.1 kN), (2) 4810 lb (21.4 kN), (3) 3780 lb (16.8 kN), and (4) 3370 lb (15.0 kN).

EXAMPLE 5.15: SPLIT RINGS Using the 2½-in (63.5-mm) split-ring chart, find the spacing between two split rings arranged in a line parallel to the grain and loaded parallel to grain at (1) 100 percent load, (2) 85 percent load, (3) 70 percent load, (4) 50 percent load.

SOLUTION: Use Fig. 5.34*b*. Values given below have been obtained by linearly interpolating along the horizontal axis between 100 percent of load (represented by 0° angle of load-to-grain curve) and 50 percent of the full-load curve.

ANSWERS: (To next highest ¼ in): (1) 6¾ in (171 mm), (2) 6 in (152 mm), (3) 5 in (127 mm), (4) 3½ in (88.9 mm).

EXAMPLE 5.16: SPLIT RINGS Determine the minimum spacing parallel to the grain for 4-in (102-mm) split rings if the spacing perpendicular to the grain is given as 3 in (76.2 mm) (Fig. 5.47). The split rings are loaded to 75 percent of their full-load capacity at an angle of load to grain of 30°.

SOLUTION: Use Fig. 5.35*b*. The solution is obtained as shown by the heavy lines on Fig. 5.47 for Example 5.16, which is a reproduction of Fig.5.35*b* and which is described below. The parallel to grain spacing is obtained by finding the intersection of the perpendicular to grain spacing line (3 in) with a radial line from the origin

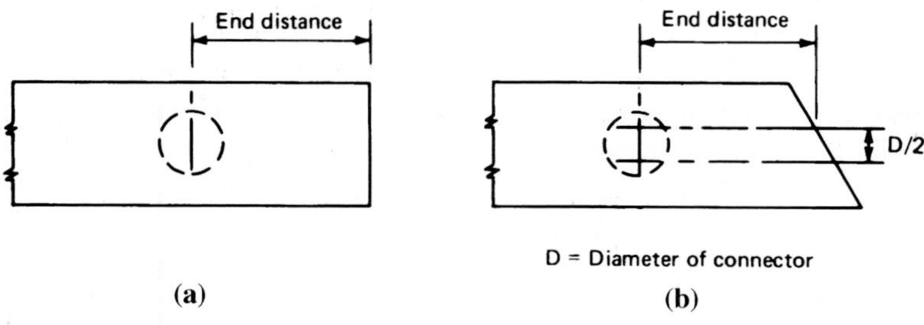

FIG. 5.46 End distances.

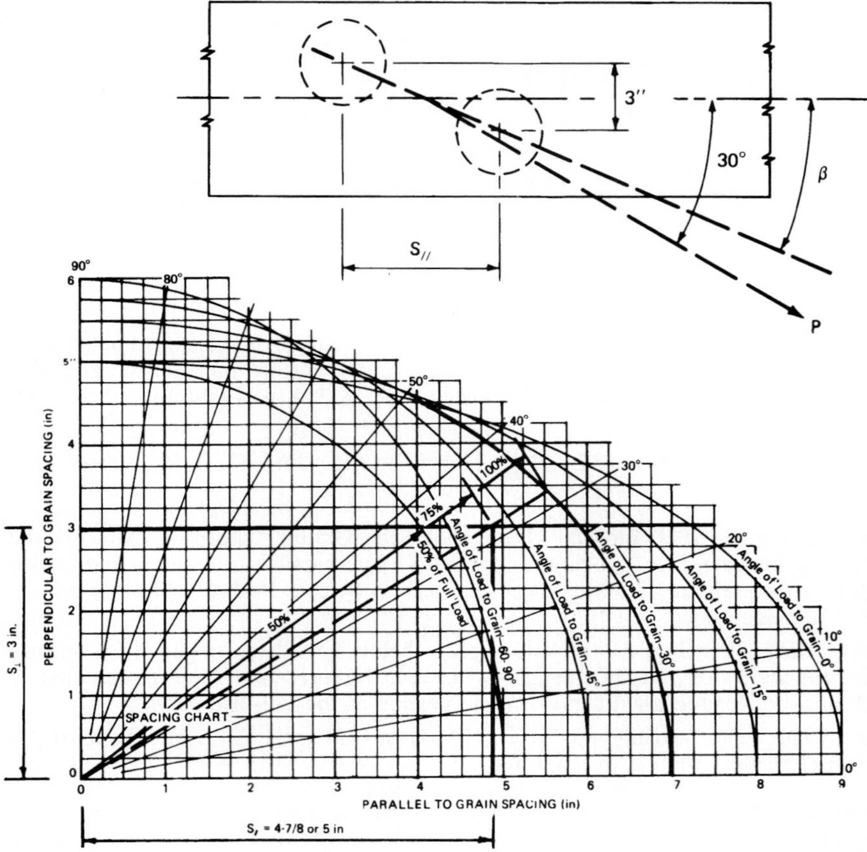

FIG. 5.47 Example 5.16.

(0, 0) to the angle of load to grain line of 30°. The radial line is positioned so that the distance on the radial line between 50 percent of full-load curve and 100 percent of full-load curve, which is the angle of load-to-grain curve of 30 percent in this example, is bisected by the 3-in perpendicular spacing line. The parallel-to-grain spacing is then obtained by projecting down to the parallel-to-grain spacing axis.

ANSWER: $S_{\|} = 5$ in (to next higher ¼ in) (127 mm).

EXAMPLE 5.17: SPLIT RING, LAG BOLT, ANALYSIS Find the allowable load for a 4-in (102-mm) split ring fastened by a ¾- by 6-in (19.0- by 152-mm) lag screw (Fig. 5.48). Wood is seasoned Douglas fir and remains dry in service. Assume loading is dead load plus snow load and that load is applied parallel to grain.

SOLUTION: Wood group B (Table 5.25).

Penetration: $6 - 1.5 = 4.5$ in.
Diameters of penetration $= 4.5/0.75 = 6.0$.

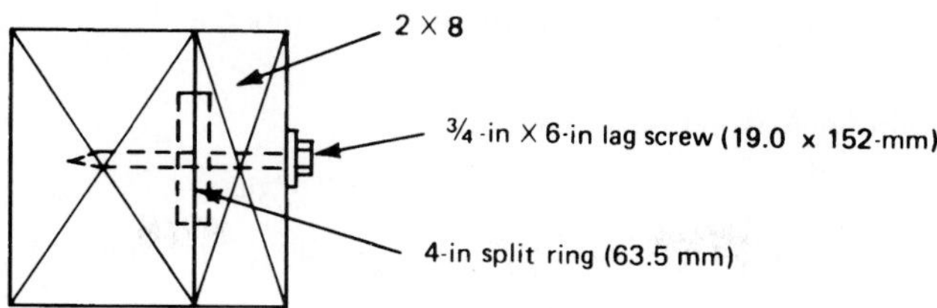

FIG. 5.48 Example 5.17.

$$P \text{ (allowable)} = 5160 \text{ lb} \qquad \text{(see Fig. 5.35}a\text{)}$$

$$\text{Penetration depth factor } C_d = 0.75 + \frac{6.0 - 3.5}{8.0 - 3.5} \times 0.25$$

$$= 0.889 \quad \text{(Table 5.24)}$$

$$P \text{ (adjusted)} = P \text{ (allowable)} \times C_D \times C_M \times C_d$$

$$P \text{ (adjusted)} = 5160 \times 1.15 \times 1.0 \times 0.889$$

$$= \underline{5275 \text{ lb}} \text{ (23.5 kN)}$$

EXAMPLE 5.18: SHEAR PLATES, PARALLEL TO GRAIN LOAD, DESIGN A 4 by 6 spliced with ⅜-in (9.52-mm)-thick metal side plates and 4-in (102-mm) shear plates with ¾-in (19.0-mm) bolts is shown in Fig. 5.49. Wood is seasoned dense No. 1 & Btr. Douglas fir and will remain dry in service. Load is due to the combination

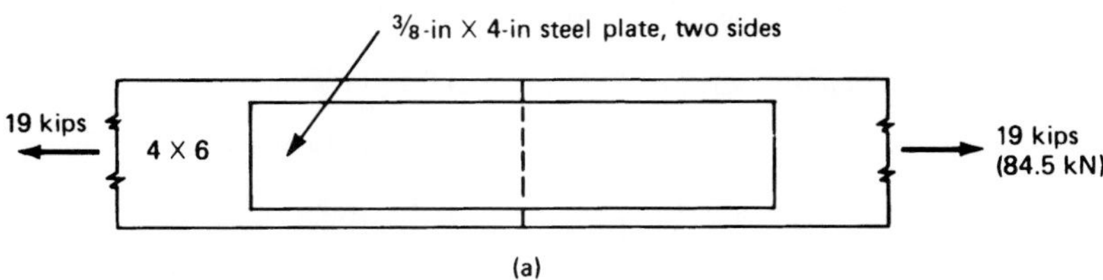

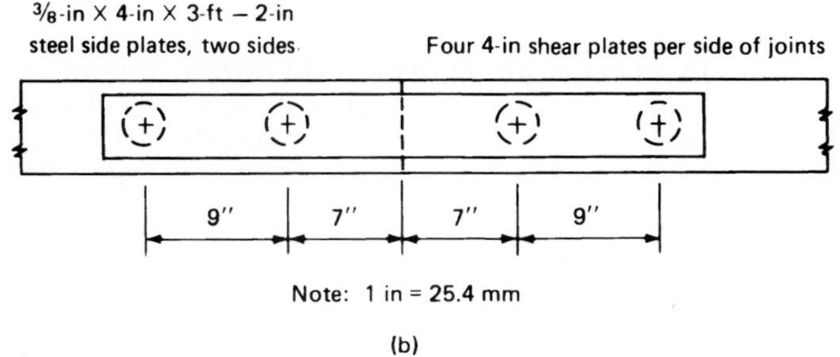

FIG. 5.49 Example 5.18.

of dead, snow, and wind loads. Determine the number and placement of shear plates.

SOLUTION: Group A wood (see Table 5.25).

$$P \text{ (allowable)} = 4970 \text{ lb} \qquad \text{(see Fig. 5.38}a\text{)}$$

$$P \text{ (adjusted)} = 4970 \times C_D \times C_M = 4970 \times 1.60^* \times 1.00$$

$$= 7950 \text{ lb per shear plate}^\dagger$$

$$\text{Number required} = \frac{19{,}000}{7950} = 2.39$$

Use four 4-in shear plates per side of joint.

$$\text{Percent full load} = \frac{2.39}{4} \times 100 = 60 \text{ percent}$$

Net section:

$$\text{Net area} = 19.25 - 6.93 = 12.3 \text{ in}^2 \qquad \text{(see Table 5.31)}$$

$$F_t \text{ (allowable)} = 775 \text{ lb/in}^2 \qquad \text{(See Table A.6)}$$

$$F_t \text{ (adjusted)} = 775 \times C_D \times C_M \times C_F = 775 \times 1.6 \times 1.00 \times 1.3$$

$$= 1612 \text{ lb/in}^2$$

$$\text{Required area} = \frac{19{,}000}{1612} = 11.8 \text{ in}^2 < 12.3 \text{ in}^2 \qquad \text{OK}$$

Placement: From Fig. 5.38*b* for 60 percent of full load.

Spacing parallel to grain = 6.0 in (152 mm)

End distance = 3½ in (114 mm)

Edge distance = 2¾ in (69.8 mm)

These are all minimum values, and spacing values for full capacity of shear plates are recommended if possible without a large increase in cost. Since little cost would be added in this example by providing longer steel side plates, the values for 100 percent capacity of the shear plates are used. See Fig. 5.49*b*.

EXAMPLE 5.19: SHEAR PLATES IN SLOPING END GRAIN Determine the number of 4-in shear plates when placed back to back in the end grain of a pair of glulam arches to transfer vertical shear force of 2900 lb which results from an unbalanced snow load on the roof (Fig. 5.50). Assume the arches are Douglas fir with a roof slope of 6 in 12.

---

*The design must be checked for all possible load combinations, and the load duration factor used for any one load combination should be the highest value of all those in the combination.

†For a 4-in (102-mm) shear plate, the maximum allowable wind load regardless of species, thickness of member, and number of faces with shear plates is 6630 lb.

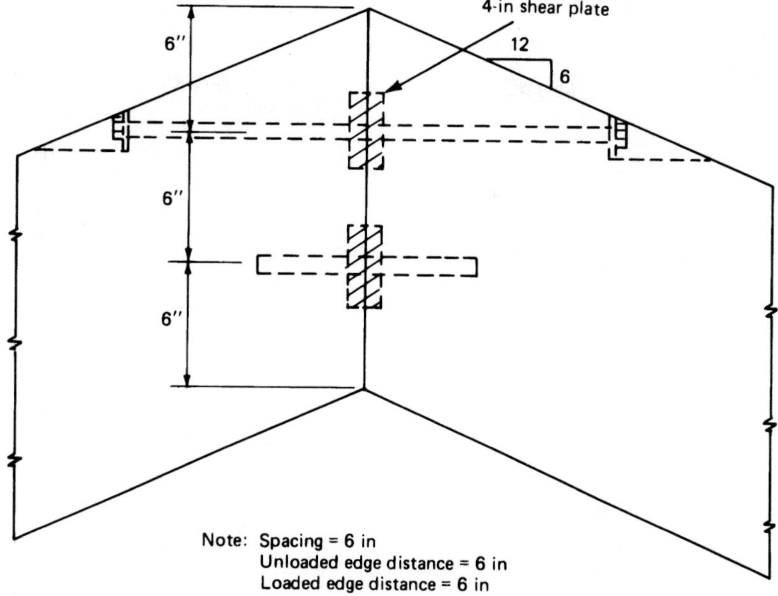

FIG. 5.50 Example 5.19.

SOLUTION: Group B wood (see Table 5.25).

$$P_{\parallel} \text{ (allowable)} = 4360 \times 1.15 = 5014 \text{ lb}$$

$$P_{\perp} \text{ (allowable)} = 3040 \times 1.15 \times 0.60^{*} = 2098 \text{ lb}$$

$$P_{\alpha} = \frac{P_{\parallel}P_{\perp}}{P_{\parallel} \sin^2 \alpha + P_{\parallel} \cos^2 \alpha}$$

where α = the least angle formed between a sloping surface and the general direction of the wood fibers (i.e., the acute angle between the axis of the cut and the general direction of the fibers; sometimes called the slope of the cut).

$$P_{63.4^\circ} = \frac{5014(2098)}{5014 \sin^2 63.4^\circ + 2098 \cos^2 63.4^\circ}$$

$$= 2375 \text{ lb per shear plate}$$

$$\text{Number required} = \frac{2900}{2375} = 1.22$$

ANSWER: Use two 4-in (102-mm) shear plates.

EXAMPLE 5.20: SPLIT RINGS, PERPENDICULAR TO GRAIN, ANALYSIS Determine the allowable load Q for the joint shown in Fig. 5.51. Wood is kiln-dried [19 percent maximum moisture content (m.c.)], dense, select, structural southern pine.

*The 0.60 reduction factor accounts for the shear plate being placed in the end grain rather than in the side grain.

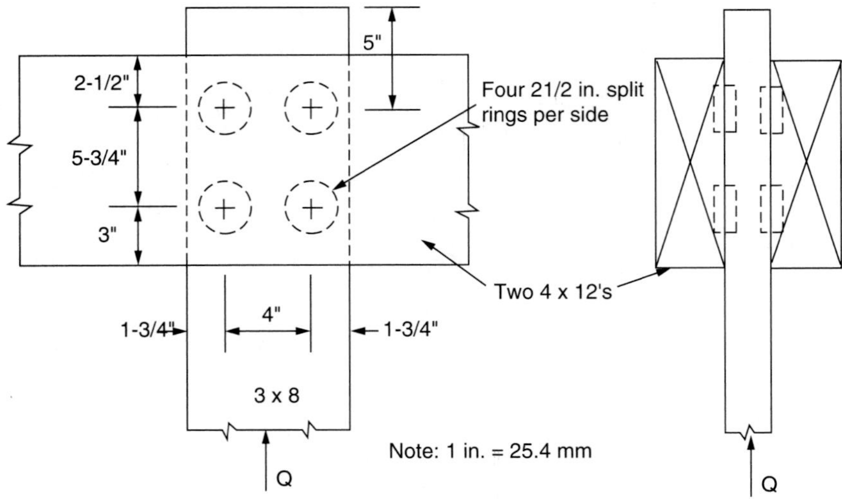

FIG. 5.51 Example 5.20.

The joint is used in a dry service condition and is subjected to a load combination of dead and wind loads.

SOLUTION: Group A wood (see Table 5.25).

$$P_{\parallel} \text{ (allowable)} = 3160 \text{ lb/SR*}$$

$$P_{\parallel} \text{ (allowable)} = 2280 \times \text{lb/SR*}$$

$$P_{\parallel} \text{ (adjusted)} = 3160 \times C_D \times \text{number of SRs}$$

$$= 3160 \times 1.6 \times 8 = \underline{40{,}500 \text{ lb}}$$

$$P_{\perp} \text{ (adjusted)} = 2280 \times C_D \times \text{number of SR}$$

$$= 2280 \times 1.60 \times 8 = \underline{29{,}200 \text{ lb}}$$

Vertical member placement of split rings.

	Required spacing for 100 percent†	Actual spacing	Percent full load*
End distance	4½	5	100
Edge distance	1¾	1¾	100
Spacing parallel to grain	6¾	5¾	85

*From Fig. 5.34*b*.
†From Fig. 5.34*a*.

Q (allowable) = 33,600 × lowest percent load = 40,500 × 0.85 = 34,400 lb.
Horizontal member placement:

	Required spacing for 100 percent*	Actual spacing	Percent full load*
End distance		Not applicable	
Edge distance			
Loaded	2¾	2½	95
Unloaded	1¾	2¼	100
Parallel to grain spacing	3½	4	100
Perpendicular to grain spacing	4¼	5¾	100

*From Fig. 5.34*b*.

Q (allowable) = 24,300 × lowest percent load = 29,200 × 0.95 = 27,700 lb.
Check net section: 3 × 8.

$$A_{net} = 7.35 \times 2.5 - 2 \times 3.16 = 11.8 \text{ in}^2$$

$$F_t = 1350 \times C_D = 1350 \times 1.6 = 2160 \text{ psi}$$

$$P = A^{net} \times F_t = 11.8 \times 2160 = 25{,}500 \text{ lb}$$

Check horizontal shear (notched beam): Two 4 × 12s.

$$V = \frac{2F_V b d_e}{3}$$

$$F_V = 100 \times C_D \times 1.5 = 100 \times 1.6 \times 1.5 = 240 \text{ psi}$$

$$V = 2(240)\,(3.5)\,(11.25 - 1.5)/3 = 5460 \text{ lb}$$

Check horizontal shear: Two − 4 × 12's

$$V = \frac{2F_V b d}{3}$$

$$F_V = 100 \times C_D = 100 \times 1.6 = 160 \text{ psi}$$

$$V = 2(160)\,(3.5)\,(11.25)/3 = 4200 \text{ lb}$$

Assuming Q is equally carried by ends of member:

$$Q = 4200 \times 2 = \underline{8400 \text{ lbs}} \text{ (controls)}$$

$$Q \text{ (controlling lowest value)} = 8400 \text{ lb (37.4 kN)}$$

EXAMPLE 5.21: SPLIT RING, TRUSS JOINT, DESIGN Determine the number and placement of 2½-in (63.5-mm) split rings needed to transfer the forces shown through the joint in Fig. 5.52. Assume wood is seasoned No. 2 dense southern pine which will remain dry in service. Forces are due to a combination of dead plus snow loads.

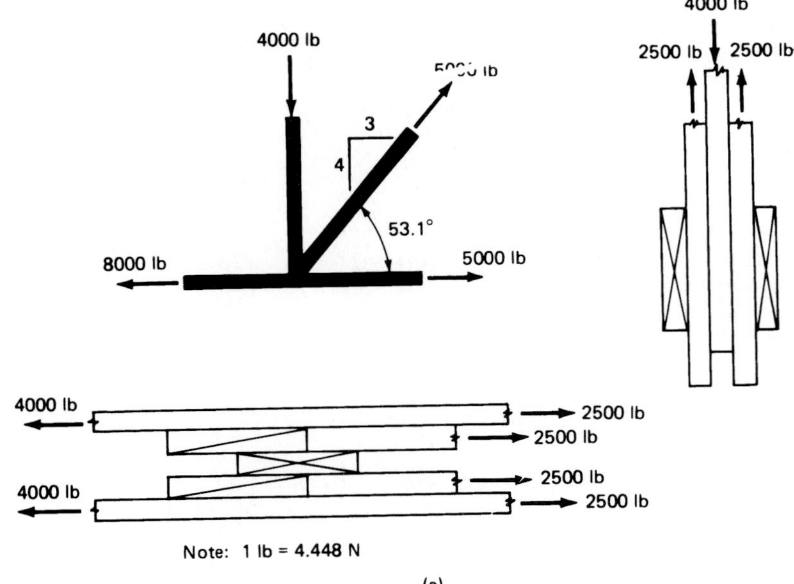

FIG. 5.52 Example 5.21.

SOLUTION: Allowable stress (Supplement NDS[5]):

$$F_t = 775(1.15) = 891 \text{ psi}$$

$$F_c = 1750(1.15) = 2012 \text{ psi}$$

Trial area of members, in^2

Chord: $A = 4000/891 = 4.49$. Try 2×6 (SR—one face).

Vertical: $A = 4000/2012 = 1.99$. Try 2×6 (SR—two faces).

Diagonal: $A = 2500/891 = 2.80$. Try 2×6 (SR—two faces).

Try 2½-in SR, group A (see table 5.25).

Load transfer:*

1. Chord to diagonal: 1500 lb at 53.1° (per face).
   Value/SR = 1960(1.15) = 2250 lb.
   Number required = 1500/2250 = 0.67. use one.
   Percent full load = (0.67/1.00)100 = 67 percent.
2. Vertical to diagonal: 2000 lb at 36.9° (per face).
   Value/SR = 2120(1.15) = 2440 lb.
   Number required = 2000/2440 = 0.82. Use one.
   Percent full load = (0.82/1.00)100 = 82 percent.

*All values for allowable load of 2½-in split rings (SR) obtained from Fig. 5.34*a*.

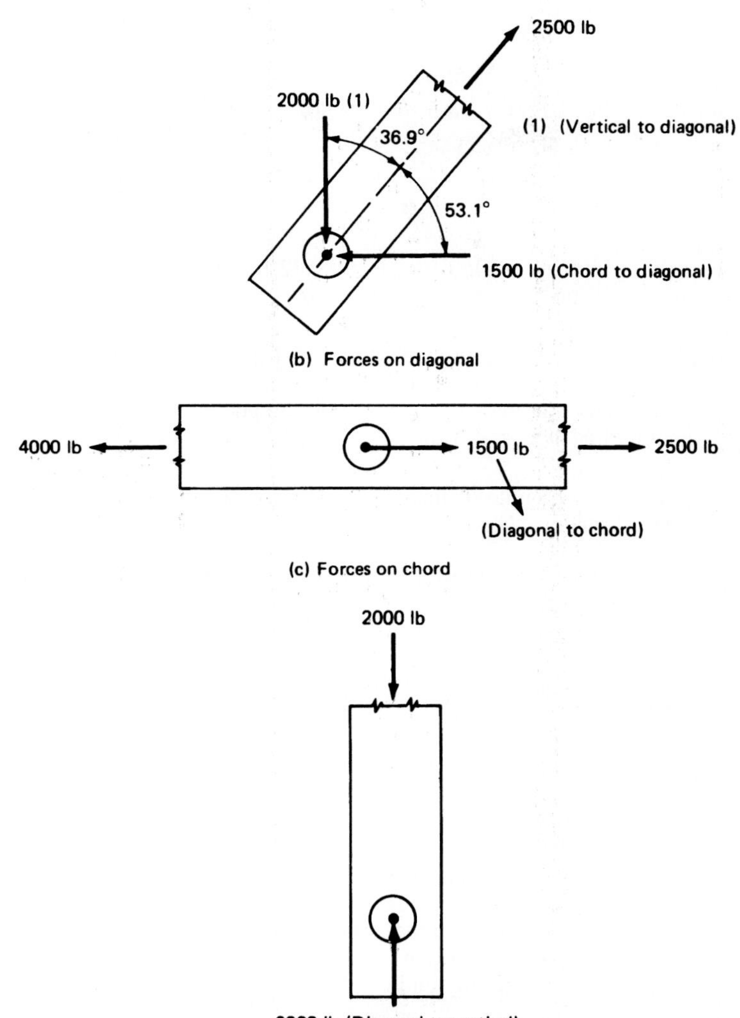

FIG. 5.52 Example 5.21. *(Continued)*

3. Diagonal to chord: 1500 at 0° (per face).
Value/SR = 3160(1.15) = 3630 lb.
Percent full load = (1500/3630)100 = 41 percent.

4. Diagonal to vertical: 2000 lb at 0° (per face).
Value/SR = 2430(1.15) = 2790 lb.
Percent full load = (2000/2790)100 = 72 percent.

Net section:*

1. Vertical = 8.25 − 2.60 = 5.65 in^2 > 1.99. OK
2. Diagonal = 8.25 − 2.60 = 5.65 in^2 > 2.80. OK
3. Chord = 8.25 − 1.71 = 6.54 in^2 > 4.49. OK

Placement†

1. Vertical:
   Diagonal to vertical: angle of load = 0°; 72 percent full load. Edge distance = 1¾ in. End distance = 3½ in.
2. Diagonal:
   Chord to diagonal: angle of load = 53.1°; 67 percent full load. Edge distance = 1¾ in. End distance = 3¼ in.
   Vertical to diagonal: angle of load = 36.9°; 82 percent full load. Edge distance = 1¾ in. End distance = 4¼ in.
3. Chord:
   Diagonal to chord angle of load = 0°; 41 percent full load. Edge distance = 1¾ in. End distance = NA.

FINAL DESIGN: All members should be 2 by 6 in (38.1 by 139.7 mm). Connectors should be 2½ in (63.5 mm) SR, one per face.

5.11 MOMENT-RESISTANT CONNECTIONS

5.11.1 Introduction

Moment-resistant connections are most often used to join members of arches and rigid frames in cases where shipping full-size structural units is not practical or economical. Rigid connections are needed when the designer decides to maintain continuity or to provide a fixed reaction.

A rigid connection must be designed to resist thrust P, bending moment M, and transverse shear V. It is also necessary to maintain alignment of the connected parts. The two most important types of rigid connections are the rigid-plate and the multiple-plate connection.

5.11.2 Rigid-Plate Connection

The rigid-plate connection consists of two steel plates, one on each side of the members being connected, which are tied together by bolts and/or shear plates and bolts, as shown in Fig. 5.53.

The distances p and g are the pitch and gauge of the shear plates, respectively, and e and c are the end distances to the wood and steel plates, respectively.

---

*All projected areas for split rings and bolts obtained from Table 5.31.
†All distances obtained from Fig. 5.34*b*.

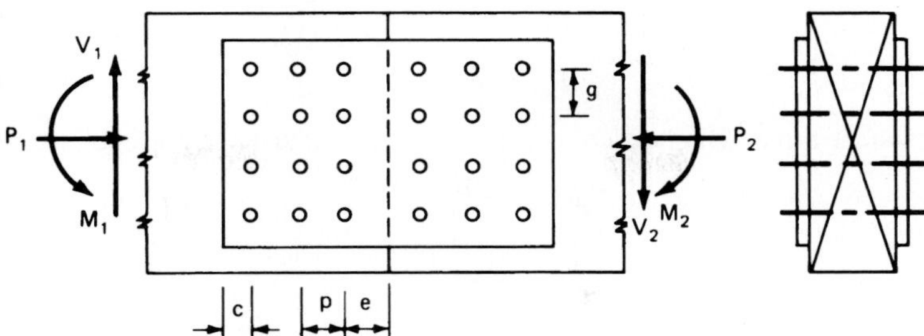

FIG. 5.53 Rigid-plate connection.

The forces and moments acting on the free-body diagram shown in Fig. 5.53 are determined by an elastic analysis of the structure. It is assumed that the steel plates have sufficient capacity to transmit these forces and moments through the joint. The true distribution is highly indeterminate; however, satisfactory results can be obtained if it is assumed that deformations of the plate are small (assumed to be a rigid plate) and that the effects of the various forces and moments may be superimposed linearly. The theory for the solution of this type of connector joint can be found in many textbooks on strength of materials and steel design and will not be restated here. The formulas needed are given.

Care must be exercised in using a wide rigid plate because a significant reduction in the moisture content of the wood member could cause the member to split through a row of connectors due to shrinkage.

Equations Needed. The x and y components of the force on a connector caused by the bending moment M are

$$F_{xm} = \frac{My_a}{\Sigma r_i^2} \tag{5.9}$$

$$F_{ym} = \frac{Mx_a}{\Sigma r_1^2} \tag{5.10}$$

and

$$\Sigma r_i^2 = \Sigma x_i^2 + \Sigma y_i^2 \tag{5.11}$$

x_i and y_i are the distances in the x and y directions from the center of gravity of the connector group to each of the connectors. Distances x_a and y_a are from the center of gravity to the connectors under consideration.

The force on each connector due to the thrust P is

$$F_{xp} = \frac{P}{n} \tag{5.12}$$

where n = the total number of connectors. The force on each connector due to the transverse shear is

$$F_{yv} = \frac{V}{n} \tag{5.13}$$

The resulting force components acting on the connector are

$$F_{xA} = F_{xm} + F_{xp} \tag{5.14}$$

$$F_{yA} = F_{ym} + F_{yv} \tag{5.15}$$

The resultant force acting on connector A can be calculated by using

$$R_A = \sqrt{F_{xA}^2 + F_{yA}^2} \tag{5.16}$$

$$\theta_A = \tan^{-1}\frac{F_{yA}}{F_{xA}} \tag{5.17}$$

The connection design is adequate if the maximum value of R is less than the allowable force for the connector for the angle θ.

5.11.3 Multiple-Plate Connection

A multiple-plate connection is shown in Fig. 5.54. It may be desirable to use the multiple-plate connection when bending moments are large, since a larger lever arm is obtained when flange plates are used. The contribution that a web plate makes to the resisting moment is small and may be neglected. The reverse is true for resisting the transverse shear force V. In this case, the web plate connectors carry most of the transverse shear and the flange plate connectors contribute very little. In the design procedure, it is assumed that the longitudinal force P is distributed to all connectors equally.

An alternative to the above use of side-mounted flange plates is to use cover plates with lag screws. In this case, the cover plates carry an even higher percentage of the moment and the web plates take nearly all the shear. Lag screws must have adequate penetration. The multiple-plate connection will avoid some of the problems that may be encountered with shrinkage when wide splice plates are used.

EXAMPLE 5.22: MULTIPLE-PLATE CONNECTION Assume that the forces and moments shown must be transferred through the joint by a multiple-plate connection (Fig. 5.55). Also assume that a trial design has been made on the number and placement of 4-in (102-mm) shear plates, as shown in Fig. 5.55*a*. Determine the force acting on each shear plate, and check to see if it is within allowable values assuming that the loading results from a combination of dead and snow load. The joint has been placed in a horizontal-vertical orientation for convenience during analysis.

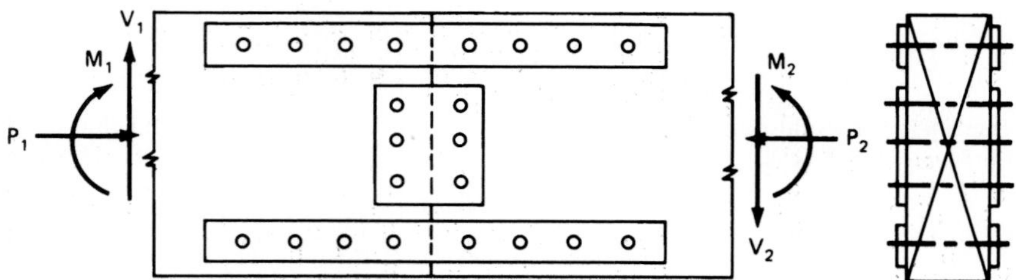

FIG. 5.54 Multiple-plate connection.

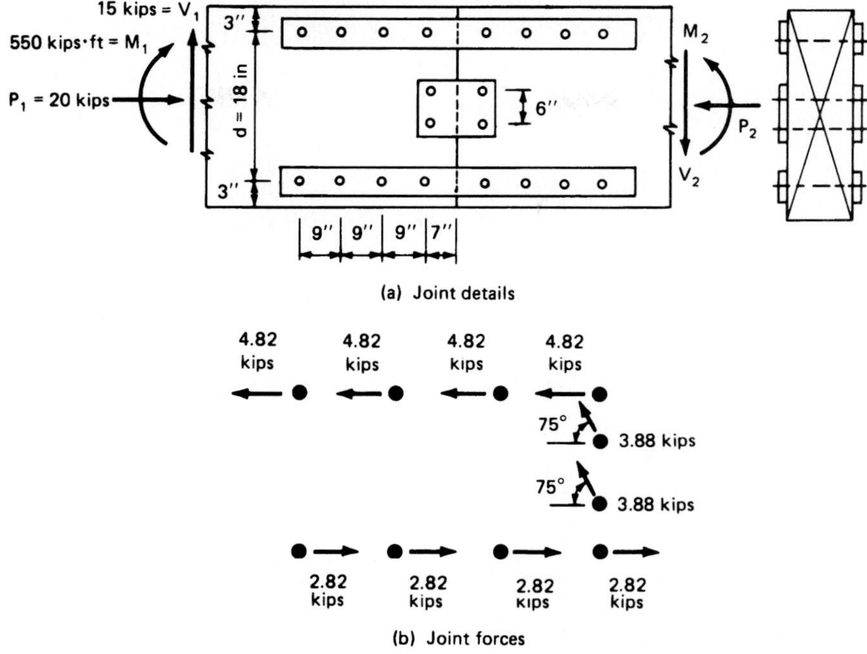

FIG. 5.55 Example 5.22.

Equations Needed. The force on connectors at the top flange is

$$F_T = \frac{M}{n_1 d} + \frac{P}{n}$$

where n = total number of connectors on one side of joint
n_1 = total number of connectors in top or bottom flange plates on one side of joint
d = distance between centroids of top and bottom rows of connectors

The force on connectors at the bottom flange is

$$F_B = \frac{M}{n_1 d} - \frac{P}{n}$$

The forces on the connectors at the web plate are

$$F_x = \frac{P}{n} \qquad \text{and} \qquad F_y = \frac{V}{n_2}$$

where n_2 = total number of connectors in web plate on one side of joint:

$$F_w = \sqrt{F_x^2 + F_y^2} \qquad \theta = \tan^{-1} F_y/F_x$$

SOLUTION:

$$F_T = \frac{550}{2 \times 4 \times 18} + \frac{20}{(2 \times 2 \times 4) + (2 \times 2)}$$

$$F_T = 3.82 + 1.00 = 4.82 \text{ kips (18.6 kN)}$$

$$F_B = 3.82 - 1.00 = 2.82 \text{ kips (10.9 kN)}$$

$$F_x = 20/20 = 1.0 \text{ kip}$$

$$F_y = 15/4 = 3.75 \text{ kips}$$

$$F_w = \sqrt{1.00^2 + 3.75^2} = 3.88 \text{ kips (15.0 kN)}$$

$$\theta = \tan^{-1}\frac{3.75}{1.00} = 75°$$

All forces acting on the connectors in the multiple-plate joint are shown in Fig. 5.55*b*.

Forces Acting on Connectors. Compare results with the allowable load for a 4-in shear plate. Assume group B wood, with a member thickness of more than 3½ in, and use Fig. 5.38*a*.

$$Q_1 = 4.32 \times 1.15 \times 1.11 = 5.51 \text{ kips (24.5 kN)} \qquad \theta = 0°$$

Note: When steel side plates are used instead of wood, the design values for 4-in shear plates loaded parallel to grain may be increased 18, 11, 5, and 0 percent for species groups A, B, C, and D, respectively. However, NDS limits the maximum design value for a 4-in shear plate with ¾-in bolts for all load combinations, except those including wind load, to 4400 lb. No additional adjustment factors apply:

$$Q_1 = 4.40 \text{ kips (19.6 kN)}$$

$$Q_2 = 3.12 \times 1.15 = 3.59 \text{ kips (16.0 kN)} \qquad \theta = 75°.$$

Therefore, shear plates in a flange plate and the web shear plates are overstressed, and it will be necessary to increase the number per side of joint. The steel plates can now be designed, and it would be proper to assume that all bending and thrust are carried by flange plates and that all shear is carried by the web plate.

5.11.4 Comments on the Accuracy of the Design Procedure

The design procedure used for rigid connections is conservative, particularly for the rigid-plate joint. This can best be explained by noting the behavior of a connector as shown in Fig. 5.42. The load-slip curve is nonlinear; thus a large load level on a connector will be accompanied by a large deformation, and any increase in load will be accompanied by an additional large deformation. This ductile behavior would allow all connectors in a rigid-plate joint to attain high levels of stress, not just those most highly stressed. A factor of safety calculated by using the load on the joint when the most highly loaded connector reaches its design load will most likely be less than the factor of safety obtained if the ultimate load the joint can sustain were used.

A group reduction factor for a rigid plate or multiple-plate connection is probably not warranted for at least one or more of the following three reasons. First, the number in a row for most practical joints is most likely small. Second, the load-reduction factor of NDS is based on analytical results for a joint loaded only parallel to a row of fasteners or connectors and also parallel to the grain of the wood. Third, a design based on the rigid-plate theory is probably conservative.

5.12 MISCELLANEOUS CONNECTORS

5.12.1 Connectors Pressed into Wood

Toothed Rings. The toothed ring is stamped from 16-gauge hot-rolled sheet steel, bent to form a corrugated sharp-toothed annular band, and welded into a ringlike fastener. Toothed ring diameters range from 2 to 4 in. The ring height is $\frac{15}{16}$ in, which allows a penetration of $\frac{15}{32}$ in into each face of adjacent members (see Fig. 5.56).

The toothed ring is installed by pressing the ring into adjoining faces by a press or by tightening a high-strength bolt. The uncertainty of how much the ring is pressed into each face makes it difficult to assign reasonable design values. Toothed rings are no longer manufactured in the United States, and their use is not recommended.

Spike Grids. Spike grids have pointed square tapered teeth protruding from both sides and are made of galvanized steel. They are available in flat, circular, flat square, and single- and double-curved square shapes (see Fig. 5.57). The flat grid is used to connect overlapping flat members. The single-curved grid is used to connect a flat to a round or semiround member. The double-curved grid is used to connect two round members.

The circular grid is $3\frac{1}{4}$ in (82.6 mm) in diameter and $1\frac{1}{8}$ in (28.6 mm) wide from tooth point to tooth point. The flat and curved grids are $4\frac{1}{8}$ in (105 mm) square and $\frac{15}{16}$ in (23.8 mm) wide from tooth point to tooth point.

Spike grids are installed by pressing together the members to be joined and are designed to transmit shear loads. The required bolt is not assumed to transmit any shear. Design values can be obtained from Ref. 14.

5.13 CONNECTORS OF THIN-GAUGE STEEL PLATE

5.13.1 Introduction

A number of manufacturers make connectors of thin-gauge steel plate. Typically, the connectors are zinc-coated and 12 to 20 gauge in thickness. Often they are the most economical way of connecting members. Some of the more commonly used

FIG. 5.56 Tooth ring.

connectors are joist hangers, framing anchors, and truss plates (metal-plate connectors).

5.13.2 Metal-Plate Connectors

Truss plates are flat steel plates with protruding teeth (see Fig. 5.58). The teeth are typically forced into the wood by a press, and one plate is installed in each face of a wood member. Their greatest use is for gusset plates in prefabricated roof and floor trusses.

Plates are typically proprietary devices, and allowable load values are not readily available. The manufacturer of the metal gusset plate obtains approval of its design from building code agencies. Generally, the design for trusses using metal plate connectors is carried out by the plate manufacturer, the truss manufacturer, or by specialized consultants. Usually the designer can obtain truss plans by contacting the truss manufacturer.

The sizing of metal-plate connectors is typically based on an allowable load for the connector in terms of pounds per square inch. Allowable values, although not typically available, are in the range of 80 to 200 lb/in^2 (551 to 1376 kPa), with

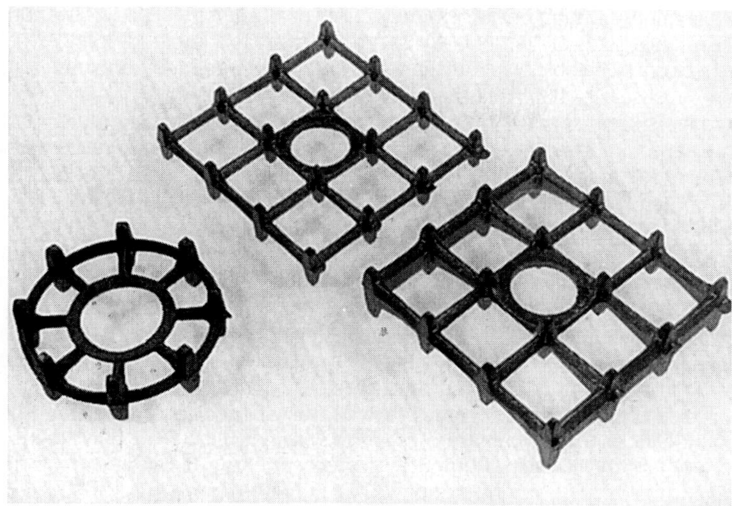

FIG. 5.57 Spike grids: single curve, flat, and circular.

FIG. 5.58 Truss plates.

the lower value applying to gross areas and lower-density wood. The 200 would be for southern pine or Douglas fir and for net areas. Angle of load to grain has some effect on allowable loads of metal-plate connectors, and adjustments for load duration and fire-retardant treatment also need to be made.

If wood is treated with fire-retardant chemicals, it is recommended that the designer obtain appropriate reduction factors for allowable load values by contacting the manufacturer of the fire-retardant chemical and/or the Truss Plate Institute. It is recommended that care be exercised in the selection of the fire-retardant chemicals to be used, since some will cause corrosion of galvanized-steel plates, in which case it would be necessary to use stainless-steel plates. Again, it is recommended that the manufacturer of the fire-retardant chemical and/or the Truss Plate Institute be contacted.

The net area of a plate is obtained by considering as inactive all plate area within ½ in (12.7 mm) of the member end measured parallel to the member and ¼ in (6.35 mm) along edges measured perpendicular to grain.

The Truss Plate Institute specifies that all trusses used to verify design be tested by loading. These trusses must withstand the design dead load plus 2½ times the design live load for at least 10 minutes. Based on a long duration of load, the truss may have a factor of safety in the range of 1.3 to 1.6. Further discussion on metal-gusset-plate trusses can be found in Chap. 6.

5.13.3 Joist Hangers and Framing Anchors

Catalogs are available[15,16] which show the configuration and give all dimensions of joist hangers, framing anchors, and other light-gauge connectors, several of which are shown in Figs. 5.59 and 5.60.

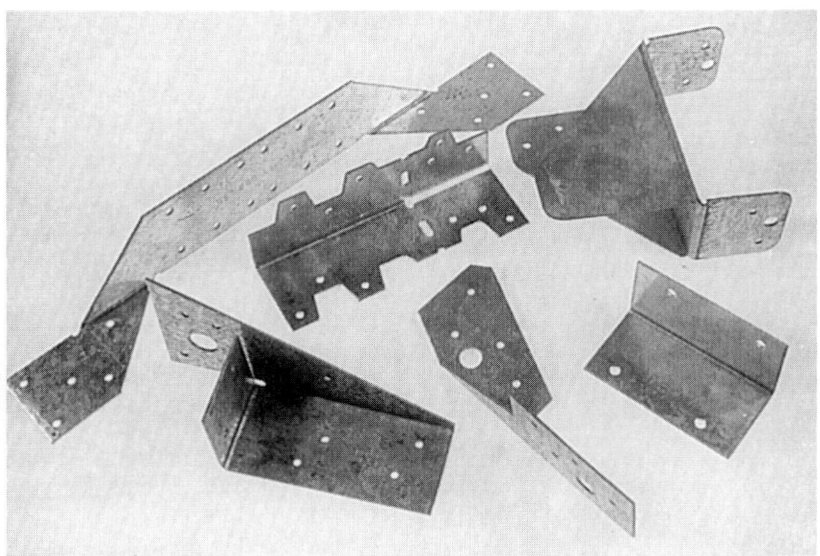

FIG. 5.59 Framing anchors.

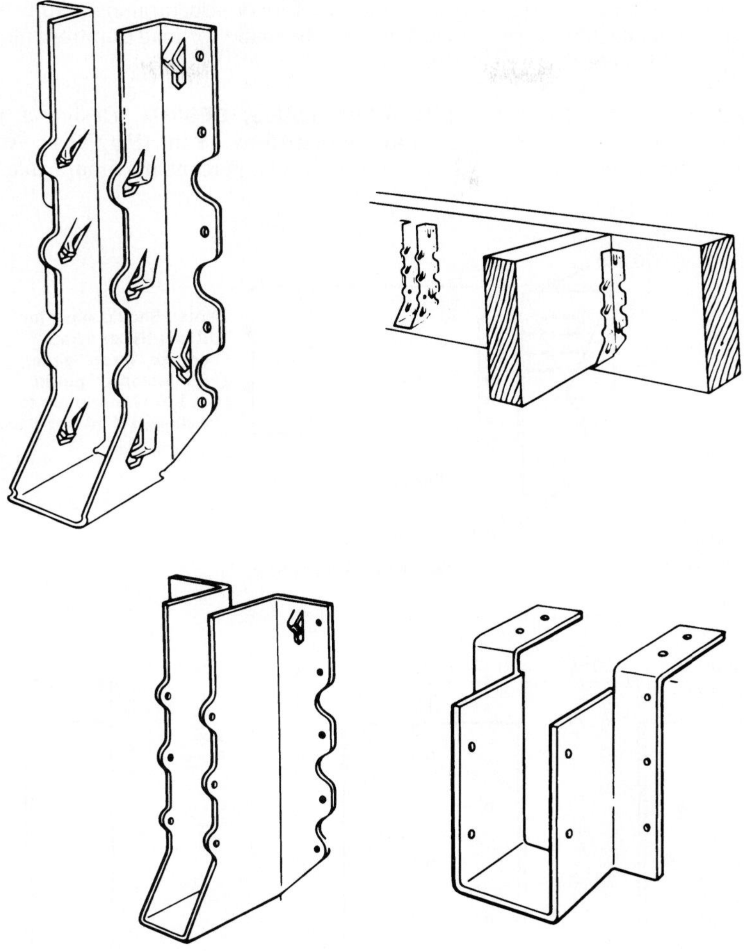

FIG. 5.60 Joist hangers.

Joist hangers and framing anchors are designed to reduce difficulties and uncertainties of nailing and to provide considerably stronger shear connections than are practically feasible otherwise. These connectors also serve to help locate and seat wood members accurately.

Framing anchors as shown in Fig. 5.59 can be used to fasten studs to plates and trussed rafters and rafters to plates. Joist hangers are used as shown in Fig. 5.60 to attach joists to headers.

The literature also provides allowable loads for the connectors. Values given have typically received approval by one or more model codes such as the *Uniform Building Code.*[2] However, this should be verified before specifying a connector.

Generally, in designs using such connectors, it is only necessary to compare allowable values, after adjustments, with end reactions, the lateral load, and / or the uplift values obtained during analysis of the structure or structural unit. Adjustments of allowable connector values typically need to be made for load duration, moisture content, and fire-retardant treatment.

EXAMPLE 5.23: PURLIN-TO-GIRDER JOINT, NAILS, DESIGN Design a purlin hanger to attach a purlin (3 by 12 in) to a girder (6 by 18 in) (Fig. 5.61). Assume that the purlin is seasoned No. 2 southern pine (19 percent maximum m.c.), the

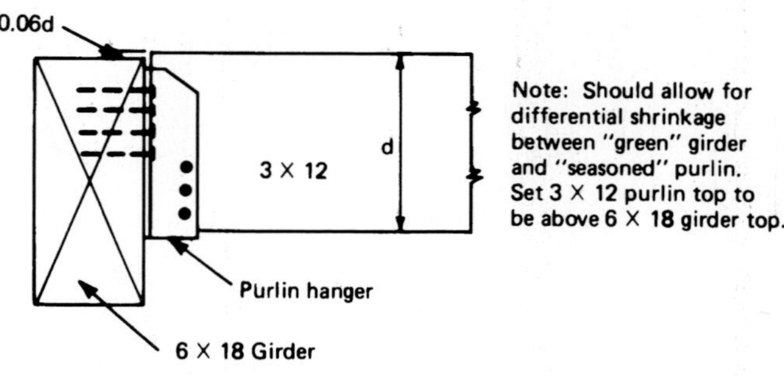

(a) Nail placement: Girder and purlin

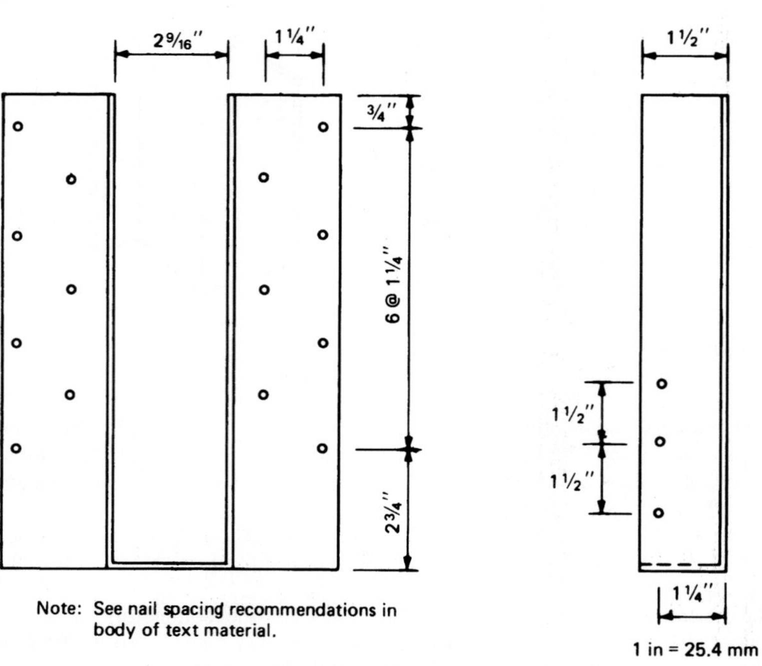

(b) Nail placement: Purlin hanger

FIG. 5.61 Example 5.23.

girder is surfaced green No. 2 SR southern pine, and the joint is subjected to dry conditions of use. The purlin has an end reaction of 1600 lb (7.12 kN) which results from a load combination of dead plus roof loads (roof load C_D = 1.25).

SOLUTION: $F_{c\perp}$(allowable) = 660 lb/in² (Supplement to NDS[5]).
Note: No. C_D adjustment is applicable for compression perpendicular to grain for sawn timber when values are based on a deformation limit.

Length of bearing required = 1600/(660 × 2.5) = 0.97 in. Use 1½ in.

Number of nails required to transfer load from the purlin hanger into the girder: Specific gravity is 0.55. Try 12d common wire nails.

$$P \text{ (allowable)} = 129 \text{ (see Table 5.5}a\text{).}$$

$$P \text{ (adjusted)} = 129 \times C_D \times C_M$$

$$= 129 \times 1.25 \times 0.75 = 121 \text{ lb per nail.}$$

$$\text{Number required} = 1600/121 = 13.2 \text{ nails}$$

Use fourteen 12d common wire nails.

Uplift resistance of purlin to purlin hanger connection. Use six 6d common wire nails.

$$P \text{ (allowable)} = 83 \text{ lb (see Table 5.3).}$$

$$P \text{ (adjusted)} = 83 \times C_D \times C_M$$

$$= 83 \times 1.60^* \times 1.0 = 133 \text{ lb per nail.}$$

$$\text{Uplift value} = 6 \times 133 = 798 \text{ lb (3.55 kN).}$$

5.13.4 Clamping Plates

Two types of clamping plates are available as shown in Figs. 5.62 and 5.63. The 5¼-in (133-mm) square plate is made of 16-gauge (15.9-mm) sheet steel and has integral triangular teeth protruding ⅝ in (15.9 mm) from both faces. The heavier 8-in (203-mm)-wide flanged plate has integral triangular teeth protruding from one face in the opposite direction of the two side flanges. Clamping plates are designed for wood-to-wood connections and are used where it is important to limit the amount of movement between members. They were developed for use in maintaining the spacing of ties on open-deck railroad structures. Clamping plates are installed by pressing or driving one set of teeth into the wood, using a special driving plate to protect the second set of teeth in the case of flat clamping plates. The flanges of the flanged clamping plates may be nailed to the sides of the member over which the flanges cantilever.

5.13.5 Nail Plates

A true nail plate is the Swiss Menig plate shown in Fig. 5.64. It has a large number of 0.0666 in (1.69-mm)-diameter nails, pointed at both ends, spaced 5⁄16 in (7.94

*Assume C_D for wind load.

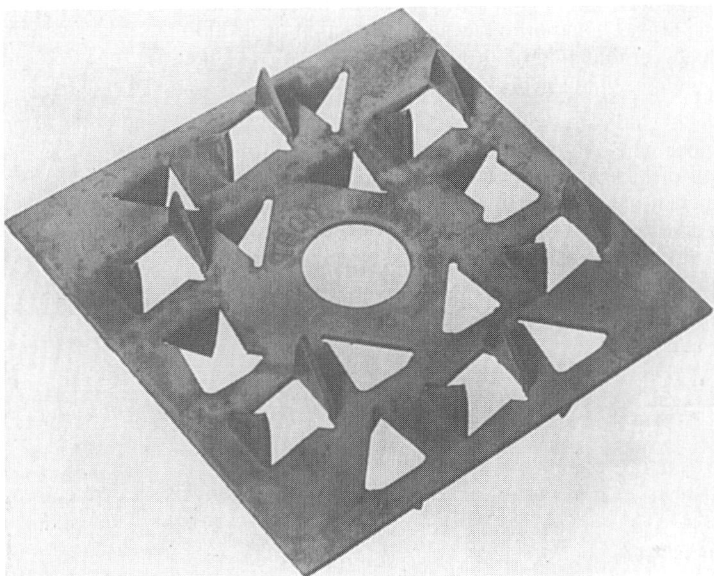

FIG. 5.62 Plain clamping plate.

mm) on centers, and protruding ⅜ in (9.52 mm) from both faces of the plate. The plate consists of three layers—solid glass-fiber-reinforced plastic, metal foil, and foamed plastic—of ⅛ in (3.17 mm) overall thickness in the installed compressed stage.

This plate is installed with platen presses and is used in the same manner as pronged and toothed sheet-metal plates, with the nails designed to transmit shear loads in wood-to-wood joints. The plate has been used successfully in small and large wood trusses and other structures in Europe.

5.13.6 Plain and Deformed Sheet-Metal Nail-On Plates

Plain and deformed 14-gauge (1.90-mm) and heavier sheet-metal nail-on plates were used extensively prior to the introduction of pronged and toothed sheet-metal plates (see Fig. 5.65). These are still used in Europe by some designers to transmit large forces and/or moments from one member to the next. If the plates are not prepunched, the desired nail locations are shown by slight indentations in the plate, or if the plate is not premarked or predrilled, the nails can be placed where desired.

These nail-on plates are installed by locating them properly and driving appropriate nails through them into the wood members. Care must be taken in the selection of the thickness of the plate and the nails to be used since if common wire nails are used with a thick plate, the nail heads can pop off when driven tightly against the plate. The nail-on plates are designed to transmit shear loads from the wood member through the nails to the metal plate which is in turn transferred to the bolt placed through the center of the plate.

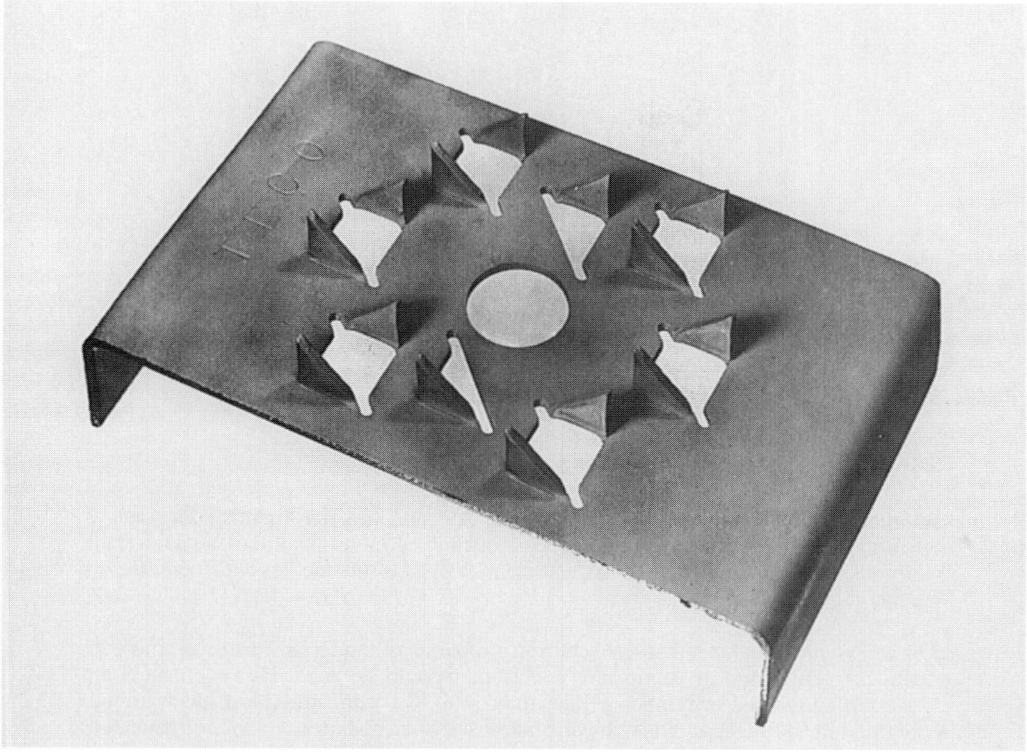

FIG. 5.63 Flanged clamping plate. *(Courtesy of Dr. E. George Stern.)*

FIG. 5.64 Swiss Menig plate.

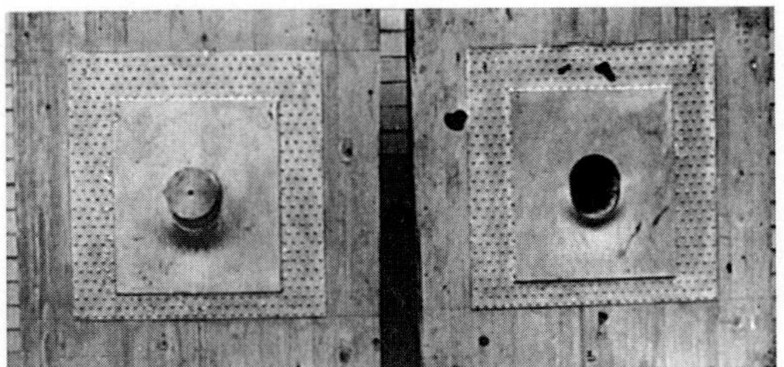

FIG. 5.65 Plain sheet-metal nail-on plate with 850 holes.

5.14 CHOICE OF FASTENERS

5.14.1 Structural Considerations

Balanced Deformations. It is not considered good practice to intermix sizes or types of connectors in a joint because the difference in slippage (stiffness) of each can cause an overload on the stiffest connectors before the less-stiff connectors receive significant load.

Thickness of Lumber. Most structural lumber is 1½ in (38.1 mm) or more in thickness; therefore, any connector or fastener could be used. However, nails are less commonly used in lumber greater than 1½ (38.1 mm) thick. For heavy timber construction, bolts, split rings, shear plates, and special-purpose timber connectors such as beam hangers and post caps are recommended.

Type of Load. Vibratory loads or those which cause a stress reversal may influence the choice of type of fastener or connector. Bolts have less of a tendency to wear or work loose than do nails, and shear plates and split rings will out-perform bolts.

Size and Type. It is generally better to use the same size and type of fastener or connector throughout a structural subunit such as a truss in order to maintain uniform magnitudes of slippage at all joints per unit of force.

5.14.2 Cost and Construction Considerations

Number of Fasteners and Connectors. The fewer the number of fasteners and connectors, in general, the lower the cost.

Uniform Size and Type of Fastener or Connector. Maintaining a single size and type will reduce overall cost, since it will reduce labor cost. It also reduces the chance of error.

Labor Cost. Labor is a large part of the total cost of many structures. It may range from approximately 25 to 50 percent or more of the total cost.

Assembly and Erection. Bolts do not require separation of the members for installation whereas using shear plates or split rings will require separation of members to install. Flexible structural components must be properly supported and braced during construction.

5.15 JOINT DESIGN: GENERAL CONSIDERATIONS

5.15.1 Shrinkage and Swelling

Wood shrinks as it dries and swells when it gains moisture. Little shrinkage or swelling takes place in wood parallel to grain (generally much less than 1 percent). However, in the perpendicular to grain direction, commonly referred to as *across the grain,* the magnitude of shrinkage or swelling will be many times that of parallel to grain. Therefore, in the design of joints it is necessary that proper consideration be given to movements caused by shrinkage and swelling of wood members.

5.15.2 Tension Perpendicular to Grain

The ultimate strength of wood in tension perpendicular to grain is extremely low. If possible, it is desirable to avoid loading wood in tension perpendicular to grain. If it cannot be avoided, then careful consideration must be given to the type and placement of fasteners and connectors.

5.15.3 Moisture Content

Wood, when maintaned at low moisture contents, will function satisfactorily for many years. However, if it becomes wet, its useful life can be very limited. This can be a very critical problem for joints of wood structures, and the expected in-service moisture content needs to be given due consideration during the design of the joint.

5.15.4 Typical Connections

Some of the connections typically used in wood construction are shown in Figs. 5.66 through 5.72. They are shown merely to demonstrate some of the types of connections in use and some of the factors that need to be considered in their design.

Beam to Steel Column. A U bracket, as shown in Fig. 5.66, is attached to a steel column by welding. The length of the bracket must be sufficient to satisfy $F_{c\perp}$ and to provide adequate end distance for the bolts. The distance a should be made large enough to satisfy edge distance requirements and small enough so that across-grain shrinkage is not a problem as the wood dries to its equilibrium moisture content. The bolts can be designed to provide resistance to uplift, in which case a is the effective depth in calculations for shear.

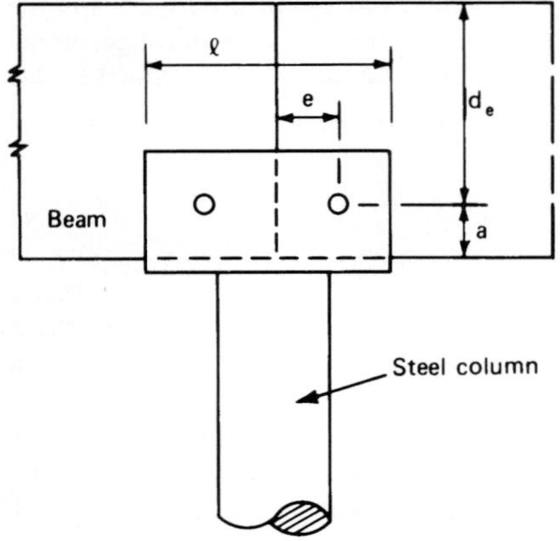

FIG. 5.66 Beam to steel column.

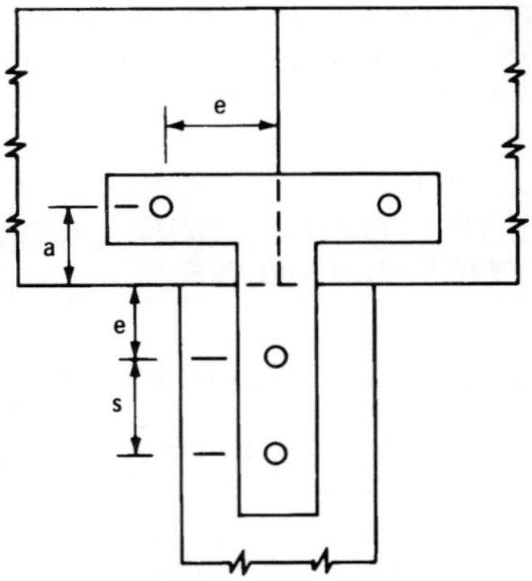

FIG. 5.67 Beam to wood column, T bracket.

Beam to Wood Column, T Bracket. If the end reactions of the beam are relatively small, it may be satisfactory to place beams directly on a wood column, as shown in Fig. 5.67 ($F_{c\perp}$ must be satisfied). A T bracket can be used to resist any uplift forces that may occur in the joint. Requirements for end distance and spacings for bolts must be adequate, and the edge distance should meet the requirement discussed earlier in this section.

Beam to Wood Column, U Bracket. If the end reactions of the beams are large, then it may be necessary to provide additional bearing length to satisfy compression perpendicular to grain requirements. This can be done by providing a U bracket as shown in Fig. 5.68. All requirements for end and edge distances and spacing must also be satisfied.

Beam Saddle. A convenient method of transferring the load from one flexural member to another is by the use of a saddle-type connection as shown in Fig. 5.69. The area in compression perpendicular to grain must be checked for both the sup-

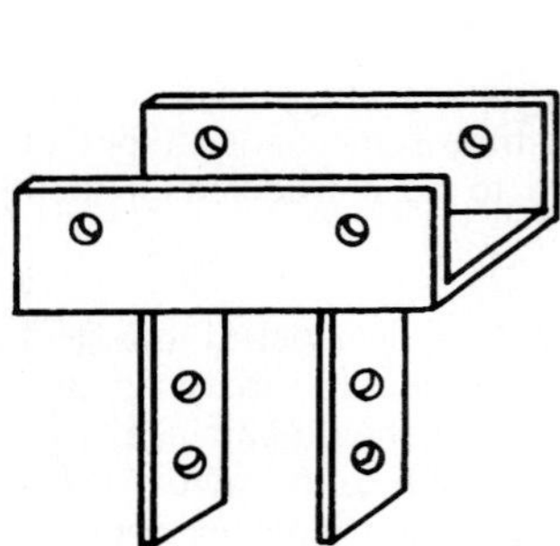

FIG. 5.68 Beam to wood column, U bracket.

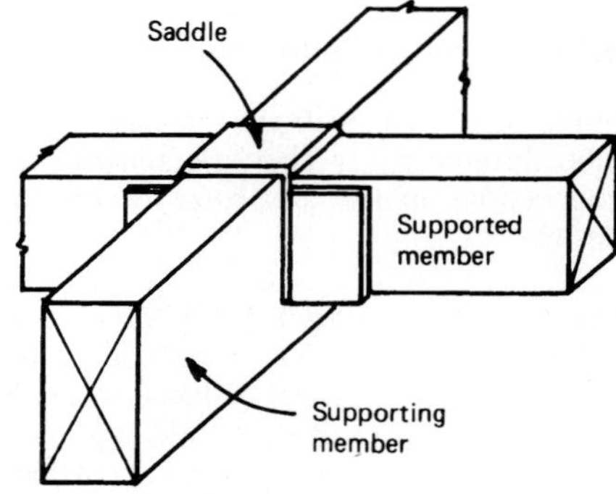

FIG. 5.69 Beam saddle.

ported and supporting members. The placement of all bolts in the supported members should satisfy all minimum requirements for end and edge distance. In addition, shrinkage of the wood as it dries to its equilibrium moisture content should be considered in the design, particularly as it relates to the placement of bolts and the vertical positioning of the supported member in relation to the supporting beam.

Hanger, Beam Face. As shown in Fig. 5.70, a purlin is supported by a hanger attached to the face of a beam. The design of this connection needs to satisfy requirements for compression stress perpendicular to the grain and for end and edge distance for the purlin. For the beam, bolts are loaded perpendicular to the grain and must be designed to transfer the end reaction of the purlin to the beam. It is desirable to place these bolts near the top of the beam but not in its most highly stressed fibers. Conversely, bolts in the purlin should be located near the bottom of this member. This placement should minimize tension perpendicular to grain stresses which can result due to load and shrinkage. Edge distances and spacing requirements also must be satisfactory. For relatively heavy loads, possible torsional stresses in the beam should be considered.

Uplift Connection. An angle bracket is commonly used to anchor a beam to a concrete or masonry wall, as shown in Fig. 5.71. End and edge distances must satisfy minimum requirements, and the effective depth in shear calculations for uplift force is d_e.

Cantilever Beam Hanger. A saddle-type beam connection with a tension tie can be used to support the suspended span on the cantilever as shown in Fig. 5.72. It is necessary that the saddle have adequate length so that compression perpendicular to grain stresses do not exceed allowable values. The tension tie should be placed as shown, and adequate end and edge distances should be provided. Bolts of adequate size to transfer the expected tensile forces should be used.

Preengineered Timber Connectors. Many types of preengineered timber connectors are commercially available. These are manufactured from heavy-gauge steel and steel plate. Several are shown in Figs. 5.73 through 5.80. These are typically used with solid wood members of nominal thickness of 4 in (102 mm) or more

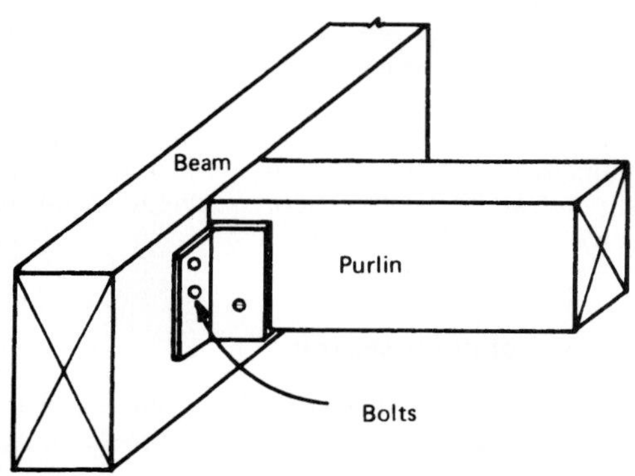

FIG. 5.70 Hanger beam face.

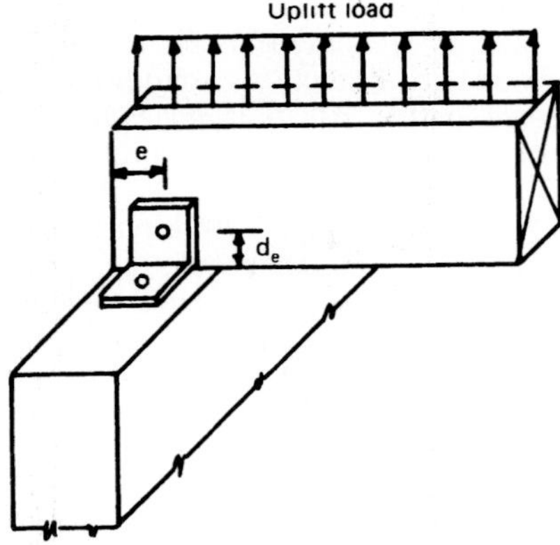

FIG. 5.71 Uplift connection.

and also with glulam members. As with thin-gauge steel plate connectors, their purpose is to increase the allowable magnitude of load transfer, to ease the construction of the joints, and to improve the alignment of members.

Column bases serve to anchor the bottom of the column to the concrete slab. At the same time, the column base shown in Fig. 5.73 serves to effectively separate the wood from the concrete, thereby preventing the potential passage of moisture from concrete to wood as a result of capillary action.

Column caps as shown in Fig. 5.74 are used to attach a beam to the top of the column.

Hold-downs can be used to anchor the corners of shear walls to the foundation (see Fig. 5.75).

Beam seats serve the purpose of attaching beams, girders, or joists to masonry or concrete walls, as shown in Fig. 5.76.

Purlin hangers and beam hangers as shown in Figs. 5.77 and 5.78 allow purlins or beams to be attached to the supporting member. It is important to consider the torsion that may be imparted to the supporting member if purlin hangers are placed on only one side of the supporting member.

Saddles as shown in Fig. 5.79 serve to support flexural members (purlins, beams, etc.) coming from two sides. They provide a more balanced load on the supporting member thereby reducing the twisting (torsion) of the supporting member.

Hinge connectors as shown in Fig. 5.80 are used to support cantilever beams. It is important that a horizontal tie be provided as shown for the purpose of tying the two members together. This is especially important where seismic action is probable. The location of the tie is also important due to shrinkage which will most likely occur in service.

5.15.5 Dos and Don'ts of Joint Design

Figures 5.81 through 5.95 show some potential problems that may occur in the design of joints in wood. Each is described very briefly and the recommended correction is given.

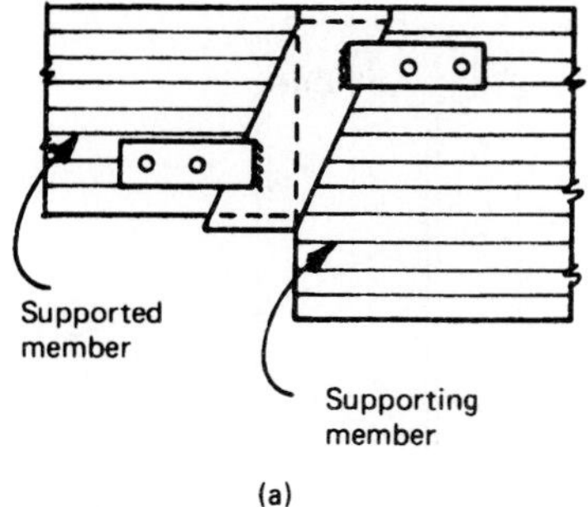

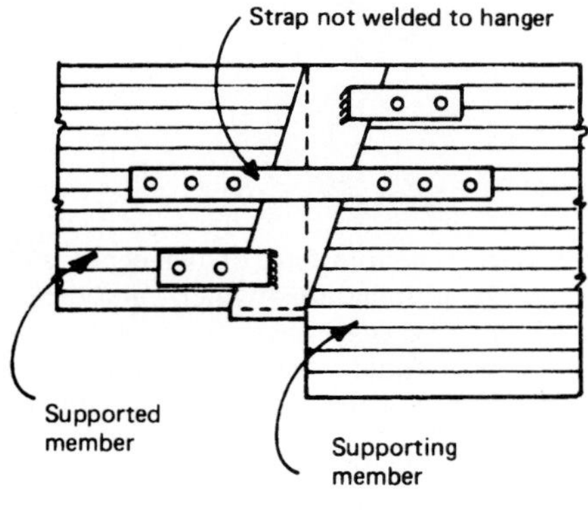

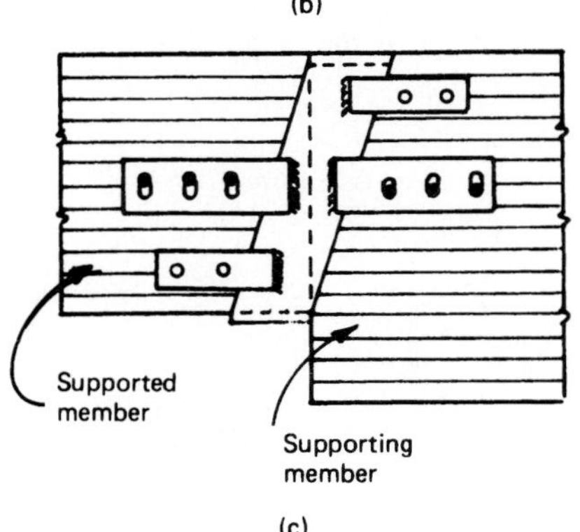

FIG. 5.72 Cantilever beam hangers. (*a*) The vertical reaction of the supported member is carried by the side plates and transferred in bearing perpendicular to grain to the supporting member. The rotation due to the eccentric loading is resisted by the bolts through the tabs at the top and bottom. The connector may be installed with the top (and bottom) bearing plates dapped into the members to obtain a flush surface or may be installed without daps. Notching on the tension side should be minimized. (*b*) Where horizontal forces must be resisted by a hinge connection, loose tension ties may be installed on both sides of the beam. The tie shown is not fastened to the cantilever hanger. (*c*) If tension ties are fastened to the cantilever hanger, vertically slotted holes are required in the tie and careful location of the bolts in the end of the slot farthest from the bearing seat is required to prevent splitting due to shrinkage and seating deformations. Bolts in slotted holes should be hand-tightened only to permit movement.

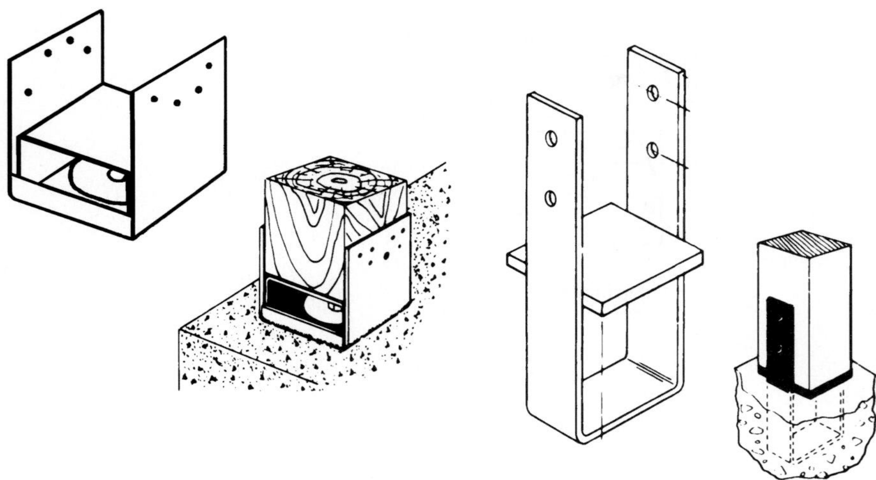

FIG. 5.73 Column bases.

Notched End (Fig. 5.81). Cutting a notch on the bottom side of the beam will reduce its load-carrying capacity significantly. The ultimate load which can be carried by a beam notched to one-half its depth may be only one-quarter or less of that which can be carried by an unnotched beam of equal size. The recommended correction would be to not notch the beam. See Chap. 4 for a discussion of this as related to the design of a beam.

End Cut Across Grain (Fig. 5.82). Placing a member on a plate as shown, although not as apparent, is little different than cutting a notch on the underside of the beam as shown in Fig. 5.81. A better placement of the sloping member is to place point *B* directly over point *A*.

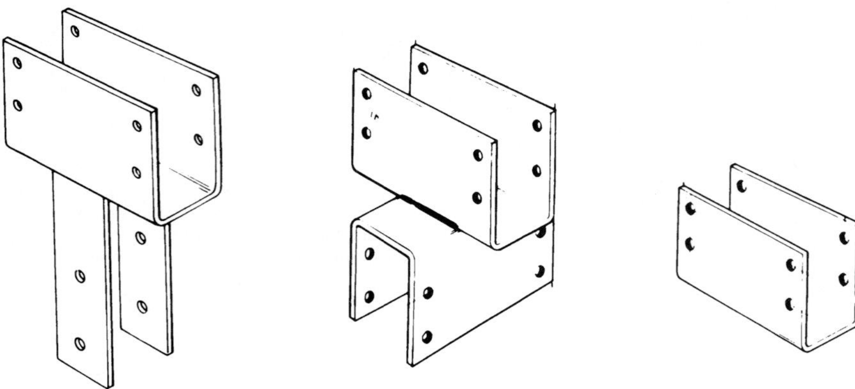

FIG. 5.74 Column caps.

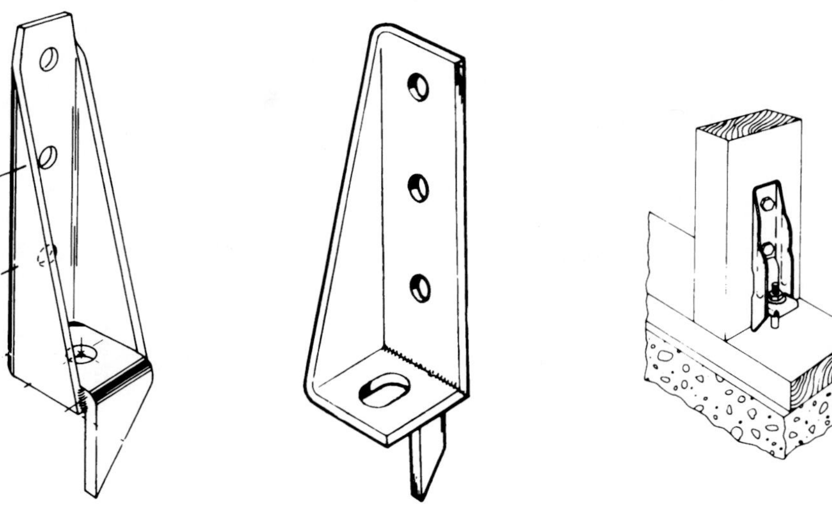

FIG. 5.75 Hold-downs.

Suspended Load (Fig. 5.83). Supporting a load on a connector placed near the bottom of the member will cause tensile stress perpendicular to the grain which may cause the beam to split as shown. It would be better design practice to attach the connectors or fasteners some distance above the neutral axis of the member.

Support in Upper Half of Beam (Fig. 5.84). This is similar to Fig. 5.81 in that it causes tensile stress perpendicular to the grain and may split the beam as shown. Changing the clip angle so that bolts are placed near the bottom of the supported beam but are still located near the top of the supporting girder will correct this problem.

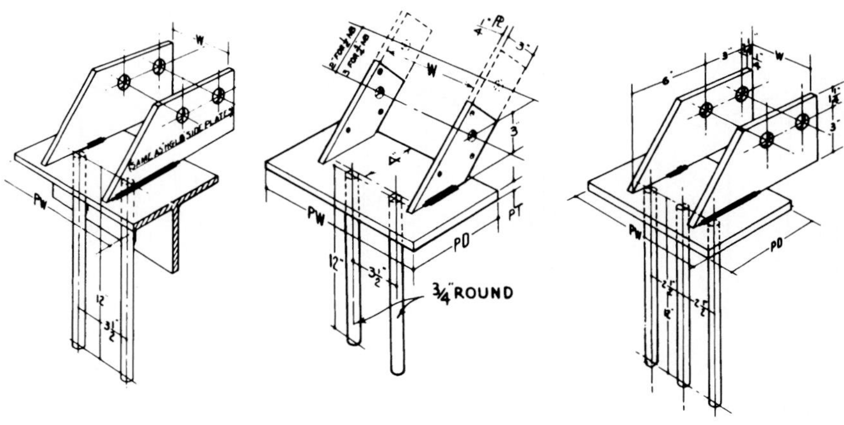

FIG. 5.76 Beam seats.

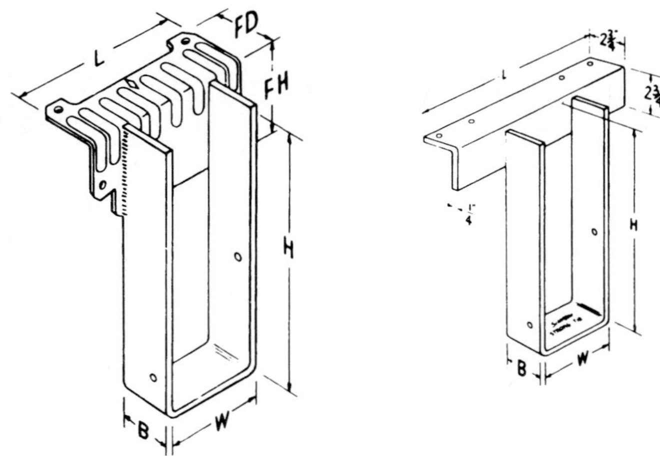

FIG. 5.77 Purlin hangers.

Long Splice Plate (Fig. 5.85). Most wood members, although seasoned when placed, still have a moisture content above the equilibrium moisture content they will attain in service. Therefore, if long splice plates are used as shown, the members will try to shrink, but the rigid splice plates will not permit shrinkage to occur, thus causing the wood to split. A solution for this problem would be to use only short splice plates or two separate plates on each side, one near the top and one near the bottom.

Top Restraint—Deep Beam (Fig. 5.86). The rigid wall to which the clip angles are attached causes the same problem as the long splice plates of Fig. 5.85. The split could be avoided by not placing a bolt in the beam at the top clip angle. The clip angles would still prevent rotation of the end of the beam.

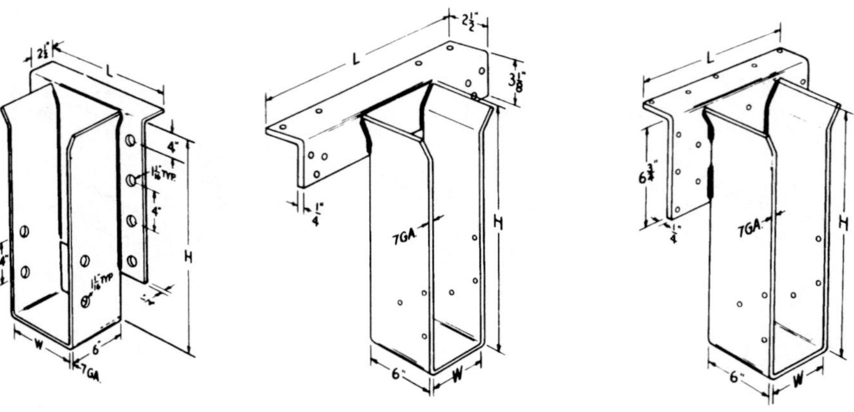

FIG. 5.78 Beam hangers.

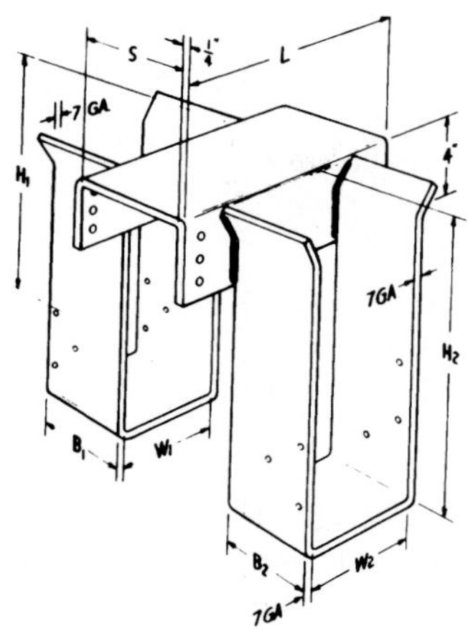

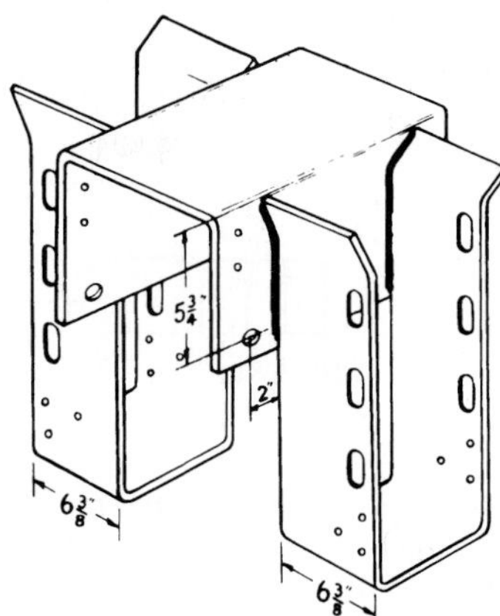

FIG. 5.79 Saddles.

Top Restraint (Fig. 5.87). As the beams bend, their tops will move apart and possibly cause a split in the beams as a result of pulling on the bolts. Slotting the holes in the splice plates would allow the bolts to move with the bending of the beams.

Notched Tension Side (Fig. 5.88). This is similar to cutting a notch on the bottom side at the end of a simple span beam as shown in Fig. 5.81. The notch is serious for any continuous or cantilever beam and particularly so for glulam beams, since the tension laminations are critical in the performance of the member.

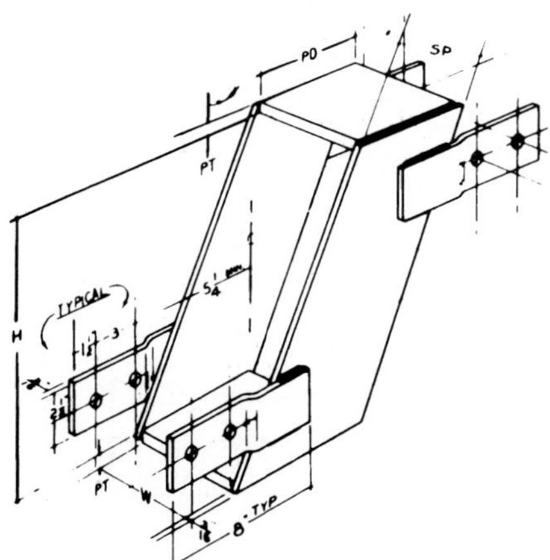

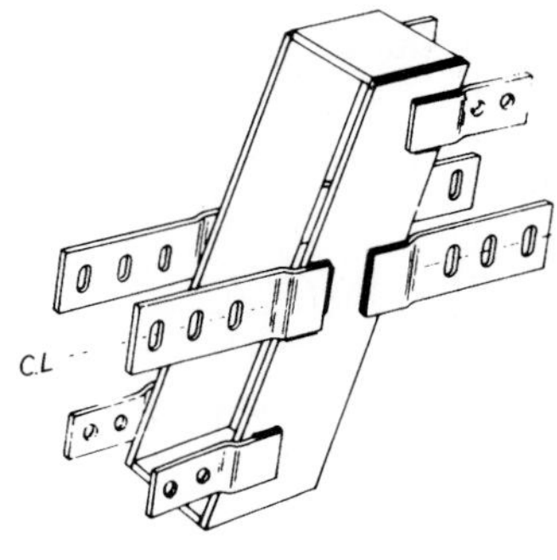

FIG. 5.80 Hinge connections.

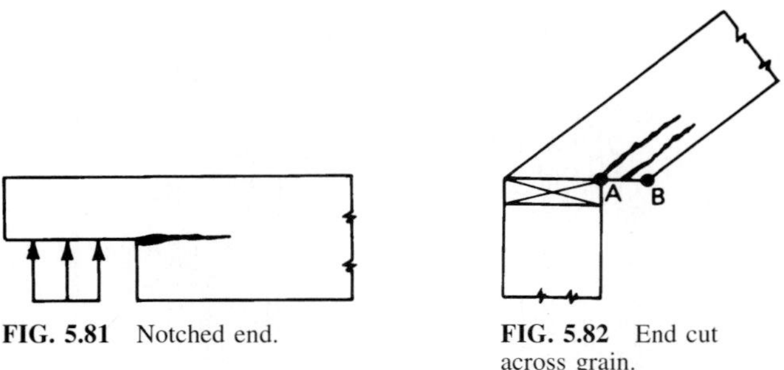

FIG. 5.81 Notched end.

FIG. 5.82 End cut across grain.

Column Encased in Concrete (Fig. 5.89). Some designers try to conceal the bases of columns. If the concrete is in contact with the ground, moisture will most likely migrate into the lower portion of the wood and cause decay. The solution to this problem is to place the base of the column on a base plate located on the top of the finished floor.

Cantilever Beam with Bottom Ties (Fig. 5.90). A tension connection has been provided by placing bolts along a single line. As the supporting beam shrinks, the saddle wants to move downward. However, the tension bolts in the cantilever member restrain movement and a split can develop. This can be corrected by placing the tension tie at the top of the cantilever member (see Fig. 5.72).

Arch or Column in Closed Box (Fig. 5.91). The end of a member is placed in a closed steel box in which moisture can accumulate and cause swelling and, if the wood is not preservatively treated, decay. This hazard can be reduced by providing weep holes, weep slots, or any other method which permits the drainage of the water from the steel box.

Top Restraint by Nails (Fig. 5.92). This is similar to Fig. 5.86 in that a deep beam is restrained at the top and rests on the hanger at the bottom. Since large spikes or nails are used in place of bolts, designers often feel that the spikes or nails cannot develop sufficient force to cause wood to split as it seasons in service. However, large spikes can in fact develop forces of sufficient magnitude to cause the beam to split. If the spikes were placed near the bottom, shrinkage could take place without restraint.

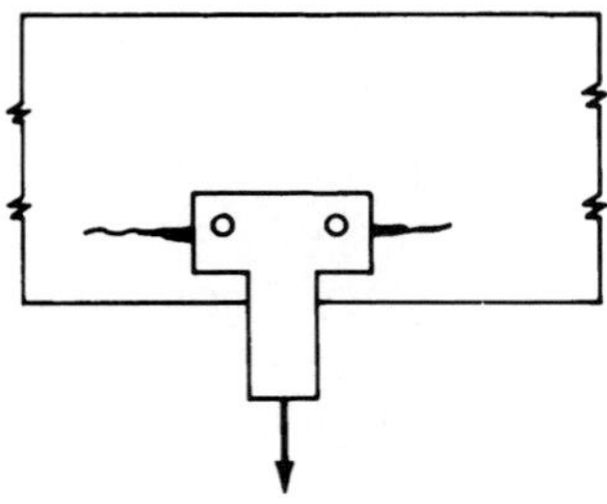

FIG. 5.83 Suspended load.

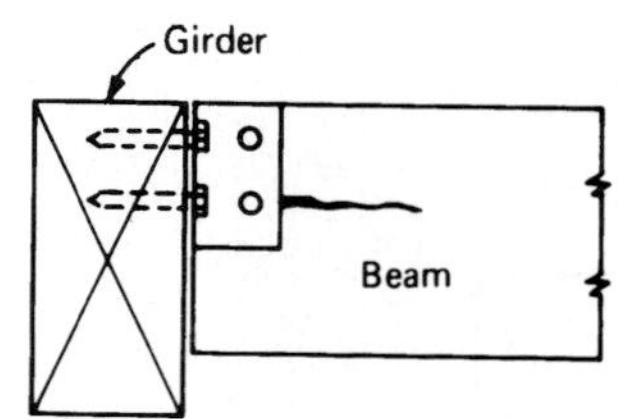

FIG. 5.84 Support in upper half of beam.

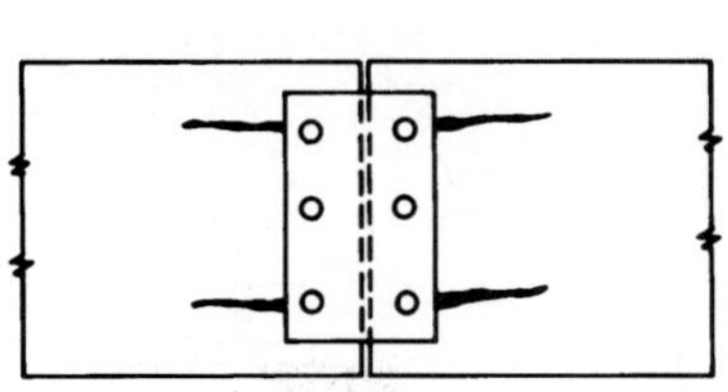

FIG. 5.85 Long splice plate.

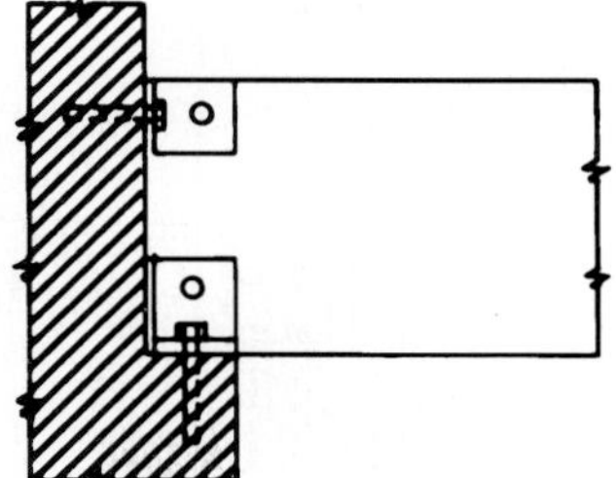

FIG. 5.86 Top restraint—deep beam.

Fixed-Angle Gusset (Fig. 5.93). A connection for a truss is fabricated from steel plates. The steel gusset has a fixed angle between truss diagonals as a result of welding. Some angular change takes place between the diagonals as the truss deflects under load. However, the fixed gusset restrains the diagonals from rotating and may cause them to split along the row of bolts. This can be corrected by providing separate gusset plates for attaching each diagonal.

Beam to Girder, Free to Rotate (Fig. 5.94). A girder supporting a beam on only one side, if not restrained, may rotate and fail. A horizontal tie between the beam and girder at the bottom of the hanger is recommended.

Eccentric Joints (Fig. 5.95). If the center lines of members of a joint do not intersect at a point (see Fig. 5.95*a*), then considerable shear and moment may exist, and tensile stress perpendicular to the grain of the wood could be high. The combined stresses may cause failure. In Fig. 5.95*b*, the right diagonal may cause high tensile stresses perpendicular to the wood grain. Neither of the joints shown in Fig. 5.95 should be used unless an appropriate analysis is made or tests are employed to ensure that the joint will perform satisfactorily under design loads.

5.15.6 Shear in Joints

Shear parallel to the grain may be critical at joints where a shear force must be carried by one of the members. It may be particularly critical in joints which are

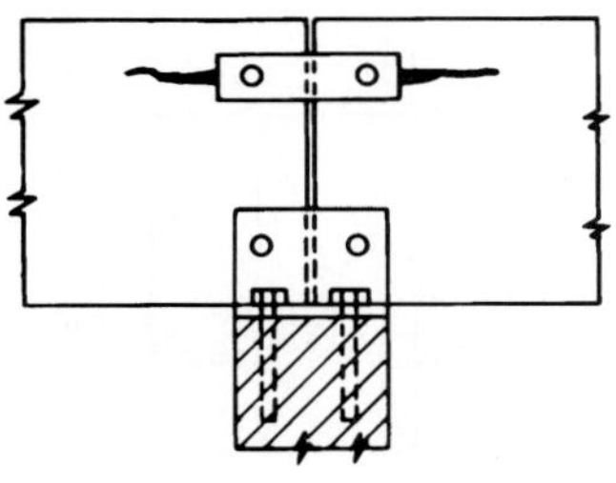

FIG. 5.87 Top restraint.

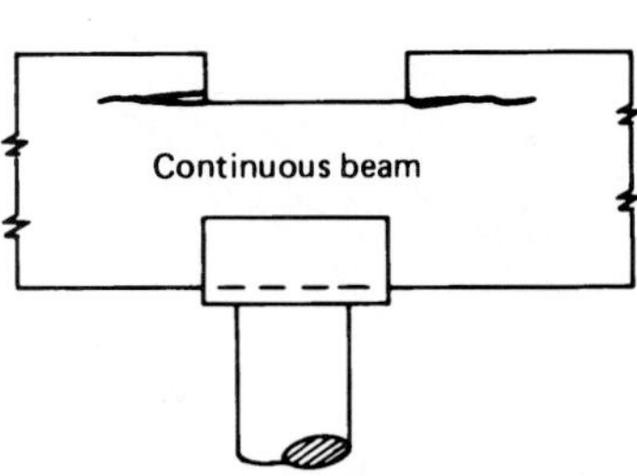

FIG. 5.88 Notched tension side.

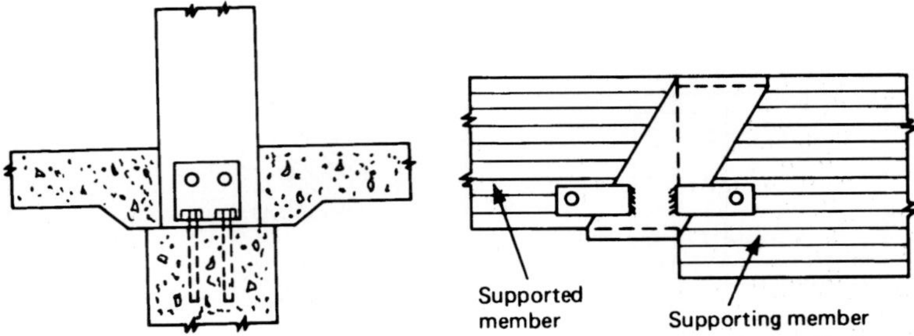

FIG. 5.89 Column encased in concrete.

FIG. 5.90 Cantilever beam with bottom ties.

located near the end of the member. Figure 5.96 shows some typical joints in which shear must be checked. The shear stress f_v may be calculated by using the following formulas:

1. When the joint is at least 5 times the depth of the member from its end, the shear stress should be calculated using the formula

$$f_v = \frac{3V}{2bd_e} \tag{5.18}$$

and the allowable shear stress may be increased by 50 percent. In addition, the shear stress calculated using the gross cross-sectional area of the member should not exceed the allowable shear stress parallel to grain.

2. When the joint is less than 5 times the depth of the member from its end, the shear stress should be calculated using the formula

$$f_v = \frac{3V}{2bd_e}\left(\frac{d}{d_e}\right) \tag{5.19}$$

and the allowable design shear stress may not be increased by 50 percent.

V is calculated for both Eqs. (5.18) and (5.19) by using recognized procedures of engineering mechanics. For a connector, d_e is the depth of the member less the

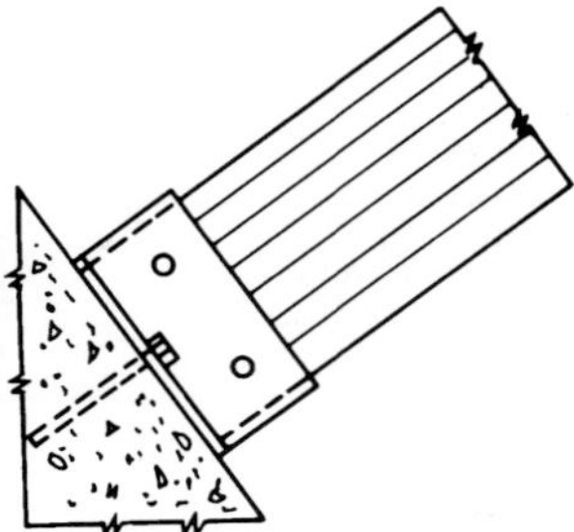

FIG. 5.91 Arch or column in closed box.

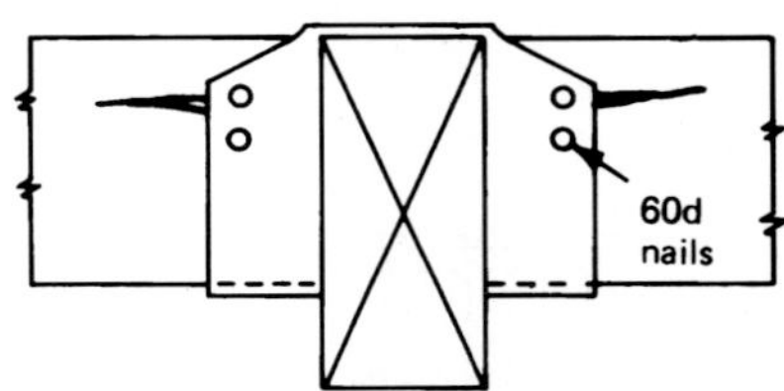

FIG. 5.92 Top restraint by nails.

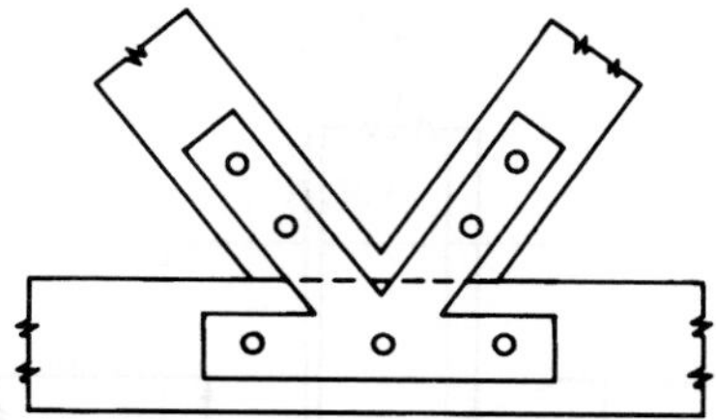

FIG. 5.93 Fixed-angle gusset.

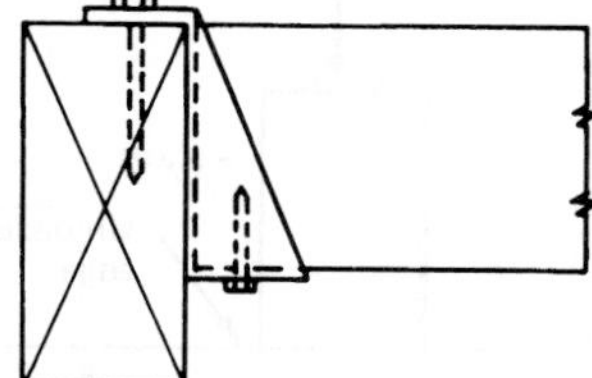

FIG. 5.94 Beam to girder, free to rotate.

distance from the unloaded edge of the member to the nearest edge of the nearest connector. For bolts or lag screws, d_e is measured from the center of the bolt hole (see Fig. 5.96). V is the transverse shear force, and b and d are, respectively, the breadth and depth of the member.

EXAMPLE 5.24 The joint shown is fabricated using Douglas fir–larch No. 2 (Fig. 5.97). The wood remains dry in service. The load combination is dead plus snow. Determine the horizontal shear stress, and determine if it is less than the allowable value. Four-inch (102-mm) split rings are used.

SOLUTION: $d = 13.25$ in, $d_e = 13.25 - 0.78 = 12.47$ in, and $\ell/d = 16/13.25 < 5$; thus Eq. (5.19) applies:

$$f_v = \frac{3V}{2bd_e}\left(\frac{d}{d_e}\right) = \frac{3 \times 2700 \times 13.25}{2 \times 3.5 \times 12.47 \times 12.47}$$

$$= 98.6 \text{ psi (703 kPa)}$$

$$F_v = 95 \times 1.15 = 109 \text{ psi (751 kPa)} 98.6 \text{ psi} \qquad \text{OK}$$

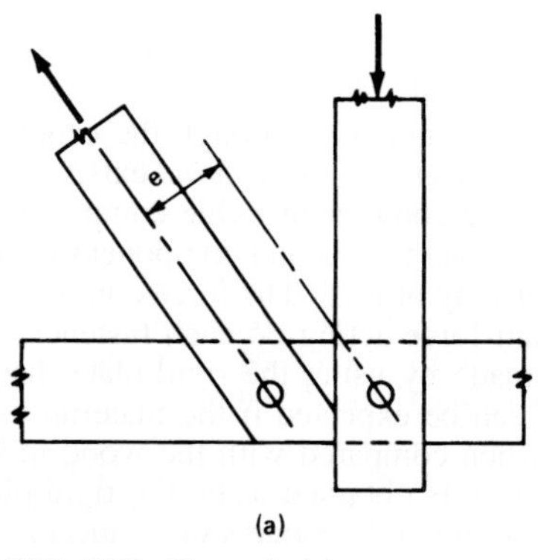

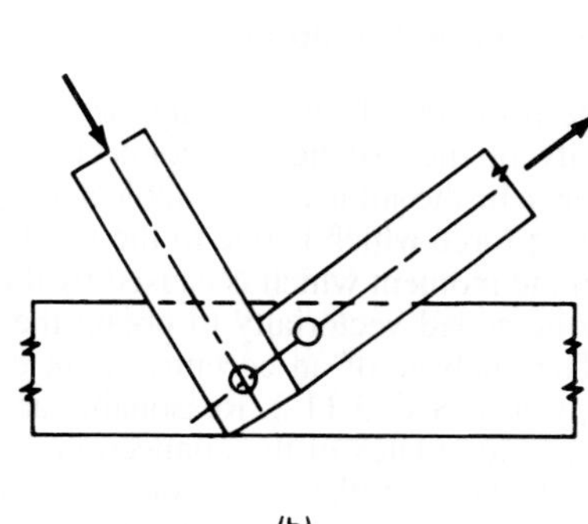

FIG. 5.95 Eccentric joints.

TABLE 5.29 Group Action Factors C_g for Bolt or Lag Screw Connections with Steel Side Plates* for $D = 1$ in, $s = 4$ in, $E_{wood} = 1{,}400{,}000$ psi, $E_{steel} = 30{,}000{,}000$ psi

		Number of fasteners in a row										
A_m/A_s	A_m, in²	2	3	4	5	6	7	8	9	10	11	12
12	5	0.97	0.89	0.80	0.70	0.62	0.55	0.49	0.44	0.40	0.37	0.34
	8	0.98	0.93	0.85	0.77	0.70	0.63	0.57	0.52	0.47	0.43	0.40
	16	0.99	0.96	0.92	0.86	0.80	0.75	0.69	0.64	0.60	0.55	0.52
	24	0.99	0.97	0.94	0.90	0.85	0.81	0.76	0.71	0.67	0.63	0.59
	40	1.00	0.98	0.96	0.94	0.90	0.87	0.83	0.79	0.76	0.72	0.69
	64	1.00	0.99	0.98	0.96	0.94	0.91	0.88	0.86	0.83	0.80	0.77
	120	1.00	0.99	0.99	0.98	0.96	0.95	0.93	0.91	0.90	0.87	0.85
	200	1.00	1.00	0.99	0.99	0.98	0.97	0.96	0.95	0.93	0.92	0.90
18	5	0.99	0.93	0.85	0.76	0.68	0.61	0.54	0.49	0.44	0.41	0.37
	8	0.99	0.95	0.90	0.83	0.75	0.69	0.62	0.57	0.52	0.48	0.44
	16	1.00	0.98	0.94	0.90	0.85	0.79	0.74	0.69	0.65	0.60	0.56
	24	1.00	0.98	0.96	0.93	0.89	0.85	0.80	0.76	0.72	0.68	0.64
	40	1.00	0.99	0.97	0.95	0.93	0.90	0.87	0.83	0.80	0.77	0.73
	64	1.00	0.99	0.98	0.97	0.95	0.93	0.91	0.89	0.86	0.83	0.81
	120	1.00	1.00	0.99	0.98	0.97	0.96	0.95	0.93	0.92	0.90	0.88
	200	1.00	1.00	0.99	0.99	0.98	0.98	0.97	0.96	0.95	0.94	0.92
24	40	1.00	0.99	0.97	0.95	0.93	0.89	0.86	0.83	0.79	0.76	0.72
	64	1.00	0.99	0.98	0.97	0.95	0.93	0.91	0.88	0.85	0.83	0.80
	120	1.00	1.00	0.99	0.98	0.97	0.96	0.95	0.93	0.91	0.90	0.88
	200	1.00	1.00	0.99	0.99	0.98	0.98	0.97	0.96	0.95	0.93	0.92
30	40	1.00	0.98	0.96	0.93	0.89	0.85	0.81	0.77	0.73	0.69	0.65
	64	1.00	0.99	0.97	0.95	0.93	0.90	0.87	0.83	0.80	0.77	0.73
	120	1.00	0.99	0.99	0.97	0.96	0.94	0.92	0.90	0.88	0.85	0.83
	200	1.00	1.00	0.99	0.98	0.97	0.96	0.95	0.94	0.92	0.90	0.89
35	40	0.99	0.97	0.94	0.91	0.86	0.82	0.77	0.73	0.68	0.64	0.60
	64	1.00	0.98	0.96	0.94	0.91	0.87	0.84	0.80	0.76	0.73	0.69
	120	1.00	0.99	0.98	0.97	0.95	0.92	0.90	0.88	0.85	0.82	0.79
	200	1.00	0.99	0.99	0.98	0.97	0.95	0.94	0.92	0.90	0.88	0.86
42	40	0.99	0.97	0.93	0.88	0.83	0.78	0.73	0.68	0.63	0.59	0.55
	64	0.99	0.98	0.95	0.92	0.88	0.84	0.80	0.76	0.72	0.68	0.64
	120	1.00	0.99	0.97	0.95	0.93	0.90	0.88	0.85	0.81	0.78	0.75
	200	1.00	0.99	0.98	0.97	0.96	0.94	0.92	0.90	0.88	0.85	0.83
50	40	0.99	0.96	0.91	0.85	0.79	0.74	0.68	0.63	0.58	0.54	0.51
	64	0.99	0.97	0.94	0.90	0.85	0.81	0.76	0.72	0.67	0.63	0.59
	120	1.00	0.98	0.97	0.94	0.91	0.88	0.85	0.81	0.78	0.74	0.71
	200	1.00	0.99	0.98	0.96	0.95	0.92	0.90	0.87	0.85	0.82	0.79

*Tabulated group action factors (C_g) are conservative for $D < 1$ in or $s < 4$ in.
Source: This table provided courtesy of the American Forest and Paper Association, Washington, D.C.

TABLE 5.30*a* Wet-Service Factors C_M for Connections

Fastener Type	Condition of wood*		Wet-service factor C_M
	At time of fabrication	In service	
Split-ring or shear-plate† connectors	Dry	Dry	1.0
	Partially seasoned	Dry	‡
	Wet	Dry	0.8
	Dry or wet	Partially seasoned or wet	0.67
Bolts or lag screws	Dry	Dry	1.0
	Partially seasoned or wet	Dry	§
	Dry or wet	Exposed to weather	0.75
	Dry or wet	Wet	0.67
Laterally loaded drift bolts or drift pins	Dry or wet	Dry	1.0
	Dry or wet	Partially seasoned or wet, or subject to wetting and drying	0.7
Wood screws	Dry or wet	Dry	1.0
	Dry or wet	Exposed to weather	0.75
	Dry or wet	Wet	0.67
Common wire nails, box nails or common wire spikes			
Withdrawal loads	Dry	Dry	1.0
	Partially seasoned or wet	Wet	1.0
	Partially seasoned or wet	Dry	0.25
	Dry	Subject to wetting and drying	0.25
Lateral loads	Dry	Dry	1.0
	Partially seasoned or wet	Dry or wet	0.75
	Dry	Partially seasoned or wet	0.75
Threaded, hardened steel nails	Dry or wet	Dry or wet	1.0
Metal connector plates	Dry	Dry	1.0
	Partially seasoned or wet	Dry or wet	0.8

TABLE 5.30*a* Wet-Service Factors C_M for Connections *(Continued)*

**Conditions of wood* are defined as follows for determining wet service factors for connections:

Dry wood has a moisture content $\leq$ 19%.

Wet wood has a moisture content $\geq$ 30% (approximate fiber saturation point).

Partially seasoned wood has 19% $<$ moisture content $<$ 30%.

Exposed to weather means that the wood will vary in moisture content from dry to partially seasoned, but is not expected to reach the fiber saturation point at times when the connection is supporting full design load.

Subject to wetting and drying means that the wood will vary in moisture content from dry to partially seasoned or wet, or vice versa, with consequent effects on the tightness of the connection.

†For split-ring or shear-plate connectors, moisture content limitations apply to a depth of ¾ in below the surface of the wood.

‡When split-ring or shear-plate connectors are installed in wood that is partially seasoned at the time of fabrication but that will be dry before full design load is applied, proportional intermediate wet service factors shall be permitted to be used.

§When bolts or lag screws are installed in wood that is wet at the time of fabrication but that will be dry before full design load is applied, the following wet service factors, C_M, shall apply:

Arrangement of bolts or lag screws	C_M
One fastener only, or Two or more fasteners placed in a single row parallel to grain, or Fasteners placed in two or more rows parallel to grain with separate splice plates for each row	1.0
All other arrangements	0.4

When bolts or lag screws are installed in wood that is partially seasoned at the time of fabrication, but that will be dry before full design load is applied, proportional intermediate wet service factors shall be permitted to be used.

Source: This table provided courtesy of the American Forest and Paper Association, Washington, D.C.

TABLE 5.30*b* Modification Factors for Laterally Loaded Bolts and Lag Screws in Timber Seasoned in Place

Factors apply when wood is at or above the fiber saturation point (wet) at time of fabrication but dries to a moisture content of 19 percent or less (dry) before full design load is applied. For wood partially seasoned when fabricated, adjusted intermediate values may be used.

Arrangement of bolts or lag screws	Type of splice plate	Modification factor
One fastener Two or more fasteners placed in a single line parallel to grain Fasteners placed in two or more lines parallel to grain with separate splice plates for each line	Wood or metal	1.0
All other arrangements	Wood or metal	0.4

TABLE 5.31 Total Projected Area (in^2) of Connectors and Bolts

For use in determining net section

Connectors		Bolt diam., in	Placement of connectors	Lumber thickness, inc				
No.	Size, in			1½	2½	3½	5½	7½
			Split rings					
1	2½	½	One face	1.71	2.27	2.84	3.89	5.02
		½	Two faces	2.60	3.16	3.73	4.78	5.91
2	4	¾	One face	3.01	3.86	4.64	6.16	7.79
		¾	Two faces	4.85	5.66	6.47	8.00	9.62
			Shear plates					
1	2⅝	¾	One face	2.00	2.81	3.62	4.14	6.77
		¾	Two faces	2.81	2.68	4.43	5.96	7.58
1	2⅝LG*	¾	One face	1.87	2.68	3.50	5.02	6.65
		¾	Two faces	2.56	3.38	4.19	5.71	7.34
2	4	¾	One face	3.24	4.05	4.87	6.39	8.01
		¾	Two faces	—	6.11	6.93	8.45	10.07
2-A	4	⅞	One face	3.33	4.27	5.21	6.97	8.84
		⅞	Two faces	—	6.25	7.19	8.95	10.82

Note: 1 in = 25.4 mm.
*LG = light-gauge

TABLE 5.32 Applicability of Adjustment Factors for Connections

		Load-duration factor*	Wet-service factor†	Temperature factor	Group action factor	Geometry factor‡	Penetration-depth factor‡	End-grain factor‡	Metal side plate factor‡	Diaphragm factor‡	Toenail factor‡
Bolts	$Z' = Z$	C_D	C_M	C_t	C_g	C_Δ	•	•	•	•	•
Lag screws	$W' = W$	C_D	C_M	C_t	•	•	•	C_{eg}	•	•	•
	$Z' = Z$	C_D	C_M	C_t	C_g	C_Δ	C_d	C_{eg}	•	•	•
Split-ring and shear-plate connectors	$P' = P$	C_D	C_M	C_t	C_g	C_Δ	C_d	•	C_{st}	•	•
	$Q' = Q$	C_D	C_M	C_t	C_g	C_Δ	C_d	•	•	•	•
Wood screws	$W' = W$	C_D	C_M	C_t	•	•	•	•	•	•	•
	$Z' = Z$	C_D	C_M	C_t	•	•	C_d	C_{eg}	•	•	•
Nails and spikes	$W' = W$	C_D	C_M	C_t	•	•	•	•	•	•	C_{tn}
	$Z' = Z$	C_D	C_M	C_t	•	•	C_d	C_{eg}	•	C_{di}	C_{tn}
Metal plate connectors	$Z' = Z$	C_D	C_M	C_t	•	•	•	•	•	•	•
Drift bolts and drift pins	$W' = W$	C_D	C_M	C_t	•	•	•	C_{eg}	•	•	•
	$Z' = Z$	C_D	C_M	C_t	C_g	C_Δ	C_d	C_{eg}	•	•	•
Spike grids	$Z' = Z$	C_D	C_M	C_t	•	C_Δ	•	•	•	•	•

*The load-duration factor C_D shall not exceed 1.6 for connections.

†The wet-service factor C_M shall not apply to toe-nails loaded in withdrawal.

‡Specific information concerning geometry factors C_Δ, penetration depth factors C_d, end-grain factors C_{eg}, metal side plate factors C_{st}, diaphragm factors C_{di}, and toenail factors C_{tn} is provided in Parts VIII, IX, X, XI, XII and XIV of the NDS.[5]

Source: This table provided courtesy of the American Forest and Paper Association, Washington, D.C.

TABLE 5.33 Temperature Factors C_t for Connections

In-service moisture conditions	C_t		
	$T \leq 100°F$	$100°F < T \leq 125°F$	$125°F < T \leq 150°F$
Dry	1.0	0.8	0.7
Wet	1.0	0.7	0.5

Source: This table provided courtesy of the American Forest and Paper Association, Washington, D.C.

TABLE 5.34 Dowel Bearing Strength for Nail or Spike Connections

Species combination	Specific gravity G^*	Dowel bearing strength F_e, pounds per square inch (psi)
Southern pine	0.55	5550
Douglas fir–larch	0.50	4650
Hem-fir	0.43	3500
Spruce-pine-fir	0.42	3350

Note: 1 lb/in^2 = 6.895 kPa.

*Specific gravity based on weight and volume when oven dry.

Source: This table provided courtesy of the American Forest and Paper Association, Washington, D.C.

TABLE 5.35 Dowel Bearing Strength for Wood Screw Connections

Species combination	Specific gravity G^*	Dowel bearing strength F_e, pounds per square inch (psi)
Southern pine	0.55	5550
Douglas fir–larch	0.50	4650
Hem-fir	0.43	3500
Spruce-pine-fir	0.42	3350

Note: 1 lb/in^2 = 6.895 kPa.

*Specific gravity based on weight and volume when oven dry.

Source: This table provided courtesy of the American Forest and Paper Association, Washington, D.C.

5.36 Dowel Bearing Strength for Lag Screw Connections

Species combination	Specific gravity G*	Dowel bearing strength, pounds per square inch (psi)											
		$F_{e\parallel}$	$F_{e\perp}$ $D = 1/4$ in	$F_{e\perp}$ $D = 5/16$ in	$F_{e\perp}$ $D = 3/8$ in	$F_{e\perp}$ $D = 7/16$ in	$F_{e\perp}$ $D = 1/2$ in	$F_{e\perp}$ $D = 5/8$ in	$F_{e\perp}$ $D = 3/4$ in	$F_{e\perp}$ $D = 7/8$ in	$F_{e\perp}$ $D = 1$ in	$F_{e\perp}$ $D = 1\,1/8$ in	$F_{e\perp}$ $D = 1\,1/4$ in
Southern pine	0.55	6150	5150	4600	4200	3900	3650	3250	2950	2750	2550	2400	2300
Douglas fir–larch	0.50	5600	4450	4000	3650	3400	3150	2800	2600	2400	2250	2100	2000
Hem-fir	0.43	4800	3600	3200	2950	2700	2550	2250	2050	1900	1800	1700	1600
Spruce-pine-fir	0.42	4700	3450	3100	2850	2600	2450	2200	2000	1850	1750	1650	1550

Note: 1 lb/in^2 = 6.895 kPa.
*Specific gravity based on weight and volume when oven dry.
Source: This table provided courtesy of the American Forest and Paper Association, Washington, D.C.

5.37 Dowel Bearing Strength for Bolted Connections

Species combination	Specific gravity G*	Dowel bearing strength, pounds per square inch (psi)					
		$F_{e\parallel}$	$F_{e\perp}$ D = ½ in	$F_{e\perp}$ D = ⅝ in	$F_{e\perp}$ D = ¾ in	$F_{e\perp}$ D = ⅞ in	$F_{e\perp}$ D = 1 in
Southern pine	0.55	6150	3650	3250	2950	2750	2550
Douglas fir–larch	0.50	5600	3150	2800	2600	2400	2250
Hem-fir	0.43	4800	2550	2250	2050	1900	1800
Spruce-pine-fir	0.42	4700	2450	2200	2000	1850	1750

Note: 1 lb/in^2 = 6.895 kPa.
*Specific gravity based on weight and volume when oven dry.
Source: This table provided courtesy of the American Forest and Paper Association, Washington, D.C.

REFERENCES

1. *Wood Handbook: Wood as an Engineering Material,* Agricultural Handbook No. 72, rev. Aug. 1974, Forest Products Laboratory, U.S. Department of Agriculture, Washington, D.C., 1987.
2. *Uniform Building Code,* International Conference of Building Officials, Whitter, Cal., 1991.
3. *Timber Design and Construction Handbook,* Timber Engineering Co., McGraw-Hill Book Co., New York, 1956.
4. R. J. Hoyle, *Wood Technology in the Design of Structures,* 3d ed., Mountain Press Publishing Co., Missoula, Mont., 1973.
5. *National Design Specification for Wood Construction,* rev. ed., American Forest and Paper Association, Washington, D.C., 1991.
6. J. A. Scholten, *Strength of Wood Joints Made with Nails, Staples, or Screws,* Research Note FPL 0100, U.S. Department of Agriculture, Washington, D.C., March 1965.
7. *Structural Wood Research: State-of-the-Art and Research Needs,* American Society of Civil Engineers, New York, 1984.
8. N. S. Perkins, *Plywood Properties Design and Construction,* American Plywood Association, Tacoma, Wash., out of print.
9. *Plywood Design Secification,* American Plywood Association, Tacoma, Wash., Dec. 1983.
10. C. O. Cramer, "Load Distribution in Multiple-Bolt Tension Joints," *J. Struct. Div. ASCE* **94**(ST5):1101–1117 (May 1968).
11. M. J. Samsalone and R. N. White, *End-Grain Dowel Connections in Laminated Timber: Monotonic, Repeated, and Sustained Load Behavior,* Research Report No. 84-6, Cornell Univ., Ithaca, N.Y., March 1984.
12. G. W. Trayer, *The Bearing Strength of Wood Under Bolts,* Tech. Bull. No. 332, U.S. Department of Agriculture, Washington, D.C., Oct. 1932.
13. J. A. Scholten, *Timber-Connector Joints. Their Strength and Design,* Tech. Bull. No. 865, U.S. Department of Agriculture, Washington, D.C., March 1944.
14. *Design Manual for TECO Timber Connector Construction,* Publ. No. 109, Timber Engineering Co., Colliers, W.V., 1973.
15. *Structural Wood Fasteners,* Publ. No. 101, Timber Engineering Co., Colliers, W.V., 1983.
16. *Rough Carpentry Wood Framing Systems,* Catalog No. 85H-1, Simpson Company, San Leandro, Calif., 1985.

CHAPTER 6
TRUSSES

Trus Joist MacMillan

6.1 THE WOOD TRUSS INDUSTRY—AN OVERVIEW

Although wood trusses have been used for centuries, the emergence of engineered, mass-produced, prefabricated, lightweight wood or wood-steel composite trusses has significantly altered the basic design philosophy of this industry. Prior to the evolution of these lightweight truss systems, the wood truss was considered a relatively complex and labor-intensive structural component. Typically, wood trusses used in commercial construction were heavy solid sawn or glued-laminated timber trusses fabricated on site or in a laminating plant from detailed engineering designs. Commonly referred to as a *girder truss framing system,* these trusses were usually placed from 12 to 20 ft (3.66 to 6.10 m) on center with dimension lumber purlins framing between them, as illustrated by Fig. 6.1. Other relatively long clear-span framing systems which utilize timber trusses include trussed arches, portal frames, and rigid bents.

Some of the common heavy timber truss configurations used are shown in Fig. 6.2. These trusses can be constructed of individual planar components, i.e., all web members and chords occurring in the same plane, or can be of a multiple-member design, wherein the chord members consist of two pieces with the web members placed between them. In either case, the members can be joined by a variety of techniques; however, bolts or bolts used in conjunction with timber connectors (shear plates or split rings) with either steel or wood side plates are most commonly observed.

The king- or queen-post truss forms a unique example of timber truss construction by combining a heavy timber compression chord with a steel rod or cable tension chord. These chords are customarily joined by vertical steel pipe webs. Figure 6.3 shows an example of this truss configuration. (See Chap. 10 for an additional example.)

Although most often associated with building construction, the heavy timber truss also has been used effectively in timber bridge construction. The early covered bridges commonly used some form of heavy timber truss as the main structural load-carrying element. The protection from direct exposure to the elements afforded by the external covering of these structures has allowed many of these trusses to

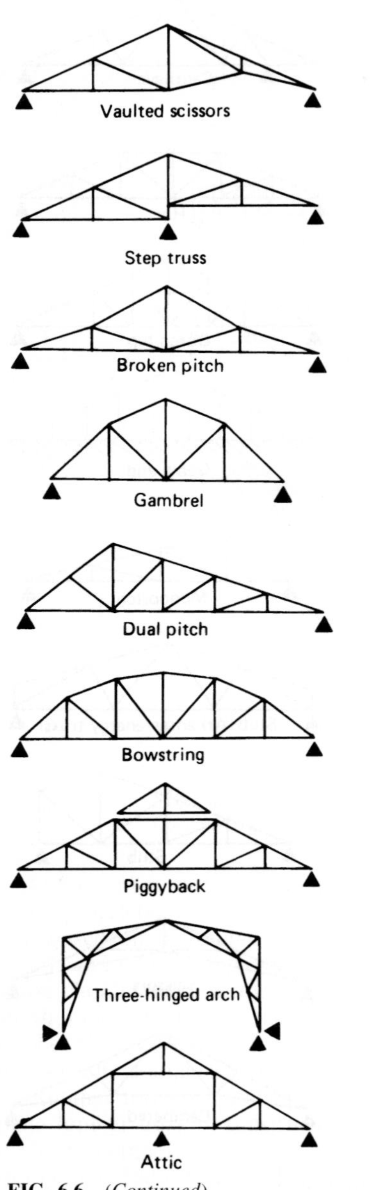

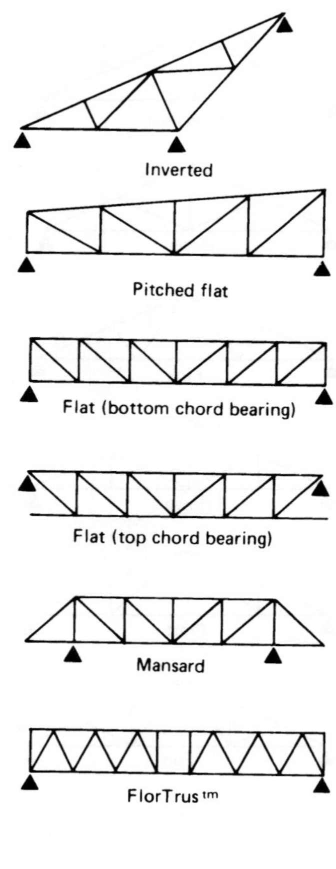

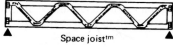

FIG. 6.6 (*Continued*)

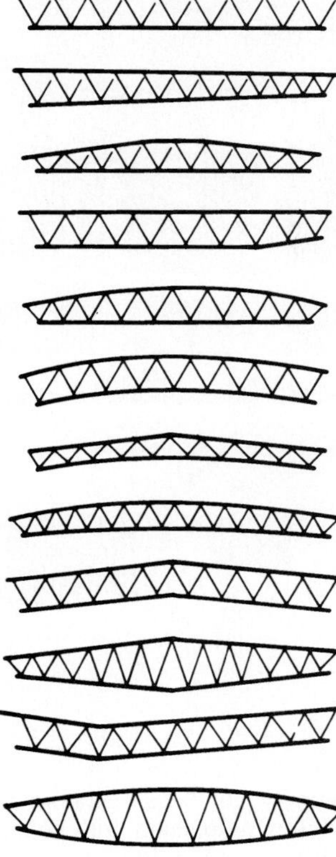

FIG. 6.7 Composite truss profiles. (*Courtesy Trus Joist MacMillan, Boise, Idaho.*)

In addition, these manufacturers commonly maintain internal manufacturing quality-control programs to ensure the structural integrity of these trusses.

While used primarily in applications with relatively close on-center spacings, i.e., 48 in (121.9 cm) or less, lightweight lumber or composite trusses also can be used in a girder truss framing system with some limitations. In order to use these trusses at on-center spacings of 8 ft (2.4 m) or more, it is common practice to tie two or more of them together in such a way that their individual capacities are additive. Figure 6.9 illustrates a method of combining multiple lightweight trusses to form a girder truss. The specific framing details will dictate the actual load distributions among the trusses thus joined. If these framing details apply loads to one side of the multiple trusses, it would be improper to consider equal load sharing. Experience has shown that three lightweight trusses are the maximum number that can easily and effectively be joined in this fashion.

Normally, multiple lightweight trusses built up as a girder truss are used in a floor or roof system where it is necessary to frame around openings created by skylights, chimneys, and stairwells or where a large concentrated load, such as from a rooftop unit, requires a greater truss capacity to carry the load. Multiple light-

FIG. 6.8 Composite lumber-metal parallel chord trusses. *(Courtesy Hydro-Air Co., St. Louis, Mo.)*

weight trusses tied together may not be as economical as a heavy timber truss because of the cost and difficulty associated with connecting them together, but it is a possible design alternative.

6.2 TRUSS SYSTEM LOADING

The minimum design loads to be resisted by any structural member or assembly are normally set forth by the governing code authority, with the designer of record having the final responsibility of selecting the proper loads for each structural application. In addition to specifying these minimum design loads, the governing codes also indicate minimum combinations of loads to be considered for each design situation. While these loads and combinations of loads are common to all structural materials or systems, the manner in which they are applied or resisted may be unique to a specific material or system.

In wood truss systems, loads may be applied to the chords in a variety of ways, such as directly through the decking as uniformly distributed loads; as a series of relatively closely spaced concentrated loads, as from joists spanning perpendicular to the truss; or as concentrated loads from purlins spaced 48 in (121.9 cm) on center or greater. The following loads or loading considerations are discussed as they specifically affect the design and performance of wood truss systems.

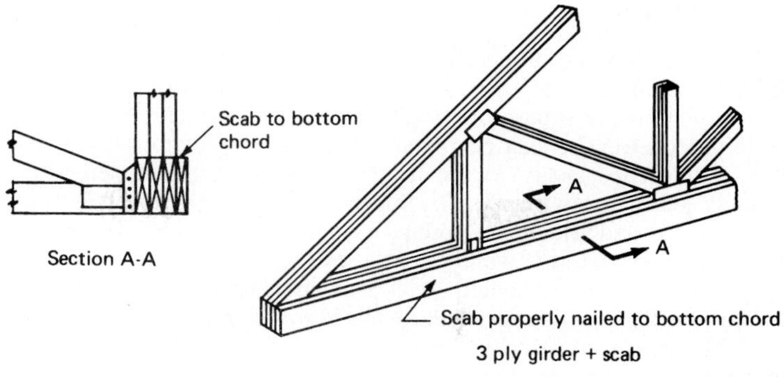

No. of 10 D common wire nails per tie-in truss for multi-ply grider chords (see Notes 2 and 3)

Total load, lb/ft²	2-ply chord			3-ply chord					
	2nd to 1st			2nd to 1st			3rd to 2nd		
	20′	30′	40′	20′	30′	40′	20′	30′	40′
25-35	4	5	7	5	7	9	2	4	5
36-45	4	6	8	6	8	11	3	4	6
46-55	5	8	10	7	10	13	4	5	7
56-65	6	9	12	8	12	16	4	6	8

FIG. 6.9 Multiple trusses tied together. *Notes:* (1) Nails for southern pine and Douglas fir only. (2) Nailing schedule applies to chord where load ties in. Loads assumed to tie in 24 in o.c. maximum. (3) Nailing schedule based on a duration of load factor of 1.15. (4) Other chords and webs as well as those of multi-ply nongirders require 10 nails on 12-in centers.

6.2.1 Dead Loads

The dead load imposed on a structural member is the weight of all the component building materials in a structural assembly supported by the structural member. The weight in pounds per square foot (newtons per square meter) of materials common to building construction can be found in various publications, as given in the Appendix, "Reference Data." While most dead loads are assumed to be uniformly distributed loads, loads imposed by mechanical systems are often applied as concentrated loads and should be applied at panel points wherever possible. Interior partition walls or exterior walls bearing on the ends of cantilevers may result in additional uniformly distributed loads or concentrated loads acting on the truss depending on the positioning of the walls in relationship to the truss-framing system. Consideration must be given to proper detailing of roof-wall and floor-wall connections to ensure that non-load-bearing partitions do not become load-bearing walls as the trusses deflect under in-service loading.

6.2.2 Live Loads

The live loads imposed on a structural member are those loads which are due to the use and/or occupancy of the structure. Floor live loads are those due to human occupancy, furniture, materials stored on the floor, etc. The minimum recommended uniformly distributed design live loads for various uses and occupancies are listed in the governing building codes. In some applications, a wood floor truss may actually be subjected to several different uniform loads over a single span, such as a truss supporting an office loading over part of its span and corridor loading over the remainder of the span. Similarly, trusses spanning continuously over two or more spans also must be evaluated for unbalanced loading acting on alternate spans in addition to full balanced loading on all spans to determine the maximum stress conditions for each truss component, i.e., webs, chords, and joints.

In addition to these uniformly distributed loads, the applicable code also may require that the floor be designed to carry a minimum concentrated load. This concentrated load must be considered to be positioned on a wood truss in a manner that will produce the maximum stress conditions in the truss members.

Roof live loads are those minimum loads established by the building codes to provide for temporary loadings which the roof must support, such as workers, equipment, and materials. Roof live loads and snow loads are not considered additive; rather, that which produces greater stresses governs the design.

6.2.3 Snow Loads

The subject of proper and adequate snow-load design is one that has received considerable attention. Snow loads on roofs can vary according to geographic location, climate, site exposure, shape and type of roof, whether the building is heated or not, and of course, from one year to the next. Virtually all major building codes now recognize the need to design for these variable snow-loading conditions. Ground snow loads generally form the basis for the determination of the resultant roof snow loads, and ASCE 7-93, *Minimum Design Loads for Buildings and Other Structures,*[1] provides ground snow loads by geographic area.

Of particular concern in the design of wood truss systems are drifting snow loads or accumulations such as may occur on a low roof located adjacent to a higher roof plane. This drift condition may result in a triangular load distribution being superimposed on the normal roof loading over a portion of the length of a roof truss spanning perpendicular to this high-low roof plane intersection. This condition is illustrated in Fig. 6.10. For trusses spanning parallel to the high-low roof plane intersection, the resultant additive load is a uniformly distributed load with a maximum intensity for the truss located closest to this roof plane interface. This effect is shown in Fig. 6.11. In either case, the wood trusses must be designed to support the governing maximum loading condition with all truss components sized accordingly.

Of a similar nature is snow accumulation or ice buildup in valleys of adjacent pitched roofs which can result in other than uniformly distributed loads acting on the roof trusses. Unbalanced snow loads as required by the codes in the case of wood truss applications involving multiple-span members must be considered because they may create higher stresses or possible stress reversals in the truss elements and their joints. Unbalanced snow loads can occur in other ways, such as on a cantilevered truss used to create a roof overhang or in a gable roof application where snow may accumulate on only one side of the roof peak. The effects of unheated attic spaces or highly insulated roofs also should be considered because they can result in uneven snow accumulations.

ASCE 7-93[1] provides detailed explanations of snow load analysis for virtually all roof conditions and configurations which may be encountered. Further information on roof snow loads can be found in "Roof Snow Loads in Canada."[2]

6.2.4 Wind Loads

The application of wind loads on the exterior surfaces of a building causes wind pressures and/or suctions on the building which result in forces being imposed on the structural members. Considerable research has been conducted to evaluate wind effects on various structures, and this has resulted in the establishment of design pressure coefficients that account for building shape and wind direction. Each of the major building code agencies has addressed the issue of wind design by providing various minimum wind pressures for a given geographic location on the basis of historical recurrence and the height above the ground. Wind-load pressures and/or suctions can have the effect of imposing uplift loads on roof trusses. In lightweight wood truss systems, the net uplift loads (uplift load minus the structure dead load) may result in stress reversals of the truss components and uplift reactions at the bearing locations. Similarly, wide overhangs created by cantilevered trusses may result in negative reactions at bearings, with wind loading causing possible stress reversals in web and chord members.

6.2.5 Seismic Loads

Seismic stresses are treated as the result of laterally applied horizontal forces, and vertical forces to a lesser extent, applied at each floor or roof level above the base. These forces are assumed to come from any horizontal direction so as to create the maximum loading effect on the structure. As with wind loads, a particular concern

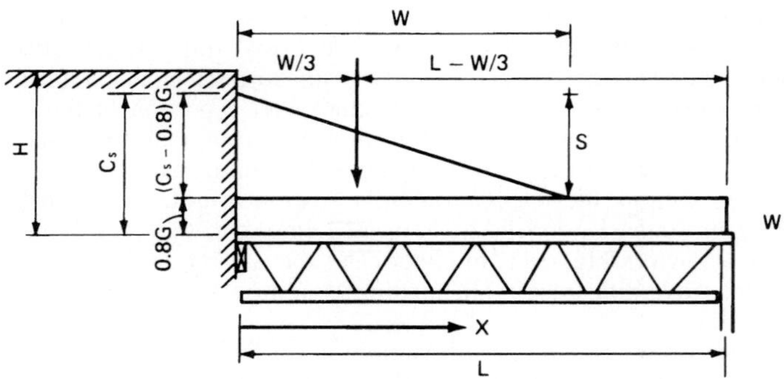

FIG. 6.10 Snow load diagram for trusses perpendicular to wall.

Calculation procedures:

1. Calculate $C_s = 15H/G$, where G = ground snow load

$$0.80 \leq C_s \leq 3.00$$

2. Calculate S = snow drift weight in pounds per lineal foot $= (C_s - 0.8)G$

3. Calculate maximum reaction per lineal foot of bearing wall R. Let

$$W = 0.8G + \text{dead load (lb/ft)}$$

$$R = \frac{W_u L}{2} + \frac{SW}{2} - \frac{SW^2}{6L} \text{ (lb/ft)}$$

4. Calculate the location X of maximum bending moment from the drifted end of the truss. Let

$$T = (W + S)\, W/S$$

$$X = T - \sqrt{(T^2 - 2WR/S)}\text{(ft)}$$

5. Calculate maximum moment M (assuming 12-in o.c. spacing)

$$M = RX - \frac{(W + S)X^2}{2} + \frac{SX^3}{6W} \text{ (ft·lb/ft)}$$

6. Determine maximum allowable truss spacing by comparing calculated shear and moment with shear and moment capacity of selected truss.

in wood truss systems is that the connection between the truss and its supporting structure is capable of resisting the lateral forces induced by seismic deformations.

6.2.6 Erection Loads

A common problem related to the installation of wood trusses is the lack of proper consideration given to erection loads and the effects of these loads on the trusses.

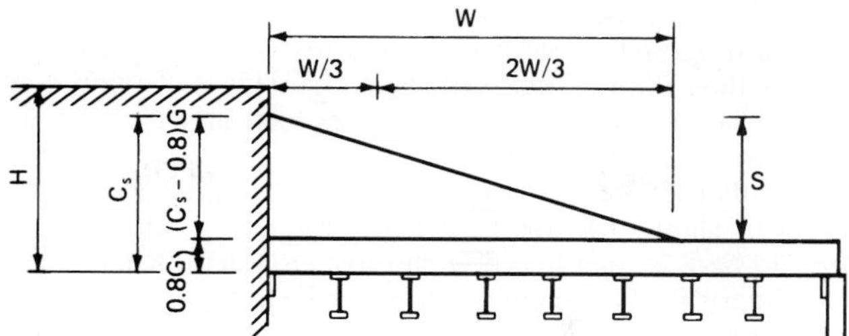

FIG. 6.11 Snow-load diagram for trusses placed parallel to wall.

Calculation procedures:

1. Calculate $C_s = 15H/G$, where G = ground snow load

$$0.80 \leq C_s \leq 3.0$$

2. Calculate the weight of the drift per lineal foot as

$$W_T = \frac{(C_s - 0.8)(G)(W)}{2}$$

3. Determine the number of additional trusses required by dividing the weight of the drift W_T by the capacity of one truss in pounds per lineal foot.

4. Locate the additional trusses such that they adequately support the drift load. As a general guideline, ⅔ of the additional trusses should be located in the area designated $W/3$ above, and the remaining trusses in the area designated $2W/3$.

A typical construction practice is to place partial or complete bundles of sheathing material on trusses after they have been erected but prior to the complete installation of sheathing. These erection loads can result in relatively significant top chord compressive stresses which can induce buckling of an improperly braced compression chord. These erection stresses must be accounted for by using an adequate lateral bracing system, ensuring that it is properly installed during the erection sequence, and clearly defining the maximum allowable construction loads which can be placed on the truss system. Erection bracing is discussed in more detail in Sec. 6.8. Care also must be given to the methods used to lift the trusses into position so as not to overstress the unbraced truss compression chords or to create excessive stress reversals in the truss members.

6.2.7 Ponding

In the design of flat or nearly flat roofs, special consideration should be given to the potential for ponding of rainwater. Roof collapses which were directly attributed to water ponding on the roof have occurred, involving virtually all types of building materials.

When ponding of water occurs, for whatever reason, deflection is initiated and may continue at a progressive rate because the work energy of the ponding water is initially greater than the resistance of the truss. This deflection continues until equilibrium is reached between the added water load and the truss resistance or until failure occurs.

Ponding is usually a greater problem for roofs with long-span structural members than for roofs with short-span trusses, since the relative stiffness of a long-span system is likely to be less than that of a short-span system. Roofs with large areas tributary to a primary flexural member (truss or beam) are, in general, more susceptible to ponding than roofs with small areas tributary to a primary flexural member. Ponding problems are not necessarily limited by geographic location, although the frequency of occurrences seems to be higher in areas where relatively low design live loads are used. Failures have occurred in semiarid regions, since rainstorms of high intensity may occur, even though the annual rainfall in these regions is small. Although roofs in colder climates are generally designed for relatively high live loads which increase the stiffness of the system, unusual weather conditions can occur that may result in the blockage of drainage paths due to packed snow or ice. In such cases, the ponding load becomes additive with the existing snow or ice on the roof.

While actually a part of the overall building design rather than a loading provision, providing an adequate slope to roofs—whether by cambering the truss, sloping the top chord, or varying bearing elevations—and making provisions for an adequate drainage system help minimize most potential ponding problems. While flat roofs can be designed to resist overloads due to ponding, this requires very stiff members and hence larger members than would be required if ponding were not allowed to occur. Such roofs may be less economical, and the designer must exercise the utmost care in structural calculations and control in the overall design to adequately allow for intentional ponding.

6.2.8 Other Loads

Most typically, nonuniform or concentrated loads are imposed on wood truss systems through the installation of mechanical equipment. Section 6.4.3 provides a detailed discussion of the application of loads from sprinkler systems. Point loads may be imposed on floor systems through interior load-bearing columns. Line loads and/or concentrated loads may be imposed on floor and roof trusses by suspended folding partitions and on floors by load-bearing walls. When possible, all such loads should be applied to the wood truss at panel point locations. Figure 6.12 illustrates the use of wood sleepers to distribute the concentrated load of a mechanical unit to the upper chord panel points. When applying concentrated loads to panel point locations, the allowable compression perpendicular to grain stresses should not be exceeded. Mechanical units or other loads suspended from the bottom chords of trusses also should be applied at the panel point locations. Figure 6.13 is illustrative of loads applied to truss bottom chords. When supporting movable partition loads, the anticipated truss deflections become a primary design consideration to ensure proper performance of the supported partition.

In bridge trusses, loads imposed by moving vehicles become the governing loads. These loads may be applied in the form of concentrated wheel loads or as uniform lane loadings depending on which creates the maximum stresses in the

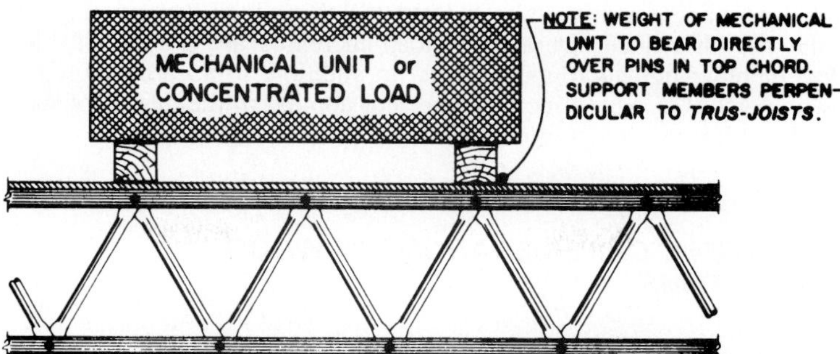

FIG. 6.12 Support details for roof-mounted equipment. (*Courtesy Trus Joist Macmillan, Boise, Idaho.*)

truss. AASHTO's *Standard Specifications for Highway Bridges*[3] establishes the minimum loading criteria for highway and pedestrian bridges.

6.2.9 Duration of Load

The duration of stress or time-dependent effect of load on the strength of wood is discussed in Secs. 1.3.8 and 2.3. The normal design working stresses listed for lumber have been adjusted to provide for a 10-year accumulative load duration. These normal (10-year duration) load stresses are commonly used for floor truss applications. In wood roof trusses, these stresses may generally be increased by 15 percent for snow-load applications (2-month load duration), 25 percent for non-snow-load roof applications (7-day load duration), and 60 percent for wind or seismic applications (10-minute duration), although some codes may not allow the full magnitude of these adjustments.

A unique situation exists when roof loads are superimposed on a floor system through intermediate bearing walls or columns. In these applications, load combinations which both include and exclude the roof live load must be checked. Du-

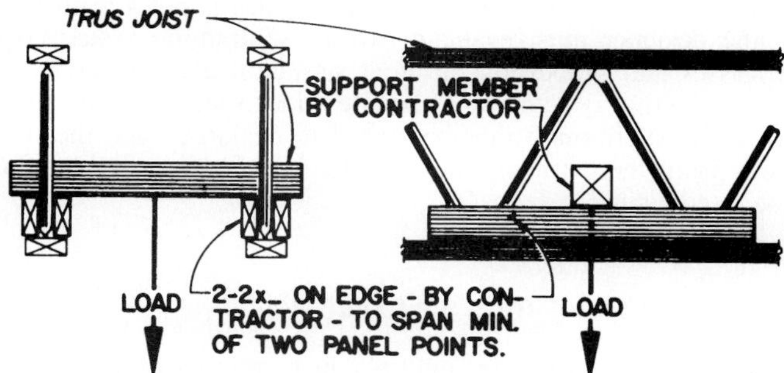

FIG. 6.13 Support details for loads supported from truss bottom chord. (*Courtesy Trus Joist MacMillan, Boise, Idaho.*)

ration-of-load increases are applicable only to those load combinations which include the roof live load. Duration-of-load increases are not applicable to steel members or other nonwood components. In addition, in accordance with the provisions of AASHTO,[3] these increases are not applied in the design of wood members used in highway bridge construction.

6.3 ECONOMIC CONSIDERATIONS IN WOOD TRUSS SYSTEMS

Transferring an architectural concept into reality challenges the designer to determine the most efficient and cost-effective means to cover the required floor and roof spaces while maintaining the desired architectural features. A number of design considerations must be evaluated to accomplish this task using a wood truss framing system. While these considerations are often interrelated, they individually affect the overall cost-effectiveness of the truss system.

6.3.1 Heavy Timber Truss Systems

Two variables have primary influence on the cost of heavy timber truss applications. The first is the overall architectural appearance to be achieved, while the second is the structural efficiency of the truss spacing and related subframing. If the roof system is to be exposed as an architectural feature, wood decking is often specified. The thickness of decking required is dependent on the truss spacing, and the interrelationship of truss spacing and deck thickness has a direct influence on system cost. While a wider spacing of the trusses results in fewer trusses, the increased deck thickness and subsequent cost increase may offset any savings derived from the reduced number of trusses. While structural glued-laminated timber trusses have a higher cost than solid sawn timber trusses, they offer advantages over solid sawn members in that they can be supplied in various architectural appearances, have generally higher strength characteristics resulting in smaller member sizes, and are more dimensionally stable. However, in some cases, the designer is attempting to create the so-called heavy timber appearance, and solid sawn timbers produce this desired architectural effect.

If the trusses are not to be exposed or appearance is not a primary design consideration, the designer must evaluate various subframing systems spanning between the trusses and supporting different structural deck materials to determine the most cost-effective system. Again, while wider spacing of the trusses requires fewer trusses, the subframing members need to be larger, and the relatively high end reactions from these trusses may require heavier foundations, thus affecting overall system cost.

6.3.2 Lightweight Wood Truss Systems

The decisions facing the designer multiply in repetitive-member lightweight prefabricated truss applications. Each decision-making step must be evaluated not only individually but also with respect to its effect on other design variables as it affects overall systems costs. Some of the primary design parameters to be evaluated with respect to their structural efficiency and cost-effectiveness in a lightweight wood truss system are the following:

1. *The design loads and the deflection requirements of the truss system:* While the minimum design loads and deflection criteria to be applied in a specific design situation are normally specified by the governing building code, the designer may want to consider more stringent load and deflection criteria. While designing to these more restrictive criteria may result in an increased system cost, the possible benefits of improved floor performance may justify this added cost. A further discussion of this aspect of truss design is given in Sec. 6.5.

2. *The maximum desired clear span of the wood truss system:* It is generally recognized that shorter-span systems result in less overall cost than those with relatively long spans. As design spans decrease, lighter and shallower trusses or deeper trusses spaced farther apart may be used with an attendant cost savings to the system.

3. *The maximum spacing of the wood truss system:* Generally, an increase in truss spacing results in cost savings because of the requirement of a minimum number of trusses. However, the maximum spacing may be dictated by other considerations. As truss spacing increases, the thickness of decking required to span between trusses increases, with a corresponding increase in deck costs. The choice of ceiling construction also may control the truss spacing. In the case of a conventional suspended ceiling, a truss spacing of 48 in (121.9 cm) on center or more can be accommodated. However, if the designer intends to use a direct applied drywall ceilng, a maximum spacing of 24 in (61.0 cm) on center is dictated. The cost and architectural consideration of the ceiling construction thus become an integral part of the overall wood truss system costs.

4. *The depth of the wood truss system:* For a given span, spacing, and loading condition, generally as the depth of the truss increases, so does its ability to carry heavier loads. However, this increased depth may require higher support walls to be constructed to maintain interior height clearance requirements, thus adding additional building costs.

5. *The location of interior load-bearing elements:* The positioning of interior load-bearing walls or columns also can affect the wood truss system. Interior load-bearing columns supported by the wood truss system can result in relatively high concentrated loads being applied to the trusses and may require multiple trusses designed as a girder to support this load. Similarly, load-bearing walls supported by the wood truss system may require additional trusses if the walls are positioned parallel to the truss span, or stronger trusses positioned at a closer on-center spacing may be required to support these walls if they are placed perpendicular to the truss span. In either case, the supporting truss system has higher costs associated with it when required to support these loads, and alternative framing schemes not requiring such support by the trusses should be evaluated to optimize the structural system cost.

6. *The routing of mechanical systems through the truss support structure:* The extent of mechanical systems which are located within the truss structure may require deeper trusses and larger panels or openings than would be needed to carry the actual design loads. In some instances, the mechanical system layout may have an influence on the actual direction in which the trusses are to span, thus affecting system costs.

7. *Foundation and wall support considerations:* While conventional wood or steel stud walls or masonry walls and their normal wall foundations are usually adequate to carry the loads imposed by uniformly spaced lightweight wood trusses, the use of widely spaced trusses such as in girder trusses may result in concentrated end reactions which require separate support columns in the wall construction and associated heavier footings.

8. *Rooftop or suspended mechanical units:* The placement of mechanical units also can influence the design and cost of the truss systems. These units, either placed on the roof or suspended from the trusses and located near the midpoint of the truss span, may require additional trusses for support or a stronger and thus more costly truss design. Placement of these loads near bearing walls may permit the use of the truss systems as designed for normal uniformly distributed loads with no increase in truss size or quantity.

It becomes readily apparent that the interrelationship of these design considerations makes any general conclusion regarding the economic advantages of one truss system over another virtually impossible. However, the manufacturers of the lightweight wood and wood-steel composite trusses have developed a wealth of technical information in the form of design load tables which greatly assist the designer. A typical load table is illustrated by Table 6.1. In these tables, the depth of the truss, the span, and the allowable load the truss can carry while meeting specified deflection criteria are given. Combining these types of data with the maximum allowable spacing of the trusses arrived at from other design considerations and applying the relative costs of various decking materials allow the designer to establish the total cost of a wood truss system that achieves specific structural and architectural criteria.

It is suggested that the manufacturers of the engineered, lightweight prefabricated wood trusses be contacted in the conceptual stage of a project for assistance in making economic assessments of various possible framing schemes, as many of them have established so-called best systems for given design criteria.

6.4 FIRE AND LIFE SAFETY IN BUILDINGS

All model building codes contain extensive requirements pertaining to fire and life-safety considerations. These provisions involve all aspects of the building design but are strongly influenced by the type of structural materials used, i.e., combustible or noncombustible. The following sections briefly discuss the fire and life-safety issues most commonly associated with wood or wood-steel composite trusses.

6.4.1 Type of Construction

Generally, the building codes of North America permit wood trusses in heavy timber, ordinary, and frame construction classifications. A more detailed discussion of construction classification may be found in Chap. 2, "Preliminary Design Considerations." Worth note here is that wood trusses may only be used in the heavy timber classification when all members of the truss meet the minimum size requirement of that classification.

Ordinary and frame constructions are typically subdivided into protected (fire-resistive) and nonprotected categories. Because of the minimum member size required, heavy timber construction is assumed to have a fire endurance in keeping with the occupancies, building size, etc. allowed by the building codes.

Protected or fire-resistive construction, when required for a particular building, requires the trusses to be part of an assembly having the specified fire-endurance rating. Fire-endurance assembly ratings are established by laboratory test. Tests on assemblies which include lightweight wood trusses have usually been sponsored by individual manufacturers and pertain only to the specific truss or trusses of that manufacturer. An example of such an assembly is shown in Fig. 6.14. Numerous similar tested assemblies are listed in the fire-resistive assemblies publications of Underwriters Laboratories, Inc. Others may be found in manufacturers' literature and research reports published by various building code authorities.

6.4.2 Fire and Draft Stopping

Unless properly fire- and draft-stopped, the truss space located between the structural decking and the ceiling construction can act as a horizontal chimney with consequent rapid spread of flame and smoke. Adherence to building code requirements and careful detailing are necessary to ensure adequate fire and draft stopping.

6.4.3 Sprinkler Systems and Wood Truss Design

The addition of an approved automatic sprinkler system to a building permits modification to be made to the basic fire provisions of the building codes. Allowable areas and heights of buildings may be increased and in some codes fire endurance requirements may be reduced. In wood truss construction incorporating a ceiling, it is generally necessary to install sprinkler heads both in the concealed truss space and below the ceiling construction.

When supported by the trusses, sprinkler systems can impose substantial structural loads. While small branch lines usually can be accounted for as additional uniformly applied dead load, main lines may require reduced truss spacing or additional trusses to support these loads. Table 6.2 gives approximate wet-line weights for sprinkler systems depending on the diameter of the pipe.

Spacing of sprinkler line supports varies with diameter. The resulting concentrated loads can be a controlling criterion in the design of lightweight prefabricated trusses. Connections must be capable of resisting certain horizontal forces as well as vertical loads. Moreover, all connectors must be of an approved type. Generally, the horizontal forces and approved connections are those given in Standard NFPA 13 National Fire Protection Association.[4]

Some lightweight wood truss manufacturers can provide recommendations and approved details particularly suited to their products. In any case, sprinkler loads and connections must be considered for their effect on wood truss design.

In considering the structural effects of a sprinkler system, a frequent problem is not having the final sprinkler system layout at the time of the structural design. However, preliminary layouts and maximum line sizes usually can be obtained and appropriate allowances provided in the wood truss design. Unfortunately, a number of contractors and designers have suffered the embarassing and costly situation (not

TABLE 6.1 A Typical Load Table

Depth	20		22		24		26		28		30		32		34		36		38		40		Depth
	100% TL	115% TL	100% TL	115% TL	100% TL	115% TL	100% TL	115% TL	100% TL	115% TL	100% TL	115% TL	100% TL	115% TL	100% TL	115% TL	100% TL	115% TL	100% TL	115% TL	100% TL	115% TL	
Span	100% LL	125% TL	100% LL	125% TL	100% LL	125% TL	100% LL	125% TL	100% LL	125% TL	100% LL	125% TL	100% LL	125% TL	100% LL	125% TL	100% LL	125% TL	100% LL	125% TL	100% LL	125% TL	Span
20	291	331	318	358	344	377	350	381	350	385	350	389	350	393	341	392	331	381	322	370	311	358	20
	259	361	308	373		377		381		385		389		393		397		401		402		389	
22	246	280	269	306	291	332	313	344	318	347	318	350	318	353	318	357	318	360	314	362	305	350	22
	200	307	238	336	279	340		344		347		350		353		357		360		361		353	
24	208	238	229	261	249	284	268	306	287	316	291	319	292	321	292	324	292	326	292	329	292	320	24
	157	262	188	287	221	307	254	313		316		319		321		324		326		329		322	
26	175	203	195	225	213	245	232	264	248	283	265	292	269	294	269	297	269	299	269	301	269	291	26
	125	222	151	245	177	269	205	287	234	290	264	292		294		297		299		301		293	
28	152	177	168	196	185	214	201	228	217	245	232	265	246	272	250	274	250	276	250	277	250	267	28
	102	192	122	213	145	234	168	250	192	268	217	270	242	272		274		276		277		271	
30	132	154	147	171	162	188	177	203	191	219	204	234	217	248	230	254	233	256	233	257	233	252	30
	84	168	101	187	119	204	139	223	159	238	180	250	202	252	224	254		256		257		252	
32	116	135	129	149	142	165	154	179	167	194	179	206	189	221	200	234	209	238	219	240	218	231	32
	69	147	84	163	100	179	116	195	133	212	151	225	170	235	189	237	208	238		240		237	
34	102	119	113	132	125	145	136	158	146	171	156	183	167	195	177	205	185	215	194	225	200	208	34
	58	130	71	144	84	158	98	173	113	187	128	199	144	213	161	222	177	223		225		219	
36	90	105	100	117	110	128	119	140	129	151	139	161	148	171	157	182	166	190	173	202	181	195	36
	49	115	60	127	71	141	83	153	96	166	109	178	123	188	137	199	152	208	167	211		205	
38	81	95	89	104	97	115	106	125	114	134	123	144	132	153	140	163	148	170	155	181	162	183	38
	42	104	51	115	61	126	71	137	82	147	94	158	106	167	119	178	131	187	145	196	158	192	
40		87	83	96	91	105	99	115	106	124	113	132	121	141	128	148	135	157	142	164	149	166	40
		95	44	105	53	115	62	126	71	135	81	145	92	154	103	163	114	170	126	179	138	179	
42					84	97	91	106	98	114	104	122	112	130	118	137	124	143	131	150	136	155	42
					46	106	54	116	62	125	71	133	80	141	90	149	100	156	110	164	121	166	
44					74	86	80	94	86	101	93	108	99	115	105	122	112	129	118	135	124	142	44
					40	95	47	103	54	111	62	118	70	127	79	133	88	141	97	147	106	153	
46						76	73	83	79	90	84	96	90	102	96	109	101	116	106	122	113	130	46
						85	41	91	48	98	55	105	62	112	70	119	78	126	86	133	94	140	

48						70		75	72	82	76	89	81	95	87	100	92	106	97	112	103	119	48
						77		83	42	89	48	96	55	102	62	109	69	117	76	123	84	130	
50										76	71	81	75	86	81	92	85	98	90	103	95	109	50
										82	43	89	49	94	55	100	61	106	68	112	75	118	
52										70		75	69	80	75	84	80	90	82	95	87	100	52
										75		81	44	86	49	92	55	98	61	104	67	109	
54										63		66		74	68	78	74	83	77	88	82	92	54
										70		77		82	44	86	49	91	55	96	60	100	
56										60		65		70	62	73	68	77	73	81	76	86	56
										64		70		76	40	79	44	83	49	89	54	93	
58												59		64		67	65	71	68	77	71	80	58
												67		69		73	40	77	45	83	49	87	
60												55		62		64		68	63	71	67	75	60
												60		67		68		73	40	77	45	81	
62												53		56		60		63		67	61	70	62
												57		61		65		69		72	41	76	
64												51		55		59		62		63		67	64
												56		60		62		65		69		74	
66												47		50		53		56		60		63	66
												54		55		58		61		65		68	
68												45		47		51		54		57		59	68
												49		52		55		59		62		65	
70												43		45		49		51		55		56	70
												47		51		53		58		60		61	

Notes:

1. Straight line interpolation may be made between depths and spans.
2. Values shown are the maximum allowable load capacities of the trusses in pounds per lineal foot (PLF) based on simple span, uniformly loaded conditions, and assume roof applications have provisions for positive drainage (1/8" per foot slope minimum). This table may also be used for bottom chord bearing trusses (maximum bottom chord slope of 1"/12") with or without cantilevers – at one or both ends. Cantilevers are limited to 1/3 of the main span provided the inboard shear is limited to 2,500 pounds. Contact your Trus Joist MacMillan representative for other conditions.
3. Values in teal shaded areas may be increased 7% for repetitive member usage if the criteria on page 29 is met.
4. Tapered and pitched profiles are available. Contact your Trus Joist MacMillan representative for additional information.

To size floor trusses:
Check both live load (100% LL) and total load (100%TL). When live load is not shown, total load will control. Total load values limit deflection to L/240. Live load values are based on "NON-RESIDENTIAL FLOOR DEFLECTION LIMIT" shown on page 12 and assume a nailed floor system. Live load (100% LL) values may be increased with a glue-nailed floor system, contact your Trus Joist MacMillan representative for assistance.

To size roof trusses:
Check the appropriate snow load area (115% TL) or non-snow load area (125% TL) value to determine the maximum allowable total load. Total load (115% TL and 125% TL) values limit truss deflection to L/180.

Consult local codes to verify deflection limits required for specific applications.

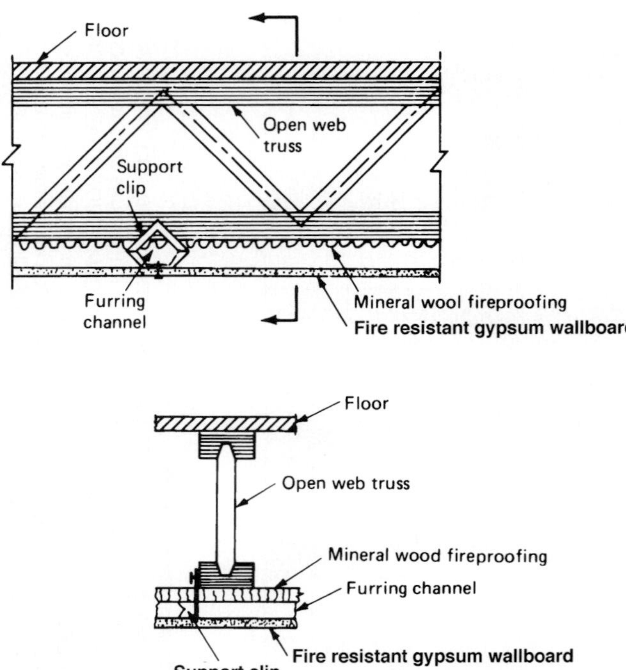

FIG. 6.14 One-hour fire-rated floor truss assembly.

TABLE 6.2 Approximate Wet-Line Weights for Sprinkler Systems

	Schedule 40, std. pipe, lb/ft		Schedule 10, thin wall, lb/ft	
Size of pipe	Dry	Wet	Dry	Wet
1	1.7	2.1		
1¼	2.3	3.0		
1½	2.7	3.6		
2	3.7	5.2	2.7	3.8
2½	5.8	7.9	3.5	5.9
3	7.6	10.8	4.3	8.0
3½	9.2	13.5	5.0	11.2
4	10.9	16.4	5.6	14.5
5	14.8	23.5	7.8	20.0
6	19.2	31.7	9.3	26.2
8	28.6	50.8	16.9	40.1
10	40.5	74.6		

only with wood trusses but with other structural framing systems) of having a structural system in place before considering sprinkler system loads. It is essential that these loads and their connections be considered before final truss layout and design.

6.4.4 Fire-Retardant-Treated (FRT) Wood Trusses

The use of FRT wood in trusses generally reduces fire insurance rates. Some codes allow limited use of such members in noncombustible construction types. However, the fire-retardant treatments cause a significant reduction in the allowable strength properties of wood, and in certain cases the chemicals used in this process can cause corrosion of the metal connectors. Allowable design values, including connector design values, are available from the company providing the treatment and redrying service. It is particularly important to provide for adequate ventilation in roof systems using FRT wood combined with high-temperature environments. Some truss manufacturers do not recommend the use of fire-retardant treatments with their products. More detail on these issues can be found in Chap. 2.

6.5 ROOF AND FLOOR TRUSS SYSTEM PERFORMANCE

Satisfactory performance of a wood truss system is dependent on its ability to (1) resist all design loads which may be applied during the life of the structure with sufficient consideration of possible overloads, (2) provide adequate stiffness to maintain both short- and long-term deflections within acceptable limits, and (3) minimize movements, vibrations, and noise which may be objectionable to human occupants.

6.5.1 Resistance to Loads

While minimum design loads are set forth by the governing building codes, the final design loads for each specific structural application are established by the designer based on experience and judgment. These specified design loads thus become the maximum anticipated loads to be carried by the wood truss system during the life of the structure.

Resistance to overloads or unanticipated loads thus becomes a factor-of-safety consideration. The tabulated design values set forth in the referenced design standards for the various materials used in a wood or wood-steel composite truss incorporate specific factors of safety. However, because of the interaction of the various materials and connection details used in an individual truss combined with effects of decking, bridging, and bracing, it is difficult, if not impossible, to assess the factor of safety of the total system and thus its inherent capability to resist overloads.

In the case of prefabricated lightweight wood trusses, the manufacturers gain acceptance through the governing code authorities based on a thorough review of test data and design evaluation. Inherent in these data are appropriate factor-of-safety considerations for the truss component materials and the truss itself. Integral to these code acceptances are the requirements for internal quality-control programs to ensure structural integrity. In the case of metal gusset plate lumber trusses, the code acceptances are limited to an evaluation of the plate connections only and not the fabricated truss, which compounds the definition of a factor of safety for the truss itself.

Generally, a system of relatively closely spaced trusses, i.e., 24 in (61.0 cm) or less on center as used in a repetitive-member system, is accepted as performing more effectively than an individual truss in resisting loads due to the inherent load-sharing aspects of the system itself. In addition, the possibility of a weak member occurring in a given truss system is offset to a degree by the probability that a stronger member will be located adjacent to it, thus helping to resist the imposed loads. In the case of an individual heavy timber truss application, additional concern in the selection of maximum design loads may be warranted, since system overload redundancies are less likely to be present than in a closely spaced truss system.

6.5.2 The Resistance to Short- and Long-Term Deflections

A wood truss system deflects under loading, with the deflections being time-dependent relative to the creep and set characteristics of the truss components. The proper design of wood truss systems should limit these short- and long-term deflections to acceptable bounds through material selection, connection design, and truss proportions. In addition, camber provisions should be incorporated in the truss design to account for these anticipated deflections. *Deflection* is defined as the vertical movement of the truss under load, whereas *camber* is that vertical curvature manufactured into the truss to offset the calculated deflections and thus eliminate possible sagging of the truss below a level line under service loads. *Creep* is the movement or deflection which occurs over time under continued loading. *Set* is the permanent deflection which remains after loads are removed and is caused by inelastic deformations between the wood fibers and slip or yielding at the truss joints.

The deflection limits for wood truss systems set forth by various building code authorities and standards are separately specified for roof and floor systems. The limits for roof systems generally are directed to ensure adequate drainage with additional consideration for possible distress of ceiling materials which may be directly applied to the truss chords.

Typically, roof live-load deflections are limited to $\ell/360$ (where ℓ = clear span) for those applications receiving a plaster ceiling and $\ell/240$ for designs requiring the use of more flexible ceiling coverings such as drywall. In most cases, this deflection limit is set at $\ell/180$ when the overall building design provides a positive roof slope for drainage and where this amount of deflection will not cause distress to the roof construction itself.

In addition to these general deflection criteria, designers also should evaluate roof truss deflections for special conditions such as a truss system supporting a glass window wall or skylight which may require highly restrictive deflection limitations. Roof trusses supporting movable or folding partitions generally require more restrictive deflection limitations to ensure the long-term operation of these partitions. Another example where deflection may be of primary design importance would be in the design of a flat or nearly flat roof where ponding of rainwater may occur and a relatively stiff system is warranted. Overall evaluation of the deflection characteristics of the truss system also should take into account the deflection of the decking material spanning between trusses.

In heavy timber truss applications, the primary deflection concerns are to minimize distress to other roof construction materials and to eliminate detrimental visual effects which would be associated with an appearance of sagging or deflection of the bottom chord below a level plane. It is essential to appraise the degree of slip or set in the joints of any wood truss using mechanical connection devices in assessing the overall deflection performance of the truss.

Camber of wood roof trusses is often provided to assist in ensuring proper drainage, for appearance, and to offset creep or set due to long-term loading. Specification of camber must be carefully evaluated to ensure that it does not cause framing problems as may occur at a mismatch of adjoining roof planes or the inability to create a straight fascia line at a building overhang. A commonly used guideline for lightweight, repetitive-member truss systems is to provide camber equal to 1½ times the calculated dead-load deflection to allow for both initial set plus long-term creep deformation. Another suggested camber policy often used is to camber for dead-load deflection plus one-half the live-load deflection. The final responsibility for proper roof truss camber lies with the building designer.

These camber recommendations also may be applied to heavy timber trusses. For heavy timber trusses, the deflection is typically calculated using the method of virtual work. For multiple, timber-connected trusses, the camber C in inches may be determined as

$$C = \frac{K_1 L^3}{h} + \frac{K_2 L^2}{h} \tag{6.1}$$

where h = truss rise, ft
L = truss span, ft
K_1 = 0.000032 for all truss configurations
K_2 = 0.000632 for bowstring trusses or
K_2 = 0.0028 for pitched or parallel-chord trusses

Floor truss systems require more restrictive deflection limitations based on the desirability of stiff floors as a human response issue. A live-load deflection limit of $\ell/360$ has been universally applied for many years. However, for the longer spans achieved using lighter truss systems which have evolved through advancements in wood truss technology, this criterion becomes questionable. A suggested deflection criterion based on occupancy satisfaction for these longer spans, beyond 20 ft (6.1 m), is to limit live-load deflections to $\ell/480$ for residential floors and $\ell/600$ for nonresidential floors. While this type of criterion has not been adopted by the governing building code authorities, it has been applied in numerous building applications with apparent success in minimizing objectionable floor deflections.

A composite action between floor sheathing and the truss system is achieved through proper nailing schedules and to a greater extent by the addition of a field application of elastomeric adhesive as a connection between the sheathing and the trusses. Some prefabricated wood truss manufacturers have conducted tests of this composite action and established composite-action design procedures accounting for this additional deflection resistance. Elastomeric adhesives have generally been limited to floor-system applications, since they are not considered effective in reducing roof deflections because of their thermal/creep characteristics.

As with roof truss systems, the possibility of creep or set should be considered in floor-system design, with particular attention to the potential deformations associated with mechanical joint connections such as may occur in a metal gusset plate truss. A floor truss system which takes a significant set over time can be objectionable in appearance and may cause separations at partition moldings, cracks in interior walls, or possible distress in ceiling construction. For repetitive-member systems, both roof and floor, it is advisable to provide additional trusses to support concentrated loads such as may be caused by the installation of heating and ventilating equipment and by partitions to equalize deflections of the truss system.

The camber of wood floor truss systems is somewhat less critical than that of roof trusses, since drainage is obviously not a concern and, in general, these trusses are inherently stiffer than roof trusses because of their more restrictive deflection criteria and the generally higher loads used in their design. A recomended camber policy is to provide floor trusses with a camber equal to 1½ times the anticipated dead-load deflection, thus accounting for initial deflection and long-term creep from permanent loads. If the floor system is more likely to sustain heavy long-term live loads such as in warehouses or libraries, it is recommended that camber requirements be increased accordingly.

6.5.3 Human Response to Floor Performance

Considerable research related to human response to movements and/or vibrations in floor systems has been conducted. While this research has not resulted in revised guidelines regarding deflection limitations, it has underscored the need to provide relatively stiff floor systems to overcome human objections to floor movements. The dynamic loadings and subsequent responses to these loadings in the form of movement as may be encountered in floor systems is a complex subject, and the spectrum of human response to these dynamic effects is even more complex. In addition to floor movements induced by loadings, noises in the floor system, such as squeaks which may occur because of movement between mechanical fasteners such as nails attaching the floor sheathing to the trusses, are also objectionable. To minimize these potential human objections to the performance of wood truss floor systems, the following items are suggested as a chesklist to be considered by the designer:

1. Good workmanship in the field during the installation of the trusses is most critical, particularly in ensuring that all bridging and bracing are properly installed and that required bracing conditions are satisfied. This can only be ensured by adequate field inspection by the designer, truss supplier, and building official.
2. Total uniform live-load deflection as a criterion of performance may not be as significant as the movement and/or vibration induced in the floor by the dynamic loadings of a person walking across the floor. Applying conventional live-load deflection criteria as required by the code authorities may not eliminate this concern.
3. A floor system which provides composite action between the sheathing and supporting trusses such as with a nailed-glued system acting in conjunction with an effective bridging system helps minimize these objectionable movements. In addition to minimizing floor movements, the nailed-glued system also results in fewer noise (squeak) objections.
4. Thicker sheathing for a given span condition provides greater stiffness between trusses with better dampening characteristics. A double-layer system or an equivalent single-layer material helps to reduce floor movements.

5. Bottom chords of trusses should be laterally restrained to eliminate torsional vibrations and rotation.
6. An unloaded or lightly loaded floor system generally does not perform as well as a heavier loaded system because of the dampening effect which the loads have on floor vibrations.
7. Structural discontinuities between separate living occupancies in multioccupancy structures should be provided.
8. Carpeting or other resilient floor coverings help reduce objectionable vibrations and noise. However, they also can aggravate the movement of unattached less stable objects on the floor.
9. In general, human sensitivity to floor performance increases as the cost and sophistication of the use of the facility increases.
10. As a general rule, once people become sensitized to the poor performance of a floor system, it is very difficult to desensitize them through remedial modifications of the system. Thus the initial human response to a floor system becomes of significant importance.

The preceding issues relate primarily to field experiences rather than specific engineering issues and as such are not addressed by the building code authorities. However, how a floor performs with respect to human perception of that floor's response to dynamic loads is a critical design consideration.

6.6 ADDITIONAL ROOF AND FLOOR WOOD TRUSS SYSTEM REQUIREMENTS

Wood floor and roof truss systems must be designed to perform in an integrated manner with other structural elements of an overall building system. Provision for support of the truss system, adequate anchorage, lateral support, and bracing of these structural elements must be evaluated within the overall scheme of stability of the total structure. Because buildings are so varied in size and shape with a virtually infinite array of structural framing schemes possible, these specific support requirements and bearing details for wood truss systems must become the responsibility of the building designer.

6.6.1 Bearing Details and Anchorage Requirements

Essential to the performance of wood trusses is adequate support and attachment at the bearing locations. Inadequate attention to bearing details is probably the greatest factor associated with the failure of lightweight prefabricated repetitive-member wood truss systems. These support and anchorage inadequacies may be categorized into three problem areas:

1. Insufficient capacity of the support structure to resist truss reactions
2. Insufficient bearing between truss and support members
3. Improper attachment details, particularly with respect to uplift forces

Perhaps the technological developments achieved in the design and fabrication of repetitive-member lightweight prefabricated wood truss systems have not had matching developments relative to the structural support of the products. These lightweight trusses are often utilized in relatively long span applications, creating greater reactions than would be realized with more conventional 2 × __ or other framing systems. One result has been structural inadequacies in ledger support details and attachments and insufficient support capabilities of walls, headers, and beams. This problem becomes most evident in situations where conventional framing methods have been extrapolated routinely to accommodate the longer spans without adequate engineering verification.

Prefabricated trusses are normally manufactured to a predetermined specified span dimension. Hence it is imperative that the supporting structure be constructed to tolerances that match the span dimensions of this prefabricated truss. If these dimensional requirements are not met in the field, concessions may be made or poor judgment used regarding bearing modifications, resulting in inadequate bearing support for the trusses. Field inspection by a qualified manufacturer's representative, building inspector, or the design professional is thus necessary to ensure bearing support adequacy.

Lightweight wood roof truss systems are susceptible to the effects of net uplift forces which may develop during periods of high winds. Inadequate bearing attachment to resist these forces may result in either folding one bay of trusses over the next bay or simply lifting an entire bay off the supporting structure. The applicable codes establish minimum design wind uplift forces, and proper structure design should include adequate anchorage of the trusses at their support to resist these reactions. This anchorage requirement must be carried to total structure resolution. Some manufacturers of prefabricated lightweight wood trusses have developed standard bearing details with accompanying load capacities as an aid to the designer in ensuring that adequate bearing provisions are provided for all possible design loads.

6.6.2 Lateral Support Considerations

The required lateral support to resist buckling of the compression chords of lightweight repetitive-member wood truss systems is most often provided by the sheathing material which is directly attached to the top chord members of the truss. While the top chord is generally the compression chord of a truss, special consideration needs to be given to provide adequate lateral bracing to the bottom chords of trusses for cantilever conditions, for trusses spanning continuously over two or more spans, or when wind loading causes a net uplift loading to the truss, since under these varied conditions, the bottom chord becomes the compression chord over part or all of its length.

A plywood or other wood-based panel product acting as a structural diaphragm provides excellent lateral support for the trusses using simple mechanical connection to the top chord members. The addition of an elastomeric adhesive in addition to the mechanical fastening of the panel product to the top chords further enhances this lateral support. Other types of decking or cladding materials also can be designed to provide this lateral support. Solid sawn or laminated tongue-and-groove decking of various sizes can provide effective lateral support to the top chords. However, it is essential that in addition to the attachment of the decking to the trusses, care be taken to ensure that each course of the decking be attached to the adjacent course such that an integral diaphragm is formed. Again, application of an adhesive to the tongue-and-groove joint of this decking can significantly increase the diaphragm resistance values of this type of decking. Reference may be made to *Diaphragm Construction and Design with Potlatch Lock-Deck Decking*[5] for specific diaphragm values for a nailed–glued-laminated timber deck system.

Joists or stringers framing across or between the top chord members of the trusses at relatively close on-center spacing with a decking material attached directly to these subframing members also can provide sufficient lateral bracing. This requires that the deck itself provide suitable diaphragm stability and that the attachment of the stringers to the trusses be adequate to provide the top chord restraint to the extent presumed in the truss design.

The use of heavy timber decking or purlins spanning between trusses is quite common in designs using heavy timber trusses which generally have wide on-center spacings. However, heavy timber deck and/or purlin framing also can be used in systems utilizing lightweight prefabricated trusses spaced at 6 to 8 ft (1.83 to 2.44 m) on center or with multiple trusses tied together to form girder trusses at greater on-center spacings. Regardless of the type of truss, the requirements for adequate bracing of the compression chords are the same.

As general guidelines, when heavy timber decking is nailed directly to the truss chords or when roof joists are set between the top chords with the decking nailed directly to the joists and chords, the least dimension of the top chord is taken as the depth of the chord. Similarly, when roof joists are set on top of the compression chord and securely attached to the chord and to blocking set between the joists with an adequate diaphragm attachment to the joists and blocking, the least dimension can again be taken as the depth of the chord.

For other conditions, the least dimension should be taken as the width of the top chord. When decking or blocking between roof purlins does not provide continuous lateral support of the top chord, the unbraced length for determining lateral buckling characteristics should be taken as the spacing between purlins. The truss should then be analyzed as a beam column in accordance with the provisions of the *National Design Specification for Wood Construction*.[6]

While sometimes used in conjunction with wood roof trusses, corrugated metal decking may not provide adequate lateral restraint to the top chords. The nailing or screw attachment to the truss is normally made through the top of the corrugation rather than at the valley to enhance watertightness. The inherently longer nails or screws required by this connection detail do not necessarily provide the required lateral support to the truss. In addition, corrugated decking in itself may not provide required diaphragm resistance. A preferred detail is thus to provide a light plywood or wood panel sheathing material under the corrugated decking.

There are various "composite wood fiber" decking materials available that may be used in conjunction with wood truss framing. While these materials provide excellent vertical-load-carrying capacity, their ability to transfer lateral loads is significantly less than that of other common wood deck products. Some of the manufacturers of these products have performed diaphragm testing and provide recommended attachment details with corresponding load capacities. However, numerous lateral stability problems have been associated with wood truss systems using this type of deck because of improper or insufficient mechanical attachment of the deck to the truss chords. The requirement of relatively large nails or spikes to penetrate these thick—2 in (5.08 cm) or more—decking materials also causes potential splitting problems in the wood chords. The designer is thus cautioned that care be given to attachment detailing and required diaphragm strengths when using the wood fiber deck products in conjunction with wood trusses.

Lateral support requirements provided for lower chord members when loaded in compression are additional design considerations. Directly attached ceiling or soft materials may not be sufficient to provide adequate lateral restraint, and other methods must be considered by the designer.

6.6.3 Bridging and Bracing

Bridging in truss systems is installed to provide vertical-load sharing between trusses. Bracing in truss systems is used to provide lateral stability and alignment to the system or its component members, either as temporary bracing during construction and/or as a permanent-bracing requirement. With proper provision, temporary bracing may fulfill permanent-bracing requirements, and indeed bridging members may fulfill some of the bracing requirements.

The purpose of bridging may differ for roof and floor systems. In roof systems, real loadings tend to be somewhat uniform or uniformly varying, with obvious exceptions such as rooftop heating and ventilating equipment or the occasional maintenance personnel loadings. Thus bridging in roof systems is primarily provided to give structural redundancy to the system; i.e., a weaker truss is thus partially supported by stronger trusses adjacent to it.

The extent of load transfer to be provided with wood roof truss systems is not clearly understood. In some cases, an ultimate load transfer required per bridging line is specified with a maximum spacing of bridging lines given. Another philosophy of viewing load transfer requirements is to require greater load transfer capability for truss systems which have less reliability. For example, a truss system of relatively low grades of visually graded lumber manufactured with minimal quality-control provision should have a more extensive bridging system than a truss system utilizing a high grade of machine stress-rated lumber fabricated under a more restrictive quality-control system. This essentially indicates that the more reliable and predictable the truss, the less the redundancy is needed.

It is relatively easy to provide effective bridging and thus load transfer to trusses which are spaced closely together. It is more difficult to provide effective bridging to trusses which are spaced 8 ft (2.44 m) or more on center. Hence the building designer generally considers these trusses to have little redundancy with respect to load sharing.

The load-sharing requirements between trusses of a floor system have greater significance in transferring concentrated loads than with a roof system. The purpose or objective of floor system bridging tends to shift to floor performance regarding deflection and vibration characteristics rather than being a purely structural concern. Again, there are few guidelines for establishing load transfer requirements. The typically closer on-center spacing of floor trusses makes it easier to achieve effective load transfer, and indeed, it can be demonstrated that sheathing applied directly to the top chords provides significant transfer, acting as a tension tie between trusses.

Bridging details can be of several types. Strongback bridging is accomplished by extending a light solid sawn joist, typically 2 by 4 in or 2 by 6 in, through the trusses at a panel point location of either the top or bottom chord with some form of mechanical attachment between the bridging and the chord. Metal or wood cross-bridging is often used, but the attachment detail becomes quite critical because slip at the mechanical connectors can render this type of bridging virtually ineffective. A combination of strongback and cross-bridging has been utilized for deeper trusses with greater on-center spacings. The strongbacks are typically provided at both top and bottom chord members, with cross-bracing then installed between these strongbacks. Another type of bridging used which is generally less effective is to provide a flat 2 × __ member laid across the top of the bottom chords and mechanically attached thereto to act in tension as the truss deflects.

Erection bracing is discussed in detail in Sec. 6.8. The permanent bracing required for wood truss systems can satisfy two purposes: (1) bracing of the total structure which incidentally is located within the truss system (such as with seismic ties or diaphragm bracing) and (2) bracing to stabilize the individual trusses or their components. As discussed previously, this latter bracing type is provided primarily to stabilize the compression members of the trusses, including web members acting in compression, or to stabilize the bottom chord tension members from lateral movements. This bottom chord stabilization is recommended when a directly applied ceiling is not utilized and is highly beneficial where eccentricities exist in the panel point connection of the first bottom chord panel point of top-chord-bearing trusses (see also Sec. 6.6.2).

The sizing and connection requirements for bracing systems are highly judgmental. Standard wood engineering design principles are applied in this design as guidelines for ℓ/d ratios, etc. A load criterion often referenced is to provide lateral support members capable of resisting 2 percent of the compressive force acting in the compression chord. This rule applies when the chord members are in true alignment. If the members are misaligned or otherwise deviate from a straight line, the additional eccentric forces generated must be resolved. The frequency with which this lateral stabilizing is to be provided along the compression chord is left to the judgment of the designer. However, it is obvious that the chord member must have adequate buckling stability between supports to carry the design loads.

6.7 ANALYSIS AND DESIGN OF WOOD TRUSSES

As discussed in Sec. 6.1 and shown in Figs. 6.2, 6.6, and 6.7, because of the wide variety of wood materials and related technology available, there are virtually unlimited variations of profile and capacity in today's wood trusses. Because of the wide range of possibilities, the often proprietary nature of light-truss standards, and ready availability of timber truss standards, a complete coverage of wood truss design procedures is not practical in this book.

It is of course possible to design wood trusses based on sound engineering practice, with reference to wood design and connector values as found in the *National Design Specification for Wood Construction*[6] and elsewhere and to the applicable standards of steel and other component materials. A brief discussion of analytic methods usually employed and some of the considerations in wood truss design are given in Sec. 6.7.5. The wood truss designer is advised to consider connection details most carefully, since, as in most types of structures, it is in such details that design errors leading to in-service problems most frequently occur.

It is anticipated that the building designer intending to rely on the truss supplier for design input will find value in the discussion of Sec. 6.7.3. The illustrative examples in Sec. 6.7.6 are intended to provide some guidance for designers wishing to do their own truss analysis or those wishing to review or check such designs as provided by a truss manufacturer.

6.7.1 Design Standards

Lightweight factory-manufactured trusses are designed and produced in accordance with standards which are often wholly or partially proprietary in nature. The metal gusset plate truss industry has two general design standards promulgated by the TPI. These are the *Design Specification for Metal Plate Connected Wood Trusses,* TPI-85,[7] and the *Design Specification for Metal Plate Connected Parallel Chord Wood Trusses,* PCT-80.[8] TPI-85 is applicable only to pitched truss designs, while other more complex configurations must be designed under standards established by a particular plate manufacturer.

Large sawn timber or glulam trusses are often designed in accordance with standards found in the *Timber Construction Manual* of the American Institute of Timber Construction.[9] Those desiring further information on proprietary design methods should refer to manufacturers' literature or make direct inquiries to the engineering staff of such organizations.

6.7.2 Typical Spans and Proportions

The common prefabricated lightweight wood trusses typically span from 15 to 50 ft (4.57 to 15.24 m) at spacings from 12 to 48 in (30.48 to 121.92 cm) on center. However, trusses of this type capable of much greater spans and of wider on-center spacings are available from some manufacturers. There is no span-depth ratio limit for these trusses; rather, their dimensions are controlled by the strength and stiffness of the materials and connections used. The range of span-depth ratios typically encountered for prefabricated lightweight wood trusses is given in Table 6.3. However, an example of design innovation is a relatively light trussed arch of parallel laminated veneer lumber chords combined with tubular steel webs used to clear span 400 ft over the football stadium of the University of Idaho, as shown in Fig. 6.15.

Heavy timber trusses, including those fabricated from either solid sawn timber or glued-laminated members, have been used in spans of 150 ft and more in both building and bridge applications. In buildings, such trusses are normally spaced from 10 to 25 ft (3.048 to 7.62 m) on center. The profiles of heavy timber trusses are typically determined by considerations of appearance, clearance, and overall structure configuration. Experience has shown that for common profiles, greatest

TABLE 6.3 Typical Range of Span-Depth Ratios of Wood Trusses

Type	Range of span-depth ratios
Lightweight	10 to 20
Timber bowstring	6 to 8
Double pitched	5 to 6
Parallel chord	8 to 10

FIG. 6.15 University of Idaho Stadium Cover. (*Courtesy Trus Joist MacMillan, Boise, Idaho.*)

design efficiency and economics are attained when span-depth ratios are limited approximately to the ranges in Table 6.3.

6.7.3 Preliminary Design

Considered here are common types of trusses used in buildings only, since applications such as bridge trusses, long-span trussed arches, or other complex applications require additional considerations unique to the particular project. The building designer must first have an awareness of products, materials, and manufacturing facilities available to service the project. In the case of long spans or deep profiles, investigation into possible shipping problems is advisable. When shipping of the trusses as a preassembled unit is not practical, members must be assembled on the job site, which requires considerations of available space, proper scheduling, and perhaps the practicality of field assembly of certain details. For example, a glued splice may require controlled temperature and pressure, which are difficult to achieve in field conditions.

Whatever the type of truss considered, the best source of design information for estimating is those who supply, design, and/or fabricate wood trusses. If information is not at hand, a few telephone calls generally secure the desired literature. Many suppliers, manufacturers, and fabricators provide preliminary design and cost-estimating services.

Most manufacturers of prefabricated lightweight trusses publish literature which includes load-span tables, truss dimensions, and typical details which can be used for layout. Special profiles and associated details are often available on request.

When it is desirable to determine timber truss sizing on a preliminary basis, the following procedure can be used, but the results give only an approximation of required profile and member sizes. For a final design, procedures such as discussed in Sec. 6.7.4 and 6.7.5 should be followed.

1. *Consult Table 6.3 for typical span-depth ratio and determine trial dimension of the truss.*

2. *Select a trial spacing:* Primary considerations are usually based on economics and appearance. Review the discussions of Sec. 6.3. Select a desired deck from Chap. 7 or available literature, or determine purlin and panel system using Chaps. 4 and 7.

3. *Determine approximate maximum member forces for uniform total load (here it is assumed that the load is applied uniformly to the top chord):* For bowstring and double-pitched profiles,

$$R = \frac{WL}{2} \tag{6.2}$$

where W = total load, lb per lineal foot
L = span, ft
θ = Angle at intersection of top and bottom chords at the support (see illustration)
$C = R/\sin\theta$
$T = R/\tan\theta$

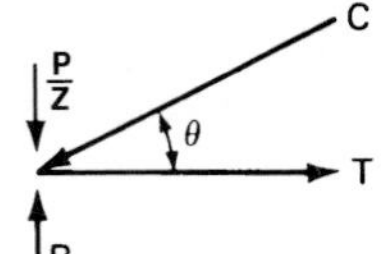

Depending on actual geometry, forces may be somewhat higher in other truss panels, but ignoring the half-panel point load $P/2$ in determining the magnitudes of C and T usually compensates for this. For parallel chord profiles,

$$T = C = \frac{WL^2}{8D} \tag{6.3}$$

where D is truss depth in feet measured between centerlines of chords.

4. *Select approximate chord member sizes:* For tension chord area selection, increase force T by 20 percent to allow for reduction of section at connections. For compression chord area selection, increase force C by 35 percent to allow for added bending stresses and possible reductions of member ℓ/d.

Trial member sizes are selected for sawn timbers by using allowable tabulated design values from *Design Values for Wood Construction,* a supplement to the NDS.[6] For glued-laminated timbers, tabulated design values are also given in the NDS[6] Supplement. Note that the tabulated design values for glued-laminated timber as given in Table 5B of the NDS[6] Supplement are those for members with axial, rather than bending, as the primary load stresses. Whether sawn or glued-laminated timbers are to be used, it may be advisable to check the local supply of available grades and species at the preliminary design stage. Tabulated design values are multiplied by all applicable adjustment factors as given in Table 2.3.1 in the NDS.[6]

5. *Estimate deflection characteristics:* For this purpose, beam equations may be used as described below. For greater accuracy, the modulus of elasticity should be decreased 10 percent to account for deformation in web members and for set in mechanical connections. The deflections calculated in this fashion are usually of sufficient accuracy to determine truss camber desired or required slope to ensure roof drainage. For uniform load, the maximum deflection is

$$\Delta = \frac{5wL^4}{384EI} \tag{6.4}$$

where w = total load, pounds per lineal inch
L = span, in
E = modulus of elasticity, pounds per square inch, from tables (reduced 10 percent)

and

$$I = \frac{ad^2}{2} \tag{6.5}$$

where a is the average of top and bottom chord areas in square inches, and d is the depth between the centerlines of the chords in inches. For other than parallel profiles, the average depth may be used to determine d, which will be somewhat conservative. A more accurate estimate is attained by calculating the average moment of inertia for the profile.

The foregoing applies equally well should a truss be designed using dimension lumber rather than timbers.

An example of this preliminary design procedure is as follows:

Assume a sawn timber truss, double-pitched profile, spaced 8 ft (2.44 m) o.c. (a tongue-and-groove wood deck is to be used over the trusses).

Span: L = 40 ft (12.2 m).

L/D = 5.

D = 8 ft (2.44 m) (at center).

Dead load = 15 lb/ft^2 (718 Pa).

Snow load = 30 lb/ft^2 (1436 Pa) (load duration factor of 1.15 is applicable).

w = 45(8) = 360 lb/ft.

$R = wL/2$ = 7200 lb

θ = 21.8°.

Adjusted tension:

$$T = \frac{7200(1.2)}{\tan 21.8°} = 21{,}600 \text{ lb}$$

Adjusted compression:

$$C = \frac{7200(1.35)}{\sin 21.8°} = 26{,}170 \text{ lb}$$

Assume that No. 1 Douglas fir–larch is the best grade available in sizes greater than nominal 2 × __ material.

Bottom chord tension: Determine the allowable tension value F_t':

$$F_t' = F_t \times C_D \times C_F \qquad \text{(see NDS Table 2.3.1)}$$

$$= 675(1.15)(1.3)^* = 1009 \text{ lb/in}^2$$

*Size factor is based on a 6-in-wide member.

Required area:

$$A_r = \frac{21600}{1009} = 21.40 \text{ in}^2$$

Try 4 × 6 in:

$$A = 3.5(5.5) = 19.25 \text{ in}^2 \qquad \text{NOT SUFFICIENT}$$

Try 4 × 8 in:

$$A = 3.5(7.25) = 25.38 \text{ in}^2$$

Reevaluate the allowable stress based on 8-in-wide member:

$$F_t' = 675(1.15)(1.2) = 932 \text{ lb/in}^2$$

$$A_r = \frac{21{,}600}{932} = 23.19 \text{ in}^2 < 25.38 \text{ in}^2$$

Top chord compression: Determine the compression design value F_c^*:

$$F_c^* = F_c \times C_D \times C_F$$

$$= 1450(1.15)(1.1) = 1834 \text{ lb/in}^2$$

$$A_r = \frac{26{,}170}{1834} = 14.27 \text{ in}^2$$

Use a 4 × 6 in top chord:

$$A = 19.25 \text{ in}^2 > 14.25 \text{ in}^2$$

Estimate the deflection: Average depth is approximately 48 in, assuming a zero depth at bearing:

$$d = 48 - \frac{5.5 + 7.25}{2} = 41.62 \text{ in}$$

$$a = 3.5\left(\frac{5.5 + 7.25}{2}\right) = 22.31 \text{ in}^2$$

$$I = \frac{a \cdot d^2}{2} = \frac{22.31(41.62)^2}{2} = 19325 \text{ in}^4$$

From Table 4A of the NDS,[6] Supplement $E' = E = 1.7 \times 10^6$ lb/in²; reduce 10 percent to effective $E' = 1.53 \times 10^6$ lb/in²:

$$L = 40(12) = 480 \text{ in}$$

$$w = \frac{360}{12} = 30 \text{ lb/in}$$

$$\Delta = \frac{5wL^4}{384E'I} = \frac{5(30)(480)^4}{384(1.53 \times 10^6)(19{,}325)}$$

$$= 0.70 \text{ in (17.8 mm) at total load (0.47 in (11.9 mm) at live load)}$$

These deflection values should be compared with acceptable in-service deflections based on structure use.

6.7.4 Typical Analysis of Wood Trusses

Discussions of the truss as a structural member abound in texts of structural analysis. Of course, the pure theoretical truss with loads applied only at frictionless pins is as difficult to achieve with wood as with other materials. However, when certain design principles are followed, such as symmetry of joint fasteners about the centerlines of the member, tests and experience have shown that results are satisfactory. Therefore, wood truss analysis usually proceeds with a theoretically pure truss analysis coupled with an evaluation of secondary stress in individual members and design of the connections. It is the orthotropic nature of wood and special connections which have evolved that leads to somewhat unique considerations in wood truss design.

As noted, the first step in wood truss analysis is usually the assumption of a simple planar truss with loads applied at panel points. Pure axial member forces can be determined by the method of joints, method of sections, graphic analysis, or use of one of the many computer programs available, with truss type members specified. Bending moments are added to axial forces when the member is loaded transversely.

Probably the most commonly used procedure for determining truss member forces by manual calculation is the *method of joints*. This method of analysis, which is described in detail in numerous textbooks on structural analysis, lends itself well to trusses that are not very complicated, such as simple-span planar statically determinate trusses.

Another method used to determine the member forces in a truss is the use of a *graphic force polygon,* or *Maxwell diagram,* as developed by James Maxwell in 1864. Figure 6.16 illustrates the graphic force polygon method of truss analysis. Again, this procedure is discussed in detail in numerous engineering reference books and will not be repeated herein.

The *method·of sections* is also very useful for manually calculating forces in the members of statically determinant trusses. It can be used very quickly to find the force in any member of the truss when performing a check on the forces determined by another method and is particularly useful for verifying computer output. It also can be used to do a complete truss analysis.

A popular analytic method of calculating the deflection of a truss is the *method of virtual work.* The concept assumes that an imaginary (virtual) unit load is applied at the point for which the deflection is to be calculated and in the direction of the desired deflection. This unit load is used to determine the deflection by equating the external virtual work to the internal virtual work. The *external virtual work* is

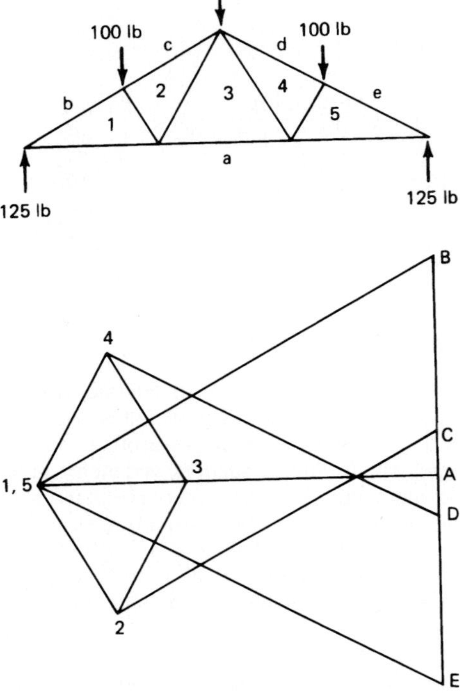

FIG. 6.16 Maxwell diagram: graphic force polygon.

the unit virtual load times the unknown deflection. The *internal virtual work* is equal to the sum of the products of the virtual force in each member caused by the unit virtual load times the deformation of each member due to the actual loads. Thus

External virtual work = internal virtual work

$$1 \times \Delta = \Sigma \frac{uSL}{AE} \tag{6.6}$$

where A = cross-sectional area of truss member, in^2 (cm^2)
L = length of member, in (cm)
E = modulus of elasticity of material, lb/in^2 (Pa)
S = force in member created by actual load, lb (N)
u = force in member created by the unit virtual load, lb (N)
Δ = deflection, in (cm)

For example, determine the vertical deflection at point L_2 in the truss shown in Fig. 6.17*a* due to the loads shown. It is assumed that all members of the truss have

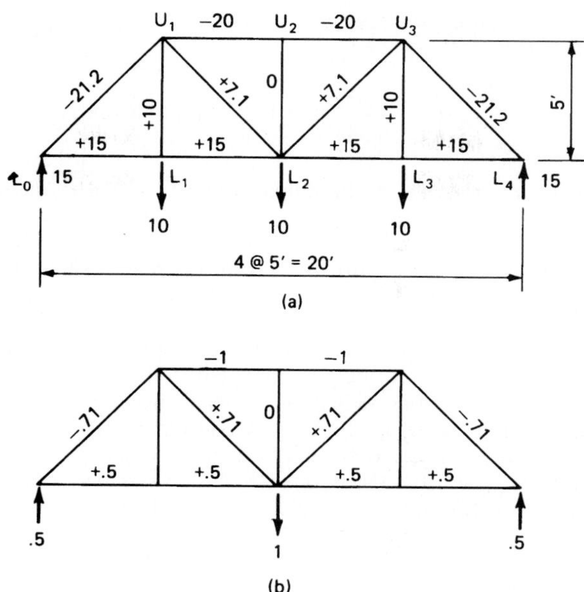

FIG. 6.17 Truss forces: virtual work method of truss deflection. (*a*) Forces in each member of the truss due to real loads. (*b*) Forces due to virtual unit loads. *Note:* All loads and forces are in kips.

a cross-sectional area of 10 in² (6.45 cm²) and that the wood has a modulus of elasticity of 1.8 × 10⁶ lb/in² (12,410 MPa).

Apply a unit virtual force in the vertical downward direction at point L_2 as shown in Fig. 6.17*b*. It is generally most convenient to place these data in table form, as shown below. For this example, the midspan deflection is calculated to be 0.42 in (1.07 cm), which can be compared with acceptable deflections for the intended use of the truss.

Member	L/A, 1/in	S, kips	u, kips	SuL/A, kips²/in
$L_0 - L_2$	12	+12	+0.5	90
$L_0 - U_1$	8.5	−21.2	−0.71	128
$U_1 - U_2$	6	−20	−1	120
$U_1 - L_2$	8.5	+7.1	+0.71	43
				381

Note: 1 in = 25.4 mm; 1 lb/ft² = 47.88 Pa; 1 ft = 0.3048 m.

$$A = 10 \text{ in}^2/\text{each truss member}$$

$$E = 1.8 \times 10^6 \text{ lb/in}^2$$

$$\Delta = \Sigma \frac{SuL}{AE}$$

$$= 2\left(\frac{381{,}000}{1{,}800{,}000}\right) = 0.423 \text{ in } (10.7 \text{ mm})$$

This example demonstrates a simplified application of the method of virtual work. Since the truss is symmetrical, only half the members were listed in the calculation, and the sum of SuL/AE for these members is multiplied by 2. Also, the truss members experiencing zero stress from the real loads to the truss can be omitted. If the modulus of elasticity is the same for all members, it may be left out of the calculations until the final step. For trusses that are not symmetrical, the procedure can be used as demonstrated in the example, except that all members whose product of Su is not zero must be included in the summation.

The preceding virtual work deflection analysis usually considers only axial stresses. In applications where deflection is considered critical, some judgment should be applied not so much to consider effects of other stresses but to account for uncertain effects of set in connections which depends on the number and type of connections, fabrication tolerances, etc. Also, published wood stiffness values are averages, and some variation might be anticipated. Creep in wood members occurs under conditions of constant load and eventually reaches about 50 percent of instantaneous dead load deflection.

In reality, real loads and the method of their application, relative member stiffness, joint fixities, support conditions, etc. all have an effect on the true member stresses and deformations. The wood truss is not unique in this respect, except that member connections are sometimes neither fixed nor pinned; rather, some partial fixity occurs in the typical connection details. This partial fixity will result in a somewhat conservative design for most pitched trusses with the opposite effect for most parallel chord trusses when secondary stresses are not considered.

Allowable wood member stresses coupled with more or less standard connection details and design procedures have been shown by test and experience to perform satisfactorily without consideration of the very complex true stresses which occur. Attention to connection details is the key to satisfactory performance.

In cases of unusually complex configurations or loadings, or when unconventional connections seem called for, more precise analytic methods should be used. Stiffness matrix solutions and finite-element analysis may be used in such cases. However, due to the variable and orthotropic nature of wood stiffness and strength, finite-element characteristics must be selected with great care, or results can be misleading. Chapter 1 should be consulted for the various elastic constants.

Related to the analysis of simple or complex wood truss configurations, a computer program which may be of interest to designers is PPSA 4. PPSA is the acronym for Purdue Plane Structures Analyzer, a software program which was developed at Purdue University with the cooperation of the U.S. Forest Products Laboratory specifically for the analysis of plane wood structures. The program uses a stiffness method to determine member forces and includes the design provisions of NDS[6] for analysis of member stresses. Other special features of the program are the ready introduction of eccentricity in joints and the use of "fictitious members" to simulate the effect of partial joint fixities on members' stresses. An illustration of truss analysis using PPSA is given in Example 6.1 in Sec. 6.7.6.

The lightweight wood truss industry utilizes many computer programs usually developed specifically to analyze one particular version of these factory-produced units. Many of these programs are proprietary, but some are available to design professionals. The potential purchaser of such a program should seek assurances that it contains the latest provisions of applicable design standards.

6.7.5 Design Considerations and Procedures

In general, the following discussions are applicable to any wood truss. Detailed procedures given tend toward the sawn timber or glued-laminated truss members, since most lightweight trusses are factory-produced and are designed in accordance with standards of that industry. Of course, design considerations are essentially the same for a custom-designed and fabricated wood truss of 2 × __ dimension lumber, and such trusses are fairly common. Usually, they satisfy an architectural as well as structural need but may not be economical for purely structural uses when compared with factory-produced trusses.

Geometry. Regardless of profile, the final truss geometry will be determined by member stresses and joint details. For the purpose of trial layout, experience suggests that glued-laminated trusses usually have panel sizes in the range of 8 to 12 ft (2.44 to 3.66 m), and sawn timber truss panels tend to be somewhat smaller, depending on member size.

Panel layout should consider location of chord splices and length of compression webs. Occasionally, otherwise redundant vertical webs are added to reduce compression chord panel length.

Parallel chord profiles normally have diagonal webs at an angle of 40° to 55° from the horizontal. In considering the geometry of a bowstring truss, it should be noted that maximum chord forces occur under uniform load, but maximum web forces usually occur under unbalanced load, which also may reverse stresses in some members from the uniform load condition.

Support Details. Support details are typically a part of an end-joint detail. The considerations in design of such details are many and can be a function of the overall structure. Some of the usual issues are the compression perpendicular to grain-bearing stress, tiedown requirements to resist uplift forces, and connection requirements to provide lateral stability for the supporting structure. In some cases, ties to resist seismic and wind forces deserve special attention and should be considered from the standpoint of alternate load combinations to be analyzed. If the truss is bottom-bearing and the first web is not vertical, the required end distance of the bottom chord may need to be increased depending on the slope of the web and the magnitude of the parallel to grain forces at that point. If a truss bears directly on a chord member, the compression perpendicular to grain stress must be checked.

Long-span trusses and certain profiles, such as scissor trusses, should include an analysis of their lateral deformation under load. For example, consider a bowstring truss spanning 100 ft (30.48 m) under a uniform load. The bottom chord tensile stress in such a truss is nearly uniform along its full length, so the chord elongation is easily approximated. If the tensile stress is 1250 lb/in^2 (8.62 MPa) and the modulus of elasticity is 1.7×10^6 lb/in^2 (11.7 GPa), the chord will elongate 0.9 in (22.9 cm). Such movement must be absorbed by the support structure or allowed for in a "frictionless" support detail. If the support structure is quite rigid, thrust will develop, thus altering the calculated member forces, and this must be allowed for in the truss analysis.

Chord Design. The design of a truss tension chord is normally straightforward. Members in tension can be sized based on the magnitude of load they are carrying and their allowable tension parallel to grain stress. The required net area is thus given as

$$A_{\text{net}} = \frac{P}{F_t} \tag{6.7}$$

where P is the magnitude of the tensile force in pounds, and F_t is the allowable tension parallel to grain stress in pounds per square inch.

It should be noted that any area of wood cross section removed by connectors cannot be included in the net area required. Thus the final tension chord design must allow for this area reduction.

Tension chord members of wood trusses may have in-service loads directly applied to them. Typical of such loads are the weight of a ceiling, small mechanical units, and fire sprinkler systems supported from bottom chords. While it is recommended that all loads supported by tension chords be located at a panel point, this may not always be possible, and bending moments may be introduced into the bottom chords. Such additional loads must be accounted for by designing and sizing the bottom chords as combined bending and axial tension members in accordance with the provisions of NDS.[6] An illustration of this type of analysis is presented in Example 6.6 in Section 6.7.6.

The top chord of a truss can become a tension member due to wind uplift loading or cantilever configurations. In any case, all load cases must be analyzed particularly to check for stress reversals.

When possible, tension chords should be continuous members to avoid expensive splices. Where these chords are continuous, they should be analyzed accordingly when transverse loads are applied.

The compression chord usually carries most of the external loads, most often applied as uniformly distributed loads along the panel length. When, as is usual, the chord is continuous over several panels, it should be first evaluated as a continuous beam with the panel points assumed to be nonyielding supports. The reactions thus determined become the panel-point loads used in the axial force analysis of the truss. The bending moments induced by uniform loading along the panel length are included in the combined stress analysis. Judgment must be used to evaluate the effect of splices, since they may result in partial fixity. Splices can be designed to resist moments, but details with mechanical connectors will take some "set," partially releasing the moment. When uncertainties exist, the conservative approach is to perform two or more analyses, alternately fixing and releasing the joint, the design then being based on the greatest stresses found. When appropriate, loading of alternate panels should be considered.

Stability of the compression chord is critical, both normal to and in the plane of the truss. The depth-to-thickness ratio of the chord member(s) and the deck system used determines the degree of lateral stability. When $d/t \leq 5$ (where d is the depth of the chord and t is the width of the chord) and the decking is designed as a structural diaphragm and is continuously attached to the chord, the chord is assumed to be totally restrained laterally. When purlins are placed on top of the chord and adequately fastened, the effective length of the chord for lateral analysis is the purlin spacing. Ratios of $d/t > 5$ should be avoided unless purlins are in hangers, in which case the depth of the chord below the purlin should be no more than three times the thickness of the chord. Again, the effective length is the purlin spacing. When considering the allowable stress for any laterally unbraced lengths, assume the chord to be a simple column under uniform axial stress equal to the maximum total stress (combined axial and bending) in the member. The analysis proceeds with the applicable simple pinned end column formulas of NDS.[6]

For example, combined compression and bending stresses are checked by the following equation.

$$\left(\frac{f_c}{F'_c}\right)^2 + \frac{f_b}{F'_b\left[1 - \left(\frac{f_c}{F_{cE1}}\right)\right]} \leq 1.0 \qquad (6.8)$$

where f_c and f_b are the calculated axial and bending stresses. F'_c and F'_b are corresponding allowable stresses based on lateral stability, as considered above. The moment magnification term $[1 - (f_c/F_{cE1})]$ includes F_{cE1}, the critical buckling design value in the plane of bending.

The combined axial and bending stresses at the center of the compression chord panel also must be evaluated. Consider first an initially straight laterally restrained chord, continuous over several panel points, with uniform transverse load and some axial force. The free body of such a panel is shown in Fig. 6.18.

Obviously, the panels are in reality a series of interconnected beam columns supported at panel points and free to deflect in the plane of the truss. At first glance, the effective length appears to be the distance between points of contraflexure for a fixed-fixed beam ($\ell_e = 0.58L$). However, because of the so-called $P\Delta$ effect, it can be shown that the effective length increases with increasing load, and of course, the stresses are nonlinear with load. The truss designer wishing to pursue this complicated analysis should first find the effective length under load and then refer to NDS, Section 15.4, "Wood Columns with Side Loads and Eccentricity."

Normally, in sawn timber and glued-laminated truss design, the complexities of the preceding are avoided by assuming a conservative effective length (panel point to panel point) and proceeding with the design on a simple column basis. The authors of this chapter recommend the following factors for the simple design procedure, where ℓ_e (effective length) $= KL$, with L being the panel length:

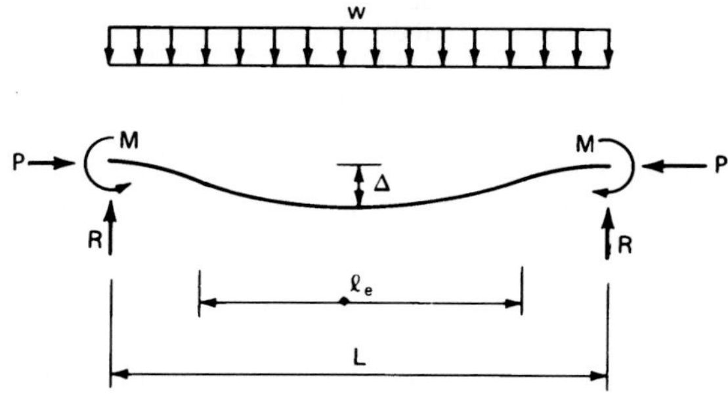

FIG. 6.18 Compression chord of truss subjected to axial and flexural stresses.

Panel end condition	K
Fixed-fixed	0.9*
Fixed-pinned	1.1*
Pinned-pinned	1.5

*When adjacent panels have similar loading. For panels loaded alternately (skip loading), use $K = 1.5$.

While a member continuous over a panel point is in effect "fixed," truly fixed mechanical connections are difficult to achieve in wood, and where splices occur, a pinned assumption is usually appropriate.

Eccentricity is usually considered only in curved or radiused top chord members such as occur in bowstring trusses, and the moments introduced by this eccentricity should be distributed in the same manner as the moments caused by externally applied loads are. The curvature factor C_c as discussed in Chap. 2 should be applied to the allowable bending stress for these curved top chords. In addition, curved top chord members subjected to bending moment have radial stresses induced which must be considered in the final design. Example 6.5 in Sec. 6.7.6 illustrates these various design requirements for bowstring trusses.

The lightweight prefabricated wood truss industry has approached the effective panel length problem in various ways. Apparently, those using simple design procedures normally use an effective length factor of 1.0 regardless of end conditions. The metal gusset plate design standard for pitched trusses, TPI-85,[7] incorporates effective lengths which were determined by a nonlinear evaluation within PPSA (see Sec. 6.7.4). Another method for determining the maximum safe panel length has been developed based on nonlinear ultimate load analysis, testing, and computer modeling. However, this method requires that panel fixity or end moments be known along with the statistical parameters of the chord stiffness and strength.

Design of Wood Truss Web Members. Provided joint details are such that end fixity need not be considered, the web members are designed as simple tension or compression members (considering, of course, the possibility of stress reversal under varying loading conditions). The effective length of compression webs is taken from center to center of the end-panel points, and the member is designed as a pinned column. Consideration must be given to buckling about both axes of compression web members; sometimes long compression webs are restrained by a secondary bracing system to prevent buckling out of the truss plane. The reader is referred to Chap. 3 for a complete discussion of column design.

Design of Wood Truss Connections. Truss joints can be connected by a variety of fasteners. Design values for various types of connectors available are given in Chap. 5. Careful and practical detailing is of extreme importance to ensure that the connection will be properly fabricated and will perform in accordance with design calculations. Regardless of the method used, the joints should always be detailed to avoid eccentricity.

Although a wide variety of connections can be devised, all have similar general design considerations. Always keep in mind that the analysis used to determine the forces and moments to be resisted in the connection may be related to the connection itself, for example, the degree of fixity assumed in the truss analysis must be consistent with the connection detail. In the following, general guidelines and a few specific dos and don'ts are presented regarding truss joint design.

Heavy Timber Truss Joints. The most common type of joint used in heavy timber trusses is a bolted connection using steel side plates, though wood side plates are sometimes used. A number of pitfalls related to this type of joint can be avoided by remembering the principles of consistent deformation for all components and materials and for all conditions to which the connection may be subjected. The use of steel side plates, while common, economical, and practical, can lead to in-service problems. The thermal characteristics and dimensional changes of wood with moisture variation, particularly across the grain, are greatly dissimilar to the characteristics of steel. The large steel side plates and multiple connector rows of Fig. 6.19*a* can lead to splitting of the truss member as cross-grain tension is induced by shrinking or swelling with moisture change. This can be avoided by the use of multiple straps as Fig. 6.19*b*. In all wood truss connections, it must be recognized that moisture content at the time of fabrication may be quite different from that in use, and that in-service equilibrium moisture also may fluctuate seasonally. For discussion of moisture effect in wood dimensions and properties, see Chap. 1.

When high forces are to be resisted at a joint, the use of shear plates is recommended. The once common use of split rings sometimes resulted in the splitting of wood members because of differential dimensional changes; moreover, it is a difficult joint to fabricate and fit together in the field.

A single large connector plate, as shown in Fig. 6.20*a*, while commonly used, should be avoided. A degree of fixity occurs, and the couple generated between the two web connectors produces cross-grain tension which may split the web end. Also, differential stiffness between the chord and side plates can induce unanticipated stress in the chord connectors. Figure 6.20*b* shows one possible arrangement to avoid these potential problems.

For both Figs. 6.19*b* and 6.20*b*, the recommended steel plate details at first glance seem more complicated than their single-member counterparts. However, the multiple-strap details typically use less steel, and fabrication tolerances are less critical because of the lesser number of connectors in a given component. Of course, steel side plates must be designed in accordance with appropriate standards, with checks made on bolt bearing, net section tension, end and edge distance, and stability in compression members.

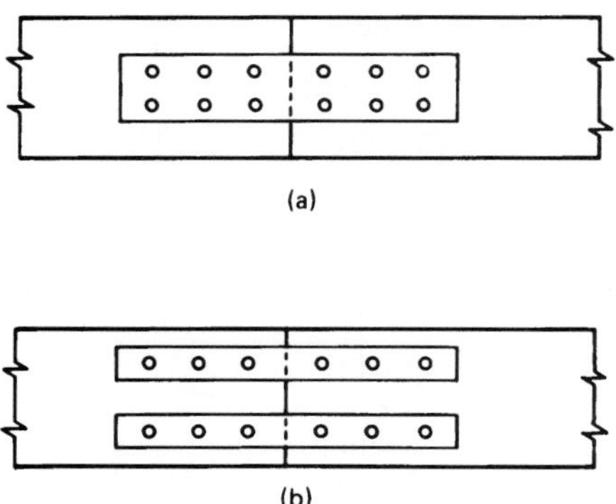

FIG. 6.19 Tension splice details.

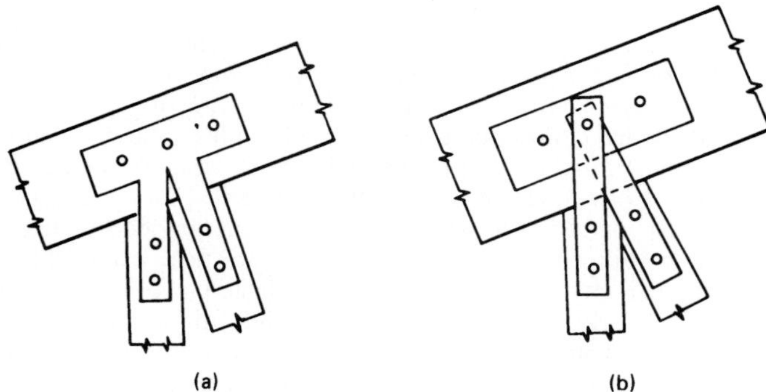

FIG. 6.20 Top chord panel-point joint details.

The preceding discussions make reference to cross-grain tension stresses. These are both the least understood and lowest-strength characteristic of wood and should be avoided whenever possible. The eccentric connection of Fig. 6.21 induces very complex tension and shear stresses and secondary bending moments and must be expected to perform poorly unless forces are very low. Of course, cross-grain tension does occur in certain connection configurations but is allowed for in the connector values of Chap. 5, which are based on test results.

A rather special connection sometimes required in truss chords is one designed to resist moment as well as shear and axial force. Because of some of the uncertainties which will be discussed, it is recommended that such splices be located at sections of minimum moment. The moment and forces to be resisted at a given section are in themselves somewhat uncertain because they may vary or even reverse with loading conditions other than uniform loading. Even under uniform load, the moment may change with increased load (see discussion on design of compression chords). However, for the general case of maximum member forces occurring under uniform top chord load, it is usually adequate to locate a compression chord splice at the panel quarter point and to design the splice for the maximum axial force and shear at the section and for either a positive or negative moment equal to 50 percent of the fixed-end moment at the panel point. Examples of moment connections are given in Chap. 5.

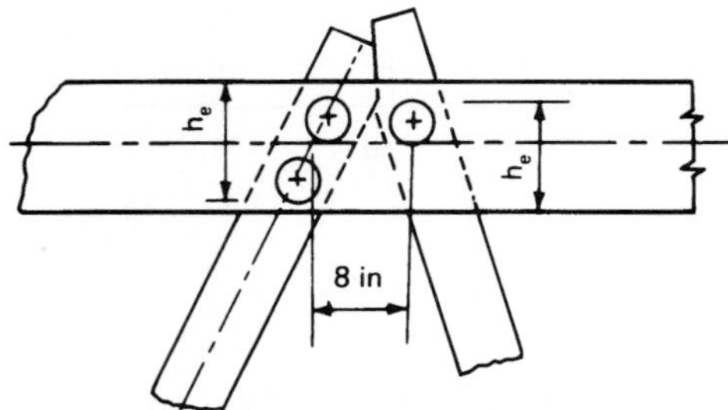

FIG. 6.21 Eccentric panel-point joint—to be avoided in practice.

Plate Truss Joints. Following is a brief discussion of the general considerations in designing truss connections with toothed metal gusset plates. For more information, TPI-85[7] and PCT-80[8] should be consulted.

Wood members must be cut accurately and be in full contact in each joint. The manufacturers of each plate type and configuration publish the basic plate design values, established by test in accordance with TPI-85.[7] Basic design values are adjusted for duration of load, except that the steel plates must be checked for net section tension and shear. Lumber moisture content is to be between 7 and 19 percent. Treated lumber, particularly with fire retardants, may require significant reductions in design stresses. Some treatment chemicals have caused corrosion in steel plates, and any particular application should be checked for this possibility. Tests establish values for plates loaded parallel, perpendicular, and at 45° to the wood grain.

Compression joints can be designed to carry 50 percent of the force in direct wood-to-wood bearing, with due regard to grain angle. Tension joints use the tension design value for the metal plate adjusted for the plate tension efficiency (net section). All plated joints must be designed to carry a minimum of 375 lb (1670 N) of axial force per member, and plates must always be installed on both sides of a joint. Plate capacities are given in pounds per square inch (kilopascals) depending on grain angle. A particular plate may be rated by either the net or the gross area method. For plates rated by the net area method, deduct ½ in (1.27 cm) end distance measured parallel to the grain and ¼ in (0.6 cm) edge distance measured perpendicular to the grain when determining the area of plate coverage. No exclusions for end and edge distance are applied when using the gross area method.

Multiple-Member Trusses. Wood trusses can be designed using multiple members. Symmetry in all connections is the primary design consideration, with the various arrangement possibilities depending on the particular truss configuration. A special consideration is the design of compression members, which may be limited by the *l/d* of individual members or may be designed as spaced columns in accordance with Chap. 3.

For a typical five-thickness multiple-member truss, there are two possible basic member arrangements, assuming that the chord members are each composed of two pieces. One arrangement places the chords on the outside and is most often used at the ends of flat trusses. The other places the chord members between the web members and is most often used at the ends of pitched trusses. In Fig. 6.22, the relative positions of the members are indicated by the numbers 1 through 5, position 1 being on the near side of the truss and position 5 on the far side.

The arrangement with the chords in positions 2 and 4 is most desirable at the end of a pitched truss in order that the heel joint may be made with splice plates

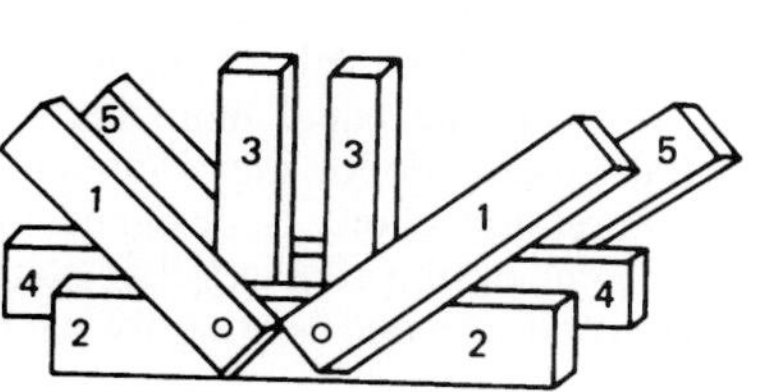

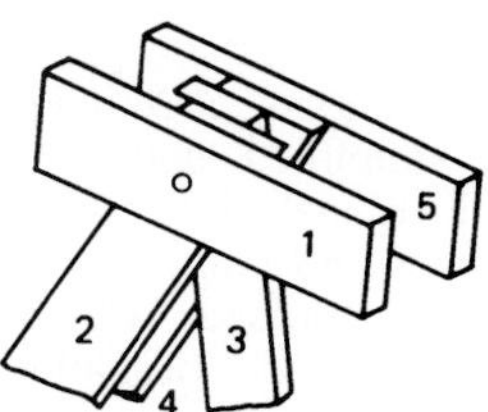

FIG. 6.22 Multiple-member joint layup.

in positions 1, 3, and 5. Toward the center of the span, the chord members may be lap-spliced to positions 1 and 5 with the web members in positions 2, 3, and 4.

The arrangement with chords in positions 2 and 4 also can be used for flat Pratt and Howe trusses, but simpler joint details usually result if the chords are in positions 1 and 5. Chords in positions 2 and 4 are desirable for the flat Warren-type truss or other trusses in which the web members intersect the chord at about the same angle.

The compression-web members of the Belgian and flat Howe trusses are usually double members, while the tension members are usually single. The compression-web members of the flat Pratt truss, on the other hand, are usually single chord members, while the tension members are usually double.

6.7.6 Typical Truss Design Examples

Design examples are presented in the following sections to illustrate the wide range of designs which may be encountered in practice. These include (1) the design of a metal gusset plate truss illustrating output as may be obtained from a proprietary plate manufacturer or from the use of PPSA, (2) the design of a proprietary wood-steel composite truss, and (3) the designs of several different common configurations of heavy timber trusses.

The examples have been selected to identify and illustrate the key design considerations unique to the specific type of truss indicated. The range of details analyzed in each example varies, since certain design considerations are common to several of these truss analyses, and repetition would be redundant.

EXAMPLE 6.1: METAL PLATE WOOD TRUSS DESIGN BY TPI DESIGN SPECIFICATIONS The design of pitched top chord metal plate connected wood trusses conforms to the *Design Specification for Metal Plate Connected Wood Trusses,* TPI-85,[7] published by the Truss Plate Institute. This design guide contains information on materials, member design procedures, plate evaluation, full-scale load test information, and appendices dealing with design loads, bracing, connector plate test method and evaluation, effective shear resistance tests for truss plates, design aids, and other technical information related to the design of this type of wood truss. The axial force design procedure assumes the members to be pin-connected. For uniformly distributed loads, the top chord moments are determined based on the assumptions that the chord has a continuous slope, is continuous over the web supports, and is pinned only at member ends where the pitch of the chord changes abruptly. Both panel-point and midpoint moments are calculated based on $M = WL^2/8$ multiplied by appropriate adjustment factors which take into consideration the truss profile and the effective length of the panels. These factors have been derived from many years of experience and intensive investigation using more sophisticated truss-modeling procedures such as matrix methods. In general, the use of these simplified modification factors to determine panel moments results in a conservative analysis for nonparallel chord trusses. Following computation of the axial forces and panel moments, the compression chord is designed as a beam column in accordance with NDS.[6] Proper joint design requires that plates are installed on both sides of a joint and there is wood-to-wood bearing for each member meeting at a joint.

The design example herein was supplied by Alpine Engineered Products, a proprietary manufacturer of metal truss plates. The span is 28 ft (8.53 m) overall with a pitched configuration truss spaced at 24 in (61 cm) on center and designed to support a live load of 30 lb/ft^2 (1.44 kPa), a dead load of 7 lb/ft^2 (0.34 kPa), and a ceiling load (applied to the bottom chord) of 10 lb/ft^2 (0.48 kPa). The 2- by 4-in bottom chord is horizontal. The web members are 2 by 4 in. The design output, shown in Fig. 6.23, includes the lumber specifications, axial member forces, plate specifications, design loads, truss spacing, truss dimensions, permanent bracing requirements, plate positioning, and general notes. Similar design data can be generated for a parallel-chord metal plate–connected wood truss by following the guidelines presented in *Design Specification for Metal Plate Connected Parallel Chord Wood Trusses,* PCT-80,[8] by the Truss Plate Institute.

PPSA Analysis. As noted in Sec. 6.7.4, PPSA is the acronym for Purdue Plane Structures Analyzer, a computerized wood engineering system developed at Purdue University in cooperation with the U.S. Forest Products Laboratory at Madison, Wisconsin. The system uses a matrix method of analysis based on traditional structural theory. The member forces are determined by the stiffness method of analysis based on a virtual energy formulation. The theoretical structure is made up of prismatic elastic members that are either pinned or rigidly connected to dimensionless joints. An unlimited number of plane frames, arches, trusses, continuous beams, etc., can be analyzed and checked against certain built-in design considerations.

The example calculation shown here is an analysis of a typical metal plate-connected wood truss example by TPI specifications. Figure 6.24 illustrates the joint and member numbering and coordinate system for this truss as used in the PPSA program. The output includes a reprint of the input and includes the member lengths (determined by the program from the input data). Under "Results" it lists the reactions, strength analysis, member and actions, interaction analysis results, shear stress analysis, and deflection analysis including maximum member deflections and point displacements. The data for this example are given in Table 6.4. The program also contains the option of outputting incremental member shear, moment, and deflection data for the increment size specified by the user.

EXAMPLE 6.2: COMPOSITE WOOD-STEEL OPEN WEB. A leading manufacturer of proprietary composite wood-steel open web trusses is Trus Joist MacMillan. These trusses consist of steel tubing web members interconnected to wood chords using a steel pin placed at the neutral axis of the chord. The wood chord used in these trusses may range from a single horizontal 2- by 4-in top and bottom member to vertical double 2- by 6-in top and bottom chords. These are illustrated in Fig. 6.24 shows one of these truss configurations. The following example illustrates the design of such a truss using vertical double 2- by 4-in chords identified as a TJM™ TM by Trus Joist MacMillan.

Assume a design span of 50 ft (15.24 m) with uniformly distributed live and dead loads of 30 lb/ft^2 (1.44 kPa) and 18 lb/ft^2 (0.86 kPa) respectively. Assume the trusses are to be spaced 48 in (120 cm) on center. For these design assumptions, a 42-in (106.6-cm) parallel chord TJM is selected. A copy of the computer output for this design is shown in Table 6.5.

For this design the input consists of the span condition (simple span), span, truss profile, slope, depth, Truss series, top and bottom chord end distances, bearing conditions (top or bottom), bearing hardware, spacing, live load, total load, and camber requirements. Besides the input section there are three other main sections: (1) truss data including allowable load deflection and camber, (2) member force diagram, and (3) manufacturing information. In this example, with the bearing hardware chosen and a span of 50 ft (15.24 m), the bearing pin-to-pin span is 49 ft 11

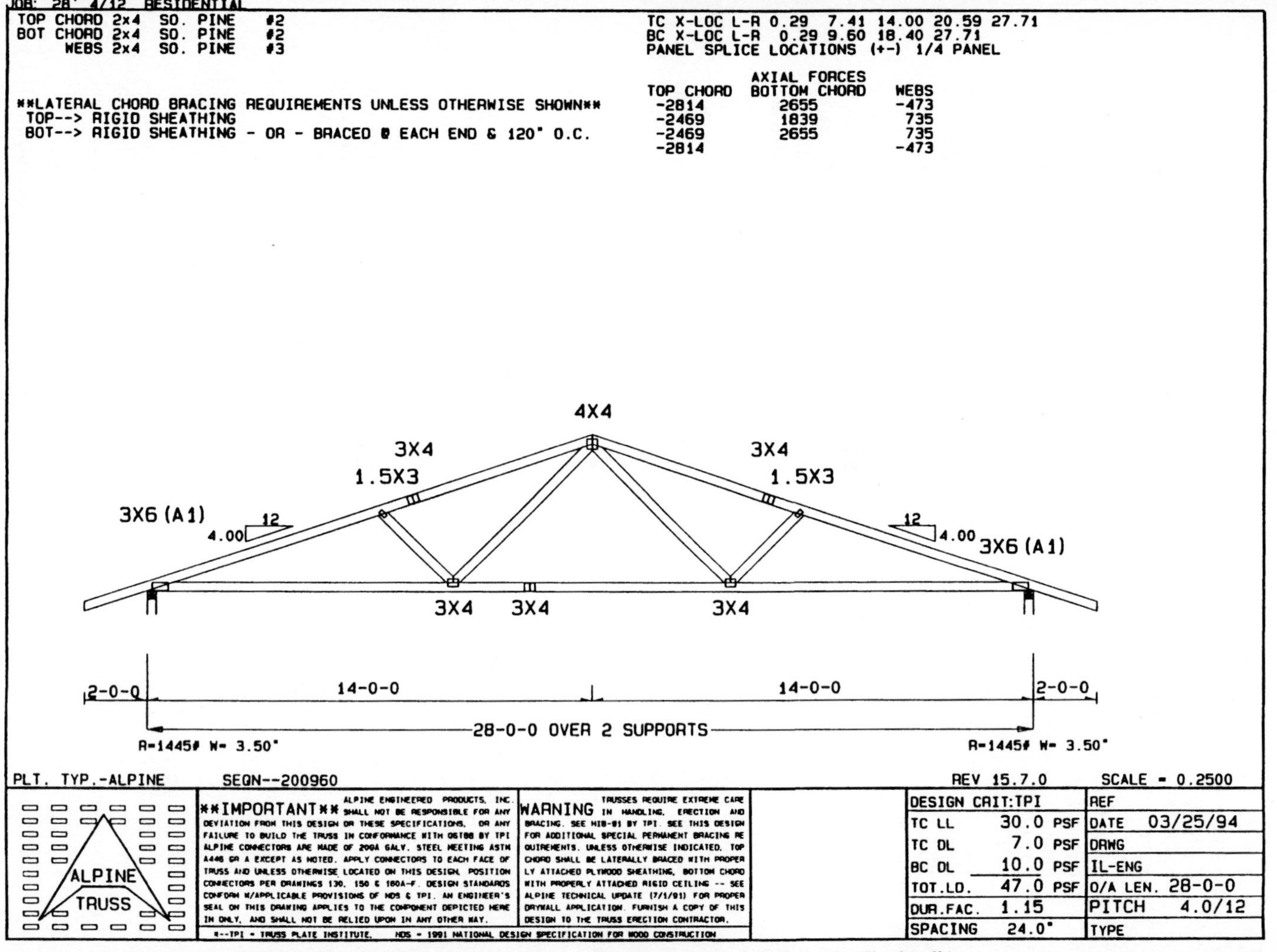

FIG. 6.23 Design example. *(Courtesy of Alpine Engineered Products, St. Charles, Il.)*

```
*************** ALPINE ENGINEERED PRODUCTS INC.   ******15.7.0*****

JOB: 28' 4/12  RESIDENTIAL

DESIGN CRIT    TPI               REF
TC LIVE LOAD  30.0 PSF           DATE        03/25/94
TC DEAD LOAD   7.0 PSF           SEQN        200960
BC DEAD LOAD  10.0 PSF           IL-ENG
       TOTAL  47.0 PSF           O/A LEN.    28- 0- 0
DUR. FACTOR    1.15              PITCH       4.00/ 0.00/12
SPACING       24.0"              TYPE        COMN

/------------------ 19.69' ----------------/
/------------ 14.00' ----------/
/----- 8.31' -----/
                                 .3.
                           .. /   \ ..
                       ..   /       \     ..
                .2.       /           \       .4.
            ..     \     /              \     /     ..
       ..           \   /                \   /           ..
1--------------------7-------------------6--------------------5
X=  0.00                                              X= 28.00
W= 3.50"                                              W= 3.50"
R=  1444                                              R=  1444
/--------- 12.00' ---------/

 ID   PITCH ------LUMBER------   AXL  BND  CSI  LOC    PL   RQ   LOAD
TC 1  4.00 2X4   SP  #2         0.20 0.71 0.91 1- 2  6.85 0.75  74.0
TC 2  4.00 2X4   SP  #2         0.15 0.67 0.82 2- 3  6.85 0.75  74.0
TC 3 -4.00 2X4   SP  #2         0.15 0.67 0.82 3- 4  6.85 0.75  74.0
TC 4 -4.00 2X4   SP  #2         0.20 0.71 0.91 4- 5  6.85 0.75  74.0

BC 2  0.00 2X4   SP  #2         0.53 0.40 0.93 5- 6  9.05 1.00  20.0
BC 1  0.00 2X4   SP  #2         0.53 0.40 0.93  6    9.05 1.00  20.0
 NOTE---PLYWOOD FACTOR USED FOR TOP CHORD WHERE APPLICABLE

L-(SCARF /  HEEL /  SEAT)**R-(SCARF /  HEEL /  SEAT)**BUTT CUT**RBF
    0.81'    3.94"   0.00"     0.81'    3.94"   0.00"    0.25"  1.15

TC AXIAL FORCES
 1        2        3        4        5
 / -2814 / -2469 / -2469 / -2814 /

BC AXIAL FORCES
 1        7        6        5
 /  2655 /  1839 /  2655 /

--WEBS TO BE 2X4 SP  #3         UNLESS OTHERWISE NOTED---
 WEB   FORCE   SIZE  ----GRADE-----  BRACES

2- 7   -473
3- 7    735
3- 6    735
4- 6   -473
```

```
                        ALPINE     PLATES
CH=510  WB=448  WB=411  WB=372  DS= 600 MT= 735  ED=1
          REFER TO DRAWING FOR APPLICABLE PLATES
       NON-SPLICE           SPLICE         INTER-PANEL SPLICE
JT     PLATE JT TYPE      PLATE JT TYPE      PLATE    LOCATION
1       NA           *     3X6  0- 1          NA          1- 2
2 *   1.5X3  1-50          5X6  1- 3   *      3X4     #   2- 3
3       NA           *     4X4  2- 8   *      3X4     #   3- 4
4 *   1.5X3  1-50          5X6  1- 3          NA          4- 5
5       NA           *     3X6  0- 1          NA          5- 6
6 *     3X4  2-51          5X6  2- 8          NA          6- 5
7 *     3X4  2-51          5X6  2- 8   *      3X4         7- 6
   ALPINE    PL.AREA (1 MEM--BOTH FACES) =   242.0 SQ.IN.

 * = THIS PLATE USED IN CALCULATING PLATE AREA
NA = THIS JOINT IS NOT ALLOWED
 # = LOCATE INTER-PANEL SPLICE WITHIN ONE FOOT OF QUARTER POINT

JT     X-LOC    Y-LOC    LOAD   #MEM   MAPPINGS
1       0.29     0.15     512     2     2  7
2       7.41     2.64     507     3     3  7  1
3      14.00     4.84     488     4     4  6  7  2
4      20.59     2.64     507     3     5  6  3
5      27.71     0.15     512     2     6  4
6      18.40     0.15     181     4     7  3  4  5
7       9.60     0.15     181     4     1  2  3  6

                      DEFLECTIONS (INCHES)
     -----LIVE LOAD-----       -----DEAD LOAD-----
JT   XDEFL   YDEFL   L/XXX     XDEFL   YDEFL   L/XXX
5     0.06   *BRG*    ***       0.03   *BRG*    ***
6     ---    -0.19   L/999      ---    -0.11   L/999
7     ---    -0.19   L/999      ---    -0.11   L/999
1     0.00   *BRG*    ***       0.00   *BRG*    ***
```

FIG. 6.23 *(Continued).*

TABLE 6.4 Data Example Using PPSA *(Courtesy of K2 Engineering, Granger, Indiana.)*

```
************************************************
***                                          ***
***    PURDUE PLANE STRUCTURES ANALYZER 4.00 ***
***                                          ***
***              COPYRIGHT (1993)            ***
***         PURDUE RESEARCH FOUNDATION       ***
***                                          ***
***   THIS PROGRAM IS INTENDED TO FACILITATE ***
***   THE  ANALYSIS  OF WOOD STRUCTURES.  IT ***
***   GIVES AN ACCURATE REPORT OF STRUCTURAL ***
***   RESPONSE OF THE INPUT ANALOG.          ***
***   ACCURACY OF THE ANALOG AND INTERPRETA- ***
***   TION  OF  STRUCTURAL ADEQUACY ARE THE  ***
***   RESPONSIBILITY OF THE USER.            ***
***                                          ***
************************************************
 PPSA4 ANALYSIS OF A METAL PLATE TRUSS
==============================================================================


 NUMBER OF NODES                          = 14

 NUMBER OF MEMBERS                        = 25

 NUMBER OF ROLLER SUPPORTS                =  1

 NUMBER OF PINNED SUPPORTS                =  1

 NUMBER OF FIRL SUPPORTS                  =  0

 NUMBER OF FIXED SUPPORTS                 =  0

 NUMBER OF LOADING ARRANGEMENTS           =  1


 TABLE I            ALLOWABLE MEMBER STRESSES IN PSI
                          NORMAL LOAD DURATION

 MEMBER  USE         ALLOWABLE                                  MODULUS OF
 GROUP   TYPE   BEND    COMP    TENS     WIDTH     DEPTH     ELASTICITY

   1     S      1420.   1430.   780.     1.500     5.500  .1500E+07
   2     SI      750.    830.   450.     1.500     3.500  .1200E+07
   3     SI     1275.   1435.   750.     1.500     3.500  .1300E+07
```

in (15.21 m). The total load deflection is 1.193 in (30.3 mm) and the truss will be cambered during manufacturing for the total load deflection of 1.909 in (48.5 mm) as recommended in Table 6.6 or as specified by the truss designer.

The design process selects a joist pattern or geometry that complies with the input, stress, and fabrication limitations. The member force analysis is done by a displacement method using matrix analysis. The material component selection is optimized and the software checks the following controls:

1. Parallel-to-grain pin bearing
2. Perpendicular-to-grain pin bearing
3. Hankinson formula at the connections
4. Compression web check including ℓ/r

TABLE 6.4 Data Example Using PPSA *(Courtesy of K2 Engineering, Granger, Indiana.)* *(Continued)*

TABLE II NODE COORDINATES

NODE NO.	X-COORD (IN)	Y-COORD (IN)
1	.000	.000
2	75.000	25.000
3	100.000	.000
4	150.000	50.000
5	200.000	.000
6	225.000	75.000
7	300.000	.000
8	300.000	100.000
9	375.000	75.000
10	400.000	.000
11	450.000	50.000
12	500.000	.000
13	525.000	25.000
14	600.000	.000

TABLE III MEMBER LAYOUT

MEMBER NUMBER	NEGATIVE END NODE	NEGATIVE END CONDITION	POSITIVE END NODE	POSITIVE END CONDITION	MEMBER GROUP
1	1	PNND	2	RIGD	1
2	2	PNND	4	RIGD	1
3	4	PNND	6	RIGD	1
4	6	PNND	8	RIGD	1
5	8	PNND	9	RIGD	1
6	9	PNND	11	RIGD	1
7	11	PNND	13	RIGD	1
8	13	PNND	14	RIGD	1
9	1	RIGD	3	PNND	1
10	3	RIGD	5	PNND	1
11	5	RIGD	7	PNND	1
12	7	RIGD	10	PNND	1
13	10	RIGD	12	PNND	1
14	12	RIGD	14	PNND	1
15	2	PNND	3	PNND	2
16	3	PNND	4	PNND	2
17	4	PNND	5	PNND	2
18	5	PNND	6	PNND	2
19	6	PNND	7	PNND	2
20	7	PNND	8	PNND	3
21	7	PNND	9	PNND	2
22	9	PNND	10	PNND	2
23	10	PNND	11	PNND	2
24	11	PNND	12	PNND	2
25	12	PNND	13	PNND	2

TABLE IV REACTION CONDITIONS

NODE NUMBER	REACTION TYPE	HORIZ DISPL	VERT DISPL
1	ROLL	1.00	.00
14	PIN	.00	.00

TABLE 6.4 Data Example Using PPSA *(Courtesy of K2 Engineering, Granger, Indiana.) (Continued)*

TABLE V MEMBER PROPERTIES

MEMBER NUMBER	LENGTH (IN)	IN PLANE COLUMN (IN)	PRP PLANE COLUMN (IN)	BEAM LENGTH (IN)
1	79.057	.000	.000	.000
2	79.057	.000	.000	.000
3	79.057	.000	.000	.000
4	79.057	.000	.000	.000
5	79.057	.000	.000	.000
6	79.057	.000	.000	.000
7	79.057	.000	.000	.000
8	79.057	.000	.000	.000
9	100.000	.000	.000	.000
10	100.000	.000	.000	.000
11	100.000	.000	.000	.000
12	100.000	.000	.000	.000
13	100.000	.000	.000	.000
14	100.000	.000	.000	.000
15	35.355	.000	.000	.000
16	70.711	.000	.000	.000
17	70.711	.000	.000	.000
18	79.057	.000	.000	.000
19	106.066	.000	.000	.000
20	100.000	.000	.000	.000
21	106.066	.000	.000	.000
22	79.057	.000	.000	.000
23	70.711	.000	.000	.000
24	70.711	.000	.000	.000
25	35.355	.000	.000	.000

LOADING 1

THE LOAD DURATION FACTOR IS 1.15

TABLE VI B
THE STRUCTURE HAS UNIFORM LOADS AS FOLLOWS

MEMBER NUMBER	HORIZ COMP (PLI)	VERT COMP (PLI)
1	.000	-7.670
2	.000	-7.670
3	.000	-7.670
4	.000	-7.670
5	.000	-7.670
6	.000	-7.670
7	.000	-7.670
8	.000	-7.670
9	.000	-.330
10	.000	-.330
11	.000	-.330
12	.000	-.330
13	.000	-.330
14	.000	-.330

******************************** RESULTS ********************************

TABLE 6.4 Data Example Using PPSA *(Courtesy of K2 Engineering, Granger, Indiana.) (Continued)*

TABLE VII REACTIONS

REACTION NODE	HOR. COMP. (LBS)	VERT. COMP. (LBS)	MOMENT (IN-LBS)
1	.004	2400.001	.000
14	-.024	2400.016	-.001
SUM OF LOADS	.000	-4800.000	-.144E+07
SUM OF REACTS	-.020	4800.017	.144E+07
DIFFERENCE	.020	.017	9.375

*** STRENGTH ANALYSIS ***

TABLE VIII MEMBER END ACTIONS

MEMBER NUMBER	LOCATION	AXIAL (LBS)	SHEAR (LBS)	MOMENT (IN-LBS)
1	NEG END	6718.697	272.865	.000
	POS END	-6536.787	272.865	.000
2	NEG END	6263.926	272.865	.000
	POS END	-6082.016	272.865	.000
3	NEG END	5074.812	272.865	.000
	POS END	-4892.901	272.865	-.000
4	NEG END	3885.695	272.865	.000
	POS END	-3703.785	272.865	-.000
5	NEG END	3703.785	272.865	.000
	POS END	-3885.695	272.865	.000
6	NEG END	4892.922	272.865	.000
	POS END	-5074.833	272.865	.002
7	NEG END	6082.057	272.865	.000
	POS END	-6263.967	272.865	-.000
8	NEG END	6536.832	272.865	.000
	POS END	-6718.742	272.865	-.001
9	NEG END	-6287.624	16.500	.000
	POS END	6287.624	16.500	.000
10	NEG END	-5391.762	16.500	.000
	POS END	5391.762	16.500	.000
11	NEG END	-4495.884	16.500	-.002
	POS END	4495.884	16.500	.000
12	NEG END	-4495.876	16.500	-.002
	POS END	4495.876	16.500	.000

TABLE 6.4 Data Example Using PPSA *(Courtesy of K2 Engineering, Granger, Indiana.) (Continued)*

TABLE VIII — MEMBER END ACTIONS

MEMBER NUMBER	LOCATION	AXIAL (LBS)	SHEAR (LBS)	MOMENT (IN-LBS)
13	NEG END	-5391.762	16.500	-.000
	POS END	5391.762	16.500	.000
14	NEG END	-6287.646	16.500	-.000
	POS END	6287.646	16.500	.000
15	NEG END	610.133	.000	.000
	POS END	-610.133	.000	.000
16	NEG END	-656.812	.000	.000
	POS END	656.812	.000	.000
17	NEG END	938.552	.000	.000
	POS END	-938.552	.000	.000
18	NEG END	-734.358	.000	.000
	POS END	734.358	.000	.000
19	NEG END	1266.973	.000	.000
	POS END	-1266.973	.000	.000
20	NEG END	-1824.766	.000	.000
	POS END	1824.766	.000	.000
21	NEG END	1266.964	.000	.000
	POS END	-1266.964	.000	.000
22	NEG END	-734.355	.000	.000
	POS END	734.355	.000	.000
23	NEG END	938.566	.000	.000
	POS END	-938.566	.000	.000
24	NEG END	-656.832	.000	.000
	POS END	656.832	.000	.000
25	NEG END	610.143	.000	.000
	POS END	-610.143	.000	.000

5. Tension web check
6. Combined bending and compression at the connections
7. Combined flexural and axial tension loading on a panel
8. Combined flexural and axial compression loading on a panel (includes ℓ/d)

The lumber grade and the locations for changes in pin size and web gauge and diameter are included in the material selection process to optimize material usage while satisfying design criteria.

EXAMPLE 6.3: PITCHED CHORD TIMBER EXAMPLE Design a pitched-chord fan truss as shown in Fig. 6.25, given the following conditions. Assume all truss components will be single-piece glulam members arranged in a planar configuration.

TABLE 6.4 Data Example Using PPSA *(Courtesy of K2 Engineering, Granger, Indiana.) (Continued)*

TABLE IX NDS-91 INTERACTION ANALYSIS

USING MAX MOMENT AND MAX FORCE

MEMBER NUMBER - TYPE	ADDNL INFO	INT VAL	LOC FROM NEG END M (IN)	LOC FROM NEG END P (IN)	STRESS BENDING (PSI)	STRESS AXIAL (PSI)	L/D
1-S		1.102	39.53	.00	713.12	-814.39	14.374
2-S		1.022	39.53	.00	713.12	-759.26	14.374
3-S		.840	39.53	.00	713.12	-615.13	14.374
4-S		.693	39.53	.00	713.12	-470.99	14.374
5-S		.693	39.53	79.06	713.12	-470.99	14.374
6-S		.840	39.53	79.06	713.12	-615.13	14.374
7-S		1.022	39.53	79.06	713.12	-759.27	14.374
8-S		1.102	39.53	79.06	713.12	-814.39	14.374
9-S		.883	50.00	100.00	54.55	762.14	18.182
10-S		.762	50.00	100.00	54.55	653.55	18.182
11-S		.641	50.00	100.00	54.55	544.96	18.182
12-S		.641	50.00	100.00	54.55	544.95	18.182
13-S		.762	50.00	100.00	54.55	653.55	18.182
14-S		.883	50.00	100.00	54.55	762.14	18.182
15-SI		.127	35.36	35.36	.00	-116.22	8.081
16-SI		.242	70.71	70.71	.00	125.11	16.162
17-SI		.234	70.71	70.71	.00	-178.77	16.162
18-SI		.270	79.06	79.06	.00	139.88	18.070
19-SI		.481	106.07	106.07	.00	-241.33	24.244
20-SI		.403	100.00	100.00	.00	347.57	22.857
21-SI		.481	106.07	106.07	.00	-241.33	24.244
22-SI		.270	79.06	79.06	.00	139.88	18.070
23-SI		.234	70.71	70.71	.00	-178.77	16.162
24-SI		.242	70.71	70.71	.00	125.11	16.162
25-SI		.127	35.36	35.36	.00	-116.22	8.081

TABLE IXA MEMBER ANALYSIS DATA

MEMBER NUMBER	LENGTH (IN)	FINAL ADJUSTED STRESSES FAXIAL (PSI)	FBEND (PSI)	FBEND PRIME (PSI)	IN PLANE L/D	EFFECTIVE LENGTHS PERP PLANE L/D	BENDING LENGTH
1	79.057	-1279.81	1633.00	1633.00	14.37	.00	.00
2	79.057	-1279.81	1633.00	1633.00	14.37	.00	.00
3	79.057	-1279.81	1633.00	1633.00	14.37	.00	.00
4	79.057	-1279.81	1633.00	1633.00	14.37	.00	.00
5	79.057	-1279.81	1633.00	1633.00	14.37	.00	.00
6	79.057	-1279.81	1633.00	1633.00	14.37	.00	.00
7	79.057	-1279.81	1633.00	1633.00	14.37	.00	.00
8	79.057	-1279.81	1633.00	1633.00	14.37	.00	.00
9	100.000	897.00	1633.00	1633.00	18.18	.00	.00
10	100.000	897.00	1633.00	1633.00	18.18	.00	.00
11	100.000	897.00	1633.00	1633.00	18.18	.00	.00
12	100.000	897.00	1633.00	1633.00	18.18	.00	.00
13	100.000	897.00	1633.00	1633.00	18.18	.00	.00
14	100.000	897.00	1633.00	1633.00	18.18	.00	.00
15	35.355	-917.83	862.50	862.50	8.08	.00	.00
16	70.711	517.50	862.50	862.50	16.16	.00	.00
17	70.711	-764.23	862.50	862.50	16.16	.00	.00
18	79.057	517.50	862.50	862.50	18.07	.00	.00
19	106.066	-501.48	862.50	862.50	24.24	.00	.00
20	100.000	862.50	1466.25	1466.25	22.86	.00	.00
21	106.066	-501.48	862.50	862.50	24.24	.00	.00
22	79.057	517.50	862.50	862.50	18.07	.00	.00
23	70.711	-764.23	862.50	862.50	16.16	.00	.00
24	70.711	517.50	862.50	862.50	16.16	.00	.00
25	35.355	-917.83	862.50	862.50	8.08	.00	.00

TABLE 6.4 Data Example Using PPSA *(Courtesy of K2 Engineering, Granger, Indiana.) (Continued)*

TABLE X SHEAR STRESS ANALYSIS

MEMBER	MAX. SHEAR STRESS (PSI)	LOC. FROM NEG. END (IN)	MEMBER LENGTH (IN)
1	49.61	.000	79.057
2	49.61	.000	79.057
3	-49.61	79.057	79.057
4	-49.61	79.057	79.057
5	49.61	.000	79.057
6	49.61	.000	79.057
7	-49.61	79.057	79.057
8	-49.61	79.057	79.057
9	3.00	.000	100.000
10	3.00	.000	100.000
11	-3.00	100.000	100.000
12	-3.00	100.000	100.000
13	-3.00	100.000	100.000
14	-3.00	100.000	100.000
15	.00	35.355	35.355
16	.00	70.711	70.711
17	.00	70.711	70.711
18	.00	79.057	79.057
19	.00	106.066	106.066
20	.00	100.000	100.000
21	.00	106.066	106.066
22	.00	79.057	79.057
23	.00	70.711	70.711
24	.00	70.711	70.711
25	.00	35.355	35.355

*** DEFLECTION ANALYSIS ***

TABLE XI MAXIMUM MEMBER DEFLECTIONS

MEMBER	MAX. DEFL. (IN)	LOC. FROM NEG. END (IN)	MEMBER LENGTH (IN)
1	-.508	79.057	79.057
2	-.746	52.705	79.057
3	-.865	42.823	79.057
4	-.882	36.234	79.057
5	-.965	42.823	79.057
6	-.948	36.234	79.057
7	-.829	26.352	79.057
8	-.590	.000	79.057
9	-.664	100.000	100.000
10	-.838	100.000	100.000
11	-.862	62.500	100.000
12	-.862	37.500	100.000
13	-.838	.000	100.000
14	-.664	.000	100.000
15	-.619	35.355	35.355
16	-.485	70.711	70.711
17	-.711	70.711	70.711
18	-.177	79.057	79.057
19	-.697	106.066	106.066
20	.131	.000	100.000
21	-.512	.000	106.066
22	-.425	.000	79.057
23	-.526	.000	70.711
24	-.670	.000	70.711
25	-.434	.000	35.355

TABLE 6.4 Data Example Using PPSA *(Courtesy of K2 Engineering, Granger, Indiana.) (Continued)*

TABLE XII NODE DISPLACEMENTS

NODE NUMBER	DISPL. HORIZ. OR IN DIR. OF ROLLER (IN)	DISPLACEMENT VERTICAL (IN)	DISPLACEMENT ROTATIONAL (RADIANS)
1	-.261	.000	-.708E-02
2	-.115	-.573	-.291E-02
3	-.211	-.664	-.218E-02
4	-.089	-.775	.203E-02
5	-.167	-.838	-.608E-03
6	-.097	-.852	.367E-02
7	-.131	-.855	-.273E-03
8	-.131	-.828	.497E-02
9	-.164	-.852	.414E-02
10	-.094	-.838	.130E-02
11	-.172	-.775	.544E-02
12	-.051	-.664	.620E-02
13	-.146	-.573	.708E-02
14	.000	.000	.120E-01

FIG. 6.24 Composite wood-metal truss.

TABLE 6.5 Computer Output Example 6.2

```
Name: EXAMPLE 2              Location: ---------                Order #:  7-94-9000      4 FEBRUARY 94     12:01:41
Building Code: ICBO                                                       Horizontal                      Repetitive
Qty.     Type       Series      Profile        Depth(s)                   Pin to Pin                      Members
  1       A          TJM        PARALLEL       42.00"                     49'-11.00"                      NOT USED
Slope Perpendicular to Trusses:  0.250"/ft

----------------------------------- APPLICATION  LOADS  AND  TRUSS  DEFLECTIONS ---- LOAD GROUP # 1 @  48.0"  O.C.
Snow Roof        115% Stress   Live Load:  30.0 Psf        Dead Load:  18.0 Psf

Live Load Defl.:  1.193"  OR L/  502     Total Load Defl.:  1.909"  OR L/  314    Mid Span Camber:  1.313"  OR L/  456

****-------------   TRUSS CAPACITY MEETS OR EXCEEDS THE DESIGN LOAD REQUIREMENTS DESCRIBED ABOVE     --------------****
IMPORTANT! The  analysis  presented  below  is  output  from  software  developed  by   TRUS  JOIST  MacMILLAN.
Allowable  product  values  shown  are  in  accordance  with  current  TRUS  JOIST  MacMILLAN   materials  and
design  values.  TRUS  JOIST  MacMILLAN  engineering  has  verified  the  analysis.  The  input  loads  and
dimensions  have  been  provided  by  others  and  must  be  verified  and  approved  for  the  specific  application
by  the  design  professional  for  the  project.   Truss  design  values  have  been  accepted  by  the  following
agencies: CABO, ICBO, SBCCI, BOCA, NBCC, LAC AND OSA

--------------------------------------------- BUILDING  DIMENSIONS --------------------------------------------
                   Left Bearing                  Face to Face of                Right Bearing
                   Width  =                      Bearings  =                    Width   =

---------------------------------------------- TRUSS  INFORMATION ---------------------------------------------
    Left Clip: Z-CLIP                            Right Clip: Z-CLIP                                 Left         Right
    Reactions (Max/Min): 4888/ 1833 Lbs.          4888/ 1833 Lbs.           Top Chord Pin to End    6.00"        6.00"
    Bearings:  TOP PIN# 1                        TOP PIN# 12                Btm Chord Pin to End   28.79"       28.79"
    Top Chord Length = 50'-11.00" of          2- 2 X 4  2400FB MSR
    Btm Chord Length = 49'-10.00" of          2- 2 X 4  2400FB MSR

NOTE: Truss member forces listed are based on Load Group #1 Total Loads, as described above

   38.656   9 panels at 57.9653"                                                        38.656
   |-------|-------------------------------------------------------------------------|-------|
   B -3625 * -7593 *-12462 *-15945 .-18033 .-18730 .-18033 .-15945 *-12462 * -7593 * -3625 B
        -4947    -4613    -3479    -2315    -1159      -1     1158     2312     3483     4592     6027
Web# 1   2   3   4   5   6   7   8   9  10  11  11  10   9   8   7   6   5   4   3   2   1
     6027     4592     3483     2312     1158      -1    -1159    -2315    -3479    -4613    -4947
         *  4831 * 10367 * 14554 . 17337 . 18730 . 18730 . 17337 . 14554 * 10367 *  4831 *
   |---|-------|-------------------------------------------------------------|-------|---|
 28.98 38.613   8 panels at 57.9000"                                       38.613     28.98

(B) Truss Bearing Point               (*)     1 " Dia. Pin Location
(.)   5/8 " Dia. Pin Location          (-) Compressive Force
-------------------------------------------- WEB  INFORMATION -------------------------------------------------
Web Colors: 13ga.= Yellow, 14ga.= Green, 16ga.= Red, 18ga.= Black, 19ga.=Blue
Web#    Dia.-ga.  Holes  Length        Web#    Dia.-ga.  Holes  Length           Web#    Dia.-ga.  Holes  Length
 1      1.50013*  Large   48.19         4      1.50013   Large   48.19            8      1.50016   Small   48.19
 2      1.50013   Large   39.70         5, 6   1.50016   Large   48.19            9-11   1.12516   Small   48.19
 3      1.50014   Large   48.19         7      1.50016   Trans   48.19


@MUF:start          TRUS JOIST MacMILLAN     4 FEBRUARY 94      12:01:41              MANUFACTURING V3.10
@MUF:job             7-94-9000    DELAWARE PLANT            ICBO                      DEPTHS
@MUF:type                                 *  TYPE A          TJM          PARALLEL     42.00"
@MUF:appl           EXAMPLE 2             *  TOP TO TOP  BEARING          ROOF   115%              PR. LOAD = 192.0
@MUF:camber         ---------             *  BRG TO BRG SPAN = 49'-11.00"                         CAMBER =  1.313"
@MUF:reqd                                 *    1 REQD       51 LF/TRUSS       51 TOTAL L.F.    SPCG=  48.00" OC

@MUF:brdg           SHOP NOTES: 0 ROW(S) OF CHORD BRIDGING REQD AT:
@MUF:access                     MAIN TRUSS TYPE
@MUF:access                     ------ PRELIMINARY DESIGN ONLY ------

@MUF:brghdw         BEARINGS: TOP PIN# 1      Z-CLIP                          TOP PIN# 12     Z-CLIP

                     B --- * --- * --- * ---  . ---  . ---  . ---  . --- * --- * --- * --- B
                      1   / 3   / 5   / 7   / 9   /11   /10   / 8   / 6   / 4   / 2   /
                        \ 2   \ 4   \ 6   \ 8   \10   \11   \ 9   \ 7   \ 5   \ 3   \ 1
                          * --- * --- * ---  . ---  . ---  . ---  . ---  . --- * --- * --- *
@MUF:pins           ( * )     1"     DIA. PIN LOCATION      TOP  4@1"        4@5/8"      4@1"
@MUF:pins           ( . )     5/8"   DIA. PIN LOCATION      BTM  3@1"        5@5/8"      3@1"
                    -----------------------------------------------------------------------------------------
@MUF:chdlbr         TOP CHORD           1 REQD        2- 2 X 4 2400FB MSR                TOTAL LGTH=  50'-11.00"
@MUF:chdpin         LEFT END TO PIN =   6.00"          PIN TO PIN = 49'-11.00"         RIGHT PIN TO END =  6.00"
@MUF:chdpnl         PANELS:          1 AT 38.6562    9 AT 57.9653    1 AT 38.6562
                    ACCUMULATIVE PANEL LIST   FT. & IN.   RIGHT TO LEFT
                     0  6.00   3  8.66   8  6.62  13  4.59  18  2.55  23  0.52  27 10.48  32  8.45  37  6.41
                    42  4.38  47  2.34  50  5.00  50 11.00

@MUF:chdlbr         BTM CHORD           1 REQD        2- 2 X 4 2400FB MSR                TOTAL LGTH=  49'-10.00"
@MUF:chdpin         LEFT END TO PIN =  28.79"          PIN TO PIN = 45'- 0.43"         RIGHT PIN TO END = 28.79"
                    CAMBER SETTINGS:     0.0436              0.0653             0.0436
@MUF:chdpnl         PANELS:          1 AT 38.6127    8 AT 57.9000    1 AT 38.6127
                     2  4.79   5  7.40  10  5.30  15  3.20  20  1.10  24 11.00  29  8.90  34  6.80  39  4.70
                    44  2.60  47  5.21  49 10.00
                    -----------------------------------------------------------------------------------------
                     7-94-9000    TYPE: A                                   # PINS; S=     9, L=    14          ROOF
                    TUBE FTG  1.12516=    26' 1.50016=    35' 1.50014=     9' 1.50013=    25'
                    WEB#     DIA.-GA.  HOLES  LENGTH    QTY         WEB#    DIA.-GA.  HOLES  LENGTH    QTY
@MUF:tbg             1       1.50013*  LARGE   48.19      2          5,6    1.50016   LARGE   48.19      4
@MUF:tbg             2       1.50013   LARGE   39.70      2          7      1.50016   TRANS   48.19      2
@MUF:tbg             3       1.50014   LARGE   48.19      2          8      1.50016   SMALL   48.19      2
@MUF:tbg             4       1.50013   LARGE   48.19      2          9-11   1.12516   SMALL   48.19      6      @MUF:end
```

TABLE 6.6 Recommended Deflection Limits for Trusses

		Recommended camber*	Min. recommended camber*
Roof	Snow load location:		
	Flat roofs	TLΔ	DL + ½ LLΔ
	Sloped roofs (⅛ in per foot—minimum)	DLΔ + ½ LLΔ	DLΔ + ¼ LLΔ
	Short-span residential flat roofs	DLΔ + ½ LLΔ	DLΔ + ¼ LLΔ
	Non-snow-load locations: all roofs	1½ DLΔ	1¼ DLΔ
Floor	All floors	1½ DLΔ	DLΔ

Note: Movable partition loads are not to be considered in this policy.
*DLΔ = dead-load deflection; LLΔ = live-load deflection; TLΔ = total-load deflection.

Design Assumptions

Span = 48 ft center to center of supports.

Truss spacing = 12 ft center to center.

Panel point spacing = 12 ft.

Pitch = 4/12.

The truss layout is as shown in the figure. The bottom chord of the truss is assumed to be braced laterally at 12-ft intervals, and the top chord is assumed to be braced laterally at the panel points by the stringers. It should be noted that this

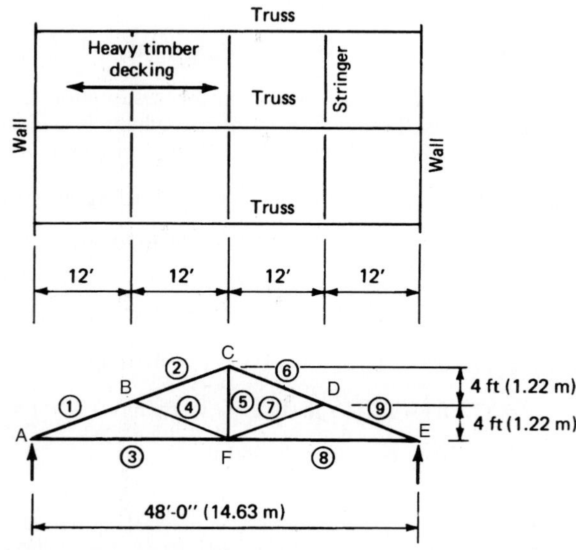

FIG. 6.25 Building plan and truss geometry for Example 6.3.

is a conservative assumption, since the heavy timber decking will be nailed directly to the compression chord thus providing additional lateral stability.

Truss Loading

Dead load (DL) = 15 lb/ft² } (applied to horizontal projection of roof
Snow load (SL) = 20 lb/ft² } framing)
Wind load (WL) = 25 lb/ft² (applied as shown on load diagram).

Material Property Assumptions. All truss components will be glulam Douglas fir using stress combination A-2. The tabulated design values for these combinations per NDS[6] Supplement are as follows:

F_t = 1250 lb/in².
F_c = 1900 lb/in².
F_b = 1700 lb/in².
F_v = 165 lb/in².
$E = 1.7 \times 10^6$ lb/in².
$F_{c\perp}$ = 560 lb/in².
Steel plates to be ASTM A36.
Steel bolts to be ASTM A307.

In order to achieve the desired architectural effect, the designer has specified a minimum member size of 5⅛ × 6 in.

Determine member forces assuming pinned joints: Calculate the panel-point loads P as follows: For the snow load plus dead load,

$$\text{Panel points } A \text{ and } E\text{: } P_A = P_B = (12 \text{ ft})(6 \text{ ft})(15 \text{ lb/ft}^2 + 20 \text{ lb/ft}^2) = 2520 \text{ lb}$$

$$\text{Panel points } B, C, \text{ and } D\text{: } P_B = P_c = P_D = 2P_A = 5040 \text{ lb}$$

Note: The preceding calculations are based on the assumption that all loads are applied to the panel points through the stringers, which is a desirable framing system because it results in negligible bending of the top chord.

For the wind load plus dead load, with the wind load acting as a suction force,

$$\text{Panel point } A\text{: } P_A = (12 \text{ ft})(12 \text{ ft}) \frac{[(15 \text{ lb/ft}^2) - (25 \text{ lb/ft}^2)(0.75)^*]}{2} = -270 \text{ lb}$$

$$\text{Panel point } B\text{: } P_B = (12 \text{ ft})(12 \text{ ft})[(15 \text{ lb/ft}^2) - (25 \text{ lb/ft}^2)(0.75)^*] = -540 \text{ lb}$$

$$\text{Panel point } D\text{: } P_D = (12 \text{ ft})(12 \text{ ft})[(15 \text{ lb/ft}^2) - (25 \text{ lb/ft}^2)(0.70)^*] = -360 \text{ lb}$$

$$\text{Panel point } E\text{: } P_E = (12 \text{ ft})(6 \text{ ft})[(15 \text{ lb/ft}^2) - (25 \text{ lb/ft}^2)(0.70)^*] = -180 \text{ lb}$$

$$\text{Panel point } C\text{: } P_C = -270 + (-180) = -450 \text{ lb}$$

*It is assumed that WL coefficients are based on height of structure, exposure, roof slope, direction of wind, etc. The designer is referred to the applicable building code for the determination of these coefficients for any specific design case.

Member Forces for Load Case I. For a full SL plus DL*

Member	Force, lb	Member	Force, lb
1	−23,900	6	−15,900
2	−15,900	7	−7,970
3	+22,700	8	+22,700
4	−7,970	9	−23,900
5	+5,040		

Member Forces for Load Case II. For a full unbalanced snow load on half of truss plus DL (unbalanced SL + DL)*

Member	Force, lb	Member	Force, lb
1	−19,400	6	−11,400
2	−11,400	7	−3,420
3	+18,400	8	+14,000
4	−7,970	9	−14,800
5	+3,600		

Member Forces for Load Case III. For WL plus DL*

Member	Force, lb	Member	Force, lb
1	+2,280	6	+1,420
2	+1,420	7	+569
3	−2,160	8	−1,890
4	+854	9	+1,990
5	−450		

Summary of Member Forces Based on Pinned Joints

Member	DL + SL*, lb	DL + USL, lb	DL + WL, lb
1 TC	−23,900	−19,400	+2,280
2 TC	−15,900	−11,400	+1,420
3 BC	+22,700	+18,400	−2,160
4 W	−7,970	−7,970	+854
5 W	+5,040	+3,600	−450
6 TC	−15,900	−11,400	+1,420
7 W	−7,970	−3,420	+569
8 BC	+22,700	+14,000	−1,890
9 TC	−23,900	−14,800	+1,990

*+ = tension; − = compression.

A review of the preceeding axial forces indicates that full DL + SL controls member sizing. However, the designer is cautioned to evaluate the effects of stress reversals which occur due to WL + DL loading.

Determining Peliminary Size of Truss Members: Check the top chord. The maximum compression force occuring in the top chord is

$$P_{TC} = 23{,}900 \text{ lb}$$

Try a 5⅛- by 5-in glulam member:

$$A = 30.75 \text{ in}^2 \qquad \text{and} \qquad S = 30.75 \text{ in}^3$$

Check the top chord as an unbraced column between panel points:

$$\ell_2 = \sqrt{12^2 + 4^2} = 12.65 \text{ ft} \quad \text{or} \quad 151.8 \text{ in}$$

Therefore,

$$\frac{\ell_e}{d} = \frac{152}{5.125} = 29.62$$

Determine the column-stability factor C_p:

$$C_p = \frac{1 + (F_{cE}/F_c^*)}{2c} - \sqrt{\left(\frac{1 + (F_{cE}/F_c^*)}{2c}\right)^2 - \frac{F_{cE}/F_c^*}{c}}$$

$$\text{where } F_{cE} = \frac{K_{cE}\,E'}{(l_e/d)^2} = \frac{0.418\,(1.7 \times 10^6)}{(29.62)^2} = 810 \text{ psi}$$

$$F_c^* = F_c \times C_D = 1900\,(1.15) = 2185 \text{ psi}$$

$$c = 0.9$$

$$\frac{F_{cE}}{F_c^*} = \frac{810}{2185} = 0.371$$

$$\text{Thus, } C_p = \frac{1 + 0.371}{2\,(0.9)} - \sqrt{\left[\frac{1 + 0.371}{2\,(0.9)}\right]^2 - \frac{0.371}{0.9}} = 0.352$$

Determine the allowable compression design value F_c':

$$F_c' = F_c^* \times C_p = 2185\,(0.352) = 769 \text{ psi}$$

$$f_c = \frac{23{,}900}{30.75} = 777 \text{ psi} \approx 769 \text{ psi}$$

Since $f_c \approx F_c'$ for the 5⅛- by 6-in size, it may not be adequate to resist the stresses once the gross cross section has been reduced for connectors. Increase the size to 5⅛ by 7½ in.

Check the bottom chord. The maximum tension force in the bottom chord is

$$T_{BC} = 22{,}700 \text{ lb}$$

Determine the allowable tension design value F_t':

$$F_t' = F_t \cdot C_D$$

$$= 1250\ (1.15) = 1437\ \text{lb/in}^2$$

The minimum cross-sectional area is

$$A_{\text{reg}} = \frac{22{,}700}{1437} = 15.79\ \text{in}^2$$

Use a 5⅛- by 7½-in member for preliminary sizing

$$A = 5.125(7.5) = 38.44\ \text{in}^2$$

While this section is somewhat larger than required, it accounts for the gross section reduction which will occur at the connections and the possible moment induced in the bottom chord due to truss deflection.

Check the web members. The maximum tension and compression forces are

$$T_{\max} = +\ 5040\ \text{lb} \qquad \text{and} \qquad P_{\max} = -7970\ \text{lb}$$

Try 5⅛- by 6-in members. Check compression web 4 as an unbraced column using the critical least dimension for buckling:

$$\ell_e = \sqrt{12^2 + 4^2} = 12.65 f_t = 152\ \text{in}$$

$$\frac{\ell_e}{d} = 29.62\ \text{in}$$

As before, $C_p = 0.352$ and $F_c' = 769\ \text{lb/in}^2$, so

$$f_c = \frac{7970}{30.75} = 259\ \text{lb/in}^2 < F_c' = 769\ \text{lb/in}^2$$

Check tension web:

$$f_t = \frac{5040}{30.75} = 164\ \text{lb/in}^2 < F_t' = 1437\ \text{lb/in}^2$$

Design Connections. Connections are designed on the assumption that they will be pinned and not significantly resist rotation. As per the designer's specifications, all member sizes are at least 5⅛ by 6 in nominal in section. All connections are designed so as to have concentric lines of force to avoid possible problems caused by secondary moments resulting from eccentricities.

Design of Heel Connections. Use 4-in-diameter shear plates with ¾-in bolts. Determine the number of connectors required in the bottom chord.

The capacity of a 4-in shear plate with steel side plates, ¾-in bolt, using species group B, loaded parallel to grain per NDS[7] or Chap. 5 is

$$P' = P \times C_D \times C_g \times C_{ST}$$

$$= 4320(1.15)(1.11)C_g = 5514C_g$$

However, the maximum load cpacity for a 4-in shear plate is 4400 lb. This will control the application, so

$$P' = 4400 \text{ lb}$$

Number of shear plates required is

$$\frac{22{,}700}{4400} = 5.2$$

Try six shear plates with ¼- by 4½-in side plates.

Check the side plates:

$$A_{\text{gross}} = (0.25)(4.5)(2.0) = 2.25 \text{ in}^2$$

$$A_{\text{net}} = (0.25)(2)(4.5 - 0.81) = 1.85 \text{ in}^2$$

$$\text{Allowable capacity (gross)} = 0.60F_y A_{\text{gross}}$$

$$= (22{,}000)(2.25)$$

$$= 49{,}500 \text{ lb} > 22{,}700 \text{ lb}$$

$$\text{Allowable capacity (net)} = 0.50F_u A_{\text{net}}$$

$$= (29{,}000)(1.85)$$

$$= 53{,}650 \text{ lb} > 22{,}700 \text{ lb}$$

Check group action for three fasteners in a row. Obtain the group action factor C_g from Chap. 7 of the NDS[6]:

$$\text{Area of main member } A_M = 5.125(7.5) = 38.43 \text{ in}^2$$

$$\text{Area of side plates } A_s = 0.25(4.5)(2) = 2.25 \text{ in}^2$$

$$\frac{A_M}{A_s} = \frac{38.43}{2.25} = 17.08$$

$$C_g = 0.96$$

Verify that the shear-plate maximum load limit controls:

$$5414(0.96) = 5197 \text{ lb} > 4400 \text{ lb}$$

Note: The preceding analysis assumes that both minimum end distance and minimum fastener spacing are provided; i.e., end distance = 7 in and fastener spacing = 9 in if 100 percent of load capacity is used.

Check end-grain bearing of top chord on heel back plate. Assume a 4½-in-high heel plate. Using Hankinson's formula (see Sect. 5.5 or Appendix J of the NDS[6]):

$$F'_{c\theta} = \frac{F'_g \times F'_{c\perp}}{F'_g \sin^2 \theta + F'_{c\perp} \cos^2 \theta}$$

where $\theta = 18.4°$
$F'_{c\perp} = F_{c\perp} = 560 \text{ lb/in}^2$
$F'_g = F'_c = F_c \times C_D = 1900(1.15) = 2185 \text{ lb/in}^2$

$$\text{Thus } F'_{c18.4} = \frac{2185(560)}{2185 \sin^2 (18.4) + 560 \cos^2 (18.4)}$$

$$= 1695 \text{ lb/in}^2$$

$$f_c = \frac{23{,}900}{5.125(4.5)} = 1036 \text{ lb/in}^2 < 1695 \text{ lb/in}^2$$

Assume that one ¾-in bolt is used in the top chord to resist tension under WL + DL uplift loading. The nominal design values of the bolt in Douglas fir–larch with ¼-in steel side plates for a member having a thickness of 5⅛ in and loaded parallel to grain or perpendicular to grain are as follows (see Table 8.3D in the NDS[6]):

$$Z_{\parallel} = 3170 \text{ lb} \qquad \text{and} \qquad Z_{\perp} = 1800 \text{ lb}$$

For tension in the top chord due to WL + DL:

$$T_{TC} = 2280 \text{ lb}$$

Allowable bolt design value Z':

$$Z' = Z \times C_D \times C_\Delta$$

Determine the geometry factor C_Δ: Assume that the actual end distance is 4½ in. The end distance required for full load is = $7D$ = 5¼ in:

$$C_\Delta = \frac{4\frac{1}{2}}{5\frac{1}{4}} = 0.86$$

$$Z' = 3170(1.60)(0.86) = 4362 \text{ lb} > 2280 \text{ lb}$$

For wind uplift tension on the bolt due to WL + DL:

$$T_{\text{bolt}} = 990 \text{ lb}$$

Determine the geometry factor C_Δ: Assume that the actual end distance provided is 3½ in. The end distance required for full load is 5¼ in:

$$C_\Delta = \frac{3\frac{1}{2}}{5\frac{1}{4}} = 0.67$$

Allowable bolt design value Z':

$$Z' = \frac{3170(1800)(1.60)(0.67)}{3170 (\sin^2 71.6) + 1800 (\cos^2 71.6)} = 2016 \text{ lb} > 990 \text{ lb}$$

Note: The side plates should be checked for buckling under compressive load caused by DL + WL. If buckling is found to be critical, a tie bolt should be installed.

Recheck the tension chord for net section reduction caused by 4-in shear plates and ¾-in bolts.

$$A_{\text{gross}} = 5\tfrac{1}{8} \times 7\tfrac{1}{2} \text{ in} = 38.44 \text{ in}^2$$

$$\text{Projected area of connector units} = 8.25 \text{ in}^2$$

Therefore,

$$\text{Net section} = 38.44 - 8.25 = 30.19 \text{ in}^2$$

$$f_t = \frac{22{,}700}{30.19} = 752 \text{ lb/in}^2 < F_t' = 1437 \text{ lb/in}^2$$

Design of Web Connections. Side plates should be connected to all web members using a minimum of two bolts.

Determine the number of bolts for attachment of the web members: The maximum web forces are

$$T = +5040 \text{ lb} \qquad (\text{DL} + \text{SL})$$

$$P = -7970 \text{ lb} \qquad (\text{DL} + \text{SL})$$

For field erection purposes, use ¾-in bolts, as were used in conjunction with 4-in shear plates. The nominal design value of a ¾-in bolt used in 5⅛-in-wide Douglas fir–larch loaded parallel to grain with steel side plates is 3170 lb. The allowable bolt design value Z' is

$$Z' = Z \times C_D \times C_g$$

$$= (3170)(1.15)(1.0) = 3645 \text{ lb}$$

$$T = \frac{5040}{3645} = 1.38 \qquad (\text{req. 2 bolts})$$

$$P = \frac{7970}{3645} = 2.19 \qquad (\text{req. 3 bolts})$$

Three ¾-in bolts are sufficient for side plate to web connection of all web members. This assumes a minimum end distance of seven bolt diameters (5¼ in) and minimum spacing of four bolt diameters (3 in).

Check web-to-chord connection at joint B:

$$P = -7970 \text{ lb} \qquad (\text{DL} + \text{SL})$$

$$P_T = P \cos 36.8°$$

$$= -7970 \cos 36.8° = -6382 \text{ lb}$$

$$P_N = P \sin 36.8°$$

$$= -7970 \sin 36.8° = -4774 \text{ lb}$$

The allowable design values of a single 4-in shear plate with ¾-in bolts are

$$P' = 4320(1.15) = 4968 \text{ lb} > 4400 \text{ lb} \qquad \text{(use 4400 lb)}$$

$$Q' = 3000(1.15) = 3450 \text{ lb}$$

Try two 4-in shear plates. Allowable design value parallel to grain is

$$P' = 2(4400) = 8800 \text{ lb} > 6382 \text{ lb}$$

Allowable design value perpendicular to grain is

$$Q' = 2(3450) = 6900 \text{ lb} > 4774 \text{ lb}$$

As with the heel connection, use ¼- by 4½-in steel plates.

Check the compression chord for net section reduction caused by a 4-in shear plate and a ¾-in bolt connector unit.

$$A_{gross} = 5\tfrac{1}{8} \times 7\tfrac{1}{2} \text{ in} = 38.44 \text{ in}^2$$

$$\text{Projected area of connector unit} = 8.25 \text{ in}^2$$

Therefore,

$$\text{Net section} = 30.19 \text{ in}^2$$

$$f_c = \frac{23{,}900 \text{ lb}}{30.19 \text{ in}^2} = 791 \text{ lb/in}^2 < 810 \text{ lb/in}^2$$

Webs to Bottom Chord Connections. The largest imbalance of bottom chord forces occurs for DL + USL and governs this design. The connector must be adequate to carry this imbalance in the parallel-to-grain direction.

$$\text{Net horizontal force} = 18{,}400 - 14{,}000 \text{ lb} \qquad \text{(DL + USL)}$$

$$= 4400 \text{ lb}$$

Use two 4-in shear plates with a ¾-in bolt:

$$\text{Allowable design value} = (4400)(2)$$

$$= 8800 \text{ lb} > 4400 \text{ lb}$$

Although the connection is overdesigned, the consistent use of similar hardware reduces fabrication and assembly costs and minimizes possible assembly mistakes in the field.

Check Ridge Connection. The geometry of the ridge saddle is determined by the required end distance of bolts A under DL + WL conditions resulting in tension of the top chord. The maximum tension force to be resisted by bolt A is 2280 lb (DL + WL).

The nominal design value for a ¾-in bolt is 3170 lb parallel to grain, as previously determined. The allowable design value is

$$Z' = Z \times C_D \times C_\Delta$$

with a minimum end distance of 5¼ in. Assume that bolts are located 3½ in from the end of the compression chord to minimize connector steel requirements. The geometry factor, then, is

$$C_\Delta = \frac{3\frac{1}{2}}{5\frac{1}{4}} = 0.67$$

$$Z' \;\; 3170(1.60)(0.67) = 3398 \text{ lb} > 2280 \text{ lb}$$

Determine the bearing area required for the top plates. Maximum tension load in member 5 is 5040 lb. Therefore,

$$A_{req} = \frac{5040 \text{ lb}}{560 \text{ lb/in}^2} = 9.0 \text{ in}^2$$

The maximum load to be resisted by bolt B is 5040 lb. This load will be transmitted through the steel only.

The allowable design value for two 4-in shear plates with ¾-in bolt in double shear is 8800 lb, which is >5040 lb. The design of the strap checked on the heel connection with a higher load, and this is therefore acceptable.

$$\text{Allowable bearing load on } \tfrac{1}{2}\text{-in material} = 32.6 \text{ kips}$$

Check Buckling Capacity of Steel Side Plates. Typical plate is ¼ by 4½ in by varying length. Use A36 steel.

At heel connection,

$$\ell = 21.5 \text{ in} \qquad r = \frac{d}{\sqrt{12}} = \frac{0.25}{\sqrt{12}} = 0.0722$$

$$\text{Therefore } \frac{K\ell}{r} = \frac{(1)(21.5)}{0.0722} = 298 > 200 \qquad \text{WHICH IS THE ALLOWABLE VALUE}$$

Solve for maximum ℓ:

$$\text{Set } \frac{K\ell}{r} = 200$$

$$\ell_{max} = \frac{(200)(0.0722)}{1}$$

$$= 14.44 \text{ in (say 14.25 in)}$$

Therefore, check as long column, from Table 3-36 of the AISC *Manual of Steel Construction,*[10]

$$\text{Allowable stress} = 3.73 \text{ kips/in}^2$$

$$\text{Actual stress} = 2280 \text{ lb/(2)(4.5)(0.25)}$$

$$= 1.01 \text{ kips/in}^2 < 3.73 \text{ kips/in}^2$$

At diagonal web, as before,

$$\ell_{max} = 14.25 \text{ in}$$

Therefore, for the long column,

$$\text{Allowable stress} = 3.73 \text{ kips/in}^2$$

$$\text{Actual maximum stress} = \frac{7970 \text{ lb}}{2(4.5)(0.25)}$$

$$= 3.54 \text{ kips/in}^2 < 3.73 \text{ kips/in}^2$$

It has been shown that the maximum unsupported length of a tie strap is 14¼ in. Therefore, any tie strap having greater than 14¼-in bolt spacing in adjoining members is tied together with a ¾-in through bolt at a maximum of 14¼-in intervals.

Check Weld Sizes. At heel connection,

$$F_{max} = 22{,}700 \text{ lb} \qquad (\text{DL} + \text{SL})$$

$$\text{Weld force} = \frac{22.7}{(2)(4.5)} = 2.52 \text{ kips/in}$$

Assume ³⁄₁₆-in fillet weld with E70 electrode:

$$\text{Allowable shear stress} = (0.3)(70 \text{ kips/in}^2) = 21 \text{ kips/in}^2$$

$$q_{allow} = 0.707(D)(21)$$

$$= (0.707)(3/16)(21)$$

$$= 2.78 \text{ kips/in} > 2.52 \text{ kips/in}$$

Therefore, use ³⁄₁₆-in fillet welds for heel connection.

At ridge connection, assume a ³⁄₁₆-in fillet weld with E70 electrode:

$$\text{Weld force} = 2.4 \text{ kips}/2\ell$$

$$\text{Allowable shear stress} = 2.78 \text{ kips/in}$$

$$\text{Required weld length} = \frac{2.4 \text{ kips}}{(2.78 \text{ kips/in})(2)} = 0.43 \text{ in}$$

Therefore, use a ³⁄₁₆-in fillet weld for the ridge connection.

EXAMPLE 6.4: PARALLEL CHORD TIMBER TRUSS Design a parallel chord truss as shown in Fig. 6.26 given the span and loading conditions shown. Assume that loads are applied directly to the top chord through heavy timber decking, thus bracing the chord continuously. Assume that the top chord consists of two continuous-length members spliced at midspan. Therefore, panel forces and moments are based on a four-span continuous-beam analysis under uniformly distributed load with the panel points acting as unyielding supports. Further assume that all truss components will be solid sawn timbers using double members for the top and bottom chords and single members for the webs. For purposes of demonstrating

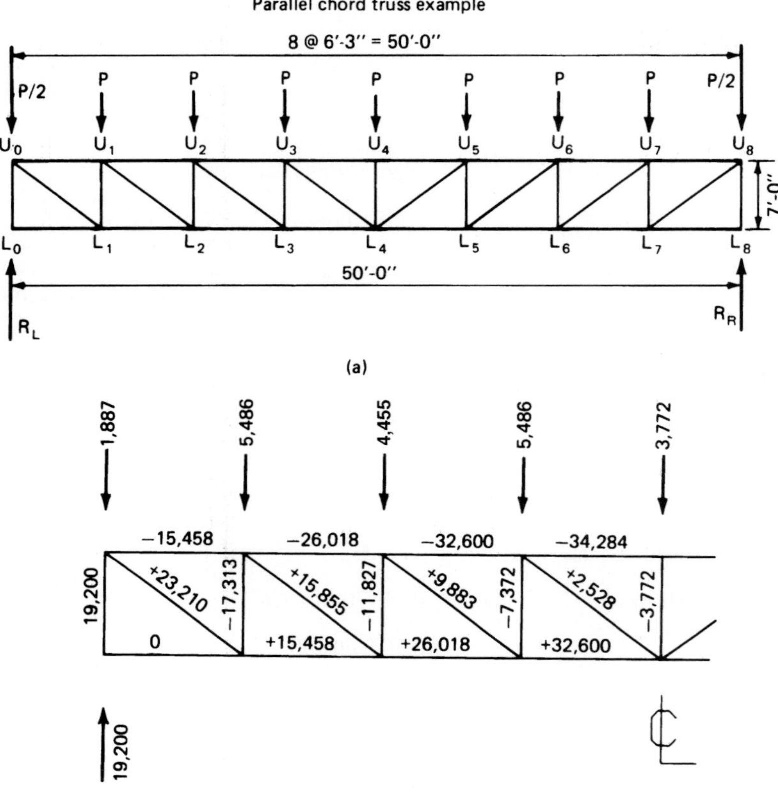

FIG. 6.26 (*a*) Geometry of parallel chord truss and (*b*) member forces. *Note:* All loads and forces are in pounds.

the analysis procedure only full snow load plus dead load is considered in this example. Refer to Example 6.3 for other possible loading conditions.

A truss depth of 84 in (213.36 cm) measured center to center of the top and bottom chord members was selected. The member forces were determined by the method of joints, and the deflection was calculated by the virtual work method. The member sizing is based on the material selection given in the example assuming seasoned untreated lumber in a dry use service condition and a duration of load of 1.15 (i.e., snow loading). The joint connection design is not discussed but would be similar to the connection designs illustrated in Examples 6.3 and 6.5.

Parallel Chord Truss Configuration and Loading. Assume the following:

Trusses are spaced at 16 ft (4.88 m) on center.

Dead load (DL) = 18 lb/ft^2 (0.86 kPa).

Snow load (SL) = 30 lb/ft^2 (1.43 kPa).

Total load (TL) = 48 lb/ft^2 (2.29 kPa).

A uniformly distributed design load is applied to each truss: $w = 48(16) = 768$ lb/ft (11.2 kN/m).

Panel-point loads shown in Fig. 6.26*b* were determined based on the assumption that the top chord consists of two four-span continuous members spliced at the truss centerline.

End reaction $R = 19{,}200$ lb.

Midspan bending moment $M = 240{,}000$ ft·lb.

Determine Member Forces by Method of Joints. (See Fig. 6.26*a* and *b* for member identification and loading.)

$$(U_0L_1)_V = 19{,}200 - 1887 = 17{,}313 \text{ lb}$$

$$(U_0L_1)_H = (U_0L_1)_V \tan\theta = 15{,}458 \text{ lb}$$

$$U_0U_1 = (U_0L_1)_H = 15{,}458 \text{ lb compression}$$

$$U_0L_1 = \sqrt{(17{,}313)^2 + (15{,}458)^2} = 23{,}210 \text{ lb tension}$$

$$U_1L_1 = (U_0L_1)_V = 17{,}313 \text{ lb compression}$$

$$L_1L_2 = (U_0L_1)_H = 15{,}458 \text{ lb tension}$$

$$(U_1L_2)_V = U_1L_1 - P = 17{,}313 - 5486 = 11{,}827 \text{ lb}$$

$$(U_1L_2)_H = (U_1L_2)_V \tan\theta = 10{,}560 \text{ lb}$$

$$U_1U_2 = U_0U_1 + (U_1L_2)_H = 15{,}458 + 10{,}560 = 26{,}018 \text{ lb compression}$$

$$U_1L_2 = \sqrt{(11{,}827)^2 + (10{,}560)^2} = 15{,}855 \text{ lb tension}$$

$$L_2L_3 = L_1L_2 + (U_1L_2)_H = 15{,}458 + 10{,}560 = 26{,}018 \text{ lb tension}$$

$$U_2L_2 = (U_1L_2)_V = 11{,}827 \text{ lb compression}$$

$$(U_2L_3)_V = U_2L_2 - P = 11{,}827 - 4455 = 7372 \text{ lb}$$

$$(U_2L_3)_H = (U_2L_3)_V \tan\theta = 6582 \text{ lb}$$

$$U_2U_3 = (U_2L_3)_H + U_1U_2 = 6582 + 26{,}018 = 32{,}600 \text{ lb compression}$$

$$U_2L_3 = \sqrt{(7372)^2 + (6582)^2} = 9883 \text{ lb tension}$$

$$L_3L_4 = L_2L_3 + (U_2L_3)_H = 26{,}018 + 6582 = 32{,}600 \text{ lb tension}$$

$$U_3L_3 = (U_2L_3)_V = 7372 \text{ lb compression}$$

$$(U_3L_4)_V = U_3L_3 - P = 7372 - 5486 = 1886 \text{ lb}$$

$$(U_3L_4)_H = (U_3L_4)_V \tan\theta = 1684 \text{ lb}$$

$$U_3U_4 = U_2U_3 + (U_3L_4)_H = 32{,}600 + 1684 = 34{,}284 \text{ lb compression}$$

$$U_3L_4 = \sqrt{(1886)^2 + (1684)^2} = 2528 \text{ lb tension}$$

$$U_3U_4 = U_4U_5 = 34{,}284 \text{ lb}$$

$$U_4L_4 = P = 3772 \text{ lb compression}$$

$$(U_5L_4)_V = P - (U_3L_4)_V = 3772 - 1886 = 1886 \text{ lb}$$

$$(U_5L_4)_H = (U_5L_4)_V \tan\theta = 1684 \text{ lb}$$

$$L_4L_5 = L_3L_4 = 32{,}600 \text{ lb tension}$$

$$U_5L_4 = 2528 \text{ lb tension}$$

See Fig. 6.26*b* for summary of member forces.

Tabulated Design Values. Assume select structural Douglas fir–larch members (used at 19 percent maximum moisture content) are to be used for all truss members. The tabulated design values given in the NDS Supplement,[6] "Design Values for Wood Construction," are as follows:

$$F_t = 1000 \text{ lb/in}^2$$

$$F_c = 1700 \text{ lb/in}^2$$

$$F_b = 1450 \text{ lb/in}^2$$

$$F_v = 95 \text{ lb/in}^2$$

$$E = 1.9 \times 10^6 \text{ lb/in}^2$$

$$F_{c\perp} = 625 \text{ lb/in}^2$$

Assume the truss consists of double-member top and bottom chords and single-member webs.

Determine the size of the bottom chord members:

$$\text{Maximum tension force} = 32{,}600 \text{ lb}$$

Allowable tension design value F'_t:

$$F'_t = F_t \times C_D \times C_F \qquad (\text{assume } C_F = 1.2, \text{ width} = 8 \text{ in})$$

$$= 1000(1.15)(1.2) = 1380 \text{ lb/in}^2$$

$$\text{Area required } A_r = \frac{32{,}600}{1380} = 23.62 \text{ in}^2$$

Try two 3- by 8-in members. Assume that one line of ¾-in bolts will be used at connections (bolt holes = 13⁄16 in).

$$\text{Net area} = 2(2.5)(7.25 - 0.81) = 32.20 \text{ in}^2$$

$$f_t = \frac{32{,}600}{32.20} = 1023 \text{ lb/in}^2 < F'_t = 1380 \text{ lb/in}^2$$

Determine the size of the top chord members: Since the compression chord is subject to both axial compression and bending stresses, it must be analyzed as a beam column in accordance with the NDS.[6] Determine the allowable compression design value F'_c:

$$F'_c = F_c \times C_D \times C_F \times C_p$$

where C_F = 1.05 for 8-in-wide members
C_p = 1.0 (Since loads are applied to the top chord through heavy timber decking, it is assumed that the top chord is continuously laterally braced.)

Thus $$F'_c = 1700(1.15)(1.05)(1.0) = 2053 \text{ lb/in}^2$$

Try two 3- by 8-in members, net size = 2.5 by 7.25 in. Assume no torsional strength such that each chord member acts independently and resists one-half the applied stresses.

Determine the allowable bending design value F'_b:

$$F'_b = F_b \times C_D \times C_L \times C_F$$

where C_L = 1.0
C_F = 1.2

Thus $$F'_b = 1450(1.15)(1.0)(1.2) = 2001 \text{ lb/in}^2$$

Determine the maximum axial compression stress at center panels (U_3U_4 and U_4U_5):

$$f_c = \frac{34{,}284}{2(2.5)(7.25)} = 946 \text{ lb/in}^2$$

Determine the maximum bending stress based on four-span continuous beam analysis:

$$M_{\max} = 3213 \text{ ft·lb}$$

$$f_b = \frac{M}{S} = \frac{3213(12)(6)}{2(2.5)(7.25)^2} = 880 \text{ lb/in}^2$$

Check combined bending and axial compression:

$$\left(\frac{f_c}{F'_c}\right)^2 + \frac{f_b}{F'_b\left[1 - \left(\frac{f_c}{F_{cE1}}\right)\right]} \le 1.0$$

where $$F_{cE1} = \frac{K_{cE} \cdot E'}{\left(\frac{\ell_{e1}}{d_1}\right)^2} = \frac{0.3(1.9 \times 10^6)}{\left(\frac{75}{7.25}\right)^2} = 5326 \text{ lb/in}^2$$

Thus $$\left(\frac{946}{2053}\right)^2 + \frac{880}{2001\left[1 - \left(\frac{946}{5326}\right)^2\right]} = 0.75 < 1.0$$

Since unity check is only 75 percent of capacity, members are OK for net area and net section reductions due to fasteners, by inspection.

Determine Size of Web Members. Tension webs: Use same size for all members.

$$\text{Maximum tension force in member } U_0L_1 = 23{,}210 \text{ lb}$$

$$A_R = \frac{23{,}210}{1380} = 16.82 \text{ in}^2$$

Try a 4- by 8-in member; net size = 3.5 by 7.25 in. Assume ¾-in bolt for net section reduction at connectors.

$$\text{Net area} = 3.5(7.25 - 0.81) = 22.54 \text{ in}^2$$

$$f_t = \frac{23{,}210}{22.54} = 1030 \text{ lb/in}^2 < F'_t = 1380 \text{ lb/in}^2$$

Compression webs: The maximum compression force is in member U_0L_0 = 19,200 lb. Try a 4- by 8-in member. Check as an unbraced column with $\ell_e = 84$ in.

Determine the column stability factor C_p:

$$C_p = \frac{(1 + F_{cE}/F_c^*)}{2c} - \sqrt{\left[\frac{1 + F_{cE}/F_c^*}{2c}\right] - \frac{F_{cE}/F_c^*}{c}}$$

where
$$F_{cE} = \frac{K_{cE}E'}{(\ell_e/d)^2} = \frac{0.3(1.9 \times 10^6)}{(84/3.5)^2} = 990 \text{ lb/in}^2$$
$$F_c^* = F_c \times C_D \times C_F = 1700(1.15)(1.05) = 2053 \text{ lb/in}^2$$
$$\frac{F_{cE}}{F_c^*} = \frac{990}{2053} = 0.482$$
$$c = 0.8$$

Thus,
$$C_p = \frac{1 + 0.482}{2(0.8)} - \sqrt{\left[\frac{1 + 0.482}{2(0.8)}\right]^2 - \frac{0.482}{0.8}} = 0.42$$

Determine the allowable compression design value F'_c:

$$F'_c = F_c^* \times C_p = 2053(0.42) = 864 \text{ lb/in}^2$$

For a ¾-in bolt with a 13⁄16-in hole,

$$A_{\text{net}} = 3.5(7.25 - 0.81) = 22.54 \text{ in}^2$$

$$f_c = \frac{19{,}200}{22.54} = 852 \text{ lb/in}^2 \approx 864 \text{ lb/in}^2$$

Note: At the designer's option, all the same size web members could be used based on aesthetic considerations. Otherwise, design of the other webs would proceed as shown above for member U_0L_0.

Truss Deflections. Determine flat Pratt truss deflections at panel point L_4 by the virtual work method.

Member	L/A, 1/in	S, kips	u, kips	SuL/A, kips^2/in
		Top chord (two 3 × 8s, A = 36.25 in^2)		
U_0U_1	2.07	−15.5	−0.45	+14.4
U_1U_2	2.07	−26.0	−0.89	+47.9
U_2U_3	2.07	−32.6	−1.34	+90.4
U_3U_4	2.07	−34.3	−1.79	+127.1
		Bottom chord (two 3 × 8s, A = 36.25 in^2)		
L_0L_1	2.07	0	0	0
L_1L_2	2.07	+15.5	+0.45	+14.4
L_2L_3	2.07	+26.0	+0.89	+54.7
L_3L_4	2.07	+32.6	+1.79	+120.8
		Comp webs (4 × 8, A = 25.375 in^2; 4 × 6, A = 19.25 in^2)		
U_0L_0 (4 × 8)	3.31	−19.2	−0.50	+31.8
U_1L_1 (4 × 8)	3.31	−17.3	−0.50	+28.6
U_2L_2 (4 × 6)	4.36	−11.8	−0.50	+25.7
U_3L_3 (4 × 6)	4.36	−7.4	−0.50	+16.1
U_4L_4 (4 × 6)	4.36	−3.7	0	0
		Tension webs (one 4 × 8, A = 25.375 in^2)		
U_0L_1	4.44	+23.2	+0.67	+69.0
U_1L_2	4.44	+15.8	+0.67	+47.0
U_2L_3	4.44	+9.8	+0.67	+29.2
U_3L_4	4.44	+2.5	+0.67	+7.4

$$\Delta L_4 = \Sigma \frac{SuL}{AE} \qquad \Delta L_4 = \frac{2(724.5)(1000)}{1,900,000} = 0.763 \text{ in}$$

$$\frac{\ell}{\Delta L_4} = 50 \times \frac{12}{0.763} = 787 > 360 \qquad \text{OK}$$

EXAMPLE 6.5: BOWSTRING TIMBER TRUSS EXAMPLE Design a bowstring truss as shown in Fig. 6.27*a* given the span and loading conditions shown. Assume loads are transmitted to the top chord through wood I beams spaced 48 in on center

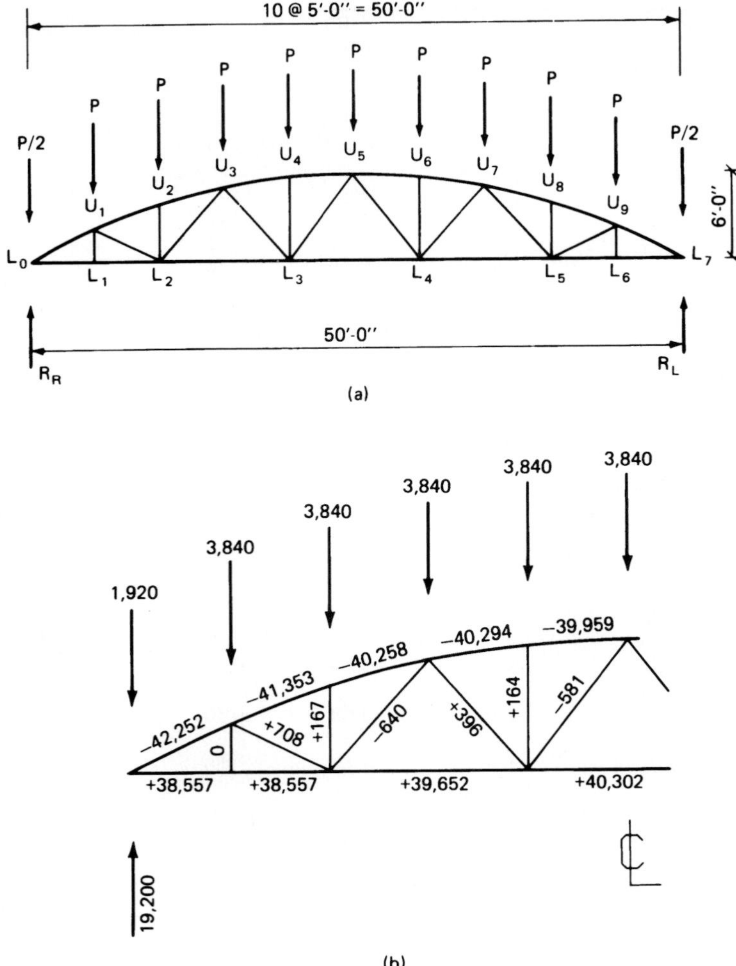

FIG. 6.27 Bowstring truss. (*a*) Geometry; (*b*) member forces. *Note:* All loads and forces are in pounds.

which also act as the lateral bracing. Further assume that the top chord consists of a series of interconnected simple-span members which results in a conservative analysis. An alternative analysis procedure is to consider the top chord to act as a continuous beam with the panel points acting as rigid supports. Assume all truss components will be single-piece glulam members arranged in a planar configuration. Only full snow load plus dead load is considered in this example for purposes of illustrating the analysis procedure. Refer to Example 6.3 for other possible loading conditions.

As shown in Fig. 6.27*a*, a bowstring truss with a centerline-to-centerline depth of 72 in (182.9 cm) was selected with a circular top chord having a radius of 55 ft (16.8 m). The member forces were determined by the method of joints, and the deflection was calculated by the virtual work method. The member sizing is based on the material selection given in the example for seasoned, untreated lumber in a dry use service condition and a duration of load of 1.15 (i.e., snow load). In addition, for the curved top chord glulam beam member, the moment induced by the eccentricity is included in the analysis as is an analysis of the radial stress induced.

Bowstring Truss Configuration and Loading. Trusses are spaced at 16 ft (4.88 m) on center.

Dead load (DL) = 18 lb/ft^2 (0.86 kPa).

Snow load (SL) = 30 lb/ft^2 (1.44 kPa).

Total load (TL) = 48 lb/ft^2 (2.30 kPa).

Design loads are applied to the horizontal projection of the roof system.

Therefore, the uniformly distributed design load w is applied to each truss: w = 48(16) = 768 lb/ft (11.2 kN/m); panel-point loads P = 768(5) = 3840 lb (17.1 kN); and end reaction R = 768(25) = 19,200 lb (85.4 kN).

Midspan bending moment M = 768(50)^2/8 = 240,000 ft·lb.

Calculation of Member Forces by Method of Joints. For joint L_1:

$$b_1 = B - R + \sqrt{R^2 - \left(\frac{L}{2} - 5\right)^2} = 2.241 \text{ ft}$$

$$Q_1 = \tan^{-1}\frac{2.241}{5} = 24.140°$$

$$L_0U_1 = \frac{19{,}200 - 1920}{\sin Q_1} = 42{,}252 \text{ lb compression}$$

$$L_0L_1 = 42{,}252 \cos Q_1 = 38{,}557 \text{ lb tension}$$

$$L_1L_2 = L_0L_1 = 38{,}557 \text{ lb tension}$$

$$U_1L_1 = 0$$

For joint U_1:

$$b_2 = B - R + \sqrt{R^2 - \left(\frac{L}{2} - 10\right)^2} = 3.918 \text{ ft}$$

$$Q_2 = \tan^{-1}\frac{3.918 - 2.240}{5} = 18.546°$$

$$\Sigma F_y = 0 \downarrow (+)$$

$$(\sin Q_2)U_1U_2 + (\sin Q_1)U_1L_2 + 3840 - (\sin Q_1)(42{,}252) = 0$$

$$0.318U_1U_2 + 0.409U_1L_2 = 13{,}440 \text{ lb} \tag{6.9}$$

$$\Sigma F_x = 0 \rightarrow (+)$$

$$(\cos Q_1)U_1L_2 + (\cos Q_1)(42{,}252) - (\cos Q_2)U_1U_2 = 0$$

$$0.913U_1L_2 - 0.948U_1U_2 = 38{,}557 \text{ lb} \tag{6.10}$$

Substituting Eq. (6.9) into Eq. (6.10),

$$U_1L_2 = 708 \text{ lb tension}$$

$$U_1U_2 = 41{,}353 \text{ lb compression}$$

Note: As an alternative to the use of simultaneous equations as required by the method of joints, truss forces could be determined by the method of sections.

For joint U_2:

$$b_3 = B - R + \sqrt{R^2 - \left(\frac{L}{2} - 15\right)^2} = 5.085 \text{ ft}$$

$$Q_3 = \tan^{-1}\frac{5.085 - 3.918}{5} = 13.131°$$

$$Q_4 = \tan^{-1}\frac{5.085}{5} = 45.481°$$

$$\Sigma F_x = 0 \rightarrow (+)$$

$$(\cos Q_2)(41{,}353) - (\cos Q_3)U_2U_3 = 0$$

$$U_2U_3 = 40{,}258 \text{ lb compression}$$

$$\Sigma F_y = 0 \downarrow (+)$$

$$(\sin Q_3)U_2U_3 + 3840 - (\sin Q_2)(41{,}353) = U_2L_2$$

$$U_2L_2 = 167 \text{ lb tension}$$

For joint L_2:

$$\Sigma F_y = 0 \downarrow (+)$$

$$(\sin Q_4)L_2U_3 - 167 - (\sin Q_1)(708) = 0$$

$$L_2U_3 = 640 \text{ lb compression}$$

$$\Sigma F_x = 0 \rightarrow (+)$$

$$L_2L_3 - 38{,}557 - (\cos Q_1)(708) - (\cos Q_4)(640) = 0$$

$$L_2L_3 = 39{,}652 \text{ lb tension}$$

For joint U_3:

$$b_4 = B - R + \sqrt{R^2 - \left(\frac{L}{2} - 20\right)^2} = 5.773 \text{ ft}$$

$$Q_5 = \tan^{-1} \frac{5.773 - 5.085}{5} = 7.834°$$

$$\Sigma F_y = 0 \downarrow (+)$$

$$(\sin Q_5)U_3U_4 + (\sin Q_4)U_3L_3 + 3840 - (\sin Q_3)(40{,}258) - (\sin Q_4)(640) = 0$$

$$0.136U_3U_4 + 0.713U_3L_3 = 5762 \qquad (6.11)$$

$$\Sigma F_x = 0 \rightarrow (+)$$

$$(\cos Q_4)U_3L_3 - (\cos Q_5)U_3U_4 + (\cos Q_3)40{,}258 + (\cos Q_4)(640) = 0$$

$$0.701U_3L_3 - 0.991U_3U_4 = -39{,}654 \qquad (6.12)$$

Substituting Eq. (6.11) into Eq. (6.12),

$$U_3L_3 = 396 \text{ lb tension}$$

$$U_3U_4 = 40{,}294 \text{ lb compression}$$

For joint U_4:

$$Q_6 = \tan^{-1} \frac{6.0 - 5.773}{5} = 2.600°$$

$$\Sigma F_x = 0 \leftarrow (+)$$

$$(\cos Q_6)U_4U_5 - (\cos Q_5)(40{,}294) = 0$$

$$U_4U_5 = 39{,}959 \text{ lb compression}$$

$$\Sigma F_y = 0 \downarrow (+)$$

$$U_4L_3 + (\sin Q_5)(40{,}294) - 3840 - (\sin Q_6)(39{,}959) = 0$$

$$U_4L_3 = 164 \text{ lb tension}$$

For joint L_3:

$$Q_7 = \tan \frac{6.0}{5.0} = 50.194°$$

$$\Sigma F_y = 0 \downarrow (+)$$

$$(\sin Q_7)L_3U_5 - 164 - (\sin Q_4)(396) = 0$$

$$L_3U_5 = 581 \text{ lb compression}$$

$$\Sigma F_x = 0 \rightarrow (+)$$

$$L_3L_4 - 39{,}652 - (\cos Q_4)(396) - (\cos Q_7)(531) = 0$$

$$L_3L_4 = 40{,}302 \text{ lb tension}$$

See Fig. 6.27*b* for summary of member forces.

Tabulated Design Values. Assume southern pine structural glued-laminated timber members; use combination A-47 for tension chord and webs and combination 24F-V3 for compression chord. The tabulated design values for these combinations, per NDS[6] supplement, are as follows:

Stress	Comb. A-47, lb/in^2	Comb. 24F-V3,* lb/in^2
F_t	1200	1150
F_c	1900	1700
F_b	1400	2400
F_v	200	200
E	1.4×10^6	1.8×10^6; 1.6×10^6†
$F_{c\perp}$	560	650

*Combination 24F-V3 is selected for compresson chord since it acts as a beam column, whereas combination A-47 is used for webs and tension chord which are loaded only in axial tension or compression.

†First value listed is for E in bending. Second value listed is for E in axial loading.

Assume the truss consists of single-member glulam chords and webs.

Determine size of bottom chord members:

$$\text{Maximum tension force} = 40{,}302 \text{ lb}$$

Determine the allowable tension value F_t':

$$F_t' = F_t \times C_D = 100(1.15) = 1380 \text{ lb/in}^2$$

$$\text{Area required } A_r = \frac{40{,}302}{1380} = 29.20 \text{ in}^2$$

Try a 3- by 12-in glulam member. Assume that two lines of ¾-in machine bolts will be used for the tension chord splice connection.

$$A_{net} = 3[12 - 2(0.81)] = 31.14 \text{ in}^2 > A_r = 29.20 \text{ in}^2$$

Note: It may be necessary to recheck this value if a different arrangement of connectors is used.

Determine size of top chord member: Because of curvature of the top chord, a moment is induced due to the eccentricity of the axial force line from a straight line between panel points. This eccentricity is calculated by

$$\text{Eccentricity} = R - \frac{\sqrt{4(R)^2 - (\text{panel length})^2}}{2}$$

$$= 55 - \frac{\sqrt{4(55)^2 - (5)^2}}{2} = 0.057 \text{ ft}$$

The moment induced by eccentricity M_e is

$$M_e = 42{,}252(0.057) = 2408 \text{ ft·lb (negative moment)}$$

Determine the midpanel moment based on the assumption of uniform loading:

$$M_u = \frac{wL^2}{8} = \frac{768(5)^2}{8} = 2400 \text{ ft·lb (positive moment)}$$

However, note that the design load is applied through subframing spaced 48 in o.c. Assume that a subframing member falls at the center of a panel:

$$M_p = \frac{PL}{4} = \frac{[48(4)(16)](5)}{4} = 3840 \text{ ft·lb (positive moment)}$$

The moment due to the subframing load acts opposite the moment induced by eccentricity of axial load. Conservatively, the larger of the two will be used.

Estimate the top chord size based on the maximum moment and axial force. Assuming 1½-in laminations, the curvature factor is

$$C_c = 1 - 2000\left(\frac{t}{R}\right)^2 = 1 - 2000\left(\frac{1.5}{660}\right)^2 = 0.99$$

Assuming a depth of 12 in or less,

$$F_b^* = F_b \times C_D \times C_c \times C_v = 2400(1.15)(0.99)(1.0) = 2732 \text{ lb/in}^2$$

$$F_c^* = F_c{\cdot}C_D = 1700(1.15) = 1955 \text{ lb/in}^2$$

Therefore, estimate section modulus and area required

$$S_{\text{est}} = \frac{3840(12)}{2731} = 16.87 \text{ in}^3$$

$$A_{\text{est}} = \frac{42{,}252}{1955} = 21.6 \text{ in}^2$$

Try a 3- by 12-in member:

$$S = 72.00 \text{ in}^3 \qquad A = 36.00 \text{ in}^2$$

Check the 3- by 12-in member for combined bending and axial compression in accordance with the NDS.[6]

Determine the allowable compression value F'_c: It is assumed that the subframing acts as lateral bracing for the top chord.

$$F'_c = F^*_c \times C_p$$

where $C_p = \dfrac{1 + (F_{cE}/F^*_c)}{2c} - \sqrt{\left[1 + \dfrac{(F_{cE}/F^*_c)}{2c}\right]^2 - \dfrac{(F_{cE}/F^*_c)}{c}}$

$$F_{cE} = \frac{K_{cE} \cdot E'}{(\ell_e/d)^2} = \frac{0.418(1.8 \times 10^6)}{(48/3)^2} = 2939 \text{ lb/in}^2$$

$$\frac{F_{cE}}{F^*_c} = \frac{2939}{1955} = 1.50$$

$$c = 0.9$$

$$\text{Thus, } C_p = \frac{1 + 1.5}{2(0.9)} - \sqrt{\left[\frac{1 + 1.5}{2(0.9)}\right]^2 - \frac{1.5}{0.9}} = 0.88$$

$$F'_c = 1955(0.88) = 1714 \text{ lb/in}^2$$

Determine the allowable bending vaue F'_b:

$$F'_b = F^*_b \times C_L \qquad \text{or} \qquad F'_b = F^*_b \times C_V$$

where $C_L = \dfrac{1 + (F_{bE}/F^*_b)}{1.9} - \sqrt{\left[\dfrac{1 + (F_{bE}/F^*_b)}{1.9}\right]^2 - \dfrac{(F_{bE}/F^*_b)}{0.95}}$

$$F_{bE} = \frac{K_{bE} E'}{(R_B)^2}$$

$$R_b = \sqrt{\frac{\ell_e d}{(b)^2}} = \sqrt{\frac{1.80(48)(12)}{(3)^2}} = 10.73$$

$$F_{bE} = \frac{0.609(1.8 \times 10^6)}{(10.73)^2} = 9516 \text{ lb/in}^2$$

$$\frac{F_{bE}}{F^*_b} = \frac{9516}{2731} = 3.48$$

$$C_L = \frac{1 + 3.48}{1.9} - \sqrt{\left(\frac{1 + 3.48}{1.9}\right)^2 - \frac{3.48}{0.95}} = 0.98$$

$$C_V = K_L\left(\frac{21}{L}\right)^{1/x}\left(\frac{12}{d}\right)^{1/x}\left(\frac{5.125}{b}\right)^{1/x} \leq 1.0$$

$$= 1.09\left(\frac{21}{5}\right)^{1/20}\left(\frac{12}{12}\right)^{1/20}\left(\frac{5.125}{3}\right)^{1/20} = 1.20 \qquad \text{(Use 1.0)}$$

Thus $\qquad F'_b = 2731(0.98) = 2676 \text{ lb/in}^2 \qquad$ (controls since $C_V > C_L$)

Therefore, combined loading gives

$$\left(\frac{f_c}{F'_c}\right)^2 + \frac{f_{b1}}{F'_{b1}[1 - (f_c/F_{cE1})]} \leq 1.0$$

$$\left[\frac{(42{,}252/36.00)}{1714}\right]^2 + \frac{[3840(12)/72.00]}{2676\left\{1 - \left[\frac{(42{,}252/36.00)}{2939}\right]\right\}} = 0.87$$

Check the radial stress:

$$f_r = \frac{3M}{2R} = \frac{3(3840)}{2(55)(36)} = 3 \text{ lb/in}^2 < F'_{rt}$$

where

$$F'_{rt} = \frac{F'_v}{3} = \frac{F_v C_D}{3}$$

Note: Radial stresses are usually quite low for this type of member and are OK by inspection.

Determine Size of Web Members: Maximum tension force in member U_1L_2 = 708 lb.

$$A_{\text{net req}} = \frac{708}{1380} = 0.51 \text{ in}^2$$

Use a 3- by 4½-in glulam member as minimum size based on architectural considerations. If $f_t \simeq F'_t$, the designer should recheck stresses based on the net area of tension web based on connectors used.

Maximum compressive force in member L_2U_3 = 640 lb.

Determine the allowable compressive stress F'_c:

$$F'_c = F_c \times C_D \times C_P$$

where $C_P = \frac{1 + (F_{cE}/F^*_c)}{2c} - \sqrt{\left[\frac{1 + (F_{cE}/F^*_c)}{2c}\right]^2 - \frac{(F_{cE}/F^*_c)}{c}}$

$$F_{cE} = \frac{K_{cE}E'}{(\ell_e/d)^2} = \frac{0.418(1.4 \times 10^6)}{[7.0(12)/3]^2} = 746 \text{ lb/in}^2$$

$$F^*_c = F_c C_D = 1900(1.15) = 2185 \text{ lb/in}^2$$

$$\frac{F_{cE}}{F^*_c} = \frac{746}{2185} = 0.341$$

$$c = 0.9$$

Thus

$$C_P = \frac{1 + 0.341}{2(0.9)} - \sqrt{\left(\frac{1 + 0.341}{2(0.9)}\right)^2 - \frac{0.341}{0.9}} = 0.33$$

$$F'_c = 2185(0.33) = 712 \text{ lb/in}^2$$

$$A_r = \frac{640}{712} = 0.9 \text{ in}^2$$

Therefore, use 3- × 4½-in glulam.

Check web U_5L_3 as an unbraced column, using a 3- by 4-½ in glulam member:

$$\text{Slenderness ratio } \frac{\ell_e}{d} = \frac{7.81(12)}{3} = 31.24 < 50$$

$$F_{cE} = \frac{K_{cE}E'}{(\ell_e/d)^2} = \frac{0.418(1.4 \times 10^6)}{(31.24)^2} = 600 \text{ lb/in}^2$$

$$\frac{F_{cE}}{F_c^*} = \frac{600}{2185} = 0.275$$

$$C_P = \frac{1 + 0.275}{2(0.9)} - \sqrt{\left(\frac{1 + 0.275}{2(0.9)}\right)^2 - \frac{0.275}{0.9}} = 0.26$$

$$F_c' = 2185(0.26) = 579 \text{ lb/in}^2$$

$$f_c = \frac{581}{3(4.5)} = 43 \text{ lb/in}^2 < 579 \text{ lb/in}^2$$

Bottom chord heel connections:

Maximum tension force at heel = 38557 lb

For 3-in-thick southern pine glulam member, with ¼-in steel side plates, load applied parallel to the grain, the nominal design value Z of a ¾-in bolt in double shear is

$$Z = 3300 \text{ lb} \qquad \text{(see NDS}^6\text{ Table 8.3D)}$$

The allowable bolt design value Z' is

$$Z' = Z \times C_D \times C_g = 3300(1.15)C_g = 3795C_g$$

This assumes that all bolt spacing and edge distances are in accordance with Fig. 5.27 or Section 8.5 of the NDS.[6]

The number of bolts required is

$$\frac{39{,}557}{3795} = 10.4$$

Therefore, try twelve ¾-in bolts arranged in two rows of six each.

Check the bolt capacity with group action:

$$\text{Area of main member } A_m = 3(12) = 36 \text{ in}^2$$

Area of side plates, assuming ¼- by 12-in plates, is

$$A_s = 2(0.25)(12) = 6 \text{ in}^2$$

Therefore,

$$\frac{A_m}{A_s} = \frac{36}{6} = 6 \qquad \text{(outside the range of Table 5.29 or Table 7.3.6C of the NDS}^6\text{)}$$

$$C_g = \left\{\frac{m(1 - m^{2n})}{n[(1 + R_{EA}m^n)(1 + m) - 1 + m^{2n}]}\right\}\left(\frac{1 + R_{EA}}{1 - m}\right)$$

(Refer to Equation 7.3-1 in the NDS.[6])

where $n = 6$

$$E_m \times A_m = (1.4 \times 10^6)(36) = 50.4 \times 10^6$$

$$E_s \times A_s = (30 \times 10^6)(6) = 180 \times 10^6$$

$$R_{EA} = \frac{E_m A_m}{E_s A_s} = \frac{50.4}{180} = 0.28$$

$$u = 1 + \gamma\left(\frac{s}{2}\right)\left(\frac{1}{E_m A_m} + \frac{1}{E_s A_s}\right)$$

$$= 1 + (270{,}000)\left(\frac{3}{2}\right)\left(\frac{1}{50.4 \times 10^6} + \frac{1}{180 \times 10^6}\right) = 1.067$$

$$m = u - \sqrt{u^2 - 1} = 1.067 - \sqrt{(1.067)^2 - 1} = 0.89$$

Thus

$$C_g = \left(\frac{0.89(1 - 0.89^{2\times6})}{6\{[1 + 0.28(0.89)^6](1 + 0.89) - 1 + 0.89^{2\times6}\}}\right)\left(\frac{1 + 0.28}{1 - 0.89}\right) = 0.94$$

Connection capacity = 12(3795)(0.94) = 42,626 lb > 39,557 lb OK

Assume bottom chord center splice connection at midspan:

Tension force at splice = 40,302 lb.

Allowable design value for ¾-in bolts Z' is

$$Z' = 3795 \times C_g$$

Use 12 bolts in two rows of 6 bolts each. Assume the same steel side plates, spacing, and edge distance as used for the heel connection.

Allowable joint value = 42,626 lb > 40,302 lb OK

Check the capacity of web to chord connection based on the use of one ¾-in bolt. For 3-in-thick southern pine glulam member with ¼-in steel side plates, the allowable design values for a ¾-in bolt in double shear is

$$Z'_{\parallel} = 3300(1.15) = 3795 \text{ lb}$$

$$Z'_{\perp} = 1330(1.15) = 1530 \text{ lb}$$

By inspection, the maximum web force is 708 lb, which is less than $Z'_{\perp} = 1530$ lb, which is the minimum load that a ¾-in bolt will carry. Therefore, it is not necessary to further evaluate each web to chord connection. However, the following calculation illustrates the design procedure:

Maximum force occurs in member $U_1L_2 = 708$ lb.
Angle of load to grain = 24.14°.

Allowable design value of ¾-in bolt at 24.1° is

$$Z'_{24.1} = \frac{3795(1530)}{3795(\sin^2 24.1) + 1530(\cos^2 24.1)} = 3044 \text{ lb} > 708 \text{ lb}$$

Determine Deflection at Panel Point U_5 by Virtual Work Method:

Member	L/A, 1/in	S, kips	u, kips	SuL/A, kips²/in
		Top chord (3 × 12 glulam, A = 36.0 in²)		
L_0U_1	1.826	−42.25	−1.22	94.12
U_1U_2	1.758	−41.35	−1.35	98.14
U_2U_3	1.711	−40.26	−1.31	90.24
U_3U_4	1.682	−40.29	−1.75	118.59
U_4U_5	1.668	−39.96	−1.74	115.98
		Bottom chord (3 × 12 glulam, A = 36.0 in²)		
L_0L_1	1.667	+38.56	+1.12	71.95
L_1L_2	1.667	+38.56	+1.12	71.95
L_2L_3	3.332	+39.65	+1.48	195.54
L_3L_4(½)	1.667	+40.03	+2.06	137.46
		Web members (3 × 4.5 glulam, A = 13.5 in²)		
L_1U_1	2.241	0	0	0
U_1L_2	4.870	+0.70	+0.18	0.62
U_2L_2	3.483	+0.17	+0.13	0.08
L_2U_3	6.339	−0.64	−0.28	1.14
U_3L_3	6.339	+0.40	+0.37	0.94
U_4L_3	5.132	+0.16	+0.14	0.11
L_3U_5	6.942	−0.58	−0.52	2.09
			Total	998.95

$$\Delta U_5 = \Sigma \frac{SuL}{AE} = \frac{2(998.95)(1000)}{1{,}700{,}000} = 1.17 \text{ in}$$

$$\frac{\ell_e}{\Delta U_5} = 50 \times \frac{12}{1.17} = 510 > 360$$

EXAMPLE 6.6: PITCHED CHORD CANTILEVERED TRUSS EXAMPLE Design a pitched top chord truss as shown in Fig. 6.28 given the span and loading conditions shown. Assume that loads are applied directly to the top chord through heavy timber decking which provides continuous lateral bracing. Assume that the lower chords are braced laterally at midspan by horizontal struts tied to the building end walls.

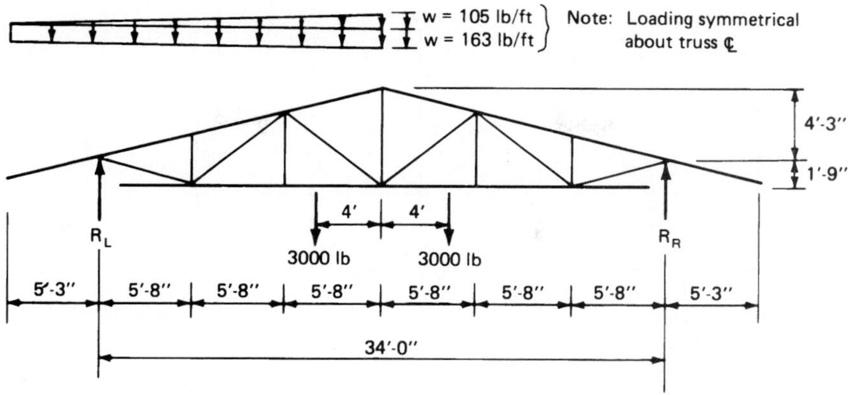

FIG. 6.28 Pitched-chord cantilever truss geometry.

Assume that the top chords are three-span continuous members with a cantilever extension at the bearing ends. Assume that the bottom chord is a four-span continuous member. In both cases, the panel points are considered to act as unyielding supports.

Further, assume that all wood truss components will consist of single-piece glulam members arranged in a single plane with steel side plates at all connections. Only full snow load plus dead load is considered in this example. Refer to Example 6.3 for other possible loading conditions.

Assume that the top and bottom chords are southern pine combination 24F-V3 and the web members are combination A-47. The tabulated design values for these combinations from the NDS[6] Supplement are as follows:

Stress	Comb. A-47, lb/in²	Comb. 24F-V3,* lb/in²
F_t	1200	1150
F_c	1900	1700
F_b	1400	2400
F_v	200	200
E	1.4×10^6	1.8×10^6; 1.6×10^6†
$F_{c\perp}$	560	650

*Combination 24F-V3 is selected for tension and compression chords since these members are subjected to combined axial and bending stresses, whereas combination A-47 is used for webs which are only subjected to axial stresses.

†First value listed is for E in bending; second value listed is for E in axial loading.

Based on the assumption that the top and bottom chords act as continuous members, panel-point loads and resultant member forces as obtained from a computer analysis are shown in Fig. 6.29.

Determine the size of the bottom chord:

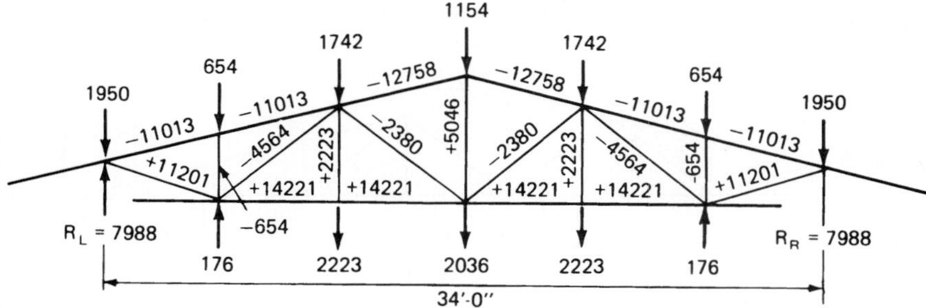

FIG. 6.29 Computer results: pitched-chord cantilever truss. *Note:* All loads, reactions, and member forces are given in pounds.

$$\text{Maximum tension force} = 14{,}221 \text{ lb}$$

$$\text{Maximum bending moment} = 2262 \text{ ft·lb}$$

Try a 3- by 9-in glulam member.

For purposes of determining the section properties, assume that a single line of ¾-in bolts with 4-in shear plates in each face of the chord will be used for all required connections as follows:

Projected area of 4-in shear plate and bolt is 6.52 in^2.

$$A_{\text{net}} = 3(9) - 6.52 = 20.48 \text{ in}^2$$

$$S_{\text{net}} = \frac{3(9)^2 - 2(0.64)(4)^2 - 1.72(0.81)^2}{6} = 36.90 \text{ in}^3$$

Analyze the bottom chord as a combined tension and bending member in accordance with the NDS.[6]

Determine the allowable tension value F'_t:

$$F'_b = F'_t \times C_D = 1200(1.15) = 1380 \text{ lb/in}^2$$

Determine F'_b:

$$F'_b = F_b{\cdot}C_D{\cdot}C_V \qquad \text{or} \qquad F'_b = F_b{\cdot}C_D{\cdot}C_L$$

where $C_V = K_L\left(\frac{21}{L}\right)^{1/x}\left(\frac{12}{d}\right)^{1/x}\left(\frac{5.125}{b}\right)^{1/x} \le 1.0$

$K_L = 1.0$

$L = 5$ ft-8 in $= 5.67$ ft (assume panel length as a conservative estimate)

$$C_V = 1.0\left(\frac{21}{5.67}\right)^{1/20}\left(\frac{12}{9}\right)^{1/20}\left(\frac{5.125}{3}\right)^{1/20} = 1.11 \qquad \text{(use 1.0)}$$

$$C_L = \frac{1 + (F_{cE}/F_c^*)}{1.9} - \sqrt{\left[\frac{1 + (F_{cE}/F_c^*)}{1.9}\right]^2 - \frac{(F_{cE}/F_c^*)}{0.95}}$$

$$R_B = \sqrt{\frac{\ell_e d}{b^2}} = \sqrt{\frac{5.67(12)(9)}{3^2}} = 8.25$$

$$F_{bE} = \frac{K_{bE}E'}{R_B^2} = \frac{0.609(1.8 \times 10^6)}{8.25^2} = 16{,}111 \text{ lb/in}^2$$
$$F_b^* = F_bC_D = 2400(1.15) = 2760 \text{ lb/in}^2$$
$$\frac{F_{bE}}{F_b^*} = \frac{16{,}111}{2760} = 5.84$$
$$C_L = \frac{1 + 5.84}{1.9} - \sqrt{\left(\frac{1 + 5.84}{1.9}\right)^2 - \frac{5.84}{0.95}} = 0.99$$

Thus $F_b' = F_b^* \times C_L = 2760(0.99) = 2732 \text{ lb/in}^2$ (controls, since $C_L < C_V$)

Determine actual stresses f_t and f_b:

$$f_t = \frac{14{,}221}{20.48} = 694 \text{ lb/in}^2$$

$$f_b = \frac{2262(12)}{36.90} = 736 \text{ lb/in}^2$$

Check combined loading:

$$\frac{f_t}{F_t'} + \frac{f_b}{F_b'} \leq 1.0$$

$$\frac{694}{1380} + \frac{736}{2732} = 0.77 < 1.0$$

$$\frac{f_b - f_t}{F_b'} \leq 1.0$$

$$\frac{736 - 694}{2732} = 0.02 < 1.0$$

Determine size of top chord:

Maximum compression force = 12,758 lb

Maximum bending moment = 984 ft·lb

Try a 3- by 7½-in glulam member.
Determine the section properties:

$$A_{net} = 3(7.5) - 6.52 = 15.98 \text{ in}^2$$

$$S_{net} = \frac{3(7.5)^2 - 2(0.64)(4)^2 - 1.72(0.81)^2}{6} = 24.52 \text{ in}^3$$

Analyze the top chord as a beam column in accordance with the NDS.[6] The top chord is continuously laterally braced by the heavy timber roof decking.
Determine the allowable compression value F_c':

$$\frac{\ell_e}{d} = \frac{5.67(12)}{(\cos 14)(7.5)} = 9.33$$

$$F'_c = F_c \times C_D \times C_P$$

where $C_P = \dfrac{1 + (F_{cE}/F^*_c)}{2c} - \sqrt{\left[\dfrac{1 + F_{cE}/F^*_c}{2c}\right]^2 - \dfrac{(F_{cE}/F^*_c)}{c}}$

$$F_{cE} = \frac{K_{cE}E'}{(\ell_e/d)^2} = \frac{0.418(1.8 \times 10^6)}{9.33^2} = 8637 \text{ lb/in}^2$$

$$F^*_c = 1700(1.15) = 1955 \text{ lb/in}^2$$

$$\frac{F_{cE}}{F^*_c} = \frac{8637}{1955} = 4.42$$

$$c = 0.9$$

$$C_P = \frac{1 + 4.42}{2(0.9)} - \sqrt{\left(\frac{1 + 4.42}{2(0.9)}\right)^2 - \frac{4.42}{0.9}} = 0.97$$

Thus $\qquad F'_c = 1955(0.97) = 1901 \text{ lb/in}^2$

Determine the allowable bending vaue F'_b:

$$F'_b = F_b \times C_D \times C_L \qquad \text{or} \qquad F'_b = F_b \times C_D \times C_V$$

By inspection,

$C_L = 1.0$ (The top chord is continuously laterally braced.)

$C_V \geq 1.0$ (This is evident, since all dimensions of the top chord panel are smaller than the tension chord and $K_L = 1.0$.)

Therefore,

$$F'_b = 2400(1.15) = 2760 \text{ lb/in}^2$$

Determine the actual stresses f_c and f_b:

$$f_c = \frac{12{,}758}{15.98} = 798 \text{ lb/in}^2$$

$$f_b = \frac{984(12)}{24.52} = 482 \text{ lb/in}^2$$

Check combined loading:

$$\left(\frac{f_c}{F'_c}\right)^2 + \frac{f_{b1}}{F'_{b1}[1 - (f_c/F_{cE1})]} \leq 1.0$$

$$\left(\frac{798}{1901}\right)^2 + \frac{482}{2760[1 - (798/8637)]} = 0.37 < 1.0$$

Check top chord extension:

Shear:
$$V = 999 \text{ lb}$$

$$f_V = \frac{1.5(999)}{15.98} = 94 \text{ lb/in}^2$$

$$F'_V = F_V \times C_D = 200(1.15) = 230 \text{ lb/in}^2$$

Bending:
$$M = 2439 \text{ ft·lb}$$

$$f_b = \frac{2439(12)}{24.52} = 1194 \text{ lb/in}^2$$

Note: The compressive edge of the top chord is unbraced throughout the length of the extension. Thus the designer must check C_L. The volume factor C_V, however, will be 1.0 as before.

$$C_L = \frac{1 + (F_{bE}/F_b^*)}{1.9} - \sqrt{\left[\frac{1 + (F_{bE}/F_b^*)}{1.9}\right]^2 - \frac{(F_{bE}/F_b^*)}{0.95}}$$

where
$$R_B = \sqrt{\frac{\ell_e \cdot d}{b^2}} = \sqrt{\frac{1.33(5.25)(12)(7.5)}{(\cos 14°)(3)^2}} = 8.48$$

$$F_{bE} = \frac{K_{bE}E'}{R_B^2} = \frac{0.609(1.8 \times 10^6)}{(8.48)^2} = 15{,}233 \text{ lb/in}^2$$

$$F_b^* = F_b C_D = 2400(1.15) = 2760 \text{ lb/in}^2$$

$$\frac{F_{bE}}{F_b^*} = \frac{15{,}233}{2760} = 5.52$$

Thus
$$C_L = \frac{1 + 5.52}{1.9} - \sqrt{\left[\frac{1 + 5.52}{1.9}\right]^2 - \frac{5.52}{0.95}} = 0.99$$

$$F'_b = F_b^* \times C_L = 2760(0.99) = 2730 \text{ lb/in}^2$$

$$f_b = 1194 \text{ lb/in}^2 < F'_b = 2730 \text{ lb/in}^2$$

Deflection:

$$\Delta_{TL} = 0.29 \text{ in (7.4 mm)} < \frac{2\ell}{240} = 0.53 \text{ in (13.5 mm)}$$

Therefore, a 3- by 7½-in top chord is OK

Determine size of web members: Observe that the diagonals have larger tension and compression forces than the verticals. The diagonals, too, are longer. Size the webs based on the diagonals.

$$\text{Maximum tension force} = 11{,}201 \text{ lb}$$

Try 3- by 6-in glulam.

$$A_{net} = 3(6) - 6.52 = 11.48 \text{ in}^2$$

$$f_t = \frac{11{,}201}{11.48} = 976 \text{ lb/in}^2$$

$$F'_t = F_t \times C_D = 1200(1.15) = 1380 \text{ lb/in}^2 > f_t = 976 \text{ lb/in}^2$$

$$\text{Maximum compression force} = 4564 \text{ lb}$$

$$\frac{\ell_e}{d} = \frac{7.31(12)}{3} = 29.24 < 50$$

$$f_c = \frac{4564}{11.48} = 398 \text{ lb/in}^2$$

$$F'_c = F_c \times C_D \times C_P$$

where $C_P = \frac{1 + (F_{cE}/F^*_c)}{2c} - \sqrt{\left[\frac{1 + (F_{cE}/F^*_c)}{2c}\right]^2 - \frac{(F_{cE}/F^*_c)}{c}}$

$$F_{cE} = \frac{K_{cE} \cdot E'}{(\ell_e/d)^2} = \frac{0.418(1.4 \times 10^6)}{(29.24)^2} = 684 \text{ lb/in}^2$$

$$F^*_c = F_c \cdot C_D = 1900(1.15) = 2185 \text{ lb/in}^2$$

$$\frac{F_{cE}}{F^*_c} = \frac{684}{2185} = 0.313$$

$$c = 0.9$$

Thus $C_P = \frac{1 + 0.313}{2(0.9)} - \sqrt{\left(\frac{1 + 0.313}{2(0.9)}\right)^2 - \frac{0.313}{0.9}} = 0.30$

$$F'_c = 2185(0.30) = 656 \text{ lb/in}^2 > f_c = 398 \text{ lb/in}^2$$

Therefore, use 3- by 6-in members for all webs.

The design of the connections would be similar to those used in Examples 6.3 and 6.5.

6.8 ERECTION OF WOOD TRUSS SYSTEMS

The successful erection of wood truss systems includes (1) common good workmanship construction practices, (2) concerns for the safety of the workers, and (3) protection of the structural integrity of the trusses. Essential to this procedure are planning and scheduling, proper handling equipment, experienced workers and supervisors, and a proper work site environment. As with all wood construction materials, wood trusses must be properly stored and protected from the environment until installed and covered in the structure.

The prefabricated lightweight repetitive-member wood truss members have the characteristic of being relatively unstable until finally stabilized in the structure by attachment to the diaphragm or permanent bracing. Figure 6.30 illustrates the distortion that may occur in the compression chord when erection bracing has not been installed. These trusses have been referred to as "spaghetti trusses" and will distort laterally to a great extent if proper handling equipment is not utilized. Their strength

FIG. 6.30 Lateral buckling of unbraced compression chord.

is clearly in the braced upright position. Aside from the safety aspects with such distortions, the structural integrity of the trusses can be seriously affected. Metal gusset plate connections are particularly susceptible to such abuse. Likewise, impact forces from improper shipping and off-loading from the truck are to be avoided.

Although collapse is not unique to the material, the erection of wood truss systems has been plagued with a high percentage of structural collapses during erection. Quite simply, the problem can be summarized as (1) inadequate supervision, (2) failure to follow instructions or to heed warnings, and (3) ignorance of the factors causing buckling of unbraced compression members. Detailed installation instructions to those in the field and elaborate warning procedures such as contained in the TPI publication *Bracing Wood Trusses: Commentary and Recommendations*[11] have not thwarted the continuation of these accidents. Unfortunately, debris remaining after collapse during the erection phase is so fragmented that an accurate assessment of the failure mechanism is difficult to pinpoint. The impact forces of such a collapse can create fractures at "apparent defects," which more likely than not are not the cause of the event. The culprit almost always is inadequate bracing.

Possible events or combinations of events leading to collapse of a wood truss system during erection can be characterized as follows:

1. Truss-handling equipment at the job site is inadequate.
2. Installation instructions from the truss manufacturer are ignored and typically found later in the contractor's office or construction trailer.

3. The trusses are hastily placed on the supporting walls or beams with the intention to brace the system later.
4. The trusses are left unbraced or inadequately braced for a long period of time.
5. Temporary bracing that does exist is inadequately attached to the trusses and is not tied off to an adequate support.
6. Large bundles of sheathing materials are placed on the trusses as concentrated loads.
7. Compression chords of the trusses "snake" out of alignment into buckling modes consistent with bracing lines.
8. Workers attempt to straighten the chord members by disconnecting a brace which is under load, or collapse occurs without this assistance.
9. After a collapse, bracing members which may have been supplied by the truss manufacturer are found still in their bundles on the job site.

Clearly, other factors may contribute to the problem on specific installations, and all the preceeding factors are not required for collapse. Buckling-induced forces are cumulative and rapidly become large. Efforts to straighten trusses must be preceded by reducing buckling forces through unloading the trusses or other means. The problem of inadequate supervision and failure to follow instructions or to heed warnings is not pursued in this writing and is left for the responsible parties and authorities.

Laypeople do not understand the factors of compression buckling and instability and only vaguely envision that the top chord members of trusses may buckle laterally under load. The trusses look safe to them. Workers generally report that "the trusses tipped over" or that "the trusses just suddenly failed." The snap or cracking noise which they report is wrongly attributed to the truss failing, not the failure of the inadequate bracing connection. Unless a contractor has technical expertise or has experienced such an event, there is typically an overestimate of the load-carrying capability of the system and an underestimate of the buckling characteristics and the stability requirements.

Compression buckling and the related forces of instability can be evaluated through standard engineering analysis procedures. Estimates can be made of construction loadings such as the weights of materials, weights and actions of workers and their equipment, wind, and other construction live loadings. Buckling of compression chord members with various loadings and bracing spacings has been evaluated by Hoyle[12] specifically for wood trusses. Parameters in this evaluation include the Euler factors plus the torsional rigidity of the truss. The compression forces in a truss chord vary along its length from a low value at each end to a maximum value at its midlength, as opposed to the constant force in the Euler column. For this loading condition, it has been shown that the critical buckling force in the compression chord is approximately twice that of the Euler prediction when torsional resistance is ignored, bracing is provided only at end supports, and the load on the span is uniform. If bracing at midspan, the critical buckling load is six times the Euler value, and if bracing is provided at the quarter points and at midspan, the critical buckling load is more than 10 times that of the end-braced-only case. Torsional rigidity of wood trusses varies with truss type and has been shown to increase the critical buckling force in the compression chord from 10 to more than 300 percent. Individual manufacturers should be contacted for these factors.

The developed forces at the bracing points vary from the theoretical value of zero for the perfectly aligned compression chord member to very large cumulative forces with significant misalignment or distortions. Proper construction practice and required dimension controls for nailing of sheathing tend to limit the misalignment, and under such limitations the range of bracing loads is 2 to 5 percent of the chord forces.

Obvious, but not always considered, is the fact that bracing members must have their forces resolved. Trusses simply braced to each other may collapse as a unit. Figure 6.31 illustrates the possible buckling mode that may occur when a series of trusses are braced to each other but not adequately tied to a rigid wall or other braced system. Figure 6.32 illustrates the use of diagonal bracing in the plane of the roof to resist the lateral buckling force components.

Thus it is possible to design an adequate bracing system for wood truss erection with stated limits or loading assumptions. The building designer is encouraged to pursue such an analysis, particularly to get a feel for the results and the factors thereof.

All too often this evaluation, the design of a bracing system, is ignored. The bracing requirement is left to the subjective judgment of the contractor or the workers, who are untrained in the analysis of trusses.

The importance of bottom chord restraint in truss stability has been shown to be significant, particularly for pitched profile trusses and in cases of concentrated loads such as workers on the trusses. Such bracing should be provided as the trusses are set in place. Figure 6.33 illustrates a system of lateral bracing used for bottom chord stability. The lateral bracing shown at approximately 45° is often used only at the end bays. In many cases, temporary erection bracing in the plane of the bottom chord is left in place after erection is completed to function as permanent bracing. Some truss manufacturers may have further stability performance information based upon testing and, additionally, may further provide specific bracing materials.

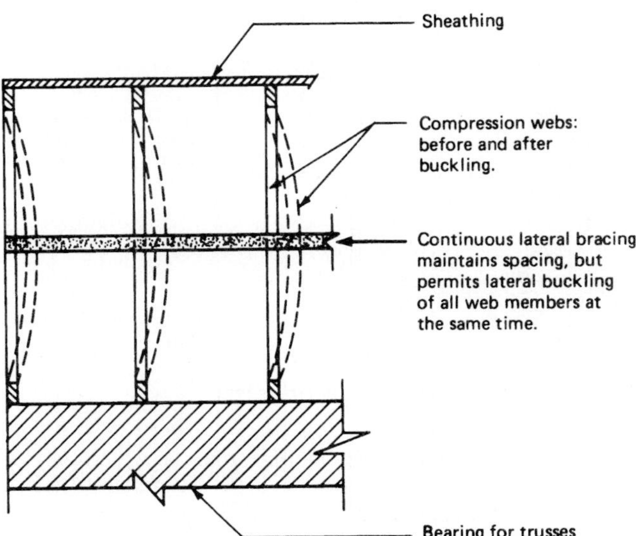

FIG. 6.31 Buckling of mode of compression chord when lateral bracing is not tied to a braced system.

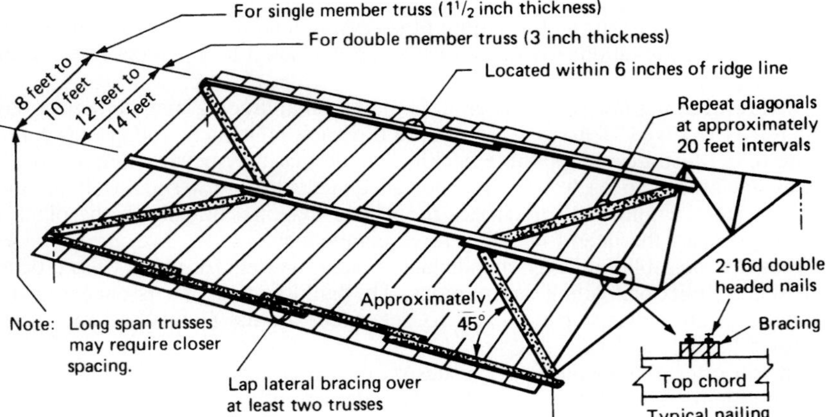

FIG. 6.32 Typical diagonal bracing system for a compression chord. *(Courtesy of Truss Plate Institute, Madison, Wisc.)*

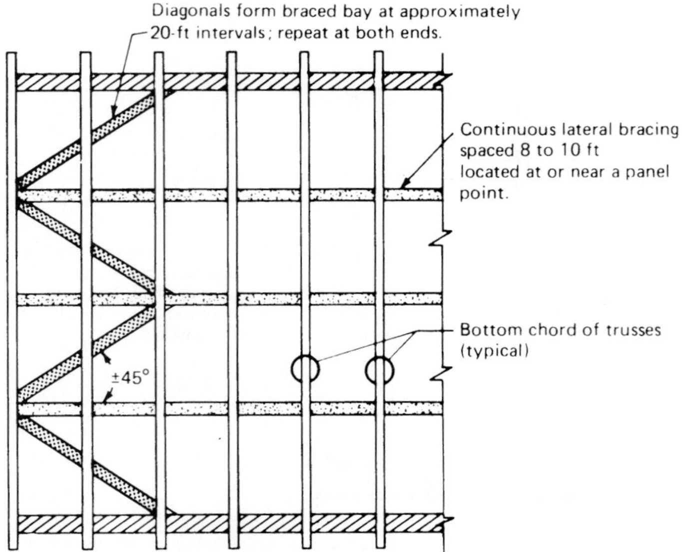

FIG. 6.33 Typical bottom chord erection bracing. *(Courtesy Truss Plate Institute, Madison, Wisc.)*

Several schemes of erection that have proved to be successful follow:

1. Erection of individual trusses which either have bracing units preattached or are systematically tied to a bracing system as erection proceeds.
2. Erection of braced modules of several trusses which are preassembled on the ground at an assembly location. An example of this system is shown in Fig. 6.34.
3. Erection of totally or partially sheathed modules of trusses are preassembled on the ground in an assembly location as illustrated in Fig. 6.35.

The erection of braced or sheathed modules is often prejudged erroneously as uneconomical. The efficiencies of preassembly in a jig on the ground and the accuracies that can thus be achieved in layout as well as the rapid erection of modules and inherent safety of keeping workers on the ground may well prove both economical and highly stable.

Heavy timber trusses require special erection considerations with regard to adequacy of attachment of bracing members be they cables, struts, or other ties. An alternative erection procedure for these larger trusses is to utilize a shoring system. Unique truss designs such as scissor trusses and structures involving compression rings require erection provisions designed by an experienced erector-engineer.

Proper installation of wood truss systems requires careful workmanship, attention to detail, and inspection to ensure compliance with design assumptions. Field problems frequently observed include improper attachment of sheathing to the trusses, inadequate support and attachment at the bearings, cutting or notching of the truss members, and damaged trusses resulting from improper handling, all potentially leading to truss system collapses during erection.

FIG. 6.34 Erection of a braced truss module.

FIG. 6.35 Erection of a plywood-sheathed truss module.

6.9 IN-SERVICE PROBLEMS

In-service problems associated with wood truss systems are as varied as the structures which use them and can range from a performance-type complaint such as a "bouncy floor system" to a structural collapse. Solutions to these problems, of necessity, must be tailored to fit the specific problem at hand and are thus difficult to generalize. Designer preference, economics, availability of materials, aesthetics, and many other variables enter into the decision-making process regarding how to remedy an in-service distress condition.

Although a comprehensive examination of field problems associated with wood trusses is beyond the scope of this handbook, some general principles and procedures may be applied to in-service problem situations. The designer should be aware that, quite often, field problems precipitate controversies, or even legal action, between the involved parties. Since the cause of the problem, or sometimes even the problem itself, is often obscure, a fact-finding investigation by trained engineering personnel is recommended as the initial step in formulating a solution.

Each probable cause should be viewed as equally likely, and the investigator must then attempt to gather supporting documentation for each case. Analysis and engineering deduction applied to the documented data should then identify the most likely cause of the problem. Once the problem and its likely cause have been established, alternative solutions may be developed and recommended as the final step in the investigation procedure. Obviously, such an investigation may be time-consuming and costly, but the learning benefits of these forensic investigations combined with the resolution of the problem can lead to improved future design guidelines. The following two in-service problems have been selected to illustrate the range of situations which might be encountered and how each could be resolved through the application of accepted engineering principles.

6.9.1 Truss Arching

Dimensional changes in wood trusses caused by in-service moisture content cycling can produce negative effects in the performance of the trusses. If the top chord of the wood roof truss is located above the insulation material, the moisture content of the top chord during the winter may increase relative to that of the bottom chord, causing the top chord to lengthen slightly. As a result, the truss will arch upward assuming the web-to-chord connections remain sound. The shrinking or swelling of normal wood along the grain, due to changes in moisture content, is very small, so that even when the above phenomenon occurs, it is generally not objectionable. However, some abnormal types of wood, such as juvenile wood, compression wood, or wood with a high slope of grain, tend to have a greater propensity to shrink and swell parallel to the length of the member. If the lumber used in the top chords of a truss consists of any of these abnormal types, truss arching may become noticeable. Although this arching generally will not damage the truss structurally, it may cause it to lift away from interior non-load-bearing partitions, thus causing cracking of the drywall and interior finishing at the interface between the ceiling and the partition. The recommended solution to this potential problem is to allow for this possible arching action of the truss in the design of the interior finish and connection of the truss to the wall system. Various methods of accomplishing this interface connection to allow for this anticipated movement have been developed.

6.9.2 Repair / Reinforcement of Heavy Timber Roof Trusses

In evaluating the condition of in-service heavy timber roof trusses, a common condition encountered is some form of distress to the tension chord. The severity of this distress can range from minor splitting, usually propagating from the web-to-chord connections, to a complete structural failure of the tension chord.

Although the cause of the distress can be attributed to many different factors, one of the primary areas of concern is related to the reduction in allowable tension parallel to grain stresses which has been imposed on structural timber members. For wood trusses designed and built prior to about 1970, the current allowable tension parallel to grain stress may be as much as 50 percent less than the values originally used in design. This reduction is most severe for the larger timber sizes and has been applied to stresses for both solid sawn timbers and glued-laminated members.

Compounding the potential for an overstress condition in the tension chords of heavy timber trusses created by this reduction in allowable tension parallel to grain stresses is the fact that many of these trusses were fabricated using timbers that because of their size had not been kiln-dried and often had moisture contents in excess of 20 percent. As these large members dry to achieve an in-service equilibrium moisture content, often as low as 6 to 8 percent, shrinkage can occur such that severe shrinkage stresses are induced in the member, particularly at the joints. This is most pronounced at joints in which more than one bolt axis with shear plate or split ring timber connectors is used in that these joints are relatively rigid and tend to restrict movement.

Distress can occur at the net section of the tension chord, at the heel connection, or at the tension splices. One solution which has been used successfully to relieve this type of distress is to reinforce the tension chords by installing steel tension rods or cables along the sides of the wood chords to carry these excess tension forces. The bowstring truss configuration has been one of the most widely used applications of heavy timber truss design because of its economy in spans which range from 50 to over 200 ft (15.24 to 60.1 m). The following example illustrates the design of tension reinforcement for this particular truss configuration.

Assume a bowstring with the configuration and span shown in Fig. 6.36 (chord forces shown are in pounds).

Assume the total design load is 1044 lb/ft (15.24 kN/m) or the load per panel point is 6264 lb (27.9 kN) based on uniformly spaced top chord panels having a simple span of 6 ft (1.83 m).

$R_{\text{left}} = R_{\text{right}} = 31{,}320$ lb (139.5 kN).

Assume the tension chord consists of double 3 × 8 select structural Douglas fir–larch members having the following allowable tension parallel to grain values F_t':

Per 1991 NDS[6] (supplement dated 1991): $F_t' = F_t \times C_F \times C_D = 1000(1.2)(1.15) = 1380$ lb/in²

Per 1962 NDS (assumed year of design): $F_t' = 1900(1.15) = 2185$ lb/in²

Check the capacity of the tension chord at the net section based on the 1962 tension parallel to grain value and the 1991 value.

Assume that the web members are attached to the tension chord with two ¾-in (1.9-cm) machine bolts, then:

$$\text{Gross area} = 2(2.5)(7.25) = 36.25 \text{ in}^2 \ (5.62 \text{ cm}^2)$$

$$\text{Area of holes} = 2(0.8125)(2.5) = 4.06 \text{ in}^2 \ (0.63 \text{ cm}^2)$$

$$\text{Net area} = 32.19 \text{ in}^2 \ (4.99 \text{ cm}^2)$$

Per 1962 design:

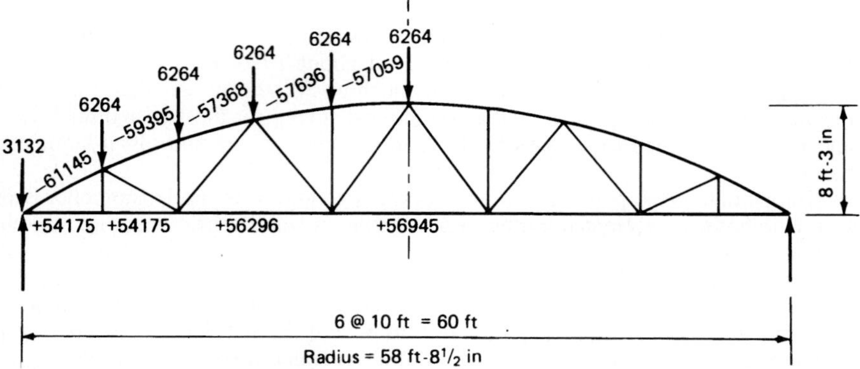

FIG. 6.36 Bowstring truss geometry and load diagram. *Notes:* (1) Truss is symmetrical about its centerline both in geometry and loading. (2) All member forces and loads are given in pounds.

$$f_t = \frac{56{,}945}{32.19} = 1769 \text{ lb/in}^2 < F'_t = 2185 \text{ lb/in}^2$$

Per 1991 design:

$$f_t = \frac{56{,}945}{32.19} = 1769 \text{ lb/in}^2 > F'_t = 1380 \text{ lb/in}^2$$

$$\text{Overstress in tension} = \frac{1769}{1380} = 1.28 \text{ or } 28 \text{ percent based on 1991 design values}$$

$$\text{Tension capacity of chords} = 1380(32.19) = 44{,}422 \text{ lb } (197.6 \text{ kN})$$

$$\text{Tension overload} = 56{,}945 - 44{,}422 = 12{,}523 \text{ lb } (55.7 \text{ kN})$$

Use steel tie rods located on each side of the tension chord at the approximate neutral axis of the chord to carry the overload. Assume A-36 steel:

$$F_t = 22 \text{ kips/in}^2 \ (15.2 \text{ kN/cm}^2)$$

$$E = 29 \times 10^6 \text{ kips/in}^2$$

$$\frac{P_{\text{wood}}}{A_{\text{wood}} \times E_{\text{wood}}} = \frac{P_{\text{steel}}}{A_{\text{steel}} \times E_{\text{steel}}}$$

$$\frac{44{,}422}{32.19(1.8 \times 10^6)} = \frac{12{,}522}{A_{\text{steel}}(29 \times 10^6)}$$

$$A_{\text{steel}} = 0.563 \text{ in}^2 \text{ (stress area at root of thread)}$$

Try two ¾-in ϕ tie rods:

$$\text{Area at root of thread} = 2(0.334) = 0.668 \text{ in}^2$$

$$f_t = \frac{12{,}523}{0.668} = 18{,}747 \text{ lb/in}^2 < F_t = 22{,}000 \text{ lb/in}^2$$

If it is assumed that the tension chord can no longer carry load, all the tensile forces must be carried by the steel tie rods. In this case, the required tie rod sizes are determined as follows:

$$A_{\text{steel}} = \frac{56{,}945}{22{,}000} = 2.59 \text{ in}^2$$

Try two 1½-in ϕ tie rods:

$$\text{Area} = 2(1.41) = 2.82 \text{ in}^2$$

$$f_t = 20{,}193 \text{ lb/in}^2 < F_t = 22{,}000 \text{ lb/in}^2$$

The attachment of the tie rods to the existing truss can be accomplished in a number of ways. Most heavy timber trusses have a steel heel plate connection, and the tie rods can be attached directly to this heel plate by welding a channel to the heel plate and then welding the tie rods to the channel. If the end of the truss is accessible, a steel plate can be attached to the end of the truss, assuming that allowable end-grain-bearing stresses are not exceeded, and the tie rod threaded through holes drilled in the extension of this plate past the edges of the timber chords. Turnbuckles or sleeve nuts can then be used to tension the rods properly. Steel angles or other similar support devices can be attached to the timber chords to provide intermediate support as required to maintain the tension rods in the horizontal plane of the neutral axis of the timber chords. Since it may be difficult to install these rods, the use of steel cables may be a better solution. Regardless of whether rods or cables are used, they must be positioned in such a manner that the tensioning of them does not result in a downward force on the truss which could cause failure.

The designer also should evaluate the structural capacity of the heel connection and the tension splices. If the capacity of either of these is exceeded, these overloads should be compared with the overload of the tension chord itself, and the steel tension rods should be designed to carry the maximum overload. Top chords should be checked for combined bending and compression stresses, allowing for eccentricities caused by the curvature of the top chord. In general, as shown in this example, the web forces are relatively low. However, the designer should particularly look for any unusual loadings applied to the webs. One example might be the attachment of a load-carrying ledger to the webs to support an adjacent roof area. This type of loading could be particularly detrimental to the capacity of the web-to-chord connection.

It is obvious that any number of typical in-service distress conditions and their applicable solution could have been illustrated. The two examples presented were selected to indicate the breadth of problems which may be encountered ranging from the less severe performance type problem to the complete structural collapse condition of a truss component.

REFERENCES

1. *Minimum Design Loads for Buildings and Other Structures,* ASCE 7-93, American Society of Civil Engineers, New York, N.Y., 1993.
2. D. A. Taylor, "Roof Snow Loads in Canada," *Can. J. Civil Eng.* **7**(1), March 1980.
3. *Standard Specifications for Highway Bridges,* American Association of State Highway and Transportation Officials, Washington, D.C., 1993.
4. *Standard for the Installation of Sprinkler Systems,* Standard NFPA 13, National Fire Protection Association, Boston, 1987.
5. *Diaphragm Construction and Design with Potlatch Lock-Deck Decking,* Potlatch Corp., Lewiston, Idaho, 1985.
6. *National Design Specification for Wood Construction and Supplement,* American Forest and Paper Products Association, Washington, D.C., 1991.
7. *Design Specification for Metal Plate Connected Wood Trusses,* TPI-85, Truss Plate Institute, Madison, Wisc., 1985.
8. *Design Specification for Metal Plate Connected Parallel Chord Wood Trusses,* PCT-80, Truss Plate Institute, Madison, Wisc., 1980.

9. *Timber Construction Manual,* 4d ed., American Institute of Timber Construction, Englewood, CO, 1994.

10. *Manual of Steel Construction,* 8th ed., American Institute of Steel Construction, Chicago, Ill., 1980.

11. *Bracing Wood Trusses: Commentary and Recommendations,* BWT-76, Truss Plate Institute, Inc., Madison, Wisc., 1976.

12. Robert J. Hoyle and Harold C. Sorensen, "Stability and Bracing of Parallel Chord Wood Trusses," *Forest Products Journal* **36**(1):74–80, Feb. 1986.

CHAPTER 7
STRUCTURAL WOOD PANELS

Thomas E. McLain, Ph.D.

7.1 STRUCTURAL PANEL CHARACTERISTICS

7.1.1 Types of Structural Panels

Wood-based panel products have been utilized successfully as structural and decorative materials for over 50 years. Recent improvements in technology have expanded the types of panel products which can be labeled as *structural*. This term is used to mean that one of the intended functions of the panel product is to successfully resist the actions of externally applied forces on the panel for a specific application.

All wood-based structural panels are composite materials. That is, they are a composite of wood elements such as veneer, particles, flakes, or fibers and some form of adhesive. *Plywood* is the most commonly known structural product and is a glued assembly of thin sheets of wood called *veneer*. *Particleboard* is a combination of wood particles and adhesive and has found wide acceptance as floor underlayment, manufactured home decking, and many specialty applications. *Waferboard* is a variant of particleboard with flakes as the basic wood element. Other forms of this product have wood strands or flakes in layers oriented in different directions through the thickness of the panel. These *oriented strand boards* (OSB) compete strongly with plywood in the light-frame residential and commercial marketplace. A hybrid product, called *composite plywood* or *composite panel* is available which features face veneers with oriented strand or random particle-flake cores. COM-PLY, a proprietary trademark of APA, is an example of this type of product.

There are many other types of panel products available (often without added adhesive) which may have some structural capability such as hardboard, medium-density fiberboard, and insulation board. For example, wood fiber insulation boards contribute significantly to the racking strength of wall systems. However, these products are not generally intended to be structural in nature except as a by-product of their specific function in a building or system. No specific structural contribution is assumed.

Note: In all example problems, SI units are only provided for given data and final problem answer or answers. No intermediate values or data are expressed in SI units.

7.1.2 Typical Applications

Structural wood panels are typically used as sheathing to provide a strong, stiff covering over some relatively flexible and weak framework. In new residential and commercial construction, wood panels are most often used as roof sheathing and decking, floor decking and underlayment, wall sheathing, and exterior siding. Additionally, plywood is used in the manufacture of structural subsystems such as stressed-skin panels, built-up beams or columns, and other modular assemblies.

Because plywood has traditionally been the most used structural panel material, plywood performance has become the standard by which other panel products are judged. Many of the products described in Sec. 7.1.1 can compete favorably with plywood both economically and in performance. Because of the many new products entering the marketplace, the designer should be keenly aware of the advantages and disadvantages of alternative panels. Particular attention should be paid to three areas. First, an accurate and complete specification of all the requirements of the material in terms of its necessary function and the environment in which it has to provide service must be developed. Second, accurate and reliable information (or assurance) of the expected properties and/or performance of the material must be obtained as input to a sound engineering design. Third, the material must be evaluated, not only in a strict engineering sense but also in terms of economics, ease of installation and maintenance, availability, and the potential consequences of its failure.

7.1.3 Panel Product Standards

Because of the many choices the designer has with panel products, standards have been developed to ensure product quality and reliability. Standards for wood-based panel products are voluntary and have been developed by interested parties. However, building codes, lending agencies, or governments often utilize standards in a legal sense to ensure an acceptable level of service and safety to the public. Consequently, the designer should be aware of the potential use of these "mandatory" standards for a specific application.

There are two types of standards for wood-based panel products. The first is a commodity (or product) standard which describes what may be used in the manufacture of a panel product. It may state some minimum properties that the product must have to be acceptable, but these are usually only loosely tied to performance. The *Voluntary Product Standard for Construction and Industrial Plywood,* PS1-83,[1] and the American National Standard *Mat-Formed Wood Particleboard,* ANSI A208.1-93,[2] are, in part, examples of this type of standard. The second type of standard specifies a level of performance of a product in service, and in a specific application it generally does not attempt to regulate how the manufacturer should make the product. For panel products, laboratory tests have been specified which have a direct relationship with the expected end use of the material. For example, one test developed by the American Plywood Association for roof and floor panels[3] simulates the actions of the heel of a construction worker or the load transmitted by a leg of a piece of furniture to the panels.

Plywood product standard PS1-83[1] includes both types of standards concepts. Panels may be certified as meeting PS1-83 quality requirements either by an inspection of the manufacturing process or by periodic performance tests of random samples of finished panels.

The American Plywood Association (APA) has promulgated performance standards for all wood-based panels for sheathing and floor applications. These have been accepted by the major model codes through a National Evaluation Service report (NER-108)[4] issued by the Council of American Building Officials (CABO). The standards do not specify plywood but encompass any wood-based panels that meet the performance criteria. Performance standards continue to receive greater emphasis and will simplify many design decisions allowing selection between numerous alternatives on a common basis. In 1992, a new performance standard for wood-based structural-use panels was established as a Voluntary Product Standard PS 2-92.[5]

Several trade associations and manufacturers provide excellent, up-to-date information on the characteristics and uses of panel products. The interested designer may wish to contact one of the sources listed in Sec. 7.7. In particular, APA and The Engineered Wood Association offers a wealth of information and practices on the structural use of wood panels.

7.2 PLYWOOD PROPERTIES

7.2.1 Description of Plywood

Despite the influx of the new panel products, plywood will continue to be a commonly used panel product for *structural* use. In addition, the performance of newer panel products is often judged against that of plywood. Consequently, this section has been developed to explain the various properties and uses of plywood.

Plywood is a panel or sheet product composed of thin sheets of veneer, or plies. Plywood always has an odd number of layers, each layer consisting of one or more plies. These layers are glued together with the grain of adjacent layers placed at right angles to one another (Fig. 7.1). The face layers are oriented with their grain parallel to the long dimension of the panel, with the crossbands thus having their grain parallel to the short sides of the panel.

Plywood is manufactured in sheets or panels with 4 by 8 ft (1.22 by 2.44 m) as a generally standard size. Other sizes may be available for specific types of plywood, although widths other than 4 ft (1.22 m) are rare. The tolerance for length

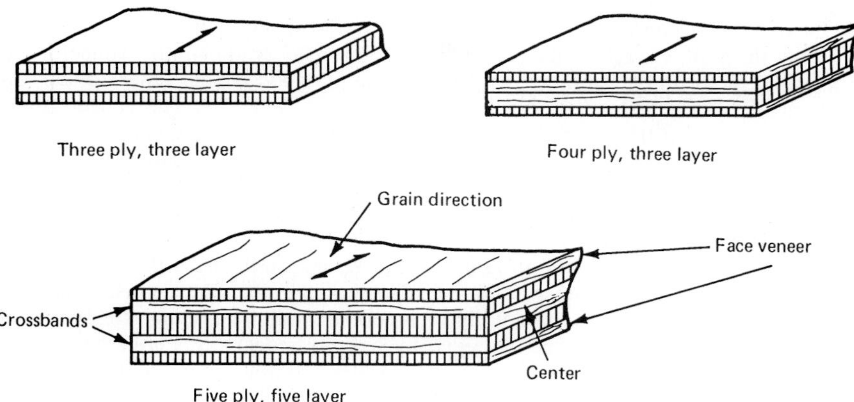

FIG. 7.1 Layered nature of plywood.

and width dimensions of a plywood panel is +0 in and $-\frac{1}{16}$ in (1.6 mm).[1] This tolerance standard allows for some change in panel dimension with varying moisture conditions when gaps are left between panels in a sheathing application. Plywood is available in a number of thicknesses from ¼ (6.4) to 1⅛ in (28.6 mm) and greater, with tolerance varying by size. For *sanded* panels, the tolerance is $\pm\frac{1}{64}$ in (0.40 mm) for thicknesses of ¾ in (19 mm) or less or ±3 percent for ¾ in (19 mm) thick. For *unsanded, touch-sanded,* and *overlaid* panels, the tolerance is $\pm\frac{1}{32}$ in (0.8 mm) for thicknesses of $\frac{13}{16}$ in (20.6 mm) or less or ±5 percent for larger thicknesses.

Many variables in the composition of plywood affect its properties and performance as a structural panel. These include

1. Number and thickness of the layers and plies
2. Species of veneer (may not all be the same)
3. Grain orientation of the plies
4. Quality or grade of veneer
5. Type of adhesive

Combinations of these variables enable the manufacturer to tailor the product for specific uses. Hence many different types of plywood are available. Thus designers must understand something of the composition of plywood to select the appropriate panel for a specific application.

7.2.2 Veneer and Adhesive

The thin sheets of wood that are laminated to form plywood are usually rotary-peeled. That is, a long knife, acting somewhat like a potato peeler, peels the veneer from a spinning log. The veneer is then clipped to size and rapidly dried to a low moisture content. Some repairs may be made to upgrade the quality of the sheet. With one type of repair called *plugging,* a defect such as a knot or pitch pocket is cut out and patch fit into the remaining hole. Smaller sheets of veneer may be joined or spliced together to form the necessary sizes. Veneer to be used in core stock may be strung or stitched together with nylon string or thread.

The sheet of veneer is then visually graded. The grade of the veneer is an important factor in determining the grade of the plywood panel. Veneer grades are designated by a letter and are briefly summarized in Table 7.1. The veneer grades are constructed so that a grade C veneer may be upgraded by repair to grade A. Similarly, grade D veneer may be upgraded to grade B. Hence similarities in terms of strength and stiffness exist between grades A and C and also between grades B and D veneer. Grade C-plugged veneer is an upgrade of C that does not meet all the requirements of grade A.

The type of adhesive used to laminate the veneers influences the durability of the resulting panel. The most common adhesives are phenolic resins, which are synthetic adhesives that cure under high temperature and must be hot-pressed. They are waterproof and will not be degraded by microorganisms. Phenolic resins may be extended or thinned by mixing them with water and other ingredients to produce a lower-cost adhesive that has some water resistance but is not waterproof.

TABLE 7.1 Veneer Grades (PS1-83)

Grade	Description
A	Smooth and paintable. Neatly made repairs permissible (max. 18). Also used for natural finish in less demanding applications.
B	Solid surface veneer. Some repairs, minor splits, and tight knots to 1 in across grain are permitted.
C-plugged	Improved C veneer with widths of splits limited to ⅛ in and knotholes and open defects limited to ¼ by ½ in. Repairs permitted.
C	Knotholes to 1 in, tight knots to 1½ in permitted. Occasional knotholes to 1 in across grain and some to 1½ in, providing total width of all knots and knotholes within specified limits. Limited splits permitted. Minimum veneer permitted in Exterior-type plywood. Stitching permitted.
D	Permits knots and knotholes with widths up to 2½ in and ½ in larger under specified limits. Limited splits and stitching permitted. Limited to Exposure 1 panels.

Source: Adapted from Ref. 15. Used with permission.

7.2.3 Plywood Physical Characteristics

Solid wood, and particularly veneer, has different strength and stiffness properties along the grain than across it. A sheet of veneer stressed in tension may be over 100 times stronger parallel to grain than perpendicular to grain. The modulus of elasticity across the grain is approximately one-thirty-fifth of that parallel to grain.

By cross-laminating, plywood can be made more homogeneous in terms of strength properties than a sheet of solid wood of the same thickness. However, there will still be a strong and a weak orientation to a panel. This is a result of the plies with grain parallel to the stress having greater resistance than those perpendicular to the stress. Because there is a greater thickness of veneer placed parallel to the face grain, the strong direction is parallel to the face grain of the panel with the weak orientation 90° from that (see Fig. 7.1). Additionally, the cross-sectional properties are different in the two orientations (see Sec. 7.2.5).

Wood is a hygroscopic material and will change dimensions when the surrounding air changes relative humidity and temperature. It is very anisotropic in shrinking and swelling characteristics, and dimensional changes across the grain are many times greater than parallel to grain. Because of plywood's cross-banded nature, plywood in-plane swelling is much less than that of solid wood and is usually less than 2 percent when a dry panel is saturated. Swelling through the thickness is similar to that of solid wood (2 to 5 percent dry to green) and varies with species. For normal construction, swelling problems can be virtually eliminated by providing a ⅛-in (3-mm) gap between panel edges and ends. These values should be doubled if the moisture content is expected to be high in service. The use of panel clips, which are used to minimize deflection differences between adjacent panels, may help in ensuring adequate spacing.

Plywood also has many of the advantages and properties of solid wood, such as light weight [$\approx$ 35 lb/ft^3 (640 kg/m^3)], ease of working, high strength-to-weight ratio, and ease in fastening. Additionally, plywood is split-resistant and has excellent shock absorbancy characteristics. Like wood, plywood is an insulator and has low thermal conductivity when dry. It is also an electrical insulator (dielectric) when

TABLE 7.6 Effective Section Properties for Plywood *(Continued)*

Face plies of different species groups from inner plies (includes all product standard grades except Marine and Structural I)

			Stress applied parallel to face grain				Stress applied perpendicular to face grain			
Nominal thickness, in	Approximate weight, lb/ft^2	Effective thickness for shear t_s, in	Area A, in^2/ft	Moment of inertia I, in^4/ft	Effective section modulus KS, in^3/ft	Rolling shear constant Ib/Q, in^2/ft	Area A, in^2/ft	Moment of inertia I, in^4/ft	Effective section modulus KS, in^3/ft	Rolling shear constant Ib/Q, in^2/ft
Touch-sanded panels										
½-T	1.5	0.342	2.698	0.083	0.271	4.252	1.159	0.006	0.061	2.746
$^{19}/_{32}$ & ⅝-T	1.8	0.408	2.354	0.123	0.327	5.346	1.555	0.016	0.135	3.220
$^{23}/_{32}$ & ¾-T	2.2	0.439	2.715	0.193	0.398	6.589	1.622	0.032	0.219	3.635
1⅛-T	3.3	0.839	4.548	0.633	0.977	11.258	4.067	0.272	0.743	8.535

TABLE 7.6 Effective Section Properties for Plywood *(Continued)*

Structural I and Marine

			Stress applied parallel to face grain				Stress applied perpendicular to face grain			
Nominal thickness, in	Approximate weight, lb/ft^2	Effective thickness for shear t_s, in	Area A, in^2/ft	Moment of inertia I, in^4/ft	Effective section modulus KS, in^3/ft	Rolling shear constant Ib/Q, in^2/ft	Area A, in^2/ft	Moment of inertia I, in^4/ft	Effective section modulus KS, in^3/ft	Rolling shear constant Ib/Q, in^2/ft
Unsanded panels										
5/16-U	1.0	0.356	1.619	0.022	0.126	2.567	1.188	0.002	0.029	6.037
3/8-U	1.1	0.371	2.226	0.041	0.195	3.107	1.438	0.003	0.043	7.307
15/32 & 1/2-U	1.5	0.535	2.719	0.074	0.279	4.157	2.175	0.012	0.116	2.408
19/32 & 5/8-U	1.8	0.707	3.464	0.154	0.437	5.685	2.742	0.045	0.240	3.072
23/32 & 3/4-U	2.2	0.739	4.219	0.236	0.549	6.148	2.813	0.064	0.299	3.540
7/8-U	2.6	0.776	4.388	0.346	0.690	6.948	3.510	0.131	0.457	4.722
1-U	3.0	1.088	5.200	0.529	0.922	8.512	5.661	0.270	0.781	6.435
1 1/8-U	3.3	1.118	6.654	0.751	1.164	9.061	5.542	0.408	0.999	7.833
Sanded panels										
1/4-S	0.8	0.342	1.280	0.012	0.083	2.009	0.626	0.001	0.013	2.723
11/32-S	1.0	0.365	1.280	0.026	0.133	2.764	0.751	0.001	0.023	3.397
3/8-S	1.1	0.373	1.680	0.038	0.177	3.086	1.126	0.002	0.033	4.927
15/32-S	1.4	0.537	1.947	0.067	0.246	4.107	2.168	0.009	0.093	2.405
1/2-S	1.5	0.545	1.947	0.078	0.271	4.457	2.232	0.014	0.123	2.725
19/32-S	1.7	0.709	3.018	0.116	0.338	5.566	2.501	0.034	0.199	2.811
5/8-S	1.8	0.717	3.112	0.131	0.361	5.934	2.751	0.045	0.238	3.073
23/32-S	2.1	0.741	3.735	0.183	0.439	6.109	3.126	0.085	0.338	3.780
3/4-S	2.2	0.748	3.848	0.202	0.464	6.189	3.745	0.108	0.418	4.047
7/8-S	2.6	0.778	3.952	0.288	0.569	7.539	4.772	0.179	0.579	5.046
1-S	3.0	1.091	5.215	0.479	0.827	7.978	5.693	0.321	0.870	6.981
1 1/8-S	3.3	1.121	5.593	0.623	0.955	8.841	5.724	0.474	1.098	8.377

TABLE 7.6 Effective Section Properties for Plywood *(Continued)*

Structural I and Marine

			Stress applied parallel to face grain				Stress applied perpendicular to face grain			
Nominal thickness, in	Approximate weight, lb/ft^2	Effective thickness for shear t_s, in	Area A, in^2/ft	Moment of inertia I, in^4/ft	Effective section modulus KS, in^3/ft	Rolling shear constant Ib/Q, in^2/ft	Area A, in^2/ft	Moment of inertia I, in^4/ft	Effective section modulus KS, in^3/ft	Rolling shear constant Ib/Q, in^2/ft
Touch-sanded panels										
½-T	1.5	0.543	2.698	0.084	0.282	4.511	2.486	0.020	0.162	2.720
$^{19}/_{32}$ & ⅝-T	1.8	0.707	3.127	0.124	0.349	5.500	2.799	0.050	0.259	3.183
$^{23}/_{32}$ & ¾-T	2.2	0.739	4.059	0.201	0.469	6.592	3.625	0.078	0.350	3.596

Note: 1 in = 25.4 mm; 1 ft = 0.3048 m.
Source: From Ref. 9. Used with permission.

TABLE 7.7 Guide to Allowable Stress Table

Plywood grade	Grade stress level (for Table 7.8)	Species group	Surface
	Exterior applications		
APA-rated sheathing Ext.[c]	S-1[d]	See "Key to Span Rating" (Table 7.7a)	Unsanded
APA Structural I rated sheathing Ext.	S-1[d]	Group 1	Unsanded
APA Structural II[b] rated sheathing Ext.	S-1[d]	See "Key to Span Rating" (Table 7.7a)	Unsanded
APA-Rated Sturd-I-Floor Ext.[c]	S-2	See "Key to Span Rating" (Table 7.7a)	Touch-sanded
APA Underlayment Ext. and APA C-C-plugged Ext.	S-2	As specified	Touch-sanded
APA B-B Plyform Class I or II[b]	S-2	Class I use Group 1; Class II use Group 3	Sanded
APA Marine Ext.	A face and back use S-1; B face or back use S-2	Group 1	Sanded
APA appearance grades Ext.	A or C face and back use S-1[f]; B face or back use S-2	As specified	Sanded
	Interior or protected applications		
APA-rated sheathing Exp. 1 or 2[c]	S-3[a]	See "Key to Span Rating" (Table 7.7a)	Unsanded
APA Structural I rated sheathing Exp. 1	S-2	Use Group 1	Unsanded
APA Structural II[b] rated sheathing Exp. 1	S-2	See "Key to Span Rating" (Table 7.7a)	Unsanded
APA-rated Sturd-I-Floor Exp.1 or 2[c]	See "Key to Span Rating" (Table 7.7a)	Touch-sanded	
APA Underlayment Int.	S-3[a]	As specified	Touch-sanded
APA C-D-plugged Int. Exp. 1, 2	S-3[a]	As specified	Touch-sanded
APA appearance grades Int, Exp. 1,2	S-3[a]	As specified	Sanded

[a]When exterior glue is specified, i.e., Exposure 1, stress-level 2 (S-2) should be used.

[b]Check local suppliers for availability of Structural II and Plyform Class II grades.

[c]Properties and stresses apply only to APA-rated Sturd-I-Floor and APA-Rated Sheathing manufactured entirely with veneers.

[d]C face and back must be natural unrepaired; if repaired, use stress-level 2 (S-2).

Source: Adapted from Ref. 9. Used with permission.

TABLE 7.7a Key to Span Rating and Species Group

(For panels with span rating as across top, and thickness as at left, use stress for species group given in table.)

Thickness, in	Span rating (APA-rated sheathing grades)							
	12/0	16/0	20/0	24/0	32/16	40/20	48/24	
					Span rating (Sturd-I-Floor grades)			
					16 o.c.	20 o.c.	24 o.c.	48 o.c.
5/16	4	3	1	—	—	—	—	—
3/8	—	—	4[c]	1	—	—	—	—
15/32 & 1/2	—	—	—	4[c]	1[a]	—	—	—
19/32 & 5/8	—	—	—	—	4[c]	1	—	—
23/32 & 3/4	—	—	—	—	—	4[c]	1	—
7/8	—	—	—	—	—	—	3[b]	—
1 1/8	—	—	—	—	—	—	—	1[d]

[a]Thicknesses not applicable to APA-rated Sturd-I-Floor.
[b]For APA-rated Sturd-I-Floor 24 o.c., use group 4 stresses.
[c]For Structural II, use Group 3 stresses.
[d]C face and back must be natural unrepaired; if required, use stress-level 2 (S-2).
Source: Adapted from Ref. 9. Used with permission.

or shear in the plane of the panel, results from shear generated in panels in flexure from loads applied normal to a face. When this failure occurs, the wood fibers appear to roll over one another giving rise to the name. A rolling shear constant Ib/Q is tabulated in columns 7 and 11 of Table 7.6. Multiplication of this constant and the allowable shear stress in the panel will yield the maximum allowable shear force.

7.2.6 Allowable Design Stresses

Allowable design stresses and stiffness values are presented in Table 7.8 and are a function of grade stress level (grade of plywood), the in-use environmental condi-

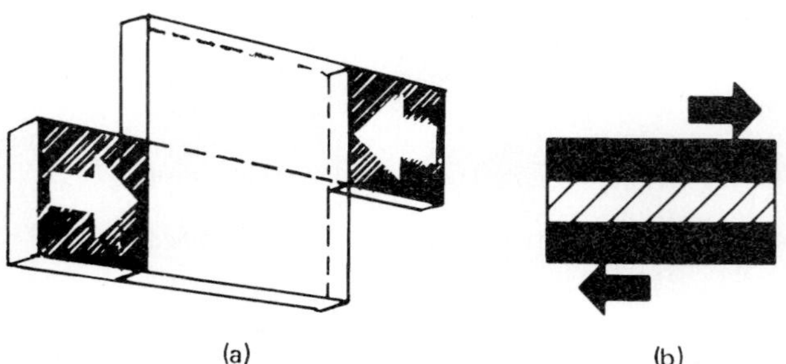

FIG. 7.3 Types of shear in plywood. (*a*) Shear through thickness; (*b*) rolling shear. *(Adapted from Ref 9.)*

TABLE 7.8 Allowable stresses for plywood (lb/in^2) conforming to U.S. Product Standard PS1-83*

Type of stress	Species group of face ply	Grade Stress Level†				
		S-1		S-2		S-3
		Wet	Dry	Wet	Dry	Dry only
Extreme fiber stress in bending F_b and tension in plane of plies F_t (face grain parallel or perpendicular to span; at 45° to face grain use $\frac{1}{6}F_t$)	1	1430	2000	1190	1650	1650
	2, 3	980	1400	820	1200	1200
	4	940	1330	780	1110	1110
Compression in plane of plies F_c (parallel or perpendicular to face grain; at 45° to face grain use $\frac{1}{3}F_c$)	1	970	1640	900	1540	1540
	2	730	1200	680	1100	1100
	3	610	1060	580	990	990
	4	610	1000	580	950	950
Shear through the thickness F_v (parallel or perpendicular to face grain; at 45° to face grain use $2F_v$)	1	155	190	155	190	160
	2, 3	120	140	120	140	120
	4	110	130	110	130	115
Rolling shear (in the plane of plies) F_s (parallel or perpendicular to face grain; at 45° to face grain use $1\frac{1}{3}F_s$)	Marine & Structural I	63	75	63	75	—
	All others‡	44	53	44	53	48

TABLE 7.8 Allowable stresses for plywood (lb/in^2) conforming to U.S. Product Standard PS1-83*
(Continued)

Type of stress	Species group of face ply	Grade Stress Level†				
		S-1		S-2		S-3
		Wet	Dry	Wet	Dry	Dry only
Modulus of rigidity G (shear in plane perpendicular to plies	1	70,000	90,000	70,000	90,000	82,000
	2	60,000	75,000	60,000	75,000	68,000
	3	50,000	60,000	50,000	60,000	55,000
	4	45,000	50,000	45,000	50,000	45,000
Bearing (on face) $F_{c\perp}$ perpendicular to plane of plies	1	210	340	210	340	340
	2, 3	135	210	135	210	210
	4	105	160	105	160	160
Modulus of elasticity in bending in plane of plies E (face grain parallel or perpendicular to span)	1	1,500,000	1,800,000	1,500,000	1,800,000	1,800,000
	2	1,300,000	1,500,000	1,300,000	1,500,000	1,500,000
	3	1,100,000	1,200,000	1,100,000	1,200,000	1,200,000
	4	900,000	1,000,000	900,000	1,000,000	1,000,000

*Stresses are based on normal duration of load and on common structural applications where panels are 24 in or greater in width.

†See Table 7.7 for guide. To qualify for stress-level S-1, gluelines must be exterior and only veneer grades N, A, and C (natural, not repaired) are allowed in either face or back. For stress-level S-2, gluelines must be exterior and veneer grade B. C-plugged, and D are allowed on the face or back. Stress-level S-3 includes all panels with interior or intermediate gluelines.

‡Reduce stresses 25 percent for three-layer (four-ply panels over ⅝ in thick). Such layups are possible under PS1-83 for APA-rated sheathing, APA-rated Sturd-I-Floor, Underlayment, C-C plugged, and C-D-plugged grades over ⅝ through ¾ in thick.

Source: From Ref. 9. Used with permission.

tions, and the species group. Actual stresses computed using the section properties from Table 7.6 may not exceed the allowable design values modified for duration of load, width, panel construction, and end-use conditions.

The grade stress level is a function of the veneer quality and the adhesive used in the panel. Table 7.7 should be used as a guide for selecting the correct level. *Dry* conditions apply to plywood under service conditions which are continuously dry and where the equilibrium moisture content will be less than 16 percent. *Wet* conditions are for applications exposed to weather or where the equilibrium moisture content is 16 percent or greater.

The values in Table 7.8 are for a normal duration of loading of 10 years. They may be modified for other periods using the guidelines of Chap. 2, on load-duration factors. If plywood is treated with fire-retardant chemicals, then there may be a reduction in strength and stiffness. These reductions should be obtained from the supplier of the treating and redrying service. Other properly applied preservative treatments do not affect strength or stiffness values.

If plywood is used in widths of 24 in (610 mm) or less, the values should be reduced for an increased chance of a strength-reducing defect in a critical location. This reduction should vary linearly from 0 percent at 24 in (610 mm) of width to 50 percent at 8 in (203 mm) of width or less.

EXAMPLE 7.1 What is the maximum uniformly distributed live load that can be safely supported by a ½-in (12.7-mm) group 1 Underlayment plywood (Exposure 1) nailed to 2 × 6s spaced 16 in (406 mm) on center (o.c.) with the span parallel to the face grain? (See Fig. 7.4.) What is the value if the spans are perpendicular to the face grain? (Assume dry service conditions, normal load duration, and a deflection limitation of span/360.)

From Tables 7.6, 7.7, and 7.8 (grade stress level = S2, species group = 1, touch-sanded):

	Span parallel to face grain	Span perpendicular to face grain
I, in^4/ft	0.083	0.006
KS, in^3/ft	0.271	0.061
Ib/Q, in^2/ft	4.252	2.746
F_b, lb/in^2	1650	1650
F_s, lb/in^2	53	53
E, lb/in^2	1.8×10^6	1.8×10^6

For panels placed with face grain parallel to span (perpendicular to supports), use equations for three-span continuous beam when supports are 32 in or less on center. Two-span equations are used for greater support spacings. These equations are found in the Appendix (Sec. 7.7.2).

For plywood placed with face grain perpendicular to span (parallel to supports), the three-span condition is used for spacings of 16 in or less, two spans for 24 in, and one span for greater than 24-in spacing.

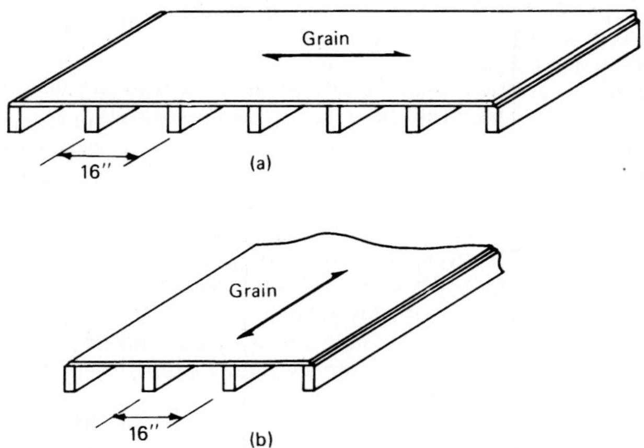

FIG. 7.4 Strong and weak orientation of a plywood panel.

Span Parallel to Face Grain. Maximum bending load (three spans, ℓ_1 = o.c. spacing):

$$w(\text{bending})\ \text{lb/ft}^2 = \frac{120F_b(KS)}{\ell_1^2} = \frac{120(1650)(0.271)}{(16)^2} = 210\ \text{lb/ft}^2$$

Maximum shear load [ℓ_2 = clear span (in) = 16 − 1.5 = 14.5]:

$$w(\text{shear}) = \frac{20F_s(Ib/Q)}{\ell_2} = \frac{20(53)(4.252)}{14.5} = 311\ \text{lb/ft}^2$$

Maximum deflection load (ℓ_3 = clear span + support width factor. This factor is 0.25 for 2-in nominal, 0.625 for 4-in nominal framing. ℓ_3 = 14.5 + 0.25 = 14.75):

$$w(\text{def}) = \frac{1743EI\Delta_b}{\ell_3^4} = \frac{1743(1.8 \times 10^6)(0.083)(16/360)}{(14.75)^4} = 244\ \text{lb/ft}^2$$

Note that if ℓ_1 ÷ panel thickness was less than 20, then the deflection due to shear may be significant. See Appendix (Sec. 7.7.2).

Maximum load = 210 lb/ft² (10.05 kPa) (bending governs).

Span Perpendicular to Face Grain. Maximum bending load (three spans):

$$w(\text{bending}) = \frac{120(1650)(0.061)}{(16)^2} = 47.2\ \text{lb/ft}^2$$

Maximum shear load:

$$w(\text{shear}) = \frac{20(53)(2.746)}{14.5} = 201\ \text{lb/ft}^2$$

Maximum deflection load:

$$w(\text{def}) = \frac{1743(1.8 \times 10^6)(0.006)(16/360)}{(14.75)^4} = 17.6 \text{ lb/ft}^2$$

Maximum load = 17.6 lb/ft^2 (846 Pa) (deflection governs).

Note that changing the orientation of the panel caused a significant reduction in the maximum allowable uniform load. This is why span ratings are valid only for panels oriented with face grain parallel with the span. Orientation perpendicular to span is generally very inefficient and not recommended. It also may be disallowed by building code. An exception to this is in panelized roof systems (Sec. 7.4).

7.2.7 Mechanical Fastenings

Many different types of mechanical fasteners have been used successfully with plywood and other similar panel products. For most applications, nails, staples, wood screws, or bolts are sufficient. In sheathing applications, a fastening schedule is usually specified rather than using individual joint ultimate strengths. These fastening schedules are based on test results and commonly successful construction practice. They will typically specify the type of fastener to be used and the maximum spacing between fasteners. Most building codes and regulatory agencies specify sheathing fastening to be used in specific applications.

The strength of mechanically fastened plywood joints depends on the type of plywood and the substrate to which it is to be fastened. Table 7.9 indicates some ultimate test loads for fasteners used with plywood. These are *not* design loads and must be reduced by an appropriate factor which typically varies from two to four.[6,17]

Design values and other specifications for some pneumatic or mechanically driven staples and nails are given in National Evaluation Report, NER-272.[6] This report contains fastening specifications for structural panels used in walls, floors, and roofs, including shear walls and diaphragms. Other specific design values may be found in the *National Design Specification for Wood Construction*[7] or local building codes.

Table 7.10 indicates some general recommendations for the size and type of nails and wood screws by plywood thickness. Recommended or required fastening schedules should always take precedence over this table for specific applications such as the design of structural diaphragms or shearwalls. For conventional light-frame construction, nails and screws should be spaced 6 in (152 mm) apart at panel edges. Panel fasteners should be a minimum of ⅜ in (9.5 mm) from panel edges. H-shaped panel clips (ply clips) are commonly used for supporting panel edges in roof construction. They may be used in place of lumber blocking or tongue-and-groove edges. When required, one clip is generally placed between each support except for 48-in (1220-mm) spans where two are required to function as effective edge support. Maximum allowable span may decrease if effective edge support is not provided (see Table 7.17).

7.3 OTHER COMPOSITE STRUCTURAL PANELS

7.3.1 Particleboards

Particleboard panel products consist of wood particles in the form of flakes, strands, wafers, chips, shavings, fibers, etc. that are combined with synthetic resins or some other bonding system. In mat-formed particleboard, the mixture of wood particles

TABLE 7.9 Ultimate Fastener Loads

Nails				
Plywood thickness, in	Ultimate lateral loads in Douglas fir lumber, lb per common nail[a,b]			
	6d	8d	10d	16d
5/16	275	305	—	—
3/8	275	340	—	—
1/2	—	350	425	—
5/8	—	350	425	445
3/4	—	—	410	445

Wood screws[c,d]						
Depth of threaded penetration, in	Ultimate withdrawal loads, lb					
	Screw size					
	#6	#8	#10	#12	#14	#16
3/8	145	165	195	125	—	—
1/2	210	190	205	340	355	—
5/8	325	330	355	430	445	—
3/4	390	370	420	480	535	—
1	—	—	—	600	715	740

Bolts[e,f]					
Bolt diameter, in	Plywood thickness, in	Face grain direction	Plywood end distance, in	Plywood edge distance, in	Ultimate lateral load, lb
1/2	5/16	90°	4	2	2400
	1/2	0°	3	1	4740
		90°	3	1	4570
	5/8	0°	3	1½	5400
		90°	3	1½	4320
	3/4	0°	4	1½	5280
		90°	4	3	5630
3/4	1/2	0°	4	2	7800
		90°	4	1¾	6900
	5/8	0°	4	1½	8070
		90°	4	1½	6900
	3/4	0°	6	1½	7920
		90°	6	1½	8650

[a]Assume 3/8-in edge distance.

[b]For galvnized casing nails, multiply tabulated values by 0.6.

[c]Plywood is all group 1, with screws driven perpendicular to face of panel.

[d]Values may be increased 10 percent for sheet-metal screws.

[e]Values are for all-group 1 plywood gussets on both sides of 3 × 3 green Douglas fir lumber with bolt loaded in double shear.

[f]Table shows the minimum plywood end and edge distances required to develop the plywood's full bolt-bearing strength. For lesser end and edge distances, with a minimum of 50 percent that tabulated, the ultimate load may be assumed directly proportional to the tabulated end or edge distance. For maximum strength, spacing between adjacent rows of bolts should be twice the tabulated edge distance.

Source: From Refs. 6, 16, and 17. Used with permission.

TABLE 7.10 General Guidelines for Fastening Plywood Panels with Nails and Screws

Fastener	Plywood thickness, in			
	3⁄8	1⁄2	5⁄8	3⁄4
Nails:				
Common	6d	6d	8d	8d
Finish	4d	6d	8d	8d
Wood screws:				
Min. size	#6	#6	#8	#8
Min. length, in	1	1 1⁄4	1 1⁄4	1 1⁄2
Drill size:				
Shank, in	9⁄64	9⁄64	11⁄64	1⁄8
Root, in	3⁄32	3⁄32	11⁄64	1⁄8

Note: 1 in = 25.4 mm.
Source: Adapted from Refs. 8, 16, and 17.

and binders is laid down in a mat which is hot-pressed to increase the density of the mat and cure the adhesive. The particles may be oriented to some degree to provide some directionality of strength properties along and across the panel. Oriented particles may be laid down in orthogonal layers similar to plywood veneer. Different types of particles may be used in the same panel to improve surface properties and create a more layered particle product.

Standards. Particleboard panel products may be manufactured under a voluntary standard, ANSI A208.1-1979, *Mat-Formed Wood Particleboard.*[2] This standard covers the physical and mechanical property requirements for grades of mat-formed board. The only structural particleboard produced under this standard is manufactured house decking. The National Particle Board Association should be contacted for recommended use of this product.

Composite panel products may be manufactured to meet the American Plywood Association's performance standard PRP-108 or the U.S. Voluntary Product Standard PS2-92. (See Sec. 7.1.3.) If the panel meets the requirements for structural adequacy, dimensional stability, and bond durability, it may qualify as an APA performance-rated structural-use panel as sheathing, Structural 1 sheathing, or single floor. This rating indicates that the panel is sufficient for the specified application and not that the different products all have the same properties.

Waferboard. Waferboard is an exterior bonded structural panel product that has largely been replaced by oriented strand board but may still be available in some areas. It is made of wood flakes whose length in direction of the grain is at least 1¼ in (31.8 mm) and is bonded with a phenolic adhesive. Wafers are usually randomly oriented to make an in-plane isotropic panel. However, they may be deliberately aligned to increase the strength and stiffness properties parallel to alignment. Those perpendicular to alignment are reduced in this case.

Allowable properties for waferboard have been established by the Structural Board Association (Canadian agency). These properties and associated product applications have been approved for use in the United States through a National Evaluation Service report assigned to the Structural Board Association.

FIG. 7.5 Composite panel products. *(Courtesy of the American Plywood Association.)*

Oriented Strand Board (OSB). OSB is a panel product that is comprised of strandlike particles of wood that are directionally oriented. Three to five layers of these strands are arranged in a panel at right angles to one another. This makes the panel more homogeneous in its in-plane properties and improves dimensional stability and fastening characteristics. OSB panels may be rated under the APA performance specifications for sheathing applications. Oriented strand material also may be used as corestock in composite plywood.

7.3.2 Composite Panels

This panel product has been commercially available for several years and is a composite of veneer and wood-based materials. Typically, the grain direction of the face veneer is in the long direction of the panel. The grain of the reconstituted wood core may be oriented at 90° to the face veneer and could be one of several types of reconstituted wood. Oriented strand cores are common. These products are marketed under a variety of names, but Comply, an APA proprietary trade name, is common. These products are usually rated under the APA performance specifications or PS2-92.

7.4 STRUCTURAL SHEATHING APPLICATIONS

7.4.1 Sheathing Applications

By their very nature, panel products are efficient in providing both surface coverage and strength requirements in frame construction. This section discusses typical applications of panel products as sheathing-type load-carrying elements. Loads are assumed to act normal to the panel surface as opposed to diaphragms or shearwall-type loadings.

Historically, the most common wood panel product for floor, wall, and roof sheathing has been plywood. Other composite panels can be used, since the function of the panel is the same in the sheathing system regardless of its composition. In recent years, composite panels and OSB have become very common in the structural-use panel market. This is the primary reason for the advent of performance standards for panel products. Other panel types described in Sec. 7.3 are commonly allowed for specific nonstructural applications.

Plywood and panels with directional characteristics are normally used in the strong direction and are assumed to be continuous over two or more spans. One exception is in stressed-skin panel systems, where the weak direction is often employed (see Sec. 7.6). These recommendations conform to most building codes but may differ with requirements of specific localities.

7.4.2 Flooring Systems

Panel products may have several different uses in a flooring system. As a subfloor in a two- or more-layer floor system, the sheathing is connected directly to the joists or beams that provide the major system support. In this system, an underlayment is also used on top of the subfloor to provide a smooth surface for floor coverings and for additional strength and stiffness. Wood-strip flooring, lightweight concrete, or other coverings with some structural capacity may preclude the need for underlayment. A combined subfloor and underlayment such as APA's Sturd-I-Floor is a single-layer product which serves as both subfloor and underlayment.

Performance requirements for floor sheathing are usually established by the building code, lending institution, or government agencies. Minimum requirements are generally specified for deflection between joists or beams under a uniform or concentrated load. Additionally, the sheathing should safely support all design uniform loads and any specified concentrated loads. There are differences in requirements between agencies.

Subfloor. The sheathing grades of plywood are frequently used as subflooring. These include PS1-83 plywood grades C-D Exposure 1 and C-C Exterior. APA-rated sheathing (Exposure 1 or 2) is designed specifically for this application and may include performance-rated composite panels. The span rating is a guide to the use of a panel in a specific application. Table 7.11 indicates thickness, spans, and nailing requirements for typical subflooring. If lightweight or gypsum concrete is to be used over the subfloor, then panels marked 42/20 may be used when joists are spaced 24 in o.c. (610 mm). A 32/16 index is the minimum that should be used for 16-in (406-mm) spacing. All recommended spans assume the panel to be continuous over two or more spans with grain of face veneer parallel to the span.

The free edges of the subfloor should be tongue and groove (T&G) or supported by blocking unless a separate underlayment layer is installed with joints offset from those of the subfloor. Lightweight concrete or wood-strip flooring also may preclude edge support.

Many code agencies accept particle- and waferboards for use as subfloors or combined subfloor and underlayment. This acceptance will vary by locality. Typical recommendations are a maximum span of 16 in (406 mm) for ⅝-in (15.9-mm) and $^{21}/_{32}$-in (16.7-mm) panels and a 19.2-in (488-mm) span for ¾-in (19.0-mm) panels. The edges must be T&G or otherwise supported.

Underlayment. This layer provides a smooth surface for nonstructural floor coverings and increases floor stiffness. It also must have sufficient hardness to resist indentation during normal use. Either plywood as shown in Table 7.12 or grade PBU particleboard is typically used. Underlayment-grade plywood has C-plugged

TABLE 7.11 Subflooring[a] (APA-Rated Sheathing, C-D Int., C-C Ext.)

Panel span rating (or group number)	Panel thickness, in	Maximum span, in	Nail size and type	Nail spacing	
				Panel edges	Intermediate
24/16[b]	$^{7}/_{16}$	16	6d common	6	12
32/16	$^{15}/_{32}$, ½, ⅝	16[c]	8d common[d]	6	12
40/20	$^{19}/_{32}$, ⅝, ¾, ⅞	20[b,e]	8d common	6	12
48/24	$^{23}/_{32}$, ¾, ⅞	24	8d common	6	12
60/32	⅞	32	8d common	6	12

Note: 1 in = 25.4 mm.

[a]For subfloor recommendations under ceramic tile, refer to Ref. 9 for recommendations. For subfloor recommendations under gypsum concrete, contact floor topping manufacturer.

[b]Other code approved fasteners may be used.

[c]Span may be 24 in if $^{25}/_{32}$-in wood-strip flooring is installed at right angles to joists.

[d]6d common nail permitted if panel is ½ in or thinner.

[e]Span may be 24 in if $^{25}/_{32}$-in wood-strip flooring is installed at right angles to joists, or if a minimum 1½ in of lightweight concrete is applied over panels.

Source: From Ref. 9. Used with permission.

TABLE 7.12 Plywood Underlayment

Plywood grades and species group[a]	Application	Minimum plywood thickness, in	Fastener size and type	Fastener spacing,[b] in	
				Panel edges	Intermediate
APA-rated Sturd-I-Floor ($^{19}/_{32}$ in or thicker)	Over smooth subfloor	$^1/_4$	3d × 1$^1/_4$-in ring-shank nails,[c,d] min. 12$^1/_2$-gauge (0.099-in) shank diameter	3	6 each way
Underlayment Exposure 1, Ext. cc-plugged, Ext.	Over lumber subfloor or other uneven surfaces[e]	$^{11}/_{32}$		6	8 each way

Note: 1 in = 25.4 mm.

[a]When thicker underlayment is desired, APA-rated Sturd-I-Floor may be specified. For $^1/_4$-in thickness, A-C Ext. may be substituted.

[b]If green framing is used, space fasteners so that they do not penetrate framing.

[c]Use 16-gauge staples for $^{11}/_{32}$-in and thicker plywood. Crown width $^3/_8$ in for 16-gauge, and $^3/_{16}$ in for 18-gauge staples, with length sufficient to penetrate completely through, or at least $^5/_8$ in into, subflooring.

[d]Use 3d ring-shank nails also for $^1/_2$-in panels and 4d ring-shank nails for $^5/_8$- or $^3/_4$-in panels.

[e]For underlayment recommendations under ceramic tile, refer to ANSI Standard A108 or contact the APA.

Source: From Ref. 8. Used with permission.

face veneer and spliced inner plies to resist indentation. Plywood underlayment is laid down in the same direction as the plywood subfloor so that the grain of the face veneer is perpendicular to the joists. However, the end joints and side joints should be staggered with respect to the subfloor panels. Particleboard is quite commonly used for underlayment and is typically applied at right angles to a plywood subfloor. The required thickness of underlayment may be specified by code or by the type of surface it covers. Underlayment should be installed immediately before the finish flooring to minimize damage during construction. It also should be water resistant if used in a high-moisture-content area such as a bathroom.

Combined Subfloor and Underlayment. It may be economical to use a panel product that will serve as both subfloor and underlayment. Labor savings are possible, but good continuity between panels is necessary and either 2-in (51-mm) wood blocking or tongue-and-groove edges are required at panel edges between supports.

The American Plywood Association has a proprietary product called Sturd-I-Floor which is grademarked with a span rating. This rating assumes a minimum uniform live load of 100 lb/ft^2 (4.79 kPa) and a $1/360$ span deflection limit for a maximum span less than or equal to 32 in (813 mm). Typical recommendations for use are shown in Table 7.13. Composite panels are acceptable under Sturd-I-Floor grademark. A special panel product, Sturd-I-Floor 48 o.c. (formerly called 2-4-1), is recommended for spans of 32 or 48 in (813 mm or 1.22 m). It is $1\frac{1}{8}$ in (28.6 mm) thick and should be used with 4-in nominal width joists only if the span is 48 in (1.22 m). The allowable uniform live load in this case is 55 lb/ft^2 (2.63 kPa). If the spans are 32 in (813 mm), nominal 2-in-wide framing may be used, and the allowable load will increase.

In recent years, OSB has been accepted by all major code authorities in the United States and Canada for some applications. This product has some excellent characteristics if used properly (see Sec. 7.3) and is accepted in some areas as combined subfloor-underlayment, subflooring, or underlayment. Local building codes should be checked for its acceptability in a specific area. Typically, a $5/8$-in (15.9-mm) or thicker panel is required for 16-in (406-mm) spacing and a $3/4$-in (19.0-mm) or thicker panel for 19.2-in (488-mm) spans. Nailing requirements are similar to those for plywood.

Glued Floor Systems. To enhance the performance of the floor system, the sheathing layer may be field-glued to the joists or beams. This enables the sheathing and joists to function as a T beam, resulting in a significant increase in floor stiffness and, potentially, load capacity. Glued floors result in increased stiffness and fewer squeaks, nail popping, and costly callbacks for repairs. Both single- and multiple-layer floors may be glued, but panels with tongue-and-groove edges are most favored. The adhesives should meet performance specifications such as APA's AFG-01 and be easily installed in the field. The contractor must see that OSB panels with sealed surfaces and edges are compatible with the glue.

Heavy-Duty Plywood Floors. PS1-83 plywood can be used to support loads that are heavier than those assumed in the span-rating system. Table 7.14 indicates some recommended live loads. This table is to be used only for plywood meeting the requirements of PS1-83. This means performance-rated panels may be used *only* if they are marked PS1-83. Composite panels are not considered in this table. The

TABLE 7.13 APA-Rated Sturd-I-Floor Use Recommendations[a]

Span rating (maximum joist spacing), in	Minimum panel thickness,[b] in	Fastening: glue-nailed[c]			Fastening: nailed-only		
		Nail size and type	Spacing, in		Nail size and type	Spacing, in	
			Supported panel edges	Intermediate supports		Supported panel edges	Intermediate supports
16	19/32	6d deformed-shank[d]	12	12	6d deformed-shank	6	12
20	19/32	6d deformed-shank[d]	12	12	6d deformed-shank	6	12
24	23/32	6d deformed-shank[d]	12	12	6d deformed-shank	6	12
24, 32	7/8	8d deformed-shank[d]	6	12	8d deformed-shank	6	12
48 (2-4-1)	1 1/8	8d deformed-shank[e]	6	[f]	8d deformed-shank[e]	6	12

Note: 1 in = 25.4 mm.

[a]Special conditions may impose heavy traffic and concentrated loads that require construction in excess of the minimums shown.

[b]Panels in a given thickness may be manufactured in more than one span rating. Panels with a span rating greater than the actual joist spacing may be substituted for panels of the same thickness with a span rating matching the actual joist spacing. For example, 19/32-in-thick Sturd-I-Floor 20 o.c. may be substituted for 19/32-in-thick Sturd-I-Floor 16 o.c. over joists 16 in on center.

[c]Use only adhesives conforming to APA specification AFG-01 with plywood and composite panels, applied in accordance with the manufacturer's recommendations.

[d]8d common nails may be substituted if deformed-shank nails are not available.

[e]10d common nails may be substituted with 1 1/8-in panels if supports are well-seasoned.

[f]Space nails 6 in apart for 48-in spans and 12 in apart for 32-in spans.

Source: From Ref. 8. Used with permission.

TABLE 7.14 PS1 Plywood Recommendations for Uniformly Loaded Heavy-Duty Floors[a] (Deflection Limited to $1/240$ of Span)

Uniform live load, lb/ft^2	Center-to-center support spacing, in (nominal 2-in-wide supports unless noted)					
	12	16[b]	20[b]	24[b]	32	48[c]
50	32/16, 16 o.c.	32/16, 16 o.c.	40/20, 20 o.c.	48/24, 24 o.c.	48 o.c.	48 o.c.
100	32/16, 16 o.c.	32/16, 16 o.c.	40/20, 20 o.c.	48/24, 24 o.c.	48 o.c.	$1\frac{1}{2}$[d]
150	32/16, 16 o.c.	32/16, 16 o.c.	40/20, 20 o.c.	48/24, 48 o.c.	48 o.c.	$1\frac{3}{4}$,[e] 2[d]
200	32/16, 16 o.c.	40/20, 20 o.c.	48/24, 24 o.c.	48 o.c.	$1\frac{1}{8}$,[e] $1\frac{3}{8}$[d]	2,[e] $2\frac{1}{2}$[d]
250	32/16, 16 o.c.	40/20, 24 o.c.	48/24, 48 o.c.	48 o.c.	$1\frac{3}{8}$,[e] $1\frac{1}{2}$[d]	$2\frac{1}{4}$[e]
300	32/16, 16 o.c.	48/24, 24 o.c.	48 o.c.	48 o.c.	$1\frac{1}{2}$,[e] $1\frac{5}{8}$[d]	$2\frac{1}{4}$[e]
350	40/20, 20 o.c.	48/24, 48 o.c.	48 o.c.	$1\frac{1}{8}$,[e] $1\frac{3}{8}$[d]	$1\frac{1}{2}$,[e] 2[d]	
400	40/20, 20 o.c.	48 o.c.	48 o.c.	$1\frac{1}{4}$,[e] $1\frac{3}{8}$[d]	$1\frac{5}{8}$,[e] 2[d]	
450	40/20, 24 o.c.	48 o.c.	48 o.c.	$1\frac{3}{8}$,[e] $1\frac{1}{2}$[d]	2,[e] $2\frac{1}{4}$[d]	
500	48/24, 24 o.c.	48 o.c.	48 o.c.	$1\frac{1}{2}$[d]	2,[e] $2\frac{1}{4}$[d]	

Note: 1 in = 25.4 mm.

[a]Use plywood with T&G edges, or provide structural blocking at panel edges, or install a separate underlayment.

[b]A-C group 1 sanded plywood panels may be substituted for span rated Sturd-I-Floor panels ($1/2$-in for 16 o.c.; $5/8$-in for 20 o.c.; $3/4$-in for 24 o.c.).

[c]Nominal 4-in-wide supports.

[d]Group 1 face and back, any species inner plies, sanded or unsanded, single layer.

[e]All-group 1 or Structural 1 plywood, sanded or unsanded, single layer.

Source: From Ref. 8. Used with permission.

table assumes that the plywood is continuous over two or more spans in the strong direction.

EXAMPLE 7.2 A light-duty storage area is to be built over a series of offices. The floor of this area will function as the office ceiling and will be exposed with no finish covering. A single-layer floor is to be used over 2 × 8 joists spaced 16 in (406 mm) o.c. with the face grain perpendicular to the supports. The local building code authority mandates a design live load of 125 lb/ft^2 (5.98 kPa). What PS1-83 plywood or performance-rated panel could be used?

APA-rated Sturd-I-Floor is designed for combined subfloor-underlayment application. Table 7.15 shows that for a 16-in (406-mm) joist spacing and greater than 100-lb/ft^2 (4.79-kPa) design live load, a 20 on-center span-rated Sturd-I-Floor panel or APA-rated sheathing with a 32/16 index will suffice. If a finish floor is to be installed on these panels, then a thin underlayment panel should be added.

Table 7.14 indicates another alternative for the floor panel. If PS1 plywood is specified, then APA-rated sheathing with a span index of 32⁄16 or 16 on-center Sturd-I-Floor can be used instead. Note that by Specifying a PS1 trademark, you are requiring an all-veneer panel product.

7.4.3 Roof Sheathing

Performance requirements for structural roof sheathing typically require a deflection limit of 1⁄180 of the span between rafters and beams for total load and $\ell/240$ for live load only. Plywood meeting the requirements of PS1-83 and structural-use panels conforming to PS2-92 also meet some requirements for resistance to concentrated loads.

Minimum allowable live loads for PS1-83 plywood roof deckings are tabulated in APA publications. Because of the increased use of structural-use panels for roof-sheathing applications, it is more practical to use Table 7.16 to assess the allowable live load. These values are, in general, conservative for PS1-83 plywood but are appropriate for panels conforming to PS2-92.

For low-slope roofs, a stiffer deck than recommended in Table 7.16*a* is needed to ensure good performance of builtup, single-ply, or modified bitumen roofing.

TABLE 7.15 Recommended Uniform Floor Live Loads for APA-Rated Sturd-I-Floor and APA-Rated Sheathing with Long Dimension Perpendicular to Supports

Sturd-I-Floor span rating	Sheathing span rating	Maximum span, in	Allowable live loads, lb/ft^2*, Joist spacing, in: 12	16	20	24	32	40	48
16 oc	24/16, 32/16	16	185	100					
20 oc	40/20	20	270	150	100				
24 oc	48/24	24	430	240	160	100			
32 oc	60/32	32		430	295	185	100		
48 oc		48			460	290	160	100	55

*10 lb/ft^2 dead load assumed. Live-load deflection limit is $\ell/360$.

TABLE 7.16a Recommended Uniform Roof Live Loads for APA-Rated Sheathing[c] and APA-Rated Sturd-I-Floor with Long Dimension Perpendicular to Supports[c]

Panel span rating	Minimum panel thickness, in	Maximum span, in		Allowable live loads,[d] lb/ft² — Spacing of supports center-to-center, in							
		With edge support[a]	Without edge support	12	16	20	24	32	40	48	60
APA-rated sheathing[c]											
12/0	5/16	12	12	30							
16/0	5/16	16	16	70	30						
20/0	5/16	20	20	120	50	30					
24/0	3/8	24	20	190	100	60	30				
24/16	7/16	24	24	190	100	65	40				
32/16	15/32	32	28	325	180	120	70	30			
40/20	19/32	40	32	—	305	205	130	60	30		
48/24	23/32	48	36	—	—	280	175	95	45	35	
60/32	7/8	60	48	—	—	—	305	165	100	70	35
APA-rated Sturd-I-Floor[f]											
16 o.c.	19/32	24	24	185	100	65	40				
20 o.c.	19/32	32	32	270	150	100	60	30			
24 o.c.	23/32	40	36	—	240	160	100	50	30	25	
32 o.c.	7/8	48	48	—	—	295	185	100	60	40	
48 o.c.	1-3/32	60	48	—	—	—	290	160	100	65	40

[a]Tongue-and-groove edges, panel edge clips (one midway between each support, except two equally spaced between supports 48 in on center), lumber blocking, or other. For low-slope roofs, see Table 7.16*b*.

[b]24 in for 15/32- and 1/2-in panels.

[c]Includes APA-rated sheathing/ceiling deck.

[d]10 lb/ft² dead load assumed.

[e]Applies to panels 24 in or wider.

[f]Also applies to C-C plugged grade plywood.

TABLE 7.16*b* Recommended Maximum Spans for APA Panel Roof Decks for Low-Slope Roofs*

Long panel dimension perpendicular to supports and continuous over two or more spans

Grade	Minimum nominal panel thickness, in	Minimum span rating	Maximum span, in	Panel clips per span† (number)
APA rated sheathing	15⁄32	32/16	24	1
	19⁄32	40/20	32	1
	23⁄32	48/24	48	2
	7⁄8	60/32	60	2

*Low-slope roofs are applicable to builtup, single-ply, and modified bitumen roofing systems. For guaranteed or warranted roofs, contact membrane manufacturer for acceptable deck.

†Edge support also may be provided by tongue-and-groove edges or solid blocking.

This is reflected in the recommendation shown in Table 7.16*b*. Typical fastening recommendations are shown in Table 7.17. Increased nail schedules may be required in high wind areas.

Preframed Roof Panels Preframed panels can save time and labor in some construction applications. Roof sections of structural-use panels as shown in Fig. 7.6 are fastened to lumber joists either on- or off-site using production-line methods. Spans of 8 to 12 ft (2.44 to 3.66 m) are usually the most practical but are often

TABLE 7.17 Recommended Minimum Fastening Schedule for APA Panel Roof Sheathing

Panel thickness, in	Nailing*‡§		
		Spacing, in	
	Size	Panel Edges	Intermediate
5⁄16 to 1	6d	6	12
1⅛, 1¼	8d or 10d†	6	12‡

Note: 1 in = 25.4 mm. More fasteners may be required in high wind areas.

*For stapling asphalt shingles to 5⁄16-in and thicker panels, use stables with a 5⁄16-in minimum crown width on a 1-in leg length. Space according to shingle manufacturers recommendations.

†Use common smooth- or deformed-shank nails with panels to 1 in thick. For 1⅛- and 1¼-in panels, use 8d deformed-shank or 10d common smooth-shank nails.

‡For spans 48 in or greater, space nails 6 in at all supports.

§Other code-approved fasteners may be used.

Source: From Ref. 8. Used with permission.

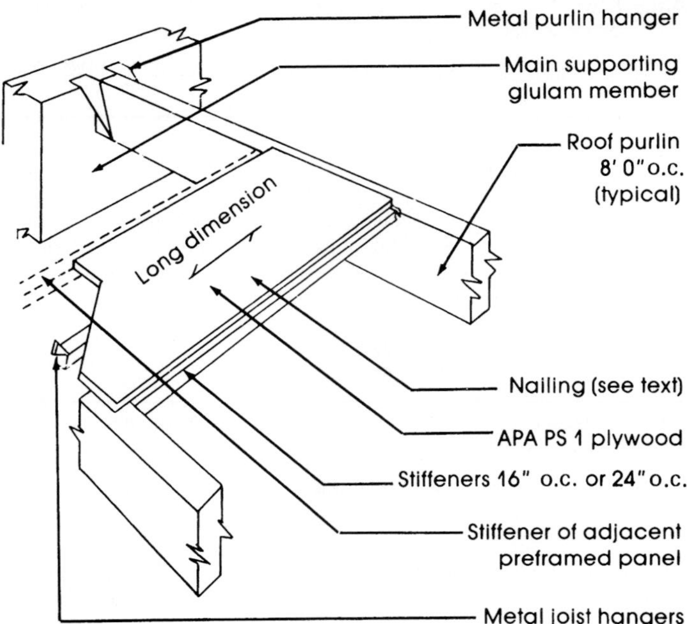

FIG. 7.6 Preframed roof panel. *(Courtesy of the American Plywood Association.)*

larger. PS1-83 plywood panels are used with face grain parallel to support stiffeners which are usually 16- or 24-in (406- or 610-mm) o.c. Because of the orientation of the panel, span ratings cannot be used. Table 7.18 indicates some recommendations for APA rated sheathing including PS1-83 plywood.

Panel roof deck systems can also function as diaphragms with relatively slight design modifications. See Chap. 8 or Ref. 8 for more details.

7.4.4 Wall Sheathing Applications

Plywood is commonly used in wall construction to provide structural rigidity or to provide both rigidity and aesthetic characteristics. In the first case, plywood is used as an underlayer on which siding, brickwork, or other materials are attached. It is generally used at corners to provide racking resistance but may cover the entire structure. In this mode it distributes the wind load to the wall framing members. APA-rated sheathing shown in Table 7.19 is appropriate as are the PS1-83 plywood grades of C-D Exposure 1 or C-C Exterior. The face grain may be applied in either direction. Shearwall action described in Chap. 8 will require blocking at panel edges.

Plywood is also available as a single-layer or surface panel which may have a variety of textures or patterns in the face and yet perform as a structural element. APA 303 siding may be applied directly to studs or to a nonstructural panel sublayer and will provide the strength and rack resistance necessary to eliminate the cost of

TABLE 7.18 Recommended Roof Loads (lb/ft²) for APA-Rated Sheathing with Long Dimension Parallel to Support[e,f] (OSB, Composite, and 5-Ply/5-Layer Plywood Panels Unless Otherwise Noted)

Panel Grade	Thickness, in	Span rating	Maximum span, in	Load at maximum span: Live	Load at maximum span: Total
APA-rated Structural I sheathing	7/16	24/0, 24/16	24[d]	20	30
	15/32	32/16	24	35[a]	45[a]
	1/2	32/16	24	40[a]	50[a]
	19/32, 5/8	40/20	24	70	80
	23/32, 3/4	48/24	24	90	100
APA-rated sheathing	7/16[b]	24/0, 24/16	16	40	50
	15/32[b]	32/16	24[d]	20	25
	1/2[b]	24/0, 32/16	24[d]	25	30
	19/32	40/20	24	40[c]	50[c]
	5/8	32/16, 40/20	24	45[c]	55[c]
	23/32, 3/4	40/20, 48/24	24	60[c]	65[c]

Note: 1 in = 25.4 mm; 1 lb/ft² = 47.88 Pa.
[a]For 4-ply plywood marked PS1, reduce load by 15 lb/ft².
[b]Composite panels must be 19/32 in or thicker.
[c]For composite and 4-ply plywood panels, reduce load by 15 lb/ft².
[d]Solid blocking recommended at panel ends for 24-in span.
[e]For guaranteed or warranted roofs, contact membrane manufacturer for acceptable deck.
[f]Provide edge support.
Source: From Ref. 8. Used with permission.

TABLE 7.19 APA Panel Wall Sheathing* (APA-Rated Sheathing Panels Continuous over Two or More Spans)

Panel span rating	Maximum stud spacing, in	Nail size‡	Maximum nail spacing,† in: Panel edges	Maximum nail spacing,† in: Intermediate
12/0, 16/0, 20/0, or Wall-16 o.c.	16	6d for panels ½-in thick or less; 8d for thicker panels	6	12
24/0, 24/16, 32/16, or Wall-24 o.c.	24			

Note: 1 in = 25.4 mm.
*See requirements for nailable panel sheathing when exterior covering is to be nailed to sheathing.
†Common, smooth, annular, spiral-thread, or galvanized box; other code-approved fasteners may be used.
Source: From Ref. 8. Used with permission.

diagonal bracing or a structured sublayer. Medium-density overlay (MDO) also provides this advantage as well as that of a smooth, paintable surface. Reference 8 or the APA, as well as local code authorities, should be consulted for details.

7.5 PLYWOOD-LUMBER BEAMS

7.5.1 Description

Plywood may be combined with lumber or glued-laminated timbers (glulam) to form I- or box-shaped beams. These nailed and glued flexural members have a very high strength-to-weight ratio and are commonly used for 20- to 80-ft (6.10- to 24.4-m) spans. They may be straight or cambered and consist of one or more vertical plywood webs joined to dry lumber flanges (see Fig. 7.7). The lumber flanges are designed to carry most of the bending moment, and the plywood is designed to carry the shear stresses. Stiffeners are used between flanges to prevent web buckling and to transfer bearing forces.

The plywood and lumber are joined with adhesives using clamps, presses, nails, or other means to obtain necessary pressure for proper bonding. Only positive

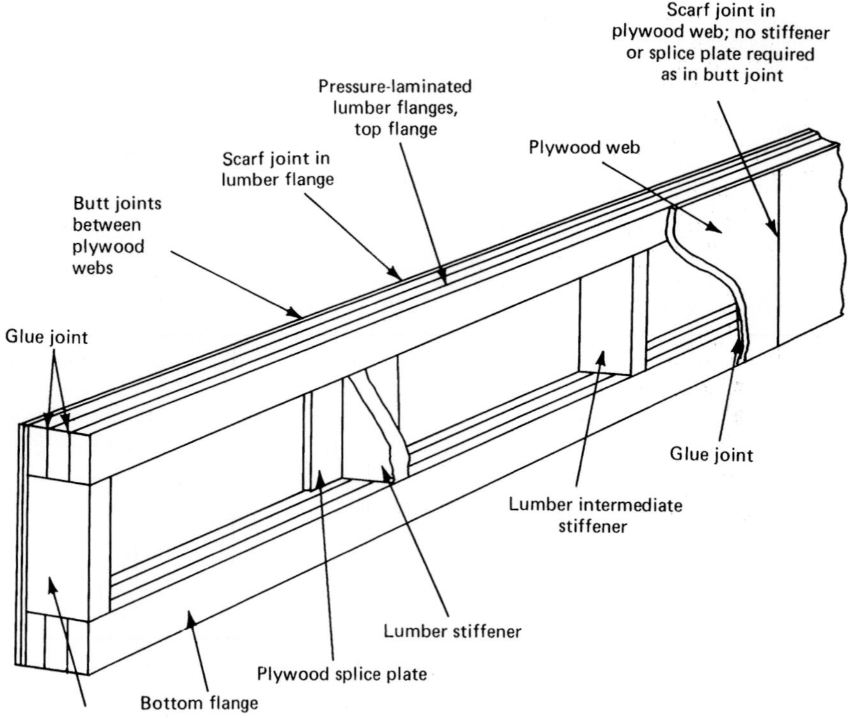

FIG. 7.7 Plywood-lumber beam. (*Courtesy of the American Plywood Association.*)

mechanical pressure (not nails) can be used in lumber flanges of more than one lamination. End joints in flanges and webs may require scarf or finger joints for splicing.

7.5.2 Beam Geometry

Figure 7.8 indicates common beam cross-sectional geometries. Types A, B, and C are box beams, and only type C may not be nail-glued. I beams require pressure gluing and generally do not have the loading capacity or torsional rigidity of the other types.

Because of nonuniform distribution of moments and shear forces along a beam, the cross section need not be prismatic. This is common with box beams and often results in more web material placed in the outer portion of the length to resist the greatest shear. I beams are usually prismatic.

A popular lumber-plywood beam shown as type TJI in Fig. 7.8 is an I joist with a laminated veneer lumber flange manufactured by the Trus Joist Corporation. The web is typically ⅜-in (9.52-mm) plywood that is inserted into a groove cut in the center of the wide face of the flange. All adhesives used in the plywood, flange, and web-flange connection are waterproof. The design characteristics of this product are available from the manufacturer (see Appendix, Sec. 7.7.1).

7.5.3 Flange and Web Design Properties

Flange Properties. Axial tension or compression allowable stresses (not bending allowable stresses) for the lumber flange are determined for the specific grade of lumber or for the glulam combination to be employed. These are modified for applicable durations of load. If two or more pieces of lumber are to be laminated together, the relative location of the joints may affect the design stresses. Full design stresses may be used for properly made scarf or finger joints as outlined in the *Plywood Design Specification* (*PDS*).[9] Butt joints may be used in the flanges, but some reduction in the effective cross-sectional area is necessary. If the butt joints in the two adjoining laminations are spaced 50 times the lamination thickness t apart, the full cross-sectional area of one lamination may be used. Other spacings

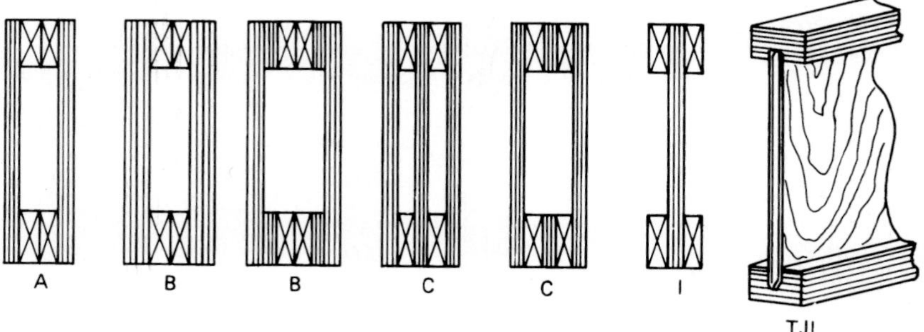

FIG. 7.8 Typical plywood-lumber beam cross sections. (*Adapted from Ref. 10. TJI is a proprietory product of Trus Joist MacMillan Corporation.*)

will require some reduction as specified in the *PDS*.[9] The APA specification on the fabrication of plywood beams[10] requires that butt joints be spaced $30t$ apart in adjoining laminations and $10t$ apart in nonadjoining ones. This results in an effective cross-sectional area of 90 percent of one layer for a two-lamination flange or 90 percent of two layers for a three-lamination flange. *The allowable stress in tension for butt-jointed members in multiple laminated flanges is 80 percent of that for the grade*. This is in addition to any reduction in effective area.

Web Properties. The plywood webs will contribute to the beam moment of inertia a thickness equal to that of the layers of veneer with grain parallel to the beam length. This thickness is equal to one-twelfth the tension or compression area found in column 4 or 8 of Table 7.6. Scarf joints of 1/8 slope will transmit 100 percent of axial or bending stresses. A slope of 1/5 (which is the limit) or flatter transmits 75 percent of tension or bending stress and 100 percent compression stress.

Butt joints backed by a glued plywood splice plate with its grain perpendicular to the joint may be used. The plate should be equivalent in thickness and quality to the web. The capacity of the joint in tension and bending is shown in Table 7.20. Values are reduced proportionally for shorter plates. There is no reduction in compression strength for plates of the lengths shown in the table. No reduction in panel shear strength is necessary if the glued plywood splice plate is at least 12 times as long as the panel thickness.

Adhesive. The box or I beam is designed as a rigid entity, and any mechanical fasteners used for gluing pressure are not assumed to contribute to its capacity. Adhesives for a dry or wet exposure must conform to the minimum specifications found in *PDS* Supplement 2.[10]

7.5.4 Design Procedures

The following steps are necessary in the design of a lumber-plywood beam. The designer usually knows the load, span, deflection criteria, environmental conditions,

TABLE 7.20 Maximum Allowable Flexural and Tension Stresses for Plywood with Butt Joints

Plywood thickness, in	Length of splice plate, in	Maximum stress, lb/in²: All Struc. I grades	Group 1	Group 2 and Group 3	Group 4
¼	6				
5⁄16	8	1500	1200	1000	900
⅜ sanded	10				
⅜ sanded	12				
15⁄32 and ½	14	1500	1000	950	900
19⁄32, ⅝	16	1200	800	750	700
23⁄32, and ¾					

Note: 1 in = 25.4 mm; 1 lb/in² = 6.895 kPa.
Source: From Ref. 9. Used with permission.

and any architectural or manufacturing considerations such as beam depth or appearance restrictions and material availability:

1. Given the above, determine a trial size using approximate methods.
2. Determine the bending moment and the required section properties.
3. From horizontal shear, determine plywood thickness.
4. From the shear at the flange-web joint, choose adequate dimension and geometry to meet rolling shear criteria.
5. Determine section necessary to meet deflection requirements. Also determine necessary camber if required.
6. Determine size and spacing of bearing and intermediate stiffeners.
7. Determine the details of any necessary splices.
8. Determine requirements for lateral supports.

See Example 7.3 for additional details of these steps.

EXAMPLE 7.3 Design a box beam to function as a roof beam over a simple span of 26 ft (7.92 m). The beam should be less than 24 in (610 mm) deep, and its allowable deflection under total load is to be less than $\ell/240$. Dry service conditions are expected. The snow-load and dead-load combination governs with a total design load of 220 lb/ft (3.21 kN/m). The dead load is 80 lb/ft (1.17 kN/m). Scarf-jointed 2 × 6 or 2 × 8 lumber (kiln-dried, 15 percent maximum moisture content, select structural spruce-pine-fir) is available, as are several thicknesses of C-D Exposure 1 unsanded plywood (grademarked PS1-83).

Trial Section. To estimate a trial size, assume the flanges carry all the bending moment and the webs carry all the shear. Typically, beam depth-to-span ratios range from 1/8 to 1/12, but others are possible. The depth should be selected to minimize waste when the webs are cut from the plywood sheet. This favors 12-, 16-, and 24-in depths. Often splice plates may be cut from the trim if these depths are inappropriate.

Depth: $h = \frac{1}{12}$ (26 ft) = 26 in; try 24 in for minimum waste and to meet problem restrictions.

To approximate the required area of the lumber flanges use

$$A = \frac{M}{Fh_1} \tag{7.1}$$

where A = net area of flange after accounting for butt joints, in^2
M = bending moment, in·lb
F = allowable tension or compression stress, lb/in^2
h_1 = center-to-center distance between flanges, in

$$M = \frac{w\ell^2}{8} = \frac{220(26)^2}{8}(12) = 223{,}100 \text{ in}\cdot\text{lb}$$

$$h_1 = 24 \text{ in} - 5.5 \text{ in} = 18.5 \text{ in (assumes a } 2 \times 6 \text{ flange trial)}$$

$$F = F_t = 675 \times 1.3 \times 1.15$$

$$= 1009 \text{ lb/in}^2$$ (Select structural S-P-F allowable tension strength for 2 × 6 width, adjusted for load duration[14]),

$$A = \frac{223{,}100}{1025(18.5)} = 11.76 \text{ in}^2$$

Since the area of the two 2 × 6s is 16.5 in^2, this trial appears satisfactory. The flange depth should be at least 4 times the adjoining web thickness at each glueline to ensure enough area for shear transfer. This is necessary to ensure that rolling shear stresses in the plywood do not control the design. Lumber which is 2 × 6 in should be satisfactory for any reasonable plywood thickness.

The plywood web thickness t is estimated from

$$t = \frac{5V}{4hF_v} \tag{7.2}$$

where V = maximum shear force, lb
h = total beam depth, in
F_v = allowable shear stress through thickness, lb/in^2

$$V = \frac{w\ell}{2} = \frac{220(26)}{2} = 2860 \text{ lb}$$

$$h = 24 \text{ in (trial)}$$

$$F_v = 190 \times 1.15$$

$$= 218.5 \text{ lb/in}^2$$ (Group 1 species, dry condition. Stress level = S-2 from Table 7.8)

$$t = \frac{5(2860)}{4(24)(218.5)} = 0.682 \text{ in}$$

This is the total effective thickness for shear and should be compared with column 3 of Table 7.6. (Remember, two webs!)

For the available unsanded panels, two webs of ¾-in C-D Exposure 1, with a span rating of 48/24 (group 1 species) are necessary.

Section Properties. Properly manufactured scarf-jointed lumber is necessary because of the closeness of the trial design. A new trial section would have to be developed if butt joints were to be used (see Sec. 7.5.2).

Net moment of inertia (see Fig. 7.9) is

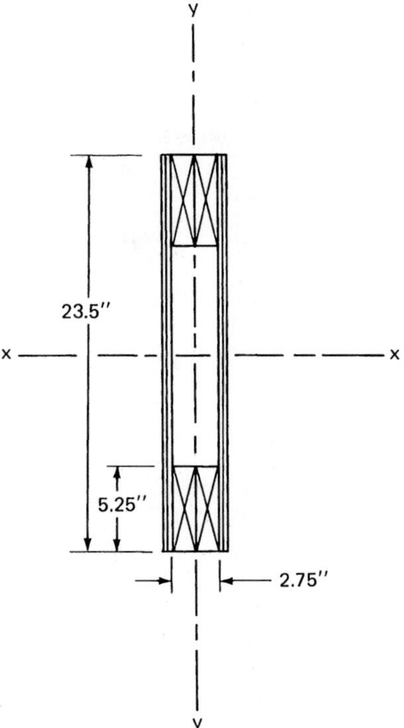

FIG. 7.9 Example 7.3.

$$I \text{ (flanges)} = \frac{b}{12} [h^3 - (h - 2d)^3] \tag{7.3}$$

where b = flange width = 2.75 in (assumes ⅛ in of each lam width is removed for surfacing prior to gluing)
d = flange depth = 5.25 in (¼ in removed for postassembly surfacing)
h = beam depth less ½ in for resurfacing = 23.5 in (if $h - 24$ in, assume ⅜ in)

$$I \text{ (flanges)} = \frac{2.75}{12} [(23.5)^3 - (23.5 - 2 \times 5.25)^3] = 2471 \text{ in}^4$$

$$I \text{ (each web)} = \frac{t^*h^3}{12} = \frac{0.271(23.5)^3}{12} = 293 \text{ in}^4$$

where t^* is 3.247/12 = 0.271 as described in Sec. 7.2.5. This value represents the total thickness of all plies that are parallel to face grain.

Note that the surfacing allowances are those recommended by the American Plywood Association and may vary by manufacturer. Assume that splice plates to transmit shear are used at plywood joints staggered 24 in apart. Thus one web member is considered to contribute to the bending resistance.

$$I\text{ (net)} = 2471 + 293 = 2764\text{ in}^4\ (1.151 \times 10^{-3}\text{ m}^4)$$

$$I\text{ (total)} = 2471 + 2 \times 293 = 3057\text{ in}^4\ (1.273 \times 10^{-3}\text{ m}^4)$$

The total I ignores the effect of butt joints and will be used to check webs, joints, and deflection.

The flange depth is greater than 4 times the panel thickness, so there is enough area for shear transfer.

First area moment Q:

$$Q\text{ (flanges)} = bd\left(\frac{h}{2} - \frac{d}{2}\right) = 2.75(5.25)\left(\frac{23.5}{2} - \frac{5.25}{2}\right) = 131.7\text{ in}^3$$

$$Q\text{ (web)} = t^*\left(\frac{h}{2}\right)\left(\frac{h}{4}\right)\text{ (number of webs)} = 0.271\,\frac{23.5^2}{8}\,(2) = 37.41\text{ in}^3$$

$$Q = 131.7 + 37.4 = 169.1\text{ in}^3\ (2.771 \times 10^{-3}\text{ m}^3)$$

Check for Bending

$$\text{Allowable moment} = M = \frac{F_t I_{\text{net}}}{0.5h} \tag{7.4}$$

where $0.5h$ is used for symmetrical cross sections, and the actual distance from the neutral axis to the flanges should be used for other geometries.

$$M = \frac{1025(2764)}{0.5(23.5)} = 241{,}100\text{ in·lb}$$

$$241{,}100\text{ in·lb (27.24 kN·m)} > 223{,}100\text{ in·lb (25.21 kN·m)} \qquad \text{OK}$$

If bending governs, then either web splicing may be used to increase the I or the size of the flanges may be increased.

Check for Shear. Shear through the thickness:

$$\text{Allowable shear force} = \frac{F_v I(\text{total})(\Sigma t)}{Q} \tag{7.5}$$

where Σt is the summation of web effective thickness for shear (column 3, Table 7.6).

$$V = \frac{(218.5)(3057)(2 \times 0.445)}{169.1}$$

$$= 3515\text{ lb (15.53 kN)} > 2860\text{ lb (12.72 kN)} \qquad \text{OK}$$

Rolling shear at the flange-web glueline:

$$V = \frac{2F_s dI_t}{Q\text{ (flange)}} \tag{7.6}$$

where F_s is allowable plywood rolling shear stress reduced by 50 percent for shear concentration (lb/in²).

$$V = \frac{2(0.5 \times 53 \times 1.15)(5.25)(3057)}{131.7}$$

$$= 7428 \text{ lb } (33.03 \text{ kN}) > 2860 \text{ lb } (12.72 \text{ kN}) \qquad \text{OK}$$

If the beam had more than two webs, then the shear can be computed using

$$V = \frac{F_s d I_t}{Q \text{ (flange)}} \left(\frac{\Sigma t_s}{t_s}\right) \tag{7.7}$$

where Σt_s is the sum of all web shear thicknesses at the section (in), and t_s is the shear thickness of the outer web (in). This assumes that the first statical moment is tributary to each web in proportion to its thickness.

Deflection. Shear deflection may be a significant factor in the design. There are two methods to calculate total deflection.

1. *Approximation:* Multiply the bending deflection by a correction factor based on the span-to-depth ratio:

Span-to-depth ratio	Correction factor
10	1.5
15	1.2
20	1.0

Interpolation is permitted. The deflection should be computed using the flange material elastic modulus and I (total).

2. *Sum of bending and shear deflections:* If deflection is critical, a better estimate of deflection may be needed. A refined method which sums the bending and shear deflections is shown in Sec. 7.7.3 of the Appendix of this chapter. This refined method should be used before changing member sizes if the approximated deflection is near the allowable limit.

$$\Delta = \frac{5w\ell^4 \text{ (correction factor)}}{384EI \text{ (total)}} \tag{7.8}$$

The span-to-depth ratio = 13. Therefore, the correction factor = 1.32. Then

$$\Delta = \frac{5(220/12)(312)^4(1.32)}{384(1.50 \times 10^6)(3057)} = 0.65 \text{ in } (16.4 \text{ mm})$$

$$0.65 \text{ in } (16.4 \text{ m}) - \frac{\ell}{240} = 1.30 \text{ in } (33.0 \text{ mm}) \qquad \text{OK}$$

Camber may be provided to counteract dead load and creep deflection as well as provide some pitch to the roof for additional drainage.

Normally, creep is accounted for by providing a camber equal to 1.5 times the dead load deflection. In this problem, that represents ¼ in (6.35 mm) which would be ignored or overshadowed by the pitch requirements. Potential ponding of water should be avoided by providing adequate roof pitch in addition to camber.

Bearing Stiffeners. Bearing stiffeners are fitted between webs and flanges to distribute concentrated loads and prevent web buckling. Stiffeners at the end of the beam should be the same width as the flanges and have a dimension parallel to the flange adequate to meet the following two criteria.

Compression Perpendicular to Grain. The stiffeners should be able to transmit the support reaction to the flange. This is met by providing a stiffener with sufficient cross-sectional area to meet the compression perpendicular to grain criterion:

$$X = \frac{P}{F_{c\perp} b} \tag{7.9}$$

where X = depth of stiffeners parallel to flange
P = reaction or, not of concentrated load
$F_{c\perp}$ = allowable stress in compression perpendicular to grain (not adjusted for duration of load[7]
b = flange width (also stiffener width)

$$X = \frac{2860}{425(2.75)} = 2.45 \text{ in } (62.2 \text{ mm})$$

Rolling Shear. The support reaction also should be transmitted to the web through rolling shear at the web-stiffener glueline:

$$X = \frac{P}{2hF_s} = \frac{2860}{2(23.5)(53 \times 0.5 \times 1.15)} = 2 \text{ in } (51 \text{ mm}) \tag{7.10}$$

A pair of 2 × 4s properly surfaced to 1.375 in each would suffice for end stiffeners.

Intermediate stiffeners should be added to improve web stability. There is no easy way to calculate their location, but nominal 2-in-thick lumber spaced at 48-in (1220-mm) or less intervals should be sufficient. They should be glued to the webs.

Lateral Stability. To determine lateral bracing requirements, the ratio of I_x/I_y is calculated and compared with those in Table 7.21.

$$I_x = I \text{ (total)} = 3057 \text{ in}^4$$

$$I_y = I \text{ (flanges)} + I \text{ (webs)}$$

$$= \frac{2(5.25)(2.75)^3}{12} + \frac{2[0.227 + 3.247(1.75)^2]23.5}{12}$$

$$= 58.03 \text{ in}^4$$

$$\frac{I_x}{I_y} = \frac{3057}{58.03} = 52.68$$

Therefore, compression flanges should be fully restrained.

TABLE 7.21 Recommendations for Lateral Bracing of Plywood-Lumber Beams

I_x/I_y	Provision for lateral bracing
Up to 5	None required
5 to 10	Ends held in position at bottom flanges at supports
10 to 20	Beams held in line at ends (both top and bottom flanges restrained from horizontal movement in planes perpendicular to beam axis)
20 to 30	One edge (either top or bottom) held in line
30 to 40	Beam restrained by bridging or other bracing at intervals of not more than 8 ft
More than 40	Compression flanges fully restrained and forced to deflect in a vertical plane, as with a well-fastened joist and sheathing, or stressed-skin panel system

Note: 1 ft = 0.3048 m.
Source: From Ref. 10. Used with permission.

7.6 GLUED STRESSED-SKIN PANELS

7.6.1 Description

Plywood and lumber also can be combined to form a flat, shallow assembly designed to resist flexural stress from loads applied normal to the panel surface. These stressed-skin panels are not unique to wood construction and have been used in aircraft, ships, and vehicles as well as buildings. They are a particularly efficient form of construction when material cost or weight is a consideration. They are usually prefabricated in a factory and are manufactured with a precision and quality that minimizes field installation time and trouble.

Stressed-skin panels may be flat or curved and are often used in folded-plate or curved-roof structures as well as in wall and floor systems. They may be either hollow web components (Fig. 7.10) or a sandwich with a lightweight core. Polystyrene or polyurethane foams or paper honeycombs have been used in the latter case. In curved panels, plywood may be used as a core material as well as for the skins. References 11 and 12 provide specific details of these types of panels. This section will focus on the common lumber-webbed panel.

The stressed-skin plywood-lumber panel gains its efficiency from having the plywood skin take most of the bending stresses while also performing as sheathing. The lumber webs space the skins, thereby increasing the moment of inertia; they also carry the shear stresses. Panels may be one- or two-sided or have lumber T-flanges. In any event, the lumber members or stringers are rigidly connected to the flanges so that the panel functions as a series of built-up beams. Elastomeric adhesives have been used in panels subject to impact loads or stress concentration. However, there is no simple way of designing panels with elastic connections, and their use is somewhat limited to trial-and-error applications. The design methods described in this section assume that the flanges and webs are rigidly connected.

7.6.2 Fabrication Notes

The size of an individual panel is governed by either the application or the sizes of available plywood and lumber. The lumber stringers could be multiple-member laminates or scarf-jointed, but generally this is not economical or practical to accomplish. For specific cases, this generality may not hold, but usually the length

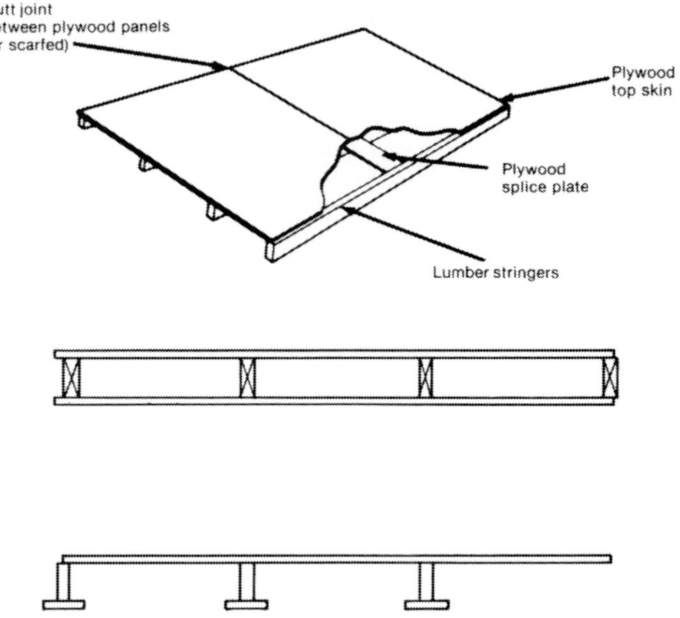

FIG. 7.10 One-sided, two-sided, and T-flange stressed-skin panels. (*Adapted from Ref. 13.*)

of the panel is limited to the available length of the lumber. The plywood skins may be spliced or scarfed to provide the necessary surface area. The plywood splicing recommendations are the same as in Table 7.20. Scarf joints of 1 in 8 or flatter transmit full allowable stress. A slope of 1 in 5 transmits 75 percent of the allowable stress, and steeper joints are not recommended. Finger joints may be used if supported by test data. While PS1-83 plywood is currently recommended for use in stressed-skin panels, successful designs with structural composite panels will inevitably evolve.

Some bridging or blocking is generally required in stressed-skin panels. Blocking will support splice plates for joining skins, distribute concentrated loads, and align stringers during construction. Headers provide the same function at the ends of the panel. Blocking may be notched to provide ventilation. If panels are used in a pitched roof with stringers perpendicular to the support rafters, blocking must be used to improve racking resistance. One-sided panels may require bridging for lateral stability purposes.

The plywood on the bottom of a two-sided panel may be of a variety of decorative forms for aesthetics. If appearance is a factor, 5⁄16 in (7.94 mm) should be the minimum thickness to avoid a wavy appearance. Usually the plywood is applied with face grain parallel to the stringers which negates use of span ratings.

The lumber web members and the plywood or lumber flanges are rigidly connected with casein, phenol, resorcinol, or melamine adhesives. Only kiln-dried lumber is used. The choice of adhesive is particularly important when wet-use in-service conditions are expected, and only waterproof adhesives should be used in these applications. Either Interior or Exterior plywood may be used depending on the moisture condition in service. Lumber-plywood panel assemblies are often slightly unsymmetrical in cross section to provide an effective tongue-and-groove arrangement for mating with other panels (see Fig. 7.10). The tongue, or male stringer, may be increased in width to provide rolling shear area and a nailing surface when mated to an adjacent panel. The groove, or female stringer, is recessed in from the edge of the skins and may be reduced in thickness, since the stringer in the mating panel will carry some of the load.

7.6.3 Design Considerations

The properties of the lumber stringer should be those recommended by Section 5 of the *Plywood Design Specification*[9] and may be modified for load duration and moisture content. Lumber stringers are normally surfaced for gluing and should be considered 1⁄16 in (1.59 mm) smaller in depth (perpendicular to gluing surface) for one-sided panels and 1⁄8 in (3.18 mm) smaller for two-sided and T-flange panels.

Section Properties. Stressed-skin panels are generally assumed to be in flexure with the span parallel to the stringer. For a rigidly glued composite of plywood and lumber with differing elastic properties, a transformed section must be computed. That is, the effective width of the lumber web is "transformed" on the basis of the ratio of the stringer MOE to the stringer skin MOE. Skins of differing stiffnesses also should be transformed to a reference stiffness. This gross moment of inertia I_g based on the transformed section assumes that the full width of the panel is effective. This section property is used for deflection and shear calculations. See Example 7.4.

In computing the bending stress, only the cross section of material with grain parallel to the span is considered effective. The area covered by an unspliced butt joint is ineffective, as is any area not covered by a splice plate (i.e., that area immediately over the stringer). Plywood in stressed-skin panels is usually oriented with face grain parallel to stringers.

Plywood that is rigidly connected to lumber stringers may have an effective width for bending stress purposes that is less than the actual width. This is because thin plywood may dish toward the neutral axis if the stringers are widely spaced. Limitations are placed on the effective width in accordance with a basic spacing b shown in Table 7.22.

If a clear distance between stringers is less than b, no reduction is necessary. If it is exceeded, the distance between stringers that is considered effective is limited. Figure 7.11 outlines these limitations. The maximum clear distance between stringers is limited to twice the basic spacing. Note that the section properties may be different for deflection and bending stress calculations.

For computation of the rolling shear stress, it is necessary to compute a statical moment of the area outside the critical shear plane. Since rolling shear is a cross-grained shear, the critical plane lies in the cross-grained layer nearest the neutral axis. The critical statical moment Q_s is for the parallel to stringer plies outside of that plane, as shown in Fig. 7.12. For an unsymmetrical panel, the value of Q_s for the top skin is usually the largest. Table 7.23 gives the values of the variables shown in Fig. 7.12. Q_s is found by multiplying the area from Table 7.23 by the distance d_s.

TABLE 7.22 Basic Spacing b for Various Plywood Thicknesses

	Basic spacing b, in*			
	Face grain ‖ to stringers		Face grain ⊥ to stringers	
Plywood thickness, in	3-, 4-, 5-ply 3-layer	5-, 6-ply 5-layer	3-, 4-, 5-ply 3-layer	5-, 6-ply 5-layer
Unsanded panels				
5⁄16	**12**	—	**13**	—
3⁄8	**14**	—	**17**	—
15⁄32, 1⁄2	**18**	22	**21**	27
19⁄32, 5⁄8	**23**	28	**22**	31
23⁄32, 3⁄4	**31**	32	**29**	31
Sanded panels				
1⁄4	**9**	—	**10**	—
11⁄32	**12**	—	**13**	—
3⁄8	**19**	—	**15**	—
15⁄32	**19**	22	**18**	24
1⁄2	**20**	24	**19**	26
19⁄32	—	**27**	—	**28**
5⁄8	—	**28**	—	**30**
23⁄32	—	**33**	—	**34**
3⁄4	—	**35**	—	**36**
Touch-sanded panels				
1⁄2	**19**	24	**21**	27
19⁄32, 5⁄8	**26**	28	**24**	29
23⁄32, 3⁄4	**32**	34	**28**	36
1 1⁄8 (2-4-1)	—	**55**	—	**55**

*Use value in boldface for plywood thickness and orientation unless another layup is specified and available.

Source: From Ref. 13. Used with permission.

Horizontal shear in the lumber stringers also may govern the design. For this computation, a different statical moment Q_v is required. This value includes all parallel to stringer material above or below the neutral axis that is computed for deflection purposes. This involves a transformed section based on the properties of the plywood skin and may be found from

$$Q_v = Q\text{ (skin)} + \frac{E\text{ (stringers)}}{E\text{ (skin)}} \times Q\text{ (stringers)} \tag{7.11}$$

This computation is outlined further in Example 7.5.

EXAMPLE 7.4 Determine the gross and net flexural stiffnesses of the 4-ft (1.22-mm)-wide stressed-skin panel shown in Fig. 7.13. What would be the change in stiffness if the bottom skin is replaced by 1 × 4 flanges (Fig. 7.14)?

Effective width W_e		For deflection calculations	For bending stress calculations
One-sided panels	Panels less than 3 in deep		
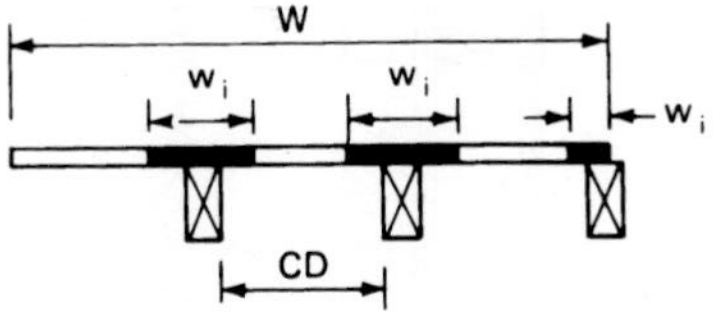 W; w_i; w_i; w_i; CD	(a) $CD > b$	$W_e = \Sigma w_i$ where w_i = stringer width† + 0.25b on each side	$W_e = \Sigma\, w_i$ where w_i = stringer width† + 0.25b each side
	(b) $CD < b$	$W_e = W$	$W_e = W$
	All others		
b = basic spacing (Table 7.23)	(a) $CD > b$	$W_e = W$	$W_e = \Sigma w_i$ where w_i = stringer width† + 0.5b on each side
	(b) $CD < b$	$W_e = W$	$W_e = W$
Two-sided panels	Panels less than 3 in deep		
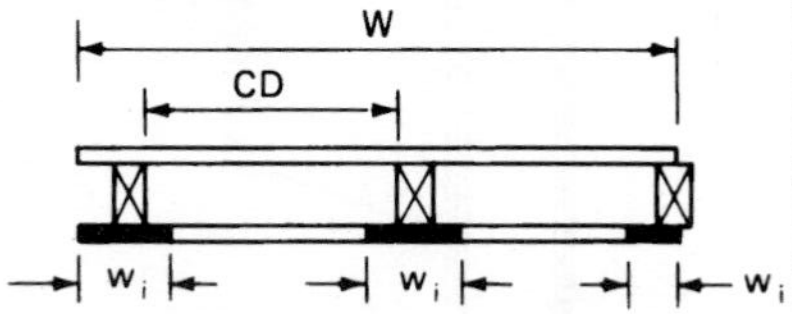 W; CD; w_i; w_i; w_i	(a) $CD > b$	$W_e = W$	$W_e = \Sigma w_i$ where w_i = stringer width† + 0.5b on each side
	(b) $CD < b$	$W_e = W$	$W_e = W$
	All others		
b = basic spacing (Table 7.23)	(a) $CD > b$	$W_e = W$	$W_e = \Sigma w_i$ where w_i = stringer width† + 0.5b on each side
	(b) $CD < b$	$W_e = W$	$W_e = W$

†Except for exterior stringers where available width is as shown.

FIG. 7.11 Effective width of the skins of stressed-skin panels.

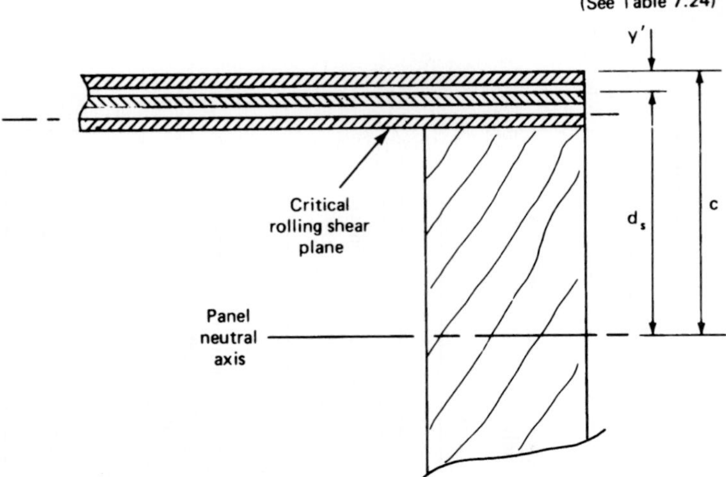

FIG. 7.12 Location of critical rolling shear plane. *(Adapted from Ref. 13.)*

Component Properties. Four-ply ½-in PS1-83 Structural I (unsanded):

$$A_{//} = 2.719 \text{ in}^2/\text{ft}$$

$$I_{//} = 0.074 \text{ in}^4/\text{ft}$$

$$I_{\perp} = 0.012 \text{ in}^4/\text{ft}$$

$$E = 1.8 \times 10^6 \text{ lb/in}^2 \times 1.10^*$$

$$F_b = 1650 \text{ lb/in}^2$$

5⁄16-in APA-rated sheathing 20/0 Exposure 1:

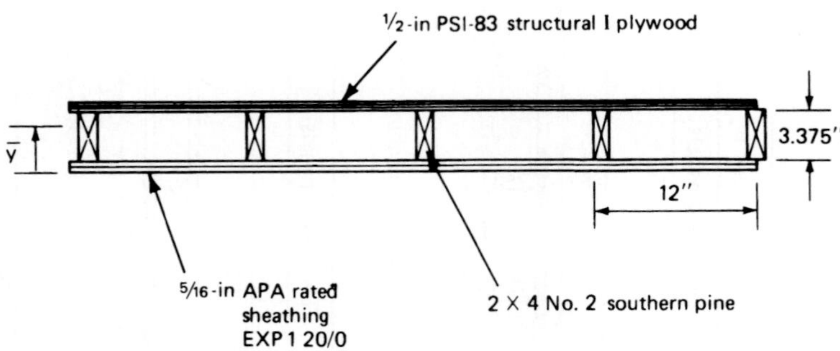

FIG. 7.13 Example 7.4.

*These factors remove the allowance for shear deformation from allowable design values. See the section following this example.

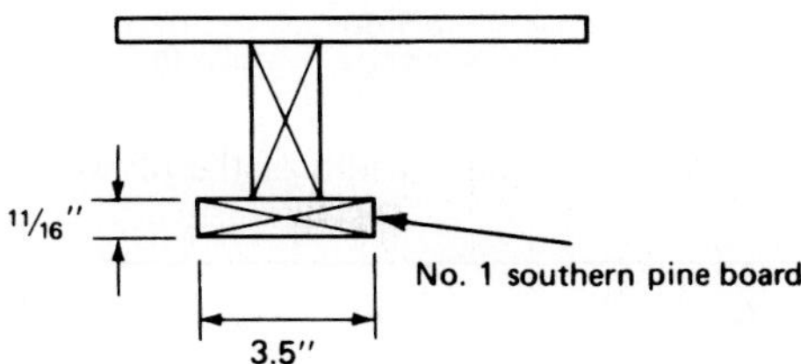

FIG. 7.14 Lumber flange—Example 7.4.

$$\mathbf{A}_{//} = 1.491\ in^2/ft$$

$$\mathbf{I}_{//} = 0.022\ in^4/ft$$

$$\mathbf{I}_{\perp} = 0.001\ in^4/ft$$

$$\mathbf{E} = 1.8 \times 10^6\ lb/in^2 \times 1.10^*$$

$$\mathbf{F}_b = 1650\ lb/in^2$$

2 × 4 No. 2 KD southern pine

$\mathbf{b} = 1.5\ in$ $\quad \mathbf{d} = 3.375\ in$ *(depth reduced* ⅛ *in for surfacing)*

$$\mathbf{E} = 1.6 \times 10^6\ lb/in^2 \times 1.03^* = 1.648 \times 10^6\ lb/in^2$$

$$\mathbf{F}_b = 1725\ lb/in^2 \text{ (repetitive use assumed)}$$

$$\text{Transformed width of lumber} = 1.5\ in \times \frac{1.6 \times 1.03}{1.8 \times 1.10} = 1.25\ in$$

$$\mathbf{I}\ (2 \times 4) = \frac{1.25(3.375)^3}{12} = 4.00\ in^4$$

$$\mathbf{A}\ (2 \times 4) = 1.25(3.375) = 4.22\ in^2$$

Gross Stiffness. First find the neutral axis y using the area moment method:

	$A_{//}$		y	$yA_{//}$
Top skin	4(2.719) =	10.876	3.938	42.83
Lumber	5(4.22) =	21.100	2.000	42.20
Bottom skin	4(1.491) =	5.964	0.156	0.93
		37.94		85.96

$$\bar{y} = \frac{yA_{//}}{A_{//}} = \frac{85.96}{37.94} = 2.27 \text{ in}$$

I_g can be computed assuming the entire width of the plywood skins is effective.

	$I_{//}$		$A_{//}$	d^*	$I_{//} + A_{//} d^2$
Top skin	4(0.074) =	0.296	10.876	1.67	30.63
Lumber	5(4.00) =	20.00	21.10	0.27	21.54
Bottom skin	4(0.022) =	0.088	5.964	2.11	26.64
					I_g = 78.81 in^4

*d = 3.938 − 2.27 = 1.67 in

$$(EI)_g = 1.98 \times 10^6(78.81) = 1.560 \times 10^8 \text{ lb·in}^2 \ (4.476 \times 10^3 \text{ N·mm}^2)$$

Remember, the section has been transformed to one of equal flexural properties.

Net Stiffness. The difference between the net and gross section properties depends on the effective width of the skins. For this problem, the clear spacing = 12 − 1.5 = 10.5 in. From Table 7.22 we see that the b values are 22 in for the top skin and 12 in for the bottom skin. Since our clear spacing is less than these values, the entire width is effective. Hence I (gross) = I (net).

If the bottom skin was of ¼-in (6.35-mm) plywood (b = 10), the effective width of the bottom layer would be 48 − 4(10.5 − 10) = 46 in, or 3.83 ft. Thus the values of $A_{//}$ and $I_{//}$ for plywood skins would be computed using 3.83 rather than 4.0 in the above calculations.

There will only be four T-flange stringers per panel, since the fifth one is integral to the adjacent panel. Assuming that the lumber web and lumber flange have the same properties, I_g and I_n are computed as shown.

$$\text{Transformed width of the flange} = 3.5 \frac{1.6 \times 1.03}{1.8 \times 1.10} = 2.91 \text{ in}$$

$$\text{Depth} = 3/4 - 1/16 \text{ in for surfacing} = 0.69 \text{ in}$$

$$I\ (1 \times 4) = \frac{2.91(0.69)^3}{12} = 0.080 \text{ in}^4 \text{ per piece}$$

$$A\ (1 \times 4) = 2.91(0.69) = 2.008 \text{ in}^2$$

Gross Moment of Inertia I_g

	$A_{//}$		y, in	$yA_{//}$, in^3
Top skin	4(2.719) =	10.880	4.313	46.92
Web	4(4.22) =	16.880	2.375	40.09
Flange	4(2.008) =	8.032	0.344	2.76
		35.79		89.77

$$\bar{y} = \frac{89.77}{35.79} = 2.508 \text{ in}$$

	I_o, in^4		d, in	$I_o + Ad^2$, in^4
Top skin	4(0.074) =	0.296	1.804	35.69
Web	4(4.00) =	16.00	0.133	16.30
Flange	4(0.080) =	0.320	2.164	37.93
				I_g = 89.92 in^4 (3.732 × 10^7 mm^4)

Net Moment of Inertia I_n Since the full width of the flange is effective, $I_n = I_g$.

Allowable Stresses and Deflections. For stressed-skin panels, the published values of plywood and lumber elastic moduli should be increased 10 and 3 percent, respectively. This increase removes the allowance for shear deformation inherent in the published values. Shear deformation is considered separately in stressed-skin panels. The lumber values published in the *National Design Specification for Wood Construction*[7] should be used with appropriate modifications. Repetitive member bending values may be used if stringer spacing is 24 in (610 mm) or less, and there are at least three members. The modulus of rigidity G may be taken as 0.06 of the true stringer bending MOE.

Plywood allowable stresses are those shown in Table 7.8 modified for end-use conditions, splices, etc. There is an additional reduction to guard against buckling of the skins. This reduction factor is shown in Fig. 7.15 and is applicable to both tension and compression allowable stresses, but *not* to rolling shear.

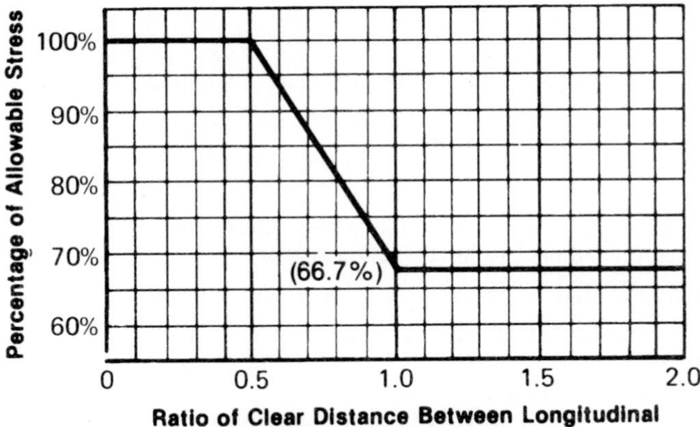

FIG. 7.15 Percentage of reduction of plywood allowable stress as a function of framing spacing in a stressed-skin panel. (*From Ref. 13. Used with permission.*)

The allowable rolling shear stress F_s for the critical shear over exterior stringers should be reduced by 50 percent for stress concentrations. Allowable stresses at the interior stringers are not subject to this reduction. See Example 7.5.

The allowable deflection of the panels is limited to that allowed by the applicable building code. However, the APA recommends the following limitations in lieu of other guidance.

	Live load only	Dead + live load
Floor panels	$\ell/360$	$\ell/240$
Roof panels	$\ell/240$	$\ell/180$

Camber may be included in the design and should be at least 1.5 times the dead load deflection. Roof panels should be designed to prevent ponding.

The top skins also should be checked for deflection between stringers. For two-sided panels, the equation for a fixed-end beam should be used. For one-sided panels with four stringers, a three-span equation should be used. If the face grain is parallel to the stringers, the perpendicular moment of inertia should be used.

7.6.4 Design Procedures

Lumber-plywood stressed-skin panels are designed on a trial-and-error basis. Some recommendations for typical panel configurations are available from the APA[8] or from fabricators. The following steps should be used for analysis or design for a specific application. It is assumed that the designer knows the load, span, deflection criteria, environmental conditions, regulatory guidelines, component properties, and availability of materials.

1. After selecting a trial size, compute the section properties for deflection computations.
2. Determine allowable load based on deflection including that of the top skin.
3. Compute section properties for bending stress.
4. Determine allowable load based on bending stress including the necessary skin or lumber splices.
5. Determine the statical moment for rolling shear, and determine the allowable load based on the allowable rolling shear stress.
6. Determine the statical moment for lumber horizontal shear and allowable load based on this property.
7. If the panel is to be used in a wall, buckling or compression should be checked as well as combined bending and axial load.

Specific designs may require a check of other factors than those outlined above. Example 7.5 should be used as a guide for the details of the above steps.

If all materials in the panel have similar moduli of elasticity, an approximate design method outlined in Ref. 13 may be used. However, the final trial sizes should be checked with a more thorough analysis.

EXAMPLE 7.5 Determine the maximum snow load that can be resisted by the two-skin panel in Example 7.4 if the simply supported span ℓ is 12 ft (3.66 mm) in length. Assume the dead load is 10 lb/ft^2 (479 Pa) and the APA deflection limits ($\ell/240$) for that criterion are applicable.

Material properties:

Lumber: $F_b = 1725 \text{ lb/in}^2 \times 1.15 = 1980 \text{ lb/in}^2$ (13.9 MPa)

$E = 1.6 \times 10^6 \text{ lb/in}^2$ (11.0 GPa)

Plywood: $F_b = 1650 \text{ lb/in}^2 \times 1.15 = 1900 \text{ lb/in}^2$ (13.1 MPa)

$E = 1.8 \times 10^6 \text{ lb/in}^2$ (12.4 GPa)

Allowable Load Based on Deflection. Shear deflection is calculated as a separate value in this computation because it is frequently significant. This is why the effect of shear was removed from the elastic moduli. The equation below reflects two components—total deflection equals bending plus shear deflections.

$$\Delta \text{ (total)} = \frac{5w\ell^4}{384EI_g} + \frac{0.15w\ell^2}{AG} \tag{7.12}$$

This equation is valid for uniform or quarter-point loading. It can be rewritten in a form that is more consistent with the units of the available properties:

$$w_\Delta = \frac{1}{Cl(7.5\ell^2/EI_g + 0.6/AG)} \tag{7.13}$$

where w_Δ = allowable load based on deflection, lb/ft^2
l = span length, ft
EI_g = gross stiffness of the 4-ft-wide panel, lb·in^2
A = actual total cross-sectional area of all stringers and T flanges, if applicable, in^2
C = factor for allowable deflection, usually 360 for floors, 240 for roofs
G = modulus of rigidity of the stringers (it may be assumed to be 0.06 times the true stringer MOE), lb/in^2

If the panel width is different than 4 ft, the number 7.5 in the preceding equation should be factored by the ratio of actual width to 4 ft. The shear deflection component Δ_s by itself is given by

$$\Delta_s = \frac{1.8P\ell}{AG} \tag{7.14}$$

where P is total panel load. For a central concentrated load, the shear deflection is twice this quantity. For a uniformly loaded cantilever, the multiplication factor is 4.

For this problem, $\ell/240$ is the governing deflection criteria and

$$w_\Delta = \frac{1}{240(12)\left[\dfrac{7.5(12)^2}{1.560 \times 10^8} + \dfrac{0.6}{21.1(98{,}900)}\right]}$$

$$= 48.2 \text{ lb/ft}^2 \text{ (live load only)}$$

The "dead-load plus live-load" criteria also should be checked. In this example, the live-load deflection governs. Therefore, $w_\Delta = 48.2 + 10 = 58.2$ lb/ft² (2.79 kPa) for live load and dead load.

Top Skin Deflection. This is a two-skin panel, so the fixed beam equation is used:

$$\Delta \text{ (top)} = \frac{w \text{ (top)}(CD)^4}{384EI(12)} \tag{7.15}$$

where CD = clear span between stringers, in
E = MOE of top skin, unadjusted for shear, lb/in²
I = moment of inertia, in direction perpendicular to stringer, in⁴/ft
w (top) = maximum load based on top skin deflection, lb/ft²

Using $CD/240$ as the criterion:

$$w \text{ (top)} = \frac{384(1.8 \times 10^6)(0.014)(12)}{(240)(10.5)^3} = 418 \text{ lb/ft}^2 \text{ (20.0 kPa)}$$

For single-sided panels with four stringers, the following equation would be used:

$$\Delta = \frac{4w(CD)^4}{581EI(12)} \tag{7.16}$$

Extreme Fiber Bending Stresses. The top and bottom skins are checked to ensure that they will take the compressive and tension stresses, respectively. The net moment of inertia I_n is used in the calculations.

For the top skin, $F_c = 1540 \times 1.15 = 1770$ lb/in². From Fig. 7.15 there is no reduction because the stringer spacing is less than that given by Table 7.22.

For the bottom skin, $F_t = 1650 \times 1.15 = 1900$ lb/in². Using Table 7.22 and Fig. 7.15, the reduction factor for spacing is 0.75. Thus $F_t = 1900 \times 0.75 = 1425$ lb/in².

$$F = \frac{Mc}{I} = \frac{48w_b\ell^2c}{8I_n} \tag{7.17}$$

or

$$w_b = \frac{8FI_n}{48c\ell^2}$$

where c is the distance from neutral axis to extreme fiber (in) and

$$w\ (b, \text{top}) = \frac{8(1770)78.81}{48(12)^2(4.19 - 2.3)} = 85.41 \text{ lb/ft}^2 \text{ (4.09 kPa)}$$

$$w\ (b, \text{bottom}) = \frac{8(1425)(78.81)}{48(12)^2(2.27)} = 57.3 \text{ lb/ft}^2 \text{ (2.74 kPa)}$$

If this were a single-skin panel, the maximum stress in the stringer would be compared to the repetitive member allowable bending stress.

Splice Plate Design. Plywood may be available in 4- by 12-ft (1.22- by 3.66-m) sheets, which would eliminate the need for designing a splice, but this size is not common. For this problem it is assumed that 4- by 8-ft (1.22- by 2.44-m) sheets are available and a splice will be needed 4 ft (1.22 m) in from one end. Plywood splice plates will be used since finger and scarf joints are generally uneconomical.

The splice plate is usually ½ in (12.7 mm) narrower than the clear distance between stringer and is long enough (on the tension side) to meet the allowable stress requirements of Table 7.20 (see Fig. 7.16). The required length from Table 7.20 is 8 in (203 mm) for the 5⁄16-in panel, providing a maximum $F_t = 1200 \times 1.15 = 1380$ lb/in². Lumber blocking should be used beneath the plate unless the skins are prespliced. If blocking exists, the basic spacing distance b need not be considered. If there is no blocking, the combined skin and plate thickness should be used to determine b from Table 7.22, and a new I_g should be computed.

The allowable stress is modified by

$$F_p = F_t \times \frac{\text{sum of plate widths}}{\text{panel width}} \tag{7.18}$$

For the problem,

$$F_p = 1380 \times \frac{4 \times 10}{48} = 1150 \text{ lb/in}^2$$

The maximum load based on the tension splice existing at the point of maximum moment is

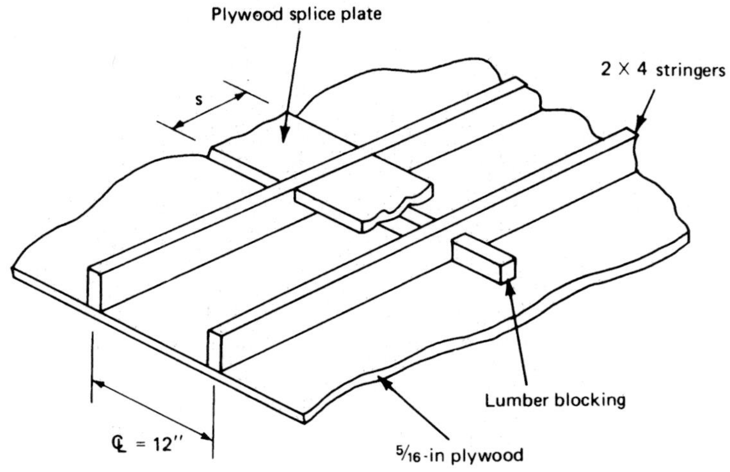

FIG. 7.16 Splice-plate details.

$$w_p = \frac{8F_p I_g}{48c\ell^2} \tag{7.19}$$

$$= \frac{8(1150)(1.560 \times 10^8)}{48(2.3)(12)^2(1.98 \times 10^6)} = 45.6 \text{ lb/ft}^2 \text{ (2.18 kPa)}$$

The compression splice can be designed in an analogous manner except that the full F_c (from Table 7.8) can be used if the splice meets the same length requirements as for tension shown in Table 7.20. It could be sized down if the analysis shows less strength is necessary.

The preceding method assumes that the splice is at the point of maximum moment. In the example problem, the splice is not located at that point, but at one-third the length of the span. The moment at the splice location is eight-ninths of the maximum, assuming a uniformly distributed load. Hence the maximum design load is

$$w_p = \frac{9}{8}(45.6) \text{ lb/ft}^2 = 51.3 \text{ lb/ft}^2 \text{ (2.46 kPa)}$$

Rolling Shear. The statical moment Q_s for the top skin will govern and is computed using Table 7.23. The face grain of the top skin is parallel to the stringers.

For ½-in Structural I plywood (unsanded), the area = 5.81 in² per 4-ft-wide panel and $y' = 0.0606$ in per 4-ft-wide panel. The value of c is obtained by using the neutral axis computed for the gross moment of inertia:

$$c = (5/16 + 3\,3/8 + 1/2) - 2.27 = 1.92 \text{ in}$$

$$d_s = c - y' = 1.92 - 0.0616 = 1.86 \text{ in}$$

$$Q_s = Ad_s = 5.81(1.86) = 10.8 \text{ in}^3 \text{ per 4-ft-wide panel}$$

The allowable stress in rolling shear for the outboard stringer is one-half that for the interior stringers because of the likelihood of stress concentrations. The equation for shear stress,

$$f_s = \frac{VQ_s}{I_g t} \tag{7.20}$$

is used to determine the allowable load. For a 4-ft (1.22-m)-wide panel over a simple span,

$$w_s = \frac{2I_g \Sigma F_s t}{4Q_s \ell} \tag{7.21}$$

where w_s is the allowable load based on rolling shear stress in pounds per square foot, and $\Sigma F_s t$ is the sum of the product of allowable rolling shear stress and glueline width for each stringer in pounds per inch.

TABLE 7.23 Area and y' for Computing Statical Moment Q_s (see Fig. 7.12)

Plywood thickness, in	Structural I Grades				All other panels			
	Face grain ∥ to stringers		Face grain ⊥ to stringers		Face grain ∥ to stringers		Face grain ⊥ to stringers	
	Area,* in^2	y', in	Area,* in^2	y', in	Area,* in^2	y', in	Area,* in^2	y', in
Unsanded panels								
5/16	3.22	0.0335	4.75	0.149	3.00	0.0375	2.64	0.149
3/8	4.46	0.0465	5.75	0.180	3.72	0.0465	3.19	0.180
15/32, 1/2	5.42	0.0565	8.70	0.227	4.60	0.0575	4.03	0.227
19/32, 5/8	9.22	0.176	11.0	0.305	4.64	0.0580	5.14	0.289
23/32, 3/4	11.2	0.176	11.3	0.352	5.57	0.0580	6.25	0.352
Sanded panels								
1/4	2.54	0.0265	2.51	0.121	2.54	0.0265	1.39	0.121
11/32	2.54	0.0265	3.00	0.168	2.54	0.0265	1.67	0.168
3/8	3.36	0.0350	4.50	0.184	3.36	0.0350	2.50	0.184
15/32	3.89	0.0405	9.01	0.231	3.89	0.0405	5.00	0.231
1/2	3.89	0.0405	10.1	0.246	3.89	0.0405	5.64	0.246
19/32	8.69	0.193	10.0	0.293	6.32	0.156	5.56	0.293
5/8	9.07	0.207	11.0	0.309	6.53	0.151	6.11	0.309
23/32	11.6	0.262	12.5	0.356	7.92	0.220	6.95	0.356
3/4	12.1	0.278	15.0	0.371	8.19	0.233	8.32	0.371
Touch-sanded panels								
1/2	4.56	0.0475	9.95	0.226	4.56	0.0475	4.64	0.224
19/32, 5/8	7.92	0.174	11.2	0.279	4.38	0.0685	6.24	0.279
23/32, 3/4	10.4	0.177	14.5	0.345	5.06	0.0790	8.06	0.345
1-1/8 (2·4·1)	—	—	—	—	12.5	0.354	16.2	0.542

Note: 1 in = 25.4 mm.
*Area based on 48-in-wide panel. For other widths, use a proportionate area.
Source: From Ref. 13. Used with permission.

$$F_s t = 75 \times 1.15 = 86.2 \text{ lb/in}^2$$

$$\Sigma F_s t = 3(86.2)(1.5) + \frac{86.2}{2}(1.5) + \frac{86.2}{2}(0.75) = 485 \text{ lb/in}$$

$$w_s = \frac{2(78.81)(485)}{4(10.8)(12)} = 147 \text{ lb/ft}^2 \text{ (7.04 kPa)}$$

Horizontal Shear. Horizontal shear for the lumber is checked in a similar manner after computing the statical moment Q_v.

$$Q \text{ (stringers)} = 5\left(1.5 \times 1.42 \times \frac{1.42}{2}\right) = 7.56 \text{ in}^3$$

Then, since $c = 1.92$ in = distance from neutral axis to top,

$$Q \text{ (skin)} = A(c - \tfrac{1}{2} \text{ skin thickness})$$

$$= 4(2.175)(1.67) = 14.5 \text{ in}^3$$

$$Q_v = 14.5 + \frac{1.60 \times 7.56}{1.98} = 20.6 \text{ in}^3$$

From the *National Design Specification for Wood Construction,*[7] $F_v = 95 \times 1.15 = 109$ lb/in². The maximum load for a simply supported, 4-ft-wide panel is

$$w_v = \frac{2I_g F_v \Sigma t}{4Q_v \ell} \tag{7.22}$$

where w_v is the allowable load based on horizontal shear in pounds per square foot, and Σt is the sum of stringer widths in inches. Then

$$w_v = \frac{2(78.81)(109)(5 \times 1.50)}{4(20.6)(12)} = 130 \text{ lb/ft}^2 \text{ (6.24 kPa)}$$

Design Summary. The maximum snow load that can be placed on the panel is the minimum of those computed.

$$w_\Delta = 48.2 \text{ lb/ft}^2 \text{ (2.31 kPa)}$$

$$w \text{ (top)} = 418 \text{ lb/ft}^2 \text{ (20.0 kPa)}$$

$$w\ (b, \text{top}) = 85.4 \text{ lb/ft}^2 \text{ (4.08 kPa)}$$

$$w\ (b, \text{bottom}) = 57.3 \text{ lb/ft}^2 \text{ (2.78 kPa)}$$

$$w_p = 51.3 \text{ lb/ft}^2 \text{ (2.46 kPa)}$$

$$w_s = 147 \text{ lb/ft}^2 \text{ (7.04 kPa)}$$

$$w_v = 130 \text{ lb/ft}^2 \text{ (6.24 kPa)}$$

Thus the design is limited by the live-load deflection of the panel to 48.2 lb/ft²

(2.31 kPa). Deflection is usually the limiting case in stressed-skin panels and should always be checked first in any trial-and-error design.

7.6.5 Wall Panels

While stressed-skin panels are most often used in roof and floor systems, they also may be used as wall elements. In this mode they can be designed as columns subject to compression alone or designed for combined compression and bending. Generally, the thickness of the panel will be chosen on the basis of aesthetics, insulation, sound isolation, or special service needs. The panels also should be checked for the structural criteria.

Pin-end connections should be assumed, since it is difficult to achieve a higher level of fixity. For compression only, the allowable axial load P_a (in pounds) is the smaller of

$$P_a = F_c A$$

and

$$P_a = \frac{3.619EI_g}{144L^2} \tag{7.23}$$

where L = unsupported vertical height of panel, ft
F = allowable compressive stress for plywood skins c, lb/in²
A = total area of stringer and skins with grain parallel to the axial load, in²

For combined loading,

$$\frac{P}{P_a} + \frac{(M/S)}{F_c} \leq 1.0 \tag{7.24}$$

where P = total axial load, lb
M = allowable bending moment on panel, in·lb
S = panel section modulus referenced to compression side = I (net)/c, in³
F_c = allowable parallel to grain compression stress of plywood, lb/in²

Note that P_a and F_c can be adjusted for load duration.

7.6.6 Curved Panels

Stressed-skin panels also may be curved to function as either flexural members or as arch segments. The difference between the two classifications is the development of horizontal thrust at the supports in the arch segment. Arch panels are usually constructed with spaced ribs and may either be a fixed-fixed arch or a two- or three-hinged arch. The subject of arches is treated in more detail in Chap. 9.

The APA recommends panels of medium curvature (3/1 to 8/1 span-to-rise ratios)[11] as the most practical. There are limits on the bending radii of plywood panels when they are dry as shown in Table 7.24. Some fractures may occur at this recommended minimum with typical plywood. Tighter radii may be achieved with wetting or steaming.

The design of spaced-rib arch and flexural curved panels is very similar to that of flat stressed-skin panels. One significant difference is the reduction in allowable

TABLE 7.24 Minimum Bending Radii for Dry Plywood Panels

Panel thickness, in	Minimum radii for panels bent, ft	
	Across grain	Parallel to grain
$\frac{1}{4}$	2	5
$\frac{5}{16}$	2	6
$\frac{11}{32}$, $\frac{3}{8}$	3	8
$\frac{15}{32}$, $\frac{1}{2}$	6	12
$\frac{19}{32}$, $\frac{5}{8}$	8	16
$\frac{23}{32}$, $\frac{3}{4}$	12	20

Note: 1 in = 25.4 mm; 1 ft = 0.3048 m.
Source: From Ref. 9. Used with permission.

stress for curvature. The allowable unit stress in bending, tension, and compression parallel to grain should be multiplied by the following factor:

$$C_c = 1 - 2000\left(\frac{t}{R}\right)^2 \tag{7.25}$$

where t is the distance between extreme fibers of plies parallel with the stress for one lamination in inches, and R is the radius of curvature to the centerline of the member.

The ratio t/R should not exceed $\frac{1}{100}$ for hardwoods and southern pine, nor $\frac{1}{125}$ for all other softwoods. All other reductions described in Sec. 7.6.3 are to be in effect, if appropriate.

When a curved member is subject to a bending moment, radial stress (either tension or compression) is induced. The maximum radial stress in a curved panel may be given as

$$f_r = \frac{3}{2}\frac{M}{Rbh} \tag{7.26}$$

where f_r = radial stress, lb/in^2
M = bending moment on a width of panel equal to rib spacing, in·lb
R = radius of curvature to centerline of member, in
b = width of rib or stringer, in
h = overall depth of panel, in

The maximum radial stress should not be greater than one-half the allowable rolling shear stress for radial tension or the allowable bearing stress for radial compression. This radial stress should also not exceed the allowable values for lumber if it is used for the ribs. More information on the design of arches may be found in Chap. 9 and on the design and fabrication of plywood curved panels in Ref. 11.

7.6.7 Other Stressed-Skin-Type Panel Products

The stressed-skin concept utilizes strong, relatively thin sheets designed to carry the tension and compression stresses due to bending. These skins are separated by a core designed to space the skins and carry the shear. Lumber cores in the form of stringers have been described in the preceding sections. However, other materials such as foams or paper honeycombs are used as well. These products are often called sandwich panels, and their design is detailed in Ref. 12.

In the design of flat or curved sandwich panels, it is assumed that the core does not contribute to the bending stiffness of the panel. The section properties are thus determined assuming that only the skins are effective. These types of panels are often used in walls or other systems where combined bending and compression conditions exist. Hence, global and local buckling effects must be checked as well as bending and shear stresses. Radial stresses in curved sandwich panels should be kept below one-third of the allowable shear stress of the core. Bearing stresses may also be important in sandwich panels, and points of contact with concentrated loads or reactions should be carefully designed.

Multiple layers of plywood may be glued together to form a solid plywood curved panel. The interior plywood may be glued over the full area of the skins or only in strips to reduce fabrication costs. Specific details on the design of these panel types is found in Ref. 11.

7.6.8 Applications

Glued plywood structural components have many advantages during and after construction. High strength-to-weight ratio, efficient use of materials, uniform size, production-line quality, and reduced overall construction time can be claimed by these products.

Stressed-skin panels are commonly used in roof and floor systems over 12- to 32-ft (3.66- to 9.75-m) spans. Two-sided panels may be premanufactured with insulation installed, and the bottom skin may be a ready-to-finish ceiling. One-sided panels offer the advantage of allowing easy installation of a mechanical service system.

Folded-plate structures (Fig. 7.17) utilize either nailed or glued plates in a shell system that relies on its shape to support the horizontal and vertical forces. Those structures can be used in spans up to 100 ft (30.5 m) or more. Panel thickness is governed by rafter spacing and shear adjacent to the rafter supports. The panels are prefabricated and are readily assembled in the field using either common or specially designed connectors and bearing hardware. The horizontal thrust of the plates is taken at the end walls and/or with horizontal tie-rods. Specific design details of this type of plywood diaphragm are given in Ref. 14. Further discussion of diaphragms is found in Chap. 8.

Folded plates also may be designed to radiate out from an unsupported apex to supporting exterior walls or other supports near the building perimeter. Another form of construction which uses this type of plate is a space frame such as shown in Fig. 7.18.

Space frames usually incorporate a combination of plates with interact to support vertical loads without beams or trusses. The webs or skin of the shell structure transmit shear to the boundaries by diaphragm action.

FIG. 7.17 Multiple-folded-plate structure. *(Courtesy of the American Plywood Association.)*

FIG. 7.18 Plywood space-frame structure. *(Courtesy of the American Plywood Association.)*

7.7 APPENDIX

7.7.1 Sources of Further Information

1. American Plywood Association, P.O. Box 11700, Tacoma, Wash. 98411.
2. National Particleboard Association, 18928 Premiere Court, Gaithersburg, Md. 20879-1569.
3. Canadian Wood Council, 85 Albert St., Ottawa, Canada K1P 6A4.
4. Structural Board Association, 45 Sheppard Avenue, Willowdale, Ontario, Canada M2N 5W9.

7.7.2 Equations for Computing Panel Uniform Load Capacity

The American Plywood Association has recommended that the following formulas be used in computing the capacity of panel products subject to uniform loads normal to the face of the panel.

When the face grain of the panel is perpendicular to the supports (span parallel to face grain), the three-span beam equations are used for spacings of 32 in (813 mm) or less. Two-span formulas are used for greater support spacings. For spans oriented perpendicular to face grain, the three-span condition is used for spacings 16 in (406 mm) or less, two-span formulas for 24-in (610-mm) spacings, and one span for greater than 24-in (610-mm) spacings.

Bending Stress

One span:
$$w_b = \frac{96F_bKS}{\ell_1^2}$$

Two spans:
$$w_b = \frac{96F_bKS}{\ell_1^2}$$

Three spans:
$$w_b = \frac{120F_bKS}{\ell_1^2}$$

where w_b = uniform load based on allowable bending stress, lb/ft^2
F_b = allowable bending stress, lb/in^2
KS = effective section modulus, in^3/ft
ℓ_1 = span center-to-center of adjacent supports, in

Shear Stress

One span:
$$w_s = \frac{24F_s(Ib/Q)}{\ell_2}$$

Two spans:
$$w_s = \frac{19.2F_s(Ib/Q)}{\ell_2}$$

Three spans:
$$w_s = \frac{20F_s(Ib/Q)}{\ell_2}$$

where w_s = uniform load based on allowable shear stress, lb/ft^2
F_s = allowable shear stress, lb/in^2
Ib/Q = rolling shear constant, in^2/ft
ℓ_2 = clear span (center-to-center span between adjacent supports minus support width), in

Deflection

All conditions:

$$w_b = \frac{\Delta\ (\text{allowable})}{\Delta_b + \Delta_s}$$

where w_b = uniform load for allowable deflection, lb/ft^2
Δ (allowable) = allowable deflection, in
Δ_b = bending deflection for 1 lb/ft^2 uniform load, in
Δ_s = shear deflection for 1 lb/ft^2 uniform load (for optional computation see below), in

If the shear deflection is computed separately from bending deflection, then the modulus of elasticity used in the bending deflection equations should be increased 10 percent. For most cases it is sufficient to approximate the total deformation by calculating only the bending deformation using an unadjusted elastic modulus.

One span:

$$\Delta_b = \frac{w\ell_3^4}{921.6EI}$$

Two spans:

$$\Delta_b = \frac{w\ell_3^4}{2220EI}$$

Three spans:

$$\Delta_b = \frac{w\ell_3^4}{1743EI}$$

where Δ_b = bending deflection, in
w = uniform load, lb/ft^2
E = modulus of elasticity, lb/in^2
I = effective moment of inertia, in^4/ft
ℓ_3 = clear span + sw
sw = support width factor, equal to 0.25 in (6.35 mm) for 2-in nominal framing and 0.625 in (15.9 mm) for 4-in nominal framing

All conditions:

$$\Delta_s \cong \frac{wCt^2\ell_2^2}{1270EI}$$

where Δ_s = shear deflection, in
C = constant = 120 if face grain is perpendicular to supports, or
= 60 if face grain is parallel to supports
t = nominal panel thickness, in
E = unadjusted modulus of elasticity, lb/in^2

7.7.3 Refined Method for Calculating Deflection of Plywood-Lumber Beams

The total deflection may be determined as a sum of deflection due to bending and that due to shear. When calculating bending deflection, the modulus of elasticity of the flange lumber should be increased by 3 percent to eliminate shear effects. The total moment of inertia I (total) should be used regardless of any butt joints.

The shear deformation Δ_s is calculated from

$$\Delta_s = \frac{KC}{AG}$$

where K = factor from Fig. 7.19 determined from beam geometry or from equation in Fig. 7.20
C = loading factor from Fig. 7.20
A = cross-sectional area (using effective shear thickness t_s from Table 7.6)
G = web shear modulus, Table 7.8

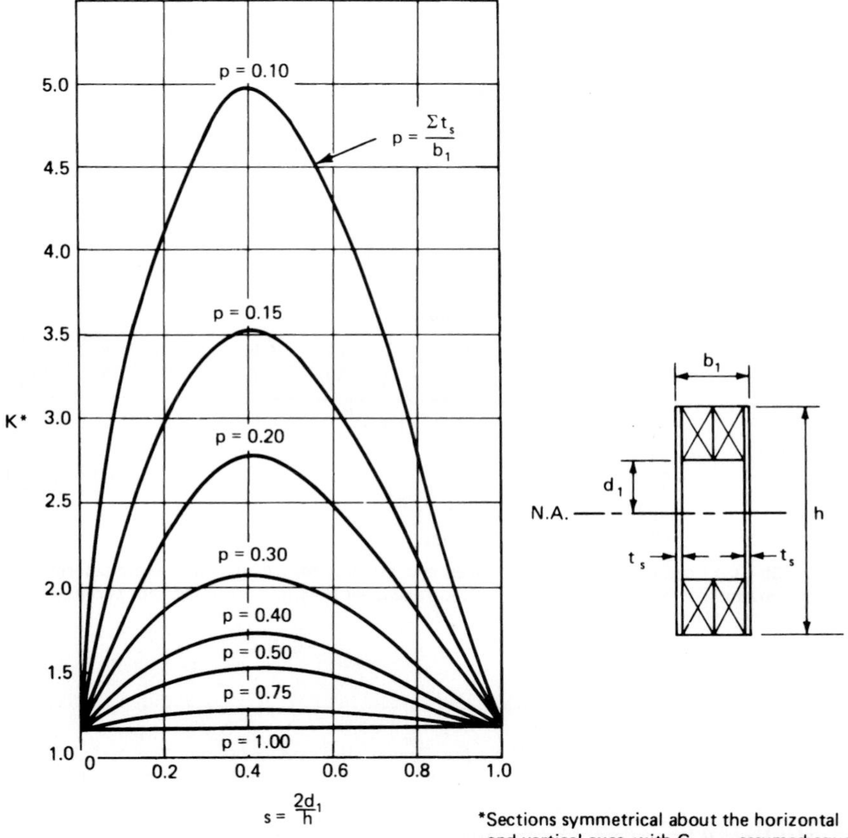

FIG. 7.19 Section constant K for plywood lumber beams. *(From Ref. 10. Used with permission.)*

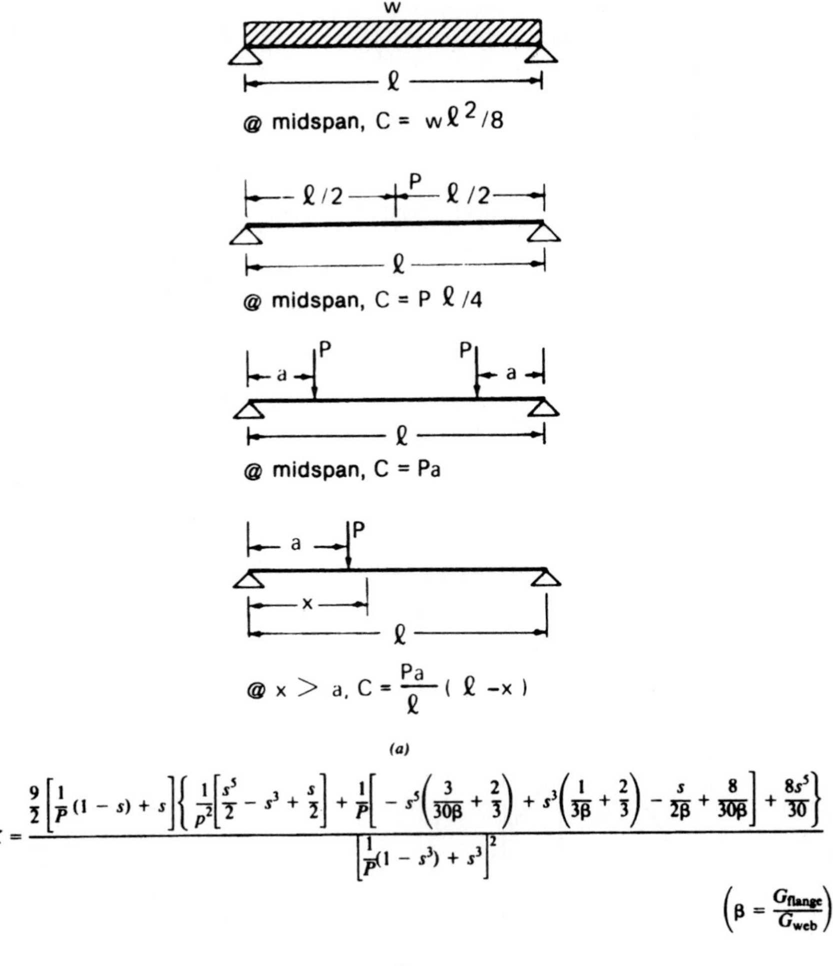

$$K = \frac{\frac{9}{2}\left[\frac{1}{P}(1-s)+s\right]\left\{\frac{1}{P^2}\left[\frac{s^5}{2}-s^3+\frac{s}{2}\right]+\frac{1}{P}\left[-s^5\left(\frac{3}{30\beta}+\frac{2}{3}\right)+s^3\left(\frac{1}{3\beta}+\frac{2}{3}\right)-\frac{s}{2\beta}+\frac{8}{30\beta}\right]+\frac{8s^5}{30}\right\}}{\left[\frac{1}{P}(1-s^3)+s^3\right]^2}$$

$$\left(\beta = \frac{G_{flange}}{G_{web}}\right)$$

(b)

FIG. 7.20 (*a*) Load coefficients and (*b*) section constant *K* for calculation of shear deformation in plywood lumber beams. See also Fig. 7.19. *(Adapted from Ref. 10. Used with permission.)*

REFERENCES

1. *Voluntary Product Standard PS1-83 for Commercial and Industrial Plywood,* U.S. Department of Commerce, National Institute of Standards and Technology, Gaithersburg, Md., 1983.
2. *Mat-Formed Wood Particleboard,* American National Standard ANSI A208.1-93, American National Standards Institute, New York, N.Y., 1993.
3. *Performance Standards and Policies for Structural Use Panels,* APA PRP-108, American Plywood Association, Tacoma, Wash., 1991.

4. *APA Structural Use Panels,* National Evaluation Service Committee Report No. NER-108, Council of American Building Officials, Falls Church, VA, 1983.
5. Voluntary Product Standard PS2-93, *Performance Standard for Wood-Based Structural-Use Panels,* U.S. Department of Commerce, National Institute of Standards and Technology, Gaithersburg, Md., 1993.
6. *Pneumatic or Mechanical Driven Staples, Nails, P-Nails and Allied Fasteners for Use in All Types of Building Construction,* National Evaluation Service Committee Report No. NER-272, Council of American Building Officials, Falls Church, VA, 1989.
7. *National Design Specification for Wood Construction,* American Forest and Paper Association, Washington, D.C., 1991.
8. *APA Design/Construction Guide, Residential and Commercial Construction,* American Plywood Association, Tacoma, Wash., 1993.
9. *Plywood Design Specification,* American Plywood Association, Tacoma, Wash., 1939.
10. *Design and Fabrication of Glued Plywood-Lumber Beams,* Plywood Design Specification Supplement No. 2, American Plywood Association, Tacoma, Wash., 1992.
11. *Design and Fabrication of Plywood Curved Panels,* Plywood Design Specification Supplement No. 1, American Plywood Association, Tacoma, Wash., 1990.
12. *Design and Construction of Plywood Sandwich Panels,* Plywood Design Specification Supplement No. 4, American Plywood Association, Tacoma, Wash., 1990.
13. *Design and Fabrication of Plywood Stressed-Skin Panels,* Plywood Design Specification Supplement No. 3, American Plywood Association, Tacoma, Wash., 1990.
14. *Plywood Folded Plates—Design and Details,* APA Laboratory Report No. 121, American Plywood Association, Tacoma, Wash., 1971.
15. *Grades and Specifications: APA Product Guide,* American Plywood Association, Tacoma, Wash., 1992.
16. *Fastener Loads for Plywood—Screws,* APA Technical Note No. 830, American Plywood Association, Tacoma, Wash., 1985.
17. *Fastener Loads for Plywood—Bolts,* APA Technical Note No. E825, American Plywood Association, Tacoma, Wash., 1989.

CHAPTER 8
DIAPHRAGMS AND SHEARWALLS

E. F. Diekmann, S.E.

8.1 SECTION LIMITATIONS

All structures are subjected to lateral forces generated by the wind. Buildings in specific geographic locations may additionally be subjected to lateral forces generated by the movement of their foundations during an earthquake. Other lateral forces such as those caused by earth pressure or blast loads also may act on buildings. The design concepts discussed herein are applicable in designing the resistance system of a building with wooden elements for any lateral force, and minimal emphasis will be given to the specific source of the lateral force.

The magnitude of the lateral force caused by either wind or earthquake which must be considered in a design as acting on the building as a whole or on the building's components is defined by the applicable building code. A large volume of technical literature is available to assist the design engineer in applying the code to specific design situations. The applicable forces will simply be given in the examples used, since it is assumed that the designer either already has the necessary skill to determine the forces for a specific design situation or will refer to the appropriate literature for the needed assistance to develop this skill.

Wall, floor, and roof subsystems, sheathed with wood products such as boards or plywood, can be designed to function within the total building system to resist lateral forces in addition to supporting vertical loads. These subsystems are commonly referred to as *shearwalls* (vertical elements) and *diaphragms* (horizontal elements). A critical consideration in the proper functioning of diaphragms and shearwalls is the connections needed to ensure that these elements act as integral units and that these units in turn are interconnected with the building as a whole to ensure the proper functioning of the entire structure. The detailed design of wood components and their connections is the subject of other chapters of this handbook. This chapter will consequently focus on the methods for determining the magnitude of forces on the elements of diaphragms and shearwalls and on the connections

Note: All SI units shown for sawn lumber are for the actual net dimensions corresponding to the nominal dimension indicated. In all example problems, SI units are only provided for given data and the final problem answer or answers. No intermediate values or data are expressed in SI units.

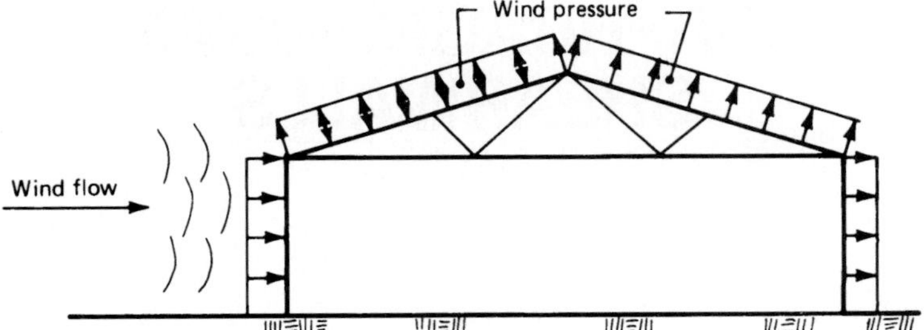

FIG. 8.1 Wind forces on a building cross section.

between elements. Once these forces are known, the design of the elements or connection proceeds according to the wood engineering principles discussed in other chapters.

8.2 WIND-FORCE FUNDAMENTALS

Figure 8.1 shows a cross section of a simple structure subjected to wind forces. Procedures in various design references, e.g., ASCE 7-93, permit the determination of the magnitude in pounds per square foot of the inward force (positive) on the windward wall and the outward force (negative) on the leeward wall. Additional forces are generated normal to the sloping roof surfaces.

Figure 8.2*a* shows the wind force acting on a segment of wall. It should be apparent that the wall as shown will fall over from the action of the wind unless designed to cantilever from the base. The wall is shown as subjected to both the

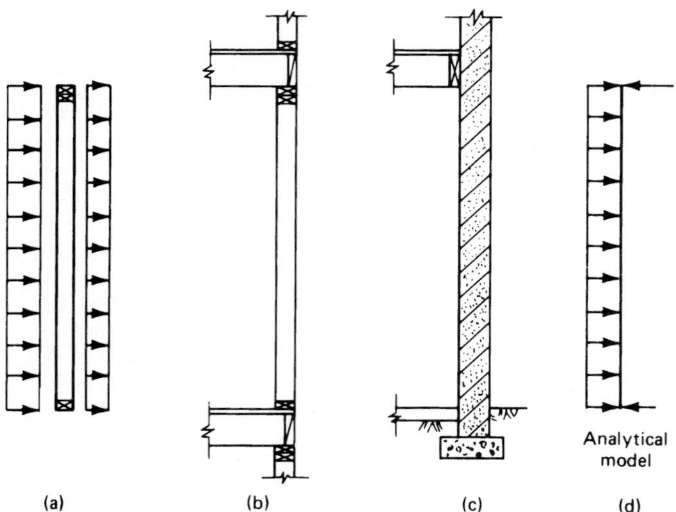

FIG. 8.2 Wind forces on a wall segment.

windward and leeward wind pressures. These pressures normally would be considered independently on a given building wall; however, in open structures as defined by the various building codes these pressures would in fact be additive. The types of buildings in which diaphragms and shearwalls are typically found have walls which are designed to span vertically, as illustrated in Fig. 8.2*b* and *c*, and only walls of this type will be considered in this section. Figure 8.2*d* shows the analytical model typically assumed for these types of walls.

Next consider a 1-ft^2 area of the sloping roof as shown in Fig. 8.3 acted on by a wind pressure F_w applied normal to the slope. The roof has a weight W (lb/ft^2), while the wind force has a vertical component $F_w/\cos\theta$ and a component parallel to the plane of the roof $F_w \tan\theta$. When the wind pressure is inward (positive), the roof deadweight and the vertical component of the wind pressure are additive. When the wind pressure is outward (negative), the roof deadweight and the vertical component of the wind pressure oppose each other. The outward pressure may in some design circumstances be larger than the weight of the roof itself, resulting in a net uplift loading of the framing system. The roof must therefore have sufficient anchorage to the walls and possibly on into the foundations to engage sufficient weight to offset this upward component of wind pressure. The vertical components of wind pressure will be ignored in the example designs of roof diaphragms because these components do not directly impact the design of the diaphragm itself.

The slope component of the wind force is of specific interest because it is this component for which the diaphragm must be designed. Figure 8.4 shows the slope component of the wind force F acting along a slope length ℓ. The force v per unit slope length would be F/ℓ (lb/ft). The horizontal component F_h of the force would be $F\cos\theta$, and the horizontal projection ℓ_h of the slope length ℓ would be $\ell\cos\theta$. The force v per unit of horizontal projection would be F_h/ℓ_h or $(F\cos\theta)/\ell\cos\theta$, which equals F/ℓ as given earlier. Thus it makes no difference analytically whether the computations use slope lengths and the force component along the slope or use the horizontal force component and the horizontal projection of the roof. In practice, the horizontal force component and projection are typically used.

8.3 EARTHQUAKE FORCE FUNDAMENTALS

Figure 8.5 shows a cross section of a simple building subjected to earthquake forces. During an earthquake, the ground displaces and an inertial force is generated in the elements of the structure according to the principle that this force is equal to the mass of the element times the acceleration, i.e.,

$$F = ma \tag{8.1}$$

The mass is defined as the weight W divided by the acceleration of gravity g. The acceleration a due to the earthquake motion is given in building code formulas as a percentage of g so that the formula for the inertial force generated in an element of a building reduces to

$$F = \frac{W}{g} \times \% \times g = \%W \tag{8.2}$$

This fundamental approach makes it possible to calculate a seismic force per square foot of building element which need not differ in its analytical treatment from the force (pressure) per square foot generated by the wind.

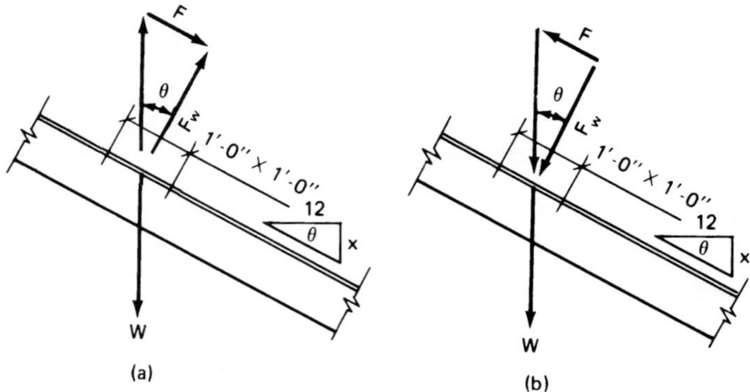

FIG. 8.3 Wind forces on a sloping roof. (*a*) Negative pressure; (*b*) positive pressure.

Figure 8.5 indicates the ground motion solely as a horizontal motion. Earthquake ground motion may have a vertical component as well. This vertical component is currently almost always ignored in the seismic design of buildings, although the vertical weight on a building element is sometimes reduced to reflect a vertical acceleration when making stability calculations for the element.

Figure 8.6 is a plan view of a simple rectangular building acted on by a total design force F_D. This total force is the sum of the wind pressure forces or seismic forces on each element of the structure and can act on the building in any direction. This total design force can be resolved into a component force transverse to the structure F_t and a component force longitudinal to the structure F_ℓ. F_t and F_ℓ act simultaneously on the structure, and each as a component would be smaller than the total design force F_D. Current practice is to calculate the transverse and longitudinal design forces and to design the structure for each force acting independently. The transverse and longitudinal design forces are most often not the same, de-

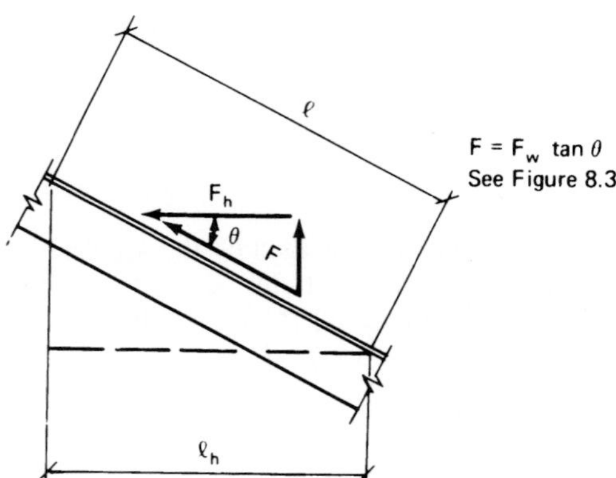

FIG. 8.4 Wind force component in plane of roof diaphragm.

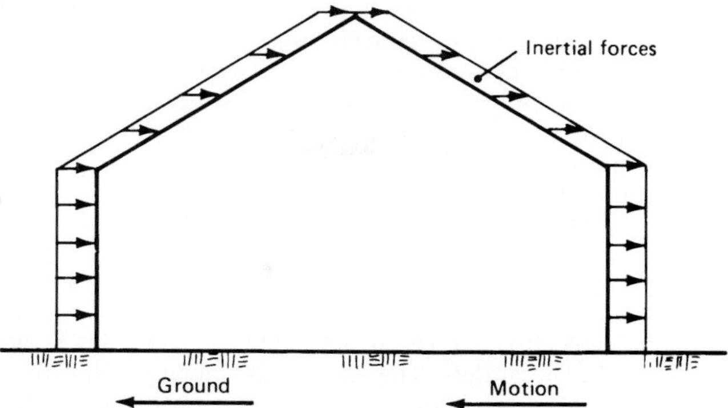

FIG. 8.5 Earthquake forces on a building cross section.

pending on code requirements. It is assumed that a structure capable of resisting the design force acting alone along each of the structure's principal axes will be able to resist the smaller components of a real force acting simultaneously along each axis.

8.4 DIAPHRAGMS

8.4.1 Diaphragm Principles

The walls shown in Fig. 8.2*b* and *c* require reactions at the top and bottom to prevent their collapse. These reactions are normally provided by the foundation, floors, and/or roof of the structure. To provide these reactions, the floors and roof

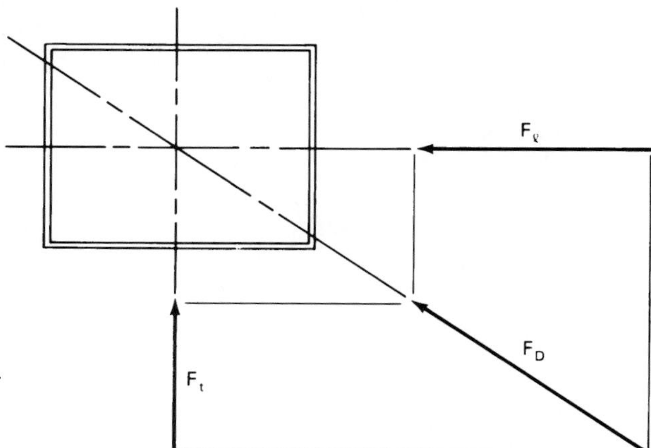

FIG. 8.6 Total design force on a building.

of the structure must have sufficient strength and rigidity in their plane to carry the wall reactions to vertical bracing elements oriented parallel to the applied load which in turn transfer the imposed force to the foundations. Any forces generated on or within the floor or roof itself are additive to the reactions from the walls in determining the total in-plane force to be carried. A floor or roof which is designed to carry in-plane forces is referred to as a *diaphragm.*

Floor and roof subsystems sheathed with wood products, such as boards or plywood, can be designed to function in the manner just described, i.e., to work as diaphragms. The needed vertical bracing elements frequently consist of solid-sheathed walls. Walls which carry in-plane forces are referred to as *shearwalls.* Figure 8.7 illustrates these components in an idealized rectangular-shaped building.

Diaphragms are typically analyzed using the same principles as are employed in the design of steel-plate girders. The analogy is shown graphically in Fig. 8.8.

The flange, often called the *chord,* of the diaphragm could be the double top plate of a wood-frame wall, a continuous wood or steel ledger on the face of a masonry or concrete wall, a reinforced concrete or masonry beam, or special re-

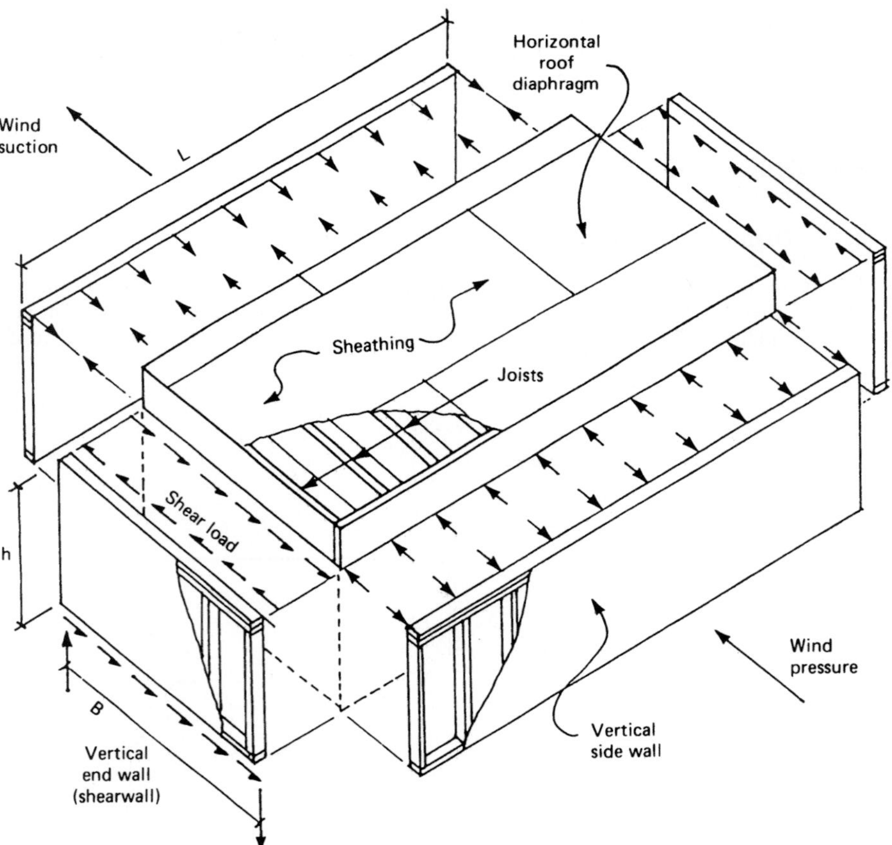

FIG. 8.7 Typical diaphragm and shearwall framing interrelationship.

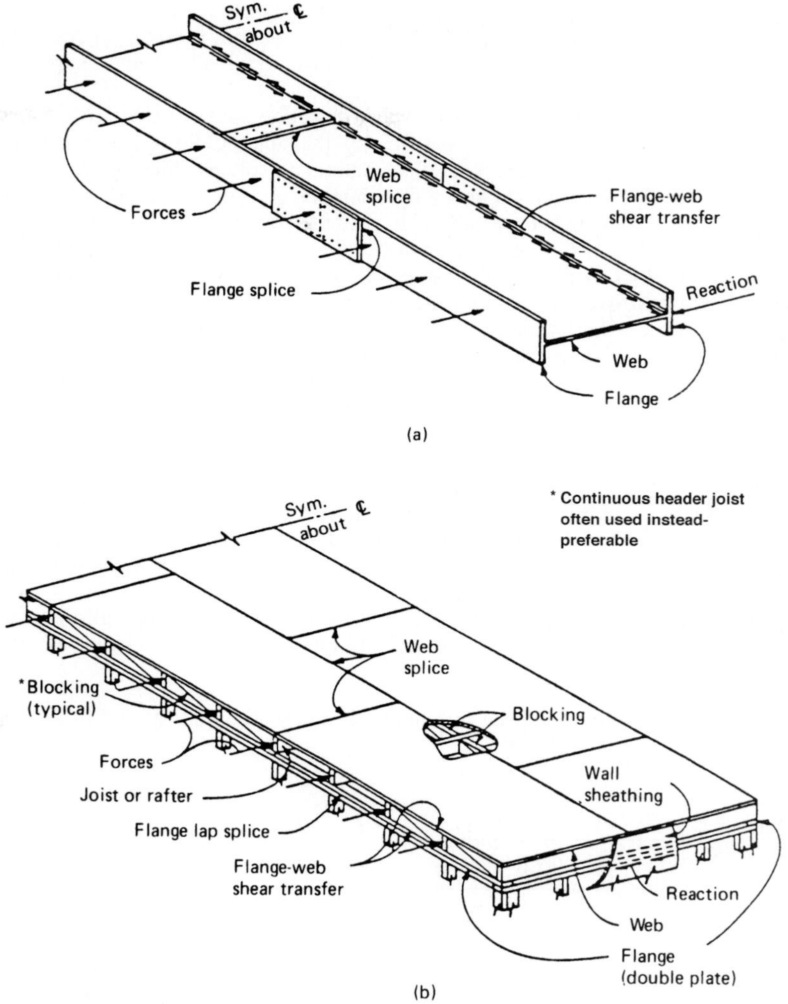

FIG. 8.8 Girder analogy for diaphragm. (*a*) Built-up steel girder; (*b*) plywood-sheathed diaphragm. *(Reprinted with permission of Applied Technology Council.[4])*

inforcing in reinforced concrete or masonry walls. The web of the diaphragm is the sheathing material, typically plywood, as shown in Fig. 8.8*b*. The web elements of blocked diaphragms are spliced over framing members, and provision for the stress transfer between the web and the flange must be made.

The flanges (chords) of diaphragms are normally designed to provide all the resistance to the flexural stresses in the diaphragm; i.e., the bending contribution of the web is neglected. The force in the flanges, therefore, is equal to the moment in the diaphragm divided by the distance between centerlines of the flanges. The flange force determined by this procedure is the upper limit of the force and is conservative. The flanges must be appropriately connected for this computed force at any joints in the flanges, and both tension and compression forces must be provided for at such splice connections because the load on the diaphragm is reversible.

The webs of diaphragms, like the webs of girders, are considered to carry the shearing stresses induced in the member by the applied forces. The size of the available web material will dictate the location of splices. Steel-girder webs are generally one piece for the depth of the member and are often one piece for the length of the girder. Wood-sheathed diaphragms virtually never have one-piece webs for either dimension because of material size limitations and must be spliced frequently. A blocked plywood-sheathed diaphragm is one in which all plywood panel edges occur over, and are nailed to, framing members. The blocking to meet the designation *blocked diaphragm* is, in fact, a splicing plate.

The forces applied to diaphragms are usually uniform along the length of the diaphragm, and therefore, the critical shear condition for diaphragms without openings occurs at the reactions, i.e., at the shearwalls. The critical shear condition dictates the thickness and boundary nailing of the diaphragm sheathing.

EXAMPLE 8.1 It is assumed for this illustration that the exterior walls contain the vertical bracing and that a force is applied in both the longitudinal and lateral directions as a result of some action, such as wind. Analysis has resulted in a determination of the design load along each axis. These design loads normally act in either direction on the structure (see Fig. 8.9*a*).

The load must be carried by the diaphragm (beam) to the end walls (reactions). As previously discussed, two simplifying assumptions will permit this diaphragm to be analyzed (see Fig. 8.9*b*):

1. The bending moment will be resisted entirely by a couple formed in the boundary members.

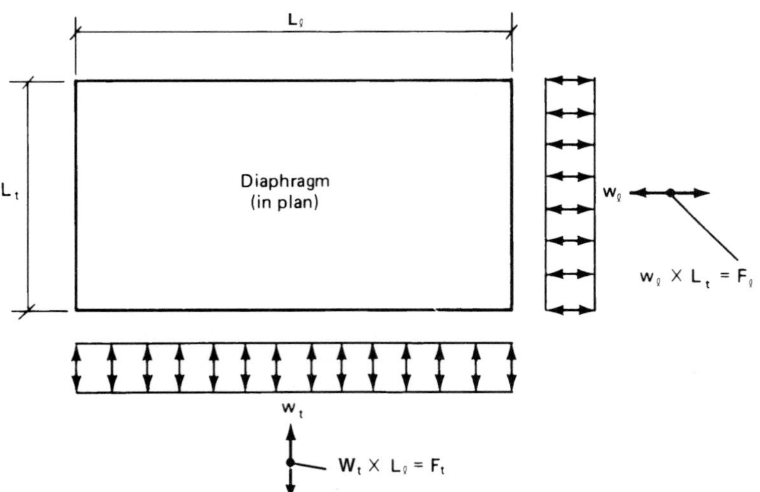

FIG. 8.9*a* Forces acting on a diaphragm.

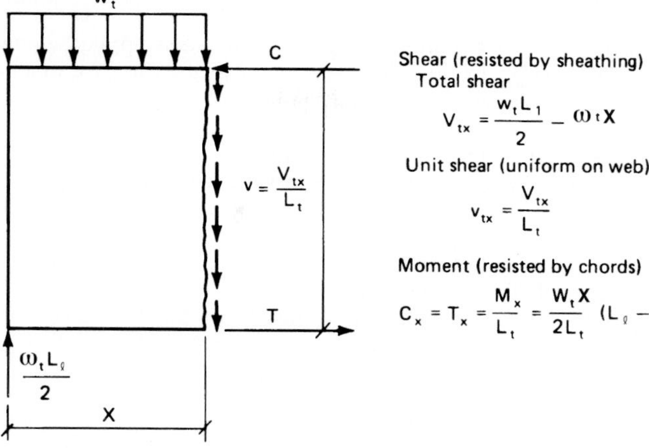

FIG. 8.9*b* Diaphragm free body.

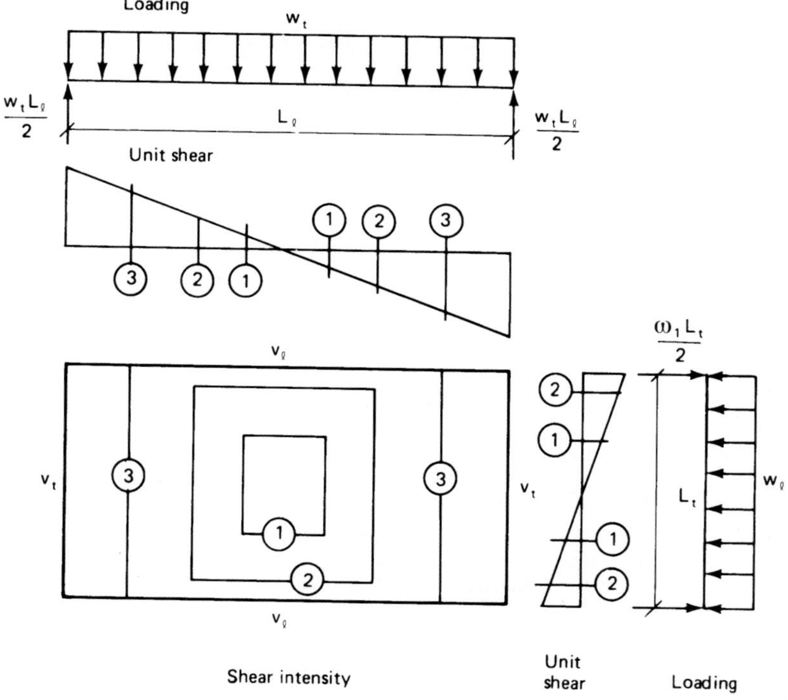

FIG. 8.9*c* Shear plot for diaphragm.

2. The shear will be distributed and carried uniformly by the sheathing.

The necessity of designing most diaphragms for loads applied along each principal axis results in zones of differing shear intensities within the diaphragm. Joining points of equal shear intensity results in shear contours for the diaphragm, as shown in Fig. 8.9*c*. The shear capacity of diaphragms varies with the spacing of the connectors used in securing the diaphragm sheathing to the framing (see Table 8.2). The boundary between the differing shear intensity zones is usually shown on construction drawings to correspond to the design location at which the fastener spacing must be altered in keeping with the dictates of the shear intensity.

A basic precept in engineering is that the moment in a beam at any point can be determined by calculating the area under the plot of the total shear along the beam from the end of the beam to the point of interest. It is this moment that is divided by the diaphragm depth to determine the chord force at that point. In the design of a diaphragm, the unit shear V/d is of primary interest because it determines the fastener spacing which must be used in a particular diaphragm zone. A plot of unit shear for a diaphragm is thus a plot of total shear divided by depth. It follows that calculating the area under the unit shear V/d plot for a diaphragm from the end of the diaphragm to the chord location of interest will produce directly the chord force at that point (see Fig. 8.9*d*).

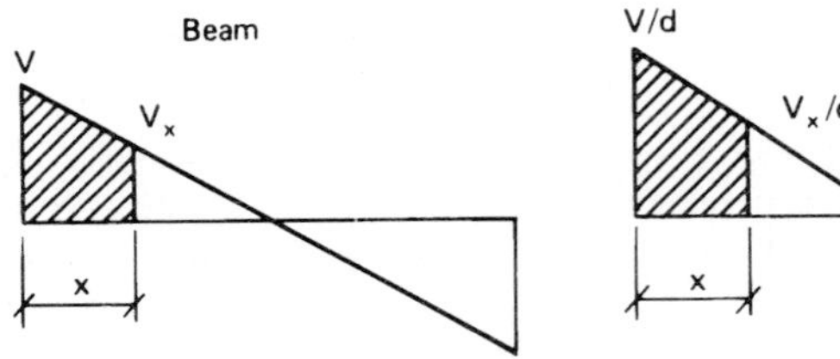

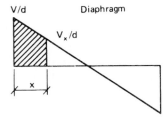

FIG. 8.9*d* Shear plot for beam and diaphragm.

Total shear plot
Moment

$$M_x = \frac{x}{2}(V + V_x)$$

Unit shear plot
Area

$$A = \frac{x}{2}\left(\frac{V}{d} + \frac{V_x}{d}\right) = \frac{x}{2d}(V + V_x) \tag{8.3}$$

Chord force at point x

$$\frac{Mx}{d} = \frac{x}{2d}(V + V_x)$$

The preceding formulas for diaphragm analysis are based on basic beam theory. Basic beam theory also can be applied to diaphragms in other ways. Assume the diaphragm is a beam consisting of the two chords and the web sheathing as shown in Fig. 8.10. The stress in the chords can be computed as $f = Mc/I$, where M = moment at point in diaphragm under study, $c \approx d/2$ for chord, and I = moment of inertia. The moment of inertia would consist of the contribution of the web and the chords. A basic assumption for diaphragms is that the web does not take moment; therefore, to be consistent, the web contribution to the moment of inertia is taken as zero. The moment of inertia for the chords in the diaphragm is defined as $2(Ay^2 + I_0)$, where y in this case is $d/2$. The moment of inertia of the chord about its centroid I_0 is extremely small for most diaphragms (where d is many feet) and can be ignored. The formula for bending stress can then be written as

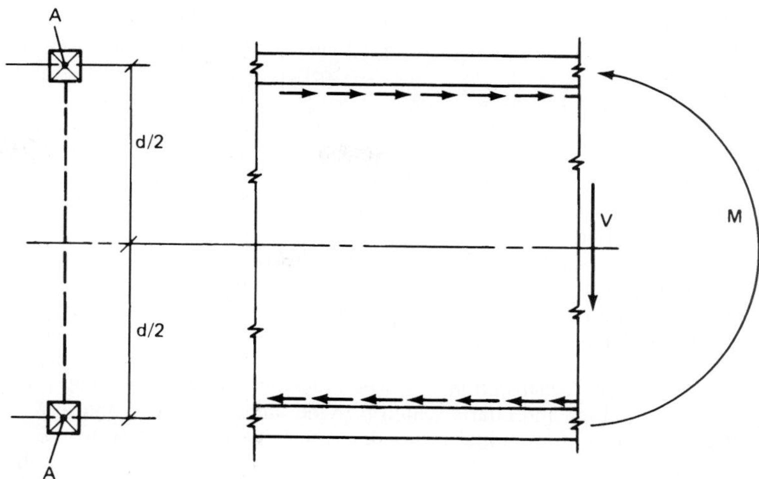

FIG. 8.10 Diaphragm equivalent beam.

$$f = \frac{M(d/2)}{2[A(d/2)^2]} = \frac{M}{Ad} \tag{8.4}$$

This formula, written to give the force in the chord rather than the stress, becomes $Af = Md$, which was the formula for the chord force previously given.

The formula for determining the connection per unit of length between the web of a beam and its flange is $v = VQ/I$, and this formula also can be applied to the web to chord attachment of a diaphragm. The statical moment of inertia Q is defined as $A(d/2)$ for the diaphragm in Fig. 8.10. The shear between the chord and web is then

$$v = \frac{V(Ad/2)}{2[A(d/2)^2]} = \frac{V}{d} \tag{8.5}$$

The total shear V divided by the depth of the diaphragm d was the unit shear in the diaphragm. The attachment of the chord to the diaphragm at a particular point has to be made for the shear in the diaphragm at the same point.

8.4.2 Diaphragm Deflections

Proper design of plywood diaphragms for wind or earthquake forces should include an analysis of the deflections of the diaphragm to ensure that it performs as intended. While past focus has been placed on the shear strength of the diaphragm, as wood-framed buildings have gotten larger and more complex, the magnitude of deflections has become of greater importance. The deflection of a uniformly loaded rectangular blocked-plywood diaphragm can be approximated from the following formula:

$$\Delta = \frac{5vL^3}{8EAd} + \frac{vL}{4Gt} + 0.188Le_n + \frac{\Sigma\Delta_c x_s}{2d} \tag{8.6}$$

where Δ = calculated deflection at the centerline, in
v = maximum shear due to design loads in direction under consideration, lb/ft
L = diaphragm length, ft
d = diaphragm depth, ft
E = elastic modulus of the flange material, lb/in^2
A = area of flange cross section, in^2
G = modulus of rigidity of plywood (assumed as 110,000 lb/in^2 for the derivation)
t = effective thickness of plywood for shear, in
e_n = nail deformation for a given load on a nail, in
x_s = distance to splice from support, ft
Δ_c = individual chord splice slip, in

Plywood Diaphragm Construction,[1] *Plywood Design Specification,*[2] and UBC Standard 25-9[3] have tables and charts which provide values for G, t, and e_n.*

In the formula, the individual terms determine the contribution to the total deflection of the chord elongation (bending), shear, nail slip, and chord-splice slip, respectively. The derivation of the terms is discussed in the *Guidelines for the Design of Horizontal Wood Diaphragms.*[4]

8.4.3 Diaphragm Types

The earliest designed diaphragms utilized board sheathing laid diagonally. These diaphragms were regarded analytically as analogous to a truss with the boards acting as web members. Board sheathing is no longer used extensively in wood-frame construction. Panel products, particularly plywood, have largely replaced individual boards for roof, floor, and wall sheathing. The change has been beneficial in an engineering sense to wood-frame construction because a panel product will inherently provide stronger and stiffer diaphragms than those made of boards and can be engineered for high capacity. Information on the design of board diaphragms can be found in Ref. 5.

Plywood sheathing panels have directional characteristics due to the grain orientation of the individual veneers which have been glued together to make up the panel (see Chap. 7). It is customary, since plywood is stronger and stiffer parallel to the panel's long dimension, to install plywood sheathing with the panel's long axis perpendicular to the framing members. There are exceptions to this practice, such as in the panelized roof discussed in Sec. 7.4.3. It is also customary to offset the end joints in adjacent rows of panels. (See case 1 in Table 8.2.) The end joints are to occur over framing members. Plywood sheathing panels are typically 8 ft long, and to minimize cutting and waste, this requires a spacing of framing members which cycles with 8 ft. Common framing member spacings are thus 12 in (305 mm) (eight per panel), 16 in (406 mm) (six per panel), and 24 in (610 mm) (four per panel). Other spacings include 48 in (1220 mm) (two per panel), 32 in (813 mm) (three per panel) and 19.2 in (488 mm) (five per panel).

Testing of plywood-sheathed assemblies as diaphragms has shown that panel thickness, panel layout, and the relationship to framing member orientation, framing

*Values for t and G also can be obtained from Tables 7.6 and 7.8, respectively. Values for e_n can be obtained from Table 8.2. References 1, 3, and 6 also contain information on values for t, G, and e_n.

member size, fastener size, and spacing all influence the shear carrying capacity of a diaphragm. These findings have been incorporated into tables developed by the American Plywood Association and adopted by building codes (see Tables 8.2 through 8.5).

Other panel-sheathing product manufacturers have followed the lead of the plywood industry in testing their products in diaphragm applications and have obtained building code recognition of the diaphragm shear capacity of their products. Tables 8.4 and 8.5 are representative of code approvals of such products. Plywood is used in the examples in this section. The design principles are equally applicable to the other panel-sheathing products.

The long edges of the panels pose two separate design considerations. The first involves loads applied normal to the panel surface. A load on one panel, particularly a concentrated load near the panel edge, can cause the loaded panel to deflect relative to the adjacent panels. This problem is customarily overcome by providing a tongue-and-groove edge joint on panels used for floor sheathing. Because of the relative cost of a tongue-and-groove joint and the common use of thinner panels for roof sheathing, tongue-and-groove plywood is not typically used in roof construction. Roof panel edges requiring support typically have this support provided by using ply clips or supporting wood members called *edge blocking.* Supporting wood members also can be provided for panels used in floors which lack a tongue-and-groove joint. The need to take some design action for loads applied normal to

TABLE 8.1 e_n Values (in) for Use in Calculating Diaphragm Deflection Due to Nail Slip (Structural I)*

Load per nail, lb	Nail designation		
	6d	8d	10d
60	0.012	0.008	0.006
80	0.020	0.012	0.010
100	0.030	0.018	0.013
120	0.045	0.023	0.018
140	0.068	0.031	0.023
160	0.102	0.041	0.029
180	—	0.056	0.037
200	—	0.074	0.047
220	—	0.096	0.060
240	—	—	0.070

*Increase e_n values 20 percent for plywood grades other than Structural I.

Values apply to common wire nails.

Load per nail = maximum shear per foot divided by the number of nails per foot at interior panel edges.

Decrease values 50 percent for seasoned lumber.

Source: Reproduced from the 1985 edition of the *Uniform Building Code,* copyright © 1985, with the permission of the publisher, the International Conference of Building Officials.

Panel Grade	Common Nail Size	Minimum Nail Penetration in Framing (inches)	Minimum Nominal Panel Thickness (inch)	Minimum Nominal Width of Framing Member (inches)	Blocked Diaphragms: Nail Spacing (in.) at diaphragm boundaries (all cases), at continuous panel edges parallel to load (Cases 3 & 4), and at all panel edges (Cases 5 & 6)[b]				Unblocked Diaphragms: Nails Spaced 6" max. at Supported Edges[b]	
					6	4	2-1/2[c]	2[c]	Case 1 (No unblocked edges or continuous joints parallel to load)	All other configurations (Cases 2, 3, 4, 5 & 6)
					Nail Spacing (in.) at other panel edges (Cases 1, 2, 3, & 4)					
					6	6	4	3		
APA STRUCTURAL I grades	6d	1-1/4	5/16	2	185	250	375	420	165	125
				3	210	280	420	475	185	140
	8d	1-1/2	3/8	2	270	360	530	600	240	180
				3	300	400	600	675	265	200
	10[d]	1-5/8	15/32	2	320	425	640	730	285	215
				3	360	480	720	820	320	240
APA RATED SHEATHING, APA RATED STURD-I-FLOOR and other APA grades except Species Group 5	6d	1-1/4	5/16	2	170	225	335	380	150	110
				3	190	250	380	430	170	125
			3/8	2	185	250	375	420	165	125
				3	210	280	420	475	185	140
	8d	1-1/2	3/8	2	240	320	480	545	215	160
				3	270	360	540	610	240	180
			7/16	2	255	340	505	575	230	170
				3	285	380	570	645	255	190
			15/32	2	270	360	530	600	240	180
				3	300	400	600	675	265	200
	10d[d]	1-5/8	15/32	2	290	385	575	655	255	190
				3	325	430	650	735	290	215
			19/32	2	320	425	640	730	285	215
				3	360	480	720	820	320	240

(a) For framing of other species: (1) Find specific gravity for species of lumber in Table 5.2. (2) Find shear value from table above for nail size for Structural I panels (regardless of actual grade). (3) Multiply value by 0.82 for species with specific gravity of 0.42 or greater, or 0.65 for all other species.

(b) Space nails maximum 12 in. o.c. along intermediate framing members (6 in. o.c. when supports are spaced 48 in. o.c.).

(c) Framing at adjoining panel edges shall be 3-in. nominal or wider, and nails shall be staggered where nails are spaced 2 inches o.c. or 2-1/2 inches o.c.

(d) Framing at adjoining panel edges shall be 3-in. nominal or wider, and nails shall be staggered where 10d nails having penetration into framing of more than 1-5/8 inches are spaced 3 inches o.c.

Notes: Design for diaphragm stresses depends on direction of continuous panel joints with reference to load, not on direction of long dimension of sheet. Continuous framing may be in either direction for blocked diaphragms.

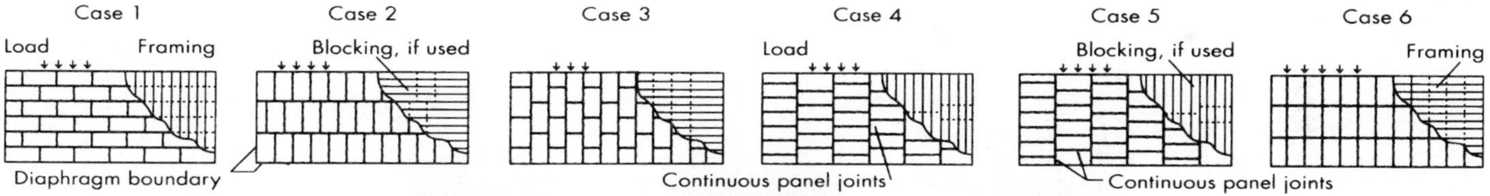

Case 1
Load
Framing
Diaphragm boundary
Case 2
Blocking, if used
Case 3
Case 4
Load
Continuous panel joints
Case 5
Blocking, if used
Continuous panel joints
Case 6
Framing

APA
RATED SHEATHING
40/20 19/32 INCH
SIZED FOR SPACING
EXPOSURE 1
000
NER-QA397 PRP-108
HUD-UM-40C

APA
RATED SHEATHING
STRUCTURAL I
32/16 15/32 INCH
SIZED FOR SPACING
EXTERIOR
000
PS 1-83 C-C
NER-QA397 PRP-108

APA
RATED SHEATHING
24/0 3/8 INCH
SIZED FOR SPACING
EXPOSURE 1
000
STRUCTURAL I RATED
DIAPHRAGMS - SHEAR WALLS
NER-QA397 PRP-108
HUD-UM-40C

Source: Reprinted with permission of the APA-The Engineered Wood Association.

TABLE 8.3 Allowable Shear in Pounds per Foot for High-Load Horizontal Blocked Diaphragms with Framing of Douglas Fir, Larch, or Southern Pine* for Wind or Seismic Loading†

Panel grade‡ and minimum nominal thickness, in	Fastener		Minimum nominal width of framing member, in	Lines of fasteners	Cases 1 and 2§					
					Fastener spacing per line at boundaries, in					
					4		2½		2	
					Fastener spacing per line at other panel edges, in					
	Type	Minimum penetration in framing, in			6	4	4	3	3	2
APA Structural I plywood $^{23}/_{32}$	10d common nails	$1^5/_8$	3	2	650	870	940	1230	—	—
			4	2	755	980	1080	1410	—	—
				3	940	1305	1375	1810	—	—
	14 gauge staples	2	3	2	600	600	840	900	1040	1200
			4	3	840	900	1140	1350	1440	1800
Rated sheathing APA C-D C-C	10d common nails	$1^5/_8$	3	2	645	870	935	1225	—	—
			4	2	750	980	1075	1395	—	—
				3	935	1305	1370	1510	—	—
Structural II $^{23}/_{32}$	14 gauge staples	2	3	2	600	600	820	900	1020	1200
			4	3	820	900	1120	1350	1400	1510

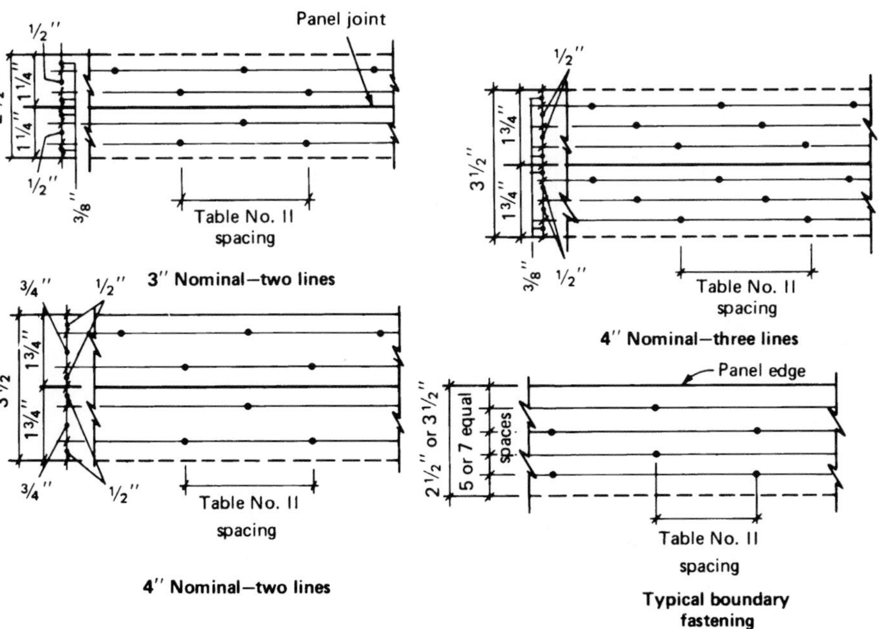

Note: Space panel end and edge joints ⅛ in. Reduce spacing between lines of nails as necessary to maintain minimum ⅜-in fastener edge margins. Minimum spacing between lines is ⅜ in.

*Allowable shear values for fasteners in framing members of other species set forth in Table 25-17-J of the UBC Standards shall be calculated for all grades by multiplying the values for fasteners in Structural I by the following factors: group III, 0.82, and group IV, 0.65.

†Fastening along intermediate framing members: Space nails 10 in on center for floors and 12 in on center for roofs, except 6 in on center for spans greater than 32 in.

‡Plywood conforming to UBC standard No. 25-9; other panels conforming to NER-108.

§This table gives shear values for cases 1 and 2. The values shown are applicable to cases 3 and 4, provided fasteners at all continuous panel edges are spaced in accordance with the boundary fastener spacing and provided the maximum shear is limited to 1200 lb/ft.

Source: Reprinted with permission of the APA-The Engineered Wood Association.

TABLE 8.4 Allowable Shear in Pounds per Foot for Horizontal Particleboard Diaphragms with Framing of Douglas Fir–Larch or Southern Pine*

Panel grade	Common nail size	Minimum nail penetration in framing, in	Minimum nominal panel thickness, in	Minimum nominal width of framing member, in	Blocked diaphragms				Unblocked diaphragms	
					Nail spacing (in) at diaphragm boundaries (all cases), at continuous panel edges parallel to load (cases 3 & 4), and at all panel edges (cases 5 & 6)				Nails spaced 6 in max. at supported edges	
					6	4	2½†	2†	Case 1 (no unblocked edges or continuous joints parallel to load)	All other configurations (cases 2, 3 4, 5, & 6)
					Nail spacing (in) at other panel edges (cases 1, 2, 3, & 4)					
					6	6	4	3		
2-M-W	6d	1¼	5/16	2	170	225	335	380	150	110
				3	190	250	380	430	170	125
			3/8	2	185	250	375	420	165	125
				3	210	280	420	475	185	140
	8d	1½	3/8	2	240	320	480	545	215	160
				3	270	360	540	610	240	180
			7/16	2	255	340	505	575	230	170
				3	285	380	570	645	255	190
			½	2	270	360	530	600	240	180
				3	300	400	600	675	265	200
	10d	1⅝	½	2	290	385	575	655†	255	190
				3	325	430	650	735	290	215
			5/8	2	320	425	640	730†	285	215
				3	360	480	720	820	320	240
2-M-3	10d	1⅝	¾	2	320	425	640	730†	285	215
				3	360	480	720	820	320	240

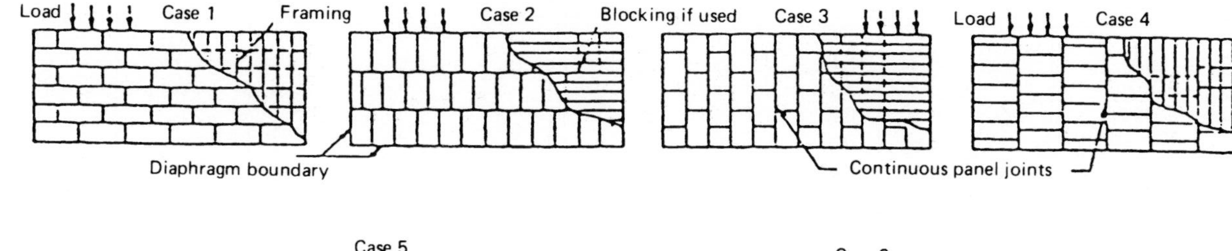

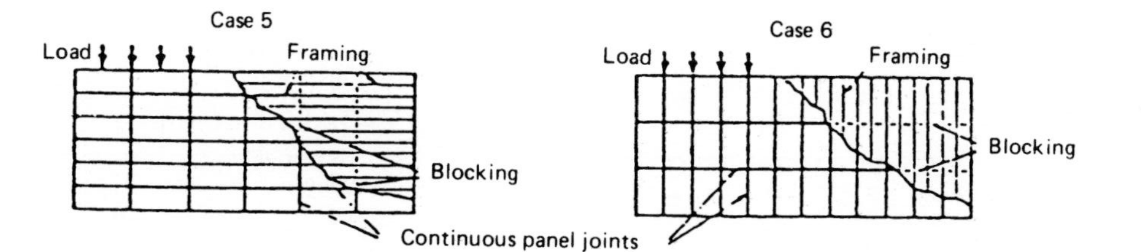

Note: Framing may be located in either direction for blocked diaphragms.

*These values are for short-time loads due to wind or earthquake and must be reduced 25 percent for normal loading. Space nails 10 in on center for floors and 12 in on center for roofs along intermediate framing members.

Allowable shear values for nails in framing members of other species set forth in Table 25-17-J of UBC Standards shall be calculated for all grades by multiplying the values for nails by the following factors: group III, 0.82, and group IV, 0.65.

†Framing shall be 3-in nominal or wider and nails shall be staggered where nails are spaced 2 or $2\frac{1}{2}$ in on center, and where 10d nails having penetration into framing of more than $1\frac{5}{8}$ in are spaced 3 in on center.

Source: Reproduced from the 1985 edition of the *Uniform Building Code,* copyright © 1985, with the permission of the publisher, the International Conference of Building Officials.

TABLE 8.5 Allowable Shear in Pounds per Foot Horizontal TWA ANSI Waferboard Diaphragms with Framing of Douglas Fir–Larch or Southern Pine*§¶

Panel grade	Common nail size	Nail penetration in framing, in	Minimum nominal panel thickness, in	Minimum nominal width of framing member, in	Blocked diaphragms				Unblocked diaphragms	
					Nail spacing (in) at diaphragm boundaries (all cases), at continuous panel edges parallel to load (cases 3 & 4), and at all panel edges (cases 5 & 6)†				Nails spaced 6 max. at supported edges†	
					6	4	2½‡	2‡	Case 1 (no unblocked edges or continuous joints parallel to load)	All other configurations (cases 2, 3, 4, 5, & 6)
					Nail spacing (in) at other panel edges (cases 1, 2, 3, & 4)					
					6	6	4	3		
Type 2-M-W	6d	1¼	5/16	2	170	225	335	380	150	110
				3	190	250	380	430	170	125
			3/8	2	185	250	375	420	165	125
				3	210	280	420	475	185	140
	8d	1½	3/8	2	240	320	480	545	215	160
				3	270	360	540	610	240	180
			7/16	2	255	340	505	575	230	170
				3	285	380	570	645	255	190
			1/2	2	270	360	530	600	240	180
				3	300	400	600	675	265	200
	10d	1⅝	1/2	2	290	385	575	655	255	190
				3	325	430	650	735	290	215
			5/8	2	320	425	640	730	285	215
				3	360	480	720	820	320	240

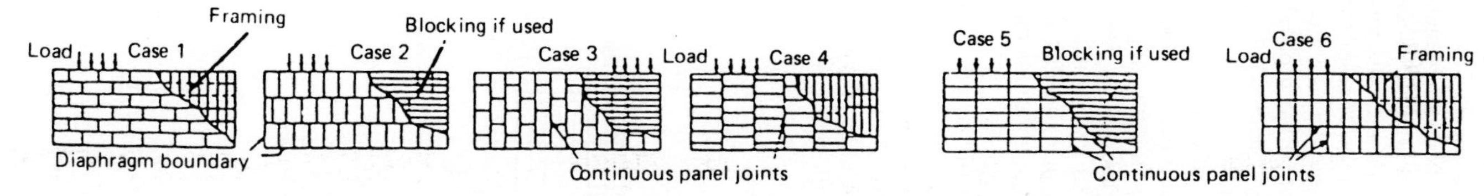

Note: Design for diaphragm stresses depends on direction of continuous panel joints with reference to load, not on direction of long dimension of sheet. Continuous framing may be in either direction for blocked diaphragms.

*For framing of other species: (*a*) Find specific gravity in Table 5.2, (*b*) find shear value from table for nail size, and (*c*) multiply value by 0.82 for species with specific gravity of 0.42 or greater, or 0.65 for all other species.

†Space nails 12 in o.c. along intermediate framing members for roofs and 10 in o.c. for floors.

‡Framing at panel edges shall be 3-in nominal or wider, and nails shall be staggered where nails are spaced 2 or 2½ in o.c. and where 10d nails having penetration into framing or more than 1⅝ in are spaced 3 in o.c. Exception: Unless otherwise required, 2-in nominal framing may be used where full nailing surface width is available and nails are staggered.

§These values are for short duration of loads due to wind or earthquake and must be reduced 25 percent for normal loading.

¶The maximum span-to-width ratio is 4 to 1.

Source: Reproduced from the 1985 edition of the *Uniform Building Code,* copyright © 1985, with the permission of the publisher, the International Conference of Building Officials.

the panel, along the panel edges for certain combinations of panel thickness and member spacing, is covered by requirements in building codes that panel edges be "blocked." Panels which do not need edge support can be left unblocked.

The second design consideration involves the in-plane loads between panels functioning as part of a diaphragm. In-plane loading parallel to a joint between panel edges causes one panel to displace relative to the adjacent panel. This displacement can be minimized by attaching the edge of one panel to the edge of the adjacent panel in some manner. Various techniques have been employed, the most common being to place a secondary wood member below the joint between panels and to nail each panel edge into this common member. Diaphragm tests have established that assemblies with panel edges interconnected to each other in this manner have greatly enhanced in-plane shear capacities. Diaphragms are thus referred to as *blocked* or *unblocked* depending on the presence or absence of attachment between panels for in-plane shear transfer. Various methods of achieving an edge attachment between panels are shown in Fig. 8.11. The use of the same terminology, blocked and unblocked, for both in-plane and normal load considerations has caused confusion on occasion. It is important to keep in mind that the loadings are different with the two types of blocking, and the design solutions may be correspondingly different.

Since most panel products will swell as the moisture content of the panel increases, it is recommended that all panels be laid with gaps at their ends and edges. For plywood, a spacing of ⅛ in (3.18 mm) is recommended for all edges, and other panel products may require different gaps. The producer's literature should be consulted. Since panels are manufactured with tolerances that do not allow the panel to exceed the 8-ft (2.44-m) and 4-ft (1.22-m) dimensions, some allowance is indi-

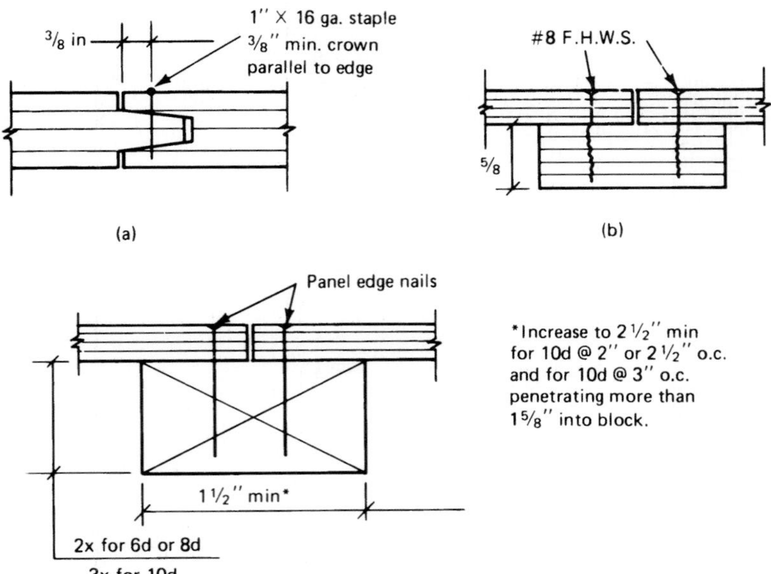

FIG. 8.11 Diaphragm edge blocking. (*a*) 1⅛-in T&G plywood; (*b*) ⅜- or ½-in panel; (*c*) all panel thicknesses.

rectly provided for spacing between panels. In long or wide structures it may be necessary to cut an occasional panel in order to maintain the recommended spacing between panels and to keep their edges properly centered over framing and blocking members.

8.4.4 Restrictions on Diaphragm Use

The depth-to-span ratios of wood diaphragms are limited. These limits are given in Table 8.6 and are usually applied not only to the diaphragm as a whole but also to individual segments of a diaphragm, such as, for example, the solid areas adjacent to openings. The depth is taken in the direction of the load, and the span is the distance between supports providing the diaphragm reactions.

Wood diaphragms are restricted in their application in buildings where an eccentricity between the center of the applied load and the resisting element(s) causes the diaphragm to want to rotate in plane about a vertical axis. The usual situation involves a building with an all-glass facade and solid walls on each side and at the back (see Fig. 8.12). The restrictions are as follows:

In buildings of wood-frame construction where rotation is provided for, the depth of the diaphragm normal to the open side shall not exceed 25 ft (7.62 m) nor two-thirds the diaphragm width, whichever is the smaller depth. Straight sheathing shall not be permitted to resist shears in diaphragms acting in rotation.

Exceptions

1. *One-story wood-framed structures with the depth normal to the open side not greater than 25 ft (7.62 m) may have a depth equal to the width.*
2. *Where calculations show that diaphragm deflections can be tolerated, the depth normal to the open end may be increased to a depth-to-width ratio not greater than 1.5/1 for diagonal sheathing or 2/1 for special diagonal-sheathed or plywood diaphragms. In masonry or concrete buildings, lumber and plywood diaphragms shall not be considered as transmitting lateral forces by rotation.*

8.4.5 Typical Diaphragm Design Examples

EXAMPLE 8.2 A 64-ft- (19.5-m)-long building with solid end walls, which are to act as shearwalls, is loaded as shown in Fig. 8.13. Both the negative [8 lb/ft^2 (117 N/m^2)] and positive [12 lb/ft^2 (175 N/m^2)] wind loads on vertical walls are shown on the building cross section (see Fig. 8.13*a*). Determine the critical design loads

TABLE 8.6 Maximum Diaphragm Dimension Ratios

Material	Maximum span-to-depth ratio
1. Diagonal sheathing, conventional	3/1
2. Diagonal sheathing, special	4/1
3. Plywood, nailed all edges	4/1
4. Plywood, blocking omitted at intermediate joints	4/1

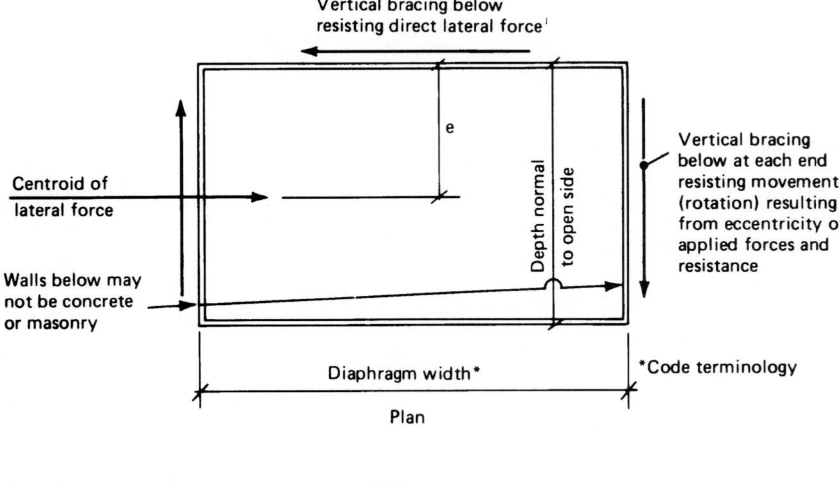

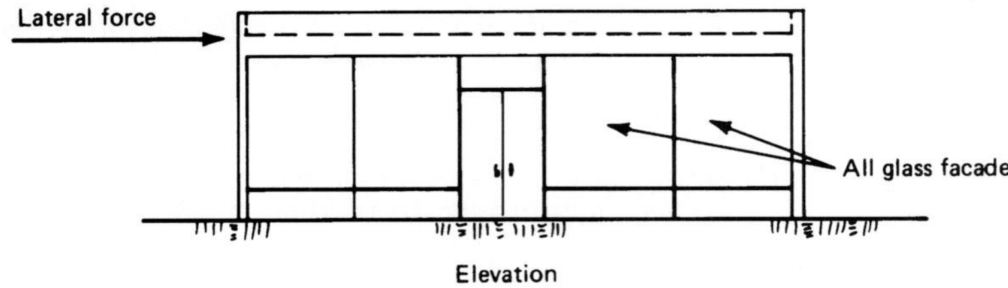

FIG. 8.12 Building subject to rotation.

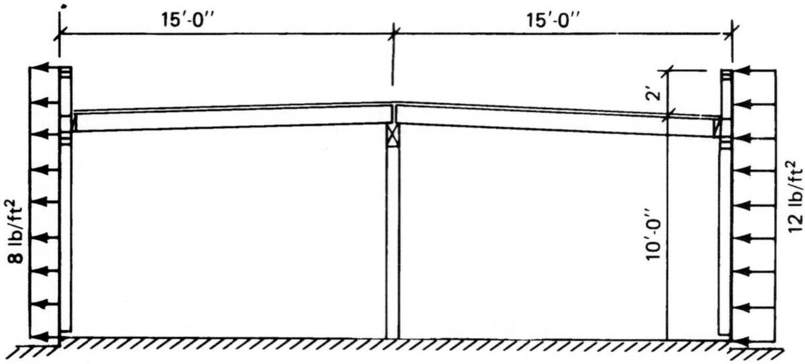

FIG. 8.13*a* Building cross section.

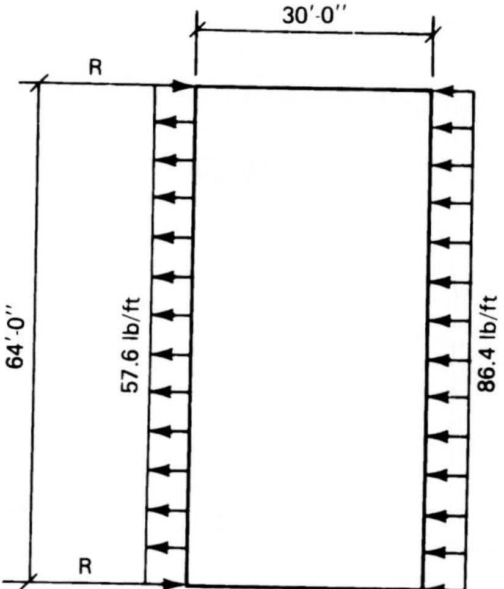

FIG. 8.13*b* Wall load schematic. **FIG. 8.13*c*** Plan view diaphragm and loads.

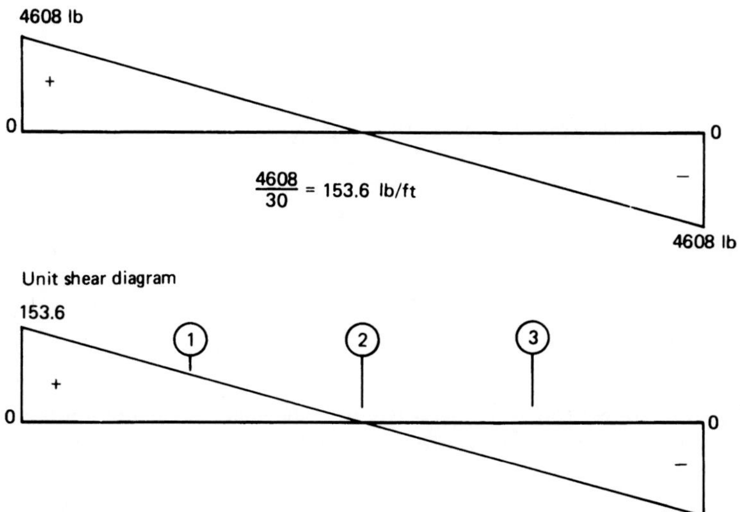

FIG. 8.13*d* Diaphragm shear diagrams.

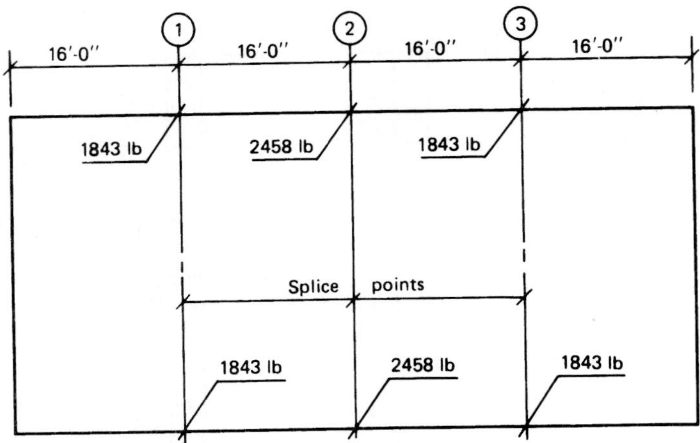

FIG. 8.13*e* Chord splice locations and forces.

for the roof diaphragm of this building. Assume that splices are needed at 16-ft (4.88 m) centers.

Determine Loads on Diaphragm (See Fig. 8.13*b*.)

$$\text{Reactions at roof: } R = \frac{w(12)^2}{2(10)} = 7.2w$$

$$\text{Windward: } R_w = 7.2(12) = 86.4 \text{ lb/ft}$$

$$\text{Leeward: } R_e = 7.2(8) = \underline{57.6 \text{ lb/ft}}$$

$$\text{Total} = 144 \text{ lb/ft}$$

Determine Diaphragm Reactions (See Fig. 8.13*b*.)

$$\frac{WL}{2} = \frac{144(64)}{2} = 4608 \text{ lb}$$

Determine Diaphragm Unit Shear (See Fig. 13*d*)

$$v = \frac{V}{d} = \frac{4608}{30} = 153.6 \text{ lb/ft}$$

Determine Chord Forces at Splice Points. The general equation for the moment at any location in a beam subject to a uniformly distributed load is

$$M = \frac{wx}{2}(\ell - x)$$

Assume all moment is carried by the flanges (chords) of the beam (diaphragm), and solving for this chord force, the equation becomes

$$F = \frac{wx}{2d}(\ell - x)$$

where F is the chord force, and d is the width of diaphragm.

The chord force can then be calculated at each splice point (see Fig. 8.13*e*). At points 1 and 3:

$$F_1 = F_3 = \frac{144(16)}{2(30)}(64 - 16) = 1843 \text{ lb } (8.198 \text{ kN})$$

At point 2:

$$F_2 = \frac{144(32)(64 - 32)}{2(30)} = 2458 \text{ lb } (10.93 \text{ kN})$$

Alternately, as discussed in Sec. 8.4.1, the chord forces may be determined by calculating the area under the unit shear diagram from the end of the beam to the chord splice point of interest. At points 1 and 3:

$$F = (153.6 + 76.8)(16)(\tfrac{1}{2}) = 1843 \text{ lb } (8.198 \text{ kN})$$

At point 2:

$$F = (153.6)(32)(\tfrac{1}{2}) = 2458 \text{ lb } (10.93 \text{ kN})$$

EXAMPLE 8.3 Design a roof diaphragm for a 32- by 48-ft (9.75- by 14.6-m) gable roof building as shown in Fig. 8.14*a*. Assume a wind loading of 130 lb/ft (1.90 kN/m) applied at the roof line as shown in Fig. 8.14*b*. The exterior walls are to be used as the shearwalls, and the double 2- by 4-in (38.1- by 88.9-mm) plates of these walls will act as chords for the roof diaphragm. Assume that roof and wall sheathing is $^{15}/_{32}$-in (11.9-mm) plywood nailed with 8d common wire nails and that Douglas fir–larch No. 2 will be used for 2- by 4-in plates. $F_t = 575 \times 1.5 \times 1.6 = 1380$ lb/in^2 (9.63 N/m^2).

North-South Design. Determine the maximum diaphragm shear:

$$R = \frac{48}{2}(130) = 3120 \text{ lb}$$

$$v = \frac{3120}{32} = 97.5 \text{ lb/ft}$$

Select a plywood and framing layout for case 1; see Table 8.2.

v (allow) = 240 lb/ft for an unlocked diaphragm with 8d nails spaced at 6 in centers on all supported edges.

$$v = 97.5 < 240 \qquad \text{OK}$$

Determine the chord force:

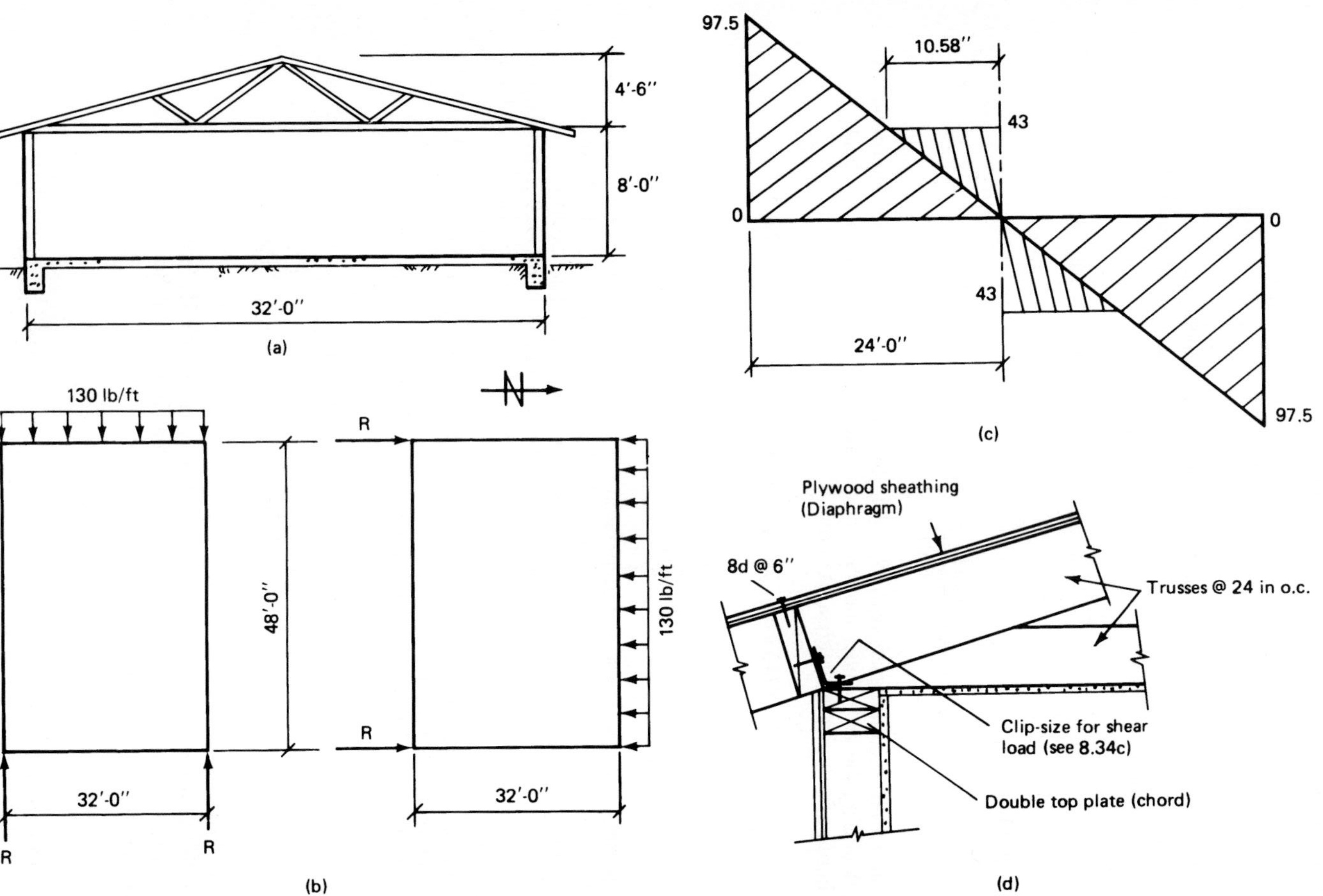

FIG. 8.14 (*a*) Building cross section; (*b*) roof diaphragm loadings; (*c*) diaphragm and chord shear distribution; (*d*) diaphragm-chord eave detail.

$$M \text{ (at centerline)} = \frac{w\ell^2}{8} = \frac{130(48)^2}{8} = 37{,}440 \text{ lb} \cdot \text{ft}$$

$$\text{Chord force} = \frac{37{,}440}{32} = 1170 \text{ lb (5204 N)}$$

$$< 1380 \times 5.25 = 7245 \text{ lb} \qquad \text{OK}$$

This assumes that all bending in the diaphragm is carried by chords of the diaphragm.

East-West Design. Determine the maximum diaphragm shear:

$$R = \frac{32}{2}(130) = 2080 \text{ lb}$$

$$v = \frac{2080}{48} = 43.3 \text{ lb/ft}$$

Based on the selection of case 1 for the plywood and framing layout in the north-south design, it would be case 3 for the east-west design.

v_a (allow) = 180 lb/ft for an unblocked diaphragm with 8d nails spaced at 6 in centers on all supported edges. Therefore,

$$V = 43.3 < 180 \qquad \text{OK}$$

Determine the chord force:

$$M \text{ (at centerline)} = \frac{w\ell^2}{8} = \frac{130(32)^2}{8} = 16{,}640 \text{ lb} \cdot \text{ft}$$

$$\text{Chord force } \frac{16{,}640}{48} = 347 \text{ lb (1543 N)}$$

$$< 1380 \times 5.25 = 7245 \text{ lb} \qquad \text{OK}$$

Design Comments. The dimensions of the structure and the general magnitude of the loading in this example are consistent with a single-family residence in an area having a 70 mi/h (113 km/h) design wind speed. The calculations indicate no special framing or nailing of sheathing is required to achieve effective diaphragm action. While the calculated chord force at midlength of the north and south walls is of sufficiently high magnitude to justify special detailing of any splices in the double plate, it is also low enough to suggest that the building might survive the design loading without special splices. These results offer some insight into why single-family residences have performed satisfactorily under all but extreme wind loadings. For details on the design of splices using mechanical fasteners, the designer is referred to Chap. 5.

Detail Considerations for the Connection of Diaphragm to Chord. In order for the diaphragm to function properly, the plywood sheathing (web) must be attached to the top plate (chord) to transfer the north-south boundary shear in the diaphragm to the shearwall. This shear as calculated was 97.5 lb/ft (1.42 kN/m).

Also, there must be an attachment to transfer the east-west design load to the north-south walls of 43 lb/ft (628 N/m). These two conditions combine to necessitate a minimum connection requirement of 43 lb/ft (628 N/m) over the middle

21.16 ft (6.45 m) of the north-south walls and an increasing requirement on the remaining portion of these walls as illustrated in Fig. 8.14*c* and calculated here:

$$L = \frac{43}{97.5}(24) = 10.58 \text{ ft } (3.19 \text{ m}) \text{ from centerline}$$

Figure 8.14*d* illustrates a typical detail for the transfer of diaphragm shears to the wall framing.

8.4.6 Special Diaphragm Elements

Subdiaphragms. Loads on a diaphragm frequently are imposed on the diaphragm by walls along the diaphragm's edge. These loads may come from wind pressures on the walls or from the inertial forces of the walls which are generated by the response of the building to the earth movement in an earthquake. Special consideration should be given to how these localized forces are anchored and distributed into the sheathing of the diaphragm. Reliance should not be placed for anchorage on the connectors attaching the sheathing to the framing members. These attachments may already be working at or near capacity in carrying the diaphragm shear, and imposition of the localized wall load on these same connectors may result in a premature failure of the diaphragm.

Current practice for the anchorage of masonry or concrete walls requires such walls to be anchored to the diaphragm for a minimum of 200 lb/ft (2.92 kN/m) or for the computed component force, whichever is larger. If the anchorages are more than 4 ft apart, the compatibility of the wall and the diaphragm between anchorages is to be investigated. Continuous ties are also required between the diaphragm chords to distribute the localized forces into the diaphragm. In many buildings it is not feasible to have continuous ties every 4 ft across the width of a building. The solution to such a design problem is to select a portion of the main diaphragm adjacent to the wall being anchored and to design that portion as a special diaphragm to perform the anchorage function. Such a selected portion of the main diaphragm is referred to as a *subdiaphragm.* The span-to-depth limitations applied to diaphragms are also applied to subdiaphragms. The subdiaphragms then span between the continuous ties between chords.

Example 8.4 illustrates the use of a subdiaphragm to anchor a concrete wall. The principle can be used to anchor any type of concentrated load. The design intent is to anchor the particular building component adequately to prevent a localized failure. Since the unit wind or earthquake design loading on a component is normally larger than the design loading on the entire structure, it is assumed that the anchorage problem can be addressed independently of the whole building design. This permits the subdiaphragm to be designed for the anchorage loads alone, and the subdiaphragm can then be designed as a part of the main diaphragm without considering possible additive features of the two loadings. The most severe design conditions considered independently would govern the connection design within the subdiaphragm. The subdiaphragm concept was introduced into design practice following the 1972 San Fernando earthquake in California which demonstrated weaknesses in the design approaches being used to anchor masonry and concrete walls. The concept awaits the test of experience, and this experience may prove that some combining of main and subdiaphragm design forces is necessary.

The subdiaphragm concept should not be regarded as applicable only to loads applied at the edges of a diaphragm. It is equally applicable to other types of problems. The concept is used in Example 8.5, a wood-frame building in which an upper-floor shearwall terminates on a floor, a situation which requires the floor diaphragm to transfer the shear from the base of the upper shearwall to shearwalls below offset laterally from the wall above.

EXAMPLE 8.4 Design an anchorage system using a subdiaphragm to anchor a concrete wall in a seismic zone 4. See Fig. 8.15*a* and *b*. For seismic zone 4, $Cp = 0.30$.

Design load:

$$V = CpW = 0.30(100) = 30 \text{ lb/ft}^2 \ (1.44 \text{ kN/m}^2)$$

Reaction at roof:

$$F = \frac{Vh^2}{2h_r} = \frac{30(28)^2}{2(25)} = 470 \text{ lb/ft} \ (6.87 \text{ kN/m})$$

1. *Select subdiaphragm depth:* Assume the glulam beams are used as the ties across the building; then the subdiaphragm reaction at the beam is

$$R = \frac{FS}{2} = \frac{470(20)}{2} = 4700 \text{ lb}$$

The subdiaphragm depth should be selected to coincide with the framing spacing.

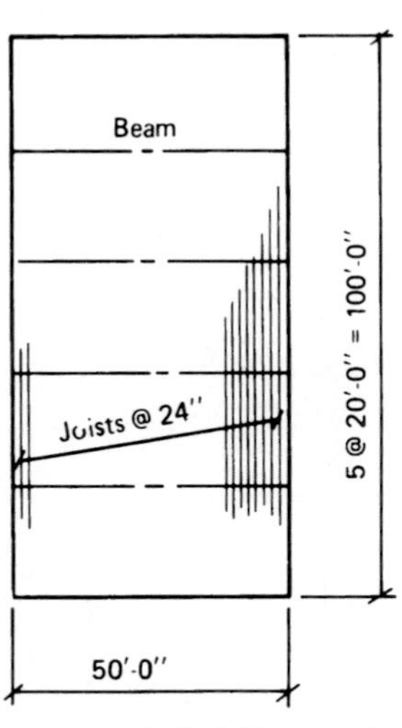

FIG. 8.15*a* Roof plan.

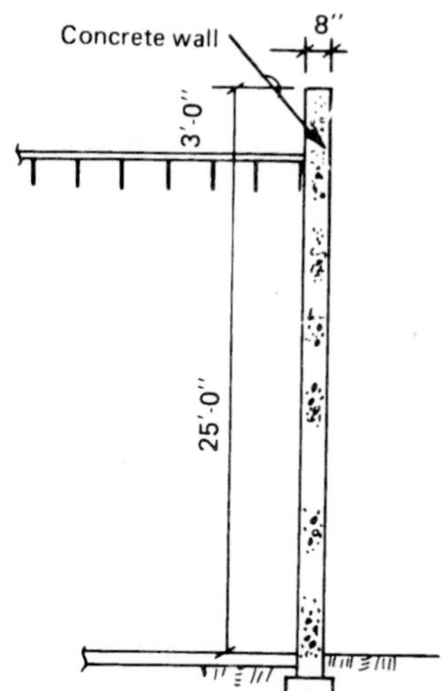

FIG. 8.15*b* Wall section.

In this case, the 50-ft dimension for the depth of the building includes the 8-in thickness of the walls. Try a 5-ft, 4-in diaphragm depth (see Fig. 8.15*c*).

$$\text{Span-to-depth ratio} = 20/5.33 = 3.75 < 4.0 \qquad \text{OK}$$

Unit shear:

$$u = 4700/5.33 = 882 \text{ lb/ft}$$

Referring to Table 8.2 indicates that this value exceeds the listed allowable shear capacity of ½-in APA rated sheathing. Therefore, the subdiaphragm needs to be designed with greater depth. Try a 7-ft, 4-in diaphragm depth (see Fig. 8.15*c*).

Unit shear:

$$v = 4700/7.33 = 641 \text{ lb/ft}$$

Table 8.2 indicates that this value of unit shear is obtainable if 15⁄32-in APA rated sheathing is used.

2. *Detailed analysis:* Anchorage load to sheathing along line of anchor is

$$L_s = \frac{F \times \text{spacing}}{\text{depth diaphragam}} = \frac{470(4)}{7.33} = 256 \text{ lb/ft}$$

Nail spacing along anchor line (use 10d common nail):

$$S_n = \frac{L_s}{Z \times C_D \times C_{di}}$$

$$= \frac{256}{90(1.6 \times 1.1)} = 1.62$$

where S_n = nails required per foot
Z = lateral capacity of nail
C_D = load duration factor
C_{di} = increase allowed in lateral capacity of nails used in diaphragm

Nail spacing:

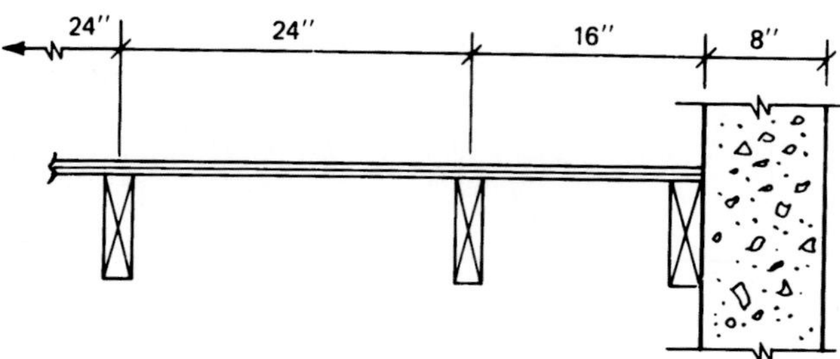

FIG. 8.15*c* Framing details at wall.

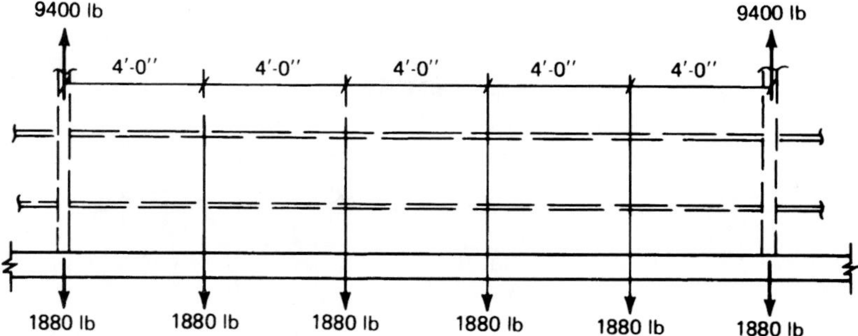

FIG. 8.15*d* Subdiaphragm loading schematic.

$$S = \frac{12}{1.62} = 7.41 \text{ in (188 mm)}$$

Use 10d common nails at 6 in on center

3. *Refined diaphragm shear analysis:* Since the subdiaphragm is actually loaded by four concentrated loads as shown in Fig. 8.15*d*, the unit shear in the diaphragm is as shown in Fig. 8.15*e*. For a maximum unit shear of 512 lb/ft (7.48 kN/m), Table 8.2 indicates that for a loading case 3 with $^{15}\!/_{32}$-in (11.9-mm) APA rated sheathing, the nailing needs to be 10d common nails at $2\frac{1}{2}$ in (63.5 mm) at the diaphragm edges and continuous panel edges and 4 in (102 mm) at other panel edges for a blocked diaphragm.

Note: It is permissible to extrapolate between values in Table 8.2. For 3-in (76.2-mm) edge spacing:

$$\text{Diaphragm edge nailing capacity} = 385 + \frac{4 - 3}{4 - 2.5}(575 - 385) = 385 + 167$$

$$= 512 \text{ lb/ft (7.38 kN/m)}$$

$$\geq \text{maximum unit shear}$$

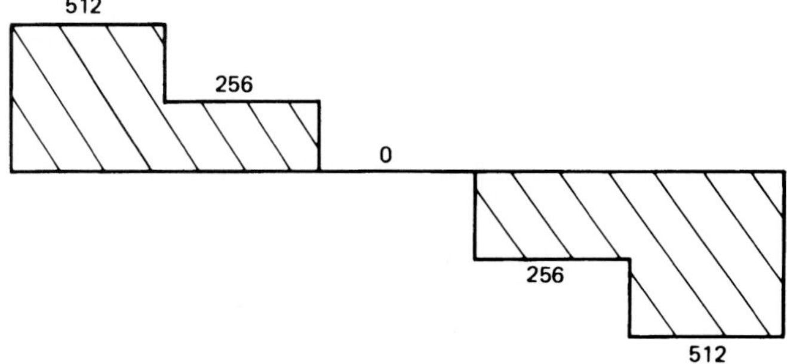

FIG. 8.15*e* Wall/subdiaphragm anchorage detail.

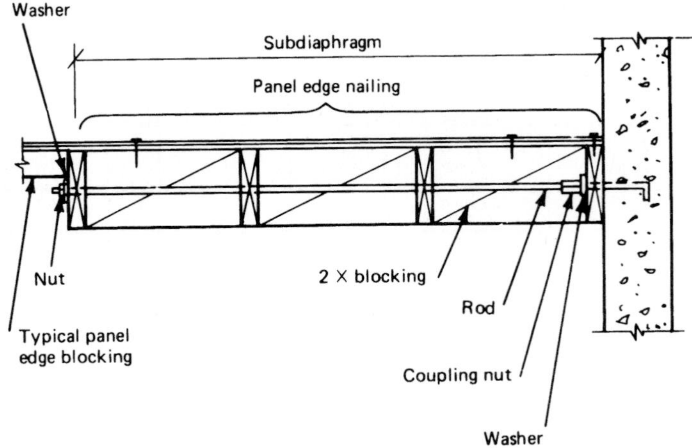

FIG. 8.15*f* Subdiaphragm shears and nailing response..

Therefore use of 10d common nails at 3 in on center is satisfactory. Details of the subdiaphragm are shown in Fig. 8.15*f* and *g*.

EXAMPLE 8.5 Consider a shearwall which terminates on the floor shown on Fig. 8.16*a* and transfers a 5100-lb (22.7-kN) lateral force to the floor. The floor which is to act as a diaphragm has a uniform load of 140 lb/ft (2.04 kN/m) applied to its edge. The loading at the diaphragm is shown in Fig. 8.16*a*, and 2-in nominal floor joists are assumed to be spaced 16 in on center.

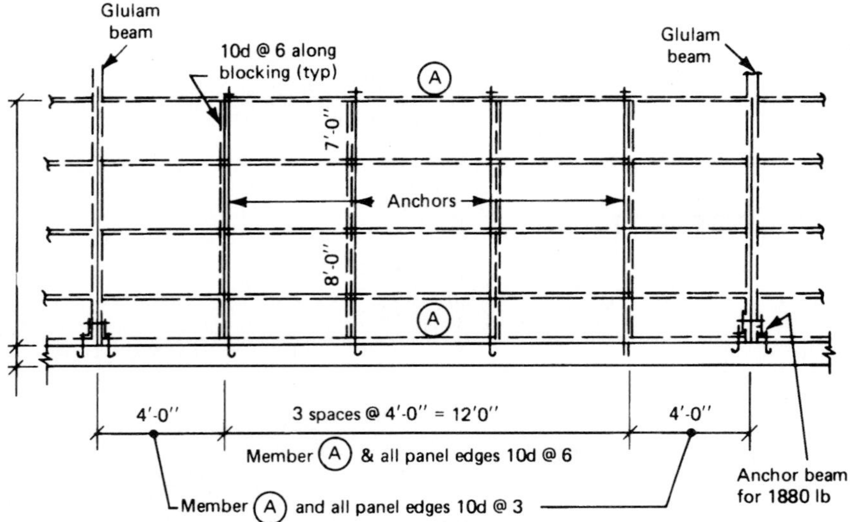

FIG. 8.15*g* Subdiaphragm panel and nailing layout.

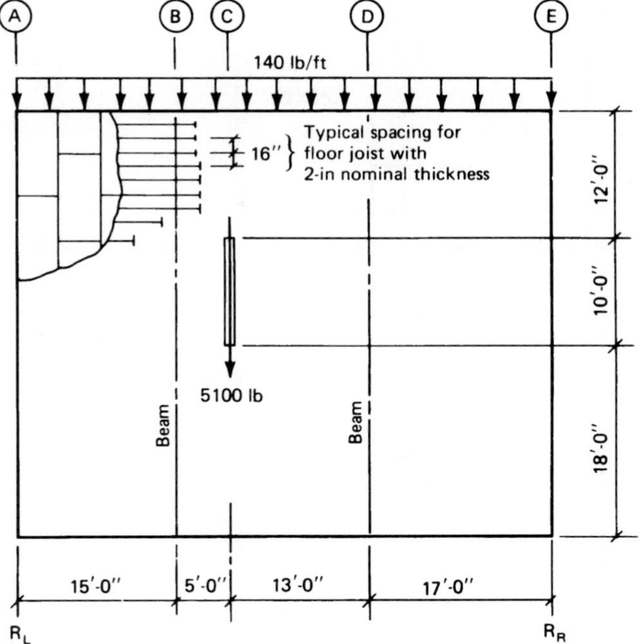

FIG. 8.16*a* Plan view diaphragm and loads.

Reactions:

$$R_L = \frac{140 \times 50 \times 25}{50} + \frac{5100 \times 30}{50} = 6560 \text{ lb}$$

$$R_R = \frac{140 \times 50 \times 25}{50} + \frac{5100 \times 20}{50} = 5540 \text{ lb}$$

Unit shears are shown in Fig. 8.16*b*, and the full depth of the diaphragm is considered to be effective. The values are calculated as follows:

Due to 5100-lb load:

$$V_1 = 3060/40 = 76.5 \text{ lb/ft}$$

$$V_2 = 2040/40 = 51.0 \text{ lb/ft}$$

Due to 140-lb/ft load:

$$V_3 = 140 \times 25/40 = 87.5 \text{ lb/ft}$$

A comparison of the calculated unit shears with the allowable shears in Table 8.2 for an unblocked diaphragm, case 3, indicates that the computed maximum unit shear of 164 lb/ft (2.40 kN/m) ($V_1 + V_3$) is well below the allowable value of 190 lb/ft (2.78 kN/m) for unblocked 15⁄32-in (11.9-mm) sheathing nailed with 10d nails. The comparison is even more favorable along the line of the shearwall from above,

Diaphragm unit shear due to shearwall loading

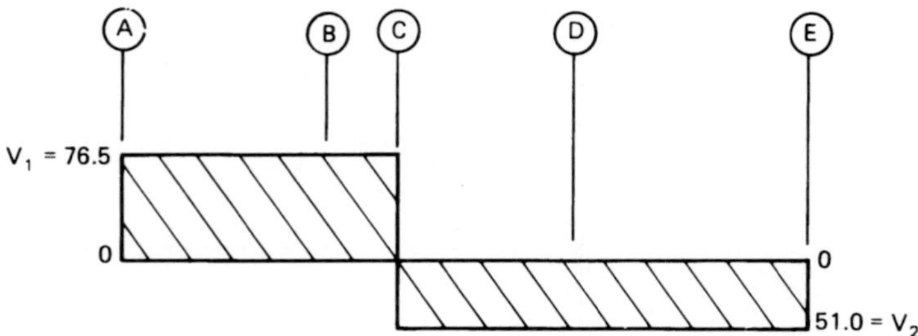

Diaphragm unit shear due to tributary loading

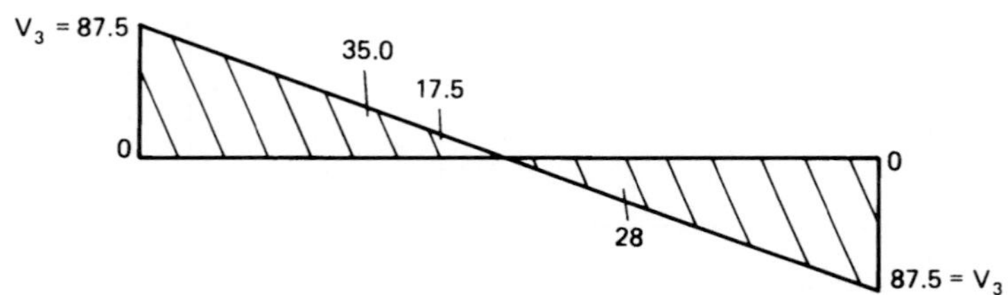

Total diaphragm unit shear

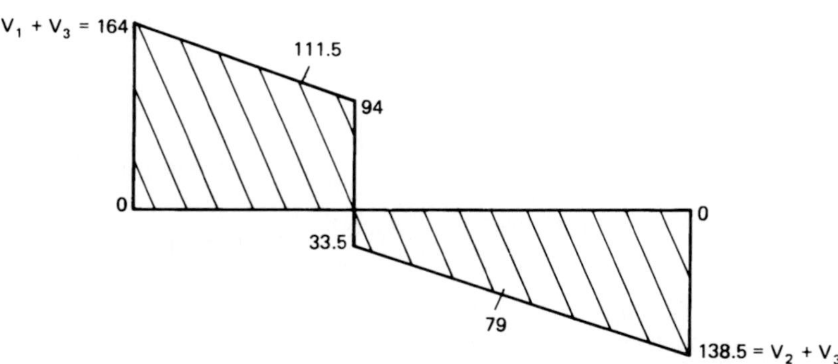

FIG. 8.16*b* Unit shear diagrams for diaphragm.

i.e., at grid line C in Fig. 8.16*a*. These calculations assume that the 5100-lb (22.7-kN) load from the wall is somehow transmitted to the diaphragm over the full 40-ft (12.2-m) depth of the diaphragm. If the shearwall from above is only attached along its 10-ft (3.05-m) length, the unit shear is 306 lb/ft (4.47 kN/m) to the left of the line of the wall and 204 lb/ft (2.98 kN/m) to the right. There is also a unit shear of 17.5 lb/ft (256 N/m) along the shearwall line resulting from the load applied to the diaphragm itself (see line C in Fig. 8.16*b*). The total unit shear of 323.5 lb/ft (4.73 kN/m) adjacent to the left side of the shearwall is greater than the 190 lb/ft (2.78 kN/m) allowable, indicating that some design measures need to be taken to ensure proper functioning of the diaphragm.

One potential solution is to provide an element in the diaphragm below and longer than the shearwall to distribute the load into the diaphragm. The diaphragm capacity available to resist the shearwall loading is 190 − 17.5 = 172.5 lb/ft (2.52 kN/m). The length of the distributor required is 306 × 10/172.5 = 17.74 ft (5.41 m). Since the joists are laid out perpendicular to the direction of any distributing element, it would be difficult to insert such an element into the framing system.

An alternate solution would be to select a depth of diaphragm at least as long as the shearwall and to design the selected segment as a subdiaphragm spanning between the beams. The joists at 16 in o.c. (406 mm) would suggest a subdiaphragm depth of 10 ft, 8 in (3.25 m) or 12 ft, 0 in (3.65 m). Blocking of the diaphragm is also indicated. A blocked diaphragm using 15⁄32-in sheathing with 4-in edge nailing using 10d nails with an allowable shear of 385 lb/ft provides the required shear. Assume a 12-ft subdiaphragm depth as shown in Fig. 8.16*c*. As shown in Fig. 8.16*d*, the unit shear to the left of the wall would vary from 324.5 lb/ft at the wall to 342 lb/ft at the beam, and the unit shear to the right of the wall would vary from 100.5 lb/ft at the wall to 146 lb/ft at the beam. These shear values can be transferred with 4-in edge nailing and a blocked diaphragm as assumed since an unblocked diaphragm will provide a stress capacity of only 255 lb/ft. In calculating these values, it has been assumed that the 140-lb/ft uniform load is applied to the overall diaphragm and that it is carried by the full depth of the diaphragm and not by the subdiaphragm alone.

At the beams, the reactions from the subdiaphragm are distributed through the full depth of the diaphragm. The subdiaphragm should be attached to the beam on line *B* to transfer a reaction of 4103 lb, and it should be attached to the beam on

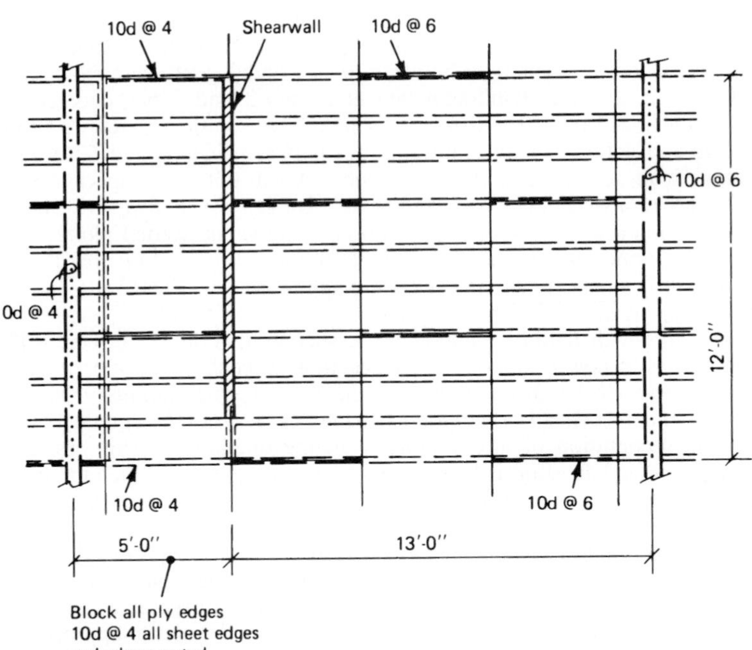

FIG. 8.16*c* Subdiaphragm panel and nailing layout.

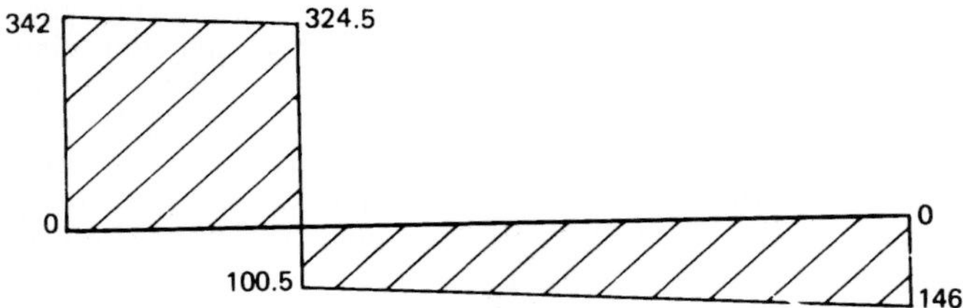

FIG. 8.16*d* Subdiaphragm unit shear diagram.

line *D* to transfer a reaction of 1753 lb. The beams in turn should be attached to the sheathing to transfer 102.6 lb/ft (4103/40) and 43.8 lb/ft (1753/40), respectively. In theory, since the 5100-lb wall reaction is already being carried by the sheathing of the subdiaphragm, the subdiaphragm need only be attached to the beams to resist 3060/12 − 76.5 lb at line *B* and 2040/12 − 51 ft at line *D*.

Collectors or Drag Struts. One of the initial assumptions presented for diaphragm design was that the shear in the diaphragm web was uniform across the diaphragm depth. This assumption implies that loads are introduced into the diaphragm across the full depth of the web and the reactions remove load from the diaphragm web in a similar manner. Examples 8.4 and 8.5 dealt with design approaches utilizing subdiaphragms, and using continuous ties between diaphragm chords is an approach to achieve that end.

It is a fairly common occurrence for buildings to have plan irregularities and for shearwalls to be located in offset walls. Figure 8.17 shows a building with such a plan irregularity. The diaphragm between lines 1 and 2 does not contact the shearwall on line 2, and the diaphragm between lines 2 and 3 has contact with the shearwall on line 2 only between lines *A* and *B*. A solution to such a problem is to provide a structural member along line 2 between lines *B* and *C* to which the diaphragms can be attached. Such a member which collects diaphragm load and drags it back to a shearwall is referred to as a *collector* or a *drag strut,* both terms being in common usage. Note that a similar member is needed along line *B* for lateral loads applied longitudinally on the building. Collectors or drag struts occur most frequently at the junction between diaphragms and shearwalls and are discussed further in Sec. 8.5.4.

Diaphragms with multiple support lines, such as that shown in Fig. 8.17, raise the question as to how to determine the reactions at each of the support lines. The traditional approach has been to assume the diaphragm is infinitely flexible. The diaphragm under such an assumption behaves as a series of simple beams; i.e., there is no recognition of any continuity in the diaphragm. This assumption is clearly in error, and an effort is being made to use an approach which by implication considers the diaphragm as a fully rigid body. There is some experimental evidence to support this approach, at least for diaphragms with an overall length-to-depth ratio of no more than 2. Rigid diaphragm analysis is well developed for concrete buildings but is not developed for wood buildings, at least partially because of a lack of information on how to determine the proper stiffness of wood shearwalls, an essential part of a complete rigid diaphagm analysis. Another approach is illustrated in Ref. 7.

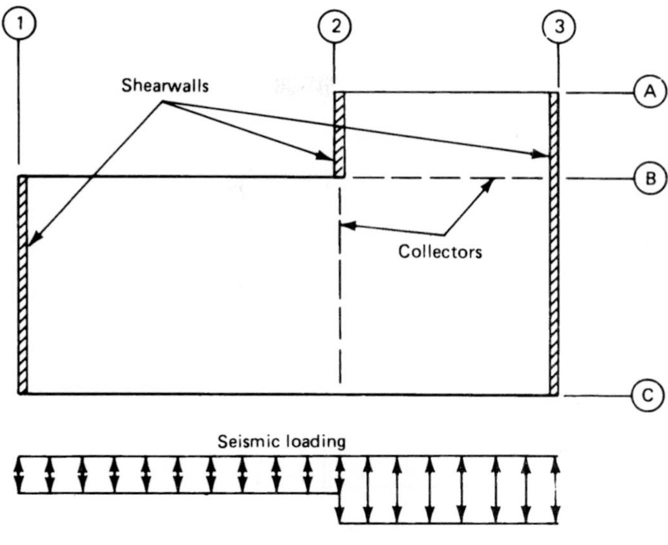

FIG. 8.17 Collectors at offset walls.

Openings and Discontinuities. Most diaphragms are penetrated by other building elements, such as pipes, ducts, elevators, stairwells, and skylights. As the penetrations get larger in proportion to the overall diaphragm length and depth, increasingly large secondary effects are introduced into the diaphragm. These effects change the unit shear distributions in the diaphragm web around the opening caused by the penetration and require the introduction of collectors to collect and then redistribute direct forces and shears from the secondary effects. A simple analytical approach to such design problems has been developed, but no attempt at experimental verification has yet been undertaken. A single example is presented here to demonstrate the suggested approach. A further example and limited discussion can be found in Ref. 6. Reference 7 discusses the theory in greater detail and applies the theory in several examples.

EXAMPLE 8.6 Figure 8.18*a* gives a plan view of a diaphragm with an unsymmetrically positioned opening. The diaphragm is loaded along each edge as noted, a design loading which occurs on a flat-roofed building under wind loading.

The analysis which follows parallels the presentation given in Ref. 6.

1. The diaphragm is first analyzed without consideration of the opening to obtain chord and web forces.

Line 1:

$$R = V_1 = \frac{wL}{Z} = \frac{170(80)}{2} = +\ 6800 \text{ lb or } +\ 227 \text{ lb/ft}$$

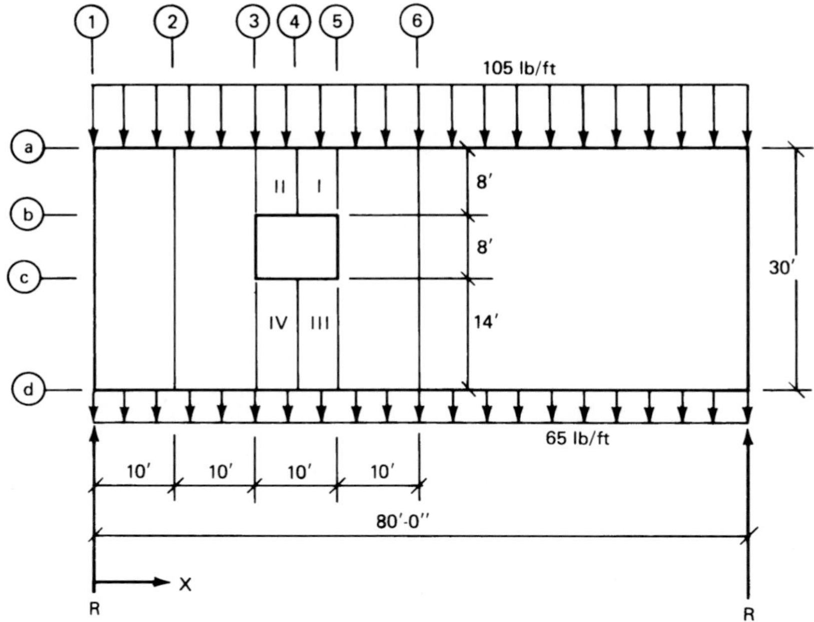

FIG. 8.18a Plan view of diaphragm with an unsymmetrically positioned opening.

Line 2:

$$V_2 = w\left(\frac{L}{2} - x\right) = 170\left(\frac{80}{2} - 10\right) = +\ 5100 \text{ lb or } +\ 170 \text{ lb/ft}$$

$$M_2 = \frac{wx}{2}(L - x) = \frac{170(10)}{2}(80 - 10) = 59{,}500 \text{ ft·lb}$$

$$F_2 = \frac{M}{30} = \frac{59{,}500}{30} = 1983 \text{ lb compression} \qquad \text{at } a$$

$$F_2 = 1983 \text{ lb tension} \qquad \text{at } d$$

Line 3:

$$V_3 = w\left(\frac{L}{2} - x\right) = 170\left(\frac{80}{2} - 20\right) = +\ 3400 \text{ lb or } +\ 113 \text{ lb/ft}$$

$$M_3 = \frac{wx}{2}(L - x) = \frac{170(20)}{2}(80 - 20) = 102{,}000 \text{ ft·lb}$$

$$F_3 = \frac{102{,}000}{30} = 3400 \text{ lb compression} \qquad \text{at } a$$

$$F_3 = 3400 \text{ lb tension} \qquad \text{at } d$$

Line 4:

$$V_4 = 170\left(\frac{80}{2} - 25\right) = +\ 2550 \text{ lb or } +\ 85 \text{ lb/ft}$$

$$M_4 = \frac{170(25)}{2}(80 - 25) = 116{,}875 \text{ ft·lb}$$

$$F_4 = \frac{116{,}875}{30} = 3896 \text{ lb compression} \qquad \text{at } a$$

$$F_4 = 3896 \text{ lb tension} \qquad \text{at } d$$

Line 6:

$$V_6 = 170\left(\frac{80}{2} - 40\right) = 0$$

$$M_6 = \frac{170(40)}{2}(80 - 40) = 136{,}000 \text{ ft·lb}$$

$$F_6 = \frac{136{,}000}{30} = 4533 \text{ lb compression} \qquad \text{at } a$$

$$F_6 = 4533 \text{ lb tension} \qquad \text{at } d$$

2. The assumption is now made that a diaphragm with openings behaves similarly to a vierendeel girder. Such an assumption produces points of contraflexure in the diaphragm at midlength (line 4) of the openings and results in diaphragm segments I, II, III, and IV being statically determinant.

A further assumption needs to be made that the diaphragm segment stiffnesses are proportional to their depth in the direction of load. The total diaphragm shear of 2550 lb along line 4 is proportioned accordingly with $^{8}/_{22}$ (36%), 927 lb, carried above the opening and $^{14}/_{22}$ (64%), 1623 lb, carried below.

The shears and chord forces at the edges of the opening are determined using free-body diagrams as shown in Fig. 8.18*b*.

Segment I:

$$F_4 = 3896 \text{ lb compression} \qquad \text{at } a \text{ and } F_4 = 0 \qquad \text{at } b$$

$$V_4(ab) = \frac{8}{22}V_4 = \frac{8}{22}(2550) = 927 \text{ lb or } 116 \text{ lb/ft}$$

$$V_4(ab) = 927 - 105(5) = 402 \text{ lb or } 50 \text{ lb/ft}$$

$$F_5 = \frac{927(5) + 3896(8) - 105(5)(2.5)}{8} \qquad \text{at } a$$

$$= 4311 \text{ lb compression}$$

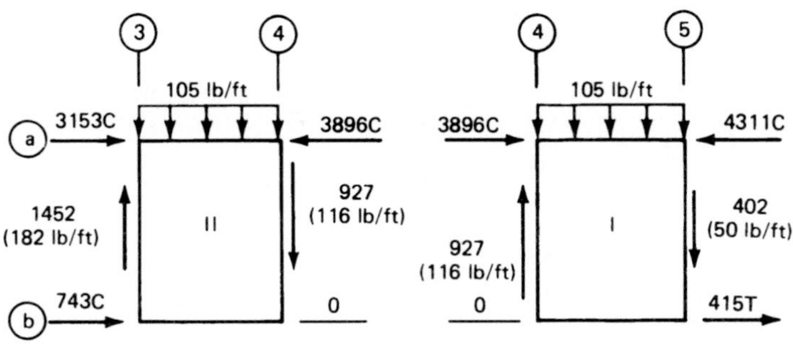

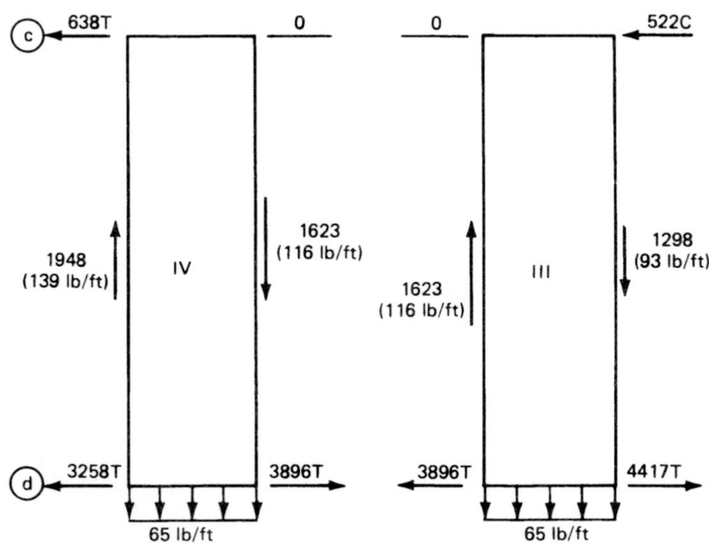

FIG. 8.18*b* Diaphragm segment free bodies.

$$F_5 = \frac{927(5) - 105(5)(2.5)}{8} \qquad \text{at } b$$

$$= 415 \text{ lb tension}$$

Statics check: $H = 0,\ 3896 + 415 - 4311 = 0$
Segment II:

$$F_4 = 3896 \text{ lb compression} \qquad \text{at } a \text{ and } F_4 = 0 \qquad \text{at } b$$

$$V_4(ab) = 927 \text{ lb or } 116 \text{ lb/ft}$$

$$V_3(ab) = 927 + 5(105) = 1452 \text{ lb or } 182 \text{ lb/ft}$$

$$F_3 = \frac{927(5) + 105(5)(2.5) - 3896(8)}{8} \qquad \text{at } a$$

$$= 3153 \text{ lb compression}$$

$$F_3 = \frac{927(5) + 105(5)(2.5)}{8} \qquad \text{at } b$$

$$= 743 \text{ lb compression}$$

Statics check: $\Sigma H = 0$, $3153 + 743 - 3896 = 0$
Segment III:

$$F_4 = 0 \quad \text{at } c \quad F_4 = 3896 \text{ lb tension} \quad \text{at } d$$

$$V_4(cd) = \frac{14}{22}V_4 = \frac{14}{22}(2550) = 1623 \text{ lb or } 116 \text{ lb/ft}$$

$$V_5(cd) = 1623 - 5(65) = 1298 \text{ lb or } 93 \text{ lb/ft}$$

$$F_5 = \frac{1623(5) - 65(5)(2.5)}{14} \qquad \text{at } c$$

$$= 522 \text{ lb compression}$$

$$F_5 = \frac{1623(5) + 3896(14) - 65(5)(2.5)}{14} \qquad \text{at } d$$

$$= 4418 \text{ lb tension}$$

Statics check: $\Sigma H = 0$, $3896 + 522 - 4418 = 0$
Segment IV:

$$F_4 = 0 \quad \text{at } c \quad F_4 = 3896 \text{ lb tension} \quad \text{at } d$$

$$V_4(cd) = 1623 \text{ lb or } 116 \text{ lb/ft}$$

$$V_3(cd) = 1623 + 5(65) = 1948 \text{ lb or } 139 \text{ lb/ft}$$

$$F_3 = \frac{1623(5) + 65(5)(2.5)}{14} \qquad \text{at } c$$

$$= 638 \text{ lb tension}$$

$$F_3 = \frac{3896(14) - 1623(5) - 65(5)(2.5)}{14} \qquad \text{at } d$$

$$= 3258 \text{ lb tension}$$

Statics check: $\Sigma H = 0$, $3258 + 638 - 3896 = 0$

3. Net changes to the chord forces due to the opening in the diaphragm are determined by comparing the chord forces at the various points with and without openings, as shown in the table below:

Diaphragm location		Chord forces,* lb		
Line	Point	Without opening	With opening	Net change
3	*a*	3400C	3153C	247T
	b	0	743C	743C
	c	0	638T	638T
	d	3400T	3258T	142C
5	*a*	4250C	4311C	61C
	b	0	415T	415T
	c	0	522C	522C
	d	4250T	4417T	167T

*C = compression; T = tension.

4. The net changes in the chord forces due to the opening must be distributed into the diaphragm sheathing beyond the opening through the plywood fastenings. How far beyond the opening the force should be distributed remains a question. The designer should consider, in deciding how to distribute beyond the opening, the ease of installing collectors and the level of the resultant unit shear intensity. In no case should the distance beyond the opening be taken as less than the diaphragm depth divided by the appropriate depth-to-width ratio of the diaphragm because the area alongside the hole is used as a subdiaphragm spanning between the chords of the main diaphragm and is subjected to the same depth-to-width ratios as the main diaphragm itself. In this example the distance beyond the opening on each side has been set at 10 ft. The width-to-depth ratio is thus 30/10 = 3/1. This is acceptable since Table 8.6 would permit a ratio of up to 4/1. This assumption results in the unit shear diagrams depicted in Fig. 8.18*c*.

5. Resultant shears in the diaphragm are obtained by combining the net unit shears due to the opening with the shears for the diaphragm without openings.

Diaphragm location		Shear, lb/ft		
Line	Point	Without openings	Due to openings	Resultant shear
2	*a-b*	+170	−24.7	+145
	b-c	+170	+49.6	+220
	c-d	+170	−14.2	+156
3	*a-b*	+113	−24.7	+88
	b-c	+113	+49.6	+163
	c-d	+113	−14.2	+99
5	*a-b*	+57	−6.1	+51
	b-c	+57	+35.4	+92
	c-d	+57	−16.7	+40

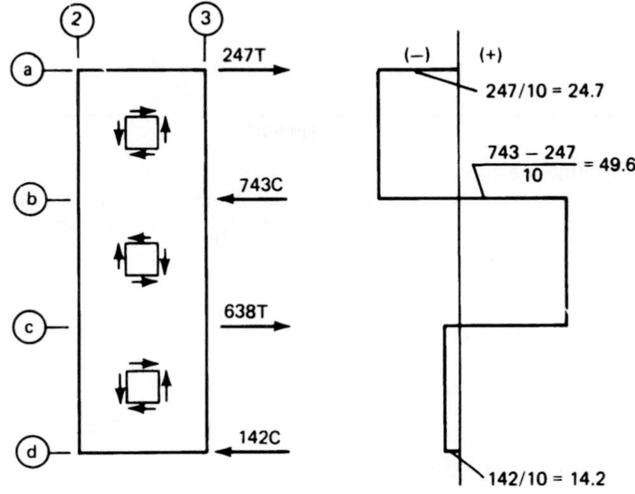

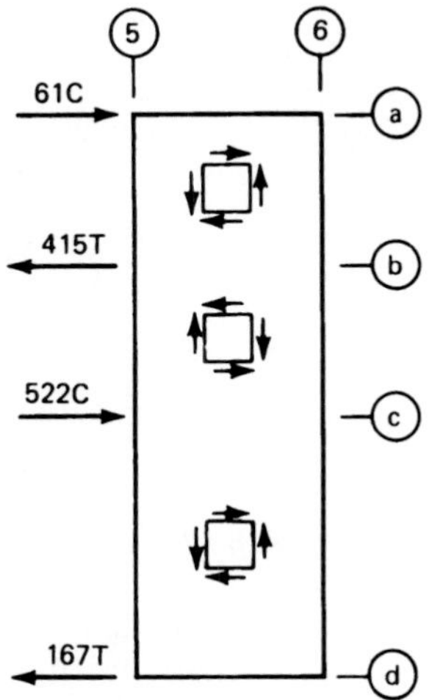

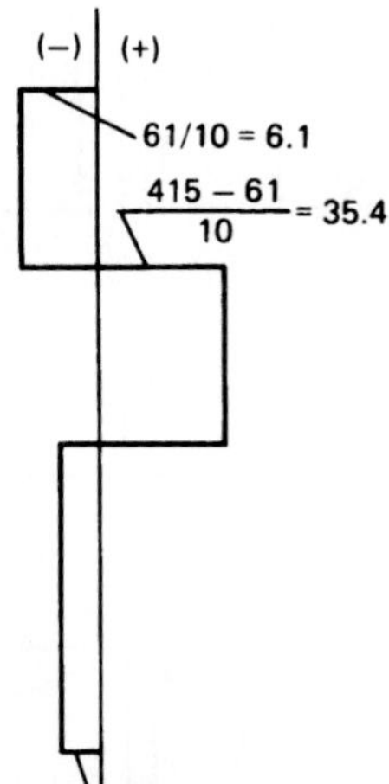

FIG. 8.18c (*Continued*)

6	*a-b*	+0	−6.1	−6
	b-c	+0	+35.4	+35
	c-d	+0	−16.7	−17

6. To determine the forces in the framing members bordering the openings, unit shears along each side of the member are combined (see Fig. 8.18*d*). The slight differences in numerical results are due to rounding of the unit shears.

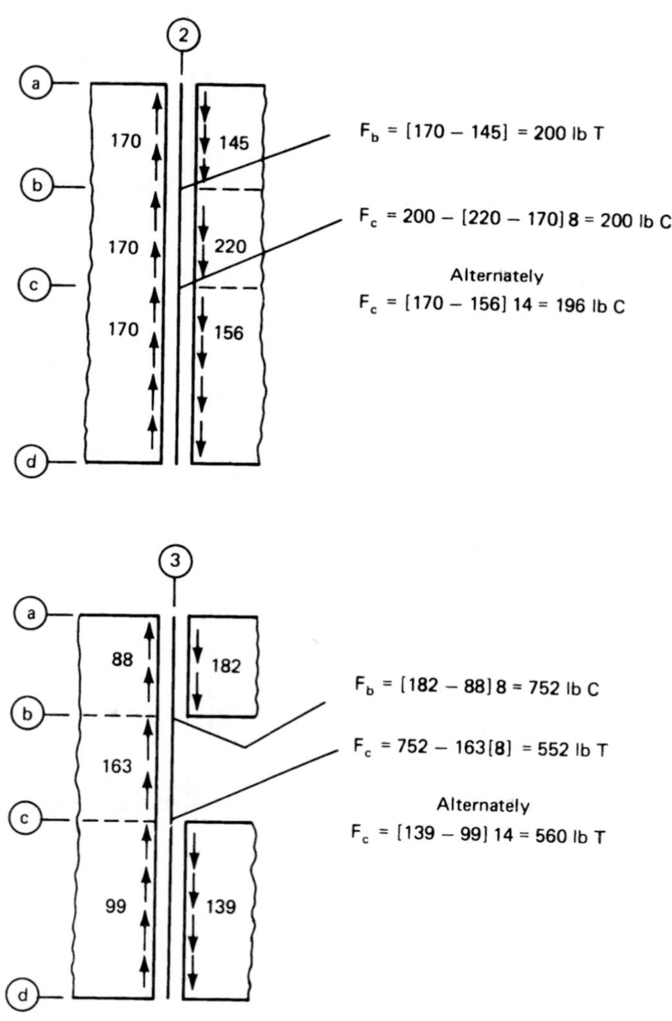

FIG. 8.18*d* (*Continued*)

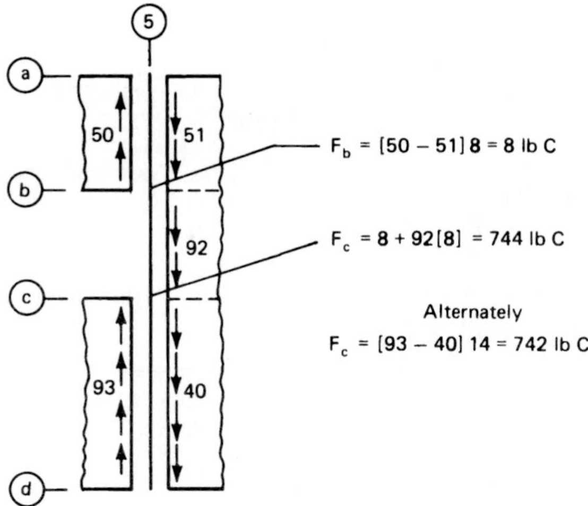

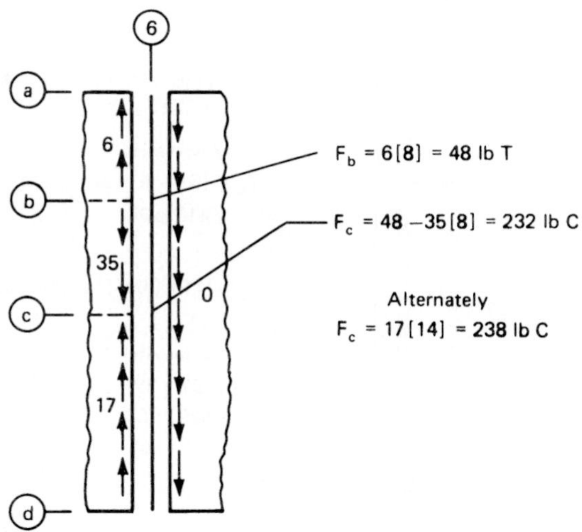

FIG. 8.18*d* (*Continued*)

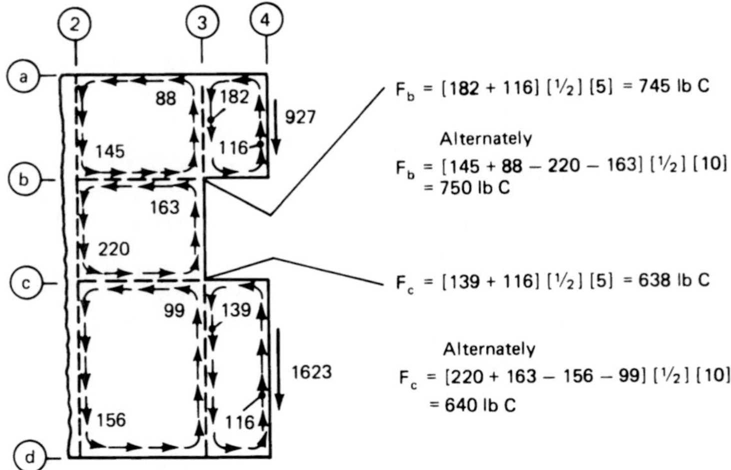

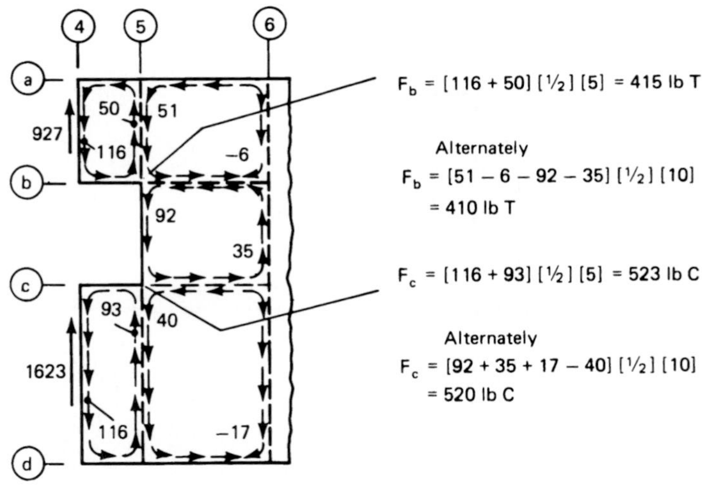

FIG. 8.18*d* (*Continued*)

8.5 SHEARWALLS

8.5.1 Shearwall Principles

Diaphragm action provides in-plane stiffness to a floor or roof which enables the floor or roof to carry forces imposed on it to the vertical bracing elements which in turn carry the forces down to the foundations. One type of vertical bracing element, and the type found in most wood-frame buildings, is a wall with in-plane rigidity referred to as a *shearwall.*

Shearwalls are regarded for design purposes as vertical cantilever beams, and their analysis is simplified by the same assumptions which were applied to diaphragms. These assumptions are that the wall's sheathing is assumed to carry all the shear imposed on the beam uniformly distributed across the length of the wall and that the moment induced in the beam is resisted by a couple applied to members at the boundary of the wall. Figure 8.19 shows the usual design assumptions.

Static equilibrium of the shearwall shown in Fig. 8.19 requires that the wall have a tension anchorage at the uplifting end. In practice, such an anchorage will be needed at each end of the wall, since the lateral load can be imposed in either direction along the wall. This tension anchorage is referred to as the *tiedown.* The solution to the overall design problem requires that direct weight equal to the tension uplift be available for anchorage or that the tiedown engage a member of sufficient strength to engage the needed weight in turn.

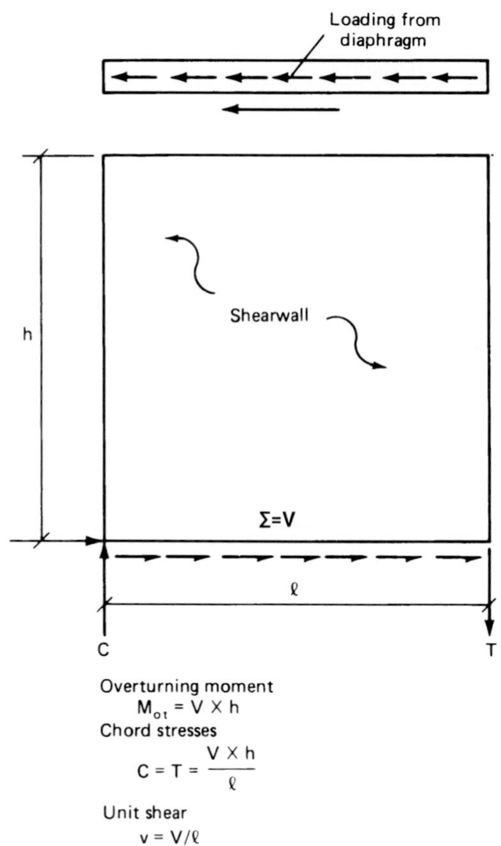

FIG. 8.19 Shearwall free-body diagrams.

The basic design approach to shearwall stability is shown in Fig. 8.19. Most testing of shearwalls has been carried out in accordance with the basic stability requirements indicated by using a tiedown to the testing machine base or laboratory floor. In actual construction conditions where the shearwalls also may be bearing walls supporting substantial building dead load, it is advantageous to utilize the dead load to provide overturning stability and to minimize or eliminate the need for tiedowns. Consider Fig. 8.20. The wall is exactly in equilibrium, and the shear in the panel sheathing would currently be computed as shown.

Unfortunately, the analysis shown in Fig. 8.20, while accurate as to the overall stability of the wall, is not accurate with respect to the shear distribution on the panel sheathing. The problem arises from the fact that the vertical load is actually imposed on the stud framing behind the panel sheathing and can only be introduced into the panel sheathing as it is transferred by mechanical fasteners from the stud framing. Figure 8.21 has been constructed on the assumption that 2000 (8 × 250) lb (8.896 kN) of vertical load noted in Fig. 8.20 is carried by seven studs [six spaces at 16 in (406 mm)] behind the panel sheathing. Figure 8.22*a* through *f* shows successive free bodies which examine the stability requirements *of the panel sheathing* as dictated by the uniform vertical load distribution assumed in Fig. 8.20. The

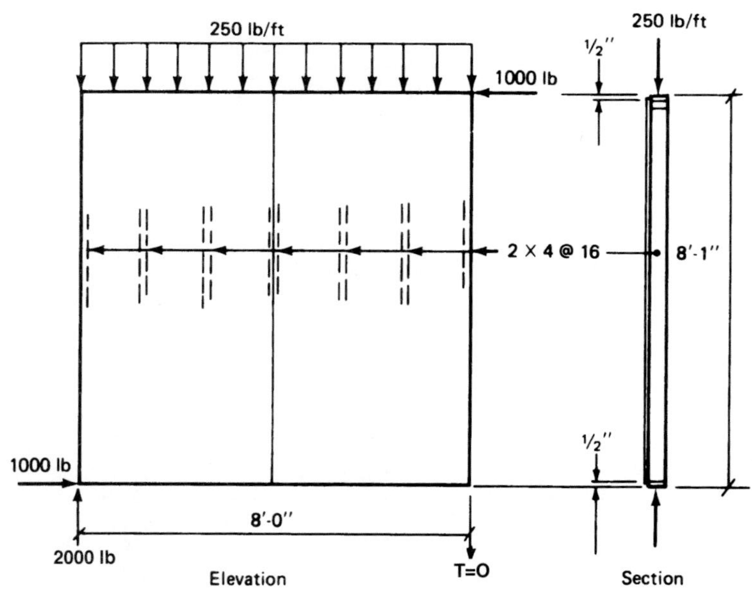

Stability check

Overturning moment

$M_{ot} = 1000\ (8) = 8000$ ft lb

Resisting moment

$M_r = 250\ (8)^2/2 = 8000$ ft lb

Unit shear

$v = V/\ell = 1000/8 = 125$ lb/ft

FIG. 8.20 Shearwall loading.

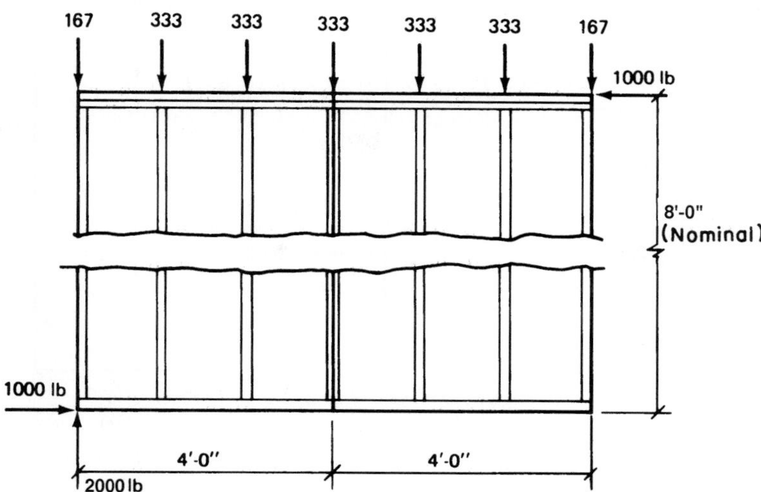

FIG. 8.21 Equivalent external shearwall loading.

slight variations between computations are caused by the rounding off of numbers in the computations.

The detailed analysis indicates that the wall is stable against overturning as the initial calculations showed. However, the detailed analysis also indicates that the shear in the sheathing is not a uniform 125 lb/ft (1.83 kN/m) as previously calculated but is rather a variable amount between 21 (307) and 229 lb/ft (3.34 kN/m). The difference between 229 (3.34) and 125 lb/ft (1.83 kN/m) is not insignificant. Thus shearwalls which rely for overturning stability on vertical load from the framing must be analyzed in detail in order to determine the maximum shear in the panel sheathing.

The more accurate analysis permits an evaluation of several questions of interest. At the studs which are not at the edge of the panels, the introduction of the vertical load into the panel to achieve panel stability requires the nails between stud and panel to transfer the 333 lb per stud to the panel. The minimum interior panel nailing consists of nails at 12 in (305 mm) on center, and this will position a minimum of seven nails between panel and stud. The load per nail will be 333/7 = 47.6 lb (212 N). This load per nail will be well within the capacity of the nails used to attach panel sheathing, so no special nailing will be required.

Considering the vertical joint between the two 4-ft-wide panels, the panel on the right transfers a shear of 104 lb/ft (1.52 kN/m) into the stud, while the panel on the left transfers a shear of 146 lb/ft (2.13 kN/m). Expressed in another way, the panel on the right carries 833 lb (3.70 kN) [833/8 = 104 lb/ft (1.52 kN/m)], while the panel on the left has to transfer this load plus another 333 lb (1.48 kN) [1166/8 = 146 lb/ft (2.13 kN/m)]. The panel edges would have to be nailed accordingly.

If the soleplate for the wall is one piece, then the attachment to the foundation or floor below for the 1000-lb (4.4486-kN) applied load can be made anywhere along its length. If, however, there is a splice in the soleplate, then the connection for each piece of the plate would have to relate to the shear imposed on that piece

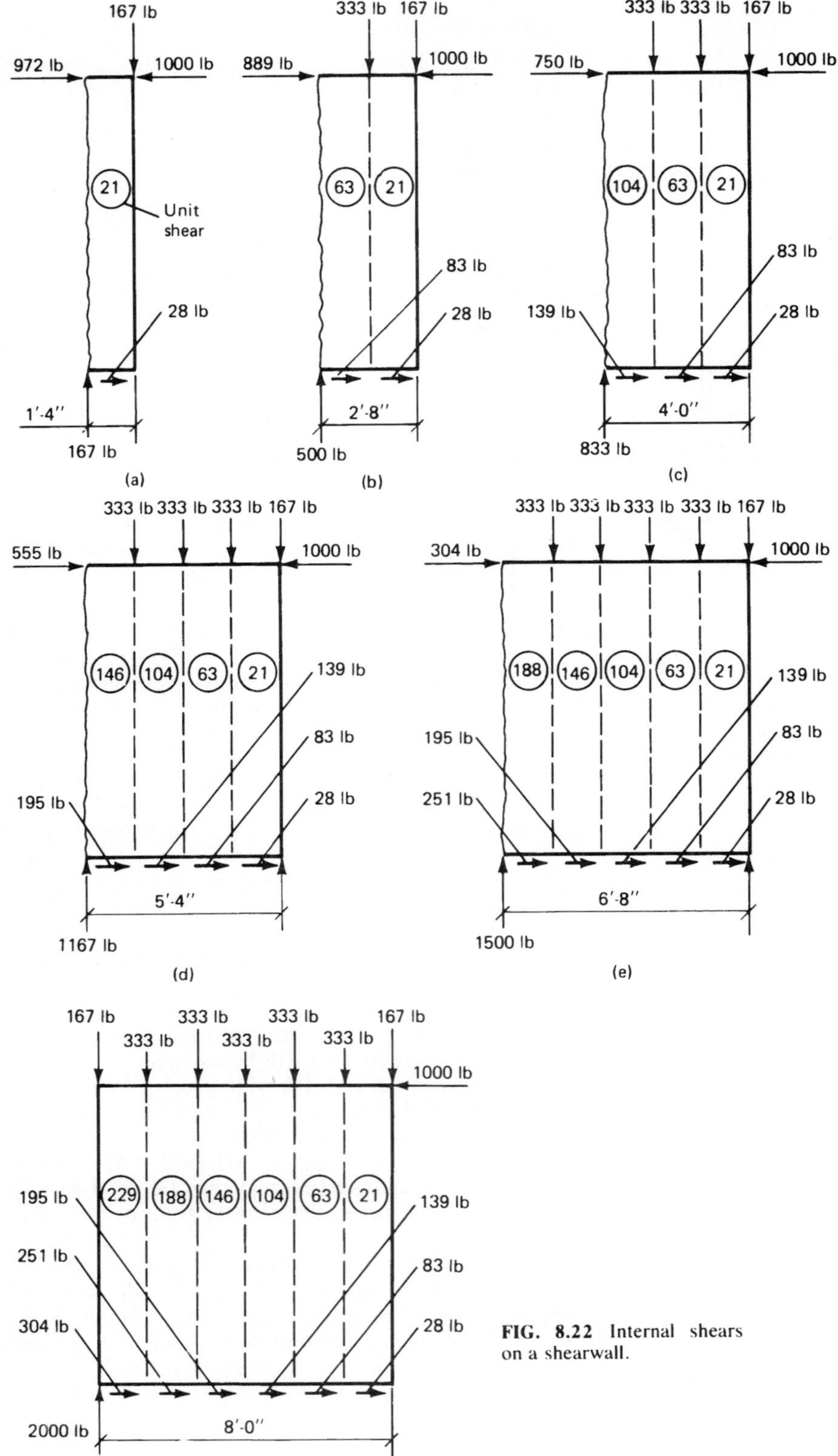

FIG. 8.22 Internal shears on a shearwall.

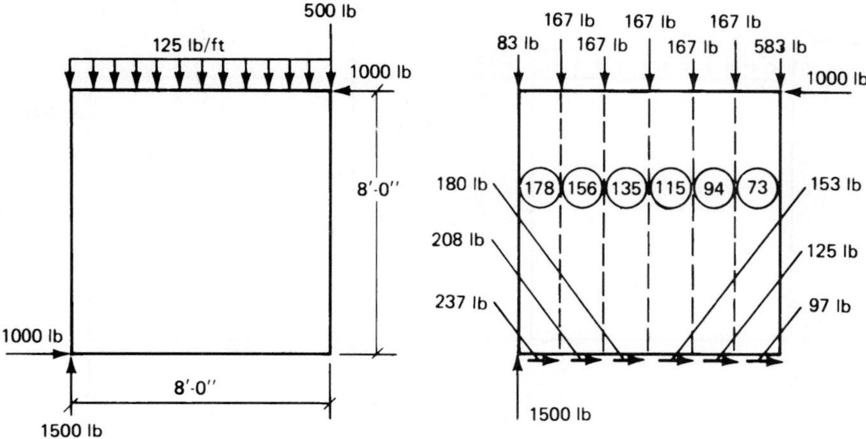

FIG. 8.23 External loading and internal shears on a shearwall.

by the plywood sheathing. Similar considerations are involved with any splices in the top plate to which the sheathing is attached.

Figures 8.23 and 8.24 show other load distributions and the results of detailed analysis of the forces induced in the shearwall. The results in Fig. 8.25 are particularly interesting because they illustrate that a uniform shear distribution in the sheathing can occur only if there is a load or tiedown at the end of the wall to provide a resistance at least equivalent to that required for the basic wall without vertical load as initially discussed. Any other distribution of vertical loading results in an uneven shear distribution in the sheathing and its fastenings.

Figure 8.25 is an illustration of a shearwall which requires a tiedown. It is assumed the tiedown provides only the load needed to ensure stability, 1000 lb

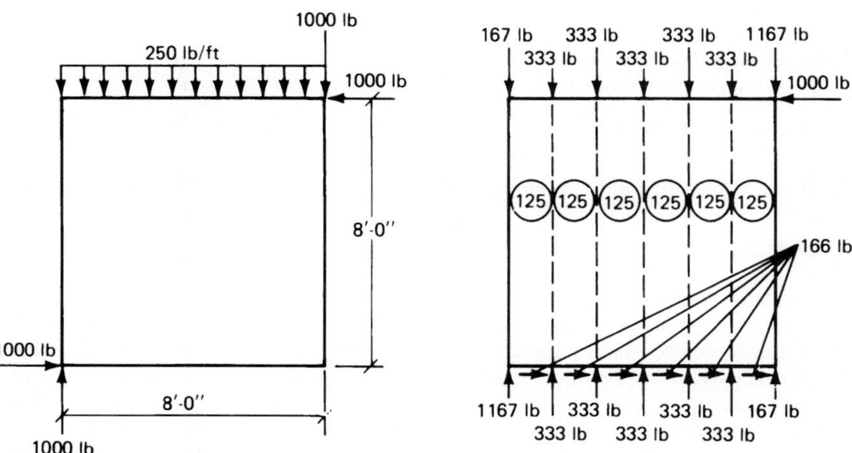

FIG. 8.24 Forces acting on a weightless shearwall.

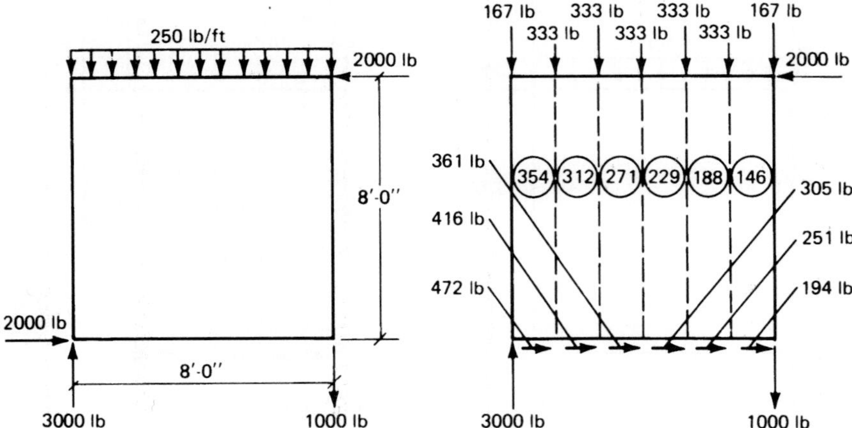

FIG. 8.25 Forces acting on a shearwall under vertical load.

(4.448 kN) in this case. For physical reasons, such as slip in the tiedown connections, it is probable the weight on the wall would be engaged before the tiedown was fully loaded, so this is a reasonable analytical estimate of the wall's behavior. Note that although there is a tiedown at the wall's end, the shear is not uniform in the sheathing and its connections.

Section 8.4.1 presented the basic concepts in the use of diaphragms in a lateral resistance system. The diaphragms receive the lateral force generated at the walls and at the diaphragm itself and transfer these forces in beam action to the vertical bracing elements which terminate at the foundations. The effectiveness of the system depends not only on the structural integrity of the diaphgrams but also on achieving an effective transfer of the forces from the diaphragm to the vertical bracing.

There are five force transfers that may occur at the intersection of a diaphragm and a vertical bracing element:

1. Support vertical live and dead loads (Fig. 8.26).
2. Transfer local forces normal to wall (Fig. 8.27).
3. Transfer shear parallel to wall from diaphragm sheathing to shearwall sheathing (diaphragm shear) (Fig. 8.28).
4. Transfer shear from diaphragm sheathing to diaphragm chord (chord shear) (Fig. 8.29).
5. Transfer wall shears from wall above, if any, to wall below (Fig. 8.30).

These force transfers may involve a number of different materials and members oriented in a variety of ways reflecting the building configurations. The myriad possibilities are presented in greater detail in Refs. 4 and 9. In broad classifications, the materials will be wood or masonry (concrete), and the members may butt to a through wall or sit on a wall below. Typical framing details for each of the force transfers considered are individually illustrated in Figs. 8.26 through 8.30.

Various devices have been used to provide the necessary tiedown to the structure or foundation below the end of the shearwall. These devices have evolved until

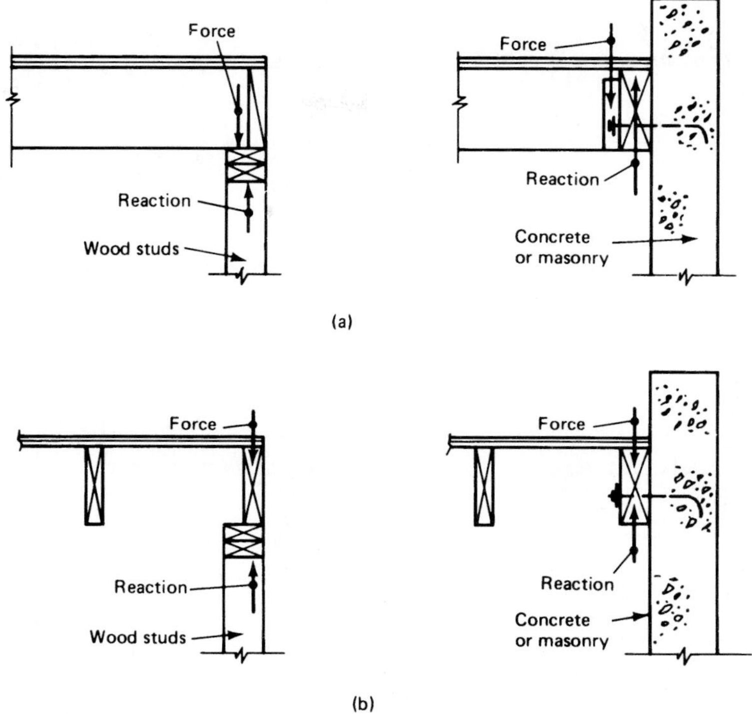

FIG. 8.26 Vertical load schematic for shearwall. (*a*) Joists perpendicular to supports; (*b*) joists parallel to supports.

hardware is now commercially available in capacities up to about 18,000 lb (80.06 kN). Such individual tiedown capacities can be more than doubled by utilizing the standard commercial device on each side of the post (chord) at the end of the shearwall and thereby placing the bolts to the post in double shear. The tiedown device may produce an eccentric load on the post to which it attaches, and the post should be analyzed for combined axial tension and bending as discussed in Chap. 4. As tiedown loads increase, the tiedown post becomes increasingly critical, and tiedowns on both sides of the post may be desirable and/or necessary in order to avoid the bending caused by the eccentricity of a tiedown on only one side of the post. It is necessary to provide suitable resistance to the tiedown force. Provision of such resistance is beyond the scope of this handbook. Details of a typical tiedown on a shearwall are shown in Fig. 8.31.

It is currently assumed for simplicity and convenience that the load on any particular fastener securing the shearwall sheathing to the framing is parallel to the panel edge and that only the edge fasteners ensure panel stability. This assumption is in keeping with the basic assumption that the sheathing does not contribute to the moment resistance of the shearwall. In fact, individual sheathing panels have significant in-plane bending capacity, and panels under shear loads rotate as rigid bodies. All the fasteners in a panel contribute to panel stability, and the fasteners are loaded with force components both parallel and perpendicular to the panel

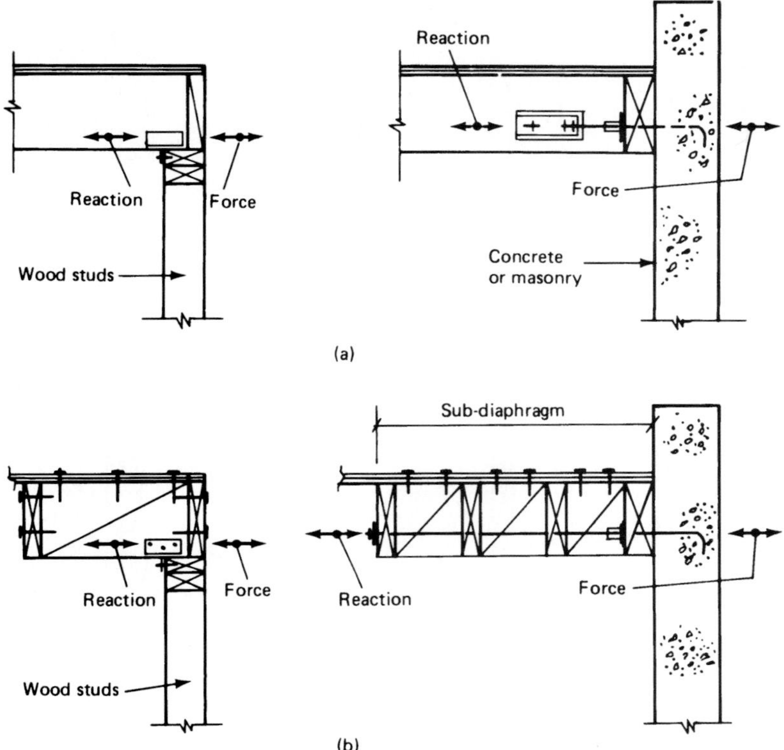

FIG. 8.27 Framing details for anchorage of forces normal to wall. (*a*) Joists perpendicular to supports; (*b*) joists parallel to supports.

edges. These force components combine to form the real force on a given fastener. This more accurate theory is discussed in Ref. 9. Analysis of shearwall tests indicates that shearwalls can be safely designed using the simplifying assumption as to load direction on individual fasteners presented here. Application of more accurate theories may ultimately lead to more efficient designs and to an ability to better model and predict performance, thereby saving on the cost of the large-scale testing currently being used to obtain shearwall design values.

8.5.2 Shearwall Types

The earliest designed shearwalls utilized board sheathing laid diagonally. This practice was largely discontinued as wood panel products, such as plywood, became available. Only plywood shearwalls will be presented here, although other structural panel products as discussed in Chap. 7 also may be used in shearwall designs.

The in-plane capacity of a sheathing panel on a wood-frame wall is presumably affected by the same variables that affect a diaphragm. However, the published shear values for plywood-sheathed walls are based on tests of wall segments 8 by

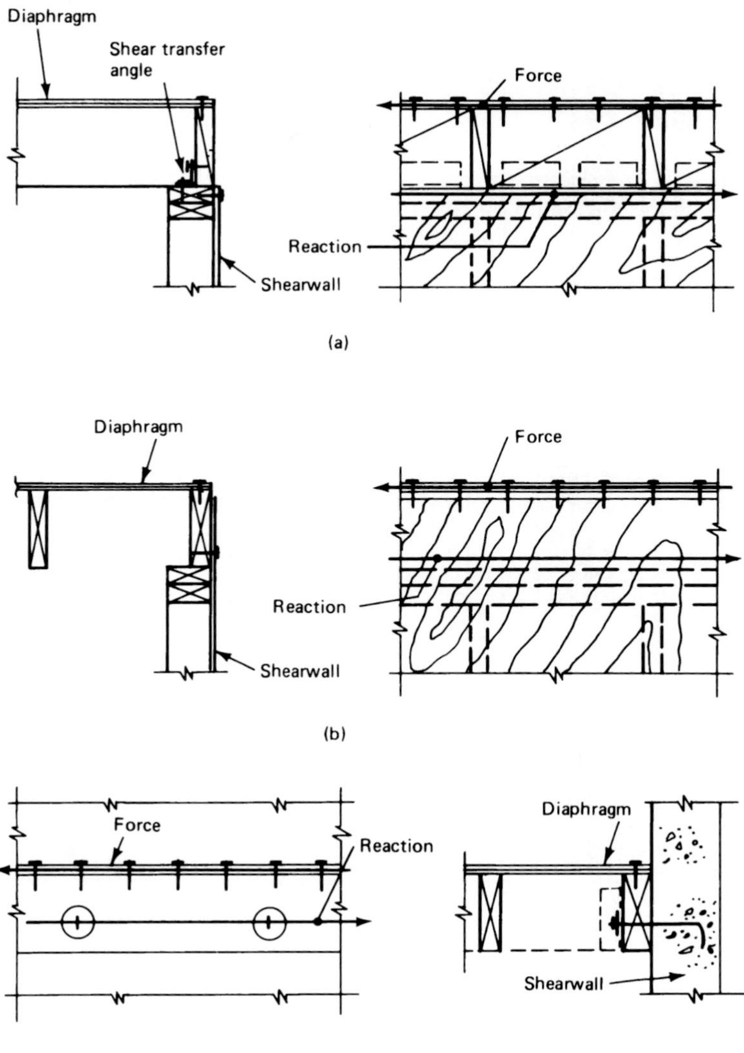

FIG. 8.28 Framing details for transfer of shear parallel to wall from diaphragm to wall. (*a*) Joists perpendicular to wall; (*b*) joists parallel to wall; (*c*) joists parallel or perpendicular to wall.

8 ft (2.44 by 2.44 m) with 2- by 4-in (38.1- by 88.9-mm) studs and the plywood panels nailed on all edges to framing members automatically producing a blocked shearwall. Thus the published values shown in Tables 8.7 through 8.9 for the shear capacity of any wall-sheathing panel product do not include a value for an unblocked panel.

TABLE 8.7 Recommended Shear in Pounds per Foot for APA Panel Shear Walls with Framing of Douglas Fir–Larch or Southern Pine[a] for Wind or Seismic Loading[b]

Panel Grade	Minimum Nominal Panel Thickness (in.)	Minimum Nail Penetration in Framing (in.)	Panels Applied Direct to Framing					Panels Applied Over 1/2" or 5/8" Gypsum Sheathing				
			Nail Size (common or galvanized box)	Nail Spacing at Panel Edges (in.)				Nail Size (common or galvanized box)	Nail Spacing at Panel Edges (in.)			
				6	4	3	2[(e)]		6	4	3	2[(e)]
APA STRUCTURAL I grades	5/16	1-1/4	6d	200	300	390	510	8d	200	300	390	510
	3/8	1-1/2	8d	230[(d)]	360[(d)]	460[(d)]	610[(d)]	10d[(f)]	280	430	550	730
	7/16			255[(d)]	395[(d)]	505[(d)]	670[(d)]		—	—	—	—
	15/32			280	430	550	730		—	—	—	—
	15/32	1-5/8	10d[(f)]	340	510	665	870	—	—	—	—	—
APA RATED SHEATHING; APA RATED SIDING[(g)] and other APA grades except species Group 5	5/16 or 1/4[(c)]	1-1/4	6d	180	270	350	450	8d	180	270	350	450
	3/8			200	300	390	510		200	300	390	510
	3/8	1-1/2	8d	220[(d)]	320[(d)]	410[(d)]	530[(d)]	10d[(f)]	260	380	490	640
	7/16			240[(d)]	350[(d)]	450[(d)]	585[(d)]		—	—	—	—
	15/32			260	380	490	640		—	—	—	—
	15/32	1-5/8	10d[(f)]	310	460	600	770	—	—	—	—	—
	19/32			340	510	665	870	—	—	—	—	—
APA RATED SIDING[(g)] and other APA grades except species Group 5			Nail Size (galvanized casing)					Nail Size (galvanized casing)				
	5/16[(c)]	1-1/4	6d	140	210	275	360	8d	140	210	275	360
	3/8	1-1/2	8d	160	240	310	410	10d[(f)]	160	240	310	410

Source: Reprinted with permission of the APA-The Engineered Wood Association.

(a) For framing of other species: (1) Find specific gravity for species of lumber in Table 5.2.
(2)(a) For common or galvanized box nails, find shear value from table above for nail size for STRUCTURAL I panels (regardless of actual grade). (b) For galvanized casing nails, take shear value directly from table above. (3) Multiply this value by 0.82 for species with specific gravity of 0.42 or greater, or 0.65 for all other species.

(b) All panel edges backed with 2-inch nominal or wider framing. Install panels either horizontally or vertically. Space nails maximum 6 inches o.c. along intermediate framing members for 3/8-inch and 7/16-inch panels installed on studs spaced 24 inches o.c. For other conditions and panel thicknesses, space nails maximum 12 inches o.c. on intermediate supports.

(c) 3/8-inch or APA RATED SIDING-16 oc is minimum recommended when applied direct to framing as exterior siding.

(d) Shears may be increased to values shown for 15/32-inch sheathing with same nailing provided (1) studs are spaced a maximum of 16 inches o.c., or (2) if panels are applied with long dimension across studs.

(e) Framing at adjoining panel edges shall be 3-inch nominal or wider, and nails shall be staggered where nails are spaced 2 inches o.c.

(f) Framing at adjoining panel edges shall be 3-inch nominal or wider, and nails shall be staggered where 10d nails having penetration into framing of more than 1-5/8 inches are spaced 3 inches o.c.

(g) Values apply to all-veneer plywood APA RATED SIDING panels only. Other APA RATED SIDING panels may also qualify on a proprietary basis. APA RATED SIDING-16 oc plywood may be 11/32-inch, 3/8-inch or thicker. Thickness at point of nailing on panel edges governs shear values.

Typical Layout for Shear Walls

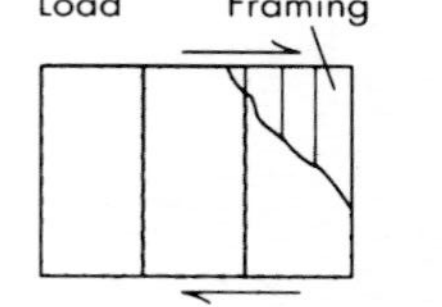

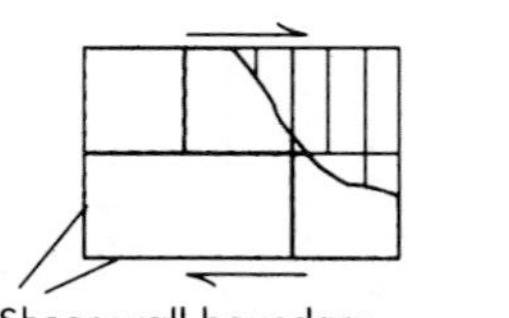

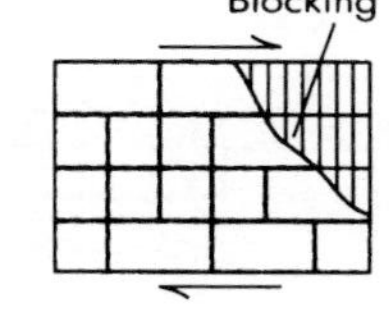

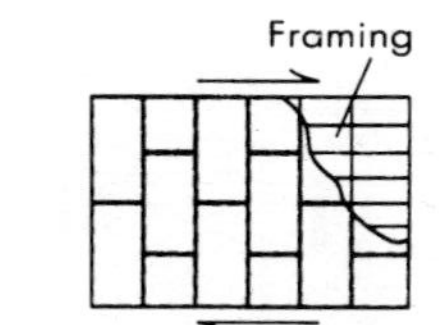

Source: Reprinted with permission of the American Plywood Association.

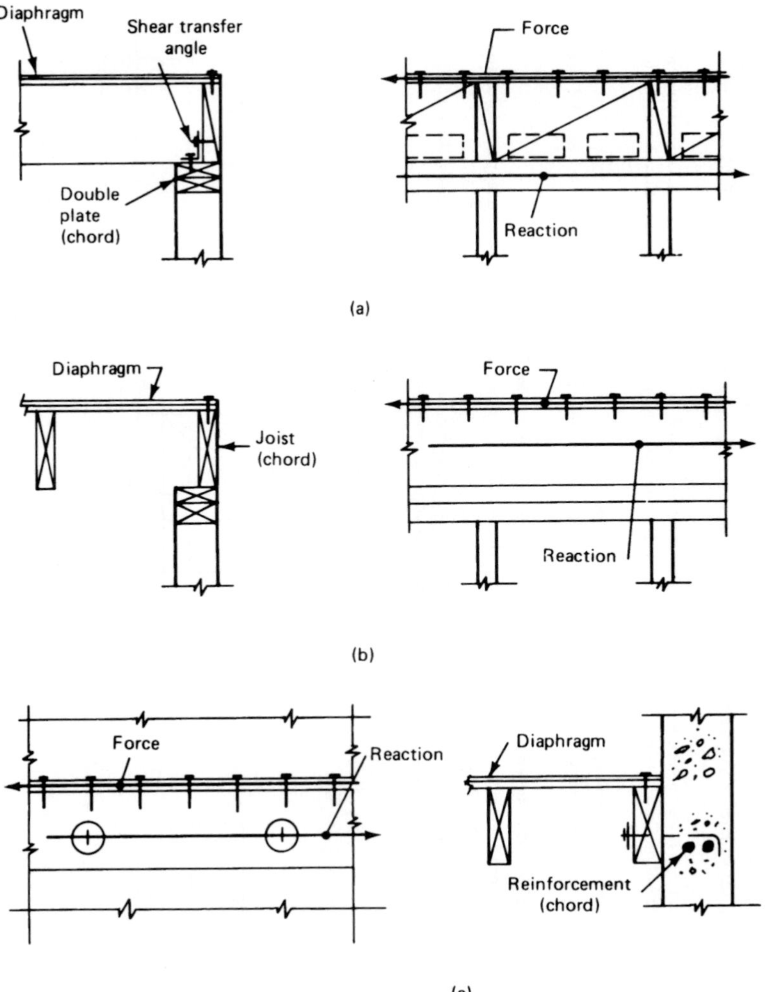

FIG. 8.28 Framing details for transfer of diaphragm edge shear to diaphragm chord

FIG. 8.29 Framing details for transfer of diaphragm edge shear to diaphragm chord. (*a*) Joists perpendicular to wall; (*b*) joists parallel to wall; (*c*) joists parallel or perpendicular to wall.

Most wood-frame residential buildings have 8-ft ceilings, a height which matches laboratory test panels and which lends itself to orienting 4- by 8-ft (1.22- by 2.44-m) sheets with the long axis vertical. When walls are taller than 8 ft (2.44 m), it is desirable to lay the plywood sheets with the long axis vertical and to stagger the horizontal joints similar to diaphragm case 1, Table 8.2. However, it is somewhat easier not to stagger the sheet joints as in diaphragm case 5, Table 8.2, and this is the usual practice. As previously noted, all panel edges on a shearwall

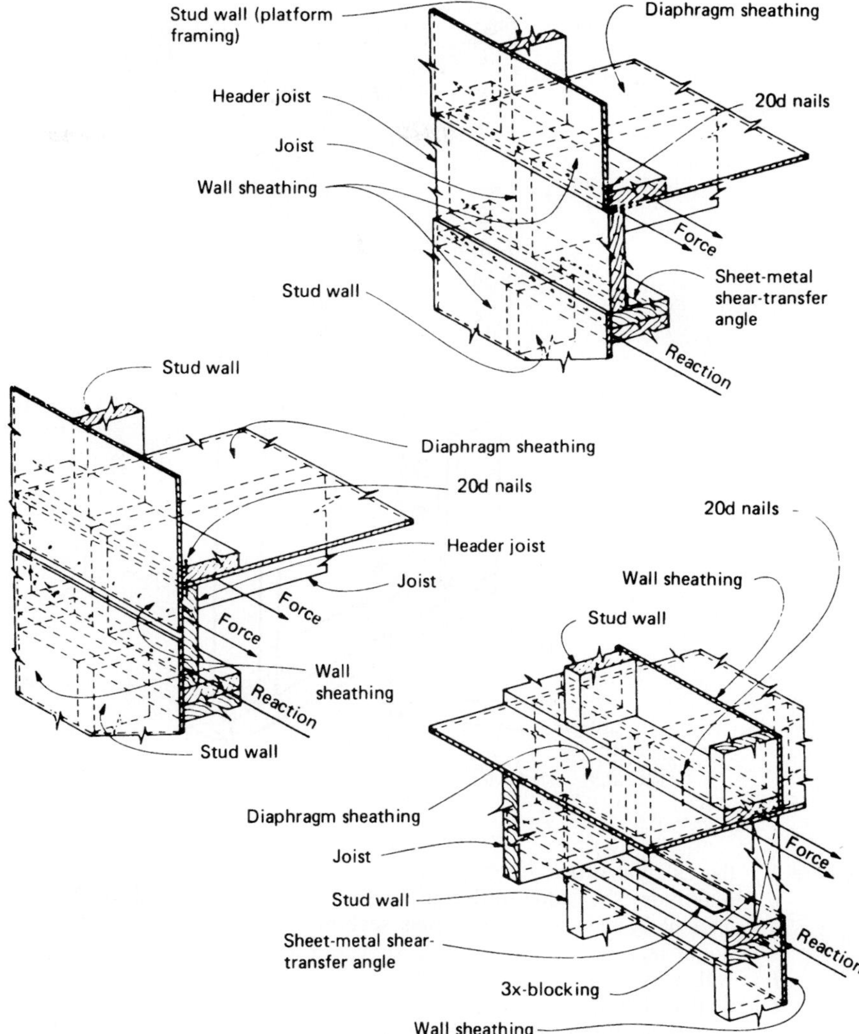

FIG. 8.30 Framing details for transfer of shear stress in shearwalls across an intervening diaphragm. *(Reprinted with permission of Applied Technology Council.[4])*

must be nailed, and this necessitates wood blocking at any panel edge not nailable to other wall framing members.

The deflection of a blocked plywood shearwall uniformly nailed throughout may be calculated by use of the following formula:

$$\Delta = \frac{8vh^3}{EAb} + \frac{vh}{Gt} + 0.376\,he_n + d_a \tag{8.7}$$

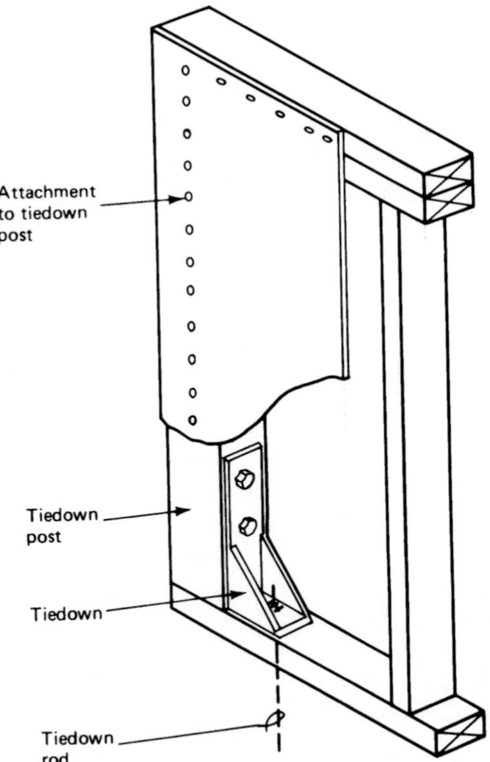

FIG. 8.31 Tiedown detail.

where Δ = the calculated deflection, in
v = maximum shear due to design loads at the top of the wall, lb/ft
A = area of boundary element cross section (vertical member at shearwall boundary), in^2
h = wall height, ft
b = wall width, ft
d_a = deflection due to anchorage details (rotation and slip at tiedown bolts)
E = elastic modulus of boundary element (vertical member at shearwall boundary), lb/in^2
G = modulus of rigidity of plywood, lb/in^2
t = effective thickness of plywood for shear, in
e_n = nail deformation, in

Plywood Diaphragm Construction,[1] *Plywood Design Specification,*[2] and UBC Standard 25-9[3] have tables and charts which provide values for G, t, and e_n.

In the formula, the individual terms determine the contribution to the total deflection of the boundary member elongation (bending), shear in the plywood, nail slip, and anchorage slip, respectively.

TABLE 8.8 Allowable Shear for Wind or Seismic Forces in Pounds per Foot for Particleboard Shear Walls with Framing of Douglas Fir–Larch or Southern Pine*§

Panel grade	Minimum nominal panel thickness, in	Minimum nail penetration in framing, in	Panels applied direct to framing					Panels applied over ½ in gypsum sheathing				
			Nail size (common or galvanized box)	Nail spacing at panel edges, in				Nail size (common or galvanized box)	Nail spacing at panel edges, in			
				6	4	3	2†		6	4	3	2†
2-M-W	5/16	1¼	6d	180	270	350	450	8d	180	270	350	450
	3/8			200	300	390	510		200	300	390	510
	3/8	1½	8d	220‡	320‡	410‡	530‡	10d	260	380	490†	640
	7/16			240‡	350‡	450‡	585‡	—	—	—	—	—
	½			260	380	490	640	—	—	—	—	—
	½	1⅝	10d	310	460	600†	770	—	—	—	—	—
	5/8			340	510	665†	870	—	—	—	—	—

*All panel edges backed with 2-in nominal or wider framing. Panels installed either horizontally or vertically. Space nails at 6 in on center along intermediate framing members for ⅜-in panel installed with the long dimension parallel to studs spaced 24 in on center and 12 in on center for other conditions and panel thicknesses. These values are for short-time loads due to wind or earthquake and must be reduced 25 percent for normal loading.

Allowable shear values for nails in framing members of other species set forth in Table 25-17-J of UBC Standards shall be calculated for all grades by multiplying the values for common and galvanized box nails by the following factors: group III, 0.82, and group IV, 0.65.

†Framing shall be 3-in nominal or wider and nails shall be staggered where nails are spaced 2 in on center, and where 10d nails having penetration into framing of more than 1⅝ in are spaced 3 in on center.

‡The allowable shear values may be increased to the values shown for ½-in-thick sheathing with the same nailing, provided: (*a*) The studs are spaced a maximum of 16 in on center, or (*b*) the panels are applied with the long dimension perpendicular to studs.

§Where plywood is applied on both faces of a wall and nail spacing is less than 6 in on center on either side, panel joints shall be offset to fall on different framing members, or framing shall be 3-in nominal or thicker and nails on each side shall be staggered.

Source: Reproduced from the 1985 edition of the *Uniform Building Code*, copyright © 1985, with the permission of the publisher, the International Conference of Building Officials.

TABLE 8.9 Allowable Shear for Wind or Seismic Forces in Pounds per Foot for TWA ANSI Waferboard Shear Walls with Framing of Douglas Fir–Larch or Southern Pine*§

Panel grade	Minimum nominal panel thickness, in	Minimum nail penetration in framing, in	Panels applied direct to framing					Panels applied over ½ in gypsum board				
			Nail size (common or galvanized box)	Nail spacing at panel edges, in				Nail size (common or galvanized box)	Nail spacing at panel edges, in			
				6	4	3	2†		6	4	3	2†
Type 2-M-W	5/16	1¼	6d	180	270	350	450	8d	180	270	350	450
	3/8			200	300	390	510		200	300	390	510
	3/8	1½	8d	220‡	320‡	410‡	530‡	10d	260	380	490†	640
	7/16			240‡	350‡	450‡	585‡					
	½			260	380	490	640					
	½	1⅝	10d	310	460	600†	770	—	—	—	—	—
	5/8			340	510	665†	870	—	—	—	—	—

*All panel edges backed with 2-in nominal or wider framing. Panels may be installed either horizontally or vertically. Space nails at 6 in on center along intermediate framing members for ⅜- and 7/16-in panels installed on studs spaced 24 in o.c. For other conditions and panel thicknesses, space nails 12 in o.c. on intermediate supports. These values are for short-time loads due to wind or earthquake and must be reduced 25 percent for normal loading.

For framing of other species: (*a*) Find species group of lumber in Table 5.2, (*b*) find shear value from table for nail size, (*c*) multiply this value by 0.82 for species with specific gravity of 0.42 or greater, or 0.65 for all other species.

†Framing at panel edges shall be 3-in nominal or wider and nails shall be staggered where nails are spaced 2 in o.c., and where 10d nails having penetration into framing of more than 1⅝ in are spaced 3 in o.c. Exception: Unless otherwise required, 2-in nominal framing may be used where full nailing surface width is available and nails are staggered.

‡The allowable shear values may be increased to the values shown for ½-in-thick sheathing with the same nailing, provided the studs are spaced a maximum of 16 in on center

§The maximum height-width ratio is 3½ to 1.

Source: Reproduced from the 1985 edition of the *Uniform Building Code,* copyright © 1985, with the permission of the publisher, the International Conference of Building Officials.

TABLE 8.10 Maximum Shearwall Dimension Ratios

Material	Maximum height-width ratios
1. Diagonal sheathing, conventional	2/1
2 Diagonal sheathing, special	3½/1
3. Plywood and particleboard, nailed all edges	3½/1
4. Plywood and particleboard, blocking omitted at intermediate joints	2/1

8.5.3 Restrictions on Shearwall Use

Shearwalls are restricted in the ratio of their height to in-plane length. Table 8.10 sets out these limiting ratios. These ratios are generally interpreted as applying to both single and multistory buildings using the total wall height for multistory buildings. Unsuccessful efforts have been made to develop an engineering consensus on how to apply these ratios to multistory buildings in which the shearwalls do not align vertically between floors and/or the wall lengths vary between floors. It is suggested that the wall length for a wall on a given story, regardless of how it aligns with other shearwalls, be at least as long as the limiting ratios would require if the walls did align. Figure 8.32 illustrates this suggestion.

The exact source and rationale for these limiting ratios is unknown. It is believed they represent engineering judgments as to the length of shearwall required to limit story drift under lateral loading to a reasonable amount.

Wood-sheathed shearwalls are considered to be relatively flexible. This initially led to confining their use in bracing buildings with concrete or masonry walls to buildings of only one story. This restriction has subsequently been modified to permit wood shearwalls to be used to brace two-story buildings with masonry or concrete walls provided the following restrictions are observed.

1. Wall heights shall not exceed 12 ft (3.66 m).
2. Horizontal diaphragms shall not be considered to transmit lateral forces by rotation or cantilever action.
3. Deflections of horizontal and vertical diaphragms shall not permit per-story deflections of supported masonry or concrete walls to exceed 0.005 times each story height.

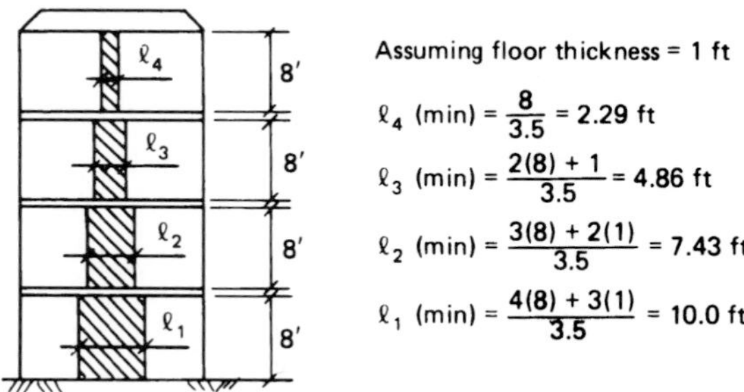

ℓ4
ℓ3
ℓ2
ℓ1
8′
8′
8′
8′
Assuming floor thickness = 1 ft
ℓ_4 (min) = $\frac{8}{3.5}$ = 2.29 ft
ℓ_3 (min) = $\frac{2(8) + 1}{3.5}$ = 4.86 ft
ℓ_2 (min) = $\frac{3(8) + 2(1)}{3.5}$ = 7.43 ft
ℓ_1 (min) = $\frac{4(8) + 3(1)}{3.5}$ = 10.0 ft

FIG. 8.32 Height-to-width ratios for multistory shearwalls.

4. Structural panel sheathing in horizontal diaphragms shall have all unsupported edges blocked. Plywood sheathing for both stories of vertical shearwalls shall have all unsupported edges blocked and for the lower story walls shall have a minimum sheathing thickness of ½ in (12.7 mm).
5. There shall be no out-of-plane horizontal offsets between the first and second stories of panel shearwalls.

8.5.4 Typical Shearwall Designs

EXAMPLE 8.7 Analysis had determined that a shearwall is subjected to the loads shown (Fig. 8.33). The plywood is ⅜ in in APA-rated sheathing. The nails will be 8d common wire. Select the appropriate nail spacing, and determine the tiedown requirements.

$$\text{Average unit shear } v = 2000/6 = 333 \text{ lb/ft}$$

Load (2000 lb) applied to left:

$$\begin{aligned} &\text{Gross uplift:} \quad 10(333) &&= -3330 \text{ lb} \\ &\text{Wall weight:} \quad 200(6)\tfrac{1}{2} &&= +\ \ 600 \text{ lb} \\ &\text{Concentrated load:} && \quad \underline{+\ \ 800 \text{ lb}} \\ &\qquad\qquad\qquad \text{Total} &&= -1930 \text{ lb} \end{aligned}$$

Compression:

$$C = 333(10) + 400 + \tfrac{1}{2}(6)(200) = 4330 \text{ lb}$$

Unit shear:

$$\text{Left edge } (4330 - 400)/10 = 393 \text{ lb/ft}$$

$$\text{Right edge } (1930 + 800)/10 = 273 \text{ lb/ft}$$

Load (2000 lb) applied to right:

$$\begin{aligned} &\text{Gross uplift:} \quad 10(333) &&= -3330 \text{ lb} \\ &\text{Wall weight:} \quad 200(6)\tfrac{1}{2} &&= +\ \ 600 \text{ lb} \\ &\text{Concentrated load:} && \quad \underline{+\ \ 400 \text{ lb}} \\ &\qquad\qquad\qquad \text{Total} &&= -2330 \text{ lb} \end{aligned}$$

Compression:

$$C = 333(10) + 800 + \tfrac{1}{2}\ 6(200) = 4730 \text{ lb}$$

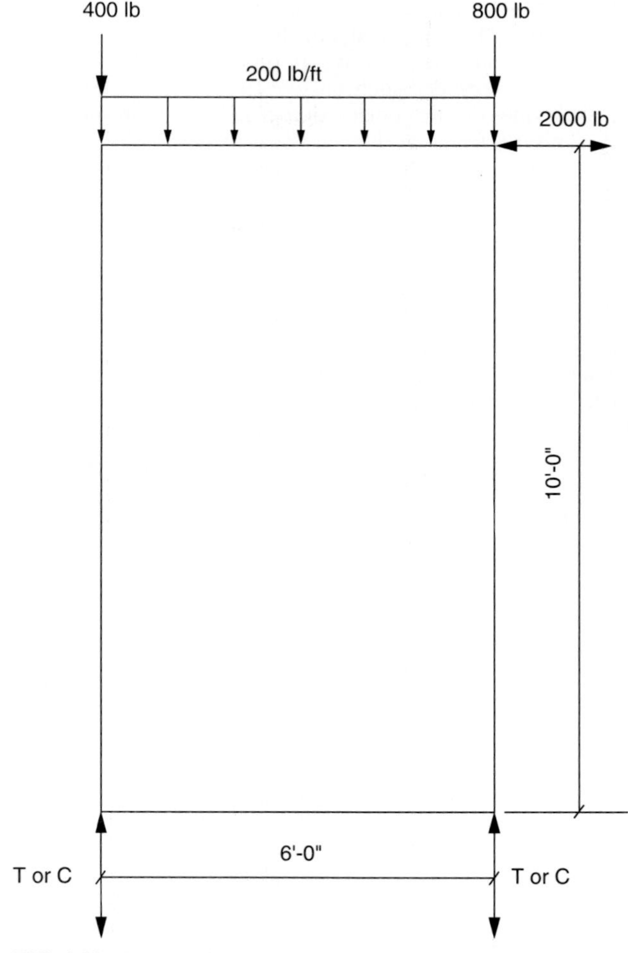

FIG. 8.33 Example 8.7.

Unit shear:

$$\text{Left edge } (2330 + 400)/10 = 273 \text{ lb/ft}$$

$$\text{Right edge } (4730 - 800)/10 = 393 \text{ lb/ft}$$

Referring to Table 8.7, ⅜-in plywood nailed with 8d common wire nail has a unit shear capacity as follows:

Nail spacing (in)	6	4	3	2
Unit shear (lb)	260*	380*	490*	640*

Use ⅜-in plywood, 8d common wire nails at 3 in on center.

*Increased values for 15⁄32 in sheathing for studs 16 in on center.

Select tiedowns at each end with 2330 lb minimum capacity.

Design Comments. The calculated unit shear of 393 lb/ft exceeds the allowable unit shear for 8d common wire nails at 4 in on center of 380 lb/ft by 3.3 percent. Most designers would consider such an overstress permissible. Mistakes in nail placement at panel edges during construction usually result in some edge nails being ineffective; this, in turn, suggests that selection of the more conservative 3-in nail spacing is appropriate. The maximum unit shear at 393 lb/ft exceeds the 333 lb/ft average value by 18 percent.

Although the analysis indicates that the two tiedowns could be of different capacities, the usual practice would be to use the same size at each location to simplify procurement and job layout.

EXAMPLE 8.8 Given the shearwall with loadings shown (Fig. 8.34), the large concentrated load is from a beam framing onto a post in the wall. The plywood is $^{15}/_{32}$-in APA-rated sheathing. The nails will be short 10d common wire nails. Select the appropriate nail spacing(s) and pattern(s), and determine the tie down requirements.

$$\text{Average unit shear } v = 4000/10 = 400 \text{ lb/ft}$$

Load (4000 lb) applied to left:

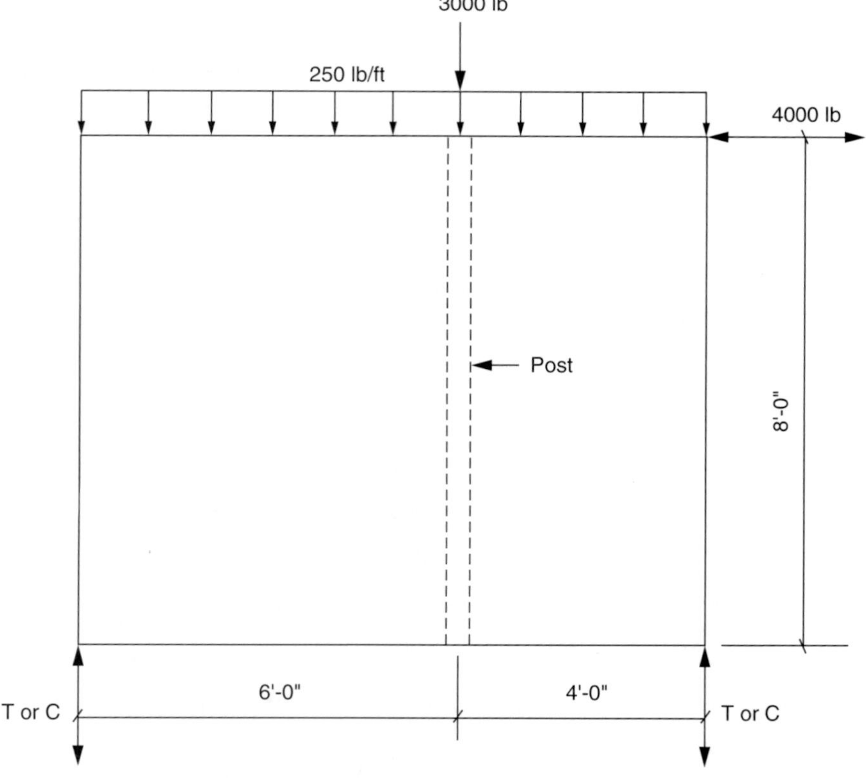

FIG. 8.34 Example 8.8.

Gross uplift: 8(400) = −3200 lb

Wall weight: 250(10)½ = +1250

Post load: 3000(6)/10 = +1800

Total = − 150 lb

Compression:

$$C = 150 + 250(10) + 3000 = 5650 \text{ lb}$$

Unit shear:

Left edge 5650/8 = 706 lb/ft

Left side post [5650 − 6(250)]/8 = 519 lb/ft

Right side post [5650 − 3000 − 1500]/8 = 144 lb/ft

Right edge 150/8 = 19 lb/ft

Load to right:

Gross uplift: 8(400) = −3200 lb

Wall weight: 250(10)½ = +1250 lb

Post load: 3000(4)/10 = +1200 lb

Total = − 750 lb

Compression:

$$C = 8(400 + 250(10)(½) + 3000\ (6/10) = 6250 \text{ lb}$$

Unit shear:

Left edge: 750/8 = 941 lb/ft

Left side post: [750 + 6(250)]/8 = 281 lb/ft

Right side post: (750 + 3000 + 1500)/8 = 656 lb/ft

Right edge: 6250/8 = 781 lb/ft

Referring to Table 8.7, 15⁄32-in plywood nailed with 10d common wire nails has a unit shear capacity as follows:

Nail spacing (in)	6	4	3	2
Unit shear (lb/ft)	310	460	600	770

Use ½-in plywood and 10d common wire nails at 2 in on center. Provide tiedown with 750 lb minimum capacity at each end of the wall.

The post needs to be attached to the sheathing for 3000 ÷ 8 = 375 lb/ft. The designer must specify this attachment, 10d nails at 4 in o.c.

8.5.5 Special Shearwall Elements

Shearwalls with Openings. Most walls in a wood-frame structure are penetrated by doors and windows. Such openings interfere with the uniform distribution of shear along the wall, and this raises the question of how to analyze such a nonuniform element. Figure 8.35 shows a building wall which is to be designed as a shearwall and which is subjected to a total shear V. The usual design assumption would involve ignoring the wall segments above the door and window and similarly ignoring the wall segment below the window. The shear wall then consists of three sections of lengths L_1, L_2, and L_3. The further assumption is made that the rigidity of these sections is directly proportional to their length. The unit shear in the section is then $V/(L_1 + L_2 + L_3)$, and the total shear on any one panel is its length divided by the sum of the section lengths times V.

For L_1, this would give

$$V_1 = \frac{L_1}{L_1 + L_2 + L_3} V \tag{8.8}$$

Each wall section can then be designed as a separate cantilevered wall.

While the technique just described is simple, it is obviously not correct; the framing above and below the openings must influence the overall behavior of the shearwall. The solution just discussed might require six tiedowns, one at each end of each wall section, and the problems and costs attendant with these devices suggest the need of an alternate approach.

Assume the wall shown in Fig. 8.36. Several assumptions might be made as a basis for an analysis reflecting the presence of the openings. The first assumption would be to ignore the shallow framing above the openings and to assume the solid wall sections cantilever from a wood base the height of the opening sill. The overturning would still be taken out through tiedowns into the foundation. The outcome of these assumptions and resultant analysis is shown in Fig. 8.37. The outcome has little to recommend it over an assumption of free-standing wall sections.

A more promising approach would seem to be to anchor the overturning in the continuous wall section below the sill. Figure 8.38 shows the outcome of an analysis based on such an approach using the same approach used for a diaphragm with a hole.

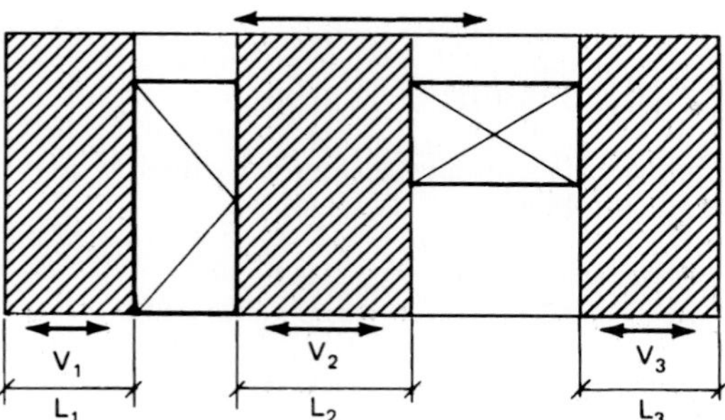

FIG. 8.35 Shearwall with openings.

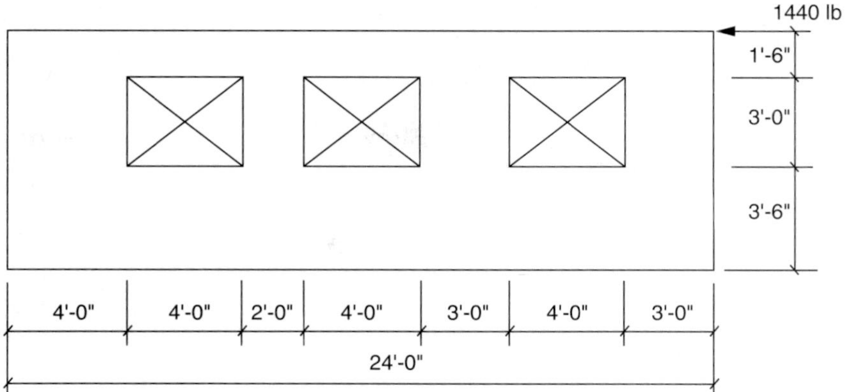

FIG. 8.36 Shearwall with openings.

A further refinement would reflect the presence of the framing above the openings. If an assumption is made that inflection points occur at midheight of the openings in the solid wall sections, an analysis can be made using the superposition approach. The various steps and final shear distributions in the various wall sections are shown in Figs. 8.37 through 8.40. A detailed study of the lower right corner of the wall is shown in Fig. 8.41. While this method provides an analysis of a shearwall containing openings, the assumptions made are very broad, and some error must be present. Tests are currently in progress on shearwalls with openings to either confirm the suitability of this approach or suggest modifications or another method for more accurately approaching these problems.

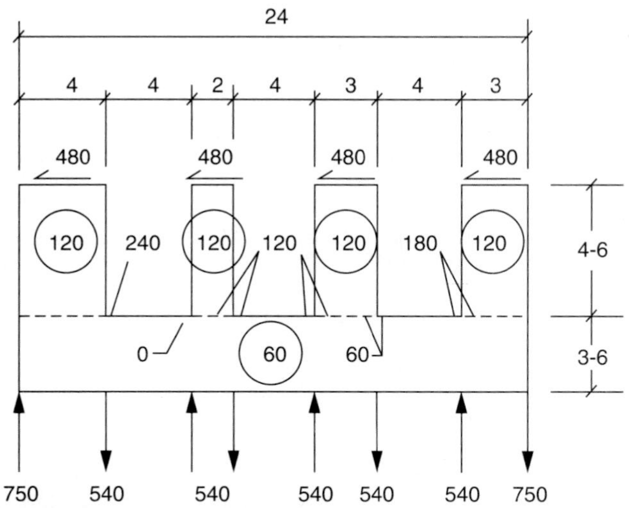

FIG. 8.37 Internal forces and shears, case 1.

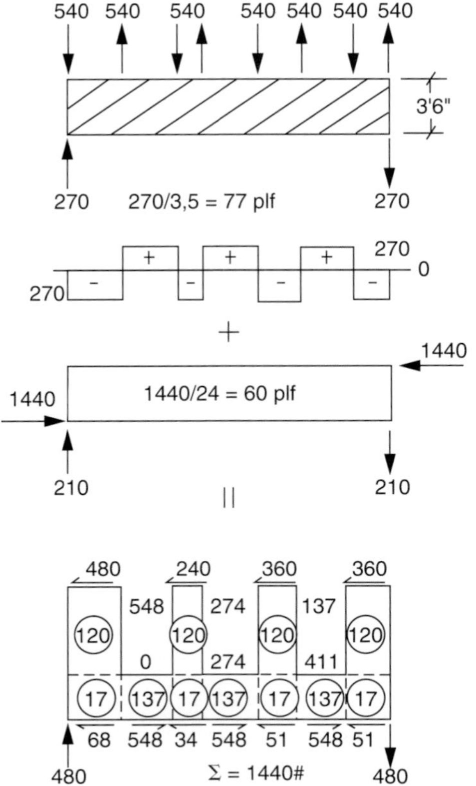

FIG. 8.38 Internal forces and shears; wall below windows taken into account.

Collectors. It frequently happens that the available length of the shearwall is less than the depth of the diaphragm attached to it, as illustrated by Fig. 8.42*a*.

In such cases it is necessary to extend the effective length of the shearwall by providing a member along which the diaphragm is attached and which in turn is attached to the shorter length of the shearwall. The terminology applied to such a member is not unanimously agreed on; however, *collector* is perhaps the most common designation, but *drag* or *drag strut* are also used.

In Fig. 8.42*a*, assume the total shear in the diaphragm at line *A* is 3000 lb (13.34 kN). The unit shear is then 3000/30 or 100 lb/ft (1.46 kN/m). The unit shear in the selected shearwall between lines 2 and 3 is 3000/10 = 300 lb/ft (4.38 kN/m). The shear flow along the collector can be plotted as shown in Fig. 8.42*b*.

The force in the collector can be easily calculated at any point of interest. For example, assuming the collector is comprised of three 10-ft-long segments, i.e., jointed at lines 2 and 3, the force at each of these joints can be calculated as 100(10) = 1000 lb (4.448 N). As drawn, the force would be tension at line 2 and compression at line 3. Two feet to the right of line 2, the force would be

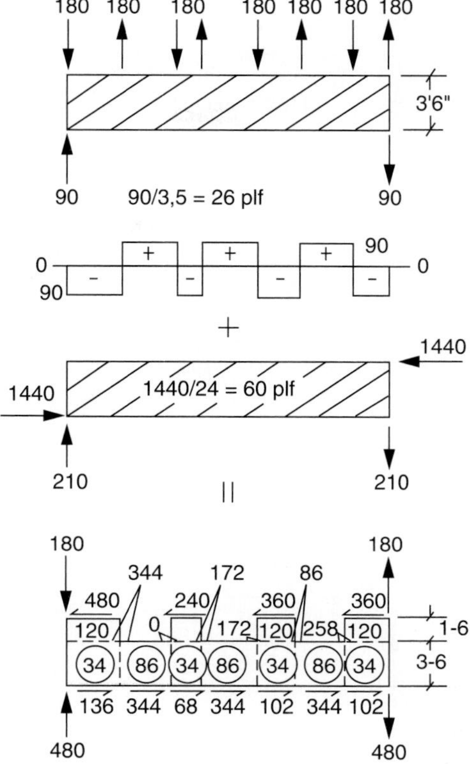

FIG. 8.39 Internal forces and shears on bottom segment of wall.

$$F_1 = 100(10) + 200(2) = 600 \text{ lb } (2.67 \text{ N}) \text{ (tension)}$$

The plot also can be used to select splice points at which the forces are minimized. In this case, the theoretical collector force is zero midway between lines 2 and 3:

$$F_2 = -100(10) + 200(5) = 0$$

EXAMPLE 8.9 A wall of a building with openings for a door and windows as shown in Fig. 8.43*a* is to be designed as a shearwall. The forces to be resisted by the wall panels, collector, and tiedowns are to be determined. Vertical loading on the wall is assumed to be negligible. The shear force from the roof diaphragm is 200 lb/ft (2.92 kN/m).

1. *Load to shear panels:* Total shear:

$$V = 200(36) = 7200 \text{ lb } (32.0 \text{ kN})$$

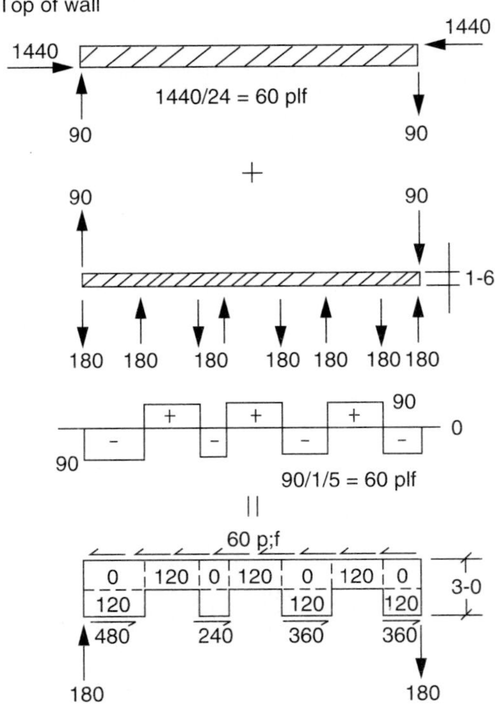

FIG. 8.40 Internal forces and shears on top segment of wall.

Unit shear on wall:

$$v = \frac{7200}{4 + 2 + 3 + 4} = 554 \text{ lb/ft } (8.09 \text{ kN/m})$$

Load per panel:

Panel 1: $554(4) = 2216$ lb (9.856 kN)

Panel 2: $554(2) = 1108$ lb (4.928 kN)

Panel 3: $554(3) = 1662$ lb (7.392 kN)

Panel 4: $554(4) = 2216$ lb (9.856 kN)

2. *Tiedown requirement:* Check panel 1 as shown in Fig. 8.43*b*:

$$T = \frac{2216(8)}{4} = 4432 \text{ lb } (19.71 \text{ kN})$$

Design comment: Note that the tiedown force divided by the panel height is the same as the horizontal unit shear, or $4432/8 = 554$ lb/ft (8.09 kN/m). This has to be true for the panel to be in static equilibrium. The tiedown requirements on the

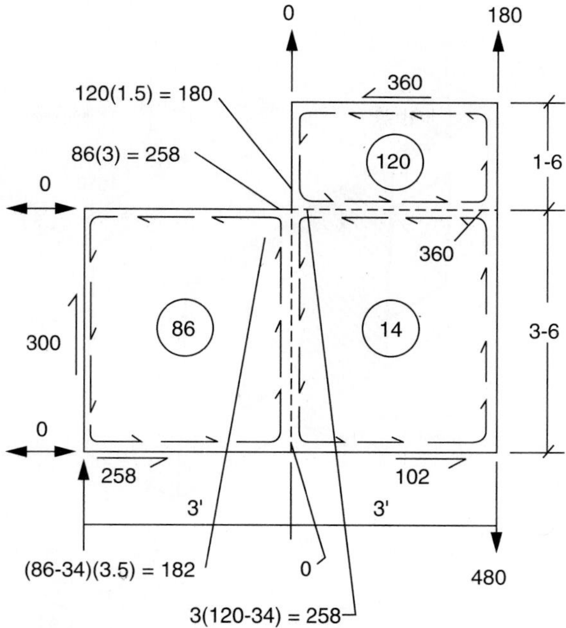

FIG. 8.41 Equilibrium of segment of shearwall with an opening.

other panels are therefore also 4432 lb (19.71 kN). A second panel will be checked to verify the validity of this observation. See Fig. 8.43*b*, panel 2.

$$T = \frac{1108(8)}{2} = 4432 \text{ lb } (19.71 \text{ kN})$$

3. *Collector forces:* Design comment: A member needs to be provided to collect the shear from the roof diaphragm and to redistribute the force this collects into the shearwalls below. The plot in Fig. 8.43*c* shows the net shear intensities per foot along the length of the collector and the total force in the collector at specific points. The shear intensity in the collector above the shearwalls is the difference between the unit load added by the diaphragm and the unit load subtracted by the resistance of the shearwall. Collector splice locations can be picked to coincide with the theoretical locations where the total force is zero. Alternately the force at any splice location can be determined by summing the applied and resisting shears from the end of the collector to the location of interest.

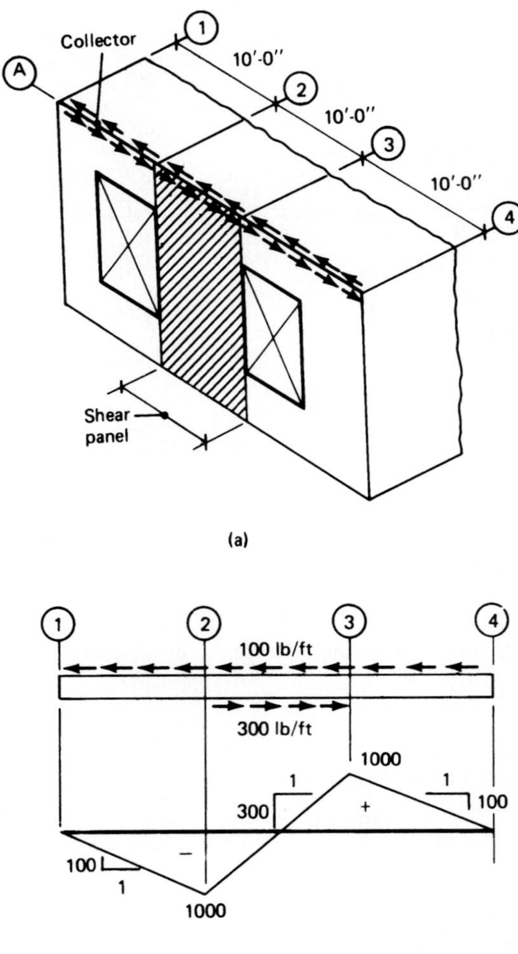

FIG. 8.42 (*a*) Collector at shearwall; (*b*) shear distribution along a collector.

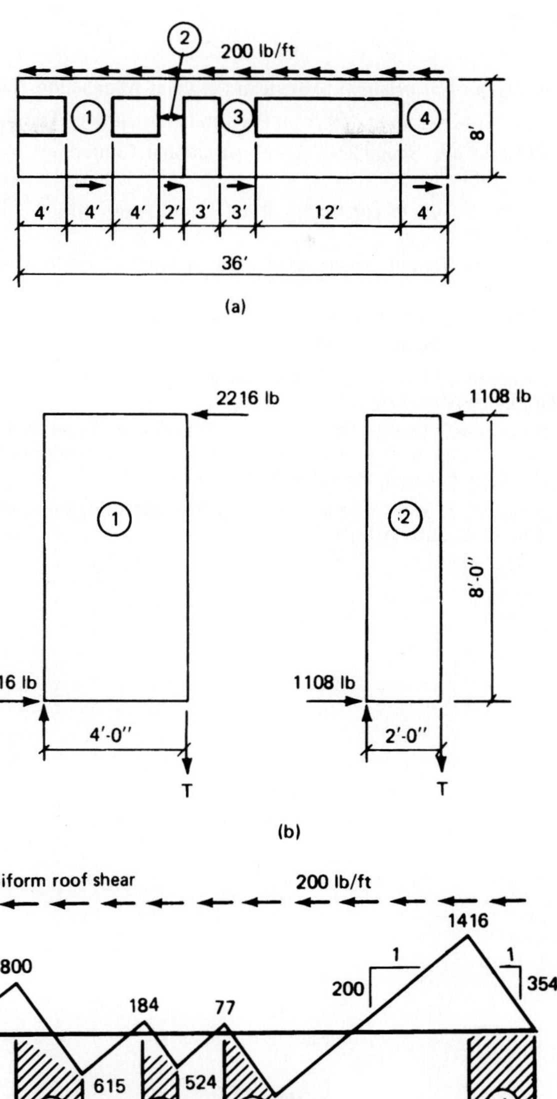

FIG. 8.43 (*a*) Shearwall elevation; (*b*) shearwall panel stability; (*c*) diaphragm–collector–shear panel interaction.

REFERENCES

1. *Plywood Diaphragm Construction,* American Plywood Association, Tacoma, Wash., 1970.
2. *Plywood Design Specification,* American Plywood Association, Tacoma, Wash., 1986.
3. *Uniform Building Code Standards 25-9,* International Conference of Building Officials, Whittier, Calif., 1988.
4. *Guidelines for the Design of Horizontal Wood Diaphragms,* Applied Technology Council, Berkeley, Calif., 1981.
5. *Timber Construction Manual,* American Institute of Timber Construction, Wiley, New York, 1974.
6. John R. Tissell and James R. Elliott, *Plywood Diaphragms,* Research Report 138, American Plywood Association, Tacoma, Wash., 1981.
7. Edward F. Diekmann, "Design of Wood Diaphragms," *Materials Education* **8:**1–2, Pennsylvania State University, 1986.
8. Edward F. Diekmann, "Design Details for the Transfer of Forces in Wood Diaphragms to Vertical Elements," *Proceedings of a Workshop on Design of Horizontal Wood Diaphragms,* Applied Technology Council, Berkeley, Calif., 1979.
9. R. L. Tuomi and W. J. McCutcheon, "Racking Strength of Light-Frame Walls," *J. Struct. Div. ASCE* **104**(ST7), July 1978.

CHAPTER 9
ARCHES AND DOMES

Robert K. Kaseguma, P.E.

9.1 INTRODUCTION

One of the primary advantages of glued-laminated (glulam) wood is that the laminations can be bent to various curvatures with their grain oriented essentially parallel to the length of the member. One common use of curved glulam members is in the fabrication of arches and domes. Arches may take any of several configurations, with some of the more common shapes shown in Figs. 9.1 and 9.3.

As is apparent from these figures, the ability to curve glulams to almost any arch shape, subject to practical considerations, allows the designer of a building much architectural freedom not easily matched by other structural materials. Some of the practicel considerations are the minimum radius of curvature based on the thickness of the laminations used and the species of wood, the ability to cover the structural members with a covering such as wood sheathing, and the cost of the framing. It is generally recommended that t/R shall not exceed 1/100 for hardwoods and southern pine and 1/125 for other softwoods, where t is the thickness of the lamination and R is the bending radius.

In practice, a smaller ratio is used for the most common laminating species because of breakage during the forming; for southern pine the ratio typically used is 1/112 and for Douglas fir, 1/150. Thus the laminating industry utilizes a minimum bending radius of 7 ft 0 in for ¾-in net laminations for southern pine and 9 ft 4 in for ¾-in laminations for Douglas fir.

9.2 ARCHES

9.2.1 Three-Hinged Arches

The majority of glulam arches are of the three-hinged type rather than the two-hinged type. These three-hinged arches are statically determinate, and the reactions can be found easily from the equations of static equilibrium. They are easier to erect than two-hinged arches and utilize simpler connections. Two of the three hinges are located at the supports, and the third hinge is located within the member,

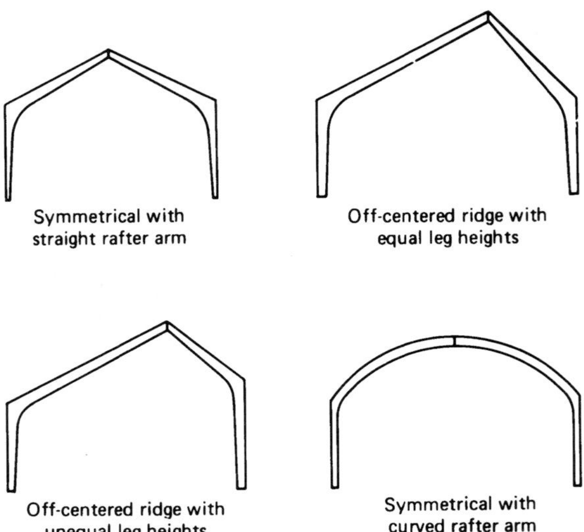

FIG. 9.1 Typical Tudor arch profiles.

usually at the peak. The most common of all the three-hinged types is the Tudor arch, which is used in churches, gymnasiums, and recreational buildings.

Most arches are symmetrical about the centerline, but the designer has considerable freedom in the placement of the interior hinge, which can result in unsymmetrical spans or unequal leg heights and pitches on each side of the centerline, as illustrated in Fig. 9.1. In addition to these arches being used in a conventional paired configuration, such as in a rectangular building, it is common to use them in what is termed a *cross-vault configuration,* where the arch halves frame from the corners of a building to a central compression ring. The building may have any number of sides, but this configuration is often used in four-, six-, and eight-sided structures. Again, as with the traditional opposing paired Tudor arch configuration, the compression hub or ring may be offset from the building center, thus creating many unique shapes. Figure 9.2 illustrates some of these possible building configurations. No matter what the complexity of the shape is, it is still possible to calculate reactions from the conditions of static equilibrium.

The constraints on the shape and size of the arch are primarily those of manufacturing and transportation. The depth of the member may be too large to fit through a stationary planer used to surface the sides of the arch, or the arch shape may be such that it may be too high or wide to be transported on the highways or by rail. It is possible to utilize moment splices at interior joints to permit transporting the members, but moment splices are relatively expensive and do create the possible problem of increasing the deflection of the structure because of the initial slippage in the connectors of the splice. An example of the design of a moment splice for a Tudor arch is given in Sec. 9.2.6. Other typical examples of the variety of shapes possible with three-hinged arches are shown in Fig. 9.3.

The circular shape (Fig. 9.3*a*) is used commonly where large, clear spans are required, such as in athletic field houses or gymnasiums. The circular arches are often supported on concrete buttresses that are either designed as freestanding to resist the vertical and horizontal reactions or with a tension tie across the span to resist the horizontal thrust. The circular shape is quite efficient structurally for

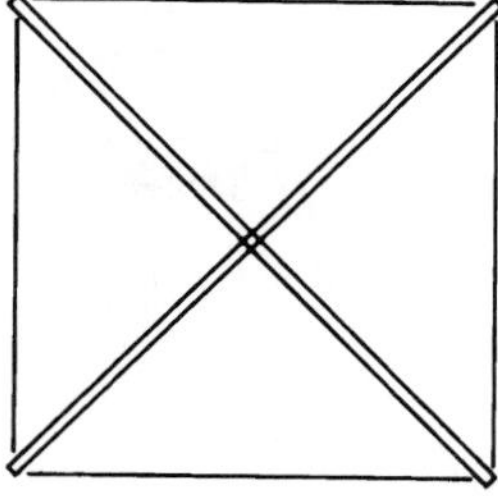

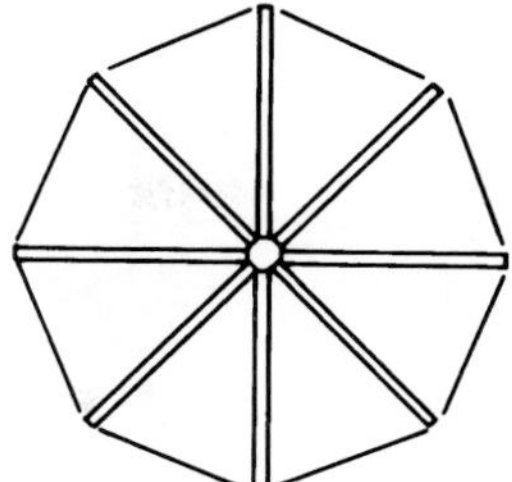

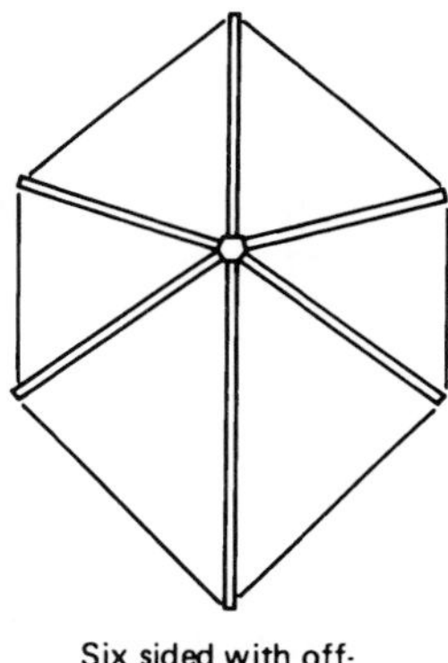

FIG. 9.2 Possible building configurations. Typical plan views of cross-vault arch framing.

vertical uniform loads because the equilibrium polygon is not too different from the circular shape, thus introducing little moment. This is particularly true for rise-to-span ratios in the 0.1 to 0.3 range. The other advantage of the circular arch with a low rise-to-span ratio is that the half-arch shipping width or height is small, thus allowing easier transportation to the job site.

The parabolic shape (Fig. 9.3*b*) is not used commonly by designers. The advantage of the parabolic shape is that it is structurally efficient in resisting vertical uniformly distributed loads, since the equilibrium polygon is a parabola which results in zero moment at all sections of the arch. If a parabolic arch is utilized, the designer should be aware of limitations on the minimum bending radius at the peak of the arch. If the bending radius is too small, the cost of the arch may be very high because of the cost of using thinner laminations than the standard nominal 1 in, which is laminated at a net thickness of 0.75 in or as low as 0.67 in. It is possible to calculate the minimum radius of curvature at the apex of a parabolic arch, given the span and rise of the arch, from

$$R = \frac{L^2}{8T} \tag{9.1}$$

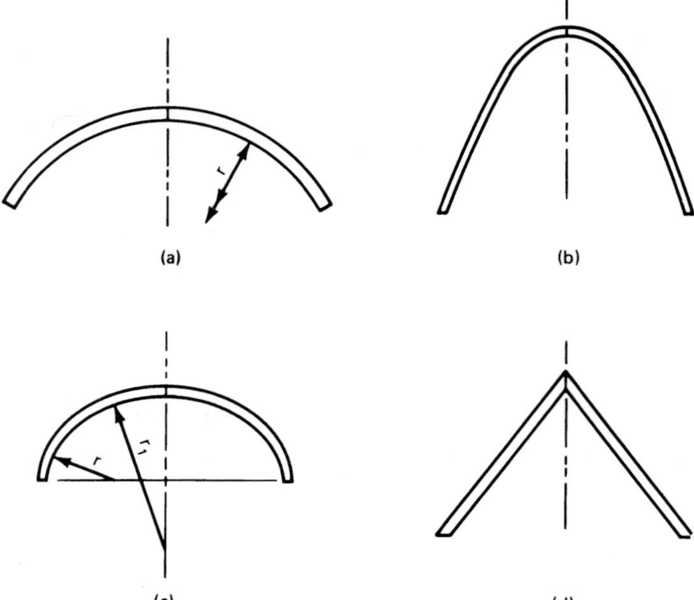

FIG. 9.3 Other three-hinged arch profiles. (*a*) Circular shape; (*b*) parabolic shape; (*c*) three-centered arch; (*d*) A frame.

where R = minimum radius of curvature, feet
T = total rise of arch, feet
L = span of arch, feet

The three-centered arch (Fig. 9.3*c*) is an approximation to an ellipse using circles for the approximation. This arch shape is not often used by designers unless they require a certain height clearance within the building over that provided by a circular arch. An example would be for use as a tennis court enclosure. This shape is not as structurally efficient as the circular or parabolic shapes. The three-centered arch has the disadvantage of having a flat spot at the peak, which creates a potential roofing problem. The minimum radius of curvature also should be checked for problems relating to the bending of the laminations. Because of the curvature of the arch, it is possible that the gaps at the top of the wood decking may be too large to bridge over with roofing materials. This problem also could occur on circular and parabolic arches.

The A-frame or tepee arch (Fig. 9.3*d*) is often used in recreational homes and buildings and in storage buildings for chemicals and fertilizers. The shape is easy to manufacture because it involves no bending of the laminates and is relatively efficient, structurally. An advantage of the shape for bulk storage is that the angle of repose of the stored material can be matched by the arch pitch.

A disadvantage of all the shapes depicted in Fig. 9.3 is that they spring from the ground at an angle other than vertical, and this can cause difficulty in the placement of doors or windows other than at the end walls.

9.2.2 Three-Hinged Tudor Arch

There are various ways in which to design a Tudor arch. The most sophisticated way would be by using a computer program which could handle various loadings and compute all the deflections. To date, most designers do not have access to a program that analyzes Tudor arches, so most arches are still designed by "manual" methods with the aid of calculators. A designer should be aware that a computer or calculator can compute answers to many decimal places, but the variability of the material and the arbitrary assignment of live loads must be kept in mind in determining the overall accuracy of the analysis.

A semigraphic approach to arch design is a "manual" method which combines the advantages of the graphic and the algebraic methods. This method will be illustrated by an example. It should be kept in mind that if an absolute minimum arch design were used from a stress standpoint, it is highly probable that the deflections would be objectionable.

The following steps will be taken to design a three-hinged Tudor arch:

Step 1. Establish the arch geometry, loading, and material specifications. Calculate the corresponding reactions.

Step 2. Determine the arch base design.

Step 3. Determine the lower tangent depth.

Step 4. Make a preliminary upper tangent point depth selection.

Step 5. Make a preliminary peak depth selection.

Step 6. Lay out the preliminary arch profile.

Step 7. Tabulate moments.

Step 8. Make a combined bending and axial stress unity check.

Step 9. Determine the arch peak dimension.

Step 10. Calculate the arch deflections.

EXAMPLE 9.1: DESIGN OF A TUDOR ARCH Given: laminating combination for southern pine 24F-V2 with the following tabulated stresses per 1991 NDS:

$F_b = 2400$ lb/in^2 (16,547 kPa) $F_c = 1600$ lb/in^2 (11,031 kPa)

$F_v = 200$ lb/in^2 (1379 kPa) $F_{c\perp} = 650$ lb/in^2 (4481 kPa)

Assume that laminations other than outer laminations may be in compression.

$$E = 1{,}700{,}000 \text{ lb/in}^2 \text{ (11,721,500 kPa)}$$

Assume a lamination thickness of 0.75 in (19.05 mm). Assumed arch geometry:

Span = 40 ft 0 in (12.192 m).

Leg height = 10 ft 0 in (3.048 m).

Roof pitch = 6 on 12.

Leg is laterally unsupported from base to knee.

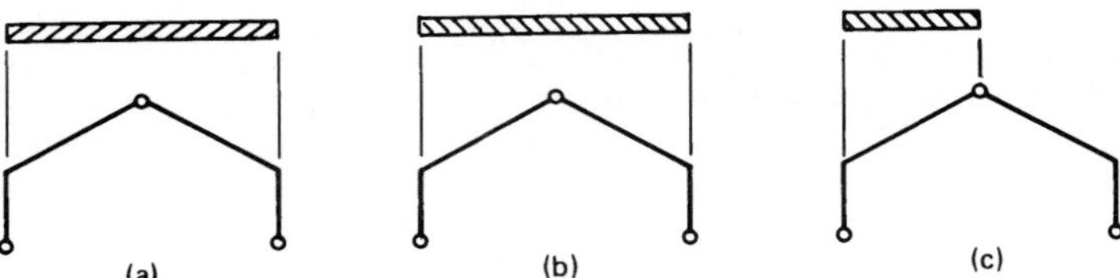

FIG. 9.4 Loading cases for Tudor arch (Example 9.1). (*a*) Dead load; (*b*) snow load; (*c*) unbalanced snow load.

Loading data:

Spacing of arches = 16 ft 0 in (4.877 m).

Dead load = 15 lb/ft^2 (718.2 Pa) on horizontal projection.

Snow load = 30 lb/ft^2 (1436.4 Pa) on horizontal projection.

Unbalanced snow load = 30 lb/ft^2 (1436.4 Pa) on horizontal projection.

See Fig. 9.4 for these loading cases.

Step 1: Determine Arch Geometry and Loading, Calculate Reactions. Equations are available for the most common load cases on three-hinged arches, as given in the *Timber Construction Manual.*[2] For preliminary design purposes, it is sufficiently accurate to use the out-to-out span dimension for the structural span and the total rise to the peak of the arch for the structural rise. Figure 9.5 illustrates the variables to be used in the equations to calculate the vertical reactions and the horizontal thrusts for the various load cases. If the equations cannot be located in

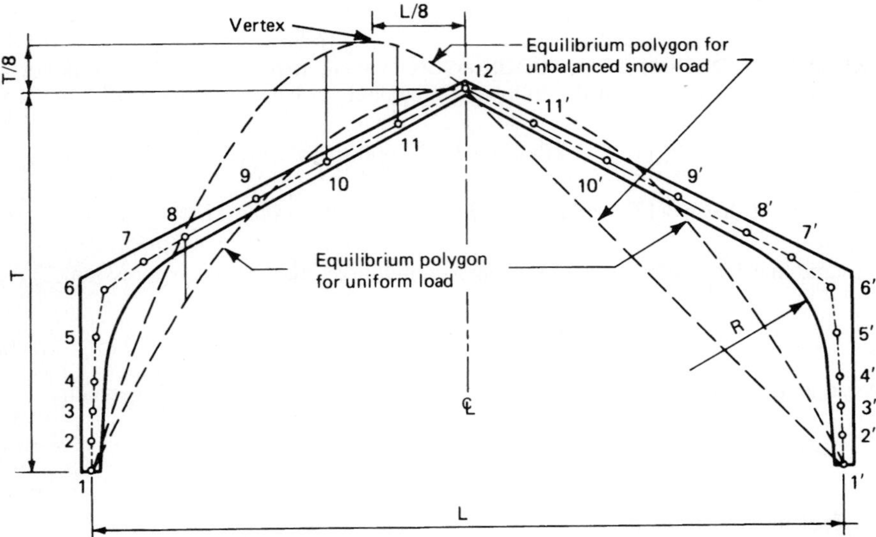

FIG. 9.5 Preliminary arch profile and equilibrium polygons.

a textbook, they can be calculated from the equations of statics $\Sigma F_x = 0$, $\Sigma F_y = 0$, and $\Sigma M_z = 0$.

Case A: For uniformly distributed dead load:

$$V = 0.5wL = 0.5 \times 240 \times 40 = 4800 \text{ lb}$$

$$H = \frac{VL}{4T} = \frac{4800 \times 40}{4 \times 20} = 2400 \text{ lb}$$

Case B: For uniformly distributed snow load (by proportion):

$$V = 4800 \times (30/15) = 9600 \text{ lb}$$

$$H = 2400 \times (30/15) = 4800 \text{ lb}$$

Case C: For full unbalanced snow load on left half:

$$V_L = \tfrac{3}{8}wL = 0.375 \times 480 \times 40 = 7200 \text{ lb}$$

$$V_R = \tfrac{1}{8}wL = 0.125 \times 480 \times 40 = 2400 \text{ lb}$$

$$H_L = H_R = \frac{wL^2}{16T} = \frac{480 \times 40 \times 40}{16 \times 20} = 2400 \text{ lb}$$

Two load combinations will be calculated. The first combination is dead load plus uniformly distributed snow over the full span. The second combination is dead load plus full snow load over one-half the span.

Combination 1:

$$V = 14{,}400 \text{ lb} \qquad H = 7200 \text{ lb}$$

Combination 2:

$$V_L = 12{,}000 \text{ lb} \qquad V_R = 7200 \text{ lb} \qquad H_L = H_R = 4800 \text{ lb}$$

By inspection, it is apparent that the load in combination 1 is more critical for designing the base and lower tangent because the vertical and horizontal reactions are greatest for this load combination.

Step 2: Base Design. Design the base of the arch for the maximum horizontal thrust of 7200 lb for load combination 1. A trial width of the arch is assumed as $b = 5$ in. Calculate the base depth based on the allowable horizontal shear stress $F_V = 200 \times 1.15 = 230 \text{ lb/in}^2$ as for snow loading:

$$d = \frac{1.5H}{bF_V} = \frac{1.5 \times 7200}{5 \times 230} = 9.4 \text{ in}$$

Try 10 in:

$$f_V = \frac{1.5 \times 7200}{5 \times 10} = 216 \text{ lb/in}^2 \qquad \text{OK}$$

Step 3: Lower Tangent Design. An approximation for the lower tangent location above the base for a minimum bending radius for southern pine of 7 ft 0 in can be found graphically. The exterior profile of the arch is laid out in Fig. 9.6. Using a radius of 8 ft 4 in, the lower tangent is located at $y = 4.85$ ft. The radius of 8 ft 4 in assumes a preliminary lower tangent depth of 1 ft 4 in and is the sum of 1 ft 4 in and 7 ft 0 in. The moment at the lower tangent is calculated to be

$$M_{LT} = 4.85 \times 12H = 4.85 \times 12 \times 7200 = 419{,}040 \text{ in·lb}$$

Because combined axial and bending stresses exist at the lower tangent, to find the depth required at the lower tangent for bending, use an allowable bending stress of 1855 lb/in². This value is calculated as follows:

$$F'_b = 2400 \times 1.15 \times 0.84 \times 0.8 = 1855 \text{ lb/in}^2$$

where 1.15 = increase for load duration as for snow
0.84 = curvature factor for a 7-ft bending radius and 0.75-in-thick lamination
0.8 = arbitrary reduction for combined axial and bending stress effects

$$f_b = \frac{6M}{bd^2}$$

or

$$d = \sqrt{\frac{6M}{1855b}} = \sqrt{\frac{6 \times 419{,}040}{1855 \times 5}} = 16.46 \text{ in}$$

Try 17.25 in, assuming lamination multiples of 0.75 in. Make a preliminary combined stress unity check. Recall that the leg is laterally unsupported from the base to the knee, or effective length = 10 ft, and therefore $\ell_e/d = (10 \times 12)/5 = 24 < 50$(OK) and $K_e = 1.0$:

$$F_{cE}: \quad \frac{K_{cE}E'}{(\ell_2/d)^2} = \frac{0.418 \times 1{,}700{,}000}{(24)^2} = 1234 \text{ lb/in}^2$$

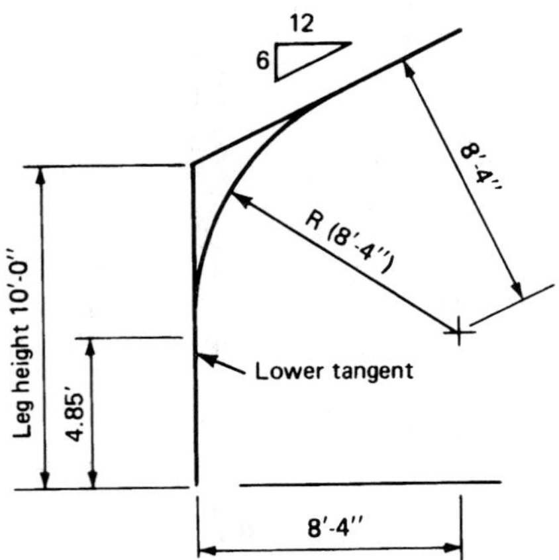

FIG. 9.6 Preliminary arch layout to locate lower tangent.

$$F_c^* = F_c \times C_D = 1600 \times 1.15 = 1840 \text{ lb/in}^2$$

$$\frac{F_{cE}}{F_c^*} = \frac{1234}{1840} = 0.671$$

$$C_p = \frac{1 + (F_{cE}/F_c^*)}{2c} - \sqrt{\left[\frac{1 + (F_{cE}/F_c^*)}{2c}\right]^2 - \frac{(F_{cE}/F_c^*}{c}}$$

$$= \frac{1 + 0.671}{2 \times 0.9} - \sqrt{\left[\frac{1 + 0.671}{2 \times 0.9}\right]^2 - \frac{0.671}{0.9}} = 0.587$$

$$F'_c = F_c^* \times C_p = 1840 \times 0.587 = 1080 \text{ lb/in}^2$$

Since F'_c is less than the allowable compressive stress parallel to grain of $1600 \times 1.15 = 1840$ lb/in^2, use $F'_c = 1080$ lb/in^2.

Combined stress unity check at lower tangent:

$$\left(\frac{f_c}{F'_c}\right)^2 + \frac{f_{b1}}{F'_{b1}[1 - (f_c/F_{cE1})]} \leq 1.0$$

$$f_{b1} = \frac{6 \times 419{,}040}{5 \times 17.25^2} = 1690 \text{ lb/in}^2$$

$$F'_b = 2400 \times 1.15 C_c$$

where C_c is the curvature factor calculated as

$$C_c = 1 - 2000\left(\frac{t}{R}\right)^2 = 1 - 2000\left(\frac{0.75}{7 \times 12}\right)^2 = 0.84$$

Hence

$$F'_{b1} = 2400 \times 1.15 \times 0.84 = 2318 \text{ lb/in}^2$$

$$f_c = \frac{14{,}400}{5 \times 17.25} = 167 \text{ lb/in}^2$$

$$F_{cE1} = F_{cE} = 1234 \text{ lb/in}^2$$

$$\left(\frac{167}{1080}\right)^2 + \frac{1690}{2318[1 - (167/1234)]} = 0.024 + 0.843 = 0.867 < 1.0 \qquad \text{OK}$$

Note that in the bending portion of the unity check the volume factor was not taken into account to reduce the allowable stress.

The volume factor for a glulam beam is given as

$$C_v = K_L\left(\frac{21}{2}\right)^{1/x}\left(\frac{12}{d}\right)^{1/x}\left(\frac{5.125}{b}\right)^{1/x}$$

where K_L, L, d, and b represent the loading condition coefficient, the span length in feet, the depth of the member in inches, and the width of the member in inches, and x is a coefficient of 20 for southern pine and 10 for all other species. $K_L = 1.0$ for uniformly distributed load.

Step 4: Preliminary Upper Tangent Depth Selection. In this example it is assumed that the knee of the arch will be integrally glued with the balance of the half-span and will not have to be mechanically fastened to the half-span. The upper tangent can usually be made 1.5 to 4 in less in depth than the lower tangent depth if stress is the governing factor for vertical, uniformly distributed loads. This is because the vertical distance from the upper tangent to the equilibrium polygon is less than the distance from the lower tangent to the base. If the arch is loaded with triangular loads or wind loads, the upper tangent depth may be the same as the lower tangent depth or larger. For the upper tangent a preliminary depth of 17.25 − 2.25 = 15 in is selected.

Step 5: Preliminary Peak Depth Selection. The preliminary peak depth is taken as 1.5 times the width of the arch or one-half the depth of the upper tangent, whichever is larger. In this instance, both depths are 7.5 in, so a preliminary peak depth of 8 in is selected. The actual peak depth will be determined by the structural requirements of the rafter.

Step 6: Layout of Preliminary Arch Profile. Having established the base depth at 10 in, the lower tangent depth at 17.25 in, the upper tangent depth at 15 in, and the peak depth at 8 in, it is now possible to sketch the profile of the arch and the neutral surface as shown in Fig. 9.5. In order to design the upper tangent and the peak of the arch, it is necessary to know the bending moments and axial forces at several points along the neutral surface of the arch. The accuracy of the design will be improved as the number of points used is increased. The number of points utilized is also influenced by the span of the arch, with more points needed on the large spans. Usually 12 points per half-span will suffice, where point 1 is the base and point 12 the peak.

The points are located on the neutral surface of the arch, as indicated on Fig. 9.5. It is sufficiently accurate to draw the arch to scale at ¼, ⅜, or ½ in = 1 ft 0 in, depending on the size of the arch span, and to scale the x and y coordinates from the sketch. The moments and axial forces are calculated at all the points and used to determine the structural depths required. For the load cases selected, uniformly distributed dead load and uniformly distributed snow load, the equilibrium polygon is a parabola with the bases at points 1 and 1′ and the vertex at point 12. Various methods are available by which to draw a parabola, and the parallelogram method was used for this example. The method is explained in basic drawing texts such as *Technical Drawing.*[3] The curves for load cases A and B are shown in Fig. 9.5. For the full unbalanced live load, case C, the apex of the parabola shifts to the loaded side of the span at a location $L/8$ to the left of point 12 and $T/16$ above point 12. Using point V as the vertex, a new parabola is drawn from point V to point 1. The portion of the parabola from V to point 12 (the peak) can be drawn from symmetry. On the unloaded half-span from the peak, point 12 to the base, point 1′, the equilibrium polygon is a straight line.

Step 7: Tabulation of Moments. Utilizing the reactions for load cases A, B, and C and the equilibrium polygons from Fig. 9.5, the moments at each of the points can be determined and tabulated. For example, at point 8, which is approximately at the upper tangent, the moment for uniformly distributed dead load is the scaled distance vertically down from point 8 to the equilibrium polygon multiplied by the thrust for dead load, or 3.5 ft × 2400 lb = 8400 ft·lb. The moment for uniformly distributed live load is 3.5 ft × 4800 lb = 16,800 ft·lb. The moment for unbalanced live load on the loaded side is the vertical distance up to the equilibrium polygon of -0.33 ft × 2400 lb = -792 ft·lb. In general, for vertical loads, the vertical distance from the point on the neutral surface to the equilibrium polygon is multiplied by the horizontal thrust for the particular case to calculate the bending moment at the point. For horizontal loads, such as for wind load, the horizontal distance from the point on the neutral surface to the equilibrium polygon is multiplied by the vertical reaction for the particular load case to calculate the bending moment at the point.

The selection of the signs for the moments is arbitrarily set such that the moments that cause the inside face, or soffit, of the arch to be in compression are positive moments. The moments for this example are tabulated in Table 9.1.

Step 8: Combined Stress Unity Check. All points on the arch are subject to bending moments and axial forces. The axial force at point 8 is determined by laying out the slope of the arch rafter at point 8 and the slope of the equilibrium polygon on the same layout. In this example for uniformly distributed live load, the thrust is 4800 lb, the slope of the rafter is 27° (angle A) off the horizontal, and the slope of the equilibrium polygon (angle B) is 62.5° off the horizontal. The vertical shear at point 8 is $\tan B \times H = 1.92 \times 7200 = 13{,}831$ lb. The resultant of H and the vertical shear V is $R = 15{,}593$ lb.

TABLE 9.1 Moments at All Points for All Loadings

Point	Case A M_{DL}, ft·lb	Case B M_{SL}, ft·lb	Case C M_{USL}, ft·lb	Combination 1 $M_{DL} + M_{SL}$, ft·lb	Combination 2 $M_{DL} + M_{USL}$, ft·lb
1	0	0	0	0	0
2	3,600	7,200	3,600	10,800	7,200
3	6,408	12,816	6,408	19,224	12,816
4	10,000	20,000	10,000	30,000	20,000
5	14,400	28,800	14,000	43,200	28,400
6	19,200	38,400	16,400	57,600	19,200
7	13,200	26,400	6,000	39,600	19,200
8	8,400	16,800	−800	25,200	7,600
9	1,200	2,400	−10,600	3,600	−9,400
10	−2,400	−4,800	−14,000	−7,200	−16,400
11	−2,800	−5,600	−10,400	−8,400	−13,200
12	0	0	0	0	0
11′	−2,800	−5,600	4,008	−8,400	1,208
10′	−2,400	−4,800	8,000	−7,200	5,600
9′	12,000	2,400	12,000	3,600	13,200
8′	8,400	16,800	16,800	25,200	25,200
7′	13,200	26,400	18,600	39,600	31,800
6′	19,200	38,400	20,200	57,600	39,400
5′	14,400	28,800	14,800	43,200	29,200
4′	51,000	20,000	10,200	30,000	20,200
3′	6,408	12,816	6,600	19,224	1,300
2′	3,600	7,200	2,200	10,800	5,800
1′	0	0	0	0	0

Note: 1 ft·lb = 1.355 N·m.

$$\text{Angle } C = \text{angle } B - \text{angle } A = 62.5° - 27° = 35.5°$$

The axial force at point 8 is

$$\cos 35.5° \times 15{,}593 = 12{,}594 \text{ lb}$$

The shear at point 8 is

$$\sin 35.5° \times 15{,}593 = 9055 \text{ lb}$$

See Fig. 9.7 for a summary of these forces at point 8.

A unity check can now be performed. Assume that the rafter arm is continuously laterally braced by roof decking, thus classifying it as a short column:

$$f_b = \frac{6 \times 25{,}000 \times 12}{5 \times 15^2} = 1600 \text{ lb/in}^2$$

$$F'_b = 2400 \times 1.15 \times 0.84 = 2318 \text{ lb/in}^2$$

$$f_c = \frac{P}{A} = \frac{12{,}594}{5 \times 15} = 168 \text{ lb/in}^2$$

$$F'_c = 1600 \times 1.15 = 1840 \text{ lb/in}^2$$

$$\left(\frac{f_c}{F'_c}\right)^2 + \frac{f_{b1}}{F'_{b1}[1 - (f_c/F_{cE1})]} = \left(\frac{168}{1080}\right)^2 + \frac{1600}{2318[1 - (168/1234)]}$$

$$= 0.024 + 0.799 = 0.823 < 1.0 \qquad \text{OK}$$

The unity checks are carried out for all the points on the arch for load combinations 1 and 2. In many cases it is not necessary to carry out the entire unity check by evaluating the moment at a critical point and by simply checking the bending stress only.

Step 9: Determination of Peak Depth. By inspection of Fig. 9.5 it appears that the moments due to unbalanced load may affect the design of the rafter because of the vertical distance between the arch axis and the equilibrium polygon for load

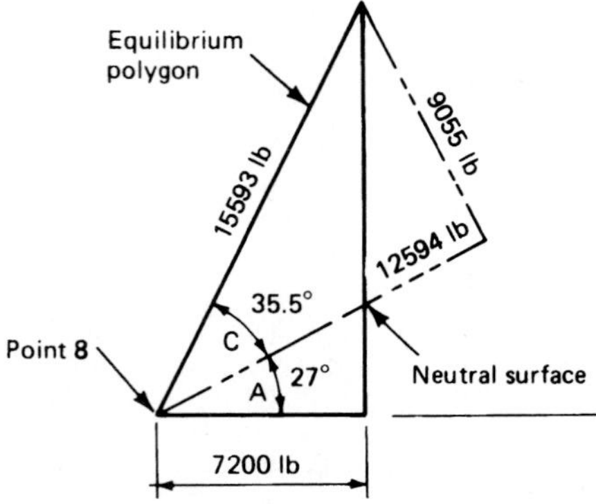

FIG. 9.7 Calculation of axial force at point 8.

case C. A check of the moments due to dead load plus full unbalanced snow load (on the loaded side), load combination 2, should be made.

At point 10,

$$M_{LLU} = -8 \times 2400 \times 12 = -230{,}400 \text{ in·lb}$$

$$M_{DL} = -1 \times 2400 \times 12 = -28{,}800 \text{ in·lb}$$

$$M_T = 259{,}200 \text{ in·lb}$$

$$d = \sqrt{\frac{6M}{bF_b}} = \sqrt{\frac{6 \times 259{,}200}{5 \times 2400 \times 1.15 \times 0.9}} = 11.19 \text{ in}$$

At point 11,

$$M_{LLU} = -4.25 \times 2400 \times 12 = -122{,}400 \text{ in·lb}$$

$$M_{DL} = -1 \times 2400 \times 12 = -28{,}800 \text{ in·lb}$$

$$M_T = 151{,}200 \text{ in·lb}$$

$$d = \sqrt{\frac{6 \times 151{,}200}{5 \times 2400 \times 1.15 \times 0.9}} = 8.5 \text{ in}$$

Thus the sizes selected are adequate to provide the required depths in the rafter.

Note: A factor of 0.9 was arbitrarily used to reduce the allowable bending stress to account for the effect of combined bending and axial stresses. For a more accurate analysis, a unity check should be performed.

Step 10: Calculation of Arch Deflection. There are instances where the designer must calculate the deflection of the Tudor arch at certain points on the arch due to specific restrictions, such as clearance between the leg and the wall construction or vertical deflection of the peak to match a rigid end wall. Thus the two points on the arch that are typically checked are the vertical deflection of the peak and the horizontal deflection of the knee area at the top of the wall. The unit-load method is used to calculate these deflections. By one application of the unit load, only the deflection component in the direction of the unit load at its point of application can be determined. The example problem will be checked for vertical deflection at the crown for load combination 1 and for horizontal deflection at the knee for the same load combination.

The full arch span is divided into 22 segments labeled A through K and K' through A'. The depth of the segment is taken as the average depth of the section between adjacent points. For the vertical deflection at the peak, a unit load is placed at the peak directed vertically downward, as shown in Fig. 9.8. If the arch profile has changed from the preliminary sizes of Fig. 9.5, the arch should be redrawn with the final sizes before calculating the deflections. Since the profile has not changed significantly, the equilibrium polygons can be traced on the new drawing of Fig. 9.8.

The moments at stations A through A' are tabulated for load combination 1 by multiplying the vertical distance from the station to the equilibrium polygon for uniformly distributed load over the full span times the horizontal thrust of dead

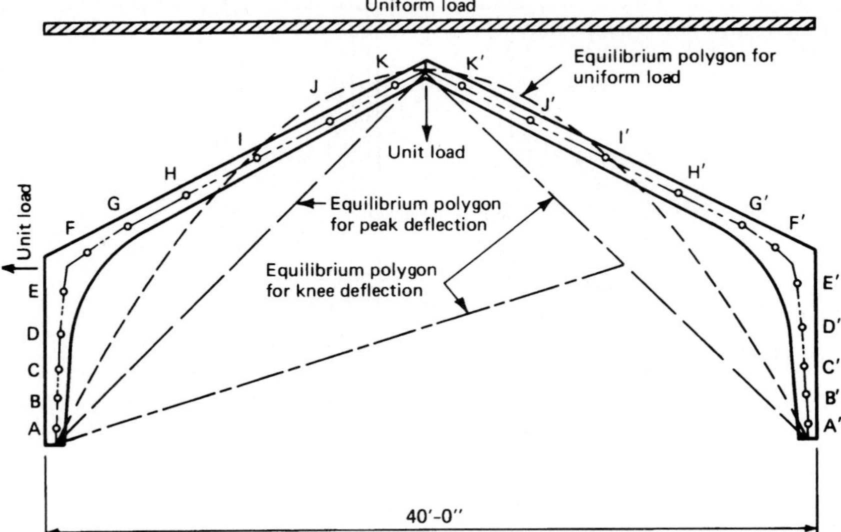

FIG. 9.8 Final arch profile for deflection calculations.

load plus snow load of 7200 lb. Since the loading of the full span is symmetrical about the centerline of the span and the unit load is symmetrical for the full span, it is necessary to compute only the half-span values and multiply these results by 2. The tabulated values are found in Table 9.2 with a resulant vertical deflection under full snow plus dead load of 1.23 in. The designer must compare this deflec-

TABLE 9.2 Deflection Calculations for Vertical Deflection

Station	M, in·lb	m, in	s, in	I, in^4	Mms/I, lb/in
A	−57,600	−6.75	18	720	9,720
B	−194,400	−13.5	18	915.4	51,605
C	−317,088	−21.5	18	1,143.3	107,332
D	−453,600	−32.0	27	1,707	229,590
E	−604,800	−44.5	30	5,070	159,252
F	−554,400	−49.0	30	5,070	160,743
G	−374,112	−45.0	30	1,406	359,211
H	−151,200	−36.0	50	1,143	238,110
I	32,400	−25.5	50	915	−45,148
J	108,000	−15.0	50	555	−145,946
K	64,800	−5.0	50	213	−76,056
					1,048,413

Vertical deflection at peak = 2 × 1,048,413/1.7 × 10^6 = 1.23 in.

Note: 1 in·lb = 0.113 N·m.

tion with the overall performance of the structure to determine whether it is satisfactory.

To calculate the horizontal deflection near the knee at station *E*, apply the unit load at station *E* in the horizontal direction in which the deflection is anticipated. If the assumption is invalid, the sign of the deflection will be negative. Calculate the vertical reactions and thrusts due to the unit load as in Fig. 9.9. Although the moments due to uniformly distributed load (loading combination 1) are symmetrical, the unit load is not symmetrical, which necessitates tabulating the moments, unit moments, and so on, for both half-spans. This tabulation is given in Table 9.3. In this example, the calculated deflection is 0.68 in, which must be evaluated in consideration of its effect on the contiguous wall construction.

The knee area, which encompasses the area between the lower and the upper tangents, is critical in controlling the vertical deflection at the peak and the horizontal deflection of the knee. Since this area is subjected to the highest moments, an increase in either tangent depth greatly influences the amount of deflection. In cases where the outer portion of the knee is removed during fabrication for shipping clearance or planer clearance, the deflection of the arch may become the critical factor in the design. The stress in the arch in the knee area should be checked when the outer portion of the knee is removed.

9.2.3 Three-Hinged Tudor Arch with Steeply Pitched Roof

The same basic design steps are followed in the analysis of a Tudor arch of steep pitch as those for an arch with a flat pitch, but the loading cases may be more complex for the steeply pitched roof. The design of a Tudor arch with a steeply pitched roof is illustrated in Example 9.2.

EXAMPLE 9.2: DESIGN OF THREE-HINGED TUDOR ARCH WITH STEEP ROOF PITCH The deflection calculation is omitted in this example, but the procedure is the same as that followed in Example 9.1. In most designs, the calculation of the loads to satisfy the governing code is a critical part of the actual design, as is illustrated in this example.

Given: laminating combination for Douglas fir 24F-V3 with the following tabulated allowable design stresses per AITC 117[1] for dry-use conditions:

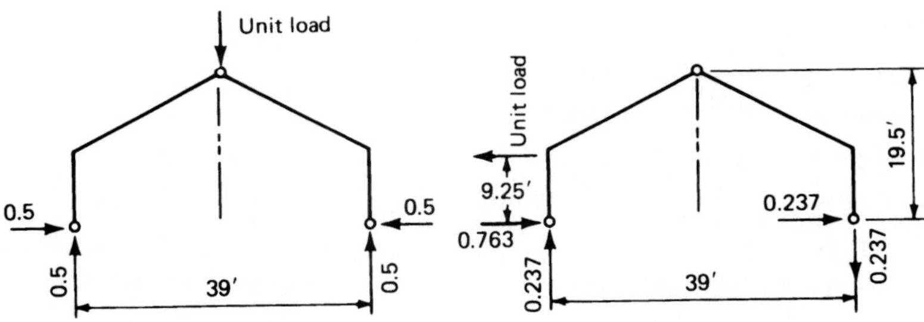

FIG. 9.9 Application of unit loads.

TABLE 9.3 Deflection Calculations for Knee Area

Station	M, in·lb	m, in	s, in	I, in^4	Mms/I, lb/in
A	−57,600	−7.63	18	720	10,987
B	−194,400	−26.2	18	915.4	100,152
C	−317,088	−35.74	18	1,143.3	178,421
D	−453,600	−51.8	27	1,707	371,649
E	−604,800	−73.2	30	5,070	261,961
F	−554,400	−77	30	5,070	252,596
G	−374,112	−67.5	30	1,406	538,817
H	−151,200	−55.5	50	1,143	367,087
I	32,400	−40	50	915	−70,820
J	108,000	−32.75	50	555	−318,649
K	64,800	−8.30	50	213	−126,253
K'	64,800	2.6	50	213	39,549
J'	108,000	7.35	50	555	71,513
I'	32,400	12.33	50	915	21,830
H'	−151,200	17.3	50	1,143	−114,425
G'	−374,112	21.1	30	1,406	−168,430
F'	−554,400	23.23	30	5,070	−76,205
E'	−604,800	21.8	30	5,070	−78,016
D'	−453,600	15.9	27	1,707	−114,078
C'	−317,088	11	18	1,143	−54,929
B'	−194,400	6.4	18	915.4	−24,465
A'	−57,600	2.13	18	720	−3,067
					1,065,221

Deflection near knee = 1,065,221/(1.7 × 10^6) = 0.68 in.

Note: 1 in·lb = 0.113 N·m.

F_b = 2400 lb/in^2 (16,547.4 kPa) F_c = 1600 lb/in^2 (11,031.6 kPa)

F_v = 165 lb/in^2 (1137.6 kPa) $F_{c\perp}$ = 385 lb/in^2 (4482 kPa)

E = 1,700,000 lb/in^2 (12,410,000 kPa)

Assume a lamination thickness of 0.75 in (19 mm).

Assume that the wall construction is such that the walls laterally brace the arch legs and permit the legs to take a uniformly distributed horizontal wind load.

Assumed arch geometry:

Span = 40 ft 0 in (12.19 m).

Leg height = 10 ft 0 in (3.05 m).

Roof pitch = 12 on 12.

Arch spacing = 16 ft 0 in (4.88 m).

Step 1: Determine Arch Geometry and Loading, Calculate Reactions. Loading data: Assume the governing code is the *Uniform Building Code* (UBC). For the assumed location, the loadings are:

No snow load.

Minimum live load = 12 lb/ft^2 (574.6 Pa) as applied to the horizontal projection.

Dead load = shingles and felt 3 lb/ft^2 (143.6 Pa) plus rigid insulation 2.5 lb/ft^2 (119.7 Pa) plus 3 in wood decking 8 lb/in^2 (383 Pa) plus arch (assumed) 1.5 lb/ft^2 (71.8 Pa); i.e., total dead load = 15 lb/ft^2 (718.2 Pa).

The calculated dead load of 15 lb/ft^2 is the actual weight per square foot of roof. In order to place this weight on the horizontal projection, the dead load must be divided by the cosine of the roof pitch:

$$\text{Dead load} = \frac{15}{\cos 45°} = 21.2 \text{ lb/ft}^2$$

$$w_{LL} = 12 \times 16 = 192 \text{ lb/ft} \qquad w_{DL} = 21.2 \times 16 = 339.2 \approx 340 \text{ lb/ft}$$

The basic wind speed is given as 80 mi/h. From the UBC,

$$p = C_e C_q q_s I$$

where p = design wind pressure, lb/ft^2

C_e = combined height, exposure, and gust factor coefficient, as given in Table 23-G of UBC

C_q = pressure coefficient for portion of structure under consideration, as given in Table 23-H of UBC

q_s = wind stagnation pressure at the standard height of 30 ft, as given in Table 23-F of UBC

I = importance factor, as set forth in sec. 2311(h) of UBC

For this example,

$$C_e = 1.2$$

$$C_{q1} = 0.8 \text{ for windward wall (inward)}$$

$$C_{q2} = 0.4 \text{ for windward roof (inward)}$$

$$C_{q3} = 0.7 \text{ for leeward roof (outward)}$$

$$C_{q4} = 0.5 \text{ for leeward wall (outward)}$$

$$q_s = 17 \text{ lb/ft}^2 \qquad I = 1.15$$

$$p_1 = 1.2 \times 0.8 \times 17 \times 1.15 = 18.77 \text{ lb/ft}^2$$

$$p_2 = 1.2 \times 0.4 \times 17 \times 1.15 = 9.38 \text{ lb/ft}^2$$

$$p_3 = 1.2 \times 0.7 \times 17 \times 1.15 = 16.42 \text{ lb/ft}^2$$

$$p_4 = 1.2 \times 0.5 \times 17 \times 1.15 = 11.73 \text{ lb/ft}^2$$

The uniformly distributed wind loads are

$$w_1 = p_1 \times 16 = 300.3 \text{ lb/ft}$$

$$w_2 = p_2 \times 16 = 150 \text{ lb/ft}$$

$$w_3 = p_3 \times 16 = 262.7 \text{ lb/ft}$$

$$w_4 = p_4 \times 16 = 188 \text{ lb/ft}$$

The total uniform wind loads as applied to the walls and roof planes are

$$W_1 = 300.3 \times 10 = 3003 \text{ lb}$$

$$W_2 = 150.0 \times 28.28 = 4242 \text{ lb}$$

$$W_3 = 262.7 \times 28.28 = 7429.2 \text{ lb}$$

$$W_4 = 188 \times 10 = 1880 \text{ lb}$$

The reactions for the uniformly distributed vertical loads, i.e., dead and minimum live loads, are

$$V_{DL} = 0.5wL = 0.5 \times 340 \times 40 = 6800 \text{ lb}$$

$$H_{DL} = \frac{V_{DL}L}{4T} = \frac{6800 \times 40}{4 \times 30} = 2267 \text{ lb}$$

$$V_{LL} = 0.5wL = 0.5 \times 192 \times 40 = 3840 \text{ lb}$$

$$H_{LL} = \frac{V_{LL}L}{4T} = \frac{3840 \times 40}{4 \times 30} = 1280 \text{ lb}$$

The reactions for the wind loading will be found from the three equations of static equilibrium $\Sigma F_x = 0$, $\Sigma F_y = 0$, and $\Sigma M_z = 0$. Prepare a sketch of the arch profile with the wind loads applied, as shown in Fig. 9.10.

$$\Sigma M_A = 0 = +40V_B - (3003 \times 5) - (4242 \times 21.21)$$
$$+ (7429.2 \times 7.07) - (1880 \times 5)$$

$$V_B = 1546.6 \text{ lb}$$

$$\Sigma F_y = 0 = +V_B - V_A - 4242 \cos 45° + 7429.2 \cos 45°$$

$$V_A = 3800.3 \text{ lb}$$

$$\Sigma M_C \text{ (right)} = 0 = +(1546.6 \times 20) - 30H_B$$
$$+ (7429.2 \times 14.14) + (1880 \times 25)$$

$$H_B = 6099 \text{ lb}$$

$$\Sigma M_C \text{ (left)} = 0 = -(3800.3 \times 20) + 30H_A - (3003 \times 25) - (4242 \times 14.14)$$

$$H_A = 7035 \text{ lb}$$

Check with $\Sigma F_x = 0$:

$$\Sigma F_x = -7035 - 6099 + 3003 + 4242 \cos 45° + 7429.2 \cos 45° + 1880 \approx 0$$

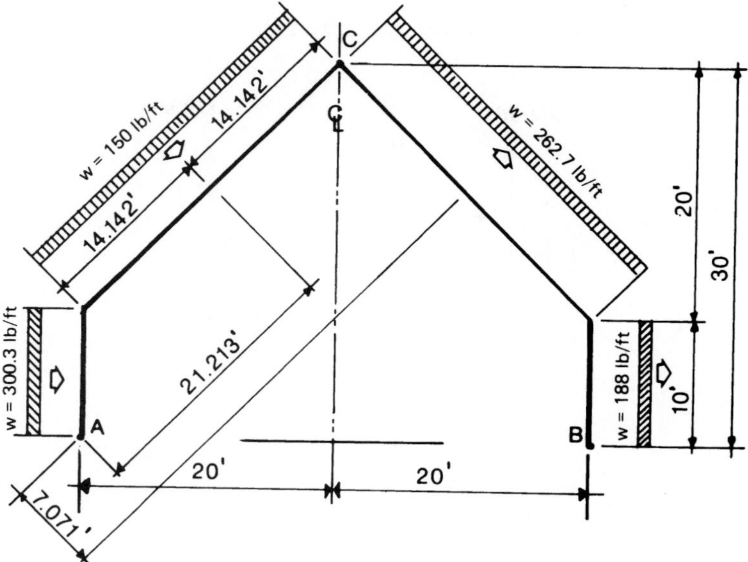

FIG. 9.10 Arch profile with wind loads applied (Example 9.2).

The loading combinations to be checked are (1) dead load plus minimum live load and (2) dead load plus wind load. The free-body diagrams for the two loading combinations are shown in Fig. 9.11 for combination 1 and in Fig. 9.12 for combination 2.

By inspection of the reactions for loading combinations 1 and 2, it is apparent that the maximum thrust of 8366 lb occurs at the leeward base for loading combination 2 (dead load + wind load). This thrust will affect the base, the lower tangent, and possibly the rafter design.

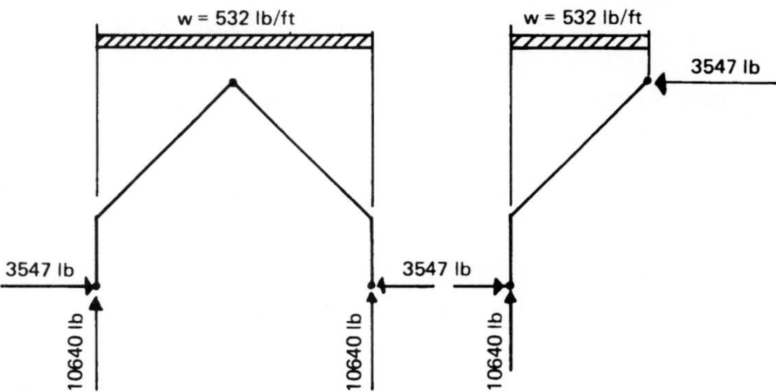

FIG. 9.11 Free-body diagrams for loading combination 1.

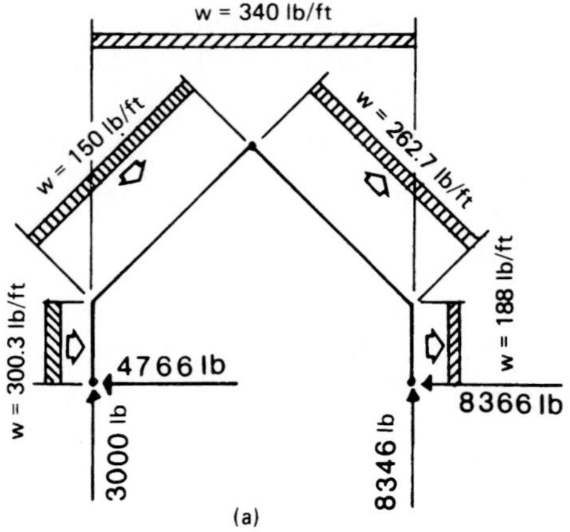

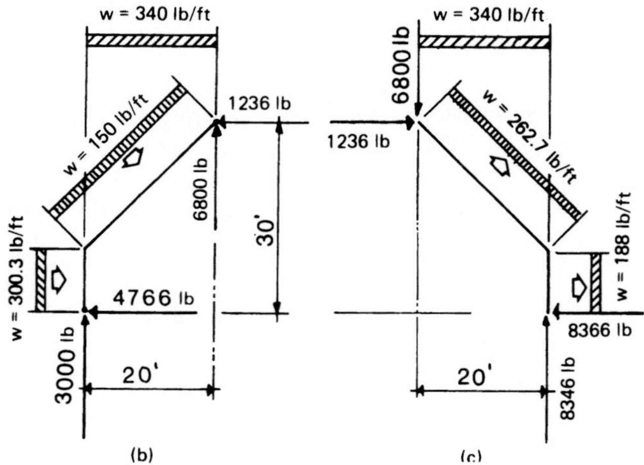

FIG. 9.12 Free-body diagrams for loading combination 2.

Step 2: Base Design

$$d = \frac{1.5H}{bF_V}$$

Assume that $b = 5.125$ in wide and

$$F_V = 1.60 \times 165 = 264 \text{ lb/in}^2$$

Hence

$$d = \frac{1.5 \times 8366}{5.125 \times 264} = 9.27 \text{ in}$$

Try 12 in.

Step 3: Lower Tangent Design. For Douglas fir use a trial radius of 10 ft 8 in to determine the location of the lower tangent. The 10-ft 8-in dimension is arrived at by adding 1 ft 4 in to the minimum bending radius of 9 ft 4 in for Douglas fir and 0.75-in thickness laminations. The 1 ft 4 in is an arbitrary amount to add to approximate a tangent depth of 1 ft 4 in. This portion of the arch is drawn to scale in Fig. 9.13. The distance up from the base to the lower tangent point is scaled as 5.58 ft. Then

$$M_{LT} = 5.58 \times 8366 \times 12 = 560{,}187 \text{ in·lb}$$

$$d = \sqrt{\frac{6M_{LT}}{F'_b b}} = \sqrt{\frac{6 \times 560{,}187}{3145 \times 5.125}} = 14.44 \text{ in}$$

Try 16½ in for ¾-in laminations.

For wind loading use $F'_b = 3145$ lb/in², which allows for an increase for wind loading but reduces the allowable stress for some axial stress:

$$F'_b = 2400 \times 1.60 \times 0.91 \times 0.90 = 3145 \text{ lb/in}^2$$

where 1.60 = load duration factor for wind loading
0.91 = curvature factor
0.90 = the arbitrary factor to allow for combined bending and axial stresses

Since the leg is laterally braced by the wall, $\ell_e/d = 0$ and it is classified as a short column:

$$F'_c = 1600 \times 1.60 = 2560 \text{ lb/in}^2$$

Calculate the volume factor:

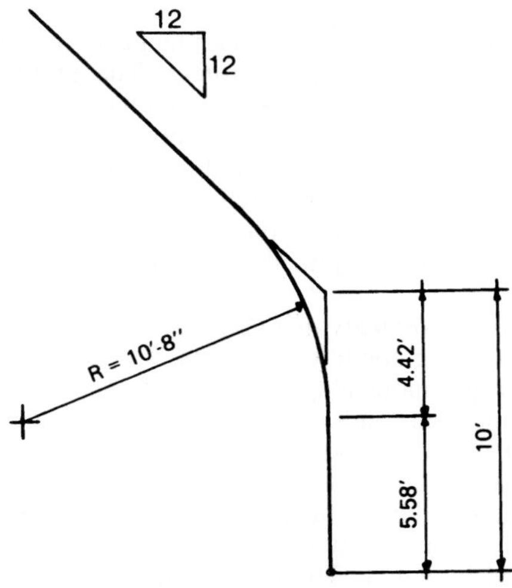

FIG. 9.13 Location of lower tangent point.

TABLE 9.4 Point Coordinates for Example 9.2

Joint	x, ft	x', ft	y, ft	y', ft
1	19.5	0	0	29.0
2	19.42	0.08	5.5	23.5
3	19.0	0.5	9.5	19.5
4	16.58	2.92	12.42	16.58
5	13.50	6.0	15.5	13.5
6	11.0	8.5	18.0	11.0
7	8.0	11.5	21.0	8.0
8	5.0	14.5	24.0	5.0
9	2.25	17.25	26.75	2.25
10	0	19.5	29.0	0
11	2.25	17.25	26.75	2.25
12	5.0	14.5	24.0	5.0
13	8.0	11.5	21.0	8.0
14	11.0	8.5	18.0	11.0
15	13.5	6.0	15.5	13.5
16	16.58	2.92	12.42	16.58
17	19.0	0.5	9.5	19.5
18	19.42	0.08	5.5	23.5
19	19.5	0	0	29.0

Note: 1 ft = 0.3048 m.

The axial compression is

$$9755 \cos (68.7° - 45°) = 8932 \text{ lb}$$

This calculation is shown graphically in Fig. 9.15*b*.

2. *Moment and axial force at point 13 for dead load plus wind load:* First, isolate the right half of the arch as a free body, as shown in Fig. 9.16, and work from point 10 at the peak down to point 13 to calculate the moments and axial force as shown in Fig. 9.16*a*:

$$M_{13} = +(1236 \times 8) - (6800 \times 8) - \frac{340 \times 8^2}{2} + \frac{267.7 \times 11.314^2}{2} = -38{,}572 \text{ ft·lb}$$

The shear at point 13 is

$$V_{13} = -6800 - (340 \times 8) + (11.314 \times 262.8) \sin 45° = 7420 \text{ lb}$$

$$H_{13} = 1236 + (11.314 \times 262.8) \cos 45° = 3339 \text{ lb}$$

For a thrust of 3339 lb and vertical shear of 7420 lb, the resultant is

$$\sqrt{3339^2 + 7420^2} = 8137 \text{ lb}$$

The angle of the resultant from the horizontal is

TABLE 9.5 Moments and Axial Forces for Example 9.2

	Combination 1 (DL + LL)		Combination 2 (DL + WL)	
Point	Moment, ft · lb	Axial force, lb	Moment, ft · lb	Axial force, lb
1	0	−10,640	0	−3,000
2	−18,657.4	−10,592	+21,913	−3,000
3	−28,440.0	−10,374	+33,229	−3,000
4	−17,521.0	− 8,932	+45,265	− 52
5	+ 176.8	− 7,774	+58,085	+ 688.4
6	+ 7,381.0	− 6,834	+49,679	+1,290.0
7	+12,701.0	− 5,705	+43,809	+2,011.0
8	+11,084.0	− 4,389	+32,182	+2,752.0
9	+ 6,917.0	− 3,354	+16,477	+3,393.4
10	0	− 2,508	0	+3,935.0
11	+ 6,917.0	− 3,354	−12,049	−3,640.0
12	+11,084.0	− 4,389	−26,251	−6,884.0
13	+12,701.0	− 5,705	−38,572	−7,597.0
14	+ 7,381.0	− 6,834	−49,958	−8,327.0
15	− 176.8	− 7,774	−58,208	−8,928.0
16	−17,521.0	− 8,932	−66,723	−9,668.0
17	−28,440.0	−10,374	−66,848	−8,345.0
18	−18,657.4	−10,592	−43,182	−8,345.6
19	0	−10,640	0	−8,345.6

Note: 1 ft · lb = 1.356 N · m; 1 lb = 4.45 N.

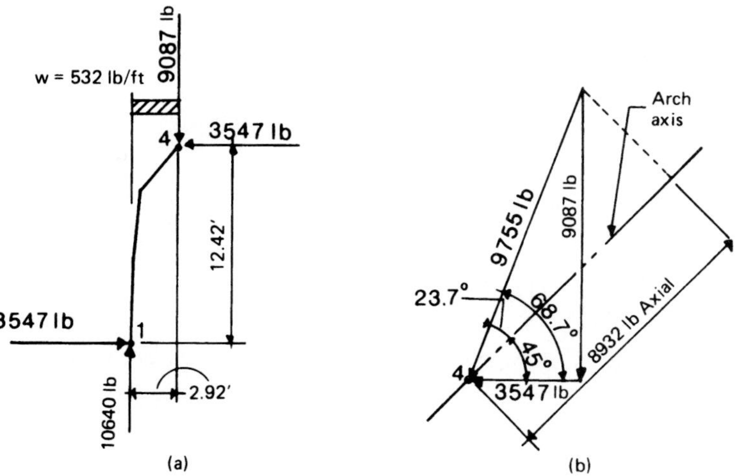

FIG. 9.15 (*a*) Free-body diagram and (*b*) force diagram at point 4.

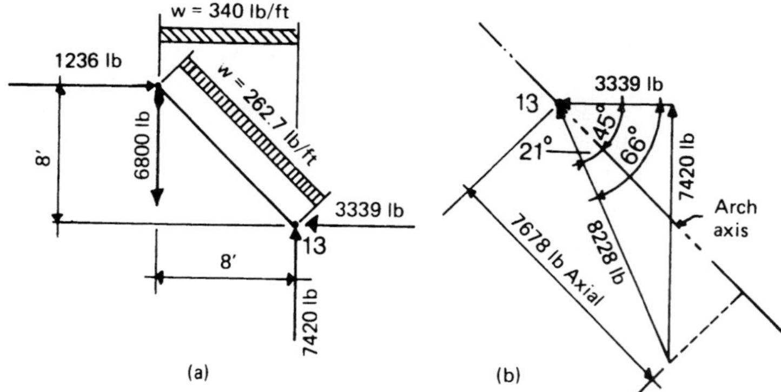

FIG. 9.16 (*a*) Free-body diagram and (*b*) force diagram at point 9.

$$\arctan\left(\frac{7420}{3339}\right) = 66°$$

The axial compression is

$$\cos\,(66° - 45°)\ 8137 = 7597 \text{ lb}$$

In similar fashion, all the points on the arch are checked for the two loading combinations. Because of symmetry, only one-half of the arch has to be checked for the balanced uniformly distributed loading of dead load plus minimum live load. The results of the moment and axial force computations are tabulated in Table 9.5.

A negative moment indicates tension on the inner face or soffit of the arch. A negative axial force indicates compression.

Step 8: Combined Stress Unity Check. By reviewing Table 9.5, it can be determined that the maximum moment in the rafter is at point 16 for loading combination 2, dead load plus wind load. Since the rafter arm is of constant cross section, it will be necessary to check only this point.

$$M = -66{,}723 \text{ ft·lb}$$

$$\text{Axial force} = -9668 \text{ lb}$$

$$f_b = \frac{6 \times 66{,}723 \times 12}{5.125 \times 16.5^2} = 3443 \text{ lb/in}^2 < F'_b = 2400 \times 1.60 = 3840 \text{ lb/in}^2 \qquad \text{OK}$$

$$f_c = \frac{9668}{5.125 \times 16.5} = 114 \text{ lb/in}^2$$

The volume factor C_v was previously calculated to be 0.94. The curvature factor is

$$C_c = 1 - 2000\left(\frac{t}{R}\right)^2 = 1 - 2000\left(\frac{0.75}{112}\right)^2$$
$$= 0.91$$

Hence

$$F'_{b1} = 2400 \times 1.60 \times 0.94 \times 0.91 = 3285 \text{ lb/in}^2$$

Unity check:

$$\left(\frac{f_c}{F'_c}\right)^2 + \frac{f_{b1}}{F'_{b1}\,[1 - (f_c/F_{cE1})]} \leq 1.0$$

$$\left(\frac{114}{1080}\right)^2 + \frac{3443}{3285\,[1 - (114/1778)]} = 0.011 + 1.120 = 1.131 < 1.0 \qquad \text{NG}$$

Therefore, increase depth to 19.5 in and recalculate:

$$f_b = \frac{6 \times 66{,}723 \times 12}{5.125 \times 19.5^2} = 2465 \text{ lb/in}^2 < 3840 \text{ lb/in}^2 \qquad \text{OK}$$

$$f_c = \frac{9668}{5.125 \times 19.5} = 96.7 \text{ lb/in}^2$$

The volume factor C_v must be recalculated:

$$C_v = 1.0\left(\frac{21}{28.28}\right)^{1/10}\left(\frac{12}{19.5}\right)^{1/10}\left(\frac{5.125}{5.125}\right)^{1/10} = 0.92$$

The curvature factor $C_v = 0.91$. Hence

$$F'_{b1} = 2400 \times 1.60 \times 0.92 \times 0.91 = 3215 \text{ lb/in}^2$$

$$F_{cE1} = \frac{0.418 \times 1{,}800{,}000}{[28.28 \times (12/19.5)]^2} = 2484 \text{ lb/in}^2$$

Unity Check:

$$\left(\frac{96.7}{1080}\right)^2 + \frac{2465}{3215\,[1 - (96.7/2484)]} = 0.806 < 1.0 \qquad \text{OK}$$

Use 5⅛- × 19.5-in glulam section.

Step 9: Determination of Peak Depth. By reviewing Table 9.5 again, it can be seen that points 5 and 15 have approximately the same moments, 58,085 and 58,208 ft · lb, respectively. The moments are relatively high in the rafter due to the combined dead load and wind load, and the peak depth is typically made the same depth as the upper tangent depth:

$$f_b = \frac{6 \times 58{,}208 \times 12}{5.125 \times 19.5^2} = 2151 \text{ lb/in}^2 < F'_b = 2400 \times 1.60 \times 0.95 = 3648 \text{ lb/in}^2$$

Since $f_b/F'_b = 0.59 < 1.0$, the member is OK for unity check by inspection.

Because of the stress reversal in the rafter due to wind load on the windward and leeward sides, the rafter should be made a constant depth to permit tension laminations to be placed on the soffit side of the arch as well as on the top. If the rafter arm is tapered, it is difficult to attain high tensile strength without using multiple tension laminations. Because of this criterion, the laminating combination will be changed from 24F-V3 to 24F-V8, a combination using a balanced layup of laminations, thus providing the same allowable bending stresses on both the top and the bottom of the member.

Step 10: Calculation of Arch Deflection. This step is not performed for this example, but the procedure is the same as that followed in Example 9.1 to calculate the arch deflection at a specific point for a specified loading.

9.2.4 Three-Hinged Circular Arch

Fewer steps are required for the design of three-hinged circular arches than for three-hinged Tudor arches because of the simpler shape of the circular arch and the cross section usually being constant. Once the maximum required depth is found, no further points have to be checked, since the entire arch is set to the maximum depth. The basic steps taken to design a circular arch are as follows:

Step 1. Determine the geometry of the arch, given the span and the radius of curvature or rise of the arch.

Step 2. Calculate the arch reactions due to the various load cases either from the published equations,[4] or from the three equations of statics: $\Sigma F_x = 0$, $\Sigma F_y = 0$, and $\Sigma M_z = 0$.

Step 3. Calculate and tabulate the moments and the axial forces at selected points along the arch profile.

Step 4. Determine the required cross section at the point of maximum moment found in Step 3. Using this trial section, perform a combined bending and axial compression stress unity check at this point. Several points that may control the design should be given the unity check.

EXAMPLE 9.3: DESIGN OF THREE-HINGED CIRCULAR ARCH Given: laminating combination for southern pine 24F-V2 with the following tabulated allowable stresses per NDS for dry-use conditions:

$$F_b = 2400 \text{ lb/in}^2 \text{ (16,547 kPa)}$$

$$F_c = 1600 \text{ lb/in}^2 \text{ (11,031 kPa)}$$

$$F_v = 200 \text{ lb/in}^2 \text{ (1379 kPa)}$$

$$F_{c\perp} = 650 \text{ lb/in}^2 \text{ (4482 kPa)}$$

$$E = 1{,}700{,}000 \text{ lb/in}^2 \text{ (11,721,500 kPa)}$$

Assume a lamination thickness of 1.5 in (38 mm).

Assumed arch geometry:

Span $L = 100$ ft (30.5 m);

Radius of curvature $R = 100$ ft (30.5 m);

Rise $T = R - \frac{1}{2}\sqrt{4R^2 - L^2} = 100 - \frac{1}{2}\sqrt{4 \times 100^2 - 100^2} = 13.4$ ft (4.09 m).

Loading data: Assume loading to be similar to that of the *Building Officials Conference of America (BOCA) Code.*

Spacing of arches = 20 ft on center (6.1 m).

Basic ground snow load = 30 lb/ft^2 (1436.5 Pa) on horizontal projection.

Dead load = 20 lb/ft^2 (957.7 Pa) on horizontal projection.

In this instance, due to the relatively flat pitch, the dead load of the roof is taken to be the same as that on the horizontal projection.

The arches are assumed to be braced against lateral buckling by the roof construction consisting of joists and plywood sheathing, nailed directly to the top of the arch.

Step 1: Calculate Loads and Basic Geometry for Arch. For load case *A*, dead load, $w = 20 \times 20 = 400$ lb/ft.

For load case *B*, uniform snow load, $w = 0.8 \times 30 \times 20 = 480$ lb/ft. The uniformly distributed balanced roof snow load is determined as 0.8 times ground snow load.

For load case *C*, assume an unbalanced triangularly distributed load on one-half of the span. The basic ground snow load is multiplied by 2 at the eave. Unbalanced snow load $w = 30 \times 2 \times 20 = 1200$ lb/ft. These loads are illustrated in Fig. 9.17.

The arch will be designed for two loading combinations:

1. Uniformly distributed dead load plus uniformly distributed snow load
2. Uniformly distributed dead load plus unbalanced triangularly distributed snow load

The arch is divided into equal segments on the arc for purposes of determining the location of stations or joints along the neutral surface of the arch. The number of subdivisions is arbitrary, with the greater number of subdivisions resulting in greater accuracy in the final design. In this example, the number of total segments for the full span is set at 12, which is a central angle of 5° for each arc segment. The layout is shown in Fig. 9.18.

The coordinates of each station are calculated and tabulated in Table 9.6. A typical calculation for a station is as follows:

For station 9, working from the arch centerline, the central angle is 10°:

$$y' = R - R\cos 10° = 1.5192 \text{ ft} \qquad y = T - y' = 13.3975 - 1.5192 = 11.8783 \text{ ft}$$

$$x = R\sin 10° = 17.3648 \text{ ft} \qquad x' = \frac{L}{2} - x = 50 - 17.3648 = 32.6352 \text{ ft}$$

This procedure is carried out for points 1 through 13 and is tabulated in Table 9.6.

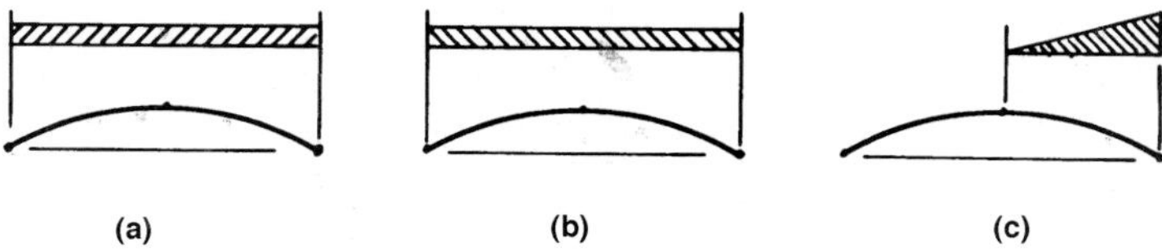

FIG. 9.17 Loading cases for Example 9.3. (*a*) Case *A*, dead load; (*b*) case *B*, snow load; (*c*) case *C*, unbalanced snow load.

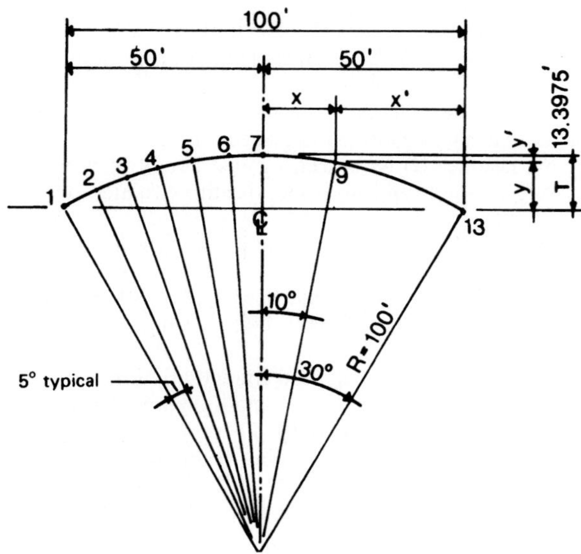

FIG. 9.18 Subdivision of arch (Example 9.3).

Step 2: Compute Reactions. Loading case *A* (Fig. 9.17*a*) for uniformly distributed dead load:

$$V = 0.5wL = 0.5 \times 400 \times 100 = 20{,}000 \text{ lb}$$

TABLE 9.6 Point Coordinates for Example 9.3

Joint	x, ft	x', ft	y, ft	y', ft
1	50	0	0	13.397
2	42.26	7.74	4.03	9.37
3	34.20	15.80	7.37	6.03
4	25.88	24.12	9.99	3.41
5	17.36	32.64	11.88	1.52
6	8.72	41.28	13.02	0.38
7	0	50	13.40	0
8	8.72	41.28	13.02	0.38
9	17.36	32.64	11.88	1.52
10	25.88	24.12	9.99	3.41
11	34.20	15.80	7.37	6.03
12	42.26	7.74	4.03	9.37
13	50	0	0	13.397

Note: 1 ft = 0.3048 m.

$$H = \frac{VL}{4T} = \frac{20{,}000 \times 100}{4. \times 13.3975} = 37{,}320 \text{ lb}$$

Loading case B (Fig. 9.17*b*) for uniformly distributed snow load:

$$V = 0.5wL = 0.5 \times 480 \times 100 = 24{,}000 \text{ lb}$$

$$H = \frac{VL}{4T} = \frac{24{,}000 \times 100}{4 \times 13.3975} = 44{,}784 \text{ lb}$$

Loading case C (Fig. 9.17*c*) for unbalanced triangularly distributed snow load:

$$W = \frac{w(L/2)}{2} = 1200 \times 0.5 \times 50 = 30{,}000 \text{ lb}$$

$$\Sigma M_A = 0 = +100V_{13} - 30{,}000\,[50 + \tfrac{2}{3}(50)], \qquad V_{13} = 25{,}000 \text{ lb}$$

$$\Sigma F_y = 0 = +25{,}000 - 30{,}000 + V_1$$

$$V_1 = 5000 \text{ lb}$$

$$\Sigma M_C = 0 = +50V_1 - 13.3975H_1 + (5000 \times 50) - 13.3975H_1$$

$$H_1 = H_{13} = 18{,}660 \text{ lb}$$

Load combination 1, dead load plus uniformly distributed snow load:

$$V_1 = V_{13} = 20{,}000 + 24{,}000 = 44{,}000 \text{ lb}$$

$$H_1 = H_{13} = 37{,}320 + 44{,}785 = 82{,}105 \text{ lb}$$

Load combination 2, dead load plus unbalanced snow load:

$$V_1 = 20{,}000 + 5000 = 25{,}000 \text{ lb}$$

$$V_{13} = 20{,}000 + 25{,}000 = 45{,}000 \text{ lb}$$

$$H_1 = H_{13} = 37{,}320 + 18{,}660 = 55{,}980 \text{ lb}$$

By inspection of the reactions for the two loading combinations, it is apparent that the maximum reactions are due to load combination 1.

Step 3: Calculation of Moments and Axial Forces. By utilizing the coordinates of the points from Table 9.6 and the reactions calculated in step 2, calculate the moments and the axial force at all the points.

Two of the points are illustrated as examples, and the results for the balance of the points are given in Table 9.7.

1. *Point 3 for loading combination 1:* See Fig. 9.19*a* for the free-body diagram used to calculate the bending moment.

$$\Sigma M_3 = (44{,}000 \times 15.8) - (82{,}105 \times 7.37) - \frac{880 \times 15.8^2}{2} = -19{,}755 \text{ ft·lb}$$

The vertical shear at point 3 is found by summing the forces in the y direction:

TABLE 9.7 Moments and Axial Forces for Example 9.3

	Combination 1 (DL + SL)		Combination 2 (DL + UNBAL SL)	
Point	Moment, ft · lb	Axial forces, lb	Moment, ft · lb	Axial force, lb
1	0	−93,149	0	−60,980
2	−16,605	−90,130	− 44,025	−59,993
3	−19,547	−87,747	− 67,359	−58,994
4	−14,974	−85,202	− 72,631	−58,047
5	− 7,923	−83,515	− 62,083	−57,205
6	− 2,180	−82,461	− 37,467	−56,507
7	0	−82,105	0	−55,981
8	− 2,180	−82,461	+ 47,040	−55,715
9	− 7,923	−83,515	+ 90,683	−56,097
10	−14,974	−85,202	+116,834	−57,539
11	−19,547	−87,747	+114,625	−57,522
12	−16,605	−90,130	+ 76,772	−64,825
13	0	−93,149	0	−70,981

Note: 1 ft · lb = 1.356 N · m; 1 lb = 4.45 N.

$$\Sigma F_y = +44{,}000 - (880 \times 15.8) - V_3 = 0$$

$$V_3 = 30{,}096 \text{ lb}$$

$$H_3 = 82{,}105 \text{ lb (horizontal thrust)}$$

The resultant is

$$\sqrt{30{,}096^2 + 82{,}105^2} = 87{,}447 \text{ lb}$$

directed 20.1° off the horizontal. Since the tangent to the curve at point 3 is 20°

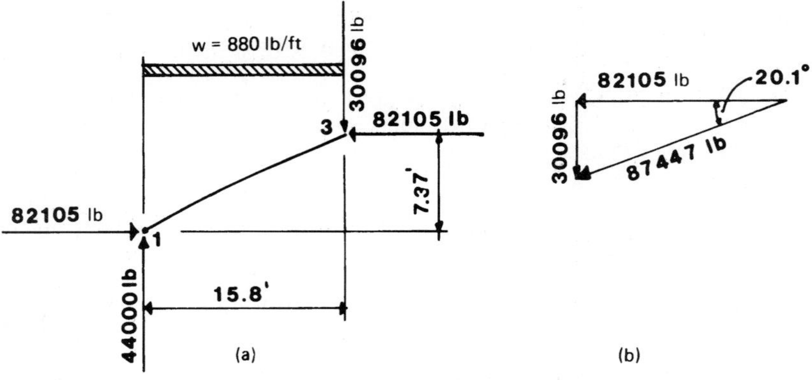

FIG. 9.19 Axial force at point 3. (*a*) Free-body diagram; (*b*) force diagram.

off the horizontal, or approximately equal to 20.1°, the axial compression can be taken as 87,447 lb. See Fig. 9.19*b* for the graphic layout.

2. *Point 9 for loading combination 2:* The free-body diagram shown in Fig. 9.20*a* was used to calculate the bending moment at point 9. This loading is a little unusual in that a triangular load is combined with a uniform load. The magnitude of the triangularly distributed load at point 9 is denoted by z. By using the proportion $1200/50 = z/x$, we find $z = 24x$ for any value of x. In this instance,

$$z = 24 \times 17.36 = 417 \text{ lb/ft}$$

$$W_1 = \tfrac{1}{2} \times z \times 17.36 = 3619 \text{ lb}$$

$$W = 400 \times 17.36 = 6944 \text{ lb}$$

$$\Sigma M_9 = +(5000 \times 17.36) + (55{,}981 \times 1.52) - \frac{400 \times 17.36^2}{2}$$

$$-(3618 \times \tfrac{1}{3} \times 17.36) = 90{,}683 \text{ ft·lb}$$

The vertical shear at point 9 is found from

$$\Sigma F_y = +5000 - 3618 - 6944 + V_9 = 0$$

$$V_9 = 5562 \text{ lb}$$

$$H_9 = 55{,}981 \text{ lb horizontal thrust}$$

The resultant is

$$\sqrt{5562^2 + 55{,}981^2} = 56{,}257 \text{ lb}$$

and the angle off the horizontal is 5.68°. The slope of the tangent to the curve at point 9 is 10°. To find the axial compression, subtract the angle of the resultant from the angle of the arch axis, take the cosine of the resulting angle, and multiply by the resultant:

$$\text{Axial compression} = \cos(10° - 5.68°)56{,}257 = 56{,}097 \text{ lb}$$

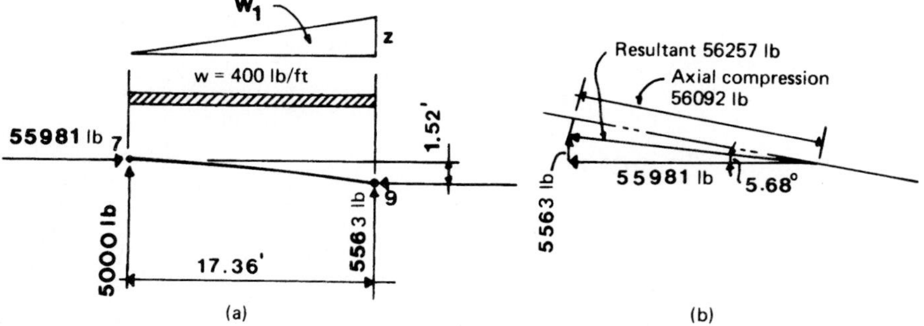

FIG. 9.20 Axial force at point 9. (*a*) Free-body diagram; (*b*) force diagram.

This procedure is carried out for all points under both loading combinations, and the results are tabulated in Table 9.7.

Negative moments indicate compression on the soffit or inner face. Negative axial forces indicate compression.

Step 4: Design of Arch. Reviewing Table 9.7, it can be ascertained that the maximum bending moment occurs at point 10 for loading combination 2. Design the arch for the bending moment and axial force at this point:

$$M = 116{,}834 \text{ ft·lb}$$
$$\text{Axial force} = 57{,}539 \text{ lb}$$

1. *First trial section:* The first trial section can either be estimated based on engineering judgment or be found by selecting a section modulus S based on an allowable bending stress F'_b of 2484 lb/in^2 based on $F'_b = 2400 \times 1.15 \times 0.90$, where 1.15 is the duration of load increase as for snow loading and 0.90 is an arbitrary factor selected to allow for combined bending and axial stresses,

$$S = \frac{M}{F'_b} = \frac{116{,}834 \times 12}{2484} = 564.4 \text{ in}$$

Since $S = bd^2/6$ and $d = \sqrt{S \times 6/b}$, and assuming $b = 5$ in, then $d = \sqrt{564.4 \times 6/5} = 26$ in. Try $d = 27$ in, based on $1\frac{1}{2}$-in laminations:

$$f_b = \frac{6 \times 116{,}834 \times 12}{5 \times 27^2} = 2308 \text{ lb/in}^2$$

At this point in the design, the allowable axial compressive stress F'_c is unknown and must be calculated. The allowable compressive stress is the lesser of the tabulated allowable compressive stress parallel to grain and that based on the effective ℓ_e/d ratio of the arch. The effective length is taken as the straight-line distance from the base hinge to the peak hinge in inches. The depth d is the depth of the section in inches. In this example it is assumed that lateral buckling of the section in the x–x direction is not a design consideration, since it is continuously laterally braced by decking.

The distance from the base hinge to the peak hinge is

$$\ell = \sqrt{50^2 + 13.39^2} = 51.76 \text{ ft or } 621.1 \text{ in}$$

$$\frac{\ell}{d} = \frac{621.1}{27} = 23.0$$

$$F_c^* = F_c \times C_D = 1600 \times 1.15 = 1840 \text{ lb/in}^2$$

$$F_{cE1} \frac{K_{cE}E'}{(\ell_e/d)^2} = \frac{0.418\ (1{,}700{,}000)}{(23.0)^2} = 1343 \text{ lb/in}^2$$

$$\frac{F_{cE1}}{F_c^*} = \frac{1343}{1840} = 0.730$$

$$C_p = \frac{1 + 0.730}{2 \times 0.9} - \sqrt{\left(\frac{1 + 0.730}{2 \times 0.9}\right)^2 - \frac{0.730}{0.9}} = 0.574$$

$$F_c' = F_c C_D C_p = 1600 \times 0.15 \times 0.574 = 1056 \text{ lb/in}^2$$

$$f_c = \frac{P}{A} = \frac{57{,}539}{5 \times 27} = 426 \text{ lb/in}^2$$

$$\left(\frac{426}{1056}\right)^2 + \frac{2308}{2484[1 - (426.2/1343)]} = 0.163 + 1.362 = 1.52 > 1.0 \qquad \text{NG}$$

This trial section is overstressed; therefore, a new cross section must be selected.

2. *Second trial section:* Select a 6.75- by 28.5-in section.

Note: The designer can increase either the depth or the width of the member. However, it is recommended that a depth-to-width ratio of ≤6 be maintained. Therefore, both the width and depth of the member have been increased.

$$f_b = \frac{6 \times 116{,}834 \times 12}{6.75 \times 28.5^2} = 1534 \text{ lb/in}^2$$

$$f_c = \frac{57{,}539}{6.75 \times 28.5} = 299.1 \text{ lb/in}^2$$

$$\frac{\ell_e}{d} = \frac{621.1}{28.5} = 21.79$$

$$F_{cE} = \frac{0.418\ (1{,}700{,}000)}{(21.79)^2} = 1496 \text{ lb/in}^2$$

$$F_c^* = 1600 \times 1.15 = 1840 \text{ lb/in}^2$$

$$\frac{F_{cE}}{F_c^*} = \frac{1496}{1840} = 0.813$$

$$C_p = \frac{1 + 0.813}{2 \times 0.9} - \sqrt{\left(\frac{1 + 0.813}{2 \times 0.9}\right)^2 - \frac{0.813}{0.9}} = 0.685$$

$$F_c' = 1600 \times 1.15 \times 0.685 = 1260 \text{ lb/in}^2$$

$$\left(\frac{299.1}{1260}\right)^2 + \frac{1534}{2484[(1 - 299.1)/1496]} = 0.056 + 0.772 = 0.828 < 1.0 \qquad \text{OK}$$

Use a section size of 6.75 by 28.5 in for the arch.

On a circular arch of relatively large span (>150 ft), it is common to use true hinged connections at the bases and the peak. These hinged connections consist of side and back plates welded together and joined to each other with pins to provide a true hinge. There is usually very little vertical shear leading to horizontal shear at these connections as the usual stress is compression parallel to grain. On smaller spans (<150 ft) there may be a flat cut and a vertical cut at the bases to accommodate a steel base shoe. In this case, the arch base should be checked for horizontal shear.

9.2.5 Two-Hinged Circualr Arch

Two-hinged circular arches are not commonly used except for small spans because of limitations of shipping length, width, or height. In addition, two-hinged arches are statically indeterminate, and the analysis procedure is thus more complicated than that used for the three-hinged arch design. The two hinges are located at the supports, with no hinge within the arch itself. As noted, the arch is indeterminate, and the axial and shearing deformations are neglected in the analysis. A virtual work method such as the dummy unit load method is commonly used to determine the horizontal thrust for this arch shape. Computer programs based on the stiffness or matrix displacement method are also used to analyze these indeterminate arches. It is possible to provide a moment splice within the span to overcome the problem of shipment, but the cost of the splices is relatively high, and erection of the full arch section may be difficult on large spans due to the weight of the member and the required reach of the cranes. Equations and curves for computing horizontal reactions for circular two-hinged arches were compiled by Schofield and O'Brien[4] for four different loading cases. With their equations and curves it is also possible to find the locations of the maximum moment. Their curves were tabulated for various rise-to-span ratios. Cornforth and Childs[5] developed equations for the plastic design of steel two-hinged circular arches. Given only the geometry of the arch and the design loading, it is possible to calculate the reactions and the moments for these arches in closed form. For example, take the case of an arch subjected to a uniform load, as shown in Fig. 9.21.

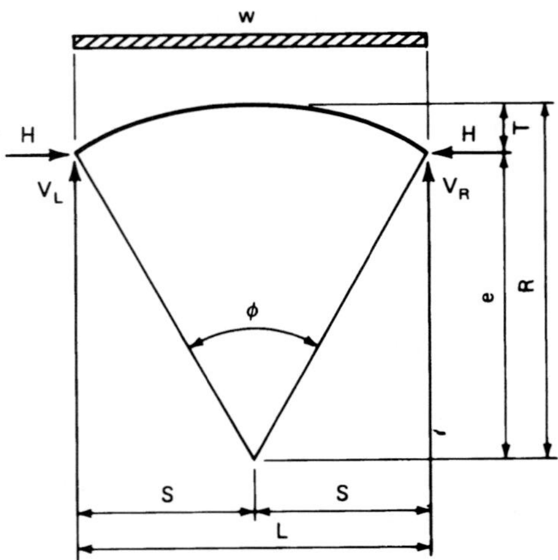

FIG. 9.21 Two-hinged circular arch with nomenclature.

$$V_L = V_R = wS$$

$$H = \left(\frac{w}{2}\right) \frac{\frac{4}{3}S^3 + e\phi(R^2/2 - S^2) - e^2S}{\phi(R^2/2 + e^2) - 3eS}$$

where all terms are as shown in Fig. 9.21.

EXAMPLE 9.4: DESIGN OF CIRCULAR TWO-HINGED ARCH. Assume the following arch geometry and loading conditions:

$$L = 100 \text{ ft } (30.48 \text{ m})$$

$$S = 50 \text{ ft } (15.24 \text{ m})$$

$$T = 13.3975 \text{ ft } (4.08 \text{ m})$$

$$R = 100 \text{ ft } (30.48 \text{ m})$$

$$e = 86.6025 \text{ ft } (26.40 \text{ m})$$

$$w = 1000 \text{ lb/ft } (14.594 \text{ kN/m})$$

$$\phi = 1.0472 \text{ rad}$$

Assume the following allowable stresses for a southern pine combination 48 from AITC 117[1]:

$$F_b = 1900 \text{ lb/in}^2 \qquad F_c = 2200 \text{ lb/in}^2 \qquad E = 1{,}700{,}000 \text{ lb/in}^2$$

Allowable increase for short-duration loading is 15 percent, as for snow. Assume a trial cross section of 5 by 20.625 in.

$$V_L = V_R = \frac{1000 \times 100}{2} = 50{,}000 \text{ lb}$$

$$H = \left(\frac{1000}{2}\right)$$

$$\times \frac{(\frac{4}{3} \times 50^3) + (86.6025 \times 1.0472)(100^2/2 - 50^2) - (86.6025^2 \times 50)}{1.0472(100^2/2 + 86.6025)^2 - (3 \times 86.6 \times 50)}$$

$$= 92{,}315 \text{ lb}$$

After calculating the vertical and horizontal reactions, the design or analysis of two-hinged circular arches is similar to that of three-hinged circular arches. The moments, axial forces, and shears can be calculated from the equations of statics. See Table 9.8 for arch coordinates. For example, at station 3 in Fig. 9.22,

$$M_3 = (50{,}000 \times 11.74) - (92{,}315 \times 5.78) - \frac{1000 \times 11.74^2}{2} = -16{,}083 \text{ ft·lb}$$

TABLE 9.8 Point Coordinates for Example 9.4

Station	x, ft	x', ft	y, ft	y', ft
1	50	0	0	13.40
2	44.23	5.77	3.08	10.32
3	38.26	11.74	5.78	7.62
4	32.14	17.86	8.09	5.31
5	25.87	24.13	9.99	3.41
6	19.50	30.5	11.48	1.92
7	13.04	36.96	12.54	0.86
8	6.52	43.48	13.18	0.22
9	0	50.00	13.40	0

Note: 1 ft = 0.3048 m.

The vertical shear at station 3 is

$$50{,}000 - (1000 \times 11.74) = 38{,}260 \text{ lb}$$

The resultant is

$$\sqrt{38{,}260^2 + 92{,}315^2} = 99{,}929 \text{ lb}$$

The axial force is approximately equal to the resultant, 99,929 lb. This is usually true with uniform loads because the thrust line, which is parabolic, is not too far off the member axis, which is circular.

This procedure is carried out for all stations, and the results are tabulated in Table 9.9. From inspection of Table 9.9, it can be seen that the maximum moment occurs at station 3 and is 16,083 ft·lb. The accompanying axial force is 99,929 lb. The sign of the moments changes between stations 5 and 6, which indicates that

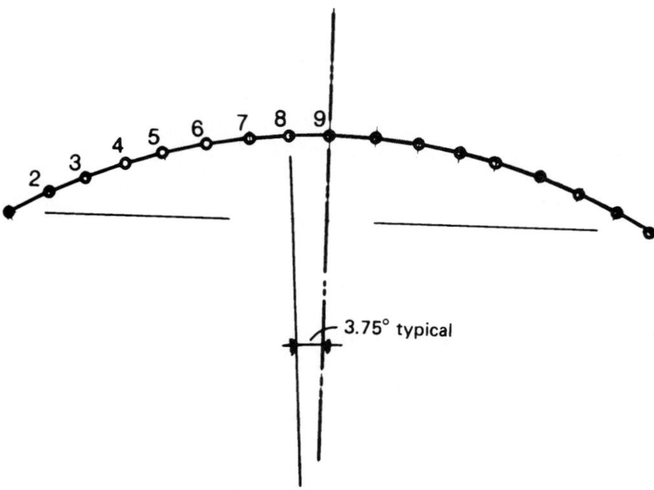

FIG. 9.22 Subdivision of arch (Example 9.4).

TABLE 9.9 Moments and Axial Forces for Example 9.4

Station	Moment, ft·lb	Axial force, lb
1	0	104,986
2	−12,477	102,364
3	−16,083	99,929
4	−13,318	97,750
5	−6,855	95,871
6	99	94,352
7	7,349	93,231
8	12,033	92,545
9	0	92,315

Note: 1 ft·lb = 1.356 N·m; 1 lb = 4.45 N.

the point of zero moment or contraflexure is between stations 5 and 6. By assuming that the point of contraflexure is at station 6, the column length ℓ used in determining the allowable compressive stress for an unbraced column will be on the conservative side. The column length is calculated using the straight-line distance from the base to station 6. It is assumed that the arch is laterally braced against buckling by decking directly attached to it. Thus the unbraced depth is 20.625 in.

$$L = 11.475 + 30.5 = 32.6 \text{ ft}$$

$$\frac{\ell}{d} = \frac{32.6 \times 12}{20.625} = 18.97$$

$$F_c^* = F_c C_D$$

$$= 2200 \times 1.15 = 2530 \text{ lb/in}^2$$

$$F_{cE1} = \frac{K_{cE}E'}{(\ell_e/d)^2} = \frac{0.418(1{,}700{,}000)}{18.97} = 1975 \text{ lb/in}^2$$

$$\frac{F_{cE}}{F_c^*} = \frac{1975}{2530} = 0.781$$

$$C_p = \frac{1 + 0.781}{2(0.9)} - \sqrt{\left[\frac{1 + 0.781}{2(0.9)}\right]^2 - \frac{0.781}{0.9}} = 0.656$$

$$F_c' = F_c^* C_p = 2530 \times 0.656 = 1660 \text{ lb/in}^2$$

$$F_{b1} = F_b C_D C_v$$

$$C_v = 1.0\left(\frac{21}{32.6}\right)^{1/20}\left(\frac{12}{20.625}\right)^{1/20}\left(\frac{5.125}{5.0}\right)^{1/20}$$

$$= 0.953$$

$$F'_{b1} = 1900 \times 1.15 \times 0.953 = 2082 \text{ lb/in}^2$$

$$f_c = \frac{P}{A} = \frac{99{,}929}{5 \times 20.625} = 969 \text{ lb/in}^2$$

$$f_{b1} = \frac{6M}{bd^2} = \frac{6 \times 16{,}083 \times 12}{5 \times 20.625^2} = 544 \text{ lb/in}^2$$

Combined stress check:

$$\left(\frac{f_c}{F'_c}\right)^2 + \frac{f_{b1}}{F'_{b1}[1 - (f_c/F_{cE1})]} \leq 1.0$$

$$\left(\frac{969}{1660}\right)^2 + \frac{544}{2082[1 - (969/1975)]} = 0.857 \leq 1.0 \qquad \text{OK}$$

The designer should also check the arch section for shear at base and crown, radial stresses, and deflection.

9.2.6 Two-Hinged Tudor Arch

The two-hinged Tudor arch as shown in Fig. 9.23 is not often utilized by designers. The primary reasons for this are that it is a difficult shape to erect, and the moment connections are relatively expensive. Usually the arch has a large span with high legs, and the pitch of the roof is low. In many cases, the arch is too cumbersome and heavy to erect as one unit, which necessitates that the center beam portion is erected on scaffolding, and the moment connections are made in the air. Typically, when encountered with the need for this arch geometry, i.e., a high leg combined with a low pitch, thus making the arch too large for transportation as a single half-arch section, the designer will introduce a hinge at the peak. The arch can then be analyzed as a three-hinged arch with a moment splice introduced as required for shipping purposes. The following design example illustrates the somewhat unique features associated with the design of a moment splice for a Tudor arch. The moment splice, if possible, should be located as closely as possible to the point of minimum bending moment. This location will be a compromise between the max-

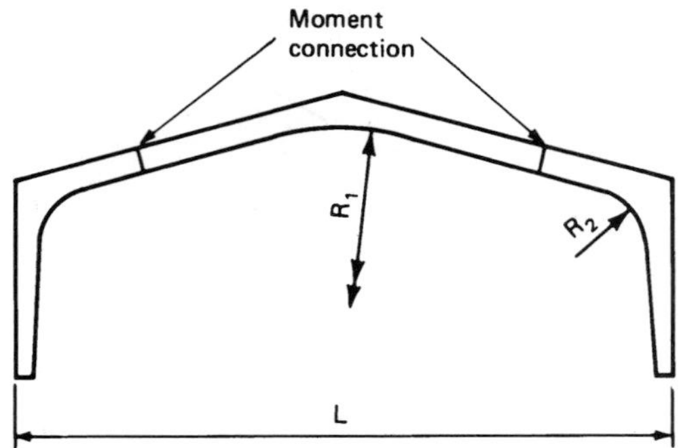

FIG. 9.23 Two-hinged Tudor arch.

imum shipping width or height and the least moment for a variety of load combinations. It also should be kept in mind that the member may be subjected to erection stresses at the splice, which may be completely different than those caused by dead, wind, and live loads.

As discussed in Chap. 5, there are several approaches to the design of a moment splice.

1. Resist the axial forces due to direct tension or compression and bending moments by the steel connections only
2. Resist the compressive axial forces due to direct compression and bending moment by direct bearing on the wood and resist the tensile force with steel strap and connectors

If the axial forces are tensile, or compressive but of small magnitude, approach 1 is preferable. If the axial forces are compressive and of large magnitude in relation to the bending moment, approach 2 is a more economical choice since it reduces the steel requirements appreciably.

In most applications the forces at a moment splice are moment, axial tension or compression, and shear. The usual methods of structural analysis apply in computing the magnitude of the combined stresses due to bending and axial forces. The most efficient way to handle the bending moments is to make the resisting moment arm the largest dimension possible. This is normally accomplished by placing the steel straps at the top and bottom faces of the cross section. Usually the top plate is routed into the top face, which results in a flush surface for the decking attachment while the bottom plate is mounted flush on the bottom face. The steel plates are usually attached with lag bolts combined with shear plates. It should be noted that a moment splice will not be as rigid as the member was prior to being cut. This is due to inelastic slippage in the bolts and connectors, which will result in some initial movement in the connection when first loaded.

EXAMPLE 9.5: DESIGN OF MOMENT SPLICE FOR A TUDOR HALF-ARCH TOO LARGE TO BE SHIPPED IN ONE PIECE At the splice location (Fig. 9.24), the maximum forces are

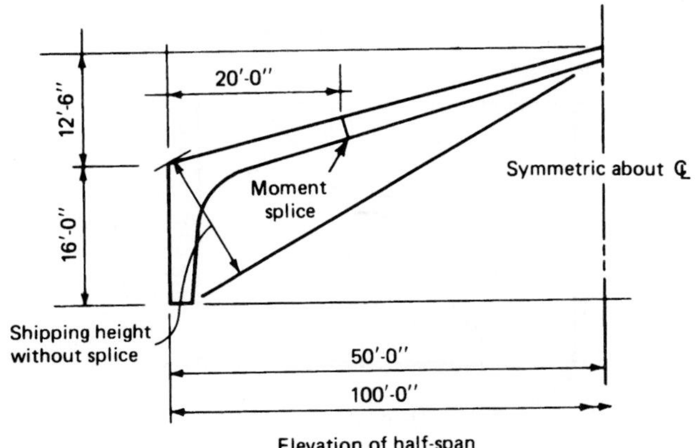

FIG. 9.24 Moment splice location on Tudor arch (Example 9.5).

$$\text{Moment} = 508{,}000 \text{ in·lb } (57{,}396.3 \text{ N·m})$$

$$\text{Axial compression} = 39{,}000 \text{ lb } (306.9 \text{ kN})$$

$$\text{Shear} = 11{,}700 \text{ lb } (52 \text{ kN})$$

Assume that the following allowable unit stresses are applicable:

$$F'_b = 2200 \times 1.15 = 2530 \text{ lb/in}^2 \ (17{,}443.7 \text{ kPa})$$

$$F'_c = 1500 \times 1.15 = 1725 \text{ lb/in}^2 \ (11{,}893.5 \text{ kPa})$$

Assume an effective arch section of 8.75 × 30.5 in at the splice location. $A = 266.9 \text{ in}^2$, $S = 1356.6 \text{ in}^3$.

Step 1: Determine Bending and Axial Stresses

$$f_b = \frac{M}{S} = \frac{508{,}000}{1356.6} = 374.5 \text{ lb/in}^2$$

$$f_c = \frac{P}{A/2} = \frac{39{,}000}{266.9/2} = 146.1 \text{ lb/in}^2$$

Combined compressive stress:

$$f_c = 374.5 + 146.1 = 520.6 \text{ lb/in}^2$$

Combined tensile stress:

$$f_t = 374.5 - 146.1 = 228.4 \text{ lb/in}^2 \qquad \text{(see Fig. 9.25)}$$

Step 2: Locate Neutral Axis

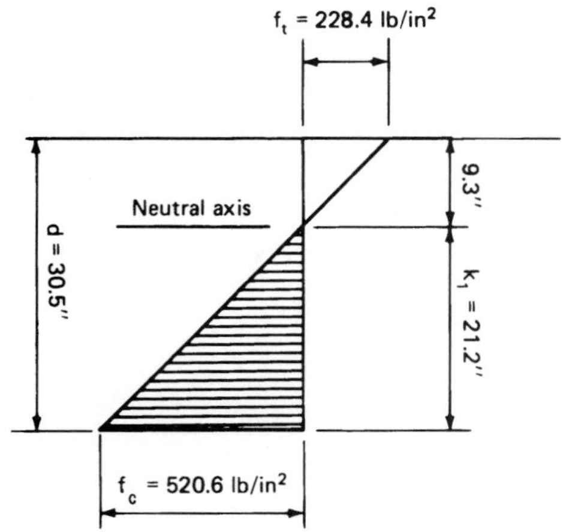

FIG. 9.25 Diagram of combined stresses.

$$k_1 = \frac{f_c d}{f_t + f_c} = \frac{520.6 \times 30.5}{228.4 + 520.6} = 21.2 \text{ in} \qquad \text{(see Fig. 9.25)}$$

$$C = \tfrac{1}{2} \times 520.6 \times 21.2 \times 8.75 = 48{,}286 \text{ lb}$$

$$T = \tfrac{1}{2} \times 228.4 \times 9.3 \times 8.75 = 9277 \text{ lb}$$

In theory, the tensile force should be located at 9.3/3 = 3.1 in down from the top of the member, but a conservative solution is to design for 9277 lb at the top of the member.

Step 3: Determine Tension Resistance Requirements. For a group II species, 4-in shear plate, and a ⅞-in-diameter lag bolt the allowable load parallel to grain is 4320 × 1.15 × 1.11 = 5514 lb (see Chap. 5). The number of shear plates required is

$$\frac{T}{5514} = \frac{9277}{5514} = 1.68$$

Use 2 shear plates. This is OK for group action of fasteners in a row by inspection, since for two or less connectors in a row, there is no reduction in load.

The required end-distance spacing is 7 in for tension. The required spacing between 4-in-diameter shear plates loaded parallel to grain is 9 in. See Fig. 9.26 for the positioning of shear plates.

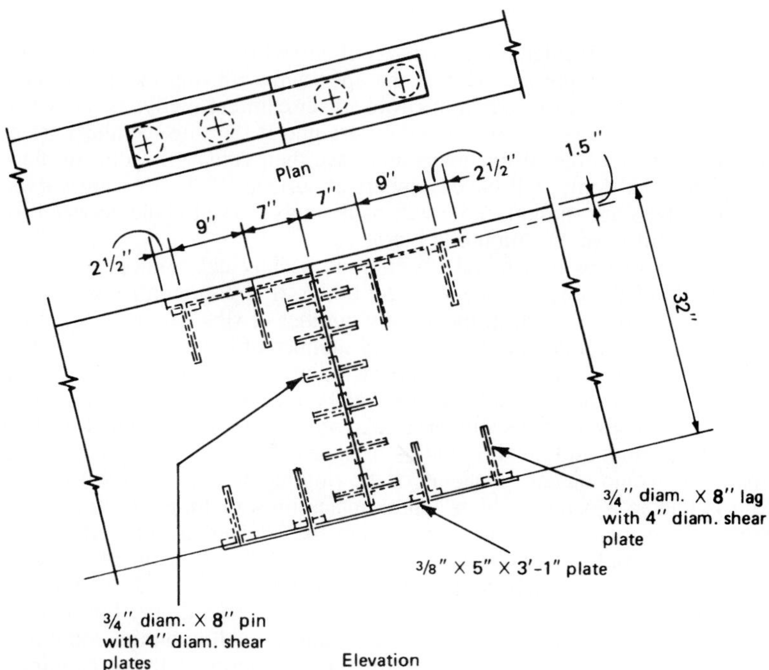

FIG. 9.26 Moment splice detail.

The net area of the steel strap is (5 − 0.875)0.375 = 1.55 in^2. The tensile stress in the steel strap is 9277/1.55 = 6000 lb/in^2, which is OK.

Step 4: Determine Compressive Force Requirements. Theoretically, no positive connection is required on the compressive side of the joint, but for purposes of erection and alignment, a steel strap is used. In this case, the compressive steel is made the same dimension as the tensile steel. The compression plate between the butting ends of the members was omitted because the compressive stress $f_c < 0.75F_c$.

Step 5: Determine Vertical Shear Resistance Requirements. The vertical shear at the joint is 11,700 lb. The allowable load on a 4-in-diameter shear plate loaded perpendicular to grain in end grain is 3000 × 0.6 × 1.15 = 2070 lb per shear plate. The number of shear plates required (on one side of the joint) is 11,700/2070 = 5.65 shear plates; use 6. The depth of the arch may need to be increased to accommodate the required connectors.

It is important that deep steel side plates not be used in moment splices to carry the vertical shear or moment because of the possibility of the wood shrinking or expanding due to moisture conditions while the steel plates remain dimensionally stable, which can result in serious splitting of the wood. The details of this moment splice are illustrated in Fig. 9.26.

9.3 DOMES

9.3.1 Dome Geometry and Design

The radial rib, or Schwedler, dome consists of curved rib members that extend from the base ring to a compression ring at the apex and with ring members that are at different elevations and extend from rib to rib circumferentially, as shown in Fig. 9.27. The ring members may be curved or straight. If the ring members are curved to the same radius as the rib members and have their center of radius at the center of the sphere, the dome will have a spherical surface. If the ribs are curved, but the ring members are straight, there will be a singly curved plane between the ribs and the roof will have an "umbrella" look.

The number of ribs in a radial rib dome is usually determined by considering the magnitude of the circumference of the dome. It is common to set the number of ribs at 24 or 36, although in theory any number of ribs can be used. If the ribs are supported by columns, the location and number of columns will be influenced by the location and number of doors and windows. The number of ring members is often dictated by the material used to sheathe the roof. Since the roof surface is curved, wood domes are typically sheathed with 2-in (nominal) wood deck, which has a practical minimum bending radius of approximately 80 ft. Depending on the live load, this would dictate a spacing of the ring members of 5 to 8 ft because the decking is laid in a pattern which approximates lines of longitude for the sphere. Other sheathing materials could be used, but the choices are limited because the sheathing must conform to the curved shape. The design principles and design procedures for the radial rib dome can be found in Ref. 2 and are not repeated here. The radial rib dome is often designed not as a true dome, but as a hybrid. The hybrid dome is designed to take the unbalanced loading on the dome by bending stresses in the ribs. In the "true" dome there is theoretically no bending stress in the ribs due to axial loads because the loads are assumed to be applied at the

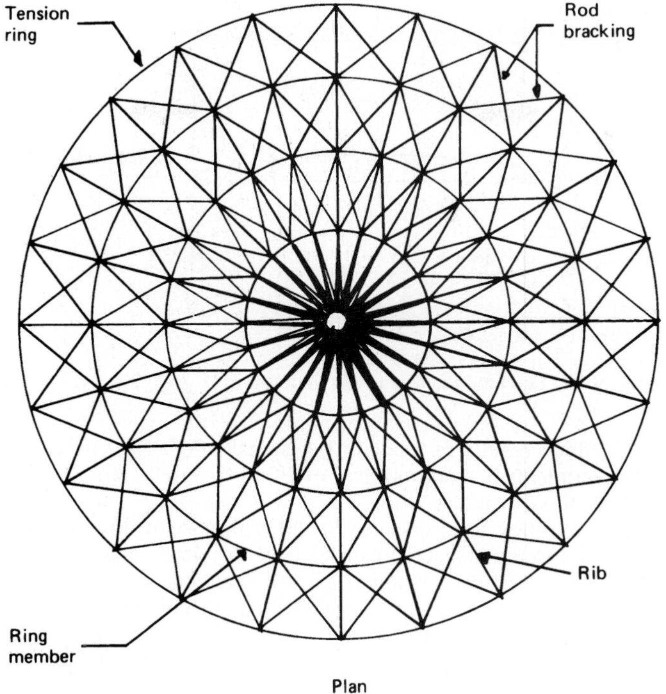

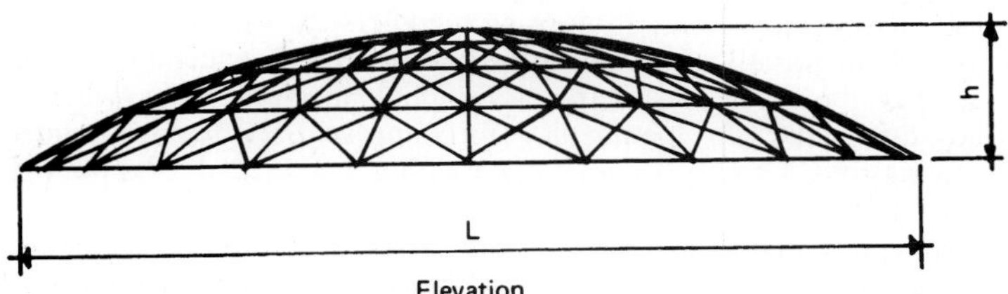

FIG. 9.27 Radial rib dome.

node points of the dome. The node points are at the intersections of the ring members and the ribs, and of the ribs to the compression ring and the base ring. Since the "true" dome is designed as a space truss, no bending moments would be expected in the ribs. The bending stresses are due to the eccentricity of the axial loads caused by the curvature of the members. Bending moments are also caused by the lateral loads on the members. For example, as shown in Fig. 9.28, the curved ring member on a radius of 100 ft has an eccentricity of 3.846 in. Assuming an axial compression in the member of 80,000 lb, the moment due to eccentricity is −307,693 in·lb. Assume that at the same time the member is subjected to a lateral

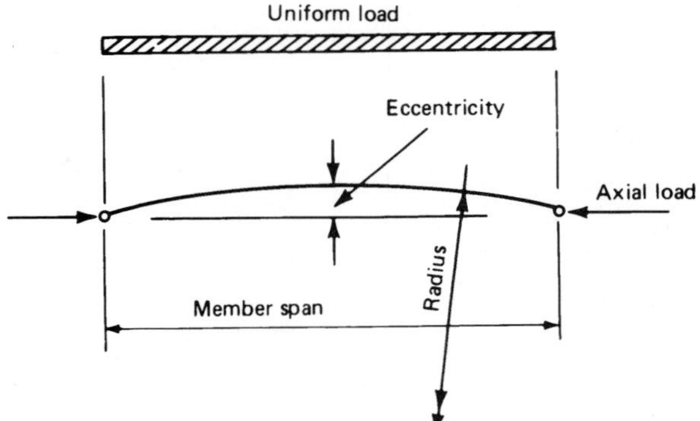

FIG. 9.28 Eccentric moments due to curvature.

load of 270 lb/ft, which results in a bending moment of 103,680 in·lb. The combined effect of the moments is a net moment of −204,013 in·lb, since the moments negate each other in this particular case.

The hybrid dome is often used because of the high cost of utilizing × bracing on the "true" dome for unbalanced loading. In the hybrid design, the ribs are designed as three-hinged circular arches to carry the unbalanced loads from wind or unbalanced live load by bending and axial stresses in the ribs. The cost of the material for the × bracing and to erect this material is quite high. Further research is required on the necessity of this × bracing to carry a realistic unbalanced load. It is possible that this bracing may be eliminated if the sheathing is capable of resisting, in shear, the axial forces taken by the rods. The problem is complex because of the orthotropic nature of the sheathing and the attachment of the sheathing to the members.

The connections of the ring members to the ribs are critical because the magnitude of the axial compression in the ring members can become large. Since there is a component of force that causes shear between the connection and the side of the rib member, this force must be taken by the connectors, as shown in Fig. 9.29. In a "true" dome, the ring member to rib connection also has to connect to the steel × bracing rods. Usually a gusset plate with a hole drilled for a pin for a clevis can be welded to the connection, as shown in Fig. 9.29.

An advantage of the radial rib dome is that it is relatively straightforward to design because it is statically determinate. Other advantages are that the connections are relatively simple and the members are not difficult to fabricate. The erection of the dome is not overly complicated, although care has to be taken to stabilize the dome during erection to keep it from "spinning" about its center vertical axis pole, particularly when the supports are on columns. Often two adjacent ribs and the ring members between them are connected on the ground and erected as a unit to help stabilize the rib members and to keep them from "rolling" around the axis from the base to the peak due to the eccentricity from curvature.

Many of the disadvantages of the radial rib dome have been eliminated by use of triangulated timber domes identified as Varax* and Triax* patterns, as shown in

*Varax is a registered trademark of Western Wood Structures: Triax is a registered trademark of Unit Structures, Inc.

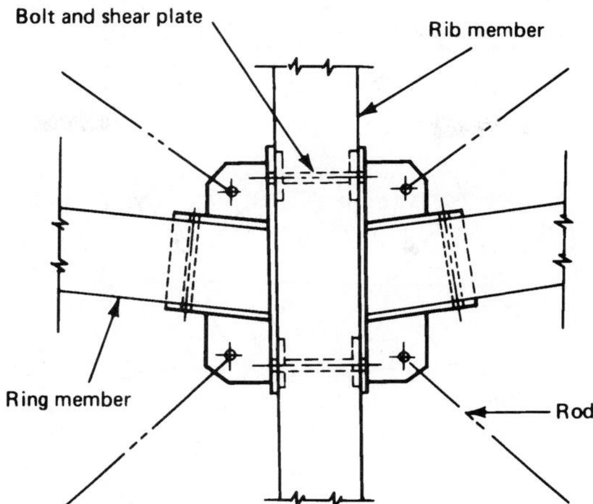

FIG. 9.29 Radial rib dome connection.

Figs. 9.30 and 9.31, respectively. With these domes, the maximum length of the rib members can be controlled by the number of sectors and the frequency of the dome. The number of sectors in a dome is the number of equal pie-shaped patterns that is repeated in 360°. The frequency of the dome is determined by counting the number of times the line representing the edge of the sector is divided. For example, in Fig. 9.30 for the Varax dome, lines *A* to *B* and *C* to *B* represent sector lines. The sector lines are divided three times, which sets the frequency of this dome at 3. For both the Varax and the Triax patterns shown in Figs. 9.30 and 9.31, the number of sectors is 6 and the frequency is 3. The Varax and Triax domes have a similar triangulated pattern but the method of generating the geometry is different, which results in completely different lengths of members for the two patterns. In general, the Varax dome joint placement is determined by setting the transition ring height at a constant elevation. The transition ring is the first ring of joints up from the base ring. This ring is called a *transition ring* because the members that connect from the transition ring to the base ring do not follow the great circle generation pattern of the members above the transition ring. The balance of the joint locations are determined by the intersection of great circles, as shown in Fig. 9.30. The Triax dome joint configuration is generated by setting the equilateral triangular pattern on a plane at the elevation of the bases, as shown in Fig. 9.31. By passing rays from the center of the sphere through the grid intersections to the surface of the sphere, the nodes or joints are located. The rib members form triangles from node to node. They are curved to the radius of the sphere.

The complex geometry of these domes results in a large set of simultaneous equations that are impossible to solve by manual calculation. Some approximations can be made for the ribs by manual calculation for uniform loadings at the supports, but the calculations for unbalanced loading become impossible unless computerized. The key to these triangulated domes are the steel hubs at the interior joints or nodes and at the supports. Most hubs are proprietary with the manufacturer of the dome, and the design of the dome is usually performed by the manufacturer or the manufacturer's agent.

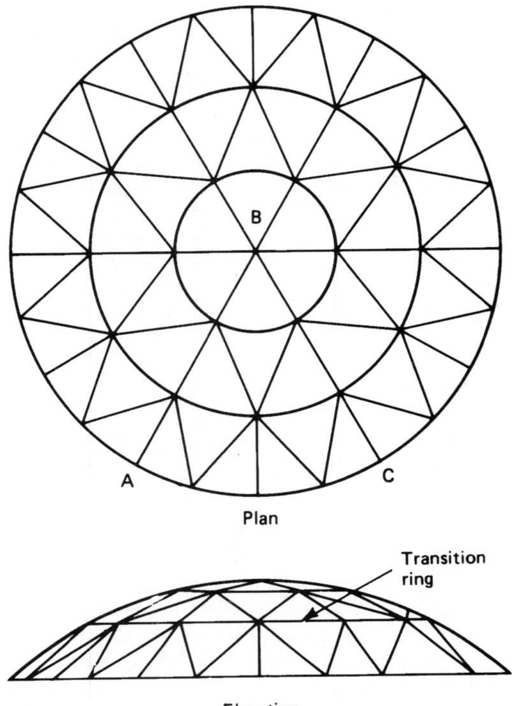

FIG. 9.30 Varax dome geometry.

loads placed at the nodes, or joints. The intermediate purlins are also curved to the radius of the sphere, the same as the main ribs. Although the dome is designed as a space truss, the design of the individual rib members has to take into account the curvature of the member, the lateral loading from the purlins or sheathing, and the axial tension or compression due to the space truss action. Although it is conservative to assume that the ends of the ribs are pinned for purposes of determining bending moments in the ribs, some designers apply partial fixity at the ends of the ribs to account for the rib-to-hub connection. The magnitude of the axial forces is usually high, and the rib members must be checked for the effect of the eccentric moment caused by the curvature of the rib and the axial force. For an accurate analysis of the rib, the member should be designed as a beam column with initial eccentricity, as covered by Timoshenko and Gere.[6]

9.3.2 Dome Erection

Several schemes have been devised to erect the triangulated domes. One early method used was to erect the center portion of the dome on the ground and to pull it up through the outer portion of the dome, which was already in place. The

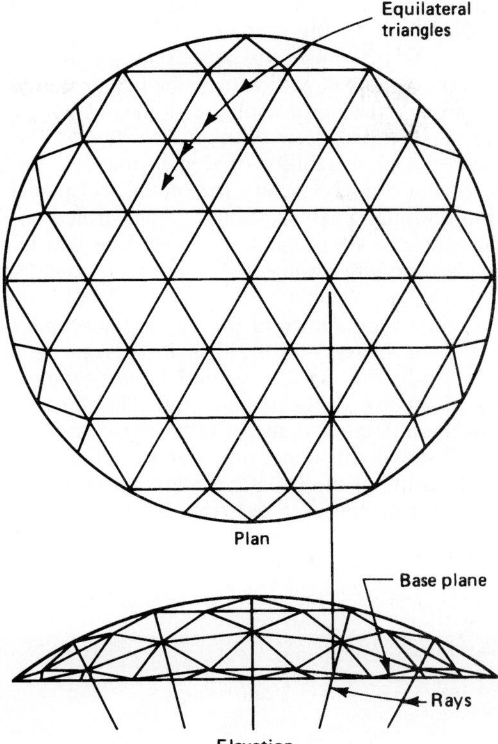

FIG. 9.31 Triax dome geometry.

difficulty was that the raising of the center part had to be executed carefully, with all exterior lift points elevated at the same time. To accomplish this it was necessary to have gin poles at the outer support points with attached tackle to raise the center portion of the dome. In addition, it was necessary to have a crane available to raise the apex to the dome to help lift the center portion and help prevent it from spreading. The present practice is to start at the exterior of the dome and erect preassembled segments of the triangulated sections by crane. Gin poles with attached tackle are used to raise the hubs to the proper elevations. It is usually not necessary to support all the hubs on the first tier of hubs since the triangulated pattern becomes somewhat self-supporting as the erection proceeds. As the erection commences toward the center of the dome, the need for gin poles for additional support decreases until they are no longer necessary.

9.3.3 Dome Buckling

A serious concern in the design of low-rise domes (rise-to-span ratio ≤ 0.15) of large span (>250 ft) is the possibility of snap-through buckling. This mode of buckling is a form of structural failure in which structural instability occurs as a result of geometric deformations. This instability occurs at the global level rather than at a local or member level. A low-rise dome of large span typically undergoes large deflections and exhibits highly nonlinear behavior. As the loads are applied, the structure becomes less stiff. When the stiffness of a joint reaches zero, this joint can no longer carry additional load without a sudden change of position. The critical joint will displace through the surface of the dome, leaving a depression in the surface. This behavior is called *snap-through buckling* of the dome. A detailed discussion of the aspects of instability of domes may be found in Smith.[7] The nonlinear analysis for buckling is usually performed by specialists in the field. A global, not local, snap-through analysis should be performed on low-rise large-span domes. Domes that appear to be adequate to carry dead and live loads with linear analysis may be inadequate when subjected to nonlinear analysis for snap-through buckling.

Two examples of very large domes of the Varax pattern are the city of Tacoma, Washington dome and the University of Northern Arizona dome at Flagstaff. The Tacoma dome is currently the world's second largest-diameter wood dome and spans 520 ft with a 150-ft rise above its base ring. The third largest wood dome is the University of Northern Arizona dome, which spans 506 ft and rises 112 ft above the supports. Fig. 9.32 shows this dome under construction. An example of a large radial-rib dome is the dome at the Montana State University Fieldhouse in Bozeman. This dome is 300 ft in diameter and rises 50 ft 8 in.

FIG. 9.32 Ensphere at Flagstaff, Arizona.

9.4 RESEARCH

The AITC has sponsored research at Colorado State University (CSU) to investigate the structural behavior of Tudor arches. Gutkowski and Goodman[8] used orthotropic finite-element techniques to determine the stresses in the arches, primarily in the knee area between the lower and upper tangents. Although additional research is needed, the preliminary findings indicate that there is relatively straight-line distribution of stress throughout the depth of the member at the tangent points, but the variation of stress through the knee section is not a straight-line. As in pitched and tapered curved beams, radial stresses were found to exist in the knee. Under gravity vertical loading, the radial stress is compression and normally is not significant when compared with allowable stresses. However, under certain wind loads, the radial stress is tension perpendicular to grain and can become a design factor due to the relatively low allowable stress for wood loaded in this mode. An ancillary result of this original research was an investigation of stress behavior of nonprismatic members, which would apply to the leg and upper arm portions of the arches and to tapered beams and pitched and tapered curved beams.

In the research by Dewey, Gopu, and coworkers,[9,10] a challenge is made of the applicability of the interaction equation to orthotropic materials used in pitched and tapered curved beams, arches, and tapered beams. They propose that the designs be based on a maximum-stress theory rather than interaction, which is based on the energy of distortion theory of failure.

As the cost of computers, their peripherals, and software continue to decline, design engineers are becoming involved with more complex structural designs. One of these types of structures that involve wood structural members is the space frame. Particularly with unsymmetrical framing plans, the lateral deflection of the entire framing system may become a problem due to sidesway. A part of the problem is caused by the system not being a "true" space frame because the purlins, when utilized with arches, are seldom designed as tensile or compressive members in addition to being designed as beams. If the roof covering, such as the wood decking or plywood, were utilized in the analysis in conjunction with the framing members, the magnitude of the lateral deflections could be reduced appreciably. The tensile and compressive forces in the purlins also could be reduced. The finite-element method can be utilized to perform complex analyses of these systems, which involve framing members and their connections as well as the roof diaphragm and its connection. Foschi[11] demonstrated that this analysis is feasible. In order to take advantage of the "skin" in reducing lateral movement and, in some instances, reducing sizes, it will be necessary to develop values for various roof coverings and load slip values for various connectors. Since most design professionals do not have access to orthotropic finite-element programs, or the time to utilize them, it will be necessary to develop design procedures that can approximate the actual behavior of the structure. Many materials competitive to wood are already utilizing the "skin" for bracing and to decrease the amount of material in the framing members. The trend is for larger and larger enclosed sporting arenas, particularly in the colder climates. The triangulated dome is ideal for this type of structure because each individual rib can be easily handled and shipped on the highways or by rail. The wood dome is very cost-competitive with other dome systems. Although the initial cost of the wood dome may be higher than that of the inflatable or tensile fabric domes, when the operating costs for the air system and the cost of heating or cooling these types of fabric domes are taken into account, the wood dome becomes very cost-competitive. In addition, it is often difficult to hang heavy concentrated loads, such as scoreboards, from the fabric dome. The cost of petroleum-based products, of which the fabric of these domes is made, may rise significantly in the future, which would make the wood dome an even more viable alternative. With modern technologic advancement, the future for long-span wood domes appears unlimited.

REFERENCES

1. *Standard Specifications for Structural Glued Laminated Timber of Softwood Species,* AITC 117, American Institute of Timber Construction, Vancouver, Wash., 1987.
2. American Institute of Timber Construction, *Timber Construction Manual,* 4th ed., Wiley, New York, 1994.
3. Giesecke, Mitchell, Spencer, Hill, and Dygoon, *Technical Drawing,* Macmillan, New York, 1980, p. 113.
4. W. F. Schofield and W. H. O'Brien, *Modern Timber Engineering,* 3d ed., Southern Pine Association, New Orleans, La., 1949.
5. R. C. Cornforth and S. B. Childs, "Computer Analysis of Two-Hinged Circular Arches," *J. Am. Soc. Civil Eng.* **ST2:**319 (Apr. 1967).
6. S. P. Timoshenko and J. M. Gere, *Theory of Elastic Stability,* 2d ed., McGraw-Hill, New York, 1961.
7. G. R. Smith, Jr., "A Nonlinear Static Analysis for Spherical Truss Domes," Ph.D. dissertation, Dept. of Civil Engineering, North Carolina State University, Raleigh, 1971.
8. R. M. Gutkowski and J. R. Goodman, "Progress Report on Analysis and Design of Laminated Timber Tudor Arches," Dept. of Civil Engineering, Colorado State University, Ft. Collins, June 1978 (unpublished).
9. G. R. Dewey, R. M. Gutkowski, J. R. Goodman, and J. Bodig, *Analysis and Testing of Single- and Double-Tapered Glulam Beams,* Structural Research Rep. 25, Dept. of Civil Engineering, Colorado State University, Fort Collins, Nov. 1979.
10. V. K. A. Gopu, J. R. Goodman, M. D. Vanderbilt, E. G. Thompson, and J. Bodig, *Behavior and Design of Double-Tapered Pitched and Curved Beams,* Structural Research Report 16, Dept. of Civil Engineering, Colorado State University, Fort Collins, Jan. 1976.
11. R. O. Foschi, "Analysis of Wood Diaphragms and Trusses: Part I: Diaphragms," *Can. J. Civil Eng.* **4**(3):345 (1977).

CHAPTER 10
MISCELLANEOUS WOOD STRUCTURES

Michael A. Ritter, P.E.
D. W. Ebeling, P.E.

10.1 WOOD BRIDGES

10.1.1 Introduction

Wood was probably the first material used by humans to construct a bridge. Although in the twentieth century concrete and steel replaced wood as the major material for bridge construction, wood is still widely used for short- and medium-span bridges. Of the bridges listed in the National Bridge Inventory with spans longer than 20 ft (6.10 m), approximately 8 percent, or 37,030 bridges, are made entirely of wood and 11 percent, or 51,422 bridges, use wood as one of the primary structural materials. The strength, lightweight, and energy-absorbing properties of wood are features that are desirable for bridge construction. Wood is capable of supporting short-term overloads without adverse effects, and contrary to popular belief, large wood members provide good fire-resistance qualities that meet or exceed those of other materials in severe fire exposures. From an economic standpoint, wood is competitive with other materials on a first-cost basis and shows advantages when life-cycle costs are compared. Wood bridges can be constructed in virtually any weather conditions without detriment to the material. The material is not damaged by continuous freezing and thawing and resists harmful effects of deicing agents, which cause deterioration in other bridge materials. Wood bridges do not require special equipment for installation and normally can be constructed without highly skilled labor. They also present a natural and aesthetically pleasing appearance, particularly in natural surroundings.

The misconception that wood provides a short service life has plagued wood as a construction material. Although wood is susceptible to decay or insect attack under specific conditions, it is inherently a very durable material when protected from moisture. Many covered bridges built during the nineteenth century have lasted over 100 years because they were protected from direct exposure to the

Note: In all example problems, SI units are provided only for given data and the final problem answer or answers. No intermediate values or data are expressed in SI units.

elements. In modern applications, it is seldom practical or economical to cover bridges; however, the use of wood preservatives has extended the life of wood used in exposed bridge applications. Using modern application techniques and preservative chemicals, wood can now be effectively protected from deterioration for periods of 50 years or longer. Treated wood requires little maintenance and no painting, which are distinct advantages over the life of the structure.

Another misconception about wood as a bridge material is that its use is limited to minor structures of no appreciable size. This belief is probably based on the fact that trees for commercial use are limited in size and are normally harvested before they reach maximum size. Although tree diameter limits the size of sawn lumber, the advent of glued-laminated timber (glulam timber) some 50 years ago provided designers with several compensating alternatives. Glulam timber, which is the most widely used modern wood bridge material, is manufactured by bonding sawn lumber laminations together with waterproof structural adhesives. Thus glulam timber members are virtually unlimited in depth, width, and length and can be manufactured in a wide range of shapes. Glulam timber provides higher design strengths than sawn lumber and provides better utilization of the available wood resource by permitting the manufacture of large wood structural elements from smaller lumber sizes. Technological advances in laminating over the past four decades have further increased the suitability and performance of wood for modern highway bridge applications.

This section addresses the design of two types of glulam timber bridges: beam bridges with transverse decks and longitudinal glulam deck (slab) bridges. The material presented in the section is based on the 1992 edition of the AASHTO *Standard Specifications for Highway Bridges* (AASHTO specifications),[1] including interim specifications through 1993. When specific design requirements or criteria are not addressed by that specification, recommendations are based on referenced standards and specifications or commonly accepted design practice. Because AASHTO specifications are periodically revised to reflect new developments in bridge design, the designer should refer to the latest edition for the most current requirements. This section is not intended to serve as a substitute for current specifications.

10.1.2 Design of Glulam Timber Beam Bridges

Beam bridges consist of a series of longitudinal wood beams supporting a transverse wood deck. They are constructed of glulam timber or sawn lumber components and historically have been one of the most common and most economical types of timber bridge. For the past 25 years, beam bridges have been constructed almost exclusively from glulam timber because of the greater size and better performance characteristics glulam provides compared with sawn lumber systems. Sawn lumber beam bridges are still used to a limited degree on low-volume public and private road systems. The focus of this section will be on beam bridges constructed of glulam timber. For information regarding the design of sawn lumber beam bridges, refer to AASHTO specifications[1] and Ritter (1990).[6]

Glulam timber beam bridges consist of a series of transverse glulam timber deck panels supported on straight or slightly curved beams (Fig. 10.1). They are the most practical for clear spans of 20 to 100 ft (6.10 to 30.5 m) and are widely used on single- and multiple-lane roads and highways. Glulam timber has proved to be an excellent material for beam bridges because members are available in a range of

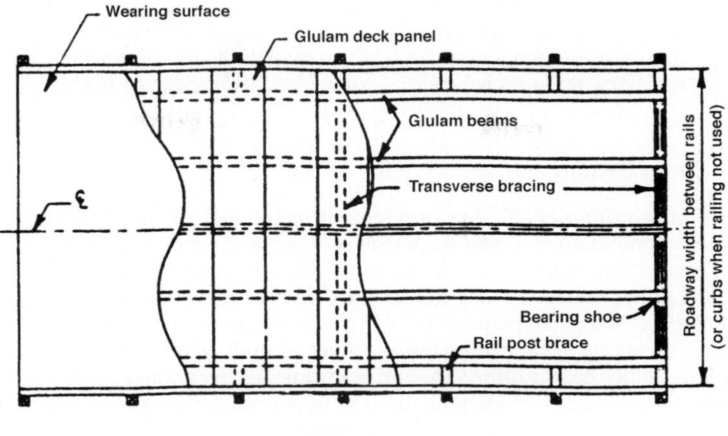

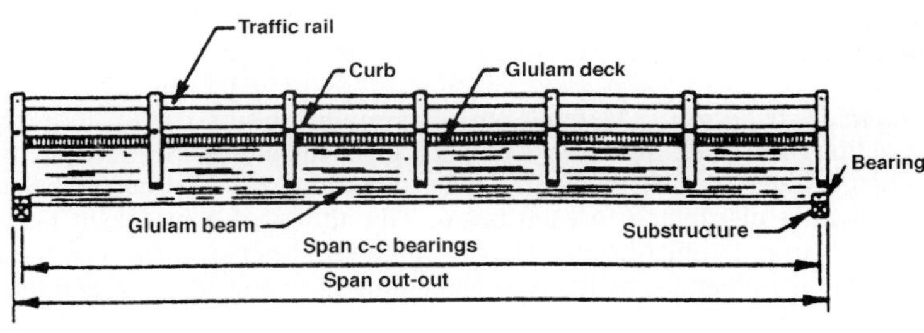

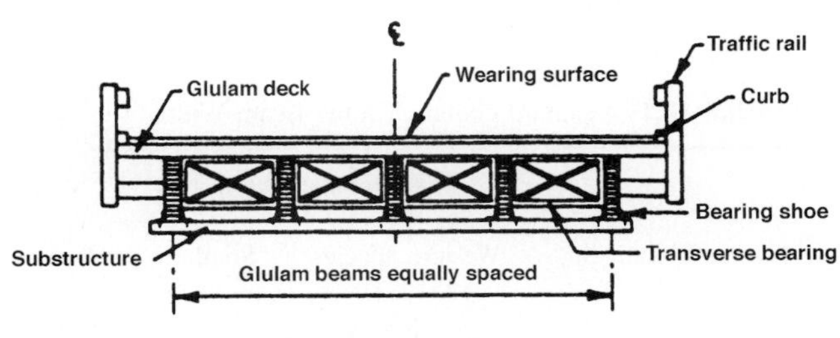

FIG. 10.1 Typical glulam beam bridge configuration.

sizes and grades and are easily adaptable to a modular or systems concept of design and construction. Although glulam timber can be custom fabricated in many shapes and sizes, the most economical structure uses standardized components in a repetitious arrangement, an approach that is particularly adaptable to bridges.

10.1.3 Beam Design

Glulam timber bridge beams are horizontally laminated members designed from the bending combinations given in AASHTO specifications[1] and the NDS Supplement.[3] These combinations provide the most efficient beam section where primary loading is applied perpendicular to the wide face of the laminations. The quality and strength of outer laminations are varied for different combination symbols to provide a wide range of tabulated design values in both positive and negative bending. Glulam timber beams offer substantial advantages over conventional sawn lumber beams because they are manufactured in larger sizes, provide improved dimensional stability, and can be cambered to offset dead-load deflection. Beams are available in standard widths ranging from 3 to 14½ in (76.2 to 362 mm) (Table 10.1) and in depth multiples of 1½ in (38.1 mm) for western species and 1⅜ in (34.9 mm) for southern pine. Beam length is usually limited by treating and transportation considerations to a practical maximum of 110 to 120 ft (33.5 to 36.6 m), but longer members may be feasible in some areas.

Live-Load Distribution. Methods for determining the maximum moment, shear, and reactions for truck and lane loads are given in the AASHTO specifications.[1] For beam bridges, the designer also must determine the portion of the total load that is laterally distributed to each beam. The ability of a bridge to laterally distribute loads to individual beams depends on the transverse stiffness of the structure as a unit and is influenced by the type and configuration of the deck and the number, spacing, and size of the beams. Load distribution also may be influenced by the type and spacing of beam transverse bracing. In view of the complexity of the theoretical analysis involved in determining lateral wheel-load distribution, the AASHTO specifications[1] give empirical methods for longitudinal beam design. The fractional portion of the total vehicle load distributed to each beam is computed as a distribution factor DF expressed in wheel lines WL per beam. The magnitude of

TABLE 10.1 Standard Glulam Timber Beam Widths

	Net finished width (in)	
Nominal width (in)	Western species	Southern pine
4	3⅛	3
6	5⅛	5
8	6¾	6¾
10	8¾	8½
12	10¾	10½
14	12¼	12¼
16	14¼	14¼

Note: 1 in = 25.4 mm.

the design forces is determined by multiplying the distribution factor for each beam by the maximum force produced by one wheel line of the design vehicle (moment, shear, reaction, and so forth). The procedures for determining distribution factors for longitudinal beams depend on the type of force and are specified separately for moment, deflection shear, and reactions.

1. *Distribution for moment.* When computing bending moments in longitudinal beams, wheel loads are assumed to act as point loads. Lateral distribution is determined by empirical methods based on the position of the beam relative to the transverse roadway section. Different criteria are given for outside beams and for interior beams; however, AASHTO requires that the load distributed to an outside beam not be less than that distributed to an interior beam.

The distribution factor for moment in outside beams is determined by computing the reaction of the wheel lines at the beam, assuming the deck acts as a simple span between beams. Wheel lines in the outside traffic lane are positioned laterally to produce the maximum reaction at the beam, but wheel lines are not placed closer than 2 ft (0.610 m) from the face of the traffic railing or curb. The distribution factor for moment for interior beams is computed from empirical formulas based on deck thickness, beam spacing, and the number of traffic lanes (Table 10.2). For glulam timber decks 6 in (152.4 mm) or more in nominal thickness, these equations are valid up to the maximum beam spacing specified in the table. When the average beam spacing exceeds the maximum, the distribution factor is the reaction of the wheel lines at the beam, assuming the flooring between beams acts as a simple span. In this case, wheel lines are laterally positioned in traffic lanes to produce the maximum beam reaction, but wheel lines in adjacent traffic lanes are separated by a minimum of 4 ft (1.219 m).

2. *Distribution for deflection.* Lateral load distribution for determining deflection is generally determined by using the same criteria specified for moment. However, AASHTO allows that for timber beam bridges with beams of equal stiffness and cross-bracing or diaphragms sufficient in depth and strength to ensure lateral distribution of loads, the deflection may be computed by considering all beams as acting together and having equal deflection.

3. *Distribution for shear.* Live-load horizontal shear in glulam timber beams is computed from the maximum vertical shear occurring at a distance from the beam

TABLE 10.2 Interior Beam Live-Load Distribution Factors for Glulam Timber Beams with Transverse Glulam Timber Decks

	Distribution factor for moment (wheel lines/beam)	
Nominal deck thickness, in	Bridges designed for one traffic lane	Bridges designed for two or more traffic lanes
4	$S/4.5$	$S/4.0$
≥ 6	$S/6.0$ (If S exceeds 6 ft, use footnote *a*)	$S/5.0$ (If S exceeds 7.5 ft, use footnote *a*)

Note: 1 ft = 0.3048 m.

[a]In this case, the distribution factor for each beam is the reaction of the wheel lines, assuming the deck between beams to act as a simple beam. S = average beam spacing (ft).

support equal to three times the beam depth ($3d$) or the span quarter point ($L/4$), whichever is less. Lateral shear distribution at this point is computed as one-half the sum of 60 percent of the shear from the undistributed wheel lines and the shear from the wheel lines distributed laterally as specified for moment. For undistributed wheel lines, one wheel line is assumed to be carried by one beam. These requirements are expressed in the following equation:

$$V_{LL} = 0.5(0.6V_{LU} + V_{LD}) \tag{10.1}$$

where V_{LL} = distributed live-load vertical shear used to compute horizontal shear, lb

V_{LU} = maximum vertical shear from an undistributed wheel line, lb

V_{LD} = maximum vertical shear from the vehicle wheel lines distributed laterally as specified for moment, lb

4. *Distribution for reactions.* Live-load distribution for end reactions is computed assuming no longitudinal distribution of wheel loads. The distribution factor for outside and interior beams is determined by computing the reaction of the wheel lines at the beam, assuming the deck acts as a simple span between beams.

Beam Configuration. One of the most influential factors on the overall economy and performance of a glulam timber bridge is the beam configuration. For a given roadway width, the spacing of beams affects size and strength requirements for both beam and deck elements and significantly influences the cost for material, fabrication, and construction. Numerous combinations of beam size and spacing are possible, and the designer must select the most economical combination that provides the required structural capacity and meets serviceability requirements. In most situations, beam configuration is based on an economic evaluation influenced by three factors: (1) site restrictions, (2) deck thickness and performance, and (3) live-load distribution to the beams.

1. *Site restrictions.* Efficient beam design favors a relatively narrow, deep section with a width-to-depth ratio of 4:1 to 7:1. In some cases, the optimal beam depth may not be practical because of vertical clearance restrictions at the site. In these situations, beam depth is limited, and the number of beams must be increased to achieve the same capacity provided by fewer, deeper beams. The most common configuration for such low-profile beam bridges uses a series of closely spaced beam groups (Fig. 10.2). In most cases, however, the longitudinal deck designs discussed in the following sections will provide a more economical design for restricted-depth crossings when span requirements permit.

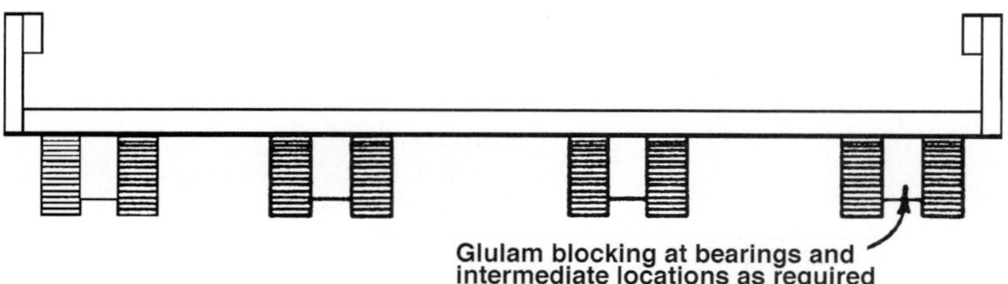

FIG. 10.2 Typical low-profile glulam beam configuration.

2. *Deck thickness and performance.* Deck thickness and performance vary with the spacing of supporting beams. As beam spacing increases, the stress and deflection of the deck increase, resulting in greater deck thickness, strength, or stiffness requirements. The thickness of glulam timber deck panels is based on standard member sizes that increase in depth in 1½- to 2-in (38.1- to 50.8-mm) increments. As a result, the load-carrying capacity and stiffness of a panel are adequate for a range of beam spacings. For example, a 6¾-in (171.4-mm) deck panel is used when the computed deck thickness is between 5⅛ and 6¾ in (130.0 and 171.4 mm). The largest effect of beam spacing on the deck occurs when the panel thickness must be increased to the next thicker panel, e.g., from 6¾ to 8¾ in (171.4 to 222.2 mm). On the other hand, considerable savings may be realized when the next smaller deck thickness can be used.

In general, the most practical and most economical beam spacing for transverse glulam timber decks supporting highway loads is between 4.5 and 6.5 ft (1.371 and 1.981 m). The maximum recommended deck overhang, measured from the centerline of the exterior beam to the face of the curb or railing, is approximately 2.5 ft (0.762 m). These values are based on deck stress and deflection considerations that may vary slightly for different panel combination symbols and configurations.

3. *Live-load distribution.* In beam design, the magnitude of the vehicle live load supported by each beam is directly related to the distribution factor computed for that beam. The higher the distribution factor (DF), the greater is the load the beam must support. Thus the value of the distribution factor gives a good indication of relative beam size and grade requirements for different configurations. It is generally beneficial to have the distribution factor for interior beams and outside beams approximately equal so that the beam sizes are equal. If there is a significant difference between interior and outside beams, different beam sizes will be required. A summary of suggested beam configurations for various bridge widths that result in the same distribution factor to interior and outside beams is given in Table 10.3. For additional information, refer to Ritter (1990).[6]

10.1.4 Deck Design

Glulam timber decks are constructed of panels manufactured of vertically laminated lumber. The panels are placed transverse to supporting beams, and loads act parallel to the wide face of the laminations. Glulam timber decks are stronger and stiffer than conventional nail-laminated lumber or plank decks, resulting in longer deck spans, increased spacing of supporting beams, and reduced live-load deflection. Additionally, glulam timber panels can be placed to provide a watertight deck, protecting the structure from the deteriorating effects of rain and snow. The two basic types of glulam timber decks are the noninterconnected deck and the doweled deck. Noninterconnected decks have no mechanical connection between adjacent panels. Doweled decks are interconnected with steel dowels to distribute loads between adjacent panels. Noninterconnected glulam timber decks are the most commonly used glulam timber deck. They are economical, require little fabrication, and are easy to install with unskilled labor and without special equipment. Because the panels are not connected to one another, each panel acts individually to resist the stresses and deflection from applied loads. Discussions in this section will be limited to noninterconnected decks, which are most common.

Noninterconnected glulam timber decks are designed from the axial glulam timber combinations given in the AASHTO specifications[1] and the NDS supplement.[3]

TABLE 10.3 Recommended Beam Spacing for Glulam Timber Beams with Transverse Glulam Timber Decks

Roadway width,* ft	Number of beams	Beam spacing, ft	Deck overhang,† ft	Moment DF, interior beams‡	Moment DF, outside beams§
		Single-lane bridges			
14	3	5.5	1.5	0.92	0.92
16	3	6.0	2.0	1.00	1.00
		Double-lane bridges			
24	5	5.0	2.0	1.00	1.00
26	5	5.5	2.0	1.10	1.10
28	5	6.0	2.0	1.20	1.20
34	6	6.0	2.0	1.20	1.20

Note: 1 ft. = 0.3048 m.

*Measured face to face of railings or of curbs when railing is not used.

†Measured from centerline of outside beam to face of railing or curbs.

‡For glulam decks 6 in or more in nominal thickness ($S/6$ for single-lane; $S/5$ for two or more lanes).

§Computed assuming the deck acts as a simple span between beams but not less than the interior beam DF.

These combinations provide the most economical and efficient layups where primary loading is applied parallel to the wide face of the laminations. Deck panels are normally 5⅛ in (130.2 mm) (5 in for southern pine) or 6¾ in (171.4 mm) thick. Increased thicknesses of 8¾ to 12¼ in (222.2 to 311.1 mm) are available but are seldom required. Panel width is a multiple of 1½ in (38.1 mm) for western species and 1⅜ in (34.9 mm) for southern pine, the net width of the individual lumber laminations. The practical width of panels ranges from approximately 30 to 55 in (0.762 to 1.397 m); however, the designer should check local manufacturing and treating limitations before specifying widths over 48 in (1.219 m). Panels can be manufactured in any specified length to be continuous across the structure. It is common practice to vary adjacent panel lengths to provide a drainage opening under curbs.

Live-Load Distribution. Load distribution for glulam timber deck panels is specified in the AASHTO Specifications[1] as a function of the wheel load width and the deck thickness. Different criteria are used for moment and deflection, as well as for shear.

1. *Distribution for moment and deflection.* In the direction of the deck span s, perpendicular to traffic, the wheel load is assumed to be uniformly distributed over a width given by the following equation (see Fig. 10.3):

$$b_t = \sqrt{0.025P} \tag{10.2}$$

where b_t = wheel load distribution width in the direction of the deck span, in
P = maximum wheel load, lb

For a 12,000-lb (53.34-kN) wheel load, b_t = 17.32 in (0.440 m).

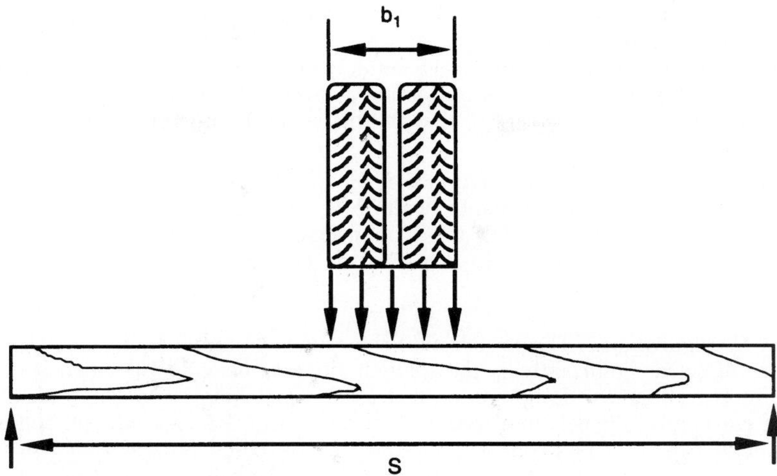

FIG. 10.3 Wheel load distribution parallel to deck span.

In the direction perpendicular to the deck span, parallel to traffic, the wheel load is distributed over an effective width equal to the deck thickness plus 15 in (381 mm), but not greater than the deck panel width (Fig. 10.4):

$$b_d = t + 15 \leq \text{actual panel width} \tag{10.3}$$

where b_d = wheel load distribution width perpendicular to the deck span, in
t = deck thickness, in

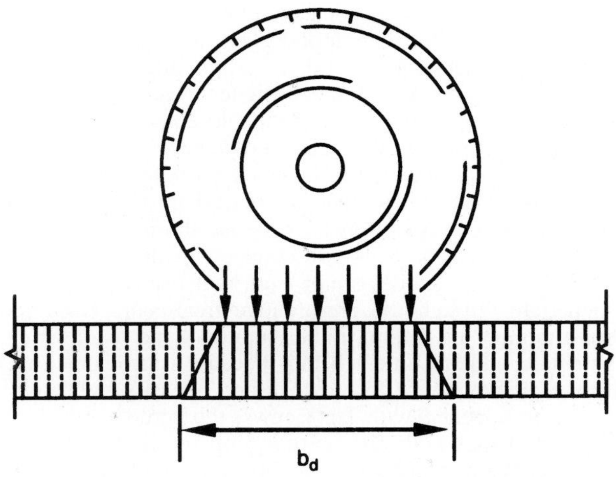

FIG. 10.4 Wheel load distribution perpendicular to deck span.

The effective deck section, defined by a deck width b_d and thickness t, is designed as a beam to resist the loads and deflection produced by one wheel line of the design vehicle. For analysis purposes, the deck is assumed to act as a simple span between beams. When the deck is continuous over more than two spans, the maximum deflection is 80 percent of that computed for a simple span to account for deck continuity.

2. *Distribution for shear.* Live-load vertical shear is computed by placing the edge of the wheel load distribution width b_t a distance from the support equal to the deck thickness t. AASHTO does not specify the distribution width for shear, but it is common practice to assume that the entire panel width is effective for horizontal shear.

Deck Configuration. The performance and economy of glulam timber deck panels can be affected significantly by the configuration and materials specified in design. The most economical design is one that uses a modular-type system with two or three standardized panels in a repetitious arrangement. Panel width and configuration are usually based on considerations for curb or railing systems with attachment points on every second or third panel. When the bridge length is not evenly divisible by the selected panel width, odd-width panels are placed on the approach ends of the deck.

10.1.5 Deck Attachment

Glulam timber decks are attached to supporting glulam timber beams with mechanical fasteners such as bolts or lag screws. The attachments must hold the panels securely and transmit longitudinal and transverse forces from the deck to the beams. They also should be easy to install and maintain and be adjustable for construction tolerances in deck alignment. The most desirable connection requires no field fabrication, where holes or cuts made after preservative treatment increase susceptibility to decay.

The performance of deck attachments is affected primarily by live-load deflection in the panels. Large deflections cause attachments to loosen from vibrations and from panel rotation about the support. The larger the deflection, the more is significant the effect. Acceptable panel deflection is difficult to quantify and should be based on the best judgment of the designer. Recommended maximum deck deflections given in this section should provide acceptable attachment performance.

Glulam timber decks are placed directly on beams without material at the deck-beam interface. Panels are attached to beams with bolted brackets that connect to the beam side or with lag screws that are placed through the deck and into the beam top. The bracket configuration uses a cast aluminum alloy bracket (Weyco bracket) that bolts through the deck and connects to the glulam timber beam in a routed slot (Fig. 10.5). It includes small teeth that firmly grip the deck and beam but do not penetrate through the preservative treatment. This bracket, which is available from a number of glulam timber suppliers and manufacturers, is the preferred attachment for glulam timber beams because it provides a tight connection, does not alter the preservative effectiveness, and is easily tightened in service.

When panels are attached with lag screws, the screws are placed through the panel and into beam tops (Fig. 10.6). It is impractical to drill beam lead holes before pressure treatment; therefore, holes must be field bored and treated before placing the screws. Lag screw attachments are not recommended because the field

FIG. 10.5 Aluminium deck bracket for attaching glulam decks to glulam beams.

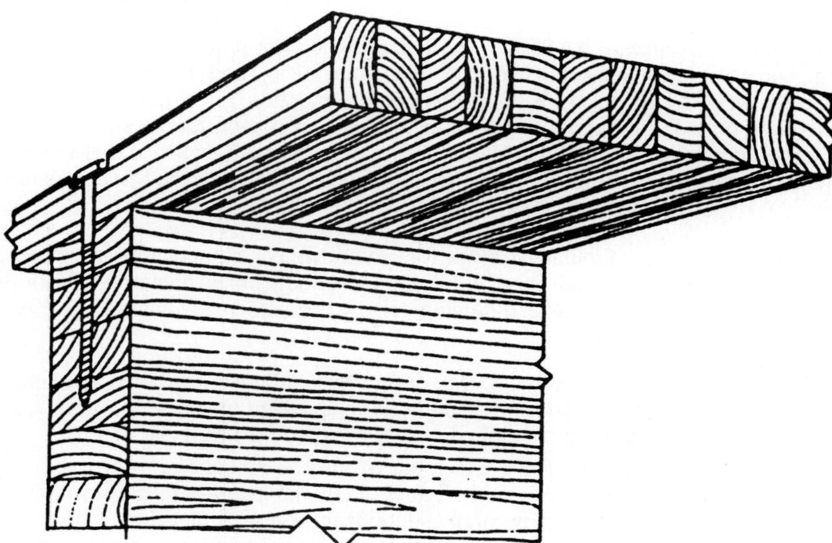

FIG. 10.6 Lag screw connection for attaching glulam decks to glulam beams.

boring increases the susceptibility to beam and deck decay, and they are not accessible for tightening if the deck is paved.

10.1.6 Design Examples

Sequential design examples are included in this section to familiarize the reader with the design procedures and requirements for glulam timber beam bridges with transverse glulam timber decks. The order of the examples is based on the most common design sequence and may vary for different applications. Specific site requirements and criteria are noted for each example. In addition, the following general criteria related to loads, materials, live-load deflection, and conditions of use are applicable.

Loads. Loads are based on the AASHTO Specification load requirements. Beam and deck design procedures are limited to AASHTO group I loads where design is routinely controlled by a combination of structure dead load and vehicle live load. For wood deck design, AASHTO special provisions for HS 20-44 and H 20-44 loads allow the use of one-axle loads of 24,000 lb (106.8 kN) or two-axle loads of 16,000 lb (71.17 kN) each, spaced 4 ft (1.219 m) apart, instead of the standard 32,000-lb (142.3-kN) axle. For most glulam timber decks, the deck panel width is 4 ft or less and the single 24,000-lb axle load [12,000-lb (53.38-kN) wheel load] is used.

Materials. Tabulated values for glulam timber are taken from the AASHTO Specifications.[1] Glulam timber material specifications are given by combination symbol; however, glulam timber also can be specified by required design values. Visually graded combination symbols are used most often, with provisions for E-rated substitution at the option of the manufacturer. *All timber components are assumed to be properly pressure-treated with an oil-type preservative after fabrication.*

Live-Load Deflection. AASHTO Specifications[1] do not require a limit for deflection but recommend that the live-load deflection not exceed 1/500 of the bridge span. Although it is recommended that these deflection guidelines be followed, deflection criteria should be based on specific design circumstances and are left to designer judgment. AASHTO does not give a recommended live-load deflection for glulam timber decks. In this section, deck deflection will be limited to a maximum value of 0.10 in (2.54 mm).

Conditions of Use. Tabulated values for glulam timber components must be adjusted for specific use conditions by all applicable adjustment factors given in the AASHTO Specifications.[1] The following criteria for adjustment factors have been used in this section.

1. *Duration of load.* Beam and deck design for combined dead load and vehicle live load are based on the 2-month load duration specified in AASHTO. Applicable tabulated design values are multiplied by a load-duration factor C_D of 1.15.

2. *Moisture content.* With the exception of glulam timber beams covered by a watertight deck, all design values for bridge components are adjusted for wet-use conditions. Based on industry recommendations, covered glulam timber beams are designed for dry-condition stresses with the exception of compression perpendicular to grain at supports, where wet-condition stress is recommended. This is based on the assumptions that a watertight deck sufficiently protects glulam timber beams from the elements and that superficial surface wetting does not cause significant increases in beam moisture content except at supports.

3. *Temperature effects and fire-retardant treatment.* Conditions requiring adjustments for temperature or fire-retardant treatment are rare in bridge applications. Design examples in this chapter do not include modification factors for temperature effect C_t or fire-retardant treatment C_R. The use of fire-retardant treatments is not permitted with glulam timber.

EXAMPLE 10.1: SIMPLE-SPAN GLULAM TIMBER BEAM BRIDGE, TWO-LANE HIGHWAY LOADING Design a glulam timber beam bridge for a length of 92 ft (28.04 m) with a center-to-center beam span of 90.5 ft (27.58 m). The bridge will have a transverse noninterconnected glulam timber deck and will carry two lanes of AASHTO HS 20-44 loading in 12 ft (3.658-m) lanes. The following provisions apply:

1. The deck wearing surface is a 3-in (76.2-mm) layer of asphalt pavement with a waterproof membrane.
2. Post and beam vehicle railing is provided with a dead load of 55 lb/ft (802 N/m). The railing extends approximately 1 ft (0.3048 m) inward from the post, and the post spacing must be 8 ft (2.438 m) or less.
3. The beam live-load deflection shall not exceed 1/500 of the beam span ($L/500$). Deck live-load deflection shall not exceed 0.10 in (2.54 mm).
4. Glulam timber is manufactured from visually graded Douglas fir.

SOLUTION: From the information given, a configuration of five beams spaced 5 ft (1.524 m) on center is selected from Table 10.3. An out-to-out deck width of 26 ft (7.925 m) will be used to accommodate the two 12-ft (3.658 m) traffic lanes and railing width (Fig. 10.7).

Beam Design. Beam design is an interactive process. A combination symbol is selected, and the beam is designed for bending, deflection, shear, and bearing requirements. Design is routinely controlled by a combination of dead load and vehicle live load given in AASHTO load group I. Transverse or longitudinal loads may be significant in some cases and also should be checked.

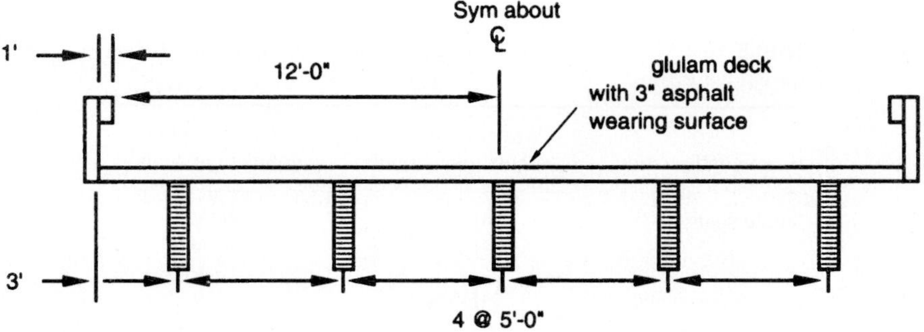

FIG. 10.7 Bridge cross section.

Select a Beam Combination Symbol. Several glulam timber combination symbols commonly used for bridge beams are given in Table 10.4. For this design, combination symbol 24F-V4, manufactured from visually graded Douglas fir, is selected for the beams. Tabulated values from the AASHTO Specifications[1] are as follows:

$$F_{bx} = 2{,}400 \text{ lb/in}^2 \ (16.55 \text{ MPa})$$

$$F_{c\perp x} = 650 \text{ lb/in}^2 \ (4.481 \text{ MPa})$$

$$F_{vx} = 165 \text{ lb/in}^2 \ (1.138 \text{ MPa})$$

$$E_x = 1{,}800{,}000 \text{ lb/in}^2 \ (12.41 \text{ GPa})$$

Determine Deck Dead Load and Dead-Load Moment. The dead load *DL* of the deck and wearing surface is computed in pounds per square foot based on AASHTO unit material weights of 50 lb/ft^3 (800.9 kg/m^3) for wood and 150 lb/ft^3 (2402 kg/m^3) for asphalt pavement. At this time, the deck thickness is unknown, so a thickness of 5⅛ in is tentatively assumed:

$$DL = \frac{(5.125 \text{ in})(50 \text{ lb/ft}^3)}{12 \text{ in/ft}} + \frac{(3 \text{ in})(150 \text{ lb/ft}^3)}{12 \text{ in/ft}} = 59 \text{ lb/ft}^2$$

The deck dead load applied to each beam is equal to the tributary deck width supported by the beam. In this case, interior beams support 5 ft (1.524 m) of deck width. Outside beams support 5.5 ft (1.676 m) of deck plus 55 lb/ft (881.0 kg/m^3) of railing dead load.

For interior beams,

$$\text{Deck } W_{DL} = (5 \text{ ft})(59 \text{ lb/ft}^2) = 295 \text{ lb/ft}$$

$$\text{Deck } M_{DL} = \frac{W_{DL}L^2}{8} = \frac{(295 \text{ lb/ft})(90.5 \text{ ft})^2}{8} = 302{,}015 \text{ ft·lb}$$

For outside beams,

$$\text{Deck } W_{DL} = (5.5 \text{ ft})(59 \text{ lb/ft}^2) + 55 \text{ lb/ft} = 380 \text{ lb/ft}$$

$$\text{Deck } M_{DL} = \frac{(380 \text{ lb/ft})(90.5 \text{ ft})^2}{8} = 389{,}037 \text{ ft·lb}$$

TABLE 10.4 Glulam Timber Combination Symbols Commonly Used for Bridge Beams

Beam configuration	Western species combination symbols	Southern pine combination symbols
Single spans	24F-V3	24F-V2
	24F-V4	24F-V3
	—	24F-V6
Continuous spans	24F-V8	24F-V5

Determine Live-Load Distribution for Moment. The live-load distribution factor DF for moment is determined in truck wheel lines WL per beam. From AASHTO tables (see Table 10.2), the distribution factor for interior beams is $S/5.0$, where S is the average beam spacing in feet:

$$DF_{\text{interior}} = \frac{S}{5} = \frac{5 \text{ ft}}{5} = 1.0WL/\text{beam}$$

For outside beams, the live-load distribution factor is determined as the reaction at the outside beam, assuming that the truck wheel line is 2 ft (0.610 m) from the rail face and the deck acts as a simple span between supports (Fig. 10.8). By examination, $DF_{\text{outside}} = 1.0WL/\text{beam}$.

Determine Live-Load Moment. The maximum moment for one wheel line of the design vehicle is computed by statics or obtained from design tables given in the AASHTO specifications[1] and other publications. For a span of 90.5 ft (27.58 m), the maximum HS 20-44 moment is 676,665 ft·lb. The live-load moment per beam is determined by multiplying the maximum moment for one wheel line by the distribution factor DF. For interior and outside beams,

$$M_{LL} = 676{,}670 \text{ ft·lb } (1.0WL/\text{beam}) = 676{,}670 \text{ ft·lb}$$

Determine Beam Size Based on Bending. Beams must be designed to satisfy the following requirement:

$$F'_b \leq \frac{M}{S_x} \qquad \text{or} \qquad S_x \geq \frac{M}{F'_{bx}}$$

The allowable beam bending stress F'_b is determined by multiplying the tabulated

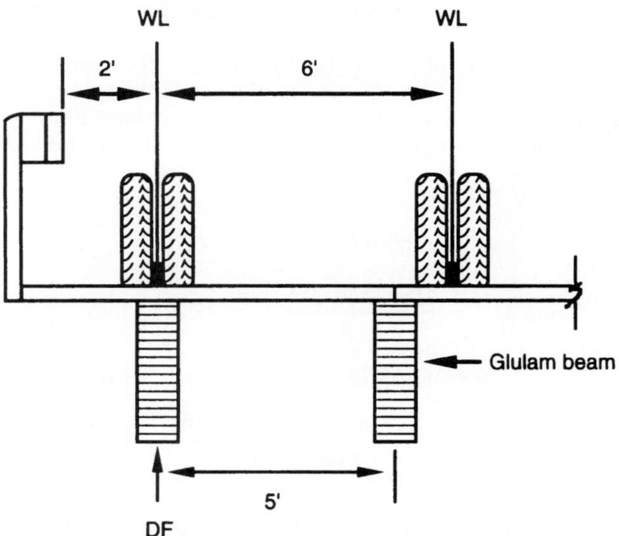

FIG. 10.8 Wheel load placement for outside beam.

bending stress F_{bx} by the wet-service factor C_M, load-duration factor C_D, and the more restrictive of the volume factor C_V or beam-stability factor C_L:

$$F'_b = F_{bx} C_M C_D (C_V \text{ or } C_L)$$

In most cases, the volume factor will control in bridge design. Thus the beam will be designed initially assuming that C_V controls, and then C_L will be checked. Per the AASHTO Specifications,[1] $C_D = 1.15$ will be used for the combination of vehicle live load and dead load. Because the glulam timber deck and asphalt wearing surface provide an essentially watertight system, protecting the beams from direct exposure to the elements, $C_M = 1.0$.

$$F'_b = F_{bx} C_M C_D C_V = 2400 \text{ lb/in}^2 (1.15)(1.0)(C_V) = 2760 \text{ lb/in}^2 (C_V)$$

$$C_V = (21/L)^{1/x}(12/d)^{1/x}(5.125/b)^{1/x} \leq 1.0$$

where $x = 10$ in C_V calculations for Douglas fir.

Initial beam design will be based on the outside beams, which have a greater required moment capacity. Beam size is unknown, and values for C_V and beam dead load must be estimated. An iterative process is followed to arrive at an acceptable beam size.

$$M = 389{,}037 \text{ ft·lb} + 676{,}670 \text{ ft·lb} + \text{beam } M_{DL} = 1{,}065{,}707 \text{ ft·lb} + \text{beam } M_{DL}$$

Generally, a beam depth-to-width ratio of 7:1 or less is preferable for bridge applications. A design aid for estimating initial values for C_V and beam weight is given in Fig. 10.9.

Assuming a beam width of 10¾ in (273 mm), $C_V = 0.67$ per Fig. 10.7 for span of 90.5 ft, and a beam for western species glulam. Similar design charts can be developed for southern pine or other species which may have a different exponent for x in the volume effect equation weight of 250 lb/ft, an initial beam size is determined:

$$F'_b = 2760(0.67) = 1849 \text{ lb/in}^2$$

$$\text{Beam } M_{DL} = \frac{(250 \text{ lb/ft})(90.5)^2}{8} = 255{,}945 \text{ ft·lb}$$

$$M = 1{,}065{,}707 + 255{,}945 = 1{,}321{,}652 \text{ ft·lb}$$

$$S_x \text{ required} = \frac{(1{,}321{,}652 \text{ ft·lb})(12 \text{ in/ft})}{1849 \text{ lb/in}^2} = 8578 \text{ in}^3$$

Entering the glulam timber beam tables (Reference Data Table A.3) for western species, a beam size of 10¾ × 70.5 in (273 × 1791 mm) provides an S_x value of

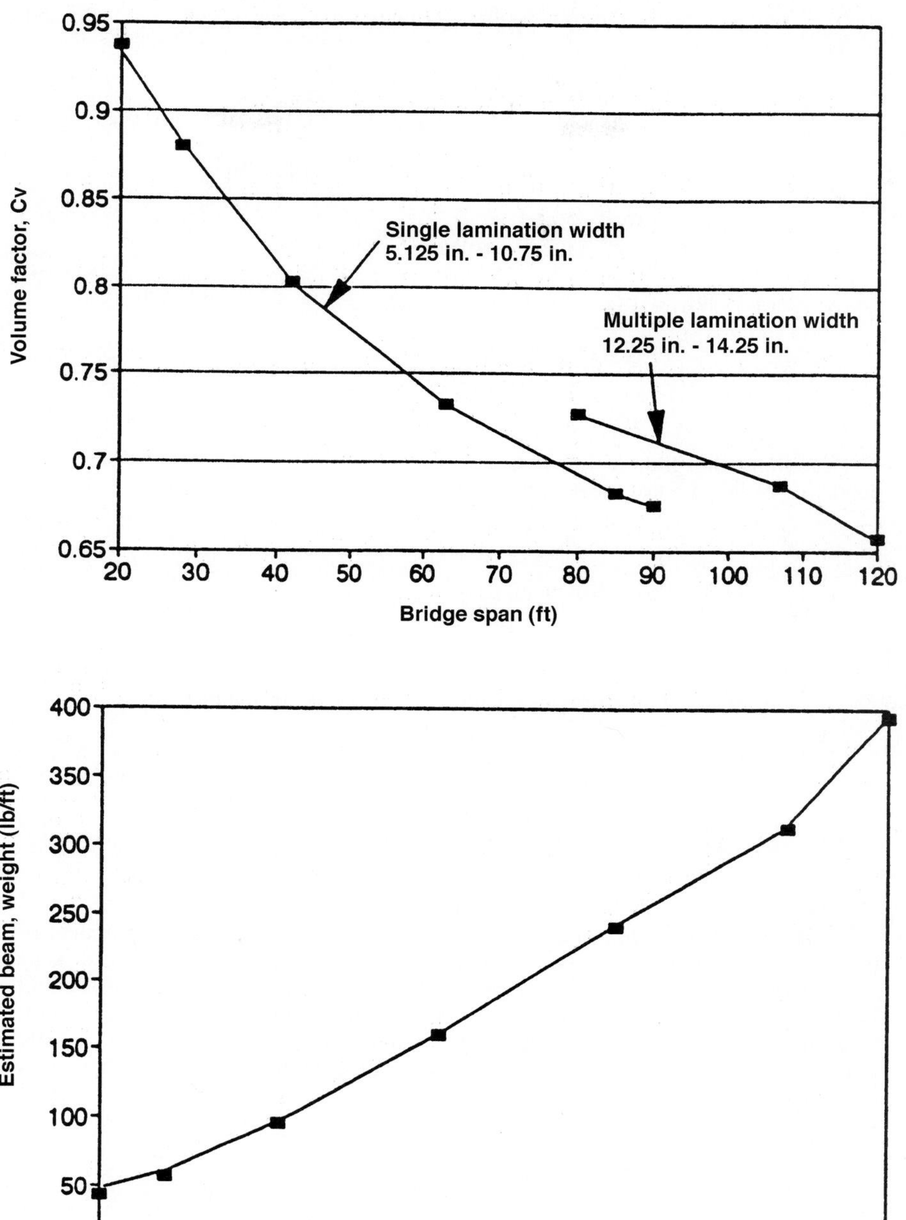

FIG. 10.9 Graphic aids for estimating initial beam volume factor and weight.

8905 in^3 and a beam weight of 263 lb/ft. Values for F'_b and M are computed and the beam size is checked:

$$C_V = (21/90.5)^{1/10}(12/70.5)^{1/10}(5.125/10.75)^{1/10} = 0.67$$

$$F'_b = 2760 \text{ ft·lb}(C_V) = 2760(0.67) = 1849 \text{ lb/in}^2$$

$$M_{DL} = \frac{(263)(90.5)^2}{8} = 269{,}254 \text{ ft·lb}$$

$$M_{TL} = 1{,}065{,}707 \text{ ft·lb} + 269{,}254 \text{ ft·lb} = 1{,}334{,}961 \text{ ft·lb}$$

$$S_x \text{ required} = \frac{(1{,}334{,}961 \text{ ft·lb})(12 \text{ in/ft})}{1849 \text{ in}^3} = 8664 \text{ in}^3$$

Examining the glulam timber beam tables (Table A.3), the next lower beam depth of 69 in will not meet design requirements. Therefore, a 10¾- × 70½-in (273 × 1790 mm) beam is selected, and the actual bending stress is computed:

$$f_b = \frac{(1{,}334{,}961 \text{ ft·lb})(12 \text{ in/ft})}{8905 \text{ in}^3} = 1799 \text{ lb/in}^2 \leq F'_b = 1849 \text{ lb/in}^2$$

The selected beam size is next evaluated for interior beam loading:

$$M = 302{,}015 + 676{,}670 + 269{,}254 = 1{,}247{,}939 \text{ ft·lb}$$

$$S_x \text{ required} = \frac{(1{,}247{,}939 \text{ ft·lb})(12 \text{ in/ft})}{1849 \text{ lb/in}^2} = 8099 \text{ in}^3$$

From the glulam timber beam tables (Table A.3), the beam depth for interior beams could be reduced by two laminations to a 10¾- by 67½-in (273 × 1714 mm) member. If this is done, provisions must be made at the bearings to account for the depth difference between interior and outside beams. In this case, a uniform beam depth is considered more economical, and a 10¾- by 70½-in (273 × 1790 mm) beam will be used for all beams. Bending stress for interior beams is computed:

$$f_b = \frac{(1{,}247{,}939 \text{ ft·lb})(12 \text{ in/ft})}{8905 \text{ in}^3} = 1682 \text{ lb/in}^2 \leq F'_b = 1849 \text{ lb/in}^2$$

The beam must next be checked for lateral stability using AASHTO requirements. Assuming a maximum spacing between points of lateral support, transverse beam bracing will be provided at the bearings and at the quarter points.

$$\ell_u = \frac{L}{4} = \frac{90.5\text{ ft}}{4} = 22.63\text{ ft}$$

$$\frac{\ell_u}{d} = \frac{(22.63\text{ ft})(12\text{ in/ft})}{70.5\text{ in}} = 3.85 \qquad \frac{\ell_u}{d} < 7$$

$$\ell_e = 2.06\ell_u = (2.06)(22.63\text{ in})(12\text{ in/ft}) = 559\text{ in}$$

$$R_B = \sqrt{\frac{(\ell_e)(d)}{b^2}} = \sqrt{\frac{(559\text{ in})(70.5\text{ in})}{(10.75\text{ in})^2}} = 18.47$$

The beam stability factor C_L is determined using $K_{bE} = 0.609$ for glulam timber. As with bending stress, $C_M = 1.0$ is assumed for E.

$$C_L = \frac{1 + (F_{bE}/F_b^*)}{1.90} - \sqrt{\frac{[1 + (F_{bE}/F_b^*)]^2}{3.61} - \frac{(F_{bE}/F_b^*)}{0.95}}$$

$$E' = E_x C_M = 1{,}800{,}000\text{ lb/in}^2(1.0) = 1{,}800{,}000\text{ lb/in}^2$$

$$F_{bE} = \frac{K_{bE}E'}{(R_B)^2} = \frac{(0.609)(1{,}800{,}000\text{ lb/in}^2)}{(18.47)^2} = 3213\text{ lb/in}^2$$

$$\frac{F_{bE}}{F_b^*} = \frac{3213\text{ lb/in}^2}{2760\text{ lb/in}^2} = 1.16$$

Thus

$$C_L = \frac{1 + 1.16}{1.90} - \sqrt{\frac{(1 + 1.1)^2}{3.61} - \frac{1.16}{0.95}} = 0.87$$

As assumed, the volume factor $C_V = 0.67$ will control over the beam stability factor $C_L = 0.87$.

Check Live-Load Deflection. Live-load deflection is checked by assuming that deflection is distributed in the same manner as bending; one beam resists the deflection produced by one wheel line. Deflection can be computed through static analysis or from coefficients provided in design tables. Using a deflection coefficient *DC* from Ritter (1990),[6] the beam moment of inertia I_x and deflection are computed for one HS 20-44 wheel line on a span of 90.5 ft (27.6 m):

$$I_x = \frac{bd^3}{12} = \frac{(10.75\text{ in})(70.5\text{ in})^3}{12} = 313{,}902\text{ in}^4$$

$$\Delta_{LL} = \frac{DC}{E'I_x} = \frac{9.06 \times 10^{11}}{E'I_x} = \frac{9.06 \times 10^{11}}{(1{,}800{,}000\text{ lb/in}^2)(313{,}903\text{ in}^4)}$$

$$= 1.60\text{ in (40.6 mm)} = L/679$$

$L/679 < L/500$, so live-load deflection is acceptable.

Check Horizontal Shear. From bending calculations, the total dead load for outside beams is 380 lb/ft (5.55 kN/m) for the deck and railing and 263 lb/ft (3.48 kN/m) for the beam, for a total of 643 lb/ft (9.39 kN/m). Neglecting loads within

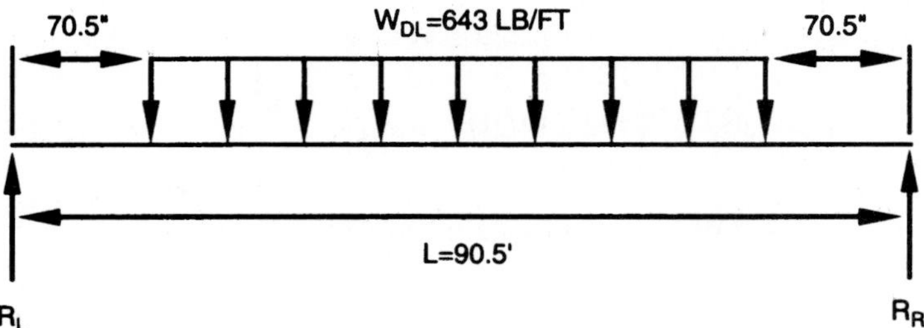

FIG. 10.10 Dead load placement for vertical shear.

a distance d = 70.5 in (1790 mm) from the supports, dead-load vertical shear is computed (Fig. 10.10):

$$V_{DL} = w_{DL}\left(\frac{L}{2} - d\right) = 643\ \text{lb/ft}\left(\frac{90.5\ \text{ft}}{2} - \frac{70.5\ \text{in}}{12\ \text{in/ft}}\right) = 25{,}318\ \text{lb}$$

Live-load vertical shear is computed from the maximum vertical shear occurring at the lesser of $3d$ or $L/4$ from the support. $3d$ controls (see below), and maximum vertical shear at that location due to one wheel line of an HS 20-44 truck (V_{LU}) is determined (Fig. 10.11):

$$3d = \frac{3(70.5\ \text{in})}{12\ \text{in/ft}} = 17.63\ \text{ft} \qquad \frac{L}{4} = \frac{90.5\ \text{ft}}{4} = 22.63\ \text{ft}$$

$$V_{LU} = R_L = 25{,}270\ \text{lb}$$

The AASHTO Specifications[1] require that live-load vertical shear be based on the maximum vertical shear due to undistributed wheel loads V_{LU} and wheel loads distributed laterally as specified for moment V_{LD}, as given by the Eq. (10.1). In this case, the distribution factor for moment equals 1.0, so the values for both V_{LU} and V_{LD} are 25,270 lb.

$$V_{LL} = 0.50[(0.60)(25{,}270\ \text{lb}) + 25{,}270\ \text{lb}] = 20{,}216\ \text{lb}$$

$$\text{Total vertical shear} = V_{DL} + V_{LL} = 25{,}318\ \text{lb} + 20{,}216\ \text{lb} = 45{,}534\ \text{lb}$$

Stress in horizontal shear is computed in accordance with AASHTO requirements:

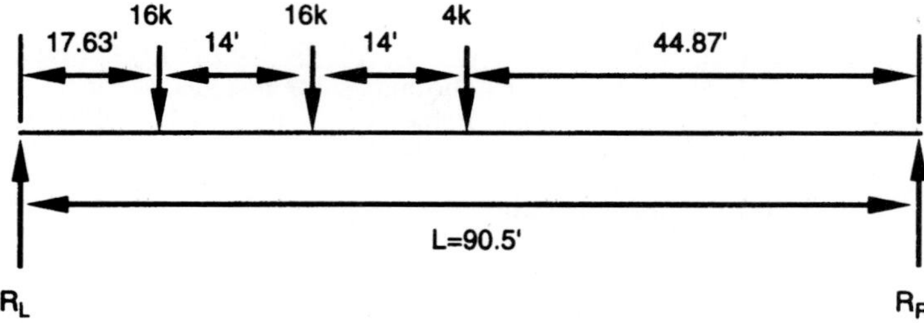

FIG. 10.11 Live load placement for vertical shear.

$$f_v = \frac{3V}{2bd} = \frac{(3)(45{,}534\ \text{lb})}{(2)(10.75\ \text{in})(70.5\ \text{in})} = 90\ \text{lb/in}^2$$

The allowable stress in horizontal shear is computed using $C_M = 1.0$ and $C_D = 1.15$:

$$F'_v = F_{vx}C_MC_D = (165\ \text{lb/in}^2)(1.0)(1.15) = 190\ \text{lb/in}^2$$

$F'_v = 190\ \text{lb/in}^2 > f_v = 90\ \text{lb/in}^2$, so the beam is satisfactory in horizontal shear.

Check Bearing Length and Stress. From the information provided, the bridge length is 92 ft (28.0 m) with a center-to-center beam span of 90.5 ft (27.6 m). Thus the bearing length at each beam end is 18 in. The bearing length and stress will be checked for the outside beams, which carry the greatest load.

For a unit dead load w_{DL} to outside beams of 380 lb/ft for the deck and railing and 263 lb/ft for the beam, the beam dead load reaction R_{DL} is computed:

$$R_{DL} = \frac{w_{DL}L}{2} = \frac{(380\ \text{lb/ft} + 263\ \text{lb/ft})(92\ \text{ft})}{2} = 29{,}578\ \text{lb}$$

The live-load beam reaction R_{LL} is the product of the maximum reaction for one wheel line of the design vehicle and the reaction *DF*. For outside beams, the reaction *DF* is the same as the moment *DF* of 1.0. From AASHTO Specification tables, the maximum reaction for one wheel line of an HS 20-44 truck on a span of 90.5 ft is 32,290 lb:

$$R_{LL} = R(DF) = (32{,}290\ \text{lb})(1.0) = 32{,}290\ \text{lb}$$

The bearing stress in compression perpendicular to grain $f_{c\perp}$ is computed for the bearing area A, which is the product of the beam width and the bearing length:

$$f_{c\perp} = \frac{R_{DL} + R_{LL}}{A} = \frac{(29{,}578\ \text{lb}) + (32{,}290\ \text{lb})}{(10.75\ \text{in})(18\ \text{in})} = 320\ \text{lb/in}^2$$

The allowable stress in compression perpendicular to grain $F'_{c\perp}$ is determined by multiplying the tabulated stress in compression perpendicular to grain $F_{c\perp x}$ by the wet-service factor C_M of 0.53:

$$F'_{c\perp} = F_{c\perp x}(C_M) = (650\ \text{lb/in}^2)(0.53) = 345\ \text{lb/in}^2$$

$F'_{c\perp} = 345\ \text{lb/in}^2 > f_{c\perp} = 320\ \text{lb/in}^2$, so the bearing stress is acceptable. A bearing configuration shown in Fig. 10.12 will be used.

Determine Camber. Per the AASHTO Specifications,[1] beam camber should be a minimum of three times the dead-load deflection but not less than ½ in. Dead-load deflection Δ_{DL} will be based on $w_{DL} = 643$ lb/ft for outside beams, but the same camber will be placed in both interior and outside beams.

From the glulam timber beam tables (Table A.3), the moment of inertia I_x for a 10¾- by 70½-in glulam timber beam is 313,902 in^4. Beam dead-load deflection is computed by the following equation:

$$\Delta_{DL} = \frac{5(w_{DL})(L^4)}{384(E')(I_x)} = \frac{(5)(643\ \text{lb/ft})(90.5\ \text{ft} \times 12\ \text{in/ft})^4}{(384)(1{,}800{,}000\ \text{lb/in}^2)(313{,}902\ \text{in}^4)(12\ \text{in/ft})} = 1.72\ \text{in}$$

The beams will be cambered 5 (127 mm) in at midspan.

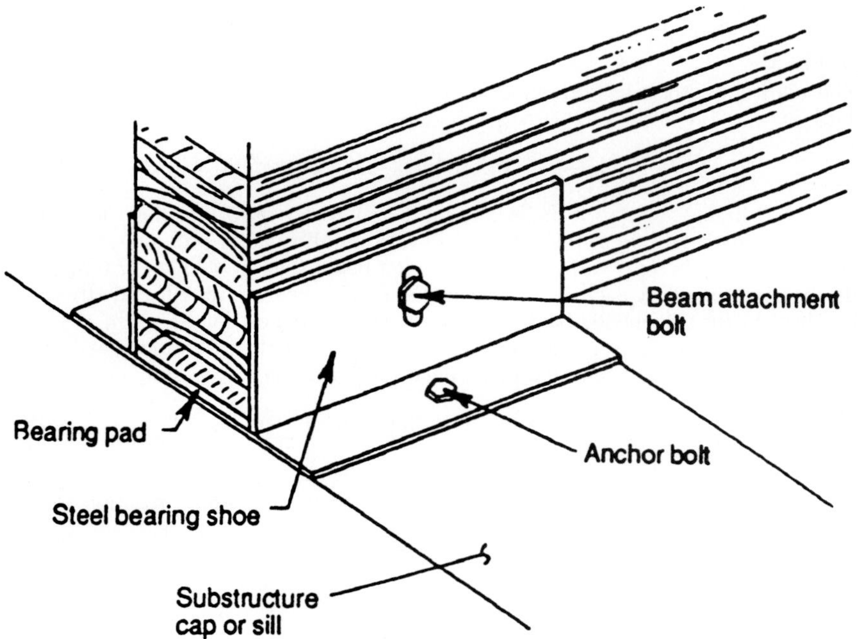

FIG. 10.12 Typical fixed-bearing configuration for glulam beams.

Deck Design. Noninterconnected glulam timber decks are designed using an interactive procedure, similar to that previously discussed for beams. The deck is assumed to act as a simple span between beams and is typically designed for bending and then checked for deflection and shear. Although deflection rather than bending may control in many applications, the acceptable level of deflection is established by the designer and may vary for different applications.

Determine the Deck Span, Design Loads, and Panel Size. Based on previous assumptions, an initial deck thickness of 5⅛ in will be used. Per the AASHTO Specifications,[1] the deck span(s) is the clear distance between supporting beams plus one-half the width of one beam, but not greater than the clear span plus the panel thickness:

$$\text{Clear distance between beams} = 60 \text{ in} - 10.75 \text{ in} = 49.25 \text{ in}$$

$$s = 49.25 + \frac{10.75 \text{ in}}{2} = 54.63 \text{ in}$$

$$\text{Clearspan} + \text{deck thickness} = 49.25 \text{ in} + 5.125 \text{ in} = 54.38 \text{ in}$$

$s = 54.38$ in will be used for design.

For HS 20-44 loading, AASHTO special provisions apply, and the deck will be designed for a 12,000-lb wheel load. Panel width for an out-to-out bridge length of 92 ft (28.0 m) will be based on an alternating repetition of panels to allow standardized panel configurations. In this case, 48-in-wide (1.22 m) panels will be used. Rail posts will be placed at the center of end panels and at the center of every second panel for a post spacing of 8 ft (2.44 m) (Fig. 10.13).

Determine Wheel Distribution Widths and Effective Deck Section Properties. The wheel load distribution width in the direction of the deck span b_t is computed using Eq. (10.2):

$$b_t = \sqrt{0.025P} = \sqrt{0.025(12{,}000 \text{ lb})} = 17.32 \text{ in}$$

Normal to the deck span, the wheel load distribution width b_d is computed using Eq. (10.3):

$$b_d = t + 15 \text{ in} = 5.125 \text{ in} + 15 \text{ in} = 20.125 \text{ in}$$

The deck will be designed with a beam of width b_d and depth t to resist the forces and deflection of one wheel load. Section modulus S_y, and moment of inertia I_y are computed using the following equations:

$$S_y = \frac{b_d t^2}{6} = \frac{(20.125 \text{ in})(5.125 \text{ in})^2}{6} = 88 \text{ in}^3 \text{ } (1.44 \text{ Kcm}^3)$$

$$I_y = \frac{b_d t^3}{12} = \frac{(20.125 \text{ in})(5.125 \text{ in})^3}{12} = 226 \text{ in}^4 \text{ } (9.41 \text{ Kcm}^4)$$

Determine Deck Dead Load. For a 5⅛-in deck and 3-in asphalt wearing surface, dead-load unit weight w_{DL} and dead-load moment M_{DL} over the effective distribution width of 20.125 in are computed:

$$w_{DL} = 20.125 \text{ in}\left[\frac{(5.125 \text{ in})(50 \text{ lb/ft}^3) + (3 \text{ in})(150 \text{ lb/ft}^3)}{1728 \text{ in}^3/\text{ft}^3}\right] = 8.2 \text{ lb/in}$$

$$M_{DL} = \frac{w_{DL}s^2}{8} = \frac{(8.2 \text{ lb/in})(54.38 \text{ in})^2}{8} = 3031 \text{ in·lb}$$

Determine Live-Load Moment. For an effective deck span less than 122 in, maximum live-load moment M_{LL} is computed for a 6-ft track width and 12,000-lb wheel load by the following equation (see Ritter[6]):

$$M_{LL} = 3000s - 25{,}983 = 3000(54.38 \text{ in}) - 25{,}983 = 137{,}157 \text{ in·lb}$$

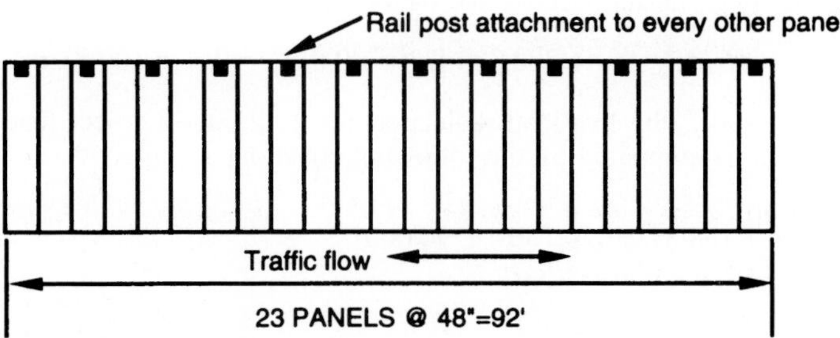

FIG. 10.13 Deck panel layout and rail post placement.

Compute Bending Stress and Select a Deck Combination Symbol. The deck is continuous over more than two spans, so bending stress f_b is based on 80 percent of the simple span moment:

$$M_{TL} = M_{LL} + M_{DL} = 3031 \text{ in·lb} + 137{,}157 \text{ in·lb} = 140{,}188 \text{ in·lb}$$

$$f_b = \frac{0.80M}{S_y} = \frac{0.80(140{,}188 \text{ in·lb})}{88 \text{ in}^3} = 1274 \text{ lb/in}^2$$

From the AASHTO glulam timber design tables for axial combinations, Douglas fir combination No. 2 is selected with the following tabulated values and wet-service factors C_M:

$$F_{by} = 1{,}800 \text{ lb/in}^2 \qquad C_M = 0.80$$

$$F_{vy} = 165 \text{ lb/in}^2 \qquad C_M = 0.875$$

$$E_y = 1{,}700{,}000 \text{ lb/in}^2 \qquad C_M = 0.833$$

From the AASHTO Specifications,[1] the allowable bending stress F'_b is equal to the tabulated bending stress F_{by} times the wet-service factor C_M, load-duration factor C_D, and bending size factor C_F:

$$F'_b = F_{by}C_MC_DC_F$$

Per the AASHTO Specifications,[1] the value of C_D is 1.15 and C_F is computed by the following equation:

$$C_F = \left(\frac{12}{t}\right)^{1/9} = \left(\frac{12}{5.125 \text{ in}}\right)^{1/9} = 1.10$$

The allowable deck bending stress is computed:

$$F'_b = F_{by}C_MC_DC_F = (1800 \text{ lb/in}^2)(0.80)(1.15)(1.10) = 1822 \text{ lb/in}^2$$

$f_b = 1{,}274$ lb/in^2 is substantially less than $F'_b = 1{,}822$ lb/in^2, and a lower grade glulam timber combination symbol may be feasible. However, no changes will be made until the live-load deflection is checked.

Check Live-Load Deflection. To determine the deck live-load deflection, the allowable modulus of elasticity E' is computed by multiplying the tabulated modulus of elasticity E_y by the wet-service factor C_M:

$$E' = (E_y)(C_M) = (1{,}700{,}000 \text{ lb/in}^2)(0.833) = 1{,}416{,}100 \text{ lb/in}^2$$

From Ritter (1990),[6] the live-load deflection for a 12,000-lb wheel load and 6-ft track width Δ_{WL} is computed by the following equation:

$$\Delta_{WL} = \frac{1.80}{E'I_y}(138.8s^3 - 20{,}780s + 90{,}000)$$

$$= \frac{1.80[(138.8)(54.38 \text{ in})^3 - (20{,}780)(54.38 \text{ in}) + 90{,}000)]}{(1{,}416{,}100 \text{ lb/in}^2)(226 \text{ in}^4)} = 0.12 \text{ in}$$

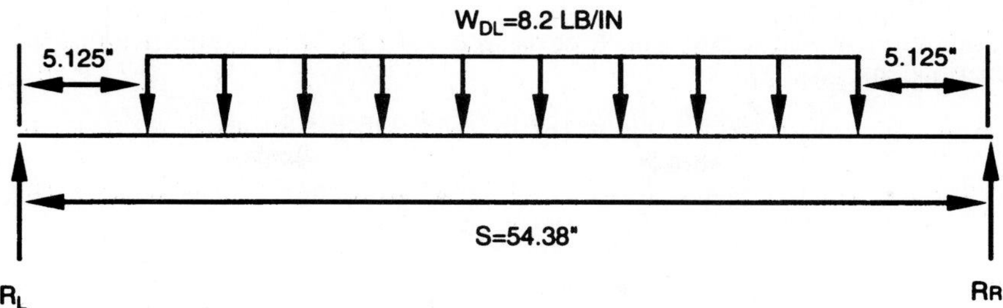

FIG. 10.14 Dead load placement for vertical shear.

The deck is continuous over more than two spans, and per AASHTO Specifications,[1] 80 percent of the simple span deflection is used to account for span continuity:

$$\Delta_{LL} = 0.80(0.12 \text{ in}) = 0.10 \text{ in}$$

The computed deflection of 0.10 in equals the maximum allowable, so the deck thickness and combination symbol are acceptable for live-load deflection. A reduction in the glulam timber combination symbol grade will reduce E', which will result in greater deck deflection. Therefore, a combination symbol No. 2 will be retained.

Check Horizontal Shear. Dead-load vertical shear is computed at a distance from the support equal to the deck thickness t, and loads acting within the distance t are neglected. For $w_{DL} = 8.2$ lb/in (Fig. 10.14),

$$V_{DL} = w_{DL}\left(\frac{s}{2} - t\right) = 8.2 \text{ lb/in}\left(\frac{54.38 \text{ in}}{2} - 5.125 \text{ in}\right) = 181 \text{ lb}$$

Live-load vertical shear is computed by placing the edge of the wheel load distribution width b_t a distance t from the support. The resultant of the 12,000-lb wheel load acts through the center of the distribution width, and live-load vertical shear V_{LL} is computed by statics (Fig. 10.15):

$$V_{LL} = R_L = \frac{(12{,}000 \text{ lb})(8.66 \text{ in} + 31.94 \text{ in})}{54.38 \text{ in}} = 8{,}959 \text{ lb}$$

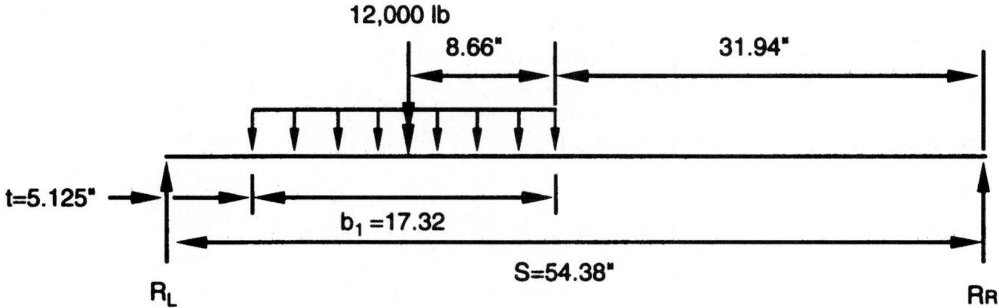

FIG. 10.15 Live load placement for vertical shear.

The applied stress in horizontal shear f_v is computed using AASHTO equations, assuming that the entire panel cross-sectional area A_p is effective in shear distribution:

$$V_{TL} = V_{DL} + V_{LL} = 181 \text{ lb} + 8959 \text{ lb} = 9140 \text{ lb}$$

$$A_p = (\text{panel width})(t) = (48 \text{ in})(5.125 \text{ in}) = 246 \text{ in}^2$$

$$f_v = \frac{1.5V}{A_p} = \frac{(1.5)(9140 \text{ lb})}{246 \text{ in}^2} = 56 \text{ lb/in}^2$$

Per AASHTO requirements, the allowable stress in horizontal shear F'_v is equal to the tabulated stress in horizontal shear F_{vy} times the wet-service factor C_M and the load-duration factor C_D. Values of C_M and C_D are 0.875 and 1.15, respectively.

$$F'_v = F_{vy}C_MC_D = (165 \text{ lb/in}^2)(0.875)(1.15) = 166 \text{ lb/in}^2$$

$f_v = 56$ lb/in^2 $< F'_v = 166$ lb/in^2, so the panel is satisfactory in horizontal shear.

Summary. The bridge superstructure will consist of five Douglas fir glulam timber beams, combination symbol 24F-V4. The beams will measure 10¾ in (273 mm) wide, 70½ in (1790 mm) deep, and 92 ft (28.04 m) long. The span center to center of bearings will be 90½ ft (27.58 m). Transverse bracing will be provided for lateral support at the bearings and at the beam quarter points. The deck will consist of 23 combination No. 2 Douglas fir glulam timber deck panels measuring 5⅛ in (130.2 mm) thick by 48 in (1.219 m) wide by 26 ft (7.925 m) long. Stresses and live load deflection are given in Table 10.5.

EXAMPLE 10.2: SIMPLE-SPAN GLULAM TIMBER BEAM BRIDGE, ONE-LANE HIGHWAY LOADING Design a glulam timber beam bridge with a span of 47 ft (14.32 m) measured center to center of bearings and a length of 48 ft (14.63 m). The bridge will have a transverse noninterconnected glulam timber deck and will carry AASHTO HS 20-44 loading in a single lane, 14 ft (4.267 m) wide. The following provisions apply:

1. The deck wearing surface is a 3-in (76.2-mm) layer of wood plank.

TABLE 10.5 Summary of Design Values for Example 10.1

Design value	Outside beams	Interior beams	Deck
f_b	1799 lb/in^2	1682 lb/in^2	1274 lb/in^2
F'_b	1849 lb/in^2	1849 lb/in^2	1822 lb/in^2
Δ_{LL}	1.60 in = $L/679$	1.60 in = $L/679$	0.10 in
f_v	90 lb/in^2	—	56 lb/in^2
F'_v	190 lb/in^2	—	166 lb/in^2
$f_{c\perp}$	320 lb/in^2	—	N/A
$F'_{c\perp}$	345 lb/in^2	—	N/A
Δ_{DL}	1.72 in	—	N/A
Camber	6 in	6 in	N/A

Note: 1 in = 25.4 mm; 1 lb/in^2 = 6.895 kPa.

2. Post and beam vehicle railing is provided with a dead load of 45 lb/ft (656.7 N/m). The railing extends approximately 1 ft (0.3048 m) inward from the deck edge.
3. The beam live-load deflection shall not exceed 1/360 of the beam span ($L/360$). Deck live-load deflection shall not exceed 0.10 in (2.54 mm).
4. Glulam timber is manufactured from visually graded southern pine.

SOLUTION: From the given information, a configuration of three beams spaced 5.5 ft on center is selected from Table 10.3. An out-to-out deck width of 16 ft will be used to accommodate the traffic lane and railing width (Fig. 10.16).

Beam Design. Beam design will follow the same basic procedure illustrated in the preceding example.

Select a Beam Combination Symbol. A southern pine combination symbol 24F-V3 is initially selected for the beams. Tabulated values and wet-service factors are obtained from the AASHTO specifications[1]:

$$F_{bx} = 2400 \text{ lb/in}^2 \text{ (16.55 MPa)} \qquad C_M = 0.80$$

$$F_{c\perp x} = 650 \text{ lb/in}^2 \text{ (4.481 MPa)} \qquad C_M = 0.53$$

$$F_{vx} = 200 \text{ lb/in}^2 \text{ (1.380 MPa)} \qquad C_M = 0.875$$

$$E_x = 1{,}800{,}000 \text{ lb/in}^2 \text{ (12.41 GPa)} \qquad C_M = 0.833$$

Determine Deck Dead Load and Dead-Load Moment. The dead load DL of the deck and wearing surface is computed in pounds per square foot based on the AASHTO unit material weight for wood of 50 lb/ft³. At this time, the deck thickness is unknown, so a thickness of 6¾ in is assumed:

$$DL = \frac{(3 \text{ in} + 6.75 \text{ in})(50 \text{ lb/ft}^3)}{12 \text{ in/ft}} = 41 \text{ lb/ft}^2$$

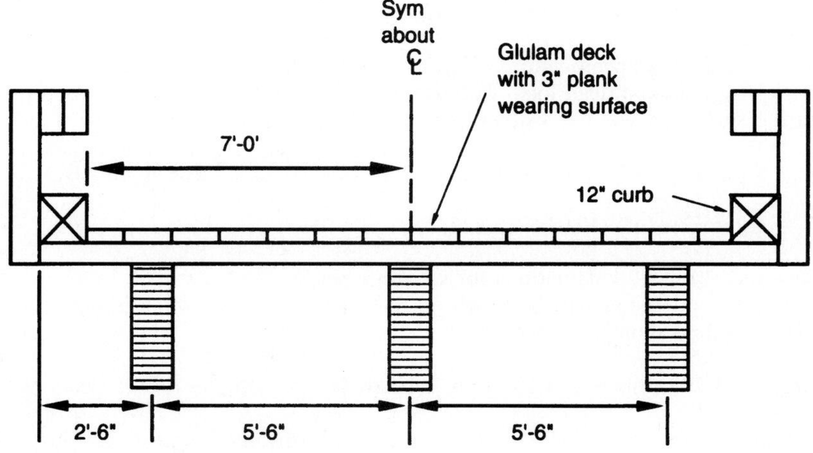

FIG. 10.16 Bridge cross section.

The deck dead load applied to each beam is equal to the tributary deck width supported by the beam. The interior beam supports 5.5 ft of deck width. Outside beams support 5.25 ft of deck plus 45 lb/ft of railing dead load.

For the interior beam,

$$\text{Deck } w_{DL} = (5.5\text{ ft})(41\text{ lb/ft}^2) = 226\text{ lb/ft}$$

$$\text{Deck } M_{DL} = \frac{w_{DL}L^2}{8} = \frac{(226\text{ lb/ft})(47\text{ ft})^2}{8} = 62{,}404\text{ ft·lb}$$

For outside beams,

$$\text{Deck } w_{DL} = (5.25\text{ ft})(41\text{ lb/ft}^2) + 45\text{ lb/ft} = 260\text{ lb/ft}$$

$$\text{Deck } M_{DL} = \frac{(260\text{ lb/ft})(47\text{ ft})^2}{8} = 71{,}793\text{ ft·lb}$$

Determine Live-Load Distribution Factors and Live-Load Moment. From Table 10.2, the live-load distribution factor for both the interior beams and the outside beams is 0.92 *WL*/beam. From AASHTO Specification tables, the maximum moment for one wheel line of an HS 20-44 truck on a span 47 ft long is 287,170 ft·lb. The live-load moment per beam is determined by multiplying the maximum moment for one wheel line by the distribution factor *DF*. For interior and outside beams,

$$M_{LL} = 287{,}170\text{ ft·lb }(0.92WL/\text{beam}) = 264{,}196\text{ ft·lb}$$

Determine Beam Size Based on Bending. The allowable beam bending stress F_b' is determined by multiplying the tabulated bending stress F_{bx} by the wet-service factor C_M, load-duration factor C_D, and the more restrictive of the volume factor C_V or beam stability factor C_L:

$$F_b' = F_{bx}C_MC_D(C_V\text{ or }C_L)$$

Per the AASHTO Specifications,[1] $C_D = 1.15$ will be used for the combination of vehicle live load and dead load. Because the glulam timber deck has a wood plank wearing surface, a wet-use value of $C_M = 0.80$ will be used:

$$F_b' = F_{bx}C_MC_DC_V = 2400\text{ lb/in}^2\ (1.15)(0.80)(C_V) = 2208\text{ lb/in}^2\ (C_V)$$

$$C_V = (21/L)^{1/x}(12/d)^{1/x}(5.125/b)^{1/x} \le 1.0$$

where $x = 20$ in C_V calculations for southern pine.

Initial beam design will be based on the outside beams, which have a slightly greater required moment capacity:

$$M_{TL} = 71{,}793\text{ ft·lb} + 264{,}196\text{ ft·lb} + \text{beam } M_{DL} = 335{,}989\text{ ft·lb} + \text{beam } M_{DL}$$

Assume a beam width of 8½ in, $C_V = 0.78$, and a beam weight of 120 lb/ft. An initial beam size is computed:

$$F_b' = 2{,}208(0.78) = 1722 \text{ lb/in}^2$$

$$\text{Beam } M_{DL} = \frac{(120 \text{ lb/ft})(47)^2}{8} = 33{,}135 \text{ ft·lb}$$

$$M = 335{,}989 + 33{,}135 = 369{,}124 \text{ ft·lb}$$

$$S_x \text{ required} = \frac{(369{,}124 \text{ ft·lb})(12 \text{ in/ft})}{1722 \text{ lb/in}^2} = 2572 \text{ in}^3$$

Entering the glulam timber beam tables for southern pine, a beam size of 8½ × 42⅝ in provides an S_x value of 2574 in³ and a beam weight of 126 lb/ft. Values for F_b' and M are computed, and the beam size is checked:

$$C_V = (21/47)^{1/20}(12/42.625)^{1/20}(5.125/8.5)^{1/20} = 0.88$$

$$F_b' = 2208(C_V) = 2208(0.88) = 1943 \text{ lb/in}^2$$

$$M_{DL} = \frac{(126)(47)^2}{8} = 34{,}792 \text{ ft·lb}$$

$$M_{TL} = 335{,}989 \text{ ft·lb} + 34{,}792 \text{ ft·lb} = 370{,}781 \text{ ft·lb}$$

$$S_x \text{ Required} = \frac{(370{,}781 \text{ ft·lb})(12 \text{ in/ft})}{1943 \text{ in}^3} = 2290 \text{ in}^3$$

Entering the glulam timber beam tables, a revised smaller beam size of 8½ × 41¼ in will meet design requirements with an S_x value of 2411 in³ and beam weight of 122 lb/ft:

$$C_V = (21/47)^{1/20}(12/41.25)^{1/20}(5.125/8.5)^{1/20} = 0.88$$

$$F_b' = 2208 \text{ ft·lb}(C_V) = 2208(0.88) = 1943 \text{ lb/in}^2$$

$$M_{DL} = \frac{(122)(47)^2}{8} = 33{,}687 \text{ ft·lb}$$

$$M_{TL} = 335{,}989 \text{ ft·lb} + 33{,}687 \text{ ft·lb} = 369{,}676 \text{ ft·lb}$$

$$S_x \text{ required} = \frac{(369{,}676 \text{ ft·lb})(12 \text{ in/ft})}{1943 \text{ lb/in}^2} = 2283 \text{ in}^3$$

Examining the glulam timber beam tables, the next lower beam depth will not meet design requirements. Therefore, an 8½- × 41¼-in beam is selected, and the actual bending stress is computed:

$$f_b = \frac{(369{,}676 \text{ ft·lb})(12 \text{ in/ft})}{2411 \text{ in}^3} = 1840 \text{ lb/in}^2 \le F_b' = 1943 \text{ lb/in}^2$$

The beam must next be checked for lateral stability using the AASHTO Specification requirements. Assuming a maximum spacing between points of lateral support, transverse beam bracing will be provided at the bearings and at centerspan:

$$\ell_u = \frac{L}{2} = \frac{47\text{ ft}}{2} = 23.5\text{ ft}$$

$$\frac{\ell_u}{d} = \frac{(23.5\text{ ft})(12\text{ in/ft})}{41.25\text{ in}} = 6.84 \qquad \frac{\ell_u}{d} < 7$$

$$\ell_e = 2.06\ell_u = (2.06)(23.5\text{ ft})(12\text{ in/ft}) = 581\text{ in}$$

$$R_B = \sqrt{\frac{(\ell_e)(d)}{b^2}} = \sqrt{\frac{(581\text{ in})(41.25\text{ in})}{(8.5\text{ in})^2}} = 18.21$$

The beam stability factor C_L is determined using $K_{bE} = 0.609$ for glulam timber. As with bending stress, wet-use conditions ($C_M = 0.833$) are assumed for E.

$$C_L = \frac{1 + (F_{bE}/F_b^*)}{1.90} - \sqrt{\frac{[1 + (F_{bE}/F_b^*)]^2}{3.61} - \frac{(F_{bE}/F_b^*)}{0.95}}$$

$$E' = E_x C_M = 1{,}800{,}000\text{ lb/in}^2\ (0.833) = 1{,}499{,}400\text{ lb/in}^2$$

$$F_{bE} = \frac{K_{bE}E'}{(R_B)^2} = \frac{(0.609)(1{,}499{,}400\text{ lb/in}^2)}{(18.21)^2} = 2754\text{ lb/in}^2$$

$$\frac{F_{bE}}{F_b^*} = \frac{2754\text{ lb/in}^2}{2208\text{ lb/in}^2} = 1.25$$

Thus
$$C_L = \frac{1 + 1.25}{1.90} - \sqrt{\frac{[1 + 1.25]^2}{3.61} - \frac{1.25}{0.95}} = 0.89$$

The volume factor $C_V = 0.88$ will control over the beam stability factor $C_L = 0.89$.

Check Live-Load Deflection. The beam moment of inertia I_x is computed, and the deflection for one HS 20-44 wheel line Δ_{WL} is computed using a deflection coefficient DC from Ritter (1990).[6] The live-load deflection Δ_{LL} is the product of Δ_{WL} and the distribution factor DF:

$$I_x = \frac{bd^3}{12} = \frac{(8.5\text{ in})(41.25\text{ in})^3}{12} = 49{,}718\text{ in}^4$$

$$\Delta_{WL} = \frac{DC}{E'I_x} = \frac{1.09 \times 10^{11}}{E'I_x} = \frac{1.09 \times 10^{11}}{(1{,}499{,}400\text{ lb/in}^2)(49{,}718\text{ in}^4)} = 1.46\text{ in}$$

$$\Delta_{LL} = \Delta_{WL}(DF) = (1.46\text{ in})(0.92) = 1.34\text{ in (34.0 mm)} = L/421$$

$L/421 < L/360$, so live-load deflection is acceptable.

Check Horizontal Shear. From bending calculations, the total dead load for outside beams is 260 lb/ft for the deck and railing and 122 lb/ft for the beam, for a total of 382 lb/ft. Neglecting loads within a distance $d = 41.25$ in from the supports, dead-load vertical shear is computed (Fig. 10.17):

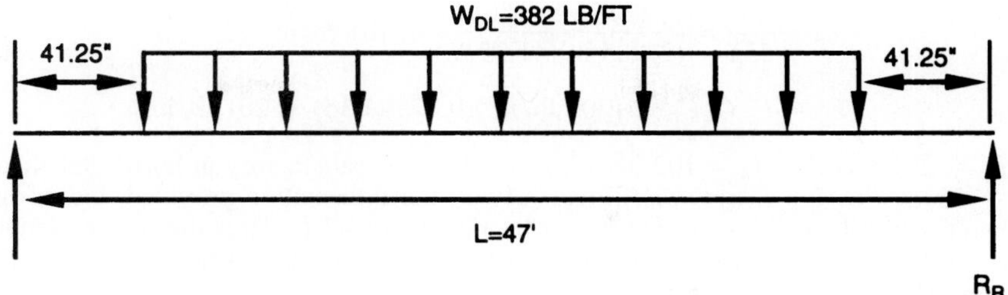

FIG. 10.17 Dead load placement for vertical shear.

$$V_{DL} = w_{DL}\left(\frac{L}{2} - d\right) = 382 \text{ lb/ft}\left(\frac{47 \text{ ft}}{2} - \frac{41.25 \text{ in}}{12 \text{ in/ft}}\right) = 7664 \text{ lb}$$

Live-load vertical shear is computed from the maximum vertical shear occurring at the lesser of $3d$ or $L/4$ from the support:

$$3d = \frac{3(41.25 \text{ in})}{12 \text{ in/ft}} = 10.31 \text{ ft} \qquad \frac{L}{4} = \frac{47 \text{ ft}}{4} = 11.75 \text{ ft}$$

$3d = 10.31$ ft controls, and maximum vertical shear at that location due to one wheel line of an HS 20-44 truck V_{LU} is determined (Fig. 10.18):

$$V_{LU} = R_L = 20{,}954 \text{ lb}$$

The distributed shear V_{LD} is the product of V_{LU} and the moment DF:

$$V_{LD} = V_{LU}(DF) = 20{,}954 \text{ lb}(0.92) = 19{,}278 \text{ lb}$$

$$V_{LL} = 0.50[(0.60)(20{,}954 \text{ lb}) + 19{,}278 \text{ lb}] = 15{,}925 \text{ lb}$$

$$\text{Total vertical shear} = V_{DL} + V_{LL} = 7664 \text{ lb} + 15{,}925 \text{ lb} = 23{,}589 \text{ lb}$$

Stress in horizontal shear is computed in accordance with AASHTO requirements. The allowable stress in horizontal shear is computed using $C_M = 0.875$ and $C_D = 1.15$:

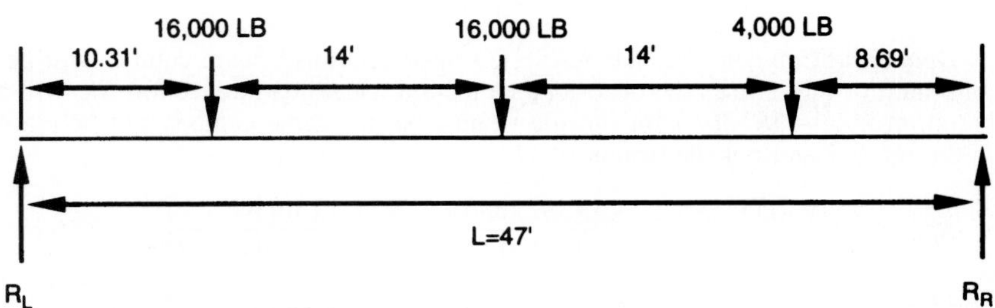

FIG. 10.18 Live load placement for vertical shear.

$$f_v = \frac{3V}{2bd} = \frac{(3)(23{,}589 \text{ lb})}{(2)(8.5 \text{ in})(41.25 \text{ in})} = 101 \text{ lb/in}^2$$

$$F'_v = F_{vx}C_M C_D = (200 \text{ lb/in}^2)(0.875)(1.15) = 201 \text{ lb/in}^2$$

$F'_v = 201 \text{ lb/in}^2 > f_v = 102 \text{ lb/in}^2$, so the beam is satisfactory in horizontal shear.

Check Bearing Length and Stress. From the information provided, the bridge length is 48 ft with a center-to-center beam span of 47 ft. Thus the bearing length at each beam end is 12 in. The bearing length and stress will be checked for the outside beams, which carry a slightly greater load.

For a unit dead load w_{DL} to outside beams of 260 lb/ft for the deck and railing and 122 lb/ft for the beam, the beam dead-load reaction R_{DL} is computed:

$$R_{DL} = \frac{w_{DL}L}{2} = \frac{(260 \text{ lb/ft} + 122 \text{ lb/ft})(48 \text{ ft})}{2} = 9168 \text{ lb}$$

From AASHTO Specification tables, the maximum reaction for one wheel line R_{WL} of an HS 20-44 truck is 28,850 lb. The live-load reaction R_{LL} is computed:

$$R_{LL} = R_{WL}(DF) = (28{,}850 \text{ lb})(0.92) = 26{,}542 \text{ lb}$$

Bearing stress in compression perpendicular to grain $f_{c\perp}$ is computed for the bearing area A:

$$f_{c\perp} = \frac{R_{DL} + R_{LL}}{A} = \frac{(9168 \text{ lb}) + (26{,}542 \text{ lb})}{(8.5 \text{ in})(12 \text{ in})} = 350 \text{ lb/in}^2$$

The allowable stress in compression perpendicular to grain $F'_{c\perp}$ is determined by multiplying the tabulated stress in compression perpendicular to grain $F_{c\perp x}$ by the wet-service factor C_M of 0.53:

$$F'_{c\perp} = F_{c\perp x}(C_M) = (650 \text{ lb/in}^2)(0.53) = 345 \text{ lb/in}^2$$

$F'_{c\perp} = 345 \text{ lb/in}^2 < f_{c\perp} = 350 \text{ lb/in}^2$, so the bearing stress exceeds the allowable by approximately 1.5 percent. In most cases, this minor difference is acceptable and within roundoff error. However, the bearing length will be extended to 13 in. The minor change in span length will have a slight conservative effect on values previously computed but will be negligible. The applied stress is computed for the revised bearing length of 13 in:

$$f_{c\perp} = \frac{R_{DL} + R_{LL}}{A} = \frac{(9168 \text{ lb}) + (26{,}542 \text{ lb})}{(8.5 \text{ in})(13 \text{ in})} = 323 \text{ lb/in}^2$$

Determine Camber. Per the AASHTO Specifications,[1] beam camber will be a minimum of three times the dead-load deflection. Dead-load deflection Δ_{DL} will be based on $w_{DL} = 382$ lb/ft for outside beams, but the same camber will be placed in the interior and outside beams.

$$\Delta_{DL} = \frac{5(w_{DL})(L^4)}{384(E')(I_x)} = \frac{(5)(382 \text{ lb/ft})(47 \text{ ft} \times 12 \text{ in/ft})^4}{(384)(1{,}499{,}400 \text{ lb/in}^2)(49{,}718 \text{ in}^4)(12 \text{ in/ft})} = 0.56 \text{ in}$$

The beams will be cambered 1¾ in (44.4 mm) at centerspan.

Deck Design. The deck will be assumed to act as a simple span between beams and will be designed for bending and then checked for deflection and shear.

Determine the Deck Span, Design Loads, and Panel Size. For the beam spacing of 5.5 ft, an initial deck thickness of 6¾ in will be used. Per the AASHTO Specifications,[1] the deck span(s) is the clear distance between supporting beams plus one-half the width of one beam, but not greater than the clear span plus the panel thickness:

$$\text{Clear distance between beams} = 66 \text{ in} - 8.5 \text{ in} = 57.5 \text{ in}$$

$$s = 57.5 + \frac{8.5 \text{ in}}{2} = 61.75 \text{ in}$$

$$\text{Clear span} + \text{deck thickness} = 57.5 \text{ in} + 6.75 \text{ in} = 64.25 \text{ in}$$

$s = 61.75$ in will be used for design.

For HS 20-44 loading, AASHTO special provisions apply, and the deck will be designed for a 12,000-lb wheel load. Panel width for an out-to-out bridge length of 48 ft will be 11 panels 48⅛ in wide and 1 panel 6⅝ in wide (Fig. 10.19).

Determine Wheel Distribution Widths and Effective Deck Section Properties. The wheel load distribution width in the direction of the deck span is computed using Eq. (10.2):

$$b_t = \sqrt{0.025P} = \sqrt{0.025(12{,}000 \text{ lb})} = 17.32 \text{ in}$$

Normal to the deck span, the wheel load distribution width is computed using Eq. (10.3):

$$b_d = t + 15 \text{ in} = 6.75 \text{ in} + 15 \text{ in} = 21.75 \text{ in}$$

Section modulus S_y and moment of inertia I_y are computed using the following equations:

$$S_y = \frac{b_d t^2}{6} = \frac{(21.75 \text{ in})(6.75 \text{ in})^2}{6} = 165 \text{ in}^3$$

$$I_y = \frac{b_d t^3}{12} = \frac{(21.75 \text{ in})(6.75 \text{ in})^3}{12} = 557 \text{ in}^4$$

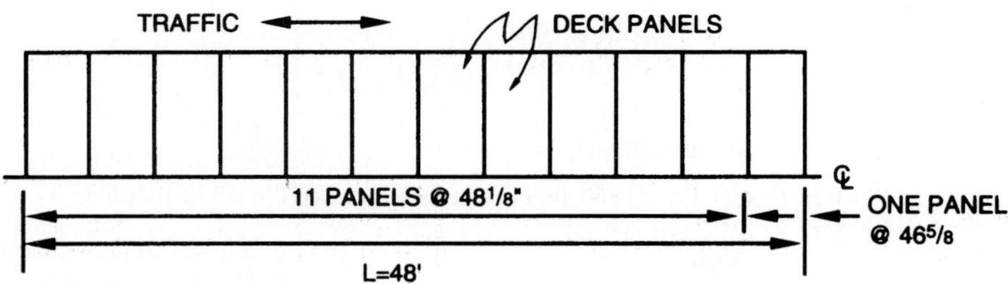

FIG. 10.19 Deck panel layout.

Determine Deck Dead Load. For a 6¾-in deck and 3-in wood plank wearing surface, dead-load unit weight w_{DL} and dead-load moment M_{DL} over the effective distribution width of 21.75 in are computed:

$$w_{DL} = 21.75 \text{ in}\left[\frac{(6.75 \text{ in} + 3 \text{ in})(50 \text{ lb/ft}^3)}{1728 \text{ in}^3/\text{ft}^3}\right] = 6.1 \text{ lb/in}$$

$$M_{DL} = \frac{w_{DL}s^2}{8} = \frac{(6.1 \text{ lb/in})(61.75 \text{ in})^2}{8} = 2907 \text{ in·lb}$$

Determine Live-Load Moment. For an effective deck span of less than 122 in, maximum live-load moment M_{LL} is computed for a 6-ft track width and 12,000-lb wheel load by the following equation (see Ritter[6]):

$$M_{LL} = 3000s - 25{,}983 = 3000(61.75 \text{ in}) - 25{,}983 = 159{,}267 \text{ in·lb}$$

Compute Bending Stress and Select a Deck Combination Symbol. The deck is not continuous over more than two spans, so bending stress f_b is based on the simple-span moment:

$$M_{TL} = M_{LL} + M_{DL} = 2907 \text{ in·lb} + 159{,}267 \text{ in·lb} = 162{,}174 \text{ in·lb}$$

$$f_b = \frac{M}{S_y} = \frac{162{,}174 \text{ in·lb}}{165 \text{ in}^3} = 983 \text{ lb/in}^2$$

From the AASHTO glulam timber design tables for axial combinations, southern pine combination No. 47 is selected with the following tabulated values and wet-service factors C_M:

$$F_{by} = 1{,}750 \text{ lb/in}^2 \qquad C_M = 0.80$$

$$F_{vy} = 175 \text{ lb/in}^2 \qquad C_M = 0.875$$

$$E_y = 1{,}400{,}000 \text{ lb/in}^2 \qquad C_M = 0.833$$

The allowable bending stress F'_b is equal to the tabulated bending stress F_{by} times the wet-service factor C_M, load-duration factor C_D, and bending size factor C_F:

$$F'_b = F_{by}C_MC_DC_F$$

Per the AASHTO specifications,[1] the value of C_D is 1.15 and C_F is computed by the following equation:

$$C_F = \left(\frac{12}{t}\right)^{1/9} = \left(\frac{12}{6.75 \text{ in}}\right)^{1/9} = 1.07$$

The allowable deck bending stress is computed:

$$F'_b = F_{by}C_MC_DC_F = (1750 \text{ lb/in}^2)(0.80)(1.15)(1.07) = 1723 \text{ lb/in}^2$$

$f_b = 983$ lb/in² is substantially less than $F'_b = 1723$ lb/in², so a lower-grade glulam timber combination symbol or deck thickness may be feasible. However, no changes will be made until the live-load deflection is checked.

Check Live-Load Deflection. The allowable modulus of elasticity E' is computed by multiplying the tabulated modulus of elasticity E_y by the wet-service factor C_M:

$$E' = (E_y)(C_M) = (1{,}400{,}000 \text{ lb/in}^2)(0.833) = 1{,}166{,}200 \text{ lb/in}^2$$

From Ritter (1990)[6] the live-load deflection Δ_{LL} for a 12,000-lb wheel load and 6-ft track width is computed by the following equation:

$$\Delta_{LL} = \frac{1.80}{E'I_y}(138.8s^3 - 20{,}780s + 90{,}000)$$

$$= \frac{1.80[(138.8)(61.75 \text{ in})^3 - (20{,}780)(61.75 \text{ in}) + 90{,}000)]}{(1{,}166{,}200 \text{ lb/in}^2)(557 \text{ in}^4)} = 0.09 \text{ in}$$

The computed deflection of 0.09 in (2.29 mm) is less than the maximum allowable, so the deck thickness and combination symbol are acceptable for live-load deflection. A reduction in the glulam timber combination symbol grade or deck thickness will result in excessive deflection. Therefore, a combination symbol No. 47 will be retained.

Check Horizontal Shear. Dead-load vertical shear is computed at a distance from the support equal to the deck thickness t, and loads acting within the distance t are neglected. For $w_{DL} = 6.1$ lb/in (Fig. 10.20):

$$V_{DL} = w_{DL}\left(\frac{s}{2} - t\right) = 6.1 \text{ lb/in}\left(\frac{61.75 \text{ in}}{2} - 6.75 \text{ in}\right) = 147 \text{ lb}$$

Live-load vertical shear V_{LL} is computed by placing the edge of the wheel load distribution width b_t a distance t from the support (Fig. 10.21):

$$V_{LL} = R_L = \frac{(12{,}000 \text{ lb})(8.66 \text{ in} + 37.68 \text{ in})}{61.75 \text{ in}} = 9{,}005 \text{ lb}$$

The applied stress in horizontal shear f_v is computed using AASHTO equations, assuming that the entire panel cross-sectional area A_p of the narrowest panel is effective in shear distribution:

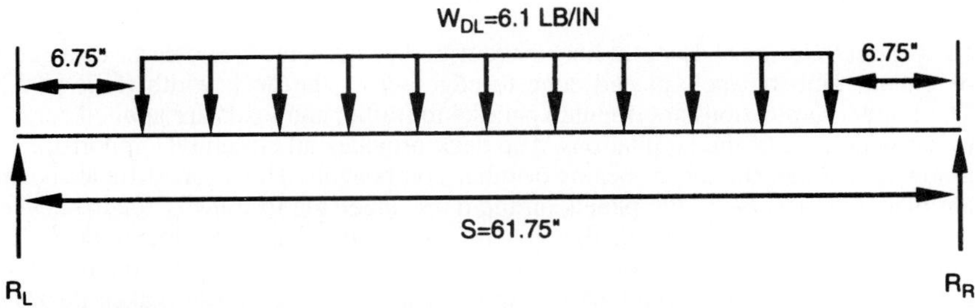

FIG. 10.20 Dead load placement for vertical shear.

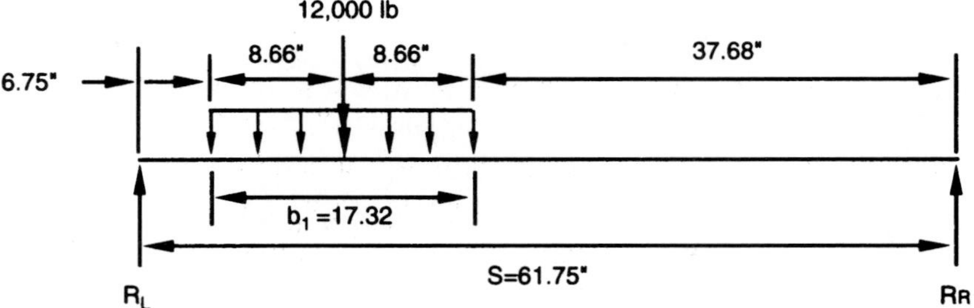

FIG. 10.21 Live load placement for vertical shear.

$$V = V_{DL} + V_{LL} = 147 \text{ lb} + 9005 \text{ lb} = 9152 \text{ lb}$$

$$A_p = (\text{panel width})(t) = (46.625 \text{ in})(6.75 \text{ in}) = 315 \text{ in}^2$$

$$f_v = \frac{1.5V}{A_p} = \frac{(1.5)(9152 \text{ lb})}{315 \text{ in}^2} = 44 \text{ lb/in}^2$$

The allowable stress in horizontal shear F'_v is equal to the tabulated stress in horizontal shear F_{vy} times the wet-service factor C_M and the load-duration factor C_D. Values of C_M and C_D are 0.875 and 1.15, respectively.

$$F'_v = F_{vy}C_MC_D = (175 \text{ lb/in}^2)(0.875)(1.15) = 176 \text{ lb/in}^2$$

$f_v = 44 \text{ lb/in}^2 < F'_v = 176 \text{ lb/in}^2$, so the panel is satisfactory in horizontal shear.

Summary. The bridge superstructure will consist of three southern pine glulam timber beams, combination symbol 24F-V3. The beams will measure 8½ in (215.9 mm) wide, 41¼ (1048 mm) deep, and 48 ft (14.63 m) long. The span center to center of bearings will be 47 ft (14.33 m). Transverse bracing will be provided for lateral support at the bearings and at the beam centerspan. The deck will consist of 12 combination No. 47 southern pine glulam timber deck panels 6¾ in (171.4 mm) thick by 16 ft (4.877 m) long. Eleven panels will be 48⅛ in (1.23 m) wide, and one panel will be 46⅝ in (1.184 m) wide. Stresses and live-load deflection are given in Table 10.6.

10.1.7 Design of Glulam Timber Longitudinal Deck Bridges

Deck Panel Design. Longitudinal glulam timber deck bridges consist of a series of glulam timber panels placed edge to edge across the deck width (Fig. 10.22). The lumber laminations are oriented parallel to traffic, and loads are applied parallel to the wide face of the laminations. The deck provides all structural support for the roadway, without the aid of beams or other components. However, stiffener beams are placed transverse to the panels on the deck underside to transfer loads between panels and give continuity to the system. Longitudinal glulam timber decks are practical for clear spans up to approximately 35 ft (10.67 m) and are equally adaptable to single- and multiple-lane crossings. The low deck profile makes them especially suitable for short-span applications where clearance below the structure is limited. The same basic configuration also can be used over transverse floorbeams

TABLE 10.6 Summary of Design Values for Example 10.2

Design value	Outside beams	Deck
f_b	1840 lb/in^2	983 lb/in^2
F'_b	1943 lb/in^2	1723 lb/in^2
Δ_{LL}	1.34 in. = $L/421$	0.09 in
f_v	101 lb/in^2	44 lb/in^2
F'_v	201 lb/in^2	176 lb/in^2
$f_{c\perp}$	323 lb/in^2	N/A
$F'_{c\perp}$	345 lb/in^2	N/A
Δ_{DL}	0.56 in	N/A
Camber	2 in	N/A

Note: 1 in = 25.4 mm; 1 lb/in^2 = 6.895 kPa.

for the construction or rehabilitation of other superstructure types. As with glulam timber beam bridges, longitudinal glulam timber deck bridges can be prefabricated in a modular system that is pressure-treated with preservatives after all required cuts and holes are made. This improves the bridge economy and longevity and reduce field erection time.

Longitudinal glulam timber deck panels are manufactured from visually graded glulam timber axial combinations given in the AASHTO specifications.[1] Combination symbols with a tabulated bending stress F_b of 1800 lb/in^2 (12.41 MPa) or less are most economical and are most commonly used. Panels are 42 to 54 in (1.067 to 1.372 m) wide in increments equal to the net lamination thickness of 1½ in (38.1 mm) for western species and 1⅜ in (34.9 mm) for southern pine. Panels can be manufactured in any length subject to local pressure-treating and transportation restrictions and are available in thicknesses that correspond to the standard glulam timber beam widths given in Table 10.1. Deck thicknesses up to 10¾ in (273.0 mm) are generally manufactured from full-width laminations (Fig. 10.23). Deck thicknesses of 12¼ and 14¼ in (311.1 and 362.0 mm) are also available but typically require multiple-piece laminations, which may be bonded or unbonded depending on specific design requirements in horizontal shear. With unbonded edge joints, tabulated horizontal shear values are assumed to be 50 percent of those for comparable panels with bonded joints.

The design criteria for glulam timber longitudinal deck bridges are given in the AASHTO Specifications[1] and are based on research and development work conducted at Iowa State University.[7] The primary emphasis of the Iowa State University studies dealt with the lateral live-load distribution characteristics for deck panel design. Empirical methods for stiffener beam design also were developed based on limitations placed on design parameters within the load-distribution studies. Additional experimental data obtained by Iowa State University subsequent to development of the load-distribution criteria should eventually provide a basis for more explicit stiffener beam design criteria rather than the empirical methods currently given in the AASHTO Specifications[1] and presented in this section.

Live-Load Distribution. Deck panels for longitudinal glulam timber deck bridges are designed as individual beams of rectangular cross section. Design is based on the maximum forces and deflection produced by the design vehicle, assuming that

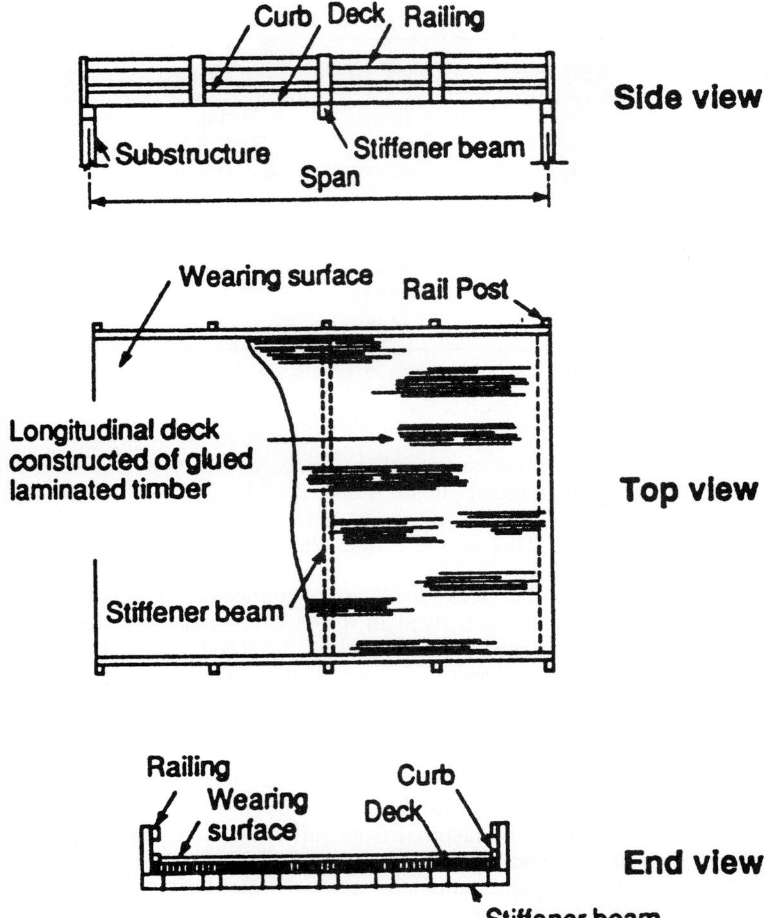

FIG. 10.22 Typical configuration for a single-lane longitudinal deck bridge.

wheel loads act as point loads in the direction of the deck span. The portion of the vehicle wheel line distributed transversely to each panel is computed as a wheel load fraction *WLF*, which is similar in application to the distribution factors used for beam design. The *WLF* represents the portion of one vehicle wheel line that is assumed to be distributed to one deck panel. The procedures for determining the *WLF* for bending, deflection, shear, and reactions follow.

1. *Distribution for moment and deflection.* For live-load moment and deflection, the *WLF* is based on the panel width and span in feet. The AASHTO Specifications[1] give *WLF* equations for bridges designed for two or more traffic lanes and for bridges designed for one traffic lane.

For bridges designed for two or more traffic lanes,

Single-piece laminations are used for deck thicknesses up to 10-1/2 inches for Southern Pine and 10-3/4 inches for western species.

Multiple-piece laminations are required for deck thicknesses of 12-1/4 inches and 14-1/4 inches.

Panel end views

FIG. 10.23 Laminating patterns for longitudinal glulam deck panels.

$$WLF = \frac{W_p}{3.75 + (L/28)} \quad \text{or} \quad \frac{W_p}{5.00} \quad \text{whichever is greater} \tag{10.4}$$

For bridges designed for one traffic lane,

$$WLF = \frac{W_p}{4.25 + (L/28)} \quad \text{or} \quad \frac{W_p}{5.50} \quad \text{whichever is greater} \tag{10.5}$$

where WLF = the portion of the maximum wheel line moment or deflection distributed to one deck panel
W_p = panel width, ft
L = length of span for simple-span bridges or length of the shortest span for continuous-span bridges, measured center to center of bearings, ft

2. *Distribution for shear.* Live-load vertical shear is based on the maximum vertical shear occurring at a distance from the support equal to three times the deck thickness ($3t$) or the span quarter point ($L/4$), whichever is less. At this location, WLF for shear is the same as that specified for moment and deflection. Horizontal shear is normally not a controlling factor in longitudinal glulam timber deck design because of the relatively large panel area.

3. *Distribution for reactions.* The WLF for live-load reactions at the supports of multiple-lane and single-lane bridges is given by the following equation:

$$WLF = \frac{W_p}{4} \geq 1.0 \tag{10.6}$$

Stiffener Beam Design. Transverse stiffener beams are placed transversely across the underside of longitudinal glulam timber decks to distribute loads and deflections among the individual panels. Stiffener beams typically consist of horizontally laminated glulam timber beams or shallow steel shapes (Fig. 10.24). The AASHTO Specifications[1] require that a stiffener beam be placed at midspan for all deck spans and at intermediate spacings not to exceed 10 ft (3.048 m). A more restrictive

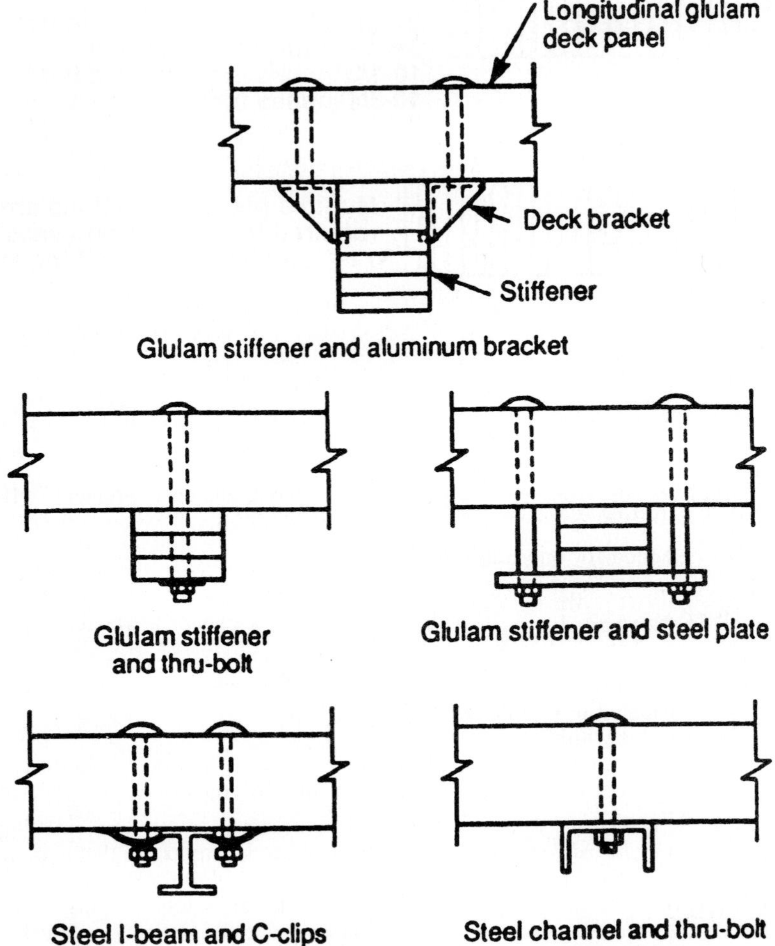

FIG. 10.24 Types of transverse stiffener-beam configurations for longitudinal glulam deck panels.

intermediate stiffener beam spacing of 8 ft (2.438 m) is recommended by industry and is used in this section. Stiffener beam design consists of sizing the beam so that the stiffness factor $E'I$ of the member is not less than 80,000 k-in^2 (551.6 GN·m^2); however, this is an approximate value that should not be significantly exceeded. Experimental and analytical tests at Iowa State University have shown that the connection may be overstressed if the stiffness factor is very large, on the order of twice the minimum value. Load distribution between panels is more effectively improved by decreasing stiffener beam spacing rather than by increasing the beam size substantially above the required minimum.

Connections between the stiffener beam and the deck panels are placed approximately 6 in from each panel edge (Fig. 10.25). The type of connection depends on the stiffener-beam material and configuration. Through-bolting is most common for glulam timber beams and steel channels. Deck brackets or steel plates are also used for glulam timber beams, and C clips are used for steel I beams. A minimum bolt diameter of 3/4 in (19.05 mm) is recommended for single through-bolt connections, while a minimum 5/8-in (15.88-mm)-diameter bolt is used for bracket connections. The type of connection is left to designer judgment, since all connector types shown in Fig. 10.24 were modeled in the Iowa State University study. However, experimental results indicate that the through-bolt type of connections provide more favorable load distribution in the panels and reduce the potential for localized stress conditions in the region of the connection to the stiffener beams. They are also more effective in reducing interpanel displacements that occur between stiffener-beam locations.

10.1.8 Design Examples

Sequential design examples are included in this section to familiarize the reader with the design procedures and requirements for longitudinal glulam timber deck bridges. These examples are based on AASHTO requirements and are valid for panels that are 42 to 54 in (1.067 to 1.372 m) wide and are provided with transverse stiffener beams. The basic sequence assumes that deck panels are initially designed

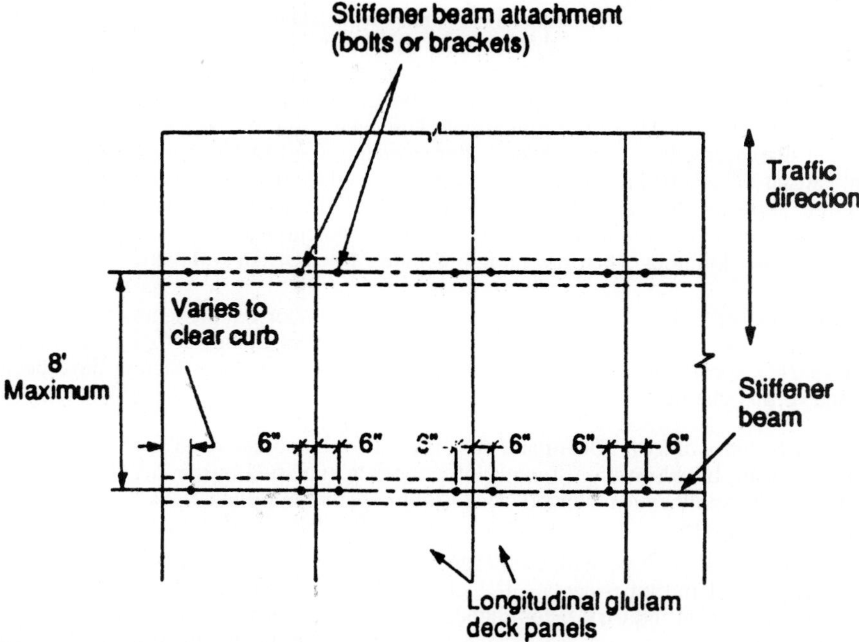

FIG. 10.25 Stiffener-beam attachment for longitudinal glulam decks.

for deflection and then checked for bending and shear. The process is iterative in nature if panel dimensions are changed at any point during the design process. After a suitable panel size and grade are determined, stiffener beams and bearings are designed.

Specific site requirements and criteria are noted for each example. In addition, the following general criteria related to loads, materials, live-load deflection, and conditions of use are applicable.

Loads. Loads are based on the AASHTO load requirements and are illustrated for AASHTO group I, where design is routinely controlled by a combination of structure dead load and vehicle live load. Other loads and load combinations also should be checked depending on site-specific conditions. AASHTO special provisions regarding reduced wheel loads for H 20-44 and HS 20-44 trucks previously discussed for transverse glulam timber decks do not apply to longitudinal decks.

Materials. Tabulated values for glulam timber are taken from tables for axial glulam timber combinations given in the AASHTO Specifications.[1] *All timber components are assumed to be properly pressure-treated with an oil-type preservative after fabrication.*

Live-Load Deflection. The AASHTO Specifications[1] do not require a limit for deflection but recommend that the live-load deflection not exceed 1/500 of the bridge span. Although it is recommended that these deflection guidelines be followed, deflection criteria should be based on specific design circumstances and are left to designer judgment. However, it is recommended that maximum panel deflection not exceed $L/360$. Because continuity from panel to panel is provided only at stiffener-beam locations, relative panel displacements do occur at locations between these beams. At this time, there is no accurate method for predicting the interpanel displacements between stiffener beams; however, with a maximum panel live-load deflection of $L/360$, Iowa State University studies indicate that the interpanel displacement will not exceed approximately 0.10 in (2.54 mm) in most applications. The 0.10-in limit on relative panel displacement is considered the maximum allowable for acceptable asphalt wearing surface performance. A further reduction in deflection is desirable to reduce the potential for minor asphalt cracks at the panel joints or when the bridge includes a pedestrian walkway.

Conditions of Use. Tabulated values for glulam timber components must be adjusted for specific use conditions by all applicable adjustment factors given in the AASHTO Specifications.[1] The following criteria for adjustment factors have been used in this chapter:

1. *Duration of load.* Beam and deck design for combined dead load and vehicle live load are based on the 2-month load duration specified in the AASHTO Specifications.[1] Applicable tabulated design values are multiplied by a load-duration factor C_D of 1.15.

2. *Moisture content.* With the exception of transverse stiffener beams used with watertight glulam timber decks, all deck components are designed for wet-use conditions. Based on industry recommendations, stiffener beams that are treated with oil-type preservatives and are located under a watertight glulam timber deck are assumed to remain within the range of dry-use conditions.

3. *Temperature effects and fire-retardant treatment.* Conditions requiring adjustments for temperature or fire-retardant treatment are not applicable in the design examples.

EXAMPLE 10.3: SIMPLE-SPAN LONGITUDINAL DECK GLULAM TIMBER BRIDGE, TWO-LANE HIGHWAY LOADING Design a longitudinal deck glulam timber bridge with a length of 26 ft (7.924 m) and a center-to-center span of 25 ft (7.62 m). The bridge will carry two lanes of AASHTO HS 20-44 loading in 12-ft (3.658-m) lanes. The following provisions apply:

1. The deck wearing surface is a 3-in (76.2-mm) layer of asphalt pavement.
2. Railing dead load is 50 lb/ft (729.6 N/m) along each deck edge, and the railing extends approximately 1 ft (0.3048 m) inward from the deck edge.
3. The deck live-load deflection shall not exceed 1/500 of the deck span ($L/500$).
4. Glulam timber is visually graded southern pine.

SOLUTION: The design of longitudinal glulam timber deck panels involves an iterative process similar to that used for beam design. In this case, with a maximum live-load deflection of $L/500$, it is likely that deflection will control the design. Therefore, the deck will be designed initially based on deflection and then checked for bending and shear.

Define the Deck Configuration and Deck Panel Width. The deck span L is the distance measured center to center of the bearings. Deck width is the roadway width plus any additional width required for curb and railing systems. With two 12-ft (3.658-m)-wide traffic lanes and a railing that projects 1 ft (0.3048 m) inward from each deck edge, an out-to-out bridge width of 26 ft (7.924 m) is required.

Panel width depends on the out-to-out structure width. Panels are 42 to 54 in (1.067 to 1.372 m) wide in multiples of 1½ in (38.1 mm) for western species or 1⅜ in (34.9 mm) for southern pine. The panels are normally designed to be of equal width, obtained by dividing the bridge width by a selected number of panels. Using southern pine glulam timber with 1⅜-in laminations, a configuration of six panels, each 52¼ in (1.327 m) wide, is selected (Fig. 10.26).

Select a Deck Panel Combination Symbol. The southern pine glulam timber combination symbols most commonly used for longitudinal decks are No. 47 and No. 48, with tabulated modulus of elasticity E values of 1,400,000 lb/in^2 (9.652 GPa) and 1,700,000 lb/in^2 (11.72 GPa), respectively. Because of the restrictive $L/500$ live-load deflection requirement for this bridge, the No. 48 combination symbol

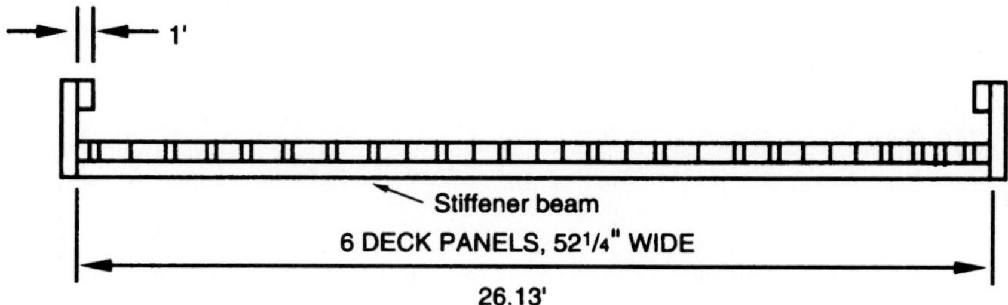

FIG. 10.26 Bridge cross section.

is selected initially because of the higher E value. Tabulated values and wet-service factors C_M for E and bending stress F_{by} are obtained from AASHTO glulam timber design tables for axial combinations:

$$F_{by} = 2000 \text{ lb/in}^2 \text{ (12.41 MPa)} \qquad C_M = 0.80$$

$$E_y = 1{,}700{,}000 \text{ lb/in}^2 \text{ (11.72 GPa)} \qquad C_M = 0.833$$

Determine the Wheel Load Fraction for Live-Load Distribution. The wheel load fraction WLF in wheel lines WL per panel is computed for a two-lane bridge using Eq. (10.4):

$$WLF = \frac{W_P}{3.75 + L/28} \quad \text{or} \quad WLF = \frac{W_P}{5} \quad \text{whichever is greater}$$

$$\frac{W_P}{3.75 + L/28} = \frac{52.25 \text{ in}/12 \text{ in/ft})}{3.75 + (25 \text{ ft}/28)} = 0.94WL/\text{panel}$$

$$\frac{W_P}{5} = \frac{52.25 \text{ in}/(12 \text{ in/ft})}{5} = 0.87WL/\text{panel}$$

$WLF = 0.94WL$/panel will be used for design.

Estimate Panel Thickness and Check Live-Load Deflection. Standard dimensions for glulam timber deck panel thickness are the same as the standard beam widths given in Table 10.1. For deflection computations, a deck panel thickness t must be estimated. An initial thickness of 12¼ in is selected, and the panel moment of inertia I_y is computed based on t and the panel width w_p in inches:

$$I_y = \frac{w_p(t)^3}{12} = \frac{52.25 \text{ in } (12.25 \text{ in})^3}{12} = 8004 \text{ in}^4$$

The allowable modulus of elasticity E' is computed per AASHTO requirements:

$$E'_y = EC_M = 1{,}700{,}000 \text{ lb/in}^2 \text{ (0.833)} = 1{,}416{,}100 \text{ lb/in}^2$$

The deflection due to one wheel line Δ_{WL} of an HS 20-44 truck is computed by statics or by coefficients given in design tables. In this case, a deflection coefficient DC is used[6]:

$$\Delta_{WL} = \frac{DC}{E'I_y} = \frac{1.11 \times 10^{10}}{(1{,}416{,}100 \text{ lb/in}^2)(8004 \text{ in}^4)} = 0.98 \text{ in}$$

The deck live-load deflection Δ_{LL} is computed by multiplying Δ_{WL} by the WLF:

$$\Delta_{LL} = \Delta_{WL}(WLF) = (0.98 \text{ in})(0.94) = 0.92 \text{ in (23.4 mm)} = L/326$$

The live-load deflection of $L/326$ exceeds the allowable $L/500$, so the panel thickness must be increased. A revised panel thickness of 14¼ in is checked using the same approach:

$$I_y = \frac{w_p(t)^3}{12} = \frac{52.25 \text{ in } (14.25 \text{ in})^3}{12} = 12{,}600 \text{ in}^4$$

$$\Delta_{WL} = \frac{DC}{E'I_y} = \frac{1.11 \times 10^{10}}{(1{,}416{,}100 \text{ lb/in}^2)(12{,}600 \text{ in}^4)} = 0.62 \text{ in}$$

$$\Delta_{LL} = \Delta_{WL}(WLF) = (0.62 \text{ in})(0.94) = 0.58 \text{ in } (14.7 \text{ mm}) = L/517$$

The live-load deflection of $L/517$ is less than the allowable $L/500$, so the panel thickness is acceptable.

Compute Panel Dead Load and Dead-Load Moment. The dead load DL of the deck and asphalt wearing surface is computed in pounds per square foot based on AASHTO unit material weights of 50 lb/ft^3 for wood and 150 lb/ft^3 for asphalt pavement:

$$DL = \frac{(14.25 \text{ in})(50 \text{ lb/ft}^3)}{12 \text{ in/ft}} + \frac{(3 \text{ in})(150 \text{ lb/ft}^3)}{12 \text{ in/ft}} = 97 \text{ lb/ft}^2$$

Railing dead load of 100 lb/ft is distributed equally over the entire deck width. An additional dead load of 10 lb/ft is added for the distributor beams and miscellaneous hardware for a total load of 110 lb/ft. The dead load per panel w_{DL} is computed for a span of 25 ft:

$$w_{DL} = \frac{(97 \text{ lb/ft}^2)(52.25 \text{ in})}{12 \text{ in/ft}} + \frac{110 \text{ lb/ft}}{6 \text{ panels}} = 441 \text{ lb/ft}$$

Panel deal-load moment M_{DL} is computed for the uniformly distributed load:

$$M_{DL} = \frac{w_{DL}L^2}{8} = \frac{(441 \text{ lb/ft})(25 \text{ ft})^2}{8} = 34{,}453 \text{ ft·lb}$$

Compute Live-Load Moment. Live-load moment M_{LL} is the product of the WLF and the moment produced by one wheel line of the design vehicle M_{WL}. From AASHTO Specification tables, the maximum moment from one wheel line of an HS 20-44 truck on a 25-ft span is 103,680 ft·lb:

$$M_{LL} = M_{WL}(WLF) = 103{,}680 \text{ ft·lb}(0.94) = 97{,}459 \text{ ft·lb}$$

Check Bending Stress. The total moment M is the sum of the dead-load and live-load moments:

$$M_{TL} = M_{DL} + M_{LL} = 34{,}450 \text{ ft·lb} + 97{,}459 \text{ ft·lb} = 131{,}909 \text{ ft·lb}$$

The deck panel section modulus S_y and the applied bending stress f_b are computed:

$$S_y = \frac{w_p(t)^2}{6} = \frac{(52{,}25 \text{ in})(14.25 \text{ in})^2}{6} = 1768 \text{ in}^3$$

$$f_b = \frac{M}{S_y} = \frac{(131{,}909 \text{ ft·lb})(12 \text{ in/ft})}{1768 \text{ in}^3} = 895 \text{ lb/in}^2$$

The allowable bending stress F'_b is computed per AASHTO requirements by multiplying the tabulated bending stress F_{by} by the wet-service factor C_M, load-duration factor C_D, and the size factor C_F. Assuming wet-service conditions and a controlling load combination of dead load and vehicle live load, the values for C_M and C_D are 0.80 and 1.15, respectively. The values of C_F and F'_b are computed:

$$C_F = \left(\frac{12}{t}\right)^{1/9} = \left(\frac{12}{14.25\text{ in}}\right)^{1/9} = 0.98$$

$$F'_b = F_{by}C_MC_DC_F = (1800\text{ lb/in}^2)(0.80)(1.15)(0.98) = 1803\text{ lb/in}^2$$

$f_b = 895\text{ lb/in}^2 < F'_b = 1803\text{ lb/in}^2$, so the deck thickness and combination symbol are satisfactory for bending.

Check Horizontal Shear. Dead-load vertical shear V_{DL} is computed at a distance t from the support, and loads acting within a distance t of the supports are neglected (Fig. 10.27):

$$V_{DL} = w_{DL}\left(\frac{L}{2} - t\right) = 441\text{ lb/ft}\left(\frac{25\text{ ft}}{2} - \frac{14.25\text{ in}}{12\text{ in/ft}}\right) = 4989\text{ lb}$$

Live-load vertical shear is computed from the maximum vertical shear occurring at the lesser of $3t$ or $L/4$ from the support:

$$3t = \frac{3(14.25\text{ in})}{12\text{ in/ft}} = 3.56\text{ ft} \qquad \frac{L}{4} = \frac{25\text{ ft}}{4} = 6.25\text{ ft}$$

$3t = 3.56$ ft controls, and maximum live-load vertical shear V_{LL} at that location is computed by multiplying the shear due to one wheel line of an HS 20-44 truck V_{WL} by the *WLF* (Fig. 10.28):

$$V_{WL} = R_L = \frac{(16{,}000\text{ lb})(7.44\text{ ft} + 21.44\text{ ft})}{25\text{ ft}} = 18{,}483\text{ lb}$$

$$V_{LL} = V_{WL}(WLF) = 18{,}483\text{ lb}(0.94) = 17{,}374\text{ lb}$$

The stress in horizontal shear f_v is computed per AASHTO requirements:

$$V = V_{DL} + V_{LL} = 4989\text{ lb} + 17{,}374\text{ lb} = 22{,}363\text{ lb}$$

$$f_v = \frac{3V}{2w_pt} = \frac{(3)(22{,}363\text{ lb})}{(2)(52.25\text{ in})(14.25\text{ in})} = 45\text{ lb/in}^2$$

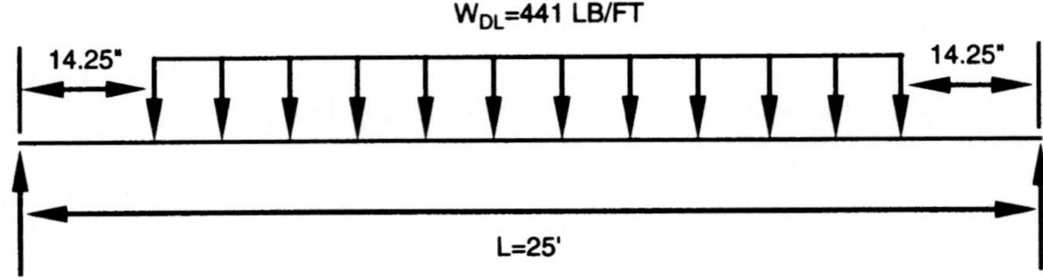

FIG. 10.27 Dead load placement for vertical shear.

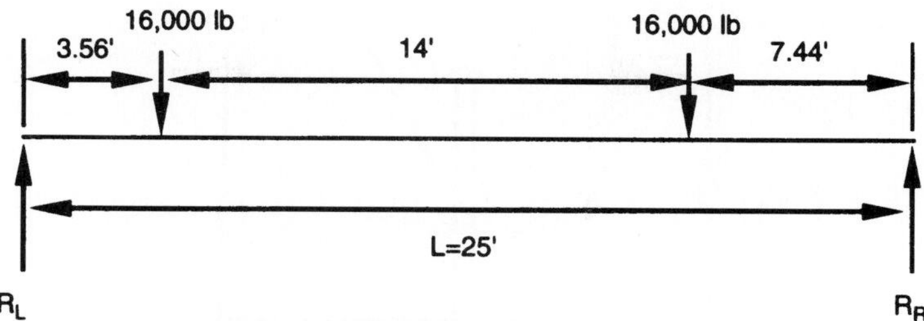

FIG. 10.28 Live load placement for vertical shear.

For a 14¼-in deck thickness, an edge layup will be used for the glulam timber deck panels. From the AASHTO tables for southern pine glulam timber axial combinations, the tabulated horizontal shear stress F_{vy} for combination No. 48 is 90 lb/in² if edge joints are not bonded and 175 lb/in² if edge joints are bonded. For this case, f_v is low, and the unbonded value will be used.

The allowable stress in horizontal shear F'_v is computed by multiplying F_{vy} by $C_M = 0.875$ and $C_D = 1.15$:

$$F'_v = F_{vy}C_MC_D = (90 \text{ lb/in}^2)(0.875)(1.15) = 91 \text{ lb/in}^2$$

$F'_v = 91 \text{ lb/in}^2 > f_v = 45 \text{ lb/in}^2$, so the deck panel is satisfactory in horizontal shear.

Determine Stiffener Beam Spacing and Configuration. The maximum recommended spacing for stiffener beams is 8 ft. For this bridge, glulam timber stiffener beams through-bolted to the deck panels (see Fig. 10.24) will be used at the span quarter points for a spacing of 6.25 ft. The size and stiffness of the stiffener beam must be sufficient to provide a minimum EI value of 80,000 k-in². Select a southern pine combination symbol No. 48 glulam timber stiffener, 5 in wide and 5½ in deep (dry-use conditions may be used for glulam timber stiffener beams if they are protected by a watertight deck):

$$E' = E_yC_M = 1{,}700{,}000 \text{ lb/in}^2 \text{ } (1.0) = 1{,}700{,}000 \text{ lb/in}^2$$

$$I = \frac{bd^3}{12} = \frac{(5 \text{ in})(5.5 \text{ in})^3}{12} = 69 \text{ in}^4$$

$$E'I = \frac{1{,}700{,}000 \text{ lb/in}^2}{1{,}000 \text{ lb/k}}(69 \text{ in}^4) = 117{,}300 \text{ k-in}^2$$

117,300 k-in² > 80,000 k-in², so 5- by 5½-in stiffener beams are satisfactory. The beams will be attached to the deck with 3/4-in-diameter bolts located 6 in from the panel edge (Fig. 10.29).

Determine Bearing Configuration and Check Bearing Stress. Bearings for longitudinal glulam timber decks are designed to resist the vertical and lateral forces in the same manner previously discussed for glulam timber beams. However, for longitudinal deck bridges, the required bearing length is normally controlled by considerations for bearing configuration rather than stress in compression perpendicular to grain. From a practical standpoint, a bearing length of 10 to 12 in is

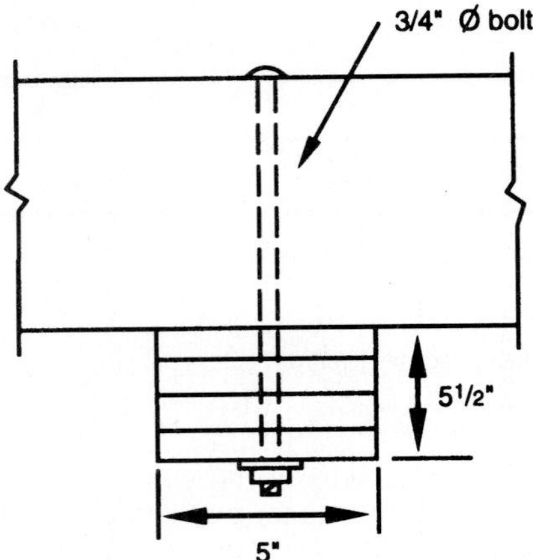

FIG. 10.29 Details of deck-beam attachment.

recommended for stability and deck attachment. In this case, a bearing length of 12 in is used.

The dead-load reaction R_{DL} is determined by assuming the panel acts as a simple beam between supports. For an out-out panel length of 26 ft,

$$R_{DL} = \frac{w_{DL}L}{2} = \frac{(441 \text{ lb/ft})(26 \text{ ft})}{2} = 5733 \text{ lb}$$

The live-load reaction R_{LL} is computed by multiplying the maximum reaction for one wheel line R_{WL} by the reaction WLF. From the AASHTO Specifications,[1] the maximum reaction for one wheel line of an HS 20-44 truck is 23,040 lb.

$$WLF = \frac{W_p}{4} = \frac{(52.25 \text{ in})(12 \text{ in/ft})}{4} = 1.09WL/\text{panel}$$

$$R_{LL} = WLF(R_{WL}) = 1.09(23{,}040 \text{ lb}) = 25{,}114 \text{ lb}$$

The applied stress in compression perpendiculat to grain $f_{c\perp}$ is computed for a length of bearing ℓ_b of 12 in:

$$f_{c\perp} = \frac{R_{DL} + R_{LL}}{w_p(\ell_b)} = \frac{5733 \text{ lb} + 25{,}114 \text{ lb}}{52.25 \text{ in } (12 \text{ in})} = 49 \text{ lb/in}^2$$

The allowable stress in compression perpendicular to grain $F'_{c\perp}$ is computed in accordance with AASHTO requirements:

$$F'_{c\perp} = F_{c\perp}(C_M) = 650 \text{ lb/in}^2(0.53) = 345 \text{ lb/in}^2$$

$f_{c\perp} = 49 \text{ lb/in}^2 < F'_{c\perp} = 345 \text{ lb/in}^2$, so a bearing length of 12 in is satisfactory. The bearing configuration shown in Fig. 10.30 will be used.

Summary. The bridge will consist of six combination No. 48 southern pine glulam timber deck panels. Each panel will measure 14¼ in thick, 52¼ in wide, and 26 ft long. Stiffener beams are combination No. 48 southern pine glulam timber,

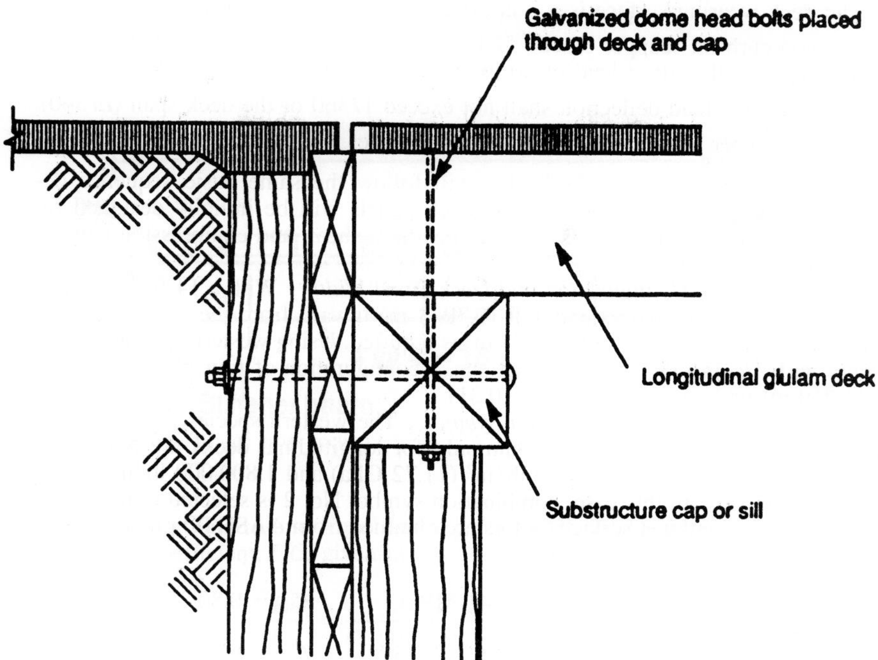

FIG. 10.30 Typical bearing configuration for longitudinal glulam timber decks.

5 in wide by 5½ in deep, placed at span quarter points. Stresses and deflection are as follows:

$$f_b = 895 \text{ lb/in}^2$$

$$F'_b = 1803 \text{ lb/in}^2$$

$$\Delta_{LL} = 0.58 \text{ in} = L/517$$

$$f_v = 45 \text{ lb/in}^2$$

$$F'_v = 91 \text{ lb/in}^2$$

$$f_{c\perp} = 49 \text{ lb/in}^2$$

$$F'_{c\perp} = 345 \text{ lb/in}^2$$

Note: 1 in = 25.4 mm; 1 lb/in^2 = 6.895 kPa.

EXAMPLE 10.4: SIMPLE-SPAN LONGITUDINAL DECK GLULAM TIMBER BRIDGE, SINGLE-LANE HIGHWAY LOADING Design a single-lane longitudinal deck glulam timber bridge with a span of 21 ft (6.401 m) center to center of bearings. The bridge is located on a low-volume road and will carry one lane of AASHTO HS 20-44 loading in a 14-ft (4.267-m) lane. The following provisions apply:

$$w_{DL} = \frac{(57.3 \text{ lb/ft}^2)(48 \text{ in})}{12 \text{ in/ft}} + \frac{70 \text{ lb/ft}}{4 \text{ panels}} = 247 \text{ lb/ft}$$

M_{DL} is computed for the uniformly distributed load:

$$M_{DL} = \frac{w_{DL}L^2}{8} = \frac{(247 \text{ lb/ft})(21 \text{ ft})^2}{8} = 13{,}616 \text{ ft·lb}$$

Compute Live-Load Moment. From AASHTO Specification tables, the maximum moment from one wheel line of an HS 20-44 truck on a 21-ft span is 84,000 ft·lb. Live-load moment M_{LL} is the product of the *WLF* and the moment produced by one wheel line of the design vehicle M_{WL}:

$$M_{LL} = M_{WL}(WLF) = 84{,}000 \text{ ft·lb}(0.80) = 67{,}200 \text{ ft·lb}$$

Check Bending Stress. The total moment M is the sum of the dead-load and live-load moments:

$$M = M_{DL} + M_{LL} = 13{,}616 \text{ ft·lb} + 67{,}000 \text{ ft·lb} = 80{,}816 \text{ ft·lb}$$

S_y and the applied bending stress f_b are computed:

$$S_y = \frac{w_p(t)^2}{6} = \frac{(48 \text{ in})(10.75 \text{ in})^2}{6} = 925 \text{ in}^3$$

$$f_b = \frac{M}{S_y} = \frac{(88{,}816 \text{ ft·lb})(12 \text{ in/ft})}{925 \text{ in}^3} = 1078 \text{ lb/in}^2$$

The allowable bending stress F'_b is computed per AASHTO requirements by multiplying the tabulated bending stress F_{by} by the wet-service factor C_M, load-duration factor C_D, and the size factor C_F. Assuming wet-service conditions and a controlling load combination of dead load and vehicle live load, the values for C_M and C_D are 0.80 and 1.15, respectively. The values of C_F and F'_b are computed:

$$C_F = \left(\frac{12}{t}\right)^{1/9} = \left(\frac{12}{10.75 \text{ in}}\right)^{1/9} = 1.01$$

$$F'_b = F_{by}C_MC_DC_F = (1800 \text{ lb/in}^2)(0.80)(1.15)(1.01) = 1673 \text{ lb/in}^2$$

$f_b = 1048 \text{ lb/in}^2 < F'_b = 1673 \text{ lb/in}^2$, so the deck thickness and combination symbol are satisfactory for bending.

Check Horizontal Shear. Dead-load vertical shear V_{DL} is computed at a distance t from the support, and loads acting within a distance t of the supports are neglected.

$$V_{DL} = w_{DL}\left(\frac{L}{2} - t\right) = 247 \text{ lb/ft}\left(\frac{21 \text{ ft}}{2} - \frac{10.75 \text{ in}}{12 \text{ in/ft}}\right) = 2372 \text{ lb}$$

Live-load vertical shear is computed from the maximum vertical shear occurring at the lesser of $3t$ or $L/4$ from the support:

$$3t = \frac{3(10.75 \text{ in})}{12 \text{ in/ft}} = 2.69 \text{ ft} \qquad \frac{L}{4} = \frac{21 \text{ ft}}{4} = 5.25 \text{ ft}$$

$3t = 2.69$ ft controls, and maximum live-load vertical shear V_{LL} at that location is computed by multiplying the shear due to one wheel line V_{WL} of an HS 20-44 truck by the *WLF* (Fig. 10.32):

$$V_{WL} = R_L = \frac{(16{,}000 \text{ lb})(4.31 \text{ ft} + 18.31 \text{ ft})}{21 \text{ ft}} = 17{,}234 \text{ lb}$$

$$V_{LL} = V_{WL}(WLF) = 17{,}234 \text{ lb}(0.80) = 13{,}787 \text{ lb}$$

The stress in horizontal shear f_v is computed per AASHTO requirements:

$$V_{TL} = V_{DL} + V_{LL} = 2372 \text{ lb} + 13{,}787 \text{ lb} = 16{,}159 \text{ lb}$$

$$f_v = \frac{3V}{2w_p t} = \frac{(3)(16{,}159 \text{ lb})}{(2)(48 \text{ in})(10.75 \text{ in})} = 47 \text{ lb/in}^2$$

For a 10¾-in deck thickness, single-piece laminations will be used for the glulam timber deck panels. From the AASHTO tables for western species glulam timber axial combinations, the tabulated horizontal shear stress F_{vy} for combination No. 2 is 145 lb/in². The allowable stress in horizontal shear F'_v is computed by multiplying F_{vy} by $C_M = 0.875$ and $C_D = 1.15$:

$$F'_v = F_{vy}C_M C_D = (145 \text{ lb/in}^2)(0.875)(1.15) = 146 \text{ lb/in}^2$$

$F'_v = 146 \text{ lb/in}^2 > f_v = 47 \text{ lb/in}^2$, so the deck panel is satisfactory in horizontal shear.

Determine Stiffener Beam Spacing and Configuration. Glulam timber stiffener beams through-bolted to the deck panels will be used at the span third points for a spacing of 7 ft. Select a western species combination symbol No. 2 glulam timber stiffener, 5⅛ in wide and 6 in deep, and apply $C_M = 0.833$;

$$E' = E_y C_M = 1{,}700{,}000 \text{ lb/in}^2 (0.833) = 1{,}416{,}100 \text{ lb/in}^2$$

$$I = \frac{bd^3}{12} = \frac{(5.125 \text{ in})(6 \text{ in})^3}{12} = 92 \text{ in}^4$$

$$E'I = \frac{1{,}416{,}100 \text{ lb/in}^2}{1000 \text{ lb/k}}(92 \text{ in}^4) = 130{,}281 \text{ k-in}^2$$

130,281 k-in² > 80,000 k-in², so 5⅛ by 6-in stiffener beams are satisfactory. The

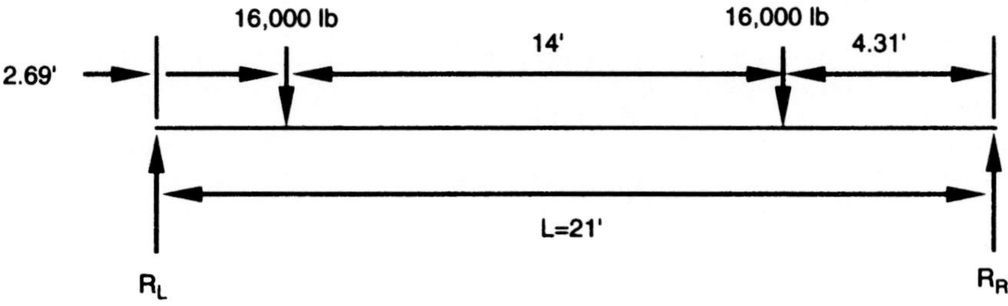

FIG. 10.32 Live load placement for vertical shear.

beams will be attached to the deck with 3/4-in-diameter bolts located 6 in from the panel edge.

Determine Bearing Configuration and Check Bearing Stress. For the given span of 21 ft, a bearing length of 12 in is selected. The dead load reaction R_{DL} is determined for a panel length of 23 ft by assuming that the panel acts as a simple beam between supports:

$$R_{DL} = \frac{w_{DL}L}{2} = \frac{(247 \text{ lb/ft})(23 \text{ ft})}{2} = 2841 \text{ lb}$$

From the AASHTO Specifications,[1] the maximum reaction for one wheel line R_{WL} of an HS 20-44 truck is 21,330 lb. The live-load reaction R_{LL} is the product of R_{WL} and the *WLF*:

$$WLF = \frac{W_p}{4} = \frac{(48 \text{ in})/(12 \text{ in/ft})}{4} = 1.00WL/\text{panel}$$

$$R_{LL} = WLF(R_{WL}) = 1.00(21{,}330 \text{ lb}) = 21{,}330 \text{ lb}$$

The applied stress in compression perpendicular $f_{c\perp}$ to grain is computed for a length of bearing ℓ_b of 12 in:

$$f_{c\perp} = \frac{R_{DL} + R_{LL}}{w_p(\ell_b)} = \frac{2841 \text{ lb} + 21{,}330 \text{ lb}}{48 \text{ in (12 in)}} = 42 \text{ lb/in}^2$$

$F'_{c\perp}$ is computed in accordance with AASHTO requirements:

$$F'_{c\perp} = F_{c\perp}(C_M) = 560 \text{ lb/in}^2(0.53) = 297 \text{ lb/in}^2$$

$f_{c\perp} = 42 \text{ lb/in}^2 < F'_{c\perp} = 297 \text{ lb/in}^2$, so a bearing length of 12 in is satisfactory. The bearing configuration shown in Fig. 10.33 will be used.

Summary. The bridge will consist of four combination No. 2 western species glulam timber deck panels. Each panel will measure 10¾ in thick, 48 in wide, and 23 ft long. Stiffener beams are combination No. 2 western species glulam timber, 5⅛ in wide by 6 in deep, placed at span third points. Stresses and deflection are as follows:

$$f_b = 1048 \text{ lb/in}^2$$

$$F'_b = 1673 \text{ lb/in}^2$$

$$\Delta_{LL} = 0.61 \text{ in} = L/413$$

$$f_v = 47 \text{ lb/in}^2$$

$$F'_v = 146 \text{ lb/in}^2$$

$$f_{c\perp} = 42 \text{ lb/in}^2$$

$$F'_{c\perp} = 297 \text{ lb/in}^2$$

Note: 1 in = 25.4 mm; 1 lb/in² = 6.895 kPa.

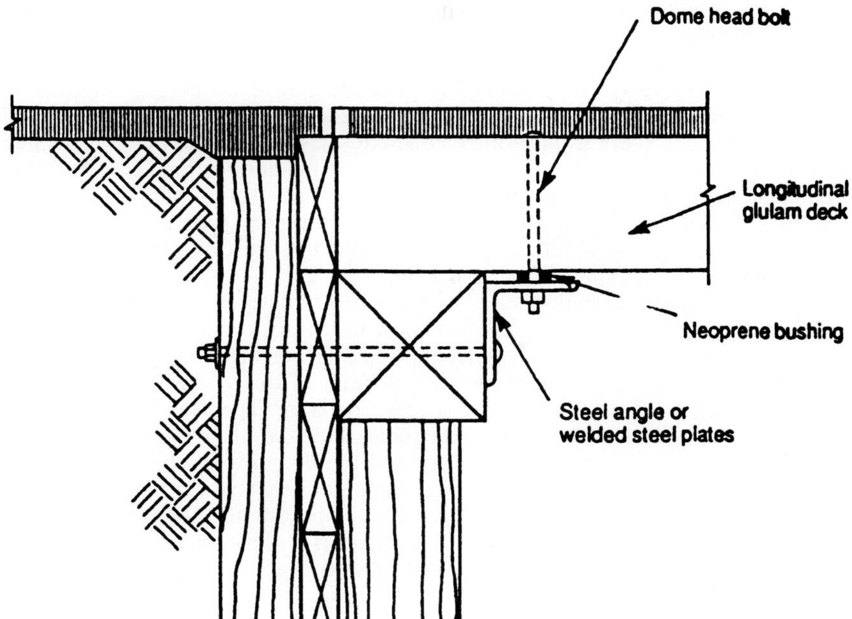

FIG. 10.33 Typical bearing configurations for longitudinal glulam decks.

10.2 CONCRETE FORMWORK

Although for multiple reuse applications wood formwork has been replaced by steel formwork to some degree and a large share of scaffolding supports are now tubular steel frames, wood is still used for a large part of the concrete forming in the United States because of its availability and ease of fabrication. As with steel, wood forms can be reused if dismantled carefully, and the material can be salvaged for future use. All formwork must be designed to support both the weight or pressure of wet concrete and all temporary construction loads, including lateral loads, until the concrete reaches a strength level at which it becomes self-supporting. The forms also must be watertight.

Formwork, particularly when used for floors and roofs, should be designed so that portions of the formwork such as beam sides or some slab soffits can be removed early, leaving the beam soffit forms with their shores or slab shores to support the main floor loads until the concrete gains greater strength. Flat slab floor forms must be removable in a sequence such that reshores can be properly placed to support the slab, control early deflections of the slab, and support additional levels of forming.

Deflections may control the spacing of the plywood supports and ties as well as the sizes of walers and joists. The deflections of concrete flatwork must be considered in determining both the camber to be built into the forms and the jacking clearance needed to allow the formwork to be decentered for removal without damaging the concrete. The following example illustrates a problem which occurred when proper camber was not used. A lightweight concrete fill was to be placed on a floor composed of plywood sheathing over wood/plywood I-beam joists supported by glulam beams. No camber was specified or furnished for the glulam beams. Normal tolerance on camber for the span involved is $\pm \frac{1}{4}$ in (6 mm). Wood/plywood I beams are not typically cambered in manufacturing. The screeds for the specified $1\frac{1}{2}$-in (38-mm)-thick concrete slabs were set at the column lines for a level floor. Due to the lack of camber of the glulam beam system and dead-load deflections, the resulting concrete slab was over 3 in (76 mm) thick at some midspans as a result of dead-load deflections. This was a considerable overrun in material quantities, and a further problem resulted because the actual dead load considerably exceeded the design dead load.

One of the most common causes of formwork failure is the lack of adequate lateral bracing. This can result in either local instability of an individual shore or instability of the entire formwork system. A line of bracing is not effective unless it is anchored to a solid support. For the stability of the system as a whole, the method used to transport the concrete is very important. The use of power buggies requires that consideration be given to the forces which result from the simultaneous action of the rapid braking of the buggy and the dumping of the concrete. This may produce large horizontal and vertical dynamic forces, which must be resisted.

The type and amount of vibration used for compacting the concrete can change the effective fluid depth on the forms. Therefore, it is recommended that the contractor plan a program for vibrating so that its effect can be included in the design loads for the forms.

Another problem often found in formwork is that shoring is not adequately supported either horizontally or vertically at its base. Adequate bearing under the shores must be provided, and the possibility of wet ground conditions at the base of the shore which can reduce the bearing capacity of the supporting material must not be neglected. Wet conditions could be due to the weather, water from form or truck washing, leakage from the forms, and so on.

Formwork must be as watertight as possible to prevent surface marring of the concrete and to prevent possible reduction in strength of the concrete due to mortar loss. Special surfaces may be required to obtain a desired architectural finish.

Once the loads are determined, the design of the formwork normally follows accepted engineering practice. Recommended design stresses for wood members in wall formwork can reasonably be increased by 25 percent, since the duration of the full concrete pressure will not exceed 7 days. For slab formwork, a 15 percent increase in allowable stresses is appropriate if the wood is to be used only once, since it would be supporting the concrete, depending on the weather and the stripping schedule, for a maximum of 14 to 28 days. For repetitive use, cumulative loading effects will eliminate any increase in allowable design stresses which would otherwise apply for a shorter single-use duration of load. If the formwork is to be exposed to moisture for any extended period of time, it is strongly recommended that the allowable design stresses be reduced to account for the wet condition of use. This is especially true for bearing stresses perpendicular to the grain.

Shoring systems will range from posts at close spacing to elaborate truss and tower systems for structures such as concrete domes, arches, and bridges. Many of the large concrete arches, hypars, and similar items built in the early 1950s used a system of wood trusses and towers for formwork support. Some of these were reused several times on the same project, and others were reused on duplicate projects.

In addition, all formwork designs must include the loads that result from construction equipment and construction workers placing and finishing the concrete. This will vary but should be at least 50 lb/ft^2 (245 kg/m^2). The formwork also may have to support other material that is to be attached to the concrete, such as stone facing or other aesthetic finishes.

Tables 10.7 through 10.10 are taken from the American Concrete Institute publication SP4.[8] Tables 10.7 and 10.8 give the maximum internal lateral pressures to be expected for column and wall forms, respectively, and are based on test results and practical experience. Tables 10.9 and 10.10 give the minimum lateral forces for wall and slab form bracing, respectively.

TABLE 10.7 Maximum Lateral Pressure for Design of Column Forms*

Rate of placement R, ft/h	Maximum lateral pressure p,†‡ lb/ft^2					
	90°F	80°F	70°F	60°F	50°F	40°F
1	250	262	278	300	330	375
2	350	375	407	450	510	600
3	450	488	536	600	690	825
4	550	600	664	750	870	1050
5	650	742	793	900	1050	1275
6	750	825	921	1050	1230	1500
7	850	938	1050	1200	1410	1725
8	950	1050	1178	1350	1590	1950
9	1050	1163	1307	1500	1770	2175
10	1150	1275	1436	1650	1950	2400
11	1250	1388	1564	1800	2130	2625
12	1350	1500	1693	1950	2310	2850
13	1450	1613	1822	2100	2490	3000
14	1550	1725	1950	2250	2670	
16	1750	1950	2207	2550	3000	
18	1950	2175	2464	2850		
20	2150	2400	2721	3000		
22	2350	2625	2979			
24	2550	2850	3000			
26	2750	3000				
28	2950					
30	3000					

Note: 1 ft = 0.305 m, 1 lb/ft^2 = 47.88 Pa, C° = (F° − 32)5/9.

*For concrete with type I cement having a unit weight of 150 lb/ft^3 and slump ≦ 4 in.

†Do not use design pressure in excess of 3000 lb/ft^2 (144 kPa) or 150 lb/ft^3 (23.6 kN/m^3) × height of fresh concrete in forms in ft (m), whichever is less.

‡3000 lb/ft^2 maximum governs.

Source: From SP4, *Formwork for Concrete,* 4th ed., American Concrete Institute, 1979,[8] by permission of the publisher. Based on ACI Committee 347 concrete pressure formula.

TABLE 10.8 Maximum Lateral Pressure for Design of Wall Forms*

Rate of placement R, ft/h	Maximum lateral pressure p,† lb/ft²					
	90°F	80°F	70°F	60°F	50°F	40°F
1	250	262	278	300	330	375
2	350	375	407	450	510	600
3	450	488	536	600	690	825
4	550	600	664	750	870	1050
5	650	712	793	900	1050	1275
6	750	825	921	1050	1230	1500
7	850	938	1050	1200	1410	1725
8	881	973	1090	1246	1466	1795
9	912	1008	1130	1293	1522	1865
10	943	1043	1170	1340	1578	1935

Note: 1 ft = 0.305 m, 1 lb/ft² = 47.88 Pa, C° = (F° − 32)5/9.

*For concrete with type I cement having a unit weight of 150 lb/ft³ and slump ≦ 4 in.

†Do not use design pressure in excess of 2000 lb/ft² (96 kPa) or 150 lb/ft³ (23.6 kN/m³) × height of fresh concrete in forms in ft (m), whichever is less.

Source: From SP4, *Formwork for Concrete,* 4th ed., American Concrete Institute, 1979,[8] by permission of the publisher. Based on ACI Committee 347 concrete pressure formula.

EXAMPLE 10.5 Design the wall forms for an 8-in (203-mm)-thick by 10-ft (3.05-m)-high concrete pour. The forms are to be filled at the rate of 5 ft (1.5 m) per hour when the air temperature is 70°F (21°C). A vibrator is to be used, but it will not be extended down into the fresh concrete more than 5 ft (1.5 m). Assume that ¾-in (19-mm) Plyform is placed on studs which are 16 in (406 mm) on center. A single plate will be used at the bottom of the form and anchored to previously poured concrete. Ties rated by the manufacturer at 2000 lb (8.9 kN) each will be used (Fig. 10.34*a*).

SOLUTION: *Tie Design.* Try ties at 24 in on center horizontally and 16 in on center vertically. The distribution of pressure on the form is obtained by using Table 10.8. From this table the tabular lateral pressure is 793 lb/ft². However, according to the footnote of the table, the maximum pressure used need not exceed 150 × 5 = 750 lb/ft², which is shown in Fig. 10.34*b*.

Check Maximum Tie Force. The force per tie is

$$750 \times 1.33 \times 2.0 = 1995 \text{ lb} < 2000 \text{ lb} \qquad \text{OK}$$

Waler Design. Assume walers are to be placed at 16-in centers vertically with studs on 16-in centers horizontally, with ties spaced at 24-in centers horizontally (Fig. 10.34*c*). The load on the waler from the stud is 750 × 1.33 × 1.33 = 1327 lb.

Figure 10.34*d* and *e* shows two possible load conditions for transferring the loads on the studs to the ties, depending on the relative lateral positioning of the studs and ties.

TABLE 10.9 Minimum Lateral Force for Design of Wall Forms

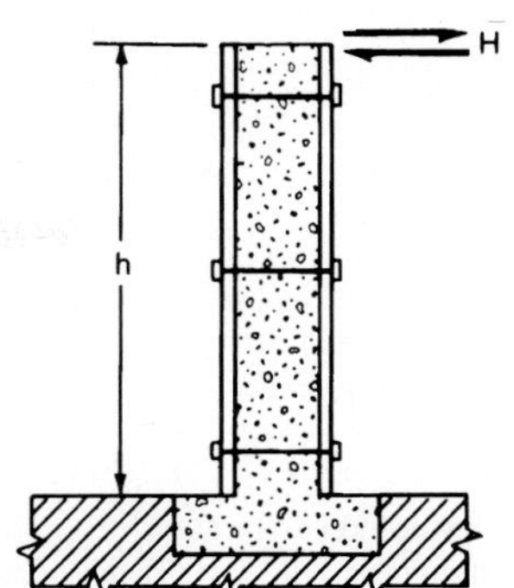

Minimum lateral force, lb/ft, applied at top of wall form in either direction.

Wall height (above grade) h, ft	Force H, lb/ft: Committee 347 minimum: 100 lb/ft or 10-lb/ft² wind	Wind force prescribed by local code,* lb/ft²: 15	20	25	30
4 or less	100	100	100	100	100
6	100	100	100	100	100
8	100	100	100	100	100
10	100	100	100	125	150
12	100	100	120	150	180
14	100	105	140	175	210
16	100	120	160	200	240
18	100	135	180	225	270
20	100	150	200	250	300
22 or more	$5.0h$	$7.5h$	$10.0h$	$12.5h$	$15.0h$
Walls below grade					
8 or less	0				
More than 8	100				

Note: 1 ft = 0.305 m, 1 lb/ft² = 47.88 N/m², 1 lb/ft = 14.6 N/m.

*Wind force prescribed by local code shall be used whenever it would require a lateral force for design greater than the minimum shown.

Source: From SP4, *Formwork for Concrete,* 4th ed., American Concrete Institute, 1979,[8] by permission of the publisher.

Assume that the alternative waler loading is selected, since all tie forces for this case are less than the 2000 lb allowable, and that all spans are assumed to be simple (on the conservative side, except in spans where waler joints are located and joint locations are unknown). The bending moments in the spans are

$$M_{AB} = M_{CD} = 1327 \times 4 = 5308 \text{ in·lb}$$

$$M_{BC} = 1327 \times 24/4 = 7962 \text{ in·lb}$$

TABLE 10.10 Minimum Lateral Force for Design of Slab Form Bracing

Minimum lateral force, lb/ft, applied along edge of slab in either direction.

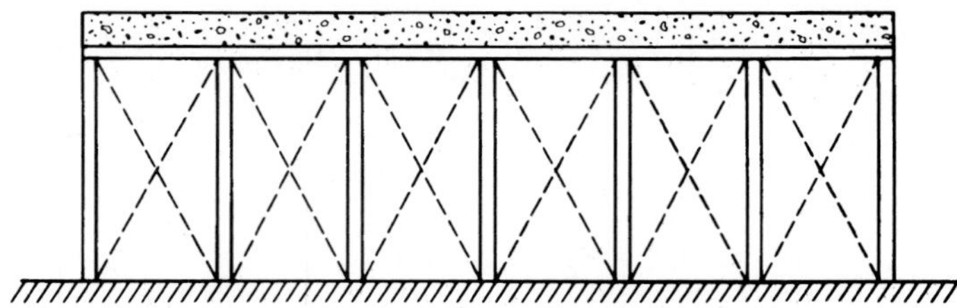

Solid slab thickness,* in	Dead load, lb/ft²	Load H,† lb/ft				
		Width of slab in direction of force, ft				
4	65	100	100	100	100	130
6	90	100	100	108	144	180
8	115	100	100	138	184	230
10	140	100	112	168	224	280
12	165	100	132	198	164	330
14	190	100	152	228	304	380
16	215	100	172	258	344	430
20	265	105	212	318	424	530

Note: 1 ft = 0.305 m, 1 lb/ft = 14.6 N/m, 1 lb/ft² (load) = 4.89 kg/m².

*Slab thickness given for concrete weighing 150 lb/ft³ (2400 kg/m³); allow 15 lb/ft² (73 kg/m²) for weight of forms. For concrete of different weight or for joist slabs or beam and slab combinations, estimate dead load per ft² (m²) and work from dead-load column, interpolating as needed on straight-line basis.

†Special conditions may require heavier bracing H.

Source: From SP4, *Formwork for Concrete,* 4th ed., American Concrete Institute, 1979,[8] by permission of the publisher.

$$M_{DE} = 663 \times 12 = 7956 \text{ in·lb}$$

Check Bending. Assuming a No. 1 grade of Douglas fir–larch having an allowable F_b of 1000 lb/in² is used [see Appendix to this book or supplement to the 1991 edition of *National Design Specifications for Wood Construction* (NDS)[2]], the required section modulus for the waler is

$$S = \frac{M}{F'_b} = \frac{7962}{1000 \times 1.25^* \times 1.15^\dagger \times 1.5^\ddagger} = 3.69 \text{ in}^3$$

Note: If forms are used under wet conditions, F_b also should be multiplied by 0.86.

S = 3.06 in³ for a single 2×4. Try two 2×4s at 16 in on center:

$$S = 3.06 \times 2 > 3.82 \text{ in}^3 \qquad \text{OK}$$

*A 7-day load-duration factor was assumed.

†A 15 percent increase in allowable stress was assumed due to the load sharing provided when three or more parallel members are placed 24 in or less on center.

‡Size-factor increase for a 4 in wide member.

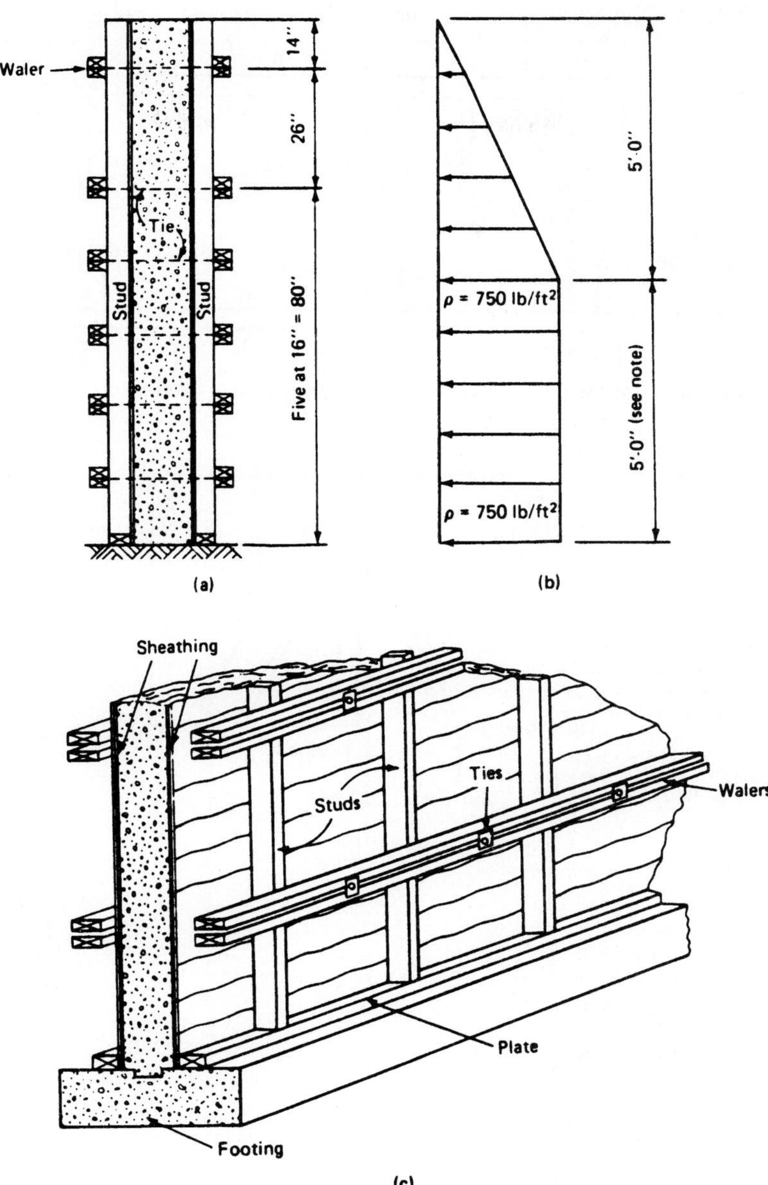

FIG. 10.34 Formwork design. (*a*) Wall form cross section; (*b*) distribution of concrete pressure on wall form; (*c*) wall forms; (*d*) possible waler load pattern; (*e*) alternative waler load pattern; (*f*) forces per foot of wall length. *Note:* Partially consolidated fluid pressure for concrete; see first footnote in Table 10.8.

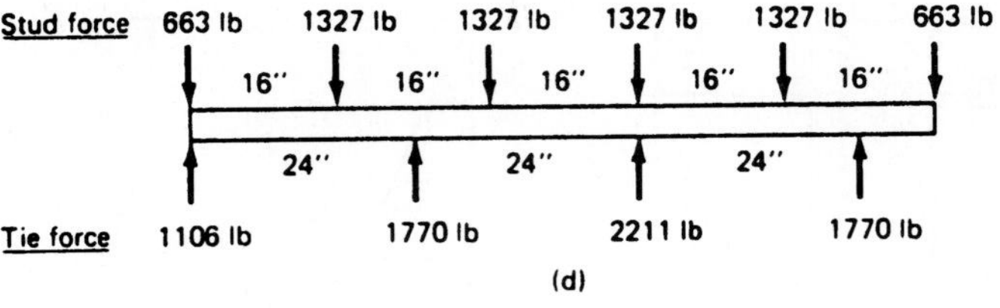

(d)

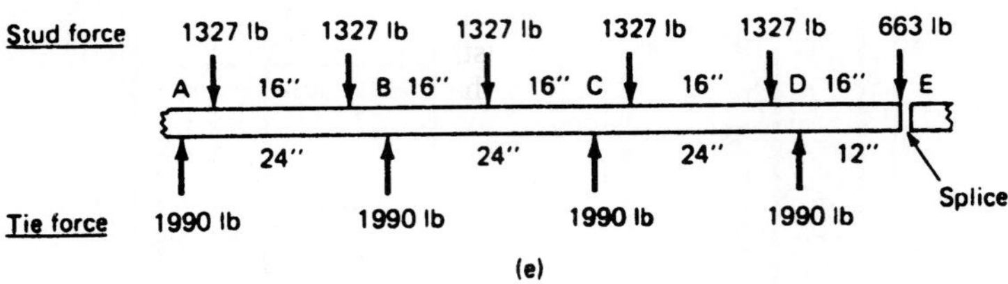

(e)

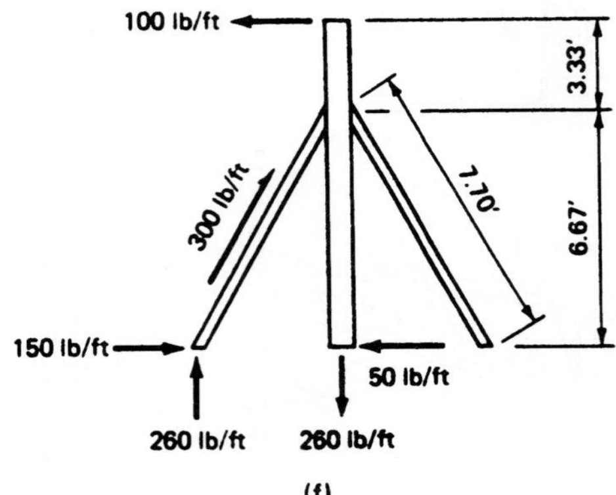

(f)

FIG. 10.34 *(Continued)*

Check Shear

$$V(\max) = 1327 \text{ lb}$$

$$f_v = \frac{1.5V}{2A} = \frac{1.5 \times 1327}{2 \times 1.5 \times 3.5} = 190 \text{ lb/in}^2$$

$$F_V = 95 \times 1.25 = 119 \text{ lb/in}^2 < 190 \text{ lb/in}^2 \qquad \text{NG}$$

Thus try two 2 × 6s:

$$f_v = \frac{1.5 \times 1327}{2 \times 1.5 \times 5.5} = 121 \text{ lb/in}^2 = 121 \simeq 119 \text{ lb/in}^2 \qquad \text{OK}$$

Check Bearing at Tie Washers (Wet Use)

$$f_{c\perp} = \frac{1990}{1.5 \times 3.0} = 442 \text{ lb/in}^2$$

$$F'_{c\perp} = F_{c\perp} C_M C_b = 625 \times 0.67 \times 1.13 = 473 \text{ lb/in}^2 > 442 \text{ lb/in}^2 \qquad \text{OK}$$

C_b is the bearing-area factor which applies when the bearing length is less than 6 in. C_M is the wet-service factor.

Stud Design. Assume that studs act as simple span beams between walers (conservative assumption) with a uniformly distributed load. The required size for a Douglas fir–larch construction grade stud having an allowable bending stress of 1000 lb/in² is

$$M = \frac{w\ell^2}{8} = \frac{750 \times 1.33 \times 16^2}{12 \times 8} = 2660 \text{ in·lb}$$

$$S = \frac{M}{F'_b} = \frac{2660}{1000 \times 1.25 \times 1.15 \times 1.5} = 1.23 \text{ in}^3$$

Try one 2 × 4 at 16 in on center:

$$S = 3.05 \text{ in}^3 > 1.23 \text{ in}^3 \qquad \text{OK}$$

Check Shear, Simple Span

$$w = 1000 \text{ lb/ft or } 83.3 \text{ lb/in}$$

$$R = 1000\left(\frac{16}{12}\right)\left(\frac{1}{2}\right) = 667 \text{ lb}$$

$$V = 667 - (3.5 \times 83.3) = 376 \text{ lb}$$

$$f_v = \frac{3V}{2A} = \frac{3 \times 376}{2 \times 1.5 \times 3.5} = 107 \text{ lb/in}^2 < 95 \times 1.25 = 119 \text{ lb/in}^2 \qquad \text{OK}$$

This is the required spacing for the bottom 5 ft of the form. The spacing for the top 5 ft can be increased as long as the load on the waler from the stud remains at 1327 lb or less.

Bracing. The form must be braced to carry the minimum 100-lb/ft lateral load at the top as determined from Table 10.9, assuming a wind force of 20 lb/ft² or less. Place braces at 4-ft centers, using a double 2 × 4 (38.1 × 88.9 mm*) nailed together with 16d nails at 12-in (305-mm) centers braced to deadmen. Braces will be placed on both sides so that they only need to act in compression. See Fig. 10.34*f* for forces:

$$f_c = \frac{300 \times 4}{2 \times 1.5 \times 3.5} = 114 \text{ lb/in}^2 \qquad \text{OK BY INSPECTION}$$

*All SI units shown for sawn lumber are for the actual net dimensions corresponding to the nominal dimensions indicated.

EXAMPLE 10.6 Design the shores and bracing for the forms shown in Fig. 10.35. The shores are 15 ft (4.57 m) long and are spaced at 4-ft (1.2-m) and 8-ft (2.44-m) centers under a 40- by 40-ft (12.2- by 12.2-m) slab which is 12 in (305 mm) thick. The concrete is to be pumped. Therefore no lateral loads will result from concrete-placing equipment.

SOLUTION: Assume a live load of 50 lb/ft² due to worker and equipment and a dead load of 150 lb/ft² for the weight of concrete plus 15 lb/ft² for the weight of forms. Therefore, the total load per shore is

$$P = (50 + 150 + 15)\,32 = 6880 \text{ lb}$$

Shore Design. Try a 4 × 4 No. 2 Douglas fir (dry-use conditions) and assume the shore has no rotational restraint at its ends (pinned ends) and that it is laterally supported at its midlength. Assume E = 1,700,000 lb/in² (11.72 GPa) and F_c = 1450 lb/in² (10.0 MPa).

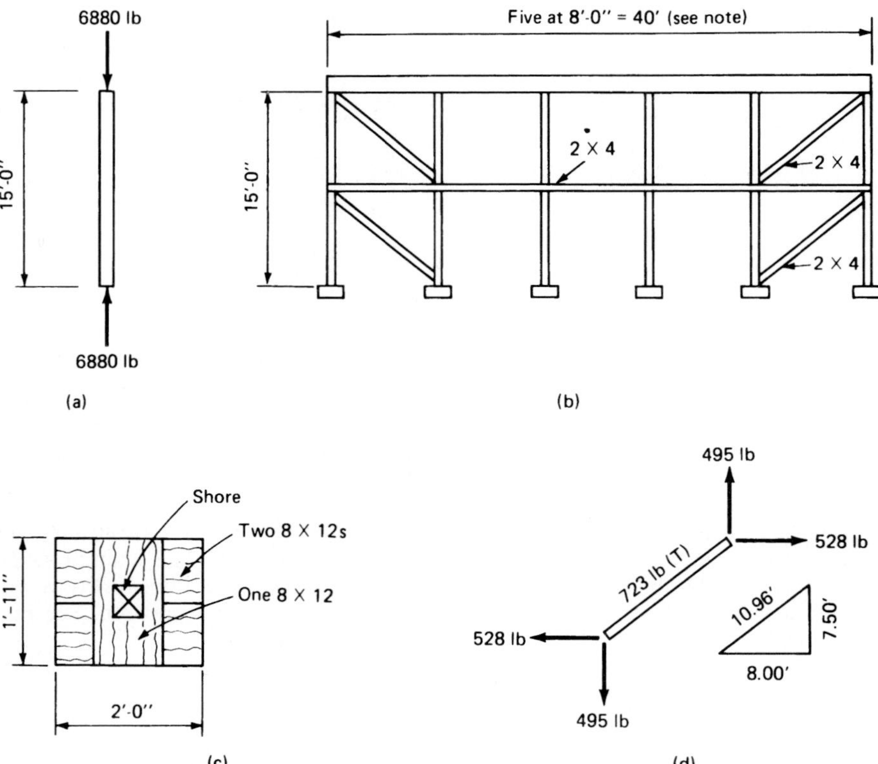

FIG. 10.35 Shore design details. (*a*) Typical shore; (*b*) elevation. (*Note:* Braced bents at 4'-0" on center.) (*c*) Base for shore; (*d*) diagonal brace—forces and dimensions.

$$\frac{\ell_e}{d} = \frac{7.5 \times 12}{3.5} = 25.7 < 50 \qquad \text{OK}$$

$$F_{cE} = \frac{K_{cE}E'}{(\ell_e/d)^2} = \frac{0.3 \times 1{,}700{,}000}{(25.7)^2} = 772 \text{ lb/in}^2$$

$$F_c^* = F_c C_D C_F = 1450 \times 1.25 \times 1.15 = 2084 \text{ lb/in}^2$$

$$C_P = \frac{1 + (F_{cE}/F_c^*)}{2c} - \sqrt{\left[\frac{1 + (F_{cE}/F_c^*)}{2c}\right]^2 - \frac{(F_{cE}/F_c^*)}{c}}$$

$$= \frac{1 + (772/2084)}{2 \times 0.8} - \sqrt{\left[\frac{1 + (772/2084)}{2 \times 0.8}\right]^2 - \frac{(772/2084)}{0.8}}$$

$$= 0.336$$

$$F_c' = F_c^* C_p = 2084 \times 0.336 = 700 \text{ lb/in}^2$$

$$P_{\text{allowable}} = F_c'A = 700 \times 3.5 \times 3.5$$

$$= 8580 \text{ lb} > 6880 \text{ lb} \qquad \text{OK}$$

Assuming an allowable soil bearing pressure of 2000 lb/ft², the required base area per shore is

$$A \text{ (required)} = \frac{6880}{2000} = 3.44 \text{ ft}^2$$

Use a 2-ft 0-in by 1-ft 11-in base, as shown in Fig. 10.2*c*.

$$A = 3.83 \text{ ft}^2 \qquad \text{OK}$$

Bracing. It is generally recommended that slab forms be braced for a minimum lateral load of 100 lb/ft of slab edge or for 2 percent of total dead load on the form (distributed as uniform load per lineal foot of slab edge), whichever is greater. Only the area of slab placed in a single pour needs to be considered,

$$F \text{ (2 percent of dead load)} = 0.02 \times 165 \times 40 = 132 \text{ lb/ft}$$

Table 10.10 is based on 2 percent dead load, with a minimum of 100 lb/ft, and will give identical results. Based on a value of 132 lb/ft, the force in a brace for the 8-ft-wide shore spacing is (Fig. 10.35*d*)

$$F = \frac{132 \times 4 \times 10.96}{8.0} = 723 \text{ lb}$$

If it is assumed that the bracing acts in tension only and that a No. 3 Douglas fir 2 × 4 will be used with F_t = 325 lb/in² (dry condition of use), then the allowable force for the 2 × 4 is

$$P = F_t C_D C_F A = 325 \times 1.25 \times 1.5 \times 5.25 = 3200 \text{ lb} > 723 \text{ lb} \qquad \text{OK}$$

Each end of the brace must be capable of transferring a force of 723 lb. (For the design of joints using fasteners and connectors, see Chap. 5). Bracing using 2 × 4s adequately fastened to the shores would be satisfactory and must be provided as shown in Fig. 10.35*b*. It is also necessary to provide bracing in the 4-ft shore spacing direction.

10.3 WOOD-METAL COMPOSITES

Wood-metal structures are typically of two types. The first is basically the combination of two beams of different materials which share in carrying the load, while the second uses the metal as a tensile reinforcement for the wood. The simplest of the first type is illustrated by a header composed of two wood 3 × 12s (63 × 286 mm) with a ⅜- by 11-in (9.5- by 279-mm) steel plate between them (Fig. 10.36). All pieces are bolted together at close intervals, and all members bear on the supports at their ends. These are typically used in situations where a deeper wood beam would not leave adequate headroom or in rehabilitation work where it is necessary to reinforce existing wood members (Fig. 10.37). In this latter case the steel plates can be positioned on the outside of the existing wood member.

When sheet steel plates are placed between lumber laminations, as shown in Fig. 10.37, and used as flexural members, they are known as *flitch beams*. They have become more economically feasible as a result of the availability of helically threaded and hardened framing nails. These nails can be hammer- and machine-driven effectively through the wood and the sheet steel plates. Other forms of wood such as glulam and laminated veneer lumber, however, have largely replaced the use of flitch beams. It is important in composite construction that the members be adequately fastened together so that both the wood and the steel deflect equally and each component material carries its proportionate share of the design load. Therefore, the fasteners or connectors must be designed to transfer the shear forces between members unless adequate bearing is provided so that loads are applied directly to both wood and steel.

EXAMPLE 10.7: COMPOSITE BEAM ANALYSIS Determine the maximum design dead load plus snow load for the composite wood-steel beam shown in Fig. 10.38*a* and *b*. Assume that the wood members are No. 2 Douglas fir and the plate is A36 steel. Also assume that the beam will remain dry in service.

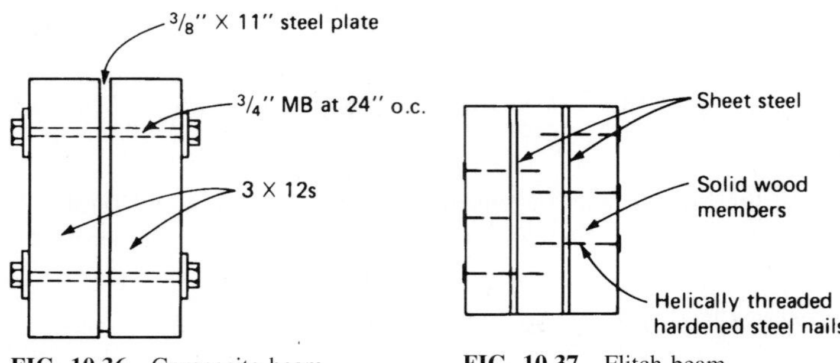

FIG. 10.36 Composite beam.

FIG. 10.37 Flitch beam.

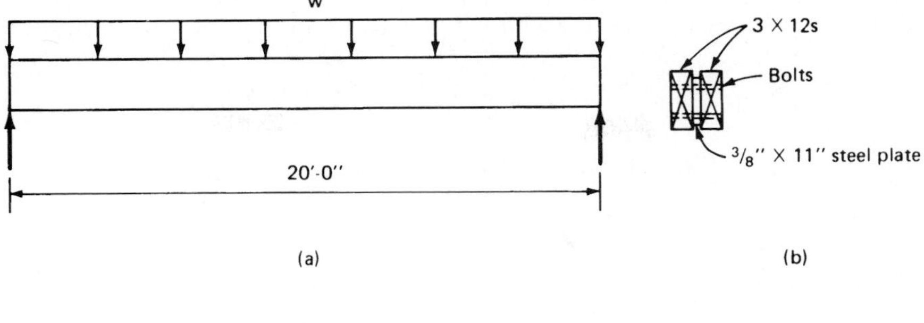

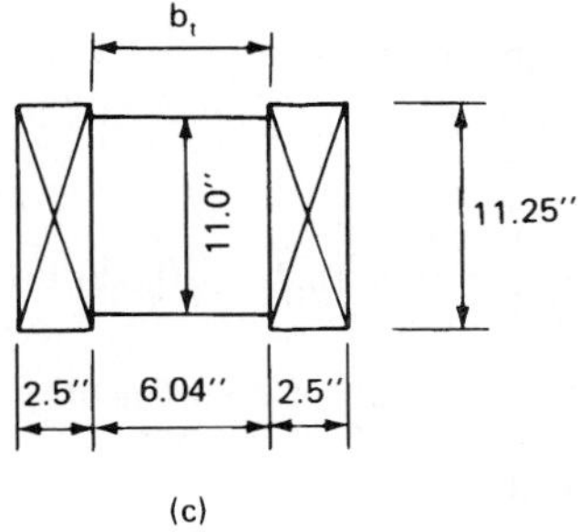

FIG. 10.38 Example 10.7: composite beam. (*a*) Beam and loading; (*b*) beam cross section; (*c*) transformed section.

SOLUTION: Allowable stresses and moduli of elasticity are as follows:

Steel	Wood
$E_s = 29 \times 10^6$ lb/in^2	$E_w = 1.8 \times 10^6$ lb/in^2
$F_{bs} = 0.66 f_y = 23{,}800$ lb/in^2	$F_{bw} = 1150$ lb/in^2
$F_{vs} = 0.4\ F_y = 14{,}400$ lb/in^2	$F_{vw} = 95$ lb/in^2

The load-duration factor for the combination of dead and snow loads is 1.15. Using the concept of transformed section and converting all steel to an equivalent wood area, the modified section is

$$n = \frac{E_s}{E_w} = \frac{29 \times 10^6}{1.8 \times 10^6} = 16.1$$

The width of the transformed steel (Fig. 10.38*c*) is

$$b_t = \tfrac{3}{8} \times 16.1 = 6.04 \text{ in}$$

The transformed section modulus is

$$I_t = 2 \times 296.6 + \frac{6.04 \times 11^3}{12} = 1263 \text{ in}^4$$

Assuming that the wood controls the design based on its flexural capacity, the allowable uniformly distributed load is

$$F'_b = \frac{Mc}{I_t}$$

$$M = \frac{F'_b I_t}{c} = \frac{1150 \times 1.15 \times 1.0 \times 1263}{11.25/2} = 296{,}900 \text{ lb·in}$$

$$M = \frac{w\ell^2}{8}$$

$$w = \frac{8M}{\ell^2} = \frac{8 \times 296{,}900}{(20 \times 12)^2} \times 12 = 495 \text{ lb/ft}$$

Check Stress in Steel

$$f_{bs} = \frac{Mc}{I_t} n = \frac{296{,}900 \times 5.5}{1263} \times 16.1 = 20{,}820 \text{ lb/in}^2 < 23{,}800 \text{ lb/in}^2$$

Therefore, the flexural stress in the wood component controls the maximum load for the moment as assumed.

Check Shearing Stress in Wood

$$V_w = 495\left(10 - \frac{11.25}{12}\right) = 4486 \text{ lb}$$

$$Q = \frac{56.25}{2}\left(\frac{11.25}{4}\right)^2 + \frac{11.0}{2} \times 6.04\left(\frac{11.0}{4}\right) = 170.5 \text{ in}^3$$

$$f_v \text{ (wood)} = \frac{VQ}{I_t t} = \frac{4486 \times 170.5}{1263 \times 11.04} = 54.8 \text{ lb/in}^2$$

$$F'_{vw} = 95 \times 1.15 = 109 \text{ lb/in}^2 > 54.8 \text{ lb/in}^2 \qquad \text{OK}$$

Check Shearing Stress in Steel

$$V_s = 495 \times 10 = 4950 \text{ lb}$$

$$f_v \text{ (steel)} = \frac{VQ}{I_t t} n = \frac{4950 \times 170.5}{1263 \times 11.04} \times 16.1$$

$$= 974 \text{ lb/in}^2 \ll 14{,}400 \text{ lb/in}^2 \qquad \text{OK}$$

Note: Steel shear stress rarely controls the design of the steel component.

Check Total Deflection

$$\Delta = \frac{5w\ell^4}{384EI_t} = \frac{5 \times 495 \times 20^4 \times 1728}{384 \times 1{,}800{,}000 \times 1263} = 0.784 \text{ in (19.9 mm)}$$

If the limit on deflection is $\ell/240$ for dead load plus applied load,

$$\Delta\ (\text{allowable}) = \frac{20 \times 12}{240} = 1.0\ \text{in}\ (25.4\ \text{mm}) > 0.784\ \text{in}\ (19.9\ \text{mm}) \qquad \text{OK}$$

Fasteners. It is also necessary that an adequate number and size of fasteners be provided in the design to ensure that both wood and steel deflect equally. For fastener design, see Chap. 5.

Summary. The maximum uniform load capacity is 495 lb/ft (7.22 kN/m) and is controlled by the flexural stress in the wood.

The preceding example is a simple combination of two materials and is given to illustrate some of the basic calculations needed in this type of composite member. Many other arrangements for combining these two materials are possible.

Examples of the use of steel to carry tensile forces in combination with a wood compression member are shown in Fig. 10.39. Figure 10.39*a* and *b* illustrates the king and queen post trusses using steel tension rods. They can serve to increase the span length or load capacity of a wood member and have been used to reinforce a two-span beam whose center support is to be removed, or to reinforce a simple-span beam of insufficient capacity for changed conditions. The kind and queen post trusses are statically indeterminate and are discussed in some textbooks. The solution is based on the elastic strain properties of the materials and the equation usually given obtains the force in the post.

The equation for the force in the post of a king post truss and for the forces in the posts of a queen post truss in which the posts are symmetrically placed about the centerline of the flexural member is

$$P = \frac{\int Mm\ dx/EI}{\Sigma u^2 L/AE + \int m^2\ dx/EI} \tag{10.8}$$

If the flexural member is divided into a finite number of elements, the integral signs may be replaced by summation signs and the equation becomes

$$P = \frac{\Sigma Mm\ \Delta x/EI}{\Sigma u^2 L/AE + \Sigma m^2\ \Delta x/EI} \tag{10.9}$$

where P = force in post of king or queen post truss
A = area of truss member
E = modulus of elasticity of truss member
L = length of truss member
M = moment at center of beam segment due to external loads without redundant member (post or posts)
m = moment at center of beam segment due to unit force in redundant member (post or posts)
u = force in truss member due to unit force applied to redundant member (post or posts)
Δx = length of beam segment
I = moment of inertia of beam segment

Usually it is not necessary to use a large number of segments for the flexural

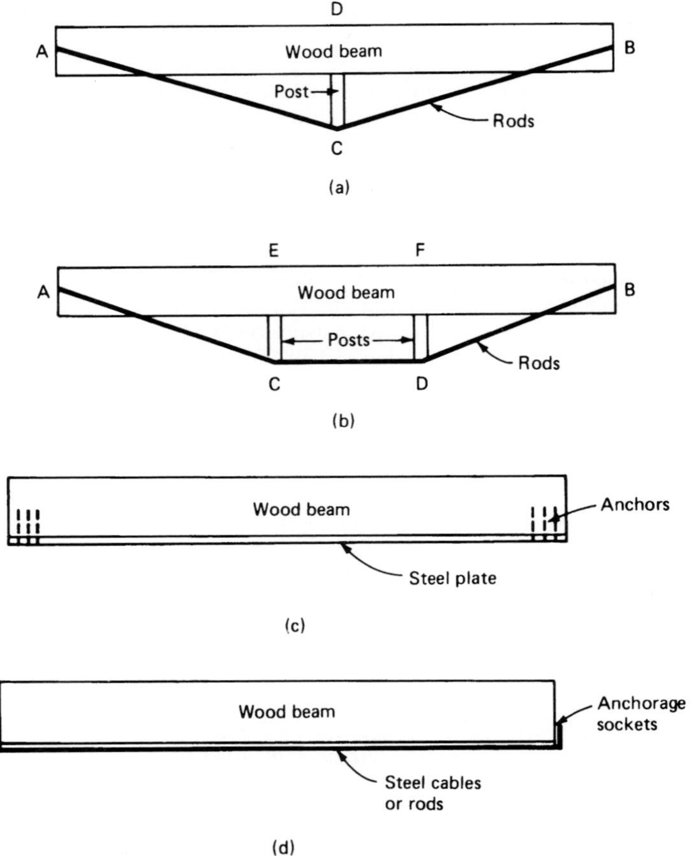

FIG. 10.39 Types of composite beams. (*a*) King post truss; (*b*) queen post truss; (*c*) composite wood-steel beam; (*d*) composite wood-cables/rods beam.

member (AB) of the king or queen truss in order to obtain accurate results, even if a variable-depth member were used, which is unlikely. Four or five segments for each half, as shown in Example 10.8, usually give satisfactory results. The term for axial strains of Eq. (10.9), $\Sigma u^2L/AE$, would involve only four terms for the king post truss, one each for members AC, CB, CD, and ADB (Fig. 10.39*a*), and due to symmetry, AC would be equal to CB. For the queen post truss, six terms would be involved.

After the force in the post or posts has been determined, the forces and moments in other members of the indeterminate structure can be calculated by using the equations of equilibrium. In general, trussed beams should have as much depth as conditions will permit in order to minimize their stresses. To accomplish this may require too much encroachment on available headroom if the king post truss shown in Fig. 10.39*a* is used. Therefore, the queen post truss of Fig. 10.39*b* or a reinforced beam as shown in Fig. 10.39*c* or *d* may be a better solution.

EXAMPLE 10.8 A loading dock 40 ft wide with a 15-ft overhang is to be converted to a simple span by removing an interior existing support and installing a new support at the free end of the overhang (Fig. 10.40*a* and *b*). A queen post truss supporting the uniformly distributed normal load of 1000 lb/ft (14.59 kN/m) is selected.

SOLUTION: To obtain a solution for this problem, it will be necessary to solve Eq. (10.9). To do this, the following assumptions are made:

1. The cross-sectional area of the tension member is assumed to be 2.00 in^2.
2. The beam is divided into 10 equal segments.
3. The moment is assumed constant throughout the segment and the value used is that at the center of the segment.
4. The cross-sectional area of the post is assumed to be 30 in^2.
5. E(wood) = 1600 kips/in^2 and E(steel) = 29,000 kips/in^2.

Figure 10.40*c* and *d* gives moments M and m, and Fig. 10.40*e* gives the axial forces u, assuming a 1-kip force exists in the posts.

Segment	M, kips·ft	m, kips·ft	Δx, ft	$Mm\ \Delta x_3$, kips^2·ft^3	$m^2\ \Delta x_3$, kips^2·ft^3	Final moments, kips·ft
1	38	1.6	4	243	10.2	12.8
2	102	4.8	4	1,958	92.2	26.4
3	150	8.0	4	4,800	256.0	24.0
4	182	11.2	4	8,154	501.8	5.6
5	198	12.0	4	9,504	576.0	16.1
Totals				24,659	1436.2	

Since the beam is symmetrical about its centerline, the values for one-half can be multiplied by 2 to obtain the values for the entire beam:

$$\frac{\Sigma Mm\ \Delta x}{EI} = \frac{24{,}659 \times 2}{EI} = \frac{24{,}659 \times 2 \times 1728}{1600 \times 3244} = 16.42 \text{ kips·in}$$

$$\frac{\Sigma m^2\ \Delta x}{EI} = \frac{1436.2 \times 2}{EI} = \frac{1436.2 \times 2 \times 1728}{1600 \times 3244} = 0.956 \text{ kips·in}$$

For axial strain energy, the queen post truss is divided into sections, as shown in Fig. 40*e*.

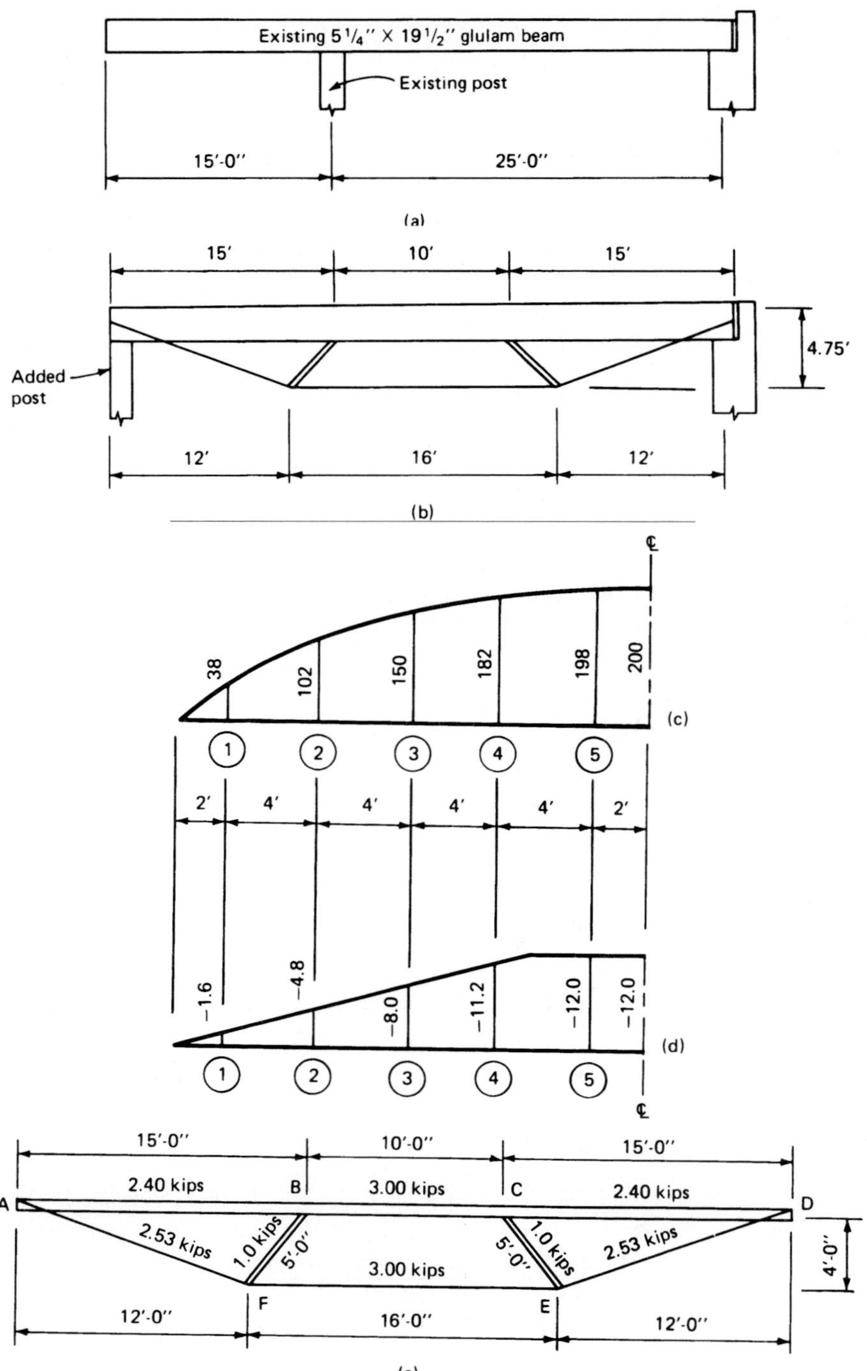

FIG. 10.40 Example 10.8. (*a*) Existing beam and supports; (*b*) modified beam, queen post truss; (*c*) moments M (kips·ft); (*d*) moments m (kips·ft); (*e*) axial forces u (kips) and dimensions.

Section	u, kips	L, in	A, in²	E, kips/in²	u^2L/AE, kips·in	Axial force Pu, kips
AB	2.40	180	102	1,600	0.00635	37.80
BC	3.00	120	102	1,600	0.00662	47.25
CD	2.40	280	102	1,600	0.00635	37.80
AF	2.53	152	2	29,000	0.01677	40.95
FE	3.00	192	2	29,000	0.02979	47.25
ED	2.53	152	2	29,000	0.01677	40.95
BF	1.0	60	30	1,600	0.00125	15.78
CE	1.0	60	30	1,600	0.00125	15.75
Total					0.08515	

Solving Eq. (10.9),

$$P = \frac{16.42}{0.08515 + 0.956} = 15.75 \text{ kips}$$

which is the axial force in each post of the queen post truss. Other forces and moments can now be calculated as follows:

$$\text{Axial force} = Pu$$

$$\text{Axial force in rod } (FE) = 15.75 \times 3.00 = 47.25 \text{ kips}$$

$$\text{Axial force in beam } (BC) = 15.75 \times 3.00 = 47.25 \text{ kips}$$

$$\text{Maximum bending moment in beam} = M - mP$$

$$M \text{ (maximum)} = 102 - 4.8 \times 15.75 = 26.4 \text{ kips·ft}$$

which occurs at point 2 in beam.

Check the sizes of the members.

Steel Rod

$$f_t = \frac{47.25}{2.0} = 23.62 \text{ kips/in}^2$$

Try A588 threaded steel rods. F_t (allowable) $= 0.33F_u$, the allowable tensile stress in threaded fasteners.

$$F_t = 0.33 \times 70 = 23.1 \text{ kips/in}^2 \approx f_t$$

Select rods to provide a steel area slightly greater than 2.0 in². Try two 1¼-in-diameter rods:

$$\text{Area} = 2.45 \text{ in}^2 \qquad \text{OK}$$

Post. Design as a pin-ended column and assume a least dimension of 5.5 in, i.e., a nominal 6- by 6-in member,

$$\frac{\ell_e}{d} = \frac{60}{5.5} = 10.9 < 50 \qquad \text{OK}$$

$$F_{cE} = \frac{K_{cE}E}{(\ell_e/d)^2} = \frac{0.3 \times 1{,}600{,}000}{(10.9)^2} = 4040 \text{ lb/in}^2$$

Assume $F_c = 1150$ lb/in² selected structure Douglas fir (posts and timbers) and a normal load duration $C_D = 1.0$.

$$F_c^* = F_c = 1150 \text{ lb/in}^2$$

$$C_p = \frac{1 + (4040/1150)}{2 \times 0.8} - \sqrt{\left[\frac{1 + (4040/1150)}{2 \times 0.8}\right]^2 - \frac{(4040/1150)}{0.8}}$$

$$= 0.932$$

$$F_c' = F_c^* C_p = 1150 \times 0.932 = 1072 \text{ lb/in}^2$$

$$P_{\text{allowable}} = F_c'A = 1072 \times 5.5 \times 5.5 = 32{,}430 \text{ lb} > 15{,}750 \text{ lb} \qquad \text{OK}$$

Beam. Design as a beam column, assuming that the top edge of the member is laterally supported by the existing roof.

Check Segment AB. The existing beam is a 5¼- by 19½-in Douglas fir glulam with allowable stresses equivalent to a 20F-V3 stress combination (see Appendix, "Reference Data Table A.3"):

$$F_b = 2000 \text{ lb/in}^2 \qquad \text{and} \qquad F_c = 1{,}000 \text{ lb/in}^2$$

$$\left(\frac{f_c}{F_c'}\right)^2 + \frac{f_{b1}}{F_{b1}'[1 - (f_c/F_{cE1})]} \leq 1.0$$

$$f_c < F_{cE1} = \frac{K_{cE}E'}{(\ell_{e1}/d_1)^2}$$

$$\frac{\ell_{e1}}{d_1} = \frac{40 \times 12}{19.5} = 24.6$$

$$F_{cE1} = \frac{0.418 \times 1{,}600{,}000}{(24.6)^2} = 1105 \text{ lb/in}^2$$

$$f_c = \frac{P}{A} = \frac{37{,}800}{99.94} = 378 \text{ lb/in}^2 < 1105 \text{ lb/in}^2 \qquad \text{OK}$$

$$F_{b1} = 2000 \text{ lb/in}^2$$

$$f_{b1} = \frac{M}{S} = \frac{27{,}400 \times 12}{324.8} = 975 \text{ lb/in}^2 < 2000 \text{ lb/in}^2 \qquad \text{OK}$$

$$\left(\frac{378}{1105}\right)^2 + \frac{975}{2000[1 - (378/1105)]} = 0.858 < 1.0 \qquad \text{OK}$$

Check Segment BC

$$f_c = \frac{47{,}250}{99.94} = 473 \text{ lb/in}^2 < 1105 \text{ lb/in}^2 \qquad \text{OK}$$

$$f_{b1} = \frac{24{,}000 \times 12}{324.8} = 887 \text{ lb/in}^2 < 1105 \text{ lb/in}^2 \qquad \text{OK}$$

$$\left(\frac{473}{1105}\right)^2 + \frac{887}{2000[1 - (473/1105)]} = 0.959 < 1.0 \qquad \text{OK}$$

In the reinforced beam shown in Fig. 10.39*c*, the metal plate can be used as a beam splice or to repair a beam damaged on its tension side. Transformed section properties are used and all wood in tension can be ignored, as is done in concrete design using the working stress method. Formulas used in the working stress method for concrete can be modified and used for a reinforced wood beam.

Another method of reinforcing the wood beam is to use steel rods or cables posttensioned to place the wood in compression (Fig. 10.39*d*). This method has been used to repair damaged beams and to reinforce beams of inadequate strength. The calculations are basically the same as for a prestressed concrete beam. The long-term creep and relaxation of the wood can only be estimated. Assume a value of 1½ to 2 times the initial elastic shortening of the wood under load. If an average of 1.75 is used,

$$\Delta = \frac{1.75fL}{E}$$

where Δ = long-term creep and deflection, in (mm)
f = average axial stress, lb/in² (Pa)
L = length, in (mm)
E = modulus of elasticity, lb/in² (Pa)

The design of the anchorages is simplified if symmetrical bearing plates are used on the ends. Manufacturing difficulties have so far prevented any common use of prestressed glulam beams in a production facility, although some experimentation has been done.[9] Such concepts as a glue joint reinforced with fiberglass or wire mesh or a steel plate glue-bonded to the wood have been considered, but additional research is needed before these concepts can be considered for production.

If posttensioning is to be done using rods or cables, it is important that these rods or cables maintain a positive upward pressure on the beam. This is best accomplished by placing spacers between the beam and the reinforcing elements so that the reinforcing elements have a slight curvature, as shown in Fig. 10.41*a*. Failure to maintain upward pressure has resulted in the failure of the beam since the prestress can introduce an additional positive moment, as exhibited by Fig. 10.41*b*.

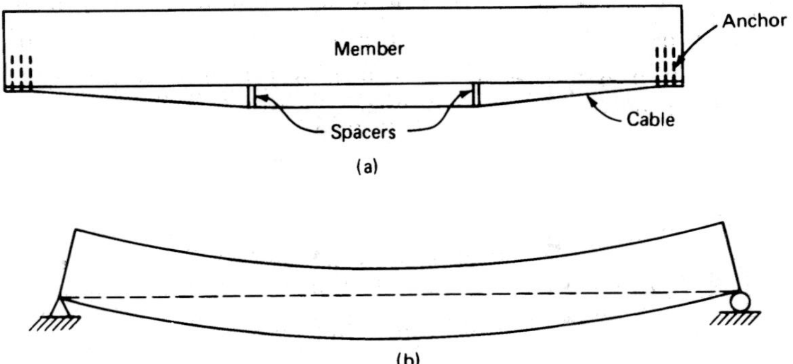

FIG. 10.41 Posttensioning tendons. (*a*) Details, posttensioning tendons; (*b*) improper placement of posttensioning tendons.

REFERENCES

1. American Association of State Highway and Transportation Officials, *Standard Specifications for Highway Bridges,* 13th ed., Washington, D.C., American Association of State Highway and Transportation Officials, 1992.
2. American Forest and Paper Association, *National Design Specification for Wood Construction,* Washington, D.C., American Forest and Paper Association, 1991.
3. American Forest and Paper Association, *Design Values for Wood Construction: A Supplement to the 1991 ed. of the National Design Specification,* Washington, D.C., American Forest and Paper Association, 1991.
4. American Institute of Timber Construction, *Glulam Bridge Systems,* Englewood, Colo., American Institute of Timber Construction, 1988.
5. American Institute of Timber Construction, AITC 117-93, *Design Standard Specifications for Structural Glued Laminated Timber of Softwood Species,* Englewood, Colo., American Institute of Timber Construction, 1993.
6. Michael A. Ritter, *Timber Bridges: Design, Construction, Inspection, and Maintenance,* EM 7700-8, Washington, D.C., U.S. Department of Agriculture, Forest Service, Engineering Staff, 1990.
7. T. J. Wipf, F. W. Klaiber, and W. W. Sanders, "Load distribution criteria for glued-laminated longitudinal timber deck highway bridges," *Transportation Research Record 1053,* Washington, D.C., National Academy of Sciences, National Research Council, Transportation Research Board, 1986, pp. 31–40.
8. "Guide to Formwork for Concrete," *ACI Struct. J.* **85**(5), 1988.
9. J. Peterson, "Wood Beam Prestressed with Bonded Tension Elements," *J. Struct. Div. Am. Soc. Civ. Eng.* **91**(ST2), 1965.
10. *Manual of Recommended Practice: Specifications for Structural Lumber,* American Railway Engineers Association, Chicago, Ill., 1985.
11. S. Timoshenko and J. N. Goodier, *Theory of Elasticity,* 3rd ed., McGraw-Hill, New York, 1970.
12. R. Gutkowski and T. G. Williamson, "Timber Bridges: State-of-the-Art," *J. Struct. Div. Am. Soc. Civ. Eng.* **109**(9), Sept. 1983.

13. *Standard for Preservative Treatment of Structural Glue Laminated Timber,* AITC 109, American Institute of Timber Construction, Vancouver, Wash., 1984.

14. *Weyerhaeuser Glulam Wood Bridge Systems,* Weyerhaeuser Co., Tacoma, Wash., 1980.

15. *Prefabricated Composite Deck Panels with Improved Fasteners,* American Wood Preservers Association Service Bureau, Springfield, VA, 1946.

16. *Western Woods Use Book,* 3d ed., Western Wood Products Association, Portland, Oreg., 1983; revised 1987.

CHAPTER 11
WOOD FOUNDATION STRUCTURES

Alfred R. Mangus, P.E.

11.1 PERMANENT WOOD FOUNDATIONS (PWF)

11.1.1 History

Timber foundations were used and recorded in engineering documents by the Romans and certainly were used long before that period in history. Untreated wood exposed to the elements deteriorates very quickly if not completely submerged in water. The Brooklyn Bridge has two 168- by 102-ft (51- by 31-m) timber casions, weighing 3600 tons, for each stone tower. Recent borings into the submerged 100-year-old timber caissons show the wood to be as sound and sapfilled as when first placed.[1] Since wood foundations are generally built in locations where fluctuations occur in the groundwater level, thus resulting in alternate wetting and drying of the wood, decay of untreated wood is a major concern. The wood located near the groundwater table is the most susceptible to decay and will deteriorate most rapidly.

In addition to the potential for decay in untreated wood foundations, there are several types of insects that attack and destroy untreated timber. These are discussed in Sec. 1.4.7. Chapter 2 provides a discussion of preservative treatments for wood construction. In 1969, the permanent wood foundation (PWF) was developed in a joint government-industry effort involving the U.S. Department of Agriculture, the American Forest and Paper Association, and the American Wood Preservers Institute. Since 1969, over 90,000 homes have been built with PWF. The PWF system uses various waterborne salts for treatment of the wood components. It should be noted that these preservative salts, in combination with moisture, will react chemically with certain metals, causing them to deteriorate rapidly. Therefore, the latest guidelines[2–4] for hardware and fastener coatings for PWFs must be followed. The organizations listed in the references should be contacted to obtain current recommendations. The PWF has been approved by all major building codes and lending agencies.

Note: In all example problems, SI units are provided only for given data and for the final problem answers. No intermediate values or data are expressed in SI units.

11.1.2 Advantages and Disadvantages

In designing a foundation, the designer should select the system which will be of greatest benefit to the owner. Reasons to consider the PWF are

1. Minimize initial foundation costs
2. Concrete may not be readily available
3. Minimize interior finish costs
4. Natural insulating characteristics of wood provide warmth to basement area
5. Lower deadweight realized with wood construction
6. Can be installed quickly and easily, with minimal mechanical equipment
7. Proven structural integrity
8. Temporary structures can be easily disassembled, relocated, and rebuilt

The construction cost of a PWF for a timber-framed structure will generally be less than that of a masonry or concrete foundation. One reason is that no masons and concrete finishers (and their equipment) will be required for the PWF system. The PWF is most cost-competitive in regions of high labor costs, since carpenters can construct an entire wood-framed structure, including the foundation. Cold-weather construction costs will be less because there will be no need for heating the foundation walls during construction. Also, furring of the finish wall will not be required because insulation and electrical wiring can be installed inside the stud wall cavity. Paneling or interior finish material can then be attached directly to the PWF stud framing.

In many rural locations, concrete is not always available at a competitive cost because acceptable aggregate must be transported to the site. Site batching also may reduce the quality of the product, and it will be more expensive than computerized batch plant concrete.

Wood is a natural insulator and reduces the amount of additional insulation required to achieve a specified *R* value. Batt-type insulation can be installed inside the stud-framed wall cavity. Thus there is no loss of interior space, which occurs in furred concrete or masonry walls.

A 6-in (15.24-cm)-thick, 8-ft (2.438-m)-high PWF wall will weigh about 80 lb/ft (119 kg/m), while a 6-in (15.24-cm) concrete wall of the same height weighs 600 lb/ft (893 kg/m). Occasionally, structures located on marginal soils which use concrete foundations will require pile foundations, while a PWF can be built without piles. Seismic forces will be less on a PWF footing than on a masonry or concrete wall because it has a lower mass. A PWF is built faster than a masonry or concrete foundation because installation of formwork and subsequent curing of the masonry are not required. Also, panelization of the wood wall panels prior to delivery to the job site minimizes on-site labor time. Since time is a major factor in building costs, minimizing construction time optimizes costs.

The PWF can be custom designed to provide optimum strength and cost by varying stud spacing, size, and wood species. Concrete and masonry block foundations used for lightly loaded wood-framed structures often have excessive structural capacity because it is not practical to construct these walls thinner than 6 in (152 mm).

PWF systems are often used for foundations to carry temporary construction loadings or construction equipment since they can be disassembled and reused. The *Handbook of Temporary Structures in Construction*[5] describes many practical applications of timber foundations in construction. The safe working loads of timber elements can be doubled for impact loading, which often occurs in construction. Because wood is relatively lightweight, it costs less to transport the material to the next construction project. Normally, one or two workers can assemble or disassemble a timber foundation.

The potential disadvantages associated with a PWF are listed below, since it is important to identify the possible misapplications of any construction concept or technique. Inappropriate application of the PWF can be detrimental to all parties involved.

1. It lacks mass to resist overturning.
2. It is impossible or impracticable to develop sufficient strength under some loading conditions.
3. Care must be taken to ensure proper contact with bearing soils.

For tall structures, the overturning force due to wind often makes concrete footings and foundations desirable because of their greater deadweight. Two-thirds of this mass can then be used in design computations to resist these overturning forces.

When heavy soil loadings or surcharge loads exist, dimensional lumber and plywood may not be adequate for footings. While treated glued-laminated (glulam) stud members and treated timber planking for sheathing could be used to carry high loads, concrete and masonry foundations will normally prove to be more economical under these conditions.

Placement of the footing plate on its gravel base so that a uniform distribution of bearing is obtained is a critical part of PWF construction. For this reason, local building codes may require a concrete footing for the PWF.

It is very important that PWF systems be adequately damp-proofed. PWF recommendations call for one layer of polyethylene film, but designers should consider specifying a higher-performance membrane when the interior finishes are vulnerable to water damage. Possible choices include 15-lb felt embedded in steep asphalt (designed for vertical surfaces) or, for better protection, one of the high-performance single-ply waterproofing membranes which incorporate layers of modified bitumens within layers of plastic film. Backfill material should be free draining to avoid trapping water against the wall, and footing drains should be provided.

11.1.3 Structural Details for Single-Column Footings

Single-column footings are frequently required for architectural reasons. Wall footings are generally more economical because they distribute the loading over a larger area, thus requiring smaller members. Four types of single-column footings are shown in Fig. 11.1. The plywood pad footing and the California plank footing are recommended for light loadings because minimal labor and materials are required for their construction. Their strength is limited by the bending forces on the wood pad or the crushing of the wood (compression perpendicular to grain) below the post. A metal post base with corrosion-resistant coating and the capacity to handle uplifting forces is recommended.

When forces are greater than the capacity of the plywood pad footing or the California plank footing, the plank pad footing could be utilized. The post is attached to the spreader beam with a metal post base, as previously described. The spreader plank transfers the forces from the post to the footing planks. Compressive

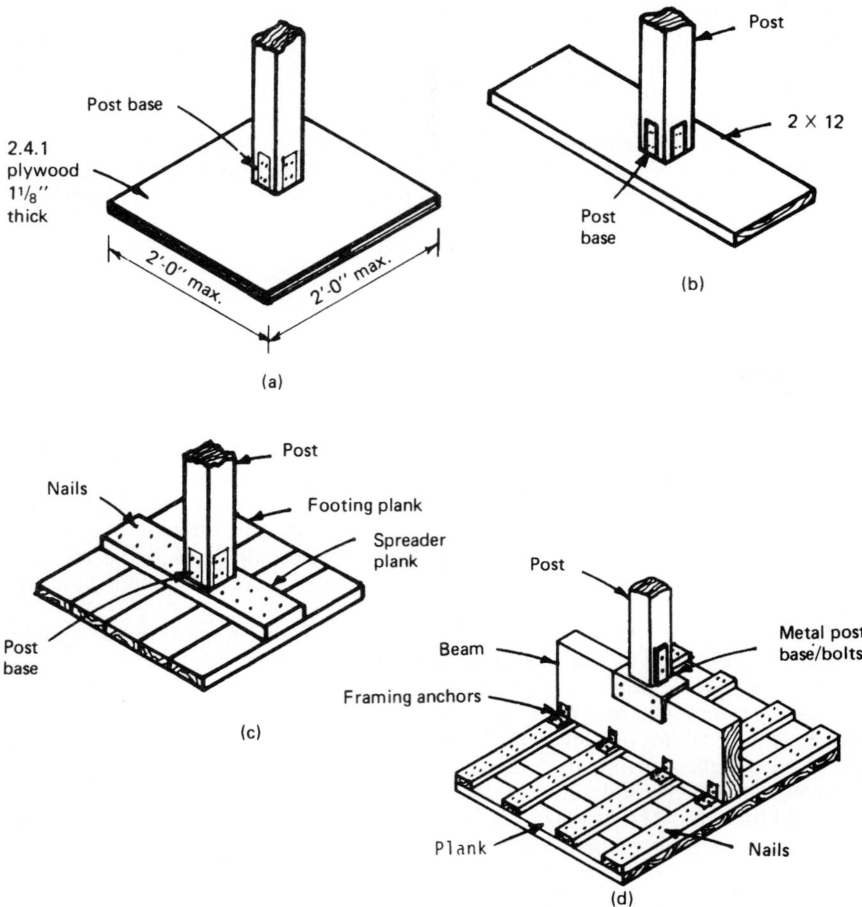

FIG. 11.1 Single-column footings. (*a*) Plywood pad footing; (*b*) California plank footing; (*c*) plank pad footing; (*d*) grillage footing. *Notes:* (1) All fasteners and connectors to have corrosion-resistant coating. (2) All lumber to be preservatively pressure-treated.

stresses perpendicular to grain in the spreader plank below the post should be checked during design. The spreader plank and the footing plank are analyzed as cantilever beams. Deflection criteria for these members often control their design. When greater forces are encountered, a grillage-type footing will be required. A steel post-to-beam bracket with a corrosion-resistant coating is used to distribute the forces such that the compressive strength perpendicular to grain of the support beam below the post is not exceeded. This type of bracket can be designed to resist the higher uplift forces on the footing. This support beam is analyzed as a cantilever member. The beam transfers the forces to the wood spreaders, and the contact area between these elements must be such that the compressive stresses perpendicular to grain are not exceeded. Sheet metal framing anchors with corrosion-resistant coating are recommended for transferring any uplift forces and to tie the elements together. The wood spreader planks are analyzed as cantilevered beams with uniform load. If the grillage footing framing becomes too complex, a concrete footing may be more economical.

EXAMPLE 11.1: PLANK PAD FOOTING Given: column = nominal 4- × 6-in (8.89- × 14-cm)* solid sawn timber post, dead load = 2000 lb (8.89 kN), live load = 4000 lb (17.78 kN), allowable soil bearing pressure = 1000 lb/ft² (47.9 kPa).

Design Properties. It is recommended that the designer specify structural lumber by allowable stresses required and not by wood species and grade if possible. However, species plays a role in the size factor C_F; thus southern pine No. 3 is selected, and C_F is included in table values. The load-duration factor for combined dead and live loads is 1.0. No reduction has been applied or is required by code for preservative treatment.

Using the *National Design Specifications* (NDS),[6] single-member bending is

$$F_b = 750 \times 1.0 = 750 \text{ lb/in}^2 \text{ (5.00 MPa)}$$

Repetitive-member bending is

$$F_b = 750 \times 1.15 = 862 \text{ lb/in}^2 \text{ (5.75 MPa)}$$

Horizontal shear is

$$F_v = 90 \times 1.0 = 90 \text{ lb/in}^2 \text{ (6.20 kPa)}$$

Compression perpendicular to grain is

$$F_{c\perp} = 565 \text{ lb/in}^2 \text{ (3.48 MPa)}$$

Modulus of elasticity is

$$E = 1{,}400{,}000 \text{ lb/in}^2 \text{ (10.34 GPa)}$$

SOLUTION: The footing size is

$$\frac{6000 \text{ lb}}{1000 \text{ lb/ft}^2} = 6 \text{ ft}^2$$

Use 2- × 3-ft footing. Check 4- × 6-in post bearing on a spreader plank. The area of a 4- × 6-in post is 19.25 in².

$$f_{c\perp} = \frac{6000 \text{ lb}}{19.25 \text{ in}^2} = 312 \text{ lb/in}^2 < 565 \text{ lb/in}^2$$

Determine the size of a 2-ft-long spreader plank, assuming that it acts as a cantilever beam. Position the 4- × 6-in post to minimize the span. The length of the cantilever portion is

$$L = \frac{(2 \text{ ft})(12 \text{ in/ft}) - (5.5\text{-in post})}{2} = 9.25 \text{ in} = 0.771 \text{ ft}$$

*All SI units shown for sawn lumber are for the actual net dimensions corresponding to the nominal dimension indicated.

The uniform load, on 3 ft of tributary area, is

$$w = (3\text{ ft})(1000\text{ lb/ft}^2) = 3000\text{ lb/ft}$$

$$V = wL = (0.771\text{ ft})(3000\text{ lb/ft}) = 2313\text{ lb}$$

The required area is

$$A_r = \frac{1.5V}{F_v} = \frac{1.5(2313\text{ lb})}{90\text{ lb/in}^2} = 38.6\text{ in}^2$$

$$M = \frac{wL^2}{2} = \frac{(3000\text{ lb/ft})(0.771\text{ ft})^2}{2} = 1156\text{ ft·lb}$$

The required section modulus is

$$S_r = \frac{M}{F_b} = \frac{(1156\text{ ft·lb})(12\text{ in/ft})}{750 \times 1.10\text{ lb/in}^2} = 16.8\text{ in}^3$$

where F_b is the allowable bending stress for a single member, and the 1.11 is to account for the 4-in-thick member used in flatwise bending. The deflection is limited to $L/360$ on applied load only. The maximum allowable deflection is

$$\frac{L}{360} = \frac{9.25\text{ in}}{360} = 0.0257\text{ in}$$

The required moment of inertia is

$$I_r = \frac{wL^4}{8E\Delta} = \frac{(3000\text{ lb/ft})(0.771\text{ ft})^4(1728\text{ in}^3/\text{ft}^3)}{8(1{,}400{,}000\text{ lb/in}^2)(0.0257\text{ in})} = 6.36\text{ in}^4$$

Therefore, check 16- × 4-in planks:

$$A_r = 38.6\text{ in}^2 < 53.38\text{ in}^2 \text{ (shear controls)}$$

$$S_r = 16.8\text{ in}^3 < 31.14\text{ in}^3$$

$$I_r = 6.36\text{ in}^4 < 54.48\text{ in}^4$$

Use a 16- × 4-in (387- × 88.9-mm) plank.

Determine the size of 3-ft-long footing planks assuming that they act as cantilevers.

$$L = \frac{(3\text{ ft})(12\text{ in/ft}) - (15.25\text{-in-wide spreader plank})}{2} = 10.38\text{ in} = 0.864\text{ ft}$$

Use 5 planks of 7.25-in (0.604-ft) width for a total width of 36.25 in, which is very close to the 36-in width assumed. The uniform load is

$$w = (1000\ \text{lb/ft}^2)(0.604\ \text{ft}) = 604\ \text{lb/ft}$$

$$V = wL = (604\ \text{lb/ft})(0.864\ \text{ft}) = 522\ \text{lb}$$

$$A_r = \frac{1.5(522\ \text{lb})}{90\ \text{lb/in}^2} = 8.70\ \text{in}^2$$

$$M = \frac{wL^2}{2} = \frac{(604\ \text{lb/ft})(0.864\ \text{ft})^2}{2} = 225\ \text{ft·lb}$$

$$S_r = \frac{(225\ \text{ft·lb})(12\ \text{in/ft})}{862 \times 1.16\ \text{lb/in}^2} = 2.79\ \text{in}^3$$

Note: Repetitive-member allowable bending stress is applicable for footing planks, and the 1.16 is to account for the 3-in plank used in flatwise bending.

The maximum allowable deflection (applied load only) is

$$\Delta = \frac{L}{360} = \frac{10.38\ \text{in}}{360} = 0.0288\ \text{in}$$

$$I_r = \frac{wL^4}{8E\Delta} = \frac{(402\ \text{lb/ft})(0.864\ \text{ft})^4(1728\ \text{in}^3/\text{ft}^3)}{8(1{,}500{,}00\ \text{lb/in}^2)(0.0288\ \text{in})} = 1.12\ \text{in}^4$$

Try 8- × 3-in planks:

$$A_r = 8.70\ \text{in}^2 < 18.13\ \text{in}^2$$

$$S_r = 2.79\ \text{in}^3 < 7.55\ \text{in}^3\ \text{(bending controls)}$$

$$I_r = 1.12\ \text{in}^4 < 9.44\ \text{in}^4$$

Therefore, use five 8- × 3-in (184- × 63.5-mm) planks (Fig. 11.1*c*). Fasten the 16- × 4-in (387- × 88.9-mm) spreader plank to each plank with 20d galvanized nails.[2–4] Framing anchors may be required if uplift forces are present and are of such magnitude that they exceed the withdrawal capacity of the 20d nails. As noted at the beginning of this example, it is recommended that the designer specify the required minimum allowable stresses and member sizes so that the contractor may supply the most economical species and grade locally available that satisfy these requirements of stress and size.

11.1.4 Structural Details for Wall Footing

Details for a crawl-space basement are shown in Fig. 11.2. Since the space is used for mechanical chase or storage only, the designer has two choices for bracing the bottom of the wall: either to use the passive soil pressure or to install a diagonal compression strut. A patented truss system is shown in Fig. 11.3. The advantages of this manufactured system are that it can be erected quickly and that the braces reduce bending moments in the floor members. Another use of the PWF is the Plen-Wood System,[7] in which the entire crawl space serves as an HVAC plenum.

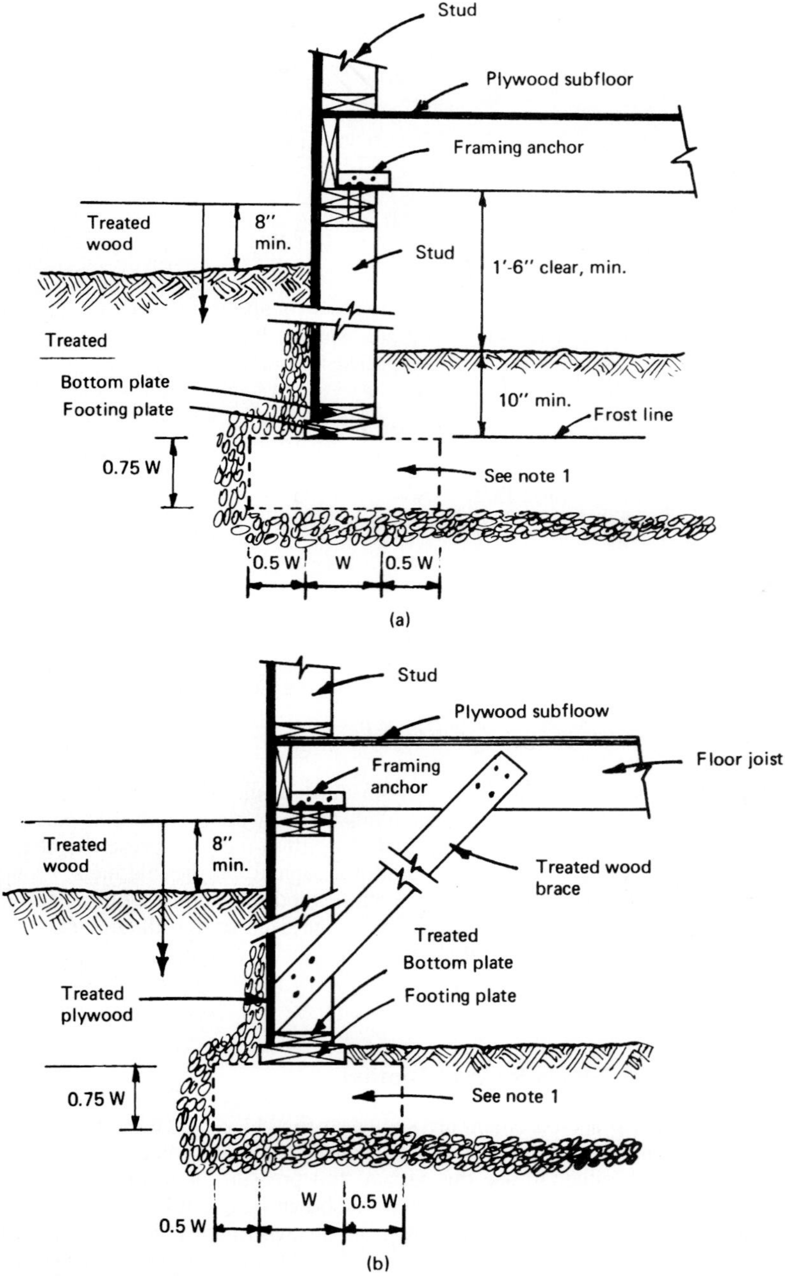

FIG. 11.2 Structural details of crawl-space walls. (*a*) Passive pressure; (*b*) compression strut. *Note:* Footing of gravel, crushed stone, coarse sand, soil cement, or concrete.

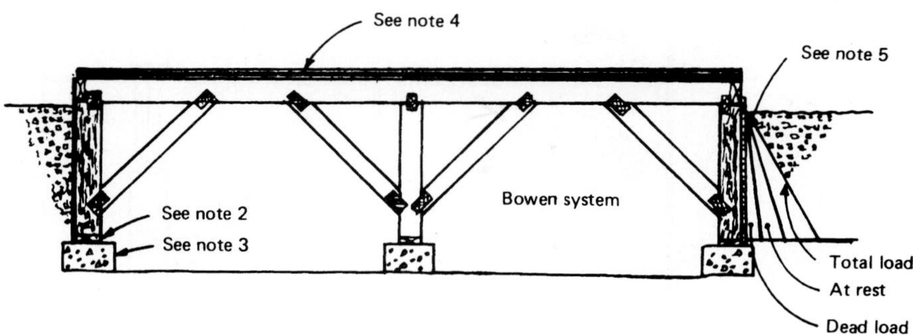

FIG. 11.3 Bowen system (PWF). *Notes:* (1) Shaded members are preservatively pressure-treated. (2) Two AWPB foundation sill plates. (3) Concrete or gravel foundation. (4) ¾-in T&G plywood or other approved sheathing. Glue and nail with 6d deformed shank or 8d common at 12 in o.c. at panel edges and 12 in o.c. at intermediate areas. (5) All-weather plywood fastened with 16-gauge × 1½ in stainless-steel staples 4 in o.c. at panel edges and 8 in o.c. at intermediate areas or 8d stainless-steel nails at 6 in o.c. at panel edges and 12 in o.c. at intermediate areas. *(Courtesy of Bowen Quality Construction. U.S. Patent 4,457,118.)*

A footing having a minimum width of twice the width of the treated timber footing plate and a thickness not less than three-quarters the width of the footing plate is constructed of gravel, coarse sand, crushed stone, soil cement, or concrete. Gravel, coarse sand, and crushed stone footings must be capable of allowing groundwater to drain away from the foundation. For soils which drain poorly, the PWF manual[2] recommends that a layer of gravel, which drains quickly, be placed as a base under the entire building. All water can be drained to a sump for removal by pump.

A contractor may prefer to pour a concrete footing in lieu of leveling gravel or crushed stone. Some local building codes may require a concrete footing. Whichever method is used, the wall must be constructed on a level surface. Stepped footings can be engineered for sloping sites.[2]

In a full-basement application, the basement floor is used to brace the bottom of the wall (Fig. 11.4). The floor can be braced by a continuous bearing wall at midspan or be capable of spanning the full width of the structure. Normally, a metal framing anchor is required to transfer the forces at the top of the wall into the first-floor system, as illustrated in Fig. 11.4. When long-span trusses are used in nonresidential buildings for the floor and roof, the designers may wish to use the double-wall system shown in Fig. 11.5. This allows readily available treated nominal 2-in (38.1-mm) studs to be used for the construction of the entire structure and more uniformly distributes the load on the footing plate.

11.1.5 Structural Design of Foundation Wall

To assist the designer, Tables 11.1 to 11.3 have been compiled to show some design sizes, soil loadings, and plywood sheathing load-carrying capacities for engineering calculations. Tables 11.1 and 11.2 can be used as guides in selecting initial wood component sizes for the design of a PWF.[8] Average equivalent fluid pressures are given in Tables 11.4 and 11.5 for various types of soils and can be used with the formulas shown. Table 11.4 gives the equations for a partially loaded basement

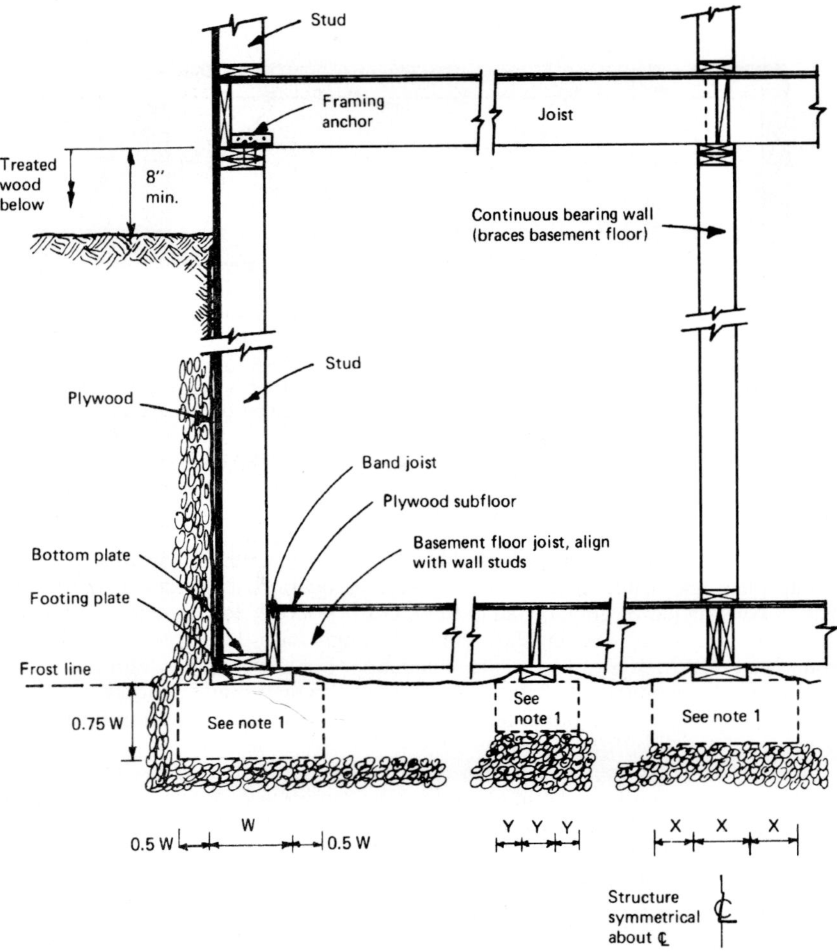

FIG. 11.4 Structural details of full basement. *Note:* Footings of gravel, crushed stone, soil cement, or concrete.

wall, while the formulas in Table 11.5 include an additional term for surcharge load such as that caused by a vehicle. The safe plywood loading chart assumes that the plywood face grain is placed perpendicular to the studs and that the plywood is continuous over two or more spans. Also, these values have been multiplied by the long-term duration load factor. The use of the tables is illustrated by the following example problem.

EXAMPLE 11.2: FOUNDATION WALL Given: basement height $D = 8$ ft (2.43 m). A typical wall cross section is shown in Fig. 11.4. Soil type is fine sandy silt; $h = 1$ ft (0.305 m). The axial force assumed to act at the centerline of the wall results

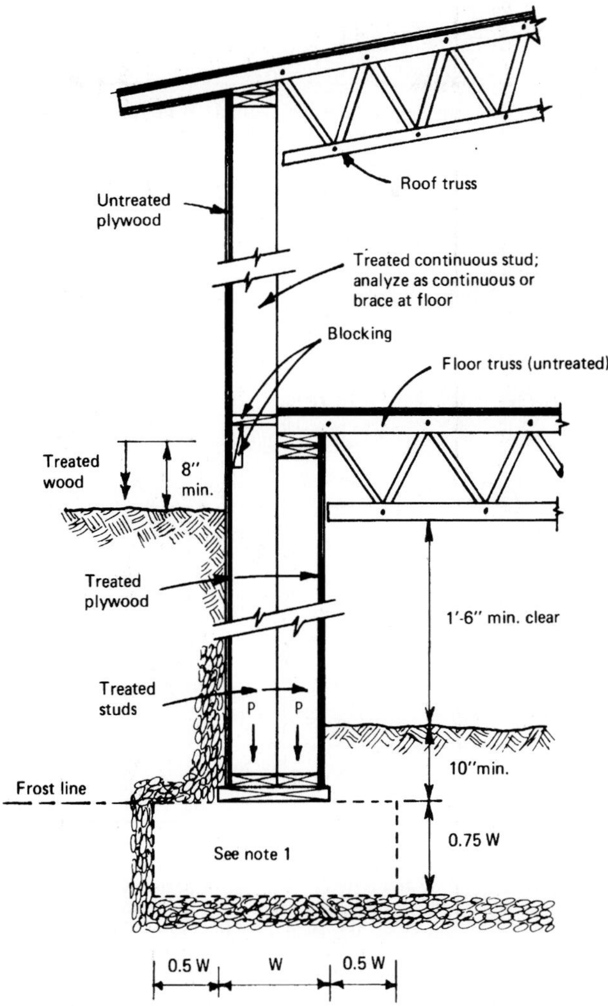

FIG. 11.5 Structural details of double-wall system, nonresidential loadings. *Notes:* (1) Footings of gravel, crushed stone, coarse sand, soil cement, or concrete. (2) Design so that floor and roof *P*s are balanced for dead and live loadings.

TABLE 11.1 Minimum Structural Requirements for Crawl-Space Wall Framing

Apply to installations with outside fill height not exceeding 4 ft and wall height not exceeding 6 ft. Roof supported on exterior walls. Floors supported on interior and exterior bearing walls.† *30 lb/ft³ equivalent fluid density soil pressure, 2000 lb/ft² allowable soil bearing pressure.*

Construction	House width, ft	Uniform load conditions, ceiling 10 lb/ft², 1st and 2d floors 50 lb/ft² live and dead					
		Roof 40 lb/ft² live, 10 lb/ft² dead			Roof 30 lb/ft² live, 10 lb/ft² dead		
		Lumber species and grade‡	Stud and plate size (nominal), in	Stud spacing, in	Lumber species and grade‡	Stud and plate size (nominal), in	Stud spacing, in
2 stories	32 or less	B	2 × 6	16	B D	2 × 6 2 × 6	16 12
	28 or less	D	2 × 6	12	D	2 × 6	12
	24 or less	D	2 × 6	12	C	2 × 6	16
1 story	32 or less	B B D	2 × 4 2 × 6 2 × 6	12 16 12	A B D	2 × 4 2 × 4 2 × 6	16 12 16
	28 or less	A D	2 × 4 2 × 6	16 16	B D	2 × 4 2 × 6	12 16
	24 or less	D	2 × 6	16	C	2 × 4	12

Note: 1 in = 25.4 mm.

*Studs and plates in interior bearing walls supporting floor loads only must be of lumber species and grade D or higher. Studs shall be 2 by 4 in at 16 in on center where supporting 1 floor and 2 by 6 in at 16 in on center where supporting 2 floors. Footing plate shall be 2 in wider than studs.

†If brick veneer is used, see page 23 of APA publication for knee wall requirements.

‡See Table 11.3 for minimum properties of lumber species and grade.

Source: From *Permanent Wood Foundations*, American Plywood Association, Tacoma, Wash., 1990.

from dead and live loads acting on the roof, floor, and walls above. Dead load = 280 lb/ft (217 kg/m); live load = 800 lb/ft (1190 kg/m).

Wood Stud Design Properties. Published NDS values for allowable stresses have been multiplied by 0.90 to account for long-term loading with the exception of the modulus of elasticity and the value of compression perpendicular to grain. No reduction in allowable stress is required by NDS for preservative treatment. Use Douglas fir–larch No. 1 and assume a width of 10 in nominal.

Allowable repetitive-member bending stress is

TABLE 11.2 Minimum Structural Requirements for Basement Walls

Wall height 8 ft. Roof supported on exterior walls. Floors supported on interior and exterior bearing walls.†‡ 30 lb/ft³ equivalent fluid density soil pressure, 2000 lb/ft² allowable soil bearing pressure.

Construction	House width, ft	Height of fill, in	Uniform load conditions, ceiling 10 lb/ft², 1st and 2d floors 50 lb/ft² live and dead: Roof 40 lb/ft² live, 10 lb/ft² dead: Lumber species and grade§	Stud and plate size (nominal), in	Stud spacing, in	Roof 30 lb/ft² live, 10 lb/ft² dead: Lumber species and grade§	Stud and plate size (nominal), in	Stud spacing, in
2 stories	32 or less	24	D	2 × 6	16	D	2 × 6	16
		48	D	2 × 6	16	D	2 × 6	16
		72	A	2 × 6	16	A	2 × 6	16
			B	2 × 6	12	B	2 × 6	12
			C	2 × 8	16	C	2 × 8	16
			D	2 × 8	12			
		86	A*	2 × 6	12	A*	2 × 6	12
			B	2 × 8	16	B	2 × 8	16
			C	2 × 8	12	C	2 × 8	12
	24 or less	24	D	2 × 6	16	D	2 × 6	16
		48	D	2 × 6	16	D	2 × 6	16
		72	C	2 × 6	12	C	2 × 6	12
			D	2 × 8	16			
		86	A*	2 × 6	12	D	2 × 8	12
			B	2 × 8	16			
			C	2 × 8	12			
1 story	32 or less	24	B	2 × 4	16	C	2 × 4	16
			D	2 × 4	12	D	2 × 4	12
			D	2 × 6	16	D	2 × 6	16
		48	D	2 × 6	16	D	2 × 6	16
		72	A	2 × 6	16	A	2 × 6	16
			B	2 × 6	12	C	2 × 6	12
			D	2 × 8	16	D	2 × 8	16
		86	A*	2 × 6	12	A*	2 × 6	12
			B	2 × 8	16	B	2 × 8	16
			C	2 × 8	12	D	2 × 8	12
	28 or less	24	B	2 × 4	16	D	2 × 4	16
			D	2 × 4	12			
			D	2 × 6	16			
		48	D	2 × 6	16	B	2 × 4	12
		72	C	2 × 6	12	C	2 × 6	12
		86	D	2 × 8	12	A*	2 × 6	12
						B	2 × 8	16
						D	2 × 8	12
	24 or less	24	D	2 × 4	16	D	2 × 4	16
		48	B	2 × 4	12	B	2 × 4	12
		72	C	2 × 6	12	C	2 × 6	12
		86	D	2 × 8	12	A*	2 × 6	12
						B	2 × 8	16
						D	2 × 8	12

Note: 1 in = 25.4 mm.

*Length of end splits or checks at lower end of studs not to exceed width of piece.

†Studs and plates in interior bearing walls supporting floor loads only must be of lumber species and grade D or higher. Studs shall be 2 by 4 in at 16 in on center where supporting 1 floor and 2 by 6 in at 16 in on center where supporting 2 floors. Footing plate shall be 2 in wider than studs.

‡If brick veneer is used, see page 23 of APA publication for knee wall requirements.

§See Table 11.3 for minimum properties of lumber species and grade.

Source: From *Permanent Wood Foundations,* American Plywood Association, Tacoma, Wash., 1990.

TABLE 11.3 Minimum (Surfaced Dry or Surfaced Green) Properties for Species Groups and Grades as Provided in *National Design Specification*

Property	Stud and plate size (nominal), in.	Grade			
		A	B	C	D
F_b (repetitive member), lb/in^2	2 × 6	1700	1400	1100	975
	2 × 4	1950	1650	1300	1150
F_c, lb/in^2	2 × 6	1250	1000	825	700
	2 × 4	1250	975	775	675
$F_{c\perp}$, lb/in^2		385	385	245	235
F_v, lb/in^2		90	90	70	70
E, lb/in^2 × 10^6		1.7	1.6	1.3	1.1
Typical lumber grades		Douglas fir No. 1, Southern pine No. 1	Douglas fir No. 1 Southern pine No. 2	Hem-fir No. 2 Northern pine No. 2	Ponderosa pine No. 2

Note: 1 in = 25.4 mm.
Source: From *Permanent Wood Foundation: Guide to Design and Construction,* American Plywood Association, Tacoma, Wash., 1990.

TABLE 11.4 Equations for Designing Basement Walls and Equivalent Fluid Pressure for Selected Soil Types

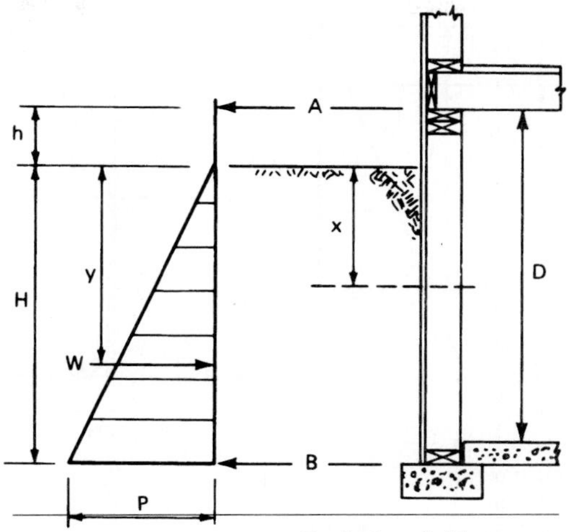

Soil type (compact)	Equivalent fluid pressure F, lb/ft²
Gravel	29
Medium sand	31
Fine sand	37
Fine sandy silt	40
Fine silt	45
Clay silt	60
Silty clay	70
Clay	90

$$W = \frac{FH^2}{2} = \frac{PH}{2} \qquad P = FH$$

$$y = \frac{2H}{3} \qquad A = \frac{WH}{3D} \qquad B = A - W$$

Maximum shear $V = B$

Point of maximum moment $x = H\sqrt{\frac{H}{3D}}$

Maximum moment $M = A\left(h + \frac{2}{3}x\right)$

where D = distance between floors
H = height of soil
F = equivalent fluid pressure

Note: 1 lb/ft² = 47.88 Pa.

TABLE 11.5 Equations for Designing Basement Walls with Surcharge Loading and Plywood Design Table

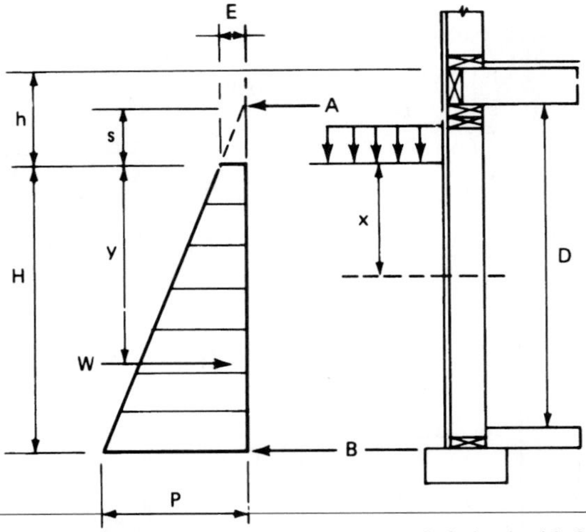

Plywood type: thickness, in (span index)	Stud spacing, in	Safe load with 3-span face grain across supports,* lb/ft^2
½, ⅝	16	155
(32/16)	24	69
⅝, ¾, ⅞	16	238
(42/20)	24	105
¾, ⅞	16	311
(48/24)	24	138
2.4.1	16	608
	24	284
1⅛	16	491
Groups 1 and 2	24	197
1¼	16	530
Groups 3 and 4	24	252

$$S = \frac{\text{surcharge(lb/ft}^2)}{\text{soil weight(lb/ft}^3)} = F(H + S) \qquad P = FH$$

$$W = \frac{H(P + E)}{2} \qquad y = \frac{H(2P + E)}{3(P + E)} \qquad A = \frac{H^2(P + 2E)}{6D}$$

Maximum shear $V = B = W - A$

Point of maximum moment: Solve for x using quadratic equation

$$\frac{(P - E)x^2}{H} + 2Ex - 2A = 0$$

$$\textit{Maximum moment } M = \frac{H^2(P + 2E)(h + x)}{6D} - \frac{X^2[3HE + x(P - E)]}{6D}$$

where D = distance between floors
H = height of soil
F = equivalent fluid pressure

Note: 1 in = 2.54 cm; 1 lb/ft^2 = 47.88 Pa.

*Plywood values have been multiplied by 0.81 for reduction due to preservation treatment plus long-duration holding.

$$F'_{b1} = 1000 \times 0.9\ 1.15 \times 1.10 = 1138 \text{ lb/in}^2 \text{ (7.85 MPa)}$$

Allowable hoizontal shear stress is

$$F'_v = 95 \times 0.9 = 86 \text{ lb/in}^2 \text{ (0.593 MPa)}$$

Allowable compression stress perpendicular to grain is

$$F'_{c\perp} = 625 \text{ lb/in}^2 \text{ (4.31 MPa)}$$

Allowable compression stress parallel to grain is

$$F'_c = 1450 \times 0.9 \times 1.0 = 1305 \text{ lb/in}^2 \text{ (9.00 MPa)}$$

Allowable modulus of elasticity is

$$E = 1{,}700{,}000 \text{ lb/in}^2 \text{ (11.72 GPa)}$$

SOLUTION: From Table 11.4, $F = 40$ lb/ft^2. Using the formulas given in Table 11.4,

$$W = \frac{FH^2}{2} = \frac{(40 \text{ lb/ft}^2)(7 \text{ ft})^2}{2} = 980 \text{ lb per ft of wall}$$

$$Y = \frac{2H}{3} = \frac{2(7 \text{ ft})}{3} = 4.67 \text{ ft}$$

$$A = \frac{WH}{3D} = \frac{(980 \text{ lb})(7 \text{ ft})}{3(8 \text{ ft})} = 286 \text{ lb per ft of wall}$$

Select a framing anchor (with a corrosion-resistant coating) which will provide a minimum load of 286 lb per foot of wall length.

The maximum shear is

$$V = W - A = 980 - 286 = 694 \text{ lb per foot of wall}$$

The required area is

$$A_r = \frac{1.5V}{F_v} = \frac{1.5 \text{ (694 lb/ft)}}{86 \text{ lb/in}^2} = 12.10 \text{ in}^2$$

Try 2- × 10-in studs at 12 in on center. Hence,

$$A = 13.88 \text{ in}^2 > A_r = 12.10 \text{ in}^2$$

Check combined bending and axial forces on studs. The point of maximum moment is

$$x = H\sqrt{\frac{H}{3D}} = (7 \text{ ft})\sqrt{\frac{7 \text{ ft}}{3 \text{ (8 ft)}}} = 3.78 \text{ ft}$$

The maximum moment is

$$M = A\left(h + \frac{2}{3}x\right) = (286 \text{ lb})\left(1 \text{ ft} + \frac{2}{3}\, 3.78 \text{ ft}\right) = 1007 \text{ ft·lb}$$

The stud is analyzed as a bending and axial compression member per NDS.[6] Plywood sheathing braces studs in their 1.5-in dimension. Therefore, the least dimension is $d = 9.25$ in.

$$\frac{\ell_{e1}}{d_1} = \frac{(8 \text{ ft})(12 \text{ in/ft})}{9.25 \text{ in}} = 10.4$$

$$F_{cE1} = \frac{K_{cE}E'}{(\ell_{e1}/d_1)^2} = \frac{0.30\ (1{,}700{,}000 \text{ psi})}{(10.4)^2} = 4715 \text{ psi}$$

$$C_p = 0.935 \qquad \text{and} \qquad F'_c = 0.935 \times 1305 \text{ psi} = 1220 \text{ psi}$$

Note: See Chap. 3 for equation for C_p.

Assuming the weight of the basement wall to be 80 lb/ft, the total load on a single stud is 280 + 800 + 80 = 1160 lb. Then

$$f_c = \frac{1160 \text{ lb}}{13.88 \text{ in}^2} = 83.6 \text{ lb/in}^2 < F_{cE1} = 4715 \text{ lb/in}^2 \qquad \text{OK}$$

$$f_{b1} = \frac{(1007 \text{ ft·lb})(12 \text{ in/ft})}{21.39 \text{ in}^3} = 565 \text{ lb/in}^2$$

Therefore, the equation for bending and axial compression in a single plane is

$$\frac{f_c}{F'_c} + \frac{f_{b1}}{F'_{b1}[1 - (f_c/F_{cE1})]} \leq 1.0$$

$$\frac{83.6}{1220} + \frac{565}{1138[1 - (83.6/4715)]} = 0.07 + 0.505$$

$$= 0.575 \leq 1.0$$

Use 2- × 10-in (3.05- × 23.58-cm) studs at 12 in (30.48 cm) on center. Check the compression stress perpendicular to grain acting on the plate:

$$f_{c\perp} = 83.6 \text{ lb/in}^2 < F_{c\perp} = 625 \text{ lb/in}^2 \qquad \text{OK}$$

Determine the required thickness of plywood. The soil pressure at base is 694 lb per foot of wall, or 694 lb/ft^2 and is Reaction B (see Fig 11.4). Extrapolating from Table 11.5, use 2.4.1 plywood for exterior of wall surface.

Size the band joist by checking compression stress perpendicular to grain. For the basement floor,

$$t_{bj} = \frac{\text{reaction } B}{f_{c\perp}} = \frac{694 \text{ lb}}{625 \text{ lb/in}^2} = 1.11 \text{ in}$$

which is the minimum depth of the band joist. Hence use the band joist having the same depth as the floor thickness.

Try a nominal 3- × 14-in footing plate. The total load on a stud is 1160 lb. Therefore, the soil pressure is

$$P_s = \frac{1160 \text{ lb}}{(1 \text{ ft})(13.25 \text{ in})(1 \text{ ft}/12 \text{ in})} = 1050 \text{ lb/ft}^2$$

Either a 3- × 14-in (6.35- × 8.89-cm) footing plate with gravel base or a concrete footing may be used.

11.2 WOOD PILE FOUNDATIONS

11.2.1 History

The use of timber piles began when humans first learned to remove branches from tree trunks and to drive the trunk into the ground with a mass. Archaeologists have uncovered sound 4000- to 5000-year-old timber piles upon which Swiss lake dwellers built homes during the Stone Age. The Phoenicians are the first people known to have used the temporary preservative technique of charring and tarring timber piles, while the Romans developed state-of-the-art pile driving, which included iron tips to protect piles during driving, as recorded by Vitruvius in 58 A.D.

Archaeologists believe that they have recently discovered one of the oak foundations for the first bridge across the River Thames in London. It was probably built about 60 A.D. by Roman legionnaires utilizing a crude rig on a barge. Timber pile driving equipment continued to improve as time passed.

Untreated timber piles supporting the Campanile of St. Mark's in Venice have been in use for over 1000 years. Untreated timber piles that are in excess of 100 years old safely support structures built throughout the United States. The growth of decay fungi requires air, free moisture, and moderate temperatures. When untreated timber piles are installed completely below the water table, air cannot reach the pile and decay will not occur. However, as a result of a gradual lowering of the water table to a level below the pile tops, decay of untreated pile foundations can result. Due to the uncertainty of the level of groundwater tables, treated timber foundations are recommended even when they are to be installed below the groundwater table. The expected engineering life of modern treated timber piling is 100 years or more. Timber piling is still the most common type of pile in use around the world.

11.2.2 Treated Timber Piles

The applicable standard for round timber piles in ASTM D 25,[9] *Standard Specifications for Round Timber Piles,* which defines the sizes, lengths, straightness, flaws, and so on. Pile circumferences are now specified by ASTM because a pile is not perfectly round (see Table 11.6), and it is easier to measure accurately the circumference rather than the diameter. Also, it is not practical to measure anything other than the circumference, except at the ends of the piles. Preservative treatments for piling are shown in Table 2.18.

The average pile length varies from 30 to 65 ft. The American Association of State Highway and Transportation Officials' (AASHTO) bridge specifications[10] permit design loads ranging from 20 to 32 tons without subsurface investigation or load tests (Table 11.7). This table is based on pole diameter rather than circumfer-

TABLE 11.6*a* Minimum Tip Circumference (Friction Piles)* for Specified Butt Circumferences, in

	Required minimum circumference 3 ft from butt, in										
Length, ft	22	25	28	31	35	38	41	44	47	50	57
20	16.0	16.0	16.0	18.0	22.0	25.0	28.0	—	—	—	—
30	16.0	16.0	16.0	16.0	19.0	22.0	25.0	28.0	—	—	—
40	—	—	—	16.0	17.0	20.0	23.0	26.0	29.0	—	—
50	—	—	—	—	16.0	17.0	19.0	22.0	25.0	28.0	—
60	—	—	—	—	—	16.0	16.0	18.6	21.6	24.6	31.6
70	—	—	—	—	—	16.0	16.0	16.0	16.2	19.2	26.2
80	—	—	—	—	—	—	16.0	16.0	16.0	16.0	21.8
90	—	—	—	—	—	—	16.0	16.0	16.0	16.0	19.5
100	—	—	—	—	—	—	16.0	16.0	16.0	16.0	18.0
110	—	—	—	—	—	—	—	—	—	16.0	16.0
120	—	—	—	—	—	—	—	—	—	—	16.0

Note: 1 in = 25.4 mm; 1 ft = 0.3048 m.

*Where the taper applied to the butt circumferences calculates to a circumference at the tip of less than 16 in, the individual values have been increased to 16 in to assure a minimum 5-in diameter at tip for purposes of driving.

Source: Timber tables, from ASTM D 25-1991.[9]

TABLE 11.6*b* Minimum Circumferences 3 ft from Butt (End-Bearing Piles) for Specified Tip Circumferences, in

	Required minimum tip circumference, in							
Length, ft	16	19	22	25	28	31	35	38
20	22.0	24.0	27.0	30.0	33.0	36.0	40.0	43.0
30	23.5	26.5	29.5	32.5	35.5	38.5	42.5	45.5
40	26.0	29.0	32.0	35.0	38.0	41.0	45.0	48.0
50	28.5	31.5	34.5	37.5	40.5	43.5	47.5	50.5
60	31.0	34.0	37.0	40.0	43.0	46.0	50.0	53.0
70	33.5	36.5	39.5	42.5	45.5	48.5	52.5	55.5
80	36.0	39.0	42.0	45.0	48.0	51.0	55.0	58.0
90	38.6	41.6	44.6	47.6	50.6	53.6	57.6	60.5
100	41.0	44.0	47.0	50.0	53.0	56.0	60.0	—
110	43.6	46.6	49.6	52.6	55.6	61.0	—	—
120	46.0	49.0	52.0	55.0	58.0	—	—	—

Note: 1 in = 25.4 mm; 1 ft = 0.3048 m.

Source: Timber tables, from ASTM D25-1991.[9]

TABLE 11.7 AASHTO Maximum Design Loads* for Timber Piles without Subsurface Investigation or Load Test

Pile diameter measured 3 ft from butt end, in	Maximum design load, tons
10	20
12	24
14	28
16	32

*Per AASHTO Table 4.3.4.5.
Source: From AASHTO specifications.[10]

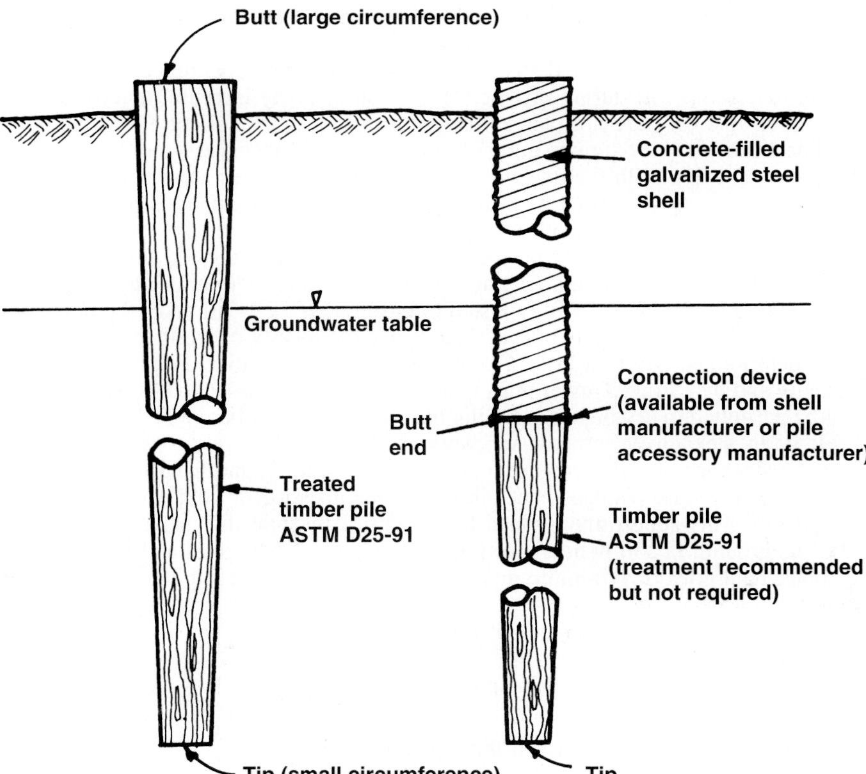

FIG. 11.6 Types of timber piles.

ence. A 70-ton design load, with an approved load test, is the largest documented in an engineering publication for a bridge foundation.[11] Piles are normally installed with the smaller diameter, or tip, down (Fig. 11.6), except where lateral loading is dominant, when used as marina guide piles, or in permafrost. The advantages of tapered timber piles driven tip down are as follows:

1. Low initial cost
2. Lightweight
3. Resistant to acidic soils
4. Can be redriven
5. Easy to cut off
6. Act as displacement piles, densifying sand
7. Larger butt to absorb driving energies
8. Easier to drive than displacement piles of constant cross section

Normally, timber piles have lower material costs than other types of piling. Costs for driving all types of piling are essentially equal.

The relatively light weight of a timber pile makes it economical to transport and allows it to be handled with minimal equipment. Timber is naturally resistant to acidic soil, while unprotected steel and concrete are not. Coatings to protect steel piling may scrape off during driving. These coatings may increase the cost of steel piles such that they are not competitive with treated timber piling.

The availability of timber piles of suitable length and size should be verified before proceeding with the design. Some of the longer sizes shown in Table 11.6 may be very expensive in terms of both material and transportation cost. Piles over 60 ft in length may be difficult to transport.

Timber piles from existing projects which are being demolished can be removed with a vibratory hammer and, if in acceptable condition, redriven for a new project. Piles reused in situ must be fully tested to ensure that they will carry the new load. Untreated piles are normally not redriven, since the quality of wood in the pile may have deteriorated due to a lack of protection by a preservative. Piles are inspected visually and by coring. Timber piles which have been water-soaked for years should not be permitted to dry before redriving because the wood fibers will become brittle.

It is an inexpensive process for workers to cut off the pile tops with a chain saw. Other types of piling require more expensive cutting and handling equipment.

Timber piles are displacement piles and thus displace or compact soils as they are driven. This action may reduce the length of the pile that needs to be driven into the ground. In soft noncompacting soils, open-end pipe piles and H-piles (non-displacement piles) may require great lengths to be driven before the required blow count is reached.

Some potential disadvantages of timber piling are

1. Timber piles are limited in length (usually 120 ft), and they are generally not practical to splice.
2. Timber piles cannot be driven through very hard soils.
3. Careful handling procedures are required, and the disposal of creosoted or other preservatively treated cutoffs may be a problem.

Timber piles need to be purchased in correct lengths. Therefore, the contractor must be experienced in ordering, and the engineer's soil information must be accurate.

Splicing means adding material to the outside of a displacement pile, which increases its driving resistance. It is very expensive to develop the full bending strength or tension strength of a spliced timber pile. Also, the splice point is a weak area in the preservative treatment system and must be properly field-treated.

Driving timber piling through soils with rock, debris, or other obstructions cannot be done without destroying the pile, unless spudding or predrilling is practicable at the site. Sometimes timber piles with a steel shoe can be driven successfully.

The handling of timber piles requires reasonable care since they can be physically damaged. Individuals sometimes unload piling from a truck by rolling, and the subsequent dropping of the pile could result in structural damage. The use of handling tools that puncture the treated part of the pile completely should not be allowed.

11.2.3 Wood Composite Piles

The wood composite pile has a bottom length of timber with a concrete-filled corrugated shell or pipe for its top section. There are three major reasons for its use. First, it extends the length beyond that of timber available. Second, it extends a shell pile beyond the length for which it is practical to drive. Third, it allows the use of untreated timber piles below the groundwater table and of concrete or other material for the top portion of the pile (Fig. 11.6).

The shell may have a constant or tapered diameter, and it is normally shorter than the timber portion. Connection devices between the two components are available from the shell manufacturer and independent piling accessory manufacturers.[12] The normal range of wood composite pile lengths is from 60 to 100 ft, with a maximum length of 150 ft. The timber pile has to be at least 50 ft long for these piles to be economical. The design loading is based on the critical timber section (see Example 11.3).

The advantage of a composite pile is that of providing a long pile at a low initial cost. A disadvantage is that in irregular ground it may be difficult to predetermine the length of the timber section before driving so that its top remains below the watertable. If this is a design concern, a treated wood pile should be used.

A second disadvantage is that the splice is a weak point in the composite pile, although the splicing of the shell section to the timber is an easy task and connection devices are available. The butt of the timber pile is larger than the shell. Thus there is little friction drag on the shell during driving and the shell is not easily damaged.

11.2.4 Design loads for Timber Piling

The two loading classifications for piles are end-bearing and friction. In either case, the pile is supported by layers of soil, and its design will be limited by either the soil or the pile. End-bearing piles transmit their loads to a hard layer, usually rock. Thus the pile strength will most often govern their load-carrying capacity. Friction piles transmit their loads by friction to the soil surrounding the piles, and their strength is most often governed by the soil. The critical section for an end-bearing pile is near its tip, while it is near the butt end for friction piles. The critical point in a pile will vary when several layers of soil are encountered and tapered piles are used (Fig. 11.7). Determining design loads for piling is a complex problem based on soil layers, pile type, timber species and size, and group pile loading.

The first step in the design procedure is to determine what soils exist and to evaluate their engineering properties. The engineer then decides if the timber piles can be installed economically and proceeds with the preliminary design of the structure. Many building codes limit the design loads of timber piles, such as those given by AASHTO in Table 11.7, but higher design values are permitted when an approved load test is performed. The designer needs to determine if it will cost more for the testing or for the installation of the additional piles required by the code. Often testing will cost more than the additional piles, particularly on small projects. A 70-ton design timber pile loading was approved by the State of Nevada for a bridge foundation because the weakest test pile did not fail until 134 tons was reached.[13] The timber species selected depends to a great degree on its availability. In the United States, hardwood is not commonly used for piling. ASTM D 2899[14] is the accepted standard used to establish allowable code design stress values (Table 11.8) for the 1991 *Uniform Building Code* version. However, a pulp mill constructed in the jungles of Brazil used a local hardwood with an unusually high

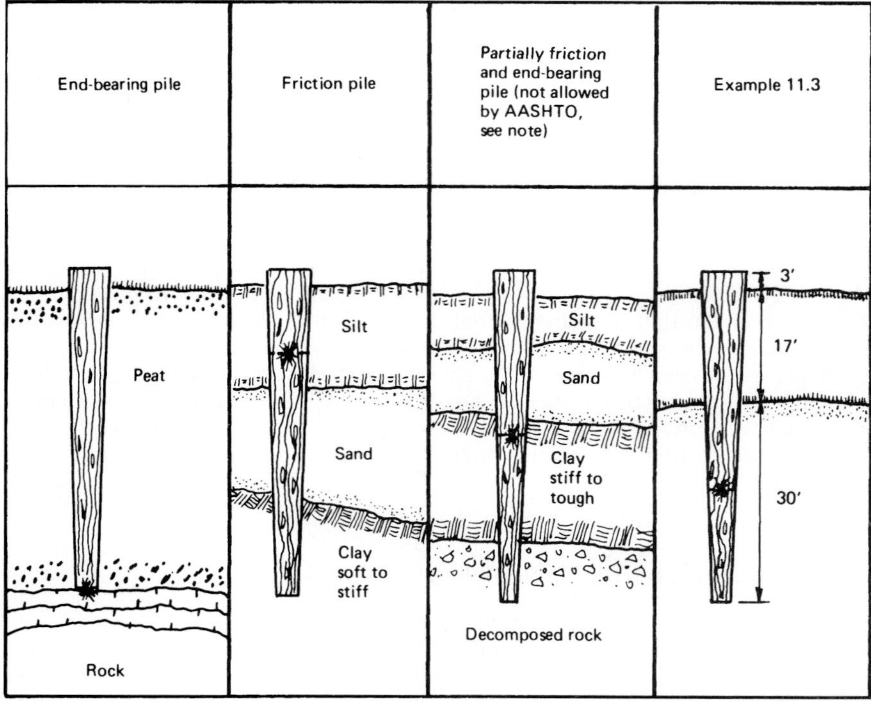

FIG. 11.7 Pile loading classifications. *Note:* See code Sec. 4.3.5.3.

TABLE 11.8 Allowable Unit Stresses for Treated Round Timber Poles and Piles,[a] lb/in^2

Values for normal load duration and wet conditions of use.

Species	Compression parallel to grain[b] F_c	Extreme fiber in bending[b] F_b	Horizontal shear F_v	Compression perpendicular to grain $F_{c\perp}$	Modulus of electricity E
Pacific Coast Douglas fir[c,d]	1250	2450	115	230	1,500,000
Southern pine[c,e]	1200	2400	110	250	1,500,000
Red oak[f]	1100	2450	135	350	1,250,000
Red pine[g]	900	1900	85	155	1,280,000

[a] The form factor of 1.18 for bending members of circular cross section is incorporated in the allowable unit stresses for extreme fiber in bending as listed within table.

[b] The allowable values listed for compression parallel to grain and extreme fiber in bending are based on load-sharing principles such as occur in a pile cluster. For piles which support their own specific load, an additional safety factor of 1.25 shall be used with compression parallel to grain values and an additional safety factor of 1.30 shall be used with extreme fiber in bending values.

[c] Design values in compression parallel to grain for Pacific Coast Douglas fir and southern pine may be increased 0.2% for each foot of length from the tip of the pile to the critical section. The increase shall not exceed 10% for any single pile. However, the increase is cumulative with the increase in section properties due to taper from the pile tip to the critical section.

[d] Pacific Coast Douglas fir includes Douglas fir from west of the crest of the Cascade Mountains in Oregon, Washington, and northern California and west of the crest of the Sierra Nevada mountains in the rest of California. For fastener design, use Douglas fir–larch design values.

[e] Southern pine values apply to longleaf, slash, loblolly, and short-leaf pines.

[f] Red oak values apply to northern and southern red oak.

[g] Red pine values apply to red pine grown in the United States. For fastener design, use northern pine design values.

Source: Reproduced from the *Uniform Building Code* 1991 ed., Copyright © 1991, with permission of the publisher, The International Conference of Building Officials, Whitter, Calif.

compressive strength of 12,000 lb/in^2, or 10 times the strength of a softwood pile.[15] Timber pile design stress values for some hardwood species from equatorial forests are shown in Table 11.9. The species shown are imported into the United States for construction purposes.

EXAMPLE 11.3: LOCATION OF CRITICAL STRESS IN PILE Determine the location of the critical section for compressive stress parallel to grain f_c in a friction pile (see Fig. 11.7, far right pile). Given:

1. Depth driven into soil is 47 ft (14.232 m). A 50-ft-long pile is used; see Table 11.6. The circumference 3 ft (914 mm) from the butt is 38 in (965 mm); the circumference at the tip is 17 in (432 mm).
2. Pile acts partially in end-bearing and partially in friction. Friction load is P_f = 79,000 lb (351.11 kN); end-bearing load is P_c = 10,000 lb (44.44 kN); total load is P_t = 89,000 lb (395.55 kN).

Note: AASHTO[10] requires that a pile be designed as a friction pile or an end-bearing pile.

3. There are two distinct layers of soil. The upper 17 ft (5.18 m) has negligible vertical capacity but can provide adequate lateral stability. For this reason, there

TABLE 11.9 Equatorial Hardwoods Imported into the United States

	Greenheart	Bongossi and Ekki	Chengal	Jarrah
Botanical name	Ocotea radiae	Bongossi Lophira alata	Balanocypus heimii	Eucalyptus marginata
Location of forest	Guyana	West Africa	Malaysia	West Australia
Resistance to abrasion	High	High	High	Medium to high
Resistance to borers	High	High	High	High
Resistance to decay	Very durable, 25 years +	Very durable, 25 years +	Very durable, 25 years +	Very durable, 25 years +
Comments	Straight grain with tendency to split; hard and heavy; difficult to work; drives well; prebore	Interlocking grain; hard and heavy; difficult to work; drives well; prebore	Interlocking grain; stable and little splitting; words and drives well; prebore	Interlocking grain; some gum pockets; stable; works and drives well; prebore
Compression parallel to grain F_c, lb/in^2	2600	3500	3440	1500
Extreme fiber in bending F_b, lb/in^2	4100	3560	3600	1800
Horizontal shear F_v, lb/in^2	450	460	360	220
Compression perpendicular to grain $F_{c\perp}$, lb/in^2	780	1348	913	520
Modulus of elasticity E, lb/in^2	2,494,000	2,010,000	2,629,000	1,490,000
Density at 50% moisture content, lb	82	82	70	63
Hardness, resistance to indentation on side grain, lb	1880	2890	2080	1280

Note: 1 lb/in^2 = 6.895 kPa.

is no change in the value of friction force, column 5 in Table 11.10. The lower 30 ft (9.14 m) can carry 79,000 lb (351.11 kN) of load through shear transfer.

4. No bending is induced in the pile; therefore $f_b = 0$. If there exists combined bending and axial loading on a pile, beam-column design procedures should be used.

SOLUTION: Circumference = πd; difference in circumference = 38 − 17 = 21 in; difference in diameters = (21 in)/π = 6.68 in. Assume the pile diameter decreases at a uniform rate along its length. The rate of change in diameter is (6.68 in)/(47 ft) = 0.142 in per foot of pile length.

Select locations along the length of pile at which compressive stresses are to be calculated and calculate the diameter of the pile. At 47 ft from pile tip,

At 45 ft from pile tip,

$$D_x = 12.10 - (2 \times 0.142) = 11.82 \text{ in}$$

The rest are calculated in a similar manner and are tabulated in column 2 of Table 11.10. Next, the cross-sectional area of the pile is calculated as shown below for each location given in column 1, and the results are tabulated in column 3 of Table 11.10.

$$A = \frac{\pi D_x^2}{4} = \frac{\pi(12.10)^2}{4} = 115.0 \text{ in}^2$$

TABLE 11.10 Location of Critical Compressive Stress in a Friction Pile for Example 11.3

Location from pile tip x, ft (1)	Diameter of pile D_x, in (2)	Cross-sectional area A_x, in² (3)	Surface area to tip A_s, ft² (4)	Friction load remaining P_{fx}, lb (5)	Total load $P_t = P_{fx} + P_c$, lb (6)	Compressive stress f_c, lb/in² (7)
47	12.10	114.8	—	79,000	89,000	775
45	11.81	109.4	—	79,000	89,000	814
40	11.09	96.6	—	79,000	89,000	921
35	10.38	84.6	—	79,000	89,000	1,052
31	9.81	75.6	—	79,000	89,000	1,177
30	9.67	73.4	59.3	79,000	89,000	1,212*
29	9.53	71.3	56.7	75,536	85,536	1,200
25	8.96	63.1	47.1	62,747	72,747	1,153
20	8.25	53.5	35.8	47,693	57,693	1,078
15	7.54	44.7	25.5	33,971	43,971	984
10	6.83	36.6	16.0	21,315	31,315	856
5	6.12	29.4	7.6	10,124	20,125	685
0	5.41	23.0	0	0	10,000	434

*Governs pile design.

The approximate equation for calculating frustrums of the cone-shaped timber pile is

$$A_s = 0.131(D_x + D_t)x$$

where A_s = surface area of tapered pile from tip to any point x feet from tip, ft^2
D_x = pile diameter at any point x feet from tip, in
D_t = pile tip diameter, in (for this example 5.41 in)
x = distance from tip of pile over which surface area is to be calculated, ft

The surface area of the pile from its tip to a point 47 ft away is

$$A_s = 0.131(12.10 + 5.41)47 = 107.8 \text{ ft}^2$$

The rest of the surface areas are calculated in a similar manner and are listed in column 4 of Table 11.10.

Assume the friction between the pile and the 30-ft layer of soil to be uniformly distributed over the surface area of the pile, as given by

$$P_{fx} = \frac{A_s P_f}{S_T}$$

where P_{fx} = cumulative load from tip of pile to point under consideration, which is x feet from tip of pile, tons
A_s = surface area, ft^2, column 4
S_T = total surface area of pile in soil capable of shear transfer, ft^2 (for this example 59.3 ft^2 from tip)
P_f = total friction load

No shear force is transferred between piles from 47 to 30 ft from tip (see given information). Thus at 30 ft from the tip,

$$P_{fx} = 79{,}000 \text{ lb}$$

At 29 ft from the pile tip,

$$P_{fx} = \frac{56.7 \times 79{,}000}{59.3} = 75{,}536 \text{ lb}$$

The remaining values in column 5 are calculated in a similar manner.

According to Table 11.8, footnote *a*, the allowable stress for Pacific Coast Douglas fir and southern pine may be increased by 0.2 percent for each foot of length from the tip of the pile to the critical section. However, the maximum increase allowed is 10 percent.

For Pacific Coast Douglas fir,

$$F_c(\text{allowable}) = 1250[1 + (30 \times 0.002)] = 1325 \text{ lb/in}^2$$

For southern pine,

$$F_c(\text{allowable}) = 1200[1 + (30 \times 0.002)] = 1272 \text{ lb/in}^2$$

Both values are for normal load duration and wet-use condition. Since the maximum value for the pile is 1212 lb/in^2 (see column 7 of Table 11.10), either species could be used.

The allowable load for a friction pile is usually controlled by the shearing strength of the soil and not by the compressive strength of the wood pile. The "critical section" in this example lies 30 ft from the pile tip, just beneath the upper soil stratum, because the upper stratum contributes no additional friction load while the pile's cross section continues to increase with the distance from the tip.

Where several soil strata of different shear strengths occur, the location of the critical section will probably not be obvious. It must be determined by calculations similar to those of this example and based on known or assumed soil properties. The load transferred to the pile is determined by using the formula

$$P_f = \Sigma a \sigma S \tag{11.1}$$

where Σ = summation of calculations for each soil stratum through which pile penetrates
a = adhesion factor between pile material and soil, normally 1.00 for tapered timber piling and cohesive soils
σ = shear strength of soil, lb/ft^2
S = surface area of pile within soil stratum, ft^2

The relationship can be more complex. If the compressibility of each soil layer differs materially from that of adjacent layers, the load transfer may not be fully effective in some strata.

If the pile is a friction pile, the allowable axial load may have to be reduced when the piles are closely spaced, since the friction on the perimeter of the pile group may be less than the sum of the values of the individual piles in the group.

Piles for single-column footings and abutments are normally driven in standard groupings, as shown in Fig. 11.8. Design aids are available which can be helpful in the selection of the optional pile spacing and the concrete footing size. Concrete pile cap design aids are available from the American Concrete Institute and the Concrete Reinforcing Steel Institute. The pile group reduction formula as given by AASHTO Sec. 4.3.4.7 is reproduced here as Eq. (11.2).

When the capacity of a group of friction piles driven into plastic material is not determined by test loading, the following Converse-Labarre formula is suggested to determine the reduction of a single-pile load for a group-pile load:

$$E = 1 - \phi \frac{(n-1)m + (m-1)n}{90mn} \tag{11.2}$$

where E = efficiency or decimal fraction of single-pile value to be used for each pile in group
n = number of piles in each row
m = number of rows in each group
d = average diameter of pile
s = center-to-center spacing of piles
$\tan \phi = d/s$, ϕ being numerically equal to angle expressed in degrees

The designer is reminded that higher load values are permitted with the test loading method.

The formulas in Fig. 11.9 can be used to determine the moment of inertia of a pile group when needed in calculations involving overturning forces.

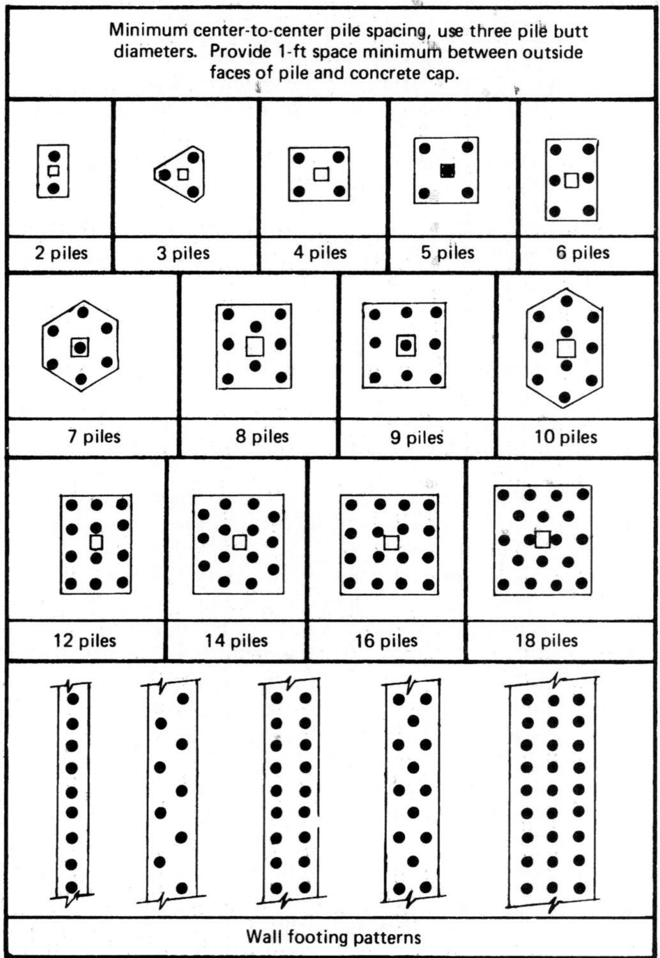

FIG. 11.8 Wood pile footing groups for concrete pile caps.

Piles may be loaded normal to their length (laterally). Table 11.11 provides for the designer an order of magnitude on lateral loads. Formulas for lateral loads on poles or piles are shown in Fig. 11.10. A nomograph which can be used to determine the length of enbedment required for a pile or pole loaded laterally when ½ in of ground motion is permitted can be obtained from Ref. 16. If bending stresses become excessive due to lateral loading on the pile, batter piles may be used. A batter pile is placed at a maximum slope of 4 to 1 (vertical to horizontal), and a part of the lateral load is supported by axial thrust. An analysis of a group of piles may be complex if the pile group supports a load combination which includes downward, uplift, and lateral loads. Additional information on piles subject to such load combinations is given in Refs. 17 to 19.

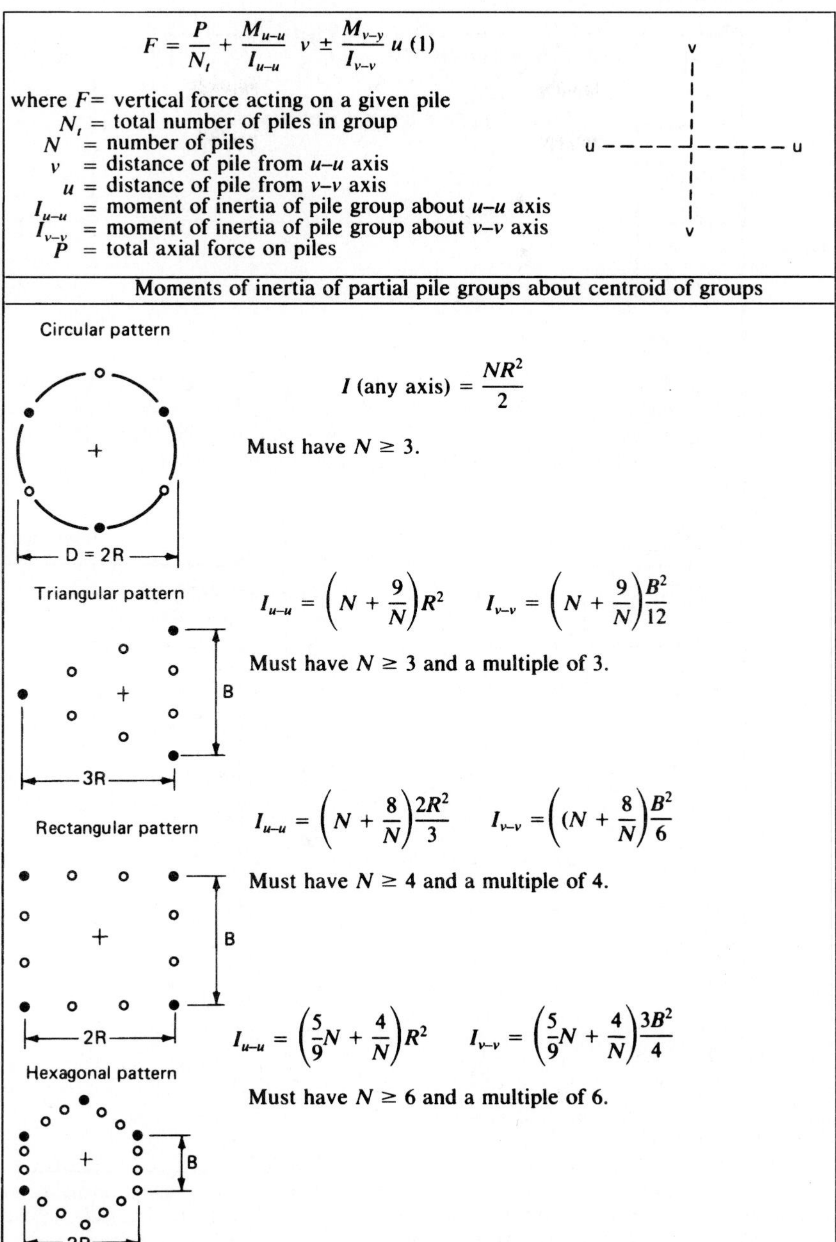

$F = \frac{P}{N_t} + \frac{M_{u-u}}{I_{u-u}} v \pm \frac{M_{v-y}}{I_{v-v}} u$ (1)
where F = vertical force acting on a given pile
N_t = total number of piles in group
N = number of piles
v = distance of pile from u–u axis
u = distance of pile from v–v axis
I_{u-u} = moment of inertia of pile group about u–u axis
I_{v-v} = moment of inertia of pile group about v–v axis
P = total axial force on piles
v
u
u
v
Moments of inertia of partial pile groups about centroid of groups
Circular pattern
I (any axis) $= \frac{NR^2}{2}$
Must have $N \geq 3$.
D = 2R
Triangular pattern
$I_{u-u} = \left(N + \frac{9}{N}\right) R^2 \quad I_{v-v} = \left(N + \frac{9}{N}\right) \frac{B^2}{12}$
Must have $N \geq 3$ and a multiple of 3.
B
3R
Rectangular pattern
$I_{u-u} = \left(N + \frac{8}{N}\right) \frac{2R^2}{3} \quad I_{v-v} = \left((N + \frac{8}{N}\right) \frac{B^2}{6}$
Must have $N \geq 4$ and a multiple of 4.
B
2R
$I_{u-u} = \left(\frac{5}{9}N + \frac{4}{N}\right) R^2 \quad I_{v-v} = \left(\frac{5}{9}N + \frac{4}{N}\right) \frac{3B^2}{4}$
Hexagonal pattern
Must have $N \geq 6$ and a multiple of 6.
B
2R

FIG. 11.9 Section properties of pile groups. (*From W. E. Wilson, "Rapid Calculation of Section Properties of Pile Groups," Civil Eng., ASCE (Nov. 1972).*)

Octagonal pattern

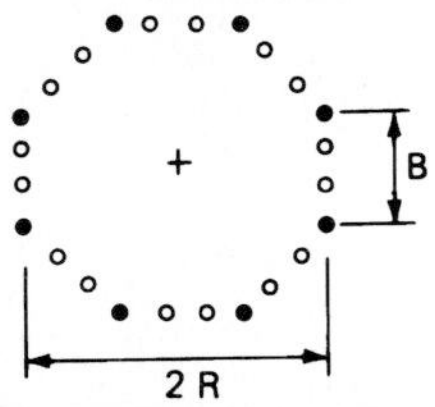

$$I_{u-u} = \left[N + 0.0572\left(N + \frac{128}{N}\right)\right]\frac{R^2}{2} \qquad I_{\geq v-v} = \left(0.77N + \frac{16}{3N}\right)B^2$$

Must have $N \geq 8$ and a multiple of 8.

B

2 R

FIG. 11.9 *(Continued)*

11.2.5 Pile-Driving Formulas

Pile-driving formulas for timber piles have not changed significantly since the beginning of this century. In 1888, the editor of *Engineering News,* A. M. Wellington, developed the formulas still used in the latest edition of the AASHTO specification, and they are given below. AASHTO does not give expressions for all types of

TABLE 11.11 Allowable Lateral Loads on Plumb Piles According to Different Authorities

Authority	Allowable lateral load on each plumb pile, tons			
New York City Building Code (1947)			1.0	
New York City Building Code (1968)			2.0	
McNulty*		Medium sand	Fine sand	Medium clay
	Free-end timber piles, 12-in diameter†	0.75	0.75	0.75
	Fixed-end timber piles, 12-in diameter	2.50	2.25	2.00
Feagin‡	Timber piles, allowable lateral displacement ¼ in		4.50	
	Timber piles, allowable lateral displacement ½ in		7.00	
Teng§	Piles in deep bed of soft silt or clays		0.50	

*J. F. McNulty, "Thrust Loading on Piles," *Soil Mech. Found. Div., Proc. ASCE* **86**(SM2), (Apr. 1956); also discussion, *ibid.* (SM4), (Oct. 1956).

†Safety factor of 3 applied to load required for ¼-in lateral displacement.

‡L. B. Feagin, "Lateral Pile Load Tests," *Trans. ASCE* **102** (1937).

§W. C. Teng, *Foundation Design,* Prentice-Hall, Englewood Cliffs, N.J., 1962, p. 227.

Source: From S. M. Johnson and T. C. Kavanagh, *The Design of Foundations for Buildings,* McGraw-Hill, New York, 1968.

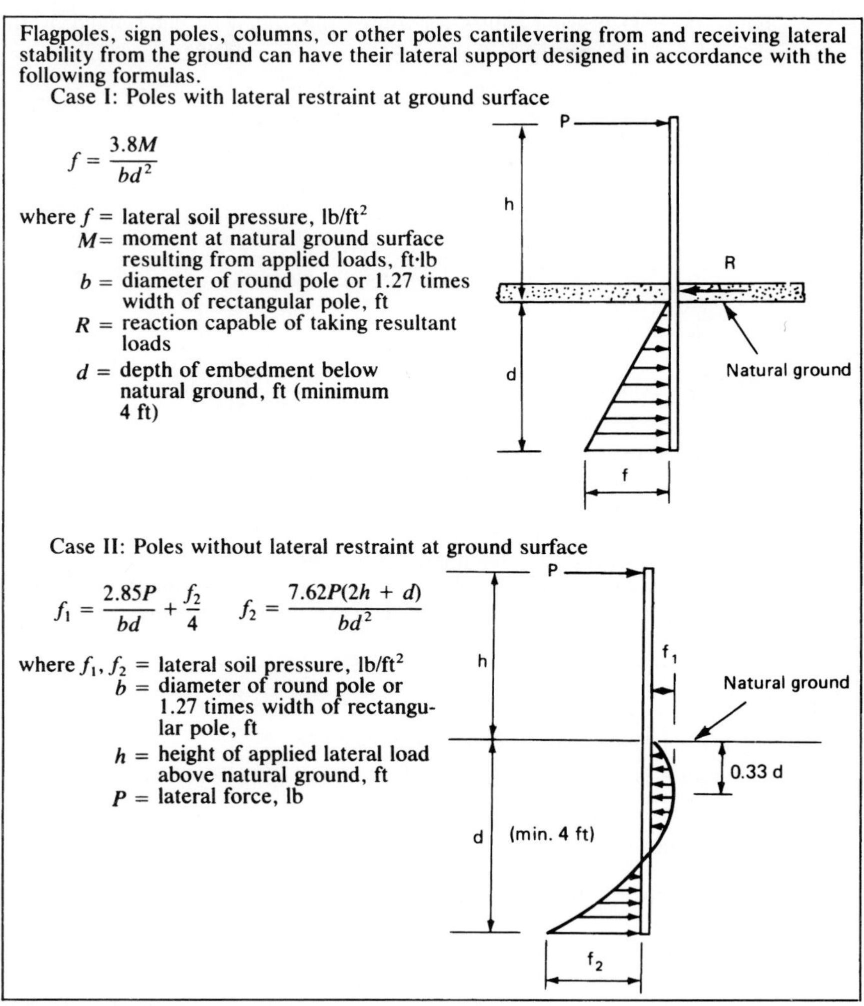

Flagpoles, sign poles, columns, or other poles cantilevering from and receiving lateral stability from the ground can have their lateral support designed in accordance with the following formulas.
Case I: Poles with lateral restraint at ground surface
$f = \frac{3.8M}{bd^2}$
where f = lateral soil pressure, lb/ft²
M = moment at natural ground surface resulting from applied loads, ft·lb
b = diameter of round pole or 1.27 times width of rectangular pole, ft
R = reaction capable of taking resultant loads
d = depth of embedment below natural ground, ft (minimum 4 ft)
P
h
R
d
Natural ground
f
Case II: Poles without lateral restraint at ground surface
$f_1 = \frac{2.85P}{bd} + \frac{f_2}{4}$ $f_2 = \frac{7.62P(2h + d)}{bd^2}$
where f_1, f_2 = lateral soil pressure, lb/ft²
b = diameter of round pole or 1.27 times width of rectangular pole, ft
h = height of applied lateral load above natural ground, ft
P = lateral force, lb
P
h
f_1
Natural ground
0.33 d
d (min. 4 ft)
f_2

FIG. 11.10 Lateral loads on poles.

hammers used in driving piles. The formula shown for single-acting steam hammers also can be used for diesel and air single-acting hammers. For double-acting hammers, the expression $H(W + Ap)$ or E, the manufacturer's rating of energy (use 90 percent of E for diesel hammers), is substituted in the AASHTO equation for double-acting steam hammers. Some hammers that are manufactured have a chart and gauge attached to the hammer, which can be used by the field inspector to calculate the equivalent energy.

Timber Pile Formulas. The following formulas are taken from AASHTO specifications.[10] Formulas given in parentheses are to be used with SI units.

When not driven to practical refusal, the bearing values of piles preferably shall be determined by load tests. In the absence of load tests or substantiated adequate pile formulas, the safe bearing values for timber piles shall be determined by the following formulas.

For gravity hammers,

$$P = \frac{2WH}{S + 1.0} \qquad \left(\frac{0.05WH}{0.0305S + 0.0076}\right)$$

For single-acting steam hammers,

$$P = \frac{2WH}{S + 0.1} \qquad \left(\frac{0.05WH}{0.0305S + 0.00076}\right)$$

For double-acting steam hammers,

$$P = \frac{2H(W + Ap)}{S + 0.1} \qquad \left(\frac{0.5H(W + Ap)}{0.0305S + 0.00076}\right)$$

where P = safe bearing capacity, lb (N)
W = weight of striking parts of hammer, lb (N)
H = height of fall, ft (m)
A = area of piston, in^2 (m^2)
p = steam pressure at the hammer, lb/in^2 (Pa)
S = average penetration per blow for the last 5 to 10 blows for gravity hammers and for the last 10 to 20 blows for steam hammers, in (m)

The preceding formulas are applicable only when

1. The hammer has a free fall.
2. The head of the pile is not broomed or crushed.
3. The penetration is reasonably quick and uniform.
4. There is no sensible bounce after the blows.
5. A follower is not used.

Twice the height of bounce shall be deducted from H to determine its value in the formula.

Unless otherwise ordered by the engineer, timber piling shall be driven to the bearing value given on the plans or in the supplemental specifications. If bearing values are not given, timber piling shall be driven to a minimum value of 20 tons (177.9 kN).

In case water jets are used in connection with the driving, the bearing capacity shall be determined by the above formulas from the results of driving after jets have been withdrawn, or a load test may be applied.

A more recently developed formula is the Hiley formula.[20] This formula, which is used in the *National Building Code of Canada* to estimate driving conditions and, when the load does not exceed 30 tons, the design capacity of piling, is

$$R = \frac{4nWH}{s + c/2} \tag{11.3}$$

where R = allowable load on pile, lb
n = efficiency of blow; see Eq. (11.4)
W = weight of striking part of hammer, lb

H = height of free fall of hammer or ram; see Eq. (11.5)
s = average penetration per blow for last 5 blows, in
c = sum of temporary elastic compressions of pile, ground, and driving head, in; see Eq. (11.6)

Hammer Efficiency n

$$n = \frac{W + e^2P}{W + P} \tag{11.4}$$

where P = weight of pile, lb
W = weight of striking part of hammer, lb
e = coefficient of restitution for iron on wood

Figure 11.11 shows values of n for an iron hammer striking on a wood cap or directly on a timber pile ($e = 0.25$) and for the steel ram of a double-acting hammer striking on a steel anvil and driving timber piles ($e = 0.4$).

Height of Free Fall H. For double-acting hammers,

$$H = \frac{h(W + AM)}{W} \tag{11.5}$$

where h = actual stroke of hammer or ram, ft
$H = h$ for drop hammer released by monkey trigger
$H = 0.9h$ for single-acting steam hammer
$H = 0.8h$ for drop hammer actuated by wire rope from friction winch
A = area of piston acted on by steam, lb/in^2
M = mean effective steam pressure, lb/in^2
W = weight of striking part of hammer, lb

Total Temporary Compression c. This may be determined by measurement during driving, or if the completed load after driving does not differ by more than 20 percent from the assumed load, it may be estimated approximately from Fig. 11.11 or by calculation from the formula

$$c = 3R\left(\frac{L}{A_1E} + \frac{0.00014}{A_2}\right) \tag{11.6}$$

where R = allowable load assumed in design, lb
A_1 = cross-sectional areas of pile, taken (for tapered wood piles) at midpoint of pile length, in^2
A_2 = bearing area (small end area) of pile, in^2
L = length of pile, in
E = modulus of elasticity in compression, lb/in^2

11.2.6 Protection of Pile Tops

Timber piles can be hit too hard with the hammer, particularly a drop hammer, causing them to split at the top or tip. This splitting, crushing, and flaring outward of the fibers resembles a broom—hence the term *brooming*. With the evolution of large hammers, caution must be used by the operator when installing piles. Three methods which can be used to protect the pile top are shown in Fig. 11.12. The

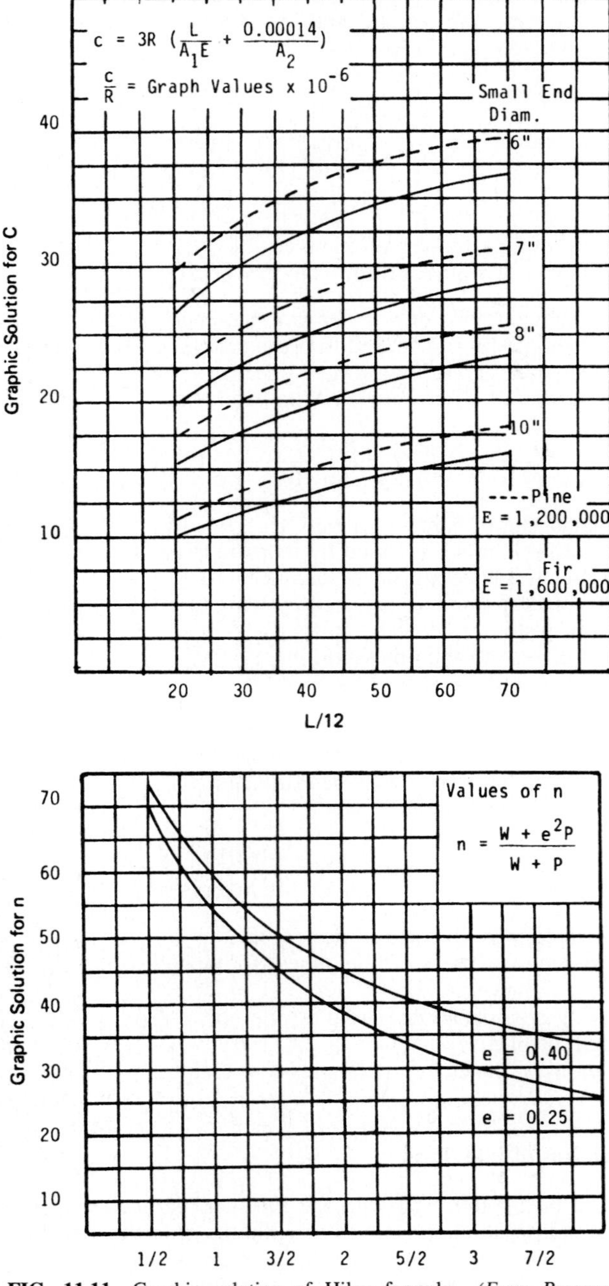

FIG. 11.11 Graphic solution of Hiley formula. (*From Pressure Treated Timber Piles, Canadian Institute of Timber Construction.*[20])

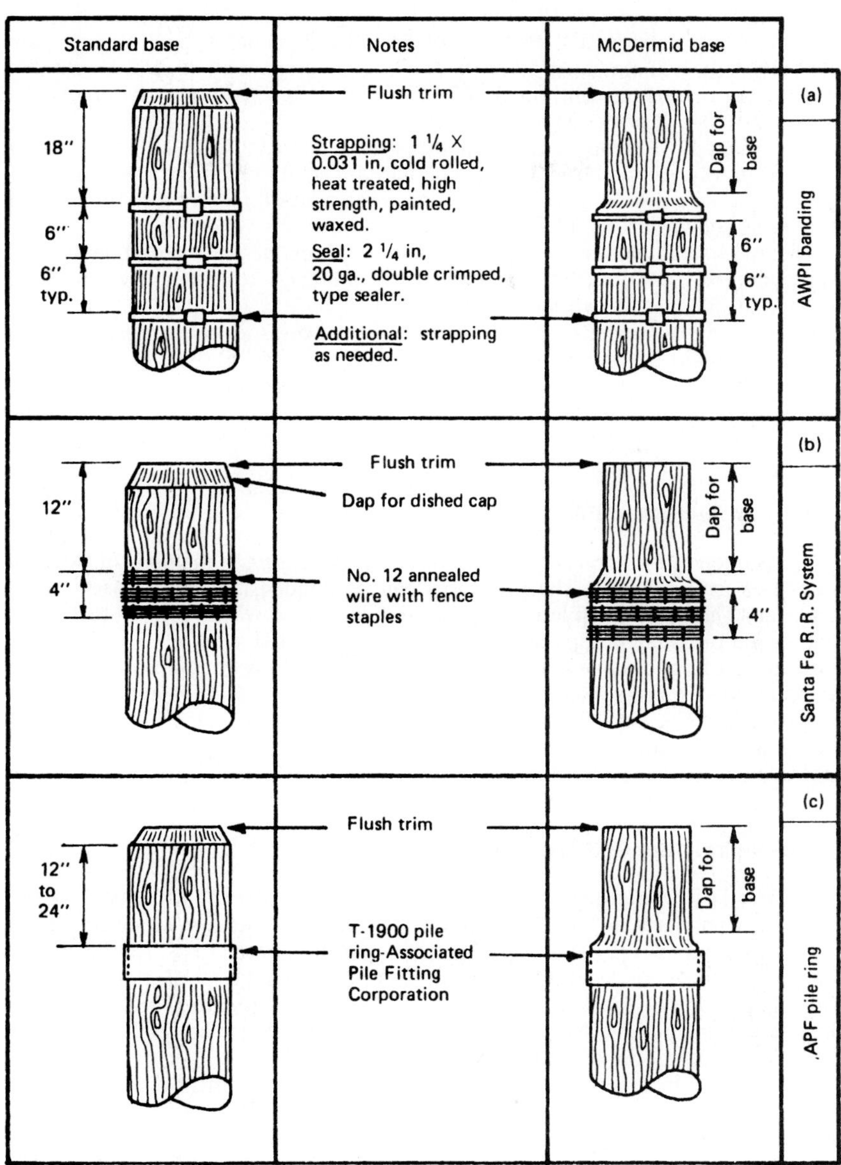

FIG. 11.12 Protection of pile tops.

American Wood Preservers Institute (AWPI) suggested the banding method, which uses steel straps, or bands, and can be installed by one worker with a clamp. Normally only two straps are used, but additional straps may be added as desired. This system is illustrated in Fig. 11.12*a* for piles to be driven with hammers using either the standard or the McDermid base.

The Santa Fe Railway developed the system of using No. 12 annealed wire wrapped tightly around the pile butt. The wire is then fastened in place using fence staples. The wire is wrapped side by side in three bands that have a combined width of 4 in, as shown in Fig. 11.12*b*.

The Associated Pile and Fitting Corporation manufacturers a carbon steel pile ring (model T-19000) that is available in 13-, 14-, and 16-in diameters to protect the tops of piles, as shown in Fig. 11.12*c*.

Overdriving of timber piles can be a problem. Any sudden decrease in driving resistance should be investigated with regard to the possibility of breakage of the pile, and if such sudden decrease in driving resistance cannot be correlated to boring data or some incident in the driving, and if the pile cannot be removed for inspection, it should be considered as cause for rejection of the pile.

11.2.7 Protection of Pile Tips

The protection of pile tips is also important and the common methods of protection are shown in Fig. 11.13. The protectors can be divided into two classes: pointed and blunt. The tip of the pile must be accurately shaped when using a steel pointed shoe or the pile may be driven eccentrically. If a pointed shoe hits a resistant rock below the surface, the pile may be driven out of line. If obstructions are anticipated, the blunt pile tip protection is recommended. Blunt tips will also not drive up into the pile fibers since the protector is of the same diameter as the pile. The cost of a pile tip is nominal when compared to the cost of redriving a pile. The AWPI steel bands can also be used at the tip.

11.2.8 Installation in Permafrost

Permafrost is frozen ground that has been at 32°F or colder for at least 2 years. It may be dry and have no ice. But the more ice it has, the more problems are created. Twenty percent of the land mass in the world has permafrost. In the northern hemisphere, this includes more than half of the land area within the political boundaries of the State of Alaska, the People's Republic of China, the U.S.S.R., Canada, Greenland, Finland, and Norway. Permafrost in the southern hemisphere is located on the continent of Antarctica.

The earliest documents discussing permafrost are the records of explorers' journeys in Siberia and northern Alaska. By the early 1900s the basic phenomenon was documented in papers written by the U.S. Geological Survey. The Russians were the pioneers and leaders in scientific research at that time because of the large populated regions of the Soviet Union that have permafrost. During World War II, all technical information developed to that date by Russian scientists and engineers was turned over to the United States and Canada as part of the Lend-Lease Act. This information was used by military and civilian engineers to assist them in the design of the Alcan highway. Much of this highway is over permafrost soils in British Columbia, the Yukon Territory, and Alaska.

After World War II, more classified research and building was done by the military in Alaska, northern Canada, and Greenland. The Distant Early Warning

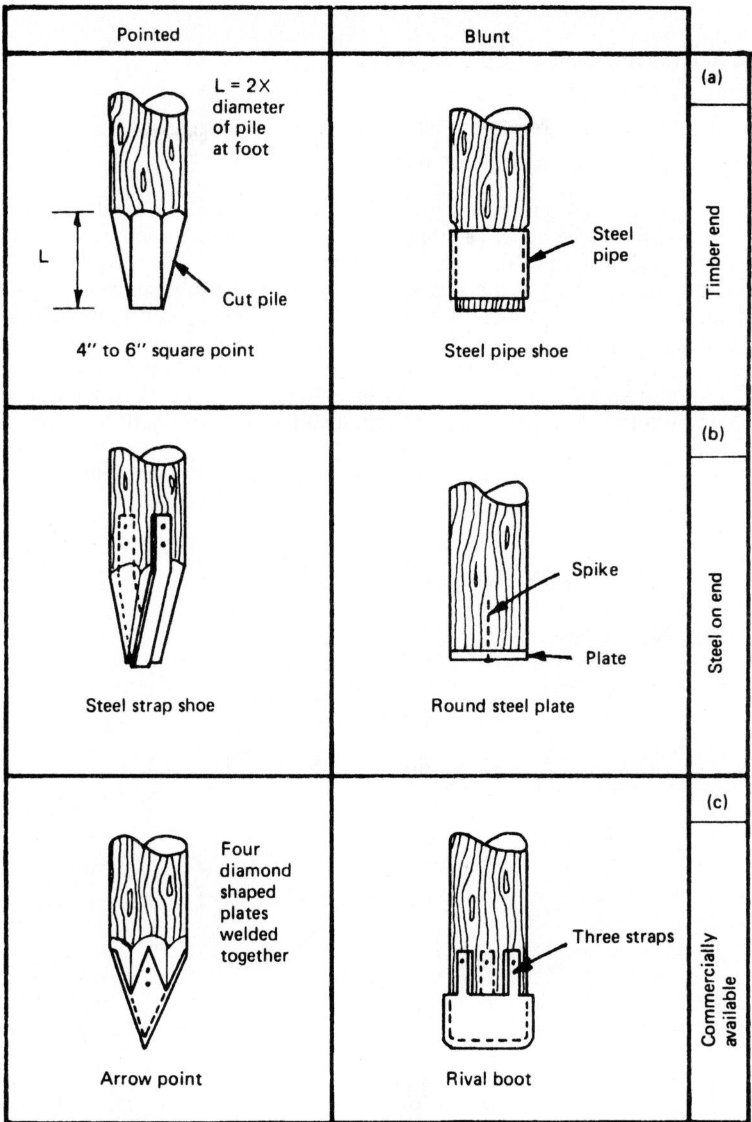

FIG. 11.13 Protection of pile tips.

(DEW) line stations were built in very remote permafrost locations. In the early 1970s the oil industry started the construction of permanent facilities in locations with continuous permafrost, and they initiated additional research and development. In addition, many northern communities benefited financially from oil exploration and have constructed more sophisticated structures for their communities. During this 80-year history, many foundation failures have occurred and continue to occur because of a lack of experience with permafrost.

Some common misunderstandings concern:

1. The actual temperature of permafrost
2. The types of soils in permafrost
3. The percentage of permafrost that is ice
4. What happens when permafrost melts

The temperature of the frozen ground varies with specific locations. The map of Fig. 11.14 shows the approximate regions of continuous permafrost and discontinuous and supermarginal permafrost in North America. The supermarginal permafrost (ground at 31°F) is the region where the most problems occur, because it only requires 1°F of warming to start thermal inbalance (constant melting until thermal balance is achieved again). Soils in permafrost areas can have layers of frozen and unfrozen soil, making geotechnical engineering complex.

Soils in permafrost include every conceivable type and are distributed in various layers and mixtures. The percentage of ice in soil varies with both location and soil type. There is no standard percentage of ice for specific soil types. When silty sand melts, the soil quickly collapses, whereas large gravel is more stable.

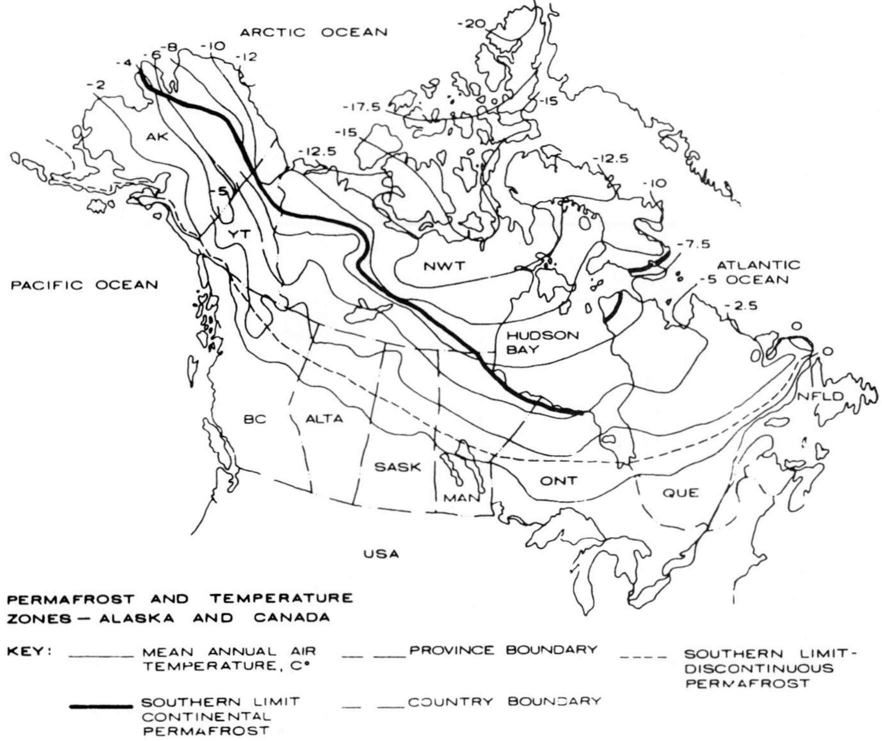

FIG. 11.14 Permafrost locations in North America. (*From R. T. Packard (ed.), Architectural Graphic Standards, 7th ed., Copyright © 1981, John Wiley & Sons, Inc., Reprinted by permission of John Wiley & Sons, Inc.*)

The type of arctic foundation shown in Fig. 11.15 has experienced the lowest rate of failure, since only the piles transfer heat into the ground. The heated or unheated structure is separated from the ground to minimize this transmission, and wind blowing from any direction will remove most of the heat radiated from the structure. Timber piles have the natural advantage of not transmitting heat as readily as steel or concrete piles.

Holes 4 to 6 in larger in diameter than the pile are augered into the permafrost (Fig. 11.16), and piles are accurately positioned butt down. Then a sand-water slurry is placed into the hole. Eventually, the sand-water, surrounded by the colder permafrost, freezes and supports the piles (friction piles) in their permanent position. This is known as the *adfreeze strength* of the soil. Normally, piles will creep with time because the ice creeps, and some designers commonly use 1 in of creep per 20 years as a maximum design value. Plastic wrapped around the pile is not very effective in preventing the active layer from gripping the pile and raising it by frost jacking. For this reason, tapered piles should have their point upward. Timber piles are most often treated with waterborne preservatives since oilborne preservatives reduce allowable adfreeze strengths. Soft rot can occur at the annual thaw zone in the active layer, which is usually the location of greatest flexural stress in the pile.

The active layer is the layer of soil above the permafrost that is not continuously frozen, and its thickness varies with building site location. The active layer consists of alternating frozen and unfrozen layers of soils. Active layers usualy consist of frost-susceptible soils (those that retain moisture) that move up and down due to water expansion when frozen. This movement exerts a force called *frost heaving,* or *frost jacking,* on any embedded items that pass through the active layer. In colder permafrost regions, the active layer is thinner. Therefore, it is practicable and de-

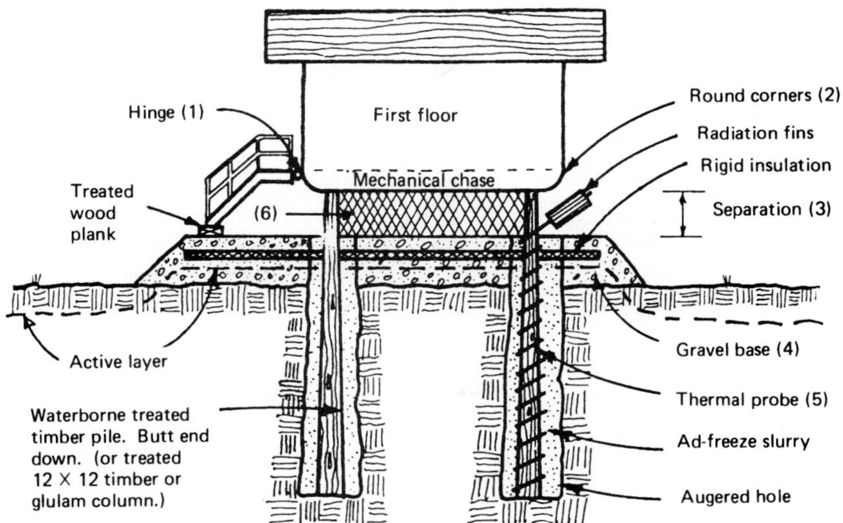

FIG. 11.15 Details of Arctic foundation. *Notes:* (1) To allow stairs to rotate with frost heaving, floating stairs, not attached to structure. (2) To minimize snow drifting. (3) Between structure and ground to prevent transmission of heat. (4) Used in continuous permafrost areas to raise active layer into gravel. (5) Required in supermarginal permafrost, spirally wrapped around pile; see Fig. 11.16. (6) Chain-link fence.

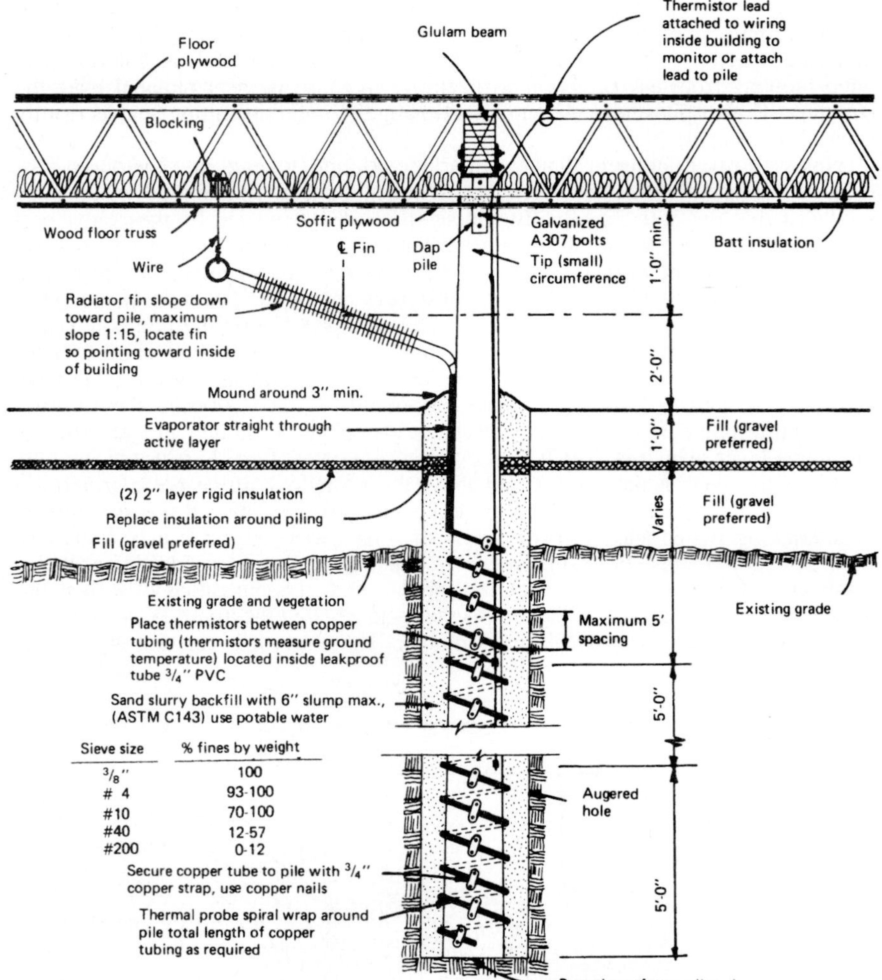

Sieve size	% fines by weight
3/8"	100
# 4	93-100
#10	70-100
#40	12-57
#200	0-12

FIG. 11.16 Timber pile with thermal probe for permafrost.

sirable to bring the active layer out of the frost-susceptible soil and into a gravel pad, which is constructed on top of the existing soils and vegetation. The existing ground and vegetation should not be disturbed because that might initiate thermal inbalance. This gravel pad may need to be only 5 ft thick in regions along the Arctic Ocean. In supermarginal permafrost, a gravel pad on top of rigid insulation board should be installed. In mild regions such as Anchorage, Alaska, relic permafrost or deep seasonal permafrost, when discovered, is purposely destroyed permanently by melting prior to construction of a structure.

An additional safety factor, which can be used to prevent thawing of the permafrost, is a patented thermal probe or "heat pipe." It is a sealed metal tube filled with a gas mixture, and it has an aluminum radiator located at the top. It removes heat from the ground and releases it into the air only when the air temperature is cooler than the ground. The heat from the ground turns the chemical into a gas, which rises to the top. The wind removes the heat, turning the gas into a liquid, which drops to the bottom of the tube. Thus it requires no fossil fuel energy to operate. Mechanical refrigeration, a system requiring energy from fossil fuel, has been used for both the correction of a temporary problem and, at times, as a permanent solution. It is a very expensive system to operate and therefore will not be discussed.

The elevated building system has been the most successful in permafrost construction because there are only two ways maintenance personnel can trigger a foundation failure. One is to prevent the flow of wind underneath the building. This can be done by attaching skirting, storing items underneath the building, or shoveling snow underneath the building, all of which block the wind needed to remove the heat from beneath the building. The second way is to damage the thermal probe system. Designers normally elevate the building as high as reasonable (36 in minimum, which allows personnel access below the entire building) and provide an architectural finish to the bottom surface. A constant clearance height between the bottom of the building and the ground will minimize snow drifting below the building. Incorporating a chain link fence around the building facade will prevent storage of material or wind-blown debris from collecting below the building. Numerous failures have occurred when maintenance personnel have not understood how the foundation system functions. Other failures have been due to incomplete soil investigations, or the lack of a correct workable solution to the foundation problem. Several types of treated wood foundations have been used successfully in the Arctic.[21]

11.2.9 Pile-to-Concrete Connections

Timber piles are usually connected to some type of concrete footing, except in pole building construction. When the top of the pile is cut to the correct elevation, it is highly recommended that the end be field-treated with preservative in accordance with the appropriate AWPA specifications. This should be done since the interior portion of the pile is not penetrated by the preservative during treatment. Thus moisture will migrate into the end grain of the wood, which will most likely result in decay of the untreated wood. Field treating should be done even if the top of the pile is to be encased in concrete. The additional cost of field treating end cuts is very small, especially when compared with the additional protection it provides.

Designers often encase the pile tops in concrete and do not provide any connection between the concrete and the piles. The connector is eliminated to save money. However, if down-drag or uplift forces were to act on the pile, a sudden failure might result. A nominal connection will provide a degree of reserve strength.

Figure 11.17 illustrates six common methods of connecting timber piles to concrete. These are used to transmit forces that result from overturning due to wind or earthquake, buoyancy pressure from groundwater, and down-drag forces on the pile. Analysis of these connections is the same as for any other timber connection. For bolts longer than about 6 in, the design load values remain constant with bolt length; therefore, the designer will have to choose between additional bolts or shear plates if large-magnitude loads must be transferred. A glulam rivet is a specially shaped nail developed in Canada which is used in several patented connections.

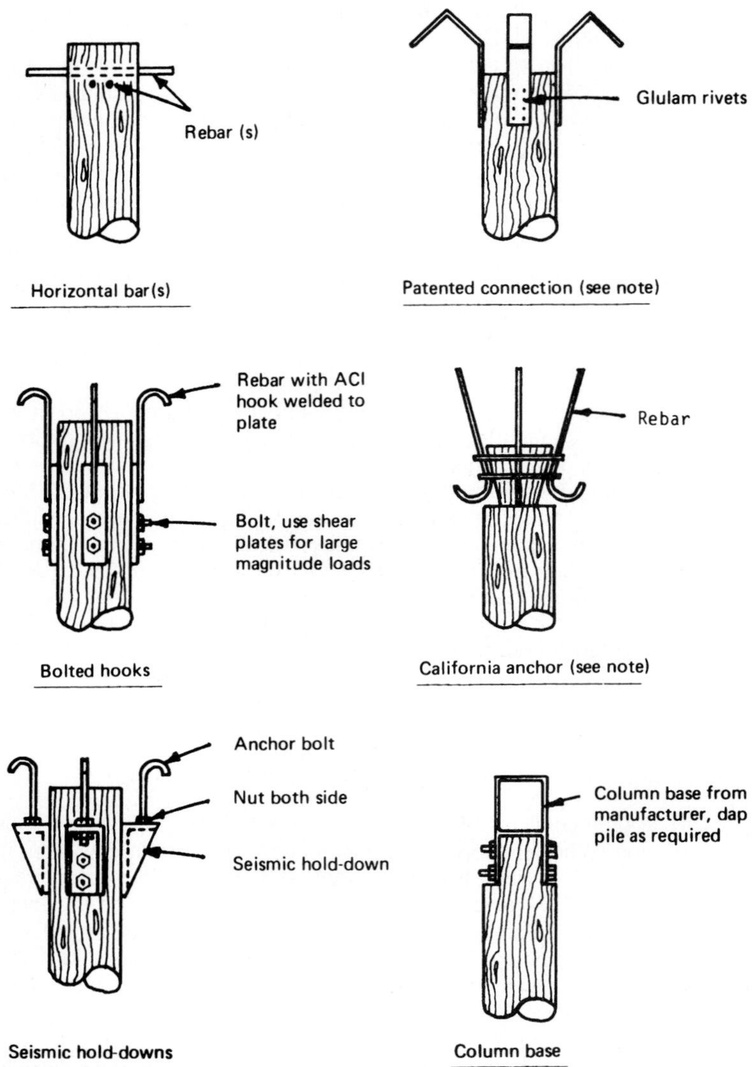

FIG. 11.17 Pile-to-concrete connections. (*Note:* The glulam rivet is a patented connection.)

The bolted hook connection with rebars welded to steel straps is used for tension load, and all design formulas for allowable tension are given by the building specifications of the American Concrete Institute. The seismic hold-down is a readily available item in western states and makes a very simple connection from both the designer's and the contractor's points of view. A nut on both sides of the bottom plate of the hold-down secures the anchor bolt during the concrete pour. The column base connection is available as a shelf item, and code-accepted design values are available. All metal fasteners and hardware should have a corrosion-resistant coating.

REFERENCES

1. "Brooklyn Bridge," *Civil Eng.,* May 1983, pp. 42–47.
2. *The All-Weather Wood Foundation System: Design, Fabrication and Installation Manual,* American Forest and Paper Association, Washington, D.C., Jan. 1986, 94 pp.
3. *Stainless Steel Fasteners (Types 304 or 316) for AWWF System,* from D475C, American Plywood Association, Tacoma, Wash., Mar. 1983.
4. *All Weather Pressure-Treated Wood Foundation,* American Wood Preservers Institute, Stevensville, Md., 1972, 24 pp.
5. R. T. Ratay (ed.), *Handbook on Temporary Structures in Construction: Engineering Standards, Designs, Practices and Procedures,* McGraw-Hill, New York, 1984, 690 pp.
6. *The National Design Specifications for Wood Construction,* American Forest and Paper Association, Washington, D.C., 1991, 125 pp.
7. *Plen-Wood System,* form K 300A, American Wood Council, Washington, D.C., 1985.
8. *APA Design/Construction Guide to Permanent Wood Foundation,* form A400M, American Plywood Association, Tacoma, Wash., 1992.
9. *Standard Specifications for Round Timber Piles,* ASTM D 25, American Society for Testing and Materials, Philadelphia, Pa., 1991.
10. *Standard Specifications for Highway Bridges,* 14th ed., American Association of State Highway and Transportation Officials, Washington, D.C. 1989, 420 pp.
11. "Highway 'First'," Engineering News in *Civil Eng.,* Dec. 1978, pp. 16.
12. Hal W. Hunt, *Design and Installation of Driven Pile Foundations,* Associated Pile and Fitting Corporation, Clifton, N.J. 1979, 218 pp.
13. W. E. Ferree, "For Economy Use STTP Seventy-Ton Timber Pile," *AE Concepts in Wood Design,* American Wood Preservers Institute, Stevensville, Md., Jul.–Aug. 1978, pp. 7–13.
14. *Method for Establishing Design Stresses for Round Timber Piles,* ASTM D 2899-86, American Society for Testing and Materials, Philadelphia, Pa., 1986.
15. E. Isaac and S. Johnson, "Pile Fields Support Prefabricated Plants Floated into Place," *Civil Eng.,* Jan. 1980, pp. 61–63.
16. *Pole Building Design,* American Wood Preservers Association, McLean, Va., 1981.
17. M. I. Brill, "Practical Formulas in Battered Pile Foundations (Without a Computer)," *Civil Eng.,* June 1972; reprinted by American Wood Preservers Institute, Stevensville, Md., 4 pp.
18. *Foundations and Earth Structures,* NAVFAC Design Manual 7.02, Naval Facilities, Engineering Command, Department of the Navy, Alexandria, Va., Sept. 1986, pp. 177–244.
19. R. D. Chellis, *Pile Foundations,* 2d ed., McGraw-Hill, New York, 1961, 704 pp.
20. *Pressure Treated Timber Piles: A Manual for Architects and Engineers,* Canadian Institute of Timber Construction, 1962, 160 pp. (CITC is not now in existence; related material can be obtained from Canadian Wood Council, Ottawa, Canada.)
21. A. R. Mangus, "35-Year Old Foundations, Thule Air Base, Greenland," *Proc. 4th Int. Conf., Cold Regions Engineering,* ASCE, Feb. 1986, pp. 106–117.
22. *Design of Pile Foundations,* Technical Engineering and Design Guide as Adapted from the U.S. Army Corps of Engineers, No. 1, ASCE, 1993.

23. *Foundations,* Pile Buck, Inc., Jupiter, Fl., 1992, 300 pp.

24. *Pile Hammer Specifications Chart,* Pile Buck, Inc., Jupiter, Fl., 1993, 6 pp.

25. *Inspector's Manual for Pile Foundations,* Deep Foundations Institute, Sparta, NJ., 1992, 47 pp.

26. *Engineering of Pile Installations,* McGraw-Hill, New York, 1983.

27. *Falsework Manual,* Office of Structure Construction, California Department of Transportation, Sacramento, Calif., 1988.

28. *Uniform Building Code Standards,* International Conference of Building Officials, Chap. 25, Whittier, Calif., 1991.

29. E. F. Diekmann, *Timber Pile Connections,* AE Concepts in Wood, American Wood Preservers Institute, Stevensville, Md., July-August, 1978.

CHAPTER 12
ADHESIVES

R. Richard Avent, Ph.D., P.E.

12.1 USES OF ADHESIVES IN WOOD CONSTRUCTION

The primary goal in engineered construction is to produce a structure that optimally combines safety, economy, function, and aesthetics. The fact that a variety of building materials are used competitively illustrates the versatility available to the designer in developing structural concepts. Wood, like other materials, has inherent advantages that make it especially attractive in specific applications. Its relative light weight to high strength ratio, ease of handling, durability, and natural beauty are widely recognized. However, wood also has its limitations. One factor that can affect the effective use of wood as a structural component is the limitation associated with attaching wood members to each other or to other materials. The relatively low bearing strength of wood combined with the possibility of cracks or splits developing at mechanical fasteners can result in connections being considered the weak link in a wood structure. However, the advent of the use of adhesives has provided an effective means of connecting a variety of wood components such that the strength of the joints may no longer necessarily be the weakest element in the structural system.

The purpose of this chapter is to provide information on the use of adhesives in wood construction. The primary topics covered are criteria for selecting adhesives, manufactured and field uses of adhesives, and repair of wood structures using adhesives.

12.1.1 Why and When to Use Adhesives

Because of the porous nature of wood, a properly applied adhesive penetrates the wood surface and forms a strong bond. Application techniques range from a simple brush coating of the surfaces and subsequent clamping to heat and pressure treatments. The most effective way to take advantage of load transfer using adhesives is through shear resistance at the bond line. The primary connection type consists

Note: In all example problems, SI units are provided only for given data and the final problem answer or answers. No intermediate values or data are expressed in SI units.

of lapped members. The most effective bond is obtained when the grain orientation of the members is parallel, as shown in Fig. 12.1*a*. With such an arrangement, bond strengths on the order of the ultimate shear strength of the wood can often be obtained. The shear transfer with a perpendicular grain orientation of members, as shown in Fig. 12.1*b*, is also effective, although the strength may not be quite as great as in case *a*. A load transfer in tension such as the butt joint shown in Fig. 12.1*c* is much less effective. The bond strength is typically on the order of the allowable tension strength of the wood for most softwoods. As a consequence, most uses of adhesives in wood construction are related to shear transfer of load. For example, rather than a butt type joint transferring tension, the joint is usually modified in a way that shear transfer of forces is obtained. The scarf or finger joints shown in Fig. 12.1*d* and *e* illustrate this approach.

One of the most important reasons for using adhesives is to construct composite systems which economize material usage. Adhesives enable different grades of wood to be assembled in the most efficient manner, minimizing the effect of defects on strength and stiffness. Also, many composite combinations are feasible only with the use of adhesives. Because a properly bonded joint can provide efficient load transfer, a full utilization of material is often possible where it would not be the case with mechanical connection devices.

Another advantage of adhesive bonding is that building components can be preassembled. Stressed-skin panels, trusses, and built-up box or I beams are typical

(a)

(b)

(c)

(d)

(e)

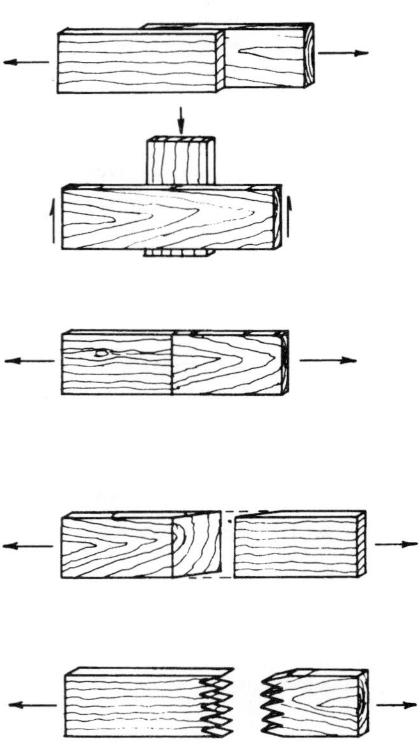

FIG. 12.1 Typical adhesive-bonded joints.

examples. Not only is on-site labor reduced, but the bonding process can be highly controlled in a factory environment.

A third advantage is that adhesive bonding increases the rigidity of the joint and enables the full strength of the materials to be utilized. Composite construction such as sandwich panels or skin-stress panels illustrate examples where full advantage of the material is taken.

Special consideration must be given to environmental conditions when using adhesives. Of particular concern are temperature and moisture. Some adhesives are sensitive to these parameters. For example, many epoxies begin to lose strength at 150°F (65.6°C), a temperature that might be found in roof sections on unusually hot days. Also, certain adhesives deteriorate in the presence of moisture. A typical example is the adhesive used in many types of interior plywood. To ensure that the adhesive is compatible with the environment, the adhesive properties must be carefully matched to the expected temperature and moisture conditions. Also, unplanned conditions, such as leaks in roofs, moisture condensation on walls, wet-dry cycles during construction, and high heat during a fire, deserve consideration in selecting the proper adhesive.

12.1.2 Structural Applications for Adhesives

Structural applications of adhesives can be categorized by the function of their application. The U.S.D.A. Forest Service[1] suggests the following five categories:

1. *Prime structural:* The adhesive contributes to strength and stiffness for the life of the structure. Typical examples include glued-laminated (glulam) beams, plywood, and various built-up systems.
2. *Semistructural:* The adhesive contributes to the stiffness for the life of the structure. Examples include the use of adhesives in floor systems and subfloors as a supplement to nailing.
3. *Temporary structural:* The adhesive provides strength and stiffness for a period shorter than the life of the structure (such as resisting racking stresses while being transported).
4. *Secondary structural:* The adhesive is used in cases where failures due to service loading would not involve life, safety, or structural integrity and would be readily recognized and easily repaired.
5. *Nonstructural:* Adhesives are used to attach accessories such as trim.

Structural applications of adhesives also can be categorized by the means of their application. The following classifications are suggested:

1. *Manufactured components:* Adhesives are applied at a plant or factory to produce a component for later shipment to the construction site. Examples range from plywood panels to major sections of modular homes.
2. *Field construction:* The adhesive is applied at the site during construction. Floor systems, gusset plates, and wood-to-concrete bonding are typical examples.
3. *Repair:* The adhesive is used to repair, strengthen, or stiffen components which have been (and usually still are) in service. Epoxy injection of deteriorated or failed timber members is a typical example.

For any structural use of adhesives, care must be taken during each phase of application. The glueline joints must be properly designed, the selection of adhesives must be compatible with the substrates and environment, and the mixing and use of bonding equipment must ensure control over all variables in the bonding process. After completion of the bonding, inspection (and possibly testing) must be performed, and care must be taken in handling the completed assembly. In most cases, the quality control needed for bonding with adhesives must be greater than that generally used in construction practice. Lack of control during any phase can lead to poor bonds and possible failure of the structure in service.

12.2 TYPES OF ADHESIVES AND THEIR PROPERTIES

A wide variety of adhesives are currently being used in the construction industry. The uninitiated can easily be overwhelmed in trying to select the best adhesive for a particular application. Described in this section are adhesives for use in both controlled and uncontrolled environments.

12.2.1 Classification of Adhesives

Material for bonding wood can be divided into two broad groups: synthetic adhesives and natural adhesives. The synthetic adhesives are usually subdivided into thermosetting and thermoplastic adhesives. Synthetic adhesives consist of specific chemicals that are mixed or reacted under controlled conditions to produce an adhesive product. A wide range of properties can be obtained with such manufacturing processes and the resulting adhesives are similar to commercial plastics in many respects.

Synthetic Thermosetting Adhesives. Thermosetting adhesives become hard, infusible, and insoluble by a chemical reaction when the proper catalyst is added to the resin. The reaction is not reversible once cure is obtained. There are three general types of thermosetting adhesives used in the wood construction industry.

Resorcinol-Formaldehyde Resins. This type of adhesive is produced from two chemicals: resorcinol, a flaky material, and formaldehyde (in water solution). Complete reaction of the components results in a fully set adhesive. Therefore, during manufacture only a portion of the needed formaldehyde is added. To prepare the adhesive for use, sufficient formaldehyde is added to allow the reaction to go to completion. The adhesive is thus normally sold as a two-component system with a liquid resin and a powdered catalyst or hardener. Phenol is sometimes added to the resorcinol-formaldehyde combination to produce a lower-cost adhesive. The disadvantage of adding phenol is that an increase in temperature, proportional to the amount of phenol, is needed for adequate curing. Resorcinol mixes are exothermic (tend to increase in temperature) after the hardener is added. Cooling may thus be required when mixing large batches. One disadvantage of the system is that assemblies bonded with resorcinol adhesives must be held under pressure during the normal cure time of 4 to 16 hours at room temperature. The resorcinols provide curable waterproof bonds that resist chemical, weather, or insect attacks. They also adhere to a variety of chemically treated woods. They provide excellent joint strength and are used frequently to bond lumber laminates. A summary of important properties is given in Table 12.1.

Melamine-Formaldehyde Resins. These adhesives are produced as a condensation product of melamine and formaldehyde. Sometimes urea is added as a cost-savings measure. Melamine resins are usually produced in powdered form. In some cases the catalyst is incorporated and only water is added, although some mixes require the catalyst and possibly a filler to be added separately. Melamines provide a strong, water-resistant bond. However, heat is required to set the adhesive (usually greater than 160°F) (71.1°C). Melamines are thus used primarily in factory-manufactured components. One of the principal uses in component manufacture is for bonding scarf and finger joints. See Table 12.1 for additional properties.

Epoxy Adhesives. The resin is produced in liquid form by the reaction of epichlorohydrin with bisphenol in the presence of sodium hydroxide. The hardener is usually a polyamine compound with specific ones selected to provide a pot life varying from a few minutes to several hours. Flexibilizers are sometimes added to one of the two components to accommodate movement. Upon curing, there is usually less than 0.2 percent shrinkage. Epoxy resins are available which cure in the presence of high moisture. The mix proportions and additives can be varied to produce a range of material characteristics. The desirable properties for epoxy resins as used for wood structures are shown in Table 12.1. Epoxy resins, in general, also exhibit the following characteristics: (1) resist acids, alkalies, and organic chemicals, (2) cure without volatile by-products, (3) cure without external heat, and (4) accept various thickening agents. Epoxies are thermosetting resins; hence once they have hardened, they will not again liquify when heated (although they may soften). Epoxies have had limited use in building construction such as bonding wood to aggregate substrates. However, epoxies are the primary materials used in the repair of wood structures.

Synthetic Thermoplastic Adhesives. Thermoplastic adhesives are usually reacted as supplied to the user. Their application involves physical change such as film forming through loss of solvent or melting and solidification upon cooling. The bonding process is generally reversible by adding solvent or by reheating. Most thermoplastics exhibit significant creep under load and are not recommended for bonded joints that are highly stressed. The following types of thermoplastics are used in building construction.

Polyvinyl-Acetate-Resin Emulsions. These resin emulsions are commonly known as "white glues." They are manufactured as an emulsion in which many small adhesive particles are suspended in a protected colloid. Most of these resins come in ready-to-use liquid form and require no mixing. Curing usually depends on a partial loss of solvent into the substrate allowing a film to form. The primary applications have been in mobile and modular home manufacturing where immediate strength and stiffening are needed but long-term strength is accommodated by nails or other fasteners. These emulsions offer the advantages of being ready to use, easy to apply, setting rapidly, and curing to a colorless bondline. However, they tend to creep under high stress and offer only fair moisture and water resistance.

Elastomeric Adhesives. These adhesives contain an elastomeric material such as natural or synthetic rubber providing a somewhat flexible bondline. The basic elastomer is present in a sufficient quantity to act as a binder. Through the use of proper compounding techniques, the flexibility of the adhesive is varied as desired. Elastomeric adhesives used in construction can be divided into two groups: contact

TABLE 12.1 Building Construction Adhesives—Physical and Working Properties, Typical Applications, and Use Conditions

Types of properties; applications and uses	Synthetic thermoset			Synthetic thermoplastic				
	Resorcinol-formaldehyde	Melamine-formaldehyde	Epoxy	Resin emulsions	Elastomeric contact	Elastomeric mastic	Hot melt	Casein
Physical form commercially available	Liquid	Liquid, powder	Liquid	Liquid, powder	Liquid	Liquid	Solid	Powder
Shipping container	Bulk, drum, pail, small cans	Drum	Drum, pail, small cans	Bulk, drum, pail, small cans	Drum, pail, small cans	Drum, pail, small cans, cartridge	Drum, pail	Drum, small cans
Shelf life at 70°F (21°C)	3 to over 9 mo	Less than 3 to over 9 mo	3 to over 9 mo	Less than 3, up to 9 mo	Less than 3, up to 9 mo	Less than 3, up to 9 mo	Over 9 mo	3 to over 9 mo
Mix additives	Catalyst or hardener	Catalyst or hardener, water, fillers, or extenders	Catalyst or hardener	None, or catalyst, or hardener and water	None	None	None	Water
Working life at 70°F (21°C)	1 to 6 h	1 to over 6 h	Under 1 to 6 h	Over 6 h	Over 6 h	1 to over 6 h	Over 6 h	1 to 6 h
Spreading equipment	Roller, spreader, brush, extruder	Roller spreader	Trowel, brush, paint roller, pressure injection equipment	Roller spreader, spray, brush, paint roller	Roller spreader, spray, curtain coater, trowel, brush, paint roller	Pressure gun, trowel, cartridge	Roller spreader, pressure gun, curtain coater	Roller spreader, extruder, brush, paint roller
Assembly time tolerance at 70°F (21°C)	60 to 90 min maximum	Up to 8 h maximum	20 min maximum	20 min maximum	60 to 90 min maximum	20 min maximum	Seconds or less	60 to 90 min maximum
Pressure application and typical pressure, lb/in^2 (kPa)	Mechanical press, nail bonding; 25 to over 100 (172 to 689)	Hydraulic press; 100 to 200 (689 to 1378)	Pneumatic clamps, nail bonding; 25 to 150 (172 to 1034)	Mechanical press; 50 to 200 (345 to 1378)	Nip rolls, air press, nail bonding; 25 to 100 (172 to 689)	Nail bonding; 25 to 100 (172 to 689)	Nip rolls, pneumatic clamps; 25 to 150 (172 to 1034)	Mechanical press, nail bonding; 25 to 200 (172 to 1378)
Adhesive cure temperature	68 to over 212°F (20 to over 100°C)	87 to over 212°F (31 to over 100°C)	Below 68 to 87°F (below 20 to 30°C)	Below 68 to over 212°F (below 20 to over 100°C)	68 to 86°F (20 to 30°C)	Below 68 to 86°F (20 to 30°C)	Above 212°F (above 100°C)	Below 68 to 86°F (below 20 to 30°C)

Cure or setting time of adhesive*	4 to 16 h; under 10 min above 212°F (100°C)	Under 10 min above 212°F (100°C)	½ to 16 h	Under ½ to 16 h	Immediate use	Immediate use or under ½ h	Immediate use	4 to 16 h
Interior and exterior applications	Primarily exterior, some interior	Primary exterior, some interior	Interior and exterior	Primary interior some exterior	Primary interior	Primary interior	Primary interior	Primary interior
Suitability for stressed joints	Yes	Yes	With mechanical fasteners only	With mechanical fasteners only	No	With mechanical fasteners only	No	Yes
Heat resistance of bondine	To 150°F (66°C)	To 150°F (66°C)	To 150°F (66°C)	To 110°F (43°C)	To 110°F (43°C)	To 110°F (43°C)	To 110°F (43°C)	To 150°F (66°C)
Strong-as-wood shear bond strength	Yes	Yes	Yes	In some instances	Usually not	Usually not	Usually not	Yes
Spread rates, lb/MGSL (N/km^2)†	50 to 100 (2395 to 4790)	35 to 50 (1677 to 2395)	35 to 50 (1677 to 2395)	35 to 50 (1677 to 2395)	35 to 50 (1677 to 2395)	200 to 300 (9580 to 14,370)	100 to 150 (4790 to 7185)	50 to 100 (2395 to 4790)
Structural timbers	Yes	—	—	—	—	—		Yes
Stressed-skin panels	Yes	Yes	—	—	—	—	—	—
Folded plates	Yes	—	—	—	—	—	—	
Ridge beams	Yes	—	—	—	—	—	—	
Box beams	Yes	—	—	—	—	—	—	Yes
Moldings	—	—	—	Yes	Yes	—	—	Yes
High-density plastic laminates	Yes	—	—	Yes	—	—	Yes	Yes
Finger and scarf joints	Yes	Yes	—	—	—	—	—	—
Sandwich panels	Yes	Yes	—	—	—	—	—	—
Treated wood	Yes	Yes	—	—	—	—	—	—
Kitchen units	—	—	—	Yes	Yes	—	—	—
Furring strips	—	—	Yes	—	Yes	—	—	—
Parquet floors	—	—	Yes	—	—	Yes	—	—
Drywall and paneling	—	—	—	Yes	Yes	Yes	—	—
Underlayment	—	—	—	Yes	—	Yes	—	Yes
Plywood floors	—	—	—	—	—	Yes	—	Yes
Gusset plates	—	—	—	—	—	Yes	—	Yes
Repair by injection	—	—	Yes	—	—	—	—	—

*Cure time here is the lapse of time at 70°F (21°C) after mating the adherends under pressure application, but before the assembly can be moved or pressure released.

†lb/MGSL is pounds of solids per thousand square feet single bondline (newtons of solids per square kilometer).

adhesives and mastics. Contact adhesives are applied to all mating surfaces and partially dried. When the mated surfaces come into contact, they adhere instantly. These adhesives produce thin gluelines suitable only for well-fitted joints because of their low viscosity at application. They are most suitably applied by spraying, roller coating, or trowel. Mastic adhesives, which are very viscous, are usually applied with a trowel or putty knife. Thick bondlines can be obtained, and the material is usually applied only to one surface. Mastics are often used in combination with nails to bond floor or wall systems to joints or studs. Either of these elastomeric adhesives is principally used where only moderate strength is required. They are easy to use, economical, and require only brief pressure during curing. Because of the volatile solvents used in these adhesives, they should be used in well-ventilated and fire-safe areas. The elastomerics may also creep in stressed joints and have low heat resistance. Properties and characteristics of elastomerics are shown in Table 12.1.

Hot-Melt Adhesives. These adhesives consist of synthetic polymers formulated with additives such as rosin and similar thermoplastic materials. The application is performed by melting the adhesive using suitable equipment and applying in molten form, at temperatures between 250 and 450°F (121 and 232°C). The adhesive sets by cooling. Hence the material must be mated quickly to ensure bond quality. Hot melts are used to install certain types of veneer bonds and to seal roof assemblies. They also have been used to quickly seal leaks during epoxy injection of structures being repaired. The hot melts are likely to creep under stress, lack solvent resistance, and do not exhibit good heat resistance. Characteristics are described in Table 12.1.

Natural Adhesives. These adhesives are derived from natural sources rather than produced synthetically. They had wide applicability prior to World War II, but have been generally replaced by synthetics. One type still used is the casein adhesive. It is a dry powder that is derived from skimmed milk and combined with several alkaline chemicals and extenders. It is usually sold as a dry blend which is prepared by mixing with water. A few minutes after mixing, the casein usually becomes quite thick. A stand time is then allowed during which the mix viscosity gradually reduces. After agitation, the adhesive is ready for use. Although pressure is required during setting, the caseins cure at normal temperatures as well as temperatures near freezing. They are currently used on an occasional basis for on-site bonding jobs. Caseins offer the advantages of high bond strength, rigid bond lines, resistance to temperature variation, setting capabilities at low temperatures, and good gap-filling properties. The disadvantages are the need to prepare the mix and allow for "stand time," susceptibility to microorganism attack, and poor resistance to moisture exposure.

A second type of natural adhesive is the animal adhesive. While one of the oldest adhesives known, it has generally been replaced by synthetics with superior properties. It is now used only occasionally for special bonding jobs.

12.2.2 Selection of an Adhesive

With the wide choice of adhesives available, the selection of the most suitable adhesive can be difficult. The following factors should be considered before making a selection.

Durability. Durability is usually associated with two environmental aspects: temperature and moisture. Many adhesives tend to weaken when exposed to either excessive heat or moisture. Some adhesives are only sensitive to these effects during application and curing. However, care must be taken to match the adhesive to the environmental application.

Strength and Stiffness. An effectively glued connection requires certain strength and stiffness characteristics. An evaluation of these requirements may necessitate a structural analysis of the system. A knowledge of the basic bond strength for various loading conditions may also be needed. For structural applications this information is often unavailable. In such cases bondline strength tests are recommended. A number of standard test procedures are available to evaluate strength. An expert should be consulted for guidance when such information is not provided by the manufacturer.

Methods of Application. Selection of an adhesive may well depend on the method of application. Factors to consider are surface conditions, moisture content of wood, temperature at time of application, equipment required, setting time, and final cure time. Some adhesives can be spread, sprayed, or rolled. Others require special means of application. Manufacturers' guidelines should be carefully followed for a successful bond.

Physical and Working Properties. The wide variety of properties may play a crucial role in adhesive selection. Preparation may range from ready-to-use to water dispersion to the addition of catalysts or hardeners. Viscosity also varies greatly with consistency, ranging from that of lightweight oil to being thick and puttylike. The pot life (the time from mixing to initial set) may range from a few minutes to weeks. Storage or shelf life (time from purchase to use) may also vary considerably. Other important properties include odor during use, fire hazard during application, health hazards from human contact, and potential for staining.

Cost Considerations. The actual price of the adhesive is often a poor indicator of total cost. Price after mixing in solution offers a better comparison. However, the amount required on the bond line also must be taken into account. The measurement frequently used is pounds of adhesive mix needed to bond 1000 ft^2 (92.9 m^2) of single-glueline surface [lb/MSGL (N/km^2)]. Many manufacturers list a range of spread rate in their technical literature and on labels. Use of these data allows the engineer to predict adhesive cost accurately. Even this cost may be misleading since labor cost can often be the major pricing component. Mix and surface preparation, application equipment, and fabrication costs can be the deciding factors in a cost analysis of adhesive-bonded construction.

Selection Guide. To provide the designer with guidance in selecting the most suitable adhesive, Table 12.1, taken from Ref. 1, is provided. This table catalogs the general physical and working properties of various adhesive types along with typical application and use conditions. It provides only general guidelines, however, and manufacturers' instructions should be followed closely when using any product.

12.2.3 Bonding Characteristics to Substrates

The substrate is the material to which the adhesive is applied. Obviously, the bonding characteristics of the adhesive are affected by the substrate. Too often adhesive manufacturers provide information on the strength of the adhesive without reference to the substrate. While providing general insight into the adhesive characteristics, such information is of little use in an engineering analysis. There are several substrate properties that are important to the bonding process. Many of these are related to the density of the wood. Density is the weight per unit volume of the wood. In general, the greater the density, the higher the strength properties and the modulus of elasticity. On the other hand, porosity decreases with an increase in density.

Porosity. While good bonding does not require the substrate to be porous, the bonding of porous substrates is easier than that of nonporous ones. When adhesive penetrates the pores, the area of surface contact between adhesive and adherend is increased. In addition, the relationship between adhesive and substrate at the microlevel may change, that is, from shear to bearing. Since wood used in construction is usually porous, excellent bonding results can be obtained. However, porosity can occasionally produce problems such as excessive migration of the adhesive from the glueline, resulting in a joint with an inadequate film of adhesive.

Surface Properties. Often the strength of the bond depends on the wettability of the substrate by the adhesive solvent. Also important are smoothness and surface fit. Of primary importance is the cleanliness of the surface. Deposits of oil, airborne contaminants, or wood extractives may severely reduce the bonding effectiveness.

Dimensional Stability. Adhesives must be compatible with the expected dimensional changes of the substrate. Wood, for example, has greater dimensional variability across the grain than longitudinal to the grain. Grains of substrates oriented perpendicular to each other may have differing expansion characteristics. Often adhesives are tested with the perpendicular grain arrangement to assess the glueline compatibility. Usually dimensional problems can be minimized by care in construction of mechanical constraints.

12.2.4 Methods of Preparation and Application

Methods of preparation vary considerably. Some adhesives come ready to use, others require mixing with water, while some require mixing with catalysts or hardeners. In all cases, the manufacturers provide mixing instructions which should be followed carefully. Methods of application may be less clearly described by manufacturers. Adhesives are often pumped in various ways. Air pumps allow even high-viscosity adhesives to be pumped. A positive screw conveyer pump will also handle high-viscosity materials. Low-viscosity materials are often handled with a positive rotary pump or a peristaltic pump. Centrifugal pumps are are also used.

The simplest way to apply low-viscosity adhesives is by squeeze can, bottles, or sprinkler cans. More expensive devices are used to (1) control the amount of adhesive, (2) control adhesive placement, and (3) minimize labor costs. Devices such as push boxes, pressurized caulking guns, or air guns give varying degrees of control. Spreaders are often used to obtain a uniform spread along with spray applications and certain coatings.

12.3 COMPUTATION OF DESIGN STRESSES FOR BONDED WOOD ELEMENTS

In the design of adhesive bonded timber, the engineer has traditionally taken one of two approaches. In the first case, the adhesive selected for use is stronger and more durable than the adherends under all load and end use conditions. For such cases, the adhesive is not a design factor. However, the process of selecting such an adhesive may be quite difficult and require extensive testing and evaluation. The alternative approach is to develop a set of design stress criteria which enable the engineer to both rationally analyze and design the component. This approach requires not only analytical procedures to predict the actual stress conditions at critical points of the bonding surface, but a set of allowable stresses for comparison.

Most references in the literature address adhesive design in a qualitative manner. Descriptions usually concentrate on schemes for minimizing stress concentrations, tension bond stresses, or joint eccentricity. Absent from the literature is a discussion of allowable design parameters for adhesives. Thus most adhesive joints have historically been designed empirically. The approach of proportioning on the basis of prototype tests works well for mass production as found in certain manufactured components such as plywood, scarf joints, or laminated beams. However, for many applications in building construction, this approach is time-consuming, expensive, and often overly conservative. The adhesive-using community has not adopted a design stress approach for bonded joints and the design codes do not specify allowable stresses for adhesive-bonded timber. The codification process will develop slowly because of the multiplicity of adhesives available. An outline of parameters to consider in developing design stress criteria is given in the following sections.

12.3.1 Methodology for Computing Allowable Stresses for Adhesives Bonded to Wood

Computation of the allowable stress for an adhesive bonded to a wood joint involves several parameters. Generally a basic strength is determined experimentally for a given adhesive and wood species and then reduced for various effects. The most important of these effects are variability factor, exposure conditions, duration of load, aging, and bond configuration conditions. In addition, certain parameters may be included in the allowable stress computations if they are excluded from the actual design stress computations for a given loading condition and bond configuration. Typical examples of such parameters include glueline thickness, grain orientation, overlap length, and bond configuration. An allowable glueline stress F_g can thus take the following form:

$$F_g = \text{mean stress} \times \text{applicable modification factors } f_1 \text{ to } f_5$$

where f_1 = variability factor
f_2 = exposure conditions factors
f_3 = duration of load factor
f_4 = aging factor
f_5 = bond configuration factors

The basic mean stress can be determined from short-term specimen testing. The type of test depends on the specified bond conditions, but generally is either a shear, a tension, or a combined stress specimen. The variability factor is used to reflect the scatter of test results. To be consistent with the procedures for determining the mechanical properties of lumber, the ASTM D 2915 guidelines[2] are recommended. Thus the mean stress should be reduced to the 5 percent exclusion value, or a value that is exceeded by 95 percent of the specimens. ASTM D 2915 describes the methodology for computing this value.

The exposure condition factors depend on the expected end use of the bonded member. Parameters that might be included are high temperature (short-term exposure), high moisture (short-term exposure), fire resistance, cold temperatures, chemical reagent exposure, microbiologic exposure, insect attack, mold exposure, and cyclic loading (fatigue).

The duration-of-load factor is used to correlate the test specimen short-term load rate (usually 5 to 10 min) to the long-term loading expected in service. It has been demonstrated that wood exhibits a decrease in ultimate strength as a function of load-duration time. A similar relationship is needed for adhesives bonded to wood. The conventional procedure of applying a constant load and leaving specimens to fail at successive stress levels is time-consuming and thus not often used. The Prot method[3] can be used to approximate the load-duration effect in a much shorter time period. This method uses an increasing rate of stress to failure as a means of predicting the load-duration effect.

The aging factor is also time-consuming to determine experimentally. Thus quite often an accelerated aging test is utilized to approximate this effect. These tests usually consist of successive soaking, boiling, and drying cycles. Since little information exists on correlating accelerated aging to actual aging effects for adhesives, this factor is usually an approximation.

Finally, the bond configuration factor is sometimes incorporated into the allowable stress formulation. This factor reflects the effect of stress concentrations and other variations which are a function of the arrangement of the bonded members. Lap length, shape of bonded surfaces, and glueline thickness are such parameters that might be considered.

Codes or standards are not available which provide allowable stress information for adhesives bonded to wood. However, to illustrate the procedure for determining allowable stress values, an epoxy (Sikadur Hi-Mod LV) will be used. This epoxy has been used in the field repair and rehabilitation of wood structures and is manufactured by the Sika Chemical Company of Lyndhurst, N.J. Although the design of an adhesive joint may be based on one or more of three stress conditions (shear, bending, and tension), shear is by far the most common condition encountered in construction. Therefore, only the allowable shear stress is developed here. The basic specimen test to determine the mean shear stress is a single-lap shear test. Although several tests are available, the most widely used is ASTM D 905.[4] The wood species selected was No. 2 KD southern pine with the grain orientation parallel. For an evaluation of the allowable bond shear stress, 100 specimens from three lots were tested. Using the same statistical procedures as are used for evaluating the allowable stresses of structural lumber, ASTM D 2915,[2] the data in Table 12.2 were obtained. The variability factor is the 5 percent exclusion limit (EL) if the percent difference between EL and the lower tolerance limit (TL) is less than 5 percent. Otherwise, a value of 1.05TL is used. Taking the ratio of 1.05TL and the average bond shear stress yields a variability factor of 0.302. For dry-use conditions, the exposure conditions factor is 1.0. The duration of load factor was obtained through a conventional load-duration test. The results indicated that the standard load-duration curve for wood[5] provides an excellent measure of that effect on the epoxy-bonded

TABLE 12.2 Statistical Data for Computing the Shear Bond Strength of No. 2 KD Southern Pine with Sikadur Hi-Mod LV Adhesive

Strength of characteristic	Stress, lb/in^2
Average bond shear stress	1312
Confidence interval for the mean (95% level)	1228 to 1396
Standard deviation	422
5% exclusion limit	584
Lowest tolerance limit for the 5% exclusion limit	377

Note: 1 lb/in^2 = 6.89 kPa.

joints. Extrapolating the 5-min specimen load tests to a 10-year normal load duration yields a load-duration factor of 0.60. The aging factor is taken as unity based on a correlation between accelerated aging tests and exterior aging conducted over a 4-year period.

The bond configuration factor requires special attention. Experimental tests[6] on various bonded lapped members have shown that the bond strength varies directly with the ratio of lap length to member thickness. In addition, the average failure shear stress on a small shear block specimen is significantly larger than the average failure stress on a large bonded joint of dimensioned lumber. The size factor between a standard shear block and a lapped nominal 2- by 6-in (38.1- by 139.7-mm)* joint [with 5½-in (139.7-mm) lap length] has been found to be 2. Applying the reciprocal of this parameter as a shape reduction factor gives a bond configuration factor of 0.5. The allowable glueline shear stress is thus

$$F_g^P = 1312 \times 0.302 \times 1 \times 0.6 \times 0.5 = 119 \text{ lb/in}^2 \text{ (819 kPa)}$$

The lap length effect was determined by tests on bonded dimension lumber.[6] Based on tests over a wide range of lap length to thickness ratios ℓ/t in which the previous adjustment factors were made, the following formula for allowable glueline shear stress has been developed:

$$F_g^P = \tfrac{2}{3} F_v \ell/t \tag{12.1}$$

where F_v is the allowable shear stress for the wood species as tabulated in the NDS specifications.[5] Using $\ell/t = 2$ for a standard shear block and $F_v = 90$ lb/in^2 (620 kPa) for No. 2 southern pine for dry use and normal load duration, Eq. (12.1) gives $F_g = 120$ lb/in^2 (827 kPa). Thus an excellent correlation is obtained between the independent test results when adjusted to allowable stress values.

The resulting allowable stress formula is for parallel-to-grain orientation and shear between the lapped members. Similar computations can be made for members with perpendicular-to-grain orientation. The resulting formula is

$$F_g^Q = \tfrac{1}{3} F_v \ell/t \tag{12.2}$$

For other grain orientations the use of Hankinson's formula is recommended:

*All SI units shown for sawn lumber are for the actual net dimensions corresponding to the nominal dimension indicated.

$$F_g = \frac{F_g^P F_g^Q}{F_g^P \sin^2 \theta + F_g^Q \cos^2 \theta} \tag{12.3}$$

where θ is the acute angle between grain lines of the lapped members.

In the example presented here, variations of the actual bond stress are incorporated into the allowable stress formulas. For example, a typical shear stress variation is shown in Fig. 12.2. The stress is relatively uniform except for the stress concentrations at the leading and trailing edges of the joint. Failure of such joints begins at these concentrations and spreads over the joint. The magnitude of the stress concentrations is primarily a function of the lap length to member thickness ratio. In addition, such parameters as load eccentricities may produce some tension bond stresses as well as shear stresses. Since adjustment is made for these effects in the allowable stress formulas, the actual stress can be computed as the average shear stress with tensile stresses neglected. The appropriate formula for the actual shear stress in a lapped adhesive-bonded joint is

$$f_g = \frac{V}{A} \tag{12.4}$$

where V is the shear force on the lapped surface and A is the surface area of the lapped joint.

12.4 BUILT-UP COMPONENTS USING ADHESIVES

A wide variety of adhesive-bonded manufactured components are available for use in the construction industry. Such prefabricated components are often more eco-

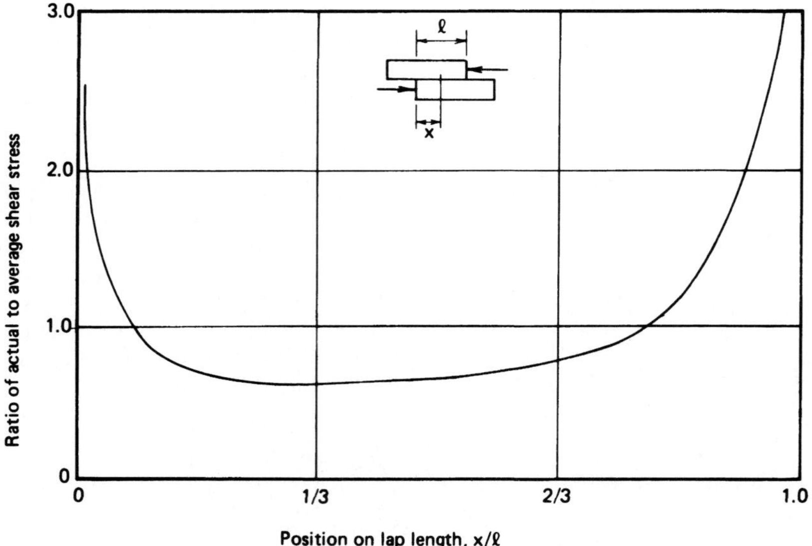

FIG. 12.2 Typical line shear stress distribution of lapped joint (angle of load to grain = 0°).

nomical than conventional construction, and their use may reduce the overall construction time. Typical examples range from relatively standard components such as plywood and glulam timbers to more specialized structural components such as stressed-skin and sandwich panels, trusses, box beams, I beams, and folded plates. Design procedures for such structural components are described in other chapters. Only design aspects associated with adhesive strength are discussed here. However, before discussing design, mention should be made of plant facilities.

For plant bonding of components, the fabrication and storage areas should be dry and temperature controlled. The lumber used is usually stress graded and has restrictions on dimensional variations, cross-grain, knots and knotholes, twist, cup, and moisture content. The surfaces to be bonded are often resurfaced to ensure contact over the entire mating surface and to minimize dimensional variations. Such resurfacing also ensures dimensional uniformity, which is essential for proper installation and performance. The adhesive to be selected must possess adequate structural characteristics for the particular application and must possess required working and curing properties.

Design computations for glued composite systems are often based on the use of the transformed section concept. The moduli of elasticity of the skins and stringers are usually different; thus transforming the section enables standard design procedures to be utilized. Specific types of manufactured components are discussed in the following sections. For the formulas presented, the following symbols are used, as shown in Fig. 12.3:

a = Joist spacing or panel width
b = Joist or stringer width
d = Joist or stringer depth
E = Modulus of elasticity; subscript s denotes joist or stringer flexural modulus, subscripts 1 and 2 denote top and bottom skin compressive modulus, and F denotes top and bottom skin flexural modulus
h = Distance between centroids of principal moment-carrying components
n = Number of stringers in panel
t = Thickness of skins or facings
V = Maximum shear per width for panels or maximum shear for beams
w = Thickness of web

12.4.1 Joists with Sheathing

A standard framing system consisting of plywood sheathing and lumber joists as shown in Fig. 12.3a is sometimes bonded with an adhesive to provide increased strength and stiffness. The bondline shear stress formula is given in Table 12.3. This formula is based on the assumption that the system acts as a one-way beam in the joist direction and that the ends are simply supported. The unbonded bending stiffness coefficient $(\mathrm{EI})_u$ represents the effect of the sheathing and joist acting independently, while the rigidly bonded coefficient $(\mathrm{EI})_b$ includes the composite behavior. The bondline shear stress f_g should be compared with the allowable value when designing such built-up members.

EXAMPLE 12.1 Determine the glueline shear stress for a bonded floor system (dry use) consisting of 2- by 8-in (38.1- by 184-mm) No. 2 southern pine joists spaced at 16 in (406 mm) on centers with ⅝-in (15.9-mm) sanded species group 2 plywood

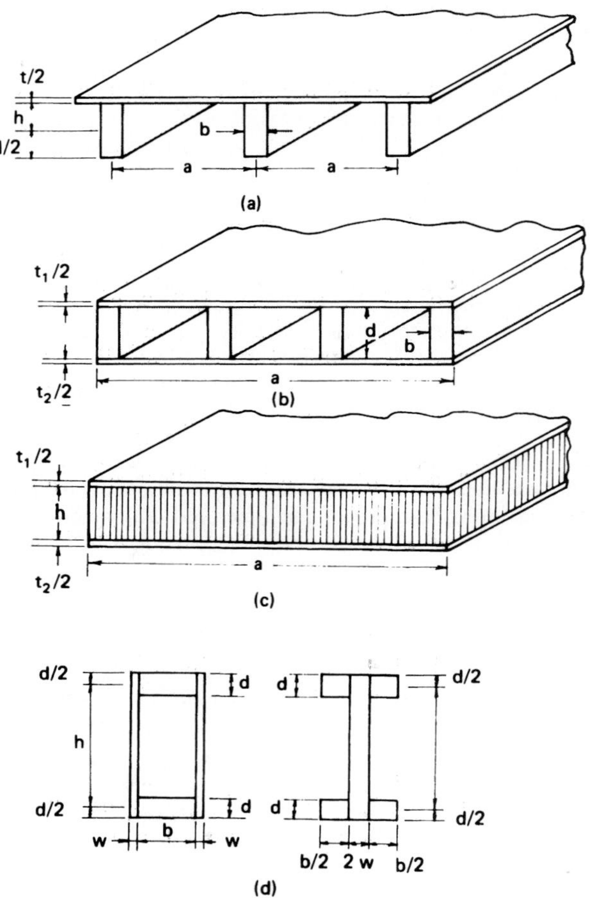

FIG. 12.3 Adhesive-bonded panel and beam systems. (*a*) Joists with sheathing; (*b*) stressed-skin panels; (*c*) sandwich panel; (*d*) Built-up beams.

(dry use, grade-stress level S-1) laid with the face grain direction perpendicular to the joist direction. Assume that plywood edges are bonded so that the sheathing is completely effective. Use a 40-lb/ft^2 (1916-Pa) uniformly distributed loading with a joist span of $L = 12$ ft (3.66 m).

SOLUTION: The following data are found in the *Plywood Design Specification* (PDS)[7] and the *National Design Specification for Wood Construction* (NDS):[5] Effective plywood flexural stiffness (which includes effects of shear deformation):

$$E_{1F} = 1.5 \times 10^6 \text{ lb/in}^2 \ (10.3 \times 10^6 \text{ kPa})$$

Compressive modulus of elasticity ($1.1 \times E_{1F}$ to exclude shear effects):

TABLE 12.3 Bondline Shear Stress Formulas for Adhesive-Bonded Components with Variations in Modulus of Elasticity

Type of construction	Unbonded bending stiffness $(EI)_u$	Rigidly bonding bending stiffness $(EI)_b$	Bondline shear stress f_g
Joists with sheathing	$\frac{1}{12}(E_{1F}at^3 + E_s bd^3)$	$\frac{E_1 at_1 E_s bdh^2}{E_1 at_1 + E_s bd} + (EI)_u$	$\frac{V}{bh}\left[1 - \frac{(EI)_u}{(EI)_b}\right]$
Stressed-skin panels	$\frac{1}{12}(E_{1F}a{t^3}_1 + E_{2F}a{t^3}_2 + nE_s bd^3)$	$\frac{[4E_1 at_1 E_2 at_2 + nE_s bd(E_1 at_1 + E_2 at_2)]h^2}{4(E_1 at_1 + E_2 at_2 + nE_s bd)} + (EI)_u$	$\frac{V[E_1 at_1(2E_2 at_2 + E_s nbd)h]}{2nb(E_1 at_1 + E_2 at_2 + E_s nbd)(EI)_b)}$
Sandwich panels	$\frac{1}{12}(E_{1F}a{t^3}_1 + E_{2F}a{t^3}_2)$	$\frac{E_1 at_1 2E_2 at_2 h^2}{E_1 at_1 + E_2 at_2} + (EI)_u$	$\frac{V}{ah}\left[1 - \frac{(EI)_u}{(EI)_b}\right]$
Built-up box or I beams	$\frac{1}{6}[Ebd^3 + E_w w(h + d)^3]$	$\frac{1}{2}Ebdh^2 + (EI)_u$	$\frac{V}{2dh}\left[1 - \frac{(EI)_u}{(EI)_b}\right]$

$$E_1 = 1.65 \times 10^6 \text{ lb/in}^2 \ (11.4 \times 10^6 \text{ kPa})$$

Joist modulus of elasticity:

$$E_s = 1.6 \times 10^6 \text{ lb/in}^2 \ (11 \times 10^6 \text{ kPa})$$

$$a = 16 \text{ in (406 mm)}$$

$$b = 1.5 \text{ in (38.1 mm)}$$

$$d = 7.25 \text{ in (184 mm)}$$

$$h = 3.94 \text{ in (100 mm)}$$

$$t = 0.625 \text{ in (15.9 mm)}$$

The maximum shear force is

$$V = \frac{wa}{2} = 40 \times 12 \times \frac{16}{12} \times \frac{1}{2} = 320 \text{ lb}$$

Substituting into the joist and sheathing formulas of Table 12.3 gives

$$(\text{EI})_u = \frac{1}{12}\left[(1.5 \times 10^6 \times 16 \times 0.625^3) + (1.6 \times 10^6 \times 1.5 \times 7.25^3)\right]$$

$$= 76.7 \times 10^6 \text{ lb·in}^2 \ (220 \times 10^9 \text{ N·mm}^2)$$

$$(\text{EI})_b = \frac{1.65 \times 10^6 \times 16 \times 0.625 \times 1.6 \times 10^6 \times 1.5 \times 7.25 \times 3.94^2}{(1.65 \times 10^6 \times 16 \times 0.625) + (1.6 \times 10^6 \times 1.5 \times 7.25)} + (76.7 \times 10^6)$$

$$= 208 \times 10^6 \text{ lb·in}^2 \ (597 \times 10^9 \text{ N·mm}^2)$$

$$f_g = \frac{320}{1.5 \times 3.94}\left(1 - \frac{76.7 \times 10^6}{208 \times 10^6}\right)$$

$$= 34.2 \text{ lb/in}^2 \ (235 \text{ kPa})$$

12.4.2 Stressed-Skin Panels

Stressed-skin panels are composites of stringers with top and bottom plywood skins. Flat stressed-skin panels are designed to act like built-up I beams with the skins resisting the bending moment stresses and the stringers resisting the shear stresses. Curved stressed-skin panels act like arch or shell-like structures. A typical flat panel is shown in Fig. 12.3*b*. The shear stress at the bondline between skin and stringer is given in Table 12.3.

EXAMPLE 12.2 Determine the bondline shear stress for a stressed-skin panel of the same configuration as in Example 12.1, except that the ⅝-in (15.9-mm) plywood is applied to both top and bottom of the stringers.

SOLUTION: For this case,

$$a = 16 \text{ in } (406 \text{ mm})$$

$$n = 2$$

$$E_{2F} = 1.5 \times 10^6 \text{ lb/in}^2 \; (10.3 \times 10^6 \text{ kPa})$$

$$E_2 = 1.65 \times 10^6 \text{ lb/in}^2 \; (11.4 \times 10^6 \text{ kPa})$$

$$t_1 = t_2 = 0.625 \text{ in } (15.9 \text{ mm})$$

$$h = 7.875 \text{ in } (200 \text{ mm})$$

and all other variables remain unchanged. Using the formulas from Table 12.3,

$$\begin{aligned}
(\text{EI})_u &= \frac{1}{12}[(1.5 \times 10^6 \times 16 \times 0.625^3) + (1.5 \times 10^6 \times 16 \times 0.625^3) \\
&\quad + (2 \times 1.6 \times 10^6 \times 1.5 \times 7.25^3) \\
&= 1.53 \times 10^6 \text{ lb·in}^2 \; (439 \times 10^9 \text{ N·mm}^2)
\end{aligned}$$

$$\begin{aligned}
(\text{EI})_b &= \frac{\begin{array}{c}\{(4 \times 1.65 \times 10^6 \times 16 \times 0.625 \times 1.65 \times 10^6 \times 16 \times 0.625) \\ + (2 \times 1.6 \times 10^6 \times 1.5 \times 7.25) \times [(1.65 \times 10^6 \times 16 \times 0.625) \\ + (1.65 \times 10^6 \times 16 \times 0.625)]\}3.94^2\end{array}}{\begin{array}{c}4[(1.65 \times 10^6 \times 16 \times 0.625) + (1.65 \times 10^6 \times 16 \times 0.625) \\ + (2 \times 1.6 \times 10^6 \times 1.5 \times 7.25)\end{array}} \\
&\quad + 153 \times 10^6 \\
&= 281 \times 10^6 \text{ lb·in}^2 \; (807 \times 10^9 \text{ N·mm}^2)
\end{aligned}$$

$$\begin{aligned}
f_g &= \frac{\begin{array}{c}320(1.65 \times 10^6 \times 16 \times 0.625)[(2 \times 1.65 \times 10^6 \times 16 \times 0.625) \\ + (1.6 \times 10^6 \times 2 \times 1.5 \times 7.25)]3.94\end{array}}{\begin{array}{c}(2 \times 2 \times 1.5)[(1.65 \times 10^6 \times 16 \times 0.625) + (1.65 \times 10^6 \times 16 \times 0.625) \\ + (1.6 \times 10^6 \times 2 \times 1.5 \times 7.25)]281 \times 10^6\end{array}} \\
&= 7.86 \text{ lb/in}^2 \; (54.2 \text{ kPa})
\end{aligned}$$

12.4.3 Sandwich Panels

A sandwich panel is an assembly consisting of a lightweight core laminated between two plywood facings, as shown in Fig. 12.3*c*. The core material may consist of resin impregnated paper honeycomb, a rigid plastic foam, or a combination of the two. Structural sandwich panels can be designed for axial and transverse loading. For such panels, the bondline stress is given in Table 12.3.

12.4.4 Built-up Beams

Wood-plywood box or I beams are popular because of their efficient use of materials to optimize strength. Two examples are shown in Fig. 12.3*d*. The use of adhesives is essential to the successful performance of such components. The bond shear stress formula is given in Table 12.3 with the dimensions shown in Fig. 12.3*d*. *E* is the elastic modulus of the lumber flanges and *Ew* is the compression modulus of the webs.

EXAMPLE 12.3 Determine the bondline shear stress for a built-up I beam as shown in Fig. 12.3*d* with the following properties:

$$d = 1.5 \text{ in (38.1 mm)}$$

$$h = 9.75 \text{ in (248 mm)}$$

$$b = 7 \text{ in (178 mm)}$$

$$2w = \tfrac{3}{4} \text{ in (19 mm)}$$

$$E = 1.8 \times 10^6 \text{ lb/in}^2 \ (12.4 \times 10^6 \text{ kPa})$$

$$E_w = 1.3 \times 10^6 \text{ lb/in}^2 \ (8.96 \times 10^6 \text{ kPa})$$

$$V = 1200 \text{ lb (5330 N)}$$

SOLUTION: The stiffness and stress values obtained from the formulas in Table 12.3 are

$$(\text{EI})_u = \tfrac{1}{6}[(1.8 \times 10^6 \times 7 \times 1.5^3) + (1.3 \times 10^6)\ \tfrac{3}{8}\ (9.75 + 1.5)^3]$$

$$= 123 \times 10^6 \text{ lb·in}^2 \ (353 \times 10^9 \text{ N·mm}^2)$$

$$(\text{EI})_b = (\tfrac{1}{2} \times 1.8 \times 10^6 \times 7 \times 1.5 \times 9.75^2) + (123 \times 10^6)$$

$$= 1021 \times 10^6 \text{ lb·in}^2 \ (2930 \times 10^9 \text{ N·mm}^2)$$

$$f_g = \frac{1200}{2 \times 1.5 \times 9.75}\left(1 - \frac{123 \times 10^6}{1021 \times 10^6}\right)$$

$$= 36.1 \text{ lb/in}^2 \ (249 \text{ kPa})$$

12.4.5 Other Applications

Adhesives are increasingly being used in both modular and field construction. In addition to those applications previously described, successfully bonded structural elements include gusset plates on trusses and rigid frames; wall, floor, and roof systems; and folded plate structures. Adhesives also offer a convenient method of attaching wood to concrete or masonry. However, design procedures are not well established for these applications and must be treated on an individual basis.

12.5 REPAIR OF DAMAGED STRUCTURES USING EPOXY ADHESIVES

12.5.1 Introduction

The repair of structures requires an engineering evaluation similar to that applied in the initial design of these structures. While this statement may seem obvious, quite often little engineering analysis is used in developing a repair contract. The origin of this approach may be associated with replacement techniques of repair. If damaged members are replaced by new identical members, then the original strength should be restored. No engineering is required to make this determination. However, if repairs involve member augmentation such as stitch bolting or gluing, the degree of restoration cannot be determined without analysis. In fact, without knowing the degree of strength restoration associated with a given repair method, it would be difficult to decide whether to use the method or not. The purpose of this section is to provide analytical techniques for predicting the strength of epoxy-repaired timber structures. It is assumed that the designer has a basic understanding of the mechanics of material behavior. Included are methods of stress analysis for epoxy-repaired joints and procedures for determining allowable stresses for bonded members.

12.5.2 Structural versus Nonstructural Epoxy Repair

Epoxy repair can be divided into two categories: structural and nonstructural. Nonstructural applications include waterproofing, crack sealing to prevent interior deterioration, and cosmetic repairs. Early epoxy repair applications tended to be of this type. It soon became evident that epoxy repair was also structurally effective. The technique was thus used in structural applications as well. However, there are significant differences in methodology for structural and nonstructural repairs. In nonstructural repairs, the cracks are usually well defined and the goal is to simply provide a seal. Epoxy repair for this situation is relatively simple and success can often be measured by checking for air or water tightness.

For structural repairs, the cracks are often less well defined and internal damage may be present. In addition, the crack sizes may range from microcracks to 1 in or larger. To ensure adequate strength, it is necessary to inject epoxy into all cracks and voids. Thus high pressures are required and any leaks that may occur can reduce the structural effectiveness. In general, the successful sealing of cracks prior to epoxy injection is of paramount importance to contain the epoxy in the crack or joint. The sealing and injection procedure must be performed differently and more carefully than would be needed for nonstructural repairs. Many contractors do not appreciate these differences and as a result, the quality of structural repairs ranges the full spectrum from unacceptable to excellent. An additional problem is the difficulty in inspecting this type of structural repair. Inspection procedures have not been developed to completely determine the degree of penetration of epoxy.

This lack of appreciation of the differences between structural and nonstructural repairs coupled with a lack of structural testing to verify repair strength has meant that engineers are lacking in analytical tools to decide on when and how to repair wood members using epoxy. The primary purpose of this section is to provide such analytical tools.

12.5.3 Types of Epoxy Repair

Epoxy repair of timber is applicable primarily in structural or semistructural applications. Based on this classification, the types of epoxy repair can be conveniently typed as follows, where *A* indicates prime structural and *B* indicates semistructural:

Type A-1: Epoxy injection of cracked and split members at truss joints

Type A-2: Epoxy injection and reinforcement of decayed or insect-damaged wood

Type A-3: Splicing and epoxy injection of broken members

Type A-4: Epoxy injection of delaminated or damaged glulam timbers

Type B-1: Epoxy injection of longitudinal cracks and splits in truss members away from joints.

Type B-2: Repair of bearing surfaces using epoxy gel

12.5.4 Repair Mechanism

Early attempts at epoxy repair were aimed only at filling the cracks themselves with epoxy. However, because of the low viscosity of epoxy (similar to a thin paint), it was found to be extremely difficult to contain the epoxy within the damaged zones. The epoxy readily flowed from the cracks into the lapped surfaces between the members. It was thus necessary to seal the edges of all lapped surfaces in order to contain the epoxy. Since damage was often found in only one member of a multimember joint, early repairs also were attempted in which only the lapped members adjacent to the cracked member were sealed. However, the epoxy flowed through the bolt holes and leaked out at unsealed areas. In order to inject epoxy effectively into the damaged area, it was necessary to seal the entire joint, including all lapped areas, bolt holes, grooves, and notches. Upon epoxy injection of such sealed joints, the epoxy penetrates not only the cracked and damaged area, but the voids between lapped surfaces as well. This bonding of lapped surfaces provides an effective transfer of axial force through shear stresses at the glueline. Typically, a mechanical connector produces high stress concentrations at the bearing points between the connector and the wood. Assuming that a sufficient amount of lapped surface is available, a highly effective stress distribution is obtained for epoxy-bonded lapped members. As a consequence, an epoxy-repaired joint may often be stronger than the original joint. However, a number of variables may affect the strength after epoxy repair.

12.5.5 Steps in Epoxy Repair Procedure

There are four basic steps in the epoxy repair procedure. Each step is described in the following paragraphs.

Special Member Preparations. The preparation of the repair area can range from little to extensive. Individual judgment is necessary to determine the preparations required. The following items should be considered prior to any epoxy repair.

Shoring and Jacking. In cases where excessive damage or deterioration has occurred, it may be necessary to shore the members to prevent additional movement during repair or to jack members back to a more normal position. Three reasons for considering jacking are (1) to relieve stresses, (2) to close large cracks, and (3) to remove excessive sag. Jacking to relieve stresses will probably be unsuccessful and is not recommended. While it is difficult to completely close cracks by jacking, it may be possible to minimize the opening and thus reduce the amount of sealing and epoxy injection required. The primary reason to jack a truss before repairing would be to remove excessive sag. A traditional guide to excessive deflections has been based on sag-span ratios exceeding 1/240. Should this value be exceeded, jacking should be considered. If jacking is necessary, extreme caution should be exercised to prevent stress reversals which could cause member failures, especially in the vicinity of the jacking points. Jacking forces should always be applied at panel points. The differential movement also may damage attachments such as roofing. In general, a structural analysis of the system should be conducted to determine the maximum jacking force that is permissible. If jacking is necessary, gauges to measure the jacking forces should be utilized during the operation. A preferred method to truss jacking is to jack against the roof purlins. Such a procedure decreases truss deflections by unloading the truss and yet avoids potential stress reversal problems in the truss.

Addition of Splice Plates. For some repairs it may be necessary to add splice plates. The primary example is the case of a broken member. The epoxy repair technique is most effective for lapped joints in which the epoxy is injected between the lapped surfaces to provide shear resistance. For broken members, splices are tack nailed on both sides of the broken member to be later injected with epoxy. Since most failures occur at joints that already consist of lapped members, it is generally not necessary to provide additional splice plates.

Removal of Moisture Source. For moist or decayed sections the moisture source must be eliminated to protect the member from further deterioration. While epoxy formulations exist which adhere in moist environments, the presence of moisture may mean that decay will continue in encapsulated or adjacent areas and result in continued deterioration. If the moisture content exceeds 20 percent, the member should be dried out before repair and the source of the high moisture eliminated. For roof members, any roof leaks should be repaired so that continued moisture intrusion will not contaminate the repaired member.

Reinforcement. For severely decayed members, reinforcing elements may be necessary. Holes are drilled and fiberglass reinforcing rods inserted to form either a strong connector pattern between sound and unsound wood, or a stiffening internal truss or frame for increasing the load-carrying capacity. Epoxy injection will bond the reinforcing members to the surrounding wood to provide increased strength. Since little experimental evidence is available, this procedure should not be used without careful engineering analysis.

Cleaning. The area to be repaired should be thoroughly cleaned. All dust and debris should be cleared so that a good bonding surface is provided. An air jet from a compressed air source has been found to be very effective for this purpose.

Joint Sealing. The area to be repaired must be completely sealed on the exposed surfaces except for injection and bleeding ports. The success of the repair depends to a large degree on the effectiveness of the sealing. The sealant used should be a high-viscosity epoxy with a puttylike consistency (referred to as a *gel*). The usual steps in the sealing process are as follows.

Port Setting. The placing of ports serves three purposes. A means is provided for (1) injecting epoxy into the interior of the damaged area, (2) venting the air which is displaced by the epoxy during the injection process, and (3) determining the penetration of the epoxy into the damaged area.

Materials. One of the most common materials used for ports is ¼-in (6.3-mm)-diameter copper tubing. Also frequently used is small-diameter [¼- to ⅜-in (3- to 9.5-mm)] standard pipe. Plastic tubing also has been used successfully. The primary requirements for port material are that it should be compatible with the injection equipment, that it should be bondable with the epoxy gel, and that it can be sealed or closed during the injection itself.

Placement of Ports. Ports are placed by drilling holes of a diameter identical to the outside diameter of the port. The port is inserted into the hole and sealing gel is applied around the port. The depth of the hole depends on its location and type. Recalling that the key to a successful epoxy repair is ensuring penetration into all lapped surfaces, the ports should be placed to maximize this penetration. Alternative placement methods are shown in Fig. 12.4. One method is to place the port at the juncture of the lapped surfaces as illustrated by port type A in Fig. 12.4. The hole is drilled at an angle to the surface while ensuring that it includes the lap area. The depth of the hole should extend approximately ¼ in (6.3 mm) beyond the interface. The second method is to drill holes perpendicular to the lapped surfaces, as illustrated by port type B in Fig. 12.4. This method allows easier installation and the penetration of multiple lap planes by drilling the hole deeper. The

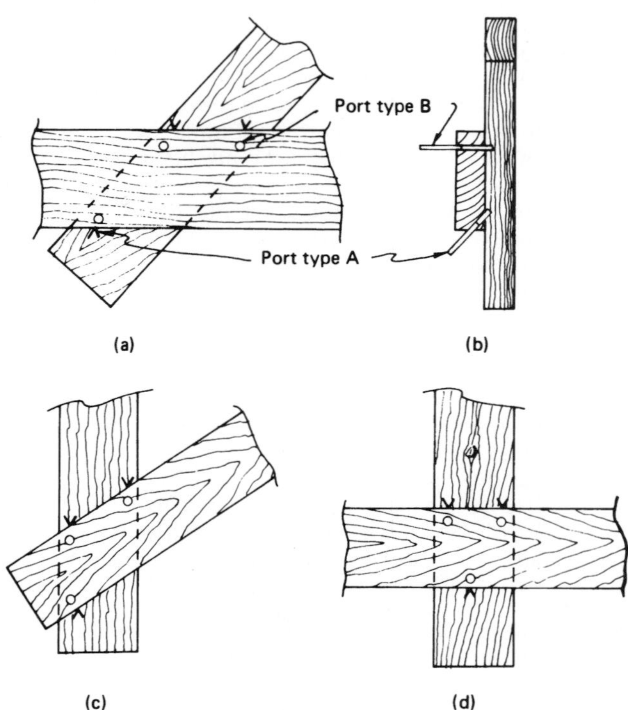

FIG. 12.4 Alternate methods of setting injection ports.

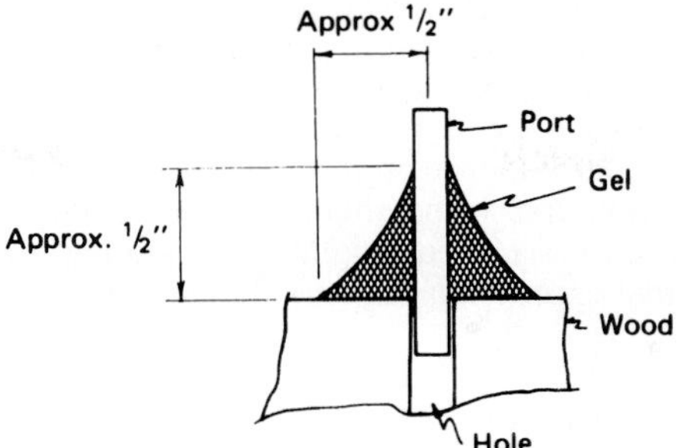

FIG. 12.5 Cross section showing gel buildup around port.

hole should be drilled deep enough to penetrate the lapped surfaces to be repaired. For either method the port should be inserted only approximately ¼ in (6.3 mm) into the hole. After placement, the port should be sealed with gel. The gel should be built up around the port, as shown in Fig. 12.5. It is important to build up the gel to prevent leaking during injection and capping.

Location and Number of Ports. The minimum number of ports for a single lapped surface is three. Two ports are usually placed at the top and one at the bottom, as shown in Fig. 12.4. However, placement may vary depending on the shape of the lapped surfaces. For members oriented at an angle to the grain, three ports per lapped surface are usually sufficient. Hence the total number of ports would be 3 times the number of lapped surfaces at a joint. However, for parallel to grain members such as splices, the lap area may be long enough to justify additional ports. It is recommended that two ports per lapped surface be provided (one top and one bottom) for every 2 ft (0.61 m) of length of spliced members. One other location for ports is at cracks and splits. It is recommended that single ports be placed at the extreme ends of all longitudinal splits, with additional ports placed at 3-ft (0.91-m) increments.

Lap Joint and Crack Sealing. All cracks, lap joints, bolts, open holes, and defects must be completely sealed with gel. This sealing is usually performed using putty knives and trowels. The gel must be thick enough to span the openings and withstand pressures of 40 to 80 $\mathrm{lb/in^2}$ (275 to 552 kPa). A cross section of a crack covered with gel is shown in Fig. 12.6. The thickness h of the gel at the crack should be approximately equal to the crack thickness t. The gel is usually spread ¼ to 1 in (6.3 to 25.4 mm) wide on either side of the crack. For cracks wider than

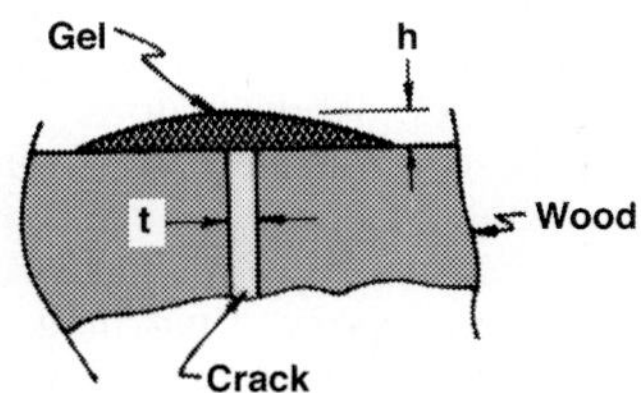

FIG. 12.6 Gel applied over a longitudinal crack.

⅜ in (9.5 mm), a fiberglass cloth can be placed over the crack and covered with gel. This procedure prevents the gel from penetrating too deeply into the crack and provides a stiffening effect once the gel has hardened. Care should be taken to apply the gel to the surface only. Forcing gel deeply into cracks may obstruct the injection epoxy and could prevent it from filling the voids. The gel is significantly weaker than the injection epoxy and should not be counted on for strengthening the repaired joint. Special care should be taken in sealing the following since experience has shown that leaks often occur at these points:

1. At sharp corners

2. At openings greater than ¼ in (6.3 mm)

3. Around bolts and washers

4. Around ports

The entire joint or damaged area must be completely sealed. The injection epoxy has a viscosity similar to thin paint and will seek the path of least resistance when injected. Any small opening will leak enough so that the injection cannot continue without sealing the leak.

Leak Testing. It is recommended that joints be leak-tested before injection. A suitable procedure is to use compressed air. All ports, except one venting port and injection port, should be temporarily capped. Compressed air [at 25-lb/in^2 (172-kPa) pressure] is then forced into the joint. The joint is coated with a soap film and observed for bubbles. All leaks are marked and repaired after the film has dried. While leak testing may seem tedious, experience has shown that the time spent in leak testing is more than compensated for by expedited injection. In addition, the joint has a higher repaired strength when leaking is minimized.

Hairline Cracks. In some cases, the deterioration has resulted in a number of hairline cracks which are difficult to detect visually. Should leak testing reveal a large number of such cracks, it is recommended that the entire damaged area be painted with a thick epoxy paint. This application fills hairline cracks and small holes not generally visible.

Epoxy Injection. The next step is to pressure inject a low-viscosity two-component epoxy into the sealed joint through the injection ports (Fig. 12.7). This can usually be done by attaching the nozzle of the injection gun to a single port (usually the lowest) and letting the other ports serve as vents. As epoxy fills the joint, the venting ports leak epoxy and are sealed off. After all ports are sealed, epoxy injection should be continued to ensure penetration into the fibers. Care should be taken not to inject with too much pressure or the seals might break. A nozzle pressure of 40 lb/in^2 (276 kPa) maximum is recommended. When possible, the entire joint should be injected from a single port.

Port Capping. Various methods can be used to seal off ports during injection. One method is to lightly tap wooden golf tees into the port. Copper tubing can be bent or squeezed closed with pliers. Wooden dowels also can be inserted. The primary caution is that the seals should not be broken in the process.

Leaking During Injection. Should a leak develop during the injection process, quick-drying patching cement can be applied. Since it is essential to finish the injection before the initial set of the epoxy, a patching cement with a 2- to 3-min pot life is needed. Hydraulic cements which can be mixed with water work well. Hot-melt glues have also been used successfully. Because of the porous nature of

FIG. 12.7 Epoxy injection in progress.

wood, leaking will occur on occasion. No injection should be attempted without a supply of patching compound on hand.

Injection Equipment. Injection is usually accomplished with automatic equipment, although hand equipment can be used. Typically, two positive displacement pumps geared to the specified mix ratio feed the separate components into a nozzle. Mixing is accomplished by forcing the epoxy through static mixing brushes in the nozzle. As long as the flow is not interrupted for more than a few minutes, injection can progress for hours without damage to the nozzle.

Finishing. The initial cure time for many epoxies is 2 to 5 hours. Final cure is usually accomplished in several days. After curing, any temporary supports may be removed. If aesthetics are important, the injection ports are removed and the sealing gel is sanded smooth. Paint can then be applied to finish the repair.

12.5.6 Dimensional Factors Affecting Strength of Epoxy-Repaired Joints

In a stress analysis of epoxy-repaired joints, the engineer is faced with a number of variables. Primary among these is the multitude of joint configurations. Quantities such as number of members, lap area, grain orientation, and the number of mechanical connectors may vary considerably. Other important variables include member thickness, age of wood, and crack width between lapped surfaces. A comprehensive analytical and experimental testing program has been conducted to evaluate these factors. Based on the results of analytical and experimental studies, the following conclusions were reached.

Degree of Damage. Since epoxy repair is primarily used to provide shear resistance in lapped members, the degree of damage is usually unimportant. As long as there are adequate lapped surfaces for bonding, the strength of the joint can be restored completely. The major exception is decay. It is quite difficult to restore the structural integrity of decay-damaged wood using epoxy, and such effort requires unusual care and expertise.

Effect of Mechanical Connectors. All joints in wooden trusses must have some form of connector. Generally, in older trusses, mechanical connectors such as bolted connections, split-ring connectors, and tooth-plate connectors were used. Often it will be found that some of these connectors may have been left out, or in extreme cases, the members of the joint may have deteriorated to a point where the connectors may have fallen out. Since the structure being repaired may have a variable number and arrangement of connectors, it is important to know what effect the connector will have on the capacity of the repaired joint. Based on a series of load tests of epoxy-injected joints with and without split rings, it was found that the connector contributed little to the strength of the joint after the repairs were made. From observation of failure, the glueline must fail (or at least deform significantly) before the load can be transferred to the rings. If the load required to make the glueline fail is greater than the split ring capacity, then the split rings will fail immediately after the glueline fails. Thus split rings would be effective only if the ring capacity was larger than the glueline capacity. Since in most repair situations the ring capacity is less than the glueline capacity, the effect of mechanical connectors on the joint strength is small. A similar condition would exist with other mechanical connectors such as bolts or toothed plates.

Width and Length of Overlap. It has been generally established that the failure stress of a bonded lap joint is not affected by the width of overlap. However, bond shear stress varies significantly with respect to lap length. The variation in strength due to lap length can be accounted for by selecting allowable bondline stresses based on lap length. The thickness of the outside members was found to have a negligible effect on the average failure stress. See Sec. 12.3.1 for recommended magnitudes of allowable stresses associated with the lap length effect.

Effect of Grain Orientation. Experimental results have indicated that a proportional decrease in ultimate load capacity occurs as the grain angle varies from 0 to 90° in lapped joints loaded in shear. Therefore allowable stress criteria must include the effect of grain orientation. The recommended procedure is to use Hankinson's formula as given in Eq. (12.3).

Effect of Glueline Thickness. Based on theoretical studies, the glueline thickness has been found to be an important variable in obtaining the strength of bonded joints. However, experimental results indicate that glueline thickness has a much smaller effect on strength than theoretical studies have indicated. The effect is so small as to be considered negligible in epoxy-repaired joints. This conclusion is particularly useful since the glueline thickness usually varies in actual truss joints and would be difficult to measure.

12.5.7 Strength Evaluation of Epoxy-Repaired Joints

In order to predict the expected capacity of an epoxy-repaired truss, two things are needed. First, for a given set of loadings, a method of calculating the intensity and distribution of stress over the glueline is required. Second, a means of determining

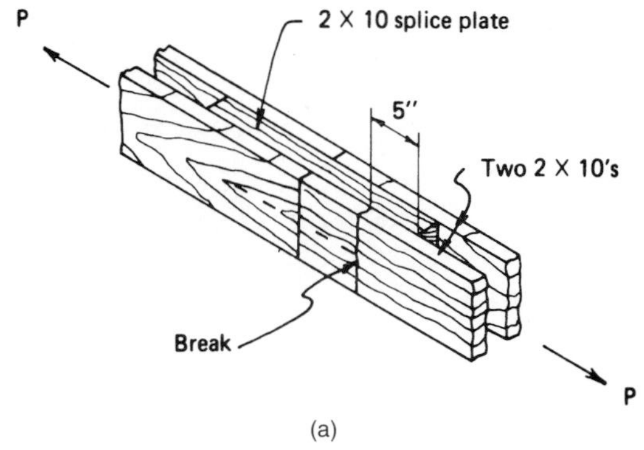

(a)

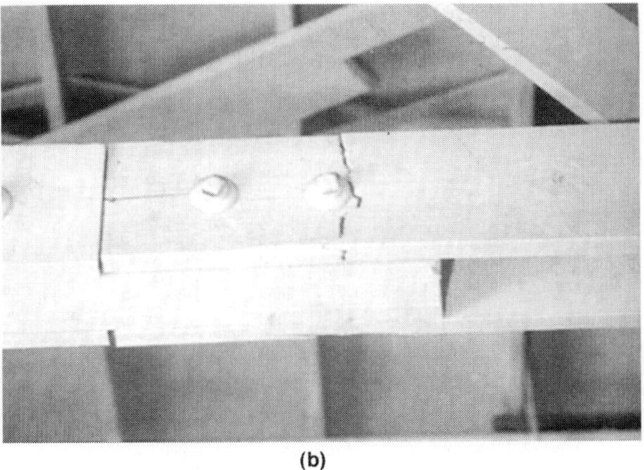

(b)

FIG. 12.10 Example 12.6. Broken member at a double chord tension space (1 in = 25.4 mm).

EXAMPLE 12.7 Determine the repaired strength of the joint with the member forces as shown in Fig. 12.8, which is to be epoxy-injected to repair longitudinal end splits. The members are all 2 by 12 in (38.1 by 286 mm) of No. 2 Douglas fir south. Thus F_v = 90 lb/in^2 (620 kPa) and C_a = 0.50.

SOLUTION: The capacity of each member can be determined as follows. Member 1 is controlled by single shear having perpendicular-to-grain orientation with member 2. For single shear, $t = 2 \times 1.5 = 3.0$ in (76 mm) and $\ell/t = 11.25/3 = 3.75$. Using Eq. (12.6*b*),

$$F_g^Q = \frac{1}{3} \times 0.5 \times 90 \times 3.75 = 56.25 \text{ lb/in}^2 \text{ (388 kPa)}$$

and the allowable load on member 1 is

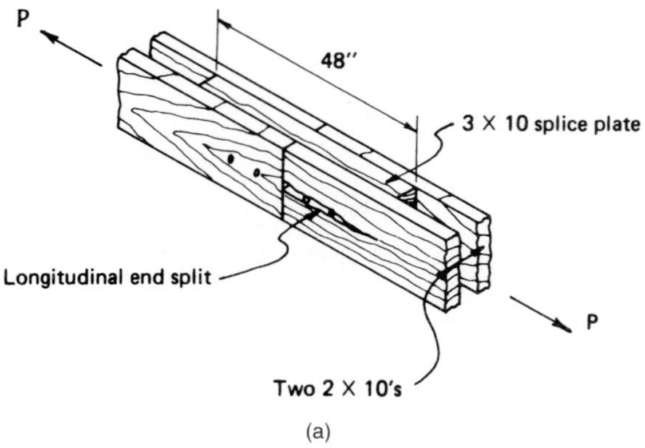

(a)

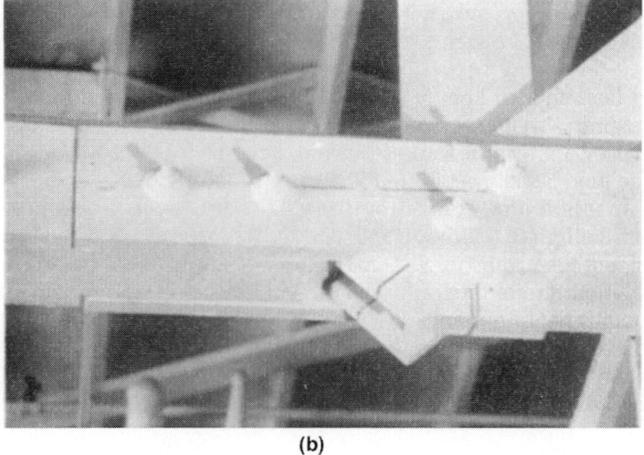

(b)

FIG. 12.9 Example 12.5. Longitudinal split at the splice of a double chord tension member (1 in = 25.4 mm).

SOLUTION: Compute the allowable glueline shear stress between chord and splice plate over the 5-in (127-mm) lap length. Since the repaired joint will be in double shear, $\ell/t = 5/2.5 = 2$, $C_a = 1$, and $F_v = 90$ lb/in² (620 kPa). From Eq. (12.6),

$$F_g^P = \frac{2}{3} \times 1 \times 90 \times 2 = 120 \text{ lb/in}^2 \text{ (827 kPa)}$$

The load capacity of the double chord member based on glueline strength is found from multiplying allowable stress by shear area,

$$P = 120 \times 2 \times 5 \times 9.25 = 11{,}100 \text{ lb (49.4 kN)}$$

The joint capacity based on member strength is computed for comparison. The splice plate controls and the capacity is the same as computed in the previous example, $P = 11{,}500$ lb (51.2 kN). Thus epoxy repair will restore the joint to 97 percent of original strength.

$$F_g = \frac{2}{3} C_a F_v \frac{\ell}{t} \quad \text{for members with grain orientation parallel} \qquad (12.6a)$$

$$F_g = \frac{1}{3} C_a F_v \frac{\ell}{t} \quad \text{for members with grain orientation perpendicular} \qquad (12.6b)$$

where F_v is the allowable horizontal shear stress for the given species and C_a is the wood species factor. Values of C_a have been compiled from test results using Sikadur Hi-Mod LV epoxy[6] and a wood moisture content of less than 12 percent. For some commonly used species, the following values of C_a are recommended: southern pine, C_a = 1.0; California redwood, C_a = 0.50; Douglas fir, C_a = 0.50; Ponderosa pine, C_a = 1.40; and western hemlock, C_a = 0.67. The recommended C_a values for California redwood, Douglas fir, and western hemlock are lower than values typically found in glulam construction. These differences are attributable to the type of glue used, lack of surface preparation, and the effect of injection as opposed to pressure/temperature gluing procedures.

EXAMPLE 12.5 Determine the repaired strength of the double chord tension member splice with 2½-in (63.5-mm) split rings shown schematically in Fig. 12.9*a*. This type of damage is typical of that found in old timber trusses, as illustrated in Fig. 12.9*b*. A longitudinal end split has occurred through the connector pattern of one chord member. All material is No. 2 southern pine.

SOLUTION: The allowable glueline stress is computed from Eq. (12.6*a*) using $C_a = 1$, $F_v = 90$ lb/in² (620 kPa), and $\ell/t = 24/2.5 = 9.6$. The allowable stress is thus

$$F_g^P = \frac{2}{3} \times 90 \times 9.6 = 576 \text{ lb/in}^2 \text{ (3969 kPa)}$$

The tensile load capacity P based on glueline strength is computed by multiplying the double shear lap area by F_g^P to yield

$$P = 576 \times 24 \times 9.25 \times 2 = 256{,}000 \text{ lb (1138 kN)}$$

The tensile strength is computed based on a net section through the wood members. The 3 × 10 splice plate has a smaller section than the chord members and will control. The net section through the splice plate with a 2½-in split ring connector on each face is $A_n = (2.5 \times 9.25) - (2 \times 1.10) = 20.9$ in². This area multiplied by the allowable tension stress as taken from NDS[5] for mixed southern pine yields the allowable tensile capacity

$$P = 20.9 \times 550 = 11{,}500 \text{ lb (51.2 kN)}$$

Comparing the strength of the connection based on glueline shear stress and member tensile stress shows that the epoxy repair will restore the joint to full capacity.

EXAMPLE 12.6 Consider a tension splice in which a break has occurred in the member, as shown schematically in Fig. 12.10*a*. An actual joint showing similar damage is illustrated in Fig. 12.10*b*. All material is No. 2 mixed southern pine. Determine the expected strength after repair.

On the face of member 3, the resultant stress is parallel to the grain and is given by

$$f_g^P = \frac{5660}{179} = 31.6 \text{ lb/in}^2 \text{ (218 kPa)}$$

The approach of using the average shear stress in the computation of actual stress ignores the effect of stress concentrations, member force eccentricities, and the shape of the lapped surface area. Research has shown that only the stress concentration effect is significant and should be taken into account by the proper selection of allowable stress.

Computation of Allowable Glueline Stress. The strength of an epoxy-repaired joint may be governed by either the glueline strength or the member strength. If the glueline has greater capacity than the member itself, strength computations must be based on the member strength in either tension or compression, as appropriate. Allowable stresses for wood members can be obtained from the NDS.[5] The selection of allowable glueline stresses is not as convenient since there are no industry publications that provide allowable glueline stresses. However, based on experimental evidence, allowable stresses can be determined. For Sikadur Hi-Mod LV epoxy, the methodology for computing allowable stresses has been described previously and values were given by Eqs. (12.1) and (12.2).

12.5.8 Additional Factors Affecting the Behavior of Epoxy-Repaired Joints

In addition to the basic strength considerations, several factors may influence the load-carrying capacity of epoxy-repaired joints. These factors are primarily environmental and should be evaluated as applicable.

Effect of Timber Age. The bond strength of a limited amount of 30- to 40-year-old southern pine has been compared to that of new wood. Statistically, the bond strength of old wood was slightly higher than that of new wood. Tests and actual repair applications have indicated that no unusual effects are found when repairing old timber.

Wood Species. Most experimental research on epoxy repair has been conducted using southern pine lumber. However, many other species are often found in timber construction. Over the last 30 years, Douglas fir, southern pine, Ponderosa pine, western hemlock, and California redwood have constituted the bulk of structural lumber produced in the United States. To apply the previous formulas to species other than southern pine, a wood species factor C_a should be incorporated, which reflects the differences between glueline strength and wood shear strength for various species. The allowable glueline stress F_g for any of the tabulated wood species is thus

$$P = 56.25 \times 11.25^2 = 7120 \text{ lb } (31.6 \text{ kN})$$

This load is significantly higher than the actual load from Fig. 12.8. Members 2, 3, and 4 form a three-member double shear joint with a grain orientation of 45°. For the perpendicular-to-grain component, $\ell/t = 11.25/1.5 = 7.5$ and

$$F_g^Q = \frac{1}{3} \times 0.5 \times 90 \times 7.5 = 112 \text{ lb/in}^2 \text{ (776 kPa)}$$

Similarly, the parallel to grain component has a lap length $\ell = 11.25/\sin 45° =$ 15.9 in (404 mm), $\ell/t = 15.9/1.5 = 10.6$, and

$$F_g^P = \frac{2}{3} \times 0.5 \times 90 \times 10.6 = 318 \text{ lb/in}^2 \text{ (2190 kPa)}$$

Using Eq. (12.3),

$$F_g = \frac{318 \times 112}{318 \sin^2 45° + 112 \cos^2 45°}$$

$$= 166 \text{ lb/in}^2 \text{ (1140 kPa)}$$

The glueline strength for member 3 is

$$P = 166 \times 15.9 \times 11.25 \times 2 = 59{,}400 \text{ lb (264 kN)}$$

This value is much larger than the actual force from Fig. 12.8. An epoxy repair of this joint would therefore restore the joint to its original design capacity.

Load-Duration Effect. Tests have shown that wood can carry significantly larger loads over a short time period than over a longer period. This behavior is referred to as the load-duration effect, and a load-duration adjustment factor is commonly used in timber design. The NDS[5] specifies that design allowable stresses should be modified based on the expected duration of the maximum load intensity. The load-duration adjustment factors are given by NDS in graphic form. A series of double shear joints have been partially loaded to evaluate the load-duration effect of epoxy bondlines. Results of these tests indicate that the NDS load-duration curve is conservative. Based on these results, it is recommended that the same load-duration adjustment factors be used for epoxy-repaired wood as are used for the wood itself.

Effects of Extreme Temperature and Fire on Epoxy-Repaired Joints. The effect of temperature variation on the strength of epoxy repair can be divided into two categories. First is the effect of temperature changes due to natural environmental causes. For the continental United States, temperature changes from 0 to 125°F are reasonable expected variations, and this magnitude of temperature change should not have an adverse effect on the strength of most epoxies.

The second major temperature effect to be considered is fire resistance. It is well established that most epoxies begin to "soften" at 150 to 250°F (65.5 to 121°C), and their strength rapidly decreases. However, it is also well known that wood is one of the best thermal insulators of all structural materials. For example, the thermal conductivity of an average softwood (measured in Btu·in/(h·ft^2·°F) or J·mm/(h·m^2·°C) is $0.8 \times 0.643 \times 10^3$, while that of concrete is $12.6 \times 10.1 \times 10^3$, and steel is 312 × 251 × 10³. The question to be answered is: How well does the wood insulate the epoxy?

An important aspect to be considered in a discussion of fire resistance is the ultimate goal to be achieved. Of primary importance is that a fire will not weaken the structure so rapidly as to cause collapse, which will hamper escape and fire-fighting attempts. Wood (especially heavy timber) exhibits exceptional properties in such cases. As the wood chars on the outside, the char forms a protective thermal barrier which retards further deterioration. Wood also distorts very little at high temperature. Thus it is unlikely that walls will be toppled, as happens often with some other materials. In general, the weakening of a primary structural component would be considered a failure. However, in epoxy repair of timber the situation is somewhat different. Typically, the damaged structure has not collapsed but obvious distress is present such as cracks and splits. Many epoxy repairs are performed in place without temporary support of the members. The damaged members are therefore supporting the dead loading during repair and the epoxy will not be stressed until additional live loads are applied to the structure. Epoxy repair thus serves two functions: it provides increased load capacity above the dead-load level, and it prevents further deterioration of the member through crack propagation. If the epoxy is weakened during a fire, the structure will, at worst, revert to its original condition before repair. If the structure was functioning prior to repair, then this residual capacity would remain as the epoxy deteriorates during the early portion of a fire. The evaluation of an epoxy-repaired structure during a fire should thus be tempered with a consideration of the condition of the structure prior to repair.

A comprehensive testing program for evaluating the effects of high heat on epoxy-repaired joints has been conducted.[8] Based on these tests and a theoretical extrapolation of results, an approximate fire rating for various joint configurations has been obtained. An approximate fire rating based on these results and the ASTM E 119 standard[9] fire curve is shown in Fig. 12.11.

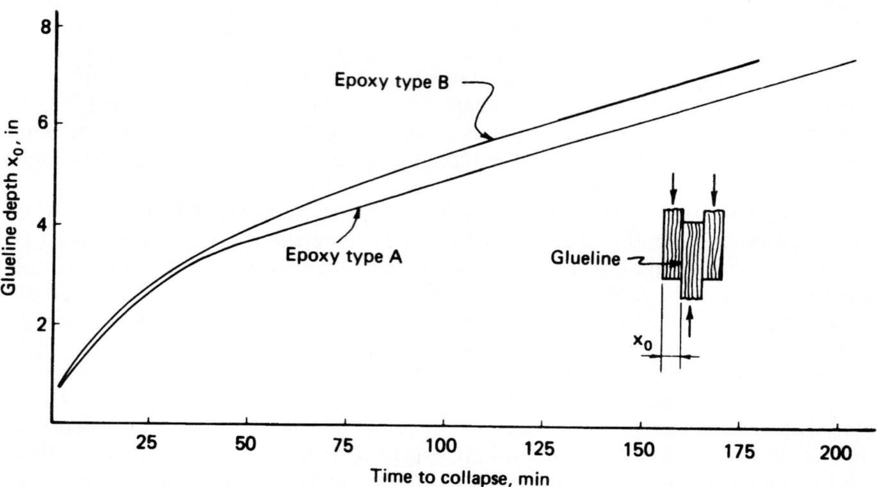

FIG. 12.11 Approximate fire rating for epoxy-repaired joints exposed to ASTM E-119[9] standard fire curve in terms of distance from exposed face to glueline.

Effects of Weathering and Decay on the Epoxy Repair of Timber. Wood can be an extremely durable material. However, the durability depends on the surrounding environment. Examples can be found of wood that has endured for centuries after being buried underground, submerged under water, or fully exposed to weather. In contrast, the same type of wood exposed to a different environment may vanish without a trace in just a few years. One convenient way to classify environmental effects on wood is by the forms of energy producing the effect. Excluding insects, fungi, and animals, the energy effects on wood can be classified as thermal, light, mechanical, and chemical. For enclosed structures, the most serious risk usually comes from the thermal source of intense heat due to an accidental fire. For exterior wood structures the most serious risk comes from a combination of light, chemical, and mechanical effects, usually referred to as *weathering*. Although some decay may result from the weathering process, a distinction is usually made between the two. Decay, which results from excessive moisture over an extended period, can lead to rapid deterioration in wood and result in a phenomenon quite different from that observed in the weathering process.

Two types of tests[10] on southern pine have been conducted to evaluate weathering effects: an accelerated pressure, soaking, and drying procedure on small shear blocks and a long-term exposure of full-sized joints to natural weathering. The results of these tests indicate that glueline strength is maintained well when subjected to weathering. It is therefore recommended that the usual precautions in maintenance of exposed wood be used to protect epoxy-repaired joints.

In a related study, severely weathered and decayed joints were epoxy-repaired and tested. For both lightly and heavily damaged weathered material that was subsequently epoxy-repaired, the strength of the repaired joints compared favorably with that of undamaged material. It is thus concluded that seriously deteriorated timber can be epoxy-repaired. However, it should be noted that such repairs are difficult for five reasons:

1. All deteriorated joints may not be detectable from a visual inspection, especially around interior mechanical connectors.
2. Deterioration may extend outward from the joint, where repaired strength may not be restorable to original strength by epoxy repair.
3. The epoxy repair process for seriously deteriorated joints can be extremely difficult, especially the joint sealing before injection.
4. If the source of deterioration is not removed, recurrence of the problem is likely.
5. Without completely drying the area to be repaired, encapsulated moisture may continue to deteriorate the repaired joint.

When practical, it is usually better to replace seriously weathered and decayed timber. However, epoxy repair can be used in situations where it is necessary to maintain the original structural elements. In such cases it would be advisable to consult someone knowledgeable in the field of timber repair for guidance in the initial inspection to locate the deterioration, establish repair recommendations, and provide inspection during repair.

12.5.9 Quality Control to Ensure Adequate Repair

One of the major difficulties associated with the epoxy repair procedure is quality control. Engineering inspection is one measure. However, it may prove difficult to verify whether epoxy has completely penetrated the damaged area. This concern is often emphasized by the fact that workers may have relatively little experience with wood as opposed to concrete repairs. The following procedures are recommended for ensuring a satisfactory epoxy repair.

Epoxy Samples. In many cases, laboratory testing is not possible for wood repair in contrast to concrete repair, where test cylinders can be taken. This lack of quality control can result in serious problems for epoxy-repaired members. Many epoxies are very sensitive to mix proportions. One type of injection equipment consists of two positive displacement pumps driven by a single motor geared to obtain the proper mix. The two epoxy components are mixed at the nozzle. Thus a fairly continuous flow prevents hardening of the epoxy in the nozzle. However, crimped lines, malfunctioning pumps, or line blockages can sometimes occur. In severe cases, the epoxy will not harden at all, but in other cases, the problem may result in soft spots within joints. Frequent collecting of small samples which are allowed to cure in containers such as paper cups will verify whether the epoxy is hardening as expected, and this should be done routinely. It is recommended that a sample be taken before the injection of each joint with a notation as to the specific point being repaired. Should the epoxy not harden properly, the joint should be repaired by an alternative method, such as member replacement or steel reinforcement.

Shear Block Specimens. The detection of weak but hardened materials is much more difficult. One method is to inject shear block specimens at the beginning of operations and periodically thereafter, such as after the repair of every fifth member. A shear specimen (Fig. 12.12) is cut into four shear blocks after curing, and each is tested in single shear. The failure stress level should be approximately equal to the ultimate strength of the wood [approximately 600 to 800 lb/in² (4.1×10^3 to 5.5×10^3 kPa) for southern pine]. This level of shearing strength indicates a high-quality bond.

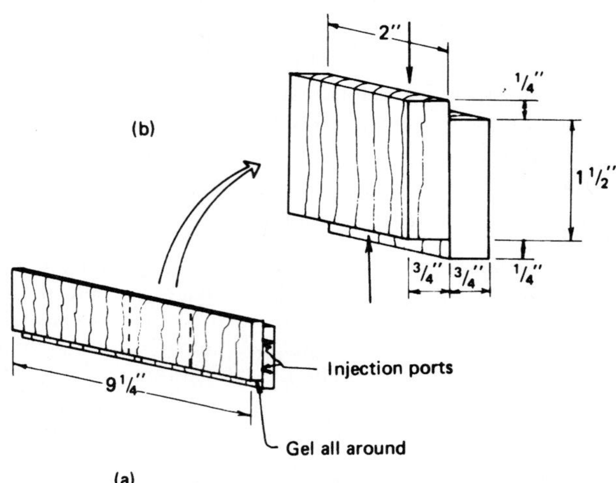

FIG. 12.12 Quality-control specimens for shear block tests. All dimensions in inches (1 in = 25.4 mm).

Coring. Another quality-control problem is determining epoxy penetration into voids. Coring techniques have been developed, but none has proved completely satisfactory. The coring devices either are time-consuming, thus allowing for only spot checks, or destroy the sample, making it difficult to detect the epoxy.

REFERENCES

1. R. H. Gillespie, D. Countryman, and R. F. Blomquist, *Adhesives in Building Construction,* U.S.D.A. Agriculture Handbook 516, Feb. 1978.
2. *Standard Method for Evaluating Allowable Properties for Grades of Structural Lumber,* D 2915-74 (Reapproved 1980), American Society for Testing and Materials, Philadelphia, Pa., 1980.
3. A. F. Lewis, R. A. Kinmonth, and R. P. Kreahling, "Long Term Strength of Structural Adhesive Joints," *J. Adhesion* **3:**249–257, 1972.
4. *Standard Test Method for Strength Properties of Adhesive Bonds in Shear by Compression Loading,* D 905-44 (Reapproved 1981), American Society for Testing and Materials, Philadelphia, Pa., 1981.
5. *National Design Specification for Wood Construction,* National Forest and Paper Association, Washington, D.C., 1991.
6. R. R. Avent, "Design Criteria for Epoxy Repair of Timber Structures," *J. Struct. Eng. ASCE* **112**(2):222–240, Feb. 1986.
7. *Plywood Design Specifications,* American Plywood Association, Tacoma, Wash., 1987.
8. R. R. Avent and C. A. Issa, "Effect of Fire on Epoxy-Repaired Timber," *J. Struct. Eng. ASCE* **110**(12):2858–2875, Dec. 1984.
9. *Book of ASTM Standards,* E-119, vol. 14, American Society for Testing and Materials, Philadelphia, Pa., 1980.
10. R. R. Avent, "Decay, Weathering and Epoxy Repair of Timber," *J. Struct. Eng. ASCE* **111**(2):328–342, Feb. 1985.

APPENDIX
REFERENCE DATA

Keith F. Faherty, Ph.D., P.E. and Thomas G. Williamson, P.E.

TABLE A.1 Nominal and Minimum-Dressed Sizes of Boards, Dimension, and Timbers
The thicknesses apply to all widths and all widths to all thicknesses

	Thicknesses, in			Face widths, in		
		Minimum dressed			Minimum dressed	
Item	Nominal	Dry	Green	Nominal	Dry	Green
Boards	1	3/4	25/32	2	1 1/2	1 9/16
	1 1/4	1	1 1/32	3	2 1/2	2 9/16
	1 1/2	1 1/4	1 9/32	4	3 1/2	3 9/16
				5	4 1/2	4 5/8
				6	5 1/2	5 5/8
				7	6 1/2	6 5/8
				8	7 1/4	7 1/2
				9	8 1/4	8 1/2
				10	9 1/4	9 1/2
				11	10 1/4	10 1/2
				12	11 1/4	11 1/2
				14	13 1/4	13 1/2
				16	15 1/4	15 1/2
Dimension	2	1 1/2	1 9/16	2	1 1/2	1 9/16
	2 1/2	2	2 1/16	3	2 1/2	2 9/16
	3	2 1/2	2 9/16	4	3 1/2	3 9/16
	3 1/2	3	3 1/16	5	4 1/2	4 5/8
				6	5 1/2	5 5/8
				8	7 1/4	7 1/2
				10	9 1/4	9 1/2
				12	11 1/4	11 1/2
				14	13 1/4	13 1/2
				16	15 1/4	15 1/2
	4	3 1/2	3 9/16	2	1 1/2	1 9/16
	4 1/2	4	4 1/16	3	2 1/2	2 9/16
				4	3 1/2	3 9/16
				5	4 1/2	4 5/8
				6	5 1/2	5 5/8
				8	7 1/4	7 1/2
				10	9 1/4	9 1/2
				12	11 1/4	11 1/2
				14	—	13 1/2
				16	—	15 1/2
Timbers	5 and thicker	—	1/2 off	5 and wider	—	1/2 off

Note: 1 in = 25.4 mm.
Source: From *National Design Specification for Wood Construction,* courtesy of the American Forest and Paper Association, Washington, D.C.

TABLE A.2 Sectional Properties of Standard Dressed (S4S) Sizes

Nominal size $b \times d$, in	Standard dressed size (S4S) $b \times d$, in	Area of section A, in^2	Moment of inertia I, in^4	Section modulus S, in^3	Approximate weight* in pounds per linear foot of piece when weight of wood per cubic foot equals: 25 lb	30 lb	35 lb	40 lb	45 lb	50 lb
1 × 4	¾ × 3½	2.625	2.680	1.531	0.456	0.547	0.638	0.729	0.820	0.911
1 × 6	¾ × 5½	4.125	10.398	3.781	0.716	0.859	1.003	1.146	1.289	1.432
1 × 8	¾ × 7¼	5.438	23.817	6.570	0.944	1.133	1.322	1.510	1.699	1.888
1 × 10	¾ × 9¼	6.938	49.466	10.695	1.204	1.445	1.686	1.927	2.168	2.409
1 × 12	¾ × 11¼	8.438	88.989	15.820	1.465	1.758	2.051	2.344	2.637	2.930
2 × 4	1½ × 3½	5.250	5.359	3.063	0.911	1.094	1.276	1.458	1.641	1.823
2 × 6	1½ × 5½	8.250	20.797	7.563	1.432	1.719	2.005	2.292	2.578	2.865
2 × 8	1½ × 7¼	10.875	47.635	13.141	1.888	2.266	2.643	3.021	3.398	3.776
2 × 10	1½ × 9¼	13.875	98.932	21.391	2.409	2.891	3.372	3.854	4.336	4.818
2 × 12	1½ × 11¼	16.875	177.979	31.641	2.930	3.516	4.102	4.688	5.273	5.859
2 × 14	1½ × 13¼	19.875	290.775	43.891	3.451	4.141	4.831	5.521	6.211	6.901
3 × 4	2½ × 3½	8.750	8.932	5.104	1.519	1.823	2.127	2.431	2.734	3.038
3 × 6	2½ × 5½	13.750	34.661	12.604	2.387	2.865	3.342	3.819	4.297	4.774
3 × 8	2½ × 7¼	18.125	79.391	21.901	3.147	3.776	4.405	5.035	5.664	6.293
3 × 10	2½ × 9¼	23.125	164.886	35.651	4.015	4.818	5.621	6.424	7.227	8.030
3 × 12	2½ × 11¼	28.125	296.631	52.734	4.883	5.859	6.836	7.813	8.789	9.766
3 × 14	2½ × 13¼	33.125	484.625	73.151	5.751	6.901	8.051	9.201	10.352	11.502
3 × 16	2½ × 15¼	38.125	738.870	96.901	6.619	7.943	9.266	10.590	11.914	13.238
4 × 1	3½ × ¾	2.625	0.123	0.328	0.456	0.547	0.638	0.729	0.820	0.911
4 × 2	3½ × 1½	5.250	0.984	1.313	0.911	1.094	1.276	1.458	1.641	1.823
4 × 4	3½ × 3½	12.250	12.505	7.146	2.127	2.552	2.977	3.403	3.828	4.253
4 × 6	3½ × 5½	19.250	48.526	17.646	3.342	4.010	4.679	5.347	6.016	6.684
4 × 8	3½ × 7¼	25.375	111.148	30.661	4.405	5.286	6.168	7.049	7.930	8.811

4 × 10	3½ × 9¼	32.375	230.840	49.911	5.621	6.745	7.869	8.933	10.117	11.241
4 × 12	3½ × 11¼	39.375	415.283	73.828	6.836	8.203	9.570	10.938	12.305	13.672
4 × 14	3½ × 13¼	46.375	678.475	102.411	8.047	9.657	11.266	12.877	14.485	16.094
4 × 16	3½ × 15¼	53.375	1034.418	135.66	9.267	11.121	12.975	14.828	16.682	18.536
6 × 6	5½ × 5½	30.250	76.255	27.729	5.252	6.302	7.352	8.403	9.453	10.503
6 × 8	5½ × 7½	41.250	193.359	51.563	7.161	8.594	10.026	11.458	12.891	14.323
6 × 10	5½ × 9½	52.250	392.963	82.729	9.071	10.885	12.700	14.514	16.328	18.142
6 × 12	5½ × 11½	63.250	697.068	121.229	10.981	13.177	15.373	17.569	19.766	21.962
6 × 14	5½ × 13½	74.250	1127.672	167.063	12.891	15.469	18.047	20.625	23.203	25.781
6 × 16	5½ × 15½	85.250	1706.776	220.229	14.800	17.760	20.720	23.681	26.641	29.601
6 × 18	5½ × 17½	96.250	2456.380	280.729	16.710	20.052	23.394	26.736	30.078	33.420
6 × 20	5½ × 19½	107.250	3398.484	348.563	18.620	22.344	26.068	29.792	33.516	37.240
6 × 22	5½ × 21½	118.250	4555.086	423.729	20.530	24.635	28.741	32.847	36.953	41.059
6 × 24	5½ × 23½	129.250	5948.191	506.229	22.439	26.927	31.415	35.903	40.391	44.878
8 × 8	7½ × 7½	56.250	263.672	70.313	9.766	11.719	13.672	15.625	17.578	19.531
8 × 10	7½ × 9½	71.250	535.859	112.813	12.370	14.844	17.318	19.792	22.266	24.740
8 × 12	7½ × 11½	86.250	950.547	165.313	14.974	17.969	20.964	23.958	26.953	29.948
8 × 14	7½ × 13½	101.250	1537.734	227.813	17.578	21.094	24.609	28.125	31.641	35.156
8 × 16	7½ × 15½	116.250	2327.422	300.313	20.182	24.219	28.255	32.292	36.328	40.365
8 × 18	7½ × 17½	131.250	3349.609	382.813	22.786	27.344	31.901	36.458	41.016	45.573
8 × 20	7½ × 19½	146.250	4634.297	475.313	25.391	30.469	35.547	40.625	45.703	50.781
8 × 22	7½ × 21½	161.250	6211.484	577.813	27.995	33.594	39.193	44.792	50.391	55.990
8 × 24	7½ × 23½	176.250	8111.172	690.313	30.599	36.719	42.839	48.958	55.078	61.198
10 × 10	9½ × 9½	90.250	678.755	142.896	15.668	18.802	21.936	25.069	28.203	31.337
10 × 12	9½ × 11½	109.250	1204.026	209.396	18.967	22.760	26.554	30.347	34.141	37.934
10 × 14	9½ × 13½	128.250	1947.797	288.563	22.266	26.719	31.172	35.625	40.078	44.531
10 × 16	9½ × 15½	147.250	2948.068	380.396	25.564	30.677	35.790	40.903	46.016	51.128
10 × 18	9½ × 17½	166.250	4242.836	484.896	28.863	34.635	40.408	46.181	51.953	57.726
10 × 20	9½ × 19½	185.250	5870.109	602.063	32.161	38.594	45.026	51.458	57.891	64.323
10 × 22	9½ × 21½	204.250	7867.879	731.896	35.460	42.552	49.644	56.736	63.828	70.920
10 × 24	9½ × 23½	223.250	10274.148	874.396	38.759	46.510	54.262	62.014	69.766	77.517

TABLE A.2 Sectional Properties of Standard Dressed (S4S) Sizes (*Continued*)

Nominal size $b \times d$, in	Standard dressed size (S4S) $b \times d$, in	Area of section A, in²	Moment of inertia I, in⁴	Section modulus S, in³	Approximate weight* in pounds per linear foot of piece when weight of wood per cubic foot equals: 25 lb	30 lb	35 lb	40 lb	45 lb	50 lb
12 × 12	11½ × 11½	132.250	1457.505	253.479	22.960	27.552	32.144	36.736	41.328	45.920
12 × 14	11½ × 13½	155.250	2357.859	349.313	26.953	32.344	37.734	43.125	48.516	53.906
12 × 16	11½ × 15½	178.250	3568.713	460.479	30.946	37.135	43.325	49.514	55.703	61.892
12 × 18	11½ × 17½	201.250	5136.066	586.979	34.939	41.927	48.915	55.903	62.891	69.878
12 × 20	11½ × 19½	224.250	7105.922	728.813	38.932	46.719	54.505	62.292	70.078	77.865
12 × 22	11½ × 21½	247.250	9524.273	885.979	42.925	51.510	60.095	68.681	77.266	85.851
12 × 24	11½ × 23½	270.250	12437.129	1058.479	46.918	56.302	65.686	75.069	84.453	93.837
14 × 14	13½ × 13½	182.250	2767.922	410.063	31.641	37.969	44.297	50.625	56.953	63.281
14 × 16	13½ × 15½	209.250	4189.359	540.563	36.328	43.594	50.859	58.125	65.391	72.656
14 × 18	13½ × 17½	236.250	6029.297	689.063	41.016	49.219	57.422	65.625	73.828	82.031
14 × 20	13½ × 19½	263.250	8341.734	855.563	45.703	54.844	63.984	73.125	82.266	91.406
14 × 22	13½ × 21½	290.250	11180.672	1040.063	50.391	60.469	70.547	80.625	90.703	100.781
14 × 24	13½ × 23½	317.250	14600.109	1242.563	55.078	66.094	77.109	88.125	99.141	110.156
16 × 16	15½ × 15½	240.250	4810.004	620.646	41.710	50.052	58.394	66.736	75.078	83.420
16 × 18	15½ × 17½	271.250	6922.523	791.146	47.092	56.510	65.929	75.347	84.766	94.184
16 × 20	15½ × 19½	302.250	9577.547	982.313	52.474	62.969	73.464	83.958	94.453	104.948
16 × 22	15½ × 21½	333.250	12837.066	1194.146	57.856	69.427	80.998	92.569	104.141	115.712
16 × 24	15½ × 23½	364.250	16763.086	1426.646	63.238	75.885	88.533	101.181	113.828	126.476
18 × 18	17½ × 17½	306.250	7815.754	893.229	53.168	63.802	74.436	85.069	95.703	106.337
18 × 20	17½ × 19½	341.250	10813.359	1109.063	59.245	71.094	82.943	94.792	106.641	118.490
18 × 22	17½ × 21½	376.250	14493.461	1348.229	65.321	78.385	91.450	104.514	117.578	130.642
18 × 24	17½ × 23½	411.250	18926.066	1610.729	71.398	85.677	99.957	114.236	128.516	142.795

Note: 1 in = 25.4 mm; 1 in^2 = 645.2 mm^2; 1 in^3 = 16.39 × 10^3 mm^3; 1 in^4 = 416.2 × 10^3 mm^4; 1 lb/ft^3 = 16.02 kg/m^3.

*Weight in lb·ft^3 = 62.4 $\{G/[1 + G(0.009)\ \text{m.c.}]\}\ [1 \times (\text{m.c.}/100)]$. (For G see Table 5.2.)

Source: From *National Design Specification for Wood Construction,* courtesy of the American Forest and Paper Association, Washington, D.C.

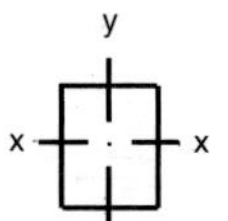

TABLE A.3 Section Properties of Structural Glued-Laminated Timber*

Number of 1½-in. laminations	Depth d, in	Area A, in²	x-x axis		y-y axis		Volume per ft, ft³	Weight, lb/ft		
			S_x, in³	I_x, in⁴	S_y, in³	I_y, in⁴		DFL† (35 lb/ft³)	SP† (36 lb/ft³)	HF/CR† (27 lb/ft³)
3⅛-in width‡										
2	3	9.375	4.688	7.031	4.883	7.629	0.07	2.3	2.3	1.8
3	4.5	14.06	10.55	23.73	7.324	11.44	0.10	3.4	3.5	2.6
4	6	18.75	18.75	56.25	9.766	15.26	0.13	4.6	4.7	3.5
5	7.5	23.44	29.30	109.9	12.21	19.07	0.16	5.7	5.9	4.4
6	9	28.12	42.19	189.8	14.65	22.89	0.20	6.8	7.0	5.3
7	10.5	32.81	57.42	301.5	17.09	26.70	0.23	8.0	8.2	6.2
8	12	37.50	75.00	450.0	19.53	30.52	0.26	9.1	9.4	7.0
9	13.5	42.19	94.92	640.7	21.97	34.33	0.29	10.3	10.5	7.9
10	15	46.88	117.2	878.9	24.41	38.15	0.33	11.4	11.7	8.8
11	16.5	51.56	141.8	1170	26.86	41.96	0.36	12.5	12.9	9.7
12	18	56.25	168.8	1519	29.30	45.78	0.39	13.7	14.1	10.5
13	19.5	60.94	198.0	1931	31.74	49.59	0.42	14.8	15.2	11.4
14	21	65.62	229.7	2412	34.18	53.41	0.46	16.0	16.4	12.3
15	22.5	70.31	263.7	2966	36.62	57.22	0.49	17.1	17.6	13.2
16	24	75.00	300.0	3600	39.06	61.04	0.52	18.2	18.7	14.1
17	25.5	79.69	338.7	4318	41.50	64.85	0.55	19.4	19.9	14.9
18	27	84.38	379.7	5126	43.95	68.66	0.59	20.5	21.1	15.8
19	28.5	89.06	423.0	6028	46.39	72.48	0.62	21.6	22.3	16.7
20	30	93.75	468.8	7031	48.83	76.29	0.65	22.8	23.4	17.6

Depth movement in multiples of 1⅜ in are common for glulam members manufactured using southern pine.

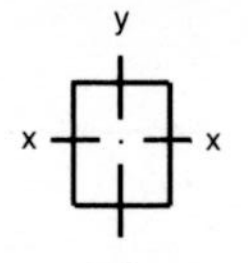

TABLE A.3 Section Properties of Structural Glued-Laminated Timber* *(Continued)*

Number of 1½-in. laminations	Depth d, in	Area A, in²	x-x axis: S_x, in³	x-x axis: I_x, in⁴	y-y axis: S_y, in³	y-y axis: I_y, in⁴	Volume per ft, ft³	Weight, lb/ft: DFL† (35 lb/ft³)	Weight, lb/ft: SP† (36 lb/ft³)	Weight, lb/ft: HF/CR† (27 lb/ft³)
					5⅛-in width‡					
2	3	15.38	7.688	11.53	13.13	33.65	0.11	3.7	3.8	2.9
3	4.5	23.06	17.30	38.92	19.70	50.48	0.16	5.6	5.8	4.3
4	6	30.75	30.75	92.25	26.27	67.31	0.21	7.5	7.7	5.8
5	7.5	38.44	48.05	180.2	32.83	84.13	0.27	9.3	9.6	7.2
6	9	46.12	69.19	311.3	39.40	101.0	0.32	11.2	11.5	8.6
7	10.5	53.81	94.17	494.4	45.96	117.8	0.37	13.1	13.5	10.1
8	12	61.50	123.0	738	52.53	134.6	0.43	14.9	15.4	11.5
9	13.5	69.19	155.7	1051	59.10	151.4	0.48	16.8	17.3	13.0
10	15	76.88	192.2	1441	65.66	168.3	0.53	18.7	19.2	14.4
11	16.5	84.56	232.5	1919	72.23	185.1	0.59	20.6	21.1	15.9
12	18	92.25	276.8	2491	78.80	201.9	0.64	22.4	23.1	17.3
13	19.5	99.98	324.8	3167	85.36	218.7	0.69	24.3	25.0	18.7
14	21	107.6	376.7	3955	91.93	235.6	0.75	26.2	26.9	20.2
15	22.5	115.3	432.4	4865	98.50	252.4	0.80	28.0	28.8	21.6
16	24	123.0	492.0	5904	105.1	269.2	0.85	29.9	30.7	23.1
17	25.5	130.7	555.4	7082	111.6	286.0	0.91	31.8	32.7	24.5
18	27	138.4	622.7	8406	118.2	302.9	0.96	33.6	34.6	25.9
19	28.5	146.1	693.8	9887	124.8	319.7	1.01	35.5	36.5	27.4
20	30	153.8	768.8	11,530	131.3	336.5	1.07	37.4	38.4	28.8
21	31.5	161.4	847.5	13,350	137.9	353.4	1.12	39.2	40.4	30.3
22	33	169.1	930.2	15,350	144.5	370.2	1.17	41.1	42.3	31.7
23	34.5	176.8	1017	17,540	151.0	387.0	1.23	43.0	44.2	33.2
24	36	184.5	1107	19,930	157.6	403.8	1.28	44.8	46.1	34.6

6¾-in width										
2	3	20.25	10.12	15.19	22.78	96.89	0.14	4.9	5.1	3.8
3	4.5	30.38	22.78	51.26	34.17	115.3	0.21	7.4	7.6	5.7
4	6	40.50	40.50	121.5	45.56	153.8	0.28	9.8	10.1	7.6
5	7.5	50.62	63.28	237.3	56.95	192.2	0.35	12.3	12.7	9.5
6	9	60.75	91.12	410.1	68.34	230.7	0.42	14.8	15.2	11.4
7	10.5	70.88	124.0	651.2	79.73	269.1	0.49	17.2	17.7	13.3
8	12	81.00	162.0	972.0	91.12	307.5	0.56	19.7	20.3	15.2
9	13.5	91.12	205.0	1384	102.5	346.0	0.63	22.1	22.8	17.1
10	15	101.3	253.1	1898	113.9	384.4	0.70	24.6	25.3	19.0
11	16.5	111.4	306.3	2527	125.3	422.9	0.77	27.1	27.8	20.9
12	18	121.5	364.5	3280	136.7	461.3	0.84	29.5	30.4	22.8
13	19.5	131.6	427.8	4171	148.1	499.8	0.91	32.0	32.9	24.7
14	21	141.8	496.1	5209	159.5	538.2	0.98	34.5	35.4	26.6
15	22.5	151.9	569.5	6407	170.9	576.7	1.05	36.9	38.0	28.5
16	24	162.0	648.0	7776	182.3	615.1	1.13	39.4	40.5	30.4
17	25.5	172.1	731.5	9327	193.6	653.5	1.20	41.8	43.0	32.3
18	27	182.3	820.1	11,070	205.0	692.0	1.27	44.3	45.6	34.2
19	28.5	192.4	913.8	13,020	216.4	730.4	1.34	46.8	48.1	36.1
20	30	202.5	1013	15,190	227.8	768.9	1.41	49.2	50.6	38.0
21	31.5	212.6	1117	17,580	239.2	807.3	1.48	51.7	53.2	39.9
22	33	222.8	1225	20,220	250.6	845.8	1.55	54.1	55.7	41.8
23	34.5	232.9	1339	23,100	262.0	884.2	1.62	56.6	58.2	43.7
24	36	243.0	1458	26,240	273.4	922.6	1.69	59.1	60.8	45.6
25	37.5	253.1	1582	29,660	284.8	961.1	1.76	61.5	63.3	47.5
26	39	263.3	1711	33,370	296.2	999.5	1.83	64.0	65.8	49.4
27	40.5	273.4	1845	37,370	307.5	1038.0	1.90	66.4	68.3	51.3
28	42	283.5	1984	41,670	318.9	1076.4	1.97	68.9	70.9	53.2
29	43.5	293.6	2129	46,300	330.3	1114.9	2.04	71.4	73.4	55.1

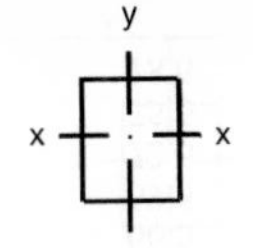

TABLE A.3 Section Properties of Structural Glued-Laminated Timber* (*Continued*)

Number of 1½-in. laminations	Depth d, in	Area A, in²	x-x axis S_x, in³	x-x axis I_x, in⁴	y-y axis S_y, in³	y-y axis I_y, in⁴	Volume per ft, ft³	Weight, lb/ft DFL† (35 lb/ft³)	Weight, lb/ft SP† (36 lb/ft³)	Weight, lb/ft HF/CR† (27 lb/ft³)
					10¾-in width					
27	40.5	435.4	2939	59,510	780.0	4193	3.02	105.8	108.8	81.6
28	42	451.5	3160	66,370	808.9	4348	3.14	109.7	112.9	84.7
29	43.5	467.6	3390	73,740	837.8	4503	3.25	113.7	116.9	87.7
30	45	483.8	3628	81,630	866.7	4659	3.30	117.6	120.9	90.7
31	46.5	499.9	3874	90,070	895.6	4814	3.47	121.5	125.0	93.7
32	48	516.0	4128	99,070	924.5	4969	3.58	125.4	129.0	96.7
33	49.5	532.1	4390	108,700	953.4	5124	3.70	129.3	133.0	99.8
34	51	548.3	4660	118,900	982.3	5280	3.81	133.3	137.1	102.8
35	52.5	564.4	4938	129,600	1011	5435	3.92	137.2	141.1	105.8
36	54	580.5	5224	141,100	1041	5590	4.03	141.1	145.1	108.8
37	55.5	596.6	5519	153,100	1069	5746	4.14	145.0	149.1	111.9
38	57	612.8	5821	165,900	1098	5901	4.26	148.9	153.2	114.9
39	58.5	628.9	6132	179,300	1127	6056	4.37	152.9	157.2	117.9
40	60	645.0	6450	193,500	1156	6212	4.48	156.8	161.2	120.9
41	61.5	661.1	6776	208,400	1184	6367	4.59	160.7	165.3	124.0
42	63	677.3	7111	224,000	1213	6522	4.70	164.6	169.3	127.0
43	64.5	693.4	7454	240,400	1242	6677	4.82	168.5	173.3	130.0
44	66	709.5	7804	257,500	1271	6833	4.93	172.4	177.4	133.0
45	67.5	725.6	8163	275,500	1300	6988	5.04	176.4	181.4	136.1
46	69	741.8	8530	294,300	1329	7143	5.15	180.3	185.4	139.1
47	70.5	757.9	8905	313,900	1358	7299	5.26	184.2	189.5	142.1
48	72	774.0	9288	334,400	1387	7454	5.38	188.1	193.5	145.1
49	73.5	790.1	9679	355,700	1416	7609	5.49	192.0	197.5	148.1
50	75	806.3	10,080	377,900	1444	7764	5.60	196.0	201.6	151.2

Note: 1 in = 25.4 mm; 1 in² = 645.2 mm²; 1 in³ = 16.39 × 10³ mm³; 1 in⁴ = 416.2 × 10³ mm⁴; 1 lb/ft³ = 16.02 kg/m³.

* For use with straight or slightly cambered members. Depths based on multiples of 1½-in-thick laminations.

† DFL = Douglas fir–larch; SP = southern pine; HF = hem-fir; CR = California redwood.

‡ Normal widths are 3⅛ and 5⅛ in for western softwood glued-laminated timbers and 3 and 5 in for southern pine glued-laminated timbers. To determine alternative section properties, multiply A, S, and I_x values for 3⅛-in widths by 3/3.125 and for 5⅛ in widths by 5/5.125.

Source: From *National Design Specifications for Wood Construction,* courtesy of the American Forest and Paper Association, Washington, D.C.

TABLE A.4 Weight of Materials—Roofs and Floors

Refer to local building code for live-load design requirements

Composition roofing, lb/ft²	
2-15 lb and 1-90 lb	1.7
3-15 and 1-90 lb	2.2
3 ply and gravel	5.6
4 ply and gravel	6.0
5 ply and gravel	6.5

Douglas fir sheathing, lb/ft²	
(Based on 36 lb/ft³)	
⅜-in plywood	1.1
½-in plywood	1.5
⅝-in plywood	1.8
¾-in plywood	2.3
1⅛-in plywood	3.4
1-in sheathing	2.3
2-in decking	4.3
3-in decking	7.0
4-in decking	9.3

Miscellaneous decking materials, lb/ft²	
Tectum (1 in thick)	2.0
Insulrock (1 in thick)	2.7
Poured gypsum (1 in thick)	6.5
Vermiculite concrete (1 in thick)	2.6
Petrical (1 in thick)	2.7
Corrugated galvanized steel	
16 ga.	2.9
20 ga.	1.8
22 ga.	1.5
24 ga.	1.3

Rigid insulation, lb/ft²	
Temlock (1 in thick)	1.2
Cork (1 in thick)	0.7
Gold Bond (1 in thick)	1.5
Styrofoam (1 in thick)	0.2
Foamglass (1 in thick)	0.8
Rigid Fiberglas (1 in thick)	1.5

Roll or batt insulation, lb/ft²	
Rock Wood (1 in thick)	0.2
Glass Wool (1 in thick)	0.3
ALPOL (1 in thick)	0.1

Floors, lb/ft²	
Hardwood (nominal 1 in)	4.0
Concrete (1 in thick):	
Regular	12.0
Lightweight	6.0 to 10.0
Linoleum or soft tile	1.5
¾-in ceramic or quality tile	10.0

Ceilings, lb/ft²	
Acoustical fiber tile	1.0
½-in gypsum board	2.2
⅝-in gypsum board	2.8
Plaster (1 in thick)	8.0
Metal suspension system (inc. tile)	1.8
Wood suspension system (inc. tile)	2.5

Wood framing members, lb/ft²

Nominal size	Joist spacing, in: 12	16	24
2 × 4	1.4	1.1	0.7
2 × 6	2.2	1.7	1.1
2 × 8	2.9	2.2	1.5
2 × 10	3.7	2.8	1.9
2 × 12	4.4	3.3	2.2

Wood framing members, lb/ft	
3 × 6	2.4
4 × 6	5.0
4 × 8	6.8
4 × 10	8.6
4 × 12	10.4

Weight of sprinkler systems

Size of pipe, in	Dry, lb/ft	Wet, lb/ft
1	1.7	2.1
1¼	2.3	3.0
1½	2.7	3.6
2	3.7	5.2
2½	5.8	7.9
3	7.6	10.8
3½	9.2	13.5
4	10.9	16.4
5	14.81	23.5
6	19.2	31.7
8	28.6	50.8
10	40.5	74.6

Truss weight (approximate)

Chord size: Top	Bottom	lb/ft of truss length	For truss spacing of 24-in centers, lb/ft²
2 × 4	2 × 4	5.2	2.6
2 × 6	2 × 4	6.1	3.1
2 × 6	2 × 6	6.9	3.5
2 × 8	2 × 6	7.8	3.9
2 × 8	2 × 8	8.5	4.3
2 × 10	2 × 8	9.3	4.7
2 × 10	2 × 10	10.0	5.2
2 × 12	2 × 10	10.9	5.5
2 × 12	2 × 12	11.6	5.8

Note: 1 in = 25.4 mm; 1 lb = 0.4536 kg; 1 lb/ft = 1.488 kg/m; 1 lb/ft² = 4.882 kg/m².

TABLE A.5 Amount of Camber for Glulams (in)

	Radius,* ft				Radius,* ft		
Span, ft	1600	2000	3000	Span, ft	1600	2000	3000
6	1/16			56	2 15/16	2 3/8	1 9/16
7	1/16	1/16		57	3 1/16	2 7/16	1 5/8
8	1/16	1/16	1/16	58	3 1/8	2 1/2	1 11/16
9	1/16	1/16	1/16	59	3 1/4	2 5/8	1 3/4
10	1/8	1/16	1/16	60	3 3/8	2 11/16	1 13/16
11	1/8	1/16	1/16	61	3 1/2	2 13/16	1 7/8
12	1/8	1/8	1/16	62	3 5/8	2 7/8	1 15/16
13	3/16	1/8	1/16	63	3 3/4	3	2
14	3/16	1/8	1/8	64	3 13/16	3 1/16	2 1/16
15	3/16	3/16	1/8	65	3 15/16	3 3/16	2 1/8
16	1/4	3/16	1/8	66	4 1/16	3 1/4	2 3/16
17	1/4	3/16	1/8	67	4 3/16	3 3/8	2 1/4
18	5/16	1/4	3/16	68	4 5/16	3 7/16	2 5/16
19	5/16	1/4	3/16	69	4 7/16	3 9/16	2 3/8
20	3/8	5/16	3/16	70	4 5/8	3 11/16	2 7/16
21	7/16	5/16	1/4	71	4 3/4	3 3/4	2 1/2
22	7/16	3/8	1/4	72	4 7/8	3 7/8	2 9/16
23	1/2	3/8	1/4	73	5	4	2 11/16
24	9/16	7/16	5/16	74	5 1/8	4 1/8	2 3/4
25	9/16	1/2	5/16	75	5 1/4	4 1/4	2 13/16
26	5/8	1/2	5/16	76	5 7/16	4 5/16	2 7/8
27	11/16	9/16	3/8	77	5 9/16	4 7/16	2 15/16
28	3/4	9/16	3/8	78	5 11/16	4 9/16	3 1/16
29	13/16	5/8	7/16	79	5 7/8	4 11/16	3 1/8
30	7/8	11/16	7/16	80	6	4 13/16	3 3/16
31	7/8	3/4	1/2	81	6 1/8	4 15/16	3 1/4
32	15/16	3/4	1/2	82	6 5/16	5 1/16	3 3/8
33	1	13/16	9/16	83	6 7/16	5 3/16	3 7/16
34	1 1/16	7/8	9/16	84	6 5/8	5 5/16	3 1/2
35	1 1/8	15/16	5/8	85	6 3/4	5 7/16	3 5/8
36	1 3/16	1	5/8	86	6 15/16	5 9/16	3 11/16
37	1 5/16	1	11/16	87	7 1/8	5 11/16	3 13/16
38	1 3/8	1 1/16	3/4	88	7 1/4	5 13/16	3 7/8
39	1 7/16	1 1/8	3/4	89	7 1/16	5 15/16	3 15/16
40	1 1/2	1 3/16	13/16	90	7 5/8	6 1/16	4 1/16
41	1 9/16	1 1/4	13/16	91	7 3/4	6 3/16	4 1/8
42	1 5/8	1 5/16	7/8	92	7 15/16	6 3/8	4 1/14
43	1 3/4	1 3/8	15/16	93	8 1/8	6 1/2	4 5/16
44	1 13/16	1 7/16	15/16	94	8 5/16	6 5/8	4 7/16
45	1 7/8	1 1/2	1	95	8 7/16	6 3/4	4 1/2
46	2	1 9/16	1 1/16	96	8 5/8	6 15/16	4 5/8
47	2 1/16	1 11/16	1 1/8	97	8 13/16	7 1/16	4 11/16
48	2 3/16	1 3/4	1 1/8	98	9	7 3/16	4 13/16
49	2 1/4	1 13/16	1 3/16	99	9 3/16	7 3/8	4 7/8
50	2 3/8	1 7/8	1 1/4	100	9 3/8	7 1/2	5
51	2 7/16	1 15/16	1 5/16	101	9 9/16	7 5/8	5 1/8
52	2 9/16	2	1 3/8	102	9 3/4	7 13/16	5 3/16
53	2 5/8	2 1/8	1 3/8	103	9 15/16	7 15/16	5 5/16
54	2 3/4	2 3/16	1 7/16	104	10 1/8	8 1/8	5 7/16
55	2 13/16	2 1/4	1 1/2	105	10 5/16	8 1/4	5 1/2

**Note:*

$$R = \left[\frac{4\,(\text{camber})^2 + (\text{span})^2}{8\,(\text{camber})}\right] \div 12$$

where camber and span are to be given in inches and R = radius of curvature in feet.

Example: span = 52 ft × 12 = 624 in, camber = 2 in.

$$R = \left[\frac{4\,(2)^2 + (624)^2}{8\,(2)}\right] \div 12 = 2028 \text{ ft} \approx 2000 \text{ ft}$$

ADJUSTMENT FACTORS FOR TABLE A.6

Size Factor C_F

Tabulated bending, tension, and compression parallel to grain design values for dimension lumber 2 to 4 in thick shall be multiplied by the following size factors:

Size Factors C_F

Grades	Width, in	F_b Thickness 2 & 3 in	F_b Thickness 4 in	F_t	F_c
Select Structural, No. 1 & Btr. No. 1, No. 2, No. 3	2, 3, 4	1.5	1.5	1.5	1.15
	5	1.4	1.4	1.4	1.1
	6	1.3	1.3	1.3	1.1
	8	1.2	1.3	1.2	1.05
	10	1.1	1.2	1.1	1.0
	12	1.0	1.1	1.0	1.0
	14 and wider	0.9	1.0	0.9	0.9
Stud	2, 3, 4,	1.1	1.1	1.1	1.05
	5, 6	1.0	1.0	1.0	1.0
Construction & Standard	2, 3, 4	1.0	1.0	1.0	1.0
Utility	4	1.0	1.0	1.0	1.0
	2, 3	0.4	—	0.4	0.6

Repetitive Member Factor C_r

Bending design values F_b for dimension lumber 2 to 4 in thick shall be multiplied by the repetitive member factor C_r = 1.15, when such members are used as joists, truss chords, rafters, studs, planks, decking or similar members which are in contact or spaced not more than 24 in on centers, are not less than 3 in number and are joined by floor, roof or other load distributing elements adequate to support the design load.

Flat-Use Factor C_{fu}

Bending design values adjusted by size factors are based on edgewise use (load applied to narrow face). When dimension lumber is used flatwise (load applied to wide face), the bending design value E_b also shall be multiplied by the following flat use factors:

Flat-Use Factors C_{fu}

Width, in	Thickness 2 & 3 in	Thickness 4 in
2, 3	1.0	—
4	1.1	1.0
5	1.1	1.05
6	1.15	1.05
8	1.15	1.05
10 and wider	1.2	1.1

Wet-Service Factor C_M

When dimension lumber is used where moisture content will exceed 19 percent for an extended time period, design values shall be multiplied by the appropriate wet service factors from the following table:

Wet-Service Factors C_M

F_b	F_t	F_V	$F_{c\perp}$	F_c	E
0.85*	1.0	0.97	0.67	0.8†	0.9

*When $(F_b)(C_F) \leq 1150$ psi, $C_M = 1.0$
†When $(F_c)(C_F) \leq 750$ psi, $C_M = 1.0$

Shear Stress Factor C_H

Tabulated shear design values parallel to grain have been reduced to allow for the occurrence of splits, checks, and shakes. Tabulated shear design values parallel to grain F_v shall be permitted to be multiplied by the shear stress factors specified in the following table when length of split or size of check or shake is known and no increase in them is anticipated.

A.15

Shear Stress Factors C_H

Length of split on wide face of 2-in (nominal) lumber	C_H	Length of split on wide face of 3-in (nominal) and thicker lumber	C_H	Size of shake* in 2-in (nominal) and thicker lumber	C_H
No split	2.00	No split	2.00	No shake	2.00
½ × wide face	1.67	½ × narrow face	1.67	⅙ × narrow face	1.67
¾ × wide face	1.50	¾ × narrow face	1.50	¼ narrow face	1.50
1 × wide face	1.33	1 × narrow face	1.33	⅓ × narrow face	1.33
1½ × wide face or more	1.00	1½ × narrow face or more	1.00	½ × narrow face or more	1.00

*Shake is measured at the end between lines enclosing the shake and perpendicular to the loaded face.

ADJUSTMENT FACTORS FOR TABLE A.7

Appropriate size adjustment factors have already been incorporated in the tabulated design values for most thicknesses of southern pine and mixed southern pine dimension lumber. For dimension lumber 4-in thick, 8-in, and wider (all grades except Dense Structural 86, Dense Structural 72, and Dense Structural 65), tabulated bending design values F_b shall be permitted to be multiplied by the size factor C_F = 1.1. For dimension lumber wider than 12-in (all grades except Dense Structural 86, Dense Structural 72, and Dense Structural 65), tabulated bending, tension, and compression parallel to grain design values for 12-in wide lumber shall be multiplied by the size factor $C_F = 0.9$. When the depth d of Dense Structural 86, Dense Structural 72, or Dense Structural 65 dimension lumber exceeds 12-in, the tabulated bending design value F_b shall be multiplied by the following size factor:

$$C_F = (12/d)^{1/9}$$

Repetitive Member Factor C_r

Bending design values F_b for dimension lumber 2 to 4 in thick shall be multiplied by the repetitive-member factor C_r = 1.15, when such members are used as joists, truss chords, rafters, studs, planks, decking or similar members which are in contact or spaced not more than 24 in on centers, are not less than 3 in number, and are joined by floor, roof, or other load-distributing elements adequate to support the design load.

Flat-Use Factor C_{fu}

Bending design values adjusted by size factors are based on edgewise use (load applied to narrow face). When dimension lumber is used flatwise (load applied to wide face), the bending design value F_b also shall be multiplied by the following flat use factors:

Flat-Use Factors C_{fu}

	Thickness	
Width, in	2 & 3 in	4 in
2, 3	1.0	—
4	1.1	1.0
5	1.1	1.05
6	1.15	1.05
8	1.15	1.05
10 and wider	1.2	1.1

Wet-Service Factor C_M

When dimension lumber is used where moisture content will exceed 19 percent for an extended time period, design values shall be multiplied by the appropriate wet-service factors from the following table (for Dense Structural 86, Dense Structural 72, and Dense Structural 65, use tabulated design values for wet-service conditions without further adjustment):

Wet-Service Factors C_M

F_b	F_t	F_V	$F_{c\perp}$	F_c	E
0.85*	1.0	0.97	0.67	0.8†	0.9

*When $(F_b)(C_F) \leq 1150$ psi, $C_M = 1.0$
†When $F_c \leq 750$ psi, $C_M = 1.0$

Shear Stress Factor C_H

Tabulated shear design values parallel to grain have been reduced to allow for the occurrence of splits, checks, and shakes. Tabulated shear design values parallel to grain F_v shall be permitted to be multiplied by the shear stress factors specified in the following table when length of split or size of check or shake is known and no increase in them is anticipated. When shear stress factors are used for southern pine, a tabulated design value of $F_V = 90$ psi shall be assigned for all grades of southern pine dimension lumber. Shear stress factors shall be permitted to be linearly interpolated.

Shear Stress Factors C_H

Length of split on wide face of 2-in (nominal) lumber	C_H	Length of split on wide face of 3-in (nominal) and thicker lumber	C_H	Size of shake* in 2-in (nominal) and thicker lumber	C_H
No split	2.00	No split	2.00	No shake	2.00
½ × wide face	1.67	½ × narrow face	1.67	⅙ × narrow face	1.67
¾ × wide face	1.50	¾ × narrow face	1.50	¼ narrow face	1.50
1 × wide face	1.33	1 × narrow face	1.33	⅓ × narrow face	1.33
1½ × wide face or more	1.00	1½ × narrow face or more	1.00	½ × narrow face or more	1.00

*Shake is measured at the end between lines enclosing the shake and perpendicular to the loaded face.

TABLE A.7 Design Values for Visually Graded Southern Pine Dimension Lumber

Tabulated design values are for normal load duration and dry service conditions, unless specified otherwise. (Use with Table A.7 Adjustment Factors.)

Species and commercial grade	Size classification	Design values in pounds per square inch (psi)						Grading Rules Agency
		Bending F_b	Tension parallel to grain F_t	Shear parallel to grain F_V	Compression perpendicular to grain $F_{c\perp}$	Compression parallel to grain F_c	Modulus of Elasticity E	
Southern Pine								
Dense Select Structural		3050	1650	100	660	2250	1,900,000	SPIB
Select Structural		2850	1600	100	565	2100	1,800,000	
Non-Dense Select Structural		2650	1350	100	480	1950	1,700,000	
No. 1 Dense		2000	1100	100	660	2000	1,800,000	
No. 1	2–4 in thick	1850	1050	100	565	1850	1,700,000	
No. 1 Non-Dense		1700	900	100	480	1700	1,600,000	
No. 2 Dense	2–4 in wide	1700	875	90	660	1850	1,700,000	
No. 2		1500	825	90	565	1650	1,600,000	
No. 2 Non-Dense		1350	775	90	480	1600	1,400,000	
No. 3		850	475	90	565	975	1,400,000	
Stud		875	500	90	565	975	1,400,000	
Construction	2–4 in thick	1100	625	100	565	1800	1,500,000	SPIB
Standard		625	350	90	565	1500	1,300,000	
Utility	4 in wide	300	175	90	565	975	1,300,000	
Dense Select Structural		2700	1500	90	660	2150	1,900,000	SPIB
Select Structural		2550	1400	90	565	2000	1,800,000	
Non-Dense Select Structural		2350	1200	90	480	1850	1,700,000	
No. 1 Dense		1750	950	90	660	1900	1,800,000	
No. 1	2–4 in thick	1650	900	90	565	1750	1,700,000	
No. 1 Non-Dense		1500	800	90	480	1600	1,600,000	
No. 2 Dense	5–6 in wide	1450	775	90	660	1750	1,700,000	
No. 2		1250	725	90	565	1600	1,600,000	
No. 2 Non-Dense		1150	675	90	480	1500	1,400,000	
No. 3		750	425	90	565	925	1,400,000	
Stud		775	425	90	565	925	1,400,000	

Dense Select Structural		2450	1350	90	660	2050	1,900,000	SPIB
Select Structural		2300	1300	90	565	1900	1,800,000	
Non-Dense Select Structural		2100	1100	90	480	1750	1,700,000	
No. 1 Dense	2–4 in thick	1650	875	90	660	1800	1,800,000	
No. 1		1500	825	90	565	1650	1,700,000	
No. 1 Non-Dense	8 in wide	1350	725	90	480	1550	1,600,000	
No. 2 Dense		1400	675	90	660	1700	1,700,000	
No. 2		1200	650	90	565	1550	1,600,000	
No. 2 Non-Dense		1100	600	90	480	1450	1,400,000	
No. 3		700	400	90	565	875	1,400,000	
Dense Select Structural		2150	1200	90	660	2000	1,900,000	SPIB
Select Structural		2050	1100	90	565	1850	1,800,000	
Non-Dense Select Structural		1850	950	90	480	1750	1,700,000	
No. 1 Dense	2–4 in thick	1450	775	90	660	1750	1,800,000	
No. 1		1300	725	90	565	1600	1,700,000	
No. 1 Non-Dense	10 in wide	1200	650	90	480	1500	1,600,000	
No. 2 Dense		1200	625	90	660	1650	1,700,000	
No. 2		1050	575	90	565	1500	1,600,000	
No. 2 Non-Dense		950	550	90	480	1400	1,400,000	
No. 3		600	325	90	565	850	1,400,000	
Dense Select Structural		2050	1100	90	660	1950	1,900,000	SPIB
Select Structural		1900	1050	90	565	1800	1,800,000	
Non-Dense Select Structural		1750	900	90	480	1700	1,700,000	
No. 1 Dense	2–4 in thick	1350	725	90	660	1700	1,800,000	
No. 1		1250	675	90	565	1600	1,700,000	
No. 1 Non-Dense	12 in wide	1150	600	90	480	1500	1,600,000	
No. 2 Dense		1150	575	90	660	1600	1,700,000	
No. 2		975	550	90	565	1450	1,600,000	
No. 2 Non-Dense		900	525	90	480	1350	1,400,000	
No. 3		575	325	90	565	825	1,400,000	

TABLE A.7 Design Values for Visually Graded Southern Pine Dimension Lumber *(Continued)*

Tabulated design values are for normal load duration and dry service conditions, unless specified otherwise. (Use with Table A.7 Adjustment Factors.)

Species and commercial grade	Size classification	Design values in pounds per square inch (psi)						Grading Rules Agency
		Bending F_b	Tension parallel to grain F_t	Shear parallel to grain F_V	Compression perpendicular to grain $F_{c\perp}$	Compression parallel to grain F_c	Modulus of Elasticity E	
Southern Pine		(Dry-service conditions—19% or less moisture content)						
Dense Structural 86	2–4 in thick	2600	1750	155	660	2000	1,800,000	SPIB
Dense Structural 72		2200	1450	130	660	1650	1,800,000	
Dense Structural 65	2 in & wider	2000	1300	115	660	1500	1,800,000	
Southern Pine		(Wet-service conditions)						
Dense Structural 86	2½–4 in thick	2100	1400	145	440	1300	1,600,000	SPIB
Dense Structural 72		1750	1200	120	440	1100	1,600,000	
Dense Structural 65	2½ in & wider	1600	1050	110	440	1000	1,600,000	

Notes: (1) ***Lumber dimensions.*** Tabulated design values are applicable to lumber that will be used under dry conditions such as in most covered structures. For 2- to 4-in-thick lumber the *dry* dressed sizes shall be used (see Table A.1) regardless of the moisture content at the time of manufacture or use. In calculating design values, the natural gain in strength and stiffness that occurs as lumber dries has been taken into consideration as well as the reduction in size that occurs when unseasoned lumber shrinks. The gain in load-carrying capacity due to inceased strength and stiffness resulting from drying more than offsets the design effect of size reductions due to shrinkage. (2) *Stress-rated boards.* Information for various grades of southern pine stress-rated boards of nominal 1, 1¼, and 1½ in thickness, 2 in and wider, is available from the Southern Pine Inspection Bureau (SPIB) in the *Standard Grading Rules for Southern Pine Lumber.* (3) *Spruce pine.* To obtain recommended design values for spruce pine graded to SPIB rules, multiply the appropriate design values for mixed southern pine by the corresponding conversion factor shown below and round to the nearest 100,000 psi for E; to the next lower multiple of 5 psi for F_V and $F_{c\perp}$; to the next lower multiple of 50 psi for F_b, F_t, and F_c if 1000 psi or greater, 25 psi otherwise.

Conversion Factors for Determining Design Values for Spruce Pine

	Bending F_b	Tension parallel to grain F_t	Shear parallel to grain F_V	Compression perpendicular to grain $F_{c\perp}$	Compression parallel to grain F_c	Modulus of Elasticity E
Conversion factor	0.784	0.784	0.965	0.682	0.766	0.807

Source: *Design Values for Wood Construction,* a supplement to the 1991 edition of *National Design Specification,* courtesy of the American Forest and Paper Association, Washington, D.C.

ADJUSTMENT FACTORS FOR TABLE A.8

Repetitive-Member Factor C_r

Bending design values F_b for dimension lumber 2 to 4 in thick shall be multiplied by the repetitive-member factor $C_r = 1.15$ when such members are used as joists, truss chords, rafters, studs, planks, decking, or similar members which are in contact or spaced not more than 24 in on center, are not less than 3 in number, and are joined by floor, roof, or other load-distributing elements adequate to support the design load.

Flat-Use Factor C_{fu}

Bending design values adjusted by size factors are based on edgewise use (load applied to narrow face). When dimension lumber is used flatwise (load applied to wide face), the bending design value F_b also shall be multiplied by the following flat use factors:

Flat-Use Factors C_{fu}

	Thickness
Width, in	2 in
2 & 3	1.0
4	1.1
5	1.1
6	1.15
8	1.15
10 & wider	1.2

Wet-Service Factor C_M

When dimension lumber is used where moisture content will exceed 19 percent for an extended time period, design values shall be multiplied by the appropriate wet-service factors from the following table:

Wet-Service Factors C_M

F_b	F_t	F_V	$F_{c\perp}$	F_c	E
0.85*	1.0	0.97	0.67	0.8	0.9

*when $F_b \leq 1150$ psi, $C_M = 1.0$.

Shear Stress Factor C_H

Tabulated shear design values parallel to grain have been reduced to allow for the occurrence of splits, checks, and shakes. Tabulated shear design values parallel to grain F_V shall be permitted to be multiplied by the shear stress factors specified in the following table when length of split or size of check or shake is known and no increase in them is anticipated. Shear stress factors shall be permitted to be linearly interpolated.

Shear Stress Factors C_H

Length of split on wide face of 2-in (nominal) lumber	C_H	Length of split on wide face of 3-in (nominal) and thicker lumber	C_H	Size of shake* in 2-in (nominal) and thicker lumber	C_H
No split	2.00	No split	2.00	No shake	2.00
½ × wide face	1.67	½ × narrow face	1.67	⅙ × narrow face	1.67
¾ × wide face	1.50	¾ × narrow face	1.50	¼ narrow face	1.50
1 × wide face	1.33	1 × narrow face	1.33	⅓ × narrow face	1.33
1½ × wide face or more	1.00	1½ × narrow face or more	1.00	½ × narrow face or more	1.00

*Shake is measured at the end between lines enclosing the shake and perpendicular to the loaded face.

TABLE A.8 Design Values for Mechanically Graded Dimension Lumber

Tabulated design values are for normal load duration and dry-service conditions. (Use with Table A.8 Adjustment Factors.)

Species and commercial grade	Size classification	Design values in pounds per square inch (psi)				Grading Rules Agency
		Bending F_b	Tension parallel to grain F_t	Compression parallel to grain F_c	Modulus of Elasticity E	
Machine stress rated (MSR) lumber						
900f-1.0E	2 in & less in thickness 2 in & wider	900	350	1050	1,000,000	WCLIB, WWPA
1200f-1.2E		1200	600	1400	1,200,000	NLGA, SPIB, WCLIB, WWPA
1350f-1.3E		1350	750	1600	1,300,000	SPIB, WCLIB, WWPA
1450f-1.3E		1450	800	1625	1,300,000	NLGA, WCLIB, WWPA
1500f-1.3E		1500	900	1650	1,300,000	SPIB
1500f-1.4E		1500	900	1650	1,400,000	NLGA, SPIB, WCLIB, WWPA
1650f-1.4E		1650	1020	1700	1,400,000	SPIB
1650f-1.5E		1650	1020	1700	1,500,000	NLGA, SPIB, WCLIB, WWPA
1800f-1.6E		1800	1175	1750	1,600,000	NLGA, SPIB, WCLIB, WWPA
1950f-1.5E		1950	1375	1800	1,500,000	SPIB
1950f-1.7E		1950	1375	1800	1,700,000	NLGA, SPIB, WWPA
2100f-1.8E		2100	1575	1875	1,800,000	NLGA, SPIB, WCLIB, WWPA
2250f-1.6E		2250	1750	1925	1,600,000	SPIB
2250f-1.9E		2250	1750	1925	1,900,000	NLGA, SPIB, WWPA
2400f-1.7E		2400	1925	1975	1,700,000	SPIB
2400f-2.0E		2400	1925	1975	2,000,000	NLGA, SPIB, WCLIB, WWPA
2550f-2.1E		2550	2050	2025	2,100,000	NLGA, SPIB, WWPA
2700f-2.2E		2700	2150	2100	2,200,000	NLGA, SPIB, WCLIB, WWPA
2850f-2.3E		2850	2300	2150	2,300,000	SPIB, WWPA
3000f-2.4E		3000	2400	2200	2,400,000	NLGA, SPIB
3150f-2.5E		3150	2500	2250	2,500,000	SPIB
3300f-2.6E		3300	2650	2325	2,600,000	SPIB

900f-1.2E		900	350	1050	1,200,000	NLGA, WCLIB
1200f-1.5E	2 in & less in thickness	1200	600	1400	1,500,000	NLGA, WCLIB
1350f-1.8E		1350	750	1600	1,800,000	NLGA
1500f-1.8E	6 in & wider	1500	900	1650	1,800,000	WCLIB
1800f-2.1E		1800	1175	1750	2,100,000	NLGA, WCLIB
Machine evaluated lumber (MEL)						
M-10		1400	800	1600	1,200,000	
M-11		1550	850	1650	1,500,000	
M-12		1600	850	1700	1,600,000	
M-13		1600	950	1700	1,400,000	
M-14		1800	1000	1750	1,700,000	
M-15		1800	1100	1750	1,500,000	
M-16		1800	1300	1750	1,500,000	
M-17	2 in & less in thickness	1950	1300	2050	1,700,000	
M-18		2000	1200	1850	1,800,000	SPIB
M-19	2 in & wider	2000	1300	1850	1,600,000	
M-20		2000	1600	2100	1,900,000	
M-21		2300	1400	1950	1,900,000	
M-22		2350	1500	1950	1,700,000	
M-23		2400	1900	2000	1,800,000	
M-24		2700	1800	2100	1,900,000	
M-25		2750	2000	2100	2,200,000	
M-26		2800	1800	2150	2,000,000	
M-27		3000	2000	2400	2,100,000	

Notes: (1) *Lumber dimensions.* Tabulated design values are applicable to lumber that will be used under dry conditions such as in most covered structures. For 2- to 4-in thick lumber the *dry* dressed sizes shall be used (see Table A.1) regardless of the moisture content at the time of manufacture or use. In calculating design values, the natural gain in strength and stiffness that occurs as lumber dries has been taken into consideration as well as the reduction in size that occurs when unseasoned lumber shrinks. The gain in load-carrying capacity due to increased strength and stiffness resulting from drying more than offsets the design effect of size reductions due to shrinkage. (2) *Shear parallel to grain F_V and compression prependicular to grain F_V.* Design values for shear parallel to grain F_V and compression perpendicular to grain $F_{c\perp}$ are identical to the design values given in Tables A.6 and A.7 for No. 2 visually graded lumber of the appropriate species. (3) *Modulus of elasticity E.* For any given bending design value F_b the average modulus of elasticity E may vary depending on species, timber source, or other variables. The E value included in the F_b-E grade designations in Table A.8 are those usually associated with each F_b level. Grade stamps may show higher or lower E values (in increments of 100,000 psi) if machine rating indicates the assignment is appropriate. When the E value shown on a grade stamp differs from the E value in Table A.8, the E value shown on the grade stamp shall be used for design. The tabulated F_b, F_t, and F_c values associated with the designated F_b value shall be used for design.

Source: *Design Values for Wood Construction,* a supplement to the 1991 edition of *National Design Specification,* courtesy of the American Forest and Paper Association, Washington, D.C.

ADJUSTMENT FACTORS FOR TABLE A.9

Size Factor C_F

When the depth d of a beam, stringer, post, or timber exceeds 12 in, the tabulated bending design value F_b shall be multiplied by the following size factor:

$$C_F = (12/d)^{1/9}$$

Wet-Service Factor C_M

When timbers are used where moisture content will exceed 19 percent for an extended time period, design values shall be multiplied by the appropriate wet-service factors from the following table (for southern pine, use tabulated design values without further adjustment):

Wet-Service Factors C_M

F_b	F_t	F_V	$F_{c\perp}$	F_c	E
1.00	1.00	1.00	0.67	0.91	1.00

Shear Stress Factor C_H

Tabulated shear design values parallel to grain have been reduced to allow for the occurrence of splits, checks, and shakes. Tabulated shear design values parallel to grain F_V shall be permitted to be multiplied by the shear stress factors specified in the following table when length of split or size of check or shake is known and no increase in them is anticipated. When shear stress factors are used for southern pine, a tabulated design value of F_V = 90 psi shall be assigned for all grades of southern pine. Shear stress factors shall be permitted to be linearly interpolated.

Shear Stress Factors C_H

Length of split on wide face of 5-in (nominal) and thicker lumber	C_H	Size of shake* in 5-in (nominal) and thicker lumber	C_H
No split	2.00	No shake	2.00
½ × narrow face	1.67	⅙ × narrow face	1.67
¾ × narrow face	1.50	¼ narrow face	1.50
1 × narrow face	1.33	⅓ × narrow face	1.33
1½ × narrow face or more	1.00	½ × narrow face or more	1.00

*Shake is measured at the end between lines enclosing the shake and perpendicular to the loaded face.

TABLE A.9 Design Values for Visually Graded Timbers (5 × 5 in and Larger)

Tabulated design values are for normal load duration and dry-service conditions unless specified otherwise. (Use with Table A.9 Adjustment Factors.)

Species and commercial grade	Size classification	Design values in pounds per square inch (psi)						Grading Rules Agency
		Bending F_b	Tension parallel to grain F_i	Shear parallel to grain F_V	Compression perpendicular to grain $F_{c\perp}$	Compression parallel to grain F_c	Modulus of Elasticity E	
Douglas fir-larch								
Dense Select Structural	Beams and stringers	1900	1100	85	730	1300	1,700,000	WCLIB
Select Structural		1600	950	85	625	1100	1,600,000	
Dense No. 1		1550	775	85	730	1100	1,700,000	
No. 1		1350	675	85	625	925	1,600,000	
No. 2		875	425	85	625	600	1,300,000	
Dense Select Structural	Posts and Timbers	1750	1150	85	730	1350	1,700,000	
Select Structural		1500	1000	85	625	1150	1,600,000	
Dense No. 1		1400	950	85	730	1200	1,700,000	
No. 1		1200	825	85	625	1000	1,600,000	
No. 2		750	475	85	625	700	1,300,000	
Dense Select Structural	Beams and stringers	1850	1100	85	730	1300	1,700,000	WWPA
Select Structural		1600	950	85	625	1100	1,600,000	
Dense No. 1		1550	775	85	730	1100	1,700,000	
No. 1		1350	675	85	625	925	1,600,000	
Dense No. 2		1000	500	85	730	700	1,400,000	
No. 2		875	425	85	625	600	1,300,000	
Dense Select Structural	Posts and timbers	1750	1150	85	730	1350	1,700,000	
Select Structural		1500	1000	85	625	1150	1,600,000	
Dense No. 1		1400	950	85	730	1200	1,700,000	
No. 1		1200	825	85	625	1000	1,600,000	
Dense No. 2		800	550	85	730	550	1,400,000	
No. 2		700	475	85	625	475	1,300,000	

TABLE A.9 Design Values for Visually Graded Timbers (5 × 5 in and Larger) *(Continued)*

Tabulated design values are for normal load duration and dry-service conditions unless specified otherwise. (Use with Table A.9 Adjustment Factors.)

Species and commercial grade	Size classification	Design values in pounds per square inch (psi)						Grading Rules Agency
		Bending F_b	Tension parallel to grain F_t	Shear parallel to grain F_V	Compression perpendicular to grain $F_{c\perp}$	Compression parallel to grain F_c	Modulus of Elasticity E	
Hem-fir								
Select Structural	Beams and stringers	1300	750	70	405	9250	1,300,000	WCLIB
No. 1		1050	525	70	405	750	1,300,000	
No. 2		675	350	70	405	500	1,100,000	
Select Structural	Posts and timbers	1200	800	70	405	975	1,300,000	
No. 1		975	650	70	405	850	1,300,000	
No. 2		575	375	70	405	575	1,100,000	
Select Structural	Beams and stringers	1250	725	70	405	925	1,300,000	WWPA
No. 1		1050	525	70	405	775	1,300,000	
No. 2		675	325	70	405	475	1,100,000	
Select Structural	Posts and timbers	1200	800	70	405	975	1,300,000	
No. 1		950	650	70	405	850	1,300,000	
No. 2		525	350	70	405	375	1,100,000	
Southern Pine		(Wet-service conditions)						
Dense Select Structural SR	5 × 5 in & larger	1750	1200	110	440	1100	1,600,000	SPIB
Select Structural SR		1500	1000	110	375	950	1,500,000	
No. 1 Dense SR		1550	1050	110	440	975	1,600,000	
No. 1 SR		1350	900	110	375	825	1,500,000	
No. 2 Dense SR		975	650	100	440	625	1,300,000	
No. 2 SR		650	590	100	375	525	1,200,000	
Dense Structural 86		2100	1400	145	440	1300	1,600,000	
Dense Structural 72		1750	1200	120	440	1100	1,600,000	
Dense Structural 65		1600	1050	110	440	1000	1,600,000	

Spruce-pine-fir								
Select Structural	Beams and stringers	1100	650	65	425	775	1,300,000	
No. 1		900	450	65	425	625	1,300,000	
No. 2		600	300	65	425	425	1,000,000	NLGA
Select Structural	Posts and timbers	1050	700	65	425	800	1,300,000	
No. 1		850	550	65	425	700	1,300,000	
No. 2		500	325	65	425	500	1,000,000	

Note: (1) *Lumber dimensions.* Tabulated design values are applicable to lumber that will be used under dry conditions such as in most covered structures. For 5 in and thicker lumber, the *green* dressed sizes shall be permitted to be used (see Table A.1) because design values have been adjusted to compensate for any loss in size by shrinkage which may occur.

Conversion Factors for Determining Design Values for Spruce Pine

	Bending F_b	Tension parallel to grain F_b	Shear parallel to grain F_V	Compression perpendicular to grain $F_{c\perp}$	Compression parallel to grain F_c	Modulus of Elasticity E
Conversion factor	0.784	0.784	0.965	0.682	0.766	0.807

Source: *Design Values for Wood Construction,* a supplement to the 1991 edition of *National Design Specification,* courtesy of the American Forest and Paper Association, Washington, D.C.

ADJUSTMENT FACTORS FOR TABLE A.10

Volume Factor C_v

Tabulated bending design values for loading perpendicular to wide faces of laminations F_{bxx} for structural glued laminated bending members shall be multiplied by the following volume factor:

$$C_V = K_L\,(21/L)^{1/x}(12/d)^{1/x}(5.125/b)^{1/x} \leq 1.0$$

where L = length of bending member between points of zero moment, ft
d = depth of bending member, inches
b = width (breadth) of bending member, inches. For multiple piece width layups, b = width of widest piece in the layup. Thus $b \leq 10.75$ in.
x = 20 for southern pine
x = 10 for all other species
K_L = loading condition coefficient described below:

Single-span beam	K_L
Concentrated load at midspan	1.09
Uniformly distributed load	1.0
Two equal concentrated loads at ⅓ points of span	0.96

Continuous beam or cantilever	
All loading conditions	1.0

Flat-Use Factor C_{fu}

Tabulated bending design values for loading parallel to wide faces of laminations F_{byy} shall be multiplied by the following flat use factors when the member dimension parallel to wide faces of laminations is less than 12 in:

Flat Use Factors C_{fu}

Member dimension parallel to wide faces of laminations, in	C_{fu}
10¾ or 10½	1.01
8¾ or 8½	1.04
6¾	1.07
5⅛ or 5	1.10
3⅛ or 3	1.16
2½	1.19

Wet-Service Factor C_M

When glued-laminated timber is used where moisture content will be 16 percent or greater, design values shall be multiplied by the appropriate wet service factors from the following table:

Wet-Service Factors C_M

F_b	F_t	F_V	$F_{c\perp}$	F_c	E
0.8	0.8	0.875	0.53	0.73	0.833

TABLE A.10 Design Values for Structural Glued-Laminated Softwood Timber Members Stressed Primarily in Bending[1,2,3,4,11]

(Use with Table A.10 Adjustment Factors.)

		Design values in pounds per square inch (psi)												
		Bending about *X-X* axis (loaded perpendicular to wide faces of laminations)						Bending about *Y-Y* axis (loading parallel to wide faces of laminations)					Axially loaded		
		Bending		Compression Perpendicular to Grain											
Combination symbol[4]	Species outer laminations/ core laminations[5]	Tension zone stressed in tension F_{bxx}	Compression zone stressed in tension[6] F_{bxx}	Tension face[9,10] $F_{c\perp xx}$	Compression face[9,10] $F_{c\perp xx}$	Shear parallel to grain[10] F_{vxx}	Modulus of elasticity E_{xx}	Bending F_{byy}	Compression perpendicular to grain (side faces) $F_{c\perp yy}$	Shear parallel to grain F_{vyy}	Shear parallel to grain (for members with multiple piece laminations which are not edge glued)[12] F_{vyy}	Modulus of elasticity E_{yy}	Tension parallel to grain F_t	Compression parallel to grain F_c	Modulus of elasticity E
Visually graded southern pine															
20F-V1	SP/SP	2000	1000	650	560[10]	200	1,500,000	1450	560	175	90	1,400,000	1000	1450	1,400,000
20F-V2	SP/SP	2000	1000	650	560[10]	200	1,600,000	1450	560	175	90	1,400,000	1050	1550	1,400,000
20F-V3	SP/SP	2000	1000	560[9,10]	560[10]	200	1,400,000	1600	560	175	90	1,400,000	1000	1500	1,400,000
20F-V4[7]	SP/SP	2000	1000	650	560[10]	90[10]	1,500,000	1100	470	150	75	1,300,000	725	950	1,300,000
20F-V5[8]	SP/SP	2000	2000	650	650	200	1,600,000	1450	560	175	90	1,400,000	1050	1550	1,400,000
24F-V1	SP/SP	2400	1200	650	560[10]	200	1,700,000	1500	560	175	90	1,500,000	1100	1350	1,500,000
24F-V2	SP/SP	2400	1200	650	650	200	1,700,000	1600	560	175	90	1,500,000	1100	1600	1,500,000
24F-V3	SP/SP	2400	1200	650	650	200	1,800,000	1600	560	175	90	1,600,000	1150	1700	1,600,000
24F-V4[7]	SP/SP	2400	1200	650	650	90[10]	1,700,000	1250	470	155	80	1,400,000	850	1050	1,400,000
24F-V5[8]	SP/SP	2400	2400	650	650	200	1,700,000	1600	560	175	90	1,500,000	1150	1700	1,500,000
24F-V6	SP/SP	2400	1200	650	650	200	1,700,000	1500	560	175	90	1,500,000	1150	1750	1,500,000

E-rated southern pine															
20F-E1	SP/SP	2000	1000	560[10]	560[10]	200	1,700,000	1600	560	175	90	1,500,000	1050	1600	1,500,000
20F-E2[7]	SP/SP	2000	1000	650	560[10]x	90[10]	1,600,000	1100	470	150	75	1,400,000	750	1000	1,400,000
20F-E3[8]	SP/SP	2000	2000	560[10]	560[10]	200	1,700,000	1800	560	175	90	1,500,000	1150	1700	1,500,000
24F-E1	SP/SP	2400	1200	650	560[10]	200	1,800,000	1600	560	175	90	1,600,000	1100	1750	1,600,000
24F-E2	SP/SP	2400	1200	650	650	200	1,900,000	1700	560	175	90	1,600,000	1150	1700	1,600,000
24F-E3[7]	SP/SP	2400	1200	650	650	90[10]	1,800,000	1300	470	155	80	1,500,000	950	1100	1,500,000
24F-E4[8]	SP/SP	2400	2400	650	650	200	1,800,000	2000	560	175	90	1,600,000	1250	1750	1,600,000
Visually graded western species															
20F-V2	HF/HF	2000	1000	500[10]	375[10]	155	1,500,000	1200	375	135	70	1,400,000	950	1350	1,400,000
20F-V3	DF/DF	2000	1000	650	560[10]	165	1,600,000	1450	560	145	75	1,500,000	1000	1550	1,500,000
20F-V4	DF/DF	2000	1000	590[9,10]	560[10]	165	1,600,000	1450	560	145	75	1,600,000	1000	1550	1,600,000
20F-V7[8]	DF/DF	2000	2000	650	650	165	1,600,000	1450	560	145	75	1,600,000	1000	1600	1,600,000
20F-V8[8]	DF/DF	2000	2000	590[9,10]	590[9,10]	165	1,700,000	1450	560	145	75	1,600,000	1000	1600	1,600,000
20F-V9[8]	HF/HF	2000	2000	500[10]	500[10]	155	1,500,000	1400	375	135	70	1,400,000	975	1400	1,400,000
20F-V11	DFS/DFS	2000	1000	650	500	165	1,300,000	1400	500	145	75	1,100,000	900	1400	1,100,000
20F-V12	AC/AC	2000	1000	560	560	190	1,500,000	1200	470	165	80	1,400,000	900	1500	1,400,000
24F-V2	HF/HF	2400	1200	500[10]	500[10]	155	1,500,000	1250	375	135	70	1,400,000	950	1300	1,400,000
24F-V3	DF/DF	2400	1200	650	560[10]	165	1,800,000	1500	560	145	75	1,600,000	1100	1600	1,600,000
24F-V4	DF/DF	2400	1200	650	650	165	1,800,000	1500	560	145	75	1,600,000	1150	1650	1,600,000
24F-V7[7]	DF/N3DF	2400	1200	650	560[10]	90[10]	1,700,000	1250	470	135	70	1,600,000	900	950	1,600,000
24F-V8[8]	DF/DF	2400	2400	650	650	165	1,800,000	1450	560	145	75	1,600,000	1100	1650	1,600,000
24F-V9[8]	HF/HF	2400	2400	500[10]	500[10]	155	1,500,000	1500	375	135	70	1,400,000	1000	1450	1,400,000
24F-V11	DF/DFS	2400	1200	650	560[10]	165	1,700,000	1600	500	145	75	1,400,000	1150	1700	1,400,000

TABLE A.10 Design Values for Structural Glued-Laminated Softwood Timber Members Stressed Primarily in Bending[1,2,3,4,11] *(Continued)*

(Use with Table A.10 Adjustment Factors.)

*Due to space limitations, only visually graded Western species layup combinations are shown. However, layup combinations using E-rated lumber as tabulated in the supplement to the national design specification may also be used to achieve similar beam performance characteristics.

Notes: Design values in this table are based on combinations conforming to AITC 117-87 (*Design Standard Specifications for Structural Glued Laminated Timber for Softwood Species*), by American Institute of Timber Construction, and manufactured in accordance with American National Standard ANSI/AITC A190.1-1991 (*Structural Glued Laminated Timber*). (2) The combinations in this table are intended for members stressed in bending due to loads applied perpendicular to the wide faces of the laminations (bending about *x-x* axis). Design values are tabulated, however, for loading both perpendicular and parallel to the wide faces of the laminations, and for axial loading. For combinations applicable to members loaded primarily axially or parallel to the wide faces of the laminations, see Table A.11. (3) Design values in this table are applicable to members having four or more laminations. For members having two or three laminations, see Table A.11. (4) The 24F combination for members 15 in and less in depth may not be readily available, and the designer should check availability prior to specifying. The 20F combination is generally available for members 15 in and less in depth. (5) The symbol used for southern pine is SP. (6) Design values in this column are for bending when the member is loaded such that the compression zone laminations are subjected to tensile stresses. For more information, see AITC 117-87. The values in this column may be increased 200 psi where end joint spacing restrictions are applied to the compression zone when stressed in tension. (7) These combinations are intended for straight or slightly cambered members for dry use and industrial appearance grade, because they may contain wane. If wane is omitted these restrictions do not apply. (8) The combinations are balanced and are intended for members continuous or cantilevered over supports and provide equal capacity in both positive and negative bending. (9) For bending members greater than 15 in in depth, these design values for compression perpendicular to grain are 650 psi on the tension face. (10) These design values may be increased in accordance with AITC 117-87 when the member conforms with special construction requirements therein. For more information see AITC 117-87. (11) Species groups for split-ring and shear-plate connectors should be determined by associated compression design values perpendicular to grain $F_{c\perp}$ as follows:

$F_{c\perp}$ (psi)	Species groups for split-ring and shear-plate connectors
650*	A
590 or 560	B
500	C
470 or 375	C
315	C
255	D

*For $F_{c\perp}$ = 650 psi for Douglas fir-south, use group B.

(12) The values for shear parallel to grain F_{vyy} apply to members manufactured using multiple piece laminations with unbonded edge joints. For members manufactured using single piece laminations or using multiple piece laminations with bonded edge joints the shear parallel to grain values in the previous column apply.

Source: *Design Values for Wood Construction,* a supplement of the 1991 edition of *National Design Specification,* courtesy of the American Forest and Paper Association, Washington, D.C.

ADJUSTMENT FACTORS FOR TABLE A.11

Volume Factor C_V

Tabulated bending design values for loading perpendicular to wide faces of laminations F_{bxx} for structural glued-laminated bending members shall be multiplied by the following volume factor:

$$C_V = K_L\,(21/L)^{1/x}(12/d)^{1/x}(5.125/b)^{1/x} \leq 1.0$$

where L = length of bending member between points of zero moment, ft
d = depth of bending member, inches
b = width (breadth) of bending member, inches. For multiple piece width layups, b = width of widest piece in the layup. Thus $b \leq 10.75$ in.
x = 20 for southern pine
x = 10 for all other species
K_L = loading condition coefficient described below:

Single-span beam	K_L
Concentrated load at midspan	1.09
Uniformly distributed load	1.0
Two equal concentrated loads at ⅓ points of span	0.96

Continuous beam or cantilever	
All loading conditions	1.0

Flat-Use Factor C_{fu}

Tabulated bending design values for loading parallel to wide faces of laminations F_{byy} shall be multiplied by the following flat-use factors when the member dimension parallel to wide faces of laminations is less than 12 in:

Flat-Use Factors C_{fu}

Member dimension parallel to wide faces of laminations, in	C_{fu}
10¾ or 10½	1.01
8¾ or 8½	1.04
6¾	1.07
5⅛ or 5	1.10
3⅛ or 3	1.16
2½	1.19

Wet-Service Factor C_M

When glued-laminated timber is used where moisture content will be 16 percent or greater, design values shall be multiplied by the appropriate wet service factors from the following table:

Wet-Service Factors C_M

F_b	F_t	F_V	$F_{c\perp}$	F_c	E
0.8	0.8	0.875	0.53	0.73	0.833

TABLE A.11 Design Values of Structural Glued-Laminated Softwood Timber Members Stressed Primarily in Axial Tension or Compression[1,2,8]

(Use with Table A.11 Adjustment Factors.)

				Design values in pounds per square inch (psi)												
				Axially loaded			Bending about *Y-Y* axis (loaded parallel to wide faces of laminations)							Bending about *X-X* axis (loading perpendicular to wide faces of laminations)		
				Tension parallel to grain	Compression parallel to grain		Bending			Shear parallel to grain[4]				Bending		Shear parallel to grain[4]
Combination symbol	Species[3]	Modulus of elasticity E	Compression perpendicular to grain[7] $F_{c\perp}$	2 or more laminations F_t	4 or more laminations F_c	2 or 3 laminations F_c	4 or more laminations F_{byy}	3 laminations F_{byy}	2 laminations F_{byy}	4 or more laminations (for members with multiple piece laminations)[9] F_{vyy}	4 or more laminations F_{vyy}	3 laminations F_{vyy}	2 laminations F_{vyy}	2 laminations to 15 in deep[5] F_{bxx}	4 or more laminations[6] F_{bxx}	2 or more laminations F_{vxx}
Visually graded southern pine																
45	SP	1,100,000	470	325	850	550	550	550	550	60	120	115	105	450	—	140
46	SP	1,300,000	560	900	1500	675	1450	1250	1000	90	175	165	150	1000	—	200
47	SP	1,400,000	560[7]	1200	1900	1150	1750	1550	1300	90	175	165	150	1400	1600	200
48	SP	1,700,000	650	1400	2200	1350	2000	1800	1500	90	175	165	150	1600	1900	200
49	SP	1,700,000	560[7]	1350	2100	1450	1950	1750	1500	90	175	165	150	1800	2100	200
50	SP	1,900,000	650	1550	2300	1700	2300	2100	1750	90	175	165	150	2100	2400	200
51	SP	1,700,000	560[7]	1300	1900	1600	2100	1950	1650	90	175	165	150	1750	2100	200
52	SP	1,900,000	650	1500	2200	1850	2400	2300	1950	90	175	165	150	2100	2400	200
E-rated southern pine																
53	SP	1,800,000	650	900	1900	1200	1450	1250	1000	90	175	165	150	1250	1500	200
54	SP	2,000,000	650	1100	2300	1400	1450	1250	1000	90	175	165	150	1500	1750	200
55	SP	2,200,000	650	1250	2400	1550	1650	1400	1150	90	175	165	150	1700	2000	200
56	SP	1,800,000	650	1550	1850	1700	2400	2400	2100	90	175	165	150	1800	2100	200
57	SP	2,000,000	650	1800	2400	1900	2400	2400	2400	90	175	165	150	2100	2400	200
58	SP	2,200,000	650	1800	2400	2100	2400	2400	2400	90	175	165	150	2300	2400	200

Visually graded western species																
10	DF	1,800,000	560[7]	1300	1950	1450	1950	1750	1500	75	145	135	125	1750	2100	165
11	DF	2,000,000	650	1500	2300	1700	2300	2100	1750	75	145	135	125	2100	2400	165
12	DF	1,800,000	560[7]	1400	1950	1650	2100	1950	1650	75	145	135	125	1900	2200	165
13	DF	2,000,000	650	1600	2300	1950	2400	2300	1950	75	145	135	125	2200	2400	165
14	HF	1,300,000	375[7]	800	1100	975	1200	1050	850	70	135	130	115	1100	1300	155
15	HF	1,400,000	375[7]	1050	1350	1300	1500	1350	1100	70	135	130	115	1450	1700	155
16	HF	1,600,000	375[7]	1200	1500	1450	1750	1550	1300	70	135	130	115	1600	1900	155
17	HF	1,700,000	500	1400	1750	1700	2000	1850	1550	70	135	130	115	1900	2200	155
18	HF	1,300,000	375	425	900	575	700	700	700	70	135	130	115	575	—	155
E-rated western species																
32	DF	2,200,000	650	1800	2400	2100	2400	2400	2400	75	145	135	125	2300	2400	165
62	DF	2,100,000	650	1150	2200	1500	1550	1350	1100	75	145	135	125	1600	1900	165
63	DF	2,100,000	650	1800	2400	2000	2400	2400	2400	75	145	135	125	2200	2400	165
33	HF	1,500,000	500	800	1050	950	1200	1050	850	70	135	130	115	1100	1300	155
34	HF	1,800,000	500	900	1300	1200	1450	1250	1000	70	135	130	115	1250	1500	155
35	HF	2,000,000	500	1100	1550	1400	1450	1250	1000	70	135	130	115	1500	1750	155

TABLE A.11 Design Values of Structural Glued-Laminated Softwood Timber Members Stressed Primarily in Axial Tension or Compression[1,2,8] *(Continued)*

(Use with Table A.11 Adjustment Factors.)

Notes: (1) Design values in this table are based on combinations conforming to AITC 117-87 (*Design Standard Specifications for Structural Glued Laminated Timber of Softwood Species*), by American Institute of Timber Construction, and manufactured in accordance with American National Standard ANSI/AITC A190.1-1991 (*Structural Glued Laminated Timber*). (2) The combinations in this table are intended primarily for members loaded either axially or in bending with the loads acting parallel to the wide faces of the laminations (bending about y-y axis). Design values for bending due to load applied perpendicular to the wide faces of the laminations (bending about x-x axis) are also included, although the combinations in Table A.10 are usually better suited for this condition of loading. (3) The symbol used for southern pine is SP. (4) The design values in shear parallel to grain in Table A.12 are based on members that do not contain wane. (5) The design values in bending about the x-x axis in this column are for members up to 15 in depth without tension laminations. (6) The design values in bending about the x-x axis in this column are for members having specific tension laminations and apply to members having four or more laminations. When these values are used in design and the member is specified by combination symbol, the design also should specify the required bending design value. (7) These design values may be increased in accordance with AITC 117-87 when member conforms with special construction requirements therein. For more information, see AITC 117-87. (8) Species groups for split-ring and shear-plate connectors should be determined by associated compression design values perpendicular to grain $F_{c\perp}$ as follows:

$F_{c\perp}$ (psi)	Species groups for split-ring and shear-plate connectors
650*	A
590 or 560	B
500	C
470 or 375	C
315	C
255	D

*For $F_{c\perp}$ = 650 psi for Douglas fir–south, use group B.

(9) The values for shear parallel to grain F_{vyy} apply to members manufactured using multiple-piece laminations with unbonded edge joints. For members using single-piece laminations or using multiple-piece laminations with bonded edge joints, the shear parallel to grain values tabulated in the next three columns apply.

Source:: *Design Values for Wood Construction,* a supplement of the 1991 edition of *National Design Specification,* courtesy of the American Forest and Paper Association, Washington, D.C.

TABLE A.12 Bearing Design Values Parallel to Grain F_g
Tabulated design values are for normal load duration.

Species Combination	Wet-service conditions	Dry-service conditions		
		Sawn lumber		
		5 × 5 in & larger	2–4 in thick	Glued-laminated timber
Douglas fir–larch	1350	1480	2020	2360
Hem-fir	1110	1220	1670	1940
Southern pine (dense)	1540	1690	2310	2690
Southern pine	1320	1450	1970	2300
Spruce-pine-fir	940	1040	1410	1650

Note: Wet- and dry-service conditions are defined in NDS 4.1.4 for sawn lumber and in NDS 5.1.5 for glued-laminated timber. Wet-service factors C_M have already been applied to tabulated bearing design values to reflect the appropriate moisture service conditions.

Source: *Design Values for Wood Construction,* a supplement to the 1991 edition of *National Design Specification,* courtesy of the American Forest and Paper Association, Washington, D.C.

INDEX

ABOUT THE EDITORS

KEITH F. FAHERTY holds M.S. and Ph.D. degrees in structural engineering. He is currently a professor in the Department of Civil and Environmental Engineering at Marquette University in Milwaukee, Wisconsin, where he teaches courses on wood design. He has taught a wood design course at three universities for more than 30 years. He has lectured in many of the major cities in the United States on the design and behavior of wood structures and he has chaired the American Society of Civil Engineers' (ASCE) National Committee on Wood for three years. He has done research on wood and has written chapters on the design of joints for wood structures for four major publications. He was also coeditor of the proceedings of a workshop on research needs in wood.

THOMAS G. WILLIAMSON began his professional career as an Assistant Professor of Civil Engineering at San Jose State University. He then joined the American Institute of Timber Construction (AITC) as Manager of Engineering Services. He was subsequently appointed Director of Marketing for AITC. Mr. Williamson left AITC to join LAMFAB Wood Structures, a midwest firm specializing in the design and construction of wood framed commercial structures. As Executive Vice President of LAMFAB, he was involved in the structural design of over 500 industrial, commercial and institutional structures utilizing engineered wood framing systems. Mr. Williamson left LAMFAB to rejoin AITC as Vice President of Technical Services and was subsequently appointed Executive Vice President of AITC. He is currently Executive Vice President of APA's American Wood Systems. He has presented over 100 design seminars on engineered wood construction throughout the U.S. Mr. Williamson is very active in the American Society of Civil Engineers (ASCE) having served seven years as Chair of the ASCE Committee on Wood and nine years as a member of the Structural Division Executive Committee, including a term as Chair. He also served as editor of the ASCE Journal of Structural Engineering and was General Chairman of the 1991 ASCE Structures Congress and the 1994 ASCE Annual Convention and Exposition. He currently chairs an ASCE Standards Division committee developing an LRFD Standard for Wood Construction.